P9-A5 (b) Estimated ending inventory (at cost), $16,000

P9-A6 (b) Debit to cost of goods sold, $1,395,000

P9-A7 (b) Ending inventory, $465,400

P9-B1 (a) Correct 19X5 net income, $20,840

P9-B2 (a2) Gross profit, $31,200

P9-B3 (a) Cost of goods sold, $8,380

P9-B4 (b) Earthquake loss, $39,000

P9-B5 (a) Estimated ending inventory (at cost), $120,060

P9-B6 (b) Debit to cost of goods sold, $46,110

P9-B7 (b) Ending inventory, $6,440

EDB9-1 (a1) Yes, 26.4% of total assets

BB9-1 (c) Increase in net income, $4.8 million

Chapter 10

P10-A2 Total land improvements, $84,920

P10-A3 (a3) 19X3 depreciation, $20,000

P10-A4 (a) Ford depreciation, $3,750

P10-A5 Sum-of-the-years'-digits, D

P10-A6 (c) Book value, $311,000

P10-B2 Total land improvements, $102,000

P10-B3 (a3) 19X1 depreciation, $16,000

P10-B4 (a) Cessna depreciation, $467,040

P10-B5 Sum-of-the-years'-digits, A

P10-B6 (b) Net income understated by $2,700

EDB10-1 (a) Sherwin-Williams, 45.6%

BB10-1 (d) Buildings (net), $91,833

Chapter 11

P11-A1 (b) Machinery depreciation, $54,000

P11-A2 (b2) Loss on exchange of van, $3,000

P11-A3 (a) Income after disposals and exchanges, $81,900

P11-A4 (c) Revised depletion rate per ton, $0.90

P11-A5 (b) Book value, $109,950

P11-A6 (a) Goodwill, $14,400

P11-B1 (b) Truck depreciation, $7,120

P11-B2 (b2) Loss on exchange of equipment, $3,000

P11-B3 (a) Income after disposals and exchanges, $58,100

P11-B4 (c) Revised depletion rate per ton, $0.68

P11-B5 (b) Amortization expense, $8,775

P11-B6 (a) Goodwill, $29,600

EDB11-1 (a) Mattel property, plant, and equipment, 19.6%

COMP P2 (c) Total assets, $709,850

Chapter 12

P12-A1 (b) Total current liabilities, $138,220

P12-A2 (c) Total current liabilities, $45,198

P12-A3 (c) Total current liabilities, $322,560

P12-A4 (b) Total current liabilities, $32,460

P12-A5 (b) Payroll tax expense, $3,511

P12-A6 (a) Total net pay, $9,058.10

P12-B1 (b) Total current liabilities, $264,625

P12-B2 (c) Total current liabilities, $57,378

P12-B3 (c2) Total current liabilities, $123,929

P12-B4 (b) Total current liabilities, $34,670

P12-B5 (b) Payroll tax expense, $24,960

P12-B6 (a) Total net pay, $9,658.25

EDB12-1 (a3) Boise, $281,723 surplus

Chapter 13

P13-A2 (a) Corrected owner's equity, $44,300

P13-A3 Total profit, $4,830,000

P13-A4 (a) Profit recognized in 19X3, $1,890,000

P13-A5 (a) Net income, $12,513

P13-B2 (a) Corrected owner's equity, $34,450

P13-B3 Total profit, $2,760,000

P13-B4 (b) Profit recognized in 19X2, $1,200,000

P13-B5 (a) Net income, $21,094

EDB13-1 (d1) Percentage of U.S. sales, 55.2%.

Chapter 14

P14-A1 (b) Total assets, $268,000

P14-A2 (b) Ending equity for Rambo, $81,600

P14-A3 (c) Wiley's capital balance, $2,400

P14-A4 (a3) Credit to Engle's capital account, $16,000

P14-A5 (b) Total partners' equity, $1,260,000

P14-A6 (b1) Cash balance, $50,000

P14-B1 (b) Total assets, $250,000

P14-B2 (b) Ending equity for Petty, $9,600

P14-B3 (c) Rice's capital balance, $91,600

P14-B4 (a3) Credit to Richardson's capital account, $112,000

P14-B5 (b) Total partners' equity, $265,000

P14-B6 (b1) Cash balance, $35,000

Chapter 15

P15-A1 (b) 19X3 dividends to common, $4,000

P15-A2 (b) Total stockholders' equity, $304,100

P15-A3 Total stockholders' equity, $11,980,000

P15-A4 (c) Total stockholders' equity, $196,900

P15-A5 Total legal capital, $3,111,000

P15-A6 (a) Book value per common share, $9.90

P15-B1 (b) 19X4 dividends to common, $0

P15-B2 (b) Total stockholders' equity, $557,500

P15-B3 Total stockholders' equity, $561,300

P15-B4 (c) Total stockholders' equity, $490,400

P15-B5 Total legal capital, $378,500

P15-B6 (a) Book value per common share, $16.74

ACCOUNTING
PRINCIPLES

Fourth Edition

Accounting Principles

Fourth Edition

Lanny M. Solomon
*The University of Texas
at Arlington*

Larry M. Walther
*The University of Texas
at Arlington*

Linda M. Plunkett
*University of Charleston,
South Carolina*

Richard J. Vargo
University of the Pacific

West Publishing Company
Minneapolis/Saint Paul ■ New York ■ Los Angeles ■ San Francisco

Copyediting:	Patricia A. Lewis
Indexing:	Virginia Hobbs
Composition:	Bi-Comp, Inc.
Illustration:	Randy Miyake, Miyake Illustration and Design
Cover Image:	Charles Biederman, #25, Giverny, 1972–1974
Photo Credits:	p. 6—*top left:* Michael Keller, FPG International; *top middle:* Gary Gladstone; *top right:* David Wagenaar; *bottom left:* Courtesy of Arlington Memorial Hospital, Arlington, TX; *bottom middle:* Richard Laird, FPG International.

West's Commitment to the Environment

In 1906, West Publishing Company began recycling materials left over from the production of books. This began a tradition of efficient and responsible use of resources. Today, up to 95 percent of our legal books and 70 percent of our college and school texts are printed on recycled, acid-free stock. West also recycles nearly 22 million pounds of scrap paper annually—the equivalent of 181,717 trees. Since the 1960s, West has devised ways to capture and recycle waste inks, solvents, oils, and vapors created in the printing process. We also recycle plastics of all kinds, wood, glass, corrugated cardboard, and batteries, and have eliminated the use of styrofoam book packaging. We at West are proud of the longevity and the scope of our commitment to the environment.

Production, prepress, printing and binding by West Publishing Company.

Lotus 1-2-3 is a registered trademark of Lotus Development Corporation, Cambridge, MA.
SEC-ONLINE is a registered trademark of SEC-ONLINE, Inc., Hauppauge, NY.

COPYRIGHT © 1993   **By WEST PUBLISHING COMPANY**
610 Opperman Drive
P.O. Box 64526
St. Paul, MN 55164-0526

Library of Congress Cataloging-in-Publication Data

Accounting Principles—4th ed. / Lanny M. Solomon . . . [et al.]
    p. cm.
    Rev. ed. of: Accounting Principles / Lanny M. Solomon, Richard J.
      Vargo, Larry M. Walther. 3rd ed. c1990.
    Includes index.
    ISBN 0-314-01191-9 (hard)
    1. Accounting. I. Solomon, Lanny M., 1946–   . II. Solomon,
Lanny M., 1946–   . Accounting Principles, 3rd ed.
HF5635.S688 1992
657—dc20
                                                92–26316
                                              CIP

This book is dedicated to our families:

To Nancy, Scott, and Deborah
from Lanny

To Laurie, Corbett, and Russell
from Larry

To Ron and Amanda and my dad
from Linda

To Melinda, Matthew, Blaine, and Mike
from Dick

ABOUT THE AUTHORS

Lanny M. Solomon is currently a professor of accounting at The University of Texas at Arlington. He holds a Ph.D. in accounting and information systems from Case Western Reserve University and is a certified management accountant. Professor Solomon has published articles in *The Accounting Review, Journal of Accountancy, Cost and Management*, and various journals of state CPA societies. In addition, he has presented numerous papers at technical accounting meetings. Professor Solomon is an active member of the American Accounting Association and the Institute of Certified Management Accountants, has public and industrial accounting experience, and has been the recipient of several outstanding teaching awards.

Larry M. Walther is an associate professor of accounting at The University of Texas at Arlington. He received his doctorate in accounting from Oklahoma State University and has experience with an international public accounting firm. Professor Walther is both a certified public accountant and a certified management accountant. Articles by Professor Walther have appeared in *The Accounting Review, Journal of Accountancy, Management Accounting, The Practical Accountant*, and other professional journals. He is a member of the American Accounting Association, Texas Society of Certified Public Accountants, and other professional organizations. Professor Walther has provided consulting services to a number of businesses on accounting and financial reporting matters and serves as a director of a corporation that operates in the Dallas–Fort Worth area.

Linda M. Plunkett, an associate professor of accounting at the University of Charleston, SC, received her doctorate from Georgia State University. She is a third-generation certified public accountant, with professional experience in both public accounting and private industry. Professor Plunkett has published articles in a variety of publications including *Accounting Horizons, Journal of Accountancy*, and *The Woman CPA*. She is a recent recipient of the Literary Award by the AWSCPA for her article, "Enforced Competition in the Accounting Profession: Does It Make Sense?" In addition, she has presented numerous papers at regional and national accounting meetings. She is a member of the American Accounting Association, American Woman's Society of CPAs, Academy of Accounting Historians, and other professional and academic organizations. Professor Plunkett is regarded as being very student-oriented and has won several awards for her teaching and scholarship.

Richard J. Vargo, currently a professor at the University of the Pacific, received his doctorate in accounting from the University of Washington. He has experience with an international public accounting firm. Articles by Professor Vargo have appeared in the *Journal of Accountancy, CPA Journal*, and other professional publications. He is the author of several other accounting and business books, including one prepared for the American Institute of Certified Public Accountants. Professor Vargo is actively involved in the American Accounting Association and has served as a member of both the editorial board of *The Accounting Review* and the Professional Examinations Committee. In addition, he has acted as a consultant to a number of businesses on accounting and financial reporting matters.

CONTENTS
IN BRIEF

CONTENTS

CHAPTER

Income Measurement and Adjusting Entries   91

CHAPTER

Completion of the Accounting Cycle   133

CHAPTER

5

Accounting/Reporting for Merchandising Operations   177

CHAPTER

6

Accounting Systems and Internal Control   225

CHAPTER

7

Cash and Short-Term Investments   261

CHAPTER

8

Receivables   299

CHAPTER

Inventory   335

CHAPTER

Property, Plant, and Equipment:
Acquisition and Depreciation   381

CHAPTER

11

Property, Plant, and Equipment/Natural Resources/Intangibles 417

CHAPTER

Current Liabilities and Payroll 455

CHAPTER
13

Financial Accounting and Reporting: U.S. and Global Perspectives 495

CHAPTER
14

Partnerships 543

CHAPTER

15

Introduction to Corporations   581

CHAPTER

16

Corporations: Additional Equity Issues and Income Reporting   619

CHAPTER
17
Long-Term Liabilities   633

CHAPTER
18
Long-Term Investments   717

CHAPTER

23

Process Costing, Activity-Based Costing, and Just-In-Time Production   943

CHAPTER

24

Cost-Volume-Profit Analysis   987

CHAPTER
25
Budgeting   1025

CHAPTER
26
Performance Evaluation Via Flexible Budgets and Standard Costs   1071

CHAPTER

Decision Making and Contribution Reporting   1115

CHAPTER

28

Capital Budgeting   1157

PREFACE

Accounting education has undergone considerable change in recent years. Students have been asked to comprehend a growing number of complex pronouncements; professorial complaints regarding students' reading and analytical abilities have increased; and there is evidence that we are losing our brightest classroom performers to other disciplines on campus. Furthermore, classes often contain a substantial number of students who quickly lose interest in the subject matter, which is often regarded as time-consuming and somewhat dry and boring. These are the very problems that prompted us to write the first edition of *Accounting Principles* in 1983.

A primary emphasis on these issues was sufficient for the 1980s and the very early 1990s. Further refinements are needed and have been made, however, in this, the fourth edition. Ethics, computerized information systems, globalization, high-tech manufacturing, the role of information in decision making, financial statement interpretation and use, communication skills, cases, simulations, and the ability to think and apply are collectively the current focus—key elements required to train the managers of tomorrow (accounting or otherwise). A review of the text's 28 chapters and accompanying package will find numerous revisions that reflect contemporary business practices and the thinking of prominent educators.

The authors fully agree with a recent statement by the Accounting Education Change Commission, which noted that:

> The knowledge and skills provided by the first course in accounting should facilitate subsequent learning even if the student takes no additional academic work in accounting or directly related disciplines.[1]

We feel that our fourth edition accomplishes this objective. Discussions of the concepts and rationale that underlie accounting practices are integrated at appropriate points throughout the text. Recognizing that there is more to accounting than just calculations, our end-of-chapter problem material asks students to reason, justify, explain, and apply. Combining this approach with a clear, readable, and accurate presentation results in what we believe is an enlightening presentation—one that will create a stimulating educational experience for both students *and* faculty.

SIGNIFICANT CHANGES IN THE FOURTH EDITION

On the basis of user feedback and market studies, we have made various changes in the organization and content of the fourth edition. The major changes include the following:

1 There is an added focus on ethics and the accountant. In addition to topical coverage via an appendix to Chapter 1, each chapter now con-

---

[1] "The First Course in Accounting," *Position Statement No. 2: Exposure Draft* (Torrance, Calif.: Accounting Education Change Commission, 1992), p. 3.

tains an Ethics Issue vignette (in the text's margin). The vignettes are designed to raise various points relative to conduct in business situations.

2   The presentation on special journals has been moved to an end-of-book appendix. In its place, Chapter 6 (Accounting Systems and Internal Control) has been totally rewritten to focus on computerized information systems. Portions of the chapter are coordinated with VTL, our computerized general ledger package. Furthermore, the text's overall coverage of computer applications in accounting has been expanded.

3   Coverage of international accounting issues has been moved to Chapter 13 (Financial Accounting and Reporting: U.S. and Global Perspectives). In addition, the topics of globalization and foreign competition are presented in the cost/managerial chapters.

4   Chapter 20's discussion of financial statement analysis has been heavily rewritten and now takes an annual report focus. New sections have been added about earnings quality and management and audit reports.

5   Chapter 23 has been extensively revised. To our discussion of process costing, we have added the contemporary topics of activity-based costing, just-in-time production systems, and product quality.

6   Basic presentations related to the statement of stockholders' equity and postretirement health-care benefits are now included in the text. In contrast, we have deleted a number of topics of minimal significance for beginning students (e.g., subsidiary ledgers for plant assets, purchase versus pooling-of-interests accounting, the manufacturing work sheet, process costing in a second manufacturing department, and corporate income tax regulations). Many of our deletions are based on the results of a national market survey and the growing thought that introductory accounting courses should shift toward a user (rather than preparer) orientation.

7   Most chapters now contain an Executive Briefing. These are short scenarios written by executives of high-profile businesses on the significance of particular accounting topics to their firms.

8   Each chapter (as opposed to selected chapters in previous editions) now has a summary problem and solution. Other features include a new end-of-chapter glossary, "Beyond the Basics" problems that are multiple choice in format (good preparation for those students who will be exposed to multiple-choice testing formats), and interpretive problems that focus on financial statements contained in our electronic data base.

9   We are especially excited about a new problem series entitled "Communication of Accounting Information." These problems begin by citing a business communication principle, with students being asked in many cases to apply the principle to data from real-world companies. The emphasis is on the development of writing skills rather than extensive manipulation of numbers.

10   The text now contains four comprehensive problems. The problems cover the accounting cycle (Chapter 4); short-term investments, receivables, inventory, and property, plant, and equipment (Chapter 11); corporate accounting and bonds (Chapter 17); and basic issues in cost accounting (Chapter 23).

Many features in the third edition proved popular with users. Those features, repeated in this edition, include a heavy use of real-world firms and data, excerpts from periodicals, a truly managerial section, solid problem material, and clarity and readability of presentations.

THIRD EDITION FEATURES RETAINED

Heavy Real-World Emphasis

Many accounting texts use hypothetical firms in their illustrations and examples. The authors have found that students show an increased interest in the subject matter when exposed to the accounting and financial reporting practices of real businesses. Thus, we include annual report data and "war stories" of over 100 different companies, including McDonald's, American Airlines, Apple Computer, NIKE, and The Coca-Cola Company. We have carefully selected firms from industries with which students themselves have contact. All examples were screened for appropriateness at the introductory level.

Excerpts from Periodicals

The authors have integrated excerpts from journal and newspaper articles into topical discussions in an effort to bridge the gap between academia and the business world. The selected articles relate to the subject matter at hand and were chosen (and adapted) to focus on practical, interesting applications. Excerpts are from such popular periodicals as *The Wall Street Journal*, *Forbes*, and *Business Week*. Typical examples include:

- "Pass the Vinegar and Oil, Please"
- "What's in a Name, Anyway?"
- "A College Student + Good Decisions = Million$"

A Truly Managerial Section

The final chapters of an accounting principles text are normally devoted to cost and managerial accounting topics. The usual approach is to have students calculate this and calculate that, while paying very little attention to the use or impact of the data they are generating. Our approach is to focus on the how *and* why of planning, control, performance evaluation, and decision making and to show practical applications whenever possible. This balanced presentation should appeal to a wide range of instructors, including those who currently use a separate text for managerial coverage.

Solid Problem Material

All problem material contained in this text was carefully designed to reflect current accounting principles and practices. Questions, exercises, and problems range in scope from the simple to the complex; they were written and solved by the authors to assure total coordination with the text presentation. To further ensure accuracy and reliability, we have triple-checked the *Instructor's Solutions Manual*. We are confident the end-of-chapter materials are as trouble-free as repeated multiple checking can make them. These items will provide a solid, well-rounded foundation for accounting students and a varied resource for instructors.

The problem material is divided into Series *A* and Series *B*. Instructors can therefore use one problem for illustration purposes and assign another as homework or use different problem sets in alternating semesters or quarters. Although duplication is important, the authors have not lost sight of the need for variety. Both sets contain an ample variety of material to allow instructors to approach a given topic from varying perspectives.

Clarity and Readability of Presentations

We have monitored readability throughout the text and have strived to make troublesome topics (such as adjusting entries, corporate equity, bonds, and the statement of cash flows) especially understandable to students. To eliminate differences in writing styles, one of the authors has spent countless hours integrating the same tone, approach, and manner of presentation in all 28 chapters. Accounting is a rigorous subject for most individuals. The authors recognize this fact and have worked hard to produce a clear and usable volume. Comments from users (instructors *and* students) indicate that we have, in fact, generated a readable book.

SUPPLEMENTARY MATERIALS

A complete set of supplementary materials for both student and instructor accompanies this text to help facilitate the learning and teaching of accounting.

For the Student

- **Study Guide.** A study guide, available in two volumes, has been written by Larry Walther to reinforce the material presented in the text. The Study Guide contains chapter learning objectives; a chapter synopsis; multiple-choice, two-response, and completion questions; exercises; and answers *with explanations,* as well as computer software that provides step-by-step instruction on key accounting topics.
- **Working Papers.** Two volumes of working papers have been prepared: Volume I covers Chapters 1–14 and Appendix A; Volume II covers Chapters 14–28 and Appendix B. The inclusion of Chapter 14 (Partnerships) in both volumes recognizes that this topic is covered in the first Principles course at some schools and in the second course at others. Many of the working papers are partially filled in, thereby allowing students to concentrate on accounting concepts as opposed to the pencil pushing associated with problem setup. Forms for the end-of-chapter exercises are included, and pages are now bar coded for electronic check-in. A separate book of blank working papers is available.
- **Practice Sets.** Five practice sets tie together various issues discussed in the text.

  Office Warehouse (1) is available for use after completion of Chapter 5 (merchandising operations) and Appendix A (special journal systems). This practice set concentrates on transaction recording and the accounting cycle.

  Midwest Sporting Goods (2) is a "50/50 practice set." It covers two months of operation and focuses on the accounting cycle for a merchandising business. Transactions for the first month are processed by using a manual system that features special journals; in contrast, the second month's transactions are processed on the computer. Alternative data sets are presented, allowing flexibility within a given class and from one term to the next.

Electronic Supply (3) is a computerized practice set that covers two months of activity for a merchandising business, spanning Chapters 1–9. Some "what-if" analysis may be employed. (*Note:* Added information on practice sets 2 and 3 appears in the section entitled "Computer Software.")

Hewlett-Packard Company (4) focuses on financial statement analysis. Students are asked to analyze a corporate annual report and comment on their findings.

Allied Manufacturing (5) concentrates on cost/managerial accounting. This set has students perform some basic transaction processing as well as several spreadsheet applications.

- **Using Accounting Information: An Interactive Learning Approach.** For those instructors who choose to integrate contemporary educational methods in their classes, we have designed a supplement that centers on students' abilities to extract, analyze, and apply accounting data in a variety of settings. The supplement includes decision cases, simulations and role playing exercises, readings, and other interactive experiences. These items are generic in nature, allowing use with other *Principles* texts.
- **Limited English Proficiency Manual.** Written by Elaine Kirn, language arts chair and ESL specialist at West Los Angeles College, this guide has been prepared for those students who may need extra help with reading and comprehension skills. The manual focuses on the accounting cycle.

For the Instructor

- **Annotated Instructor's Edition.** An annotated instructor's edition of the text is available to help improve teaching effectiveness. This special printing includes, by notations in the margins, Points to Emphasize, Teaching Ideas, Teaching Transparency References and Placement, and Check Figures for Exercises and Problems (more extensive than those given to students). This edition is also available in a three-ring binder.
- **Instructor's Solutions Manual.** A comprehensive, two-volume manual is available that contains the solutions to all questions, exercises, and problems. In addition, a suggested completion time and difficulty index is provided for each problem. Solutions to the practice sets are available in separate booklets.
- **Instructor's Resource Manual.** The Instructor's Resource Manual contains detailed lecture outlines that parallel the text's discussion. These outlines are especially useful for part-time instructors and graduate teaching assistants. The manual also includes suggested homework assignments and a series of short quizzes. Both hard-copy and computerized (Word Perfect) versions are available.
- **Transparencies.** A set of transparencies is free to adopters. Packaged in two boxes, the transparencies contain solutions to all exercises and problems. All are prepared in large, easy-to-read type.
- **Teaching Transparencies.** A set of over 100 teaching transparencies is free to adopters. These helpful color acetates include summaries of key narrative discussions raised in the chapter and various examples, with

an emphasis on those that are too time-consuming to present on a chalk-board. A special group of "layered" transparencies is included. These consist of overlays, allowing the instructor to demonstrate, one step at a time, the completion of a work sheet, the construction of a production cost report, and other troublesome tasks.

■ **Lecture Outline Transparencies.** The lecture outlines contained in the Instructor's Resource Manual are available on transparencies. These helpful tools add structure to a classroom presentation and allow students to focus on key points raised in each chapter.

■ **Test Bank.** A thoroughly revised test bank has been prepared. Each chapter of the text is covered via an ample selection of multiple-choice, true-false, and matching questions, along with a series of multipart exercises and essay questions. The Test Bank is available in printed and micro-computer versions. We have also included various achievement tests that take 40 to 60 minutes to complete and examine a student on approximately three chapters at a given sitting. In addition, there are two comprehensive tests.

Computer Software/Other Media

We also offer a variety of microcomputer software and other media to help both the student and the instructor.

■ **Computer-Assisted Accounting Tutorials.** Contained in the Study Guide, these tutorials present essential accounting material on a step-by-step basis. As they proceed through the lesson, students are queried on subject matter presentations through a series of two-response (e.g., yes/no, agree/disagree, logical/illogical), multiple-choice, and computational questions. The tutorials are designed for use on an IBM PC or compatible machines.

■ **Computerized Practice Sets.** Two computerized transaction-processing practice sets accompany the text. Both are compatible with the IBM PC, and each has a grading disk for the instructor.

■ **Lotus 1-2-3 Spreadsheet Exercises and Problems.** Exercises and problems from each chapter have been adapted to microcomputers by use of Lotus 1-2-3 (IBM) templates. The templates, which explore a wide variety of spreadsheet skills, are denoted by the logo shown. The related instructor materials are available to text adopters.

■ **General Ledger Software.** A general ledger software package (VTL) has been developed for use with the text and selected problems, the latter designated by the VTL logo. This package shows the power of the computer in terms of processing transactions and preparing financial statements.

■ **SEC-ONLINE Electronic Data Base.** Available on disk, this data base contains financial statements, accompanying notes, and other disclosures of many well-known, real-world companies. Special text problems have been written that ask students to obtain data about specific corporations and then perform comparative analyses.

■ **Westest.** Westest is a microcomputer test-generation package that consists of item banks on disks and the software necessary to turn them into instructor-customized examinations. Random selection of questions is available and, if desired, multiple tests may be generated simultaneously. Westest can be used on the IBM PC and compatible machines, the Apple IIe family of computers, and the Macintosh.

- **Working Paper Scanning System.** The working papers that accompany the text have been bar coded for use with light pens and accompanying software. This unique feature will greatly assist instructors who collect and check homework.
- **Presenter by SoftCraft.** This software is a self-contained classroom delivery system for use with a microcomputer and overhead projector. Learning objectives, detailed discussion outlines, teaching illustrations, and Lotus templates have been designed for each of the chapters. If desired, Presenter also gives the instructor the option of creating an original lecture system.
- **Videotapes.** Tutorial tapes covering key points in various chapters are available for lab settings. Additional video vignettes are available to supplement lectures.

ACKNOWLEDGMENTS

A project of this nature and magnitude is a team effort, entailing much cooperation, thoughtfulness, and patience. To our team members we owe a tremendous debt of gratitude. Those persons who responded to surveys, tested materials, and reviewed chapters were especially helpful with their comments and suggestions. Therefore, many thanks to the following people:

John C. Arnsparger
Red Rock Community College

James P. Bates
University of Texas—Dallas

Frank R. Beigbeder
Rancho Santiago College

J. V. Colmie
Thomas Nelson Community
College

Alan E. Davis
Community College of
Philadelphia

Donna Dietz
Concordia College

Thomas A. Gavin
University of Tennessee—
Chattanooga

Robert L. Hurt
California State Polytechnic
University—Pomona

Laura G. Jones
Wheaton College

Charles A. Konkol
University of Wisconsin—
Milwaukee

James Kopel
Black Hawk Community College

James P. Makofske
Fresno City College

E. Michelle McEacharn
Northeast Louisiana State
University

Kenneth L. Paige
Duquesne University

Paul Palmer
West Los Angeles College

Theresia M. Porter
Highland College

Linda Schaffeld
Cincinnati Technical College

Ann Snodgrass
Pellissippi Community College

Gene Sullivan
Liberty University

David Thais
Roane State Community College

Keith T. Yandoh
Jefferson Community College

Gregory C. Yost
The University of West Flordia

Survey respondents include Rebecca L. Andrews, Roane State Community College; Gerald Ashley, Grossmont College; Florence Atiase, Austin Community College; Sue Atkinson, Tarleton State University; John A. Beegle, Western Carolina University; Bonnie Jo Bilant, Western Montana College; Dorothy Binger, Tallahassee Community College; A. P. Boratgis, North Shore Community College; John C. Borke, University of Wisconsin-Platteville; William Bradberry, Bluefield State College; Kurt H. Buerger, Angelo State University; W. Glen Bushnell, De Anza College; Bruce Busta, St. Cloud State University; Gene Carlson, Brainerd Community College; W. D. Claflin, St. Clair County Community College; Bob Cluskey, Bradley University; Gilbert S. Cohen, Montgomery County Community College; John W. Coker, Belmont College; Paul Concilio, McLennan Community College; David G. Coy, Adrian College; Gene Crotty, Virginia Western Community College; Richard L. Cross, Bentley College; Patricia A. Cummins, Troy State University; Zoel W. Daughtrey, Mississippi State University; James A. Davidson, Southeastern Oklahoma State University; Alan E. Davis, Community College of Philadelphia; John W. Dawson, Christopher Newport College; Laura Denton, Maysville Community College; Paul T. De Pietro, Jr., Housatonic Community College; S. T. Desai, Cedar Valley College; Mikel W. Dexter, Southwestern College; Lorella Donlin, Black Hills State University; Roger Dufresne, Northern Essex Community College; Patricia C. Elliott, University of New Mexico; Richard D. English, Augustana College; James E. Faircloth, Georgia Southwestern College; Janice Feingold, Moorpark College; Jerry W. Ferry, University of North Alabama; James L. Ficek, Iowa Western Community College; Ralph Fritzsch, Midwestern State University; Bruce L. Fry, Butler County Community College; Michael Garms, Henry Ford Community College; Harold Gellis, York College; Lucille S. Genduso, Nova University; Rob Giacoletti, Eastern Kentucky University; Shirley Glass, Macomb Community College; William D. Goodman, Bluefield State College; Rita Grant, Grand Valley State University; Regina Grantz, Alverno College; W. Bill Greenwood, Northern Montana College; William L. Groft, Butler County Community College; Vincent D. R. Guide, Clemson University; Majorie Gunter, Birmingham–Southern College.

Rodney O. Hardcastle, Pacific Union College; Eugene Harris, Hanover College; Judy Hinshaw, New Mexico Junior College; Dolan R. Hinson, University of North Carolina–Charlotte; Thomas L. Hofmeister, Northwestern Business College; George Holdren, University of Nebraska—Lincoln; Jay S. Horton, Greenville Technical College; Barbara L. Howald, Franklin College; Spencer Howard, Blackhawk Technical College; Candace Humphrey, University of Dubuque; Inam Hussain, Indiana University Northwest; Debra Jeter, Austin Peay State University; Charles E. Johnson, Western Oklahoma State College; Kenneth H. Johnson, Georgia Southern University; Carol Jones, Amber University; Kris T. Jones, Southeastern Louisiana University; Joe Kaderabek, Baldwin Wallace College; LeRoy B. Kane, Austin Community College; William Keller, Ferris State University; Terry L. Klocke, Washington University; Marilyn Y. Knight, Saginaw Valley State University; Juene Knutel, Lake Michigan College; Ed Kraft, Southwest State University; Ray Krov, Union County College; Gerard A. Lange, St. John's University; Thomas Largay, Husson College; Larry Larson, Triton College; James Lasseter, Jr., University of South Florida; Judith A. Laux, Colorado College; Kevin Leeds, St. Peter's College; Sharon Lipham, Odessa College; William P. Lovell, Cayuga Community College; John W. McCall, Rollins College; Lois McClain, California State University—Los Angeles; Sandra Z. McClure, Pueblo Community College; Florence McGovern, Bergen Community College; John McIntyre, Bemidji State University; Christine L. McKeag, University of Evansville; L. Kevin McNelis, Eastern New Mexico University; Charles L. Martin, Jr., Towson State University; Mary Maury, St. John's University; Jim Meir, Andrew College; Andrew Miller, Hudson Valley Community College; Keith D. Moon, Daniel Webster College; Paula Mooney, Georgia Southern University; David Moore, Kankakee Community College; Gregory R. Mostyn, Mission Community College; Lloyd M. Munson, Brigham Young University—Hawaii; Susan Murphy, Monroe Community College; C. Lynn Murray, Florida Community College; Harry J. Murvin, Brandywine College of Widener University.

Paul Nieball, El Paso Community College; Deborah A. Niemer, Oakland Community College; James O'Donnell, Jr., The Katharine Gibbs School; Aileen Ormiston, Mesa Community College; Steve Pagel, Concordia Lutheran College; Al Partington, Los Angeles Pierce College; Sandra Gill Penn, Wayne State University; Robert Phillips, Radford University; David S. Pines, University of Maryland—Eastern Shore; J. Edwin Priddle, Barry University; Pat Prugh, East Central College; Alan Rainford, Greenfield Community College; Alan Ransom, Cypress College; Jane Garson Reed, Baldwin-Wallace College; Gayle M. Richardson, Bakersfield College; Diane Ritz, Northwestern Business College; Donald J. Robbins, Indiana University of Pennsylvania; Sharon L. Robinson, Frostburg State University; Georgia Roth, Jackson State Community College; Joseph B. Ruth, Jr., Mount Wachusett Community College; Alfredo Salas, El Paso Community College; Scott Sandstrom, College of the Holy Cross; N. R. Schaffner, Southwestern College; Robert Schesser, Chaffey College; Henry Schulman, Grossmont Community College; Nancy M. Scott, Abraham Baldwin College; William A. Serefin, Community College of Allegheny County; Dennis D. Shannon, Belleville Area College; J. Shepherd, University of California—Santa Cruz; Brenda F. Skornogoski, Northern Montana College; Linda McElvey Smith, Brenau College; Teresa Speck, Saint Mary's College of Minnesota; Maureen Stefanini, Worcester State College; John R. Stewart, University of Northern Colorado; Lynn Suberly, Bellevue College; William N. Sullivan, Assumption College; Richard F. Sweet, University of South Alabama; Glen Tenney, Northern Nevada Community College; Mary Tichich, The American University; Don Trent, St. Mary of the Plains College; Lina Valcarcez, Duquesne University; Joan Van Hise, Fordham University; Thomas L. Vannaman, Midland College; Arlan Van Roekel, Grand View College; Marcia Veit, University of Central Florida; Ronald L. Vogel, College of Eastern Utah; Gloria Vollmers, University of Texas—Dallas; Du Wayne Wacker, University of North Dakota; Frederick J. Walsh, Franklin Pierce College; Martin E. Ward, DeVry Institute of Technology; Mark Wilensky, College of Staten Island; Philip Wolitzer, Long Island University; Robert G. Wrenn, Los Angeles Harbor College; William Zacchaeus, St. Edward's University; and Jack Zeller, Kirkwood Community College.

A special thank you goes to Sandra Elliott, Mary Lee Hodge, Lola Rhodes (all from The University of Texas at Arlington), Ceil Fewox (Trident Technical College), Becky Herring (University of Charleston, SC), and Elizabeth Orem (Texas Tech University), who played important roles in the development of text and supplement components. Miscellaneous chores related to the book's development were performed by Galen Carpenter, Harley Courtney, Luis Otaola, Becky Pierce, Aruna Ravi, Bill Ross, Joe Sarkis, Jeffrey Tsay, Karen Turner, and Connie Weaver, all of The University of Texas at Arlington.

The assistance from West Publishing in producing this text was extremely helpful. We especially appreciate the work of Bob Horan, Janine Wilson, Mark Jacobsen, Lucinda Gatch, Ann Hillstrom, John Lindley, Andi Peters, and Bill Stryker—all of whom offered numerous suggestions and provided constant encouragement during the period that the text and ancillary materials were under development.

Comments from users are welcomed and appreciated.

Lanny M. Solomon
Larry M. Walther
Linda M. Plunkett
Richard J. Vargo

A MESSAGE TO OUR READERS . . .

You are about to begin the study of accounting, which has frequently been called the language of business. Accounting concepts and terminology are used in conversations among managers and often appear in business periodicals. A day doesn't go by, for example, without metropolitan newspapers reporting the financial happenings of major U.S. corporations.

Ask almost any professional (e.g., a company president, engineer, marketing manager, or the owner of a local restaurant) about the benefits of having a reasonable understanding of accounting and financial matters, and he or she will likely cite an improvement in job performance and/or lifestyle. The importance of accounting is perhaps best seen via the following statistics. A survey performed by the major accrediting agency of U.S. business schools asked managers to evaluate various courses to determine which ones students should stress in their studies. Accounting ranked first. (Finance and economics placed second and third, respectively.) Another study conducted by *Fortune* magazine found that many corporations preferred their chief executive officers (CEOs) to have a heavy accounting and financial background. Approximately 25% of the 800 highest paid CEOs in this country followed a financial career path while climbing to the top of the corporate hierarchy.

Over the years, many businesses have flourished because of entrepreneurial spirit and innovative ideas and products. Some companies, of course, have met with more success than others. Those organizations that have outpaced the competition have done so, in part, because of their executives' ability to understand and analyze basic accounting information. Careful study of this text will give you the foundation for developing that ability. You will be exposed to principles, practices, procedures, and applications—all of which are necessary to gain a fundamental understanding of the subject matter.

Accounting is a discipline characterized by reward and challenge. Although the introductory course in which you are enrolled may be more time-consuming and rigorous than other courses on campus, the effort you put forth today will have significant long-term benefits. The time that you spend is an investment in the future, with high returns in the years to come.

CHAPTER 1

An Introduction to Accounting

LEARNING OBJECTIVES

After studying this chapter, you should be able to:

1

List the users, uses, and limitations of accounting information.

2

Describe the accounting profession and identify accounting-related careers.

3

Explain the use of accounting principles in financial reporting.

4

Define assets, liabilities, and owner's equity, and state the relationship of these components in the accounting equation.

5

Identify the four items that cause owner's equity to change: owner investments, owner withdrawals, revenues, and expenses.

6

Describe the impact of various transactions on the accounting equation.

7

Understand the content of and prepare an income statement, a statement of owner's equity, and a balance sheet.

Most professionals recognize that accounting plays a major role in the management of any business. Companies require a system that summarizes past financial activity and communicates selected information to interested parties. Accounting is such a system. By reporting output (e.g., ending cash balances, earnings for the period, and the manufactured cost of finished products) to the appropriate individual(s), accounting gives its users the ability to make more informed economic decisions.

This process is better understood if we develop a definition of accounting, which, in itself, is not an easy task. The field is broad and the work that an accountant performs is varied. Accountants are typically involved with such diverse activities as the review of business transactions and client computer systems, tax planning, budgeting, and the analysis of long-term investment proposals. A publication from an accounting firm notes:

> Historically, [accounting] suffered from an image problem—the Bob Cratchit syndrome—which portrayed it as dull, routine work. If this view were ever true, it certainly isn't today.[1]

Observing the accountants' work and the profession of which they are members, few would find fault with the following definition: **Accounting** is a set of concepts and techniques that collectively measure, summarize, and report financial information about an economic unit. To expand, most disciplines are based on some type of theoretical framework. Accounting is no exception. The foundation for much of what accountants do is a set of underlying principles, assumptions, and practices that have been generally accepted by the accounting profession. These items are used to measure the financial activities of numerous business units ranging from Exxon Corporation to the family-owned corner market and even the local art museum. Once derived, the measurements are processed, summarized, and communicated in the form of financial reports and statistics, allowing users to make judgments about a wide variety of business matters.

Users and Uses of Accounting Information

OBJECTIVE

1

List the users, uses, and limitations of accounting information.

The audience for accounting information is large and diverse. Numerous user groups within and outside of an enterprise attempt to satisfy their needs by relying on financial disclosures (see Exhibit 1-1). For example:

Owners have invested their precious funds into a business organization. This group requires information concerning investment profitability and whether continuance in an ownership role is economically justified. Potential owners have similar information needs. These individuals desire insight about a firm's past earnings trends, likelihood for future growth, and cash flow prospects, perhaps in comparison with other enterprises in the same industry.

Creditors are those parties that provide a firm with goods, services, and financial resources by either extending credit or making loans. Included in this group are suppliers, banks, loan companies, and other lending institutions. Creditors are interested in knowing whether an organization can settle its obligations (including related interest charges) in a timely manner

---

[1] KPMG Peat Marwick, *Your Career in Professional Accounting*, p. 12.

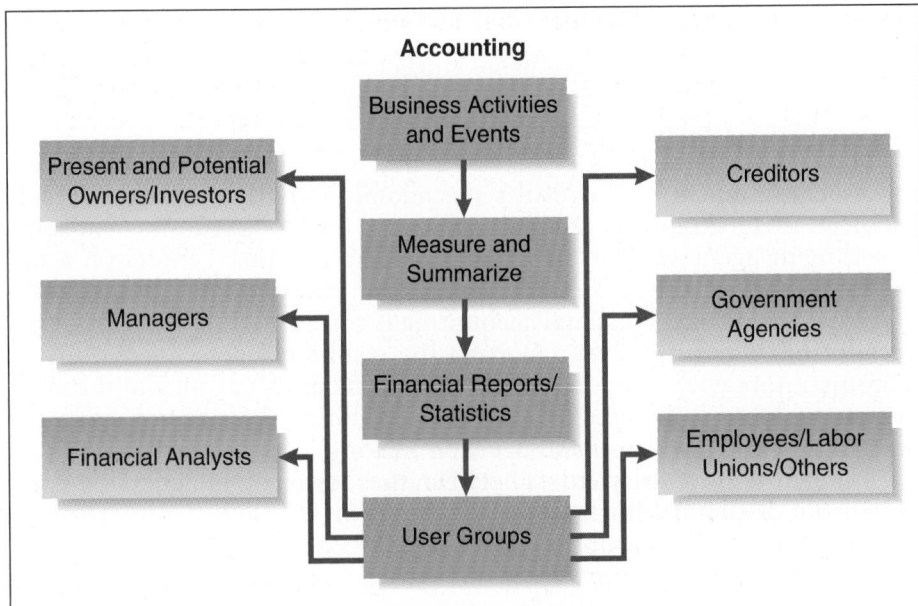

EXHIBIT 1-1
Accounting and the
Communication Process

and on scheduled dates. Thus, an enterprise's existing cash position, out-standing debts, and present and projected earnings are of utmost concern.

Managers are charged with the responsibility of meeting a company's goals and objectives. To achieve this end, managers must select from and implement various projects, evaluate performance, and, if necessary, take corrective action to bring an organization back on target. Depending on the firm involved, information needs will vary and may include product cost data and manufacturing resource requirements.

Government agencies also employ accounting information. Governmental units, along with various programs (such as Social Security and unemployment), are financed from the taxes that are paid by businesses and individuals. These taxes are frequently based on income as defined by numerous tax statutes and rulings. In addition, businesses must often comply with the financial reporting directives of certain regulatory agencies. These agencies are charged with administering a variety of legislative enactments and include the Securities and Exchange Commission (SEC), the Interstate Commerce Commission, and the U.S. Department of Labor, to name just a few.

Finally, other users include *financial analysts*, who advise their clients or employers about various investment alternatives; *employees and labor unions*, who need information to properly evaluate salary and fringe benefit packages; and customers, lawyers, and trade associations.

As you can see, accountants attempt to satisfy many different user groups and needs. Be aware that the financial reporting techniques preferred by one particular group may not adequately satisfy the needs of another. In view of this situation a neutral position is taken, with a company's financial reports having a general-purpose orientation. This orientation means that the information being disclosed is not biased to favor owners, creditors, or any other interested party.

Financial and Managerial Orientation

Accounting encompasses extensive subject matter and consists of many component parts. Two of the field's major segments are financial accounting and managerial accounting.

Financial accounting is primarily concerned with external reporting, that is, communicating the results of economic activities to parties outside the firm. Included in this group are potential owners, creditors, and some government agencies. The financial reporting function centers on a fair presentation of (1) the resources invested in an enterprise and (2) the profitability of operations. Financial accounting is complemented by **managerial accounting**, which involves reporting the results of operating activity to administrators within an organization. Because of its nature and the audience to which it is directed, managerial accounting deals heavily with the areas of planning, control, and decision making.

Although some overlap exists between these two components, there is a significant distinguishing factor with which you should be familiar—regulation. Managerial accounting is characterized by an "anything goes" philosophy. Although there are a number of widely accepted practices, a company can do whatever it pleases when reporting internally to its executives. In contrast, the financial (external) reporting environment is heavily regulated, a situation that is caused, in part, by the wide variety of businesses in our economy. It is essential that financial accounting be standardized somewhat to permit comparative analysis. Imagine the difficulties faced by a potential investor who is attempting to evaluate the economic activities of Ford Motor Company and those of The Gap, Inc. (a much smaller retailer of casual and activewear). If each company were allowed to account for its activities by employing unique, self-prescribed methods, the investor would surely face a formidable task.[2]

The private sector agency that currently oversees external reporting is the **Financial Accounting Standards Board (FASB).** Beginning operation in 1973, the FASB has studied a number of important topics and has issued various pronouncements that detail specific accounting practices. These pronouncements, called *Statements of Financial Accounting Standards,* constitute generally accepted accounting principles and are followed by virtually all large businesses in the United States. The work of the FASB will be cited throughout this text; at this point simply understand the FASB's existence and basic function.

Limitations of Accounting Information

Accounting information contains several inherent limitations. Because accounting involves the computation of dollar amounts, many people assume a great degree of precision in financial reports. As you progress through the study of accounting, you will see that numerous estimates, assumptions, and subjective judgments are required in the reporting of business activity. Further, the accountant must frequently select from among various acceptable accounting practices when determining how well an organization has performed over a period of time. Collectively,

---

[2] Even though standardization is suggested here, businesses are given some leeway in the selection of accounting practices. This fact will become apparent in later chapters.

these factors contribute to a general lack of "exactness" in the financial information disclosed by a business enterprise.

Another limitation associated with accounting information is that certain events are not conducive to monetary measurement. For example, the loss of a key manager and low employee morale often have undesirable consequences for a firm; however, placing a dollar value on these items is extremely difficult. How is an organization's profit affected, for instance, if a sales manager suddenly resigns in favor of a new position with a strong competitor? Accountants are unable to express an event such as this in economic terms and therefore use the **monetary unit assumption** when assessing performance. This assumption holds that only events and activities measurable in dollars are entered and recognized in a company's records.

A further limitation of accounting information is the fact that the measures employed do not necessarily portray true value. As we will see shortly, accounting measures are often based on cost rather than on current worth.

The preceding criticisms should not be interpreted as an indictment of accounting. Logical explanations underlie the need for these restricting factors. In addition, the accounting profession has prescribed certain standards that partially offset the limitations' negative impact. The accountant, for example, often prepares a narrative discussion describing certain nonfinancial events that have a significant bearing on the business organization. Furthermore, the profession is continually reevaluating its position to determine if changes in practices would improve the relevancy and reliability of a firm's information disclosures.

The Accountant: A Glorified Bookkeeper?

Many people tend to confuse bookkeeping with accounting. They often express the opinion that these two occupations are identical, or that the accountant is nothing more than a glorified bookkeeper. Both of these notions are incorrect.

Bookkeeping is concerned with record keeping and is composed of numerous mechanical tasks. Accountants may become involved with this type of work at times, but usually their duties are more complex and sophisticated. Accounting focuses primarily on the *use and interpretation* of information as opposed to repetitive data accumulation. In other words, the bookkeeper assists the accountant in generating the figures needed for reporting and analysis.

The profession of accounting can be traced back many centuries and has had considerable time for growth and development. Accounting and its financial and managerial reporting functions have matured considerably in response to a changing, dynamic business environment.

With this maturity comes an opportunity for well-paid and challenging careers—careers that have blossomed in the last decade for sharp, dedicated individuals. To better understand these career opportunities, a brief overview of the profession's various facets is helpful. (See Exhibit 1-2 for an accompanying pictorial presentation.)

THE ACCOUNTING PROFESSION

OBJECTIVE
2

Describe the accounting profession and identify accounting-related careers.

Using a computer to improve
efficiency . . .

Helping a small business with an
inventory problem . . .

Attending a professional development class . . .

Learning about the operation of a
hospital pharmacy . . .

Advising a client on financial
matters . . .

Explaining the features of newly
installed, automated machinery . . .

EXHIBIT 1-2
A Day in the Life of an
Accountant

Public Accounting

Firms engaged in **public accounting** render accounting services to all types
of enterprises (e.g., hotels, publishers, equipment manufacturers, and professional sports clubs). In view of the size and multiple locations of many
of their clients, several public accounting firms have offices from coast to
coast and in foreign countries. Others operate on a much smaller scale and
are established on a regional or local basis.

All of these firms, regardless of scope, employ certified public accountants (CPAs). **CPAs** are individuals who, like physicians, dentists, and
lawyers, are licensed to practice their profession. The CPA certificate is
granted to those who pass a rigorous multipart examination and meet
certain accounting experience and educational requirements.

Public accounting firms perform numerous services for their clients.

Most often their work is in the fields of auditing, income tax, and management advisory services (MAS).

Auditing

Audit work represents the major source of business for most public accounting firms, particularly those organized on the national or international level. **Auditing** involves the investigation and examination of the transactions that underlie an organization's financial reports. The investigation is conducted by an auditor, who studies the controls that have been built into a client's information-processing system for purposes of error detection and fraud prevention. In addition, the auditor performs statistical tests on accounting data to verify the data's reasonableness.

A major purpose of the audit process is to increase the credibility of the financial statements (reports) prepared by a business. The statements are sent to the owners of the business, to financial analysts, and frequently to government agencies. These parties are very much concerned that the reports result in a neutral and complete presentation of the enterprise's financial activities. The employment of an *external independent* auditor, who performs certain investigative tasks, enhances this process.

Income Tax

Public accounting firms also perform **income tax services.** These services are somewhat specialized and include much more than the preparation and filing of tax returns. In fact, many of the mechanical procedures associated with tax returns have been computerized, thus eliminating considerable drudgery for the accountant.

Tax accountants must be well versed in the many and often confusing tax laws. Not only do they determine the amount of taxes owed to federal, state, and local authorities, but tax accountants also ensure compliance with tax laws and plan for the future. They advise clients on various alternatives that might minimize taxes. The suggested courses of action are within the legal boundaries of the tax statutes and therefore center on techniques of tax avoidance, not tax evasion.

Management Advisory Services

Management advisory services (MAS) are the broadest of the services performed by public accounting firms. MAS essentially involve the operation of a management consulting practice for clients. Often the work is only indirectly related to traditional accounting matters, leading some of the larger firms to hire nonaccounting specialists for selected practice areas. Examples include physicians (if a firm has extensive involvement with hospitals), educators (if the firm does considerable work in university administration), computer experts, and engineers.

Listing all the advisory services performed by accountants is an impossible task. However, the following projects seem fairly representative: inventory control, analysis and design of information-processing systems, implementation of production-scheduling systems, cost analysis of lease-versus-buy alternatives, and assistance in product pricing.

Private Accounting

Private accounting, sometimes referred to as industrial accounting, is another major branch of the profession. Rather than perform accounting services for many different clients, a private accountant is employed by an individual business to render services exclusively for that organization. As you can imagine, there is considerable variety within this field. Typical opportunities for employment include jobs with retailers, manufacturers (in such diverse industries as petroleum and filmmaking), and service enterprises (such as airlines, lending institutions, and ski resorts).

There are several other significant distinctions between public and private accounting. For instance, there is no specific licensing procedure for private accountants. (The only accounting "license" is the CPA.) Various programs have been designed, however, to measure competence in the private field. One of the most prominent is the *Certified Management Accountant (CMA)* program, which requires candidates to pass a broad two-day examination. This test covers such disciplines as managerial finance and economics, principles of organizational behavior, business ethics, financial and managerial accounting practices, and quantitative methods. Another program has been designed to measure proficiency in internal auditing. Individuals who pass an examination and meet certain work experience requirements may receive the *Certified Internal Auditor (CIA)* designation.

Much of the work performed in the private field can be subdivided into specialized areas, including the following.

Cost Accounting

Cost accounting, an important facet of managerial accounting, deals with the collection, assignment, and interpretation of costs. Cost data are captured by an organization's information system and then assigned to various business segments and activities. Examples of such segments include territories, departments, and products. Activities, on the other hand, may encompass the design of a new advertising campaign, the operation of a summer recreation program by a city, or the implementation of a new all-day ticket plan by an amusement park. The purpose of the assignment process is to answer the age-old question, "How much does it cost?" Once cost is determined, management can proceed with an analysis of:

- Anticipated costs for various planning needs.
- Budgeted versus actual costs for control and evaluation.
- Relevant costs of different alternatives for use in decision making.
- Costs of producing goods and services for use in pricing and inventory valuation.

Internal Auditing

Large organizations often have their own personnel to review and monitor established accounting procedures and controls. The review process, which determines whether the procedures and controls are functioning as originally intended, helps to (1) safeguard the company's resources and (2) check the reliability and accuracy of the accounting information being produced. The individuals performing this work are known as **internal**

auditors. Although their duties and responsibilities are similar to those of auditors employed in public accounting (i.e., external auditors), the internal-audit orientation is somewhat different. The internal auditor focuses mainly on controls and procedures. The independent external auditor, while also investigating accounting controls, is concerned primarily with the fairness of the financial statements that are prepared by a business.

Other Activities

Depending on size, many companies engage in accounting activities other than cost accounting and internal auditing. Larger businesses maintain separate *systems departments* to design the methods, procedures, and forms needed to process accounting data. Frequently, computers are involved. In addition, many organizations have established *planning departments* that deal heavily with budgeting and forecasting. Finally, large businesses often operate their own *tax departments*. These departments offer in-house advice on various issues and engage in tax-planning activities.

Governmental/Not-for-Profit Accounting

The last major segment of the profession is composed of those accountants employed by governmental agencies and other not-for-profit organizations. Like any business, the government has numerous financial and managerial accounting needs that must be satisfied. Records must be kept, reports prepared, monies accounted for, and operations controlled and reviewed. Governmental accountants assist in all of these tasks—at the local, state, and federal levels. Accountants are employed by the Federal Bureau of Investigation to gather evidence for use in fraud cases; by state regulatory agencies to review rate increase requests of public utility companies; and by the Internal Revenue Service to examine the millions of tax returns that are filed each year. The General Accounting Office (GAO) also employs accountants to assist in its evaluations of governmental programs and agencies. The GAO's work is extremely diverse, with recent efforts including an investigation of NASA's space shuttle program and a look at the effects of competition on airfares.

Not-for-profit enterprises other than the government also have a need for accountants. Hospitals, universities, and charitable organizations require budgets and controls. In addition, selected data must be computed for use in fund raising, and an evaluation must be made to determine whether resources are being used in an efficient and effective manner. The accountant is in an excellent position to perform these tasks and help the not-for-profit organization further its role in society.

KEY UNDERLYING CONCEPTS

Earlier in the text we noted that accounting is supported by a set of underlying principles and concepts. These concepts are presented throughout the text, with an in-depth discussion contained in Chapter 13. At this particular time it is helpful to introduce the entity assumption and the

OBJECTIVE

Explain the use of accounting principles in financial reporting.

principles of historical cost and objectivity. We will then expand our discussion to focus on an entity's "financial position" and its relevance to the fundamental accounting equation. In short, the following sections provide an introduction to the manner in which accounting measures financial activity.

Entity Assumption

The **entity assumption** holds that an organization must be viewed as a unit that is separate and apart from its owners and from other firms. If this assumption were not made, personal economic activities of the owners (e.g., the purchase of a home, the payment of a spouse's medical bill) would be merged with the transactions of their businesses, thus combining the affairs of two separate and distinct units. The resulting financial statements constructed to report the business's financial health and profitability, therefore, would not be meaningful.

The entity assumption also notes that a firm should be viewed aside and apart from other firms. Imagine the difficulty of performing a detailed analysis of the computer industry if the operations of IBM could not be distinguished from those of Apple. These are two separate units and their activities must be accounted for accordingly. The entity assumption thus requires the establishment of segregated accounting systems and individual sets of financial records for each business enterprise.

There are three popular entity forms in this country. The simplest in structure is the **sole proprietorship,** which is a business owned by one individual. A step above the proprietorship is the **partnership**—an organization owned by two or more individuals and managed according to a contractual agreement among them. The third basic form of entity is the **corporation,** in which the owners are its stockholders. Most enterprises are operated as proprietorships; accordingly, our initial discussions will focus on this widespread organizational form.

Historical-Cost Principle

Accounting is based on the **principle of historical cost.** This principle holds that purchases of goods, services, and other resources are initially entered in the accounting records at acquisition cost. For example, if Stadium Manufacturing pays $200,000 to purchase a parcel of land for use as a future plant site, the land is established in the records at $200,000. Further, if the company had financed the acquisition, not only would the land be set up at this amount, but the accounting records would also reveal a $200,000 bank loan (i.e., mortgage).

The use of historical cost, while beneficial in some respects, creates an interesting accounting problem. Entering a long-term resource in the accounting records at cost at the time of acquisition is satisfactory. Maintaining that resource over its lifetime at cost, however, can result in a severe misstatement of financial condition and profitability. Picture, for instance, what has happened to the real estate market in many parts of the country over the past 10 to 15 years. Prices have risen because of inflation and other factors; yet the historical-cost basis of accounting ignores these increases in valuation. As an example, suppose the land purchased for

$200,000 is now worth $350,000. The land, nevertheless, will continue to be carried and reported at $200,000. Because of this treatment, the cost basis is criticized by many users of financial reports as not being in accord with economic reality.

Accountants have taken various steps in recent years to help overcome this deficiency, including supplemental publication of selected inflation-adjusted data. Despite the problem with historical cost, it continues to serve as the primary valuation base in accounting. One of the underlying reasons is the objectivity principle.

Objectivity Principle

Accountants strive to produce financial reports that are unbiased, thereby reducing (or eliminating) various user interpretations that may arise. One way of achieving this goal is to follow the **objectivity principle,** which holds that accounting measurements be both definite and verifiable. Although subject to some criticism, historical cost is said to meet these twin criteria.

Consider, for instance, the parcel of land in our earlier example that Stadium Manufacturing acquired for $200,000. The parcel may have cost the seller $110,000 and, at the time of Stadium's acquisition, may have been assessed for property taxes at $150,000. Further, the land may have been appraised by three independent appraisal services at $180,000, $210,000, and $230,000 to determine its "worth" when negotiations were about to occur. Which of these figures is correct? They all are. The cost of $200,000 was entered in Stadium's accounting records, however, because Stadium and the seller negotiated a transaction, agreeing that the land was to be exchanged at a price of $200,000. The use of definite cost figures helps to make accounting reports and information more objective. Conversely, appraisal or market figures can vary and often incorporate personal opinion and bias.

In addition to being definite, historical cost is also verifiable by financial experts. In our discussion of the accounting profession, we noted that auditors examine the financial reports of an enterprise to determine whether the reports result in a fair presentation of economic activity. The use of objective, cost-based information lends itself to this process. Evidence of the cost of goods, services, and resources normally exists in the form of contracts, accounting documents, and canceled checks. Furthermore, objective cost data allow different accountants who may be examining a complex transaction to reach essentially the same conclusions and report the same facts. When subjective market and appraisal values are used, this outcome would probably not occur.

**FINANCIAL POSITION
AND THE ENTITY**

Let us begin our study of the entity (and proprietorships) by focusing on a popular accounting concept called financial position. An entity's **financial position** reveals the resources owned by the business and the claims on those resources by specified parties at a particular point in time. The specified parties are the firm's creditors and owner, resulting in the relationship shown in Exhibit 1-3.

HIGHLIGHT
What's It Worth, Anyway?

Historical cost and objectivity—two accounting principles with no practical benefit? Not quite. Consider the case of Kathleen Price, who is leaning w–a–a–y back to eyeball the building looming before her: a 13-story structure of granite and bronzed glass, with a waterfall and a hundred fountains out front.

Ms. Price is about to attempt a near-impossible feat: to determine the value of this vacant edifice. Built to house the defunct Sunbelt Savings Association, it is now just another bad Texas asset turned over to the government. "Well, you know what it's not worth," the real-estate appraiser ventures, after a pause. "It's not worth what it cost to build it."

Ms. Price's problem is caused by the mid-1980s' collapse of the state's oil-based economy and real-estate market, in conjunction with the crash of the U.S. savings and loan (S&L) industry. As the federal government has sought to dispose of the real-estate assets seized from insolvent savings institutions, it has relied on the appraisers to accurately gauge those properties' values.

The stakes of the sale are enormous. Even if the government gets top dollar prices for its holdings, the S&L bailout will cost taxpayers in excess of $160 billion—a figure that seems to grow with each passing day. If properties are priced too high to sell, the holding costs—for the period the government is stuck with the unsold properties—could add tens of billions of dollars to the tab. If they are sold too cheaply, another real-estate collapse could result, sending the cost of the bailout soaring and further crippling the southwestern economy. "We're talking on the order of a couple hundred billion dollars in real-estate assets . . . so a difference of just 10% in price means big money," says a finance professor at the University of Houston.

So what's a property really worth? Appraisers rely heavily on sales of comparable properties to fix values, an expert explains. But there isn't much to go on in Texas, where there haven't been many "non-distressed" sales of late. The problem is particularly acute when it comes to raw land. In many of the state's markets, there hasn't been a single sale of undeveloped property for three or four years, and demand may not rebound for many years. So to price a parcel now, appraisers have to guess what the state's economy will look like years hence, a near-impossible task.

All the uncertainty in the market (and some problems within the appraisal profession) are leading to widely varying valuations of properties. For example, a Houston S&L executive recently complained about an apartment building his institution owned that was valued at $6.4 million by one appraiser and just $2.2 million by another. "So what am I supposed to do, split the difference?" he asked in frustration.

In another case, consider a 17-story hotel that the Federal Deposit Insurance Corporation (FDIC) had inherited near Texas A&M University. An initial appraisal declared the property was worth $7.6 million. By spending just $500,000 more to finish five additional floors under construction, the appraiser thought the new owners could sell the structure for $10 million. But four other appraisers fixed the value at no more than $1.7 million.

No sooner did the FDIC decide it would be fortunate to get the lower price than a California developer, eager to convert the building to a dormitory, snapped up the property for $3.6 million. A government official says he is happy about the higher offer. But he is concerned about what the experience says about the appraisal process. "We had four appraisals right on target, then we got a higher price," he groans. "It still bothers me" . . . and the accounting profession as well.

Source: Adapted from "Appraisers, Culprits in S&L Crisis, Are Now Key to S&L Recovery," *The Wall Street Journal,* January 24, 1990, p. 1. Reprinted by permission of *The Wall Street Journal,* © Dow Jones & Company, Inc., 1990. All rights reserved worldwide.

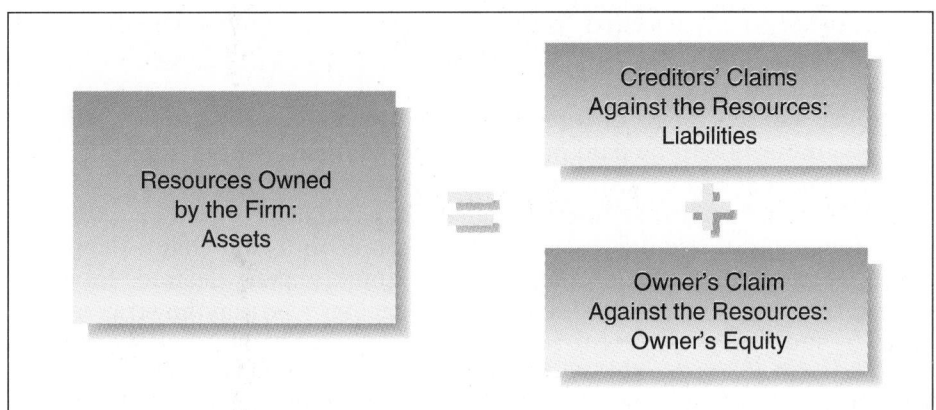

EXHIBIT 1-3
Financial Position

OBJECTIVE

4

Define assets, liabilities, and owner's equity, and state the relationship of these components in the accounting equation.

We will now expand on this relationship which, in its shortened form, is commonly referred to as the fundamental **accounting equation.** The shortened form is:

Assets = Liabilities + Owner's Equity

Assets

Assets are the economic resources owned by a company that are expected to benefit future time periods. These resources are controlled by the entity and have arisen from past transactions and events.

An organization can possess many different types of assets. Some assets, such as the cash that a business has on hand and in the bank, inventories of goods maintained for sale, buildings, land, and equipment, have a definite physical existence. In contrast, other business resources lack physical substance but are able to render benefits because they represent valuable legal rights and/or claims. Two examples are patents and receivables.

A patent, which is granted by the federal government, gives its owner the exclusive right to manufacture, use, and sell a particular product or process. Receivables, on the other hand, are the amounts that a business expects to collect on some future date. The most commonly encountered receivable, *accounts receivable,* represents the amounts due a company from its customers. This asset generally arises from the sale, on credit, of goods and services.

Liabilities

The economic obligations of an entity are known as **liabilities.** Such obligations are owed to creditors and, like assets, are created from a variety of past transactions and events. Consider, for instance, that many businesses buy goods and services on credit, with the amounts owed to be paid on a future date. These transactions give rise to a liability known as *accounts payable.* In addition, an entity may borrow funds via a loan (thereby creating a loan payable) and use the funds to acquire equipment, expand a warehouse, or purchase other assets.

Still other liabilities arise when a company has obligated itself to pay certain costs connected with normal business activities. Suppose, for example, that on December 31, the Hernandez Company owes $2,000 of employee salaries, $500 of interest, and $300 for payroll taxes. Assuming that all amounts will be paid on some future date, the company's accounting records at the end of the year would reveal liabilities entitled salaries payable, interest payable, and payroll taxes payable.

Businesses that use credit too liberally sometimes find that a liability's future settlement date approaches more quickly than desired. In other words, the obligation comes due, but the paying firm may be strapped for cash. In such cases the creditors, because they have a legal claim against the firm, can force the sale of business assets to satisfy the amounts due. As shown on page 13, it should now be clear that liabilities represent creditor claims against an entity's resources.

Owner's Equity

Owner's equity, or capital, represents the owner's stake or "interest" in the assets of a business. It is equal to the company's net assets (i.e., assets minus liabilities).

The concept of owner's equity is best explained by resetting the accounting equation in the following format:

$$\text{Assets} - \text{Liabilities} = \text{Owner's Equity}$$

Now, assume that Colorado Enterprises has assets of $50,000 and liabilities of $30,000, resulting in $20,000 ($50,000 − $30,000) of owner's equity. These figures indicate that the firm has resources that amount to $50,000 and creditor claims against those resources of $30,000. As noted earlier, should Colorado experience financial difficulties and be unable to settle its obligations, the creditors can force the sale of business assets. Law dictates that distributions be made first to the creditors, with any remaining amounts going to the owner. The owner, then, is said to have a $20,000 *residual* interest in the assets of the entity.

Tips & Techniques

Owner's equity is the mathematical difference between total assets and total liabilities, nothing more, nothing less. Many people are under the impression that equity is equivalent to cash, to be used for future spending and acquisitions. This notion is incorrect; there is *no* direct relationship between this amount and a company's cash balances.

A CLOSER LOOK AT OWNER'S EQUITY

The three components of the accounting equation—assets, liabilities, and owner's equity—change throughout the year in response to various transactions and events. To illustrate, assume the following data apply to Mansfield Builders as of December 31, 19X1:

Assets	$100,000
Liabilities	$ 30,000
Owner's equity	70,000
Total liabilities & owner's equity	$100,000

Suppose that Mansfield desires to purchase a new machine that costs $25,000. Because of insufficient cash balances, the company has arranged to finance the purchase by obtaining a $25,000 loan from the equipment dealer. This transaction results in the following figures.

Assets ($100,000 + $25,000)	$125,000
Liabilities ($30,000 + $25,000)	$ 55,000
Owner's equity	70,000
Total liabilities & owner's equity	$125,000

Assets have increased because of the machine, while liabilities have risen from the loan. It is important to notice that owner's equity has remained at $70,000. We can conclude that any transaction or event that affects both assets *and* liabilities by an equal amount has no impact on owner's equity. Similarly, a transaction that affects *only* assets (such as an acquisition of machinery for a cash payment) or *only* liabilities will leave owner's equity intact. What, then, causes this third component of the accounting equation to rise or fall?

Owner's equity will change during a time period because of four factors:

Factor	Impact on Owner's Equity
Investments by the owner	Increase
Withdrawals by the owner	Decrease
Revenues	Increase
Expenses	Decrease

OBJECTIVE

5

Identify the four items that cause owner's equity to change: owner investments, owner withdrawals, revenues, and expenses.

Investments by the Owner

The owner of an enterprise often takes personal assets and puts (invests) them in a business. Since the investment causes company assets to increase, the owner's net "interest" or equity in these assets will also increase.

Withdrawals by the Owner

A withdrawal is just the opposite of an investment; the owner is removing assets from the business (usually cash) for personal use. Withdrawals therefore decrease the equity of the owner in the firm's assets.

Revenues

Businesses pursue a variety of activities in an attempt to earn a profit. Such profit-related activities give rise to **revenues,** which are the amounts charged to customers for goods sold or services rendered. These amounts cause owner's equity to increase and, as the following list shows, may take many different forms.

Entity	Revenue Form
Toys "R" Us, Inc.	Toy sales revenue
Ryder System, Inc.	Vehicle-leasing revenue
Los Angeles Dodgers	Ticket revenue
Law firm	Fees earned

Expenses

Expenses are the costs of items and services consumed in producing revenue. Examples of expenses include the salaries and wages incurred for employee compensation, utility costs related to the use of natural gas and electricity, advertising, repairs, taxes, and interest costs on loans. Expenses, which cause owner's equity to decline, are logically called the costs of doing business—that is, the costs that arise from attracting and keeping clientele.

A careful study of the preceding examples reveals the absence of owner withdrawals. Expenses *must* be related to the revenue-generating process of the firm. Withdrawals, in contrast, arise from a totally different situation (i.e., the personal use of business assets by the owner).

Tips & Techniques

Revenues and expenses should not be equated with the cash inflows and outflows of a firm. Consider, for instance, that a company may receive cash from its owner as an investment or pay cash to acquire land (an asset). Both of these transactions affect cash; in neither case, however, is any revenue or expense involved.

Net Income/Net Loss

The revenues and expenses of a business are periodically compared to measure operating success or failure. Revenues in excess of expenses give rise to **net income.** When an individual states that a company is "making (earning) money," he or she normally means that a net income is being generated.

Companies do not always operate in a profitable manner, perhaps because of a lack of cost control or a depressed economy. Operating in an unprofitable manner means that expenses exceed revenues, creating a **net loss.**

THE ACCOUNTING EQUATION: AN EXTENDED ILLUSTRATION

To tie together a number of the concepts introduced in this chapter, we will focus on the operations of Vista Transit. Vista, a small proprietorship that provides charter transportation in the town of Oceanside, was founded on January 2 of the current year. The following sections describe the firm's January transactions and show their effect on the accounting equation.

Investment by the Owner—Ted Barto began the operation of Vista Transit on January 2 by investing $40,000 in the firm. As a result of this transaction, the company now has an asset, Cash, of $40,000. In addition, Barto has obtained a $40,000 interest (i.e., owner's equity) in the firm's assets. The items that affect owner's equity are listed individually beneath the column heading for clarity.

> **OBJECTIVE**
> **6**
> Describe the impact of various transactions on the accounting equation.

Date	Assets — Cash	= Liabilities +	Owner's Equity (+) Investments (−) Withdrawals	(+) Revenues (−) Expenses
1/2	+$40,000		+$40,000	

Purchase of Assets for Cash—Vista acquired two used vans for the business at a total cost of $34,000 on January 6. The company paid cash, thereby decreasing its remaining funds to $6,000 ($40,000 − $34,000). Notice, however, that this transaction merely shifts dollar amounts from one asset to another, leaving the total assets intact at $40,000.

Date	Assets — Cash	Vans	= Liabilities +	Owner's Equity (+) Investments (−) Withdrawals	(+) Revenues (−) Expenses
	$40,000	$ —		$40,000	
1/6	−34,000	+34,000			
	$ 6,000	$34,000		$40,000	
	$40,000			$40,000	

Generation of Revenue on Account—The firm completed two charter trips on January 12 and billed clients a total of $1,700. This transaction is representative of Vista's earnings process, causing an increase in total revenue (and owner's equity) for the entity. Furthermore, the clients have been billed and will pay at a later date. An asset, Accounts Receivable, has therefore been created because Vista has a claim against these individuals. This type of transaction is commonly known as a sale of services on account.

Date	Assets — Cash	Accounts Receivable	Vans	= Liabilities +	Owner's Equity (+) Investments (−) Withdrawals	(+) Revenues (−) Expenses
	$6,000	$ —	$34,000		$40,000	$ —
1/12		+1,700				+1,700 (Charter revenue)
	$6,000	$1,700	$34,000		$40,000	$1,700
		$41,700			$41,700	

Note: Assets are normally listed in the following order: cash, near-cash assets (e.g., receivables), and long-term resources (such as the vans). Typically, items that fall in the long-term category are sequenced in descending order of their productive lives—land first, then buildings, equipment, and so forth.

Recognition of Expense on Account—Westside Auto performed miscellaneous repairs on one of the vans on January 16. The repairs amounted to $750; Vista agreed to pay the balance due in 30 days. This transaction involves an increase in Vista's liabilities (Accounts Payable) because of the balance owed to the repair shop. In addition, $750 of expense must be recognized, which reduces owner's equity.

	Assets			= Liabilities	+	Owner's Equity	
Date	Cash	Accounts Receivable	Vans	Accounts Payable	(+) Investments (−) Withdrawals	(+) Revenues (−) Expenses	
1/16	$6,000	$1,700	$34,000	$ — +750	$40,000	$1,700 −750 (Repairs)	
	$6,000	$1,700	$34,000	$750	$40,000	$ 950	
		$41,700				$41,700	

Collection of Accounts Receivable—A $600 check from a client who was previously billed on January 12 arrived in the mail of January 21. Is this revenue for Vista? The answer is no. Vista performed the service earlier in the month, and revenue was recorded at the time the billing took place. To record the $600 again as revenue would result in a double counting. The client is paying the balance due, requiring a reduction in Accounts Receivable. This type of transaction is frequently referred to as a receipt on account.

	Assets			= Liabilities	+	Owner's Equity	
Date	Cash	Accounts Receivable	Vans	Accounts Payable	(+) Investments (−) Withdrawals	(+) Revenues (−) Expenses	
1/21	$6,000 +600	$1,700 −600	$34,000	$750	$40,000	$950	
	$6,600	$1,100	$34,000	$750	$40,000	$950	
		$41,700				$41,700	

Payment of Accounts Payable—Vista paid $400 to Westside Auto on January 27, partial payment for the repairs performed on January 16. The repairs were initially established as a liability, to be paid on a future date. Because payment is now occurring, the related account payable must be reduced. Transactions of this nature are commonly known as payments on account.

	Assets			= Liabilities	+	Owner's Equity	
Date	Cash	Accounts Receivable	Vans	Accounts Payable	(+) Investments (−) Withdrawals	(+) Revenues (−) Expenses	
1/27	$6,600 −400	$1,100	$34,000	$750 −400	$40,000	$950	
	$6,200	$1,100	$34,000	$350	$40,000	$950	
		$41,300				$41,300	

Payment of Expenses—On January 29, Vista paid $500 to its drivers, subdivided as follows: John Warren, $300; Ben Richards, $200. Each driver earned $200 of wages during the month. Warren received an extra $100 to cover the cost of advertising materials that he designed and distributed to Oceanside residents. The wage and advertising expenditures are expenses for Vista—costs incurred to generate revenue.

Date	Assets			= Liabilities +	Owner's Equity	
	Cash	Accounts Receivable	Vans	Accounts Payable	(+) Investments (−) Withdrawals	(+) Revenues (−) Expenses
1/29	$6,200 −300	$1,100	$34,000	$350	$40,000	$950 −200 (Wages) −100 (Advertising)
	−200					−200 (Wages)
	$5,700	$1,100	$34,000	$350	$40,000	$450
	$40,800				$40,800	

Sale of an Asset—Because of the entry of a new competitor in the Oceanside market, Vista decided to sell one of its vans on January 30. The van, acquired on January 6 for $14,000, was sold to a charter client for the same amount. The client paid Vista $10,000 down, with the balance owed to be remitted in two weeks. This transaction affects three different assets, calling for an increase to both Cash and Accounts Receivable and a decrease to Vans.

Date	Assets			= Liabilities +	Owner's Equity	
	Cash	Accounts Receivable	Vans	Accounts Payable	(+) Investments (−) Withdrawals	(+) Revenues (−) Expenses
1/30	$ 5,700 +10,000	$1,100 +4,000	$34,000 −14,000	$350	$40,000	$450
	$15,700	$5,100	$20,000	$350	$40,000	$450
	$40,800				$40,800	

Withdrawal by the Owner—Ted Barto withdrew $250 from the company on January 31 to meet personal living expenses. This $250 outlay results in a reduction of both Cash and owner's equity.

Date	Assets			= Liabilities +	Owner's Equity	
	Cash	Accounts Receivable	Vans	Accounts Payable	(+) Investments (−) Withdrawals	(+) Revenues (−) Expenses
1/31	$15,700 −250	$5,100	$20,000	$350	$40,000 −250	$450
	$15,450	$5,100	$20,000	$350	$39,750	$450
	$40,550				$40,550	

Tips & Techniques

As you have seen, business transactions affect the accounting equation in many different ways. Assets, liabilities, and owner's equity can each remain the same or change; there are numerous possibilities. Stated bluntly (and honestly), if your approach to learning this and subsequent material is memorization, you will be fighting a losing battle. *Successful accounting students are those who develop the abilities to reason and analyze, not memorize.*

FINANCIAL STATEMENTS

OBJECTIVE 7

Understand the content of and prepare an income statement, a statement of owner's equity, and a balance sheet.

Owners, managers, lenders, and analysts use accounting information for a variety of purposes. Much of this information is contained within formal financial reports that are prepared and distributed by companies. These reports are commonly referred to as **financial statements.**

The financial statements prepared by a business reveal various insights about the entity's operations and financial position, with one of the most important disclosures being net income. Most businesses are organized with a profit objective and strive to generate a return for their owners. Income measurement is a complex task; at this point you should understand that income is probably the single most important barometer of economic success and of utmost interest to financial statement users.

In addition to profit generation, companies seek to maintain a healthy financial position. This means that an entity has the ability to pay its debts when due, along with the potential of generating future positive cash flows. Statement users therefore pay close attention to a firm's cash and near-cash assets (i.e., liquidity) in relation to the amounts owed to creditors. Put simply, if a company is unable to meet its maturing obligations, the firm's survival as an ongoing entity could be threatened.

An entity's financial information is disclosed via four financial statements (and accompanying footnotes): the income statement, statement of owner's equity, balance sheet, and statement of cash flows. Discussion of the last statement, which shows the cash flows related to a company's operating, investing, and financing activities, is postponed until Chapter 19 because of its complex nature.

Income Statement

The **income statement** summarizes the results of operations by disclosing an entity's net income or net loss. This statement, like its counterparts, is divided into two sections: heading and body. The heading reveals the company's name, the name of the statement, and the period of time covered by the statement. The period is usually a month, a quarter, or a year. The statement's body contains detailed accounting information, in this case an itemized listing of revenues and expenses.

The income statement for Vista Transit appears on the top of Exhibit 1-4. Observe how the statement is developed from the right-most column of the extended illustration (pp. 17–19). Because revenues exceeded expenses, the business was profitable during its first month of activity.

EXHIBIT 1-4
Financial Statements of Vista
Transit

VISTA TRANSIT
Income Statement
For the Month Ended January 31, 19XX

Charter revenue		$ 1,700
Less expenses		
Repairs	$ 750	
Wages	400	
Advertising	100	
Total expenses		1,250
Net income		$ 450

VISTA TRANSIT
Statement of Owner's Equity
For the Month Ended January 31, 19XX

Beginning balance, Jan. 1		$ —
Increases		
Owner investments	$40,000	
Net income	450	40,450
		$40,450
Decreases		
Owner withdrawals		250
Ending balance, Jan. 31		$40,200

VISTA TRANSIT
Balance Sheet
January 31, 19XX

Assets		
Cash		$15,450
Accounts receivable		5,100
Vans		20,000
Total assets		$40,550
Liabilities		
Accounts payable		$ 350
Owner's equity		
Ted Barto, capital		40,200
Total liabilities & owner's equity		$40,550

complete listing of companys. assets, liabilities and owners equity at a certain time

Statement of Owner's Equity

The **statement of owner's equity** discloses the causes of change in owner's equity during the accounting period. Owner investments, owner withdrawals, and net income/loss—the last item being a "summary" of the entity's revenues and expenses—therefore comprise the heart of this financial report. Vista's statement of owner's equity appears in the middle of Exhibit 1-4. The January 31 balance of $40,200 will carry over to become the beginning owner's equity balance on February 1, 19XX.

Balance Sheet

The **balance sheet** focuses on a measure that was introduced earlier in the chapter. By revealing the resources owned by the entity and the claims on those resources by the creditors and owner of the business, the statement's emphasis is on financial position. Appropriately, the balance sheet is sometimes called the statement of financial position.

To become more specific, the balance sheet is a formalized listing of the accounting equation's components: assets, liabilities, and owner's equity. This financial report shows that the sum of the individual equity interests, the owner's and creditors', is equal to and in balance with the firm's assets; that is, assets = liabilities + owner's equity. This equality is shown for some particular *point* in time. The statement's heading therefore reflects a single date rather than a time period.

The balance sheet of Vista Transit, which appears at the bottom of Exhibit 1-4, is based on the January 31 final balances of the accounting equation illustration, with one minor exception. So that the information already contained in the income statement and statement of owner's equity is not duplicated, the January 31 (ending) owner's equity balance is reported as a single amount labeled Ted Barto, Capital.

Statement Interrelationships

The three statements that we discussed are distinct, with each presenting different types of financial information. Although they do differ, the statements are also interrelated. The income statement furnishes the necessary net income figure for the statement of owner's equity, which, in turn, provides the ending capital amount for the balance sheet.

The statements are also interrelated in another sense. The balance sheet depicts a company's financial position as of a specific date, for example, January 31 in the Vista Transit illustration. Going one step further, the company would subsequently prepare an income statement and a statement of owner's equity for February to disclose monthly activity. To complete the reporting cycle, a new balance sheet would be constructed as of February 28. It is apparent, then, that the income statement and the statement of owner's equity bridge the gap between successive balance sheets when reporting financial information.

Ethics and Reporting

Preparation of the financial statements just discussed (as well as other financial reports) requires that competent professionals exercise due care. Competence and due care are not sufficient, however, to ensure complete integrity of a company's reporting function. For example, transactions may be purposefully manipulated and records falsified to achieve personal gain. Bear in mind that when bonuses, promotions, and jobs are at stake, employees will occasionally take desperate actions to improve reported income and/or financial position.

Because of the reliance placed on financial figures, it is mandatory that employees and management maintain high ethical standards when involved with reporting activities. Such standards help to avoid the construction of misleading (i.e., fraudulent) financial statements. Businesses in general and the accounting profession in particular have worked hard in recent years to develop ethical codes of conduct. An overview of their endeavors follows in the appendix to this chapter.

ETHICS ISSUE

Should an accountant accept a financial-reporting assignment that requires skills beyond his or her present level of expertise?

APPENDIX: ETHICS AND THE ACCOUNTANT

Not too long ago, a survey was conducted of the 500 largest corporations in a five-state region.[3] The topic was **ethics:** a broad set of moral principles that groups adopt as behavior standards. The survey involved a mail questionnaire, which was completed by the firms' chief executive officers or by other senior managers. The findings were eye-opening, with a significant number of the business leaders reporting concerns. Consider that:

Thirty percent said they had inherited problems from a predecessor who was "too lenient, allowing questionable practices to become part of doing business."

Thirteen percent said they had "high concern" that employees who have access to confidential information might be misusing that information.

Nine percent were at least somewhat concerned that *directors* of their corporate boards might be profiting from inside information.

Without a doubt, ethics has become an extremely hot topic. A day rarely goes by without the media reporting that companies and employees have engaged in some type of marginal behavior—doing things that they clearly should have avoided. In an effort to address these problems, a number of businesses have implemented ethics policies. The questionnaire just cited found that 76% of the surveyed companies had done so. Further, the respondents reported that various steps had been taken to inform employees about the companies' standards.

A Case Study

An example of an ethics policy is that implemented by General Dynamics, an engineering-based manufacturer that does considerable work for the military and government.[4] The firm's program has three goals: to support individual employees in their daily business conduct; to enhance the administrative performance of the company in basic business relationships; and to build a bond of trust between the company and its customers,

---

[3] "Southwest Firms Concerned About Ethics, Survey Finds," *The Dallas Morning News,* October 10, 1989, pp. 5D, 6D.

[4] See *General Dynamics Standards of Business Ethics and Conduct, Second Edition;* and *The General Dynamics Ethics Program Update.* Both of these sources are published by General Dynamics Corporation, Falls Church, Virginia, Copyright 1988.

suppliers, employees, shareholders, and the communities in which it functions.

General Dynamics has established a series of broad-reaching standards to achieve these goals. Several of the standards follow.

- *Gifts, gratuities, and entertainment to customers*—It is a serious violation of standards for any employee to seek a competitive advantage through the use of gifts, gratuities, entertainment, or other favors. (An exception may apply in some foreign countries, where custom requires the exchange of gifts.)
- *Inside information*—Employees may not use or share inside information that is not otherwise available to the general public for any type of personal gain (e.g., trading in the stock of General Dynamics or other firms).
- *Time card reporting*—Prompt and accurate completion of time cards is essential. A cost must not be allocated to a government contract if it (the cost) is unallowable, contrary to the contract or related regulations, or otherwise improper.
- *Quality and testing*—All inspection and testing documentation that relate to design and manufacturing activities must be complete, accurate, and truthful.
- *Expense reports*—Business expenses must be properly and promptly disclosed on expense reports. Further, employees must distinguish between personal expenses, and travel and conference expenses that pertain to business activity.
- *Cash and bank accounts*—All transactions that involve cash and bank accounts must be handled in such a way as to avoid any questions of bribery, kickbacks, and any other types of illegal or improper payments.

Ethical Challenges for the Accountant

Accountants, through certain professional organizations, have developed ethical standards that pertain to financial record keeping and reporting. For example, all accountants should be objective, maintain a high degree of integrity, and not knowingly misrepresent facts to others. In addition, acts should not be committed that reflect poorly on the profession.

As discussed in the body of this chapter, accountants may be employed in such diverse areas as public accounting, industry, and government. Those involved in public practice are faced with the further ethical issue of independence. Independence requires that the accountant be free from the influence of others when performing his or her duties. Such independence, which helps to protect the public interest, must be maintained in both fact and appearance. Certain activities that may impair independence would include an accountant having a financial interest in a company for which he or she provides services; an accountant having a relative in a high-level management position with a client organization; and an accountant serving as trustee of a client organization.

Ethics also affect the managerial accountant, who faces the challenge of balancing a commitment to a particular employer with the ethical rules of the profession. As an employee, the managerial accountant has a direct financial interest in a company as the source of his or her well-being (e.g., salary, fringe benefit plans, and so forth). Consider the difficulty that would arise for the accountant when, in complying with ethical standards of the profession, the financial security of the company is endangered. This situation could occur if the accountant discloses that the employer-firm is in violation of the terms of a major loan agreement (such as the maintenance of certain financial ratios). The loan's due date could be accelerated, forcing the company to settle any outstanding balances immediately. For many businesses this action would lead to bankruptcy (and eventual unemployment for the "whistle-blower").

A Concluding Comment

Ethics is big news in the business world, with many companies and professions having established ethics programs. Unfortunately, though, such programs do little to change individuals who deliberately engage in misconduct. As far as accounting is concerned, the profession has taken steps to set ethical guidelines for its members. However, the practice of accounting is not always black and white, and no set of standards can ensure the ethical behavior of all participants. Each accountant must therefore overcome the pressures to which he or she is subject and practice the profession in an objective, moral, and dignified manner.

Who's the Most Ethical?

A nationwide survey of business people ranked the corporate ethics of various professions or occupations in the following order:

1 Accountants	9 TV repairmen
2 Dentists	10 Realtors
3 Doctors	11 Newspaper reporters
4 Officers of large corporations	12 Stockbrokers
5 Public relations practitioners	13 Union leaders
6 Lawyers	14 Politicians
7 Funeral home operators	15 TV evangelists
8 Advertising practitioners	16 Used car salesmen

Source: "Ethics Survey Ranks Accountants First," *Journal of Accountancy,* October 1989, p. 110.

END-OF-CHAPTER REVIEW

---

1 **List the users, uses, and limitations of accounting information.** Many groups use accounting information, including owners, creditors, managers, government agencies, financial analysts, and employees and labor unions. These groups study a company's earnings, the ability of an organization to settle its debts on a timely basis, the progress of a business toward meeting stated objectives, and other key issues. The information under review, however, suffers from certain inherent limi-

LEARNING OBJECTIVES: THE KEY POINTS

tations. Accounting, for example, is based on various estimates, assumptions, and subjective judgments; lacks the ability to express all events in monetary terms; and sometimes fails to portray true value.

2 Describe the accounting profession and identify accounting-related careers. The profession and its career options tend to be segmented into public, private, and governmental/not-for-profit accounting. Public accountants render accounting services, such as external auditing, tax planning, and management consulting, to other businesses. In private accounting, an individual provides accounting services for a specific organization, with the work often centering on cost accounting or internal auditing. Finally, individuals employed by not-for-profit organizations typically work for the government, hospitals, universities, and charitable institutions.

3 Explain the use of accounting principles in financial reporting. Because of the wide variety of businesses in our economy, some standardization is necessary when reporting to external parties. Financial accounting is therefore governed by a set of accounting principles that includes the monetary unit assumption, the entity assumption, and the principles of historical cost and objectivity. The monetary unit assumption holds that only events and activities measurable in dollars are recognized in a company's accounting records. The entity assumption holds that a business be viewed as a unit that is separate and distinct from its owners and from other businesses. There are three types of business entities: sole proprietorships, partnerships, and corporations. The historical-cost principle requires that goods, services, and other resources be entered in the accounting records at acquisition cost. This procedure results in an objective valuation amount at the time of acquisition; however, the meaningfulness of cost-based amounts can deteriorate over time, especially in inflationary economies. Historical cost is consistent with the objectivity principle, which holds that accounting valuations be definite and verifiable.

4 Define assets, liabilities, and owner's equity, and state the relationship of these components in the accounting equation. Assets are the economic resources of a firm that are expected to benefit future time periods. Typical examples of assets include cash, land, buildings, inventories, and equipment. Certain parties have claims on these resources. Liabilities, for instance, measure the claims on the resources by creditors. In contrast, the owner's equity is the owner's stake or "interest" in the assets of the business. The three components are related, as shown by the accounting equation: assets = liabilities + owner's equity.

5 Identify the four items that cause owner's equity to change: owner investments, owner withdrawals, revenues, and expenses. An investment by the owner occurs when the owner relinquishes personal assets to the enterprise. Such an event causes the owner's equity of an entity to increase. Conversely, an owner may remove assets from a business for personal use, causing owner's equity to fall. Owner's equity will also change as a result of revenues and expenses. Revenues, which increase owner's equity, are the amounts charged to customers for goods sold or services rendered. In contrast, expenses are the costs incurred to produce revenues (e.g., salaries, advertising, utilities, and other similar items) and thus decrease equity. If revenues exceed expenses, a net income is generated; the opposite case creates a net loss.

6 Describe the impact of various transactions on the accounting equation. A company's transactions and events affect the accounting equation in many different ways. The purchase of an asset on account, for example, will increase both assets and liabilities. The acquisition of that same asset for cash, however, will leave total assets, liabilities, and owner's equity unchanged. Finally, a withdrawal of cash out of the business will decrease both assets and owner's equity. Memorization of the impact of these transactions and events should not be attempted. Instead, it is best to reason and analyze the ultimate effect on the equation's components.

7 Understand the content of and prepare an income statement, a statement of owner's equity, and a balance sheet. The income statement reveals an entity's revenues and expenses (and associated net income or net loss) for a particular period of time. The statement of owner's equity shows the amount of change in owner's equity during the same time period covered by the income statement. This change is caused by the firm's revenues and expenses, which appear in the summarized form of net income (or loss), owner investments, and owner withdrawals. Finally, the balance sheet details a company's assets and liabilities as of a specific date. As its name implies, this financial statement shows that the sum of the assets is equal to and in balance with the individual equity interests, that is, assets = liabilities + owner's equity.

---

accounting   A set of theories, concepts, and techniques that collectively measure, summarize, and report financial information about an economic unit.

accounting equation   A mathematical relationship: Assets = Liabilities + Owner's Equity.

assets   The economic resources owned by a company that are expected to benefit future time periods.

auditing   The investigation and examination of transactions that underlie an organization's financial statements.

balance sheet   A financial statement that presents a firm's assets, liabilities, and owner's equity at a particular point in time.

bookkeeping   A discipline heavily involved with record keeping and various mechanical tasks.

certified public accountant (CPA)   An individual who is licensed by a state to practice public accounting.

corporation   A form of business organization where ownership is in the hands of investors who have acquired shares of the company's stock.

cost accounting   An area of accounting that deals with the collection, assignment, control, and evaluation of costs.

entity assumption   An assumption that a business is viewed as a unit that is separate and apart from its owners and from other firms.

ethics   A broad set of moral practices that groups follow as behavior standards.

expenses   The costs incurred in producing revenues.

financial accounting   An area of accounting concerned primarily with external reporting—that is, reporting the results of financial activities to parties outside the firm.

Financial Accounting Standards Board (FASB)   The private sector organization presently in charge of formulating standards of financial reporting in the United States.

financial position   A determination of the resources owned by a company and the claims on those resources at a particular point in time.

**KEY TERMS
AND CONCEPTS:
A QUICK OVERVIEW**

financial statements   Financial reports that are compiled and distributed by companies.

historical-cost principle   The principle of recording goods, resources, and services acquired at cost.

income statement   A financial statement that summarizes the results of a company's operation for a given time period by disclosing the revenues earned and the expenses incurred.

internal auditors   Individuals in large organizations who review and monitor the organization's accounting procedures and controls.

liabilities   Debts that are owed by an enterprise.

management advisory services (MAS)   "Consulting" services performed by public accounting firms that are often unrelated to traditional accounting matters.

managerial accounting   An area of accounting oriented toward reporting the results of operations to managers and other interested parties within an organization.

monetary unit assumption   Only those events and activities measurable in dollars are entered in a company's accounting system.

net income   The excess of a company's revenues over expenses for a given time period.

net loss   The excess of a company's expenses over revenues for a given time period.

objectivity principle   A principle requiring that accounting information be free from bias and verifiable by an independent party, such as an external auditor.

owner investments   Personal assets put into a business by the owner. The owner is relinquishing asset control and ownership to the enterprise.

owner withdrawals   The removal of assets from the business by the owner for personal use.

owner's equity (capital)   The owner's stake or "interest" in the assets of a business; equal to the company's net assets (assets minus liabilities).

partnership   A company formed by two or more persons and managed according to a contractual agreement among them.

public accounting   A branch of accounting in which an accountant provides services to all types of enterprises for fees.

revenue   Amounts charged to customers for goods sold or services rendered.

sole proprietorship   A business owned by one individual.

statement of owner's equity   A financial statement that discloses the changes in owner's equity during an accounting period.

CHAPTER QUIZ

The five questions that follow relate to several issues raised in the chapter. Test your knowledge of these issues by selecting the best answer. (The answers appear on p. 45.)

1 The principle of historical cost:

   a holds that acquisitions of goods and services should be entered in the accounting records at acquisition cost.

b results in the development of subjective financial statements.

c is ideal for use in periods of high inflation.

d is not acceptable when constructing general-purpose financial statements.

2 Apex Company had owner's equity of $32,000 on January 1, 19X2. During January, owner investments and withdrawals amounted to $15,000 and $9,000, respectively. In addition, the company generated revenues of $50,000 and expenses of $48,000. The amount of owner's equity on January 31 was:

a $8,000.   c $40,000.

b $36,000.   d $58,000.

3 John Davis recently withdrew $1,000 cash from the Davis Repair Shop, a sole proprietorship. This transaction would:

a decrease both assets and liabilities.

b decrease both assets and owner's equity.

c decrease assets and increase owner's equity.

d increase both assets and owner's equity.

4 A company's ending accounts receivable balance and the period's advertising expense would be found on which financial statements, respectively?

a Balance sheet and statement of owner's equity.

b Balance sheet and income statement.

c Income statement and balance sheet.

d Income statement and statement of owner's equity.

5 X Company had revenues, expenses, owner investments, and owner withdrawals of $45,000, $35,000, $4,000, and $1,000, respectively. The firm's net income was:

a $9,000.   c $13,000.

b $10,000.   d $14,000.

On October 2, 19XX, John Gilbert opened the Gilbert Realty Company. The following transactions occurred during the month:

SUMMARY PROBLEM

Oct. 2 Received $25,000 cash from Gilbert as an investment in the business.
      6 Received a $3,600 cash commission for services rendered on the sale of a home.
      10 Paid $400 of transportation expenses. (Gilbert uses his personal auto for business matters and bills the firm for all business expenses.)
      14 Sold another home. The commission on this sale was $3,200, but Gilbert will not receive the cash until November.
      18 Paid $900 of advertising expenses.
      23 Purchased furniture for the office at a cost of $6,500. Made a down payment of $2,000 and agreed to remit the balance owed next month.
      24 Paid utility bills of $350 for the month.
      27 Returned $600 of office furniture to the supplier. The supplier deducted the return from the amount that Gilbert owes.
      29 Paid $1,700 of salaries expense.
      30 Processed a $500 cash withdrawal for personal use.

Instructions

a Analyze the effects of these transactions on the individual elements of the accounting equation.

b Prepare an income statement for the month ended October 31.

c Prepare a statement of owner's equity for the month ended October 31.

d Prepare a balance sheet as of October 31.

Solution

a

Date	Cash	Accounts Receivable	Office Furniture	Accounts Payable	(+) Investments (−) Withdrawals	(+) Revenues (−) Expenses
		Assets		= Liabilities +	Owner's Equity	
10/2	+$25,000				+$25,000	
10/6	+3,600					+$3,600 (Commissions)
10/10	−400					−400 (Transportation)
10/14		+$3,200				+3,200 (Commissions)
10/18	−900					−900 (Advertising)
10/23	−2,000		+$6,500	+$4,500		
10/24	−350					−350 (Utilities)
10/27			−600	−600		
10/29	−1,700					−1,700 (Salaries)
10/30	−500				−500	
	$22,750	$3,200	$5,900	$3,900	$24,500	$3,450
		$31,850			$31,850	

b

GILBERT REALTY
Income Statement
For the Month Ended October 31, 19XX

Commissions		$6,800
Less expenses		
Transportation	$ 400	
Advertising	900	
Utilities	350	
Salaries	1,700	
Total expenses		3,350
Net income		$3,450

c

GILBERT REALTY
Statement of Owner's Equity
For the Month Ended October 31, 19XX

Beginning balance, Oct. 1		$ —
Increases		
Owner investments	$25,000	
Net income	3,450	28,450
		$28,450
Decreases		
Owner withdrawals		500
Ending balance, Oct. 31		$27,950

d

GILBERT REALTY	
Balance Sheet	
October 31, 19XX	
Assets	
Cash	$22,750
Accounts receivable	3,200
Office furniture	5,900
Total assets	$31,850
Liabilities	
Accounts payable	$ 3,900
Owner's equity	
John Gilbert, capital	27,950
Total liabilities & owner's equity	$31,850

ASSIGNMENT MATERIAL

QUESTIONS

Q1-1 Identify typical users of accounting information.

Q1-2 How does financial accounting differ from managerial accounting?

Q1-3 What are several of the limitations of accounting information?

Q1-4 How does bookkeeping differ from accounting?

Q1-5 Paul Martin is contemplating an investment in the Indiana Company. He has secured the firm's audited financial statements, which have been examined by a certified public accountant. How can Martin be satisfied that the statements do not present false and incorrect information to purposely mislead investors?

Q1-6 Explain the entity assumption.

Q1-7 Mr. P, the president of Fairwood Company, recently purchased a new car solely for personal use. He asked Mr. A, Fairwood's accountant, to record the car as a miscellaneous expense of the company's current accounting period. Mr. A refused. Explain the reason behind A's action.

Q1-8 Discuss the use of historical cost in the accounting process. Why is historical cost used, and what is one of its chief limitations?

Q1-9 What is meant by the term "financial position"?

Q1-10 Define the term "owner's equity."

Q1-11 What factors cause owner's equity to change during an accounting period?

Q1-12 The Harter family owns a service station in Vermont. After his first lecture in accounting principles, the youngest of the Harter sons, Teddy, decided to review the accounting records for the year just ended. He noted that net income of $15,800 was generated. At the same time the balance in the station's checking (i.e., cash) account had decreased by $5,300. Teddy felt that this situation was not possible and that a mistake had been made. Is Teddy correct? Explain and cite several examples to support your answer.

Q1-13 Thomas and Rodriguez are having a heated debate about the order in which certain items should be listed on the balance sheet. Their views are as follows:

> *Thomas*—Cash, Accounts Receivable, Equipment, Rent Expense
> *Rodriguez*—Equipment, Accounts Receivable, Rent Expense, Cash

Who is correct? Why?

Q1-14 The text suggests that the income statement should be prepared first, the statement of owner's equity second, and the balance sheet last. Explain how this order of preparation facilitates the accounting process.

Q1-15 Consider the income statement, the statement of owner's equity, and the balance sheet. Which of these statements cover(s) a period of time as opposed to a specific date?

*Q1-16 Define the term "ethics."

*Q1-17 Briefly discuss the ethical issue of independence as it relates to accountants in public practice.

EXERCISES

E1-1 *Basic concepts* **(L.O. 4)**
Jean's Marine Supply specializes in the sale of boating equipment and accessories. Identify the items that follow as an asset (A), liability (L), revenue (R), or expense (E) from the firm's viewpoint.
a The inventory of boating supplies owned by the company.
b Monthly rental charges paid for store space.
c A loan owed to Citizens Bank.
d New computer equipment purchased to handle daily record keeping.
e Daily sales made to customers.
f Amounts due from customers.
g Land owned by the company, to be used as a future store site.
h Weekly salaries paid to salespeople.

E1-2 *Basic computations* **(L.O. 4, 5)**

1-2-3

The following selected balances were extracted from the accounting records of Rossi Enterprises on December 31, 19X3:

Accounts payable	$ 3,200	Interest expense	$ 2,500
Accounts receivable	14,800	Land	18,000
Auto expense	1,900	Loan payable	40,000
Building	30,000	Tax expense	3,300
Cash	7,400	Utilities expense	4,100
Fee revenue	56,900	Wage expense	37,500

a Determine Rossi's total assets as of December 31.
b Determine the company's total liabilities as of December 31.
c Compute 19X3 net income or loss.

---

* An asterisk preceding an item indicates that the material is covered in an appendix to this chapter.

E1-3 *Impact of business transactions* (L.O. 6)

The items that follow describe the impact of a business transaction or event on the components of the accounting equation. Present an example of a transaction or event that correctly matches the described impact.

a Increase an asset and increase a liability. *by asset on credit*

b Increase one asset and decrease another asset *buy asset and putting downpayment on it.*

c Increase an asset and increase in owner's equity from a transaction or event not related to income-producing activities. *Owner put money into business*

d Increase an asset and increase in owner's equity from a transaction or event related to income-producing activities.

e Decrease an asset and decrease a liability. *returned an asset*

f Decrease an asset and decrease in owner's equity from a transaction or event not related to income-producing activities. *owner took money out of business*

E1-4 *Analysis of transactions* (L.O. 6)

Set up the following headings across a piece of paper:

Assets = Liabilities + Owner's Equity

By using "+" and "−," indicate the effect of each of the following transactions on total assets, liabilities, and owner's equity:

a Processed a $5,000 cash withdrawal for the owner.

b Recorded the receipt of May's utility bill, to be paid in June.

c Provided services to customers on account.

d Paid the current month's advertising charges.

e Purchased a $27,000 delivery truck by paying $5,000 down and securing a loan for the remaining balance.

f Received $11,000 cash from the owner as an investment in the business.

g Returned a new computer and printer purchased earlier in the month on account. The bill had not as yet been paid.

h Paid the utility bill recorded previously in (b).

E1-5 *Accounting equation; analysis of owner's equity* (L.O. 5)

Sportscar Repair revealed the financial data that follow on January 1 and December 31 of the current year.

	Assets	Liabilities
January 1	$45,000	$20,000
December 31	49,000	31,000

a Compute the change in owner's equity during the year by using the accounting equation.

b Assume there were no owner investments or withdrawals during the year. What is the probable cause of the change in owner's equity from part (a)?

c Assume there were no owner investments during the year. If the owner withdrew $17,000, determine and compute the company's net income or net loss. Be sure to label your answer.

d If owner investments and withdrawals amounted to $13,000 and $2,000, respectively, determine whether the company operated profitably during the year. Show appropriate calculations.

E1-6 *Financial statement content* (L.O. 7)

You are in the process of reviewing the income statement, statement of owner's equity, and balance sheet of the Weissman Company. On which financial statement(s) would the following information be found?

a The amount of equipment owned.
b Withdrawals by the owner.
c Interest incurred on loan payable.
d Beginning owner's equity.
e Ending owner's equity.
f Amounts owed to creditors.
g Fees earned for services rendered.
h Amounts due from customers.

E1-7 *Balance sheet preparation* (L.O. 7)
The following data relate to Preston Company as of December 31, 19XX:

Building	$44,000	Accounts receivable	$24,000
Cash	17,000	Loan payable	30,000
J. Preston, capital	65,000	Land	21,000
Accounts payable	?		

Prepare a balance sheet in good form as of December 31, 19XX.

E1-8 *Income statement concepts* (L.O. 5, 7)
Evaluate the comments that follow as being True or False. If the comment is false, briefly explain why.
a An income statement reveals the net income or net loss of an entity for a period of time as opposed to a specific date.
b Withdrawals are properly classified as an expense of doing business.
c If a company has $50,000 of revenues for March, it stands to reason that cash receipts for March must total $50,000.
d If expenses exceed revenues, a net loss has been generated.
e A computer acquired late in the year for use in the business should be disclosed on a firm's income statement.

E1-9 *Financial statement relationships* (L.O. 7)

The following information appeared on the financial statements of the Altoona Repair Company:

1-2-3

Income statement	
Total expenses	$ 64,900
Net income	7,200
Statement of owner's equity	
Beginning owner's equity balance	$113,200
Owner withdrawals	61,300
Ending owner's equity balance	70,800
Balance sheet	
Total liabilities	$ 97,000

By picturing the content of and the interrelationships among the financial statements, determine:
a Total revenues for the year.
b Total owner investments.
c Total assets.

E1-10 *Financial statement presentation* (L.O. 3, 5, 7)
The accounting records of Hickory Enterprises revealed the following selected information for the year ended December 31, 19X6:

Cash investments by the owner	$ 59,000
Services rendered to customers	86,000

Cash withdrawals by the owner   12,000
Total year-end assets   177,800

Salaries, advertising, and utilities for the year totaled $68,500. The year-end asset total included a parcel of land that had cost the company $45,000. Hickory's accountant used this amount for valuation purposes rather than the land's current market value of $75,000 (as determined by a recent real estate appraisal).

a Determine the net income to be disclosed on the company's income statement.

b Compute the increase or decrease in owner's equity during 19X6. On which financial statement would this information appear?

c Determine and justify the proper valuation for Hickory's year-end assets.

Series A

PROBLEMS

P1-A1 *Identification of transactions* (L.O. 6)
The following tabulation summarizes several transactions of the Hartford Company:

	Assets			= Liabilities	+	Owner's Equity
	Cash	Accounts Receivable	Computers	Accounts Payable		Investments/Withdrawals Revenues/Expenses
Balances	$5,000	$13,000	$29,000	$17,000		$30,000
(a)	−800					−800*
(b)	+1,900	−1,900				
(c)	−2,000					−2,000
(d)	−3,000		+10,000	+7,000		
(e)		+1,500				+1,500*
(f)			+2,500			+2,500
(g)				+900		−900*
	$1,100	$12,600	$41,500	$24,900		$30,300

Transactions in the Owner's Equity column designated with an asterisk (*) were caused by the company's income-producing activities. The $2,000 and $2,500 figures are unrelated to such activities.

Instructions

Write a brief explanation of each transaction.

P1-A2 *Basic transaction processing* (L.O. 6, 7)
On November 1 of the current year, Richard Parker established a sole proprietorship. The following transactions occurred during the month:

1 Received $19,000 from Parker as an investment in the business.
2 Paid $9,000 to acquire a used minivan.
3 Purchased $1,800 of office furniture on account.
4 Rendered $2,100 of consulting services on account.
5 Paid $300 of repair expenses.
6 Received $800 from clients who were previously billed in (4).
7 Paid $500 on account to the supplier of office furniture in (3).
8 Received a $150 electric bill, to be paid next month.
9 Processed a $600 withdrawal for Parker.

10   Received $250 from clients for consulting services rendered.
11   Returned a $450 office desk to the supplier. The supplier agreed to reduce the balance due from Parker.

Instructions

a Arrange the following asset, liability, and owner's equity elements of the accounting equation in a manner similar to that shown on page 17: Cash, Accounts Receivable, Office Furniture, Van, Accounts Payable, Investments/Withdrawals, and Revenues/Expenses. *Note:* This step is not necessary if you are using the preprinted working papers that accompany the text.
b Record each transaction on a separate line. After all transactions have been recorded, compute the balance in each of the preceding items.
c Answer the following questions for Parker:
   (1) How much does the company owe to its creditors at month-end? On which financial statement(s) would this information be found?
   (2) Did the company have a "good" month from an accounting viewpoint? Briefly explain.

P1-A3 Statement preparation (L.O. 7)
The following information is taken from the accounting records of Grimball Cardiology at the close of business on December 31, 19X1:

Accounts payable	$ 14,700	Surgery revenue	$175,000
Surgical expenses	80,000	Cash	60,000
Surgical equipment	37,000	Office equipment	118,000
Salaries expense	30,000	Rent expense	15,000
Accounts receivable	135,000	Loan payable	10,300
Utilities expense	5,000		

All equipment was acquired just prior to year-end. Conversations with the practice's bookkeeper revealed the data that follow.

Rose Grimball, capital (January 1, 19X1)	$300,000
19X1 owner investments	2,000
19X1 owner withdrawals	22,000

Instructions

a Prepare the income statement for Grimball Cardiology in good form.
b Prepare a statement of owner's equity in good form.
c Prepare Grimball's balance sheet in good form.

P1-A4 Transaction analysis and statement preparation (L.O. 6, 7)
The transactions that follow relate to Frisco Enterprises for March 19X1, the company's first month of activity.

Mar. 1   Received $20,000 cash from Joanne Burton, the owner, as an investment in the business.
      4   Rendered $2,400 of services on account.
      7   Acquired a small parcel of land by paying $6,000 cash.
     12   Received $700 from a client, who was billed previously on March 4.
     15   Paid $800 to the *Journal Herald* for advertising that ran during the first half of the month.
     18   Acquired $9,000 of equipment from Park Central Outfitters by paying $7,000 down and agreeing to remit the balance owed within the next two weeks.
     22   Received $300 from clients for services performed on this date.

24   Paid $1,500 on account to Park Central Outfitters in partial settlement of the balance due from the transaction on March 18.

28   Rented a car from United Car Rental for use on March 28. Total charges amounted to $75, with United billing Frisco for the amount due.

31   Paid $900 for March wages.

31   Processed a $600 cash withdrawal from the business for Joanne Burton.

Instructions

a   Determine the impact of each of the preceding transactions on Frisco's assets, liabilities, and owner's equity. Use the following format:

	Assets			= Liabilities +		Owner's Equity
Cash	Accounts Receivable	Land	Equipment	Accounts Payable	(+) Investments (−) Withdrawals	(+) Revenues (−) Expenses

Record each transaction on a separate line. Calculate balances only after the last transaction has been recorded.

b   Prepare an income statement, a statement of owner's equity, and a balance sheet in good form.

P1-A5 *Financial statement preparation* (L.O. 7)

On October 1, 19X6, Susan Thompson opened Thompson Decorating Services, a sole proprietorship. Susan was able to begin operations with $50,000 cash, 60% of which was acquired via an owner investment. The remaining amount was obtained from a bank loan. A review of the accounting records for October revealed the following:

- *Asset purchases*   Van, $16,000; office equipment, $4,000; and decorator (household) furnishings, $17,000. These amounts were paid in cash except for $2,100 that is still owed for the furnishings acquisition.
- *Services performed*   Total billings on account, $18,300. Clients have remitted a total of $14,200 in settlement of their balances due.
- *Expenses incurred*   Salaries, $8,700; advertising, $2,500; taxes, $150; postage, $1,800; utilities, $100; interest, $450; and miscellaneous, $200. These amounts had been paid by month-end with the exception of $700 of the advertising expenditures.

Further information revealed that Thompson withdrew $5,500 of cash from the business on October 31.

Instructions

a   Prepare an income statement for the month ended October 31, 19X6.

b   Prepare a statement of owner's equity for the month ended October 31, 19X6.

c   Prepare a balance sheet as of October 31, 19X6.

P1-A6 *Identification of income statement errors* (L.O. 7)

The following income statement was prepared by the bookkeeper of the Action Tree Service:

ACTION TREE SERVICE Profit and Loss Statement June 30, 19XX		
Revenue		
Services rendered	$34,900	
Accounts receivable	6,100	$41,000
Owner investments		16,000
Total revenue		$57,000
Less:		
Salaries expense	$15,600	
Advertising expense	3,400	
Down payment on truck	1,000	
Utilities expense	900	
Rent expense	1,200	
Tree trimming equipment	1,500	
Loan payment (includes $600 interest)	1,900	
Miscellaneous expense	12,000	
Supplies used	800	
Owner withdrawals	2,000	
Total deductions		40,300
Net loss		$16,700

Instructions

Identify and explain the errors in Action's income statement. Tell what should be done to correct the errors. (*Note:* A corrected income statement is not required.)

Series B

P1-B1 *Identification of transactions* (L.O. 6)

The following tabulation summarizes several transactions of Ciminelli's, a small restaurant:

	Assets			= Liabilities +	Owner's Equity
	Cash	Accounts Receivable	Kitchen Equipment	Accounts Payable	Investments/Withdrawals Revenues/Expenses
Balances	$10,000	$ 3,000	$100,000	$ 7,000	$106,000
(a)			+5,600	+5,600	
(b)	+800	+13,700			+14,500*
(c)	−900			−900	
(d)	−6,000				−6,000
(e)	+4,600	−4,600			
(f)			−500	−500	
(g)	−2,500				−2,500*
	$ 6,000	$12,100	$105,100	$11,200	$112,000

Transactions in the Owner's Equity column designated with an asterisk (*) were caused by the company's income-producing activities. The $6,000 figure is unrelated to such activities.

Instructions

Write a brief explanation of each transaction.

P1-B2 *Basic transaction processing* (L.O. 6, 7)

On September 1 of the current year, John McCarthy established a sole proprietorship. The following transactions occurred during the month:

1 Received $25,000 from McCarthy as an investment in the business.
2 Purchased $4,000 of office equipment on account.
3 Rendered $1,900 of services on account.
4 Paid $500 of office salaries.
5 Received a $300 electric bill, to be paid next month.
6 Paid $7,000 to acquire a used truck.
7 Processed a $900 withdrawal for McCarthy.
8 Received $650 from clients who were previously billed in (3).
9 Received $200 from clients for services rendered.
10 Paid $450 on account to the supplier of office equipment in (2).
11 Sold $350 of extra office equipment to a neighboring business for $350 cash.

Instructions

a Arrange the following asset, liability, and owner's equity elements of the accounting equation in a manner similar to that shown on page 17: Cash, Accounts Receivable, Office Equipment, Truck, Accounts Payable, Investments/Withdrawals, and Revenues/Expenses. *Note:* This step is not necessary if you are using the preprinted working papers that accompany the text.
b Record each transaction on a separate line. After all transactions have been recorded, compute the balance in each of the preceding items.
c Answer the following questions for McCarthy:
 (1) What is the total of the company's assets at month-end? On which financial statement(s) would this information be found?
 (2) What is the owner's equity of the business at month-end? On which financial statement(s) would this information be found?

P1-B3 *Statement preparation* (L.O. 7)

The following balances are taken from the accounting records of Essex and Associates at the close of its year on December 31, 19XX:

Accounts payable	$ 8,700	Miscellaneous expense	$ 3,800
Accounts receivable	18,350	Postage expense	8,400
Advertising expense	3,850	Repair expense	5,600
Cash	15,000	Salaries expense	34,000
Gloria Essex, capital	26,800*	Service revenue	65,000
Land	9,000	Utilities expense	2,500
Loan payable	5,500	Van	8,000

* This amount represents Essex's capital balance on January 1, 19XX. Owner investments and withdrawals during the year totaled $10,000 and $7,500, respectively.

The van was acquired just before the close of business on December 31.

Instructions

a Prepare Essex's income statement in good form.

b Prepare a statement of owner's equity in good form.

c Prepare Essex's balance sheet in good form.

P1-B4 *Transaction analysis and statement preparation* (L.O. 6, 7)

The transactions that follow relate to R. David Enterprises for August 19X2, the company's first month of activity.

Aug. 1 Received $22,000 cash from Roland David as an investment in the business.

6 Acquired a small parcel of land by paying $9,000 cash.

9 Rendered $3,400 of services, $300 of which were for cash and the remainder were on account.

13 Paid $900 to WBGH radio for ads that had run the previous week.

16 Received $200 from a client, who was billed previously on August 9.

19 Acquired $6,500 of computing equipment from Master Computer; made a down payment and agreed to remit the remaining $1,800 balance by September 10.

23 Received $150 from clients for services performed on this date.

26 Returned $600 of the computing equipment purchased on August 19. Master Computer agreed to reduce the balance due on September 10.

28 Processed a $700 withdrawal from the business for Roland David.

31 Paid $1,000 for August wages.

31 Received a $100 electric bill, to be paid next month.

Instructions

a Determine the impact of each of the preceding transactions on the company's assets, liabilities, and owner's equity. Use the following format:

	Assets			= Liabilities +	Owner's Equity	
Cash	Accounts Receivable	Land	Computing Equipment	Accounts Payable	(+) Investments (−) Withdrawals	(+) Revenues (−) Expenses

Record each transaction on a separate line. Calculate balances only after the last transaction has been recorded.

b Prepare an income statement, a statement of owner's equity, and a balance sheet in good form.

P1-B5 *Financial statement preparation* (L.O. 7)

On January 1, 19X3, Mike Jeffcote opened the Jeffcote Advertising Agency, a sole proprietorship. Mike was able to begin operations with $90,000 cash, one-third of which was acquired via a bank loan. The remaining amount was obtained from an owner investment. A review of the accounting records for January revealed the following:

- *Asset purchases* Land, $15,000; building, $40,000; and office equipment, $9,000. These amounts were paid in cash; however, the firm still owes $3,000 for the equipment acquisition.
- *Services performed* Total billings on account, $29,500. Clients have remitted a total of $8,400 in settlement of their balances due.
- *Expenses incurred* Salaries, $21,000; utilities, $300; taxes, $150; interest, $800; and miscellaneous, $400. These amounts had been paid by month-end with the exception of $250 of the miscellaneous items.

Further information revealed that Jeffcote withdrew $3,100 of cash from the business on January 31.

Instructions

a Prepare an income statement for the month ended January 31, 19X3.
b Prepare a statement of owner's equity for the month ended January 31, 19X3.
c Prepare a balance sheet as of January 31, 19X3.

P1-B6 *Identification of balance sheet errors* (L.O. 7)

The following balance sheet was prepared by the bookkeeper of Rapid Cleaning Service, a sole proprietorship owned by Sarah Randolph:

RAPID CLEANING SERVICE For the Year Ended December 31, 19X4	
Assets	
Amounts due from customers–November	$ 3,000
Amounts due from customers–December	11,000
Cash	5,000
Delivery van*	18,000
Inventory of cleaning supplies	1,000
Investments in the business by owner	22,000
Total assets	$60,000
Liabilities & owner's equity	
Amounts owed to others	$ 2,000
Business expenses	4,000
Loans from the bank	10,000
Net income	17,000
Sarah Randolph, capital (12/31/X3)	33,000
Total liabilities & owner's equity	$66,000

* Owned by Frank Randolph, Sarah's husband.

Instructions

Identify and briefly explain the errors in the company's balance sheet. *Note:* A corrected balance sheet is not required.

EDB1-1 *A look at financial statements: The Promus Companies* (L.O. 7)

Promus Companies is a hospitality business, heavily involved in casino gaming and hotels. The firm operates Harrah's Casinos, Embassy Suites, Hampton Inns, and Homewood Suites hotels. Collectively, Promus has over 400 facilities throughout the United States.

ELECTRONIC DATA BASE

Instructions

By using the text's Electronic Data Base, access the balance sheet and income statement of the Promus Companies and answer the questions that follow. Unless otherwise indicated, responses should be based on data for the most recent year presented.

a What is the total cost of assets owned by the firm? What are the three most significant assets owned?
b Does the company have enough cash on hand to settle its accounts payable? Briefly explain.

c Was the firm profitable? Did the company's net earnings increase or decrease from the previous year?

d How much was the firm's income tax expense (i.e., provision for income taxes)?

e What type of operation produced the greatest amount of revenue for the company?

EDB1-2 *A look at financial statements* (L.O. 7)

This problem is essentially a duplication of Problem EDB1-1. It is based on a company selected by your instructor.

Instructions

By using the text's Electronic Data Base, access the specified company's balance sheet and income statement and focus on data for the most recent year reported. Answer requirements (a)–(d) of Problem EDB1-1 along with the following:

e Suppose an investor wanted information about the cost of items and services consumed by the company in producing revenue. What financial statement should the investor review? What would he or she find for this business?

BEYOND THE BASICS

BB1-1 *Accounting information: Uses and reporting* (L.O. 1, 2, 7)

Frank Bell is an outdoors enthusiast. While employed as a personnel manager at Hansen Engineering in Denver, Frank often helped friends on camping trips and had even built a canoe for river exploration. Luckily, Frank's brother owned a sporting goods store in a neighboring suburb. This was a nice arrangement because it gave Frank access to wholesalers' catalogs, thereby enabling him to acquire specialized equipment at great savings.

Frank's love for camping, coupled with his friends' support, soon led to his resignation from Hansen Engineering and the opening of The Outdoors Store. Frank rented space in a local shopping center and purchased an extensive supply of maps and outdoor equipment. He also acquired some materials and hired a laborer to expand his canoe-building activities. The operation was financed primarily from various investments that Frank had made over the years.

An extensive advertising campaign for the store's opening proved very beneficial, and business was much better than expected. However, as the winter months approached, store traffic slowed. Frank soon realized that his operation faced a problem shared by many other firms—seasonality. In an effort to boost sales during the fall and winter, Frank conducted some market research and decided to add ski equipment and accessories to his product line.

Having resolved that issue, Frank still faced several other problems. An emergency withdrawal had left the store's cash balance at a dangerously low level. Recent canoe-building costs appeared to be skyrocketing, although Frank could not be certain because he did not have a formal costing system. In addition, upon signing the original lease at the shopping center, Frank anticipated conducting business only in the camping field. With a new venture into skiing, however, he rapidly found himself cramped for space. Finally, there was a financing issue. The outlays required for the purchases of ski equipment were more than the store's checking account could bear, creating the need for a bank loan.

In an effort to minimize operating costs, Frank had maintained the financial records for The Outdoors Store himself. Fortunately, he had completed two accounting courses at a local university before being employed by Hansen Engineering. In his own words, however, Frank admitted that "partying came before studying and I really wasn't a serious student." The bank's loan officer, in a preliminary conversation with Frank, had suggested that the store's financial statements be audited by a CPA.

Instructions

a How can accounting help Frank in the management of The Outdoors Store?

b The loan officer had suggested that the store's financial statements be audited by a CPA. Briefly explain the audit process and the rationale behind the banker's request.

c Assume the role of the loan officer. What information would she like to see before making a decision on a loan for The Outdoors Store?

d What are the basic financial statements of a business and what information do these statements report?

BB1-2 *Overview of chapter concepts: Multiple choice* **(L.O. 1, 3, 4, 5, 6)**

The following multiple-choice questions relate to various topics discussed in the chapter. Select the best answer.

1 Which of the following statements about financial reporting is incorrect?

a Accounting is based on an underlying foundation of principles, practices, and assumptions that have been generally accepted by the accounting profession.

b The private sector agency that oversees external reporting in the United States is the Securities and Exchange Commission.

c Users of financial accounting information include owners, creditors, managers, government agencies, and others.

d To the greatest degree possible, financial statements reflect amounts that are determined in an objective manner.

2 An assumption inherent in the development of financial statements holds that a business organization must be viewed as a unit that is separate and apart from its owners and from other firms. What is this assumption called?

a Entity assumption.   c Objectivity principle.

b Monetary unit assumption.   d Going-concern assumption.

3 Expert Automatic Teller recently invested in a computer system by purchasing hardware from ABM Company. To pay for the system, Expert gave ABM cash as a down payment and agreed to pay additional cash in 90 days. What is the impact of the system purchase on Expert's total assets, total liabilities, and ending owner's equity, respectively?

a Increase, no change, decrease.   c No change, increase, decrease.

b Increase, increase, no change.   d No change, increase, no change.

4 Davidson Company, a sole proprietorship, recently reported revenues of $359,000 and net income of $41,000. Nevertheless, owner's equity showed a decline of $60,000. If investments by the owner amounted to $25,000, what is the amount of owner withdrawals during the period?

a $19,000.   c $126,000.

b $101,000.   d $318,000.

5 If a company records the proceeds of a loan by increasing cash and revenues, what will be the impact on year-end liabilities, owner's equity, and the total of liabilities plus owner's equity, respectively?

    a Overstated, understated, incorrect.
    b Overstated, understated, correct.
    c Understated, overstated, incorrect.
    d Understated, overstated, correct.

6 You are in possession of a company's income statement, statement of owner's equity, and balance sheet. Which of the following could be found on at least two of the three financial statements?
    a Owner investments in the business and ending owner's equity.
    b Cash and service revenue.
    c Net income and ending owner's equity.
    d Total assets and net income.

7 Consider the following equations:

$$\text{Revenues} - Q = \text{Net Income}$$
$$\text{Net Income} + \text{Beginning Owner's Equity} - R = \text{Ending Owner's Equity}$$
$$\text{Beginning Cash Balance} + \text{Cash Receipts} - S = \text{Ending Cash Balance}$$
$$\text{Total Owner's Equity} + T = \text{Total Assets}$$

Which of the unknowns is total expenses?
    a Q.   c S.
    b R.   d T.

8 Which of the following statements is correct?
    a When a company has (1) revenues in excess of expenses and (2) owner investments in excess of owner withdrawals, it has generated net income *and* an increase in owner's equity for the period.
    b Withdrawals consume a company's cash and should therefore be deducted from revenues in the calculation of net income.
    c Additional owner investments of cash in the business increase net income.
    d Ending owner's equity equals cash on hand.

COMMUNICATION OF ACCOUNTING INFORMATION

CAI1-1 *Audience analysis: Wm. Wrigley Jr. Company* (L.O. 2, 4, 5, 7)
Communication Principle: Audience analysis is an important principle of communication. In other words, know your readers (audience) and write to fit their knowledge and interests. Tailoring the presentation to your readers' needs by choosing an appropriate vocabulary and simplified examples will help you deliver the information effectively.

■ ■ ■ ■ ■ ■ ■ ■

The Wm. Wrigley Jr. Company is best known for the manufacture and sale of chewing gum. The firm, headquartered in the historic Wrigley Building in downtown Chicago, is also involved with various candy products and flavorings. For a recent year, the company's financial statements reported the following information:

End-of-year total assets: $564 million
Net income for the period: $117 million

Wrigley has had profitable operations for a number of years.

Instructions

Assume that you are a staff accountant with Wrigley. Management has asked you to prepare lecture materials and speak to a group of sales personnel about the firm's financial statements. All sales personnel have college degrees but have very limited or no accounting knowledge. The average age is 25; attendance at the presentation is required. Management believes that job performance will improve if personnel have some knowledge of the company's financial situation. The employees may also be motivated by any encouraging data you present and pass on their enthusiasm for the company to colleagues and customers.

For their information, create easy-to-understand lecture notes that answer the questions that follow. In your word choice, examples, and format, be sure to remember the audience. Be as brief as possible, and consider that you will use the notes for an oral presentation. Although the notes should be understandable on a stand-alone basis, assume that you would fill in added details and explanations at the meeting.

a What are financial statements? Name and briefly describe the content of the financial statements on which total assets and net income would be found.

b What process was likely performed on the company's financial statements to improve their credibility? Briefly explain.

c Terminology is very important for proper communication in accounting. The terms "revenue" and "net income" are often confused.
  (1) Briefly distinguish between revenue and net income.
  (2) In all likelihood, is the firm's total revenue greater than $117 million? Why?

d The terms "asset" and "expense" are often confused.
  (1) Briefly distinguish between asset and expense.
  (2) More than likely, do the amounts owed to creditors exceed $564 million? Why?

Answers to Chapter Quiz

1 a

2 c ($32,000 + $15,000 − $9,000 + $50,000 − $48,000)

3 b

4 b

5 b ($45,000 − $35,000)

CHAPTER 2

Processing Accounting Information

LEARNING OBJECTIVES
After studying this chapter, you should be able to:

1

Identify accounts, debits and credits, journals, and their interrelationships.

2

Journalize transactions and post entries to the general ledger.

3

Describe and prepare a trial balance.

4

Determine the impact of errors on the trial balance and apply the various steps necessary to locate an error.

The businesses that operate in our economy are involved with a multitude of financial events and transactions, such as the sale of goods and services to customers, the payment of cash to creditors and employees, the acquisition of merchandise and equipment, and owner investments and withdrawals. These examples, while not all-inclusive, illustrate the variety of transactions that a company must be capable of handling and recording. Add to this variety the frequency with which these transactions occur and a genuine record-keeping problem is created.

The Vista Transit example in Chapter 1 showed that a business could process transactions by increasing and decreasing the components of the accounting equation. Although this processing method was satisfactory for illustrative purposes, some modification is necessary in a more realistic environment. It is not uncommon for an enterprise to process thousands of transactions each day. In addition, complex organizations may have dozens of asset, liability, and owner's equity elements that must be updated on a timely basis.

To illustrate the record-keeping problems of real firms, consider the Atlanta Braves and PepsiCo, Inc. The Braves, a professional baseball team owned by Turner Broadcasting System, Inc., is certainly not a giant organization by today's standards. Operating in one primary location, the club generates revenues of around $53 million and fields a team for approximately two-thirds of a year. At first glance, accounting for the Braves would not appear much more complex than the accounting required for Vista Transit. However, a deeper probe into the operations of a professional baseball club discloses the following:

- Multiple sources of revenue from gate receipts, concession operations, and the sale of broadcast rights.
- Guaranteed salaries under long-term player contracts.
- Participation in the Major League Baseball Players' Benefit Plan.

In addition, the Braves lease sports facilities. Rentals are dependent on paid attendance or revenues at sports events, subject to specified minimum amounts.

PepsiCo, considerably larger than the Atlanta Braves, has annual revenues of about $20 billion and conducts activities in three different business segments. PepsiCo's holdings and operations include the following:

Business Segment	Company
Soft drinks	Pepsi-Cola Co.
Snack foods	Frito-Lay, Inc.
Restaurants	Pizza Hut, Inc., Taco Bell, Kentucky Fried Chicken (KFC)

Manufacturing soft drinks, feeding thousands of people in restaurants, and producing snack foods are only a small part of PepsiCo's daily activities that need summarization in the firm's financial statements. Furthermore, management must have ready and efficient access to operating information for use in planning, control, and decision-making endeavors.

Whether large like PepsiCo or small like Vista Transit, all companies need the capability to produce financial statements, generate information for executives, and satisfy numerous governmental reporting requirements (such as the filing of an income tax return). In an effort to perform these varied tasks, businesses have found it beneficial to establish formalized accounting systems that operate in the following manner:

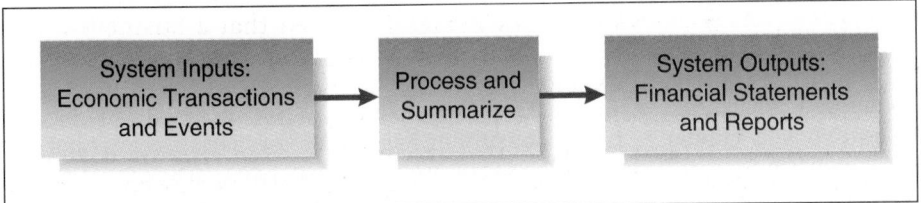

Economic transactions and events are input to an entity's system. The inputs are then translated into a specialized processing "language" (to be discussed shortly) and later summarized. These processes result in the production of numerous financial reports and outputs that assist various user groups.

Such accounting systems have long been recognized as a key ingredient to effective management. This fact was stated very succinctly by Franklin Roosevelt, who over 50 years ago noted:

> A good system of accounting, by indicating weaknesses in the structure of the business, may save thousands of dollars to investors and may even save the business itself. The development of natural resources, the exploitation of new fields of commerce, . . . keener competition, higher standards of living and greater complexities of modern business . . . have brought about a condition where an effective accounting system is as essential to the continued life of a business as production and distribution.[1]

The accounting systems found in practice today range in scope from the simple to the sophisticated. No matter how complex, virtually all systems employ four basic tools to process transactions into financial information. These tools, which improve efficiency and reduce the cost of the input-to-output conversion, are accounts, debits and credits, journals, and the chart of accounts.

Accounts

As we explained earlier in the text, transactions and events affect the fundamental accounting equation. To accumulate the information necessary for financial statement and report construction, a business must keep detailed records of its assets, liabilities, and owner's equity. Assets, for example, should be subdivided into more specific elements such as cash,

OBJECTIVE

1

Identify accounts, debits and credits, journals, and their interrelationships.

---

[1] Letter from Franklin Roosevelt to the president of the American Institute of Accountants, October 12, 1937.

HIGHLIGHT
Small Business Accounting: Bag It!

"Homer, if you don't get those invoices and checks to the office in Baton Rouge this week, you can just hang it up." Ed Simpson, the owner of a construction firm, was talking to his superintendent, Homer Huntley. Simpson had come to the construction site after repeated phone calls had failed to produce the documents needed to record expenditures and the extent of progress on the job Homer was supervising.

By the time Simpson had left the construction shack, Homer was furious. "Bookkeepers! Don't they have anything better to do than to ruin my day?" Homer then started yanking invoices, check stubs, handwritten notes, and other papers off the nails that he had driven into the shack's walls as a filing system for job records. Homer stuffed the papers into a brown grocery bag he'd been using as a trash container, folded the bag's top and fastened it with a nail, and mailed the records to the home office that night.

The preceding story is true, although the names have been changed to protect the not-so-innocent. The conflict between good accounting practice and the speedy completion of related procedures is a very real one, made more difficult by the attitudes of people like Homer Huntley. Traditional corrective efforts have sought to educate personnel about the need to keep reliable records. To a large extent, though, the efforts have been relatively unsuccessful in very small enterprises like Simpson Construction.

Brown bag bookkeeping, a small business accounting system, is alive and popular. Many extremely small businesses save check stubs, invoices, and other documents and deliver them to their trusted

CPA at year-end in grocery bags, expecting the accountant to somehow make heads or tails of the jumbled mass of papers.

One consultant has gone so far as to suggest that three classes of brown baggers exist. The Class I brown bagger, a rare commodity, uses the system in the proper manner by keeping separate bags or containers for each type of document. The documents are neatly filed in the bags in chronological order, with appropriate handwritten notes attached (e.g., a receipt from a business luncheon might contain a note such as "Ate with Tim Smith of Smith Radiator—tried to get more of his business").

A Class II bagger does not organize the documents but does annotate them properly and at least keeps them together for the accountant. Finally, there's the Class III bagger, or the ultimate in sloppiness. Documentation of business activity is generally inadequate and/or missing. Even the most skilled accountants experience trouble here, with trouble being translated into added hours on the job. Added hours, of course, generate more revenues for the CPA.

To conclude, many organizations have taken steps to ensure the adequacy of their systems, some, naturally, more than others. How does brown bag bookkeeping fit in? Although microcomputers are playing an important role in making the bagger obsolete, this type of bookkeeping system will always exist. Class I and II baggers are, as a minimum, preferable to a constant and ineffectual struggle to get the Homer Huntleys of the world to do detailed and disciplined accounting work.

Source: Adapted from "Brown Bag Bookkeeping," *Journal of Accountancy*, July 1986, pp. 122, 124, 126, 128. Reprinted with permission from the *Journal of Accountancy*, copyright © 1986 by American Institute of Certified Public Accountants, Inc. Opinions of the authors are their own and do not necessarily reflect policies of the AICPA.

accounts receivable, and equipment, with individual accountings made for each element.

The records that are kept for the individual asset, liability, and owner's equity components are known as **accounts.** If a company employs manual accounting methods, the record keeping for each account is normally performed on a separate sheet of paper. If electronic data processing is used, the account is located somewhere in a computer's memory or on a storage medium such as a tape or disk. Keep in mind that in both manual and computerized systems, the purpose of the account is the same: to accumulate (record) the increases and decreases that result from transactions. All the accounts taken together comprise a firm's **general ledger.** Essentially, the general ledger is a book that contains separate listings for each account that appears on an organization's financial statements.

The account may assume several different forms. One form is the **T-account,** so named because of its shape. A Cash T-account appears as follows:

Cash			
19XX			
2/1	1,000	2/4	450
2/12	200	2/18	290
2/24	600		**740**
1,060	**1,800**		

Observe that the T-account has both a left and a right side. The left side of any account is known as the *debit* side, and the right side is known as the *credit* side. In this particular case, Cash has entries that total $1,800 on the debit side (debits) and $740 on the credit side (credits).[2] The Cash account therefore has a debit balance of $1,060 ($1,800 − $740). If a given account has credits in excess of debits, the account would possess a credit balance.

The T-format presents a concise picture of the various transactions affecting a given account and is useful for understanding how transactions increase or decrease assets, liabilities, and owner's equity. In actual practice, however, the **running balance form of account** is encountered more frequently. Using the same information that appeared in the preceding example, we can illustrate the running balance form as follows:

Cash					**Account No. 110**
Date	Explanation	Post Ref	Debit	Credit	Balance
19XX					
Feb. 1			1,000		1,000
4				450	550
12			200		750
18				290	460
24			600		1,060

---

[2] The small boldface figures are commonly known as *footings.*

Entries on the left side of the T-account are recorded in the debit column; entries on the right side appear in the credit column.

The running balance account form offers the advantage of maintaining an up-to-date balance after each transaction. In addition, an explanation column is provided for descriptive purposes should an unusual entry arise. Normally, however, this column is left blank. The use of the posting reference (Post Ref) column will be explained shortly.

At this point you should understand the concepts of establishing an account and determining the related balance. However, two important questions have probably occurred to you:

1 Should the dollar amounts be entered as debits or credits?
2 Which amounts in the Cash account represent increases in cash and which are decreases?

The answers to these questions will become clear in the explanation of a second key accounting mechanism, debits and credits.

Debits and Credits

Debits and credits are tools used by the accountant to increase and decrease account balances. Certain accounts are debited to record an increase; that is, entries are made on the debit (left) side or in the debit column. These accounts, in turn, are credited when a reduction is needed, with entries being made on the right side (credit) or in the credit column. To keep the accounting equation balanced, other accounts employ the opposite rule; namely, increases are recorded by credits and decreases are recorded by debits. Exhibit 2-1 summarizes the debit/credit rules used in accounting.

To understand the rules, remember that the elements of the accounting equation are assets, liabilities, and owner's equity. In addition, recall that owner's equity changes, in part, from revenues and expenses. We can thus safely identify five basic account types: assets, liabilities, owner's equity, revenues, and expenses.

The balance of each account is obtained by offsetting or netting the total debits against the total credits. Certain account types tend to contain more debits than credits and will almost always possess a debit balance. Their **normal balance,** then, is a debit balance. According to Exhibit 2-1, assets and expenses fall in this category. In contrast, liabilities, owner's equity, and revenue accounts generally have more credits than debits and usually possess a credit balance.

Tips & Techniques

The preceding discussion should *not* be taken to mean that accounts always contain a normal balance. Certain accounts may, at times, carry opposite balances. For example, Accounts Receivable (an asset) could have a credit balance if a customer overpaid the amount due a business. In other cases, however, an opposite balance generally means that an error has arisen. For instance, a credit balance in Machinery (also an asset) is not possible because a company cannot have "negative" equipment.

EXHIBIT 2-1
Debit/Credit Rules

Account Type	Normal Balance	To Increase	To Decrease
Assets	Debit	Debit	Credit
Liabilities	Credit	Credit	Debit
Owner's equity	Credit	Credit	Debit
Revenues	Credit	Credit	Debit
Expenses	Debit	Debit	Credit

The normal balances of accounts correspond to the accounting equation: assets = liabilities + owner's equity. An enterprise's assets (debit balances) are matched against their ownership interests—the creditors' (credit balances) and the owner's (credit balance). Because revenues increase owner's equity, such accounts normally possess a credit balance. Expenses, conversely, have the opposite effect and generally maintain a debit balance. These relationships are shown in Exhibit 2-2.

Application of the Rules

A review of Exhibits 2-1 and 2-2 will show that to increase the balance of any asset or expense, the account must be debited. Let us focus for a moment on Six Flags, Inc., which operates a chain of amusement parks. The salaries earned by the firm's employees would be debited to the Salaries Expense account because the company's total salary expense is increasing. In contrast, credits are used to record increases in liabilities, owner's equity, and revenues. Thus, Six Flags would credit an Amusement Revenue account to record the admission fees received from visitors who enter the corporation's various facilities.

The observant accounting student should note that *the procedures to increase any account match perfectly with the account's normal balance.*

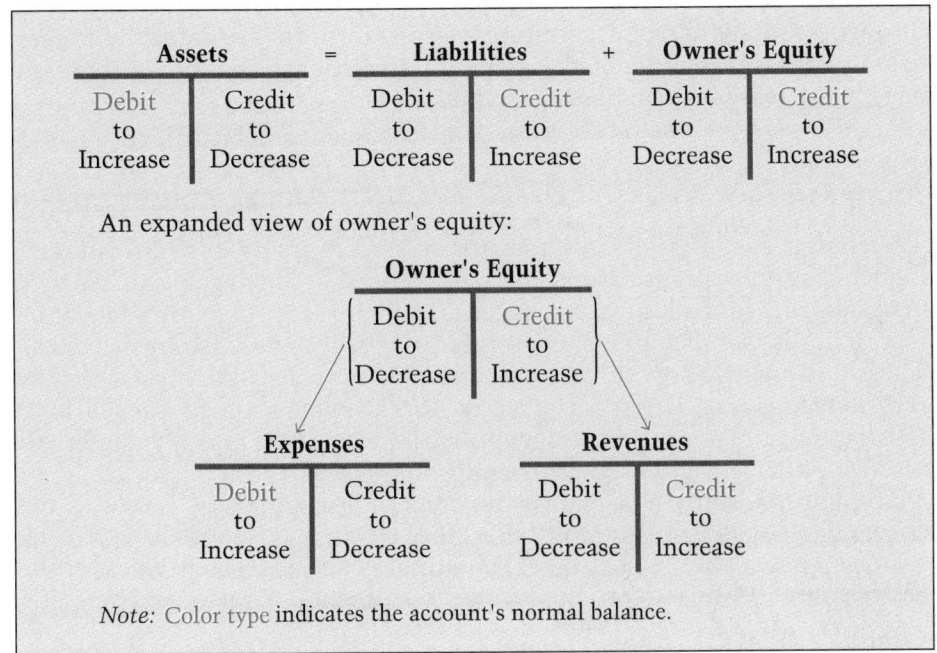

Note: Color type indicates the account's normal balance.

Therefore, once the normal balance is mastered, all you need remember is to give the account "more of the same" to record an increase. The rules to decrease, of course, would be just the opposite.

Let us return now to the two questions raised on page 52 that relate to the Cash account illustration. The answers are as follows:

1 The dollar amounts will be entered as debits or credits depending on whether the amounts increase or decrease the account. Because Cash is an asset, receipts or increases are recorded as debits. Conversely, decreases to Cash are entered on the right side as credits, or in the credit column.

2 This question has really been answered above. Debits of $1,800 ($1,000 + $200 + $600) represent increases to the Cash account; the credits ($450 and $290) are reductions.

Misconceptions about Debits and Credits

There are two common misconceptions about debits and credits. From their experiences with retail stores, many people believe that credits *always* reduce account balances. When they pay on account or return merchandise, customers are often told that their account will be credited. Because the amounts due from customers are an asset to the retail establishment, these transactions will generate credits to reduce Accounts Receivable. Keep in mind, however, that credits also increase certain account balances, specifically, liability, owner's equity, and revenue accounts.

A second misconception is that credits are good and debits are bad. This notion is incorrect. Although credits reduce your account on someone else's books ("good"), credits also increase the amounts you owe as shown in your Accounts Payable account ("bad"). Overall, then, it is a matter of perspective. Generally stated, the "good/bad" relationship has no validity and is best forgotten.

At this juncture it would be wise to thoroughly learn (repeat, *thoroughly learn*) the rules presented in Exhibits 2-1 and 2-2. These rules are used throughout the study of accounting, as they form the basis for the proper recording and processing of all business transactions. The sooner that you master the exhibits, the better off you will be.

Journals

The transactions that affect an entity arise from many different sources. Evidence of these transactions is often provided by the receipt or issuance of accounting forms known as **source documents** (e.g., inventory receiving reports, bills from suppliers, customer sales slips, and customer checks). These documents show that a transaction has occurred and thus trigger the recording process. To properly record the account changes caused by a transaction, the source document must be translated into a debit/credit format. This translation takes place in the journal.

The **journal,** sometimes called the book of original entry, serves as the entry or starting point for transactions into a company's formal accounting system. Many students feel that the journal is a needless repetition of the information contained on the source documents. This is not so. Frequently, transactions are complicated; they affect numerous accounts and are supported by voluminous paperwork that is filed in various places. The journal brings order to the recording process by summarizing a transaction's key financial data in one location. Furthermore, the summarization is done in chronological order.

The Recording Process

To record its many transactions, a business may use different types of journals. For example, sales transactions may be entered in a specialized sales journal, purchases in a purchases journal, cash receipts in a cash receipts journal, and so forth. The journal illustrated in this chapter is commonly referred to as a *two-column general journal.* It has two amount columns (debit and credit) and is used to record a variety of transactions.

Recording transactions in the journal is a three-step process known as **journalizing.** The transactions are first analyzed in terms of the accounts that are affected. Next, the appropriate debits and credits are determined. Finally, in their new debit/credit format, the transactions are formally entered in the journal.

To illustrate these procedures, let us examine the following transaction of the Wise Advertising Agency. The agency was founded on May 1 of the current year when Gary Wise invested $9,000 of personal savings into the business. Analyzing the effect of this transaction, we see that the investment increased the agency's cash balance and also owner's equity. Using the format introduced in Chapter 1, the investment would appear as follows:

$$Assets \ = Liabilities \ + \ Owner's \ Equity$$

Cash	Investments
+$9,000	+$9,000

Once the proper accounts are determined, the transaction is next translated into debits and credits. Because Cash is an asset, a $9,000 debit is needed to record the appropriate increase. As we just noted, the investment has also increased owner's equity, namely, the Gary Wise, Capital account. According to the debit/credit rules, increases to owner's equity are recorded by credits. This analysis is summarized in the following general journal entry:

Date	Accounts	Post Ref	Debit	Credit
19XX May 1	Cash		9,000	
	Gary Wise, Capital			9,000
	Owner investment			

Observe that the debits are recorded first and appear next to the date column. Credits are entered next by using a slight indentation. Finally, a short description is prepared because the general journal will eventually

OBJECTIVE

2

Journalize transactions and post entries to the general ledger.

contain a variety of transactions. The explanation notes the purpose of the entry: to record an investment by the owner. The posting reference (Post Ref) column is left blank at the time the entry is made.

Upon completion of the recording process, debits of $9,000 equal credits of $9,000, and the entry is said to be in balance. *In any transaction, the total dollar amount of the debits must equal the total dollar amount of the credits.* Naturally, this equality would not be possible if a transaction affected only one account. Accountants, however, prevent this situation from arising by employing a double-entry system of bookkeeping. With such a system, a transaction always affects a minimum of two general ledger components.

Tips & Techniques

Observe that we are really performing the same operation that was illustrated in Chapter 1—increasing and decreasing the various elements of the accounting equation. Now, however, the increases and decreases are recorded by using a system of debits and credits. The overall objective of effecting account balance changes has remained the same; only the method differs.

Chart of Accounts

Accounts in the general ledger are usually arranged in the following order: assets, liabilities, owner's equity, revenues, and expenses. Within each grouping the individual accounts are assigned a number according to the **chart of accounts**—a detailed listing of a company's accounts and associated account numbers. For example, the asset portion of a chart of accounts may appear as follows:

Assets (100s)	
Cash	101
Accounts receivable	110
Inventory	120
Land	130
Building	140
Equipment	150

Liabilities might be numbered in the 200s, owner's equity accounts in the 300s, and so on. The determination of a suitable numbering scheme is an important issue in systems design work. Sufficient gaps should be left when assigning account numbers for the possible insertion of additional accounts at a later date.

The chart of accounts is very useful in helping to determine proper transaction recording. For instance, suppose Binkert Company paid an electric bill of $1,800 on March 31. The correct analysis should reveal that Binkert's total electrical costs have increased, calling for a debit to an

EXHIBIT 2-3
Specialized Business Accounts

Firm	Account	Account Type
Philip Morris Companies, Inc.	Leaf tobacco inventory	Asset
Southwest Airlines	Deposits on flight equipment purchase contracts	Asset
Kimberly-Clark Corporation	Timberlands	Asset
The New York Times Co.	Unexpired subscriptions	Liability
Chevron Corporation	Exploration costs	Expense

expense account. Also, Cash has decreased. Therefore the following entry appears to be needed:[3]

```
Mar. 31   Utilities Expense     1,800
              Cash                        1,800
          Paid utilities bill
```

However, a review of the chart of accounts might reveal that Binkert does not use a Utilities Expense account. Rather, in view of the large sums expended for energy costs, the firm has established separate accounts for:

- Electricity expense
- Natural gas expense
- Fuel oil expense
- Telephone expense
- Water and sewer expense

Separate accounts furnish management with more detailed information. The proper entry, then, which could only be made after inspecting the chart of accounts, requires a debit to Electricity Expense.

In addition to assisting with transaction recording, the chart of accounts also reveals how organizations can differ. Although virtually every company has accounts such as Cash, Accounts Receivable, Loans Payable, Sales, and Salaries Expense, businesses often establish accounts that are attuned to their specific area of operation. A review of corporate annual reports revealed the specialized accounts listed in Exhibit 2-3.

POSTING: INTERACTION OF THE BASIC TOOLS

The journal alone is not sufficient to handle the recording process. Many transactions have affected the same account and must be grouped together (i.e., summarized) to allow for the eventual preparation of financial statements. This summarization is achieved through **posting**, a process by which transactions in the journal are transferred to accounts in the ledger. The necessary posting for the entry on May 1 of Wise Advertising appears

---

[3] This entry is recorded in general journal format. Observe the manner in which the account titles and amounts are staggered, thus duplicating the appearance of the entry in the general journal. It is not necessary to write the words "debit" and "credit" next to the accounts or amounts because this format is well recognized and understood by accountants.

in Exhibit 2-4. The circled numbers represent the order in which the posting steps are performed.

To explain: ① The transaction recorded in the journal requires a debit to Cash of $9,000. This amount is transferred to the debit column of the Cash account. ② Next, the date of the transaction (May 1) is indicated. ③ J1 is then entered in the posting reference column of the Cash account to signify that the debit was transferred from page 1 of the general journal (as opposed to one of the other journals noted earlier). This procedure is performed should the need arise to trace a ledger entry back to its origin. ④ The account number, 101, is next placed in the posting reference column of the journal. This step serves two purposes:

1 The posting reference aids in the tracing process by showing the account to which the debit was actually transferred.

2 The posting reference signifies completion of the posting process. Consequently, a blank in this column is interpreted to mean that an entry has not yet been transferred. This procedure is important; should an interruption occur, the person performing the posting can easily find the proper place to resume his or her work.

EXHIBIT 2-4
Posting Transactions from the Journal to the Ledger

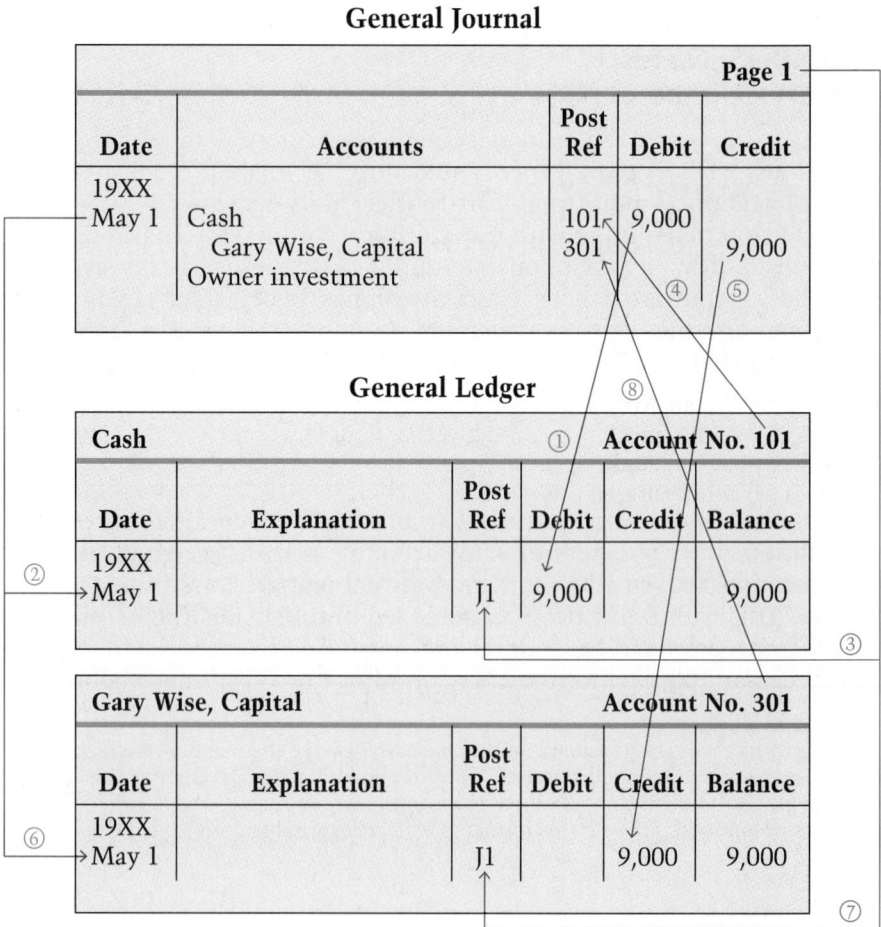

The Cash account has now been increased by $9,000. If there were additional debits in the journal entry, they, too, would be posted in this fashion.

Once the debit is posted, the credit is transferred in a similar manner. ⑤ The investment generated a credit to Gary Wise, Capital. Therefore $9,000 is posted from the journal to this account. ⑥ Next, May 1 is transferred to the date column. ⑦ The source of the entry, J1, is then entered in the ledger account. ⑧ Finally, the account to which the credit was transferred (301) is entered in the journal. The credit has now been posted and the process is complete.

Computerized Record Keeping

You have no doubt received the impression that posting (and perhaps transaction processing in general) is very procedural. This impression is correct. For this reason, even the smallest of businesses have acquired computer software to perform the necessary tasks. In many systems, ledger accounts are updated in a matter of seconds by the push of only a single key. The calculation of end-of-period balances and the preparation of financial state-

EXECUTIVE BRIEFING
The Importance of a Good Transaction Processing System

Thomas Kiernan
President, SABRE Computer Services
American Airlines, Inc.

What does an airline need to fly? Of course, you answered, "airplanes," but you probably didn't answer, "computers." Yet, in today's complex airline environment, computers are just as important as airplanes in making American Airlines fly. With over 600 aircraft, 2,500 daily departures, and 50,000 pilots, mechanics, and flight attendants, there is simply no way we could plan, schedule, and operate our airline without one of the largest transaction processing systems in the world.

American's reservation system (SABRE) today serves over 200,000 terminals and printers, handles the reservations of over 30% of the entire industry's travelers annually, and operates at the unmatched speed of up to 3,000 transactions per second. Processing and counting all these transactions is key to our success. It allows us to forecast demand, manage our revenue, and ticket our passengers. Although we have huge batch systems that handle our accounting and billing, it is our transaction processing systems that really make American fly!

And, what started as our in-house computer is now sold as a service as well. We handle the reservations of over 337 other airlines and manage the reservations of over 22,000 travel agencies in 57 countries. SABRE not only runs American, it is the core of a huge computing business that makes a fair return on investment. At American, transaction processing is at the heart of our business.

ments are both automated. Furthermore, data that possess certain characteristics (e.g., an incorrect transaction date) may be rejected by the software and then printed on an exception report for review by a manager.

Suffice it to say that computerized systems have many advantages over the manual systems that once dominated accounting practice. A major portion of Chapter 6 is thus devoted to a study of these electronic time-savers. Realize, though, that humans must still select the accounts to be debited and credited, and report users should have an understanding of information flows through a system. The computer is a powerful data-processing tool. Its output, however, is highly dependent on the principles and practices shown earlier and on forthcoming pages as well.

AN EXTENDED ILLUSTRATION

The interrelationships among debits and credits, journal entries, and ledger accounts are best viewed by means of an extended illustration. Transactions of the Wise Advertising Agency are now presented, along with the proper journal entries. You should concentrate on each transaction and its analysis *prior* to viewing the correct entry. Again, follow the process of reasoning, not memorizing.

May 1   Gary Wise invested $9,000 in the business.

Analysis   See page 55.

Entry

		Page 1
19XX		
May 1	Cash	9,000
	Gary Wise, Capital	9,000
	Owner investment	

May 5   Paid $800 of marketing and promotional costs related to the agency's opening.

Analysis   Expenses have increased; thus, Marketing Expense is debited. The Cash account (an asset) has decreased from the payment, requiring a credit.

Entry

5	Marketing Expense	800	
	Cash		800
	Paid promotional costs		

May 10   Acquired a small parcel of land for $5,500 from Knox Developers. Paid $1,000 down, with the remaining balance due in 10 days.

Analysis Land is debited to record the appropriate increase. Cash is credited due to the payment. In addition, Accounts Payable is credited for $4,500 ($5,500 − $1,000), because the amount owed to Knox, a liability, has increased.

Entry

10	Land	5,500	
	Cash		1,000
	Accounts Payable		4,500
	Acquired parcel of land; balance payable in 10 days		

Note: All necessary debits are recorded first, followed by the required credits. Observe that total debits of $5,500 equal total credits of $5,500.

performed

May 14 Billed clients for services rendered, $1,700.

Analysis The amounts due from clients have increased; thus Accounts Receivable (an asset) is debited. The revenues earned by the agency have also increased, calling for a credit to Agency Revenue.

Entry

14	Accounts Receivable	1,700	
	Agency Revenue		1,700
	Billed clients		

May 20 Paid the $4,500 balance due Knox Developers from the transaction on May 10.

Analysis The $4,500 payment has reduced Wise Advertising's cash balance and the amounts owed to creditors. Accounts Payable, a liability, is debited and Cash is credited.

Entry

20	Accounts Payable	4,500	
	Cash		4,500
	Paid Knox Developers on account		

May 23 Received $950 from clients on account.

Analysis Two assets are involved in this transaction: Cash and Accounts Receivable. Cash has increased and must be debited. Because the amounts due from clients have decreased, Accounts Receivable is credited.

Entry	23	Cash		950	
		Accounts Receivable			950
		Received cash from clients on account			

May 25   Received a $125 electric bill, due in June.

Analysis   Total expenses have increased, requiring a debit to Electricity Expense. Accounts Payable is credited to record the increase in the amounts owed to creditors.

					Page 2
Entry	19XX May 25	Electricity Expense		125	
		Accounts Payable			125
		Received May's electric bill, due in June			

May 27   Received a call from Kathy Howard, a client, stating that she had not paid her bill of May 14 because of a $100 overcharge. Wise checked the agency's records and found the client was correct.

Analysis   Refer to the entry of May 14. Accounts Receivable and Agency Revenue were each overstated by $100 and must therefore be reduced. The original entry is left intact to improve accountability.

Entry	27	Agency Revenue		100	
		Accounts Receivable			100
		Corrected error on 5/14 pertaining to Kathy Howard			

May 28   Paid office salaries of $825.

Analysis   Similar to the transaction of May 5.

Entry	28	Salaries Expense		825	
		Cash			825
		Paid May salaries			

May 30 Gary Wise withdrew $200 from the business for personal use.

Analysis Recall that withdrawals decrease owner's equity. Rather than debit Gary Wise, Capital, many companies use a separate **drawing account** to accumulate such amounts. This account, given its "negative" effect on equity, will normally contain a *debit* balance. Wise's journal entry follows.

Entry

	30	Gary Wise, Drawing		200	
		Cash			200
		Owner withdrawal			

May 31 Billed clients for services rendered, $2,500.

Analysis Similar to the transaction of May 14.

Entry

	31	Accounts Receivable		2,500	
		Agency Revenue			2,500
		Billed clients			

The linkage between these journal entries and Wise's accounts is shown in Exhibit 2-5 on pages 64–65. Observe that the company's journal now contains posting references, meaning the debits and credits have been transferred to the general ledger. By tracing the transactions from the journal to the ledger, you can see, in part, how information is processed through an accounting system. (Note: We have omitted journal entry explanations to simplify the presentation.)

Earlier in the chapter we noted that total debits must equal total credits in any given transaction. Because journal entries are transferred (posted) to the ledger, the ledger accounts (taken collectively) should contain equal debit/credit totals as well. To determine whether this equality does in fact exist, the accountant constructs a trial balance. A **trial balance** is a listing of the general ledger accounts, along with the dollar balances contained therein. Unlike the balance sheet, income statement, and statement of owner's equity, the trial balance is not a formal financial statement that is distributed to owners, creditors, and other interested parties. Simply stated, its sole use is within an organization to determine whether the accounting records are in balance.

The trial balance of the Wise Advertising Agency appears in Exhibit 2-6. This two-column report lists debit balances in the left column and credit balances in the right column. The trial balance shows that the required equality is maintained at $13,225.

TRIAL BALANCE

OBJECTIVE

3

Describe and prepare a trial balance.

EXHIBIT 2-5
General Journal and General Ledger of Wise Advertising Agency

General Journal

				Page 1	
Date	**Accounts**	**Post Ref**	**Debit**	**Credit**	
19XX					
May 1	Cash	101	9,000		
	Gary Wise, Capital	301		9,000	
5	Marketing Expense	520	800		
	Cash	101		800	
10	Land	130	5,500		
	Cash	101		1,000	
	Accounts Payable	210		4,500	
14	Accounts Receivable	120	1,700		
	Agency Revenue	410		1,700	
20	Accounts Payable	210	4,500		
	Cash	101		4,500	
23	Cash	101	950		
	Accounts Receivable	120		950	

				Page 2	
19XX					
May 25	Electricity Expense	530	125		
	Accounts Payable	210		125	
27	Agency Revenue	410	100		
	Accounts Receivable	120		100	
28	Salaries Expense	510	825		
	Cash	101		825	
30	Gary Wise, Drawing	320	200		
	Cash	101		200	
31	Accounts Receivable	120	2,500		
	Agency Revenue	410		2,500	

General Ledger

Cash   Account No. 101

Date		Post Ref	Debit	Credit	Balance
19XX					
May 1		J1	9,000		9,000
5		J1		800	8,200
10		J1		1,000	7,200
20		J1		4,500	2,700
23		J1	950		3,650
28		J2		825	2,825
30		J2		200	2,625

Accounts Receivable   Account No. 120

Date		Post Ref	Debit	Credit	Balance
19XX					
May 14		J1	1,700		1,700
23		J1		950	750
27		J2		100	650
31		J2	2,500		3,150

Land   Account No. 130

Date		Post Ref	Debit	Credit	Balance
19XX					
May 10		J1	5,500		5,500

Accounts Payable   Account No. 210

Date		Post Ref	Debit	Credit	Balance
19XX					
May 10		J1		4,500	4,500
20		J1	4,500		—
25		J2		125	125

Gary Wise, Capital   Account No. 301

Date		Post Ref	Debit	Credit	Balance
19XX					
May 1		J1		9,000	9,000

Gary Wise, Drawing   Account No. 320

Date		Post Ref	Debit	Credit	Balance
19XX					
May 30		J2	200		200

Agency Revenue   Account No. 410

Date		Post Ref	Debit	Credit	Balance
19XX					
May 14		J1		1,700	1,700
27		J2	100		1,600
31		J2		2,500	4,100

Salaries Expense   Account No. 510

Date		Post Ref	Debit	Credit	Balance
19XX					
May 28		J2	825		825

Marketing Expense   Account No. 520

Date		Post Ref	Debit	Credit	Balance
19XX					
May 5		J1	800		800

Electricity Expense   Account No. 530

Date		Post Ref	Debit	Credit	Balance
19XX					
May 25		J2	125		125

EXHIBIT 2-6
Trial Balance for Wise
Advertising Agency

WISE ADVERTISING AGENCY		
Trial Balance		
May 31, 19XX		
Cash	$ 2,625	
Accounts receivable	3,150	
Land	5,500	
Accounts payable		$ 125
Gary Wise, capital		9,000
Gary Wise, drawing	200	
Agency revenue		4,100
Salaries expense	825	
Marketing expense	800	
Electricity expense	125	
	$13,225	$13,225

OBJECTIVE

4

Determine the impact of errors on the trial balance and apply the various steps necessary to locate an error.

Equality Does Not Ensure Accuracy

Unfortunately, a trial balance with equal debit/credit totals does not always mean the accounting process was free from error. Several errors can occur that have no effect on the required equality. To illustrate, examine the transaction recorded by Wise on May 31:

May 31   Accounts Receivable   2,500
        Agency Revenue   2,500
      Billed clients

As shown by the ledger accounts, this entry increased the balance in Accounts Receivable from $650 to $3,150. Furthermore, Agency Revenue rose from $1,600 to $4,100.

Consider, for a moment, the effect of a transaction omission. If Wise's bookkeeper had failed to record and post this entry, the two accounts just cited would each be understated by $2,500. Nevertheless, the trial balance will continue to balance. Although Accounts Receivable and Agency Revenue would both be incorrect, the debit/credit equality is still maintained, now at $10,725 ($13,225 − $2,500).

To be more specific, any type of error in which debits and credits are equal will have no impact on the trial balance's balancing. In addition to transaction omission, other such errors include transaction duplication, the posting of entries to the wrong accounts, and journalizing errors (e.g., incorrect accounts and amounts within a journal entry).

Unequal Totals

Unlike the errors just noted, other errors may occur that create unequal trial balance totals. The resulting out-of-balance condition is naturally unacceptable, and the debit/credit equality must be restored.

Locating the source of an error is often very troublesome, as the trial balance is really a summarization of both the journalizing and posting processes. Mistakes can be made when (1) transactions are placed in the journal, (2) journal entries are posted to the ledger, and (3) the trial balance is constructed. It is generally suggested that one work backward through this sequence of procedures in attempting to pinpoint problems. The following steps may prove helpful:

1 Re-add the trial balance columns.

2 Calculate the difference between the debit and credit totals. If the difference is divisible by 9, there is a good chance that a transposition or a slide has occurred. A **transposition** occurs when two digits of a given number are accidentally reversed (e.g., the number 560 is listed as 650, 125 as 152, and so on). With a **slide,** the decimal point of a number is improperly moved to the left or the right (e.g., the number 895 is recopied as 8,950).

3 Calculate one-half the difference between the debit and credit totals, and then look for that amount in the trial balance. If the amount can be located, a debit balance may have been entered in the credit column or vice versa. This type of error always causes the trial balance totals to differ by twice the amount of the improperly placed account balance.

4 After thoroughly checking the trial balance, return to the ledger. Examine individual accounts by recomputing balances and looking for transpositions, slides, and debit/credit reversals.

5 Return to the journal and inspect individual entries. Trace the entries to the ledger accounts to verify the accuracy of posting.

ETHICS ISSUE

A trial balance is out of balance by a large amount, and management wants the financial statements NOW. Should an accountant temporarily "fudge" the figures to satisfy management's request?

The concepts presented in this chapter have laid the groundwork for comprehending the manner in which accounting information is produced. A transaction (or event) starts the entire process in motion. The transaction triggers the generation of a source document, which is translated into debits and credits and recorded in the journal. The entries in the journal are then transferred to accounts in the ledger by posting. Next, the trial balance is prepared to determine whether the ledger accounts are in balance. This sequence of events can be summarized as shown in Exhibit 2-7.

A BRIEF OVERVIEW

The trial balance is not the end of the process; it is only an intermediate step in the processing cycle. The next two chapters will illustrate the remaining procedures that must be performed for a transaction to find its way into a company's financial statements.

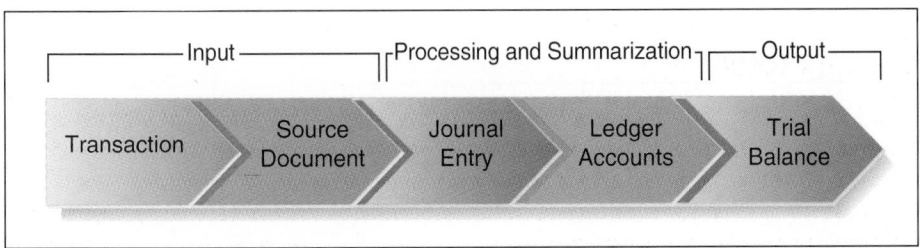

EXHIBIT 2-7
Basic Sequence in the Accounting Process

END-OF-CHAPTER REVIEW

**LEARNING OBJECTIVES:
THE KEY POINTS**

1 Identify accounts, debits and credits, journals, and their interrelationships. The transactions and events that affect a firm trigger the generation of various types of source documents, such as sales slips and receiving reports. These documents are recorded in the journal by using a debit/credit format. The debits and credits, based on the following rules, are employed to increase and decrease the individual records that are kept for accounts (e.g., Cash, Accounts Payable, Agency Revenue, and so forth).

Account Type	Normal Balance	To Increase	To Decrease
Assets	Debit	Debit	Credit
Liabilities	Credit	Credit	Debit
Owner's equity	Credit	Credit	Debit
Revenues	Credit	Credit	Debit
Expenses	Debit	Debit	Credit

The entries in the journal are then transferred to the general ledger by the posting process. The possible accounts to use when constructing journal entries are contained in a listing called the chart of accounts.

2 Journalize transactions and post entries to the general ledger. The journalizing (recording) process involves an analysis of the accounts that are affected by a transaction. Once this step is performed, the appropriate debits and credits are determined and entered in the journal. The posting process encompasses various procedures that involve the transfer of information contained in the journal to accounts in the general ledger. The major objective of posting is to summarize in one place the many transactions that may affect a given account.

3 Describe and prepare a trial balance. A trial balance is a two-column report that is used to check the equality of debits and credits in the general ledger. The procedures for construction involve classifying an account's end-of-period balance as either a debit or a credit. These amounts are then totaled to determine if the required debit/credit equality holds true.

4 Determine the impact of errors on the trial balance and apply the various steps necessary to locate an error. Numerous errors can occur when constructing a trial balance. Several of these errors, including transaction omission and transaction duplication, continue to allow total debits to equal total credits. Others, such as transpositions, slides, and debit/credit reversals, destroy the required equality. Locating an error involves performing certain tests on the trial balance figures (e.g., determining whether the difference between the debit and credit totals is divisible by 9) and, if needed, on the ledger account data. As a final step, it may be necessary to work backward to the journal to examine individual journal entries.

**KEY TERMS
AND CONCEPTS:
A QUICK OVERVIEW**

account A record that is kept for the individual asset, liability, and owner's equity components of an organization.

chart of accounts A detailed listing of a company's accounts and associated account numbers.

credit A tool used to increase and decrease account balances; also, the right-hand side of a T-account.

debit   A tool used to increase and decrease account balances; also, the left-hand side of a T-account.

drawing account   An account used to accumulate owner withdrawals from a business.

general ledger   A book or computer file that houses an entity's financial statement accounts.

journal   A chronological record that serves as the entry point for transactions into a company's formal accounting system.

journalizing   The process of recording transactions in a journal in the form of debits and credits.

normal balance   The type of balance (debit or credit) usually found in a ledger account. For example, assets usually have debit balances, liabilities normally have credit balances, and so forth.

posting   The process by which the transactions in a journal are transferred to the appropriate ledger accounts.

running balance account   An account format that offers the advantage of maintaining an up-to-date balance after each transaction is posted.

slide   An error that occurs when the decimal point of a number is improperly moved to the left or right.

source document   A document, such as an inventory receiving report, bill from supplier, or customer sales slip, that provides evidence that a transaction has occurred.

T-account   A form of account named for its shape. The left side is the debit side, and the right side is the credit side.

transposition   An error that occurs when two digits of a given number have been accidentally reversed.

trial balance   An internal report that is used to check the equality of debits and credits in the ledger.

The five questions that follow relate to several issues raised in the chapter. Test your knowledge of the issues by selecting the best answer. (The answers appear on p. 89.)

CHAPTER QUIZ

1 A credit is used in accounting to:
   a increase an asset account.   c increase a revenue account.
   b decrease a liability account.   d increase an expense account.

2 Popcorn, Inc., recently purchased some office equipment on account. The proper entry would involve a:
   a debit to Office Expense and credit to Accounts Payable.
   b debit to Office Equipment and credit to Accounts Payable.
   c debit to Office Equipment and credit to Accounts Receivable.
   d debit to Accounts Payable and credit to Office Equipment.

3 Which of the following statements is incorrect?
   a Transactions are initially recorded in the journal and then transferred to the general ledger.
   b A company's accounts are housed in the general ledger.
   c Posting is a process by which accounting information is transferred from one record to another.
   d A source document is initially translated into a debit/credit format in the general ledger.

4 The trial balance:
 a is prepared at the beginning of an accounting period.
 b checks the equality of debits and credits contained in the general ledger.
 c is prepared by extracting information directly from the journal.
 d is a formal financial statement like the balance sheet.

5 Sofa Company's trial balance will not balance if:
 a the $2,900 debit balance in the Cash account is entered in the trial balance's credit column.
 b the bookkeeper accidentally forgets to record a payment of rent in the journal.
 c a credit to Accounts Receivable is posted as a credit to Accounts Payable.
 d a $460 purchase of equipment is accidentally entered in the accounting records as $640.

SUMMARY PROBLEM

A chart of accounts and a list of transactions for operations of the Drake Company during March follow.

Cash	110	John Drake, drawing	320
Accounts receivable	120	Service revenue	410
Office equipment	130	Salaries expense	510
Accounts payable	210	Utilities expense	520
John Drake, capital	310		

Mar. 1 Received $40,000 cash from John Drake, the owner, as an investment in the business.
 18 Services rendered to date: cash, $15,500; on account, $12,200.
 20 Paid employees' salaries of $10,500.
 24 Purchased $4,000 of office equipment from Peach Equipment Company. Paid $3,200 down and agreed to remit the balance owed in 10 days.
 30 Paid the March electric bill of $175.
 31 Processed a $1,000 cash withdrawal to John Drake.

Instructions

a Record the transactions in a general journal.
b Post the transactions from the journal to the ledger.
c Prepare a trial balance as of March 31.

Solution

a

				Page 1
Date	**Accounts**	**Post Ref**	**Debit**	**Credit**
19XX				
Mar. 1	Cash	110	40,000	
	John Drake, Capital	310		40,000
	Owner investment			
18	Cash	110	15,500	
	Accounts Receivable	120	12,200	
	Service Revenue	410		27,700
	Recorded service revenue from operations			
20	Salaries Expense	510	10,500	
	Cash	110		10,500
	Paid employees' salaries			
24	Office Equipment	130	4,000	
	Cash	110		3,200
	Accounts Payable	210		800
	Purchased office equipment; balance due in 10 days			
30	Utilities Expense	520	175	
	Cash	110		175
	Paid March electric bill			
31	John Drake, Drawing	320	1,000	
	Cash	110		1,000
	Owner withdrawal			

b

Cash					Account No. 110
Date	**Explanation**	**Post Ref**	**Debit**	**Credit**	**Balance**
19XX					
Mar. 1		Jl	40,000		40,000
18		Jl	15,500		55,500
20		Jl		10,500	45,000
24		Jl		3,200	41,800
30		Jl		175	41,625
31		Jl		1,000	40,625

Accounts Receivable					Account No. 120
Date	Explanation	Post Ref	Debit	Credit	Balance
19XX Mar. 18		Jl	12,200		12,200

Office Equipment					Account No. 130
Date	Explanation	Post Ref	Debit	Credit	Balance
19XX Mar. 24		Jl	4,000		4,000

Accounts Payable					Account No. 210
Date	Explanation	Post Ref	Debit	Credit	Balance
19XX Mar. 24		Jl		800	800

John Drake, Capital					Account No. 310
Date	Explanation	Post Ref	Debit	Credit	Balance
19XX Mar. 1		Jl		40,000	40,000

John Drake, Drawing					Account No. 320
Date	Explanation	Post Ref	Debit	Credit	Balance
19XX Mar. 31		Jl	1,000		1,000

Service Revenue					Account No. 410
Date	Explanation	Post Ref	Debit	Credit	Balance
19XX Mar. 18		Jl		27,700	27,700

Salaries Expense   Account No. 510

Date	Explanation	Post Ref	Debit	Credit	Balance
19XX Mar. 20		Jl	10,500		10,500

Utilities Expense   Account No. 520

Date	Explanation	Post Ref	Debit	Credit	Balance
19XX Mar. 30		Jl	175		175

c

DRAKE COMPANY
Trial Balance
March 31, 19XX

Cash	$40,625	
Accounts receivable	12,200	
Office equipment	4,000	
Accounts payable		$ 800
John Drake, capital		40,000
John Drake, drawing	1,000	
Service revenue		27,700
Salaries expense	10,500	
Utilities expense	175	
	$68,500	$68,500

ASSIGNMENT MATERIAL

QUESTIONS

Q2-1   Briefly explain how a typical accounting system operates.

Q2-2   What is a general ledger?

Q2-3   In terms of debits and credits, liabilities are decreased by _____ , assets are increased by _____ , and revenues are increased by _____ .

Q2-4   Explain how Accounts Payable could have a debit balance.

Q2-5 Explain the relationship between the accounting equation and normal account balances.

Q2-6 Les Howard accidentally debited an expense account rather than an asset account. As a result of this error, determine whether the following items will be overstated, understated, or unaffected.
a Total assets will be _____.
b Total expenses will be _____.
c Net income will be _____.

Q2-7 What is a source document? How are source documents used in the accounting process?

Q2-8 Explain the functions of the chart of accounts.

Q2-9 A student once commented: "I don't understand the purpose of the ledger account. It seems as though the account is an unnecessary duplication of the journal." Is the student correct? Why?

Q2-10 Why is the posting reference column in the journal left blank at the time an entry is recorded?

Q2-11 What is the purpose of a trial balance?

Q2-12 What types of errors will not affect the equality of the trial balance totals?

Q2-13 A $750 debit to Cash was accidentally posted as a credit to Accounts Payable.
a Will the trial balance be in balance?
b If your answer to part (a) is "no," what will be the difference between the debit and credit totals?

EXERCISES

E2-1 *Recognition of normal balances* (L.O. 1)
The following items appeared in the accounting records of Triguero's, a retail music store that also sponsors concerts. Classify each of the items as an asset, liability, revenue, or expense from the company's viewpoint. Also indicate the normal account balance of each item.
a The albums, tapes, and CDs held for sale to customers.
b A long-term loan owed to Citizens Bank.
c Promotional costs to publicize a concert.
d Daily receipts for merchandise sold.
e Amounts due from customers.
f Land held as an investment.
g A new fax machine purchased for office use.
h Amounts to be paid in 10 days to suppliers.
i Amounts paid to a mall for rent.

E2-2 *Transaction analysis, classification* (L.O. 1)
On February 3, 19X3, Charles Lowry invested $18,000 cash in a new business called the Lowry Service Organization (LSO). Shortly thereafter, LSO purchased $6,700 of office equipment on account from a local supplier. An examination of the accounting records for February revealed that wage expenses totaled $2,200, all of which were paid in cash. LSO rendered $4,100 of services during the month and billed clients for this amount. By the end of February, clients still owed $450.

A review of the preceding data will reveal that five transactions and events occurred during the month. You are to identify these transactions and events and determine the accounts that are affected. Then, determine the account type (asset (A), liability (L), owner's equity (OE), revenue (R), or expense (E)); whether the accounts have increased or decreased; and whether the accounts must be debited or credited to record the impact of the transaction. Fill in the chart that follows (the first transaction is done as an example).

Brief Transaction Description	Accounts Affected	Account Type	Increase or Decrease	Debit or Credit
Owner investment	Cash	A	Increase	Debit
	Lowry, Capital	OE	Increase	Credit

E2-3 *Debits and credits, journals, ledgers, the chart of accounts* (L.O. 1, 2, 4)
The comments that follow were taken from the test of an accounting principles student. Do you agree with these comments or disagree? For those comments with which you disagree, briefly state the reason behind your position.
a Debits are used to decrease liability accounts.
b A trial balance with equal debit/credit totals indicates that a firm's transactions have been recorded properly.
c Transactions are normally recorded in the ledger and then posted to the journal.
d The chart of accounts is a useful device in trying to determine the proper titles of accounts to debit and credit.
e Failure to credit a revenue account will overstate total revenues on the income statement.

E2-4 *General journal and general ledger content* (L.O. 1)
St. James Services uses a general journal and general ledger to process transactions. Assume that the volume of transactions has grown in recent months and that all posting procedures have already been performed. A manager has requested that you provide the following data:
a The total amounts that clients owe the firm as of May 31.
b The accounts that were increased or decreased by a particular transaction on a specific date.
c The total cash received during May.
d The reason for a cash disbursement on May 14.
e A dated listing of all decreases to the Accounts Payable account during the month.

Evaluate the data requests of the manager independently and determine whether the requests can be answered most efficiently by a review of the company's general journal *or* the company's general ledger.

E2-5 *Basic journal entries* (L.O. 2)

Record the following transactions in general journal form. Include explanations.
a Paid advertising expenses, $600.
b Rendered $280 of services to customers on account.
c Purchased $2,600 of office equipment on account.
d Processed a $400 cash withdrawal for Angie McDonald, the company's owner.
e Received $100 from customers who were previously billed in part (b).
f Purchased land in exchange for $25,000 cash.

E2-6 Basic journal entries (L.O. 2)

The following transactions pertain to the Jennifer Royall Company:

Apr. 1 Received cash of $15,000 and land valued at $10,000 from Jennifer Royall as an investment in the business.

5 Provided $1,200 of services to Jason Ratchford, a client. Ratchford agreed to pay $800 in 15 days and the remaining amount in May.

9 Paid $250 of salaries to an employee.

14 Acquired a new computer for $3,200; Royall will pay the dealer in May.

20 Collected $800 from Jason Ratchford for services provided on April 5.

24 Borrowed $7,500 from BestBanc by securing a six-month loan.

Prepare journal entries (and explanations) to record the preceding transactions and events.

E2-7 Trial balance preparation (L.O. 3)

Brighton Company began operation on March 1 of the current year. The following account balances were extracted from the general ledger on March 31; all accounts have normal balances.

1-2-3

Accounts payable	$12,000	Interest expense	$ 300
Accounts receivable	8,800	Land	?
Advertising expense	5,700	Loan payable	26,000
Bob Brighton, capital	30,000	Salaries expense	11,100
Cash	22,500	Utilities expense	700
Fees earned	18,900		

a Determine the cost of the company's land by preparing a trial balance.

b Determine the firm's net income for the period ended March 31.

E2-8 Analysis of accounting data; errors (L.O. 1, 4)

Consider the T-account that follows, which lists selected transactions of Financial Consultants:

Accounts Receivable			
3/1	23,654	3/7	18,321
3/5	8,479	3/18	3,210
3/12	5,675	3/22	4,879
3/28	11,111		

a Determine the account's total debits, total credits, and ending balance.

b Briefly describe the type of transaction that likely occurred on March 7 and on March 28.

c A $5,675 check from a client on account was not entered in the accounting records. What is the impact of this error on the true ending accounts receivable balance?

d The firm's trial balance would not balance, with total credits exceeding total debits by $6,420. Is it possible that the Accounts Receivable account is the cause of the problem? Why?

E2-9 *Trial balance errors* (L.O. 4)

You are reviewing the month-end trial balance for Schirmer Enterprises and discover various errors (items a–f below). Identify the effect of the errors on the trial balance by using the following codes. Where appropriate, indicate the amount of the error.

1—Debits will exceed credits by $_____.
2—Credits will exceed debits by $_____.
3—Debits will be equal to credits.

a Failed to record $1,000 of service revenue charged to customers at month-end.
b Incorrectly understated the balance in the Cash account by $2,500.
c Recorded the collection of $400 on account as a debit to Cash and a debit to Accounts Receivable.
d Recorded the $5,000 balance of Equipment in the credit column of the trial balance.
e Recorded payment of the month's $700 utility bill as a $700 debit to Utilities Expense and a $70 credit to Cash.
f Recorded a $3,000 payment on account as a debit to Repairs Expense and a credit to Cash.

Series A

PROBLEMS

P2-A1 *Transaction analysis and trial balance preparation* (L.O. 1, 3)

The T-accounts that follow were taken from the books of Miller Data Processing on December 31 of the current year. Letters in the accounts reference specific transactions of the firm.

Cash			
(a)	35,000	(d)	3,000
(b)	10,000	(h)	1,500
(f)	8,000	(j)	800
(i)	400		

Accounts Receivable			
(c)	14,000	(f)	8,000

Computer Equipment			
(b)	26,000	(g)	7,000
(e)	9,000		

Accounts Payable			
(g)	7,000	(e)	9,000
(j)	800		

Loan Payable			
(h)	1,500	(a)	35,000

Miller, Capital			
		(b)	36,000

Fees Earned			
		(c)	14,000

Advertising Expense			
(d)	2,000	(i)	400

Utilities Expense			
(d)	1,000		

Instructions

a Write a brief explanation of each of the transactions (a)–(j).
b Determine the balance in each account and prepare a trial balance.

P2-A2 *T-account and trial balance preparation* (L.O. 2, 3)

Consider the following transactions of the Estrada Service Organization:

July 1 The owner, Vincent Estrada, opened a bank account in the name of the business by depositing $10,000.

6 Rendered services for cash, $3,700.

11 Purchased $450 of tools on account.

15 Rendered services on account, $1,900.

21 Paid office salaries of $1,400.

22 Purchased $9,000 of office equipment by paying $1,800 down and securing a loan payable for the remaining balance.

24 Returned $50 of the tools purchased on July 11.

27 Customers, previously billed, paid $1,550 on account.

29 Recorded the receipt of the July electric bill of $140. The bill will be paid in August.

31 Paid $1,000 for July advertising.

Instructions

a Establish T-accounts for Cash; Accounts Receivable; Tools; Office Equipment; Accounts Payable; Loan Payable; Estrada, Capital; Service Revenue; Office Salaries Expense; Utilities Expense; and Advertising Expense. Enter the transactions in the T-accounts and determine the balance of each account.
b Prepare a trial balance.

P2-A3 *Entry and trial balance preparation* (L.O. 2, 3)

Lee Adkins is a portrait artist. The following schedule represents Lee's combined chart of accounts and trial balance as of May 31.

110	Cash	$ 2,700	
120	Accounts receivable	12,100	
130	Equipment & supplies	2,800	
140	Studio	45,000	
210	Accounts payable		$ 2,600
310	Lee Adkins, capital		57,400
320	Lee Adkins, drawing	30,000	
410	Professional fees		39,000
510	Advertising expense	2,300	
520	Salaries expense	2,100	
540	Utilities expense	2,000	
		$99,000	$99,000

The general ledger also revealed account no. 530, Legal & Accounting Expense. The following transactions occurred during June:

June 2 Collected $7,500 on account from customers.

7 Sold 25% of the equipment and supplies to a young artist for $700.

10 Received a $500 bill from the accountant for preparation of last quarter's financial statements.

15 Paid $2,100 to creditors on account.

27 Processed a $1,000 cash withdrawal for personal use.

30 Billed a customer $3,000 for a portrait painted this month.

Instructions

a Record the necessary journal entries for June on page 2 of the company's general journal.

b Open running balance ledger accounts by entering account titles, account numbers, and May 31 balances. *Note:* This step is not necessary if you are using the preprinted working papers that accompany the text.

c Post the journal entries to the ledger.

d Prepare a trial balance as of June 30.

P2-A4 *Journal entries, posting, trial balance preparation* (L.O. 2, 3)

AAA Furniture Leasing was founded on February 1 of the current year to rent furniture and decorative accessories, primarily to apartment residents. The following transactions occurred during the first month of operation:

Feb. 1 James Larkin, the owner, invested $28,000 of personal funds into the business.

4 Acquired $35,000 of rental furniture from Trendsetters, Inc. Paid $10,000 down, with the remaining balance due in five equal monthly installments beginning on February 28.

10 Received $7,000 of additional financing by securing a short-term loan with United Bank & Trust.

19 Returned $2,200 of furniture to Trendsetters that was shipped in error. Trendsetters agreed to reduce the amount of the first installment due; the other installments would remain as originally negotiated.

23 Paid operating expenses as follows: salaries, $1,900; utilities, $600; and marketing, $950.

28 Paid the first installment due to Trendsetters, Inc.

28 Recorded February rental revenues as follows: cash, $2,900; on account, $3,700.

AAA has established the following accounts and account numbers:

Cash	110	James Larkin, capital	300
Accounts receivable	120	Rental revenue	400
Rental furniture	130	Marketing expense	510
Accounts payable	210	Salaries expense	520
Loan payable	220	Utilities expense	530

Instructions

a Record AAA's transactions in the general journal.

b Post the transactions to running balance ledger accounts.

c Prepare a trial balance.

P2-A5 *Journal entry preparation* (L.O. 1, 2)

On January 1 of the current year, MuniServ began operations with $100,000 cash. The cash was obtained from an owner investment by Peter Houston of $70,000 and a $30,000 bank loan. Shortly thereafter, the company acquired selected assets of a bankrupt competitor. The acquisition included land ($15,000), a building ($40,000), and vehicles ($10,000). MuniServ paid $45,000 at the time of the transaction and agreed to remit the remaining balance due of $20,000 (an account payable) by February 15.

During January, the company had additional cash outlays for the following items:

Purchases of store equipment	$4,600
Loan payment, including $100 interest	500
Salaries expense	2,300
Advertising expense	700

The January utilities bill of $200 was received on January 31 and will be paid on February 10.

MuniServ rendered services to clients on account amounting to $9,400. All customers have been billed; by month-end, $3,700 had been received in settlement of account balances.

Instructions

a   Present journal entries that reflect MuniServ's January transactions, including the $100,000 raised from the owner investment and loan.

b   Compute the total debits, total credits, and ending balance that would be found in the company's Cash account.

c   Determine the amount that would be shown on the January 31 trial balance for Accounts Payable. Is the balance a debit or a credit?

P2-A6   *Preparation of corrected trial balance* (L.O. 4)

Nettles Company was founded on January 1, 19X3. The bookkeeper was having difficulty with the December 31, 19X3, trial balance, which follows.

Cash	$ 31,300	
Accounts receivable	26,100	
Building	50,000	
Accounts payable		$ 13,200
Loan payable		55,000
Ralph Nettles, capital		25,600
Ralph Nettles, drawing	6,900	
Service revenue		71,000
Salaries expense		38,900
Utilities expense	4,100	
Advertising expense	7,600	
	$126,000	$203,700

The following facts have been called to his attention:

a   All accounts have normal balances.

b   Receipts of $2,900 from customers on account were debited to Cash and credited to Ralph Nettles, Drawing.

c   Debits in the Accounts Receivable account were incorrectly stated as $5,500 rather than $4,500.

d   The Building account includes the land on which the building is sitting. Correspondence indicates that 80% of the complex's cost is attributed to the building.

e   The December electric bill of $500, due in January, was not recorded.

f   A withdrawal of $1,200 in December was accidentally debited to Ralph Nettles, Capital. The credit was recorded correctly.

g   A $2,900 salary payment was debited to Cash and credited to Salaries Expense.

h   A $3,200 advertising bill was inadvertently recorded and paid as $2,300. The advertising agency agreed to accept the balance due in January 19X4.

i   The Miscellaneous Expense account of $1,900 was accidentally omitted from the trial balance.

j   Credits of $1,000 to the Service Revenue account were overlooked when calculating the account's balance.

Instructions

Prepare a corrected December 31, 19X3, trial balance for the Nettles Company.

Series B

P2-B1 *Transaction analysis and trial balance preparation* (L.O. 1, 3)

The T-accounts that follow were taken from the records of Bruner Enterprises on December 31 of the current year. Letters in the accounts reference specific transactions of the firm.

Cash			
(a)	20,000	(b)	500
(e)	2,400	(c)	900
(i)	1,900	(d)	10,000
(j)	3,000	(h)	1,300

Accounts Receivable			
(g)	4,000	(i)	1,900

Land			
(d)	10,000	(j)	3,000

Machinery			
(b)	4,000	(f)	2,000

Accounts Payable			
(f)	2,000	(b)	3,500
(h)	1,300		

Bruner, Capital			
		(a)	20,000

Service Revenue			
		(e)	2,400
		(g)	4,000

Utilities Expense			
(c)	600		

Salary Expense			
(c)	300		

Instructions

a Write a sentence or two describing the nature of transactions (a)–(j).
b Determine the balance in each account and prepare a trial balance.

P2-B2 *T-account and trial balance preparation* (L.O. 2, 3)

Consider the following transactions of the Lopez Service Organization:

May	1	The owner, José Lopez, opened a bank account in the name of the business by depositing $12,500.
	8	Rendered services on account, $4,000.
	16	Paid $1,000 for employee salaries.
	19	Customers, previously billed, paid $2,500 on account.
	24	Purchased $400 of office equipment on account.
	25	Rendered services for cash, $750.
	27	Paid 60% of the amount due for the equipment purchased on May 24.
	28	Purchased land for a future building site. Paid $6,000 down and secured a $14,000 loan for the remaining balance.
	28	Recorded the receipt of the May electric bill of $115. The bill will be paid in June.
	31	Paid $800 for May advertising.

Instructions

a Show how the transactions would appear in the following T-accounts: Cash; Accounts Receivable; Office Equipment; Land; Accounts Payable; Loan Payable; Lopez, Capital; Service Revenue; Advertising Expense; Salaries Expense; and Utilities Expense. Then determine the balance of each account.

b Prepare a trial balance.

P2-B3 *Entry and trial balance preparation* (L.O. 2, 3)

A review of the records of Service City revealed the following trial balance as of October 31, the end of the first month of activity. Account numbers appear in parentheses.

Cash (110)	$31,800	
Accounts receivable (120)	4,600	
Land (130)	28,000	
Accounts payable (210)		$15,700
Roger Gates, capital (310)		42,500
Service revenue (410)		39,900
Wage expense (510)	19,300	
Marketing expense (520)	10,300	
Repairs expense (530)	4,100	
	$98,100	$98,100

The following transactions occurred during November:

Nov. 3 Received $1,800 from customers on account.
7 Paid $900 of wages and $1,200 of marketing expenses.
12 Sold 75% of the land to a client for $21,000 cash.
16 Had $400 of repair work performed; agreed to pay the balance due in early December.
20 Rendered $3,500 of services on account.
28 Paid $3,900 to creditors on account.

Instructions

a Record the necessary journal entries for November on page 3 of the company's general journal.

b Open the firm's running balance ledger accounts by entering account titles, account numbers, and October 31 balances. *Note:* This step is not necessary if you are using the preprinted working papers that accompany the text.

c Post the journal entries to the ledger.

d Prepare a trial balance as of November 30.

P2-B4 *Journal entries, posting, trial balance preparation* (L.O. 2, 3)

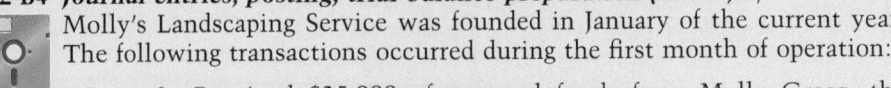

Molly's Landscaping Service was founded in January of the current year. The following transactions occurred during the first month of operation:

Jan. 2 Received $25,000 of personal funds from Molly Gregg, the owner, as an investment in the business.
4 Acquired $21,000 of office equipment from West Office Furniture by paying $6,000 down and agreeing to pay the remaining balance in three monthly installments of $5,000 each, beginning on January 31.

6   Returned a $3,000 drafting table that was purchased in error. West agreed to reduce the amount of the first installment due; the other installments would remain as originally negotiated.

10   Designed the landscaping for a new office park; collected $800.

16   Paid $2,800 to Hurst Office Management for January's rent of $1,000; Molly's portion of the utility bill, $500; and secretarial services of $1,300.

31   Paid the first installment due to West.

31   Billed clients for January consultations and design plans, $13,500.

Molly has established the following chart of accounts for her business:

110	Cash	310	Molly Gregg, capital
120	Accounts receivable	410	Landscaping revenue
130	Office equipment	510	Rent expense
210	Accounts payable	520	Secretarial expense
220	Other liabilities	530	Utilities expense

Instructions

a Record January's transactions in the general journal.

b Post the transactions to running balance ledger accounts.

c Prepare a trial balance.

P2-B5 *Journal entry preparation* (L.O. 1, 2)

VTL

On August 1 of the current year, Eclipse Enterprises began operations with $60,000 cash. The cash was obtained from a $40,000 bank loan and a $20,000 owner investment by Suzanne Peters. Shortly thereafter, the company acquired selected assets of a bankrupt competitor. The acquisition included land ($18,000), a van ($12,000), and computer equipment ($7,000). Eclipse paid $24,000 at the time of the transaction and agreed to remit the remaining balance due of $13,000 (an account payable) by September 10.

The firm rendered services to clients that amounted to $13,600, subdivided as follows: cash, $4,000; on account, $9,600. By month-end, customers still owed Eclipse $2,400. Cash outlays during August in addition to those previously mentioned were:

Wage expense	$2,100
Repairs expense	300
Loan payment, including $150 interest	700

The August utilities bill of $250 was received on August 31 and will be paid on September 3.

Instructions

a Present journal entries that reflect Eclipse's August transactions, including the $60,000 raised from the loan and owner investment.

b Compute the total debits, total credits, and ending balance that would be found in the company's Cash account.

c Determine the amount that would be shown on the August 31 trial balance for Accounts Receivable. Is the balance a debit or a credit?

P2-B6 *Correction of trial balance errors* (L.O. 4)

The bookkeeper of the Bedford Painting Company, a sole proprietorship owned by Richard DiCosola, is having trouble getting the trial balance to balance. The "latest version" showed total debits of $210,500 and total credits of $181,900. The following information is known:

1 All accounts have normal balances.
2 Two accounts were accidentally overlooked when the trial balance was prepared: Advertising Expense ($1,900) and Accounts Payable ($3,700).
3 Accounts Receivable was listed in the debit column as $15,800. A closer look at the account revealed the following:

Beginning balance	$ 18,800
Services provided on account	55,400
Customer receipts on account	(58,600)

4 A $2,200 withdrawal by DiCosola was debited to the Capital account rather than the Drawing account. The credit was recorded correctly.
5 Credits to the Cash account of $600 were overlooked when figuring the account's balance.
6 A quick glance at the trial balance found the following:

Debit column:
Equipment	$47,900
Loan payable	12,400

Credit column:
Painting revenue	78,400

7 A $300 payment for truck maintenance was debited to Repairs Expense for $3,000 and credited to Cash for $3,000.
8 The purchase of a $1,200 paint sprayer for cash was debited to Equipment; no credit was ever recorded.

Instructions

a Determine the correct totals of debits and credits that should appear on the trial balance by starting with the bookkeeper's totals and adjusting for the errors that have been made.
b Which of the following accounts would be listed in the debit column of Bedford's trial balance:

Advertising expense	Utilities payable
Warehouse	Richard DiCosola, capital
Paint inventory	Van

ELECTRONIC DATA BASE

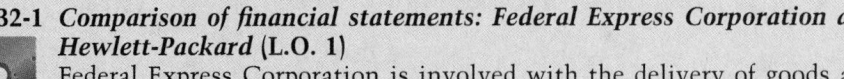

EDB2-1 *Comparison of financial statements: Federal Express Corporation and Hewlett-Packard* (L.O. 1)

SEC

Federal Express Corporation is involved with the delivery of goods and documents throughout the world. The company owns an extensive transportation fleet to perform its service. In contrast, Hewlett-Packard designs, manufactures, and services electronic products and systems. The firm is well-known among students for its calculators and computer equipment.

Instructions

By using the text's Electronic Data Base, access the balance sheet and income statement of both firms and answer the questions that follow. Unless otherwise indicated, responses should be based on data for the most recent year presented.

a Study the costs and expenses (operating expenses) reported by the two companies.

(1) Are any of the costs and expenses especially unique to each firm's type of business? Briefly explain.

(2) Comment on the amount of detail presented by the two companies. Do you see any basic differences in the manner of presentation?

(3) Compute each firm's costs and expenses (operating expenses) as a percentage of total revenues.

b Over the three years reported, which company was more profitable?

c Consider the nature of businesses in our economy (e.g., service, retail, wholesale, and manufacturing) and study the assets presented on the balance sheet. Do the assets reflect each firm's type of operation? Briefly explain.

d Each company uses long-term debt to help finance its activities. Are the amounts owed to long-term creditors approximately the same or does one company have substantially more debt than the other?

EDB2-2 *Comparison of financial statements* (L.O. 1)

This problem is a duplication of Problem EDB2-1. It is based on two companies selected by your instructor.

Instructions

By using the text's Electronic Data Base, access the specified companies' balance sheet and income statement and focus on data for the most recent year reported. Answer requirements (a)–(d) of Problem EDB2-1.

BB2-1 *Trial balance analysis and journal entry preparation* (L.O. 1, 2)

BEYOND THE BASICS

Palm Beach Enterprises renders various types of repair services. Eighty percent of the services are on account; the remaining 20% are for cash. The company purchases the equipment necessary to provide the services and finances its acquisitions via bank loans. The following information was extracted from trial balances that were prepared on April 30 and May 31 of the current year:

	April 30	May 31
Accounts receivable	$25,900	$23,000
Equipment	63,500	70,800
Loans payable (for equipment)	45,000	46,700
Repair revenue, year-to-date	55,600	68,800
Interest expense, year-to-date	2,900	3,600

Palm Beach sold $8,000 of equipment during May at cost and received cash in return. All interest charges owed to the firm's banks were paid by month-end.

Instructions

a Determine the revenues generated during May from repair services.

b Prepare journal entries to record the following:
  (1) Repair services rendered for cash during May.
  (2) Repair services rendered on account during May.
  (3) Collections on account from customers during May.

c Calculate the cost of equipment acquired during May.

d Prepare journal entries to record the following:
  (1) The equipment acquired during May.
  (2) The equipment sold during May.
  (3) May's loan payments, including interest.

BB2-2 *Overview of chapter concepts: Multiple choice* (L.O. 1, 2, 3, 4)
The following multiple-choice questions relate to various topics discussed in the chapter. Select the best answer.

1 The records that are kept for the individual asset, liability, and owner's equity components are known as accounts. The chart of accounts:
   a is also called the general ledger.
   b lists the debit/credit rules for recording various transactions in the accounts.
   c is a standardized listing of accounts (and their corresponding account numbers) that should be used by all companies.
   d may include accounts that will not be found in a particular month's trial balance.

2 Which of the following statements about debits and credits is always false?
   a Every transaction can be expressed in debit/credit form, and total debits will equal total credits.
   b The number of accounts debited throughout a period will equal the number of accounts credited.
   c For a company that has incurred expenses during the period, the total debits in a trial balance will equal the sum of the ending balances in the firm's asset accounts.
   d If accounts receivable increased during the period, services rendered on account exceeded cash collections on account.

3 Posting:
   a involves preparation of a listing of the general ledger accounts, along with the dollar balances contained therein.
   b involves application of procedures to check for the equality of debits and credits.
   c is the initial entry of a transaction into a company's formal accounting system.
   d is a process by which transactions in the journal are transferred to accounts in the ledger.

4 The four steps that follow describe the sequence of events in the accounting process, but include a critical error. Identify the first step in which the critical error occurs.
   a A transaction is evaluated and translated into debit/credit form.
   b The appropriate debits and credits are recorded in the general journal, in chronological order.
   c A trial balance is prepared.
   d The journal entries are posted to the proper general ledger accounts.

5 Wolfe Enterprises was formed and commenced operations in January. By the end of January, the general journal contained three entries. Two of the entries related to services rendered on account in the amount of $444 and $213. The other entry reflected the collection of $222 on account. How much is the balance in Accounts Receivable at month-end?
   a $435 debit.   c $657 debit.
   b $435 credit.   d $657 credit.

6 Which of the following statements is correct?
   a The excess of debits over credits in the trial balance represents a company's net income.
   b The trial balance is a formal financial statement.

c A trial balance is prepared directly from information contained in the general journal.

d If total debits equal total credits, the trial balance may nevertheless contain a variety of errors.

7 The trial balance of Tronback Company follows.

Cash	$ 1,235	
Accounts receivable	2,356	
Land	9,412	
Accounts payable		$ 2,700
Tronback, capital		10,000
Tronback, drawing	2,000	
Service revenue		11,341
Employee compensation	4,888	
Utilities	1,711	
Miscellaneous expense	2,439	
	$24,041	$24,041

What amount will Tronback report for total assets and total expenses, respectively?

a $13,003 and $4,150.

b $13,003 and $9,038.

c $13,003 and $11,038.

d $15,003 and $9,038.

8 The accountant for Audio-Matic Sound Company recently prepared an "in-balance" trial balance. The firm's auditor nevertheless managed to locate three separate errors. Which of the following errors was not among the three?

a A debit was posted as a credit.

b A journal entry was prepared that contained a transposition error, with both the debit and the credit being recorded at $360 less than the correct amount.

c A debit to Accounts Receivable was posted to the Land account.

d A cash purchase of office supplies was not entered in the accounting records.

COMMUNICATION OF ACCOUNTING INFORMATION

CAI2-1 *Writing tone: Carnival Cruise Lines* **(L.O. 1)**

Communication Principle: A polite and friendly tone is an important factor in business correspondence. In the situation that follows, you must respond in clear, nontechnical language to a confused and angry stockholder.* Before beginning, consider that any communication from a stockholder is helpful because it indicates interest and gives a firm valuable feedback. Next, consider that your response is actually a "sales" letter—a way of assuring that the stockholder feels good again about the company. You can also be confident that, unlike most sales letters, this one will be read. You have a captive and highly interested audience—the best kind!

Now, how to make the sale? The best advice is to be polite and warm. Answer the stockholder's question clearly without sounding like a textbook. Don't be too brief or too formal. The stockholder may interpret a

---

* A stockholder is an individual who has purchased shares of stock (i.e., ownership) in a corporation.

very short reply as curt and impolite and a very formal reply as cold and unfriendly. Above all, do not imply by your tone that you think the stockholder is dumb. Treat him as you would a good friend of the family, in a cordial and helpful way.

■ ■ ■ ■ ■ ■ ■ ■

Carnival Cruise Lines sells complete travel packages to people who desire a carefree vacation at sea. The company also generates revenues from hotel and casino operations in the Bahamas, although these activities are a small part of its present business.

Carnival's recent financial statements revealed balances for "typical" accounts such as Cash, Accounts Receivable, Accounts Payable, and so forth. Also disclosed were balances for two unique accounts, among others: Cash Restricted for Repayment of Long-Term Debt, and Customer Cruise Deposits. The restricted cash was listed as an asset on the balance sheet, and the deposits were listed as a liability.

These classifications are totally correct. The fact that cash is restricted as to use does not change the fact that it is an asset. The liability for cruise deposits was created when customers made advance payments for future trips. The journal entry to record the latter transactions involved a debit to the Cash account and a credit to Customer Cruise Deposits. The liability indicates that Carnival has a future obligation to either provide a service or refund the money.

You have been assigned to the stockholder relations department of Carnival Cruise Lines. As part of your job, you routinely correspond with stockholders on various matters. The letter that follows was recently received.

Dear Sir/Madam:

I own 500 shares of your stock and love to travel on your ships. However, I am disappointed with the company's recent financial statements. How can I continue to have confidence in my investment when you obviously cannot prepare a balance sheet correctly?

Please explain why Cruise Deposits appears in the liability section of the balance sheet. Deposits are obviously an asset—I send a check (an asset from my viewpoint) before the cruise departs, and you have the cash in your possession! Furthermore, the Cash Restricted for Repayment of Long-Term Debt represents a significant obligation of the company and should therefore be disclosed as a liability.

I admit that I am not an accountant, but I am not a fool either. Please straighten this out with a prompt reply.

Very truly,

James Allen

Instructions

Draft a response to James Allen.

Answers to Chapter Quiz

1 c
2 b
3 d
4 b
5 a

Income Measurement
and Adjusting Entries

LEARNING OBJECTIVES

After studying this chapter, you should be able to:

1

Explain the impact of the periodicity assumption
on accounting and income measurement.

2

Apply the principle of revenue recognition.

3

Apply the matching principle and record expenses
in the proper accounting period.

4

Calculate net income under both the accrual basis
and the cash basis of accounting.

5

Explain why the adjusting process is needed and recognize
which items typically require adjustment.

6

Prepare adjusting entries and show their impact on the financial statements.

7

Prepare an adjusted trial balance.

8

(Appendix) Describe and use the "income statement approach" of
accounting for prepaid expenses and unearned revenues.

As we move into Chapter 3, you should have some familiarity with the tools accountants use to process transactions. We saw that debits and credits record increases and decreases in the accounts that are kept by a business. In addition, we observed that entries are posted from the journal to the ledger to summarize the effect of various transactions on a given account. Finally, we noted a trial balance proves the equality of the account balances in the ledger.

You may think that we can now generate financial statements by using the information contained in the trial balance. Unfortunately, we cannot. The preparation of statements at this particular point could result in misleading reports of financial position and profitability. Although daily transactions have been entered in the journal and posted to the proper accounts, the accounting records may still not reflect the correct status of a firm's financial affairs at the end of the period.

As a very simple example, consider the procedures that accompany the acquisition of, say, $900 of office supplies. Initially, the $900 purchase price is recorded in the accounting system via a journal entry, and the supplies are placed in a storage closet. The supplies are then slowly consumed—a pen here, a box of paper clips there, and so forth. Theoretically, this usage should be recorded on a daily basis, with constant reductions being made to the Supplies account (an asset). From a practical viewpoint, however, virtually all companies keep the amount of bookkeeping at a manageable level and opt for an end-of-period update that reflects the *total* amount of consumption. Unless this updating (i.e., adjusting) procedure is performed, the ledger accounts and the resulting financial statements will be incorrect.

The updating procedure is a key issue in accounting and forms the basis for part of this chapter's discussion. Before presenting the related details, however, it is helpful to focus on the underlying rationale for the process, namely, income measurement.

INCOME MEASUREMENT

Financial statement users have a keen interest in firm performance, particularly the results of operations as expressed by the net income figure. Thus, a major objective of accounting is to derive a fair and "proper" determination of an organization's earnings for a given reporting period. Earnings measurement is a complicated task—one that accountants must wrestle with on a daily basis. Complex questions arise that relate to the identification of accounting periods, the proper point in time to recognize revenue, the appropriate moment to record an expense, and other important issues. Perhaps the best place to begin is with a discussion of income from the accountant's perspective.

The Meaning of Income

Almost all businesses are started with the objective of producing a profit, or "making money." These phrases, when put into accounting terms, mean the generation of net income.

The quest for profits is an integral part of the capitalist system. Profits (or losses) are the result of managers using the economic factors of production—land, labor, and capital—in an efficient (or inefficient) manner. Economists say that we can measure the outcome of this process in terms of being "better off." That is, profit constitutes the amount by which a business is better off at the end of a period compared to the beginning of the period. Profit would therefore represent a comparison of worth or value at two different points in time.

A determination of the degree of "better-offness" normally entails a number of subjective assumptions. For example, assume that an entity's key competitor has recently gone out of business. Presumably, the surviving entity is "better off"; however, quantifying the event involves obvious difficulties. For instance, will the surviving company attract new customers and increase its market share? Will a new business take advantage of the situation and begin operation? These events will naturally affect the survivor; determining their impact in dollars, however, is extremely troublesome. Generally stated, the economist's definition of profit is beyond the realm of what the accountant can objectively measure.

In an effort to overcome this problem, accountants have developed a different definition of income (or profit). Accounting income is measured by subtracting an organization's expenses from its revenues. Expenses and revenues arise from *transactions and events*, which are happenings that have economic consequences for a firm and are measurable in dollars. (This latter criteria is consistent with the monetary unit assumption discussed in Chapter 1.)

A company will normally experience many different types of transactions and events. One broad classification, for example, involves exchanges of assets with other entities (e.g., the sale of merchandise to customers and the payment of taxes with cash). Another group focuses on measurable *nonexchange* events, such as the financial effects of a flood loss. Overall, recording these exchange/nonexchange happenings allows the accountant to downplay the economic concept of profit. Instead, a more objective **transactions approach** is used to compute net income.

The Accounting Period

The accountant's approach to income measurement is complicated because the transactions and events that affect the financial well-being of an enterprise occur continually over the enterprise's lifetime. An in-depth analysis will find that most economic activities are ongoing; they do not cease and restart at specific times. In view of this situation, how can performance be measured? Owners, creditors, and financial analysts naturally cannot wait until the conclusion of an entity's life to assess whether a firm was successful or unsuccessful in its business endeavors. To address this situation, the accounting profession has adopted a periodicity assumption.

The **periodicity assumption** holds that for reporting purposes, an organization's life can be divided into discrete accounting periods (e.g., months, quarters, years, and so forth). When measuring annual performance, several different year-ends are available:

OBJECTIVE

1

Explain the impact of the periodicity assumption on accounting and income measurement.

Type of Year	Explanation
Calendar year	Runs from January 1–December 31.
Fiscal year	Any one-year period other than the above (e.g., July 1–June 30).
Natural business year	Ends at the conclusion of the business cycle (e.g., October 31 for a professional baseball club, which is after the play-offs and World Series). This is generally a slack period, with inventories at reduced levels and virtually all of the year's revenues and income already generated.

Although the periodicity assumption seems practical and logical, an allocation problem arises when the life of a company is broken into divisible "chunks." This problem is an outgrowth of the continuous nature of operating activity: many financial events relate to more than a single reporting period. The accounting implications of this situation are highlighted in the following case of Hilton Hotels Corporation.

Hilton generates the bulk of its revenues from furnishing room, gaming, food, and beverage services. Concentrating on the first service listed, suppose that the company received a room reservation request from a customer toward the end of May. The customer occupied the room for several days during June and, upon departure, charged the entire amount owed on a national credit card. The credit card company paid Hilton in July, after the stay was completed. Further, assume that Hilton contracted for linen and maid services during May, received those services during June, and paid its bill in July.

In view of these events, two basic questions arise for purposes of measuring financial activity. First, at what point should revenue from services be recognized: when the reservation was secured, when the room was provided, or when cash was received from the credit card company? Also, in which month should the cost of linen and maid service be recorded as an expense? To answer these questions correctly, one must understand the principles of revenue recognition and matching—the foundation for income measurement.

Revenue Recognition

OBJECTIVE

2

Apply the principle of revenue recognition

The segmentation of an entity's life into artificial reporting periods forces the accountant to address the issue of **revenue recognition.** Stated differently, the accountant must determine the proper point in time to enter revenue into the accounting records. An obvious solution might be to recognize revenue when it is earned; but exactly when does the earnings process occur? Before deciding for certain, let us explore an example with which you may be familiar. Recall that several years ago, Mazda introduced the Miata sports car. This particular item was such a hit that three-month long waiting lists developed, and dealers were commanding (and getting) prices several thousand dollars in excess of sticker. Mazda was basically assured of the revenue even before the vehicle rolled off the assembly line and hit U.S. soil. In this case, was revenue *earned* as production occurred, or when the company went through the "routine formality" of delivery to the buyer? The correct answer is debatable.

To avoid the confusion introduced by the preceding situation, the accounting profession has settled on a well-accepted guideline: *revenue is generally recognized at the time services are rendered or when goods are sold and delivered to a customer.* At this particular point, a company has concluded a major part of the economic activity related to the transaction. This point-of-sale recognition rule applies whether the customer pays cash on the spot or promises to pay in the future (or even if the customer has paid in advance).

Recall our Hilton hotel illustration. Now you can see that the revenue should be recognized in June, when the room was occupied (and the service was provided).

Expense Recognition—The Matching Principle

As noted earlier, a fair measurement of income is an important accounting objective. Because revenues *and* expenses are significant elements in this process, it logically follows that business expenses be recognized in the same period as the revenues that they helped to produce. This concept is known as the **matching principle.**

The application of the matching principle is usually straightforward, especially when there is a direct *cause and effect* relationship between costs and revenues. In our Hilton hotel example, for instance, the costs for linens and maid service should be expensed during June when the customer (guest) occupied the room, utilized these services, and generated revenue for the company. The fact that the costs were paid in July does not alter the analysis. In fact, recognition in July would create a mismatch, with revenues appearing on one month's income statement and the associated expenses on another.

Application of the matching principle can become troublesome when the relationship between costs and revenues is less direct or less strong. Consider, for instance, an entity's use of long-term assets such as equipment, machinery, and buildings. These items render benefits for a number of years. By the end of their lives, the assets are "fully consumed" because of wear and tear, obsolescence, and other factors. Consistent with the matching principle, each period benefited should be charged with an appropriate amount of expense. How much to charge is another matter—it is obviously difficult to figure the exact portion of a long-term asset (e.g., a building) that is used up in, say, one year.

To overcome this computational problem, accountants employ a systematic and rational approach and gradually expense the cost of such assets over an estimated service life. Known as *depreciation,* the mechanics of this process will be introduced shortly. Significantly, this approach is still rooted in a desire to adhere to the matching principle; however, the level of precision is not as great when compared with those costs that demonstrate strong causal relationships with associated revenues.

Accrual-Basis Accounting

The revenue and expense recognition principles just presented are fundamental to the **accrual basis of accounting.** Under the accrual basis, revenues are recognized when goods are sold or when services are rendered, and

EXHIBIT 3-1
Accrual-Basis Income
Statement for Denton
Enterprises

DENTON ENTERPRISES Income Statement—Accrual Basis For the Month Ended January 31, 19XX		
Service revenue		$30,000
Less expenses		
Operating	$10,000	
Rent	2,000	
Interest	100	
Total expenses		12,100
Net income		$17,900

expenses are recognized when incurred. Related expenses are thus matched against revenues, regardless of whether such amounts (i.e., expenses) have been paid. As an example, consider the following data of Denton Enterprises that relate to January of the current year:

■ *Services rendered*—The firm rendered $30,000 of services to clients, subdivided as follows: cash, $8,000; on account, $22,000. Customers paid $12,000 of the latter amount prior to month-end.
■ *Operating expenses*—Denton incurred $10,000 of operating expenses, of which $7,000 were paid.
■ *Rental payment*—At the beginning of January, Denton paid $6,000 for the next three months' rent.
■ *Loan*—In the middle of the month, the company secured a $20,000 loan. As of January 31, $100 of interest had been incurred, payable to the bank in February.

Denton's accrual-basis income statement appears in Exhibit 3-1.

Service revenue is $30,000 because the firm rendered services and earned $30,000 in January. The expenses incurred in producing this revenue are deducted to determine the month's net income. Note that only $2,000 ($\frac{1}{3}$ of the rental payment) is deducted as an expense—the remaining portion is applicable to future periods and will be written off in subsequent months.[1] Finally, interest of $100 is recognized because Denton had use of the loan proceeds to help finance January operations.

Cash-Basis Accounting

When measuring income, some companies select another method of accounting known as the **cash basis.** With the cash basis, revenues are recognized in the period of *receipt,* and expenses are recognized in the period of *payment.* Examine Denton's cash-basis income statement, which is shown in Exhibit 3-2.

---

[1] Accounting for such "prepayments" is explored in more depth in a later section of this chapter.

EXHIBIT 3-2
Cash-Basis Income
Statement for Denton
Enterprises

DENTON ENTERPRISES Income Statement—Cash Basis For the Month Ended January 31, 19XX		
Service revenue		$20,000
Less expenses		
Operating	$7,000	
Rent	6,000	
Total expenses		13,000
Net income		$ 7,000

Note that the statement concentrates on cash flows. Services rendered during the month, for example, total $30,000. Cash receipts from services, however, amount to only $20,000 ($8,000 + $12,000), and this is the amount recorded as revenue. Only $7,000 of the operating expenses are recognized in January; the remaining $3,000 will be recognized in future months when paid. Turning to the rental payment, the entire outflow of $6,000 is treated as January rent expense. The loan, which is a cash receipt, is not considered revenue because it has not been generated by Denton's earnings process. The $100 of interest, applicable to January, can also be ignored, because payment will not take place until February.

The cash basis of accounting is often criticized as not being in accord with economic reality. Stated simply, the receipt and disbursement of cash do not adequately measure financial activity within a given time period. This fact is apparent when examining Denton's transactions. Although the company rendered services amounting to $30,000, only those services for which cash is received in January are recognized as January revenue. As far as expenses are concerned, the firm incurred and became legally liable for $10,100 of operating and interest expense. Under cash-basis accounting, however, only $7,000 is recognized. Finally, expensing the entire $6,000 rental payment in the current month overstates Denton's "true" rent expense, because $4,000 really relates to February and March.

Overall, the cash basis does not properly match revenues and expenses. In Denton's case, for instance, several expenses that helped to generate January revenues will not be deducted until paid in future months. Furthermore, certain expenses were deducted (e.g., two months' rent) that failed to produce any revenue for the current period.

Cash and Accrual Methods in Practice

Because of the possible mismatch of revenues and expenses and the resulting misstatement of financial position, few businesses utilize a strict cash basis of accounting. The cash basis is probably employed most often in the preparation of income tax returns for individual taxpayers. The problem faced by businesses is that many companies have substantial investments in long-term assets such as buildings, machinery, and equipment. Under a strict cash basis these resources would be expensed when paid for, despite the fact that benefits are rendered for a number of years. In light of the

HIGHLIGHT
Cash-Basis Accounting and Uncle Sam

The problem with the federal government, Rep. Joseph J. DioGuardi says, is that it has too many lawyers and too few accountants. Mr. DioGuardi is an accountant. Recently, after a career spent poring over the books of private corporations, he won a seat in Congress and began studying the books of the federal government. "I'm appalled at the way we account for government spending around here," he said, his voice rising with indignation. "We're using a Mickey Mouse, cash-basis accounting system."

The New York Republican is more emphatic than most of his fellow accountants, but he isn't alone in his critique. The government's top accountant agrees. So do various other accountants, budget officials, and economists both inside and out of government. Bad accounting methods, critics say, can produce bad government policy. Because Washington focuses primarily on the cash it spends and gets each year—and the difference, or deficit, between them—its drives to cut immediate outlays can lead to actions that are penny-wise and pound-foolish.

Consider the following: Government budget proposals often include the sale of massive amounts of federal assets. Under the accounting methods used by large businesses, such asset sales would not necessarily increase income. For instance, if the assets were sold for less than the amount invested in them, a loss could arise. In contrast, under government accounting conventions, the cash raised by those asset sales would help to reduce the federal deficit, regardless of the sale price. "It's like selling your house to pay for your current spending," a Stanford University economist notes.

Further, a combination of deficit reduction goals and a cash-basis accounting system may drive Congress to raise cash or cut spending in the short run but increase costs over the long run. As an example, getting approval to buy or construct federal office space has become nearly impossible because of the big initial outlays that are involved. Such amounts, of course, would further increase the huge, present-day deficit. The outcome of this action is that the government's rent bill runs about a billion dollars a year. An accountant with the General Services Administration argues that because the government pays lower interest rates than private builders do and because it is almost certain to need the office space indefinitely, it would usually save money by owning rather than leasing. "The way it is [. . .], at the end of 20 years you end up with nothing but a bunch of canceled rent checks," he complains. [1]

Adding more fuel to the fire, the liabilities of programs such as Social Security and Medicare, which obligate the government to pay sizable benefits in the future, do not show up on the Treasury's books. Why? Under the cash basis, the amounts are not recognized until the payments take place. [2]

As one CPA observes about the cash basis, "Basically, the government is like someone who uses only a checkbook. That's not a complete picture of [. . .] financial affairs. It doesn't reflect assets, liabilities, commitments in the future. How can you run a trillion-dollar business without knowing what [the] financial position is?" [3]

Whatever the merits of arguments for accounting reform, change is occurring, albeit slowly. Accounting systems are being cleaned up, and various executive departments have taken steps to improve. Unfortunately, though, much remains to be done. [4] As DioGuardi has observed with regard to accountants in the Senate and the House, "I can't identify more than a handful in the entire history of Congress!" And, as an official from the Commerce Department notes, accounting changes aren't likely to alter the way Washington works. "[It's] politics," he says. [5]

Sources: Adapted from "Government's System of Accounting Comes Under Rising Criticism," *The Wall Street Journal*, February 3, 1986, pp. 1, 11 [1, 3, 5]; and "Restoring Fiscal Responsibility," *New Accountant*, February 1990, pp. 8–11 [2, 4]. The first article is reprinted by permission of *The Wall Street Journal*, © Dow Jones & Company, Inc., 1986. All rights reserved worldwide.

amount of dollars involved, the cash basis would severely distort reported earnings.

Most businesses that desire to use the cash basis adopt a **modified cash-basis** system, which is really a combination of both the cash and accrual methods. The cash basis is followed; however, significant expenditures that benefit multiple periods are established as assets in the accounts. As an asset's benefits are consumed, the cost is transferred to the income statement and treated as a business expense. The modified cash basis is often employed by professional practices (e.g., medical and law) and by small service organizations.

In contrast, virtually all large companies use the accrual basis of accounting. Usually, the majority of these firms' purchase, sale, and expense transactions are made on account, creating the likelihood that event occurrence and subsequent payment will take place in different periods. In view of the possible mismatch that can occur with the cash basis, the accrual method is endorsed by the accounting profession and featured throughout this text.

Financial statements that fairly present and measure economic activity cannot be produced by relying solely on information contained in the trial balance. As explained in the introduction to this chapter, many accounts need additional updating to reflect their correct status. Because of this situation, a process known as adjusting takes place at the end of the reporting period. In the **adjusting process** the accountant analyzes the various accounts that are maintained by a business. If updating is necessary, adjusting entries (adjustments) are recorded in the journal and posted to the ledger.

Frequently, the adjusting process centers on two specific situations:

1 Previously recorded multiperiod costs and revenues that must be split among two or more accounting periods.
2 Expenses that have been incurred and revenues that have been earned, but not as yet entered in the accounts.

The adjusting process is really an outgrowth of the accrual basis of accounting, with a focus on the revenues *earned* (as opposed to those received) and the expenses *incurred* (as opposed to paid).

ADJUSTING ENTRIES

OBJECTIVE
5

Explain why the adjusting process is needed and recognize which items typically require adjustment.

Multiperiod Costs and Revenues

Given the continuous nature of business activity, many of the costs and revenues encountered by a company pertain to more than a single accounting period. The three-month rental payment in the Denton Enterprises illustration is one such example. In order to measure financial activity correctly, these items must be split or allocated among the periods affected. The next few pages focus on the related allocation procedures for prepaid expenses, depreciation, and unearned revenues—common examples of multiperiod costs and revenues.

OBJECTIVE

Prepare adjusting entries
and show their impact on
the financial statements.

Prepaid Expenses

Prepaid expenses are goods and services purchased for future consumption and paid for in advance. Typical examples include such items as insurance, supplies, and rent. It is important to understand that prepaid expenses are *assets* because such amounts will benefit future accounting periods. As these assets are consumed in the process of producing revenue for a business, a portion of their cost must be written off as expense. This write-off occurs in the adjusting process and ensures a proper match of expense and revenue on the income statement.

To illustrate the required accounting, we will continue the Wise Advertising Agency example from Chapter 2. Wise had transactions during May that involved prepaid insurance and supplies.

Prepaid Insurance.   On May 1, the agency paid $480 for a two-year insurance policy. The transaction, which creates an asset known as prepaid insurance, is recorded by the following journal entry:

```
May 1   Prepaid Insurance              480
           Cash                                 480
        Purchased two-year policy
```

As each day passes, a portion of the insurance policy expires. Thus, at the end of the period, the Prepaid Insurance account must be updated by an adjusting entry.

The policy acquired provides protection for two years at a cost of $20 per month ($480 ÷ 24 months). By the end of May, $20 of the policy has been consumed; consequently, Wise must credit Prepaid Insurance. This amount represents an expense and, accordingly, total expenses are increased by a debit to Insurance Expense. Here is the necessary adjusting entry:

```
May 31   Insurance Expense                20
            Prepaid Insurance                    20
         To record expiration of one month's
         insurance coverage
```

These accounts now appear as follows:

Prepaid Insurance		Insurance Expense	
5/1 480	5/31 Adj 20	5/31 Adj 20	
(460)			

The Prepaid Insurance balance of $460 represents the 23 months of insurance that are still prepaid and is disclosed on the May 31 balance sheet in the asset section. The Insurance Expense account, which contains the one month of expired insurance at $20, appears on the May income statement.

The transfer of prepaid insurance to expense will continue in later periods. Eventually, by the end of two years, Wise will have a zero balance in the asset account. The cost of the entire policy will have been removed from the balance sheet, indicating that the firm expects no additional

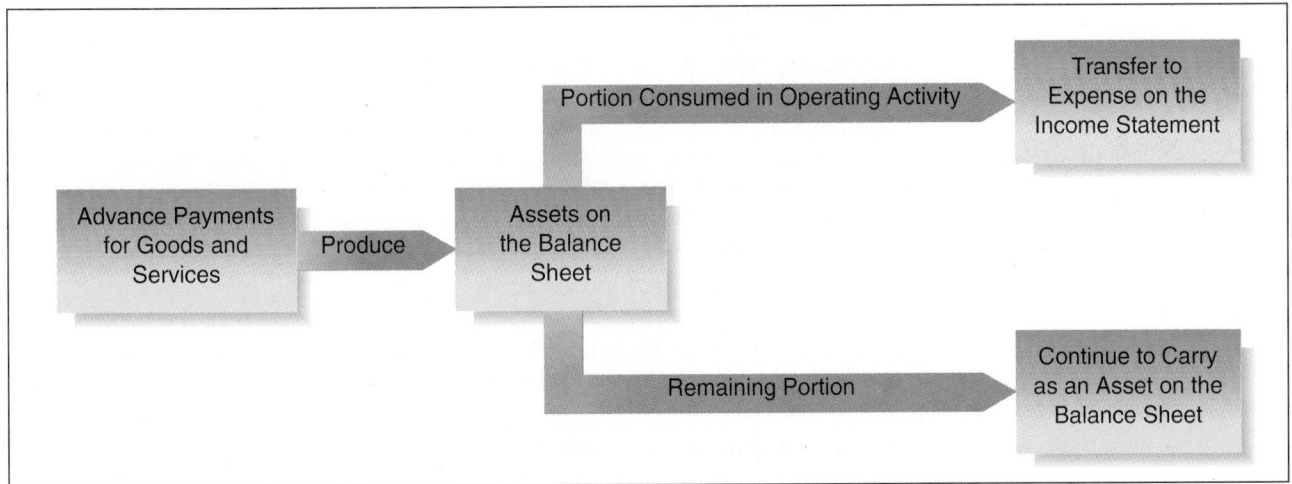

EXHIBIT 3-3
Accounting for Prepaid Expenses

future benefits from its May 1 payment. The proper accounting for prepaid expenses is shown in a generalized format in Exhibit 3-3.

Supplies. On May 4, the agency purchased $340 of supplies for cash. Because these items will be used in future periods, the purchase is recorded in an asset account as follows:

May 4   Supplies   340
        Cash   340
        Purchased supplies for cash

On May 31, Wise determined that various supplies had been consumed in operations and that items costing $260 remained on hand.

An adjusting entry must reduce the asset Supplies from $340 to $260 to reflect the amount owned at the end of the period. Because this account presently has a debit balance of $340, a credit of $80 yields the desired result. The $80 figure, which represents the portion used during May, is an expense and must be debited to Supplies Expense. The necessary adjusting entry follows.

May 31   Supplies Expense   80
        Supplies   80
        To record supplies used during
        the month

Similar to Wise's insurance transaction, the Supplies Expense balance of $80 would appear on the May income statement. The Supplies account contains a balance of $260 ($340 − $80) after adjustment and would be disclosed on the May 31 balance sheet. (For an overview of this process, see the Tips & Techniques box on p. 102.)

Depreciation

Most businesses spend relatively small amounts of money for prepaid expenses. Considerable sums are expended, however, for the acquisition of other assets, such as buildings, machinery, and equipment, that benefit multiple accounting periods. Although these assets normally assist in the revenue-producing process for a longer period of time than the typical prepaid expense, the same basic accounting practice is followed: the asset's balance is written off to expense upon consumption. This expense is called **depreciation.**

Generally speaking, accountants are unable to determine the exact portion of a long-term asset that is consumed in a given period. As a result, it is common practice to systematically expense a fraction of the asset's cost each year the asset is used. One possible approach for doing this, called the *straight-line method,* takes an equal amount of depreciation during each year of service life.

To illustrate, assume that Wise acquired a used car for cash on May 1 for use in the business. The car cost $4,500 and was estimated to have a service life of three years. The following entry was made:

May 1	Car	4,500	
	Cash		4,500
	Purchased used car		

Annual depreciation will total $1,500 ($4,500 ÷ 3 years). On a monthly basis this amounts to $125 ($1,500 ÷ 12), giving rise to the following adjusting entry on May 31:

May 31	Depreciation Expense	125	
	Accumulated Depreciation: Car		125
	To record one month's depreciation expense		

Depreciation Expense is debited and increases the agency's total expenses. Notice that the Car account is *not* credited, as accountants prefer to leave the cost of a long-term asset intact in the account where initially recorded. Thus, a separate account is established—Accumulated Depreciation: Car. This account appears as a *reduction* in the asset section of the balance sheet and is appropriately termed a **contra asset.** As its name implies, the Accumulated Depreciation account keeps a running total of the depreciation taken during the various accounting periods. The car would appear on the May 31 and June 30 balance sheets as follows:

	May 31	June 30
Assets		
⋮		
Car	$4,500	$4,500
Less: Accumulated depreciation	125	250
	$4,375	$4,250

The net figures ($4,375 and $4,250) represent the car's **book value,** or the amount that the car is carried at on the books of the business. Book value is simply the numerical difference between an asset's cost and the depreciation taken to date; it should not be equated with the value of the asset in the marketplace.

Unearned Revenues

The last of the multiperiod items to be discussed is unearned revenue. **Unearned revenue** represents future revenue that has been collected but not as yet earned. The earnings process, often called *realization,* will occur when some type of service is performed.

At the time of collection, unearned revenue represents a liability to the recipient, because goods or services are owed in return. Magazine publishers, for example, often establish an Unearned Subscription Revenue account. On receipt of a subscription, the publisher owes the subscriber a specified number of issues. As another example, airlines often report unearned revenue accounts on their balance sheets. Consider USAir Group, Inc., for instance, which owns USAir and several commuter airlines. Recently, the company reported $513 million in a liability account entitled Traffic Balances Payable and Unused Tickets. An explanation of this account was found in the following note that accompanied the financial statements:

> Passenger ticket sales are recognized as revenue when the transportation service is rendered. At the time of sale, a liability is established (Traffic Balances Payable and Unused Tickets) and subsequently eliminated either through carriage of the passenger, through billing from another carrier which renders the service or by refund to the passenger.

Returning to the Wise Advertising Agency example, assume that the firm received $10,400 on May 16 to design and run a 52-week advertising program for McConnell and Associates. The necessary work on the program began immediately. The following entry records the receipt of cash:

May 16	Cash	10,400	
	Unearned Agency Revenue		10,400
	Receipt for 52-week program		

Unearned Agency Revenue is a liability account, because Wise owes McConnell a service (advertising work). Observe that the credit increases the agency's obligations to its clients.

By the end of May, two weeks of work had been performed on the contract. Because revenue is earned at the rate of $200 per week ($10,400 ÷ 52), $400 must be recorded as Agency Revenue for inclusion on the May income statement. In addition, the amount of advertising work owed to

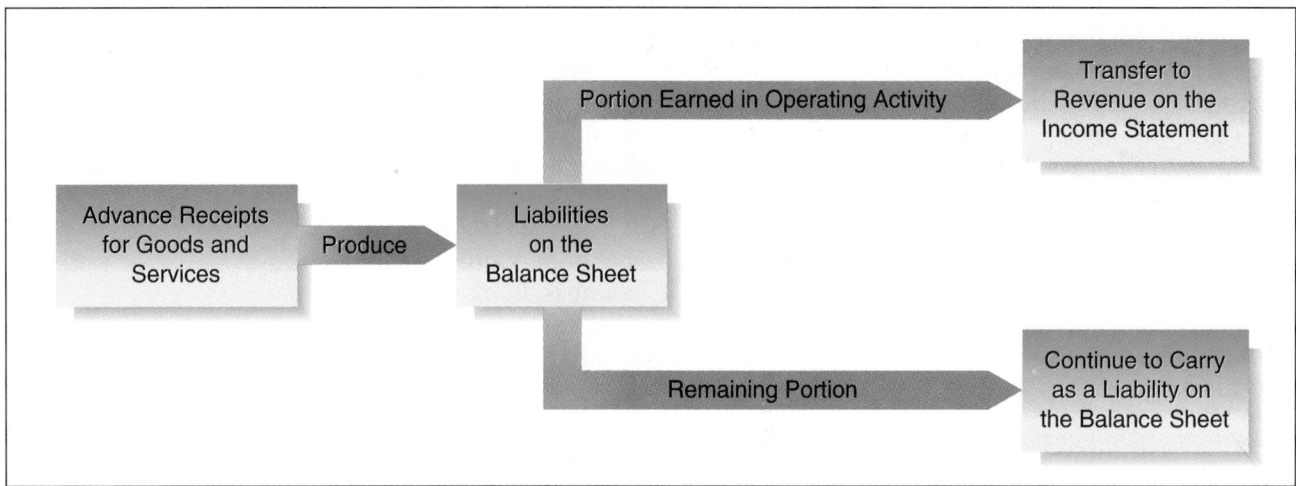

EXHIBIT 3-4
Accounting for Unearned
Revenues

McConnell has been reduced to $10,000 ($10,400 − $400) and will appear in the liability section of Wise's balance sheet. The proper updating is achieved by the following adjusting entry:

May 31 Unearned Agency Revenue   400
     Agency Revenue   400
     To record agency revenue earned
     during the month

The impact of the entry is shown by these T-accounts:[2]

Unearned Agency Revenue		**Agency Revenue**	
5/31 Adj 400	5/16 10,400		5/31 Adj 400
	(10,000)		

The preceding accounting treatment parallels that shown earlier for prepaid expenses. In this case, an appropriate amount of the liability becomes earned as services are performed, requiring a transfer of dollars from the unearned account to Agency Revenue. This process is illustrated in a generalized format in Exhibit 3-4.

Unrecorded Expenses and Revenues—Accruals

Accruals are expenses and revenues that gradually accumulate throughout an accounting period. Unlike the multiperiod costs and revenues just presented, accruals have not as yet been recorded in the accounts. As a result, an adjusting entry is needed so that these items are properly considered when the financial statements are prepared.

Accruals are consistent with the accrual basis of accounting. **Accrued expenses** are expenses that have been incurred but not as yet paid. Examples include the wages incurred by businesses during the last few days of a

---

[2] In Chapter 2, the Agency Revenue account was affected by transactions on May 14, 27, and 31. These transactions are omitted here, allowing us to focus solely on the unearned revenue concept.

month and the interest owed to creditors on loans. Both of these expenses gradually accumulate and are likely to be paid in the next reporting period. **Accrued revenues,** on the other hand, have been earned although not as yet received. Common examples of accrued revenues include the interest just mentioned (from the creditors' viewpoint), commissions earned, and unbilled revenues. As you can see, we are focusing on revenues *earned* and expenses *incurred,* and *not* on the related cash receipt or disbursement. These concepts are explored by returning to the Wise Advertising illustration.

Accrued Expenses

On May 1, the agency obtained a $6,000 loan. Payments are due on the first of each month; interest is computed at the rate of 1% per month on the unpaid balance. The proceeds from the loan are recorded in the following entry:

```
May 1   Cash                        6,000
            Loan Payable                     6,000
        Recorded loan proceeds
```

As of May 31, interest charges have been incurred because Wise has had use of the borrowed funds during the month. Although the interest will not be remitted until the first payment date on June 1, the charges arose in May and should appear on May's financial statements. Consequently, an adjusting entry is needed to update the accounts.

Interest is computed at the rate of 1% per month on the unpaid balance of the loan. May's interest thus amounts to $60 ($6,000 × 0.01). This amount represents an increase in Wise's total borrowing costs for the accounting period, requiring a debit to Interest Expense. Further, because payment does not occur until the following month, $60 must also be placed in a liability account to show the firm's obligation as of May 31. Interest Payable is therefore credited, and the adjusting entry follows.

```
May 31   Interest Expense              60
             Interest Payable                 60
         To record accrued interest for May
```

Accrued Salaries. Focusing on another accrued expense (salaries), assume that Wise's employees work a five-day week. Employees are paid once, on the last Friday of each month, and payday for May occurred on the 28th (see p. 62). As shown in the accompanying diagram, the company has incurred one day of expense (May 31) that will not be paid until the end of June.

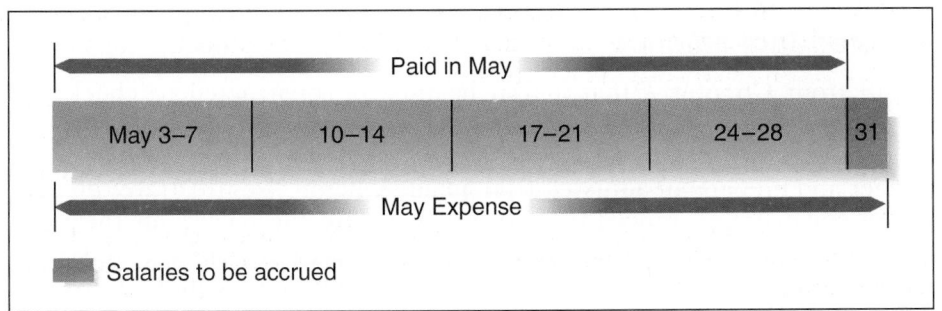

This expense properly belongs to May and must be accrued (i.e., recorded) at the end of the month by an adjustment. If salaries for May 31 amount to $50, the necessary adjusting entry is:

May 31   Salaries Expense   50
              Salaries Payable   50
         To record accrued salaries for May

The expense is debited because the agency's total salary cost has increased. Salaries Payable, a liability, is credited to reflect the added obligation of the firm as of month-end.

Accrued Revenues

To illustrate accrued revenue, assume that on May 14, Wise agreed to provide services for Holmes Corporation during the next five months. As of May 31, the agency had rendered services totaling $710. The $710 is properly considered May revenue because the service was provided during May; yet, to date, no entry has been made in the accounting records. The correct adjusting entry is as follows:

May 31   Accounts Receivable   710
              Agency Revenue   710
         To record accrued revenue for May

Accounts Receivable is debited because the amounts due from clients have increased. Also, Agency Revenue is credited to record the increase in the revenue earned from business activity.

Tips & Techniques

The adjustments required for accruals are an extension of two simple definitions. An accrued expense has been *incurred but not as yet paid,* and an accrued revenue has been *earned though not as yet received.* Given that both of these items must be entered in the accounting records at the end of the period, the adjustments may be pictured as follows:

Accrued Expense		Accrued Revenue	
Expense	XXX*	Receivable	XXX
Payable	XXX	Revenue	XXX†

* Amount incurred
† Amount earned

Adjusted Trial Balance

OBJECTIVE 7

Prepare an adjusted trial balance.

Recall from Chapter 2 that a trial balance is constructed to check the equality of debits and credits in the general ledger. To reflect the account changes that result from the adjusting entries, many companies go one step further and prepare an **adjusted trial balance.** Before we illustrate the necessary construction procedures, we must update the records of the Wise Advertising Agency for the additional transactions of May introduced in this chapter. For the required computations, study the accounts in Exhibit 2-5 and then review the tabulation that follows.

Cash: $2,625 + $10,400 (unearned revenue) + $6,000 (loan) −
    $480 (insurance) − $340 (supplies) − $4,500 (car) $13,705

Prepaid insurance: $0 + $480 (purchase on 5/1) $480

Supplies: $0 + $340 (purchase on 5/4) $340

Car: $0 + $4,500 (purchase on 5/1) $4,500

Unearned agency revenue: $0 + $10,400 (receipt on 5/16) $10,400

Loan payable: $0 + $6,000 (obtained on 5/1) $6,000

The double underlined figures (and others) are carried forward to the first two columns of Exhibit 3-5, where preparation is shown. Note that the "regular" trial balance summarizes daily transaction information only; adjusting entries are not considered. Columns 3 and 4, on the other hand, reveal the adjustments presented in the preceding discussion.

Observe that both halves of each adjustment (i.e., debit and credit) are keyed or referenced by a letter—the letter (a) in the case of insurance. The purpose of this procedure is to facilitate an examination of the adjustments by anyone who so desires. There are no rules regarding the assignment of specific letters to particular accounts.

EXHIBIT 3-5
Preparation of Adjusted Trial Balance

Account Title	Trial Balance Debit	Trial Balance Credit	Adjustments Debit	Adjustments Credit	Adjusted Trial Balance Debit	Adjusted Trial Balance Credit
Cash	13,705				13,705	
Accounts receivable	3,150		(g) 710		3,860	
Prepaid insurance	480			(a) 20	460	
Supplies	340			(b) 80	260	
Land	5,500				5,500	
Car	4,500				4,500	
Accounts payable		125				125
Unearned agency revenue		10,400	(d) 400			10,000
Loan payable		6,000				6,000
Gary Wise, capital		9,000				9,000
Gary Wise, drawing	200				200	
Agency revenue		4,100		(d) 400 (g) 710		5,210
Salaries expense	825		(f) 50		875	
Marketing expense	800				800	
Electricity expense	125				125	
	29,625	29,625				
Insurance expense			(a) 20		20	
Supplies expense			(b) 80		80	
Depreciation expense			(c) 125		125	
Accumulated depreciation: car				(c) 125		125
Interest expense			(e) 60		60	
Interest payable				(e) 60		60
Salaries payable				(f) 50		50
			1,445	1,445	30,570	30,570

EXHIBIT 3-6
Adjusted Trial Balance

WISE ADVERTISING AGENCY
Adjusted Trial Balance
May 31, 19XX

Cash	$13,705	
Accounts receivable	3,860	
Prepaid insurance	460	
Supplies	260	
Land	5,500	
Car	4,500	
Accumulated depreciation: car		$ 125
Accounts payable		125
Unearned agency revenue		10,000
Interest payable		60
Salaries payable		50
Loan payable		6,000
Gary Wise, capital		9,000
Gary Wise, drawing	200	
Agency revenue		5,210
Salaries expense	875	
Marketing expense	800	
Electricity expense	125	
Insurance expense	20	
Supplies expense	80	
Depreciation expense	125	
Interest expense	60	
	$30,570	$30,570

In several cases an account that is needed in an adjusting entry does not appear in the trial balance. When this situation occurs, the account is simply written on the lines below the trial balance. After all the adjustment information is entered, the columns are totaled to check the equality of debits and credits.

Next, the trial balance data and the adjustments are combined to yield the desired outcome. As an example, the $3,150 balance in Accounts Receivable is combined with a $710 debit (increase) from an adjusting entry, and the result ($3,860) is placed in the debit column of the adjusted trial balance. Similarly, the Prepaid Insurance balance of $480 is credited or reduced by a $20 adjustment. The account's $460 ending balance, a debit, is thus also entered in the debit column. After all extensions have been made, the columns are totaled to verify mathematical accuracy. The completed product is shown in Exhibit 3-6. Notice that for presentation purposes, all similar account types have been grouped together.

Once an adjusted trial balance is prepared, the accountant has an excellent springboard for construction of the financial statements. As you will see in Chapter 4, the data just developed serve as the foundation for a *work sheet*—a columnar form that aids in the generation of the income statement, statement of owner's equity, and balance sheet.

EXHIBIT 3-7
Prepaid Expense Adjustment Errors

Entry omitted:

Expense	XXX	
Prepaid Expense*		XXX
To record the expiration of a prepaid expense		

* An asset account

Income Statement	
Revenues	$ OK
Less expenses	Understated
Net income	$ Overstated

Statement of Owner's Equity		
Beginning balance, Jan. 1		$ OK
Add: Net income	$Overstated	
Deduct: Withdrawals	OK	Overstated
Ending balance, Dec. 31		$Overstated

Balance Sheet	
Assets	$Overstated
Liabilities	$ OK
Owner's equity	Overstated
Total liabilities & owner's equity	$Overstated

Adjustment Errors

The adjusting process is very important as far as the accountant is concerned. Failure to adjust the books properly at the end of the period will produce errors in the financial statements. To illustrate, assume that Wise's accountant failed to consider the expiration of a prepaid expense. As a result, an expense account was not debited, nor was an asset account credited. The company's expenses were not increased and are therefore understated. Because such amounts are subtracted from revenues on the income statement, the reported net income figure will be too high. Unfortunately, the problem does not stop here, given the manner in which the financial statements are linked together (see Exhibit 3-7). The overstated net income is carried forward to both the statement of owner's equity and the balance sheet. The exhibit reveals, however, that the required equality between assets and the total of liabilities and owner's equity is still maintained because of Wise's failure to credit (reduce) the appropriate asset account.

Should the adjustment error involve an accrual, a similar type of analysis can be performed. Assume, for instance, that Wise's accountant failed to make the $710 adjustment for accrued revenues. The failure to credit Agency Revenue will understate revenues on the income statement. If revenues are understated, net income will be too small. This, in turn, depresses ending owner's equity on both the statement of owner's equity and the balance sheet. The balance sheet will balance, however, because the accountant also failed to debit (increase) Accounts Receivable.

APPENDIX: AN ALTERNATIVE ACCOUNTING TREATMENT FOR PREPAID EXPENSES AND UNEARNED REVENUES

OBJECTIVE

Describe and use the "income statement approach" of accounting for prepaid expenses and unearned revenues.

The accounting treatments illustrated in the body of this chapter for prepaid expenses and unearned revenues are used by many businesses. These treatments could be called the "balance sheet approach" because the initial recording of insurance, supplies, and revenues received in advance took place in balance sheet accounts. More specifically, the acquisition of prepaid expenses entailed a debit to an asset account, while the receipt of unearned revenue generated a credit to a liability.

Under an alternative practice followed by some firms (i.e., the "income statement approach"), prepaid expenses and unearned revenues are recorded initially in income statement accounts. Prepaid expenses are immediately charged to expense when acquired, and unearned revenues are credited to revenue accounts upon collection. To illustrate these accounting alternatives, we will continue to use data from the Wise Advertising Agency example.

Accounting for Prepaid Expenses

Recall from page 100 that Wise acquired a two-year insurance policy on May 1. The $480 policy cost was recorded in an asset account entitled Prepaid Insurance, indicating use of the balance sheet method. One month of the policy expired during May, requiring a transfer of $20 ($480 ÷ 24 months) from Prepaid Insurance to Insurance Expense via an adjusting entry. These events and the resulting financial statement disclosures are summarized at the top of Exhibit 3-8.

This exhibit also reveals the proper accounting had the agency used the income statement approach. Upon acquisition, the cost of the entire policy is placed in the Insurance Expense account. It is naturally incorrect to show the full policy cost of $480 on May's income statement because the actual expense to the firm is only $20. In view of this situation, an adjusting entry is needed at the end of the month.

To achieve the desired $20 balance in Insurance Expense, this account must be reduced, or credited, by $460 ($480 − $460 = $20). The $460 figure represents the cost of the policy's forthcoming 23 months (i.e., the prepaid portion as of May 31) and is therefore debited to Prepaid Insurance. In effect, the adjustment transfers the *unused* portion of the prepayment from the expense account to an asset. The overall result of this process is one month of cost on the income statement and the remaining 23 months of cost on the balance sheet.

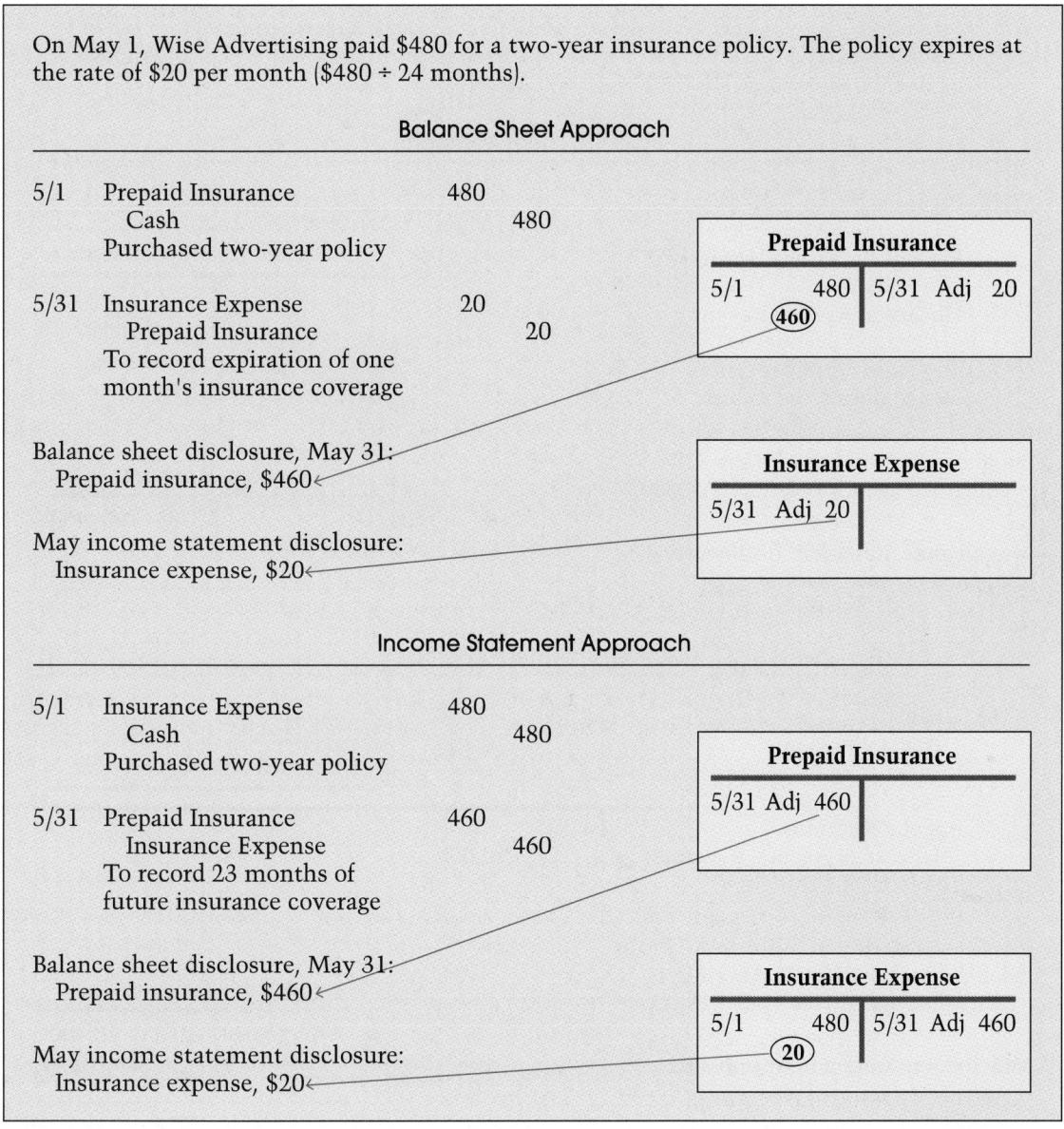

On May 1, Wise Advertising paid $480 for a two-year insurance policy. The policy expires at the rate of $20 per month ($480 ÷ 24 months).

Balance Sheet Approach

5/1	Prepaid Insurance	480	
	Cash		480
	Purchased two-year policy		

5/31	Insurance Expense	20	
	Prepaid Insurance		20
	To record expiration of one month's insurance coverage		

Prepaid Insurance

| 5/1 | 480 | 5/31 Adj | 20 |
| | (460) | | |

Balance sheet disclosure, May 31:
  Prepaid insurance, $460

Insurance Expense

| 5/31 Adj | 20 | |

May income statement disclosure:
  Insurance expense, $20

Income Statement Approach

5/1	Insurance Expense	480	
	Cash		480
	Purchased two-year policy		

Prepaid Insurance

| 5/31 Adj | 460 | |

5/31	Prepaid Insurance	460	
	Insurance Expense		460
	To record 23 months of future insurance coverage		

Balance sheet disclosure, May 31:
  Prepaid insurance, $460

Insurance Expense

| 5/1 | 480 | 5/31 Adj | 460 |
| | (20) | | |

May income statement disclosure:
  Insurance expense, $20

EXHIBIT 3-8
Alternative Accounting Methods for Prepaid Expenses

Accounting for Unearned Revenues

The alternative accounting treatment for unearned revenues is similar to that shown for prepaid expenses. We will once again utilize data from the Wise Advertising example, this time focusing on the May 16 receipt of $10,400 for a 52-week advertising program. The analysis shown earlier in the text on page 103 is summarized at the top of Exhibit 3-9.

Wise originally recorded the receipt by crediting Unearned Agency Revenue, a liability account. Because two weeks of work had been performed by month-end, the adjusting entry reflected the earnings process and transferred $400 from the liability account to Agency Revenue for inclusion on

Wise received $10,400 on May 16 to design and run a 52-week advertising program for Mc-Connell and Associates. Two weeks of work had been performed by the end of the month, resulting in $400 of revenue [($10,400 ÷ 52 weeks) × 2].

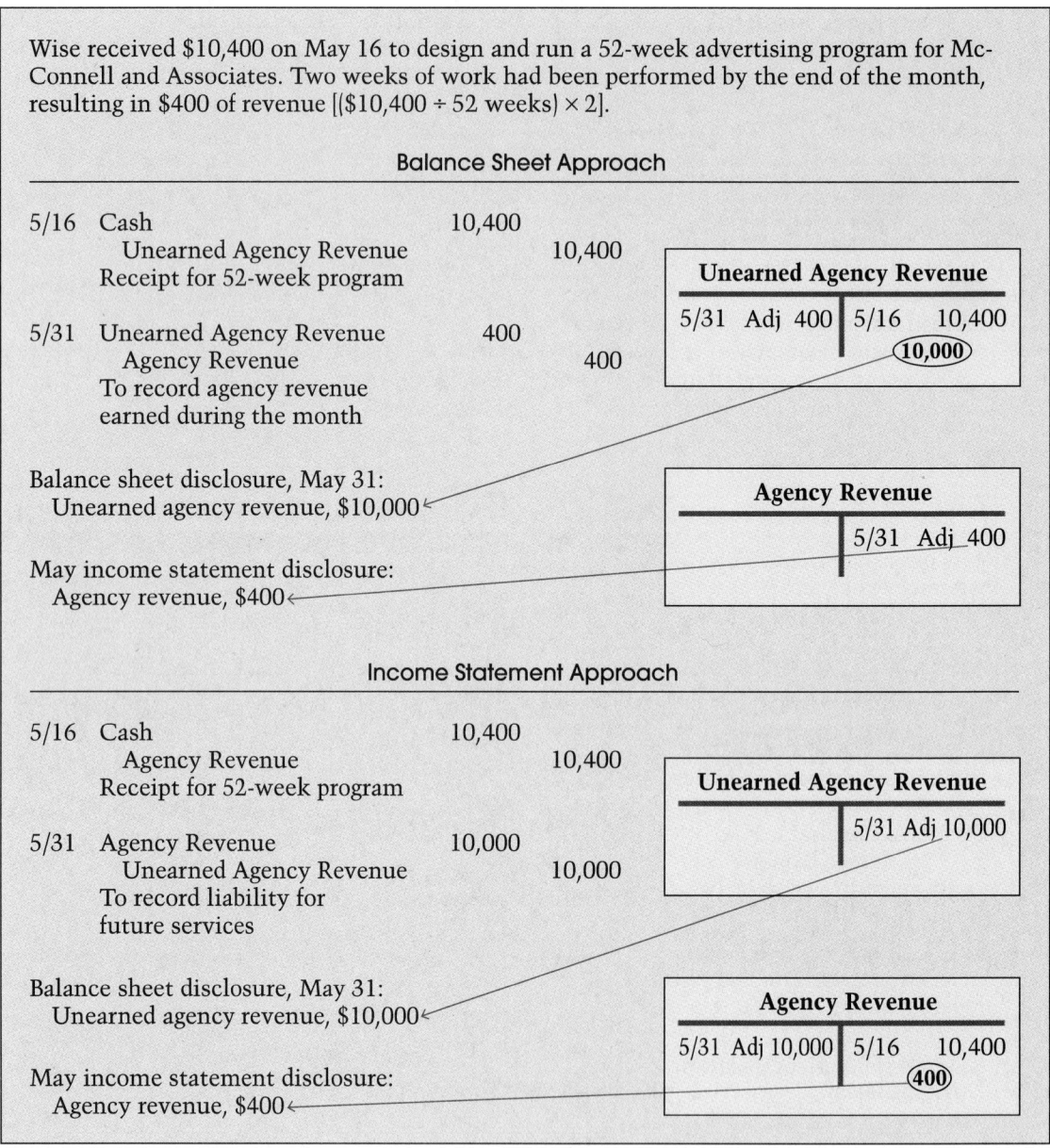

Balance Sheet Approach

5/16	Cash	10,400	
	Unearned Agency Revenue		10,400
	Receipt for 52-week program		

5/31	Unearned Agency Revenue	400	
	Agency Revenue		400
	To record agency revenue earned during the month		

Unearned Agency Revenue

| 5/31 Adj 400 | 5/16   10,400 |
| | **10,000** |

Agency Revenue

| | 5/31   Adj 400 |

Balance sheet disclosure, May 31:
   Unearned agency revenue, $10,000

May income statement disclosure:
   Agency revenue, $400

Income Statement Approach

5/16	Cash	10,400	
	Agency Revenue		10,400
	Receipt for 52-week program		

5/31	Agency Revenue	10,000	
	Unearned Agency Revenue		10,000
	To record liability for future services		

Unearned Agency Revenue

| | 5/31 Adj 10,000 |

Agency Revenue

| 5/31 Adj 10,000 | 5/16   10,400 |
| | **400** |

Balance sheet disclosure, May 31:
   Unearned agency revenue, $10,000

May income statement disclosure:
   Agency revenue, $400

EXHIBIT 3-9
Alternative Accounting Methods for Unearned Revenues

the income statement. The remaining amount of advertising work to be performed ($10,000) is disclosed on the balance sheet.

Had Wise employed the income statement method, the $10,400 collection would have been entered in an income statement account on May 16, namely, Agency Revenue. By May 31, the firm had earned a total of $400—the proper amount to disclose on the income statement. An adjusting entry is therefore needed that reduces (debits) the Agency Revenue account by $10,000 ($10,400 − $10,000 = $400). This amount is a liability for Wise because the firm owes $10,000 of future services. Appropriately, then, the adjusting entry removes the amount *yet to be earned* from the Agency Revenue account and places it in Unearned Agency Revenue. The resulting financial statement disclosures reveal the agency's liability and revenue earned at $10,000 and $400, respectively.

A Comparison of the Two Approaches

Careful study of the balance sheet and income statement approaches shows that the resulting financial statement presentations are identical. Both of these methods are found in practice, with the income statement approach being extremely popular for those items that will be *totally* consumed (or earned) in the accounting period of payment (or receipt). Such items would not require adjusting entries at the end of the period, given the income statement's adjustment focus on the amounts *unused* or *unearned*. The end result is less work at this busy time of the processing cycle.

END-OF-CHAPTER-REVIEW

1 Explain the impact of the periodicity assumption on accounting and income measurement. The periodicity assumption holds that for reporting purposes, an entity's life is divided into discrete accounting periods. These periods allow feedback to interested parties at specified intervals of time, such as a month, quarter, or a year. Because of the continuous nature of economic activities (e.g., the generation of revenue), the assumption requires that economic activities be allocated or apportioned among the periods affected.

LEARNING OBJECTIVES: THE KEY POINTS

2 Apply the principle of revenue recognition. Accountants generally use a point-of-sale rule to determine the proper time to recognize revenue in the accounting records. Revenues are usually entered in the accounts when goods are sold or when services are rendered. Both of these situations signify completion of a major part of the economic activity related to the transaction.

3 Apply the matching principle and record expenses in the proper accounting period. Expenses are entered in the accounting records in the same period as the revenues that they helped to produce. This concept, known as the matching principle, is relatively straightforward when a strong cause and effect relationship exists between revenue and expense. When such a relationship is absent, allocation methods (e.g., depreciation) are needed to charge each period with an appropriate amount of expense.

4 Calculate net income under both the accrual basis and the cash basis of accounting. With the accrual basis, revenues are recognized in the accounts when goods are sold or when services are rendered, and expenses are recognized when incurred. This method of accounting results in a better matching of revenue and expense than the cash basis. Under the cash basis, revenues are recorded in the accounts in the period of receipt, and expenses are recognized when paid.

5 Explain why the adjusting process is needed and recognize which items typically require adjustment. The adjusting process is needed because many accounts are not up-to-date at the end of the accounting period. The items that often need adjustment include previously recorded costs and revenues that must be split among two or more periods (e.g., prepaid expenses, long-term assets, and unearned revenues). Other items that require adjusting entries are accrued revenues and expenses, or revenues and expenses that have been earned or incurred in a given period but not as yet entered in the accounts.

6 Prepare adjusting entries and show their impact on the financial statements. This chapter introduced the adjustments for prepaid expenses, depreciation, unearned revenues, accrued expenses, and accrued revenues. The proper entries for these items are generalized in the following chart:

Type of Adjustment	Type of Account	
	Debited	Credited
Prepaid expense	Expense	Asset
Depreciation	Expense	Contra asset
Unearned revenue	Liability	Revenue
Accrued expense	Expense	Liability
Accrued revenue	Asset	Revenue

The omission of any of these entries would affect both the balance sheet and the income statement. The failure to debit an expense, for example, would understate expenses, overstate net income, and overstate owner's equity.

7 Prepare an adjusted trial balance. The adjusted trial balance is prepared at the end of an accounting period by combining the trial balance and a company's adjusting entries. This document is used to assist in the construction of financial statements.

8 (Appendix) Describe and use the "income statement approach" of accounting for prepaid expenses and unearned revenues. Under the "income statement approach," prepaid expenses are recorded initially in expense accounts, and unearned revenues are entered in revenue accounts. The adjusting process moves the unconsumed part of the prepaid expense from the expense account to an asset account. Similarly, the yet-to-be-earned portion of the unearned revenue is transferred from the revenue account to a liability.

**KEY TERMS
AND CONCEPTS:
A QUICK OVERVIEW**

accrual   Revenues and expenses that gradually accumulate throughout an accounting period.

accrual basis   The accounting basis that recognizes revenues when earned and, for income determination purposes, matches expenses against the revenues generated.

accrued expenses   Unpaid expenses that are matched against revenues under the accrual basis of accounting.

accrued revenues   Revenues recognized under the accrual basis of accounting as being earned although such amounts have not yet been received.

adjusted trial balance   A trial balance prepared after adjusting entries have been made and posted to the ledger accounts.

adjusting process   A process performed at the end of the period in which appropriate accounts are analyzed and updated.

book value   The amount that an asset is carried at in the accounting records—namely, cost minus accumulated depreciation.

cash basis   The basis of accounting that focuses on the cash flows connected with revenues and expenses. Revenues are recognized when received, and expenses are recognized when paid.

contra asset   An account used to reduce asset balances in the financial statements.

depreciation   The process used to allocate the cost of long-lived items of plant and equipment to the accounting periods benefited.

fiscal year   Any one-year period other than a calendar year—for example, July 1–June 30.

matching principle   The principle that expenses associated with the production of revenue are recognized in the same period that the revenue is recognized.

modified cash basis   A method that utilizes features from both the cash and accrual bases of accounting.

natural business year   A year that concludes at the end of the business cycle—for example, October 31 for a professional baseball club, which is after the play-offs and World Series.

periodicity assumption   An assumption stipulating that for reporting purposes, an entity's life can be divided into discrete time periods such as months, quarters, or years.

prepaid expenses   Goods or services purchased for future consumption and paid for in advance.

revenue recognition   The point at which revenue is entered into the accounting records; generally when goods are sold or services rendered.

transactions approach   An approach to determining and measuring net income by focusing on business transactions, which have produced changes in the entity's assets, liabilities, and/or owner's equity.

unearned revenue   Future revenue that has been collected but not as yet earned.

CHAPTER QUIZ

The five questions that follow relate to several issues raised in the chapter. Test your knowledge of the issues by selecting the best answer. (The answers appear on p. 131.)

1 The accrual basis of accounting:
   a is less popular than the cash basis with respect to use by large businesses.
   b better matches expenses and revenues than does the cash basis of accounting.
   c recognizes revenues when earned and expenses when paid.
   d recognizes revenues when received and expenses when paid.

2 Joe Hamilton contacted Denver Painting Contractors in July to paint his office building. The price was agreed on in August, the painting took place in September, and Hamilton paid Denver in October. In which month would Hamilton recognize an expense under the accrual basis of accounting? Under the cash basis of accounting?

	Accrual Basis	Cash Basis
a	July	September
b	August	September
c	September	October
d	August	October

3 The Supplies account of Design Limited contained a $3,200 balance before adjustment on December 31. If $2,400 of supplies remain on hand at year-end, the proper adjusting entry would be:

	Debit	Credit	Amount
a	Supplies Expense	Supplies	$2,400
b	Supplies Expense	Supplies	$800
c	Supplies	Supplies Expense	$2,400
d	Supplies	Supplies Expense	$800

4 Kip's Appliances sells three-month service contracts to buyers of new appliances. The $32,800 balance in the company's Unearned Service Contract Revenue account is properly classified as:

a an expense.   c an asset.
b revenue.   d a liability.

5 As of August 31, Sun Shade Auto Tinting owes $600 of interest (as yet unrecorded) to First Bank and Trust. If payment will take place on September 5, Sun Shade would classify the interest on August 31 as:

a a prepaid expense.   c an accrued expense.
b an unearned revenue.   d an accrued revenue.

SUMMARY PROBLEM

Gottom Company began operation on January 1 of the current year. The company's December 31 trial balance follows.

GOTTOM COMPANY Trial Balance December 31, 19XX		
Cash	$ 65,000	
Accounts receivable	4,200	
Office supplies	800	
Prepaid insurance	2,000	
Office furniture	16,000	
Accounts payable		$ 10,000
Paul Gottom, capital		30,000
Paul Gottom, drawing	7,400	
Service revenue		85,000
Salaries expense	24,000	
Rent expense	3,000	
Utilities expense	2,000	
Other expense	600	
	$125,000	$125,000

The following adjustment information has come to your attention:
1 Ending office supplies on hand: $300.
2 Prepaid insurance expired during the period: $1,600.
3 Depreciation expense on the furniture: $2,000.
4 Accrued salaries owed to employees: $150.

Instructions

a Prepare Gottom's required adjusting entries.
b Prepare an adjusted trial balance similar to that shown in Exhibit 3-6.

Solution

a Dec. 31   Office Supplies Expense*   500
       Office Supplies   500
      To record supplies used during the period

   31   Insurance Expense   1,600
       Prepaid Insurance   1,600
      To record expiration of insurance coverage

   31   Depreciation Expense   2,000
       Accumulated Depreciation: Office
         Furniture   2,000
      To record the period's depreciation expense

   31   Salaries Expense   150
       Salaries Payable   150
      To record accrued salaries as of year-end

      * $800 − $300.

b

	GOTTOM COMPANY Adjusted Trial Balance December 31, 19XX	
Cash	$ 65,000	
Accounts receivable	4,200	
Office supplies*	300	
Prepaid insurance†	400	
Office furniture	16,000	
Accumulated depreciation: office furniture		$ 2,000
Accounts payable		10,000
Salaries payable		150
Paul Gottom, capital		30,000
Paul Gottom, drawing	7,400	
Service revenue		85,000
Salaries expense†	24,150	
Rent expense	3,000	
Utilities expense	2,000	
Office supplies expense	500	
Insurance expense	1,600	
Depreciation expense	2,000	
Other expense	600	
	$127,150	$127,150

   * $800 − $500.
   † $2,000 − $1,600.
   ‡ $24,000 + $150.

ASSIGNMENT MATERIAL

QUESTIONS

Q3-1 Why aren't financial statements prepared directly from the account balances reported in the trial balance?

Q3-2 Explain the transactions approach to the measurement of a company's net income or net loss.

Q3-3 Present three examples of "exchange-type" transactions.

Q3-4 Differentiate between a fiscal year and a natural business year.

Q3-5 What basic accounting problem arises from dividing the life of a business into discrete periods for reporting purposes?

Q3-6 When is revenue generally recognized in the accounting records?

Q3-7 Explain the matching principle.

Q3-8 Explain when expenses and revenues are recognized under both the accrual basis and the cash basis of accounting.

Q3-9 Explain, by citing several examples, how the cash basis can result in a mismatch of revenues and expenses in a given accounting period.

Q3-10 Explain why virtually all large businesses use the accrual basis of accounting.

Q3-11 Fuller Company uses a calendar year and prepares quarterly reports for its owner. On August 1, the firm prepaid a six-month, $600 insurance premium. What is the proper amount of insurance expense to recognize for the third quarter under (a) the cash basis and (b) the accrual basis?

Q3-12 What types of items frequently require adjusting entries?

Q3-13 In reviewing the records of Yager Company, you find that three months' rent of $750 was prepaid to Savage Property Management on November 1. Both companies use the accrual basis of accounting. In view of this transaction,
   a What account and amount would you show on Yager's income statement for the month ended November 30? On Savage's income statement for the month ended November 30?
   b What account and amount would you show on Yager's November 30 balance sheet? On Savage's November 30 balance sheet?

Q3-14 What is meant by the term "depreciation"? What is the purpose of recording depreciation in the accounting records?

Q3-15 A large retailer offers service contracts with the purchase of major appliances by customers. When a contract is sold, the following entry is made:

Cash   XXX
   Unearned Service Contract Revenue   XXX
To record sale of service contract

On which financial statement and in what section would the Unearned Service Contract Revenue account appear? What is the rationale behind your answer?

Q3-16 How does an accrued expense differ from a prepaid expense?

*Q3-17 Modular Products, Inc., recently charged an outlay for prepaid advertising costs to the Advertising Expense account. Describe the adjusting entry that would be required at the end of the period.

E3-1 *Revenue and expense recognition, accrual basis* (L.O. 2, 3, 4)
Dave Morris began a law practice several years ago, shortly after graduating from law school. During 19X1, he was approached by Delores Silva, who had recently suffered a back injury in an automobile accident. Morris accepted Silva as a client, and in 19X2 proceeded with a lawsuit against Maddox Motors. The suit alleged that Maddox had knowingly sold Silva an automobile with defective brakes. Late in 19X2, the courts awarded Silva $240,000 in damages. Morris was entitled to 40% of this settlement for his fees. In 19X3, Maddox Motors paid Silva and Morris their respective shares of the judgment.

Morris incurred secretarial and photocopy charges in 19X2 of $12,000—all related to the Silva case. Of this amount, $8,000 was paid in 19X2 and the balance was paid in 19X3.

Assuming that Morris uses the accrual basis of accounting, in what year(s) should the revenue and expense amounts be recognized? Why?

E3-2 *Accrual-basis and cash-basis income computation* (L.O. 4)
Campbell's Cooking Clinic furnished the following information about its first year of operation:

- *Revenue from cooking classes*—The firm provided 14,000 hours of classroom instruction at $5 per hour. Students paid $18,000 at the time of enrollment; an additional $40,000 was subsequently collected prior to the end of the year. The remaining balance is still outstanding.
- *Lesson booklets*—The clinic purchased 1,000 lesson booklets at $4 each for use in its classes. Eighty percent of the total purchase price had been paid by year-end. A count on December 31 revealed that 400 booklets were still on hand.
- *Operating expenses*—Rent, salary, advertising, and office expenses of $15,600 had been incurred by December 31. Of this amount, $3,100 will be paid in the following accounting period.

a Compute Campbell's accrual-basis net income for the year ended December 31.
b Compute Campbell's cash-basis net income for the year ended December 31.

E3-3 *Recognition of concepts* (L.O. 5)
Ron Carroll operates a small company that books entertainers for theaters, parties, conventions, and so forth. The company's fiscal year ends on June 30. Consider the items that follow and classify each as either (1) prepaid expense, (2) unearned revenue, (3) accrued expense, (4) accrued revenue, or (5) none of the foregoing.
a Amounts paid on June 30 for a one-year insurance policy.
b Professional fees earned but not billed as of June 30.
c Repairs to the firm's copy machine, incurred and paid in June.
d An advance payment from a client for a performance next month at a convention.

---

* An asterisk preceding an item indicates that the material is covered in an appendix to this chapter.

e The payment in item (d) from the client's point of view.

f Interest owed on the company's bank loan, to be paid in early July.

g The bank loan payable in item (f).

h Office supplies on hand at year-end.

E3-4 *Analysis of prepaid account balance* (L.O. 6)

The following information relates to Action Sign Company for 19X2:

Insurance expense	$4,350
Prepaid insurance, December 31, 19X2	1,900
Cash outlays for insurance during 19X2	6,200

Compute the balance in the Prepaid Insurance account on January 1, 19X2.

E3-5 *An overview of the adjusting process* (L.O. 5, 6)

Evaluate the comments that follow as being True or False. If the comment is false, briefly explain why.

a Adjusting entries are normally recorded on the last day of the accounting period.

b The balance in an account entitled Prepaid Art Supplies would most likely be disclosed on a company's income statement.

c If $700 of a $2,900 insurance policy expired during the period, the Prepaid Insurance account should contain a $2,200 balance after adjustment.

d The Oxnard Aristocrats, a minor league baseball team, records receipts of season ticket revenue in the Unearned Season Ticket Revenue account. The proper adjusting entry to reflect revenue earned during the period would involve a credit to this account.

e The adjustment for an accrued expense involves an increase to a liability account.

E3-6 *Basic adjusting entries* (L.O. 6)

Record the adjusting entries necessary for King Company as of December 31, the end of the current accounting period.

a Accrued interest owed to the bank, $2,400.

b Insurance purchased during the year totaled $1,200. Of this amount, $800 is applicable to the next accounting period. The original $1,200 payment was recorded as a debit to Prepaid Insurance.

c King earned $200 of an $800 receipt from a client for consulting services. The receipt was initially recorded in the Unearned Consulting Revenue account.

d Sales of $224,000 were made during December. King pays the sales force a 10% commission; no commissions had been paid by the end of the month.

e Accrued interest on various amounts due King totaled $580 at year-end.

E3-7 *Accounting for prepaid expenses and unearned revenues* (L.O. 6)

Hawaii-Blue began business on January 1 of the current year and offers deep sea fishing trips to tourists. Tourists pay $125 in advance for an all-day outing off the coast of Maui. The company collected monies during January for 210 outings, with 30 of the tourists not planning to take their trips until early February.

Hawaii-Blue rents its fishing boat from Pacific Yacht Supply. An agreement was signed at the beginning of the year, and $72,000 was paid for the rights to use the boat for two full years.

a Prepare journal entries to record (1) the collection of monies from tourists and (2) the revenue generated during January.

b Calculate Hawaii-Blue's total obligation to tourists at the end of January. On what financial statement and in which section would this amount appear?

c Prepare journal entries to record (1) the payment to Pacific Yacht Supply and (2) the subsequent adjustment on January 31.

d On what financial statement would Hawaii-Blue's January boat rental cost appear?

E3-8 *Adjustment error* **(L.O. 6)**
The accountant for Stringer Services failed to adjust the Supplies account to recognize the amount consumed during March. As a result of this error, will the following items be overstated, understated, or unaffected?

a March revenues will be _____.

b March expenses will be _____.

c March net income will be _____.

d Ending owner's equity as of March 31 will be _____.

e Assets as of March 31 will be _____.

f Liabilities as of March 31 will be _____.

*E3-9 *Income statement approach, adjusting entries* **(L.O. 8)**
System Consulting had the following transactions on May 1:

- Paid $10,200 for the next six months' rent.
- Received $48,000 to render consulting services to Midtown Hospital over the next year. The services were to begin immediately.

The company records prepaid expenses and unearned revenues initially in income statement accounts.

a Record the proper journal entries on May 1.

b Record the necessary adjusting entries on May 31.

Series A

PROBLEMS

P3-A1 *Accrual and modified cash basis* **(L.O. 4)**

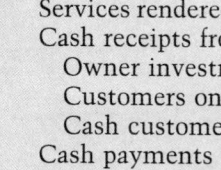

The following information pertains to Beta Company for October:

Services rendered during October to customers on account	$14,380
Cash receipts from	
Owner investment	7,000
Customers on account	5,650
Cash customers for services rendered in October	6,800
Cash payments to	
Creditors for expenses incurred during October	4,400
Creditors for expenses incurred prior to October	2,100
Monroe Equipment for purchase of new machinery on October 1	8,400
Expenses incurred during October, to be paid in future months	3,725

The machinery is expected to have a service life of five years.

Instructions

Calculate Beta's net income for October, using the following methods:

a Accrual basis of accounting.

b Modified cash basis of accounting.

P3-A2 *Adjusting entries and financial statements* (L.O. 5, 6)

The information that follows pertains to Fixation Enterprises:

1 The company previously collected $1,500 as an advance payment for services to be rendered in the future. By the end of December, one-third of this amount had been earned.

2 Fixation provided $2,500 of services to Artech Corporation; no billing had been made by December 31.

3 Salaries owed to employees at year-end amounted to $1,650.

4 The Supplies account revealed a balance of $8,800; yet only $3,300 of supplies were actually on hand at the end of the period.

5 The company paid $18,000 on October 1 of the current year to Vantage Property Management. The payment was for six months' rent of Fixation's headquarters, beginning on November 1.

Fixation's accounting year ends on December 31.

Instructions

Analyze the five preceding cases individually and determine:

a The *type* of adjusting entry needed at year-end. (Use the following code: A—adjustment of a prepaid expense; B—adjustment of an unearned revenue; C—adjustment to record an accrued expense; or D—adjustment to record an accrued revenue.)

b The year-end journal entry to adjust the accounts.

c The income statement impact of each adjustment (e.g., increases total revenues by $500).

P3-A3 *Adjusting entries* (L.O. 6)

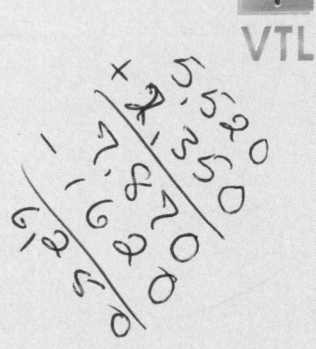

You have been retained to examine the records of Kathy's Day Care Center as of December 31, 19X3, the close of the current reporting period. In the course of your examination, you discover the following:

a On January 1, 19X3, the Supplies account had a balance of $2,350. During the year, $5,520 of supplies were purchased, and a balance of $1,620 remained unused on December 31.

b Unrecorded interest owed to the center totaled $275 as of December 31.

c All clients pay tuition in advance, and their payments are credited to the Unearned Tuition Revenue account. The account was credited for $75,500 on August 31. With the exception of $15,500, which represented prepayments for 10 months' tuition from several well-to-do families, all amounts were for the current semester ending on December 31.

d Depreciation on the school's van was $3,000 for the year.

e On August 1, the center began to pay rent in six-month installments of $21,000. Kathy wrote a check to the owner of the building and recorded the check in Prepaid Rent, a new account.

f Two salaried employees earn $400 each for a five-day week. The employees are paid every Friday, and December 31 falls on a Thursday.

g Kathy's Day Care paid insurance premiums as follows, each time debiting Prepaid Insurance:

Date Paid	Policy No.	Length of Policy	Amount
Feb. 1, 19X2	1033MCM19	1 year	$540
Jan. 1, 19X3	7952789HP	1 year	912
Aug. 1, 19X3	XQ943675ST	2 years	840

Instructions

The center's accounts were last adjusted on December 31, 19X2. Prepare the adjusting entries necessary under the accrual basis of accounting.

P3-A4 *Preparation of adjusted trial balance* (L.O. 6, 7)

The trial balance of the Warshawski Company as of December 31, 19XX, follows.

WARSHAWSKI COMPANY Trial Balance December 31, 19XX		
Cash	$ 2,100	
Accounts receivable	17,600	
Prepaid insurance	5,500	
Equipment	23,000	
Accumulated depreciation: equipment		$ 4,600
Accounts payable		3,700
Unearned service revenue		1,200
Loan payable		8,000
V. Warshawski, capital		9,900
V. Warshawski, drawing	5,000	
Service revenue		41,300
Rent expense	8,400	
Salaries expense	4,200	
Utilities expense	2,900	
	$68,700	$68,700

The following adjustment information has come to your attention:
1 Services provided but not yet billed, $6,200.
2 Insurance that expired during the period, $4,500.
3 Depreciation expense on the equipment, $1,900.
4 Unearned service revenues that have been earned during the period, $900.
5 Accrued interest on the loan payable, $800.
6 Salaries incurred but not yet paid, $1,400.

Instructions

a Prepare Warshawski's required adjusting entries in general journal form.
b Prepare an adjusted trial balance, using an approach similar to that demonstrated in Exhibit 3-5.
c Suppose that you were asked to prepare the financial statements of Warshawski Company. Would the trial balance or the adjusted trial balance be more useful in completing this assignment? Briefly explain.

*P3-A5 *Adjustment alternatives* (L.O. 6, 8)

Future Planners began operations on January 1 of the current year. A review of the company's accounting records on December 31 discovered the following:

■ The firm prepaid six months' rental charges of $5,400 on August 1 for the North Beach office. Future Planners took occupancy of the facility on September 1.
■ The company agreed to render consulting services to both the Hill Publishing Group and the Chicago Sidekicks, a professional soccer team. Hill paid $24,000 on May 1 for services to be rendered over a four-month period beginning on July 1. The Sidekicks contracted for $15,000 of

services to be rendered over a 12-month period beginning in early October. The team's total fee was collected on June 1.

The general ledger of Future Planners revealed accounts entitled Prepaid Rent, Rent Expense, Consulting Revenue, and Unearned Consulting Revenue. Future Planners uses the accrual basis of accounting and adjusts its accounting records at the end of the year.

Instructions

a Assume that Future Planners initially records prepaid expenses and unearned revenues in balance sheet accounts. Present the necessary journal entries to:
(1) Record the transactions of May 1, June 1, and August 1.
(2) Adjust the accounting records on December 31.
b Repeat part (a), assuming that prepaid expenses and unearned revenues are initially recorded in income statement accounts.
c Determine the amounts that would be disclosed on the company's year-end financial statements for Rent Expense, Prepaid Rent, Consulting Revenue, and Unearned Consulting Revenue. Base your answers on the initial recording of the preceding transactions in:
(1) Balance sheet accounts.
(2) Income statement accounts.

Series B

P3-B1 *Accrual and modified cash basis* (L.O. 4)

The following information was gathered from the records of Sinclair Consulting for April:

1-2-3

Beginning cash		$ 9,500
Add: Receipts		
From customers		
For cash services rendered in April	$ 8,000	
For services performed on account	9,600	
From Contemporary Office, Inc.	2,000	19,600
Subtotal		$29,100
Deduct: Payments		
To creditors		
For expenses incurred in April	$ 1,300	
For expenses incurred prior to April	2,800	
Owner withdrawal	5,000	
Purchase of office furniture	14,000	23,100
Ending cash		$ 6,000

During April, the company rendered $14,700 of services to customers on account and incurred $2,500 of expenses to be paid in future months. Finally, on April 1, Sinclair purchased furniture having an estimated service life of five years from Contemporary Office. One day later, Sinclair was given a cash refund upon discovery of a $2,000 billing error.

Instructions

Calculate Sinclair's net income for April, using the following methods:
a Accrual basis of accounting.
b Modified cash basis of accounting.

P3-B2 *Adjusting entries and financial statements* (L.O. 5, 6)

The information that follows pertains to Southlake Enterprises:

1 The Prepaid Insurance account contains a December 31 balance of $5,800. Conversations with the firm's accountant revealed that $4,300 of premiums had expired during the year.

2 Interest owed at year-end on loans payable to Second National Bank amounted to $8,000.

3 Southlake received $10,800 in April for use of a portion of its parking lot by a neighboring business. By December 31, $3,600 of the payment had yet to be earned.

4 Services rendered to clients during December not yet billed or collected total $3,700.

5 The Repair Supplies account had a balance on January 1 of the current year of $2,500. Purchases made during the period amounted to $700; supplies costing $1,800 remain on hand at December 31.

Southlake's accounting year ends on December 31.

Instructions

Analyze the five preceding cases individually and determine:

a The *type* of adjusting entry needed at year-end. (Use the following code: A—adjustment of a prepaid expense; B—adjustment of an unearned revenue; C—adjustment to record an accrued expense; or D—adjustment to record an accrued revenue.)

b The year-end journal entry to adjust the accounts.

c The remaining (or resulting) asset or liability after recording the adjustment (e.g., the ending balance in Prepaid Advertising is $900).

P3-B3 *Adjusting entries* (L.O. 6)

You have been called in to examine the records of Holiday Company as of November 30, 19X7, the close of the current reporting period. In the course of your examination, you discover the following:

a Building depreciation totaled $7,500 for the year.

b Prepaid Advertising has a debit balance of $6,500 on November 30, which represents payment on August 18 for uniform space in 26 issues of a weekly magazine. As of November 30, advertisements had appeared in 12 issues.

c Salaries earned by employees but unpaid by year-end amounted to $3,900.

d Holiday agreed that Auto Express could lease some extra space in Holiday's parking lot for $300 per month, effective September 1. Auto Express has yet to pay Holiday and, to date, no entry has been made in the accounting records. (Holiday uses an account entitled Lease Receivable to record such transactions.)

e The beginning balance in the Office Supplies account on December 1, 19X6, was $2,570. The account was increased during the year for purchases that amounted to $4,420, and a year-end count revealed that supplies costing $4,800 had been consumed by November 30.

f On March 1, an entry was made in the Unearned Service Revenue account for $24,000. This amount represents a receipt for eight months of services to be rendered beginning on June 1.

g A review of the Prepaid Insurance account discovered that Holiday had acquired a two-year liability insurance policy for $960 on February 1, 19X7. Another policy that cost $1,320 for six months' coverage of building contents was acquired one month later.

Instructions

The accounts were last adjusted on November 30, 19X6. Present the adjusting entries required on November 30, 19X7, under the accrual basis of accounting.

P3-B4 *Preparation of adjusted trial balance* (L.O. 6, 7)

VTL

The trial balance of the Logo Company as of December 31, 19XX, follows.

LOGO COMPANY Trial Balance December 31, 19XX		
Cash	$11,400	
Accounts receivable	7,600	
Prepaid rent	600	
Machinery	13,000	
Accumulated depreciation: machinery		$ 1,500
Accounts payable		1,150
Unearned contract revenue		1,200
Loan payable		7,000
Andrea Logan, capital		13,000
Andrea Logan, drawing	1,850	
Contract revenue		24,400
Wage expense	9,600	
Utilities expense	2,000	
Insurance expense	2,200	
	$48,250	$48,250

The following adjustment information has come to your attention:
1 Rent that expired during the period, $200.
2 Contract services provided but not yet billed, $700.
3 Unearned contract revenues that have been earned during the period, $550.
4 Wages incurred but not yet paid, $725.
5 Accrued interest on the loan payable, $150.
6 Depreciation expense on the machinery, $300.

Instructions

a Prepare Logo's required adjusting entries in general journal form.
b Prepare an adjusted trial balance, using an approach similar to that demonstrated in Exhibit 3-5.
c What is the purpose of the adjusting process at the end of the period? Briefly explain.

*P3-B5 *Adjustment alternatives* (L.O. 6, 8)

Creative Management (CM) began operations on January 1 of the current year. A review of the company's accounting records on December 31 discovered the following:

■ All advertising for the year had been prepaid. On March 1, CM paid $3,600 for space in six issues of *Artists' Monthly*, with displays to begin on May 1. In addition, on September 1, CM paid $4,800 for ads in 24 issues of *Theater Guild*. By year-end, ads had appeared in 11 issues of the latter publication.

■ The company agreed to manage a popular rock group's financial affairs for a 12-month period beginning on April 1 for a fee of $18,000. CM received the entire fee on March 1.

The firm's general ledger revealed accounts entitled Prepaid Advertising, Advertising Expense, Management Revenue, and Unearned Management Revenue. CM uses the accrual basis of accounting and adjusts its accounting records at the end of the year.

Instructions

a Assume that Creative Management initially records prepaid expenses and unearned revenues in balance sheet accounts. Present the necessary journal entries to:
   (1) Record the transactions of March 1 and September 1.
   (2) Adjust the accounting records on December 31.
b Repeat part (a), assuming that prepaid expenses and unearned revenues are initially recorded in income statement accounts.
c Determine the amounts that would be disclosed on the company's year-end financial statements for Advertising Expense, Prepaid Advertising, Management Revenue, and Unearned Management Revenue. Base your answers on the initial recording of the preceding transactions in:
   (1) Balance sheet accounts.
   (2) Income statement accounts.

EDB3-1 *Reporting periods; items that require adjustment: The Toro Company and The Reader's Digest Association* **(L.O. 1, 5)**

ELECTRONIC DATA BASE

The Toro Company, headquartered in Bloomington, Minnesota, is a leading supplier of lawn maintenance equipment and irrigation products (such as sprinkler systems). In addition to items sold under the Toro brand name, the company also manufactures Lawn-Boy and Wheel Horse products. In contrast, The Reader's Digest Association is perhaps best known for its publishing activities. *Reader's Digest* is the world's most widely read magazine, being published in 17 languages for 100 million readers.

Instructions

By using the text's Electronic Data Base, access the balance sheets of both firms and answer the questions that follow. Unless otherwise indicated, responses should be based on data for the most recent year presented.
a Determine the year-end for both companies.
b One of these year-ends is likely to be based on the firm's natural business year. Identify the company that is using the natural business year for reporting and explain the rationale behind your selection.
c Do either of the companies disclose any prepaid expenses? Comment on the amount of prepaid expenses relative to the total assets of the entity.
d Do either of the companies show relatively large amounts of unearned revenue? If so, what is the likely source of this unearned revenue and how are such amounts eventually earned?
e Companies often provide purchasers with promises to remedy defects in product quality for a stipulated period of time.
   (1) Do either of the firms provide such a promise, as evidenced by the balance sheet? Explain.
   (2) If you have answered "yes" to the above, where are such amounts presented on the balance sheet? What is the logic behind this treatment?

EDB3-2 *Reporting periods; items that require adjustment* (L.O. 1, 5)

SEC

This problem is a duplication of Problem EDB3-1. It is based on two companies selected by your instructor.

Instructions

By using the text's Electronic Data Base, access the specified companies' balance sheets and focus on data for the most recent year reported. Answer requirements (a)–(e) of Problem EDB3-1.

BEYOND THE BASICS

BB3-1 *Accrual- and cash-basis accounting, performance evaluation* (L.O. 4)

Beth Regal recently began a swimming pool chlorination service. She visits each of her clients on a weekly basis and applies chlorine gas and other chemicals to their pools. This service is not only convenient for her clientele, but is actually less costly than if the customers performed the process themselves.

Regal started her business on April 1 with a beginning cash investment of $3,000. Through various contacts, she was able to establish an initial client base of 40 customers. Customers are billed when serviced and settle their accounts in the following month. Regal charges each client $30 monthly, thereby generating a 100% markup on the $15 cost of chlorine and other supplies used. Other business expenses (gasoline, telephone, etc.) total $100 monthly and are paid when incurred.

All chemicals and supplies are purchased and paid for at the beginning of each month, the amounts acquired being based on the number of customers to be serviced. On April 1, for instance, purchases totaled $600 (40 customers × $15 each).

Regal's business has grown rapidly, as evidenced by the following data:

Month	Customers Serviced
April	40
May	80
June	160

It has become apparent that the customer base would total 320 for July.

On July 1, Regal approached you about a cash flow problem. She is unable to buy the necessary chemicals and supplies because of a lack of cash. Beth is also quite confused because a friend of hers, an accountant, has prepared monthly accrual-based financial statements that reveal the business is operating at a profit. Beth is now questioning these statements in view of the firm's present cash position.

Instructions

a Construct Regal's accrual-based income statements for April, May, and June.
b Construct Regal's cash-based income statements for April, May, and June.
c Compute the end-of-month balances for April, May, and June in the Cash, Accounts Receivable, and Supplies accounts.
d Using the information generated in parts (a)–(c), explain the pool service's dilemma.

BB3-2 *Overview of chapter concepts: Multiple choice* (L.O. 1–7)

The following multiple-choice questions relate to various topics discussed in the chapter. Select the best answer.

1 Which of the following concepts or policies would assist in the income determination process for a large company?
   a Expenses are recorded (matched) in the same period as the revenues they helped to produce.
   b For reporting purposes, an organization's life is divisible into discrete time segments.
   c Revenue is generally recognized at the time services are rendered or when goods are sold and delivered to a customer.
   d All of the above.

2 Watson Enterprises developed the following information pertaining to its first year of operation:

Services rendered for cash	$ 5,000
Services rendered on account	34,000
Collections on account	21,000
Expenses incurred and paid	25,000
Expenses incurred but not paid	22,000
Expenses prepaid	3,000

In addition, the company had collections of $10,000 for services to be rendered in a future year. Which of the following statements best describes the income reported under the accrual basis of accounting and that reported under the cash basis of accounting?
   a Accrual-basis income equals cash-basis income.
   b Accrual-basis income exceeds cash-basis income by $8,000.
   c Cash-basis income exceeds accrual-basis income by $8,000.
   d Cash-basis income exceeds accrual-basis income by $16,000.

3 Which of the following statements is incorrect?
   a Accountants generally prefer the accrual basis of accounting over the cash basis of accounting.
   b Adjusting entries are used to accrue multiperiod costs and revenues.
   c The adjusted trial balance provides an excellent springboard for financial statement preparation.
   d The failure to record an adjusting entry is likely to affect more than one financial statement.

4 United Transportation, which uses the accrual basis of accounting, recently sold a book of 40 one-way bus tickets for $80. If the purchaser rides the bus to and from home for a five-day work week, how should the $80 be reported at the end of one week's time?

	Unearned Revenue	Revenue
a	$0	$80
b	$20	$60
c	$60	$20
d	$70	$10

5 At the beginning of December, Lane Company prepaid two months' rent of $1,200. The journal entry used to record this transaction involved a debit to Cash and a credit to Prepaid Rent, both for $1,200. What journal entry should be recorded to correct and update the accounts on December 31?
   a Prepaid Rent   600
       Rent Expense   600

b	Prepaid Rent	1,800	
	Rent Expense	600	
	Cash		2,400
c	Rent Expense	600	
	Prepaid Rent		600
d	Rent Expense	1,800	
	Cash		1,200
	Prepaid Rent		600

6 Of the following accounts that are used in the adjustment process, which is most likely to be presented in the liability section of a balance sheet?
a Prepaid insurance.
b Interest receivable.
c Accumulated depreciation.
d Unearned fee revenue.

7 Which of the following statements is true?
a Total debits in the adjusted trial balance will exceed total debits in the trial balance. The difference equals the sum of the debits recorded in the adjusting process.
b The debits in the adjusted trial balance relate solely to a company's assets.
c Although expenses may be greater in the adjusted trial balance than in the trial balance, such a relationship would not hold true for revenues.
d It is unlikely that the owner's capital account would be used in the adjusting process.

8 Hughes Company omitted an adjusting entry that caused an understatement of net income. The adjusting entry probably:
a dealt with an accrued expense.
b concerned the reduction of Prepaid Insurance.
c concerned the reduction of Unearned Contract Revenue.
d dealt with recording the annual depreciation charge.

COMMUNICATION OF ACCOUNTING INFORMATION

CAI3-1 *Information presentation: Tandy Corporation (L.O. 4, 5, 6)*

Communication Principle: The presentation of information is just as critical to communication as the information itself. According to readability principles, writing should be organized and displayed in a way that is easy and fast to comprehend. Readability principles include writing short paragraphs, using ample "white space" (margins and blank space on the page), and setting off important numerical data from text so they are emphasized and easy to follow.

These guidelines will help you produce a professional-looking and readable document:

1 Write short paragraphs (averaging three to four sentences or four to six lines).
2 Use 1½-inch margins and leave some extra space between paragraphs.
3 Leave extra space before and after illustrations (e.g., tabular data) within paragraphs. Be sure to indent illustrations by using a larger left-hand margin than that used with narrative text.

■ ■ ■ ■ ■ ■ ■ ■

Tandy Corporation is America's largest specialty electronics retailer, operating over 7,000 Radio Shack stores and computer centers. Tandy also runs more than 300 McDuff and VideoConcepts stores that sell appliances along with audio and video products. In addition, the firm is heavily involved in manufacturing activities.

Given the company's diversity, it is no wonder that Tandy's financial statements report a variety of accrued expenses and unearned revenues. Examples include the following (amounts are in thousands):

Accrued payroll and bonuses	$59,841
Accrued interest expense	11,124
Deferred (unearned) service contract revenue	43,833

Instructions

You are presently taking an employment test with Tandy for an entry-level accounting position. Part of this test involves preparation of information (i.e., the answers to the following questions) that will eventually be placed in a management report. Draft sample responses that could be inserted in the report, being sure to use appropriate topic or lead-in sentences with each paragraph. Because involved computations are often hard to understand in the context of a sentence or paragraph, set off any needed calculations in tabular form.

a Briefly describe the nature of the transaction or event that gave rise to the three dollar amounts presented. Assume the reader of the final report is a relatively unsophisticated user of financial information.

b Further details are needed concerning the $43,833 year-end deferred contract revenue balance.

   (1) On what financial statement would this amount be reported? What is the rationale behind this treatment?

   (2) Would the Deferred Contract Revenue account be needed under the cash basis of accounting? Why?

   (3) Tandy had a beginning balance of $35,711 in the Deferred Contract Revenue account. If, say, $60,000 of contracts were sold during the period, how would the firm's income statement have been affected?

Answers to Chapter Quiz

1 b

2 c

3 b

4 d

5 c

CHAPTER 4

Completion of the Accounting Cycle

LEARNING OBJECTIVES

After studying this chapter, you should be able to:

1

Prepare a work sheet and the accompanying financial statements.

2

Close a set of books and prepare a post-closing trial balance.

3

Name and describe the various steps in the accounting cycle.

4

Understand the concept of an operating cycle and
construct a classified balance sheet.

5

(Appendix) Explain the concept and mechanics of reversing entries.

In the previous chapter we examined the adjusting process, which is used to update selected accounts upon conclusion of the reporting period. Chapter 3 also included an illustration showing how adjusting entries are combined with account data to derive an adjusted trial balance.

Because an entity's records now reflect all measurable activity that has occurred, we can begin to concentrate on disclosure of this activity via a formal income statement, statement of owner's equity, and balance sheet. The construction of these reports involves the simple reorganization of the information contained in the adjusted trial balance.

A natural inclination might be to assume that statement preparation is the final step in the financial reporting cycle. As you will soon see, a few additional tasks must be performed to ready a company's records for the next accounting period. These tasks include closing entries and the preparation of a post-closing trial balance. This chapter examines financial statement construction along with the preceding "housekeeping" chores. Our presentation concludes with an in-depth discussion of balance sheets, including the need for added captions within the body of this statement.

WORK SHEET

OBJECTIVE

1

Prepare a work sheet and the accompanying financial statements.

Most businesses have a large number of accounts in their general ledgers that require adjustment. To help accountants better organize their work for this process, a series of *working papers* is often prepared. These documents are used for preliminary calculations when deriving financial statement data (e.g., the cost of supplies consumed during the reporting period, a company's depreciation expense, and so forth). Generally speaking, working papers provide evidence of related computations and are useful in supporting the validity of the figures being reported.

There are many different types of working papers, with one of the most popular being the work sheet. The **work sheet** is a large columnar form that assists in the formation of an entity's financial statements. The design of the work sheet not only helps to detect mathematical errors, but it also highlights certain types of discrepancies *before* they are entered in the journal and posted to the ledger. In effect, one could view the work sheet as the accountant's "scratch pad." Proper completion of this document ensures that many end-of-period accounting procedures have been performed correctly.

Work Sheet Construction

The work sheet and the procedures for preparation will be shown by continuing the Wise Advertising Agency example from the previous chapter. The starting point for preparation is the trial balance and the end-of-period adjusting entries. These data are reproduced in Exhibit 4-1.

The amounts in the trial balance are combined with the adjustments to produce an adjusted trial balance. Notice, for instance, that the $3,150 debit balance in Accounts Receivable is increased by $710, yielding an ending account balance of $3,860. This procedure should be familiar to you; it is identical to that described in the previous chapter. A review of Exhibit 3-5 and the accompanying discussion that begins on page 106 may

WISE ADVERTISING AGENCY
Work Sheet
For the Month Ended May 31, 19XX

Account Title	Trial Balance Debit	Trial Balance Credit	Adjustments Debit	Adjustments Credit	Adjusted Trial Balance Debit	Adjusted Trial Balance Credit	Income Statement Debit	Income Statement Credit	Balance Sheet Debit	Balance Sheet Credit
Cash	13,705				13,705				13,705	
Accounts receivable	3,150		(g) 710		3,860				3,860	
Prepaid insurance	480			(a) 20	460				460	
Supplies	340			(b) 80	260				260	
Land	5,500				5,500				5,500	
Car	4,500				4,500				4,500	
Accounts payable		125				125				125
Unearned agency revenue		10,400	(d) 400			10,000				10,000
Loan payable		6,000				6,000				6,000
Gary Wise, capital		9,000				9,000				9,000
Gary Wise, drawing	200				200				200	
Agency revenue		4,100		(d) 400 (g) 710		5,210		5,210		
Salaries expense	825		(f) 50		875		875			
Marketing expense	800				800		800			
Electricity expense	125				125		125			
	29,625	29,625								
Insurance expense			(a) 20		20		20			
Supplies expense			(b) 80		80		80			
Depreciation expense			(c) 125		125		125			
Accumulated depreciation: car				(c) 125		125				125
Interest expense			(e) 60		60		60			
Interest payable				(e) 60		60				60
Salaries payable				(f) 50		50				50
			1,445	1,445	30,570	30,570	2,085	5,210	28,485	25,360
Net income							3,125			3,125
							5,210	5,210	28,485	28,485

EXHIBIT 4-1
Work Sheet of the Wise Advertising Agency

be helpful at this time. The review will not only serve as a refresher, but will also show that the Chapter 3 illustration coincides precisely with the first six columns of the work sheet. The numbers that appear in colored type (the income statement and balance sheet data) are really the only new elements to master.

Income Statement and Balance Sheet

The data in the adjusted trial balance serve as the "raw material" for a company's financial statements. Thus, each amount listed in the adjusted trial balance is transferred to either the work sheet's income statement section or balance sheet section. This process is performed on a line-by-line basis, starting at the top of the work sheet. *Revenues and expenses go to the income statement. Assets, liabilities, and owner's equity accounts, the last of which includes the drawing account, are extended to the balance sheet.* Although the drawing account does not appear on a formal balance sheet,[1] extension is necessary because withdrawals reduce owner's equity.

Financial Statement Totals

As a final step, after all amounts have been extended, the income statement and balance sheet columns are totaled. Focusing on the income statement, the credit column contains the accounts with credit balances, namely, the revenues. In contrast, the debit column contains the expense accounts. Therefore:

Total revenues (credits)	$5,210
Total expenses (debits)	2,085
Net income	$3,125

The net income figure is placed beneath the debit total and is added to bring both columns into agreement with each other.

Turning to the balance sheet, the firm's net income is entered in the credit column because revenues in excess of expenses raise owner's equity. The income of $3,125 is then combined with the other balance sheet credits, yielding a total of $28,485.

Wise generated net income during May. If the agency had operated at a loss, the procedure for balancing the statements would have been slightly different. With expenses greater than revenues, the loss would be entered in the credit column of the income statement to achieve the desired equality. On the balance sheet the net loss must reduce owner's equity. Appropriately, then, the loss would be listed in the debit column to produce the necessary impact.

Tips & Techniques

Students often take a quick glance at a completed work sheet and conclude that it is extremely complex and beyond their comprehension. As you have seen, work sheet construction is *not* difficult if viewed as a logical step-by-step process. In fact, the most troublesome elements are those introduced in Chapters 2 and 3—the generation of a trial balance that balances and determination of the proper adjusting entries.

Uses of the Work Sheet

The work sheet performs several useful functions for the accountant. As is evident from its form, the work sheet lays the groundwork for formal

---

[1] Withdrawals appear on the statement of owner's equity.

financial statement preparation. In addition, it serves as the basis for completing the adjusting process and assists in closing at the end of the accounting period.

Financial Statements

Once the work sheet is completed, the preparation of financial statements is a relatively easy task. Virtually all the information needed for this process is found in the work sheet's income statement and balance sheet sections. The income statement, for example, is simply a formalized listing of the income statement debit and credit columns.

The statement of owner's equity cannot be constructed by relying solely on the work sheet. Any investments made by the owner are already buried in the capital account, which appears in the adjusted trial balance. Consequently, it is necessary to return to the general ledger and examine the underlying detail of such transactions (see Gary Wise, Capital, in Exhibit 2-5).

Finally, the balance sheet is prepared by compiling the asset and liability figures that are listed in the balance sheet section. The drawing account of $200 is ignored, because it was used when constructing the statement of owner's equity. As you know, the balance sheet reflects end-of-period amounts. Thus, the ending figure on the statement of owner's equity is carried forward and labeled as Gary Wise, Capital. This procedure was discussed in Chapter 1 and is illustrated in Wise's financial statements, which are shown in Exhibit 4-2.

Adjusting Entries

In the previous chapter we first introduced the concept of adjustments via formal journal entries (see pp. 100 and 104 as examples). We later used the information contained in these adjustments for purposes of completing the adjusted trial balance and the work sheet. The presentation in Chapter 3 was for illustrative purposes only. In practice, accountants would first prepare the work sheet and then record data from the adjustment columns into the journal. The work sheet, therefore, serves as the basis for the updating process at the end of the period.

Like other journal entries, the adjustments are posted to the general ledger. This procedure achieves consistency with the balances that appear in the agency's financial statements. We will assume that all adjustments presented in the Wise Advertising illustration have already been journalized and posted.

The Closing Process

Discussion of the **closing process** should help tie together several loose ends. As we emphasized earlier in the text, four factors cause owner's equity to change during the period: investments, withdrawals, revenues, and expenses. The statement of owner's equity of Wise Advertising (see Exhibit 4-2) reveals an ending balance of $11,925 from these items. Interestingly, however, the capital *account* in the general ledger contains a balance of $9,000. This latter amount reflects only the investment on May 1, which was entered directly in the account. Withdrawals, on the other

> **OBJECTIVE**
>
> **2**
>
> Close a set of books and prepare a post-closing trial balance.

EXHIBIT 4-2
Financial Statements of Wise Advertising Agency

WISE ADVERTISING AGENCY
Income Statement
For the Month Ended May 31, 19XX

Agency revenue		$5,210
Less expenses		
Salaries expense	$875	
Marketing expense	800	
Electricity expense	125	
Insurance expense	20	
Supplies expense	80	
Depreciation expense	125	
Interest expense	60	
Total expenses		2,085
Net income		$3,125

WISE ADVERTISING AGENCY
Statement of Owner's Equity
For the Month Ended May 31, 19XX

Beginning balance, May 1		$ —
Increases		
Owner investments	$9,000	
Net income	3,125	12,125
		$12,125
Decreases		
Owner withdrawals		200
Ending balance, May 31		$11,925

---

hand, are located in Gary Wise, Drawing, and revenues and expenses are still housed in the accounts where initially recorded. It is naturally desirable that the ending balance reported on the statement of owner's equity (and the balance sheet) be consistent with the ending balance found in the ledger. This consistency is achieved by placing a set of *closing entries* in the accounting records at the end of the period.

Purpose.   The purpose of the closing process is twofold. First, closing corrects the just mentioned lack of agreement between the capital account and the owner's equity statement. Second, closing reduces the balances in certain accounts to zero. The income statement and the statement of owner's equity each report economic activity for a span of time. On conclusion of a given period, a business must start anew in its accumulation of information for these two financial reports. *Thus, revenue, expense, and drawing accounts must be closed, or reduced to zero, so there is no carryover*

WISE ADVERTISING AGENCY Balance Sheet May 31, 19XX		
Assets		
Cash		$13,705
Accounts receivable		3,860
Prepaid insurance		460
Supplies		260
Land		5,500
Car	$4,500	
Less: Accumulated depreciation	125	4,375
Total assets		$28,160
Liabilities		
Accounts payable		$ 125
Unearned agency revenue		10,000
Loan payable		6,000
Interest payable		60
Salaries payable		50
Total liabilities		$16,235
Owner's equity		
Gary Wise, capital		11,925
Total liabilities & owner's equity		$28,160

from one period to the next. These accounts are appropriately known as **temporary** or **nominal accounts.**

Because the balance sheet reports information at a particular point in time as opposed to a period, *balance sheet components (assets, liabilities, and ending owner's equity) are never closed.* Wise, for example, reported a cash balance of $13,705 on May 31. It would not make any sense to reduce this account to zero so that the firm could start accounting all over again on June 1. The agency has $13,705 of cash to begin June operations, not zero. Accounts whose balances are carried forward from period to period are commonly called **real accounts.**

Technique.   Most companies close their books only once a year. For illustrative purposes, however, we will demonstrate the necessary closing process for Wise Advertising on May 31, the conclusion of the agency's first month of activity.

Closing is a four-step process that requires the establishment of a new account entitled **Income Summary.** As its name implies, the Income Summary account is used to summarize the net income or net loss of a business. The four steps to closing are as follows:

1 Close all revenue accounts.

2 Close all expense accounts.

3 Close the Income Summary account.

4 Close the drawing account.

EXHIBIT 4-3
Closing Revenue Accounts

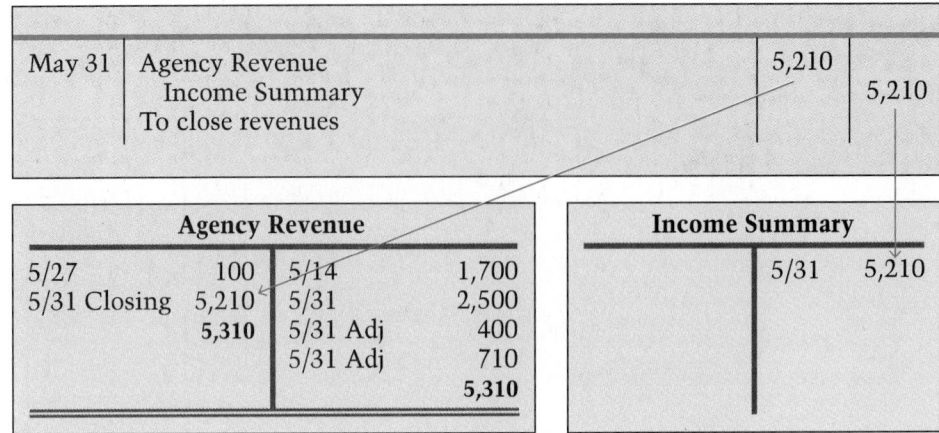

The information needed to perform these steps is obtained from the work sheet.

Closing Revenue Accounts. Revenue accounts normally possess credit balances. To reduce the accounts to zero, the closing entry debits revenue accounts for the amount of their balance and credits Income Summary. This process transfers all revenues earned to the credit side of Income Summary and is shown in Exhibit 4-3.

To explain, the Agency Revenue account contains charges from May 14, 27, and 31 (see Exhibit 2-5) and two adjusting entries (see Exhibit 4-1). The balance *prior* to closing is $5,210 ($5,310 − $100). The closing entry debits Agency Revenue for $5,210, thereby equalizing total debits and credits and reducing the account's balance to zero.

Closing Expense Accounts. The closing of expense accounts is performed in essentially the same manner. Each expense account is credited to eliminate its debit balance. The closing entry's corresponding debit, then, is to Income Summary, which transfers the expenses incurred to the debit side of this account. Rather than close the expense accounts individually, a combined or *compound journal entry* is usually employed to reduce posting. Exhibit 4-4 illustrates the proper entry and the related postings.

Closing the Income Summary Account. The Income Summary account presently contains revenues (credits) of $5,210 and expenses (debits) of $2,085. The resulting credit balance of $3,125 ($5,210 − $2,085) represents Wise's net income for May.

The next step in the closing process is to reduce, or close, the Income Summary account to zero. This is achieved by debiting Income Summary for $3,125. To complete the entry, Gary Wise, Capital, is credited because revenues in excess of expenses (i.e., net income) boost owner's equity. The necessary entry is shown in Exhibit 4-5.

In the case of a net loss, the Income Summary account would possess a debit balance prior to closing. The required closing entry, therefore, is the opposite of that just described.

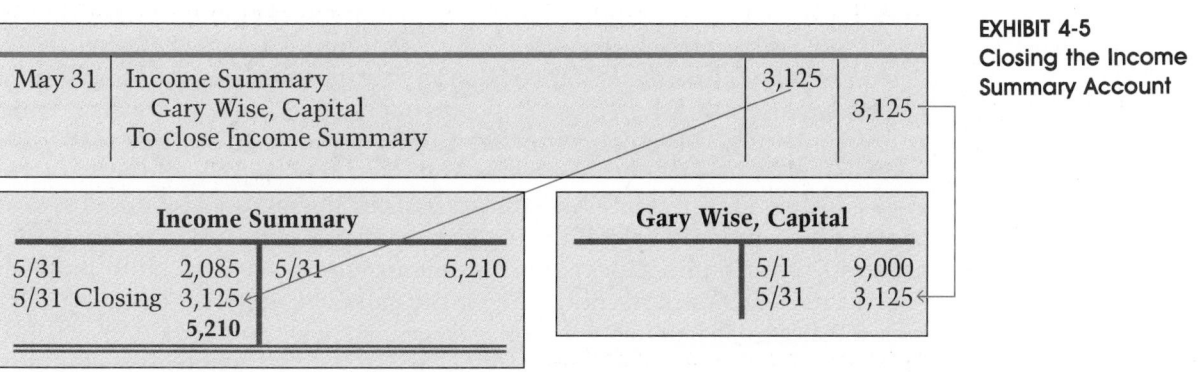

May 31	Income Summary	2,085	
	Salaries Expense		875
	Marketing Expense		800
	Electricity Expense		125
	Insurance Expense		20
	Supplies Expense		80
	Depreciation Expense		125
	Interest Expense		60
	To close expenses		

EXHIBIT 4-4
Closing Expense Accounts

Income Summary

| 5/31 | 2,085 | 5/31 | 5,210 |

Salaries Expense

5/28	825	5/31 Closing	875
5/31 Adj	50		
	875		

Supplies Expense

| 5/31 Adj | 80 | 5/31 Closing | 80 |

Marketing Expense

| 5/5 | 800 | 5/31 Closing | 800 |

Depreciation Expense

| 5/31 Adj | 125 | 5/31 Closing | 125 |

Electricity Expense

| 5/25 | 125 | 5/31 Closing | 125 |

Interest Expense

| 5/31 Adj | 60 | 5/31 Closing | 60 |

Insurance Expense

| 5/31 Adj | 20 | 5/31 Closing | 20 |

May 31	Income Summary	3,125	
	Gary Wise, Capital		3,125
	To close Income Summary		

EXHIBIT 4-5
Closing the Income Summary Account

Income Summary

5/31	2,085	5/31	5,210
5/31 Closing	3,125		
	5,210		

Gary Wise, Capital

| | | 5/1 | 9,000 |
| | | 5/31 | 3,125 |

EXHIBIT 4-6
Closing the Drawing Account

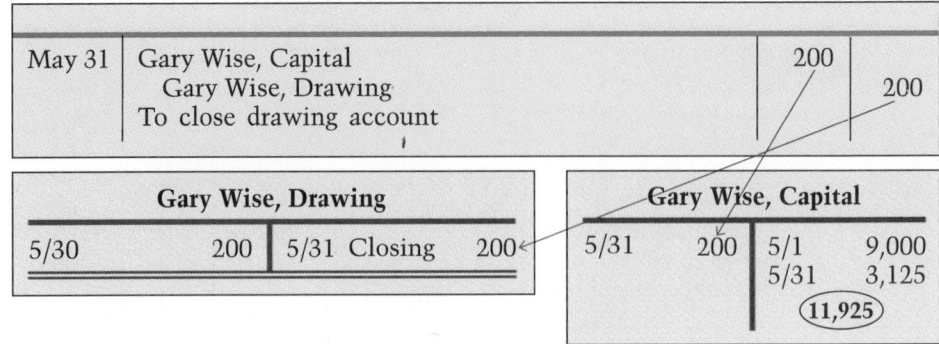

Closing the Drawing Account.   The final step in the closing process is to close the drawing account. From information that is shown in the adjusted trial balance columns of the work sheet, Wise's drawing account contains a $200 debit balance. A credit is therefore needed to reduce the account to zero. Because withdrawals decrease owner's equity, the required entry appears as shown in Exhibit 4-6.

By entering and posting this final journal entry, one completes the closing process. Observe that the revenue, expense, and drawing accounts all contain zero balances and are ready to accumulate June transactions. In addition, note that the $11,925 ending balance in Wise's capital account now agrees with the firm's financial statement disclosures as shown on pages 138 and 139.

Tips & Techniques

Notice that the drawing account is closed to Gary Wise, Capital, and *not* to Income Summary. The last account is used to summarize and collect only those elements that affect a company's profitability. Withdrawals of business assets are not expenses and are thus excluded from income computations.

An Overview.   Exhibit 4-7 presents an overview of the closing process. Throughout a period an entity's revenues, expenses, and owner withdrawals are accumulated in separate, temporary accounts for presentation in the financial statements. Upon conclusion of the reporting period these accounts have all served their temporary purposes and, accordingly, are closed. Closing transfers such balances to owner's capital, a permanent (real) element of the accounting equation.

Post-Closing Trial Balance.   Errors can occur during the closing process, just as they can in other accounting procedures. To determine whether the accounts are still in balance after the closing entries have been journalized and posted, accountants often prepare a **post-closing trial balance.** The post-closing trial balance examines ledger balances to determine if total debits equal total credits. Because this report is constructed after completion of the closing process, no balances remain in the drawing, revenue,

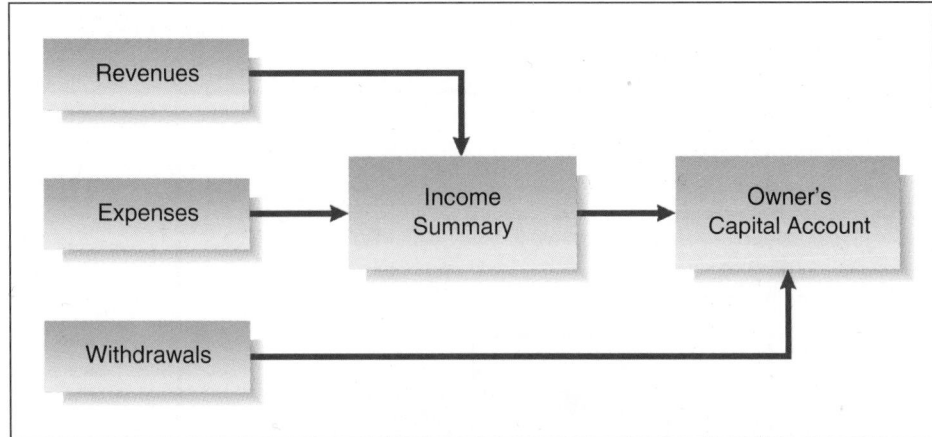

EXHIBIT 4-7
An Overview of the Closing Process

and expense accounts. In addition, the capital account has been updated to reflect these amounts. The post-closing trial balance for Wise Advertising appears in Exhibit 4-8.

A review of the material presented in this chapter and the previous two chapters reveals that we have been studying the **accounting cycle.** The cycle encompasses the various tasks performed during an accounting period to process transactions. Specifically, (1) transactions are recorded in the journal and then (2) posted to ledger accounts. To determine whether the ledger accounts are in balance, (3) a trial balance is constructed. The trial balance is updated by certain adjustments in the process of (4) preparing a work sheet. From the work sheet (5) formal financial statements are produced, and (6) adjusting entries are recorded in the journal and posted to the ledger. Finally, (7) temporary accounts are closed and (8) a post-closing

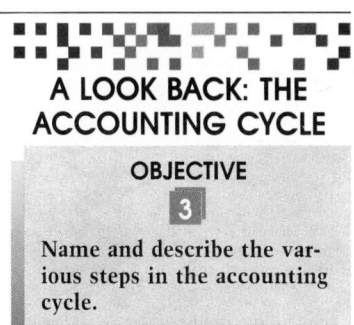

A LOOK BACK: THE ACCOUNTING CYCLE

OBJECTIVE

3

Name and describe the various steps in the accounting cycle.

EXHIBIT 4-8
Post-Closing Trial Balance

WISE ADVERTISING AGENCY Post-Closing Trial Balance May 31, 19XX		
Cash	$13,705	
Accounts receivable	3,860	
Prepaid insurance	460	
Supplies	260	
Land	5,500	
Car	4,500	
Accumulated depreciation: car		$ 125
Accounts payable		125
Unearned agency revenue		10,000
Loan payable		6,000
Interest payable		60
Salaries payable		50
Gary Wise, capital		11,925
	$28,285	$28,285

EXHIBIT 4-9
The Accounting Cycle

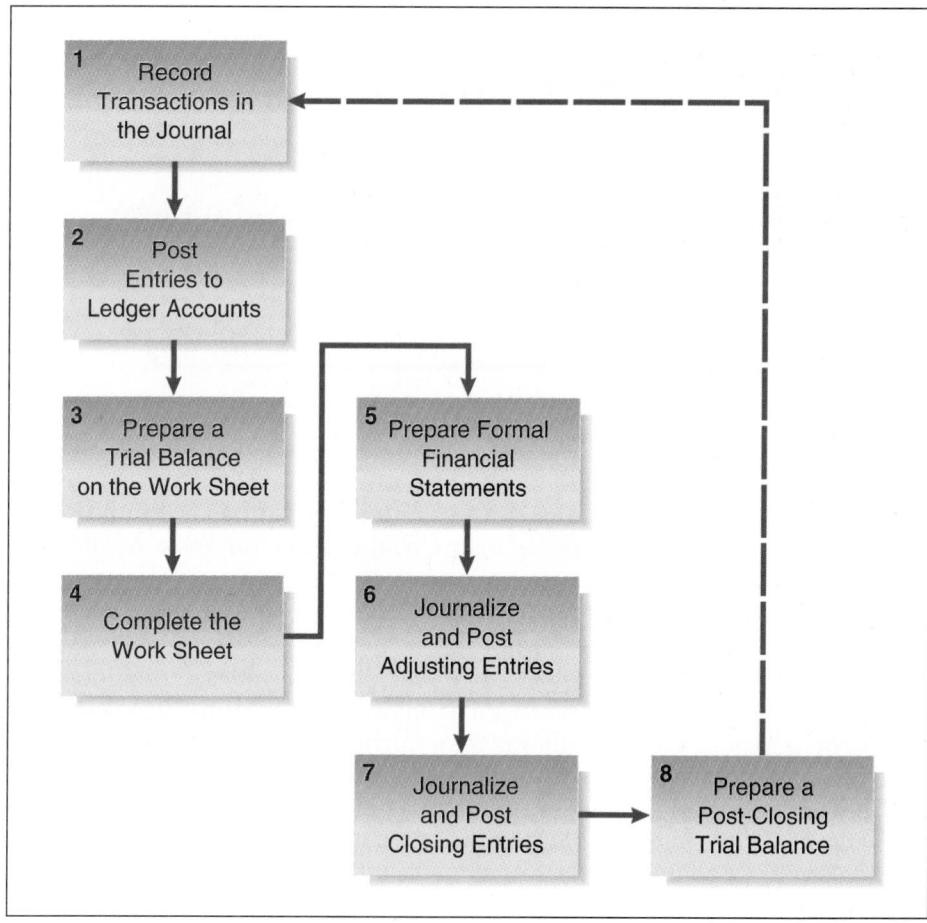

trial balance is prepared. The entire sequence, which is repeated in the next reporting period, is shown in Exhibit 4-9.

THE BALANCE SHEET

The past few chapters have shown how transactions and events eventually find their way to an entity's financial statements. Recall that financial statements comprise the output of an accounting system and, in fact, are considered by many people to be the primary objective of the accounting function. Because of their importance, we now begin an in-depth probe of the various reports prepared by a business that disclose economic activity. Our initial focus is on the balance sheet, with discussions of the other financial statements to follow in later chapters.

The balance sheet provides information about a company's assets, liabilities, and owner's equity. Such information is useful in many ways to different groups of individuals. For example, the manager of a slumping company can study the level of merchandise inventory at the end of an accounting period to judge the effectiveness of a new ordering policy. Stable inventory levels may prompt the manager to question why the ordering policy has not paralleled significant declines in sales. Creditors review the

EXECUTIVE BRIEFING
The Year-End Close: It's More Than Just the Journal Entries

Shirley Cheramy
Office Managing Partner, Century City, CA
Price Waterhouse, Certified Public Accountants

The year-end close brings with it a number of opportunities, whether you are a member of a company's financial staff or the independent accountants performing an audit. The opportunities include the time to step back and study the firm's operations for the year—that is, to look at the fundamental business, not at the journal entries that got you there. Are revenues up? Is the increase caused by price increases or by a change in product mix? How do total revenues compare to the budget and to last year? How does the new sales commission and bonus plan affect selling costs? There are lots of *business* (not accounting!) questions to answer.

Closing is also the time to look forward—how the company will do in the future, given operating results of the past year and the firm's current financial position. Such an investigation includes addressing business strategies, the competitive environment, and other nonaccounting issues.

This overview is intended to deliver a message: Take advantage of closing to understand the business. The journal entries and accounting conventions are obviously important, but the entire process involves much more. Talk to operating management; it's more fun and ensures that accounting truly reports on the period's activities.

asset and liability relationships on a balance sheet to determine the adequacy of cash balances for settling a firm's current and upcoming obligations. Creditors also analyze this financial statement to determine if the owners are investing their own capital in the business or relying on other creditors, such as banks, to finance operations. Lenders, in particular, want the owners to have a sizable stake in the business should financial problems develop.

Although the balance sheet is extremely useful, it suffers from several limitations. First, current values are seldom employed for asset valuation. As noted earlier in the text, accounting is based on the historical-cost principle. Assets are recorded in the accounts at acquisition cost and, generally, cost remains in the records until disposal (i.e., sale). Consequently, a company that acquired a parcel of land 10 years ago for $50,000 would continue to report a valuation of $50,000 even though the parcel may be currently worth several times that figure.

A second problem is that many of the assets important to the profitability and future existence of a business are not measurable in dollars. These assets, which include a good management, a skilled work force, a prime location, and business contacts and relationships, are therefore omitted from the balance sheet. No one would dispute the value of these items to a firm; yet an objective valuation for accounting purposes is extremely difficult to derive.

Statement Classification

The balance sheet in Exhibit 4-2 is adequate for an entity such as the Wise Advertising Agency. The business activities of "real-world" firms, however, tend to be more complex and involve numerous and varied accounts. Appropriately, balance sheets (and other financial statements, too) virtually always contain account classification schemes so that important relationships and subtotals can be obtained. Standard classifications improve statement utility because users can better analyze the financial relationships that are relevant and significant to them.

The balance sheet's classifications are discussed on the next few pages.

Assets

Current Assets.   **Current assets** consist of cash and those assets that management intends to convert into cash or consume in a relatively short period of time. The time period depends on the **operating cycle** of the business, that is, how long it takes a company to obtain goods for sale (i.e., inventory), sell the inventory, and ultimately collect the related receivables. Companies selling goods on credit have the operating cycle shown in Exhibit 4-10.

Most businesses have numerous operating cycles within an accounting period and use one year as the minimum time frame for classifying current assets. Be aware, however, that some firms have operating cycles well over one year in length. Examples include tobacco companies, which must cure their tobacco leaf, and liquor producers, which must age their inventory. Thus, the time period for purposes of the current asset definition is *one year or the operating cycle, whichever is longer.*

Current assets include cash, short-term investments and receivables, inventories, and prepaid expenses. These accounts are sequenced on the balance sheet in order of **liquidity,** or how close a current asset is to becoming cash. To illustrate, examine the balance sheet of The Williamsburg Company in Exhibit 4-11. Presented directly after cash is a short-term investment, the certificate of deposit. Although the certificate matures six months from the time of origination, it can be converted into cash immediately if necessary. Accounts receivable is listed next and represents claims against customers for inventory already sold or services rendered. The

EXHIBIT 4-10
Operating Cycle

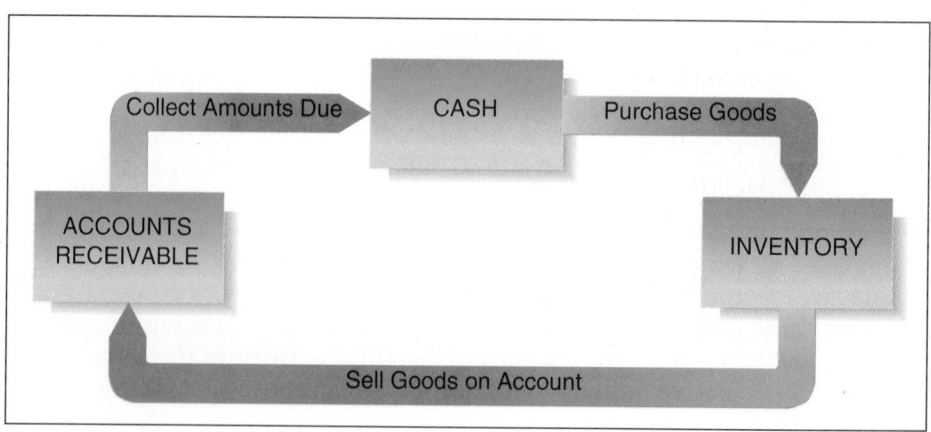

EXHIBIT 4-11

THE WILLIAMSBURG COMPANY
Balance Sheet
December 31, 19X1

Assets

Current assets			
Cash		$ 181,000	
Certificate of deposit			
(six-month maturity)		50,000	
Accounts receivable		1,389,000	
Merchandise inventory		2,375,000	
Prepaid expenses		36,000	
Total current assets			$ 4,031,000
Long-term investments			
Land (held for future use)			1,000,000
Property, plant, & equipment			
Land		$2,000,000	
Buildings	$3,000,000		
Less: Accumulated depreciation	1,250,000	1,750,000	
Equipment	$1,000,000		
Less: Accumulated depreciation	175,000	825,000	
Vehicles	$ 45,000		
Less: Accumulated depreciation	40,000	5,000	
Total property, plant, & equipment			4,580,000
Intangible assets			
Patents on inventions			40,000
Other assets			
Long-term receivables (due 19X6)			850,000
Total assets			$10,501,000

Liabilities & Owner's Equity

Current liabilities		
Accounts payable	$3,000,000	
Salaries payable	500,000	
Unearned revenues	400,000	
Current portion of mortgage payable	100,000	
Total current liabilities		$ 4,000,000
Long-term liabilities		
Mortgage payable (due 19X9)		1,500,000
Total liabilities		$ 5,500,000
Owner's equity		
Rudy Williams, capital		5,001,000
Total liabilities & owner's equity		$10,501,000

receivables are normally collected in a month or two, depending on the credit and collection practices of the firm. The merchandise inventory has yet to be sold and is presented next. Depending on the type of business involved, several months could elapse before the existing goods are purchased by customers and cash is ultimately collected. Prepaid expenses, such as rent, insurance, and supplies, commonly appear as the final current asset. Unlike receivables and inventory, prepaid expenses will not be converted to cash. They will, however, be consumed within a relatively short time.

Long-Term Investments.   The next asset classification on the balance sheet is **long-term investments.** These investments are made with the intention of being retained for a prolonged period of time. Examples include land purchased either for speculation or as a future plant site, funds set aside for a company's expansion program, and investments made to acquire other entities.

Property, Plant, and Equipment.   **Property, plant, and equipment** consists of assets that are used in the operation of a business and not held for resale to customers. These assets are tangible and have a long-term usefulness to a firm. Examples of property, plant, and equipment include land, buildings, machinery, furniture and fixtures, and vehicles. With the exception of land, the costs of assets in this category are gradually charged to expense via the depreciation process discussed in Chapter 3. Items of property, plant, and equipment are normally listed on the balance sheet in order of the length of their service lives, from the longest to the shortest. A typical presentation is shown in Exhibit 4-11.

Intangible Assets.   **Intangibles** are assets that lack physical existence; at the same time, however, these items represent valuable long-term rights to the business that has acquired or developed them. Examples include franchises, patents, copyrights, trademarks, and product formulas. Each year a portion of an intangible's cost is expensed as the asset's rights are used up or expire. This process and other issues related to intangibles are discussed further in Chapter 11.

Other Assets.   Any asset account that cannot be placed in one of the previous classifications is presented in the other assets category. For instance, The Williamsburg Company lists long-term receivables as an other asset.

Liabilities

Current Liabilities.   Generally stated, liabilities that will be liquidated within one year or the operating cycle, whichever is longer, are called **current liabilities.** Observe the consistency with the current asset definition. Examples of current liabilities include payables to suppliers and utilities, wages payable to employees, taxes payable to governmental units, and interest payable to banks. Another type of current liability is the unearned revenue discussed in Chapter 3. Unearned revenues represent cash received in advance of goods or services provided. These prepayments are liabilities until the goods or services are given in return, which usually occurs in less than a year's time.

Current liabilities are normally paid or reduced by current assets. Thus, the relationship between current assets and current liabilities is important, especially from a creditor's point of view. Creditors and other financial statement users periodically study this relationship by dividing the total current assets by the total current liabilities. The result, called the **current ratio,** provides insight into a firm's ability to pay short-term obligations on time and maintain its credit rating. Bankers and other lenders often prefer to see total current assets at least twice as large as total current liabilities. This 2 : 1 ratio essentially means that for every $1 owed and payable in the near future, a business has $2 of current assets available or soon available that can be used for payment.[2] Usually, a high current ratio is preferable to a low one. However, an abnormally high ratio may indicate that too much cash or inventory is held for the volume of business being generated. As a result, a company may be forced to forgo other more profitable investment opportunities.

The relationship between current assets and current liabilities can also be studied by focusing on **working capital,** the mathematical difference between total current assets and total current liabilities. Working capital is the amount that would remain if all current obligations were paid immediately. Thus, this figure provides an assessment of a company's ability to pay debts as the obligations come due. The amount of working capital should be sufficient to meet day-to-day expenses and provide for some expansion.

From the data shown in Exhibit 4-11, we see The Williamsburg Company's current ratio and working capital appear somewhat tenuous. The firm's current ratio is 1.01 ($4,031,000 ÷ $4,000,000), while working capital stands at only $31,000 ($4,031,000 − $4,000,000). Should an unexpected event arise, management may be forced to scramble for cash. Why? Although Williamsburg's current assets do exceed its current liabilities, observe the current asset composition. Approximately 93.4% of the current asset total is comprised of receivables and inventory, both of which will require some time until conversion into cash. Creditors may therefore be reluctant to conduct business with the firm for fear of nonpayment.

Long-Term Liabilities.   Obligations that are expected to be paid after one year or the operating cycle, whichever is longer, are classified as **long-term liabilities.** Examples of such liabilities include certain bank loans and mortgages payable.

Many long-term obligations are paid in annual installments, that is, $X per year. As a result, the portion of a long-term liability that will be paid within one year or the operating cycle is properly disclosed under the heading of "current." To illustrate, notice that Williamsburg owes $1,600,000 from a mortgage due in 19X9. The liability is split according to its payment dates: $100,000 within one year and $1,500,000 after one year.

ETHICS ISSUE

Ames, Inc., presently has a current ratio of 1.8, which is in violation of the terms of a loan agreement. Management has instructed you to immediately settle several soon-to-be-due payables, an action that will increase the ratio. Although accomplishing the ultimate objective, payment at this time will create a significant strain on cash—possibly causing insufficient funds for the week's payroll. How would you react?

---

[2] Remember that current assets include cash *and* assets that will be converted into cash in the near future (e.g., accounts receivable, inventories, and short-term investments). The exception is prepaid expenses.

Owner's Equity

As explained in Chapter 1, owner's equity represents the owner's claim against (or "interest" in) the assets of a business. The owner's equity section of the balance sheet varies with the three forms of business organization: sole proprietorship, partnership, and corporation.

Sole Proprietorship.   A **sole proprietorship** is an enterprise owned by one person. From an accounting perspective, owner investments and withdrawals, as well as the company's net income or net loss (i.e., revenues and expenses), are merged into a single account at the end of the period. For The Williamsburg Company, the account is labeled Rudy Williams, Capital. The proprietorship's balance sheet, then, will contain only one owner's equity account: the name of the owner followed by the term "Capital."

Partnership.   A **partnership** is a business owned by two or more persons, with a separate capital account established for each partner. Similar to what occurs in the proprietorship, each capital account after closing will contain a partner's investments, withdrawals, and a share of the entity's net income or net loss. Net income or net loss can be divided among the partners in any fashion. Generally, a written agreement stipulates the profit-sharing arrangements; if no written agreement exists, profits and losses are usually divided equally. Accounting problems for partnerships are presented later in the text, in Chapter 14.

Corporation.   A third form of business organization is the **corporation.** The owners, called *stockholders,* are the investors who have purchased the firm's transferable units of ownership—known as **shares of capital stock.**

Unlike sole proprietorships and partnerships, corporations do not combine owner investments, net income and net losses, and withdrawals in one capital account. Instead, shareholder investments are recorded in a Capital Stock account, and a separate account called **Retained Earnings** is used to keep track of the profits generated by management. Just as sole proprietorships and partnerships permit owner withdrawals, corporations follow a similar practice. Corporate withdrawals are termed **dividends** and represent distributions of income to the stockholders. At any point in time, then, the balance in Retained Earnings represents undistributed profits that are left (retained) in the firm.

A simplified owners' (stockholders') equity section of a corporate balance sheet would appear as follows:

Stockholders' equity	
Capital stock, 10,000 shares authorized and issued	$100,000
Retained earnings	42,500
Total stockholders' equity	$142,500

In practice, accounting for corporate equity can become quite complex. Further discussion of corporations is presented in Chapters 15 and 16.

HIGHLIGHT
All Balance Sheets Are Not Created Equal

The balance sheet of The Williamsburg Company is very representative of those prepared by many "real-world" businesses. There are notable exceptions, however, which often arise because of unique industry characteristics. Consider the following examples:

■ *Banks*—If you have occasion to review the balance sheet of a commercial bank, don't snicker because the accountants forgot to establish current and noncurrent categories. Omitting these classifications is appropriate because of the nature of a bank's assets and liabilities. For example, a financial institution's largest asset is its loans to customers (a receivable). How does one differentiate between current and noncurrent—the loans have varying terms, and when the due date arrives, there is a likelihood of renewal. As a result, loans are frequently classified by purpose—energy-related, agricultural, real estate, and so forth.

Customer deposits (a liability to a bank because such amounts are owed to clientele) also present a problem. Typically the institution's largest liability, these amounts are normally payable on demand by the customer. It therefore becomes difficult, if not impossible, to identify such sums as current or noncurrent.

■ *Utilities*—To an untrained eye, it would seem that utility companies prepare "upside down" balance sheets. In the asset section, plant and equipment is listed first, followed by current assets. On the liability side, "capitalization" (i.e., stockholders' equity and long-term obligations) heads the list and is followed by current liabilities.

The rationale for this arrangement is that utility companies have substantial investments in their plant and equipment, sometimes in the billions of dollars because of nuclear power plants. For a local or regional business, the amount of money is indeed significant. This investment is normally financed through permanent and long-term capital, such as stock issuances and various types of long-term debt. Financial statement users are particularly interested in an analysis of these sizable components over time. Evaluations of current assets and current liabilities therefore take a back seat and are positioned accordingly.

■ *Insurance companies*—Many insurance companies prepare two balance sheets. Are these firms trying to pull a fast one? Hardly! One balance sheet will likely be constructed to comply with generally accepted accounting principles. A second balance sheet, however, may be required for compliance with the various state laws that regulate the company (termed statutory accounting principles). Significant differences may arise in both asset and liability valuations.

Another interesting facet of insurance companies can be observed by reviewing the owners' equity section of the balance sheet. Frequently, the account titles would indicate that the customers own the firm. This is in fact the case. Many insurance businesses are organized as "mutual companies," meaning they are owned and controlled by the existing policyholders.

Unique—yes! Unusual—no! Those companies that have balance sheets with a special flavor invariably have financial statement users with special needs. The accounting profession has managed to tailor its reports to satisfy these users, resulting in a variety of presentations and disclosures. Stated simply, no two balance sheets are created equal.

Notes to the Financial Statements/Full Disclosure

The balance sheet classifications just discussed improve a company's presentation of financial information. For most organizations, however, further description is needed. Many business activities are complex and require some explanation—an explanation that goes beyond the numbers shown on the income statement, statement of owner's equity, and balance sheet.

In recognition of this fact, the financial statements are normally accompanied by a series of **notes** that provide an expansion on selected company information. Notes are employed to describe the details of significant accounting policies, major business events that occurred during the period, pending lawsuits, and various other facets of operation. Such information is used extensively by analysts and investors to better understand the figures being reported. See Appendix C at the end of the text, which contains the notes and financial statements of the Alberto Culver Company.

The use of notes is an example of the accounting principle of full disclosure. **Full disclosure** means that the financial statements result in a fair presentation of the facts that influence the decisions and judgment of an informed user of financial information. Such facts must be presented in a timely manner and be unbiased and understandable.

APPENDIX: REVERSING ENTRIES

OBJECTIVE
5

Explain the concept and mechanics of reversing entries.

Our presentation of the accounting cycle concluded with the construction of a post-closing trial balance. Some companies add a further step to the cycle by using reversing entries. To explain, a **reversing entry** is the exact opposite of an adjusting entry. The same accounts are involved, but the debits and credits are reversed. Reversing entries are journalized on the first day of the following accounting period and, it is important to note, are an optional bookkeeping procedure.

To illustrate the concept and purpose of reversals, assume that Houston Enterprises has a $15,000 payroll for a five-day work week. Employees are paid every Friday, giving rise to the following journal entry:

Salaries Expense	15,000	
Cash		15,000
Paid salaries for the week		

It is now December and the last payroll of the month falls due on Friday, the 26th. The journal entry just shown is recorded once again when cash is disbursed to the employees. By December 31, an additional three working days will have elapsed (Monday, December 29, through Wednesday, December 31). Houston must therefore record the following adjusting entry to properly reflect the salary expense incurred during this period:

Dec. 31	Salaries Expense	9,000	
	Salaries Payable		9,000
	To record accrued salaries		

The $9,000 adjustment is based on salaries of $3,000 per day ($15,000 ÷ 5 days).

Shortly after the adjusting process is completed, the books would be closed and the balance in the Salaries Expense account reduced to zero. The relevant expense and liability accounts would appear as follows:

Salaries Expense		
12/31 Adj	9,000	12/31 Closing 9,000

Salaries Payable	
	12/31 Adj 9,000

Note: For illustrative purposes we have omitted the weekly $15,000 debits to Salaries Expense.

Case A—No Reversing Entries

At this point Houston must decide whether it wants to utilize reversing entries. Let us first assume that the firm does *not* use reversals. As a result, our example can be completed by focusing on Friday, January 2—the next payday. Houston's $15,000 payroll would be recorded in the following manner:

```
Jan. 2  Salaries Payable            9,000
        Salaries Expense            6,000
            Cash                            15,000
        Paid salaries for the week
```

Salaries Payable is debited to eliminate the salaries owed from the previous accounting period. In addition, Salaries Expense is debited to recognize the payroll costs (i.e., an expense) related to the first two days of January ($3,000 × 2 days = $6,000).

Case B—Using Reversing Entries

We will now assume that Houston elects to use reversals. On January 1, the first day of the new accounting period, the firm will reverse the December 31 adjustment in the following manner:

```
Jan. 1  Salaries Payable            9,000
            Salaries Expense                9,000
        Reversing entry
```

The impact of this entry is best seen by studying the accompanying T-accounts:

Salaries Expense		
12/31 Adj	9,000	12/31 Closing 9,000
		1/1 Rev 9,000

Salaries Payable		
1/1 Rev	9,000	12/31 Adj 9,000

The Salaries Payable account is reduced to zero; Salaries Expense, on the other hand, contains an abnormal credit balance of $9,000. Because of its zero balance, there is no need to debit Salaries Payable when payment takes place on January 2. Instead, the *entire* disbursement is expensed, as follows:

Jan. 2	Salaries Expense	15,000	
	Cash		15,000
	Paid salaries for the week		

The $15,000 debit, when combined with the account's existing credit balance, leaves $6,000 in Salaries Expense. This amount correctly reflects Houston's salary costs for the first two days of January: $3,000 per day × 2 days = $6,000.

An Overview

A comparison of the two approaches reveals identical outcomes. Specifically, the expense is split between the accounting periods affected: $9,000 of expense is recognized in December (3 days) and $6,000 in January (2 days). Further, no balance remains in Salaries Payable, indicating that Houston has completely settled its year-end salary obligation.

As the end result is the same, why would a company use reversing entries? Although an extra journal entry is involved, reversals facilitate the bookkeeping process and reduce the chance for errors. To illustrate, briefly review Case A (no reversing entries). Observe the need to reference the year-end accrual to determine the amount of the January 2 cash disbursement that was expensed in the previous period ($9,000). In contrast, the use of reversals (Case B) allows the bookkeeper to record the normal payroll entry (namely, a debit to Salaries Expense and a credit to Cash). The possibility is therefore eliminated that errors will creep into the accounts on the subsequent payment date from the bookkeeper's failure to consider a previously recorded adjustment.

The basic reversing procedures that were shown for salaries apply to other accrued expenses as well, with similar procedures available for use with accrued revenues. Generally speaking, reversals are applied to those adjusting items that involve future cash flows. In some cases the reversing process can be employed with prepaid expenses and unearned revenues. These cases are somewhat unusual, however, and will not be discussed here.

END-OF-CHAPTER REVIEW

LEARNING OBJECTIVES: THE KEY POINTS

1 Prepare a work sheet and the accompanying financial statements. A work sheet is a columnar form that aids in the construction of financial statements. An entity's trial balance data are combined with appropriate adjustments to yield the adjusted trial balance. Each account in the adjusted trial balance is then extended to one of the work sheet's financial statement sections, with assets, liabilities, and owner's equity accounts going to the balance sheet and revenues and expenses being transferred to the income statement.

2 Close a set of books and prepare a post-closing trial balance. At the end of a reporting period, a company's temporary accounts (revenues, expenses, and drawing) are closed, or reduced to zero. Revenue accounts are debited, with a corresponding credit being made to Income Summary. Next, the individual expenses are credited and the Income Summary is debited. Income Summary, now containing the income or loss of the firm, is closed to the owner's capital account. As a final step, the drawing account is credited and charged against owner's capital. The post-closing trial balance is constructed after the closing process is completed by extracting account balances from the general ledger.

3 Name and describe the various steps in the accounting cycle. The accounting cycle consists of the various tasks performed during a period to process transactions. These tasks include journalizing, posting, construction of a trial balance, and preparation of a work sheet and formal financial statements. Also included are the recording and posting of adjusting entries, the closing process, and preparation of a post-closing trial balance.

4 Understand the concept of an operating cycle and construct a classified balance sheet. An operating cycle is the amount of time that it takes a business to buy inventory, sell that inventory to customers, and collect the related receivables. Statement classifications, such as those for current assets; long-term investments; property, plant, and equipment; intangible assets; other assets; current liabilities; long-term liabilities; and owner's equity, help make a balance sheet more useful for purposes of financial analysis.

5 (Appendix) Explain the concept and mechanics of reversing entries. Reversing entries are employed to reduce the possibility of errors in an accounting system. These entries are made on the first day of a new accounting period and are the exact opposite of previously recorded adjustments for accrued expenses and accrued revenues. It is important to note that reversals are an optional bookkeeping procedure.

**KEY TERMS
AND CONCEPTS:
A QUICK OVERVIEW**

accounting cycle The various tasks performed to process transactions, including (1) recording transactions in the journal; (2) posting; (3) preparing a trial balance, work sheet, and financial statements; (4) recording adjusting and closing entries; and (5) preparing a post-closing trial balance.

closing process A process in which the balances in all temporary accounts are transferred to the owner's capital account.

corporation An entity form whose owners have purchased shares of stock in the enterprise.

current assets Those assets that management intends to convert into cash or consume in the normal course of business within one year or the operating cycle, whichever is longer.

current liabilities Debts or obligations that will be paid within one year or the operating cycle, whichever is longer.

current ratio A measure of liquidity that relates total current assets to total current liabilities.

dividends Distributions of corporate income to the stockholders.

full disclosure principle A principle holding that an entity must provide a complete reporting of all facts important enough to influence the judgment of an informed user of financial information.

income summary An account used in the closing process to summarize the revenues and expenses of a business.

intangible assets Long-term assets that lack physical existence—for example, patents, copyrights, and trademarks.

liquidity   How close an asset is to becoming cash.

long-term investments   Investments made with the intent of being held for a long period of time.

long-term liabilities   Obligations expected to be paid after one year or the operating cycle, whichever is longer.

notes to the financial statements   A supplemental, yet integral, part of the financial statements that provides an expansion of the information contained in the body of the reports.

operating cycle   The period of time it takes a firm to buy merchandise inventory, sell the inventory, and collect the related receivables.

partnership   A business owned by two or more persons.

post-closing trial balance   An internal report that examines ledger account balances after the closing process has been completed to determine if total debits equal total credits.

property, plant, and equipment   Assets with long lives acquired for use in business operations and not held for resale to customers.

real accounts   Accounts whose balances are carried forward from period to period.

retained earnings   The undistributed income that is left in a corporation.

reversing entry   A journal entry made on the first day of the following period that is the exact opposite of an adjustment.

shares of capital stock   A corporation's transferable units of ownership.

temporary (nominal) accounts   Accounts that are reduced to zero at the end of the accounting period via the closing process.

work sheet   A columnar form that aids in the construction of the financial statements and assists in the performance of other end-of-period tasks.

working capital   The excess of total current assets over total current liabilities.

CHAPTER QUIZ

The five questions that follow relate to several issues raised in the chapter. Test your knowledge of the issues by selecting the best answer. (The answers appear on p. 175.)

1 When preparing a work sheet, the balance in the Accounts Payable account should be extended from the adjusted trial balance column to the:
a income statement debit column.   c balance sheet debit column.
b income statement credit column.   d balance sheet credit column.

2 Which of the following statements about the closing process is correct?
a Balances in income statement accounts are reduced to zero.
b The owner's capital account is updated to reflect the period's net income and owner withdrawals.
c Temporary accounts are given different treatment than real accounts.
d All of the above statements are correct.

3 Which of the following is the correct closing entry for Joe Salem's drawing account?
a Debit Joe Salem, Drawing; credit Joe Salem, Capital.
b Debit Joe Salem, Drawing; credit Income Summary.
c Debit Joe Salem, Capital; credit Joe Salem, Drawing.
d Debit Income Summary; credit Joe Salem, Drawing.

4 Which of the following accounts would not appear on a post-closing trial balance?

a Accounts Receivable.   c Loan Payable.
b Rent Expense.   d Al Jarvis, Capital.

5 The balance sheet's current asset classification:

a is normally disclosed after the property, plant, and equipment classification.
b includes cash and other assets expected to be realized or consumed within one year of the balance sheet date or the operating cycle, whichever is longer.
c includes cash and other assets expected to be realized or consumed within one year of the balance sheet date or the operating cycle, whichever is shorter.
d reports the patents and copyrights owned by a firm.

Sherry Black operates a tour service for island resorts. The company's December 31, 19X2, adjusted trial balance follows.

SUMMARY PROBLEM

SHERRY'S SHORE EXCURSIONS Adjusted Trial Balance December 31, 19X2		
Cash	$ 5,300	
Accounts receivable	13,650	
Prepaid insurance	1,100	
Building	120,000	
Accumulated depreciation: building		$ 57,650
Equipment	26,000	
Accumulated depreciation: equipment		7,200
Accounts payable		16,500
Salaries payable		7,700
Unearned service revenue		11,900
Sherry Black, capital		40,100
Sherry Black, drawing	8,500	
Service revenue		62,400
Salaries expense	13,400	
Rent expense	6,000	
Insurance expense	1,200	
Depreciation expense	8,300	
	$203,450	$203,450

Instructions

a Prepare the necessary closing entries for the year ended December 31.
b Calculate the balance in Black's capital account after closing. *Note:* There were no owner investments during the year.
c Determine the company's total current assets and total current liabilities as of December 31.
d Suppose that the company's general ledger contained the following additional accounts: Copyright, Mortgage Payable (due in 19X6), and Land Held for Future Building Site. In what sections of a classified balance sheet would these accounts appear?

Solution

a Dec. 31 Service Revenue   62,400
                   Income Summary   62,400
               To close revenues

       31 Income Summary   28,900
                   Salaries Expense   13,400
                   Rent Expense   6,000
                   Insurance Expense   1,200
                   Depreciation Expense   8,300
               To close expenses

       31 Income Summary   33,500*
                   Sherry Black, Capital   33,500
               To close Income Summary

       31 Sherry Black, Capital   8,500
                   Sherry Black, Drawing   8,500
               To close drawing account

                   * $62,400 − $28,900.

b Beginning capital, Jan. 1 $40,100
   Add: Net income   33,500
                                         $73,600
   Deduct: Owner withdrawals   8,500
   Ending capital, Dec. 31 $65,100

c Current assets
      Cash $ 5,300
      Accounts receivable   13,650
      Prepaid insurance   1,100
         Total $20,050

   Current liabilities
      Accounts payable $16,500
      Salaries payable   7,700
      Unearned service revenue   11,900
         Total $36,100

d Copyright—intangible assets; Mortgage Payable—long-term liabilities; Land Held for Future Building Site—long-term investments

ASSIGNMENT MATERIAL

QUESTIONS

Q4-1   What are the key benefits of preparing a work sheet?

Q4-2   Why is the net income amount (as derived from the income statement columns of the work sheet) also entered as a credit in the balance sheet columns?

Q4-3 Why are the adjusting entries that appear on the work sheet also recorded in the general journal?

Q4-4 What are the objectives of the closing process?

Q4-5 Which accounts are closed at the end of the accounting period and which are not closed?

Q4-6 Is the owner's drawing account closed to the Income Summary account? Why?

Q4-7 What are the differences between the adjusted trial balance and the post-closing trial balance?

Q4-8 What is meant by the term "accounting cycle"?

Q4-9 Discuss the limitations of the balance sheet.

Q4-10 Define the operating cycle. Should businesses attempt to shorten the cycle or lengthen it? Why?

Q4-11 How should current assets be organized on the balance sheet?

Q4-12 What is an intangible asset? Present three examples of intangible assets.

Q4-13 Discuss the use of the current ratio in making credit decisions.

Q4-14 Are all pertinent facts about a company disclosed directly in the body of a balance sheet and other financial statements? If not, what additional technique is used?

Q4-15 An accountant recently stated that a company's balance sheet lacked adequate disclosure. Explain the accountant's comment.

*Q4-16 What is a reversing entry? Are reversing entries a required or an optional bookkeeping procedure?

EXERCISES

E4-1 *Work sheet extensions* (L.O. 1)
The bookkeeper of Micro Shack is in the process of completing the company's work sheet for the year just ended. The following accounts appear in the adjusted trial balance:
a Accounts receivable
b Fee revenue
c Long-term payable due Lincoln Credit Corporation
d Utilities expense
e Frank Bush, drawing
f Unearned client fees
g Display equipment
h Prepaid store rent
i Frank Bush, capital

For each of the preceding items, indicate whether the account should be extended to the income statement debit column, income statement credit column, balance sheet debit column, or the balance sheet credit column. Assume that all accounts have normal balances.

---

* An asterisk preceding an item indicates that the material is covered in an appendix to this chapter.

E4-2   Preparation of financial statements (L.O. 1)

The adjusted trial balance of Apartment Finders as of December 31, 19XX, appears as follows:

Cash	$16,300	
Accounts receivable	8,900	
Prepaid advertising	2,000	
Equipment	17,500	
Accumulated depreciation: equipment		$ 4,000
Accounts payable		2,500
Commissions payable		5,000
Katie Reubens, capital		18,500
Katie Reubens, drawing	3,000	
Service revenue		37,000
Commissions expense	7,000	
Advertising expense	6,000	
Telephone expense	4,200	
Depreciation expense	2,100	
	$67,000	$67,000

Katie Reubens organized Apartment Finders on January 2, 19XX, with an initial cash investment of $18,500.

Prepare Apartment Finders' income statement and statement of owner's equity for the year ended December 31, 19XX. Also prepare the company's December 31 balance sheet, using a format similar to that shown in Exhibit 4-2.

E4-3   Overview of the closing process (L.O. 2)

Evaluate the comments that follow as being True or False. If the comment is false, briefly explain why.

a The closing process is performed after adjusting entries have been journalized and posted.

b Because they both possess a debit balance, Salaries Expense and Susan Franklin, Drawing, are treated in the same manner when accounts are closed at the end of the period.

c The Equipment account is closed at the end of the period by a debit to Income Summary and a credit to Equipment.

d If MultiTech incurred a net loss for the period just ended, the Income Summary account would contain a debit balance after the revenue and expense accounts have been closed.

e If a $4,900 balance is listed in the adjusted trial balance for Dave Miller, Capital, it stands to reason that Miller's capital account in the post-closing trial balance would be listed at $4,900 as well.

E4-4   Understanding the closing process (L.O. 2)

Examine the following list of accounts:

Interest payable	Accumulated depreciation: equipment
Alex Kenzy, drawing	Accounts payable
Service revenue	Cash
Accounts receivable	Supplies expense
Interest expense	

Which of the preceding accounts:

a Appear on a post-closing trial balance?

b Are commonly known as temporary, or nominal, accounts?

c Generate a debit to Income Summary in the closing process?

d Are closed to the capital account in the closing process?

E4-5 *Closing entries* (L.O. 2)

Gomez Company had the following adjusted trial balance on December 31:

Cash	$ 2,300	
Accounts receivable	16,500	
Prepaid insurance	1,200	
Land	40,000	
Accounts payable		$ 1,800
Miguel Gomez, capital		43,700
Miguel Gomez, drawing	2,500	
Service revenue		38,000
Rent expense	9,000	
Insurance expense	5,400	
Advertising expense	3,500	
Utilities expense	3,100	
	$83,500	$83,500

Prepare the closing entries that Gomez would record on December 31.

E4-6 *Closing entries, errors* (L.O. 2)

The closing entries that follow were prepared by a newly hired accountant of Spring Valley, a firm that specializes in real-estate property management. (*Note:* The adjusted trial balance was error-free, and all accounts had normal balances.)

Property Management Fees	235,000	
Lynn Jasper, Capital		235,000
To close revenues		
Salaries Expense	48,000	
Insurance Expense	12,000	
Depreciation Expense	13,000	
Rent Expense	15,000	
Utilities Expense	8,000	
Supplies Expense	3,000	
Interest Expense	7,000	
Income Summary		106,000
To close expenses		
Lynn Jasper, Capital	279,000	
Income Summary		279,000
To close capital account		
Income Summary	18,000	
Lynn Jasper, Drawing		18,000
To close drawing account		

Review the closing entries prepared by the new accountant and list any errors that you detect. (A corrected set of closing entries is not required.)

E4-7   *Steps in the accounting cycle* (L.O. 3)

Organize the following steps in the correct sequence of occurrence.

Step	Procedure
A	Formal financial statements are produced.
B	Transactions are posted to appropriate ledger accounts.
C	Closing entries are journalized and posted.
D	Daily transactions are recorded in the journal.
E	A post-closing trial balance is prepared.
F	Adjusting entries are entered in the journal and posted to the ledger.
G	The trial balance is updated by certain adjustments in the process of preparing a work sheet.
H	A trial balance is constructed.
I	A work sheet is completed.

E4-8   *Report interrelationships* (L.O. 1, 2)

The following selected information appeared on reports prepared by the Phantom Company:

	Trial Balance	Adjusted Trial Balance	Post-Closing Trial Balance
Cash	$15,000	$?	$?
Supplies	2,100	1,400	?
Jones, drawing	?	9,600	?
Jones, capital	?	?	51,700
Accumulated depreciation: equipment	?	31,900	?

All accounts had normal balances, and the company reported $32,700 of net income for the period.

a Briefly explain the probable reason why the Supplies account decreased by $700 from the trial balance to the adjusted trial balance.

b What balance would be disclosed for the Cash account on the adjusted trial balance?

c What balance would be disclosed for the drawing account on the post-closing trial balance?

d What balance would appear in the Income Summary account just prior to the account being closed?

e Analyze the balance in the Accumulated Depreciation account and determine whether it would likely be equal to $31,900, greater than $31,900, or less than $31,900 on the:

(1) Trial balance.

(2) Post-closing trial balance.

E4-9   *Balance sheet account classification* (L.O. 4)

The balance sheet of Packer Enterprises is similar to that appearing in Exhibit 4-11. Under which classification would each of the following appear?

a Prepaid advertising

b Portion of 30-year mortgage due in six months
c Unearned commission revenue
d Charles Packer, capital
e Receivable from Howard Gibson, due in three years
f Land purchased for speculation
g Wages payable
h Delivery vehicles
i Patents
j Accounts receivable

E4-10 *Current ratio and working capital calculations* (L.O. 4)

Selected accounts of McCormick Company, with current balances, are presented in the list that follows:

1-2-3

Accounts payable	$12,500
Accounts receivable	33,000
Accumulated depreciation	24,600
Cash	13,900
Interest payable	6,500
Loan payable, due in two months	10,000
Loan payable, due in three years	45,000
Jason McCormick, capital	36,600
Merchandise inventory	22,600
Prepaid advertising	5,300
Trademark	1,700
Unearned service revenue, to be earned next month	5,000

a Determine the current ratio.
b Calculate the company's working capital.
c If McCormick has a plan to pay off all of its accounts payable, how will working capital be affected?

*E4-11 *Reversing entries* (L.O. 5)

Burger Palace, which uses reversing entries, incurred $6,000 of wage and salary expenses during the last few days of 19X1. The company will pay these expenses on January 4, 19X2, as part of the $15,000 weekly payroll.

1-2-3

a Present the adjusting entry that is needed at the end of 19X1.
b Assuming a $740,000 balance in the Wage & Salary Expense account prior to the adjustment, present the necessary entry to close this account.
c Record the company's reversing entry on January 1, 19X2.
d Present the entry needed on January 4, 19X2.
e How much of the January 4 payroll is considered expense of 19X2?

Series A

PROBLEMS

P4-A1 *Closing entries* (L.O. 2)

The accounting records of the Fit Firm, an aerobics studio, revealed the following selected accounts on December 31 of the current year:

1-2-3

Debit balances		Credit balances	
Toni Kramer, drawing	$35,000	Toni Kramer, capital	$15,000
Salaries expense	25,000	Lesson revenue	80,400
Rent expense	6,000		
Utilities expense	2,500		
Insurance expense	3,600		
Depreciation expense	1,800		

Kramer's capital account reflects a $5,000 owner investment made on July 7.

Instructions

a Prepare the necessary closing entries for the year ended December 31.
b Compute the December 31, 19XX, balance of Kramer's capital account after the closing process has been performed.

P4-A2 *Abbreviated work sheet, financial statements, closing entries* (L.O. 1, 2)

Paul Cohen is employed in the accounting department of Crossroads Repair Company. He was in the process of completing the firm's work sheet for the year ended December 31 and had progressed through the adjusted trial balance columns. A portion of his work follows.

	Adjusted Trial Balance	
	Debit	Credit
Cash	$ 25,400	
Accounts receivable	20,700	
Repair supplies	4,300	
Prepaid rent	1,800	
Machinery	65,300	
Accumulated depreciation: machinery		$ 15,900
Accounts payable		20,800
Loan payable		16,900
Bob Goodson, capital		62,200
Bob Goodson, drawing	6,800	
Service revenue		74,600
Wages expense	40,400	
Insurance expense	2,500	
Interest expense	1,300	
Miscellaneous expense	900	
Repair supplies expense	5,200	
Rent expense	10,800	
Depreciation expense	5,300	
Interest payable		300
	$190,700	$190,700

Additional information revealed that owner investments in the firm amounted to $4,000 during the year.

Paul was recently called out of town because of a family emergency. You are his assistant and recognize that the various year-end accounting procedures must be performed on a timely basis.

Instructions

a Complete the work sheet that Paul had begun. *Note:* The preceding data should be entered in the adjusted trial balance columns. We have omitted the company's trial balance and adjustments for the sake of simplicity.
b Prepare an income statement, statement of owner's equity, and balance sheet in good form. The balance sheet should parallel the format used in Exhibit 4-2.
c Prepare the firm's closing entries.

P4-A3 Cycle, starting with work sheet (L.O. 1, 2, 3)

VTL

Trimcraft Company has the following trial balance as of December 31, 19XX:

Cash	$ 5,800	
Accounts receivable	8,200	
Prepaid insurance	2,000	
Supplies	2,700	
Equipment	89,800	
Accumulated depreciation: equipment		$ 10,000
Accounts payable		7,250
Loan payable		18,500
Lori Metcalf, capital		56,850
Lori Metcalf, drawing	4,000	
Service revenue		72,000
Salaries expense	30,500	
Rent expense	12,000	
Advertising expense	6,600	
Interest expense	3,000	
	$164,600	$164,600

Additional accounts maintained by the business include Salaries Payable, Interest Payable, Income Summary, Insurance Expense, Supplies Expense, and Depreciation Expense. Trimcraft's accountant has derived the following adjustment data:

1 Supplies on hand: $900.
2 Insurance that expired during the period: $1,300.
3 Depreciation on the equipment: $3,500.
4 Accrued interest on the loan: $400.
5 Accrued salaries incurred but not yet paid: $1,200.
6 Unrecorded service revenue, to be collected in future months: $2,200.

On March 9, 19XX, Metcalf invested $10,000 cash in the business. This event is already reflected in the figures reported in the trial balance.

Instructions

a Complete a work sheet in good form for Trimcraft Company for the year ended December 31.
b Prepare an income statement, statement of owner's equity, and balance sheet in good form. The balance sheet should be similar in format to that shown in Exhibit 4-2.
c Record Trimcraft's adjusting entries in the journal.
d Record Trimcraft's closing entries in the journal.
e Prepare a post-closing trial balance.

P4-A4 *Classified balance sheet* (L.O. 4)

Assume that the Nelson Company has the following accounts at the end of 19X1 (listed in alphabetic order):

Accounts payable	$ 6,600
Accounts receivable	13,000
Accumulated depreciation: building	52,000
Accumulated depreciation: office equipment	7,700
Building	430,000
Cash	5,500
Copyright	2,600
Interest payable	3,700
Interest receivable	1,700
Inventory	18,300
Land	50,000
Land held as a future plant site	75,000
Loan payable (due in one month)	12,000
Mortgage payable*	420,000
Office equipment	41,000
Office supplies	1,300
Pat Nelson, capital	146,300
Payable to Emery & Associates (due in 19X4)	18,000
Prepaid advertising	1,800
Receivable from employee (due in 19X3)	9,500
Salaries payable	2,000
Short-term investments	20,000
Taxes payable	6,400
Trademark	5,000

* Of this amount, $25,000 is payable within the next year.

Instructions

Prepare a classified balance sheet as of December 31, 19X1, similar in format to that shown in Exhibit 4-11.

*P4-A5 *Reversing entries* (L.O. 5)

Greenery, which began business on January 3 of the current year, renders landscaping services to both residential and commercial clients. The company's total wage expense through the most recent payday, June 26, totals $34,750. Greenery pays its employees every Friday for a five-day work week. Data for the next pay period, June 29–July 3, follow.

Date	Wage Cost Incurred
Monday, June 29	$280
Tuesday, June 30	300
Wednesday, July 1	300
Thursday, July 2	300
Friday, July 3	315

Greenery uses reversing entries.

Instructions

a Compute the company's total wage expense through June 30.

b Present the journal entries needed on June 30 to adjust and close the Wage Expense account.

c Prepare the necessary reversing entry on July 1.

d Prepare the necessary journal entry to disburse Greenery's weekly payroll on July 3.

e Repeat part (d), assuming that Greenery does not use reversing entries.

f Is it mandatory that Greenery use reversing entries? Briefly explain.

Series B

P4-B1 *Closing entries* (L.O. 2)

The income statement of Morton's Taxi Service for the year ended December 31, 19XX, follows.

1-2-3

MORTON'S TAXI SERVICE Income Statement For the Year Ended December 31, 19XX		
Taxi revenue		$144,360
Less expenses		
Salaries expense	$41,640	
Auto rental expense	12,400	
Gasoline expense	14,430	
Maintenance expense	1,500	
License expense	6,200	
Tires expense	970	
Total expenses		77,140
Net income		$ 67,220

Daniel Morton, the service's owner, had a beginning capital balance of $37,300 on January 1, 19XX. During the year he invested an additional $10,000 into the firm and withdrew $26,000.

Instructions

a Prepare the necessary closing entries for the year ended December 31.

b Compute the December 31, 19XX, balance of Morton's capital account.

P4-B2 *Abbreviated work sheet, financial statements, closing entries* (L.O. 1, 2)

Holly Knight is employed in the accounting department of Expert Systems Company. She was in the process of completing the firm's work sheet for the year ended December 31 and had progressed through the adjusted trial balance columns. A portion of her work follows.

1-2-3

	Adjusted Trial Balance	
	Debit	Credit
Cash	$ 29,200	
Accounts receivable	25,800	
Supplies	2,600	
Prepaid insurance	1,400	
Equipment	42,700	
Accumulated depreciation: equipment		$ 10,400
Accounts payable		18,000
Ray Vogel, capital		65,200
Ray Vogel, drawing	3,900	
Service revenue		56,200
Wages expense	32,100	
Advertising expense	2,400	
Rent expense	5,900	
Miscellaneous expense	1,300	
Supplies expense	800	
Insurance expense	1,100	
Depreciation expense	3,300	
Wages payable		2,700
	$152,500	$152,500

Additional information revealed that owner investments in the firm amounted to $7,000 during the year.

Holly was recently called out of town because of a family emergency. You are her assistant and recognize that the various year-end accounting procedures must be performed on a timely basis.

Instructions

a Complete the work sheet that Holly had begun. *Note:* The preceding data should be entered in the adjusted trial balance columns. We have omitted the company's trial balance and adjustments for the sake of simplicity.

b Prepare an income statement, statement of owner's equity, and balance sheet in good form. The balance sheet should parallel the format used in Exhibit 4-2.

c Prepare the firm's closing entries.

P4-B3 *Cycle, starting with work sheet* (L.O. 1, 2, 3)

Occidental Employment Service has the following trial balance as of December 31, 19XX:

VTL

Cash	$ 3,000	
Accounts receivable	6,500	
Prepaid advertising	1,600	
Office supplies	1,200	
Office equipment	17,800	
Accumulated depreciation:		
office equipment		$ 1,400
Accounts payable		2,400
Unearned service revenue		1,800
Loan payable		12,000
Yoko Nishiyama, capital		8,500
Yoko Nishiyama, drawing	10,800	
Service revenue		43,900
Salaries expense	21,100	
Rent expense	4,500	
Utilities expense	1,600	
Interest expense	1,900	
	$70,000	$70,000

Additional accounts maintained by the business include Salaries Payable, Interest Payable, Income Summary, Advertising Expense, Office Supplies Expense, and Depreciation Expense. Occidental's accountant has obtained the following adjustment data:

1 Advertising applicable to future periods: $300.
2 Office supplies used during the period: $800.
3 Depreciation on the equipment: $2,500.
4 Accrued interest on the loan: $1,200.
5 Portion of unearned service revenue that has been earned during the current period: $1,400.
6 Accrued salaries incurred but not yet paid: $1,100.

On May 26, 19XX, Nishiyama invested $5,000 cash in the business. This event is already reflected in the figures reported in the trial balance.

Instructions

a Complete a work sheet in good form for Occidental Employment Service for the year ended December 31.
b Prepare an income statement, statement of owner's equity, and balance sheet in good form. The balance sheet should be similar in format to that shown in Exhibit 4-2.
c Record Occidental's adjusting entries in the journal.
d Record Occidental's closing entries in the journal.
e Prepare a post-closing trial balance.

P4-B4 *Classified balance sheet* (L.O. 4)

VTL

Assume that Case Company has the following balance sheet accounts at the end of 19X1:

Building	$82,000
Accumulated depreciation: office furniture	800
Loan receivable (due May 19X9)	4,200
Cash	5,150
Merchandise inventory	41,570
Loan payable (due 19X8)	74,560*
Office furniture	8,000

Land held for speculation	18,320
Receivable from employee (due 19X5)	3,355
Short-term investments	22,000
J. Case, capital	40,835
Salaries payable	750
Accounts receivable	31,500
Accounts payable	52,100
Accumulated depreciation: building	19,000
Land	37,500
Payable to finance company (due June 19X2)	71,800
Patents	10,000
Prepaid insurance	900
Office supplies	750
Taxes payable	5,400

* Of this amount, $2,000 is payable within the next 12 months.

Instructions

Prepare a classified balance sheet as of December 31, 19X1, similar in format to that shown in Exhibit 4-11.

*P4-B5 *Reversing entries* (L.O. 5)

Air Shuttle, which began business on February 10 of the current year, provides a shuttle service to DFW International Airport in Dallas. The company's total wage expense through the most recent payday, August 26, totals $54,720. Air Shuttle pays its employees every Friday for a five-day work week. Data for the next pay period, August 29–September 2, follow.

Date	Wage Cost Incurred
Monday, Aug. 29	$400
Tuesday, Aug. 30	425
Wednesday, Aug. 31	425
Thursday, Sept. 1	450
Friday, Sept. 2	425

Air Shuttle uses reversing entries.

Instructions

a Compute the company's total wage expense through August 31.
b Present the journal entries needed on August 31 to adjust and close the Wage Expense account.
c Prepare the necessary reversing entry on September 1.
d Prepare the necessary journal entry to disburse Air Shuttle's weekly payroll on September 2.
e Repeat part (d), assuming that Air Shuttle does not use reversing entries.
f Determine Air Shuttle's wage expense for the first two days of September assuming the company:
   (1) Uses reversing entries.
   (2) Does not use reversing entries.

ELECTRONIC DATA BASE

SEC

EDB4-1 *Analysis of balance sheet and accompanying notes: Borden, Inc.* (L.O. 4)

Borden, Inc., is a worldwide producer of foods, nonfood consumer goods, and packaging and industrial products. The company is especially well known in the United States for its pasta, which is sold under the Creamette brand name, and various dairy products.

Instructions

By using the text's Electronic Data Base, access the balance sheet and accompanying notes of Borden and answer the questions that follow. Unless otherwise indicated, responses should be based on data for the most recent year presented.

a What are the five largest accounts presented on the balance sheet? Under what classifications do these accounts appear?

b An analysis of the balance sheet will reveal that the company is organized as a corporation. What section on the balance sheet provides such evidence, and what is the section's total?

c Did the firm's current ratio improve or deteriorate since last year? What effect did this change have on the ability to settle short-term debts on a timely basis?

d Review the summary of significant accounting policies (i.e., the first footnote in the notes that accompany the financial statements).

  (1) What is the basic purpose of this note?

  (2) What method does the company use to depreciate its property and equipment?

e In general terms, what information is presented by the firm's other note disclosures?

f By analyzing the company's quarterly financial data, determine the slowest quarter in terms of (1) revenue generation and (2) profitability.

EDB4-2 *Analysis of balance sheet and accompanying notes* (L.O. 4)

This problem is a duplication of Problem EDB4-1. It is based on a company selected by your instructor.

Instructions

By using the text's Electronic Data Base, access the specified company's balance sheet and accompanying notes and focus on data for the most recent year reported. Answer requirements (a)–(f) of Problem EDB4-1.

BB4-1 *Identification of balance sheet errors* (L.O. 4)

The following balance sheet was prepared by a staff assistant of the Orlando Company:

BEYOND THE BASICS

ORLANDO COMPANY
Balance Sheet
For the Year Ended December 31, 19X1

Assets

Current assets
Accounts receivable	$ 68,500	
Cash	27,000	
Short-term investments (cost, $20,000), at current market value	22,000	
Merchandise inventory	157,500	
Receivable from supplier (due in 19X7)	8,000	$283,000

Property, plant, & equipment
Buildings & land	$164,000	
Equipment	59,200	
	$223,200	
Plus: Accumulated depreciation	45,600	268,800

Other assets
Prepaid insurance	$ 4,100	
Estimated value of top management personnel	350,000	354,100
Total assets		$905,900

Liabilities & Owner's Equity

Current liabilities
Accounts payable	$ 43,600	
Salaries payable	18,900	
Owner withdrawals	28,000	
Patents	27,700	$118,200

Long-term liabilities
Mortgage payable (payable $10,000 per year for 35 years)	$350,000	
Owner investments	53,600	403,600

Owner's equity
Brenda Adams, capital	$200,000*	
Total payments to suppliers	184,100	384,100
Total liabilities & owner's equity		$805,900

* Excludes owner investments and withdrawals during 19X1.

Instructions

Indicate the deficiencies in the preceding financial statement. *Note:* A corrected balance sheet is not required.

BB4-2 *Overview of chapter concepts: Multiple choice* (L.O. 1, 2, 3, 4)

The following multiple-choice questions relate to various topics discussed in the chapter. Select the best answer.

1 The accountant for Milligan Insurance Company prepared a work sheet to assist in the preparation of financial statements. Unfortunately, the work sheet would not balance. Which of the following errors could have created the out-of-balance condition?

a The company failed to record the purchase of a new machine for cash.

b The company failed to record an adjusting entry for accrued salaries.

c The Unearned Agency Revenue account balance was extended from the adjusted trial balance credit column to the income statement credit column.

d The accountant failed to record the net income amount in the credit column of the balance sheet.

2 Which of the following comments about the work sheet is incorrect?

a The owner's capital balance listed on the work sheet has not as yet been updated for the current period's withdrawals and net income.

b The amount of any owner investments that occurred during the current period can be determined by studying the work sheet.

c The owner's drawing account is extended to the balance sheet debit column of the work sheet.

d Net income is recorded as a debit and net loss is entered as a credit to balance the work sheet's income statement column totals.

3 After completion of all closing entries, which of the following accounts would have a zero balance?

a Income Summary.   c Unearned Fee Revenue.

b Busch, Capital.   d Accounts Receivable.

4 The adjusted trial balance of Brookhaven Company revealed that all accounts have normal balances. Which of the following closing entries would definitely be incorrect?

a Jay Marconi, Capital   900
   Jay Marconi, Drawing   900

b Income Summary   2,000
   Jay Marconi, Capital   2,000

c Income Summary   8,000
   Delivery Equipment   8,000

d Jay Marconi, Capital   5,500
   Income Summary   5,500

5 The accounting cycle requires that certain procedures occur in a particular order. Which of the following would definitely harm a company's reporting of net income and financial position?

a A company journalized and posted closing entries without journalizing and posting the adjusting entries.

b A company prepared financial statements directly from the adjusted trial balance and then prepared the work sheet.

c A company prepared a work sheet, and journalized and posted the adjusting and closing entries prior to preparing the formal financial statements.

d After completion of the closing process, a company immediately began to record the next period's transactions in the journal. No post-closing trial balance was prepared.

6 Current assets include cash and those assets intended to be:

a converted into cash within one year or the operating cycle, whichever is longer.

b consumed within one year or the operating cycle, whichever is longer.

c used to settle current liabilities within one year or the operating cycle, whichever is longer.

d converted into cash or consumed within one year or the operating cycle, whichever is longer.

7 Certain procedures are usually followed concerning the presentation of assets on a classified balance sheet. Which of the following is not one of these procedures?
   a Current assets are generally listed in order of liquidity.
   b Long-term investments are listed in the property, plant, and equipment section.
   c Intangible assets appear before "other" assets.
   d Land is listed before buildings and equipment.

8 Ashley Company has a current ratio of 2.5 (i.e., 2.5 : 1). How would the payment of a current liability with cash affect the current ratio and total working capital, respectively?
   a Increase, no change.   c Increase, decrease.
   b Decrease, no change.   d Decrease, decrease.

COMMUNICATION OF ACCOUNTING INFORMATION

CAI4-1 *Writing clear instructions: MCI Communications* (L.O. 4)

Communication Principle: Past experience with "easy-to-assemble" products has probably shown each of us that it is difficult to write clear and concise instructions. To provide good instructions, writers must analyze their audience and determine what the reader knows and does not know. Because this knowledge requires time and, often, trial and error, the writing process may be ongoing. Good instructions are produced by authors who are flexible, ready to answer questions, and patient. The following suggestions will generally be helpful:

1 Begin with a brief overview of the entire process.
2 Review important terms.
3 Arrange steps in a logical order—chronologically or in order of importance.
4 Number the steps.
5 Write in parallel grammatical form. For instance, use short sentences beginning with active verbs (i.e., commands) such as "prepare," "include," "place," or "calculate."
6 Use examples and illustrations.

The steps that follow are editing procedures that should be employed as a writer fine-tunes and works toward the finished product:

1 Check that each activity (step) is roughly equivalent in the amount of effort required.
2 Do not include too many substeps for any one activity. Break long lists of instructions into separate activities.
3 Check that each activity is inclusive, or understandable on a stand-alone basis. Try to avoid directions such as "Refer back to Step 6 and the diagram used with Step 4."
4 Ask an independent party who is unfamiliar with the process being described to follow your instructions. If significant questions arise, some revision is in order.

■ ■ ■ ■ ■ ■ ■ ■

MCI provides a full range of telecommunications services to businesses and residential customers. The company owns and operates the world's second largest communications network, representing a gross investment of more than $8 billion. Selected accounts and balances from a recent set of the firm's financial statements, simplified for purposes of presentation, follow. (*Note:* All amounts are in millions.)

Cash	$ 183
Capital stock	1,167
Long-term debt	3,147
Other assets	1,405
Accounts payable	1,388
Accounts receivable	1,447
Retained earnings	1,173
Other long-term liabilities	340
Communications system	8,708
Miscellaneous current assets	133
Current portion of long-term debt	244
Accumulated depreciation	3,675
Short-term investments	48
Other current liabilities	790

Imagine that MCI has just hired a new computer programmer. The programmer understands the nature of assets, liabilities, and owners' (stockholders') equity, but has no knowledge about how to classify accounts on a balance sheet. You are an accountant for the company and must supervise the new employee while she develops a program to prepare a classified balance sheet.

Instructions

a Prepare written instructions that will allow the programmer to understand the content and positioning of the specific categories on a classified balance sheet.

b To give the programmer some guidance in her work, construct the balance sheet that the program should be capable of producing. The balance sheet should be dated December 31, 19X0.

Answers to Chapter Quiz

1 d

2 d

3 c

4 b

5 b

COMPREHENSIVE PROBLEM 1

Hamilton Company, which began operations on May 1, had the following transactions:

HAMILTON COMPANY

VTL

May 1 Marc Nichols, the owner, invested $9,000 cash, $12,000 of office equipment, and a building valued at $75,000 in the business. The office equipment has a service life of 5 years, and the building has a service life of 25 years.

1 Paid $240 for a four-month insurance policy.

4 Received $660 from a client to render services over the next four weeks.
6 Purchased $350 of office supplies for cash.
11 Paid $400 for various computer runs.
15 Billed clients for services rendered, $6,800.
21 Received $5,200 from clients on account.
24 Borrowed $7,000 from the bank.
25 Received the May electric bill of $100, to be paid on June 4.
26 Purchased $12,000 of new office equipment; paid $7,000 down and agreed to pay the balance in June. This office equipment will not be depreciated until June.
29 Paid wages of the office staff, $4,700.
30 Processed a $2,500 cash withdrawal for the owner.
31 Recorded $1,000 of miscellaneous expenses that were incurred in May but will be paid during June.

Hamilton's chart of accounts follows.

Cash	110	Unearned service revenue	250
Accounts receivable	120	Loan payable	260
Prepaid insurance	130	Marc Nichols, capital	310
Office supplies	135	Marc Nichols, drawing	320
Office equipment	140	Income summary	330
Accumulated depreciation:		Service revenue	410
office equipment	141	Computer service expense	510
Building	150	Wage expense	520
Accumulated depreciation:		Insurance expense	530
building	151	Office supplies expense	540
Accounts payable	210	Depreciation expense	550
Wages payable	220	Utilities expense	560
Interest payable	230	Interest expense	570
Utilities payable	240	Miscellaneous expense	580

Additional information:
1 As of May 31, accrued interest on the loan amounted to $40, while accrued wages totaled $300.
2 Since the last billing to clients on May 15, the firm had rendered $2,480 of services.
3 Hamilton has earned three weeks of revenue from the prepayment on May 4.
4 Office supplies on hand at month-end amounted to $200.
5 Hamilton must pay $1,000 of the bank loan within the next year.

Instructions

a Record the transactions of May in the general journal.
b Post the journal entries to the proper ledger accounts.
c Complete a work sheet for the month ended May 31. Be certain to analyze *all* data presented to correctly determine Hamilton's adjustments.
d Prepare an income statement, a statement of owner's equity, and a classified balance sheet in good form. The balance sheet should be similar in format to that shown in Exhibit 4-11.
e Record Hamilton's adjusting entries in the journal and post to the proper ledger accounts.
f Record Hamilton's closing entries in the journal and post to the proper ledger accounts.
g Prepare a post-closing trial balance.

CHAPTER

5

Accounting/Reporting for Merchandising Operations

LEARNING OBJECTIVES

After studying this chapter, you should be able to:

1

Account for typical transactions of sellers and buyers of merchandise.

2

Compare and contrast the gross and net methods of accounting for purchases.

3

Compute cost of goods sold and gross profit, and prepare the financial statements and work sheet for a merchandising concern.

4

Prepare the adjusting and closing entries for a merchandising enterprise.

5

Distinguish between single- and multiple-step income statements.

The bulk of the material presented in the first four chapters has focused on accounting for service enterprises. These firms are engaged in a wide variety of activities and include such entities as repair shops, advertising agencies, airlines, theaters, and professional sports clubs. Service enterprises charge a fee or commission for their services and are a rapidly growing and significant factor in our economy.

We now turn our attention to a different type of operation: the merchandising business. A merchandising firm acquires goods for resale to others (i.e., **merchandise inventory**) and is exemplified by the retailer and wholesaler. Accounting for retailers and wholesalers is not completely different from accounting for service businesses; thus, most of the material presented earlier is still applicable. The purchase and sale of inventory, however, are accompanied by and create several added complexities for the accountant. These complexities form the basis for this chapter's discussion.

MEASURING MERCHANDISING INCOME

OBJECTIVE

Account for typical transactions of sellers and buyers of merchandise.

The success of a business organization is often judged by the size of its "bottom line," or net income. A merchandising entity will be profitable if the amounts charged to customers (i.e., sales revenue) exceed the cost of merchandise sold and the operating expenses of the business. The income statement that appears in Exhibit 5-1, simplified for purposes of illustration, shows that Mid Cities Auto Parts earned 7¢ on every sales dollar ($7,000 ÷ $100,000). Further, by purchasing goods from suppliers and then selling the goods at a higher price to its customers, Mid Cities was able to generate a $52,000 gross profit.

Given this very brief overview of merchandising profitability, let us focus on the details of sales revenue, cost of goods sold, gross profit, and inventory accounting. In so doing, we will study the operations of Peachtree Jeans, an Atlanta-based wholesaler of pants, shirts, and related accessories.

EXHIBIT 5-1
Simplified Income Statement of a Merchandising Firm

MID CITIES AUTO PARTS Income Statement For the Year Ended December 31, 19XX		
Sales		$100,000
Cost of goods sold		48,000
Gross profit		$ 52,000
Expenses		
Salaries	$30,000	
Rent	12,000	
Utilities	3,000	
Total expenses		45,000
Net income		$ 7,000

Sales Revenue

The revenues of a merchandising concern are generated from its sales of inventory. The timing and measurement of these revenues are of major importance in accounting; incorrect recognition will result in inaccurate reports of financial position and earnings. An entity should enter revenue in the accounting records when ownership of the goods is transferred from the seller to the buyer. Normally, this transfer occurs at the time of sale. The amount of revenue to be recognized is determined by the transaction price, which is usually the amount of cash received or to be received.

To properly account for its revenues, a business will establish an account entitled Sales. If desired, an entity could utilize separate accounts to determine revenues by product line (e.g., Pants Sales, Shirt Sales, and Accessories Sales). Understand that the Sales account is used *strictly* to record revenues that relate to the sale of merchandise (the sale and/or disposal of other assets are recorded elsewhere). As an example, if Peachtree Jeans sold some extra office supplies for cash, Cash would be debited and Office Supplies would be credited. The Sales account is not affected.

A business must properly record both cash and credit sales. Although the exact procedures vary, the following description is representative of the practices of many companies. When a cash sale is made, a sales slip or *invoice* is completed by a clerk, who also inputs the transaction into a data-entry terminal (e.g., a cash register). At the end of the day the terminal is closed out, and the following entry is made (amount is assumed):

Apr. 3   Cash   325
    Sales   325
    Daily cash sales

Credit sales are handled in much the same fashion, with either the sales invoices or terminal providing the basis for the necessary journal entry. The use of the latter device may seem somewhat surprising; however, more and more businesses have on-line computerized record-keeping systems. Data input stations are used to capture both cash and credit sales and, as transactions occur, are capable of updating merchandise inventory records of units on hand.

To illustrate the required accounting for credit sales, assume that Peachtree Jeans sold $700 of merchandise on account to Marty's Outpost on April 7. The following entry would be needed:

Apr. 7   Accounts Receivable   700
    Sales   700
    Sale on account to Marty's Outpost

Sales Returns and Allowances

Sales of merchandise often give rise to returns. Customers frequently change their minds, find that merchandise does not fit well once they get it home, or notice defects. If an exchange of goods is neither possible nor desired, most merchandisers will grant a refund or reduce the customer's account balance. Sometimes, particularly in the case of defects or damaged goods, the seller will grant the buyer an *allowance,* that is, a price reduction as incentive to keep the item.

Once a return or allowance is authorized, the seller documents the trans-

ETHICS ISSUE

A new employee in a baseball card shop accidentally marks a rare card with a $12 (rather than $1,200) selling price. He later sells the card to an avid, 13-year-old collector. The shop's owner, realizing the error, finds the customer and requests the extra $1,188. The 13-year-old responds that "a deal is a deal." Who's to blame, and how would you handle this situation?

action on a form known as a **credit memorandum.** For a sale on account, a copy is given to the customer and a copy is forwarded to the accounts receivable department. The credit memo informs the department to credit, or reduce, a particular customer's balance.

The proper accounting treatment for sales returns and allowances is shown by the following example. Suppose that on April 16, Marty's Outpost returned $180 of shirts that it had purchased on April 7. Peachtree Jeans, the seller, would record the transaction as follows:

Apr. 16	Sales Returns & Allowances	180	
	Accounts Receivable		180
	Merchandise returned by Marty's Outpost		

The net amount of the sale is $520 ($700 − $180). Rather than reduce the Sales account by a debit, a separate account entitled Sales Returns & Allowances is established. The use of a separate account is preferable because it allows management and other readers of financial statements to easily compare the amount of returns and allowances with sales volume. This relationship, particularly if returns and allowances are sizable, provides insight into customer satisfaction (or dissatisfaction) with merchandise. In addition, an abnormally high level of returns may reveal the presence of shipping problems, such as merchandise being damaged or mishandled while en route to customers.[1]

The sales on April 3 and 7 and the return on April 16 would appear on an income statement as follows:

Revenues	
Sales	$1,025
Less: Returns & allowances	180
Net sales	$ 845

In view of this treatment (i.e., a deduction from Sales), Sales Returns & Allowances is commonly referred to as a **contra revenue** account.

Trade Discounts

Sellers frequently offer discounts to purchasers, more so to businesses than to individual consumers. One type of discount is a **trade discount.** To explain, manufacturers and wholesalers spend considerable time and money to publish catalogs of the merchandise they offer for sale. These publications often show the merchandise at a basic catalog price, or **list price.** Purchasers, however, are normally entitled to a reduction in cost and ultimately pay **invoice price,** that is, list price minus an applicable trade discount.

This procedure may seem somewhat strange. Why not just publish the invoice price in the first place? The use of trade discounts offers several distinct benefits. If a change in market conditions dictates price changes, it

---

[1] For Regina Co., the vacuum cleaner manufacturer, an abnormally high level of returns was caused by significant production problems. The firm's Housekeeper product line had a return rate that approximated 30–50% of all units sold—a factor that may have contributed to the company's filing for bankruptcy not too long ago.

is much easier (and cheaper) to quote a different trade discount than to update and reprint an entire catalog. Further, trade discounts can be altered as needed to give customers more incentive to purchase larger quantities (e.g., the larger the quantity purchased, the greater the discount).

Trade discounts are *not* entered in the accounting records; in effect, such amounts are already reflected in the actual selling prices charged by the merchant. To illustrate the proper record keeping, assume that Peachtree stocks a particular style of shirt having a list price of $25. If Peachtree received an order for 600 shirts and granted a 30% trade discount, the purchaser would be charged $10,500, computed as follows:

List price (600 shirts × $25)	$15,000
Less: 30% trade discount	4,500
Invoice price	$10,500

An invoice would be prepared for this amount, and $10,500 would be recorded in the Accounts Receivable and Sales accounts. A separate trade discounts account is not established.

Cash Discounts

When merchandise is sold on account, the seller usually gives the buyer a certain period of time to settle his or her account balance. Often, sales on account are expected to be paid within 30 days of the invoice date. Sellers, however, normally desire to collect the amounts due more rapidly to cover expenses and for purposes of investment. Consequently, to encourage prompt payment, they sometimes offer incentives called **cash discounts.** From the seller's point of view, the cash discount is termed a **sales discount.**

Cash discounts are normally stated on the invoice and expressed in the following format: 2/10, n/30 or perhaps 3/10, n/eom (see Exhibit 5-2). In both examples the first set of numbers indicates the discount rate and the discount period. The second set discloses the invoice due date. The terms of sale are read as follows:

- *2/10, n/30*—A 2% discount from the invoice price is allowed if payment is made within 10 days of the invoice date; otherwise the total invoice price is due within 30 days.
- *3/10, n/eom*—A 3% discount is allowed if payment is made within 10 days of the invoice date; otherwise the total invoice price is due by the end of the month (eom).

Several alternatives are available to account for sales discounts. The most popular approach is to record both Accounts Receivable and Sales at the total (gross) invoice price. The underlying rationale is that at the time of sale, the seller has no idea whether the discount will be taken. Later, if the buyer takes advantage of the offered price reduction, the difference between the cash received and the original amount due is recorded as a discount. In contrast, if the discount is not used, the amount paid by the customer is recorded in the same manner as any other receipt on account.

For instance, assume that Peachtree sold $1,500 of merchandise on ac-

EXHIBIT 5-2
Example of Invoice

INVOICE
Peachtree Jeans
5130 Meridian Parkway
Atlanta, Georgia 30309

Sold to: Expressway Chic   Invoice no.: 6708
         2200 Madison Blvd.   Invoice date: 4/10/X7
         Birmingham, Alabama 36296 Your order no.: B-1403
                                    Sales representative: 32

Ship to: Same
Shipped via: Overnight Freight
Shipping terms: F.O.B. Birmingham   Terms of sale: 2/10, n/30

QUANTITY	DESCRIPTION	UNIT PRICE	AMOUNT
40	Jeans--#1630	25.00	1,000.00
25	Blouse--#5800	20.00	500.00
			1,500.00

---

count to a customer on April 10, terms 2/10, n/30. The sale and subsequent cash receipt are handled as follows:

Apr. 10	Accounts Receivable	1,500	
	Sales		1,500
	Sale on account; terms 2/10, n/30		

Case A: Customer Pays on April 19 and Takes the Discount

Apr. 19	Cash	1,470	
	Sales Discounts	30	
	Accounts Receivable		1,500
	Collection on account; discount taken		

Case B: Customer Pays on April 26 and Forgoes the Discount

Apr. 26	Cash	1,500	
	Accounts Receivable		1,500
	Collection on account; discount missed		

ETHICS ISSUE

You discover that a customer accidentally paid an invoice twice. What action would you take, assuming the invoice was issued by your firm?

Observe that the sale is recorded at the total invoice price of $1,500. If the customer settles the amount due by April 20, a $30 discount ($1,500 × 0.02) can be taken and the customer will pay $1,470 ($1,500 − $30). Although only $1,470 is received, Accounts Receivable is credited for the full $1,500. This procedure reduces Accounts Receivable to zero, thereby indicating the purchaser has no further obligation to Peachtree. The $30 is debited to Sales Discounts, a contra revenue that is disclosed on the income statement as a reduction from the Sales account.

Cost of Goods Sold

Recall from Chapter 3 that accountants use the matching concept when measuring income. To explain, a business incurs various costs and expenses in the process of generating revenue. In an effort to judge profitability, the costs and expenses are matched against (i.e., subtracted from) the revenues that they helped to create (see Exhibit 5-1 as an example).

Keeping this fact in mind, let us now focus on the merchandising enterprise. A merchandising business has many different types of expenditures, perhaps the most significant being the cost of products offered for sale. To achieve a proper match on the income statement, the cost of units sold to customers during the accounting period must be deducted from net sales. This deduction is appropriately termed **cost of goods sold** and is dependent on three underlying items: (1) beginning inventory, (2) net purchases, and (3) ending inventory.

Most entities will begin an accounting period with a certain amount of merchandise held for resale to customers (termed the *beginning inventory*). Subsequently, the stock of inventory on hand is supplemented by purchases from suppliers. Combined, these two amounts represent a "pool" of **goods available for sale.** If an entity is in the very fortunate position of being able to sell all of its merchandise, the goods available for sale would correspond to the firm's cost of goods sold. Most companies, however, have some inventory remaining on hand (i.e., unsold) upon conclusion of the reporting period. Known as the *ending inventory*,[2] this amount must be considered in computing the proper dollar figure to match against net sales on the income statement. The following example shows the manner in which this is done.

Assume that Peachtree Jeans had $67,000 of inventory on hand at the start of the current accounting period. Throughout the year the firm acquired $146,000 of goods, meaning that $213,000 ($67,000 + $146,000) of merchandise was available for resale to customers. On conclusion of activity on December 31, accounting personnel checked existing stock levels in the warehouse and determined an ending inventory of $48,000. As shown in Exhibit 5-3, Peachtree has apparently sold inventory that cost the company $165,000.

The concepts presented in this exhibit have important financial statement implications. More specifically, the ending inventory figure will appear on Peachtree's December 31 balance sheet in the current asset section. Cost of goods sold, on the other hand, is deducted from net sales on the income statement. Both of these financial statements will be illustrated later in the chapter.

Accounting for Merchandise Acquisitions

Our study of cost of goods sold introduced the underlying components of beginning inventory, ending inventory, and net purchases. An in-depth discussion of the first two components is more appropriately deferred until Chapter 9. At this point, however, you should begin to understand the financial measurement and reporting problems related to merchandise acquisitions. Such acquisitions are entered in the records in accordance with the historical-cost principle.

To illustrate the necessary accounting, assume that Peachtree Jeans pur-

---

[2] The ending inventory of one accounting period becomes the beginning inventory of the following period.

EXHIBIT 5-3
Determining Cost of Goods Sold

In pictorial terms:

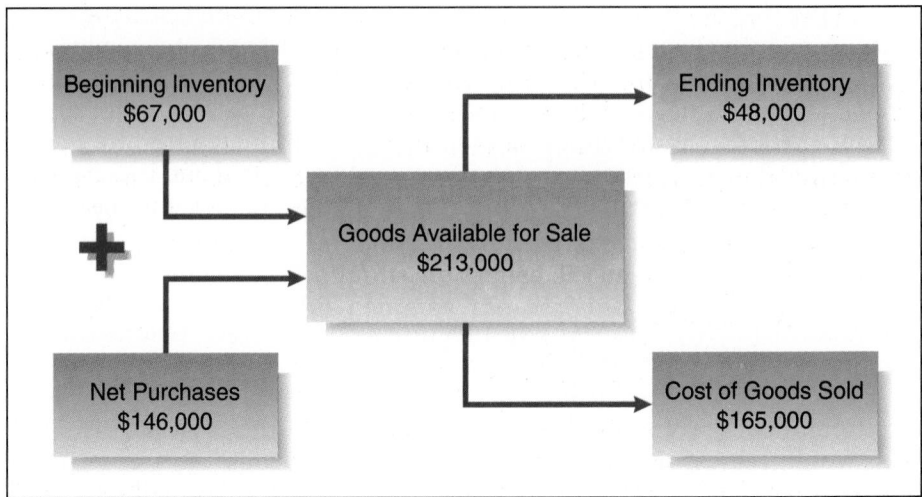

In mathematical terms:

Cost of goods sold
Beginning inventory	$ 67,000
Add: Net purchases	146,000
Goods available for sale	$213,000
Less: Ending inventory	48,000
Cost of goods sold	$165,000

chased $9,000 of merchandise on account on April 16. The entry would be as follows:

Apr. 16	Purchases	9,000	
	Accounts Payable		9,000
	Purchased merchandise on account		

The Purchases account is used to record acquisitions of goods for resale to customers. It normally has a debit balance and appears on the income statement in the cost-of-goods-sold section. The correct manner of disclosure will be shown shortly.

Tips & Techniques

Be aware that Purchases is used *solely* for merchandise. As shown earlier in the text, acquisitions of items that will be used in the business (e.g., equipment and supplies) are recorded in their own respective accounts. The acquisition of supplies, for instance, results in a debit to Supplies and has no impact on the Purchases account.

Purchases Returns and Allowances

As was true for sales, purchase transactions often involve returns and allowances. Returns and allowances are caused by many factors, including the arrival of merchandise (1) in a damaged condition, (2) much later than a requested delivery date, or (3) in error. Before a return or allowance is formally recorded in the accounts, the purchaser prepares documentation of the transaction in the form of either a letter or a **debit memorandum.** The debit memo informs the seller that its account, an account payable, has been debited (reduced) by the purchaser.

Proper accounting for purchases returns and allowances is shown by continuing the previous example. Suppose that $650 of the goods purchased on April 16 arrived past a requested delivery date. On April 30, Peachtree received authorization from the supplier and returned this merchandise. The following entry would be recorded:

Apr. 30	Accounts Payable	650	
	Purchases Returns & Allowances		650
	Returned merchandise to supplier		

The net amount of the purchase is $8,350 ($9,000 − $650). Rather than credit the Purchases account for the reduction, it is preferable to establish a separate account for returns and allowances. This procedure allows management to better examine the percentage relationship between returns and allowances and gross purchases, thus providing some insight into the effectiveness of the purchasing department. A large percentage of returns could be caused by sloppy ordering or by dealings with unreliable suppliers.

The purchase and return would appear on Peachtree's income statement as follows:

Cost of goods sold
.
.
.

Purchases	$9,000
Less: Returns & allowances	650
Net purchases	$8,350
.
.
.

Purchases Discounts

Recall that sellers frequently offer a cash discount for prompt payment of invoices. From the buyer's perspective this discount is commonly known as a **purchases discount.** If at all possible, buyers should take advantage of this potential reduction in the cost of merchandise acquired. Why? The reason becomes apparent in the example that follows.

Suppose that Peachtree acquired $10,000 of merchandise subject to terms of 2/10, n/30. Management has two options:

1 Pay $9,800 [$10,000 − ($10,000 × 0.02)] within 10 days of the invoice date.

2 Pay $10,000 within 30 days of the invoice date.

If Peachtree forgoes the discount and settles the transaction when due, the firm must pay an additional $200. The $200 outlay allows management to have the use of $9,800 for a period of 20 days (30 − 10) and may be construed as interest. For the 20-day period, then, the effective interest rate is 2.04% ($200 ÷ $9,800). Most interest rates are expressed on an annual basis of 360 days, meaning that the supplier's terms are equivalent to

36.72% ($\frac{360}{20} \times 2.04\%$)! In view of the cost, purchasers should take advantage of cash discounts even if it means borrowing money from the bank. Much cheaper financing is generally available via short-term loans.

OBJECTIVE

2

Compare and contrast the gross and net methods of accounting for purchases.

Gross Method.   A popular approach to accounting for purchases discounts corresponds to the previously illustrated method for sales discounts. Under the **gross method,** both purchases and accounts payable are recorded at the total invoice cost of the merchandise acquired. This technique is logically sound, because at the time of purchase the buyer does not always know whether the discount will be taken.

Using the gross method, let us assume Peachtree purchased $4,000 of sportswear on account from Wrangler Corporation on April 14, subject to terms of 2/10, n/30. The purchase and subsequent payment would be recorded as follows:

Apr. 14	Purchases	4,000	
	Accounts Payable		4,000
	Purchase on account; terms 2/10, n/30		

Case A: Peachtree Pays on April 23 and Takes the Discount

Apr. 23	Accounts Payable	4,000	
	Purchases Discounts		80
	Cash		3,920
	Paid on account; discount taken		

Case B: Peachtree Pays on April 27 and Forgoes the Discount

Apr. 27	Accounts Payable	4,000	
	Cash		4,000
	Paid on account; discount missed		

While Case B is straightforward, Case A needs some explanation. By paying the invoice before the 10-day discount period expires, Peachtree is entitled to an $80 discount ($4,000 × 0.02). Although only $3,920 is remitted to Wrangler, Accounts Payable is debited for the entire $4,000 because the balance is paid in full. The Purchases Discounts account is credited for the reduction in cost and is used later in deriving the net cost of merchandise acquired. It is therefore deducted from the Purchases account in the income statement's cost-of-goods-sold section.

In this particular example the discount was calculated on the basis of the $4,000 invoice cost. If any of the merchandise acquired had been returned to Wrangler prior to payment, the discount would have been figured on the net purchase only. Furthermore, discounts are computed on merchandise cost only; they are never calculated on freight charges incurred by the buyer to acquire goods.

Net Method.   Because of the high interest costs associated with missing discounts, many companies follow a policy of taking all discounts offered. In anticipation of securing these reductions in cost, businesses may follow an alternative recording procedure for purchases called the **net method.**

Under this approach, both purchases and accounts payable are recorded at the net cost of the purchase, that is, total invoice cost minus the anticipated cash discount. If the discount is taken, the liability is removed from the books in similar fashion to other payments on account. Any discounts missed, on the other hand, are entered in an account entitled Purchases Discounts Lost.

To illustrate the net method, we will use the same transaction that appeared in the previous discussion—a $4,000 purchase subject to terms of 2/10, n/30. The April 14 acquisition and subsequent payment on account would be recorded as follows:

Apr. 14	Purchases	3,920	
	Accounts Payable		3,920
	Purchase on account; terms 2/10, n/30		

Case A: Peachtree Pays on April 23 and Takes the Discount

Apr. 23	Accounts Payable	3,920	
	Cash		3,920
	Paid on account; discount taken		

Case B: Peachtree Pays on April 27 and Forgoes the Discount

Apr. 27	Accounts Payable	3,920	
	Purchases Discounts Lost	80	
	Cash		4,000
	Paid on account; discount missed		

Under Case A, since the liability is already established at the net figure of $3,920, no additional discount is recorded. With Case B, $4,000 must be paid: $3,920 for the merchandise acquired and an $80 penalty for late payment.

The Purchases Discounts Lost account appears on the income statement as an expense, not as part of cost of goods sold. The presence of a large balance in this account means that a business has missed a considerable number of discounts and often raises questions concerning managerial effectiveness. The discounts may have been lost because of carelessness in paying invoices and allowing discount periods to lapse, or perhaps because of a very tight cash position. Whatever the cause, the firm is incurring extremely high interest costs as a result, and corrective action may be needed.

Freight Charges

The acquisition of merchandise by retailers and wholesalers often gives rise to transportation charges. These charges can be significant, especially when a company deals in bulky or heavy items. Freight costs are borne by either the seller of the goods or the buyer, the exact party being determined by an order's freight terms.

Freight terms are usually expressed as F.O.B. shipping point or F.O.B. destination. **F.O.B.,** or free on board, means the seller will place the merchandise sold on board a freight carrier at no charge. Whether the seller or buyer incurs the transportation costs thereafter is dependent on "shipping point" or "destination." For example, if the terms are **F.O.B. shipping**

point, the seller's responsibility for freight stops when the goods are loaded for shipment. Thus, the buyer incurs all freight charges. In contrast, under **F.O.B. destination,** the seller's responsibility ceases when the goods arrive at their ultimate destination (e.g., the buyer's warehouse). Consequently, the seller is liable for transportation costs. These points are summarized as follows:

Terms of Shipment	Where Seller's Responsibility Ceases	Who Incurs Freight Charges
F.O.B. shipping point	At point of shipment	Buyer
F.O.B. destination	At goods' destination	Seller

The preceding treatment is consistent with the ownership of goods during the in-transit period. With F.O.B. shipping point, for example, title to merchandise legally shifts from the seller to the buyer at the time of shipment. In contrast, under F.O.B. destination, transfer of title occurs at the time of the goods' receipt.

Freight-In and Freight-Out.   As a logical outgrowth of the historical-cost principle, freight charges incurred on the *acquisition* of merchandise are treated as part of the purchase cost. Rather than bury these charges in Purchases, many firms maintain a separate account entitled Freight-in. Used only for transportation on incoming goods, Freight-in is added to the Purchases account on the income statement (see p. 190) to arrive at a net delivered cost of merchandise acquired.

To illustrate accounting for the purchaser under terms of F.O.B. shipping point, assume that Peachtree Jeans purchased $3,000 of footwear on account from Sport Shoe Company on April 22, F.O.B. shipping point. If freight charges amounted to $80, Peachtree would record the following entry:

Apr. 22	Purchases	3,000	
	· Freight-in	80	
	Accounts Payable		3,080
	Purchased merchandise; terms		
	F.O.B. shipping point		

The credit of $3,080 to Accounts Payable shows that Peachtree owes the footwear dealer for the freight. Apparently, as a matter of convenience to the purchaser, Sport Shoe prepaid the transportation costs and expects to be reimbursed. If the costs were not prepaid, Peachtree would disburse $80 to the freight company upon receipt of the goods, requiring a credit to the Cash account.

The preceding treatment applies strictly to freight on incoming merchandise. Transportation charges related to outgoing shipments (i.e., sales) are debited to a different account entitled Freight-out. Generated under terms of F.O.B. destination, such charges bear no connection to an entity's purchases and, hence, are excluded from the cost-of-goods-sold computation. Freight-out is a selling cost and is properly listed among a company's typical business expenses (such as salaries, advertising, utilities, and rent).

Merchandising businesses stock a variety of goods for resale to customers. The cost of these goods is carried in an account called Inventory or Merchandise Inventory. Interestingly, however, when we look back at the methods of recording purchases and sales that were presented earlier in the chapter, we never debited or credited the Inventory account. All merchandise acquisitions were debited to Purchases, and all sales were recorded in the Sales account. Apparently, then, the balance found in the Inventory account at the beginning of the period remains there throughout the year.[3] This type of record-keeping system is known as a **periodic inventory system.** The system is so named because the Inventory account is updated periodically, usually at year-end, to reflect the proper amount of goods owned by the firm.

The periodic system is in contrast to a **perpetual inventory system,** in which the Inventory account is directly increased for each purchase and also decreased for every sale. Many entities employ a perpetual (running) count of the units on hand to closely monitor and better control stock levels. This practice often results in improved customer service and production efficiency, as costly stockouts of merchandise and/or raw materials are avoided (or reduced). Although the perpetual method of accounting for *units* is simple, the maintenance of a running count of *dollar* values in the Inventory account creates several unique record-keeping problems. We will therefore use the periodic system for the remainder of this chapter.

INVENTORY ACCOUNTING

Thus far in the text we have concentrated on three financial statements: the income statement, statement of owner's equity, and the balance sheet. The income statement is prepared first and ties together a number of the concepts discussed in this chapter. It is therefore an appropriate place to begin.

FINANCIAL STATEMENTS OF A MERCHANDISING CONCERN

Income Statement

The income statements of a service business and a merchandising entity differ considerably. While both statements measure net income, the introduction of inventory gives rise to several modifications. See Exhibit 5-4, for example, which contains the income statement of Peachtree Jeans. (*Note:* The account balances that appear in Exhibits 5-4 through 5-7 were obtained from Peachtree's general ledger as of December 31, 19XX.)

Consistent with the matching concept, observe that the costs incurred in producing sales are deducted from the sales revenues generated. These costs are operating expenses and cost of goods sold. **Operating expenses** are expenses that arise from the principal selling and administrative activities of a business and include such items as rent, advertising, wages, utilities, and repairs.

> **OBJECTIVE**
>
> **3**
>
> Compute cost of goods sold and gross profit, and prepare the financial statements and work sheet for a merchandising concern.

---

[3] We will soon illustrate how a balance gets into the Inventory account.

EXHIBIT 5-4
Income Statement of a
Merchandising Firm

PEACHTREE JEANS
Income Statement
For the Year Ended December 31, 19XX

Revenues			
Sales			$307,000
Less: Sales discounts		$ 5,000	
Sales returns & allowances		2,000	7,000
Net sales			$300,000
Cost of goods sold			
Beginning inventory, Jan. 1		$ 67,000	
Add: Purchases	$148,000		
Freight-in	5,000		
	$153,000		
Less: Purchases discounts	$3,000		
Purchases returns &			
allowances	4,000	7,000	
Net purchases		146,000	
Goods available for sale		$213,000	
Less: Ending inventory, Dec. 31		48,000	
Cost of goods sold			165,000
Gross profit			$135,000
Operating expenses			
Rent expense		$ 15,000	
Salaries expense		61,000	
Utilities expense		11,000	
Freight-out		7,000	
Advertising expense		13,000	
Depreciation expense		10,000	
Insurance expense		9,000	
Total operating expenses			126,000
Net income			$ 9,000

Notice that cost of goods sold is subtracted from net sales to arrive at **gross profit** (sometimes called gross margin). Gross profit represents the profit that a company produces from the sale of inventory. A review of the figures in Exhibit 5-4 will show that for every dollar of net sales, Peachtree was able to earn $0.45 ($135,000 ÷ $300,000) from merchandise. This amount was used to cover operating expenses and produce a net income.[4]

---

[4] In more precise terms, the "average" sales dollar was used as follows:

Sales revenue		$1.00
Recovery of merchandise cost		
($165,000 ÷ $300,000)	$0.55	
Selling & administrative expenses		
($126,000 ÷ $300,000)	0.42	0.97
Net income		$0.03

HIGHLIGHT

Gross Profit, or "I Wonder How Much Money They're Making on Me"

Did you ever wonder how much money a store was making on a given sale? A firm's gross profit rate (gross profit ÷ net sales) provides substantial assistance in answering this question. The rate, which varies from company to company and from product to product, is dependent on numerous factors. Included among them are the anticipated level of operating expenses, the price the consumer is willing to pay, the amount of inventory spoilage, the volume of inventory sold, and management's desire to generate additional sales.

To give you an idea of how gross profit rates vary in practice, consider the data in the accompanying figure. The firms depicted have substantial investments in inventory and differ in terms of the business characteristics just cited.

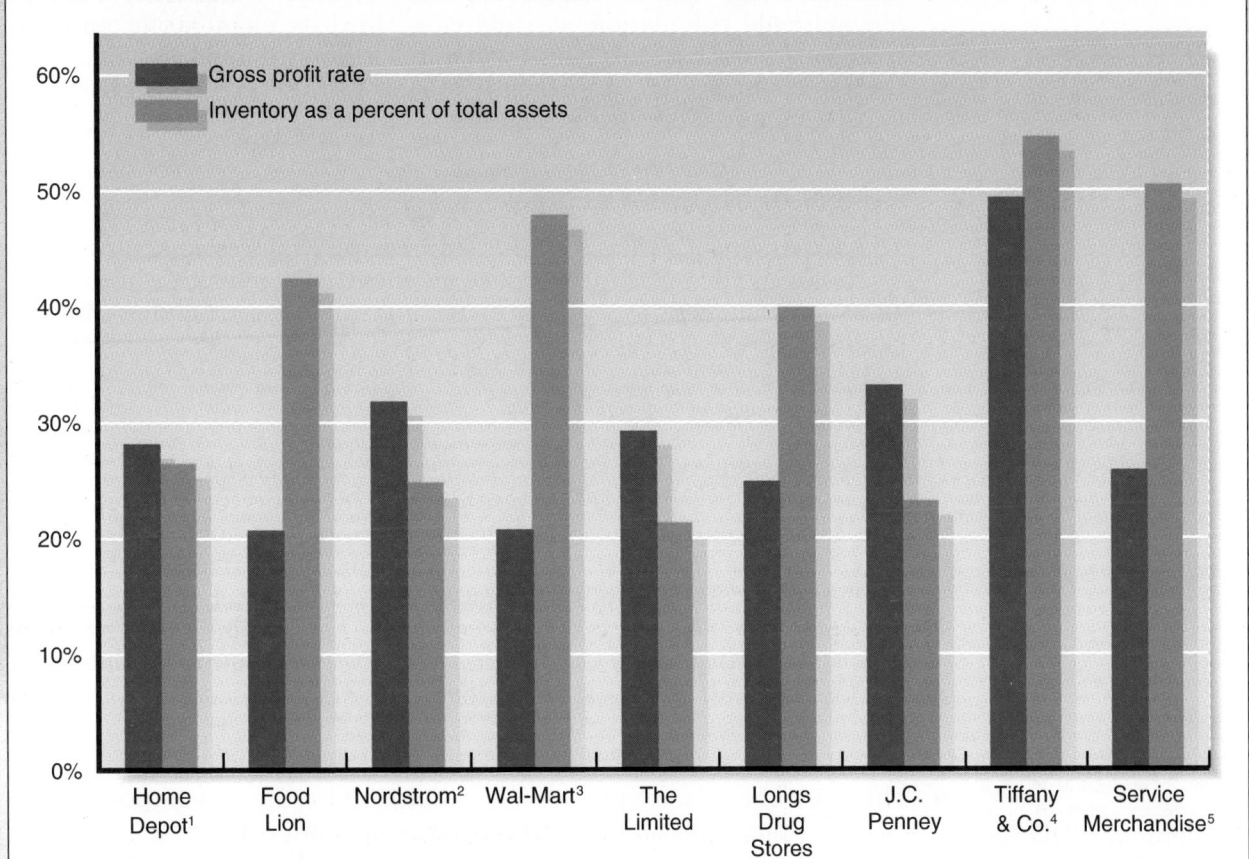

Lines of business: 1—home improvement stores; 2—department stores; 3—discount stores and warehouse clubs; 4—upscale jewelry; 5—catalog showrooms.

Note: Several alternatives are available to arrive at an inventory valuation. These alternatives produce differing results and partially account for the variations in both inventory percentages *and* gross profit rates. Inventory valuation is discussed in detail later in the text.

EXHIBIT 5-5
Statement of Owner's Equity of a Merchandising Firm

PEACHTREE JEANS	
Statement of Owner's Equity	
For the Year Ended December 31, 19XX	
Beginning balance, Jan. 1	$147,200
Add: Net income*	9,000
	$156,200
Deduct: Owner withdrawals	6,000
Ending balance, Dec. 31	$150,200

* From Exhibit 5-4.

Finally, you can now see the income statement's expansion to include the various concepts and accounts that we have been discussing. Observe that net sales is derived by subtracting discounts and returns and allowances from the Sales account. Net purchases, a key component of the cost-of-goods-sold calculation, is subdivided into its elements of purchases, freight-in, purchases discounts, and purchases returns and allowances. Furthermore, freight-out, an expense related to the sale of merchandise, is listed among the operating expenses.

Statement of Owner's Equity

The statement of owner's equity summarizes changes in the capital account during the reporting period. This financial statement is identical for both a service business and a merchandising concern and is shown in Exhibit 5-5.

Balance Sheet

The balance sheets of a service business and a merchandiser are also similar, with the exception of inventory. The inventory of a merchandising firm is an asset and, accordingly, an Inventory account appears in the statement's current asset section. The balance reported in this account represents the amount of merchandise owned upon conclusion of the reporting period ($48,000 in Peachtree's case—see Exhibit 5-3). The company's balance sheet as of December 31, 19XX, is shown in Exhibit 5-6.

GOING BEHIND THE SCENES: THE WORK SHEET

The work sheet is the underlying foundation for the preparation of financial statements. Recall that trial balance data are combined with the entries in the adjustment columns. These "updated" figures are listed in the adjusted trial balance columns and then extended on a line-by-line basis to the appropriate financial statement section (income statement or balance sheet).

It is important to note that with the exception of Inventory (and Capital), all of the accounts listed in the trial balance reflect transactions that oc-

EXHIBIT 5-6
Balance Sheet of
a Merchandising Firm

PEACHTREE JEANS Balance Sheet December 31, 19XX		
Assets		
Current assets		
Cash	$ 25,700	
Accounts receivable	19,600	
Inventory	48,000	
Prepaid insurance	4,800	
Total current assets		$ 98,100
Property, plant, & equipment		
Equipment	$124,800	
Less: Accumulated depreciation	34,800	90,000
Total assets		$188,100
Liabilities & Owner's Equity		
Current liabilities		
Accounts payable	$ 36,400	
Salaries payable	1,500	
Total current liabilities		$ 37,900
Owner's equity		
Valerie Bain, capital*		150,200
Total liabilities & owner's equity		$188,100

* From Exhibit 5-5.

curred during the period. Remember that the Inventory account under a periodic system is not affected by sales and purchases. As a result of this situation, the account's balance represents the goods on hand at the start of the year—$67,000 for Peachtree Jeans.

Two different approaches may be used when handling the beginning inventory (and also the ending inventory) on a work sheet: the closing entry method and the adjusting entry method. Both approaches produce the same outcome in the financial statements and both are widely used by accountants. The closing entry method is illustrated on the next few pages; a discussion of the adjusting entry method appears in an appendix to this chapter. *Be sure to ask your instructor which approach he or she prefers.*

The Closing Entry Method

As we will soon show, the **closing entry method** is so named because the Inventory account is updated in the closing process. Please refer to Peach-tree's work sheet, which appears in Exhibit 5-7. (*Note:* New accounts presented in this chapter are shown in capital letters.) A careful study of the exhibit will reveal that Peachtree has extended the $67,000 beginning in-

		PEACHTREE JEANS								
		Work Sheet								
		For the Year Ended December 31, 19XX								

| | Trial Balance | | Adjustments | | Adjusted Trial Balance | | Income Statement | | Balance Sheet | |
Account Title	Debit	Credit	Debit	Credit	Debit	Credit	Debit	Credit	Debit	Credit
Cash	25,700				25,700				25,700	
Accounts receivable	19,600				19,600				19,600	
INVENTORY	67,000				67,000		67,000	48,000	48,000	
Prepaid insurance	13,800			(b) 9,000	4,800				4,800	
Equipment	124,800				124,800				124,800	
Accumulated depreciation:										
equipment		24,800		(a) 10,000		34,800				34,800
Accounts payable		36,400				36,400				36,400
Valerie Bain, capital		147,200				147,200				147,200
Valerie Bain, drawing	6,000				6,000				6,000	
SALES		307,000				307,000		307,000		
SALES DISCOUNTS	5,000				5,000		5,000			
SALES RETURNS										
& ALLOWANCES	2,000				2,000		2,000			
PURCHASES	148,000				148,000		148,000			
FREIGHT-IN	5,000				5,000		5,000			
PURCHASES DISCOUNTS		3,000				3,000		3,000		
PURCHASES RETURNS										
& ALLOWANCES		4,000				4,000		4,000		
Rent expense	15,000				15,000		15,000			
Salaries expense	59,500		(c) 1,500		61,000		61,000			
Utilities expense	11,000				11,000		11,000			
FREIGHT-OUT	7,000				7,000		7,000			
Advertising expense	13,000				13,000		13,000			
	522,400	522,400								
Depreciation expense			(a) 10,000		10,000		10,000			
Insurance expense			(b) 9,000		9,000		9,000			
Salaries payable				(c) 1,500		1,500				1,500
			20,500	20,500	533,900	533,900	353,000	362,000	228,900	219,900
Net income							9,000			9,000
							362,000	362,000	228,900	228,900

EXHIBIT 5-7
Work Sheet of a
Merchandising Firm:
Closing Entry Method

ventory from the adjusted trial balance to the income statement debit column. This procedure is performed because of the inventory's use in the computation of cost of goods sold. A review of the debit column will show that, in effect, the beginning inventory is being added to net purchases to arrive at goods available for sale.

Next, as indicated by the shaded numbers, the $48,000 ending inventory count is inserted in both the income statement credit column and the balance sheet debit column. The credit allows the goods available for sale figure to be reduced by the ending inventory, to yield cost of goods sold. In contrast, the debit is needed so that Peachtree can report the year-end inventory on its balance sheet, along with the other assets owned by the firm.

Adjusting Entries

The work sheet not only assists in the construction of financial statements, but is also useful in the preparation of adjusting entries. When the beginning and ending inventories are treated in the manner just described, the adjusting entries for a merchandising concern parallel those shown earlier in the text for a service business. In Peachtree's case, for instance, the three adjusting entries for depreciation, prepaid insurance, and accrued salaries would be recorded in the journal and posted to the ledger. Please refer to Chapters 3 and 4 should you need a refresher of the proper procedures.

OBJECTIVE

4

Prepare the adjusting and closing entries for a merchandising enterprise.

Closing Entries

As before, all temporary accounts must be closed at the end of the reporting period. Such accounts would include those listed in the work sheet's income statement section, along with the drawing account. The income statement accounts with debit balances are closed in a combined journal entry by crediting each account and debiting Income Summary. New accounts presented in the chapter's discussion that have debit balances are Sales Discounts, Sales Returns & Allowances, Purchases, Freight-in, and Freight-out. Next, income statement accounts that contain credit balances are debited, with a corresponding credit to Income Summary. New accounts that fall in this category include Sales, Purchases Discounts, and Purchases Returns & Allowances.

Because Inventory is listed in both the income statement debit *and* credit columns, the account is afforded special treatment. Inventory is credited in the first entry for $67,000, a procedure that reduces the balance in the account to zero. It is then debited for $48,000 in the second entry, thereby recording (inserting) the ending balance of goods owned by the firm.

These two closing entries, along with the Inventory and Income Summary accounts, follow. Notice (1) the manner in which the Inventory account has been updated and (2) how the journal entries eventually place the company's $9,000 net income (from Exhibit 5-4) in Income Summary.

Dec. 31	Income Summary	353,000	
	Inventory		67,000
	Sales Discounts		5,000
	Sales Returns & Allowances		2,000
	Purchases		148,000
	Freight-in		5,000
	Rent Expense		15,000
	Salaries Expense		61,000
	Utilities Expense		11,000
	Freight-out		7,000
	Advertising Expense		13,000
	Depreciation Expense		10,000
	Insurance Expense		9,000
	To remove beginning inventory and close income statement accounts having debit balances		

31	Inventory	48,000	
	Sales	307,000	
	Purchases Discounts	3,000	
	Purchases Returns & Allowances	4,000	
	Income Summary		362,000
	To record ending inventory and close income statement accounts having credit balances		

Inventory			
1/1	67,000	12/31	67,000
12/31	48,000		

Income Summary			
12/31	353,000	12/31	362,000
			9,000

To complete the closing process, the Income Summary and drawing accounts are both closed to capital.

Dec. 31	Income Summary	9,000	
	Valerie Bain, Capital		9,000
	To close Income Summary		
31	Valerie Bain, Capital	6,000	
	Valerie Bain, Drawing		6,000
	To close drawing account		

INCOME REPORTING

The preceding sections of this chapter have focused primarily on facets of income measurement as related to a merchandising entity. We now turn our attention to income *reporting*, namely, financial statement presentation of operating results. A review of income statements of large U.S. companies will find considerable variation in both formats and disclosures.

Single- and Multiple-Step Statements

OBJECTIVE

5

Distinguish between single- and multiple-step income statements.

Many business enterprises prepare a **single-step income statement,** which has one section for revenues and another section for costs and expenses.[5] The single-step approach offers the advantage of simplicity, since income (or loss) before tax is determined with one step (i.e., one subtraction). Because many unsophisticated users of financial information may be confused by a detailed presentation of earnings, a large number of companies opt for this type of format. A single-step income statement of American Greetings Corporation, known for greeting cards, gift wrap, party goods, and character personalities (e.g., Ziggy and the Care Bears), appears in Exhibit 5-8.

Many other business enterprises use a **multiple-step income statement,** where accounts are presented by association so that important relation-

---

[5] Corporate entities are subject to federal income taxes, whereas sole proprietorships and partnerships are not. If desired, such amounts may be shown as a separate deduction from income.

EXHIBIT 5-8
Single-Step Income Statement

AMERICAN GREETINGS CORPORATION
Consolidated Statement of Income
For the Year Ended February 29, 1992
(in Thousands)

Net sales		$1,553,961
Other income		19,100
Total revenue		$1,573,061
Costs & expenses		
Material, labor, & other production costs	$645,951	
Selling, distribution, & marketing	556,828	
Administrative & general	186,858	
Interest	30,423	1,420,060
Income before income taxes		$ 153,001
Income taxes		55,539
Net income		$ 97,462

ships can be easily seen by readers. Merchandising firms, for example, deduct cost of goods sold from net sales to arrive at gross profit. In addition, operating expenses, other revenues and expenses, and income taxes are all segregated. Many accountants believe that specific placements and the disclosure of important subtotals (such as gross profit) make the multiple-step format more informative and useful.

The multiple-step income statement of The Waikiki Trading Company, Inc., appears in Exhibit 5-9. Note the grouping of accounts by association and the number of steps involved before net income is shown. We will now highlight several new features that relate to the firm's presentation.

Selling and Administrative Expenses

Observe that operating expenses (i.e., those that relate to normal business activities and operations) are subdivided into selling and administrative components. Selling expenses are associated with the sale of merchandise, whereas administrative costs are incurred in the management of business affairs. Certain individual expenses may need to be split between the two categories because they relate to both functional areas. An example would be depreciation on a building that houses both selling activities and executive offices.

Other Revenues and Expenses

Companies frequently incur expenses (and generate revenues) that are not directly related to normal business operations. For instance, assume that a retail store leased some extra space to a charitable organization for use as an office. The retail store would earn rental revenue and may incur some added expense (such as maintenance) as a result of the lease. On the single-step income statement, the revenue and expense would be presented as part of total revenues and total expenses, respectively. On the multiple-

EXHIBIT 5-9
Multiple-Step Income
Statement

THE WAIKIKI TRADING COMPANY, INC.
Income Statement
For the Year Ended December 31, 19XX

Revenues			
Sales			$510,000
Less: Sales discounts		$ 10,000	
Sales returns & allowances		5,000	15,000
Net sales			$495,000
Cost of goods sold			
Beginning inventory, Jan. 1		$100,000	
Add: Purchases	$120,000		
Freight-in	5,000		
	$125,000		
Less: Purchases discounts	$4,000		
Purchases returns & allowances	1,000	5,000	
Net purchases		120,000	
Goods available for sale		$220,000	
Less: Ending inventory, Dec. 31		50,000	
Cost of goods sold			170,000
Gross profit			$325,000
Operating expenses			
Selling expenses			
Advertising	$ 45,000		
Sales salaries	27,000		
Depreciation expense: building	10,000		
Depreciation expense: store equipment	13,000		
Depreciation expense: delivery vans	14,000		
Miscellaneous	8,000		
Total selling expenses		$117,000	
General & administrative expenses			
Executive salaries	$ 95,000		
Office salaries	43,000		
Insurance	18,500		
Depreciation expense: building	5,000		
Miscellaneous	12,500		
Total gen. & admin. expenses		174,000	
Total operating expenses			291,000
Income from operations			$ 34,000
Other revenues (expenses)			
Interest expense		$ (7,000)	
Gain on sale of truck		3,000	(4,000)
Income before income taxes			$ 30,000
Income taxes			10,000
Net income			$ 20,000

step statement, however, items related to the lease that affect net income would be shown in a separate nonoperating (other) category.

A careful review of Exhibit 5-9 will reveal the disclosure of interest expense in the "other" classification. The rationale for this placement is that interest (be it revenue or expense) is not derived from operating activities, such as selling a product or rendering a service. Instead it arises from a situation of either providing or securing some type of financing and is shown accordingly.

Gains and Losses

Businesses enter into a variety of earnings transactions. Many transactions are routine, such as sales to customers and payments for salaries and supplies; others, however, are not. For instance, a business may only occasionally sell a piece of equipment, a building, or a long-term investment. Market and economic conditions change over time, and management may decide that disposal is the proper course of action to follow.

Transactions that involve the sale of property, plant, and equipment or investments, as well as other events, often give rise to a gain or loss. For example, suppose that a firm purchased a $56,000 parcel of land for use as a future plant site in a companywide expansion program. At some later date the company may sell the land because of a change in plans. If the land is sold for, say, $100,000, there is a gain of $44,000 ($100,000 − $56,000) on the sale.

Gains and losses affect profitability and are therefore disclosed on the income statement. Gains increase net income, and losses cause a reduction. For businesses that use a multiple-step income statement (e.g., The Waikiki Trading Company), such gains and losses are usually placed in the other revenue (expense) category.

Income Tax Expense

Income tax expense is deducted separately from other corporate business expenses when using the multiple-step format. This treatment is justified because the amount of tax is dependent on the calculation of a company's income before tax. In Waikiki's case, for example, the company is subject to a $33\frac{1}{3}\%$ tax rate. Income taxes amounting to $10,000 ($30,000 × $33\frac{1}{3}\%$) are therefore subtracted to yield a final profit figure of $20,000.

As noted in the body of the chapter, an Inventory account maintained under a periodic system is not affected by the period's purchase and sales transactions. With Peachtree Jeans, for example, the $67,000 inventory balance from January 1 continues to be found in the account on December 31. It is therefore necessary that some updating be done to reflect the cost of goods owned by the company at year-end. This process may be performed by a series of two adjustments under the so-called **adjusting entry method.**

**APPENDIX:
THE ADJUSTING ENTRY
METHOD FOR
MERCHANDISE
INVENTORY**

Adjusting Entries for a Merchandising Business

Focus for a moment on Exhibit 5-10, the work sheet for Peachtree Jeans. (*Note:* New accounts presented in this chapter are shown in capital letters.) Three of the company's adjustments, those for depreciation (c), prepaid insurance (d), and accrued salaries (e), should look familiar. They are identical to the types of adjustments that are recorded by service businesses, a subject that was discussed in Chapters 3 and 4. A review of this material is in order should you need a refresher of the logic and procedures that underlie the entries.

Adjustments (a) and (b) are new and unique to the merchandising entity. As noted, the Inventory account must be updated to reflect the goods owned on December 31—$48,000 in Peachtree's case. In addition, because both the beginning and ending inventories are found in the cost-of-goods-sold computation on the income statement, these amounts have a direct bearing on gross profit and earnings. Recall from Chapter 4 that when end-of-period procedures are performed, the Income Summary account will eventually contain a company's net income (or net loss). Thus, in order to achieve the desired results, two adjustments are needed:

Dec. 31	Income Summary	67,000	
	Inventory		67,000
	To remove beginning inventory balance		
31	Inventory	48,000	
	Income Summary		48,000
	To record ending inventory balance		

After posting, the Inventory and Income Summary accounts would appear as shown.

Inventory					Income Summary			
1/1	67,000	12/31	67,000		12/31	67,000	12/31	48,000
12/31	48,000							

Let us complete our discussion of the merchandising company's work sheet by viewing the Inventory and Income Summary lines.

Adjustment data continue to be combined with the trial balance figures to produce the adjusted trial balance. With Inventory, the $67,000 debit in the trial balance is merged with adjustments (b) and (a), a $48,000 debit and a $67,000 credit, to yield a $48,000 debit balance. This amount is extended to Peachtree's balance sheet, as the figure represents the company's ending inventory. Turning to the Income Summary line, notice that both adjusting entry amounts are entered in the adjusted trial balance columns and then extended to the income statement section. This latter procedure is necessary because the figures represent the beginning and ending inventory balances, which, as explained earlier, are needed in cost-of-goods-sold calculations.

PEACHTREE JEANS											
Work Sheet											
For the Year Ended December 31, 19XX											

	Trial Balance		Adjustments		Adjusted Trial Balance		Income Statement		Balance Sheet	
Account Title	Debit	Credit	Debit	Credit	Debit	Credit	Debit	Credit	Debit	Credit
Cash	25,700				25,700				25,700	
Accounts receivable	19,600				19,600				19,600	
INVENTORY	67,000		(b) 48,000	(a) 67,000	48,000				48,000	
Prepaid insurance	13,800			(d) 9,000	4,800				4,800	
Equipment	124,800				124,800				124,800	
Accumulated depreciation: equipment		24,800		(c) 10,000		34,800				34,800
Accounts payable		36,400				36,400				36,400
Valerie Bain, capital		147,200				147,200				147,200
Valerie Bain, drawing	6,000				6,000				6,000	
SALES		307,000				307,000		307,000		
SALES DISCOUNTS	5,000				5,000		5,000			
SALES RETURNS & ALLOWANCES	2,000				2,000		2,000			
PURCHASES	148,000				148,000		148,000			
FREIGHT-IN	5,000				5,000		5,000			
PURCHASES DISCOUNTS		3,000				3,000		3,000		
PURCHASES RETURNS & ALLOWANCES		4,000				4,000		4,000		
Rent expense	15,000				15,000		15,000			
Salaries expense	59,500		(e) 1,500		61,000		61,000			
Utilities expense	11,000				11,000		11,000			
FREIGHT-OUT	7,000				7,000		7,000			
Advertising expense	13,000				13,000		13,000			
	522,400	522,400								
Income summary			(a) 67,000	(b) 48,000	67,000	48,000	67,000	48,000		
Depreciation expense			(c) 10,000		10,000		10,000			
Insurance expense			(d) 9,000		9,000		9,000			
Salaries payable				(e) 1,500		1,500				1,500
			135,500	135,500	581,900	581,900	353,000	362,000	228,900	219,900
Net income							9,000			9,000
							362,000	362,000	228,900	228,900

EXHIBIT 5-10
Work Sheet of a
Merchandising Firm:
Adjusting Entry Method

Closing Entries

Once the adjusting entries are journalized and posted, the accounting records may be closed. Similar to a service business, the merchandising firm closes all temporary accounts (i.e., those listed in the work sheet's income statement columns, and also the drawing account). The income statement accounts with debit balances are closed in a combined journal entry by crediting each account and debiting Income Summary. New accounts presented in the chapter's discussion that have debit balances are Sales Discounts, Sales Returns & Allowances, Purchases, Freight-in, and

Freight-out. Next, income statement accounts that contain credit balances are debited, with a corresponding credit to Income Summary. New accounts that fall in this category include Sales, Purchases Discounts, and Purchases Returns & Allowances. These journal entries and the Income Summary T-account (after posting) follow.

Dec. 31	Income Summary	286,000	
	Sales Discounts		5,000
	Sales Returns & Allowances		2,000
	Purchases		148,000
	Freight-in		5,000
	Rent Expense		15,000
	Salaries Expense		61,000
	Utilities Expense		11,000
	Freight-out		7,000
	Advertising Expense		13,000
	Depreciation Expense		10,000
	Insurance Expense		9,000
	To close income statement accounts having debit balances		
31	Sales	307,000	
	Purchases Discounts	3,000	
	Purchases Returns & Allowances	4,000	
	Income Summary		314,000
	To close income statement accounts having credit balances		

Income Summary			
12/31	67,000	12/31	48,000
12/31	286,000	12/31	314,000
	353,000	**(9,000)**	**362,000**

Observe that the Income Summary account now contains Peachtree's $9,000 net income (from Exhibit 5-4). To complete the closing process, the Income Summary and drawing accounts are both closed to Valerie Bain, Capital, in the following manner:

Dec. 31	Income Summary	9,000	
	Valerie Bain, Capital		9,000
	To close Income Summary		
31	Valerie Bain, Capital	6,000	
	Valerie Bain, Drawing		6,000
	To close drawing account		

END-OF-CHAPTER REVIEW

LEARNING OBJECTIVES: THE KEY POINTS

1 Account for typical transactions of sellers and buyers of merchandise. The chapter presents a variety of merchandising transactions, many of which are summarized in the following chart:

Type of Transaction	Journal Entry	
	Debit	Credit
Sale of merchandise on account	Accounts Receivable	Sales
Return on account of previously sold goods	Sales Returns & Allowances	Accounts Receivable
Receipt on account, minus cash discount	Cash, Sales Discounts	Accounts Receivable
Purchase of merchandise on account	Purchases	Accounts Payable
Return on account of previously acquired goods	Accounts Payable	Purchases Returns & Allowances
Payment on account, minus cash discount (gross method)	Accounts Payable	Cash, Purchases Discounts
Purchase of merchandise on account, F.O.B. shipping point, freight prepaid	Purchases, Freight-in	Accounts Payable

Be sure to remember that the Purchases and Sales accounts are used solely for merchandise transactions and not for acquisitions or disposals of other assets.

2 Compare and contrast the gross and net methods of accounting for purchases. Under the gross method, the Purchases and Accounts Payable accounts are established at the gross invoice price of merchandise acquired. Any discounts taken are credited to Purchases Discounts. With the net method, transactions are recorded at the invoice price minus any discounts that could be taken. If a discount is missed, it is charged to the Purchases Discounts Lost account.

3 Compute cost of goods sold and gross profit, and prepare the financial statements and work sheet for a merchandising concern. Cost of goods sold is calculated as follows: beginning inventory + net purchases − ending inventory. The net purchases figure is derived by adding freight-in to gross purchases and then subtracting any purchases discounts and purchases returns and allowances that occurred during the period. Gross profit, or profit from the sale of merchandise, is computed as net sales minus cost of goods sold.

The preceding items all appear on the income statement, with the ending inventory also being disclosed in the current asset section of the balance sheet. The work sheet that underlies these statements is constructed in the normal fashion, with the only new procedure involving the beginning and ending inventory figures. The procedure depends on whether a company uses the closing entry method of handling inventories or the adjusting entry method (appendix).

4 Prepare the adjusting and closing entries for a merchandising enterprise. The adjusting and closing processes update selected accounts and reduce the balance in temporary accounts to zero. With regard to inventory, the Inventory account is updated through the closing process under the closing entry method to reflect the ending balance of goods owned by the firm. This same procedure is performed with adjusting entries under the adjusting entry method. The Inventory and Income Summary accounts are used with both approaches.

5 Distinguish between single- and multiple-step income statements. The single-step income statement normally discloses all revenues in one section and all expenses (except income taxes) in another. This arrangement is said to be very easy to understand. In contrast, the multiple-step statement contains various classifications such as operating expenses and other revenues and expenses, as well as significant subtotals (e.g., gross profit). The multiple-step's format is often more informative because of added captions and disclosures.

KEY TERMS AND CONCEPTS: A QUICK OVERVIEW

adjusting entry method of handling inventory   An end-of-period procedure by which the Inventory account is updated through a series of adjusting entries.

cash discount   A discount offered to credit customers to encourage prompt payment of invoices.

closing entry method of handling inventory   An end-of-period procedure by which the Inventory account is updated through the closing process.

contra revenue   An account that is deducted from revenues and used in the computation of net revenues on the income statement.

cost of goods sold   The total cost of inventory that a company has sold during an accounting period.

credit memorandum   A document prepared by the seller for an allowance or an authorized return of merchandise.

debit memorandum   A document prepared by the purchaser for either an allowance or an authorized return of merchandise.

F.O.B. destination   Freight terms indicating that transportation charges are borne by the seller.

F.O.B. shipping point   Freight terms indicating that transportation charges are borne by the purchaser.

goods available for sale   The beginning balance of inventory plus net purchases.

gross method of recording purchases   A method of accounting for merchandise in which both Purchases and Accounts Payable are recorded at the total invoice cost of the merchandise acquired.

gross profit   Net sales minus cost of goods sold.

invoice price   List price minus applicable trade discounts.

list price   The basic catalog price for merchandise.

merchandise inventory   Goods held by a merchandising business for resale to others.

multiple-step income statement   A type of income statement in which accounts are presented by association, thereby revealing important relationships to readers.

net method of recording purchases   A method of accounting for merchandise in which both Purchases and Accounts Payable are recorded at the net cost of the purchase—that is, total invoice cost minus the anticipated cash discount.

operating expenses   Expenses that relate to the principal selling and administrative activities of a business.

periodic inventory system   A system of accounting in which purchases and sales of inventory are not recorded in the Inventory account.

perpetual inventory system   A system of accounting for inventory in which the Inventory account is respectively increased and decreased for each purchase and sale of inventory made during the period.

purchases discount A discount secured by the purchaser of merchandise for prompt payment of invoices.

sales discount A cash discount from the seller's point of view.

single-step income statement A type of income statement that has one section for revenues and another section for costs and expenses.

trade discount A discount frequently offered to customers—specifically, a reduction from the list price of merchandise.

CHAPTER QUIZ

The five questions that follow relate to several issues raised in the chapter. Test your knowledge of the issues by selecting the best answer. (The answers appear on p. 223.)

1 Which of the following statements is incorrect?
 a Sales Discounts is commonly known as a contra revenue account.
 b Net sales minus cost of goods sold equals gross profit.
 c The balance in an Inventory account that is maintained under a periodic inventory system remains constant throughout the year.
 d A trade discount is a specialized type of cash discount.

2 Which of the following accounts would not be used if a company employed the net method of recording purchases?
 a Purchases.   c Purchases Discounts Lost.
 b Purchases Discounts.   d Purchases Returns.

3 Harris Company reported the following information for the period just ended: net sales, $5,000; net purchases, $2,900; beginning inventory, $1,700; and ending inventory, $2,000. The company's cost of goods sold is:
 a $1,800.   c $2,600.
 b $2,400.   d $3,200.

4 Hospital Supply purchased $8,000 of merchandise on July 9 from Rosen Manufacturing, F.O.B. shipping point, terms 2/10, n/30. Freight charges of $200 were paid by Rosen and appear on the invoice. If Hospital Supply settled the transaction on July 17, the company would pay:
 a $7,840.   c $8,040.
 b $8,036.   d $8,200.

5 Which of the following accounts would most likely appear in the operating expense section of a multiple-step income statement?
 a Freight-out.   c Sales Discounts.
 b Freight-in.   d Interest Expense.

SUMMARY PROBLEM

The Breakfast Bar reported the following information for the period just ended:

Freight-in	$ 8,800
Purchases	349,000
Purchases discounts	6,600
Purchases returns & allowances	3,800
Sales	573,600
Sales discounts	4,000
Sales returns & allowances	11,400

An examination of the firm's Inventory account, which is maintained under a periodic system, revealed a beginning balance on January 1 of $77,200. A hand count revealed that the company owned $95,800 of inventory on December 31.

Instructions

a Compute the company's (1) net sales, (2) cost of goods sold, and (3) gross profit.
b Determine the normal balance (debit or credit) of the following accounts: Sales, Purchases Discounts, Freight-in, and Sales Returns & Allowances.
c When The Breakfast Bar makes a charge to the Freight-in account, would the transaction being recorded involve a purchase with terms of F.O.B. shipping point or F.O.B. destination? Why?

Solution

a (1) Sales $573,600
    Less: Sales discounts $ 4,000
        Sales returns & allowances   11,400   15,400
    Net sales $558,200

  (2) Beginning inventory, Jan. 1 $ 77,200
    Add: Purchases $349,000
        Freight-in   8,800
                         $357,800
    Less: Purchases discounts $6,600
        Purchases returns & allowances   3,800   10,400
    Net purchases   347,400
    Goods available for sale $424,600
    Less: Ending inventory, Dec. 31   95,800
    Cost of goods sold $328,800

  (3) Net sales $558,200
    Cost of goods sold   328,800
    Gross profit $229,400

b Credit, credit, debit, debit
c F.O.B. shipping point. The Freight-in account is used for transportation charges incurred by the buyer of merchandise, which occurs under terms of F.O.B. shipping point. With F.O.B. destination the seller incurs the charges, requiring a debit to Freight-out on the seller's accounting records.

ASSIGNMENT MATERIAL

QUESTIONS

Q5-1 J. Harrison, Inc., a furniture retailer, recently sold an old delivery truck for $7,500. Should the company's bookkeeper credit the Sales account to record this transaction? Why?

Q5-2 Explain the function and use of a credit memorandum.

Q5-3 Rather than publish catalogs that contain invoice prices, many companies follow the practice of printing list prices and then granting a trade discount to purchasers. What advantages are associated with this procedure?

Q5-4 Distinguish between a trade discount and a cash discount.

Q5-5 Explain why a purchaser should normally take advantage of cash discounts even if it means obtaining a bank loan to do so.

Q5-6 Contrast the gross and net methods of recording purchases. What is an important advantage associated with the latter approach?

Q5-7 The Gomez Company sells an item that has a list price of $1,000. Management is contemplating whether to ship the item F.O.B. shipping point or F.O.B. destination. Compare the trade discounts that would probably be quoted under the two alternatives. Which trade discount would probably be smaller? Why?

Q5-8 A student once commented: "The Freight-in account is very similar to the Purchases Returns account. Both appear in the cost-of-goods-sold section of the income statement as a reduction to determine net purchases." Evaluate the student's comment.

Q5-9 Is the Freight-out account treated differently than the Freight-in account on an income statement? Briefly explain.

Q5-10 What is the basic difference between a periodic and a perpetual inventory system?

Q5-11 Explain the difference between gross profit and net income.

Q5-12 The Ames Company sells its products at approximately 35% above cost; yet, at the end of the current year, a net loss of $15,000 was incurred. Explain how this situation is possible.

Q5-13 Systems, Inc., recently disclosed interest charges in the operating expense section of its multiple-step income statement. Do you agree or disagree with the company's reporting treatment? Why?

Q5-14 Where are gains and losses normally reported on a multiple-step income statement?

EXERCISES

E5-1 *Accounting for sales on account* (L.O. 1)
Enchanted Stones, a mail order supplier of fine gems, publishes a catalog showing list prices for its merchandise. Regular customers are entitled to trade discounts from list price; all customers are offered a 2% cash discount for payment within 10 days. Two of the company's transactions follow.

- On January 2, Helen Stephens purchased an emerald necklace having a list price of $8,500. This particular customer was not entitled to a trade discount. Stephens paid her account in full on January 8.
- On January 10, Alex Hudson purchased a package of loose diamonds on account. The list price was $12,000, subject to a 20% trade discount. Sixty percent of the diamonds were returned on January 14 because of poor color and clarity. Hudson paid his balance due on January 23.

a Prepare Enchanted's journal entries to record the preceding transactions. Assume that the customers have correctly followed the firm's cash discount policy.

b Compute the net sales from these transactions.

E5-2 *Gross and net methods of accounting for purchases* (L.O. 2)
Minnesota Flooring purchased $14,000 of merchandise on account on July 18, terms 3/10, n/30.

a Assuming that Minnesota uses the gross method of accounting for purchases, present entries to record the following:

(1) The purchase on July 18.

(2) Payment of the invoice if payment was made on July 24.

(3) Payment of the invoice if payment was made on August 15.

b Repeat instruction (a), assuming that Minnesota uses the net method of accounting for purchases.

E5-3 *Gross and net methods of accounting for purchases: An analysis* (L.O. 2)

The Software Shoppe purchased $265,000 of merchandise during the year subject to terms of 2/10, n/30. Returns to suppliers amounted to $12,000; all returns took place prior to any payments on account. An analysis of the company's records revealed a balance in the Purchases Discounts account of $1,050 at year-end. The Software Shoppe uses the gross method of accounting for purchases.

a Determine the balance in the Purchases Discounts Lost account had The Software Shoppe used the net method of accounting for purchases rather than the gross method.

b What are some possible causes of lost discounts?

c Given the company's situation, would use of the net method have been more beneficial? Briefly explain.

E5-4 *Purchases discount computations* (L.O. 1)

Bullen Plumbing Contractors made the following purchases of merchandise from suppliers A, B, C, and D during a recent month:

	A	B	C	D
F.O.B. terms	Destination	Shipping point	Shipping point	Destination
Discount offered	2/10, n/30	3/10, n/eom	2/10, n/eom	3/10, n/eom
Original purchase	$3,000	$2,500	$1,000	$1,800
Freight charges	700	400	200	350
Purchases returns	—	600	—	100

All purchases returns were made immediately upon receipt of the goods. Freight charges were initially paid by the sellers and, when appropriate, were billed to Bullen.

Determine the amount of cash that Bullen paid to each supplier if the company settled all transactions within the discount period.

E5-5 *Journal entries for buyer and seller of merchandise* (L.O. 1)

On August 6, Colbert Publishing purchased $64,000 of merchandise from Robinson Wholesale, terms 2/10, n/30, F.O.B. destination. Robinson paid freight charges of $1,800 to Roadway Express one day later. Because of a flaw in several items, Colbert returned $4,000 of merchandise on August 9. The transaction was settled on August 15.

Assuming Colbert uses the gross method of accounting for purchases, prepare journal entries to record the preceding transactions for both companies.

E5-6 *Merchandising concepts* (L.O. 1)

Evaluate the comments that follow as being True or False. If the comment is false, briefly explain why.

a Soft Rock Cafe acquired $42,000 of restaurant equipment on account for use in the business. The company should debit Purchases and credit Accounts Payable to correctly record the transaction.

b The balance in the Freight-out account should be added to the balance in Purchases to arrive at the net delivered cost of merchandise acquired.

c Cash discounts should be computed on merchandise cost only, excluding any applicable freight charges incurred on the transaction.

d The balance in an Inventory account that is maintained under a periodic system tends to fluctuate during an accounting period from an entity's purchase and sale transactions.

e Cash discounts and trade discounts are a convenient means of reducing a catalog price to invoice price.

E5-7 Basic merchandising computations (L.O. 3)

A review of the records of Riverside Mills found the following information:

Ending inventory	$ 55,000	Freight-out	$ 6,000
Sales discounts	3,200	Beginning inventory	48,000
Purchases	326,000	Utilities expense	7,800
Salaries expense	37,500	Sales	453,200
Purchases returns	4,600	Rent expense	19,000
Freight-in	2,900	Miscellaneous expense	5,400

Compute cost of goods sold, gross profit, and net income for Riverside Mills.

E5-8 Merchandising computations: Working backward (L.O. 3)

The following information was obtained from the records of Companies A, B, and C:

	A	B	C
Sales	$90,300	$51,200	$ (g)
Sales discounts	(a)	3,700	2,000
Net sales	88,400	(d)	60,700
Beginning inventory	70,000	39,500	(h)
Net purchases	99,800	(e)	15,600
Ending inventory	(b)	30,000	10,000
Cost of goods sold	62,000	33,200	(i)
Gross profit	26,400	(f)	36,800
Total expenses	(c)	11,200	41,800
Net income (loss)	9,100	3,100	(j)

Compute the amounts that are indicated by the letters (a)–(j).

E5-9 Updating the Inventory account; closing entries (closing entry method) (L.O. 4)

The following selected balances were extracted from the accounting records of Design Fantastic:

	Debit	Credit
Karen Jackson, capital		$87,500
Karen Jackson, drawing	$18,000	
Sales		99,300
Sales discounts	2,100	
Purchases	55,400	
Purchases returns		3,000
Wage expense	22,900	
Marketing expense	5,600	
Rent expense	12,000	
Utilities expense	3,700	

The company's Inventory account contains a balance of $21,800, reflecting the cost of the beginning inventory. Goods costing $27,400 remain on hand at the end of the period, December 31, 19XX.

Using the closing entry method, prepare the journal entries that are needed to update the Inventory account and close the accounting records for the year just ended.

E5-10 *Income statement computations* (L.O. 3, 5)

Selected account balances from Marshall Company for the current year include the following:

Sales	$372,000	Sales discounts	$ 1,000
Purchases	206,000	Beginning inventory	98,700
Advertising expense	11,500	Salesmen's salaries	12,600
Administrative salaries	26,300	Insurance expense	4,000
Ending inventory	94,400	Depreciation expense	15,000
Sales returns	2,800		

Forty percent of the insurance and depreciation expense relates to Marshall's sales activities. Calculate the following:
a Net revenues
b Cost of goods sold
c Gross profit
d Total selling expenses
e Total general and administrative expenses
f Net income (loss)

*E5-11 *Updating the Inventory account; closing entries (adjusting entry method)* (L.O. 5)

Refer to Exercise 5-9. Replace the last paragraph with the following and solve the exercise:

Using the adjusting entry method, prepare adjustments to update the Inventory account. Then, close the accounting records for the year just ended.

PROBLEMS

Series A

P5-A1 *Merchandising journal entries* (L.O. 1)

The Patrick Company had the following transactions during April:

Apr. 1 Sold $4,000 of merchandise on account to Campbell Company, terms 2/10, n/30.
      3 Purchased $2,500 of merchandise on account from West Enterprises, terms 3/10, n/30. The merchandise was shipped F.O.B. shipping point; freight charges amounted to $80 and were paid by West.
      7 Issued a credit memorandum for $200 to the Campbell Company for defective merchandise sold on April 1.

---

* An asterisk preceding an item indicates that the material is covered in an appendix to this chapter.

8   Received the proper amount due from Campbell Company.
10 Purchased a computer on account for business use from Bell Resources for $11,400, terms n/eom.
12 Paid the proper amount due to West Enterprises.
18 Received a purchase order from Gibbons Distributing for merchandise having a list price of $6,000. The order was subject to a 40% trade discount and terms of 1/10, n/30. Patrick shipped the merchandise F.O.B. destination and paid $40 of freight charges.
29 Received the proper amount due from Gibbons Distributing.
30 Paid the amount due to Bell Resources.

Instructions

Prepare journal entries for the April transactions, assuming Patrick uses the gross method of accounting for purchases. All terms of sale are strictly followed.

P5-A2 *Gross versus net purchases method* (L.O. 2)

Beth Dotterer runs an athletic footwear store. The store had the following purchasing activity during August:

Date	Supplier	Purchases or (Returns)	Discounts Offered
Aug. 8	Reebok	$6,200	2/10, n/30
11	Reebok	(400)	
13	NIKE	5,500	1/10, n/30

Additional information:

1 The goods returned on August 11 were part of the purchase on August 8.
2 The goods acquired from NIKE were shipped F.O.B. shipping point. Freight charges of $100 were prepaid by NIKE and appear on the invoice.
3 Beth paid Reebok on August 20 and NIKE on August 22.

Instructions

a Record the five transactions, assuming that Beth uses the gross method of accounting for purchases. All terms of sale are strictly followed.
b Record the five transactions, assuming that Beth uses the net method of accounting for purchases. All terms of sale are strictly followed.
c If you were Beth (the owner/manager), which of the two methods would you find most helpful in analyzing purchasing procedures? Briefly explain.

P5-A3 *Work sheet, adjusting entries, closing entries (closing entry method)* (L.O. 3, 4)

Jackson Simmons was in the process of completing the work sheet of Simmons Shoes for the year ended February 28, 19X3, when he was suddenly called out of town. His work follows.

	Trial Balance		Adjustments	
Account Title	Debit	Credit	Debit	Credit
Cash	15,100			
Accounts receivable	47,200			
Inventory	56,300			
Prepaid advertising	1,500			(a) 1,200
Equipment	27,600			
Accumulated depreciation:				
equipment		5,900		
Accounts payable		17,300		
Loan payable		25,000		
Jackson Simmons, capital		19,400		
Jackson Simmons, drawing	10,000			
Sales		360,400		
Sales discounts	1,900			
Purchases	185,800			
Freight-in	3,100			
Purchases returns		4,200		
Insurance expense	9,800			
Salary & wage expense	56,000			
Rent expense	15,700			
Interest expense	2,200		(b) 1,000	
	432,200	432,200		
Advertising expense			(a) 1,200	
Interest payable				(b) 1,000

A piece of paper labeled "Work Sheet Data" was found on Jackson's desk and contained the following:

1 Advertising applicable to future periods, $300.
2 Interest incurred but not yet paid, $1,000.
3 Unbilled customer sales, $800.
4 Salaries and wages incurred but not yet paid, $2,100.
5 Depreciation on the equipment, $2,600.
6 Ending inventory, $43,000.

Instructions

a Complete the work sheet that Jackson had started. Simmons Shoes uses the closing entry method for handling end-of-period inventory.
b On the basis of the work sheet that you have prepared, journalize the company's (1) year-end adjusting entries and (2) year-end closing entries.

P5-A4 *Work sheet, financial statements, and closing entries (closing entry method)* (L.O. 3, 4, 5)

Phoenix Appliance has the following trial balance as of December 31:

VTL

Cash	$ 37,200	
Accounts receivable	49,300	
Merchandise inventory	41,800	
Prepaid rent	6,400	
Store supplies	3,950	
Equipment	38,500	
Accumulated depreciation: equipment		$ 11,100
Accounts payable		16,820
Mark McGarry, capital		119,850
Mark McGarry, drawing	7,500	
Sales		227,880
Sales returns	1,570	
Sales discounts	4,360	
Purchases	91,720	
Freight-in	1,970	
Purchases returns		970
Purchases discounts		1,750
Salaries expense	51,800	
Marketing expense	11,820	
Insurance expense	10,800	
Utilities expense	3,180	
Delivery expense	16,500	
	$378,370	$378,370

Additional accounts maintained by the business include Salaries Payable, Income Summary, Rent Expense, Store Supplies Expense, and Depreciation Expense. Phoenix's accountant has derived the following data:
1 Rental prepayments expiring during the current period: $4,000.
2 Store supplies used during the period: $1,800.
3 Depreciation on the equipment: $3,700.
4 Accrued salaries: $1,900.
5 Ending inventory: $31,500.

McGarry's capital account includes $15,000 of owner investments made during the year.

Instructions

a Complete a work sheet in good form for Phoenix Appliance for the year ended December 31. The company uses the closing entry method of accounting for inventory.
b Prepare a multiple-step income statement, statement of owner's equity, and a classified balance sheet in good form. The firm's selling activities account for 70% of the salaries cost and 40% of the insurance, utilities, rent, and depreciation expense.
c Record Phoenix's adjusting entries in the journal.
d Record Phoenix's closing entries in the journal.

P5-A5 *Income statement classification* **(L.O. 5)**
Home Entertainment distributes and sells videotapes to local retailers. The categories below were extracted from the company's multiple-step income statement.
1 Revenue
2 Cost of goods sold
3 Selling expenses
4 General & administrative expenses
5 Other revenue (expense)
6 Income taxes

The following accounts appear in the general ledger:

a Marketing expense
b Sales discounts
c Warehouse equipment
d Accounting fees
e Delivery expense
f Rental revenue (from a business
   that leases extra space in the parking lot)
g Office manager's salary
h Purchases returns
i Inventory (beginning)
j Loss from traffic accident

k Interest expense
l Prepaid advertising
m Travel expense (to visit
   local retailers)
n Transportation-in
o Ray Franklin, drawing
p Interest earned on
   short-term
   investments
q Sales
r Purchases
s Commissions paid

Instructions

Classify Home Entertainment's accounts as to their proper placement on the income statement. If any of the accounts do not appear on the income statement, determine whether they appear on the balance sheet or the statement of owner's equity.

P5-A6 *Income statement preparation* (L.O. 5)

1-2-3

Presented below is financial information of the Juarez Corporation for 19XX.

Sales	$587,400
Freight-in	10,800
Loan interest expense	5,950
Interest revenue	3,800
Sales returns	4,200
Purchases returns	7,310
Gain on sale of land	18,900
Merchandise inventory (ending)	54,700
Merchandise inventory (beginning)	58,200
Loss on sale of building	24,300
Purchases	226,900
Sales discounts	9,400
Administrative expenses	
Executive salaries	61,800
Depreciation expense: buildings	23,600
Insurance expense	6,300
Miscellaneous expense	3,100
Selling expenses	
Delivery expense	17,900
Sales commissions	31,500
Advertising expense	7,250
Depreciation expense: delivery equipment	10,400
Insurance expense	3,090

The corporation is subject to a 40% income tax rate.

Instructions

a Prepare a multiple-step income statement for the year ended November 30, 19XX.
b Explain what you would have done differently if instruction (a) had called for the preparation of a single-step income statement. What benefits does the multiple-step approach offer financial statement users?

*P5-A7 **Work sheet, adjusting entries, closing entries (adjusting entry method) (L.O. 3, 4)**
Refer to Problem 5-A3.

Instructions

Follow the instructions on page 212. Assume, however, that Simmons Shoes uses the adjusting entry method for handling end-of-period inventory rather than the closing entry method.

*P5-A8 **Work sheet, financial statements, and closing entries (adjusting entry method) (L.O. 3, 4, 5)**
Refer to Problem 5-A4.

Instructions

Follow the instructions on page 213. Assume, however, that Phoenix Appliance uses the adjusting entry method of accounting for inventory rather than the closing entry method.

Series B

P5-B1 **Merchandising journal entries (L.O. 1)**

The transactions that follow occurred between Poteet Menswear and Catalina Manufacturing.

Nov. 1 Poteet purchased $5,000 of merchandise from Catalina, terms 3/10, n/30.

5 Catalina issued a $500 credit memorandum to Poteet for the return of defective goods sold on November 1.

10 Poteet paid the proper amount owed for the merchandise.

15 Catalina sold Poteet a surplus laser printer and fax machine at cost for $1,600. Terms were n/eom.

21 Poteet purchased $20,000 of Catalina's spring goods. The transaction is subject to a 40% trade discount and terms of 1/10, n/30, F.O.B. destination. Catalina paid $150 of shipping charges to Hunt Truck Lines.

Instructions

a Prepare the necessary journal entries for Poteet Menswear, assuming the company uses the gross method of accounting for purchases.
b Prepare the necessary journal entries for Catalina Manufacturing.
c Suppose that the purchase on November 1 also had $60 of freight charges, which were paid by Catalina, and terms of F.O.B. shipping point.
(1) Prepare the necessary journal entry for Poteet on November 1.
(2) Calculate the amount that Poteet would have paid on November 10 to settle the transaction.

P5-B2 **Gross versus net purchases method (L.O. 2)**
Beautiful Face operates several small cosmetics stores in shopping malls. During July, store no. 108 had the following purchases transactions:

July 7 Purchased $950 of cosmetics on account from Lovely Lady, terms 2/10, n/30. The goods were shipped F.O.B. shipping point; freight charges of $25 were prepaid by Lovely Lady and appear on the invoice.

12 Purchased $125 of store supplies on account from Atlas Office Supplies.

17   Purchased $1,400 of cosmetics on account from the Charles Norman Company, terms 1/10, n/30.
20   Paid the proper amount due to Lovely Lady.
21   Returned $200 of the cosmetics purchased on July 17 because of a shipping error made by the Charles Norman Company.
26   Paid the proper amount due to the Charles Norman Company.

Instructions

a Record the preceding transactions, assuming Beautiful Face uses the gross method of accounting for purchases. All terms of sale are strictly followed.

b Record the preceding transactions, assuming Beautiful Face uses the net method of accounting for purchases. All terms of sale are strictly followed.

P5-B3 *Work sheet, adjusting entries, closing entries (closing entry method)* **(L.O. 3, 4)**

Vicki Glazer was in the process of completing the work sheet of Runner's Supply for the year ended December 31, 19X4, when she was suddenly called out of town. Her work follows.

Account Title	Trial Balance		Adjustments	
	Debit	Credit	Debit	Credit
Cash	18,200			
Accounts receivable	25,900			
Inventory	63,100			
Prepaid insurance	4,200			(a) 1,400
Equipment	20,900			
Accumulated depreciation: equipment		7,600		
Accounts payable		23,500		
Loan payable		30,000		
Robert Edwards, capital		67,700		
Robert Edwards, drawing	18,000			
Sales		169,800		
Sales returns & allowances	900			
Purchases	87,300			
Freight-in	2,000			
Purchases discounts		1,500		
Advertising expense	5,000			
Wage expense	44,400		(b) 1,000	
Rent expense	9,600			
Interest expense	600			
	300,100	300,100		
Insurance expense			(a) 1,400	
Wages payable				(b) 1,000

A piece of paper labeled "Work Sheet Data" was found on Vicki's desk and contained the following:

1 Insurance applicable to future periods, $2,800.
2 Wages incurred but not yet paid, $1,000.
3 Depreciation on the equipment, $2,000.
4 Loan interest incurred but not yet paid, $300.
5 Unbilled customer sales, $700.
6 Ending inventory, $59,800.

Instructions

a Complete the work sheet that Vicki had started. Runner's Supply uses the closing entry method for handling end-of-period inventory.

b On the basis of the work sheet that you have prepared, journalize the company's (1) year-end adjusting entries and (2) year-end closing entries.

P5-B4 *Work sheet, financial statements, and closing entries (closing entry method)* **(L.O. 3, 4, 5)**

The Wheaton Company has the following trial balance as of December 31:

Cash	$ 24,900	
Accounts receivable	36,800	
Merchandise inventory	38,000	
Prepaid advertising	6,400	
Supplies	3,700	
Equipment	72,000	
Accumulated depreciation: equipment		$ 13,400
Accounts payable		30,600
Jerry Wheaton, capital		140,200
Jerry Wheaton, drawing	16,600	
Sales		285,900
Sales returns & allowances	5,700	
Sales discounts	2,000	
Purchases	175,100	
Freight-in	4,400	
Purchases returns & allowances		1,800
Purchases discounts		4,300
Wage expense	58,500	
Insurance expense	2,600	
Rent expense	16,500	
Freight-out	4,300	
Utilities expense	8,700	
	$476,200	$476,200

Additional accounts maintained by the business include Wages Payable, Income Summary, Advertising Expense, Supplies Expense, and Depreciation Expense. Wheaton's accountant has derived the following data:

1 Advertising applicable to future periods: $3,600.
2 Supplies on hand: $1,600.
3 Depreciation on the equipment: $4,800.
4 Accrued wages: $3,100.
5 Ending inventory: $51,600.

Wheaton's capital account includes $4,000 of owner investments made during the year.

Instructions

a Complete a work sheet in good form for the Wheaton Company for the year ended December 31. The company uses the closing entry method of accounting for inventory.

b Prepare a multiple-step income statement, statement of owner's equity, and a classified balance sheet in good form. The firm's selling activities account for 60% of the wage cost and 40% of insurance, rent, utilities, supplies, and depreciation expense.

c Record Wheaton's adjusting entries in the journal.

d Record Wheaton's closing entries in the journal.

P5-B5 *Income statement classification* **(L.O. 5)**

Welder's Supply Company sells its own inventory to area factories in addition to selling products for other companies on a commission basis. Presented below are the categories used on a multiple-step income statement.

1 Revenue

2 Cost of goods sold

3 Selling expenses

4 General & administrative expenses

5 Other revenue (expense)

6 Income taxes

The following accounts were taken from the firm's general ledger:

a Depreciation expense: office

b Freight-in

c Purchases discounts

d Depreciation expense: delivery equipment

e Sales returns

f Sales commissions (paid by Welder's Supply)

g Office supplies expense

h Inventory (ending)

i Interest expense

j Customer entertainment expense

k Sales

l Purchases

m Payroll taxes payable

n Loss from spring flood

o Freight-out

p Warren Robb, capital

q Interest revenue

r Advertising expense

s Miscellaneous expense (relates to management of the business)

Instructions

Classify the accounts of Welder's Supply as to their proper placement on the income statement. If any of the accounts do not appear on the income statement, determine whether they appear on the balance sheet or the statement of owner's equity.

P5-B6 *Income statement preparation* **(L.O. 5)**

The following information was compiled by a newly hired staff accountant of the Hanson Corporation:

Administrative expenses	$ 99,500
Advertising expense	43,500
Beginning inventory	97,100
Depreciation expense: executive offices	31,700
Depreciation expense: sales equipment	15,600
Ending inventory	76,000
Freight-in	14,200
Gain on sale of land	10,000
Insurance expense	27,000
Interest revenue	8,000

Net sales	784,000
Purchases	361,800
Purchases discounts	6,400
Sales discounts	13,600
Sales salaries expense	62,000

Additional information:

1 Administrative expenses consist of executive salaries ($85,000) and interest ($14,500).
2 Insurance expense should be allocated 70% to administration and 30% to sales.
3 Net sales was computed as follows: Sales ($757,900) − sales returns ($8,300) + freight-out ($34,400).
4 Hanson is subject to a 30% income tax rate.

Instructions

a Prepare a multiple-step income statement for the year ended September 30, 19X4. Be sure to correct any errors made by the staff accountant.
b Briefly explain what you would have done differently if part (a) had called for the preparation of a single-step income statement rather than a multiple-step statement. If you were a banker considering loaning money to Hanson Corporation, which form of income statement would you prefer to examine? Why?

*P5-B7 **Work sheet, adjusting entries, closing entries (adjusting entry method) (L.O. 3, 4)**
Refer to Problem 5-B3.

Instructions

Follow the instructions on page 217. Assume, however, that Runner's Supply uses the adjusting entry method for handling end-of-period inventory rather than the closing entry method.

*P5-B8 **Work sheet, financial statements, and closing entries (adjusting entry method) (L.O. 3, 4, 5)**
Refer to Problem 5-B4.

Instructions

Follow the instructions on page 218. Assume, however, that Wheaton Company uses the adjusting entry method of accounting for inventory rather than the closing entry method.

EDB5-1 **Merchandising profitability, income reporting: Albertson's, Inc., and Dillard Department Stores (L.O. 3, 5)**

ELECTRONIC DATA BASE

SEC

Albertson's is the sixth largest retail food/drug chain in the country. The company operates over 500 stores that are located in 17 midwestern, western, and southern states. In contrast, Dillard's is a regional group of department stores that cater primarily to middle and upper-middle income consumers. The firm has 198 stores in 18 states.

Instructions

By using the text's Electronic Data Base, access the financial statements of both companies and answer the questions that follow. Unless otherwise indicated, responses should be based on data for the most recent year presented.

a What is the largest current asset on each company's balance sheet? Is this finding somewhat expected, given the nature of the firms? Briefly explain.

b Determine the cost of goods sold for both firms. Compare each company's presentation with that shown in Exhibit 5-4 and comment on your findings.

c Determine the gross profit of both firms in dollars and as a percentage of net sales.

  (1) Consider the nature of each company's operation. Comment on what is likely causing the difference in the percentages that you calculated. (*Note:* Assume that both firms use the same methods to value inventory.)

  (2) Are there any differences in the manner of gross profit presentation on each firm's income statement? Discuss.

d Determine the income statement format (single-step or multiple-step) used by each company. Does the format affect the presentation of gross profit? Briefly explain.

EDB5-2 *Merchandising profitability, income reporting* (L.O. 3, 5)

This problem is a duplication of Problem EDB5-1. It is based on two companies selected by your instructor.

Instructions

SEC By using the text's Electronic Data Base, access the specified companies' financial statements and focus on data for the most recent year reported. Answer requirements (a)–(d) of Problem EDB5-1.

BEYOND THE BASICS

BB5-1 *Analysis of merchandising data and activity* (L.O. 3)

As part of a class project for an accounting course, Paul Davis was asked to evaluate selected income and inventory data of two companies: LaStone and Q-Mart. LaStone operates a chain of jewelry stores in upscale shopping malls throughout the country. Q-Mart, on the other hand, has five discount department stores in California and Oregon. Selected data (in thousands of dollars) from the companies' financial statements follow.

	LaStone	Q-Mart
Net sales	$3,000	$6,400
Net purchases	1,400	3,800
Beginning inventory	400	900
Ending inventory	600	700

Both LaStone and Q-Mart employ a natural business year for reporting purposes, with the year-end occurring at the slowest point in the business cycle.

Davis recently completed a finance course where his instructor talked about gross profit and the ability of a firm to manage its inventories. The instructor noted that some companies sell goods more rapidly than others and are better able to generate cash and avoid inventory financing costs than their competitors.

Instructions

Assume the role of Paul Davis and answer the following:

a Which of the two firms would probably generate a higher gross profit for each dollar of merchandise sold? Briefly explain the rationale behind your answer.

b Determine whether your answer in part (a) was correct or incorrect by calculating gross profit for the two companies and then expressing gross profit as a percentage of net sales. Round computations to one decimal place.

c Picture the movement of goods through the average LaStone and Q-Mart stores. Which of the two entities would probably move merchandise more quickly? Why?

d Analyze the preceding data and computations. Explain how it is possible for companies that sell high-profit items and those that sell low-profit items to have roughly the same rate of bottom-line income (net income ÷ net sales) for a reporting period.

e Given these firms' business cycles, would the natural business year most likely end on November 30, December 31, or January 31? Briefly explain.

BB5-2 *Overview of chapter concepts: Multiple choice* **(L.O. 1–5)**

The following multiple-choice questions relate to various topics discussed in the chapter. Select the best answer.

1 A credit memorandum is prepared by a seller of merchandise to document:
   a that a return of merchandise has been authorized and Accounts Receivable can be credited.
   b that a customer is entitled to a trade discount and Accounts Receivable can be credited.
   c that sales returns and cash discounts have caused net sales to be less than total sales.
   d that an increase in the Sales account must be recorded.

2 A $1,000 sale on account is subject to terms of 2/10, n/30. If the customer paid the correct amount on the 20th day after the sale, then:
   a the Sales account should be reduced by $20.
   b the Accounts Receivable account should be reduced by $980.
   c the amount collected would be greater than the amount entered in the Accounts Receivable account.
   d the amount collected would equal the amount entered in the Sales account.

3 Which of the following would not be used to calculate cost of goods sold?
   a Purchases discounts.   c Freight-out.
   b Ending inventory.   d Beginning inventory.

4 Which of the following characteristics is associated with both the gross and net methods of recording purchases?
   a Discounts lost can be extracted directly from the general ledger.
   b Accounts Payable is initially credited for the purchaser's maximum obligation to the supplier.
   c The cash collected will eventually equal the amount recorded in the Purchases account.
   d The initial recording of a purchase will cause both Purchases and Accounts Payable to increase by the same amount.

5 Nolte Enterprises recently purchased $2,500 of goods on account, subject to terms of 3/10, n/45. If the purchase is recorded under the gross method

and payment occurs after the discount period has lapsed:

a Accounts Payable should be reduced by $2,425 on the date of payment.

b the Purchases Discounts Lost account should be increased by $75 on the date of payment.

c only two accounts are affected on the date of payment.

d the Purchases Discounts account must be reduced by $75.

6 Treetop Company recently purchased $1,000 of merchandise on account, F.O.B. shipping point. As an accommodation to Treetop and the trucking company, the seller prepaid the $100 freight bill. As a result of this situation, Treetop should:

a debit Purchases for $1,100.

b credit Accounts Payable for $1,100.

c debit Freight-out for $100.

d credit Accounts Payable for $1,000.

7 Which of the following comments about gross profit is correct?

a Gross profit is a contemporary replacement for the term "net income."

b The proper amount of gross profit is obtainable from the Gross Profit account in the general ledger.

c Operating expenses are subtracted from gross profit in the calculation of net income.

d Gross profit is an intermediate total derived by subtracting goods available for sale from net sales.

8 Which of the following is both credited in the closing process and disclosed on a multiple-step income statement above the operating expenses section?

a Purchases returns and allowances.

b Merchandise inventory (for the ending inventory balance).

c Interest expense.

d Freight-in.

COMMUNICATION OF ACCOUNTING INFORMATION

CAI5-1 *Writing to influence: Woolworth Corporation* (L.O. 3, 5)

Communication Principle: As an accounting student, you may think that the purpose for writing most business letters is to convey information. Actually, providing factual information is only one of several objectives. Underlying the obvious informational content may be an attempt to influence.

Most information requires interpretation or comment. With interpretation, the writer guides a reader to make decisions—investment or management decisions, for instance. Most business letters are informative, but they are also persuasive; that is, they persuade us to act or feel in one way or another. Good accounting writers will understand the hidden persuasion behind the numbers they present and will "direct" the reader toward a given outcome.

■ ■ ■ ■ ■ ■ ■ ■

Woolworth Corporation is a large multinational retailer, with over 8,000 stores in 17 countries. In addition to traditional Woolworth and Woolco stores, the firm owns Foot Locker, Kinney Shoes, Kids Mart, Athletic X-Press, and over 30 other recognizable retail chains. These chains deal primarily in footwear and apparel. A review of the company's income statements for three recent years revealed the following figures (in millions of dollars):

	19X9	19X8	19X7
Sales revenues	$8,820	$8,088	$7,177
Cost of goods sold	5,759	5,333	4,714
Selling & administrative expenses	2,242	2,063	1,859

Assume that you are an employee at Woolworth's corporate headquarters. An inexperienced investment adviser has written the company for selected financial information. (She has a client who is considering investing in Woolworth.) The following information is requested:

- The company's gross profit for each year.
- Yearly gross profit as a percentage of sales revenues, along with a comment on the company's gross profit trend over time.
- The firm's rate of cost incurrence as it relates to selling and administrative costs versus cost of goods sold. That is, examine these amounts as a percentage of sales and comment on your findings. Consider the nature of the retail market in general and Woolworth's operations in particular.

Instructions

Write a letter to the investment adviser that provides the information requested. Understand that the tone and style of your response will influence the advice ultimately given to the client.

Answers to Chapter Quiz

1 d

2 b

3 c ($1,700 + $2,900 − $2,000)

4 c ($8,000 − ($8,000 × 0.02) + $200)

5 a

CHAPTER 6

Accounting Systems and Internal Control

LEARNING OBJECTIVES

After studying this chapter, you should be able to:

1

Appreciate the role and importance of a good accounting system.

2

Explain the relationship between control accounts and subsidiary ledgers.

3

Recognize the features of a typical microcomputer-based accounting system.

4

Describe the tasks performed by the general ledger, accounts receivable, and accounts payable modules.

5

Explain the nature of internal control and identify various internal control procedures.

Many individuals engaged in day-to-day business operations are concerned with the creation and flow of information. Large volumes of data must be processed into information that is usable by management and other readers of financial statements. From the material presented in the first five chapters of this text, you may think the generation of information is a relatively straightforward and simple operation. Unfortunately, many problems can arise. Managers frequently complain that (1) they lack the necessary information to perform their duties properly and (2) reports arrive too late to be useful. Furthermore, some employees are so overwhelmed with computer printouts that there is not enough time in a working day to study all the facts that flow across their desks.

The network that processes transactions and ultimately produces financial statements and other reports is known as an **accounting information system.** Such systems generate information from *data* (i.e., a variety of facts, figures, and/or transactions) for use in reporting, planning, controlling, and decision-making activities. In other words, data serve as the raw material for determining the period's income, the ending accounts receivable balance, the total cash inflows related to a proposed investment, and other key measures needed to evaluate an entity and its associated components (activities, products, and so forth).

This chapter provides an introduction to accounting systems and their related controls, the latter of which help to ensure that systems function as originally intended. By the end of our presentation, you should understand numerous systems-related issues, including how computers function in a modern accounting setting.

TRANSACTION PROCESSING

OBJECTIVE

Appreciate the role and importance of a good accounting system.

As a company expands, the volume of transactions that must be processed will increase. You can well imagine that in many situations, systems and personnel may begin to be stretched for capacity and time. This is a typical phenomenon that may actually contribute to a slowing or reversal of an entity's growth, as costly accounting errors start to decrease profitability and customer satisfaction. For example:

- Invoices may be paid twice (or cash discounts missed).
- Receivables may go unbilled for extended periods.
- The amount of cash needed to pay bills tomorrow or next week is unknown.
- The availability of items in inventory cannot be readily determined.
- The accounting department may need excessive amounts of overtime to complete seemingly routine tasks on a punctual basis.[1]

The manual accounting system that was introduced in Chapter 2 showed how transactions are processed from source documents and eventually find their way to the financial statements. Quite frankly, this type of system is cumbersome, tedious, and inefficient in high-volume opera-

---

[1] See "Computerizing an Accounting System," *DH+S Review*, October 24, 1988, pp. 7–8.

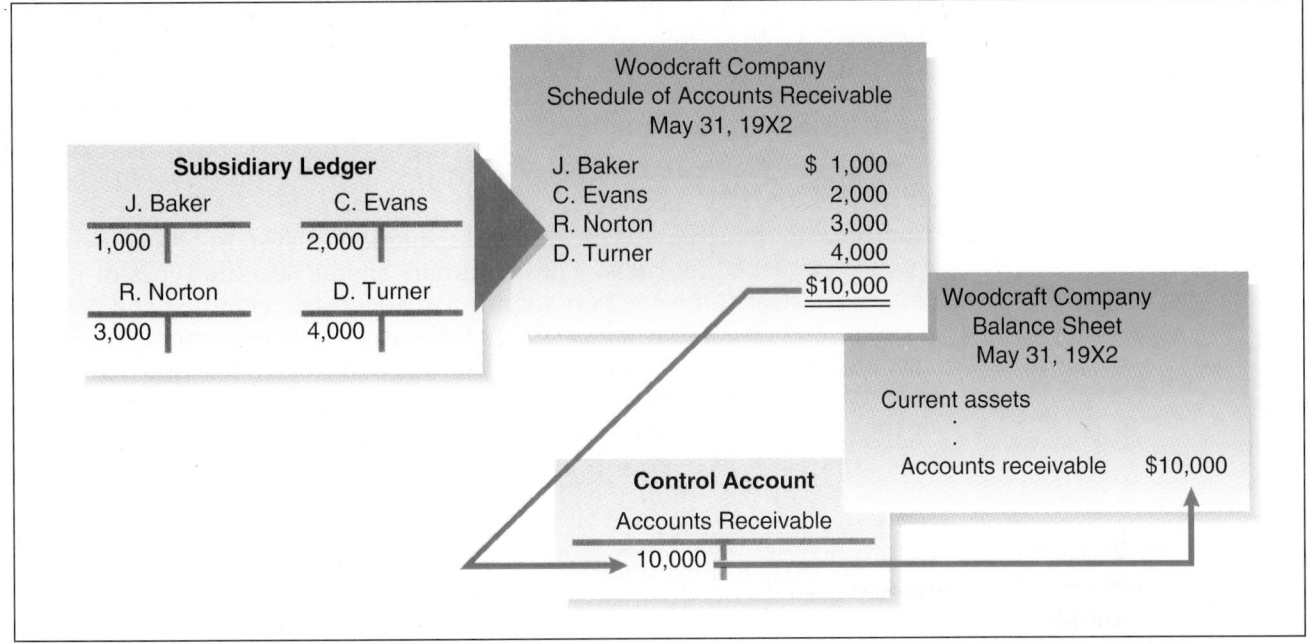

EXHIBIT 6-1
Subsidiary Ledger/Control
Account Relationships

along with the related balance. Woodcraft's schedule of accounts receivable and the preceding relationships are shown in Exhibit 6-1.

Tips & Techniques

When a credit sale or collection on account occurs, both the control account and the applicable customer account are updated. In many manual systems, for example, individual transactions are posted daily to the subsidiary ledger. The *totals* of these transactions (e.g., monthly credit sales, collections on account) are later posted to the control account.

Processing Reduction in a Manual System

The use of subsidiary ledgers is but one system refinement. Over time a company is likely to implement a variety of special features that enable the firm to better satisfy its information needs. Unfortunately, as features are added, the system is likely to become more unmanageable. Businesses must address this situation by implementing techniques that reduce the expanded amount of record keeping and detail while still providing the desired information.

A simplified example of such a technique is used by many doctors and dentists. Upon conclusion of a recent trip to a doctor's office, you may have been given a receipt that has a small strip of carbon on its back. It is likely that as the receipt was being prepared, the details of the transaction—date, patient name, amount due, and cash paid—were simultaneously being recorded (via the carbon strip) onto a summary sheet that serves as the practice's journal. Thus, the practice's daily activity in terms of revenues and cash collections can be determined quite readily. It is also likely that an individual record for the patient, made with "impression paper," is being updated at the same time.

Special Journals

Another way to achieve a meaningful reduction in system procedure is by the use of **special journals.** These journals handle specific types of recurring transactions in ways that significantly decrease recording and posting procedures. Special journals are frequently used for sales of merchandise on account, purchases of merchandise on account, cash receipts, and cash disbursements. Appendix A at the end of the text provides a detailed look at the operation of a manually maintained special journal system.

COMPUTERIZED ACCOUNTING SYSTEMS

Both the carbon strip ("write-it-once") and special journal systems are a major step forward compared to the basic general journal/general ledger system discussed earlier in the book. Nevertheless, these systems are manual in operation and lack the efficiency needed in higher-volume transaction environments. In such situations, most companies have found that computers are the answer to a variety of record-keeping problems. Computers can process data more quickly and at a lower error rate than office personnel using manual accounting systems. Stated simply, electrical circuits do not become bored, fatigued, or emotional—real pluses when it comes to productivity.

With improved efficiency via electronics comes a lower cost per transaction processed. Costs have declined in recent years to the extent that even the smallest of companies can afford computers. Hardware and software that provide adequate data processing capability can now be purchased for considerably less than the annual salary and fringe benefit outlays for one bookkeeper. Much of this affordability can be attributed to an increase in the use of small computers (commonly known as *micros*), which have minimal installation and programming costs. Prewritten, or canned, programs are available for all aspects of a company's accounting activities, including payroll, billing, and inventory control. Thus, a business that uses a microcomputer need not add a data processing specialist to its staff.

A word of caution: Yes, canned programs are readily obtainable and convenient, but no, such packages are not always satisfactory. Most programs that are available over the counter are designed for a broad range of users. Some of these packages can be modified to meet specific individual needs; others are available on an as-is basis. In general, the acquisition of quality accounting software is much like the purchase of a fine suit or dress: a reasonable amount of alteration may be required. This is not to say that functional programs cannot be obtained "off the rack" at very low cost. The comment merely suggests that most businesses are unique to a certain degree, and a customized accounting package may command a relatively high price.

ETHICS ISSUE

Your company has a very tight cash position and desperately needs an updated computerized accounting system. You can obtain illegal copies of the necessary software from a friend. What would you do?

Features of Microcomputer System Software

Computerized accounting systems tend to parallel manual accounting systems in terms of function and objective. As an example, both types of systems process transactions by using debits and credits, maintain ledger accounts, and produce financial statements and other reports for management. This is where the similarity ends, however, as the systems' form, organization, and procedures differ greatly. An entity's manual journals and ledgers are replaced by computer files that are kept on a storage medium such as a disk.[2] Posting and report preparation are automated, and the closing process is often performed by pressing a single key on the computer's keyboard. Furthermore, many computerized systems have built-in controls that examine data validity before accepting transactions as input. A transaction that erroneously contains an alphabetic character in a dollar amount field, for instance, would be rejected by the system. Automated systems also include certain maintenance routines that allow the user to add new accounts to the chart of accounts, revise financial statement formats, and perform other similar housekeeping chores.

Most system packages also subdivide the accounting process into modules. Each module handles a specific component of the overall accounting process, for example, general ledger activity, accounts receivable (sales) activity, and accounts payable (purchasing) activity. Other commonly encountered modules are used for payroll, cash management, inventory, and plant and equipment. These individual units are subsequently integrated to form a company's accounting information system.

OBJECTIVE

3

Recognize the features of a typical microcomputer-based accounting system.

The Concept of Modular Accounting

Processing modules serve to streamline the data entry process. Recording every transaction in general journal entry form is very inefficient, especially if the same type of transaction occurs with a high frequency. It is far more practical to provide a standardized format, or template, to input the necessary data. To illustrate, with the accounts receivable module, the computer may first request that the user input the *type* of transaction. Then, upon learning that a sale on account is about to be entered, the computer will display a preformatted screen design that requests only the transaction date, customer name (or number), and transaction amount. There is no need to instruct the software to debit Accounts Receivable and credit Sales, because the program is logically designed to recognize that both of these accounts must be increased. Further, you can probably imagine that the company will need to retain additional facts about the sale (e.g., billing instructions, certain customer information, and so forth). A well-designed module will capture and maintain this information in an organized and accessible format.

Modules also lead to a division of labor, in which employees specialize in

---

[2] Accounting data are stored in computers by using records and files. A *record* stores information about one employee, one inventory item, one account, and so forth. A *file*, in contrast, is a group of records. For example, all customer records taken collectively comprise the accounts receivable file.

handling one part of the overall system (say, cash receipts processing). With specialization comes increased efficiency, as employees become familiar with a job and get to know it well.

Another advantage of modules, which parallels the benefit just cited, relates to computer operations. Generally speaking, transaction processing time and program efficiency are enhanced by breaking the workload into groups of like activities. When this procedure is followed, there is no need to design complex, multipurpose packages that run numerous tests to determine whether certain routines are to be accessed. A modular environment would require less up-front data analysis since the program is designed to process only a specific type of transaction. As a logical outgrowth of this situation, program revision is usually simplified. It is normally easier to "plug in" a new, self-contained unit than to overhaul the entire system.

Accessing the Modules

The modules in a microcomputer accounting system are accessed by employing a **menu**—a listing on the computer screen of the various program options available to a user. The menu illustrated in Exhibit 6-2 shows that the system package contains separate modules for general ledger, accounts receivable, and accounts payable functions. Other options, such as payroll, would be listed here as well. Notice that another part of the screen is devoted to maintenance routines. In this particular case, routines have been designed to capture basic company information (e.g., the firm's name, end-of-period reporting dates, authorized system users, and so forth) and to terminate program operation. The bottom of the screen shows the appropriate keys that must be pressed to input selections to the computer. Once a processing module is chosen, the computer screen will reveal a new menu related to the selected alternative. This menu will include a fresh set of options that the user may elect.

An in-depth probe of the intricacies that comprise a typical accounting

EXHIBIT 6-2
Example of Main Menu

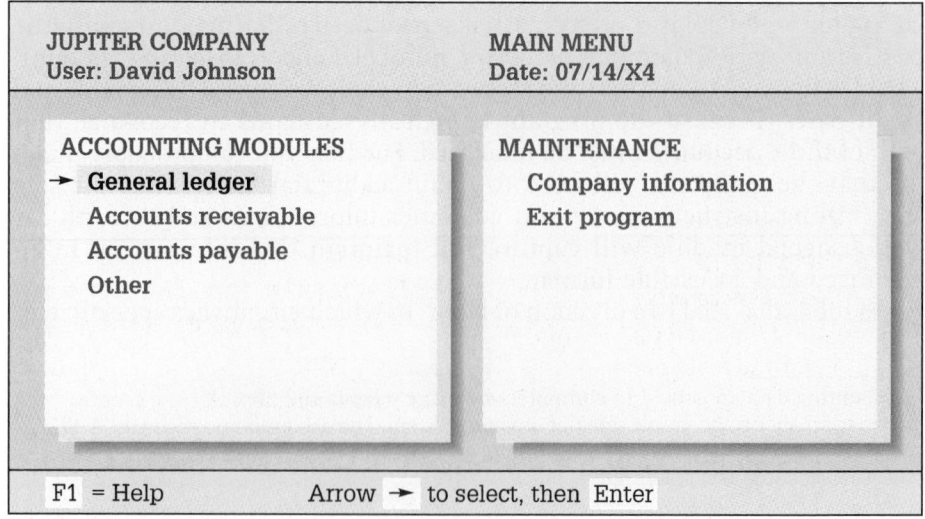

system is clearly beyond the scope of this text. However, a brief overview of several key modules will help distinguish manual-based and computer-based systems. We have selected the general ledger, accounts receivable, and accounts payable modules for further study.

General Ledger Module

Despite a name that is somewhat of a misnomer, the **general ledger module** is the heart of a computerized accounting system. This module not only houses all of the general ledger accounts, but it also provides the means by which many journal entries are entered and posted, the financial statements/reports are prepared, and the closing process is performed. Exhibit 6-3 contains a typical menu for a general ledger module.

The general ledger routine probably used most frequently is the enter/edit journal entry command. Upon selection, a screen similar to that shown in Exhibit 6-4 will appear. This screen queries the user regarding such matters as the transaction date, transaction description, accounts affected, and dollar amounts involved. Most accounting programs facilitate the input process by allowing the user to communicate with the computer via account numbers rather than account titles. Once an acceptable number is input, the correct account title appears automatically, thus saving considerable keystrokes and time.

Many software packages introduced in the past few years have an added feature known as "windows." While working within a particular segment of the program, a user can request that a superimposed listing temporarily appear on part of the current computer screen. For example, the company's chart of accounts (or portions thereof) might appear while transactions are being entered. This "window" option allows the user to quickly identify the company's account numbers without having to exit from the task presently being performed.

Other features found in most general ledger packages include input con-

> **OBJECTIVE**
>
> **4**
>
> **Describe the tasks performed by the general ledger, accounts receivable, and accounts payable modules.**

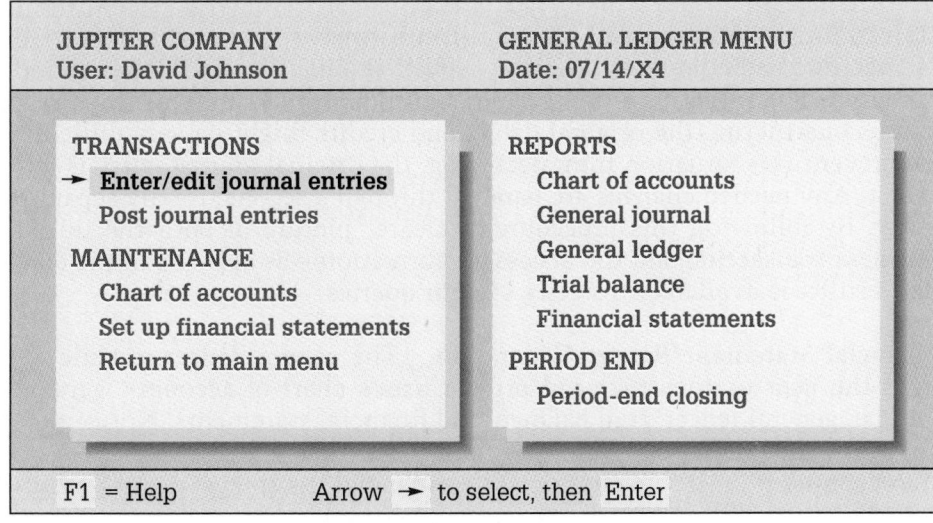

JUPITER COMPANY	GENERAL LEDGER MENU
User: David Johnson	Date: 07/14/X4

TRANSACTIONS	REPORTS
→ **Enter/edit journal entries**	Chart of accounts
Post journal entries	General journal
MAINTENANCE	General ledger
Chart of accounts	Trial balance
Set up financial statements	Financial statements
Return to main menu	PERIOD END
	Period-end closing

F1 = Help   Arrow → to select, then Enter

EXHIBIT 6-3
Example of General Ledger Menu

EXHIBIT 6-4
Example of Journal
Entry/Edit Screen

JOURNAL ENTRY — ADD MODE				
Date 07/14/X4			Reference number	723
Enter description	TO RECORD RECEIPT OF LOAN PROCEEDS			
Account	Name		Debit	Credit
101	Cash		500.00	
220	Loan Payable			500.00
Total debits should = total credits			500.00	500.00
F1 = Help F2 = Mode Enter = Record transaction				ESC = Quit

trols that reject out-of-balance journal entries. In addition, most programs assign reference numbers to individual transactions—a practice that assists in later accessing the entry from a data file should the need arise.

Edit Routines.   Occasionally, the system user may desire to correct a previously entered transaction. Some packages make this process very simple: the user selects the journal entry edit mode, keys in the appropriate reference number, and directly changes (i.e., overlays) the previously entered data. Other packages are designed so that such changes are more difficult. A special password (made available only to selected supervisors) may be required before edits can be input to the system.

Still other programs function in an entirely different manner by allowing no changes in prior entries. Instead, for purposes of control, a correcting entry is used. The reason behind this procedure relates to the nature of the *audit trail* in a computer environment. That is, unless certain routines are designed and implemented, the use of electronics (and lack of paper) hampers the ability to physically trace a transaction through a system from start to finish. You can well imagine the chaos that might arise if an irate or incompetent computer operator started to change previously entered amounts. The integrity of the system's output would surely be impaired, and reconstructing the original debits and credits might be very difficult. To prevent this situation from occurring, the original journal entry is left intact. Any needed changes are handled through a second, totally separate entry. By following this procedure, a clearer picture of both the initial business transaction and the necessary correction—as opposed to the end, *net* result—is available to satisfy system queries.

Financial Statement/Report Generation.   The general ledger module allows the user to construct and print a firm's chart of accounts, general journal, general ledger, trial balance, and financial statements. Notice that the work sheet is absent from this list. Recall that this document assists the accountant in the preparation of the financial statements and in gathering the necessary information for closing entries. Because both of these tasks are now automated, the computer has actually rendered the work sheet obsolete and unnecessary.

In many packages the preceding statements/reports can be printed either to the computer screen (for visual inspection) or on paper (hard copy). Screen printing is generally used to examine bits and pieces of the larger whole, for example, a selected journal entry or the balance in a particular account. Hard copy, on the other hand, is the preferred option for lengthier forms of feedback. Unfortunately, the nature of printed copy (bulky, heavy, and portable) and the ability of computers to generate countless reports have created a subsequent need for dealings with microfiche conversion and document-shredding services.

Closing Routine.   The final component to be discussed in the general ledger module relates to the closing of accounts. The process of closing the books is highly mechanical and, thus, easily automated. The computer simply resets the balances in temporary accounts to zero and updates the owner's capital account. Before the actual closing process is performed, a message similar to the following will often appear on the screen: "WARNING: Specific Transaction Data Will Be Lost! Are You Sure You Wish To Proceed?" If reports and statements are printed *after* closing, the income statement accounts will be void of any balances, and the trial balance will constitute a post-closing trial balance. The warning message is actually a caution against trying to perform steps of the accounting cycle in the incorrect order.

Accounts Receivable Module

Although transaction recording, account updating, and report generation can be accomplished through the general ledger module, recall that additional processing efficiencies are associated with specialization. Exhibit 6-5 reveals that a separate **accounts receivable module** can be used to process information pertaining to sales and the resulting customer account collections. This module also has the ability to produce several related documents and reports such as sales invoices, a sales journal, and a cash receipts journal. The latter two items will be explained shortly.

Recognize that the primary accounting data contained within the receivables module must interact with the general ledger module. Stated differently, data relative to changes in Accounts Receivable, Sales, and Cash from the sale of goods or services and the collection of customer balances must be imported to the general ledger module so that an up-to-date account status can be maintained. This is generally accomplished through posting or other similar processes.

Users of the accounts receivable module will normally enter sales transactions by selecting an invoice entry routine from the menu. Data would be gathered concerning the sale date, customer, items sold, transaction amount, transaction terms, and so forth. This data-entry process provides the basis for the creation of an invoice (see p. 182), a posting to the customer's subsidiary ledger account, and an overall listing of sales transactions known as a *sales journal*. Other reports that prove useful for

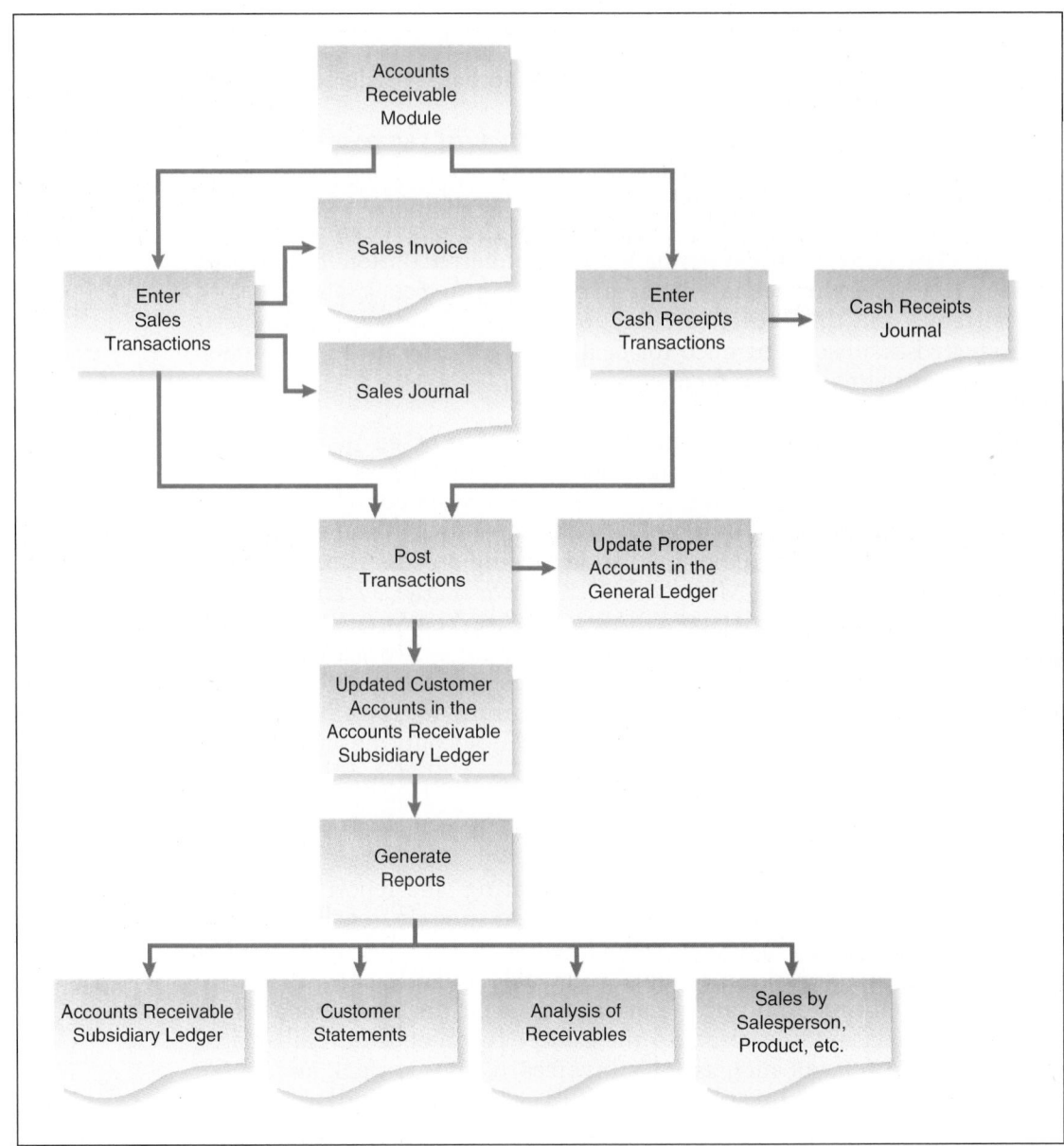

EXHIBIT 6-5
Accounts Receivable Module

management analysis can be generated as well, such as sales subdivided by salesperson, territory, and product line.

Receipts from customers on account are also entered through this module by simply selecting another option on the receivables menu. Customers' subsidiary accounts are updated for the transactions, and a compilation of collections is produced in the form of a *cash receipts journal*.[3] In addition, now that both sales and collections are known and entered, the system software can generate a detailed listing of the accounts

---

[3] As used here, the cash receipts journal lists only collections from customers on account. Business receipts from other sources (e.g., a loan) are entered in the system through the general ledger module.

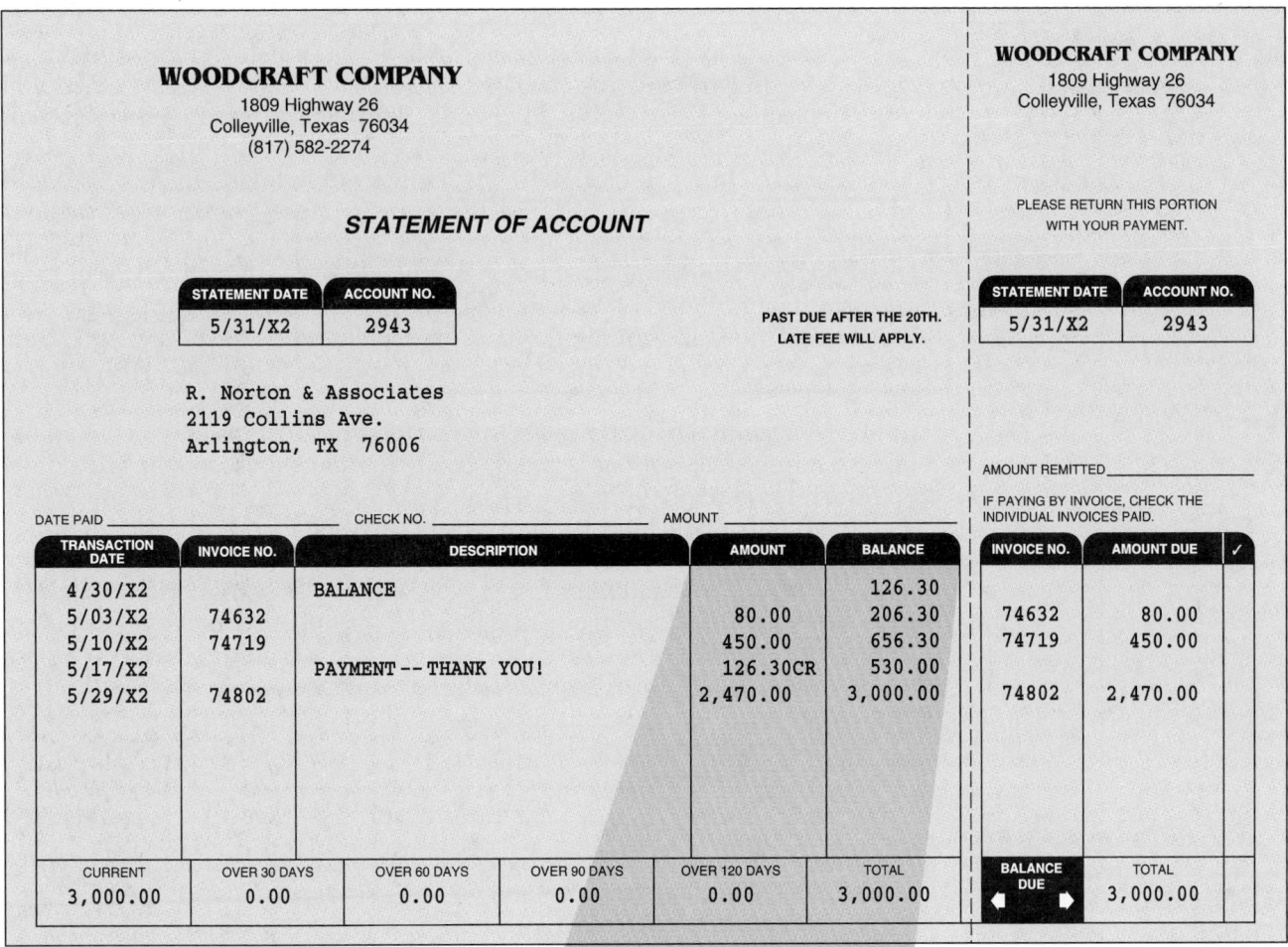

EXHIBIT 6-6
Relationship Between Customer Account Statement and Accounts Receivable Subsidiary Ledger

receivable subsidiary ledger. The information contained here parallels the monthly billing that is sent to customers in the form of an *account statement* (see Exhibit 6-6). Depending on the level of sophistication, many packages also provide an analysis of receivables to help identify delinquent accounts and various other customer statistics.

Accounts Payable Module

The accounts receivable module just discussed is very similar to the **accounts payable module,** the operation of which is depicted in Exhibit

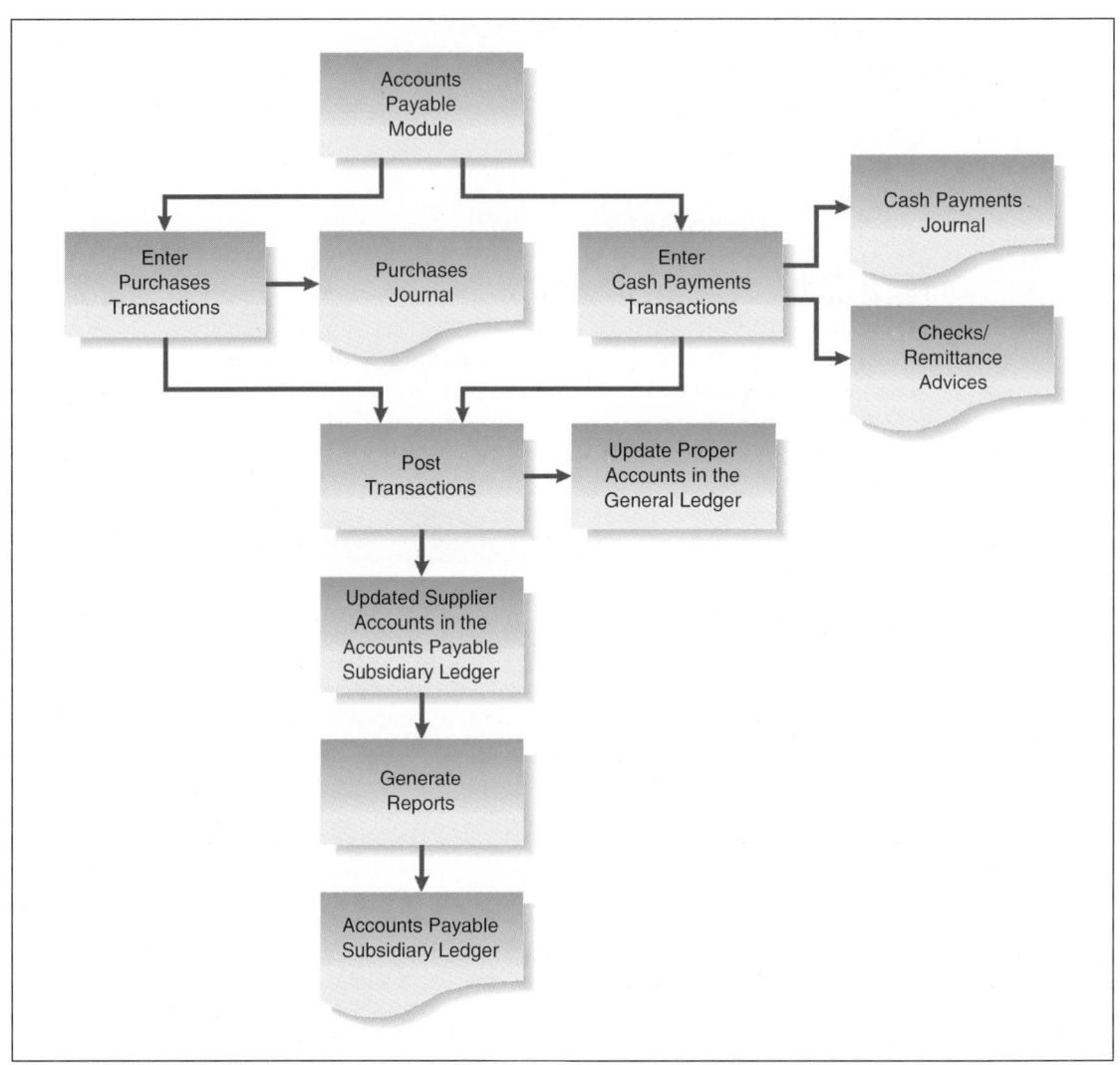

EXHIBIT 6-7
Accounts Payable Module

6-7. The accounts payable package is used to process purchases transactions along with cash payments to suppliers. As a result, vendor information and subsidiary ledger data are maintained in this segment of the system.

Output from the accounts payable module includes a *purchases journal* (a listing of all merchandise purchases on account) and a *cash payments journal*. Activity sorted by individual suppliers is shown in a subsidiary ledger, which discloses purchases, cash payments, and amounts owed at the end of the period. Many accounts payable software packages also handle the printing of checks and the attached *remittance advice* (a check stub that indicates the invoice being paid and the discount taken, if any). Such packages frequently contain built-in controls that match the invoices being processed for payment against a list of previously paid invoices. This safeguard helps ensure that the same invoice is not paid twice.

Are Computerized Systems Always the Answer?

Computerized accounting systems are not a remedy for all business problems. A company should carefully analyze its particular situation to see if in fact the computer will do more to help than to hinder. Earlier in the chapter, for example, we noted that high-speed processing networks are often accompanied by an endless string of reports and statistics. This mountain of output may not be needed and can potentially obscure important feedback, which gets lost in the shuffle. Also, in many small "mom and pop" businesses, inertia may prevail. Success in the past may lead such companies to adopt an attitude of "Don't fix what isn't broke." For these firms it is probably easier and more efficient to continue using a manual accounting system. As in any business decision, the costs and benefits must be weighed—even for those elements that are not easily quantified. An item that would definitely fall in this latter category is management's attitude toward change.

Other Microcomputer Applications

Although our discussion has focused on transaction processing systems, be aware that microcomputers are used in many other accounting applications. Micros are utilized by CPA firms to process income tax returns. In addition, through the use of special telephone hook-ups, computers can be linked to distant data bases to allow the accountant to quickly search thousands of court cases and tax laws. Such capability aids in the performance of tax research. Turning to the audit field, microcomputers are employed in numerous statistical sampling applications when examining the transactions and accounts that serve as the basis for a company's financial statements.

An innovation that has become extremely popular in recent years is the **electronic spreadsheet.** The spreadsheet is, in effect, a computerized work sheet—a series of columns and rows that are filled with report headings, financial data, and computational formulas by the user. Spreadsheets are employed to generate various types of reports (e.g., budgets and depreciation schedules) and are especially helpful in performing "what if" analysis.

Suppose, for instance, that a manager is studying an investment opportunity by using a certain set of assumptions such as projected levels of sales, expenses, cash inflows and outflows, and income tax rates. The manager may desire to study the proposal under a different set of conditions. If paper, pencil, and a calculator were the only tools available, the revised computations would take many hours to perform. By the touch of only a few computer keys, however, the essential calculations are automatically refigured. Much of the computational drudgery is therefore removed from the process, allowing more time for analysis and further "what if" scenarios.

As noted on several occasions throughout this chapter, selected controls are built into software to prevent and detect the occurrence of errors. Such controls are not used solely with sophisticated computerized systems; they

INTERNAL CONTROL

are employed with basic manual systems as well. Stated simply, virtually all processing networks contain various checks and balances to ensure that data are processed correctly and that other objectives are achieved.

The concept of internal control is actually much broader than our basic examples could possibly convey. Perhaps the best way to start is by citing a 20+-year-old report on the financial health of the Long Island Railroad, a railroad well known to those who live in and around New York City.[4] The report noted that the commuter line was losing revenue and operating in an unproductive manner largely because of a weak accounting system—so weak that the carrier was criticized as being less well managed than the average household. To become more specific:

- Cash balances had not been compared with bank statements for nearly a year, permitting an erroneous statement of cash position.
- Time sheets failed to reflect workers who arrived late and left early.
- Large amounts due the railroad hadn't been billed.
- Approximately 20,000 blank payroll checks were found in an unsecured vault; signed payroll checks were left lying on desks unprotected.
- A study of the number of tickets sold versus the number of passengers riding the trains showed an average of 670,000 free rides a month during a seven-month period.

Although the preceding situation may seem unthinkable and perhaps even laughable, similar occurrences are repeated on a daily basis in many businesses throughout the country.

Accountants recognize that designing a perfect system is an impossibility, as errors and inefficiencies will often occur when transactions are processed. A limited number of accidental errors are expected and tolerated; conversely, intentional errors via employee sabotage, fraud, and/or embezzlement are unacceptable. To minimize the probability of error occurrence and improve the credibility of financial statements and reports, features known as internal controls are designed and used by businesses. We can define **internal control** as the various measures adopted by an organization to safeguard company assets, check the reliability and accuracy of accounting information, ensure compliance with management policies, and evaluate operating performance and efficiency.

The Internal Control Structure

The control structure (i.e., framework) of a business is dependent on several factors, including the accounting system itself, the control environment, and numerous control procedures.[5] Let us focus on the latter two elements for a moment.

A company's control environment represents the combined effect of many factors that relate to the implementation and evaluation of specified

OBJECTIVE 5

Explain the nature of internal control and identify various internal control procedures.

---

[4] See "Long Island Railroad Is Said to be Losing Revenue Due to 'Weak' Accounting System," *The Wall Street Journal*, February 18, 1971, p. 10.
[5] Much of this discussion is based on "Consideration of the Internal Control Structure in a Financial Statement Audit," *Statement on Auditing Standards No. 55* (New York: American Institute of Certified Public Accountants, Inc., 1988).

firm policies. For example, the environment is influenced by anything from sound personnel practices that enable a business to attract, motivate, and compensate competent personnel, to what may be viewed as the most crucial link in setting the overall control "tone" of the entity: management's philosophy and operating style. Is management prone to take and monitor business risks? What is the company's attitude toward financial reporting? Do executives exercise care in daily operations and in meeting budget and income goals? These issues tend to reflect the overall emphasis and importance of control within a firm, as top management attitudes are often adopted and reflected at lower levels of the organizational structure.

In addition to creating a suitable control environment, a business must also establish various control procedures to ensure that company goals will be achieved. These procedures are integrated into both the control environment and accounting systems and generally include the following.

Limited Access to Assets

The safeguarding of assets is a stated objective of internal control. One way to achieve this objective is by **limiting the access to assets** to only a few authorized personnel. Limited access may take different forms. For example, customers normally are not permitted in the back of a store to roam freely through the merchandise awaiting sale. This area is reserved for employees only. Furthermore, access to a company's mainframe computer and valuable processing time and data files is usually gained only after a secret password is entered into a computer terminal. The password is known by a select few. And, finally, when many retail establishments close for business at the end of the day, the cash that has been collected is often counted in a locked room. All of these procedures are designed to ensure that assets are adequately protected from theft and unauthorized use.

Separation of Duties

Many different functions (duties) performed within a company pertain to the firm's financial activities. These duties are frequently categorized into the following broad classes:

- Transaction authorization
- Transaction recording
- Asset custody

To explain, someone must first authorize a transaction. Later the transaction must be entered in the accounting records. And finally, because virtually all transactions immediately or eventually affect an asset, an entity must control and closely monitor its valuable resources.

To achieve the stated objectives of internal control, a business must provide for an adequate **separation of duties.** Incompatible duties, namely, authorization, recording, and custody, must be performed by different employees within an organization. Such separation helps to detect errors, since different personnel will be handling different aspects of the same transaction. In effect, then, the employees will be checking each other's work, and the likelihood that an error will proceed through a system from beginning to end is reduced.

Aside from assisting in error detection, separation of authorization, recording, and custody also makes fraud and embezzlement more difficult. As an example, suppose Rhonda Martin and Joe Harrison are both employed at the same firm. Martin physically handles the company's cash receipts, while Harrison maintains the Cash account in the accounting records. An adequate separation of duties is present in this case because physical control over the asset (i.e., custody) is segregated from transaction record keeping. Imagine, however, what could happen if Harrison was laid off and Martin, in addition to her present job, also assumed Joe's duties. If she desired, Martin could steal funds from the company and then adjust the accounting records to conceal the embezzlement. Two incompatible functions have been combined, opening the door for a variety of creative schemes.

Martin would have been less inclined to embezzle in the original situation, because Harrison would be maintaining an independent record of all transactions related to Cash and, in effect, monitoring Rhonda's actions. Of course, even if duties were separated in the appropriate manner, the theft would have still been possible had both employees conspired to defraud the company. Such a conspiracy is called *collusion*.

Accountability Procedures

A business can adopt different measures to achieve financial accountability. These measures, known as **accountability procedures,** may help to pinpoint responsibility within an organization, protect the assets, or detect errors. The measures vary and depend on the size and nature of a firm. Common accountability procedures include duty authorization, prenumbered documents, and verification of records.

Duty Authorization.   Pinpointing responsibility is essential in medium and large organizations. In small businesses, the owner/manager handles many of the accounting and financial activities. In larger entities, where the tasks are too numerous for one individual to perform, the accounting duties are divided among the various employees. Each employee is authorized to perform certain functions and, as a result, is held accountable for those functions.

Frequently, the actions taken by personnel result in some form of documentation to provide the necessary basis for accountability. Did you ever observe, for example, that store clerks often initial customer checks, sales invoices, and other similar documents? These procedures assist management in pinpointing responsibility and are especially helpful should a question or problem arise. Management can quickly determine the employee involved and then take any necessary corrective action.

Prenumbered Documents.   Important forms such as checks, sales invoices, and purchase orders are usually serially prenumbered and subsequently accounted for. This practice permits the discovery of missing documents by detecting a break in the numbering scheme. An investigation can then commence to locate the source of the problem.

Verification of Records.   Another widely used accountability procedure is verification of company records by comparison with company assets. For example:

- At the end of the day, a sales-entry terminal is emptied, and the cash collected is compared against the terminal's tape.
- At the end of the month, a business compares the amount of cash in its checkbook against a statement issued by the bank.
- At the end of the annual reporting period, a firm counts inventory and compares the actual hand count against a perpetual book count.

If the comparisons do not agree, suspicions may be raised regarding errors in the recording process or possible theft.

Independent Review

Personnel changes, the introduction of certain "shortcuts" by employees to improve job efficiency, and other similar occurrences may result in established procedures not being followed. In view of this situation, businesses should continually evaluate their accounting controls to determine if the controls are functioning as originally intended. Such evaluations are commonly made by internal auditors, who are far removed from daily activities to ensure that an independent review may be rendered.

Large companies also have a thorough examination (i.e., an audit) performed by an external CPA firm. Keep in mind that the transactions processed through a system affect an entity's financial statements. Because the external CPA must express an opinion about the fairness of the statements, an evaluation of the internal controls in operation is needed.

The results of the external CPA's examination are delivered to management for use within the firm. Given the consequences of weak control systems and the reliance placed on financial statements by various user groups, management sometimes comments publicly, in a general sense, about the organization's internal control practices. As an example, the following paragraphs were excerpted from a recent annual report of the Scott Paper Company:

> . . . the Company maintains a system of internal accounting controls which is designed to provide what are believed to be reasonable assurances that assets are safeguarded, transactions are executed in accordance with the Company's authorization and financial records are reliable as a basis for preparation of financial statements. The Company is continually modifying its system of internal accounting controls in response to changes in business conditions and operations. Support for this system is provided by the Company's internal auditors through their periodic audits of Scott's operations throughout the world. . . .
>
> The Company's Board of Directors has had an Audit Committee composed solely of outside directors since 1969. This Committee reviews the Company's accounting controls and policies as well as its practices in financial reporting to shareholders and the public. It meets on a timely basis with the internal auditors, the independent accountants and Company management to review their work and to ensure that each is properly fulfilling its responsibilities. In addition, the internal auditors and independent accountants each meet periodically with the Committee, without Company management present, to discuss the results of their audit work and related matters.

Costs and Benefits

Any business can design a system with elaborate controls, but exactly how far should companies go? Should a small firm hire several additional employees just to maintain an adequate separation of duties? Should a company perform a thorough background check and take extra security precautions for an employee who, on a part-time basis, issues cash refunds to customers? For many organizations these and related questions are difficult to answer.

When designing and installing specific internal controls, the accountant must treat each business individually, because no two entities are alike. The accountant must study the errors that can occur and the probability of occurrence. Once the probability is determined, controls must be selected for which the *benefits of use exceed the costs of implementation and operation*. If this practice is followed, an organization will have a positive and financially beneficial approach to internal control.

EXECUTIVE BRIEFING
Casinos and Internal Control

Bruce Hinckley
Vice-President and Controller
Caesars World

The internal control procedures over the cash systems in a casino are extensive, similar to those of many financial institutions. In addition to being monitored by both internal and external auditors, procedures relating to cash management, integrity of the games, and credit granting policies are evaluated by state regulators. Violating or failing to comply with proper controls can result in a loss of operating license.

Furthermore, if controls are inadequate or not being followed, theft can occur. As a recent example, one of our casinos received complaints that winning football betting tickets, which were being mailed in for redemption, were not being paid. Interestingly, an investigation found that the tickets were being cashed—in the casino's sports book area.

To isolate the problem, an employee placed bets for both teams in selected games and mailed the winning tickets along with instructions as to where the proceeds were to be sent. The automated ticket system was programmed to call security if any of these tickets were redeemed in the sports book area. It turns out that the spouse of a mail room employee was apprehended, as mail room procedures allowed both easy access to winning tickets and the destruction of any accompanying correspondence. Subsequently, additional controls were installed to prevent the irregularity from recurring.

Internal Controls in a Computerized Environment

The use of computers to process accounting data has added a new dimension to internal control. Bear in mind that data are collected, processed, and stored in ways that are not visible to the human eye. This characteristic creates problems with record and file management, hard-copy documentation of system operation, and the possibility of data alteration or destruction. Unique controls must therefore be implemented in an effort to ensure data and system integrity. Thorough studies of electronic data processing (EDP) systems and the controls incorporated therein have gained so much prominence in recent years that a new specialty area has been created within the accounting profession: EDP auditing.

Tips & Techniques

A single speck of dust or a spilled cup of coffee can easily destroy the integrity of computer files. Many users therefore regularly copy data files to a backup set of disks or tapes. The copies should be stored in a secure location—preferably offsite to prevent the original files and backups from being destroyed by the same event (e.g., a fire).

Computer Fraud

The chance of fraud is a basic problem associated with EDP systems. **Computer fraud,** which involves the use of computers to aid in and conduct a fraud or embezzlement, seems to be occurring with increased frequency and may involve significant sums of money. One study of past schemes, for instance, found that the *average* loss in cases involving corporate accounting amounted to approximately $621,000! Despite intensive research, relatively little is known about computer crime. Often, for fear of embarrassment and bad publicity, knowledge of computer-related incidents remains solely within the company involved. Furthermore, only a small portion of such crime is discovered—and it is generally found by luck or accident. One fact is fairly certain though: computer misuse is often facilitated by a lack of adequate internal control in an entity's data processing network.[6]

ETHICS ISSUE

You oversee the payroll system of a huge corporation. To improve computer security, an employee has suggested hiring as a consultant an ex–computer hacker, who was once the subject of a federal investigation into computer crime. How would you react?

END-OF-CHAPTER REVIEW

1 **Appreciate the role and importance of a good accounting system.**   The network that processes transactions and ultimately produces financial statements and other reports is known as an accounting information system. The manual system introduced in earlier chapters is acceptable, but system operation becomes cumbersome as the volume of transactions grows. To avoid costly errors, late reports, and general inefficiencies, companies must adapt and add refinements to their processing methods. These refinements include "write-it-once" systems, special journals, and computer technology.

LEARNING OBJECTIVES: THE KEY POINTS

---

[6] Computer fraud is only one of the problems that businesses must face. Sabotage of data files, employees' personal use of a company's computer resources, and thefts of hardware and software further complicate the picture.

2 Explain the relationship between control accounts and subsidiary ledgers. Control accounts appear on the financial statements and are comprised of various lower level accounts. The "lower level accounts," when taken collectively, make up the subsidiary ledger. As an example, the Accounts Receivable control account on the balance sheet is supported by customer accounts contained in the subsidiary ledger. At the end of a reporting period, the balance in the control account must equal the sum of the balances in the subsidiary ledger.

3 Recognize the features of a typical microcomputer-based accounting system. Computerized accounting systems tend to parallel manual accounting systems in terms of function and objective. Both types of systems process transactions, maintain ledger accounts, and produce financial statements. However, computerized systems preserve data on storage media such as disks; automate posting, report generation, and closing routines; and have built-in logic tests to judge transaction validity. In addition, most packages divide the accounting process into modules. Typical modules include the general ledger, accounts receivable (sales), accounts payable (purchasing), payroll, cash management, inventory, and plant and equipment. These modules are integrated to comprise the complete accounting system.

4 Describe the tasks performed by the general ledger, accounts receivable, and accounts payable modules. The various accounting modules are usually accessed via a menu that lists the options available to a user. Upon entering the general ledger module, one will discover that a broad range of tasks can be performed. In addition to being used for journal entry preparation and posting, the general ledger module also provides the tools to set up the chart of accounts and close the accounting records at the end of the period. Furthermore, this module generates numerous reports and the financial statements.

The accounts receivable and accounts payable modules are used to handle tasks related to sales and purchases transactions. The receivables module allows users to prepare invoices, sales and cash receipts journals, customer statements, and reports useful for analyzing sales and collections. Similarly, the payables module is used to produce a purchases journal, cash payments journal, checks and remittance advices, and assorted reports.

5 Explain the nature of internal control and identify various internal control procedures. Internal controls are various measures that help to safeguard a company's assets, check the reliability and accuracy of the accounting information produced, ensure compliance with management policies, and evaluate operating performance and efficiency. Such controls may take many different forms, including limiting the access to assets to a few authorized personnel, maintaining an adequate separation of duties, implementing systems of authorization and approval, having prenumbered documents, and performing verifications of company records.

**KEY TERMS
AND CONCEPTS:
A QUICK OVERVIEW**

accountability procedures Internal control procedures that help to pinpoint responsibility, protect assets, or detect errors. Include duty authorization, prenumbered documents, and verification of records.

accounting information system The network that processes transactions and generates financial statements and other reports.

accounts payable module The module in a computerized accounting system that is used to process purchases transactions and cash payments to suppliers.

accounts receivable module The module in a computerized accounting system that is used to process information related to sales and the resulting account collections.

computer fraud   A scheme in which a computer is used to aid and abet in a fraud or embezzlement.

control account   A general ledger account that is composed of various subsidiary ledger accounts.

electronic spreadsheet   Computer software that resembles a huge columnar work sheet; useful in a variety of accounting applications.

general ledger module   The module of a computerized accounting system that houses the general ledger accounts. Used to enter and post journal entries, prepare financial statements, and close the accounts.

independent review   An internal control feature that involves the review and evaluation of accounting controls by an independent external auditor.

internal control   The various measures adopted by a company to safeguard assets, check the reliability and accuracy of financial information, ensure compliance with management policies, and evaluate operating performance and efficiency.

menu   A computerized listing that shows the various program options available to a user.

separation of duties   An internal accounting control that requires separation of transaction authorization, transaction recording, and asset custody.

special journals   Journals that handle specialized (specific) types of transactions (cash receipts, sales, and so forth).

subsidiary ledger   A group of lower level accounts that comprise a general ledger account.

The five questions that follow relate to several issues raised in the chapter. Test your knowledge of the issues by selecting the best answer. (The answers appear on p. 260.)

CHAPTER QUIZ

1 The Accounts Receivable control account:
   a is found in the subsidiary ledger.
   b is found in the general ledger.
   c never appears on the balance sheet.
   d serves as the basis for preparing the schedule of accounts receivable.

2 A computerized accounting system:
   a eliminates the need for internal controls.
   b is appropriate only if a company has a large, mainframe computer.
   c tends to reduce transaction processing costs in high-volume situations.
   d often gives rise to a spreadsheet, which is a listing of program options available to a user.

3 Which of the following tasks would normally be performed by a module other than the general ledger module?
   a Printing the financial statements.
   b Maintaining the chart of accounts.
   c Processing of customer account statements.
   d Processing of closing entries.

4 Which of the following is not consistent with a strong system of internal control?
   a Transaction record keeping and asset custody are handled by the same employee.

b The accounting records are audited at year-end by an external CPA.
c At the end of the day the cash collected is compared with the tape produced by the sales-entry terminal.
d A company's computer facility has a restricted, keycard employee entry system.

5 The implementation of specific internal control procedures should be considered:
a only in manual accounting systems.
b when the accounting records are in need of verification.
c when the benefits of implementation and use exceed the related costs.
d regardless of the associated costs.

SUMMARY PROBLEM

The main menu and general ledger menu for Jupiter Company appeared in Exhibits 6-2 and 6-3, respectively. Subsequently, the chapter went on to describe the accounts receivable and accounts payable modules.

Instructions

a Use the chapter narrative and the data presented in Exhibit 6-5 to develop a menu for Jupiter's accounts receivable module.
b Why is a computerized accounting system typically divided into modules?
c Briefly explain the relationship between the Accounts Receivable control account and the Accounts Receivable subsidiary ledger.

Solution

a

JUPITER COMPANY User: David Johnson	ACCOUNTS RECEIVABLE Date: 07/14/X4
TRANSACTIONS/SALES Invoice entry Post transactions **TRANSACTIONS/RECEIPTS** Cash receipts entry Post transactions **MAINTENANCE** Customer information Return to main menu	**REPORTS** Sales invoice Sales journal Cash receipts journal Customer statement Accounts receivable ledger Analysis of receivables Analysis of sales

F1 = Help   Arrow → to select, then Enter

b Modules streamline the data-entry process. For example, recurring transactions can be input in a standardized format via a template. Such an approach saves processing time and keystrokes. Modules also facilitate the division of labor, resulting in increased efficiency because of work force specialization. This practice also allows for batch processing of similar transactions, again contributing to a more efficient work environment. Finally, modular systems are easily modified without having to overhaul the complete accounting system.

c The Accounts Receivable control account is housed in the general ledger and contains a "summary" (i.e., total) of the balances due from customers. The account's balance eventually appears on a company's balance sheet. The underlying details of the amounts in the control account are contained in the Accounts Receivable subsidiary ledger. Here, individual accounts for each customer are maintained. If all procedures are properly followed, the period-end balance in the control account should coincide with the sum of the account balances in the subsidiary ledger.

ASSIGNMENT MATERIAL

QUESTIONS

Q6-1 What is a control account and where is it found?

Q6-2 Describe how a system that relies on carbon-backed impression paper can be used to reduce processing tedium.

Q6-3 What are some of the benefits of using a computerized accounting system?

Q6-4 What are some of the similarities and differences between manual accounting systems and computerized accounting systems?

Q6-5 Explain the concept of modular accounting systems. Briefly discuss several of the benefits associated with the use of modules.

Q6-6 How are modules accessed in a computerized accounting system?

Q6-7 Previously entered transactions can be edited in a variety of ways. Briefly describe some of the options that different programs may offer.

Q6-8 In a computerized environment, why must the financial statements be prepared prior to closing the accounting records?

Q6-9 What is a customer statement? What information does the statement disclose?

Q6-10 Briefly explain the meaning of internal control.

Q6-11 In general, which accounting functions should be separated because of a lack of compatibility?

Q6-12 What benefits are provided by an adequate separation of duties?

Q6-13 What is the purpose behind the serial prenumbering of important documents?

Q6-14 List several common procedures that are performed to help ensure that company accounting records are in agreement with company assets.

Q6-15 What is the purpose of the independent review, as performed by an external CPA?

Q6-16 What ultimate guideline should be used to decide the specific controls to build into a system?

Q6-17 Briefly list several of the unique control problems associated with computerized accounting applications.

EXERCISES

E6-1 *Control accounts and subsidiary ledgers* (L.O. 2)

Franklin Manufacturing maintains a subsidiary ledger of the amounts owed to individual suppliers. A review of the accounting records at the end of March revealed the following balances:

Interstate Supply	$5,800
Lincoln Corporation	1,900
Rogers & Hart	2,200

a Prepare the proper disclosure of this information on the company's March 31 balance sheet.

b Would the subsidiary ledger ordinarily serve as the source for the answer to part (a)? Explain.

c What procedure would Franklin probably follow to help ensure that the subsidiary ledger balances are relatively error-free?

d Suppose that on April 10, Franklin paid Lincoln $1,200 on account. Briefly describe what Franklin must do to keep the accounting records in balance.

E6-2 *Overview of microcomputers* (L.O. 3, 4)

Western Art Works uses a manual accounting system. The company has grown over the years, and Western is finding that the increase in volume is taxing the capacity of its system and employees. Patricia Green, the firm's CPA, has recommended the acquisition of a microcomputer to ease the record-keeping burden.

a What benefits might Western experience by acquiring a microcomputer?

b Green told management that aside from processing daily transactions, the computer could also be used in conjunction with an electronic spread-sheet. Briefly explain what a spreadsheet is and how it can be used by managers.

E6-3 *Analysis of computer output* (L.O. 3)

Lucky-K Stores recently installed a computerized accounting software package. The company's banker immediately noticed the computer-generated appearance of the monthly financial statements and asked whether the statements would differ if manual procedures had continued in use.

a Should the manner in which accounting data are gathered and compiled have any significant effect on the firm's financial statements? Briefly explain.

b Assume that the monthly financial statements included many additional schedules and reports because of the ease with which the computer generated this information. Do you see any potential problems with this "feature" of computerized accounting systems? Briefly discuss.

E6-4 *System modules and their use* (L.O. 4)

Shine Your Light Candle Store uses a computerized accounting system identical to that described in the text. The system consists of a general ledger module, accounts receivable module, and accounts payable module. Identify the module that should be used to record the following transactions or accomplish the stated tasks:

a Acquired wicks and wax on account from Wax World.

b Sold candles on account to Sally Conte.

c Prepared the month-end account statement for Joseph Lawyer, a regular customer.

d Borrowed cash from the First Interstate Bank.

e Prepared the month-end financial statements.

f Closed the accounting records at the end of May.

g Collected cash on account from Susan Davis, a customer.

h Generated a detailed listing of the amounts owed to individual suppliers.

E6-5 *Overview of systems concepts* **(L.O. 2, 3, 4)**
Evaluate the comments that follow as being True or False. If the comment is false, briefly explain why.

a A subsidiary ledger is nothing more than a detailed breakdown of a general ledger control account.

b If all procedures are properly performed, the end-of-period balance in a control account should equal the sum of the individual account balances contained in the subsidiary ledger.

c As its name implies, the sole purpose of a typical general ledger module is to house the general ledger accounts.

d To enter a journal entry, most software packages require the user to key in the full and correct account name.

e When a user enters sales transactions in the accounts receivable module, the software is likely to capture information that can be used to prepare invoices and customer statements.

E6-6 *Internal control weaknesses* **(L.O. 5)**
Sarah Stender recently opened a small jewelry store in a major shopping district. Because the business is new, Sarah could afford to hire only one employee. Marci Hopson, an accounting student from the local university, applied and got the job.

When Marci comes to work in the afternoons, Sarah usually leaves the store to run errands and take care of other business. If there are no customers, Marci updates the firm's manual accounting system and also tags jewelry in the back room. Because of this latter procedure, arriving customers may go unnoticed for a minute or two. At the end of each day, Marci verifies that the cash collected matches the amount reported on the store's sales-entry terminal. She then places the receipts in Sarah's desk, and Sarah deposits the receipts at the bank on the next business day.

Comment on any weaknesses in the jewelry store's system.

E6-7 *Internal control weaknesses* **(L.O. 5)**
Multiple Charities conducts a large door-to-door fund-raising campaign each year to assist local charitable organizations. Contributions in the form of cash and checks are received by volunteer workers who, in turn, issue an official Multiple Charities' receipt. The fund-raising campaign lasts one week.

This year the officers of Theta Theta Beta fraternity have pledged the services of the entire membership to canvass the homes in Mountain Way, a small college town located approximately 100 miles from the headquarters of Multiple Charities. On Thursday afternoon of the campaign, the brothers of Theta Theta Beta ran out of official Multiple Charities' receipts. Because it was too late to obtain an additional supply, the fraternity's treasurer designed the following form and had it printed on the chapter's copying machine. The form would be given to each contributor.

Multiple Charities

Date _____

Contributor _____

Amount Received _____

Theta Theta Beta

After dinner on Thursday, each member grabbed a handful of the forms for use in Friday's collections.

Discuss this system in terms of internal control. Does the system ensure that all contributions collected by Theta Theta Beta will be submitted to Multiple Charities? Why?

E6-8 *Separation of duties* (L.O. 5)

An important aspect of internal control is separation of duties.

a Briefly explain what is meant in accounting by "an adequate separation of duties."

b Determine whether an adequate separation of duties is present in the following cases. If the separation is adequate, label it as such. If it is inadequate, briefly state why.

(1) The warehouse foreman updates the accounting records for merchandise received.

(2) An employee who handles customer receipts also proves the equality of the balance in the Cash account with the cash balance as reported by the bank (i.e., prepares a bank reconciliation).

(3) An employee who approves customer credit also supervises the payment of supplier invoices.

PROBLEMS

Series A

P6-A1 *Subsidiary ledger/control account relationships* (L.O. 2)

Haskell Company maintains subsidiary ledger information for both accounts receivable and accounts payable. The general ledger control accounts revealed the following balances as of December 31, 19X2:

Accounts receivable	$19,900
Accounts payable	18,300

Haskell's trial balance was out of balance on this date, with total credits exceeding total debits by $2,500. The individual subsidiary ledgers revealed the following amounts due/owed:

Accounts Receivable		Accounts Payable	
Cato	$6,120	Bluebonnet	$4,000
Green	8,450	Casson	7,500
Honroe	2,500	Jackson	5,200
Jones	4,330	Moore	2,600

The additional facts below are known:
1 A $2,500 sale to Honroe occurred on the last day of the year, and the bookkeeper, in haste, forgot to post the debit to the appropriate control account.
2 Cato's subsidiary ledger account was not updated for a $1,000 sale.
3 A monthly statement received from Casson revealed a balance due of only $6,500.

Instructions

a Determine the total of the account balances in each of the subsidiary ledgers prior to any corrections.
b Evaluate the facts concerning the accounts of Cato and Casson. What appears to have happened?
c Determine the correct balance in the company's Accounts Receivable control account. Also compute the total of the corrected balances in the Accounts Receivable subsidiary ledger.
d Prepare the proper balance sheet disclosure for Haskell's accounts payable.

P6-A2 *Computerized systems; modules* (L.O. 3, 4)

Mirage Auto Paint and Body has grown rapidly and is considering the implementation of a computerized accounting system. Most services are provided on account, with an insurance company usually paying the bill. Repair parts and paint are supplied by a number of vendors, each of whom extends credit for as long as 60 days. Most other expenditures are related to purchases of equipment, payment of operating expenses, and other customary costs associated with running a small business. Mirage's bookkeeper has a reasonable understanding of accounting concepts and has maintained a manual accounting system for the past several years.

The bookkeeper has reviewed popular accounting software packages and has concluded that none are ideally suited to the company's particular needs. The owner of Mirage is willing to hire a computer consultant to develop a specialized program, and conversations with the consultant have recently begun. Thus far, the bookkeeper and consultant have agreed on the function and appearance of the main menu, general ledger module, and journal entry routine. These elements will be identical to those that appeared in the text. The appearance and functions of the accounts receivable and accounts payable modules are not yet decided.

Instructions

a What may have triggered the company's interest in a computerized accounting system?
b Prepare a list of all documents and reports that the accounts receivable and accounts payable modules should be capable of generating.
c Assume the role of the consultant and design a menu for the accounts payable module.

P6-A3 *Using a computerized general ledger* (L.O. 4)

Tri Cities Automotive, formed on January 1, 19X3, had the following transactions during the first month of activity:

Jan. 1 Received $25,000 cash from Buddy Hawkins, the owner, as an investment in the business.
  1 Acquired $6,000 of equipment, financed by a loan that bears interest at the rate of 1% per month. This loan is due in nine months.

9   Purchased $400 of supplies for cash.
12   Received $3,250 cash from a client for services rendered.
15   Paid $75 for January insurance.
23   Paid $250 for January rent.
26   Received $550 cash from a client for services rendered.
31   Received the January electric bill of $133, to be paid in February.

The company's accountant noted that adjusting entries were needed for accrued interest ($60), supplies used during the month ($150), and equipment depreciation ($100). Selected accounts (and account numbers) for Tri Cities follow.

Cash	100	Buddy Hawkins, drawing	310
Supplies	110	Service revenue	400
Equipment	120	Supplies expense	500
Accumulated depreciation	121	Insurance expense	510
Utilities payable	200	Rent expense	520
Loan payable	210	Utilities expense	530
Interest payable	220	Depreciation expense	540
Buddy Hawkins, capital	300	Interest expense	550

Instructions

Obtain a copy of the VTL accounting software that accompanies this text. Using the software's general ledger module:
a Enter Tri Cities' transactions and adjusting entries for the month.
b Post the transactions and adjusting entries to the general ledger.
c Prepare a printed listing of the journal entries and general ledger, an adjusted trial balance, and the financial statements.

P6-A4 *Internal control evaluation* (L.O. 5)

Assume that at a recent luncheon meeting, you overheard the following comments made by a group of executives sitting at the next table:
a There's no reason why a person who handles cash payments cannot also maintain the record keeping for purchases and the Accounts Payable subsidiary ledger.
b We have many internal control procedures and can therefore overlook top management's carefree attitude and sometimes irresponsible decision making.
c The design of a perfect internal control system that detects and prevents all dishonest employee actions is really possible. Top management just won't pay for it.
d Dave handles both the Accounts Receivable *and* the Accounts Payable subsidiary ledgers.
e Every week, our store managers compare the cash collected against computer runs from the sales-entry terminal.
f We save money each year by handling the evaluation of internal control ourselves. The company's internal audit department is efficient and highly competent.
g Granted, separation of duties does help to make embezzlement more difficult. I don't believe, however, that it reduces the chance for the introduction of accidental errors when processing data.

Instructions

Evaluate each of the preceding statements in terms of adequacy and/or understanding of internal control. If internal control is either lacking or misunderstood, briefly tell why.

P6-A5 *Internal control weaknesses* (L.O. 5)

The Reno Wildcats, a minor league baseball team, play at Wildcat Stadium and attract approximately 2,500 people per game. The stadium is small and antiquated, having only one entrance, one ticket booth, and no turnstiles.

All tickets are sold on the day of a game; there are no season ticket holders. Fans buy either bleacher seats for $3 or reserved seats for $4. All tickets are serially prenumbered and are sold by two cashiers located in a ticket booth outside the stadium's entrance. On entering the stadium, a fan must give a ticket to a ticket taker, who tears it in half. Half the ticket is returned to the customer to save as a rain check; the other half is tossed into a cardboard box. An exception to this procedure occurs when the Wildcats have special promotion nights (e.g., bat night). Admission for most of the attendees on these occasions is via a discount coupon in the local newspapers. In this case the coupon is shown at the ticket booth and cash is collected; however, no ticket is issued. The coupon is later surrendered and placed in the box with the ticket stubs.

The ticket operation is closed at the beginning of the fifth inning, and the contents of the cardboard box are thrown in the trash. One of the cashiers (the team's bookkeeper) counts the cash, enters the game's revenues in the accounting records, and places the receipts in his desk to await deposit the next day at the bank. The bookkeeper is known for his accuracy and attention to detail. At the end of the baseball season, for example, he performs a thorough review (i.e., audit) of the team's records to ensure proper accounting of all gate receipts.

Instructions

Identify the control weaknesses in the Wildcats' system. Explain why the items cited are weaknesses.

Series B

P6-B1 *Subsidiary ledger/control account relationships* (L.O. 2)

Abilene Company maintains subsidiary ledger information for both accounts receivable and accounts payable. The general ledger control accounts revealed the following balances as of December 31, 19X5:

Accounts receivable	$10,900
Accounts payable	12,300

Abilene's trial balance was out of balance on this date, with total debits exceeding total credits by $900. The individual subsidiary ledgers revealed the following amounts due/owed:

Accounts Receivable		Accounts Payable	
Bledsoe	$1,220	Crenshaw	$ 900
Condra	5,640	Cromer	4,350
Davis	2,450	David	2,730
Samuels	2,290	Venus	4,520

The additional facts below are known:

1 David's subsidiary ledger account was not updated for a $700 purchase.
2 A $900 purchase from Crenshaw occurred on the last day of the year, and the bookkeeper, in haste, forgot to post the credit to the appropriate control account.
3 Davis complained that his monthly statement should have revealed the following: opening balance, $0; sales (i.e., purchases) on account, $3,950;

payments on account, $2,200. A review of the accounting records found that the statement was, indeed, in error.

Instructions

a Determine the total of the account balances in each of the subsidiary ledgers prior to any corrections.
b Evaluate the facts concerning the accounts of David and Davis. What appears to have happened?
c Determine the correct balance in the company's Accounts Payable control account. Also compute the total of the corrected balances in the Accounts Payable subsidiary ledger.
d Is a monthly account statement more easily generated by using information contained in the subsidiary ledger or the control account? Briefly explain.

P6-B2 *Computerized systems; modules* **(L.O. 3, 4)**

Banner Billboard constructs highway signs throughout Texas. The company is owned by Henry Lee Harrison, who is 62 years old and close to retirement. Banner has maintained a manual accounting system for many years; however, various transaction processing problems have arisen recently and have started to cut into the firm's profitability. Given this situation and Harrison's desire for more timely, detailed operating information, a new computerized system is being considered. A consultant has recommended the use of modules to integrate flexibility and efficiency into the design, with the initial system consisting of a general ledger module, an accounts receivable module, and an accounts payable module.

Instructions

a What types of transaction processing problems may the firm be experiencing? Briefly describe.
b Harrison's bookkeeping staff is familiar with a general ledger but not a general ledger module. Prepare a description of the module's functions.
c Assume the role of the consultant and design a menu for the accounts payable module.
d Consider Harrison's age, probable computer expertise, and attitude about computers. Would you recommend the installation of a computerized system or would Banner be better off continuing with its manual procedures? Explain.

P6-B3 *Using a computerized general ledger* **(L.O. 4)**

Express Boat Repair, formed on January 1, 19X5, had the following transactions during the first month of activity:

Jan. 1 Received $15,000 cash from Keith Price, the owner, as an investment in the business.
      1 Acquired $9,000 of machinery. Paid $4,000 down and financed the remaining balance by a loan that bears interest at the rate of 1% per month. The loan is due in 10 months.
      7 Received $4,200 cash from a client for services rendered.
     12 Paid $900 for January advertising.
     16 Purchased $500 of office supplies for cash.
     21 Paid $950 for January rent.
     26 Received $650 cash from a client for services rendered.
     31 Received the January electric bill of $345, to be paid in February.

The company's accountant noted that adjusting entries were needed for accrued interest ($50), machinery depreciation ($125), and office supplies that remained on hand at month-end ($90). Selected accounts (and account numbers) for Express follow.

Cash	101	Keith Price, drawing	320
Office supplies	120	Service revenue	410
Machinery	130	Office supplies expense	500
Accumulated depreciation	131	Advertising expense	510
Utilities payable	200	Utilities expense	520
Interest payable	210	Rent expense	530
Loan payable	220	Depreciation expense	540
Keith Price, capital	310	Interest expense	550

Instructions

Obtain a copy of the VTL accounting software that accompanies this text. Using the software's general ledger module:

a Enter Express Boat Repair's transactions and adjusting entries for the month.

b Post the transactions and adjusting entries to the general ledger.

c Prepare a printed listing of the journal entries and general ledger, an adjusted trial balance, and the financial statements.

P6-B4 *Internal control evaluation* (L.O. 5)

Assume that at a recent luncheon meeting, you overheard the following comments made by a group of executives sitting at the next table. From the tone of the conversation you have determined that the executives are directors of the Drake County Stadium.

a The staff person who handles the Accounts Payable subsidiary ledger also maintains the record keeping for cash payments.

b Our recent cost-cutting moves have improved profitability. Patrons now pay the appropriate amounts to the cashier, who grants direct entry into the stadium. The elimination of ticket takers (and tickets) has led to reduced lines and faster admittance.

c Personally, I don't agree with the county's policy of having Coopers and Young, the local CPA firm, perform an annual review of our accounting procedures. Susan Randolph at the county office has been helping us for years; she thoroughly knows and understands our system and operating problems.

d Michael Dalby, our treasurer, has just been given new responsibilities. He now handles and deposits cash receipts, issues checks, and maintains all cash payments records.

e It is essential that our new data processing system provide for an adequate audit trail (i.e., the ability to trace and access accounting information). Although the benefits of doing so are marginal at best, we will be in compliance with the provisions of the Drake County systems handbook.

f Office employees should continue to initial the important documents and contracts that they have reviewed, prior to submission to the accounting and legal departments.

g To further consolidate operations, we should combine the positions of supplies receiving clerk and supplies accounting clerk. Greater efficiency will result.

Instructions

Evaluate each of the preceding statements in terms of adequacy and/or understanding of internal control. If internal control is either lacking or misunderstood, briefly tell why.

P6-B5 *Internal control weaknesses* (L.O. 5)

Jimmy's is a small neighborhood restaurant famous for its southern dinners and ice-cold beverages. The restaurant has been open for 45 years, and the present owner, a grandson of the founder, still operates just as his grandfather did.

Patrons come in the front door and seat themselves. Sometimes the single-room restaurant gets quite crowded, and patrons stand around chatting by the door while waiting for a table. Waiters usually bring them beverages and refills to make the wait more bearable.

Most of the waiters employed by Jimmy's are local college students with pleasant personalities. The waiters are instructed to be friendly and to treat the customers like family members. To maintain this congenial atmosphere, no order pads are used, and customer orders are memorized. When patrons are finished with their meals, they wait at the register for their server. The server rings up the order on a cash register (grandfather's original) and makes change. The cash register, because of its age, lacks an operator identification key.

Jimmy's does not honor credit cards, but personal checks are accepted without question. The owner pays the waiters from the register at the end of the night and then deposits the remainder of the receipts on his way home.

Instructions

a Identify the internal control weaknesses in Jimmy's system. Explain why the items cited are weaknesses.

b Suggest methods to improve the weaknesses that you found.

BEYOND THE BASICS

BB6-1 *Overview of chapter concepts: Multiple choice* (L.O. 1–5)

The following multiple-choice questions relate to various topics discussed in the chapter. Select the best answer.

1 Subsidiary accounts receivable ledgers provide detailed transaction information needed to:

a prove that the total of a company's accounts receivable control account equals the balance in the subsidiary ledger.

b identify, in one figure, the total amount due a company from its customers.

c generate customer account statements.

d list, on the balance sheet, the amounts due from each customer.

2 Which of the following does not reduce the amount of record keeping associated with transaction processing?

a Accounting software.   c "Write-it-once" systems.

b Subsidiary ledgers.   d Special journals.

3 Most accounting software divides the accounting process into specific modules. Normally, which of the following would not be considered a separate module?

a General journal.   c Accounts receivable.

b General ledger.   d Payroll.

4 Which of the following is a frequently cited advantage of dividing a computerized accounting system into separate modules?

a Reduction in errors.

b Reduction in staffing.

  c Reduction in required computer equipment.

  d Reduction in data-entry and transaction processing time.

5 A menu is best defined as:

  a a listing on the computer screen of the various program options available to a user.

  b a superimposed listing of the chart of accounts.

  c a module, or processing unit.

  d a listing of the printed output capable of being produced by a particular computer program.

6 The accounts receivable module can be used to produce:

  a customer checks.   c the cash payments journal.

  b monthly statements.   d remittance advices.

7 Controls are often designed in the accounts payable module that help to:

  a prevent paying the same invoice twice.

  b determine that equipment purchases are being properly depreciated.

  c ensure that account statements are generated on a timely basis.

  d pinpoint journal entries that have been omitted.

8 Which of the following would generally lessen the degree of internal control afforded a company?

  a Combining the duties of transaction recording and asset custody.

  b Implementing the use of serially prenumbered documents.

  c Limiting the access to assets.

  d Allowing financial information to be reviewed by an independent accountant.

CAI6-1 *A lesson in editing: United Technologies Corporation* (L.O. 5)

COMMUNICATION OF ACCOUNTING INFORMATION

Communication Principle: Accounting communications often contain long sentences and paragraphs as well as long words and abstract concepts. All of these qualities make comprehension difficult, especially for readers who are nonaccountants.

  How can we edit typical accounting writing so that it is more easily understood? First, break up long sentences and paragraphs into shorter units. Vary sentence length and aim at an average length of 18 words. Next, check your choice of terms for unnecessarily long words or words with endings such as "tion," "ity," and "ance." These suffixes often turn verbs into abstract nouns and make reading more difficult. In general, words with three or more syllables lead to increased problems for readers.

  Finally, make the writing parallel natural speaking patterns by adding personal pronouns. For instance, use the personal "we" instead of the impersonal "it" when referring to the organization or company. Before rewriting, read aloud a long, abstract, formal description to see "how it sounds." This effort will help you translate abstractions into concrete, easy-to-understand explanations.

  Much of the writing in accounting is complicated because of long sentences, word choice, and an overly formal and impersonal tone. You can make a big difference in reading ease and comprehension by changing the style into something more natural and direct. Your reader will be very appreciative of your labors.

■ ■ ■ ■ ■ ■ ■

  United Technologies Corporation (UTC) provides systems, products, and services to customers in the aerospace, defense, building, and automotive industries. The following entities are among the company's holdings: Pratt & Whitney (jet engines), Sikorsky (helicopters), Carrier (air conditioning equipment), and Otis (elevators).

UTC's annual report parallels annual reports of most other companies by containing a "standardized" statement regarding internal control. A portion of that statement follows.

> Management is responsible for the integrity and objectivity of the financial statements, including estimates and judgments reflected in them. It fulfills this responsibility primarily by establishing and maintaining accounting systems and practices adequately supported by internal accounting controls. These controls include the selection and training of management and supervisory personnel; an organization structure providing for delegation of authority and establishment of responsibilities; communication of requirements for compliance with approved accounting, control and business practices throughout the organization; business planning and review; and a program of internal audit. Management believes the internal accounting controls in use provide reasonable assurance that the Corporation's assets are safeguarded, that transactions are executed in accordance with management's authorizations, and that the financial records are reliable for the purpose of preparing financial statements.

Instructions

Assume that you have been hired to make UTC's annual report more "user friendly." Redraft the internal control statement to be more understandable to someone with little or no accounting background. (*Note:* Feel free to integrate additional internal control insights based on the text's discussion of the topic.)

Answers to Chapter Quiz

1 b
2 c
3 c
4 a
5 c

CHAPTER 7

Cash and Short-Term Investments

LEARNING OBJECTIVES

After studying this chapter, you should be able to:

1

Describe the composition of cash and explain
how cash is presented on a balance sheet.

2

Explain cash management and identify the controls and
procedures related to cash receipts and disbursements.

3

Reconcile a bank account.

4

Establish and operate a petty cash system.

5

Explain the features of a voucher system.

6

Account for short-term investments under the historical-
cost and lower-of-cost-or-market methods.

Financial statements provide a variety of information for decision making. The balance sheet, for example, is used to study relationships between the resources owned by a business and the amounts owed to creditors. Two balance sheet accounts of key interest to a number of parties are *cash* and *short-term investments*.

Cash and short-term investments are the most liquid of the current assets. Lenders, creditors, and prospective suppliers therefore compare the amounts of these assets with current liabilities when judging a firm's debt-paying ability. Investors review the cash and short-term investments of a business to gauge the funds available for dividend distributions as well as for medium- and long-term projects that are important to future profitability. Even employees are interested in cash and short-term investments, because salary increases are sometimes tied to the funds available and the balances in these two accounts. It is imperative, then, that cash and short-term investments be properly accounted for and presented in the financial statements.

CASH

OBJECTIVE

1

Describe the composition of cash and explain how cash is presented on a balance sheet.

The items reported in the Cash account on the balance sheet must be (1) acceptable to a bank for deposit and (2) free from restriction for use in satisfying current debts. **Cash** therefore includes *coins, currency, funds on deposit with a bank (checking accounts and savings accounts), checks, and money orders.* The following items are not considered to be cash for accounting purposes: certificates of deposit, postdated checks, IOUs, travel advances, and postage stamps.

1 *Certificates of deposit*—Sometimes called CDs, these are securities issued by banks that allow the investment of cash for short periods of time (six months, one year, and so forth). CDs pay a guaranteed interest rate and often contain penalty provisions should the purchaser decide to convert the securities to cash before their due date. Certificates of deposit are not considered to be cash but instead are classified as short-term investments.

2 *Postdated checks*—Postdated checks are checks that become payable on a date subsequent to the issue date. For example, suppose Buck Company issued a check to Foy Company on April 15. Buck dated the check April 22, because it lacked sufficient funds on the date of issuance. Since Foy cannot cash or deposit the check until the 22nd, the postdated check is not classified as cash. Postdated checks are receivables until the date they can be deposited.

3 *IOUs*—IOUs are written acknowledgments of debts; however, these items are not negotiable and usually cannot be used to pay off liabilities. IOUs are therefore considered to be receivables until the time of collection.

4 *Travel advances*—These amounts have been given to employees to cover out-of-pocket expenses incurred on business trips. The employees must either provide receipts for monies spent or return any unspent funds. As a result, travel advances are normally disclosed as receivables on the balance sheet.

5 *Postage stamps*—Postage stamps are usually classified as supplies or prepaid expenses.

Balance Sheet Presentation

The Cash account is listed on the balance sheet in the current asset section. For concise reporting, all cash items are normally combined and presented as a single figure.

As we noted earlier, the amount reported for cash must be available for use in satisfying current debts. Sometimes, businesses establish restricted funds to accumulate cash for specific purposes. As an example, a special fund may be created to repay money borrowed (often termed a *sinking fund*) or to expand a manufacturing plant. These funds should not be classified as current assets on the balance sheet because they are not available to settle current obligations. Likewise, amounts held in foreign banks should not be reported as current assets if governmental regulations restrict the transfer of funds out of the foreign country.

Occasionally, a bank may require that a portion of the amount lent to customers remain on deposit in the bank for the duration of the loan period. These required deposits are termed **compensating balances.** The existence of compensating balances should be fully disclosed so that financial statement users are made aware of restrictions on the funds availability.

Cash Management

Effective cash management is important to the success of any company. Care must be taken to ensure that sufficient cash is available to meet current obligations but that unnecessarily large cash balances do not remain in checking accounts. Such balances typically earn little or no interest and therefore represent a loss of earnings potential. In view of this situation, excess funds should be invested in short-term securities to earn higher rates of return or be used for new programs and projects.

The amount of cash held for daily operations varies among businesses. Consider the information that appeared in recent financial statements of Wendy's International, Maytag Corporation, and Gerber Products, as presented in Exhibit 7-1.

Wendy's major line of business is the operation of fast-food restaurants. The company's balances in cash and short-term investments (i.e., securities easily converted into cash should the need arise) constitute 76.7% of total current assets. For the other two entities, the situation is entirely different. These firms stock significant inventories for production and sale and must carry large amounts of customer receivables. As a result, combined cash and securities totals for Maytag and Gerber are substantially lower: 4.5% and 29.2%, respectively.

> **OBJECTIVE**
> **2**
> Explain cash management and identify the controls and procedures related to cash receipts and disbursements.

Cash Planning

The management of cash is subdivided into cash planning and cash control. **Cash planning systems** consist of those procedures adopted to ensure that adequate funds are available to meet normal business obligations and that any excess cash is invested. A major component of cash planning systems is the **cash budget**—an overall plan of activity that depicts cash inflows and outflows for a stated period of time. The cash budget is a very useful tool in the management of any organization, because it pinpoints

	Wendy's International		Maytag Corporation		Gerber Products	
	$	%*	$	%*	$	%*
Cash	$ 12,004	6.8%	$ 48,752	4.5%	$ 99,195	22.4%
Short-term investments	122,731	69.9	—	—	29,892	6.8
Receivables	23,049	13.1	457,773	42.5	120,960	27.4
Inventories	16,070	9.2	489,082	45.5	191,823	43.4
Prepaid expenses & other	1,829	1.0	81,026	7.5	—	—
	$175,683	100.0%	$1,076,633	100.0%	$441,870	100.0%

* Percentages calculated by the authors.

EXHIBIT 7-1
Current Asset Composition of Wendy's International, Maytag Corporation, and Gerber Products (in thousands)

when cash surpluses and shortages are likely to occur. Predicting surpluses and shortages before they take place enables a business to analyze potential high-return investments and locate low-cost sources of funds. Investment and financing decisions are thereby improved.

Cash Control

Cash control systems are the procedures adopted to safeguard an organization's funds. These systems establish adequate internal control over cash. Recall that internal control aids a company in safeguarding its assets, checking the reliability and accuracy of accounting information, promoting operational efficiency, and encouraging adherence to prescribed managerial policies. A strong cash control system is essential, given that employees and others regard cash as a very desirable asset. In addition, cash is difficult to trace because it has no readily identifiable means to establish ownership. Although currency does have serial numbers, companies make no attempt to record these numbers in view of the overwhelming amount of bookkeeping that would be required.

Internal Control for Cash. The internal control system for cash is based on the general internal control features discussed in Chapter 6. An organization should limit the access to cash to a few authorized personnel only. Furthermore, incompatible duties such as the authorization of cash transactions, the entry of cash transactions in the accounting records, and the custody of cash should be separated. Finally, the following accountability procedures should be implemented: prenumbered checks, verification of invoices prior to payment, and verification of the cash balance as reported in the general ledger. These general control features become apparent when studying typical accounting procedures for cash receipts and cash disbursements.

Receipts from Cash Sales. The control of cash receipts attempts to ensure that all cash inflows are safeguarded from the time they are received by a

HIGHLIGHT

The Height of Cash Management: The Barter System

Many different methods are available to businesses for effective cash management. A review of these methods will find one being used with increased frequency, especially by small companies. In today's high-tech, fast-paced world, that method is . . . bartering? Yes, this stone-age approach to trade is being used by cash-hungry firms that practice cash conservation by swapping—instead of buying—everything from dental work to diesel trucks.

Bartering offers companies a way to increase sales, move surplus inventory, and make use of excess capacity—all priorities in a downturn. Much of this trade occurs on organized barter exchanges, where firms pay a membership fee and accumulate "trade dollars," or credits, in return for products and services offered. Using those trade dollars, firms can then purchase goods or services offered by any other exchange members.

As an example of how this works, a Chicago-based furrier found customers for its luxury fur coats during an economic slump. In an 11-month period it bartered about $100,000 in furs. Noted the president, "I can get what I want without actually paying cash. . . . It's the only way to go when times get rough." With some of the trade dollars acquired, the president bought five 60-second spots a day for two weeks on a local radio station. Television spots also ran on hotel TV and cable.

In another case, a Connecticut wholesaler found that a customer who owed $35,000 was facing bankruptcy. "There was no way I was going to collect from the guy," the president recalls thinking. But instead of throwing in the towel, he accepted as payment $35,000 worth of baseball cards. The wholesaler then sold the cards to a local barter exchange for $35,000 of trade credits. With $10,000 of those credits, the company bought concert tickets, which it turned around and sold for cash.

While most firms barter 10% or less of their inventory, some companies use the procedure much more. A Michigan firm, which sells custom office furniture, belongs to two barter exchanges. Nearly one-third of the entity's buying and selling involves barter. In recent years the company has bartered its office furnishings to pay for printing services, maintenance work on delivery trucks, and repairs on a leaky roof. Even the company's Christmas party was catered with trade dollars.

Bartering, naturally, is not a cure-all for cash-strapped companies. Depending on the exchange, clients may be limited in their choice of products and services. And there's a danger if firms don't recognize the cash cost of a trade dollar. Businesses must still pay taxes on all sales—as if cash were received in return. The tax bill can be quite a shock.

Many say the 1984 Olympic Games helped improve the image of bartering. In one of the larger-scale examples of such trade, the Los Angeles Olympic Organizing Committee swapped the licensing rights of the Olympic logo and mascot, "Sam the Olympic Eagle," to major corporations. In return, the committee received free transportation from United Airlines, the use of 500 Buick cars from General Motors, and 250,000 rolls of film, plus processing, from Fuji Film.

Although bartering is still alien to many firms, it's clearly gaining in popularity. "Many small companies don't understand bartering because they haven't used it," says a spokeswoman of the Chicago Barter Corp. trade exchange. "But as more companies hit hard times, they'll be more open to [the idea]."

company until they are deposited in a bank account. A major source of cash inflows for many firms is cash sales. Control over cash sales is facilitated by the use of an electronic point-of-sale terminal, which requires that a salesperson record each sale in full view of the customer and provide the customer with a receipt. As the clerk enters the transaction information, the sale is simultaneously recorded on a paper tape. At the end of the business day, a store manager compares the cash collected with the total cash sales listed on the tape. The tapes are then forwarded to the accounting department and entered in the company's records. The cash is kept in a vault until deposited in the bank or picked up by an armored car service such as Brink's or Loomis.

Cash sale transactions often give rise to errors. Because of mistakes in giving change, for example, the actual cash on hand may differ slightly from the total indicated sales. If these errors are frequent, significant in amount, or traceable to the same employee, personnel adjustments may be necessary.

The accounting treatment for cash excesses and deficiencies is relatively simple. To illustrate, assume that cash sales for the Eldridge Shop on July 7 amounted to $1,247. However, cash in the terminal's drawer was only $1,237. The following entry is necessary:

Cash	1,237	
Cash Short & Over	10	
Sales		1,247
To record cash sales and cash shortage		

In contrast to the preceding entry, the Cash Short & Over account would be credited when cash in the terminal exceeds the amount of cash sales recorded. At the end of a reporting period, the net balance in Cash Short & Over is calculated. A net debit balance would be disclosed on the income statement with other miscellaneous expenses of the business, while a net credit balance is treated as miscellaneous revenue.

Receipts from Customers on Account.   Many organizations generate large inflows of cash from customer receipts on account. These inflows usually arrive in the mail, requiring a careful separation of duties. The following procedures are normally employed:

1 The daily counting of cash receipts is assigned to one person or, in large businesses, to a group of specific personnel. The personnel open the mail, prepare a list of checks received, and forward the list to the accounting department.

2 The checks are forwarded to a cashier, who prepares a deposit slip and deposits all receipts intact on a *daily* basis. Daily deposits prevent bills from being paid out of current receipts; they also minimize the amount of cash left on the premises at the end of the business day, thus reducing the possibility of large losses from theft. A duplicate deposit slip is then sent to the accounting department.

3 The accounting department compares the list of cash receipts with the deposit slip and enters the daily mail-in receipts in the accounting records. Naturally, any discrepancies between the deposit slip and the list of receipts require investigation.

Cash Disbursements. The control over disbursements includes procedures that will allow only authorized payments for actual company expenditures. A cash disbursements system with proper internal control should include the following features:

1 All significant disbursements are made by check so that a record (i.e., written evidence) exists for expenditures.

2 An organization's Cash account in the general ledger is periodically compared with the cash balance reported by the bank.

3 Certain small payments are made by using a *petty cash system.* (The operation of a petty cash system will be explained later in this chapter.)

4 Before a disbursement is made from a company's checking account or petty cash system, the expenditure is verified and approved. Verification may take the form of examining purchase orders, invoices, and receiving reports.

These procedures, like so many others, are aided by a proper separation of duties. For example, the person signing the checks should not be the same individual who prepares the checks. In addition, the comparison of a

EXECUTIVE BRIEFING
Cash Controls: McDonald's Experience

Karen Page
Director of Audit
McDonald's Corporation

There's an old saying, A sale is not a sale until the cash is in the bank. From an auditor's perspective that is so true, despite the accrual accounting concept of recognizing revenues when they are earned. At McDonald's, nearly all of our worldwide sales (about $20 billion from over 12,000 restaurants in a recent year) are in the form of cash given to an employee working a point-of-sale terminal. Cash is our most vulnerable asset, so we must have a strong system of internal controls to ensure that cash gets to the bank and not into a crewperson's or manager's pocket.

The terminal creates an audit trail of sales, sales adjustments, and cash receipts. Overrings are sales reductions made after a customer's order is totaled. How much could dishonest employees get away with by creating false overrings? Operating guidelines established with our terminal vendors suggest that overrings should not exceed 0.25% of sales. Even if one-half of allowable overrings are valid, the other half could represent $25 million in underreported sales for the McDonald's system. It is not enough that our internal control procedures require that overring slips be generated from the system, with a written explanation for the adjustment signed by the crewperson and store manager. The slip must be accompanied by a review of individual terminal activity to identify unusual or suspicious patterns. Only then can specific individuals be identified for either additional training or disciplinary action.

company's general ledger cash balance with the cash balance reported by the bank (record-keeping function) should not be performed by an employee who handles cash (custody function). Separation of duties helps in the detection of errors and also makes theft or fraud more difficult.

Bank Reconciliations

OBJECTIVE

3

Reconcile a bank account.

As previously noted, adequate internal control requires the use of checks for significant cash payments. Canceled checks and their endorsements furnish written evidence that payments have been made. In addition, checking accounts provide security and safety for the large cash balances that many businesses must carry.

As you can well imagine, a company will have many cash receipts and disbursements during a given accounting period. Because of the high frequency of transactions and the potential for error, the accuracy of the cash balance in the general ledger (or your checkbook) should be periodically examined. This process, called a **bank reconciliation,** is based on the Cash account and a document called a **bank statement.**

Bank Statements Versus Cash Accounts. Businesses and individuals receive monthly bank statements for every checking account they maintain. An example of a bank statement appears in Exhibit 7-2. Bank statements summarize the activity in a checking account and report the ending monthly balance. It is important to understand that although the Cash account of a depositor (such as Johnson Manufacturing) is an asset, the depositor's account is carried on the bank's records as a *liability*. Consequently, checks and other debits by the bank *reduce* Johnson's account, while deposits and other credits *increase* the account.

At the end of a month, the bank statement cash balance and the company's cash records will normally not agree. A major reason for this discrepancy is the timing differences associated with the use of a checking account. Timing differences result in an item being recorded on the depositor's books or the bank's books, but not both, in a given accounting period. Some of these differences arise from the operations of the Postal Service and the check-clearing procedures of the Federal Reserve System. Common examples of timing differences include the following:

1 Items reflected on the company's records but not yet reported on the bank statement, such as:
   a **Deposits in transit**—receipts entered in a firm's accounts but not yet processed by the bank. This situation often occurs when deposits are mailed. Deposits in transit are determined by comparing deposits that appear on the bank statement with deposits as reported in an organization's Cash account.
   b **Outstanding checks**—checks written by a business but not yet processed by the bank. Outstanding checks are determined by comparing checks reported on the bank statement against checks written on the company's records.

2 Items reported on the bank statement but not yet entered in the company's records, such as:
   a **Nonsufficient funds (NSF) checks**—customer checks deposited but returned because of a lack of funds. NSF checks are frequently re-

EXHIBIT 7-2
Bank Statement

FIRST CITY BANK TRUST
101 North James Ave.
Chicago, Illinois 60638

JOHNSON MANUFACTURING CORPORATION
1800 SOUTH MAIN
CHICAGO, ILLINOIS 60634

Account No.   Page No.
0008564201 _ _ _ _ _ 1 _ _

Statement Period
From   To
7/31/XX   8/31/XX

Deposits/Credits		Checks/Debits				Balance	
Date	Amount	No.	Date	Amount		Date	Amount
8/03	3,984.40	606	8/01	1,250.40		8/01	18,257.10
8/05	3,150.43	620	8/02	940.20		8/02	17,316.90
8/06	2,897.04	624	8/05	1,960.85		8/03	21,301.30
8/07	4,925.75	625	8/04	2,640.00		8/04	18,661.30
8/09	5,242.70	626	8/08	375.00		8/05	19,850.88
8/13	4,600.80 NC	627	8/08	675.18		8/06	22,747.92
8/13	75.00 IC	628	8/11	540.20		8/07	27,673.67
8/20	4,167.10	629	8/13	728.40		8/08	26,623.49
8/22	5,145.18	630	8/12	139.50		8/09	31,866.19
8/27	4,752.30	631	8/17	650.53		8/11	31,325.99
8/30	3,237.80	632	8/17	437.29		8/12	31,058.59
		633	8/20	2,147.90		8/13	35,005.99
		634	8/23	989.05		8/17	33,918.17
		635	8/22	12,785.50		8/20	35,937.37
		636	8/27	10,640.90		8/22	28,297.05
		637	8/28	2,470.80		8/23	27,308.00
		639	8/30	740.15		8/27	21,419.40
		DM	8/12	127.90		8/28	18,948.60
		SC	8/31	20.00		8/30	21,446.25
						8/31	21,426.25

Beginning Balance	Deposits/Credits		Checks/Debits		Ending Balance
	No.	Amount	No.	Amount	
19,507.50	11	42,178.50	19	40,259.75	21,426.25

Code Explanation: CM   *Credit Memo*   IC   *Interest Collection*   SC   *Service Charge*
                DM   *Debit Memo*   NC   *Note Collection*

ported on the bank statement via a debit memo notation, because the bank has reduced the depositor's account.

b Bank service charges for account processing.

c Notes receivable[1] and interest collected by the bank. The collection of a note and interest is sometimes reported with a credit memo notation because of the increase in the depositor's account balance.

d Interest earned on the account.

---

[1] A note is a written promise by an individual or company to pay a given sum of money on a specific date. Notes will be studied in detail later in the text.

In addition to timing differences, errors may cause a discrepancy between the bank statement balance and company accounting records. Errors can be made by either the company or the bank and must be corrected as quickly as possible.

The Reconciliation Process.   Several different types of reconciliations can be prepared. The most commonly encountered form results in determining the amount of cash a company has control over and reports on its end-of-period balance sheet. An example appears in Exhibit 7-3.

The exhibit reveals the thrust of a reconciliation. That is, we strive to isolate specific items that cause a difference between the depositor's records and the bank statement balance. The accountant considers these items and adjusts one cash balance or the other to bring both balances into agreement.

If the balances do not agree and the reconciling items are deemed correct, there is an excellent chance that a record-keeping error has been made. Errors must be identified and then added or subtracted on the reconciliation to arrive at the corrected cash balance. For example, if a check written by a firm for $94.50 was incorrectly entered in the accounting records as $49.50, the accounting records will be overstated by $45.00 ($94.50 − $49.50). This amount ($45) should therefore be deducted from the ending cash balance per company records, since the company's books are in error. The bank, of course, will deduct the correct amount of the transaction ($94.50) when the check is received for payment. The reconciliation, then, not only highlights timing differences but also identifies errors made by either the bank or the depositor.

Most bank reconciliations contain adjustments to both the ending cash balance per bank statement and the ending balance per company records. After the reconciliation is completed, *general journal entries must be prepared for adjustments made to company records.* These adjustments are

EXHIBIT 7-3
Illustrative Bank Reconciliation

Ending balance per bank statement	$XXX
Add: Receipts/increases entered on company records but not reported on the bank statement	XXX
	$XXX
Deduct: Disbursements/decreases entered on company records but not reported on the bank statement	XXX
Adjusted cash balance: bank	$XXX
Ending balance per company records	$XXX
Add: Receipts/increases reported on the bank statement but not entered on company records	XXX
	$XXX
Deduct: Disbursements/decreases reported on the bank statement but not entered on company records	XXX
Adjusted cash balance: company records	$XXX

These amounts must agree

necessary to update the Cash account (and others) for corrections of company errors and information already processed by the bank.

Tips & Techniques

It is important to note that no journal entries are needed for adjustments made to the ending bank statement balance. These adjustments reflect items that have already been recorded in a company's accounts; thus, no further updating is necessary. Should the reconciliation process discover that the *bank statement balance* is in error, the problem is corrected by a visit, letter, or telephone call to a bank employee.

An Example. Exhibit 7-4 contains summarized data and the bank reconciliation of Johnson Manufacturing Corporation for the month ended August 31, 19XX. It is helpful if you refer back to Johnson's bank statement (see Exhibit 7-2), which serves as the source for much of the information presented.

The reconciliation reveals two increases to the bank statement cash balance: (1) the deposit that was mailed prior to month-end but not reported by the bank and (2) the checks that were recorded by Johnson and are awaiting deposit. Johnson had control over each of these items as of August 31, and they should be included in the ending cash balance. The decrease to the bank statement cash balance was caused by checks Johnson had written that had not yet cleared the bank. The bank will receive these checks shortly, and the funds will then be deducted from the firm's account.

The increase to company records arose from the note receivable and interest, both of which appear on the bank statement. These funds are now on deposit in Johnson's bank account and must therefore be entered in the company's records. The deductions for the NSF check and service charge are also caused by items on the bank statement but not as yet in the firm's ledger. The error in recording check no. 627 was discovered during the reconciliation. Because the bank deducted the correct amount of the check, an adjustment to Johnson's records is required to bring them into agreement with those of First City.

On completion of the reconciliation, journal entries are needed for all items that affect company records. The following entries will be made on August 31:

Cash	4,675.80	
Notes Receivable		4,600.80
Interest Revenue		75.00
Note and interest collected by bank		
Accounts Receivable	127.90	
Miscellaneous Expense	20.00	
Accounts Payable	18.00	
Cash		165.90
NSF check, bank service charge, and		
error in recording check no. 627		

EXHIBIT 7-4
Data and Bank Reconciliation of Johnson Manufacturing Corporation

Data

a August 31 cash balance per bank statement, $21,426.25.

b August 31 cash balance per company records, $17,473.35.

c A customer's check for $127.90 was returned because of insufficient funds.

d A customer's note receivable for $4,600.80 plus $75.00 of interest was collected by the bank and reported on the August bank statement.

e A deposit for $1,430.00, mailed to the bank on August 30, did not appear on the bank statement.

f Monthly bank service charge, $20.00.

g Customers' checks totaling $420.00, already entered in Johnson's records, were on hand awaiting deposit.

h The following checks written by Johnson were outstanding at the end of the month:

No. 638	$410.00
No. 640	320.00
No. 641	240.00
No. 642	323.00

i Check no. 627, written for $675.18, was erroneously entered as $657.18 in the company's books. The check involved a payment to a supplier on account.

JOHNSON MANUFACTURING CORPORATION
Bank Reconciliation
August 31, 19XX

Ending balance per bank statement		$21,426.25
Add: Deposit in transit	$1,430.00	
Checks on hand	420.00	1,850.00
		$23,276.25
Deduct: Outstanding checks		
No. 638	$ 410.00	
No. 640	320.00	
No. 641	240.00	
No. 642	323.00	1,293.00
Adjusted cash balance: bank		$21,983.25
Ending balance per company records		$17,473.35
Add: Note receivable collected by bank	$4,600.80	
Interest on note	75.00	4,675.80
		$22,149.15
Deduct: NSF check	$ 127.90	
Monthly service charge	20.00	
Error in recording check no. 627	18.00	165.90
Adjusted cash balance: company records		$21,983.25

The first entry reflects the increase in cash caused by the collection of the note and $75.00 of interest. The second entry combines the company's three cash reductions. The NSF check is debited to Accounts Receivable because Johnson still has a claim against the customer for $127.90. The bank service charge is recorded as a miscellaneous expense. Finally, the error in recording check no. 627 was found to involve a payment on account; thus, Accounts Payable must be debited. These entries allow Johnson's records to reflect the true amount of cash held by the firm (see the accompanying T-account).

Cash			
8/31	17,473.35	8/31	165.90
8/31	4,675.80		
(21,983.25)	22,149.15		

An Interesting Aside: Electronic Funds Transfer. It is possible that outstanding checks will soon be a thing of the past. Checkless payment systems are emerging as a very popular device in the attempt to reduce processing time and grief. Payers, for example, enter information into a computer. The information is then transmitted electronically to the Federal Reserve System, which both decreases the payer's account and increases the payee's balance. Known as *electronic funds transfer (EFT)*, these systems typically reduce costs but at the same time dictate a need for strong computerized internal controls.

Petty Cash

Another important element in the control of cash is a **petty cash system.** Under such a system, a fund is established for use in making small payments, especially those that are impractical or uneconomical to make by check. Examples of such payments include those for minor items like coffee and other miscellaneous office needs.

A petty cash fund is created by cashing a check drawn on the company's regular checking account. The proceeds from the check, sufficient to cover payments for a short period of time (e.g., several weeks), are then placed in a petty cash box that is controlled by an individual known as the fund custodian. The custodian supervises the fund and is held accountable for any discrepancies. Assuming the petty cash fund is established at $200, the necessary journal entry is as follows:

Petty Cash	200	
Cash		200
To establish petty cash fund		

Making Disbursements from the Fund. As payments are made from the fund, the custodian completes a form known as a petty cash voucher (see Exhibit 7-5). Each voucher indicates the amount paid, the purpose of the expenditure, the date of the expenditure, and the individual receiving the money. Along with invoices and receipts, petty cash vouchers are used as evidence of disbursements.

OBJECTIVE

4

Establish and operate a petty cash system.

EXHIBIT 7-5
Petty Cash Voucher

> *Petty Cash Voucher No.* _____
>
> *Date* _____   *Payee* _____
>
> *Explanation* _____   *Account* _____
>
> _____   *Amount $* _____
>
> _____   *Approved* _____
>
> *Received Payment* _____

The completed voucher is placed in the petty cash box by the custodian. Although a payment has been made, no journal entry is recorded at this time. Preparing a formal journal entry for each disbursement would give rise to considerable bookkeeping work and posting, all for relatively small amounts. At all times the following relationship should be true:

Cash remaining in the fund	$XXX
Plus: Petty cash vouchers	XXX
Original amount of the fund	$ 200

Replenishing the Petty Cash Fund. The petty cash fund is replenished when the amount of cash in the fund becomes low. For instance, assume that a count of the petty cash on hand totaled $32.40. Vouchers revealed that the following expenses had been incurred: postage, $27.50; office supplies, $50.80; transportation, $73.40; and coffee, $15.90. The journal entry to record replenishment is as follows:

Postage Expense	27.50	
Office Supplies Expense	50.80	
Transportation Expense	73.40	
Miscellaneous Expense	15.90	
Cash		167.60
To replenish petty cash fund		

Notice that the credit is to the Cash account and not Petty Cash. Although disbursements have been made from the petty cash box, the fund is restocked by writing a check for $167.60 on the company's regular checking account. Thus, payment (and replenishment) is really from Cash.

In addition to being restocked when the fund is low, petty cash is also replenished at the end of each accounting period. This procedure is necessary because no formal journal entries have been recorded for individual fund disbursements. Replenishment requires a journal entry, thereby ensuring that expenditures are charged to the period in which they arose.

Errors in the Petty Cash Fund. Occasionally, the sum of the petty cash vouchers and cash in the fund will not equal the original fund balance. This discrepancy usually occurs because of errors made by the fund custodian, some errors in the company's favor and some against. In such cases, the Cash Short & Over account is employed. Cash Short & Over is debited to record a shortage or credited to recognize an overage at the time the fund is replenished.

Voucher System

Bank reconciliations and petty cash funds are two elements of a cash control system. A third element used by some businesses is a **voucher system,** which improves control over all disbursements made by check. As its name implies, the system is based on internal company documents known as *vouchers.* These are prenumbered forms that summarize the details of an expenditure and have supporting evidence such as invoices and paid receipts attached.[2]

The operation of a voucher system involves many detailed procedures. For example, vouchers are examined for accuracy, approved, entered in the accounting records, and then filed in an unpaid voucher file by payment date. When the payment date arrives, the disbursement is approved, paperwork is sent to the accounting department, and a check is issued. The voucher is marked "paid," the proper check number is noted, and the voucher is stored for future reference.

The Voucher System and Internal Control. The procedures just described, although burdensome at first glance, allow companies to reduce (or eliminate) improper cash outflows. Observe the use of multiple authorization and approval systems. In addition, notice that incompatible duties are separated, with the person responsible for voucher preparation not having access to the funds of the business. (Another individual or department actually prepares the checks.) By following this latter procedure, the entry of an expenditure in a firm's records is segregated from the related handling of cash. Therefore no single person or department can process a transaction through the system from beginning to end. A company's internal control is thus strengthened, assisting in error detection and making fraudulent schemes more difficult to undertake.

> **OBJECTIVE**
>
> **5**
>
> Explain the features of a voucher system.

SHORT-TERM INVESTMENTS

Without question, cash is a key asset to an entity's survival. A company may possess numerous valuable resources, but without funds to meet employee payrolls and demands for payment from important suppliers, the eventual outcome may be bankruptcy. Maintaining an abundance of cash may therefore appear to be a sensible policy. Normally, however, such action is not prudent and could actually cause an otherwise successful business to operate at a loss.

Effective cash management dictates that cash balances in excess of planned minimum levels be used to acquire securities that provide a return to the investor. Many companies therefore purchase **short-term investments** (sometimes called marketable securities), which include shares of

---

[2] The vouchers described here are more involved than and unrelated to those used in a petty cash system.

capital stock of corporations, certificates of deposit, Treasury bills, and bonds. *Treasury bills* are U.S. government obligations that pay a fixed amount of money to the purchaser after a specified number of days has elapsed (usually 91 or 182). In contrast, *bonds* are securities issued by corporations and governmental units (e.g., municipalities) when such entities desire to borrow large sums of money. With the exception of capital stock, which generates a dividend for the investor, CDs, Treasury bills, and bonds are all interest bearing.[3]

The short-term investments acquired by an organization are reported as current assets on the balance sheet if they are (1) readily salable and (2) intended to be converted into cash within the operating cycle or one year, whichever is longer. The key element in this reporting test is *managerial intent*. If management intends to convert a short-term investment into cash whenever the firm is in need of funds, the security is classified as a current asset. Securities purchased with longer-term goals in mind, such as management control or affiliation, are disclosed as long-term investments.

Recording Initial Cost and Changes in Value

OBJECTIVE

6

Account for short-term investments under the historical-cost and lower-of-cost-or-market methods.

All short-term investments are recorded initially at their acquisition price plus any other costs related to the transaction (e.g., brokerage fees). To illustrate the proper accounting, we will assume that Phillip Corporation purchased 200 shares of Allegro Corporation capital stock at $42 per share (for a total of $8,400). Brokerage fees of $50 were incurred on the purchase. This transaction would be recorded as follows:

Short-Term Investments in Stock	8,450	
Cash		8,450
Purchased 200 shares of Allegro Corporation stock		

Unlike the value of most other assets, the value of many short-term investments fluctuates continuously and can often be determined on a daily basis. Changes in the value of such investments—caused by the economy, investor expectations, earnings reports, and other factors—are readily obtainable from *The Wall Street Journal* or the business section of major metropolitan newspapers. In light of these characteristics, two alternative methods have been used to account for short-term investments: historical cost and lower of cost or market.

Historical-Cost Method

The **historical-cost method** is typically employed for short-term debt investments, such as those in bonds. Under this approach, investments are reported on the balance sheet at acquisition (historical) cost until the time of sale. Accordingly, changes in value are ignored while the securities are being held, except perhaps for disclosure in the notes to the financial statements. Any revenue from the securities (e.g., interest) is recorded as it is earned by the investor.

In recent years, some companies have abandoned historical cost in favor of lower of cost or market (to be discussed next). This latter method *must*

---

[3] Businesses frequently report highly liquid short-term investments on the balance sheet under the caption "cash and cash equivalents." Further discussion of this topic appears in Chapter 19.

be used for other specified types of securities. Such a switch has simplified record keeping by achieving consistency in accounting treatments for the various classes of investments that may be acquired.

Lower-of-Cost-or-Market Method

With the **lower-of-cost-or-market method,** valuation changes related to certain securities (e.g., shares of capital stock) are recognized and entered in the accounting records. Decreases in the market value of such securities are accounted for as losses, while recoveries in these market value declines are reported as revenue. Recoveries, however, are limited to the amount of previously recorded losses.[4]

The application of the lower-of-cost-or-market method is straightforward. The carrying value of the investment portfolio is the lower of its *aggregate* cost or market value on each balance sheet date. That is, the total cost and total market value of a firm's short-term investments are compared, and the *lower* figure is used for financial statement purposes.

To illustrate use of the lower-of-cost-or-market method for stock investments, assume that Carr Corporation acquired the following securities on January 1, 19X1:

Number of Shares	Corporation	Cost per Share	Total Cost
200 shares	Rolph Corporation	$ 50	$10,000
400 shares	Dana, Inc.	100	40,000
300 shares	Borg Corporation	75	22,500
			$72,500

The following journal entry is made to record these acquisitions:

Short-Term Investments in Stock	72,500	
Cash		72,500
Purchased Rolph, Dana, and Borg stock		

During 19X1, dividends of $4,500 were received. Dividends are revenue to the recipient and are recorded as follows:

Cash	4,500	
Dividend Revenue		4,500
To record dividends received		

Declines in Market Value. On December 31, 19X1, Carr's three securities had the following market values per share: Rolph, $48; Dana, $98; and Borg, $76. The accompanying table summarizes this information.

Security	Cost	Market*
Rolph Corporation (200 shares)	$10,000	$ 9,600
Dana, Inc. (400 shares)	40,000	39,200
Borg Corporation (300 shares)	22,500	22,800
	$72,500	$71,600

* Number of shares multiplied by market value per share.

[4] "Accounting for Certain Marketable Equity Securities," *Statement of Financial Accounting Standards No. 12* (Norwalk, Conn.: Financial Accounting Standards Board, 1975).

The table reveals that the portfolio's total market value is $900 less than cost ($72,500 − $71,600). The entry needed to record this decline in value is as follows:

Unrealized Loss on Short-Term Investments	900	
Allowance for Decline in Market Value of Short-Term		
Investments		900
To record decline in market value		

As we noted earlier, decreases in the market value of short-term investments are accounted for as losses. The loss, known as an *unrealized loss*, appears on the income statement under the other expense classification.[5] Rather than credit the Short-Term Investments account directly, one establishes an Allowance account. The Allowance for Decline in Market Value, a contra asset, is deducted from Short-Term Investments on the balance sheet as follows:

Current assets	
Short-term investments in stock	$72,500
Less: Allowance for decline in market value of short-term	
investments	900
Short-term investments at the lower of cost or market	$71,600

Notice how the balance sheet discloses more information by using a separate valuation account.

Recording Recoveries. Continuing the previous example, assume it is one year later (19X2) and that dividends of $4,800 were received. The proper entry is:

Cash	4,800	
Dividend Revenue		4,800
To record dividends received		

Now suppose that on December 31, 19X2, the market values per share were Rolph, $49; Dana, $99; and Borg, $76. This information is summarized in the accompanying table.

Security	Cost	Market*
Rolph Corporation (200 shares)	$10,000	$ 9,800
Dana, Inc. (400 shares)	40,000	39,600
Borg Corporation (300 shares)	22,500	22,800
	$72,500	$72,200

* Number of shares multiplied by market value per share.

The entry to record the recovery in market value of the portfolio from $71,600 (on December 31, 19X1) to $72,200 (on December 31, 19X2) is shown below.

Allowance for Decline in Market Value of Short-Term		
Investments	600	
Recovery in Value of Short-Term Investments		600
To record recovery in market value		

[5] In most cases, gains and losses are said to be *realized* at the time of sale. Because Carr still owns the securities, the loss is labeled "unrealized."

EXHIBIT 7-6
Comparative Financial
Statement Disclosures of Carr
Corporation

	19X2	19X1
Balance Sheet		
Current assets		
Short-term investments in stock	$72,500	$72,500
Less: Allowance for decline in market value of short-term investments	300	900
Short-term investments at the lower of cost or market	$72,200	$71,600
Income Statement		
Other revenue		
Dividend revenue	$ 4,800	$ 4,500
Recovery in value of short-term investments	600	
Other expense		
Unrealized loss on short-term investments		900

In the second and all subsequent years, losses and loss recoveries are determined by comparing the required balance in the Allowance account at the end of the year with the account's balance on the last previous balance sheet date. The previous amount in the Allowance for Decline account was $900. As of December 31, 19X2, however, the market value of the portfolio is $300 below cost ($72,500 − $72,200), which means that only a $300 balance is needed. Thus, Carr must debit the Allowance for $600 to achieve the desired result. The $600 figure represents a recovery or increase in value and is treated as revenue by the company.

The preceding events are shown in Carr's comparative financial statements for 19X1 and 19X2, portions of which appear in Exhibit 7-6.[6] Observe that if the stocks recover the remaining $300 to their original cost ($72,500), the valuation allowance would be eliminated. If the stocks continue to increase in value above $72,500, the additional increase is ignored. The lower-of-cost-or-market method would again value the securities at the lower figure, which is now the portfolio's cost.

Tips & Techniques

Recall that recoveries in portfolio value are limited to the amount of previously recorded losses. Thus, a company that recognized a $10,000 unrealized loss is limited to $10,000 of recoveries if and when the portfolio's value rebounds. If a business were allowed recoveries in excess of losses, the securities' value in the accounting records would exceed the original outlay made at acquisition.

---

[6] This example spans two years and may raise questions concerning why the securities are classified as current on the balance sheet. Ordinarily, ongoing purchases and sales would have occurred throughout this time period. We have assumed otherwise for the sake of simplicity.

Justification for Lower of Cost or Market. The lower-of-cost-or-market method is justified by the accounting convention of **conservatism,** which holds that accounting practices be employed that are least likely to overstate assets and/or net income. The use of conservatism in financial reporting became popular many years ago, primarily because of support from bankers and other lenders. These individuals review balance sheets when making loan decisions and carefully study a firm's assets and the accompanying valuations. Should assets pledged as loan security (i.e., collateral) be overvalued, the lending institution could suffer extensive losses if the borrower failed to repay the debt and the assets were seized.

A review of the discussion on the preceding pages will show the conservatism associated with lower of cost or market. When a portfolio's aggregate market value is below cost, for example, a loss is recognized for the difference. Such recognition reduces net income, and the associated Allowance account lowers the securities' balance sheet valuation to market. In contrast, the practice of ignoring increases in market value *above* cost is justified because cost will produce the lower figure for both firm assets and earnings.

END-OF-CHAPTER REVIEW

LEARNING OBJECTIVES: THE KEY POINTS

1 Describe the composition of cash and explain how cash is presented on a balance sheet. Cash includes those items that are acceptable to a bank for deposit and free from restriction for use in satisfying current debts. Specific items included in cash, which is classified as a current asset, are coins, currency, funds on deposit with a bank in checking and savings accounts, checks, and money orders.

2 Explain cash management and identify the controls and procedures related to cash receipts and disbursements. Cash management involves programs to ensure that sufficient cash is available to meet current obligations and that any excess funds are invested. Such programs, which include both cash planning and cash control, help to guard against a loss of earnings for the firm. Cash control systems are adopted to safeguard an entity's funds and involve such features as using a point-of-sale terminal, making daily deposits, having an adequate separation of duties, making all significant disbursements by check, and preparing a bank reconciliation.

3 Reconcile a bank account. A bank reconciliation involves an examination of the accuracy of the cash balance in the general ledger. Items are recognized that cause the depositor's records and the bank statement to differ. Such items, which properly appear on the bank statement but are not as yet on company records, require a journal entry on the depositor's books. The resultant figure from this process is the amount of cash that a company has control over and reports on its balance sheet.

4 Establish and operate a petty cash system. A petty cash system for small payments is established by writing a check on a company's regular checking account. As payments are made from the fund, petty cash vouchers are prepared to document each disbursement. When the fund becomes low it is replenished, and a journal entry is made to record the disbursements that have occurred. The fund is also replenished at the end of the accounting period.

5 Explain the features of a voucher system. The voucher system is a system for controlling all disbursements made by check. The system begins with the preparation of a voucher for expenditures that require a disbursement. After it has been examined for accuracy and approved, the voucher is entered in the accounting records and placed in an unpaid voucher file. When the payment date arrives, the voucher is settled by writing a check. The voucher system features various authorization and approval procedures along with a separation of duties.

6 Account for short-term investments under the historical-cost and lower-of-cost-or-market methods. Short-term investments are securities that are both readily salable and intended to be converted into cash within the operating cycle or one year, whichever is longer. Debt securities are often accounted for by using the historical-cost method, which ignores changes in the market value of securities while the securities are being held. In contrast, stock investments are accounted for by using lower of cost or market. With this approach, decreases in the aggregate market value of the investment portfolio are accounted for as losses, whereas recoveries in the portfolio's market value are reported as revenue. Recoveries, however, are limited to the amount of previously recorded losses.

KEY TERMS AND CONCEPTS: A QUICK OVERVIEW

bank reconciliation A process for determining the amount of cash that a company has control over and reports on its balance sheet.

bank statement A document that summarizes the activity in a checking account.

cash Items acceptable to a bank for deposit and free from restriction for use in satisfying current debts.

cash budget An overall plan of activity that depicts cash inflows and outflows for a stated period of time.

cash control system Procedures adopted to ensure the safeguarding of an organization's funds.

cash planning system Those procedures adopted to ensure that adequate cash is available to meet normal business obligations and that any excess cash is invested.

compensating balance A portion of an amount loaned to a customer that remains on deposit in the bank during the loan period.

conservatism A concept stipulating that when alternative valuations and measurements are possible, the alternative selected should be that which is least likely to overstate assets and/or net income.

deposit in transit Receipts entered on company records but not yet processed by the bank.

historical-cost method A method of accounting for securities by which securities are initially recorded and subsequently maintained at cost.

lower-of-cost-or-market method A method that allows investments to be accounted for at acquisition cost or market value, whichever is lower.

NSF check (nonsufficient funds) A customer's check returned by the bank because of a lack of funds.

outstanding checks Checks written but not yet processed by the bank.

petty cash system A fund used to make small payments that are impractical or uneconomical to make by check.

short-term investments   Investments made in readily marketable securities with the intention of conversion back to cash within the operating cycle or one year, whichever is longer.

voucher system   A detailed cash payments system that improves control over all cash disbursements made by check.

CHAPTER QUIZ

The five questions that follow relate to several issues raised in the chapter. Test your knowledge of the issues by selecting the best answer. (The answers appear on p. 298.)

1 Liberty had a $10,000 balance in its checking account, $15,000 in certificates of deposit, $600 of postdated checks, $200 of employee IOUs, and $900 of cash in the office safe. Further, the company had given out $500 of travel advances. The proper amount of cash to report on Liberty's balance sheet is:
a $10,900.   c $25,900.
b $11,500.   d $27,200.

2 Which of the following would not be part of an effective cash planning and control system?
a The daily deposit of cash receipts.
b The use of a cash budget.
c The use of periodic bank reconciliations.
d The assignment of cash handling and the related cash record keeping to the same employee.

3 When preparing a bank reconciliation, deposits in transit are:
a added to the balance per company records.
b subtracted from the balance per company records.
c added to the balance per bank.
d subtracted from the balance per bank.

4 Soccer, Inc., established a $200 petty cash fund. Five weeks later, the following was found in the petty cash box:

Receipts for coffee and tea	$36
Receipts for office supplies	94
Receipts for postage	?
Coins and currency	58

If the journal entry to replenish the fund contained a $2 debit to the Cash Short & Over account, the receipts for postage must have amounted to:
a $6.   c $14.
b $10.   d none of these.

5 Berry's beginning-of-year portfolio of short-term stock investments had an aggregate cost and market value of $80,000 and $75,800, respectively. The portfolio's market value increased to $84,000 by year-end. For the current reporting period, Berry should disclose:
a an unrealized loss of $4,200.   c a recovery in value of $4,200.
b a recovery in value of $4,000.   d a recovery in value of $8,200.

The Donnell Company recently hired Steve Hampton to fill a staff accounting position. On August 1, Hampton established a $400 petty cash fund. The count of petty cash on August 31 indicated that $92.30 remained in the fund. Petty cash vouchers disclosed that the following expenses were incurred during the month:

SUMMARY PROBLEM

Postage expense	$137.40
Office supplies expense	102.78
Miscellaneous selling expenses	65.52

Additionally, the following information concerning Donnell's checking account is available:

Balance per bank statement	$1,671.32
Balance per company records	1,419.99
Bank service charge	22.00
Outstanding checks	318.46
Undeposited receipts	208.70
Note and interest collected by the bank but not yet entered in the accounting records (note, $175.00; interest, $7.00)	182.00
NSF check returned by the bank with the bank statement	18.43

Instructions

a Prepare the August 1 entry to establish the petty cash fund and the August 31 entry for replenishment.

b Prepare the August bank reconciliation for the firm's checking account. Assume the balance per company records has already been reduced for the petty cash replenishment.

c Prepare the necessary journal entries related to the bank reconciliation.

Solution

a Aug.	1	Petty Cash	400.00	
		Cash		400.00
		To establish petty cash fund		
	31	Postage Expense	137.40	
		Office Supplies Expense	102.78	
		Miscellaneous Selling Expenses	65.52	
		Cash Short & Over*	2.00	
		Cash		307.70
		To replenish petty cash fund		

* Original fund		$400.00
Less: Vouchers ($137.40 + $102.78 + $65.52)	$305.70	
Cash in fund	92.30	398.00
Shortage		$ 2.00

b

		DONNELL COMPANY Bank Reconciliation August 31, 19XX
Ending balance per bank statement		$1,671.32
Add: Undeposited receipts	$208.70	
Deduct: Outstanding checks	318.46	(109.76)
Adjusted cash balance: bank		$1,561.56
Ending balance per company records		$1,419.99
Add: Note collection	$175.00	
Interest collection	7.00	182.00
		$1,601.99
Deduct: Bank service charge	$ 22.00	
NSF check	18.43	40.43
Adjusted cash balance: company records		$1,561.56

c All adjustments to company records require journal entries.

Aug. 31	Cash	182.00	
	Notes Receivable		175.00
	Interest Revenue		7.00
	Note and interest collected by the bank		
31	Miscellaneous Expense	22.00	
	Accounts Receivable	18.43	
	Cash		40.43
	Bank service charge and NSF check		

ASSIGNMENT MATERIAL

QUESTIONS

Q7-1 What items are normally included in the Cash account on the balance sheet?

Q7-2 Define the following items and describe how they are classified on the balance sheet:
a Certificate of deposit.   c IOU.
b Postdated check.   d Travel advance.

Q7-3 What is cash management? Briefly discuss the planning and control aspects of an effective cash management system.

Q7-4 What general control features should be built into a cash control system?

Q7-5 How is the Cash Short & Over account classified in the financial statements?

Q7-6 Why should cash receipts be deposited daily?

Q7-7 What is a bank reconciliation?

Q7-8 What is the effect of a bank debit memo on a depositor's account balance?

Q7-9 What are the reasons for the discrepancy between the cash balance reported on the bank statement and the cash balance in the accounting records?

Q7-10 Is a deposit in transit reported as an addition to the ending balance per bank statement or the ending balance per company records? What is the reason behind this treatment?

Q7-11 Which adjustments on a bank reconciliation require general journal entries in the accounting records?

Q7-12 Briefly discuss the purpose of a petty cash system.

Q7-13 Are journal entries made for individual disbursements from a petty cash system? Explain.

Q7-14 When is a petty cash fund replenished?

Q7-15 Briefly discuss how a voucher system results in improved internal control.

Q7-16 What are short-term investments? Why do companies make short-term investments?

Q7-17 Briefly discuss the criteria that must be met to classify a short-term investment as a current asset.

Q7-18 Describe two methods that are used to account for short-term investments. When is each method used?

Q7-19 Briefly discuss the accounting convention of conservatism, including a short description of the relationship between conservatism and the lower-of-cost-or-market method.

EXERCISES

E7-1 *Internal control: Procedures and weaknesses* (L.O. 2)

Mitzi Gifford works in the accounting department of Gaylord Consulting Services. The owner of the firm, Bob Gaylord, has given Mitzi complete authority to make business decisions for the company. Mitzi frequently approves and places purchase orders. She also maintains the general ledger, prepares the financial statements, gets and opens the mail, prepares checks for disbursements, files paid invoices, reconciles the bank account, and maintains the petty cash fund.

Bob Gaylord is the only person authorized to sign checks. After a check is prepared, Mitzi files the related invoice and then places the check in Bob's "in-box" for his signature. All checks and petty cash vouchers are serially prenumbered, and it is Mitzi's responsibility to account for all documents. An exception to this policy occurs with voided checks, which are immediately destroyed.

a Identify features that are consistent with good internal control procedures over cash disbursements.

b Identify operating procedures that may create potential control problems for the company.

E7-2 *Internal control: Procedures and weaknesses* (L.O. 2)

Consider the following independent cases:

a A cashier stole $150 from a manufacturing business and made the following journal entry in the accounting records:

Miscellaneous Expense	150
Cash	150

b Art's Market lost $12,800 (three days' cash receipts) in a robbery early Thursday morning.

c Disbursements at the alcohol rehabilitation center are made by check. To facilitate payments being made when the director is out of town, five blank, signed checks are kept in the secretary's desk.

For each of the preceding cases, indicate any apparent internal control weakness and suggest procedures that may prevent the irregularity.

E7-3 ___ *Bank reconciliations: Missing amounts* (L.O. 3)

The following independent cases relate to bank reconciliations. Compute the missing amounts, assuming that no other reconciling items exist.

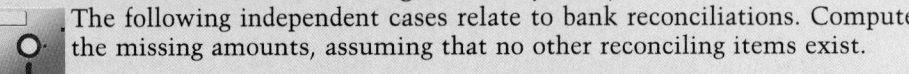

	Case A	Case B	Case C
Balance per bank	$6,000	$4,000	$?
Outstanding checks	500	2,100	1,400
Deposits in transit	2,000	?	1,000
Balance per company records	?	8,000	450

E7-4 *Items on a bank reconciliation* (L.O. 3)

You are preparing the June bank reconciliation for Advanced Systems. Identify the proper placement of items (a)–(f) on the reconciliation by using the following codes:

1—An addition to the balance per bank as of June 30.
2—A deduction from the balance per bank as of June 30.
3—An addition to the balance per company records as of June 30.
4—A deduction from the balance per company records as of June 30.

_____a Interest earned on the account during June.
_____b A company deposit taken to the bank at 3:00 P.M. on June 30, but not recorded on the June bank statement.
_____c A $3,000 deposit, entered in the company records as $300.
_____d A deposit of Advanced Design Systems, incorrectly credited to Advanced Systems' account.
_____e A customer's check returned for insufficient funds.
_____f Check no. 765, which has not yet cleared the bank.

E7-5 *Bank reconciliation and entries* (L.O. 3)

The following information was taken from the accounting records of Palmetto Company for the month of January:

Balance per bank	$6,150
Balance per company records	3,580
Bank service charge for January	20
Deposits in transit	940
Interest on note collected by bank	100
Note collected by bank	1,000
NSF check returned by the bank with the bank statement	650
Outstanding checks	3,080

a Prepare Palmetto's January bank reconciliation.
b Prepare any necessary journal entries for Palmetto.

E7-6 *Accounting for cash* (L.O. 1, 2, 3, 4)

Evaluate the comments that follow as being True or False. If the comment is false, briefly explain why.

a A petty cash fund should be replenished at the conclusion of an accounting period.

b A journal entry is needed in a company's accounting records to record both a bank service charge and the firm's outstanding checks.

c As shown on May's bank statement, the Nebraska National Bank incorrectly deducted $200 from the account of Kay's Auto Parts. When preparing its bank reconciliation, Kay's should subtract $200 from the accounting records so the adjusted cash balance (company records) will equal the adjusted cash balance (bank).

d Customer checks, money orders, and certificates of deposit are properly classified as cash on the balance sheet.

e To achieve strong internal control, a store cashier should have access to a company's accounting records for cash.

E7-7 *Petty cash fund* (L.O. 4)

The Chang Company instituted a petty cash system on March 1 to allow for the payment of small expenditures. The information that follows has come to your attention.

Mar. 1 The fund was established at $100.

31 Cash in the fund had been reduced to $11.72. The petty cash vouchers were sorted into the following expense categories, and the fund was replenished:

Warehouse supplies	$43.11
Postage	25.00
Miscellaneous	20.17
	$88.28

a Prepare the journal entry necessary to record the establishment of the fund on March 1.

b Prepare the journal entry necessary to record the replenishment of the fund on March 31.

E7-8 *Understanding a petty cash system* (L.O. 4)

Bravo Company recently established a $500 petty cash fund and recorded the following journal entry:

Petty Cash	500	
Cash		500

Petty cash vouchers were prepared as disbursements were made during the month. The individual vouchers were then recorded in the books by journal entries similar to those shown.

Supplies Expense	15	
Petty Cash		15
Postage Expense	50	
Petty Cash		50
Etc.		

Cash in the petty cash box at month-end totaled $210, and vouchers written amounted to $280. The fund was replenished for $290, with Bravo recording the following entry:

Petty Cash	280	
Cash Short & Over	10	
Cash		290

a　Identify the errors in Bravo's accounting for petty cash.
b　Despite the errors that have been made, are the ending account balances correct? Briefly explain.
c　From a bookkeeping viewpoint, criticize Bravo's method of entering petty cash vouchers in the accounting records.

E7-9　*Short-term investments: Acquisition and valuation* (L.O. 6)
You have obtained the following information from the records of Matlock Company concerning the firm's short-term investments:

		Price per Share	
Company	Number of Shares	Sept. 3	Dec. 31
Simpson	300	$20	$25
Cosby	400	30	25

a　Prepare the journal entry to record the acquisition of Matlock's short-term investments on September 3.
b　Prepare the journal entry to record the change in market value of the short-term investments as of December 31.

E7-10　*Valuation and disclosure of short-term investments* (L.O. 6)
Xenon Company, formed during 19X1, invests excess cash in stocks of utility companies. The stocks are readily salable, and management intends to sell the stocks whenever the firm is in need of cash. The accompanying table gives the cost and year-end market values of Xenon's short-term investments for 19X1 and 19X2.

	19X1	19X2
Cost	$45,000	$45,000
Market value	41,000	57,000

a　Present Xenon's journal entries in 19X1 and 19X2 to value the short-term securities at the lower of cost or market.
b　Show how the securities would appear on Xenon's 19X1 and 19X2 balance sheets.

Series A

PROBLEMS

P7-A1　*Cash on the balance sheet* (L.O. 1)

The following information has been gathered from the records of Bermuda Corporation as of December 31:

Certificate of deposit	$15,000
Reconciled balance in Center Bank checking account	1,275
Cash on hand	4,210
Employee's IOU	345
Balance in Metropolitan Trust savings account	20,100
Petty cash fund	200
Reconciled balance in American Bank checking account	6,500

Money orders on hand	400
Customer's postdated check	560
Postage stamps on hand	75

Instructions

a Compute the total cash balance to be reported as a current asset on the December 31 balance sheet.

b Describe the balance sheet treatment of the items not included in the cash balance computed in part (a).

P7-A2 *Bank reconciliation and entries* (L.O. 3)

The following selected information appeared on the October 31 bank statement of the Elshazly Company:

Beginning balance, Oct. 1	$6,068
Ending balance, Oct. 31	4,445
Miscellaneous credits	
Note collected ($5,000) and interest ($60)	5,060
Monthly interest earned	50
Miscellaneous debits	
Monthly service charge	70
NSF check from customer	550

The company's Cash account in the general ledger appeared as shown.

Cash			
Balance, 10/1	6,457	Oct. payments	9,432
Oct. receipts	3,000		

Deposits in transit on October 31 are $1,200, and checks outstanding on the same date total $1,310. In the process of determining the outstanding checks, Elshazly discovered an error. Check no. 1213, written for $860 of office supplies, was entered in the company records as $680.

Instructions

a Prepare the October bank reconciliation for the company.

b Prepare any necessary journal entries for Elshazly as of October 31.

c Determine the cash balance that Elshazly would disclose on its October 31 balance sheet.

P7-A3 *Bank reconciliation from bank statement* (L.O. 3)

The Union Company is in the process of reconciling its bank account with Metropolitan Bank and Trust for May. Union's bank statement follows.

METROPOLITAN BANK AND TRUST

UNION COMPANY   MAY BANK STATEMENT

Deposits/Credits		Checks/Debits			Balance	
Date	Amount	No.	Date	Amount	Date	Amount
					5/01	8,440
5/02	400	384	5/02	725	5/02	6,175
5/07	625	406	5/02	1,080	5/05	5,675
5/11	370	407	5/02	860	5/07	5,990
5/16	1,150	408	5/05	500	5/08	5,300
5/19	2,340	409	5/08	690	5/11	5,180
5/27	850 CM	410	5/07	310	5/12	4,750
		412	5/12	430	5/14	4,240
		413	5/11	490	5/16	5,280
		415	5/16	110	5/19	7,620
		416	5/20	665	5/20	6,955
		417	5/24	1,210	5/24	5,745
		421	5/27	800	5/27	5,795
		NSF	5/14	510	5/31	5,785
		SC	5/31	10		

CM   *Credit Memo*   NSF   *NSF Check*   SC   *Service Charge*

The credit memo represents the collection of an $830 note receivable plus $20 interest. Union's cash receipts and disbursements records for May are as follows:

Deposits		Checks Written			
5/6	$ 625	no. 408	$500	no. 417	$1,210
5/10	370	409	690	418	120
5/15	1,150	410	310	419	555
5/18	3,240	411	Void	420	440
5/31	780	412	430	421	800
	$6,165	413	490	422	80
		414	Void	423	90
		415	110	424	100
		416	665	425	200
					$6,790

An examination of the April reconciliation revealed a deposit in transit on April 30 of $400. The following checks were listed as outstanding: No. 384, $725; no. 395, $600; no. 406, $1,080; and no. 407, $860.

Instructions

a Assuming a cash balance per company records on May 31 of $4,950, prepare Union's bank reconciliation for May. Assume that any errors detected during the reconciliation process are the fault of Union's bookkeeper.

b Prepare the necessary journal entries for Union as of May 31.

P7-A4 *Petty cash fund* (L.O. 4)

United Enterprises operates a petty cash fund for small expenditures. The following information relates to August:

Aug. 1 Established the petty cash fund for $150.

12 Replenished the fund. The following items were found in the petty cash box:

Vouchers for postage	$32
Vouchers for supplies	41
Vouchers for miscellaneous expenses	29
Coins and currency	48

22 Replenished the fund. The following items were found in the petty cash box:

Vouchers for postage	$50
Vouchers for supplies	49
Vouchers for miscellaneous expenses	37
Coins and currency	10

31 Replenished the fund. The following items were found in the petty cash box:

Vouchers for postage	$43
Vouchers for supplies	36
Vouchers for miscellaneous expenses	11
Voucher stating: I owe the fund $10. Signed: Ronald Hargis (an employee)	
Coins and currency	52

Instructions

a Record the necessary journal entries on August 1, 12, 22, and 31.

b Explain the probable reasoning behind the fund replenishment on August 31 despite the presence of $52 cash in the petty cash box.

P7-A5 *Short-term investments, lower of cost or market* (L.O. 6)

1-2-3

The following schedule shows information about Jersey Company's short-term investment portfolio, all shares being acquired during 19X4:

	Delta	American	United	USAir
Number of shares	100	200	300	400
Cost per share	$50	$70	$100	$30*
Dividends per share	3	4	5	2
Market value per share, Dec. 31	60	80	90	20

* The company paid an additional $200 for brokerage fees.

Instructions

a Prepare the journal entry that Jersey made to record the purchase of USAir on February 28.

b Prepare a journal entry to record total dividends received during the year.

c Prepare a journal entry to value the securities at the lower of cost or market on December 31, 19X4.

d Show how Jersey's short-term investments would be disclosed on the year-end balance sheet.

e Suppose that USAir's market price at the end of *19X5* was $24 per share and all the other market prices remained the same.
  (1) Prepare the journal entry to properly value the securities at the end of 19X5.
  (2) How would Jersey's short-term investments be disclosed on the company's 19X5 balance sheet?

Series B

P7-B1 *Cash on the balance sheet* (L.O. 1)

The following information has been gathered from the records of Tyson Supply:

Customer's postdated check	$ 900
Reconciled balance in Pacific Bank checking account	8,040
Petty cash fund	350
Investment in Treasury bills	40,000
Certificate of deposit	20,000
Savings account balance at Meridian Federal	2,115
Postage stamps on hand	50
Employee IOU	250
Cash on hand	975

Instructions

a Compute the total cash balance to be reported as a current asset on the December 31 balance sheet.
b Describe the balance sheet treatment of the items not included in the cash balance computed in part (a).

P7-B2 *Bank reconciliation and entries* (L.O. 3)

The December 31 bank statement of Eason Company disclosed a balance of $8,400.50. On this same date the Cash account in the general ledger indicated a balance of $4,375.75. The following information has come to your attention:

1 A deposit of $903.88, mailed by Eason on December 28, was entered in the accounting records on December 29 but was not received by the bank until January 3.
2 Outstanding checks on December 31 totaled $1,400.23, computed as follows:

Checks written in November	$ 801.00
Checks written in December	599.23
	$1,400.23

3 A customer's NSF check for $325 was returned with the bank statement.
4 Eason's check no. 888 for a $9,000 machinery acquisition was entered in the accounts as $9,900.
5 Bank service charge, $25.60.
6 A note receivable of $2,950 and interest of $54 were collected by the bank but not as yet recorded in the accounts.
7 A $25 debit memo, representing a check printing charge, appeared on the bank statement.

Instructions

a Prepare a bank reconciliation for Eason Company.
b Prepare the journal entries necessary for Eason as of December 31.
c Determine the cash balance that Eason would disclose on the December 31 balance sheet.

P7-B3 *Bank reconciliation from bank statement* (L.O. 3)

The Whitlow Corporation received the accompanying bank statement for September from First City Bank & Trust.

FIRST CITY BANK AND TRUST							
WHITLOW CORPORATION				SEPTEMBER BANK STATEMENT			
Deposits/Credits		Checks/Debits			Balance		
Date	Amount	No.	Date	Amount	Date	Amount	
					9/01	10,480	
9/02	150	911	9/02	740	9/02	9,890	
9/15	2,350	912	9/04	325	9/03	9,490	
9/22	1,820	913	9/03	400	9/04	9,165	
9/27	740 CM	915	9/06	380	9/06	8,785	
9/28	2,570	916	9/08	500	9/08	8,285	
		917	9/12	480	9/12	6,965	
		918	9/12	200	9/15	9,315	
		919	9/12	640	9/18	9,105	
		920	9/18	210	9/21	8,320	
		921	9/21	370	9/22	8,690	
		922	9/22	610	9/25	7,970	
		923	9/22	840	9/26	7,670	
		924	9/26	300	9/27	8,190	
		925	9/27	220	9/28	10,280	
		926	9/25	720	9/30	9,750	
		927	9/28	480			
		929	9/30	515			
		NSF	9/21	415			
		SC	9/30	15			
CM *Credit Memo* NSF *NSF Check* SC *Service Charge*							

The credit memo represents the collection of a $700 note receivable plus $40 interest. Whitlow's cash receipts and disbursements records for September disclose the following:

Deposits		Checks Written			
9/14	$2,350	no. 915	$380	no. 924	$ 300
9/20	1,820	916	500	925	220
9/27	2,570	917	480	926	720
9/30	1,580	918	200	928	180
	$8,320	919	640	929	515
		920	210	930	720
		921	370	931	510
		922	610	932	460
		923	840		$7,855

An examination of the August reconciliation revealed a deposit in transit on August 31 of $150. The following checks were listed as outstanding: No. 890, $615; no. 911, $740; no. 912, $325; and no. 913, $400.

Instructions

a Assuming a cash balance per company records on September 30 of $9,015, prepare Whitlow's bank reconciliation for September. Assume that any errors detected during the reconciliation process are the fault of Whitlow's bookkeeper.

b Prepare the necessary journal entries for Whitlow as of September 30.

P7-B4 *Petty cash fund* (L.O. 4)

Dekalb Enterprises established a petty cash fund on July 1 to pay for small expenditures. The following schedule was prepared by Kenneth Ryan, fund custodian, to show activity for the first month:

	July 1	July 7	July 21	July 31
Cash placed in petty cash box				
To establish fund	$200	$ —	$ —	$ —
To replenish fund	—	175	180	198
Vouchers found in petty cash box for				
Postage	—	60	70	50
Store supplies	—	110	85	70
Miscellaneous	—	5	20	40

In addition to the vouchers found on July 31, the box also contained a $25 IOU signed by Ryan.

Instructions

a Record the necessary journal entries on July 1, 7, 21, and 31.

b On the basis of the preceding information and the journal entries that you prepared, do you have any concerns about Dekalb's petty cash fund in terms of control? Briefly explain.

P7-B5 *Short-term investments, lower of cost or market* (L.O. 6)

Evans Company began operations and purchased the following short-term investments in 19X7:

	Number of Shares	Cost per Share	Market Value per Share, Dec. 31
Mead, Inc.	200	$30	$35
Grace Co.	300	20	10
Russ Corp.	100	60	70

1-2-3

On March 19, 19X8, Evans purchased 400 shares of Wabash, Inc., for $5 per share, plus $100 of brokerage fees. Total dividends received during 19X8 amounted to $1,670.

Instructions

a Prepare the journal entry needed on December 31, 19X7, to value the short-term investments at the lower of cost or market.

b Show how Evans should disclose its short-term investments on the December 31, 19X7, balance sheet.

c Prepare the journal entry needed to record the purchase of the Wabash securities.

d Prepare the journal entry needed to record the dividends received during 19X8.

e Assume that by December 31, 19X8, Wabash's market value had increased to $10 per share. All other securities had the same year-end market prices as in 19X7.

(1) Prepare the journal entry to properly value the securities as of December 31, 19X8.

(2) Show how the short-term investments would be reported on the company's 19X8 balance sheet.

ELECTRONIC DATA BASE

EDB7-1 *Liquidity, short-term investments: Chiquita Brands International and Exxon Corporation* (L.O. 1, 6)

Chiquita Brands International is a marketer, distributor, and producer of fresh fruits and vegetables. The company is perhaps best known among consumers for its banana products. Exxon, in contrast, is a major force in all phases of the petroleum industry. The firm is also involved in chemicals, coal, and minerals.

Instructions

By using the text's Electronic Data Base, access the financial statements and accompanying notes of both companies and answer the questions that follow. Unless otherwise indicated, responses should be based on data for the most recent year presented.

a Determine the first two entries on each firm's balance sheet. Why are these assets listed in this position?

b Create a chart similar to that shown in Exhibit 7-1. Comment on any significant differences between the firms.

c What method is each company using to value its short-term investments (i.e., marketable securities)?

d Comment on any differences between the companies' balance sheet presentations of short-term investments and those shown in the text.

e Did either company disclose any unrealized or realized losses related to short-term investments? If not, where should this information be presented?

EDB7-2 *Liquidity, short-term investments* (L.O. 1, 6)

This problem is a duplication of Problem EDB7-1. It is based on two companies selected by your instructor.

Instructions

By using the text's Electronic Data Base, access the specified companies' financial statements and accompanying notes and focus on data for the most recent year reported. Answer requirements (a)–(e) of Problem EDB7-1.

BEYOND THE BASICS

BB7-1 *Valuation of short-term investments, conservatism* (L.O. 6)
The data that follow pertain to the short-term stock investments of five different companies.

Firm	Cost of Securities	Market Value of Securities	Balance in Allowance
Ace, Inc.	$36,900	$34,200	$ —
Baxter, Inc.	45,200	53,500	—
City Cleaning	18,500	13,600	2,900
Dakota Mining	25,800	26,500	1,800
Eastern Corp.	33,400	32,600	3,000

The "Balance in Allowance" column reflects the balance in the Allowance for Decline in Market Value of Short-Term Investments account *prior* to any necessary adjusting entries on December 31, 19X2.

Instructions

a Study the data presented and prepare the adjusting entries needed to properly value the securities at the lower of cost or market on December 31, 19X2.

b Show how these securities would appear on the December 31, 19X2, balance sheet for each of the firms.

c Generally speaking, is the lower-of-cost-or-market method consistent or inconsistent with the accounting convention of conservatism? Explain your answer by relating the proper accounting treatment for the securities investments of Ace, Inc., and Dakota Mining.

BB7-2 *Overview of chapter concepts: Multiple choice* (L.O. 2, 3, 4, 6)
The following multiple-choice questions relate to various topics discussed in the chapter. Select the best answer.

1 Sound cash disbursement control features should include each of the following except:
   a a periodic comparison of the Cash account in the general ledger with the cash balance reported by the bank.
   b significant disbursements being made by check.
   c verification and approval of disbursements by someone in a managerial capacity.
   d destruction of paid invoices to reduce the possibility of paying an invoice twice.

2 In the preparation of a bank reconciliation, which of the following items would have no impact on either the balance per bank statement or the balance per company records of Chan Corporation?
   a A customer's forged check that was rejected by the bank when deposited by Chan.
   b A deposit in transit.
   c Interest earned on an interest-bearing checking account.
   d A bank error in which the amount of a check was transposed.

3 The following data relate to Fog Company:

Cash balance per company records, 5/31	$25,500
Cash balance per bank statement, 5/31	25,500
Outstanding checks, 4/30	4,200
Outstanding checks, 5/31	3,100
Deposits in transit, 4/30	1,770

Deposits in transit, 5/31	2,331
Interest earned on account during May	124
NSF check returned with the bank statement	?

How much was the NSF check?

a $124.   c $893.

b $769.   d $1,354.

4 Ross Company recently replenished a $1,000 petty cash fund by writing a check for $730. If expense vouchers amounted to $735, the journal entry to record the replenishment would cause net income to:

a increase by $5.   c decrease by $730.

b decrease by $725.   d decrease by $735.

5 The historical-cost method of accounting for short-term investments:

a cannot be used by a company that uses the lower-of-cost-or-market method.

b is generally used with debt securities such as bonds.

c is generally used with equity securities such as stock.

d violates generally accepted accounting principles in a period of rising stock prices.

Questions 6, 7, and 8 are based on the following facts:

Spencer Company acquired the following investments during 19X1: Kirk Corporation (200 shares at $22); Kulberg Corporation (100 shares at $30); and Ostand Corporation (300 shares at $40). Per-share market values on December 31, 19X1, were Kirk, $23; Kulberg, $18; and Ostand, $40. Dividends received during the year totaled $1,500.

By the end of 19X2, Kirk and Kulberg had increased in value to $28 and $25 per share, respectively. In contrast, Ostand had declined to $39 per share. The company values its securities in accordance with generally accepted accounting principles.

6 The balance in the Allowance for Decline in Market Value account at the end of 19X1 should be:

a $0.   c $1,200.

b $1,000.   d $1,400.

7 Spencer's investment activities would increase the firm's 19X1 net income by:

a $500.   c $1,500.

b $1,000.   d $2,500.

8 The credit to the Recovery in Value of Short-Term Investments account at the end of 19X2 should be:

a $0.   c $1,000.

b $400.   d $1,400.

CAI7-1 *Writing a memo: The Dun & Bradstreet Corporation** (L.O. 2)

Communication Principle: Memos are the most frequent form of written communication used in business. This means of delivering information should be brief and direct, and the tone and style should fit the occasion and the reader. That is, serious subjects require serious and carefully phrased memos, whereas straightforward, informal messages are appropriate for regular business among colleagues.

Memos begin with To, From, Subject, and Date lines. These items allow

**COMMUNICATION
OF ACCOUNTING
INFORMATION**

---

* A continuation of this problem is found in Chapter 8 on page 333.

the communication to be quickly routed and filed. The body of a memo should start with background statements that brief the reader on the context and reason for the memo. Next, using short paragraphs, the memo should explain pertinent details or related information. It should end with forward-looking comments such as "I'd be glad to answer any questions and discuss this further. . . ."

Do not try to include too much information in a single memo or to make the memo multipurpose. Limit what you have to say and maintain a positive, natural, and polite style and tone.

■ ■ ■ ■ ■ ■ ■ ■

Dun & Bradstreet is a huge corporation involved in numerous service businesses. Among the company's activities are publishing (Moody's Investors Service), marketing services (Nielsen ratings), and corporate research. Dun & Bradstreet is also heavily involved with the compilation and sale of credit reports and maintains a data base that includes over 16 million businesses. This data base is useful in helping companies decide whether or not to extend credit to other entities.

Imagine that you work for Dun & Bradstreet in the corporate communications division, and rumors have been circulating about cash flow problems of the company. These rumors began because a newspaper article incorrectly described Dun & Bradstreet as a firm "with cash flow and credit problems" rather than as a company "that provides information about businesses having cash flow and credit problems." The following balance sheet data (in thousands) are available:

Cash	$1,026,289
Short-term investments	43,205
Accounts & other short-term receivables	1,115,500
Accounts, accrued, & other short-term payables	1,919,430

Instructions

Draft an internal memo for company employees that explains and dispels the rumors. As part of the memo, briefly describe the cash management methods that are probably used by Dun & Bradstreet to avoid cash flow problems.

Answers to Chapter Quiz

1 a ($10,000 + $900)

2 d

3 c

4 b ($200 − $36 − $94 − $2 − $58)

5 c ($80,000 − $75,800)

CHAPTER

8

Receivables

LEARNING OBJECTIVES

After studying this chapter, you should be able to:

1

Distinguish between trade and nontrade receivables.

2

Account for uncollectible receivables by using both the direct write-off and the allowance methods.

3

Calculate uncollectible accounts expense by using the income statement and balance sheet approaches.

4

Handle account write-offs and subsequent recoveries under the allowance method.

5

Account for credit card sales.

6

Demonstrate the computations and journal entries for notes receivable and interest, including discounted and dishonored obligations.

The extension of credit has been a significant factor behind economic growth in the United States. The purchase of goods and services on an installment plan, by the use of in-house charge accounts, or through bank cards such as Visa and MasterCard is a way of life for today's average business or consumer.

Businesses extend credit in order to increase sales. Frequently, however, firms concentrate on this objective and lose sight of the costs related to the credit-granting decision. Credit sales often create the need for a credit department to (1) investigate customer credit ratings, (2) approve the extension of credit, and (3) attempt to collect delinquent accounts. These activities are expensive in terms of both time and dollars.

Furthermore, companies must wait to receive monies due, and despite the offer of a cash discount, many customers still fail to settle their balances within requested time limits. Thus, businesses must often sell short-term investments and secure bank loans to obtain needed operating funds. The former action may result in the loss of future interest or dividends, while the latter will give rise to interest costs.

Another cost related to credit sales is the result of nonpayment by customers. Firms rarely collect all their accounts receivable because some customers go bankrupt, leave town, and so on. This cost of nonpayment, known as *uncollectable accounts expense,* can be especially high for an entity that has tried to increase sales by being very liberal in granting credit. Although some marginal customers may be profitable, the end result is normally increased costs and a lack of collection by the firm.

Receivables

Credit sales and other transactions give rise to **receivables,** which are claims against customers and others that arise from business operations. Receivables are reported on the balance sheet as either current or noncurrent assets until they are ultimately collected. Those amounts expected to be collected within one year or the operating cycle, whichever is longer, are classified as current assets; all other receivables are classified as noncurrent.

Receivables are subdivided into two categories: trade and nontrade. The majority of receivables are **trade receivables,** which result from the sale of products or services to customers. Trade receivables consist of accounts receivable and notes receivable. In contrast, **nontrade receivables** arise from other transactions and events and include accrued receivables, advances to employees, and deposits with utilities.

In this chapter we will concentrate on the accounting issues associated with current trade receivables. Accounting for other types of receivables is discussed elsewhere in the text.

ETHICS ISSUE

Joe has access to a major bank's computerized data base, which contains records of customer balances and loans outstanding. Joe's father has requested financial information about Susan Turner, a bank customer, for the purpose of increasing her credit limit with his business. If Joe has a close relationship with his father, what should Joe do?

OBJECTIVE

1

Distinguish between trade and nontrade receivables.

ACCOUNTS RECEIVABLE

Accounts receivable represent the amounts due an entity from credit sales of goods and services. As the figures in Exhibit 8-1 indicate, accounts receivable can be a substantial percentage of total assets for many firms.

EXHIBIT 8-1
Accounts Receivable for
Various Firms (000 Omitted)

	Compaq Computer	Harley-Davidson	Neiman Marcus	NIKE, Inc.
Net accounts receivable	$ 624,376	$ 71,517	$ 201,227	$ 521,588
Total assets	2,826,386	474,233	1,072,197	1,708,430
Net accounts receivable as a percentage of total assets	22.1%	15.1%	18.8%	30.5%

Given the magnitude of accounts receivable, proper valuation and presentation on the balance sheet are essential. In Chapter 5 we discussed a number of items related to this important asset, including trade discounts, sales discounts, and sales returns and allowances. We will now focus on one additional accounting issue: uncollectible accounts.

Despite the use of credit standards, some uncollectible accounts (often called *bad debts*) almost always arise. Uncollectible accounts have both income statement and balance sheet implications for businesses. On the income statement, for example, an "adequate" amount for bad debts expense should be matched against (deducted from) the sales revenues generated. The objective is to derive a fair measurement of net income. Turning to the balance sheet, the Accounts Receivable account should be reduced to reflect the amounts that a firm has a reasonable expectation of collecting. This latter procedure is an application of conservatism in financial reporting, which permits asset write-downs when related valuations have been diminished or impaired.

There are two methods of accounting for uncollectible accounts: the direct write-off method and the allowance method.

Direct Write-off Method

Under the **direct write-off method,** bad debts are recognized when the actual loss is confirmed. That is, when a specific customer account is deemed uncollectible, the account is written off as an expense of the period. To illustrate, assume that Bill McCracken owes the Warren Company $875. After repeated collection efforts, Warren has just learned that McCracken has filed for bankruptcy. The Warren Company would make the following entry:

Uncollectible Accounts Expense	875	
Accounts Receivable: Bill McCracken		875
To write off uncollectible account		

The direct write-off method of accounting for uncollectibles is simple and has the advantage of reporting actual losses rather than estimates. This approach presents several problems, however. Frequently, a customer's account is not deemed uncollectible until long after a sale has been made. The direct write-off method could therefore result in the recognition of sales revenue in one period and the expense related to that revenue in a later period. Thus, an improper matching of revenues and expenses would take place. Furthermore, because the write-off may occur in the future, Accounts Receivable is sometimes overstated at the end of the year of sale. Given these problems, the direct write-off approach is typically used in financial reporting by businesses that have relatively low levels of uncollectibles.

Allowance Method

The **allowance method** overcomes the objections to the direct write-off method by associating the revenue and expense in the same reporting period. Correct matching is achieved through the use of *estimates* of uncollectible accounts expense. Reasonable estimates can normally be obtained by studying a firm's past experience with bad accounts and making adjustments for current economic conditions and credit standards.

When the estimate of uncollectibles is determined, a journal entry is recorded at the end of the accounting period in the form of an adjustment. The entry involves a debit to Uncollectible Accounts Expense and a credit to an account entitled Allowance for Uncollectible Accounts.[1] Because credit policy is typically a management decision, Uncollectible Accounts Expense is usually reported on the income statement as an administrative operating expense. In contrast, the Allowance for Uncollectibles is a contra asset that is offset against Accounts Receivable on the balance sheet, as follows (amounts are assumed):

Current assets		
Accounts receivable	$19,000	
Less: Allowance for uncollectible accounts	2,600	$16,400

Offsetting the Allowance in this manner informs financial statement users of the expected **net realizable value** ($16,400), or the amount of cash expected from the collection of present customer balances. The use of this separate valuation account is required because the specific uncollectible customer accounts are unknown when the financial statements are prepared. As a result, we cannot credit individual subsidiary accounts (and the Accounts Receivable control account) at the time of bad debt estimation.

Uncollectible accounts expense can be estimated by observing historical relationships between the actual bad debts incurred and (1) sales or (2) accounts receivable. These relationships may be summarized as follows:

1 Relationship to sales (income statement approach)
  a Percentage of sales
  b Percentage of credit sales

---

[1] The Allowance account is sometimes called the Allowance for Doubtful Accounts or the Allowance for Bad Debts.

2 Relationship to accounts receivable (balance sheet approach)
  a Percentage of outstanding accounts receivable
  b Aging of accounts receivable

Relationship to Sales: Income Statement Approach

Estimating uncollectibles on the basis of sales results in current revenues being matched with the costs incurred in producing those revenues. Stated differently, the sales that ultimately give rise to the bad debts are used as the basis for the period's expense. Because of its matching emphasis, this method is commonly referred to as the **income statement approach.**

The estimate of uncollectible accounts expense may be computed on total sales or credit sales. Total sales can be used when the relationship between cash sales and credit sales is fairly stable from one period to the next. If this relationship varies substantially, use of the total figure may not be appropriate. Generally speaking, most accountants favor estimation of uncollectibles on the basis of credit sales only—a more rational approach because bad debts are not incurred on cash collections. To illustrate the income statement approach, assume that Lukin Company's sales on account for the current year total $500,000 and that uncollectible accounts have historically amounted to 3% of credit sales. The following adjusting entry for $15,000 ($500,000 × 0.03) would be made:

Uncollectible Accounts Expense	15,000	
Allowance for Uncollectible Accounts		15,000
Adjusting entry		

Relationship to Accounts Receivable: Balance Sheet Approach

Uncollectibles may also be estimated on the basis of accounts receivable. This method, known as the **balance sheet approach,** focuses on reporting receivables at net realizable value. When using the balance sheet method, we must therefore consider the previous balance in the Allowance for Uncollectibles account. For example, assume Galaxy Electronics has determined that bad accounts normally amount to 3% of the year-end accounts receivable balance. The company's records at the end of the year, prior to the adjustment for uncollectibles, disclose the following information:

Accounts receivable	$600,000
Allowance for uncollectible accounts	2,800 (credit balance)

Collections on receivables are expected to total $582,000 [$600,000 − ($600,000 × 0.03)], thereby requiring an $18,000 balance in the Allowance for Uncollectible Accounts ($600,000 − $582,000). Because $2,800 is presently in the account, an additional $15,200 ($18,000 − $2,800) must be entered to achieve the desired result. The following adjusting entry is needed:

Uncollectible Accounts Expense	15,200	
Allowance for Uncollectible Accounts		15,200
Adjusting entry		

The effect of this entry is shown in the accompanying T-accounts:

OBJECTIVE

3

Calculate uncollectible accounts expense by using the income statement and balance sheet approaches.

Uncollectible Accounts Expense		Allowance for Uncollectible Accounts	
Adj 15,200		Balance 2,800	
		Adj 15,200	
		18,000	

The resulting balance sheet presentation of Galaxy's accounts receivable appears below.

Current assets
Accounts receivable $600,000
Less: Allowance for uncollectible accounts   18,000 $582,000

Occasionally, the Allowance for Uncollectibles account may possess a debit balance.[2] Suppose, for instance, that Galaxy's Allowance account had a $3,000 *debit* balance prior to the adjustment. As the number scale in Exhibit 8-2 shows, a $21,000 adjusting entry would be necessary. The $21,000 credit to the Allowance, when combined with the $3,000 debit balance, yields the desired $18,000 outcome.

Tips & Techniques

The reported amount of expense is the focal point of the income statement approach; in contrast, the computation of net realizable value (i.e., accounts receivable valuation) is the thrust of the balance sheet method. Given the manner in which the Allowance for Uncollectibles is used to calculate net realizable value, the Allowance's balance must be considered in the adjustment process if the balance sheet approach is employed. This point is shown graphically in Exhibit 8-3.

Aging of Accounts Receivable.   Estimating bad debts as a flat percentage of outstanding accounts receivable ignores the due date of the many individual accounts that compose the total balance. The length of time a specific account has been outstanding is an important factor when assessing

EXHIBIT 8-2
Allowance for Uncollectibles: Galaxy Electronics

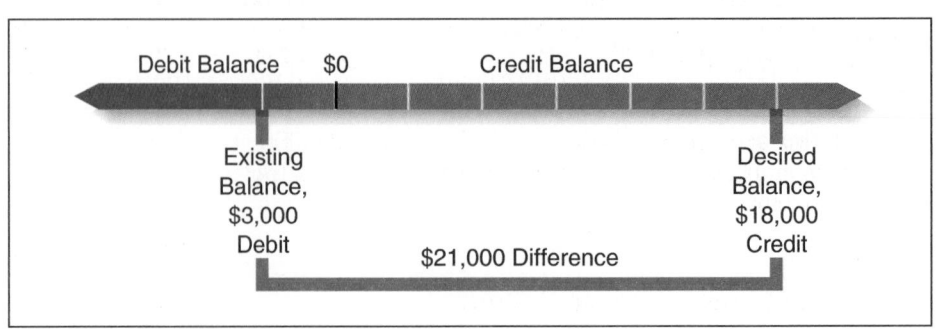

---

[2] The situations that cause a debit balance are discussed later in the chapter.

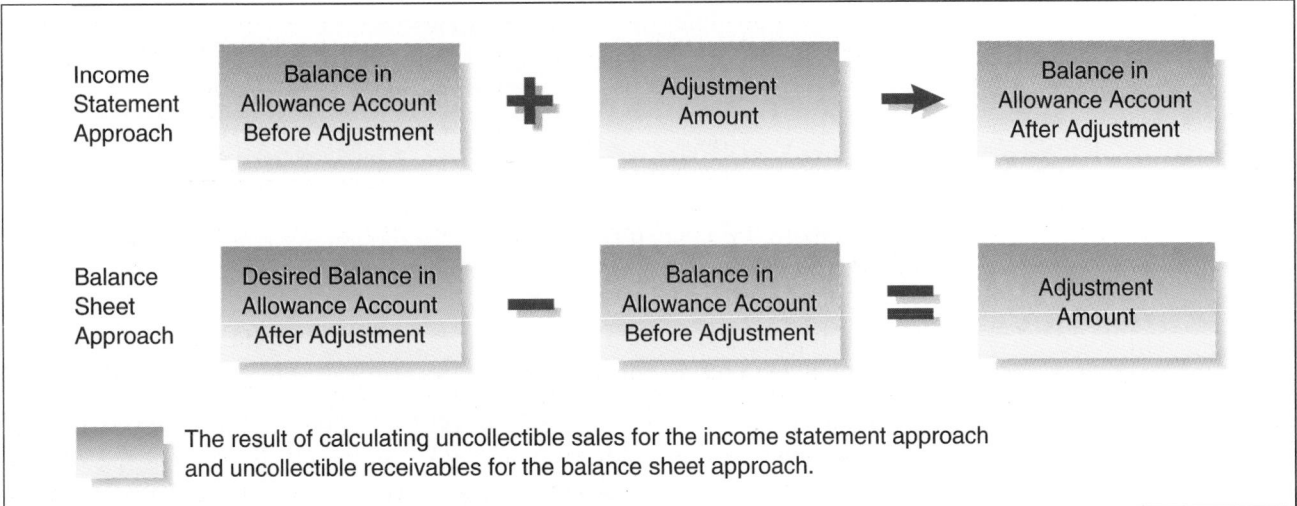

| Income Statement Approach | Balance in Allowance Account Before Adjustment | ➕ | Adjustment Amount | ➡️ | Balance in Allowance Account After Adjustment |

| Balance Sheet Approach | Desired Balance in Allowance Account After Adjustment | ➖ | Balance in Allowance Account Before Adjustment | = | Adjustment Amount |

The result of calculating uncollectible sales for the income statement approach and uncollectible receivables for the balance sheet approach.

EXHIBIT 8-3
Comparison of the Income Statement and Balance Sheet Approaches

the probability of future collection. That is, a company is more likely to collect an account that is 30 days old than to collect one that is 180 days old. To overcome this problem, accountants have developed a more sophisticated approach to estimate bad debts. This method, termed **aging accounts receivable,** categorizes individual accounts according to the length of time outstanding. A historically developed bad debts percentage is then applied to each age category to determine the estimate.

The aging process not only furnishes information for the bad debt estimate but also serves as a useful management tool. The analysis of individual accounts provides insight regarding the success or failure of a firm's credit and collection efforts. Furthermore, close monitoring of specific customer activity will determine if any changes in a customer's credit rating are necessary.

To illustrate estimation by the aging process, examine Exhibit 8-4, which contains information from the records of the Livingston Corporation. The aging of individual customer accounts indicates that the Allowance for Uncollectibles must contain a balance of $9,395 on December 31, 19XX.

As before, the previous balance in the Allowance account is considered when formulating the adjusting entry. If a review of Livingston's ledger revealed a credit balance of $2,200, then $7,195 ($9,395 − $2,200) would be needed to bring the Allowance up to the required figure. The following entry is necessary:

Uncollectible Accounts Expense	7,195	
Allowance for Uncollectible Accounts		7,195
Adjusting entry		

Writing Off Uncollectible Accounts

Under the allowance method, individual accounts are written off when they are deemed uncollectible by debiting the Allowance for Uncollecti-

OBJECTIVE
4

Handle account write-offs and subsequent recoveries under the allowance method.

EXHIBIT 8-4
Aging Schedule

LIVINGSTON CORPORATION
Aging Schedule of Accounts Receivable
December 31, 19XX

Customer	Balance, 12/31/XX	Length of Time Outstanding				
		Under 31 Days	31–60 Days	61–90 Days	91–120 Days	Over 120 Days
Clark, Inc.	$ 15,000			$6,000	$5,000	$4,000
Gibbs Manufacturing	36,000	$31,000	$ 5,000			
Madden Co.	19,500	15,000	4,500			
Nunley Co.	18,700	9,000	5,000	3,000	1,700	
Patrick Corporation	27,500	15,500	12,000			
Total	$116,700	$70,500	$26,500	$9,000	$6,700	$4,000

Estimated Uncollectibles

Age	Account Balances (from Above)	× Estimated % Uncollectible	= Estimated Amount of Uncollectibles
Under 31 days	$ 70,500	3%	$2,115
31–60 days	26,500	7	1,855
61–90 days	9,000	12	1,080
91–120 days	6,700	35	2,345
Over 120 days	4,000	50	2,000
	$116,700		$9,395

bles and crediting Accounts Receivable. Note that Uncollectible Accounts Expense is not charged again at the time of write-off; to do so would result in double counting.

In view of this treatment, the write-off of an uncollectible account does not affect the net realizable value of the accounts receivable balance. As an example, consider the following information that appeared on Harvey Company's December 31, 19X1, balance sheet:

Current assets
  Accounts receivable $140,000
    Less: Allowance for uncollectible accounts   6,780 $133,220

Assume that on January 18, 19X2, J. Waldrup's $425 balance is judged uncollectible. Thus, the entry that follows is made.

Allowance for Uncollectible Accounts   425
    Accounts Receivable: J. Waldrup   425
  To write off uncollectible account

The write-off will not have any effect on the net accounts receivable balance because the entry reduces both the Allowance and Accounts Receivable by the same amount. This result is shown at the top of the next page.

	Before	Write-off	After
Accounts receivable	$140,000	−$425	$139,575
Less: Allowance for uncollectibles	6,780	−425	6,355
	$133,220		$133,220

The process of writing off an uncollectible account places debits in the Allowance and may result in a debit balance at the end of the reporting period. This situation usually arises when a firm's estimate of expense (a credit in the Allowance account) is lower than its actual write-off experience. The debit balance is easily corrected by increasing the percentages used in the adjustment process.

Collection of an Account Previously Written Off

Occasionally, a customer whose account has been previously written off will pay the amount owed. In such cases the customer's receivable is first reestablished in the accounting records; the payment is then recorded. Continuing the previous example, assume J. Waldrup now pays $225 of his $425 balance. The following journal entries are needed:

Accounts Receivable: J. Waldrup	225	
Allowance for Uncollectible Accounts		225
To reinstate account		
Cash	225	
Accounts Receivable: J. Waldrup		225
To record collection on account		

Observe that the reinstatement entry simply reverses the entry that was made for the write-off. If collection of the entire $425 is likely, Waldrup's account would be reestablished for the full amount.

Notice that the net effect on the Accounts Receivable account is zero, because it is debited and credited for the same figure. Yet, this two-ntry procedure is preferred over one that results in a single debit to Cash and a credit to the Allowance for Uncollectibles. Why? By going back and reinstating the customer's account on the books, we are showing that an attempt has been made to pay the balance due. This action and information could be useful to management in future credit-granting decisions.

Insights into Business Operations

A study of bad debt disclosures will reveal various insights about business activities. For instance, the allowance for uncollectible accounts as a percentage of ending accounts receivable varies significantly by company. This variation is caused, in part, by the type of product being sold, customer payment habits, and a firm's credit policy. A review of recent corporate annual reports found, for example, that The Coca-Cola Company has recorded an allowance of about $4 per $100 of accounts receivable, Apple Computer about $6 per $100 of accounts receivable, and Reebok International about $10 per $100.

As more extreme cases, we cite data of URCARCO, a Fort Worth–based chain of "we finance" used-car dealerships, and several large U.S. banks.

URCARCO's primary clientele are individuals who cannot obtain financing from traditional lenders because of insufficient income, poor credit history, and other reasons. In a recent recession year, uncollectible accounts expense amounted to 54% of sales.

Turning to the banks, many of the woes experienced in the past few years by U.S. financial institutions are directly attributable to bad loans that were made by these entities. (Be aware that customer loans are receivables for these firms, to be disclosed as assets on the balance sheet.) As the following figures show ($000 omitted), the amount of uncollectible accounts expense has been staggering in some instances, severely depressing profitability.

Financial Institution	Uncollectible Accounts Expense	Net Income (Loss)
Chase Manhattan	$1,085,000	$ 520,000
Citicorp	3,890,000	(457,000)
First Chicago	440,000	116,300
Norwest Corp.	322,200	398,500
Wells Fargo & Co.	1,335,000	21,000

Credit Card Sales

OBJECTIVE 5

Account for credit card sales.

Many retailers and service establishments have found that maintaining credit departments, billing customers, and collecting accounts are costly and time-consuming processes. As a result, a large number of firms have stopped carrying their own accounts in favor of credit cards such as American Express, Visa, and MasterCard. A merchant's acceptance of these well-known cards usually offers the benefit of increased sales. In addition, the seller assumes little or no risk. If a customer does not pay his or her bill, the credit card issuer suffers the loss.

When a sale is made on one of the preceding or similar cards, the purchaser signs a multipart form, which includes a credit card draft. The draft authorizes the credit card company to pay the seller, which it generally does shortly after the sale is made. The merchant, then, experiences faster cash inflows and need no longer wait 30 or more days for customers to settle their obligations. The credit card company later bills the customer for the amount of the purchase.

In exchange for these benefits, a service charge is assessed. This charge is usually a percentage of each sale and, in essence, is a fee for the use of a credit department and customer billing services. The service charge varies and is partially determined by the seller's annual volume of credit card transactions.

Bank Card Sales Versus Nonbank Card Sales

When sales are made on bank cards, the merchant submits the credit card drafts along with daily cash receipts to the bank.[3] The bank increases the

---

[3] In many state-of-the-art systems, the transaction is "captured" electronically, and little or no paper changes hands.

EXECUTIVE BRIEFING
Managing Uncollectible Accounts: The Bottom-Line Impact

Robert Seass
Senior Vice-President and Group Controller
Dean Witter Financial Services Group

When the dust settles on the new business successes and failures over the last decade, I believe that Discover Card will be judged a clear winner. From a startup at the end of 1985, Discover Card now has over 40 million cards outstanding, 1.4 million merchant outlets, cardmember balances of $14 billion, and—to the surprise of many skeptics—a healthy profit margin.

Once the cardmember and merchant acceptance of Discover Card was assured, one of the biggest risks became exposure to losses from uncollectible accounts. Controlling credit quality is an extensive effort, from establishing credit approval standards that will minimize losses without denying credit to potentially good customers, to implementing rigorous collection efforts on delinquent accounts. Discover Card currently has more than 2,000 employees involved in such activities.

How important is managing uncollectible accounts? Some simple math provides the answer. If you start with an annualized gross yield from interest income and fees on a credit card portfolio of around 18%, from which you deduct representative funding costs of 8% and operating costs of 5%, then the difference between a 3% or a 5% annualized account write-off rate (the normal range for the bank card industry) spells the difference between a good bottom line or no bottom line. We all know the consequence of running a no return business, so at Discover Card we will continue to manage credit quality just as carefully as we know how.

seller's account; the service charge is automatically deducted and often appears on the bank statement along with other account charges. In view of this treatment, the credit card sale made on a bank card is really a cash sale.

If the transaction is on a nonbank card, the merchant normally mails the drafts to the credit card company.[4] Because reimbursement is not instantaneous, an account receivable is established for the amount of the sale. As an example, assume that Jacobs Jewelry sold $2,000 of merchandise on Charge-It, a nonbank credit card, giving rise to the following entry:

Accounts Receivable: Charge-It	2,000	
Sales		2,000
To record credit card sale		

---

[4] Credit card companies often allow merchants other alternatives, for instance, the direct deposit of drafts at designated banks. A higher service charge is usually assessed if this option is selected.

HIGHLIGHT

Diamonds, Rental Cars, Apples, and Peanut Butter

You can use them to buy expensive jewelry and to rent automobiles on out-of-town business trips. In fact, today they can be used to purchase just about anything—even a surgical procedure at the local hospital. We're talking about credit cards, those handy pieces of plastic that allow consumer survival when checking account balances run low.

Despite the widespread acceptance of credit cards, most people still can't use plastic at the supermarket. Things are beginning to change, though. Some 50 supermarket chains across the country have begun accepting Visa and MasterCard for food purchases in recent years. With many other supermarkets studying the idea, the credit card companies are pursuing one of our nation's last untapped markets.

These companies, however, face significant resistance from the supermarket industry, which has traditionally insisted on payment in cash or checks. "Supermarket chains face a big, big, big problem," says a publisher of credit card newsletters. "Their margins are too slim" to pay the fee that credit card companies charge merchants on each transaction. Also troubling to grocers is that checkout speed has become a more important marketing tool. Without the latest technology, a checkout line can be brought to a halt by a customer with a credit card as the cashier runs to the office or calls the manager to get approval.

Finally, there's the matter of psychology. "The idea of buying food on credit is a concept that stretches the credit orientation . . . of most American consumers," the publisher says. "It doesn't sound right, charging your food." Interestingly, two of the warning signs used by the National Foundation for Consumer Credit to identify possible financial overreaching are starting to use plastic to pay for things previously bought with cash, and using credit cards to pay for essentials and not paying the bills immediately. "If you're going to use a credit card as a convenience, like a check, that's fine," notes the foundation's vice-president. "But when you start paying for December's groceries in February, that starts to be a problem."

Changing demographics, though—especially the rise in the number of two-job families—have persuaded supermarkets to rethink credit cards. "One-stop shopping has tremendous appeal to people with jobs, so a lot of new items have come into supermarkets," observes an official from a grocery trade publication. Many people now buy flowers, housewares, liquor, even TV sets at the stores where they buy their groceries. "No one comes into the supermarket with $270 in cash for the television set."

More important, new technology in the form of more efficient computer terminals in checkout lanes has made the cost of processing a credit card transaction more competitive with the cost of check and cash transactions. Despite the fact that credit cards still cost more than cash and checks, the cards are affordable because new customers are attracted to the store, and cardholders' shopping baskets are fuller than they would be otherwise.

Supermarket officials whose stores have begun accepting credit cards expect the practice to spread. Just how fast is another question. [Safeway, for instance, which operates 1,100 stores, just recently started to accept plastic—but only on a piecemeal basis—in northern California. "We're] looking at it very carefully," says a spokesman. Credit cards "have a toehold," notes the trade publication executive cited earlier. "Retailers see advantages if there are items you can move that you couldn't otherwise move. But it's still not clear just how far and fast it will go."

If the service fee charged by the card company is 5%, Jacobs would update the accounting records in the following manner when the receivable from Charge-It is collected:

Cash	1,900	
Credit Card Expense	100	
Accounts Receivable: Charge-It		2,000
To record collection on account from		
credit card company		

The financial statements of many entities often reveal an asset entitled notes receivable. **Notes receivable** (sometimes called promissory notes) are written promises from clients or customers to pay a definite amount of money on a specific future date. These instruments are used in extending credit to customers and to lengthen the repayment period of outstanding accounts receivable. Notes are popular in some industries and seldom encountered in others. Exhibit 8-5 illustrates a typical promissory note.

In this particular case Precision Equipment is the **maker** of the note, namely, the person or firm that promises to pay the stipulated amount. Forseth Company is the **payee,** or the party to be paid. The stated amount (face value) of the note, $6,000, is termed the **principal.** Finally, February 9 is the **maturity date,** or the date that the note becomes due. The maturity date is computed as follows:

Term of note		60 days
Days outstanding in		
December (31 − 11)	20	
January	31	51
Days outstanding in February until maturity		9

Had the term of the note been two months (as opposed to 60 days), the maturity date would have been February 11, which is two months from the time of issue.

NOTES RECEIVABLE

OBJECTIVE 6

Demonstrate the computations and journal entries for notes receivable and interest, including discounted and dishonored obligations.

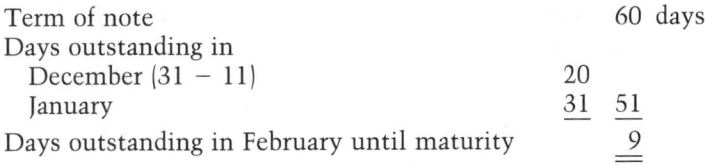

$6,000	Boise, Idaho	December 11, 19X1
Sixty days after date		we promise to
pay to the order of	Forseth Company	
Six thousand and no/100----------------------- dollars		
for value received, with interest of	12%	
payable at	First City Bank	
Due February 9, 19X2	*Michelle McGregor*	
	Precision Equipment Company	

EXHIBIT 8-5
Promissory Note

The Nature of Interest

Interest is the charge imposed on the borrower of funds. The note in Exhibit 8-5 indicates that Precision Equipment owes Forseth $6,000; however, the amount is not due until February 9, 19X2. In return for this temporary extension of credit, Forseth has become entitled to interest at a rate of 12%. Does this mean that Precision will have to pay the principal plus an additional $720 ($6,000 × 0.12)? The answer is no.

Interest rates are normally quoted on an annual basis. As a result, the term of the note would have to be extended from 60 days to a full year in order for the charge to total $720. To compute interest for a given period, the following formula is needed:

$$\text{Interest} = \text{Principal} \times \text{Rate} \times \text{Time}$$

This formula mathematically expresses the intuitive feeling that interest depends on a financial agreement's rate, amount, and duration.

To fully understand the preceding computation, it is important to know that the definition of principal is expanded somewhat to be more than just the face value of a note. Principal, as used here, is the amount on which interest is figured and may be the balance of an account receivable (in the case of finance charges), the outstanding balance of a loan, or the amount on deposit in a savings account.

Further, the formula's time element can be expressed in either days or months. In our example, for instance, interest would be calculated as follows:

$$\$6,000 \times 0.12 \times \tfrac{60}{360} = \$120$$

In many applications and for ease of computation, a year is considered to have 360 days.[5] Because the 12% rate covers an annual time frame, a factor of $\tfrac{60}{360}$ is appropriate.

Had the term of the note been three months, a factor of $\tfrac{3}{12}$ would have been employed, to yield interest charges of $180:

$$\$6,000 \times 0.12 \times \tfrac{3}{12} = \$180$$

Accounting for Notes and Interest

Notes receivable are initially entered in the accounting records at face value, requiring a debit to the Notes Receivable account. Because the note is owned by the payee firm, the associated interest is revenue. Interest revenue is recorded as it is received and as a year-end adjustment if the reporting period ends prior to the maturity date.

To illustrate, we will continue the Forseth Company example. The note in question was received on December 11, 19X1, from Precision Equip-

---

[5] Federal agencies and a number of lenders use a 365-day year.

ment, which desired to extend the repayment period of a previous purchase on account. Forseth would record the note as follows:

Dec. 11   Notes Receivable   6,000
               Accounts Receivable: Precision Equipment   6,000
          Received note in settlement of account balance

Precision has agreed to pay $6,120 on February 9: $6,000 principal plus $120 of interest ($6,000 × 0.12 × $\frac{60}{360}$). The amount due on the maturity date, principal plus interest, is commonly referred to as the **maturity value.**

Assume that December 31, 19X1, is the end of Forseth's accounting period. Although no interest has been received as of this date, 20 days' worth has been earned. Therefore, accrued interest revenue of $40 ($6,000 × 0.12 × $\frac{20}{360}$) is recorded by the following adjusting entry:

Dec. 31   Interest Receivable   40
               Interest Revenue   40
          Adjusting entry

Also on December 31 closing entries would be recorded. The interest T-accounts, after closing, would appear as follows:

Interest Receivable		Interest Revenue	
12/31 40		12/31 Closing 40	12/31 40

On February 9, 19X2, when Precision Equipment pays the note, Forseth will make the entry shown below.

Feb. 9   Cash   6,120
              Interest Receivable   40
              Interest Revenue   80
              Notes Receivable   6,000
          Collected note and interest from
          Precision Equipment

To explain, the receipt of the maturity value calls for a debit to Cash for $6,120 and a credit to Notes Receivable for the original amount of the obligation ($6,000). One-third of the $120 interest is located in the Interest Receivable account; thus, Interest Receivable must be credited for $40. The remaining $80, which has been earned during 19X2, is revenue. Observe how the adjusting entry effectively splits the interest: $40 of revenue earned in 19X1 (20 days) and $80 of revenue earned in 19X2 (40 days).

Discounting Notes Receivable

Companies frequently find that unexpected conditions dictate the need for additional cash on a short-term basis. One of the many ways to satisfy this need involves the payee's discounting a note receivable at the bank. **Discounting** allows the payee to obtain cash at the time of discounting rather than wait until the note comes due and is paid by the maker. The maker is informed to pay the bank directly on the note's maturity date, but the payee usually guarantees payment should the maker default. Consequently, during the period from the discount date to the maturity date, the note represents a **contingent (possible) liability** to the payee. Such amounts are disclosed in the footnotes to the financial statements, as opposed to the liability section of the balance sheet, because a *definite* obligation does not exist.

Since the maker is not obligated to pay the bank until maturity, the bank, in effect, is lending the discounting firm a sum of money. As in all loans, interest is charged. In this case, however, the interest is called a *discount* and is determined by the discount percentage (interest rate) assessed by the bank. At the time a note is discounted, the payee records the proceeds received and nets the discount against any interest revenue to be earned over the term of the note. The entries to record the receipt, discounting, and collection of a note receivable are illustrated in the following example.

The Details Behind Discounting

On March 10, the Kyle Corporation received a $20,000, 90-day note from Walt Dailey, a customer, in settlement of his overdue account balance. The note carried a 10% interest rate. On April 9, 30 days later, Kyle discounted the note at the bank at a 12% discount rate. The entries below are necessary to record these transactions.

Mar. 10	Notes Receivable	20,000	
	Accounts Receivable: Walt Dailey		20,000
	Received note in settlement of		
	account balance		
Apr. 9	Cash	20,090	
	Interest Revenue		90
	Notes Receivable		20,000
	Proceeds from Dailey's discounted note		

The cash proceeds from the bank are calculated as follows:

Face amount of note	$20,000
Add: Interest revenue ($20,000 × 0.10 × $\frac{90}{360}$)	500
Maturity value	$20,500
Deduct: Discount ($20,500 × 0.12 × $\frac{60}{360}$)	410
Proceeds	$20,090

The discount is based on the maturity value of $20,500, which is the value of the note to the bank. The bank subtracts the discount from the maturity value to determine the cash proceeds. Observe that the bank's discount calculation ($410) is dependent on the number of days the money will be advanced to Kyle. Because Kyle held the 90-day note for 30 days, the bank expects to be repaid in 60 days. Finally, notice that Kyle collected $20,090 for a $20,000 receivable, requiring $90 of interest revenue to be recognized. If the proceeds had been less than $20,000, the firm would have incurred interest expense. The deciding factors behind the generation of interest revenue or interest expense are the interest rate on the note, the bank's discount rate, and the holding periods involved.

If a balance sheet is prepared prior to the note's maturity date (June 8), Kyle will construct a footnote to the financial statements similar to the following:

Note E: Contingencies
On April 30, 19XX, the company was contingently liable for a discounted note receivable having a maturity value of $20,500.

The footnote is needed until June 8, at which time Dailey will either pay the bank (and thereby clear Kyle) or default.

Tips & Techniques

The formulas that follow serve to summarize many of the computations related to discounted notes receivable.

Interest = Principal × Rate × Note Term*

Maturity Value = Principal + Interest

Discount = Maturity Value × Discount Rate × Time Note Is Held by Bank*

Proceeds = Maturity Value − Discount

If the proceeds exceed the note's face value, interest revenue is generated. Conversely, the opposite situation (proceeds less than face value) gives rise to interest expense.

* Expressed as a fraction of 360 days or, if appropriate, 12 months.

Dishonoring a Note

In the event that Dailey fails to settle his $20,500 obligation, the note is said to be **dishonored.** Kyle must now pay this amount to the bank because of the contingent liability; furthermore, the company might be assessed a service charge (termed a **protest fee**). The required accounting is shown by continuing our illustration.

Assume that on June 8 the bank notified Kyle that Dailey had defaulted, and also levied a $25 protest fee. Kyle paid the amount due ($20,500 + $25 = $20,525) and recorded the following entry:

June 8   Accounts Receivable: Walt Dailey   20,525
      Cash   20,525
      To record payment to the bank from
      note default by Walt Dailey

Notice that the protest fee is not considered an expense. Rather, the total amount disbursed is charged to Accounts Receivable in hopes of future collection. If these attempts fail, the amount will be written off as an uncollectible account, using procedures discussed earlier in the chapter.

Notes Not Yet Discounted

Our example of a dishonored note focused on an obligation that had been previously discounted at the bank. It is possible, of course, that a note is dishonored at maturity while still in the possession of the payee. If Kyle

Corporation had held Dailey's note until maturity, the following journal entry would have been recorded:

June 8   Accounts Receivable: Walt Dailey   20,500
                Notes Receivable   20,000
                Interest Revenue   500
            To record dishonored note by
            Walt Dailey

Observe that the obligation's face value is transferred out of Notes Receivable and into Accounts Receivable. This procedure leaves only nonmaturing obligations in the Notes Receivable account and generates a record in the Accounts Receivable subsidiary ledger that Dailey has defaulted. Such information may be useful in future credit-granting decisions.

Furthermore, the entry reveals that any interest that has been earned is (1) recognized as revenue and (2) added to the amount due from the maker. Although this latter procedure may seem bizarre in view of the default, be aware that the payee has a valid claim against the maker not only for the face value of the note but for the interest as well.

END-OF-CHAPTER REVIEW

LEARNING OBJECTIVES: THE KEY POINTS

1 Distinguish between trade and nontrade receivables. Trade receivables result from the sale of products or services to customers and consist of accounts receivable and notes receivable. In contrast, nontrade receivables arise from other transactions and events and include accrued receivables, advances to employees, and deposits with utilities.

2 Account for uncollectible receivables by using both the direct write-off and the allowance methods. Under the direct write-off method, uncollectible accounts are recognized when the actual loss is confirmed. Use of this approach may result in a mismatch of revenue and expense on the income statement and overstated receivables on the balance sheet. With the allowance method, improved matching and receivables valuation are achieved through the use of estimates in the adjusting process. The proper adjusting entry involves a debit to Uncollectible Accounts Expense and a credit to Allowance for Uncollectible Accounts. The latter account is a contra asset that appears on the balance sheet as a deduction from Accounts Receivable.

3 Calculate uncollectible accounts expense by using the income statement and balance sheet approaches. The income statement approach to estimation involves estimates of uncollectibles that are computed on the basis of sales. This procedure results in matching current revenues with the costs incurred in producing those revenues. Alternatively, under the balance sheet approach, uncollectibles are estimated on the basis of accounts receivable, sometimes by using the aging process. This method focuses on reporting accounts receivable at net realizable value, thereby requiring that the existing balance in the Allowance for Uncollectibles account be considered when constructing the adjusting entry.

4 Handle account write-offs and subsequent recoveries under the allowance method. When a customer's account is deemed to be uncollectible, it is written off against the Allowance account. Should the customer later pay the amount due, the write-off entry is reversed and a second entry is made to record the cash collected.

5 Account for credit card sales.   Credit card sales made on bank cards (e.g., Visa and MasterCard) are similar to cash sales. Drafts deposited at the bank are credited to the depositor's account, with an appropriate service charge often appearing on the month-end bank statement. For sales on nonbank cards such as American Express, the seller normally mails the drafts to the credit card company and records a receivable for the amount due. The receivable is eliminated upon receipt of funds from the credit card company, at which time the card company's service charge is recorded as an expense.

6 Demonstrate the computations and journal entries for notes receivable and interest, including discounted and dishonored obligations.   Notes receivable are written promises from clients or customers to pay a definite amount of money on a specific date. Such obligations are recorded at face value and normally bear interest, a charge for the use of borrowed funds. Interest is computed by using the following formula: interest = principal × rate × time.

The payee may discount the note at a bank to obtain needed funds, a process that creates a contingent liability. Should the maker fail to pay the bank on the scheduled date, the payee must settle the maker's obligation. The note is said to be dishonored (i.e., not paid at maturity), giving rise to a debit to Accounts Receivable in hopes of future collection. Such a procedure is necessary for dishonored notes that have been previously discounted as well as for those that are held by a business until maturity.

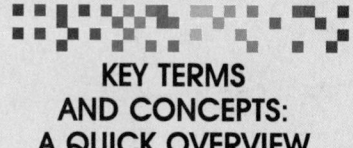

**KEY TERMS
AND CONCEPTS:
A QUICK OVERVIEW**

accounts receivable   Amounts that are due an entity from credit sales of goods and services.

aging accounts receivable   Segregation of individual accounts receivable based on the length of time outstanding; used in the balance sheet approach to estimating uncollectibles.

allowance method of uncollectible accounts   A method of accounting that employs a contra asset (Allowance for Uncollectibles) and estimates in the valuation of accounts receivable.

balance sheet approach of accounting for uncollectible accounts   A method that employs estimates of uncollectibles based on accounts receivable and focuses on reporting accounts receivable at net realizable value.

contingent liability   A potential liability whose outcome hinges on the future.

direct write-off method of uncollectible accounts   A method of accounting under which customer accounts are written off (expensed) when determined to be uncollectible.

discounting notes receivable   A means of obtaining cash by presenting notes receivable to a bank before the maturity date and receiving the maturity value minus a discount (interest) assessed by the bank.

dishonoring a note   The process of failing to pay a note receivable as of the maturity date.

income statement approach of accounting for uncollectible accounts   A method that employs estimates of uncollectibles based on total sales or credit sales.

interest   A charge made for the use of borrowed funds.

maker   The person or firm that promises to pay the stipulated amount of a note.

maturity date   The date that a note or obligation becomes due.

maturity value   The amount due on the maturity date (principal plus interest).

net realizable value   The amount of cash expected from the collection of present customer balances.

nontrade receivables   Those receivables that arise from transactions and events not directly related to the sale of goods and services.

notes receivable   Written promises owned by a firm that specify the receipt of a definite sum of money on some future date.

payee   The party to whom a note is made payable.

principal   The amount on which interest is computed.

protest fee   A bank service charge associated with dishonored notes.

receivables   Amounts that a business expects to collect at some future date from claims against customers and other parties.

trade receivables   Receivables that result from the sale of a company's products or services to customers.

CHAPTER QUIZ

The five questions that follow relate to several issues raised in the chapter. Test your knowledge of the issues by selecting the best answer. (The answers appear on p. 334.)

1 The following information is available for Hardy Company:

Credit sales during 19X8	$100,000
Allowance for uncollectibles, 1/1/X8	2,000 (credit)
Accounts written off during 19X8	4,500

Hardy estimated that uncollectibles would amount to 5% of credit sales. What amount should Hardy record as uncollectible accounts expense for the year ended December 31, 19X8?

a $3,000.   c $5,000.
b $4,500.   d $7,000.

2 An aging schedule indicated that Murphy had $12,500 of bad accounts. Yet, the adjusting entry for uncollectible accounts expense was prepared for only $6,000. This situation arose because:

a there was a $6,500 debit balance in the Allowance for Uncollectibles prior to adjustment.
b there was a $6,500 credit balance in the Allowance for Uncollectibles prior to adjustment.
c Uncollectible Accounts Expense had an existing balance of $6,500.
d $6,500 of bad accounts were written off during the period.

3 The write-off of an uncollectible account by a business that uses the allowance method:

a increases the Allowance for Uncollectibles.
b decreases the net realizable value of Accounts Receivable.
c has no effect on the net realizable value of Accounts Receivable.
d increases Uncollectible Accounts Expense.

4 On November 1, 19X6, Trendy Company received a $24,000, 3-month, 10% note receivable. How much interest revenue should be reported in 19X6 from this note, assuming that Trendy closes its books on December 31, 19X6?

a $200.   c $600.
b $400.   d $2,400.

5 When a note receivable is discounted at a bank:
  a the maker receives the maturity value of the note.
  b the payee receives the face value of the note.
  c the payee has a contingent liability to the bank.
  d the bank has a contingent liability to the payee.

The Shank Company's balance sheet revealed the following information as of January 1:

SUMMARY PROBLEM

| Accounts receivable | $75,800 | |
| Less: Allowance for uncollectible accounts | 6,500 | $69,300 |

The following transactions took place during the first quarter of the year:

Jan. 2 Received a $4,000, 60-day, 12% note from T. Abernathy in settlement of his account balance.
     18 Wrote off the $1,300 balance owed by Magna Company as uncollectible.
Feb. 11 Discounted Abernathy's note at the bank at a 15% discount rate.
     17 Received $180 from Pat Young. Young's account had been written off as uncollectible in the previous year.
Mar. 4 Received notification from the bank that Abernathy's note had been dishonored. Paid the bank the proper amount due, plus a $15 protest fee.

Shank's credit sales for the first quarter totaled $142,000.

Instructions

a Prepare journal entries for the transactions from January 2 through March 4.
b Prepare the journal entry on March 31 to adjust the Allowance account, assuming that uncollectible accounts are estimated at 3% of credit sales.

Solution

a Jan. 2 Notes Receivable 4,000
           Accounts Receivable: T. Abernathy 4,000
           Received note in settlement of
           account balance

     18 Allowance for Uncollectible Accounts 1,300
           Accounts Receivable: Magna Company 1,300
           To write off uncollectible account

Feb. 11 Cash 4,046
           Interest Revenue 46
           Notes Receivable 4,000
           Discounted note of T. Abernathy

           Calculations:
           | Face amount of note | $4,000 |
           | Add: Interest revenue ($4,000 × 0.12 × $\frac{60}{360}$) | 80 |
           | Maturity value | $4,080 |
           | Deduct: Discount ($4,080 × 0.15 × $\frac{20}{360}$) | 34 |
           | Proceeds | $4,046 |

	17	Accounts Receivable: Pat Young	180	
		Allowance for Uncollectible Accounts		180
		To reinstate account		
		Cash	180	
		Accounts Receivable: Pat Young		180
		To record collection on account		
	Mar. 4	Accounts Receivable: T. Abernathy	4,095	
		Cash		4,095
		To record payment to the bank from note default of T. Abernathy ($4,080 + $15)		
b	Mar. 31	Uncollectible Accounts Expense	4,260	
		Allowance for Uncollectible Accounts		4,260
		Adjusting entry ($142,000 × 0.03)		

ASSIGNMENT MATERIAL

QUESTIONS

Q8-1 Distinguish between trade and nontrade receivables. Give three examples of the latter.

Q8-2 Explain why uncollectible accounts have both income statement and balance sheet implications for accountants.

Q8-3 Explain how the doctrine of conservatism relates to accounting for uncollectible accounts.

Q8-4 Briefly describe the two methods that can be used to record losses from uncollectible accounts.

Q8-5 Discuss some possible deficiencies of the direct write-off method of uncollectible accounts.

Q8-6 Define the term "net realizable value" as it relates to accounts receivable.

Q8-7 Briefly describe the two general approaches that may be used for the estimation of uncollectible accounts.

Q8-8 Discuss the advantages of using aging schedules rather than a flat percentage of accounts receivable for estimates of uncollectible accounts.

Q8-9 Software International uses the allowance method of accounting for uncollectibles. What impact, if any, does the write-off of an uncollectible customer account have on the firm's net income?

Q8-10 Why do companies accept credit cards such as Visa and American Express?

Q8-11 Discuss the accounting procedures required for sales of merchandise made on nonbank credit cards in those situations where drafts are mailed to the credit card company.

Q8-12 Distinguish between the principal and maturity value of a note.

Q8-13 What is the interest computation formula? Why must a time factor be included?

Q8-14 What is the purpose behind the discounting of a note receivable?

Q8-15 Where does the payee's contingent liability appear in the financial statements when a note receivable has been discounted at a bank?

Q8-16 Artivo Company recently paid the bank a $20 protest fee, which relates to a customer's dishonored note. The bookkeeper charged the payment to Protest Fee Expense. Is this treatment correct? Why?

Q8-17 Why is Accounts Receivable increased for both the principal and interest earned when a nondiscounted note receivable is dishonored?

EXERCISES

E8-1 *Direct write-off method* (L.O. 2)

Harrisburg Company, which began business in early 19X7, reported $40,000 of accounts receivable on the December 31, 19X7, balance sheet. Included in this amount was a $550 claim against Tom Mattingly from a sale made in July. On January 4, 19X8, the company learned that Mattingly had filed for personal bankruptcy. Harrisburg uses the direct write-off method to account for uncollectibles.

a Prepare the journal entry needed to write off Mattingly's account.

b Comment on the ability of the direct write-off method to value receivables on the year-end balance sheet.

E8-2 *Allowance method: Estimation and balance sheet disclosure* (L.O. 3)

The following preadjusted information for the Maverick Company is available on December 31:

1-2-3

Accounts receivable	$107,000
Allowance for uncollectible accounts	5,400 (credit balance)
Credit sales	250,000

a Prepare the journal entries necessary to record Maverick's uncollectible accounts expense under each of the following assumptions:

(1) Uncollectible accounts are estimated to be 5% of credit sales.

(2) Uncollectible accounts are estimated to be 14% of accounts receivable.

b How would Maverick's accounts receivable appear on the December 31 balance sheet under assumption (1) of part (a)?

c How would Maverick's accounts receivable appear on the December 31 balance sheet under assumption (2) of part (a)?

E8-3 *Uncollectible account estimation: Balance sheet approach* (L.O. 3)

Folsom Company has gathered the following information to estimate bad debts by the use of an aging schedule:

Age of Receivable	Amount	Estimated Percentage Uncollectible
Under 31 days	$300,000	2%
31–60 days	140,000	8
61–90 days	60,000	30
91–120 days	30,000	40
Over 120 days	8,000	70
	$538,000	

a Determine the estimated amount of uncollectible accounts.

b Prepare the journal entry to record uncollectible accounts expense, assuming the previous Allowance for Uncollectibles account balance was
(1) $7,400 (credit).
(2) $2,900 (debit).

c Assume that the proper adjusting entry has been made in case (1) of part (b). Present the correct balance sheet disclosure of Folsom's receivables.

E8-4 *Aging of receivables* **(L.O. 3)**

1-2-3

On December 31, 19X2, the Ripley Company had $102,700 of accounts receivable and a $4,200 credit balance in the Allowance for Uncollectibles. An analysis of the firm's records found $81,700 of current receivables, along with the following activity:

	Sales on Account		Receipts on Account	
	Date	Amount	Date	Amount
Shawn Butler	Feb. 14	$ 5,300	Apr. 1	$9,000
	Mar. 1	3,700		
	Nov. 8	7,000		
Kevin O'Hara	Sept. 17	$10,000	Oct. 3	$2,000
Suzanne Wilkes	Aug. 15	$ 6,000		

All transactions pertaining to Butler, O'Hara, and Wilkes occurred during 19X2. Ripley anticipates the collection pattern that follows.

Age of Account	Estimated Percentage Uncollectible
Current	3%
31–60 days	10
61–90 days	25
91–120 days	50
Over 120 days	75

a Prepare an aging schedule and determine the balance that Ripley needs in the Allowance for Uncollectibles at the end of 19X2.

b Prepare the journal entry needed to record the estimate of uncollectible accounts.

E8-5 *Allowance method: Account write-off and collection* **(L.O. 2, 4)**
McKee Company had the following balances at the close of business on April 5:

Accounts receivable	$243,500
Less: Allowance for uncollectible accounts	17,900
	$225,600

On April 6, McKee wrote off a $4,400 receivable from Kinney Limited because the account was judged to be uncollectible. On October 6, McKee unexpectedly received a $1,000 check from Kinney. The check was accompanied by a note explaining that the company was in bankruptcy and no additional payments would be made.

a Determine the net realizable value of accounts receivable on April 5. Explain in a sentence or two what this amount represents.

b Prepare the journal entries McKee made to record:
  (1) the write-off of the Kinney account on April 6.
  (2) the payment by Kinney on October 6.
c Determine the net realizable value of accounts receivable immediately after the Kinney write-off on April 6.

E8-6 *Allowance method: Analysis of account write-off* (L.O. 4)
The Syracuse Company, which uses the allowance method of accounting for uncollectibles, has just written off the $640 balance of Providence Company. Determine the impact of the write-off (increase, decrease, or no effect) on each of the following:
a Uncollectible accounts expense
b Net income
c Accounts receivable
d Allowance for uncollectible accounts
e Net realizable value of accounts receivable

E8-7 *Credit card sales* (L.O. 5)
Compton Sales Company sold $8,400 of merchandise during August on Charge All, a national credit card. Charge All's collection fee is 4%.
a Prepare the journal entries required by Compton to record (1) credit card sales and (2) subsequent reimbursement from Charge All. Assume Charge All is not a bank card and that credit card drafts are mailed to Charge All.
b Discuss several of the benefits and problems of accepting credit cards.

E8-8 *Notes receivable and interest: Basic computations* (L.O. 6)
The following notes receivable were held by Rizzuto, Inc.:

Date of Note	Principal	Interest Rate	Term
April 3	$ 3,000	10%	2 months
June 21	10,000	12	90 days

a Determine the maturity date for each of the notes.
b Determine the interest earned on each of the notes if the notes are held until maturity.
c Assume that Rizzuto's fiscal year ends on June 30. Calculate the amount of accrued interest receivable that the company would disclose on its June 30 balance sheet.

E8-9 *Journal entries for notes receivable* (L.O. 6)
The Catton Company received a $10,000, 180-day, 12% note from Foote Enterprises on November 16, 19X6. Foote had previously purchased merchandise from Catton and wanted to extend the repayment date of the receivable. Prepare the journal entries required by Catton to record the following:
a The receipt of the note from Foote.
b Accrued interest on December 31, 19X6, the end of Catton's accounting year.
c The payment of the note by Foote on May 15, 19X7.

E8-10 *Journal entries for discounting* (L.O. 6)
On March 16 of the current year, KC Company accepted a $60,000, 60-day, 12% note on account from Niner Corporation. The note was dated March 16. On April 25, KC discounted the note at the First Street Bank at a 14% discount rate.

a Prepare the appropriate journal entry to record the receipt of the note on March 16.

b Prepare the appropriate journal entry to record the discounting on April 25.

c On May 16, KC received notification that Niner had dishonored the note. Prepare the appropriate journal entry for KC, assuming a protest fee of $15.

E8-11 *Accrued interest; dishonored notes (L.O. 6)*

The Nugget Company sells used cars. Greg Schulte, a customer, purchased a $5,000 automobile on November 1, 19X1. He paid $200 as a down payment and signed a 90-day, 18% note for the remaining balance. Prepare Nugget's journal entries to record the following:

a The sale on November 1, 19X1.

b Accrued interest on December 31, 19X1, the end of Nugget's accounting period.

c Schulte's failure to pay at maturity on January 30, 19X2.

E8-12 *Overview of notes receivable (L.O. 6)*

Evaluate the comments that follow as being True or False. If the comment is false, briefly explain why.

a Fred James gave Nancy Foster a 60-day note receivable. Foster is deemed the payee in this situation.

b A $30,000 note having a maturity value of $32,600 was discounted at a bank, with the proceeds amounting to $31,800. The maker should record $800 of interest expense on the transaction.

c A note's payee is contingently liable if the note is discounted at a bank. The maker, on the other hand, is absolutely liable.

d Protest fees are normally charged to Accounts Receivable by the paying firm.

e A note receivable of Mark Cooke that is held by Joe Swindell falls due on August 29. If the note is dishonored, Swindell should charge both the maturity value and the interest earned over the note's term to Accounts Receivable in hopes of future collection.

PROBLEMS

Series A

P8-A1 *Direct write-off and allowance methods; matching (L.O. 2, 3, 4)*

The December 31, 19X2, year-end trial balance of Targa Company revealed the following account information:

	Debits	Credits
Accounts receivable	$252,000	
Allowance for uncollectible accounts		$ 3,000
Sales		855,000
Sales returns & allowances	12,900	
Sales discounts	8,100	

Instructions

a Determine the adjusting entry for bad debts under each of the following conditions:

(1) An aging schedule indicates that $12,420 of accounts receivable will be uncollectible.

(2) Uncollectible accounts are estimated at 2% of net sales.

b On January 19, 19X3, Targa learned that House Company, a customer, had declared bankruptcy. Present the proper entry to write off House's $950 balance.

c Repeat the requirement in part (b), using the direct write-off method.

d In light of the House bankruptcy, examine the allowance and direct write-off methods in terms of their ability to properly match revenues and expenses.

P8-A2 *Allowance method: Income statement and balance sheet approaches* **(L.O. 3, 4)**

1-2-3

Tempe Company reported accounts receivable of $300,000 and an allowance for uncollectible accounts of $31,000 (credit) on the December 31, 19X2, balance sheet. The following data pertain to 19X3 activities and operations:

Sales on account	$2,000,000
Cash collections from credit customers	1,600,000
Sales discounts	50,000
Sales returns & allowances	100,000
Uncollectible accounts written off	29,000
Collections on accounts that were previously written off	2,700

Instructions

a Prepare journal entries to record the sales- and receivables-related transactions from 19X3.

b Prepare the December 31, 19X3, adjusting entry for uncollectible accounts assuming that uncollectibles are estimated to be 2% of net credit sales.

c Prepare the December 31, 19X3, adjusting entry for uncollectible accounts assuming that uncollectibles are estimated at 1% of year-end accounts receivable.

d Compute the amount of the adjusting entry in part (c) assuming that $46,000, rather than $29,000, of accounts were written off in 19X3.

P8-A3 *Allowance method; analysis of receivables* **(L.O. 3)**

1-2-3

At a January 19X2 meeting, the president of Sonic Sound directed the sales staff to "move some product this year." The president noted that the credit evaluation department was being disbanded because it had restricted the company's growth. Credit decisions would now be made by the sales staff.

By the end of the year, Sonic had generated significant gains in sales, and the president was very pleased. The following data were provided by the accounting department:

	19X2	19X1
Sales	$23,987,000	$8,423,000
Accounts receivable, 12/31	12,444,000	1,056,000
Allowance for uncollectible accounts, 12/31	?	23,000 cr.

The $12,444,000 receivables balance was aged as follows:

Age of Receivable	Amount	Percentage of Accounts Expected to be Collected
Under 31 days	$5,321,000	99%
31–60 days	3,890,000	90
61–90 days	1,067,000	80
Over 90 days	2,166,000	60

Assume that no accounts were written off during 19X2.

Instructions

a Estimate the amount of uncollectible accounts as of December 31, 19X2.
b What is the company's uncollectible accounts expense for 19X2?
c Compute the net realizable value of accounts receivable at the end of 19X1 and 19X2.
d Compute the net realizable value at the end of 19X1 and 19X2 as a percentage of respective year-end receivables balances. Analyze your findings and comment on the president's decision to close the credit evaluation department.

P8-A4 Journal entries for accounts and notes receivable (L.O. 3, 4, 6)
Nancy Wagner is the accounts receivable manager for the Georgia Southern Company. Selected information from the firm's receivables records follows.

	Balance on Sept. 30, 19X4
Customer	
T. Porter	$ 8,700
A. Snodgrass	16,000
G. Yost	7,600
Other	
Allowance for uncollectibles	14,400

The following activity took place during the last quarter of 19X4:

Oct. 2 Received a $16,000, 90-day, 10% note from A. Snodgrass in settlement of his account.
     14 Wrote off the account of G. Yost as uncollectible.
Nov. 1 Discounted the Snodgrass note at the bank. The bank's discount rate was 12%.
     23 Received a 30-day, 12% note from T. Porter in settlement of her overdue account.
Dec. 1 Sold merchandise on account to G. Gordon. Gordon issued a $12,000, 120-day, 15% note in settlement of his account.
     23 Porter dishonored her note of November 23 but promised to pay the total amount due within seven days. Because Porter is a valued customer, Wagner has agreed not to charge any additional interest or penalty.
     24 Received a $4,000 check from G. Yost in partial settlement of the balance written off in October.
     26 Received the proper amount due from Porter, as promised.
     31 Received notification from the bank that Snodgrass had paid his note in full.

31 Recorded the necessary adjusting entries for uncollectible accounts and interest related to the Gordon note.

The year-end accounts receivable balance was $119,400. Of this amount, accounts totaling $17,400 were estimated to be uncollectible.

Instructions

a Prepare journal entries for the preceding transactions and events.

b Determine the net realizable value of accounts receivable on December 31, after the adjusting process is completed.

c Wagner believes that 2% of the company's total credit sales of $980,000 may be uncollectible. Assuming the income statement method of estimation had been used instead of the balance sheet approach, prepare the journal entry to record uncollectible accounts expense.

P8-A5 *Journal entries for notes* (I..O. 6)

The following information was taken from the records of the Lima Company:

Mar. 8 Sold merchandise to R. Porter; accepted an $18,000, 120-day, 10% note.

Apr. 7 Discounted Porter's note at the bank at a 12% discount rate.

27 Received a $12,000, 90-day, 10% note from S. Taylor, a customer, in settlement of his account balance.

May 27 Discounted Taylor's note at the bank at a discount rate of 14%.

July 7 Received notification from the bank that Porter had paid her note.

26 Received notification from the bank that Taylor had defaulted on his note; paid the amount due plus a protest fee of $20. Lima informed Taylor that 15% annual interest would be charged on the face amount of the note, the interest, and the protest fee.

Aug. 10 Collected the proper amount due from Taylor, including the related interest.

16 Received a $30,000, 60-day, 12% note from Forge Manufacturing, a customer, in settlement of its past-due account.

Oct. 15 Forge Manufacturing paid the proper amount due on the note of August 16.

Instructions

a Assuming that Lima's year ends on December 31, prepare journal entries to record the transactions.

b If Lima's year ends on August 31, present the necessary adjusting entry on August 31 for accrued interest. Also, present the proper entry for the receipt of cash on October 15.

Series B

P8-B1 *Direct write-off and allowance methods; matching* (L.O. 2, 3, 4)

The December 31, 19X3, year-end trial balance of Yelland Company revealed the account information that follows.

	Debits	Credits
Accounts receivable	$90,000	
Allowance for uncollectible accounts		$ 2,500
Sales		410,000
Sales returns	10,000	
Sales discounts	8,000	

Instructions

a Determine the adjusting entry for bad debts under each of the following conditions:

(1) Uncollectible accounts are estimated at 1% of net sales.

(2) An aging schedule indicates that $12,050 of accounts receivable will be uncollectible.

b On January 13, 19X4, Yelland learned that Kaiser Distributors, a customer, had gone bankrupt. Present the proper entry to write off Kaiser's $480 balance.

c Repeat the requirement in part (b), using the direct write-off method.

d Compare the allowance and direct write-off methods by:

(1) Determining the impact on net income of the Kaiser write-off.

(2) Examining the methods' ability to match revenues and expenses.

P8-B2 *Allowance method: Income statement and balance sheet approaches* **(L.O. 3, 4)**

Huffy Company reported accounts receivable of $500,000 and an allowance for uncollectible accounts of $20,000 (credit) on the December 31, 19X4, balance sheet. The data that follow pertain to 19X5 activities and operations.

Sales on account	$7,000,000
Sales returns & allowances	400,000
Sales discounts	210,000
Cash collections from credit customers	6,000,000
Uncollectible accounts written off	19,000
Collections on accounts that were previously written off	2,500

Instructions

a Prepare journal entries to record the sales- and receivables-related transactions from 19X5.

b Prepare the December 31, 19X5 adjusting entry for uncollectible accounts assuming that uncollectibles are estimated to be 1% of net credit sales.

c Prepare the December 31, 19X5, adjusting entry for uncollectible accounts assuming that uncollectibles are estimated at ½ of 1% of year-end accounts receivable.

d Compute the amount of the adjusting entry in part (c) assuming that $34,000, rather than $19,000, of accounts were written off in 19X5.

P8-B3 *Allowance method; analysis of receivables* **(L.O. 3)**

At a January 19X4 sales meeting, the president of Phone Merchandising complained that the telemarketing staff was not closing enough business. One of the staff noted that the company policy of routing all customer calls to the credit department resulted in good prospects hanging up simply because of "slow service." The president responded that if this occurred, the salesperson should confirm the transaction and write "Code 11" on the order ticket. Code 11 items would then be shipped without credit department approval.

By the end of the year, significant gains in sales had been made, and the president was very pleased. The following data were generated by the accounting department:

	19X4	19X3
Sales	$33,945,000	$6,111,000
Accounts receivable, 12/31	18,946,000	1,127,000
Allowance for uncollectible accounts, 12/31	?	11,000 cr.

The $18,946,000 receivables balance was aged as follows:

Age of Receivable	Amount	Percentage of Accounts Expected to be Collected*
Under 31 days	$7,875,000	96%
31–60 days	6,590,000	88
61–90 days	3,450,000	72
Over 90 days	1,031,000	60

* Rates based on collection patterns in 19X2 and 19X3.

Phone Merchandising anticipates a 25% rise in uncollectibles in each of the aging categories over the levels experienced in prior years. Assume that no accounts were written off during 19X4.

Instructions

a Estimate the amount of uncollectible accounts as of December 31, 19X4.
b What is the company's uncollectible accounts expense for 19X4?
c Compute the net realizable value of accounts receivable on December 31, 19X4.
d Calculate year-end accounts receivable as a percentage of sales for both 19X3 and 19X4. (Use gross receivables, not net realizable value.) Do you feel these results are consistent or inconsistent with the company's new Code 11 sales policy? Briefly explain.

P8-B4 *Journal entries for accounts and notes receivable* (L.O. 3, 4 ,6)
The following selected transactions and events pertain to the McHale Company for the last quarter of the year:

Oct. 9 Sold merchandise to Dan Owen. Owen issued a $15,000, 60-day, 14% note in settlement of his account.

24 Discounted Owen's note at the bank; discount rate 16%.

29 Wrote off the $4,200 balance owed by Worth Company as uncollectible.

Nov. 21 Received a $2,000, 30-day, 12% note from Cindy Raymond in settlement of her past-due account balance.

28 Received $1,500 in final settlement of Doug Light's $2,400 account balance. Light's account had been written off as uncollectible in the previous year.

Dec. 9 Received notification from the bank that Owen had paid his note.

21 Raymond dishonored her note of November 21 but agreed to pay the proper amount due within five days. Management has agreed not to charge any additional interest.

26 Raymond paid her account balance in full.

31 Recorded the necessary adjusting entry for bad debts. On September 30, McHale reported an $8,200 credit balance in the Allowance for Uncollectibles account.

The Accounts Receivable account contained a balance of $92,100 on December 31. An aging schedule indicates that $8,300 of accounts receivable will be uncollectible.

Instructions

a Record the quarter's transactions and events in general journal form, assuming that McHale uses the allowance method of accounting for bad debts.

b Compute the net realizable value of accounts receivable on December 31.

c Assume that financial statements were prepared at the end of October for purposes of obtaining a bank loan. Indicate how Owen's discounted note would be reported to the loan officer.

P8-B5 *Journal entries for notes* **(L.O. 6)**

The following information on notes receivable was taken from the 19X6 records of Reckon Finance Company:

Maker	Date of Note	Principal	Rate	Note Term
F. Mart	June 16	$12,000	12%	120 days
B. Dasher	July 7	10,000	10%	90 days
B. Daniel	July 19	6,000	10%	90 days

Instructions

Prepare journal entries for Reckon to record:

a Accrued interest on the Mart note as of June 30, the end of Reckon's fiscal year.

b Receipt of Daniel's note on July 19 in exchange for land that had cost Reckon $6,000.

c Discounting of Dasher's note at the bank on August 6, at a discount rate of 12%, and

   (1) Notification on October 5, assuming that Dasher had paid the bank the proper amount due.

   (2) Notification on October 6, assuming that Dasher had defaulted on the note. Paid the proper amount due plus a $25 protest fee.

d Receipt of the proceeds from Mart's note on the October 14 maturity date.

e Dishonoring of Daniel's note on October 18.

f Collection on October 21 of the amount due from Daniel. Reckon did not charge any additional interest during this three-day period.

ELECTRONIC DATA BASE

SEC

EDB8-1 *Analysis of receivables: Ralston Purina and Hershey Foods* **(L.O. 1, 2)**

Ralston Purina manufactures pet foods and a variety of bakery products (Wonder breads and Hostess), cereals, and baby foods (Beech-Nut). The company also produces Eveready and Energizer batteries. Hershey, which is known primarily for chocolate products, also manufactures various pasta goods.

Instructions

By using the text's Electronic Data Base, access the financial statements and accompanying footnotes of both companies and answer the questions that follow. Unless otherwise indicated, responses should be based on data for the most recent year presented.

a Study the balance sheets of both firms and compute net receivables as a percentage of total assets. All other things being equal, if a severe recession hit, which firm would be most affected by slow-paying customers? Why?

b Did receivables increase or decrease?

   (1) What factors may have caused the increase or decrease?

   (2) Are any of these factors disclosed on the income statements? Briefly explain.

c Which of the companies provide supplemental information about receivables in the footnotes to the financial statements?

d Did the balance in the Allowance for Uncollectibles account increase or decrease? What would have caused the increase or decrease?

e Calculate the ending balance in the Allowance for Uncollectibles account as a percentage of the ending *gross* receivables balance. Which of the firms is more optimistic about the collection of amounts due?

EDB8-2 *Analysis of receivables: May Department Stores* **(L.O. 1, 2)**

SEC

This problem is a duplication of Problem EDB8-1. It is based on the financial statements of May Department Stores and another company selected by your instructor. May, the largest department store retailer in the country, also owns Payless ShoeSource, a chain of self-service family shoe stores.

Instructions

By using the text's Electronic Data Base, access the two companies' financial statements and accompanying footnotes and focus on data for the most recent year reported. Answer requirements (a)–(e) of Problem EDB8-1.

BB8-1 *Allowance method and errors* **(L.O. 3, 4)**

A newly hired bookkeeper recently reported an $88,000 balance in the Accounts Receivable control account of Starr Manufacturing Company. An aging schedule revealed the following:

BEYOND THE BASICS

Age	Amount	Percentage Uncollectible
Current	$40,000	1%
31–60 days	20,000	5
61–90 days	14,000	10
91–120 days	9,000	30
Over 120 days	5,000	60
	$88,000	

A detailed investigation of the bookkeeper's work discovered three items:

1 Hill Manufacturing, a customer, has entered bankruptcy proceedings. Hill has owed Starr $3,000 for the past five months; management feels there is no hope of collection.

2 An analysis of accounts in the 31–60 day category discovered the four outstanding balances that follow, all of which were verified as being correct.

Baker Concrete, Inc.	$13,500
Haxton Distributors	2,000
New Jersey Builders	4,900
ToyotaTown	4,600

3 Joe Kline's $4,000 account balance (91–120 day category) had been written off as uncollectible on October 19 by the following journal entry:

Allowance for Uncollectible Accounts	4,000	
Uncollectible Accounts Expense: Joe Kline		4,000
To write off uncollectible account		

The December 31 balance before adjustment in the Allowance for Uncollectibles account was $2,550 (credit).

Instructions

a Determine the proper accounting treatment for the account of Hill Manufacturing. Be specific.

b Was the write-off on October 19 handled correctly? If not, how would you correct the error if the books are not as yet closed?

c Determine the adjusting entry for uncollectible accounts that should be made on December 31. Assume proper handling of all preceding items.

BB8-2 *Overview of chapter concepts: Multiple choice* (L.O. 2, 3, 4, 6)
The following multiple-choice questions relate to various topics discussed in the chapter. Select the best answer.

1 Which of the following statements about the direct write-off method is false?

a The direct write-off method can result in the recognition of sales revenue in one period and expense related to that revenue in a subsequent period.

b The write-off of a customer's account balance results in a debit to Uncollectible Accounts Expense.

c The Allowance for Uncollectibles account is not used when the direct write-off method is employed.

d Sales are essentially recognized by the cash basis of accounting when the direct write-off method is used.

2 The income statement and balance sheet approaches are used to estimate uncollectible accounts. Which of the following comments applies to both of these approaches?

a The aging process is often used to obtain proper valuation amounts.

b Generally speaking, matching is improved when compared with the direct write-off method.

c The focus is on the net realizable value of accounts receivable.

d Total credit sales is commonly used as the estimation base.

3 Gonzo Company estimates uncollectible accounts at 5% of ending accounts receivable. The company's records reveal ending receivables of $2,000,000 and a $40,000 debit balance in the Allowance for Uncollectibles. Gonzo's year-end adjusting entry for bad debts would cause uncollectible accounts expense to increase by:

a $40,000.	c $100,000.
b $60,000.	d $140,000.

4 The following information pertains to Laser Company:

- Accounts receivable total $100,000, subdivided as follows: 50% are current; 30% are slightly past due; and 20% are long past due.
- Uncollectibles are: current accounts, 5%; slightly past-due accounts, 25%; and long past-due accounts, 70%.
- The balance in the Allowance for Uncollectibles prior to adjustment is $24,000, credit.

If Laser uses the aging approach to estimate bad debts, the balance in the Allowance for Uncollectibles account after adjustment should be:

a $0.

b $24,000.

c $48,000.

d some amount other than those presented above.

5 Find-a-Friend Pet Shop uses the allowance method of accounting for bad debts. The company recently wrote off the $135 balance of Karen Sorrell as uncollectible. As a result of the write-off, Find-a-Friend will experience:

a a $135 decline in income.

b a $135 decline in the net realizable value of accounts receivable.

c a $135 increase in the Allowance for Uncollectible Accounts.

d no change in total assets.

6 The collection of an account previously written off under the allowance method will involve two separate journal entries. After both of these entries are recorded:

a total accounts receivable will be unchanged.

b the Allowance for Uncollectibles account will decrease.

c uncollectible accounts expense will increase.

d uncollectible accounts expense will decrease.

7 The maturity value of a $30,000, 8% note receivable, dated December 1, 19X2, and maturing on March 31, 19X3, is:

a $30,000. c $30,800.

b $30,200. d $32,400.

8 The following facts pertain to a note receivable that was discounted at a local bank on December 1, 19X1:

Face amount: $100,000   Term: 60 days
Interest rate: 12%   Discount rate: 15%
Date of note: November 1, 19X1

The interest revenue that would be recognized at the time of discounting is:

a $0.   c $1,250.

b $725.   d $1,275.

CAI8-1 *Communicating via a press release: The Dun & Bradstreet Corporation** (L.O. 6)

COMMUNICATION OF ACCOUNTING INFORMATION

Communication Principle: Good public relations is sometimes as important an asset as cash or equipment. Relations with the public and press must be carefully cultivated, and any mistakes must be even more carefully corrected.

In the following situation, the media have made a mistake that has caused confusion both inside and outside the company. A press release is a vehicle that can be used to dispel any rumors that have arisen. Such a release should be written in a thoroughly positive style to explain and correct the situation. Under no circumstances should the media be ac-

---

*This problem is a continuation of CAI7-1; it may be used regardless of whether CAI7-1 was assigned.

cused of any intent to harm or of stupidity. Instead, in an objective and constructive way, the release should indicate the difference between what was said and what should have been said.

The press release typically begins with a background statement, referring to the date and misquote. Any mistakes are then corrected. An optimistic overview of the situation is often presented in any brief paragraphs that follow. Overall, then, the release may be used to get some extra press time for the firm. If handled properly, a situation that originally started off badly could turn into a convincing sales appeal.

■ ■ ■ ■ ■ ■ ■ ■

Dun & Bradstreet is a huge corporation involved in numerous service businesses. Among the company's activities are publishing (Moody's Investors Service), marketing services (Nielsen ratings), and corporate research. Dun & Bradstreet is also heavily involved with the compilation and sale of credit reports and maintains a data base that includes over 16 million businesses. This data base is useful in helping companies decide whether or not to extend credit to other entities.

Imagine that you work for Dun & Bradstreet in the corporate communications division, and rumors have been circulating about cash flow problems of the company. These rumors began because a newspaper article incorrectly described Dun & Bradstreet as a firm "with cash flow and credit problems" rather than as a company "that provides information about businesses having cash flow and credit problems." The following balance sheet data (in thousands) are available:

Cash	$1,026,289
Short-term investments	43,205
Accounts & notes receivable	1,115,500
Accounts, notes, accrued, & other short-term payables	1,919,430

Instructions

a Briefly describe the discounting process, a procedure the company could follow should the need arise.

b Draft a press release for newspapers, business periodicals, and wire services that explains and dispels the rumors.

Answers to Chapter Quiz

1 c ($100,000 × 0.05)

2 b ($6,500 credit + $6,000 credit = $12,500)

3 c

4 b ($24,000 × 0.10 × $\frac{2}{12}$)

5 c

CHAPTER

9

Inventory

LEARNING OBJECTIVES

After studying this chapter, you should be able to:

1

Explain the ownership issues related to goods in
transit and goods on consignment.

2

Identify the effects of inventory errors on financial statements.

Demonstrate use of the specific identification, FIFO,
LIFO, and weighted-average inventory methods.

4

Recognize the factors that are considered when selecting an inventory
method and the effects of such a selection on financial statements.

5

Apply the lower-of-cost-or-market rule of inventory valuation.

Explain the importance of inventory estimates and use
both the gross profit and retail methods.

7

Contrast the features of the periodic and perpetual inventory systems.

Not too long ago the Commerce Department reported that U.S. retailers, wholesalers, and manufacturers had $1.079 trillion of inventories—a sizable sum to say the least. These goods typically affect a number of different areas within a business. A company's finance department, for example, has the responsibility of securing operating funds and monitoring investments. Inventories, as you can see, represent a significant use of these funds. An entity's marketing function, which is concerned with maintaining a high level of customer service, wants to avoid out-of-stock situations that could result in lost sales and lost customers. The purchasing department negotiates favorable credit terms with suppliers and obtains quantity discounts by proper timing of acquisitions.

The accountant also has a keen interest in inventory. Excessive inventory investments, lost sales, lost customers, credit terms, and discounts all affect net income. Furthermore, for many firms, especially those engaged in retailing and wholesaling activities, inventories represent the largest asset on the balance sheet. These goods ultimately become a significant element on the income statement in the form of cost of goods sold.

The possession of inventory gives rise to various issues that the accountant must resolve. For example, consider Margo's Dress Shop, which overstocked a particular dress style eight months ago. Because of rapid changes in the fashion world, these dresses are now worth only a fraction of their original cost. Should Margo's continue to carry this inventory in the accounting records at original cost, or should the goods be marked down to reflect a loss in value? Focusing on another issue, we turn to the Fast-Mix Concrete Company. Throughout the year Fast-Mix has been purchasing large quantities of sand, stone, and limestone at rapidly changing prices. Each product is piled in huge mounds near the company's production facility. If Fast-Mix uses 10 tons of stone on a given day, how can the firm determine its cost? All the stone purchases have been mixed together, and employees are unable to mark or associate each ton with its acquisition cost. Should Fast-Mix use the most recent cost, the oldest cost, or an average cost? The company's selection will have a definite impact on profitability.

These questions and a number of other matters related to inventory must be addressed by accountants. This chapter focuses on inventory accounting, emphasizing the valuation of inventory on the balance sheet and the determination of cost of goods sold for the income statement.

WHAT IS INVENTORY?

When discussing merchandising businesses, we defined **inventory** as goods acquired for resale to customers. Although this definition is satisfactory for the retailer and wholesaler, it must be expanded for the manufacturer. The manufacturer, of course, does not acquire goods for resale—it makes them. Inventories, therefore, are said to include the following:

1 *Raw materials*—items to be processed into salable products.

2 *Work in process*—goods started but not as yet completed.

3 *Finished goods*—goods completed and awaiting sale.

Since most inventories are used or sold and converted into cash within the operating cycle, they are reported as current assets on the balance sheet. Inventory is usually listed immediately after accounts receivable because, in comparison with amounts due from customers, it is one step further removed from cash in terms of liquidity.

Ownership Problems

In Chapter 1, assets were defined as the economic resources owned by a firm that benefit future time periods. Let us concentrate on ownership for a moment. When the ownership of merchandise transfers to a company, the merchandise should be included as part of that company's inventory and reported on the firm's balance sheet. This principle is followed even though a business may lack physical possession of the units at the end of the reporting period—a situation that often arises with goods in transit and goods on consignment.

Goods in Transit

Goods in transit between the buyer and seller belong to the party that holds legal ownership (title) of the goods. Legal ownership, in turn, is dependent on freight terms, namely, F.O.B. shipping point and F.O.B. destination. Recall from Chapter 5 that the F.O.B. point indicates the location where the seller's responsibility for shipping ceases. As a logical extension, the F.O.B. point also indicates where (or when) legal title to the goods is transferred from the seller to the buyer. Under F.O.B. shipping point, for example, title transfers to the purchaser when the goods are shipped. Conversely, under F.O.B. destination, title passes when the goods arrive at their destination (e.g., the buyer's warehouse).

When title passes, the seller should record a sale and the buyer should record a purchase. Accordingly, inventories should be respectively reduced and increased at this time, even though the goods may still be on hand or in transit. To illustrate, suppose a company buys $10,000 of merchandise, F.O.B. shipping point, on December 29. The goods are shipped on December 30 and are in transit at the end of the purchaser's accounting year. Despite this fact, the buyer should enter a purchase in the records and include the goods in the ending inventory count because title has passed.

To simplify bookkeeping *during the year*, many companies operate on a receipt and shipment basis. Specifically, purchases are recorded when received regardless of the F.O.B. point, and sales are recognized upon shipment. If year-end in-transit shipments are significant, firms should examine their records and make appropriate account adjustments so that all merchandise owned is properly reflected in the ending inventory balance. Incorrect accounting for sales and purchases will influence inventory and often affect a host of other financial statement components. The effect of such errors is discussed in a following section.

Goods on Consignment

Some companies transfer merchandise to sales agents (to sell to potential buyers) without transferring ownership. This process is known as **consignment.** If the products on consignment are sold, the agent receives a commission. If the merchandise is not sold, the goods are returned to the supplying company (i.e., the consignor). It is important to note that the

---

OBJECTIVE

Explain the ownership issues related to goods in transit and goods on consignment.

ETHICS ISSUE

M, Inc., sells machinery to U.S. customers from a factory in Singapore. The goods are sent on cargo ships; the journey takes two weeks. To raise the current period's sales, M's marketing manager has asked you to alter some invoices to read "F.O.B. shipping point" rather than "F.O.B. destination." The manager claims that the combined sales figures for this period and the next will not be changed by this action. How would you react, knowing it is close to year-end and your bonus depends on company earnings?

consignor retains title to the transferred merchandise even though the goods are possessed by the sales agent. Consigned goods are therefore reported as part of the consignor's inventory until the time of sale and should not appear in the Inventory account of the agent.

Taking a Physical Inventory

We have determined the goods that should be reported as an asset on the balance sheet. It is now necessary to hand count these goods at the conclusion of the reporting period to derive the correct ending inventory figure. This procedure is needed because the Inventory account under a *periodic* system has not been debited or credited to reflect the individual purchases and sales made by the business. As a result, the account's year-end balance fails to reflect the cost of goods owned by the firm. The necessary information to update Inventory is not found in the formal accounting records, but is obtained by reviewing goods in transit and counting merchandise on hand and stored in warehouses.

This process, known as **taking a physical inventory,** may involve much more than "counting." Many small items (e.g., nuts and bolts) may need to be weighed, while other products, such as the amount of oil in a storage tank, must be measured. In addition, an inventory counter must determine whether the goods appearing to be in the warehouse are actually there. To explain, suppose an inventory counter observes a stack of cartons 10 across by 10 deep by 15 high. A quick conclusion at the end of a long day might be that the firm has 1,500 (10 × 10 × 15) cartons on hand. Some potential problems could exist, however: the middle of the stack might be hollow or less than 15 cartons high. Or several of the cartons may be empty. Indeed, a careful look at the inventory is required to avoid a serious misstatement. Proper inventory counts are so important that items may be counted and checked a second time to verify the accuracy of the original figure.

The inventory count, although costly and time-consuming, strengthens the credibility of the inventory figure reported on the year-end balance sheet. Even so, a physical count of inventory (and its observance by an outside independent auditor) has not always been a required practice. It took a massive fraud case to induce change. The 1937 financial statements of McKesson Corporation (formerly McKesson & Robbins) were found to contain significant amounts of fictitious inventories—all related to a fraud that had been perpetrated by the president and his brothers over a period of 12 years. The fraud was finally uncovered when an accounting executive of the company went to a warehouse to check some reported inventory and found none in existence. As an outcome of this case, generally accepted auditing standards now require the observation of physical inventory counts by audit personnel, as well as other procedures that help to avoid misstatements of assets in the financial statements.

EFFECTS OF INVENTORY ERRORS ON FINANCIAL STATEMENTS

Many errors are possible when dealing with inventory. Items may be counted incorrectly, completely omitted in the counting process, or counted twice. Furthermore, in the computation of total inventory cost, mathematical errors can be made when multiplying the number of units owned by the cost per unit. Unfortunately, these errors are carried forward

HIGHLIGHT
Pass the Vinegar and Oil, Please

The physical count is a necessary evil of trying to establish a credible inventory figure on the balance sheet. If you have ever participated in this ritual, you know exactly what we mean. Counting, moving, weighing, and measuring are truly unexciting tasks for the average businessperson. Truly unexciting, that is, unless your goal is to illegally pocket $100 million cash. Such was the case in a very complicated fraud known as the Great Salad Oil Swindle, facets of which are described below.

In the early 1960s, Allied Crude Vegetable Refining Corp. was a major player in supplying our country and others with vegetable, soybean, and cottonseed oil. The company had prospered for a time by using warehouse receipts—a credit instrument that states a certain commodity is stored in a specific place. Money is subsequently lent on the basis of the receipt and the commodity's value. Unfortunately, a code of honor prevailed, and no one thought it necessary to look behind the receipts to verify the commodities they represented. That was partly because lenders were lax, but mostly because many receipts carried the name of an American Express subsidiary and therefore seemed above suspicion.

According to receipts, Allied's refinery tanks should have contained 1.7 billion pounds of fats and oils. When someone did decide to check, only slightly more than 100 million pounds were found. The kicker: Financial institutions had lent the company at least $100 million on the basis of the 1.7 billion figure! Of course, with the tanks empty, the receipts were worthless. [1]

What happened was a complex scheme, part of which depended on overstated inventories. Ray Sadler, a former employee of Allied, admitted under oath that he had overstated inventories on many occasions during an eight- to nine-month period. A lawyer asked Sadler if it were not his job to accurately measure the contents of the tanks. "Not necessarily," he replied. "I was told to show as much oil as possible."

To determine contents, Sadler would climb atop a tank and lower a measuring tape that had a metal plate on the end. When the plate struck the surface of the oil, he would note the distance between the surface and the tank top. From this measurement, the contents could be figured. [2] The games that were played? A colleague of Mr. Sadler, Frank Vivenzio, noted that for a 54-foot tank, the quantity was overstated by 10 to 20 feet, equal to some 20% to 40% of the total tank capacity. Of the 31 tanks that Vivenzio gauged regularly, only 7 had accurate measurements. Still other tricks included mislabeling of tank contents, pumping commodities from one tank to another, and putting water in some tanks to make them appear full. (Remember, of course, what rises to the top when water and oil are mixed together.) [3] It was later revealed that some tanks were totally empty and others never existed.

From this episode you may now appreciate the importance of an accurate and objective inventory count. There is simply too much money at stake, especially with the occasional unethical businessperson who "wants to pull a fast one." In the meantime, please pass the vinegar and oil. Or on second thought, make it roquefort.

Sources: Adapted from "Content of Tanks Overstated, Allied Worker Concedes," *The Wall Street Journal,* December 18, 1963, p. 5 [2]; "Former Employe of Allied Crude Describes Four Ways to Explain 'Disappearance' of Oil," *The Wall Street Journal,* December 20, 1963, p. 6 [3]; and "Where Genius Went Wrong," *Business Week,* April 18, 1964, pp. 164–166, 171–172, 174 [1].

EXHIBIT 9-1

THE BACKERT COMPANY Income Statement For the Year Ended December 31, 19X1		
	Correct Ending Inventory of $34,000	Incorrect Ending Inventory of $32,000
Net sales	$80,000	$80,000
Cost of goods sold		
Beginning inventory	$26,000	$26,000
Add: Net purchases	59,000	59,000
Goods available for sale	$85,000	$85,000
Less: Ending inventory	34,000	32,000
Cost of goods sold	51,000	53,000
Gross profit	$29,000	$27,000
Operating expenses	20,000	20,000
Net income	$ 9,000	$ 7,000

OBJECTIVE

2

Identify the effects of inventory errors on financial statements.

ETHICS ISSUE

An accountant discovers a sizable error in last year's inventory count, which was originally verified as correct by the accountant. If disclosure will embarrass the accountant and affect the firm's profit picture, what action should be taken?

to the financial statements. Incorrect inventory determination can result in incorrect current asset valuation, net income, and owner's equity.

To understand the effect of inventory errors, we will study The Backert Company, which accidentally excluded $2,000 of goods on display in its showroom from the ending inventory count. The firm's income statement appears in Exhibit 9-1. The figures on the left are based on the correct ending inventory valuation of $34,000. In contrast, the figures on the right omit the display merchandise and use an ending inventory of $32,000.

Because of the understated ending inventory, Backert is subtracting a number that is too small from goods available for sale. The resulting cost of goods sold is therefore overstated and produces a depressed net income figure. Regrettably, the problem does not stop here. Remember that net income is closed to owner's equity. Ending owner's equity, which appears on both the statement of owner's equity and the balance sheet, is thus understated as well. The balance sheet will balance, however, because of a $2,000 understatement of inventory in the current assets section. The effects of the display merchandise error are summarized as follows:

Income Statement	
Cost of goods sold	Overstated
Gross profit	Understated
Net income	Understated
Statement of Owner's Equity	
Ending owner's equity	Understated
Balance Sheet	
Ending owner's equity	Understated
Total current assets	Understated

	Stock Number	Cost
Inventory, Jan. 1		
Watch	4618	$ 6,000
Bracelet	3207	11,000
January purchases		
Watch	4623	7,500
Watch	4624	8,100
Bracelet	3210	14,000
Bracelet	3211	18,000
		$64,600

A physical inventory of the goods on hand on January 31 revealed that three items were still in stock: the watch from the beginning of the year and the two bracelets acquired during the month. The company's ending inventory and cost of goods sold are therefore determined as shown.

Inventory, Jan. 31		
Watch (no. 4618)	$ 6,000	
Bracelet (no. 3210)	14,000	
Bracelet (no. 3211)	18,000	$38,000
Cost of goods sold		
Bracelet (no. 3207)	$11,000	
Watch (no. 4623)	7,500	
Watch (no. 4624)	8,100	26,600
		$64,600

The specific identification method offers the advantage of matching the actual cost of the units sold against sales revenues. Most businesses, though, find that the accompanying operating costs are excessive. For example, the physical tagging or coding of individual units of merchandise is impractical, if not impossible, in those situations where sales volume is high and a company's inventory consists of many (e.g., thousands of) different items. Specific identification is most feasible when sales volume is low and the cost of individual units is high. This method might therefore be used to account for jewelry, automobiles, valuable antiques, or yachts.

Cost Flow Assumptions

When specific identification is not employed, the accountant must make an assumption regarding the movement of costs through a firm's accounting system. This **cost flow assumption** pertains strictly to the *flow of cost in the accounts* and has no direct relationship to the actual *physical flow of goods*. For example, picture a company that strives to sell the oldest merchandise first because of a threat of obsolescence or spoilage. It is very possible that this same business will cost these goods at the most recent costs experienced or perhaps even an average cost.

Cost flow assumptions are used to derive computations for cost of goods sold on the income statement and ending inventory valuation on the balance sheet. The selection of an assumption is based on several different factors that will be discussed shortly. At this point, however, we wish to introduce the three most widely used cost flow assumptions in accounting: first-in, first-out (FIFO); last-in, first-out (LIFO); and weighted average.

A General Introduction to FIFO and LIFO

To introduce the FIFO and LIFO cost flow assumptions, it is helpful to visualize a chronological listing of units and their related costs. For example, a company may have an inventory of goods on hand at the beginning of the reporting period. Then, throughout the period, additional goods are acquired by purchases from the firm's suppliers. As depicted in the middle block of Exhibit 9-5, the costs that pertain to a given inventory item can be subdivided into older costs (i.e., the beginning inventory and older purchases) and recent costs (more recent purchases). Collectively, the graphic's vertical height represents goods available for sale.

As discussed earlier in the chapter, a company's goods available for sale figure is allocated between cost of goods sold and ending inventory. This allocation may be performed in several different ways. One such approach,

EXHIBIT 9-5
A Graphical Overview of FIFO and LIFO

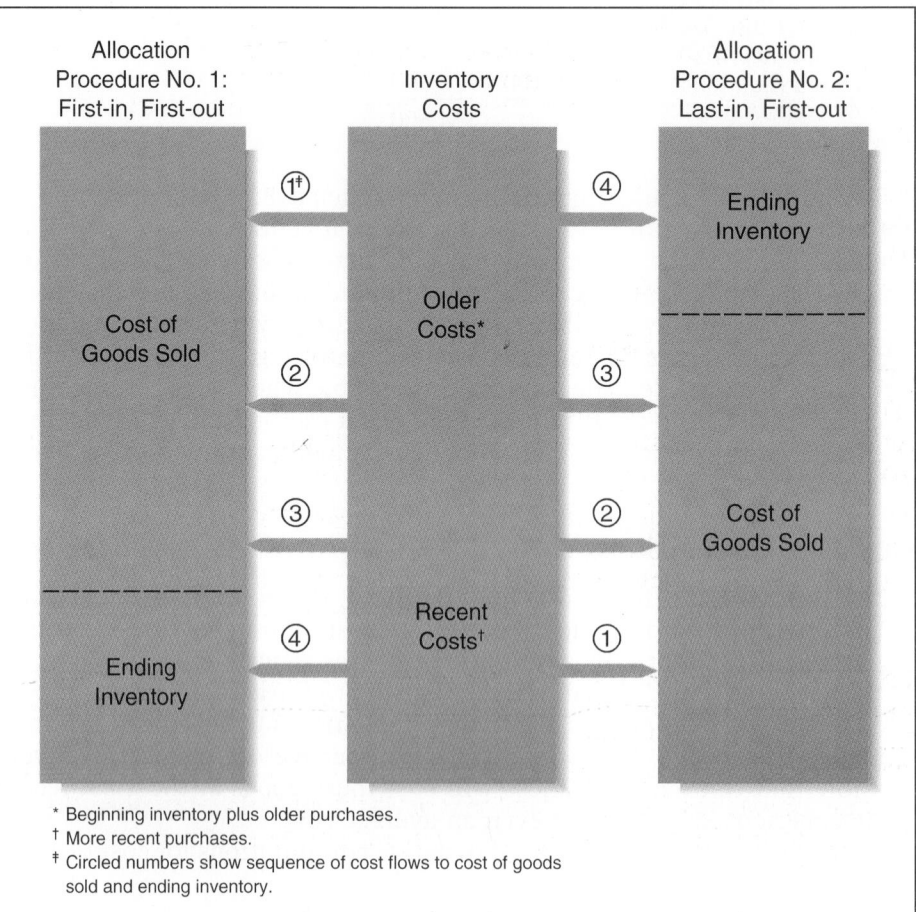

* Beginning inventory plus older purchases.
† More recent purchases.
‡ Circled numbers show sequence of cost flows to cost of goods sold and ending inventory.

known as **first-in, first-out (FIFO)**, is based on the premise that costs should be matched against revenues in the order that the costs were incurred. In other words, the oldest costs (i.e., those that were "first-in") are matched against revenues first, then the next oldest costs as the firm works forward in time, and so forth. This matching takes place in the form of cost of goods sold on the income statement. The block on the left reveals this process and shows that a company's more current costs wind up in ending inventory on the balance sheet.

The process is reversed under another acceptable approach, the **last-in, first-out (LIFO)** method. Under this procedure, costs are matched against revenues in the *reverse* order of incurrence. That is, the most recent costs incurred (i.e., the "last-in") are the first to be charged to cost of goods sold, then the next most recent, and so on. By viewing the exhibit's right-hand block, you will see that a user must go backward in time. The recent cost layers are eventually exhausted, meaning that older costs are then allocated to inventory.

First-in, First-out Calculations

To illustrate the calculations related to FIFO (and the other cost flow assumptions as well), we introduce the following data of the Tracy Company:

	Number of Units	×	Cost per Unit	=	Total Cost
Beginning inventory	3,000		$3.00		$ 9,000
Purchase (Feb. 28)	4,000		3.10		12,400
Purchase (May 15)	5,000		3.23		16,150
Purchase (Aug. 1)	1,000		3.50		3,500
Purchase (Oct. 31)	3,000		3.65		10,950
Goods available for sale	16,000				$52,000

During the year Tracy sold 11,800 units, leaving 4,200 units (16,000 − 11,800) in inventory.

The FIFO computations are most easily understood if we begin with the firm's inventory valuation, which must consist of recent purchases. The 4,200-unit ending inventory is costed in the following manner:

Most recent purchase (Oct. 31)	3,000 units × $3.65 = $10,950
Next most recent purchase (Aug. 1)	1,000 units × $3.50 = 3,500
Next most recent purchase (May 15)	200 units × $3.23 = 646
Ending inventory	4,200 units $15,096

Observe that only 200 units from the May 15 purchase are needed to complete the accounting [the other 4,800 units acquired in May (5,000 − 200) are no longer on hand].

The cost of the 11,800 units sold may now be calculated by using two different approaches. First, we can focus on the flow of the older (i.e., "first-in") costs to the income statement, as shown on the next page.

Beginning inventory	3,000 units × $3.00 =	$ 9,000
Oldest purchase (Feb. 28)	4,000 units × $3.10 =	12,400
Next oldest purchase (May 15)	4,800 units × $3.23 =	15,504
Cost of goods sold	11,800 units	$36,904

Alternatively, the company's ending inventory valuation can be subtracted from goods available for sale:

Goods available for sale (see original data)	$52,000
Less: Ending inventory	15,096
Cost of goods sold	$36,904

Last-in, First-out Calculations

Recall that under this method, the cost of older purchases is assigned to ending inventory. As the figures that follow indicate, the LIFO flow assumption produces a $12,720 inventory valuation for Tracy Company's 4,200 units on hand.

Beginning inventory	3,000 units × $3.00 =	$ 9,000
Oldest purchase (Feb. 28)	1,200 units × $3.10 =	3,720
Ending inventory	4,200 units	$12,720

Although the firm purchased 4,000 units on February 28, the cost of only 1,200 of these units is needed for inclusion in the ending inventory.
    The cost of goods sold is $39,280:

Goods available for sale (see original data)	$52,000
Less: Ending inventory	12,720
Cost of goods sold	$39,280

Weighted Average

Another inventory approach, the **weighted-average method,** recognizes that there are both high and low costs during an accounting period. Rather than focus on the time when costs are incurred (i.e., currently or in the past), an average cost is calculated by first weighting (multiplying) the cost per unit with the number of units purchased. Referring to the initial introduction of Tracy's data on page 347, observe that the outcome of this process results in $52,000—the cost of goods available for sale. The weighted-average unit cost can now be computed as shown below.

> Cost of Goods Available for Sale ÷ Units Available for Sale
>
> $52,000 ÷ 16,000 = $3.25

The unit cost of $3.25 is applied to the ending inventory as follows:

4,200 units × $3.25 = $13,650

Cost of goods sold is computed in the same manner as before, that is:

Goods available for sale	$52,000
Less: Ending inventory	13,650
Cost of goods sold	$38,350

The weighted-average method is, in effect, a compromise between FIFO and LIFO. Those who favor the weighted-average method base their argument on the belief that all goods available for sale in a period should reflect the same unit cost.

Comparison and Evaluation of Alternative Inventory Valuation Methods

The effects of using a particular cost flow assumption are summarized in Exhibit 9-6. The exhibit is based on the assumptions that sales and expenses were $125,000 and $60,000, respectively.

As you can see, each of the three methods results in reporting a different net income and ending inventory valuation. The magnitude of the differences depends on the number of units acquired and sold during the year and the extent of price changes. In light of the historical trend in purchase prices, it is possible that Tracy was experiencing an inflationary economy.

Because the last-in, first-out method charges recent (higher) costs to cost of goods sold, LIFO will usually report the lowest net income in a period of rising prices. In contrast, FIFO will report a larger net income. The results, of course, are reversed in a period of falling prices. Weighted average is a compromise between FIFO and LIFO and normally yields results somewhere between these two approaches.

All three assumptions are acceptable accounting alternatives, and each

EXHIBIT 9-6
Alternative Inventory Valuation Methods for Tracy Company

	FIFO	LIFO	Weighted Average
Sales	$125,000	$125,000	$125,000
Cost of goods sold			
Beginning inventory	$ 9,000	$ 9,000	$ 9,000
Add: Purchases*	43,000	43,000	43,000
Goods available for sale	$ 52,000	$ 52,000	$ 52,000
Less: Ending inventory	15,096	12,720	13,650
Cost of goods sold	$ 36,904	$ 39,280	$ 38,350
Gross profit	$ 88,096	$ 85,720	$ 86,650
Expenses	60,000	60,000	60,000
Net income	$ 28,096	$ 25,720	$ 26,650

* Purchases are computed by subtracting Tracy's beginning inventory from the cost of goods available for sale: $52,000 − $9,000 = $43,000.

is used extensively. A survey of large corporations revealed the data that follow.[2]

Method	Percentage of Use
FIFO	40.5%
LIFO	36.0
Average	19.2
Other	4.3

Which Method Should Be Selected?

It would be nice to generalize and state that, in certain situations, a firm should always use FIFO or LIFO or one of the other inventory valuation methods. Unfortunately, we cannot. No one approach best meets the needs and peculiarities of all businesses. Management considers several factors when selecting an inventory method, including income taxes and their related cash outlays, and financial statement presentation.

Income Taxes. In the past 15 to 20 years, LIFO has gained popularity because of overall rising prices in our economy. As just discussed, LIFO will produce lower net incomes and, thus, lower income tax payments for its users in an inflationary climate.[3] Lower taxes result in more cash available for investment purposes.

The amount of cash is dependent on several variables, such as the rate of inflation and applicable tax rates, and can be especially significant for companies that carry large amounts of inventory. As evidence, study the figures in Exhibit 9-7 that show estimated cash savings from using LIFO (as opposed to FIFO) for valuation of goods.

Financial Statement Presentation. The resulting financial statements must also be considered when selecting an inventory method. For example,

EXHIBIT 9-7
Estimated Cash Savings from LIFO

Corporation	Inventory Using LIFO (In Millions)	Inventory Using FIFO (In Millions)	Estimated Cash Savings (In Millions)*
Adolph Coors Company	$ 238.4	$ 293.9	$ 18.9
Kimberly-Clark	686.0	810.5	42.3
Quaker State Corporation	54.0	78.1	8.2
Sears, Roebuck & Co.	4,459.4	5,216.2	257.3

* Cash savings are calculated as the excess of FIFO inventory over LIFO inventory, multiplied by the 34% corporate income tax rate in effect at the time of this writing.

[2] *Accounting Trends & Techniques: 1991* (New York: American Institute of Certified Public Accountants, Inc., 1991), p. 144.
[3] According to current tax regulations, companies that use LIFO for tax purposes must also utilize LIFO for financial reporting.

the use of LIFO over long periods of time can generate a somewhat meaningless ending inventory figure on the balance sheet. Remember that the oldest costs are used as the basis for inventory valuation; consequently, units may be carried at costs incurred many years ago. In contrast, FIFO values the ending inventory at an amount close to the cost of replacement.

While producing a reasonable balance sheet valuation, FIFO frequently results in a mismatch of revenue and expense on the income statement. Cost of goods sold is determined by using older costs; revenues, on the other hand, are based on selling prices that were charged to customers during the current accounting period. The use of old costs and fairly current prices generally raises questions about the meaningfulness of the net income figure. The mechanics of LIFO tend to overcome this problem by charging an entity's most recent costs against sales. A better match is produced, leading many accountants to say that LIFO is superior to FIFO from an income measurement viewpoint.

When choosing an inventory valuation method, management must keep in mind that the income statement and balance sheet have somewhat different purposes. On the income statement, cost of goods sold should reflect a fair measure of inventory cost to be matched against revenue. The balance sheet's ending inventory valuation, on the other hand, should be consistent with the definition of a current asset and reflect the amount of resources available to meet current obligations. In sum, asset valuation and income determination are not always compatible and often result in compromises to arrive at an acceptable reporting of financial position and profitability.

Consistency in Method Application

The inventory method ultimately selected should be used consistently from one year to the next. Such a practice helps to produce financial statements that can be compared over time and is very useful when assessing trends and performing other types of analysis. Consistency should *not* be interpreted to mean that a business can never change inventory valuation methods. A change can and should be made when it is beneficial in terms of measuring economic activity, for instance, to achieve a better matching of revenues and expenses. If a change is made, the impact should be fully disclosed in the notes that accompany the financial statements.

Although inventories are generally valued at cost, circumstances sometimes arise where departures from cost are appropriate. As an example, assume that Art Nesbit, a loan officer at the First National Bank, is examining the financial statements of Tuttle Company for purposes of granting a loan. Nesbit's primary concern is Tuttle's ability to meet loan payments as the payments come due. Nesbit is also interested in the value of certain assets that might be pledged as collateral on the loan. The following disclosure appears on Tuttle's balance sheet:

Inventories: at cost $84,000

LOWER OF COST OR MARKET

OBJECTIVE
5

Apply the lower-of-cost-or-market rule of inventory valuation.

Nesbit knows that accounting is based on the principle of historical cost and that several cost assignment methods are available for inventory valuation. Because inventory levels and purchase prices have been relatively stable, the assignment method is not an issue. Nesbit's major worry is: Can the bank get $84,000 for the inventory if Tuttle defaults on the loan? Nesbit might have some difficulty with the $84,000 figure if he knew that Tuttle's merchandise had suffered considerable smoke damage from a fire; consisted of numerous perishable goods having a 6-month shelf life that were acquired 10 months ago; and was heavily loaded with fad products that are no longer popular.

Inventories are susceptible to damage, spoilage, and obsolescence. Over time the utility or usefulness of many goods declines, and a business may have to drop its selling price to ensure disposal. To achieve a better valuation of these inventory items, accountants turn to the **lower-of-cost-or-market rule.** The use of lower of cost or market is justified when the market potential for a particular product has been significantly reduced.

Measuring the Decline in Value

The decline in value of an inventory item is measured by the difference between its cost and market value. Cost is determined by any one of the methods we previously discussed: specific identification, FIFO, LIFO or weighted average. **Market value** is defined as replacement cost, or the cost that would be incurred to reproduce or repurchase the item. In the case of damaged goods, market value is the amount obtainable from disposal.[4]

To illustrate lower of cost or market, assume Tuttle stocks an electronic component that cost $170 when purchased several months ago. Because of rapidly advancing technology, the component can now be replaced for $155. Tuttle has therefore suffered a $15 decline in value on this inventory item. To value the component at the *lower* of cost or market, we would compare $170 (original cost) with $155 (market value) and choose $155 (the lower).

Application of the Lower-of-Cost-or-Market Rule

The lower-of-cost-or-market rule may be applied to each individual item in inventory. Suppose, for instance, that Tuttle's inventory consisted of the following:

Item No.	(1) Quantity	(2) Per Unit Cost	(2) Per Unit Market	(1) × (2) Total Inventory Cost	(1) × (2) Total Inventory Market	Lower of Cost or Market
101	1,000	$ 12	$ 10	$12,000	$10,000	$10,000
102	500	20	23	10,000	11,500	10,000
103	3,000	15	16	45,000	48,000	45,000
104	100	170	155	17,000	15,500	15,500
				$84,000	$85,000	$80,500

---

[4] There are exceptions to the replacement cost definition of market value. A detailed discussion of these exceptions is beyond the scope of this text.

EXECUTIVE BRIEFING
Managing Inventories to Avoid Obsolescence

Samuel Miller
Senior Vice-President of Finance and Chief
Financial Officer, Liz Claiborne, Inc.

Liz Claiborne is a leading marketer of apparel, selling over 60 million garments annually. The women's sportswear group alone, which accounts for over 50% of total revenue, has a minimum of 108 separate collections, with each collection having 12 to 25 different styles in various sizes and colors. Because this merchandise is highly seasonal and subject to fashion change, it is considered perishable and must be tightly controlled to avoid excessive markdowns. Such control is exercised through several means.

Since we plan our purchases almost a year in advance of shipment to retail store customers, we take a conservative approach and anticipate being oversold. That is, sales to individual stores are estimated and then "shaved" to reduce overall supply in the marketplace. We also use sophisticated systems to ensure timely deliveries from our manufacturers (300 factories in 35 countries). If goods arrive late to us, they will likely be marked down earlier than if normal schedules were followed. Finally, even though we plan to oversell production, we typically have some inventory left over at the end of a season. To handle these excess goods, we have opened a chain of factory outlet stores.

Conservative buying, timely deliveries, and control over distribution of excess goods are the tools we use to manage inventories. These tools limit the risk of excessive markdowns and help Liz Claiborne maintain a level of profitability that is unique in the industry.

The proper inventory valuation of $80,500 (right-hand column) is obtained by taking the lower of the cost and market figures for each inventory item. Be aware, however, that other application methods are also acceptable. For example, rather than evaluate each individual item, one can analyze the inventory as a whole. If Tuttle followed the latter approach, the inventory would be valued at $84,000. This figure is obtained by comparing the inventory's total cost ($84,000) with the total market value ($85,000) and selecting the lower amount. Turning to a third method, significant subclasses of inventory can be defined, with the lower-of-cost-or-market rule applied to each subclass. Of the three possibilities, the individual item approach results in the lowest and most conservative inventory valuation.

Once the proper valuation is determined, the accounting records must be updated. If Tuttle analyzes its four inventory items individually, a $3,500 reduction in value ($84,000 versus $80,500) is recognized. This reduction in value is a loss and is entered in the accounts as follows:

Loss Due to Decline in Inventory Value	3,500	
Inventory		3,500
To reduce inventory to lower of cost or market		

The Inventory account now contains the lower-of-cost-or-market valuation of $80,500 and is reported as such on the balance sheet. Furthermore, Tuttle's net income is reduced by the loss.

INVENTORY ESTIMATES

OBJECTIVE
6

Explain the importance of inventory estimates and use both the gross profit and retail methods.

On page 338, we noted that taking a physical inventory is a costly and time-consuming process. A physical count is mandatory, however, for determining the inventory balance that is reported in the year-end financial statements. There are numerous situations in business where an inventory valuation is needed and management desires to avoid a physical count. For these situations (and others), several inventory estimation procedures have been developed. These procedures allow the preparation of interim financial statements for periods between physical counts. In addition, the procedures allow businesses to estimate the goods on hand when physical counts are not possible. Such would be the case with disasters like tornadoes or fires, where inventories are destroyed or heavily damaged and estimates are needed for insurance claims. Estimation techniques, if they are reasonable, also permit an entity to determine the accuracy of an actual hand count. A comparison of the hand count with the estimate could reveal gross errors in the counting and valuation processes. Two widely used estimation techniques are the gross profit method and the retail method.

Gross Profit Method

The **gross profit method** estimates inventory on the basis of a company's gross profit rate, that is, gross profit expressed as a percentage of net sales. The rate, which is the key to the entire process, is developed from past transactions and adjusted for any known changes in the entity's recent profit experience. Once the rate is established, gross profit for the period can be determined by applying the rate to the current period's sales. Given this computation, we can then calculate current cost of goods sold and the estimated ending inventory.

   To illustrate, assume that Henderson Supply desires to prepare financial statements for August without taking a physical inventory. The information that follows is available for the period ended August 31.

Net sales	$80,000
Beginning inventory, Jan. 1	10,000
Net purchases	40,000
Estimated gross profit percentage	60%

Because gross profit is estimated at 60% of net sales, current gross profit is $48,000 ($80,000 × 0.60). Cost of goods sold for August therefore amounts to $32,000 ($80,000 − $48,000), and the ending inventory is found by the following computation:

Net sales		$80,000
Cost of goods sold		
Beginning inventory	$10,000	
Add: Net purchases	40,000	
Goods available for sale	$50,000	
Less: Ending inventory	?	
Cost of goods sold		32,000
Gross profit		$48,000

The August 31 inventory is estimated at $18,000 ($50,000 − $32,000).

Retail Method

Both department and discount stores carry a variety of different items that are tagged or marked with retail selling prices. Suppose it is the end of an accounting period and a department store takes a count of the inventory on hand. To determine the "value" of the goods, one need only multiply the quantities found by their readily identifiable retail prices. Unfortunately, the resulting figures cannot be used in the financial statements, which report inventories at cost or at the lower of cost or market, not selling prices. An inventory valued at retail could be converted to cost by inspecting numerous individual paid invoices and other records. This task is a rather formidable one, however, for businesses that carry large product lines. Alternatively, the retail method of inventory valuation can be employed.

The **retail method** is widely used by merchandising firms to value and/or estimate ending inventory. The method first involves determining the ending inventory at retail prices. This amount is then converted to cost on the basis of the percentage relationship between the cost and retail valuations of goods available for sale. As you will now see, the following information must be accumulated in the accounting records to perform the necessary computations:

1 The beginning inventory valued at both cost and retail amounts
2 Net purchases priced at both cost and retail
3 Net sales for the period

To illustrate the retail method, suppose that Boulder Sales Organization desires an inventory estimate as of March 31 in order to compute quarterly income. The required calculations appear at the top of the next page.

Observe that net sales are subtracted from goods available for sale to yield an ending inventory at retail of $180,000.[5] To convert this figure to cost, Boulder has computed a cost-to-retail ratio of 68%, indicating $0.68 of inventory cost for every $1.00 of retail valuation. As a result, the $180,000 estimated ending inventory is multiplied by the 68% ratio to arrive at the $122,400 cost-based valuation.

---

[5] Frequently, additional factors (such as markups and markdowns to original selling prices) are considered when computing the ending inventory at retail.

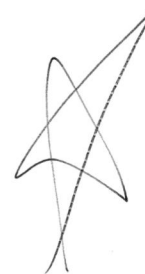

	Cost	Retail
Beginning inventory, Jan. 1	$ 60,000	$ 88,000
Net purchases, Jan. through Mar.	293,600	432,000
Goods available for sale	$353,600	$520,000
Ratio of cost to retail prices $353,600 ÷ $520,000 = 68%		
Less: Net sales		340,000
Estimated ending inventory at retail		$180,000
Estimated ending inventory at cost ($180,000 × 0.68)	$122,400	

In this example the retail method was used to obtain an interim estimate of inventory. This same method can also be employed to study a company's experience with theft and shoplifting. For instance, assume the figures in the Boulder illustration relate to a full calendar year. A physical count on December 31 has revealed an inventory of $171,000 at retail prices. Thus, Boulder has a $9,000 shortage at retail ($180,000 − $171,000), which cost the firm $6,120 ($9,000 × 0.68).

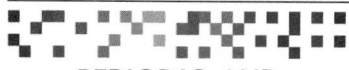

PERIODIC AND PERPETUAL INVENTORY SYSTEMS

OBJECTIVE 7

Contrast the features of the periodic and perpetual inventory systems.

Throughout this chapter and in earlier chapters, we have emphasized the **periodic inventory system.** Recall that under a periodic system, merchandise purchases are recorded in the Purchases account and sales are credited to the Sales account. These procedures result in a constant balance in Inventory throughout the year. The periodic system is frequently employed by businesses because of its minimal record-keeping requirements. This system is especially attractive for companies that (1) sell slow-moving products, (2) carry a large variety of low-cost inventory items, and (3) use manual accounting systems.

Two significant problems associated with a periodic system make it undesirable for many organizations. First, a business has no record of the number of units in stock at any given time. Remember, no entries are made to the Inventory account for acquisitions and sales. This lack of information could lead to stockouts and poor customer service. The second problem lies in the calculation of cost of goods sold. To explain, we present the following computations (the amounts are assumed):

Cost of goods sold	
Beginning inventory	$19,000
Add: Net purchases	47,000
Goods available for sale	$66,000
Less: Ending inventory	24,000
Cost of goods sold	$42,000

By subtracting the $24,000 ending inventory per the physical count, we are assuming that $42,000 of goods were sold. This assumption could be erroneous, however, because theft or errors may have occurred. Unfortunately, there is no basis for comparison, as the periodic system does not monitor the amount of inventory that *should be* on hand.

to account for the remaining 600 units, leaving 2,400 units (3,000 − 600) at $5 in stock.

After the acquisition on March 19, the company would have two layers of goods: 2,400 units at $5 and 1,600 units at $6.50. The sale on March 22nd would again be costed by using the most recent costs experienced, namely, 1,600 units at $6.50 plus 700 units from the older layer at $5. Bankston's ending inventory is therefore 1,700 units (2,400 − 700) at $5.

Normally, because of the timing of the charges to cost of goods sold, the results obtained with a LIFO perpetual system will differ from those that occur under a periodic system. With the perpetual approach, the most recent costs *at the time of each sale* are evaluated and transferred to the income statement. When a periodic system is employed, the transfer process begins with the most recent costs incurred *during the period*, namely, after all purchases have been made.

Moving Average

The average cost approach when used with a perpetual system is often called **moving average.** With this method, a new average unit cost is computed each time that inventory is purchased. This amount is later employed to determine cost of goods sold and ending inventory valuations.

Continuing the Bankston Company example, the firm's acquisition on March 10 will produce the following results:

Inventory on 3/1:	3,000 units at $5.00 =	$15,000
Purchase on 3/10:	2,000 units at $6.25 =	12,500
	5,000	$27,500

Average cost per unit: $27,500 ÷ 5,000 units = $5.50

Thus, when 2,600 units are sold on March 13, cost of goods sold will amount to $14,300 (2,600 units × $5.50) and 2,400 units (5,000 − 2,600) will be left in inventory. These latter goods will be assigned a cost of $5.50 as well, yielding an inventory valuation of $13,200 (2,400 units × $5.50).

A new average cost will be calculated on March 19 because of the purchase of 1,600 units:

Inventory on 3/13:	2,400 units at $5.50 =	$13,200
Purchase on 3/19:	1,600 units at $6.50 =	10,400
	4,000	$23,600

Average cost per unit: $23,600 ÷ 4,000 units = $5.90

To complete the example, the sale on March 22 would be costed at $13,570 (2,300 units × $5.90), while the month-end inventory of 1,700 units (4,000 − 2,300) would total $10,030 (1,700 units × $5.90).

When using the average costing approach, the difference between the perpetual and periodic systems lies in the frequency of computation. Average unit costs are calculated after each purchase with the perpetual system; in contrast, under the periodic approach, a single average cost is derived upon conclusion of the accounting period. Given the nature of the computation, ending inventory and cost of goods sold will differ between the two methods.

END-OF-CHAPTER REVIEW

LEARNING OBJECTIVES: THE KEY POINTS

1 Explain the ownership issues related to goods in transit and goods on consignment. Inventory ownership is dependent on possession of legal title to the goods, which, in turn, is dependent on freight terms. Under F.O.B. shipping point, title passes to the purchaser when goods are shipped. In contrast, under F.O.B. destination, title passes when merchandise arrives at its destination. With consignment sales, merchandise transferred to sales agents is considered part of the consignor's inventory until sold even though the goods are not in the consignor's possession.

2 Identify the effects of inventory errors on financial statements. An inaccurate inventory figure results in an incorrect income statement, statement of owner's equity, and balance sheet. For example, if the ending inventory is understated, cost of goods sold will be overstated and net income will be understated. This, in turn, produces understated amounts for both ending owner's equity and inventory. Inventory errors are counterbalanced over a two-year period because the ending inventory of one year becomes the beginning inventory of the next.

3 Demonstrate the use of the specific identification, FIFO, LIFO, and weighted-average inventory methods. With the specific identification method, the cost of the units is associated with the units themselves, often via code numbers and stickers. Because this method has limited applications, most businesses have to adopt a cost flow assumption. With the FIFO (first-in, first-out) assumption, costs are matched against revenues in the order that the costs were incurred. Thus, cost of goods sold is comprised of older costs (i.e., the "first-in"), whereas ending inventory is composed of the most recent purchase prices experienced by the firm. In contrast, the LIFO (last-in, first-out) method results in recent costs being transferred to the income statement for cost-of-goods-sold determination. Older costs therefore remain in inventory. Finally, with the weighted-average method, an average cost is calculated by dividing the cost of goods available for sale by the number of units available for sale. The unit cost is then used to compute both cost of goods sold and ending inventory.

4 Recognize the factors that are considered when selecting an inventory method and the effects of such a selection on financial statements. Income taxes are an important consideration for many businesses. Because LIFO produces lower net income and lower income tax payments than FIFO in periods of inflation, the LIFO method has gained in popularity in the past 15 to 20 years.

These flow assumptions also have different effects on the financial statements. For example, FIFO's use of the oldest costs in cost-of-goods-sold calculations produces a poor match of costs and revenues on the income statement. However, the balance sheet valuation is improved because inventories consist of fairly recent costs. The LIFO method would yield results the opposite of those just described.

5 Apply the lower-of-cost-or-market rule of inventory valuation. The lower-of-cost-or-market rule permits the write-down of inventories to market if the goods' value has been reduced because of damage, spoilage, or obsolescence. Market is generally defined as replacement cost, or the cost that would be incurred to reproduce or repurchase the item. Write-downs entail the recognition of a loss, which lowers net income, and a reduction in the recorded cost of inventory. This procedure, which produces conservative asset valuations and income figures, can be applied to individual inventory items, to subclasses of similar items, or to the inventory as a whole.

6 Explain the importance of inventory estimates and use both the gross profit and retail methods. Inventory estimates facilitate the issuance of interim financial statements and the filing of insurance claims in cases of disaster. Estimates also provide a reasonableness check of actual physical counts. With the gross profit method, inventory is estimated on the basis of a company's gross profit rate. An estimated gross profit figure is derived for use in computing cost of goods sold. Then, cost of goods sold is subtracted from goods available for sale to arrive at the estimate of inventory. In contrast, with the retail method, ending inventory is first calculated at retail prices. This figure is later converted to cost on the basis of the percentage relationship between the cost and retail valuations of goods available for sale (i.e., the cost-to-retail ratio).

7 Contrast the features of the periodic and perpetual inventory systems. With a periodic inventory system, a continual record of merchandise on hand is not maintained. The inventory at the end of the period and the related cost-of-goods-sold figure are determined on the basis of a physical count. The perpetual system, on the other hand, keeps a running record of merchandise inflows and outflows. Thus, the Inventory account is increased for acquisitions and decreased for sales. Cost of goods sold is also maintained on a continual basis, being increased when each sale occurs. The perpetual system results in improved managerial control and may be used in conjunction with a FIFO, LIFO, and average cost flow assumption.

KEY TERMS AND CONCEPTS: A QUICK OVERVIEW

consignment The process of transferring goods to a sales agent.

cost flow assumption An assumption regarding the flow of inventory costs through a firm's accounting system.

first-in, first-out (FIFO) An inventory accounting method based on the premise that costs are matched against revenues in the order of incurrence.

goods in transit Goods in the process of being transported to the buyer. Ownership is dependent on freight terms.

gross profit method .n inventory estimation method based on a company's gross profit rate—that is, gross profit expressed as a percentage of net sales.

inventory Goods acquired for resale to customers. Includes the raw materials, work in process, and finished goods of a manufacturer.

last-in, first-out (LIFO) An inventory accounting method based on the premise that costs are matched against revenues in the reverse order of incurrence.

lower-of-cost-or-market method A method whereby inventories are accounted for at acquisition cost or market value, whichever is lower.

market value The replacement cost of a unit of merchandise.

moving-average method A perpetual inventory costing system under which a new average cost is computed after each purchase.

periodic inventory system A system in which purchases and sales of inventory are not recorded in the Inventory account. The balance in the Inventory account therefore remains constant throughout the period.

perpetual inventory system A system in which the Inventory account is respectively increased and decreased for each purchase and sale of inventory made during the period.

retail method An inventory estimation method widely used by retail establishments; derives a cost-to-retail ratio and applies the ratio to the total retail value of inventory.

specific identification method   A method that requires a business to identify each unit of merchandise with the unit's cost and retain that identification until the inventory is sold.

taking a physical inventory   The process of counting or measuring the goods in a company's possession upon conclusion of an accounting period.

weighted-average method   A method of accounting under a periodic inventory system that requires the computation of a weighted-average cost for goods purchased or manufactured. The average is used to value the ending inventory and to determine cost of goods sold.

CHAPTER QUIZ

The five questions that follow relate to several issues raised in the chapter. Test your knowledge of the issues by selecting the best answer. (The answers appear on p. 380.)

1 Because of a mathematical error, the 19X8 ending inventory included goods at a $170 figure that had actually cost $710. As a result of this error:
   a net income for 19X8 is overstated.
   b net income for 19X8 is understated.
   c operating expenses for 19X8 are understated.
   d total liabilities at the end of 19X8 are overstated.

2 The inventory cost flow assumption in which the oldest costs incurred become part of cost of goods sold when units are sold is:
   a LIFO.   c weighted average.
   b FIFO.   d retail.

3 The LIFO inventory valuation method:
   a is acceptable only if a company sells its newest goods first.
   b will result in higher income levels than FIFO in periods of rising prices.
   c will result in a match of fairly current inventory costs against recent selling prices on the income statement.
   d cannot be used with a periodic inventory system.

4 Stanley Company sells two different products. The following information is available at year-end:

Inventory Item	Units	Cost Per Unit	Market Value Per Unit
A	100	$4	$6
B	200	5	3

Applying the lower-of-cost-or-market rule to each item, Stanley's ending inventory balance would be:
   a $1,000.   c $1,400.
   b $1,200.   d some other amount.

5 Which of the following accounting systems maintains a running (continuous) record of merchandising purchases and sales by inventory item?
   a Perpetual.   c Periodic.
   b Gross profit.   d Retail.

Tiger Company sells a single product and uses a periodic inventory system. The following information was extracted from the accounting records:

SUMMARY PROBLEM

Purchases	Sales
Feb. 800 units @ $4.75	1,500 units @ $ 8.50
June 600 units @ $5.50	500 units @ $10.00
Oct. 900 units @ $6.00	

The firm's beginning inventory on January 1 totaled 200 units and cost $800.

Instructions

Compute Tiger's ending inventory, cost of goods sold, and gross profit, using the following inventory valuation methods: (1) FIFO; (2) LIFO; (3) weighted average.

Solution

- Sales

      1,500 units @ $ 8.50 = $12,750
        500 units @ $10.00 =   5,000
      ─────────   ───────
      2,000 units $17,750

- Goods available for sale

      Beginning inventory   200 units @ $4.00 = $ 800
      Feb. purchase   800 units @ $4.75 =   3,800
      June purchase   600 units @ $5.50 =   3,300
      Oct. purchase   900 units @ $6.00 =   5,400
                           ───────   ────────
                           2,500 units $13,300

- Ending inventory

      Goods available for sale   2,500 units
      Less: Sales   2,000 units
                                  ───────────
      Ending inventory   500 units

- FIFO ending inventory consists of the most recent costs; therefore:

      500 units @ $6.00 = $3,000

- LIFO ending inventory consists of the oldest costs; therefore:

      200 units @ $4.00 = $ 800
      300 units @ $4.75 =   1,425
                          ────────
                           $2,225

- Weighted-average ending inventory

      $13,300 ÷ 2,500 units = $5.32 per unit

      500 units × $5.32 = $2,660

	FIFO	LIFO	Weighted Average
Sales	$17,750	$17,750	$17,750
Less: Cost of goods sold			
Beginning inventory	$ 800	$ 800	$ 800
Add: Purchases*	12,500	12,500	12,500
Goods available for sale	$13,300	$13,300	$13,300
Less: Ending inventory	3,000	2,225	2,660
Cost of goods sold	$10,300	$11,075	$10,640
Gross profit	$ 7,450	$ 6,675	$ 7,110

* Goods available for sale minus the beginning inventory.

ASSIGNMENT MATERIAL

QUESTIONS

Q9-1 What items are reported as inventory for (a) merchandising companies and (b) manufacturing companies?

Q9-2 The Potter Company purchased the following merchandise on December 28:

Supplier	Terms	Amount
Pax Company	F.O.B. destination	$1,800
James Manufacturing	F.O.B. shipping point	2,500

Both purchases were shipped December 30, but neither had been received by December 31. Should the purchases be included in Potter's December 31 ending inventory? Explain.

Q9-3 What are goods on consignment? Who has title to goods on consignment?

Q9-4 Why is it necessary to take a physical count of inventory at the end of each accounting period?

Q9-5 The Wood Company made the following mathematical error in determining the cost of its April 30 ending inventory:

Item No.	Quantity	Cost Per Unit	Total Cost
S775	150	$34	$3,100

Determine the effect of the error on the following:
a Cost of goods sold for the year ended April 30
b Operating expenses for the year ended April 30
c Net income for the year ended April 30
d Owner's equity as of April 30
e Total current assets as of April 30

Q9-6 Why are many inventory errors counterbalanced by the end of two accounting periods?

Q9-7 At the end of an accounting period, goods available for sale is segregated into two different costs. What are these two costs? Explain which of the costs is given primary emphasis by accountants.

Q9-8 Why is the specific identification method of inventory valuation used infrequently?

Q9-9 Discuss the difference between the physical flow of goods and a cost flow assumption.

Q9-10 Why has LIFO gained popularity in the past 15 to 20 years?

Q9-11 In a period of rising prices, which inventory valuation method (LIFO or FIFO) tends to result in the following?
a Highest cost of goods sold
b Lowest inventory valuation
c Highest income taxes

Q9-12 Are businesses permitted to arbitrarily change inventory valuation methods from one year to the next? Briefly explain.

Q9-13 What is meant by the term "market" as used in the phrase "lower of cost or market"?

Q9-14 Why do businesses need to estimate their inventory balances?

Q9-15 Discuss the advantages of a perpetual inventory system when compared with a periodic system.

Q9-16 Which type of inventory system, periodic or perpetual, is increasing in popularity? Briefly explain.

Q9-17 Why are two journal entries required to record a sale under a perpetual inventory system?

*Q9-18 Will the ending inventory figure computed by using a weighted-average periodic system normally agree with the figure calculated under a moving-average perpetual system? Why?

EXERCISES

E9-1 *Inventory errors and income measurement* (L.O. 2)
The income statements of Keagle Company for 19X3 and 19X4 follow.

	19X3	19X4
Sales	$100,000	$109,000
Cost of goods sold	62,000	74,000
Gross profit	$ 38,000	$ 35,000
Expenses	26,000	22,000
Net income	$ 12,000	$ 13,000

A recent review of the accounting records discovered that the 19X3 ending inventory had been understated by $4,000.
a Prepare corrected 19X3 and 19X4 income statements.
b What is the effect of the error on ending owner's equity for 19X3 and 19X4?

---

* An asterisk preceding an item indicates that the material is covered in an appendix to this chapter.

E9-2 *Specific identification method* (L.O. 3)

Boston Galleries uses the specific identification method for inventory valuation. Inventory information for several oil paintings follows.

		Painting	Cost
Jan. 2	Beginning inventory	Woods	$11,000
Apr. 19	Purchase	Sunset	21,800
June 7	Purchase	Earth	31,200
Dec. 16	Purchase	Moon	4,000

Woods and Moon were sold during the year for a total of $35,000. Determine the firm's:

a Cost of goods sold.

b Gross profit.

c Ending inventory.

E9-3 *Inventory valuation methods: Basic computations* (L.O. 3)

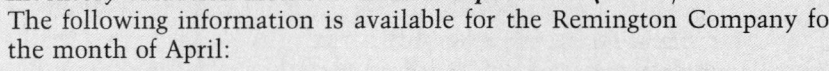

The following information is available for the Remington Company for the month of April:

Apr. 1	Beginning inventory	600 units @ $3.00
7	Purchase	1,000 units @ $3.10
17	Purchase	2,000 units @ $3.50
24	Purchase	400 units @ $4.25

On April 30, 800 units were unsold and remained in inventory. The firm uses a periodic inventory system.

Compute the ending inventory balance under each of the following valuation methods:

a First-in, first-out

b Last-in, first-out

c Weighted average

E9-4 *Inventory valuation methods: Basic computations* (L.O. 3)

The January beginning inventory of the White Company consisted of 300 units costing $40 each. During the first quarter, the company purchased two batches of goods: 700 units at $44 on February 21 and 800 units at $50 on March 28. Sales during the first quarter were 1,400 units at $75 per unit. The White Company uses a periodic inventory system.

Using the White Company data, fill in the chart that follows to compare the results obtained under the FIFO, LIFO, and weighted-average inventory methods.

	FIFO	LIFO	Weighted Average
Goods available for sale	$	$	$
Ending inventory, March 31			
Cost of goods sold			

E9-5 *Analysis of LIFO versus FIFO* (L.O. 3, 4)

Indicate whether LIFO or FIFO best describes each of the following:

a Gives highest profits when prices fall.

b Yields lowest income taxes when prices rise.

c Generates an ending inventory valuation that somewhat approximates replacement cost.

d Matches recent costs against current selling prices on the income statement.

e Comes closest to approximating the physical flow of goods of a fruit and vegetable dealer.

f Results in lowest cost of goods sold in inflationary periods.

E9-6 *Lower-of-cost-or-market rule* (L.O. 5)

The Springfield Company sells five different products. The following information is available on December 31:

1-2-3

Inventory Item	Units	Cost Per Unit	Market Value Per Unit
A	700	$3.00	$3.20
B	1,100	6.00	5.70
C	1,400	8.00	9.00
D	800	7.00	7.50
E	2,600	2.00	1.60

a Apply the lower-of-cost-or-market rule to each inventory item and determine Springfield's ending inventory balance.

b Prepare the required journal entry to reduce the inventory to the lower of cost or market.

E9-7 *Overview of inventory ownership and costing* (L.O. 1, 3, 4, 5)

Evaluate the comments that follow as being True or False. If the comment is false, briefly explain why.

a Franco purchased goods from Wholesale Supply on December 28. Although the merchandise was still in transit on December 31, Franco should nevertheless report these goods on its year-end balance sheet as an asset if the goods were sent F.O.B. shipping point.

b If a company sells its oldest goods first, the firm must use the FIFO method of inventory valuation.

c LIFO normally results in fairly current inventory costs being reported on the income statement as cost of goods sold.

d Under a weighted-average (periodic) inventory system, all goods sold during a period are costed at the same unit cost.

e Data on Olympia's inventory follow.

Item	Total Cost	Total Market
A	$15,900	$11,900
B	20,600	24,600

Olympia values its inventory on an item-by-item basis in accordance with rules stipulated by the accounting profession. Because the $4,000 loss suffered on item A is precisely offset by a $4,000 gain on item B, the company need not adjust its Inventory account at the end of the period.

E9-8 *Gross profit method and casualty loss* (L.O. 6)

Wren Electrical Company had an inventory loss on September 21, 19X9, from a hurricane. Company records kept in a safe revealed that 19X9 sales and net purchases prior to the casualty were $240,000 and $172,600, respectively. The 19X8 financial statements disclosed year-end inventory of $20,000 and a 36% gross profit rate. Management believes that the company had a similar gross profit experience during 19X9.

Determine the amount of the firm's inventory loss if goods costing $14,000 were undamaged by the storm.

E9-9   *Retail inventory method* (L.O. 6)

Abercrombie & Pearson sells designer apparel and uses the retail method of inventory valuation. The following information is available on December 31:

	Cost	Retail
Inventory, Jan. 1	$183,500	$320,000
Purchases, Jan.–Dec.	471,700	810,000
Purchases returns & allowances	8,500	15,000
Sales, Jan.–Dec.		890,000
Sales returns & allowances		18,200

Estimate the cost of the store's December 31 ending inventory.

E9-10   *Perpetual inventory systems: FIFO* (L.O. 7)

Alabama Industries had a beginning inventory on January 1 of 2,000 units that cost $6 each. Purchases and sales throughout the year were as follows:

Purchases		Sales	
Apr. 3	3,000 units @ $8.00	Apr. 9	3,500 units @ $10.00
Oct. 4	4,000 units @ $8.85	Dec. 3	3,000 units @ $11.00

The company uses a perpetual inventory system. Calculate the ending inventory valuation by using the FIFO cost flow assumption.

E9-11   *Perpetual inventory system; journal entries* (L.O. 7)

At the beginning of 19X3, Beehler Company implemented a computerized perpetual inventory system. The first transactions that occurred during 19X3 follow.

Purchases on account	
500 units @ $4	$2,000
Sales on account	
300 of the above units	2,550
Returns on account	
75 of the above unsold units	

The company president examined the computer-generated journal entries for these transactions and was confused by the absence of a Purchases account.

a Duplicate the journal entries that would have appeared on the computer printout.

b Calculate the balance in the firm's Inventory account.

c Briefly explain the absence of the Purchases account to the company president.

*E9-12   *Perpetual inventory systems: LIFO and moving average* (L.O. 7)

Refer to the beginning inventory, purchases, and sales data of Alabama Industries in Exercise 9-10. Assuming use of a perpetual inventory system, calculate the company's ending inventory valuation under the following cost flow assumptions:

a LIFO

b Moving average

Series A

P9-A1 *Inventory errors* (L.O. 1, 2)

The income statements of Diamond Company for the years ended December 31, 19X1, and 19X2 follow.

	19X1		19X2	
Net sales		$440,000		$483,000
Cost of goods sold				
Beginning inventory	$ 95,000		$109,000	
Add: Net purchases	380,000		404,000	
Goods available for sale	$475,000		$513,000	
Less: Ending inventory	109,000		127,000	
Cost of goods sold		366,000		386,000
Gross profit		$ 74,000		$ 97,000
Operating expenses		58,000		67,000
Net income		$ 16,000		$ 30,000

Diamond uses a periodic inventory system. A detailed review of the accounting records disclosed the following:

1 A review of 19X1 purchase invoices revealed that a clerk had incorrectly recorded a $12,600 purchase as $1,260.

2 A $4,800 purchase was made on December 30, 19X2, terms F.O.B. shipping point. The invoice was not recorded in 19X2 nor were the goods included in the 19X2 ending physical inventory count. Both the goods and invoice were received in early 19X3, with the invoice being recorded at that time.

3 Goods costing $3,000 were accidentally excluded from the 19X1 ending physical inventory count. These goods were sold during 19X2, and all aspects of the sale were properly recorded.

Instructions

a Prepare corrected income statements for 19X1 and 19X2.

b Determine the impact of the preceding errors on the December 31, 19X2, owner's equity balance.

P9-A2 *Inventory valuation methods: Computations and concepts* (L.O. 3, 4)

Wave Riders Surf Board Company began business on January 1 of the current year. Purchases of surf boards were as follows:

Jan.	3	100 boards @ $125
Mar.	17	50 boards @ $130
May	9	246 boards @ $140
July	3	400 boards @ $150
Oct.	23	74 boards @ $160

Wave Riders sold 710 boards at an average price of $250 per board. The company uses a periodic inventory system.

Instructions

a Calculate cost of goods sold, ending inventory, and gross profit under each of the following inventory valuation methods:

(1) First-in, first-out

(2) Last-in, first-out

(3) Weighted average

b Which of the three methods would be chosen if management's goal is to:

(1) Produce an "up-to-date" inventory valuation on the balance sheet?

(2) Approximate the physical flow of a sand and gravel dealer?

(3) Report low earnings (for tax purposes) for a separate electronics company that has been experiencing declining purchase prices?

P9-A3 *FIFO; lower of cost or market* (L.O. 3, 5)

Davenport Opticians began business on September 1 of the current year. The following purchases were made during the first few months of operation:

1-2-3

	Reading Glasses	Sunglasses	Contact Lenses
Sept. 2	1,000 @ $20	450 @ $10	2,500 @ $5
Oct. 15	750 @ $22	200 @ $15	2,000 @ $6
Dec. 6	300 @ $25		1,500 @ $7

The December 31 physical inventory count revealed the following items on hand: 650 reading glasses, 400 sunglasses, and 1,000 contact lenses. Total sales through year-end were $85,000, and operating expenses (excluding cost of goods sold) totaled $17,800. Davenport uses the FIFO inventory valuation method coupled with a periodic inventory system.

Instructions

a Compute the company's inventory as of December 31. In addition, calculate cost of goods sold and net income through the end of the year.

b Assume that the manufacturer of contact lenses announced a price decrease to $6.50. Determine the impact of the announcement on the firm's ending inventory valuation.

c Prepare the journal entry necessary to value the inventory at the lower of cost or market.

P9-A4 *Gross profit method and fire loss* (L.O. 6)

On January 28, 19X4, a fire heavily damaged the office and warehouse of Sunset Products. The following information has been obtained:

1 Sunset's condensed income statement for the year ended December 31, 19X3, is as follows:

Sales		$500,000
Cost of goods sold		
Beginning inventory	$195,000	
Add: Net purchases	325,000	
Goods available for sale	$520,000	
Less: Ending inventory	290,000	
Cost of goods sold		230,000
Gross profit		$270,000
Expenses		209,600
Net income		$ 60,400

2 Net sales and net purchases made during the first 28 days of January were $38,000 and $19,900, respectively.

3 Purchases entered in the accounting records but still in transit as of January 28 amounted to $1,700.

Sunset's insurance company agreed to reimburse the firm for the fire loss on the basis of an inventory estimate, derived by using the gross profit method. The gross profit rate will be computed by examining last year's operating results.

Instructions

a Determine the cost of inventory on hand on January 28.
b Taking your answer in part (a) into consideration, assume that goods were recovered and sold to a salvage firm for $6,000. Compute Sunset's total fire loss.
c In addition to computing fire losses, does the gross profit method have other possible uses? Explain.

P9-A5 *Retail method and inventory shrinkage* (L.O. 6)
Sarah Anne's is a children's store that specializes in novelties and clothing. A review of the store's accounting records disclosed the following information for the year ended December 31:

	Clothing		Novelties	
	Cost	Retail	Cost	Retail
Beginning inventory	$ 76,000	$146,500	$ 32,000	$ 76,800
Net purchases	496,000	953,500	164,400	414,200
Net sales		980,000		451,000

The company uses the retail inventory method.

Instructions

a Compute the cost-to-retail ratio of the firm's clothing line.
b Estimate the cost of the novelty inventory as of December 31.
c If a physical count of the novelty items on December 31 revealed an ending inventory at retail of $32,000, determine the cost of inventory shrinkage.
d On the basis of the figures that you calculated, why do you think that retail stores would likely compute cost-to-retail ratios by product line?

P9-A6 *Perpetual inventory systems: FIFO* (L.O. 7)
The Schaber Company carries parts that are in used in emergency medical situations. Given the critical nature of its business, Schaber uses a perpetual inventory system. The following information pertains to a particular heart monitor:

May 1 Beginning inventory: 100 units @ $6,800

Purchases		Sales	
May 3	50 units @ $7,100	May 7	30 units @ $11,400
18	75 units @ $7,200	14	70 units @ $11,400
25	40 units @ $7,250	20	55 units @ $11,600
		24	25 units @ $11,600
		29	20 units @ $11,700

Instructions

a Using a format similar to that of Exhibit 9-8, prepare a perpetual inventory record for the heart monitor. Schaber uses the FIFO method of inventory valuation.

b Prepare summary journal entries to record total purchases and sales.

c Assume that Schaber had used a periodic inventory system rather than a perpetual inventory system. Would the company's cost of goods sold and ending inventory differ from the amounts computed in part (a)? Why?

*P9-A7 *Perpetual inventory systems: LIFO and moving average* (L.O. 7)
Refer to the beginning inventory, purchases, and sales data of the Schaber Company in Problem 9-A6.

Instructions

a Assuming use of a LIFO cost flow assumption, prepare a perpetual inventory record for the heart monitor by using a format similar to that shown in Exhibit 9-8. (*Note:* Keep in mind that the exhibit illustrates the first-in, first-out method.)

b Assuming use of the moving-average method, determine the cost of the May 31 ending inventory and also the cost of goods sold during May.

Series B

P9-B1 *Inventory errors* (L.O. 1, 2)
The income statements of Maxum Company for the years ended December 31, 19X4, and 19X5 follow.

		19X4		19X5
Net sales		$820,000		$840,000
Cost of goods sold				
Beginning inventory	$245,000		$315,000	
Add: Net purchases	710,000		680,000	
Goods available for sale	$955,000		$995,000	
Less: Ending inventory	315,000		340,000	
Cost of goods sold		640,000		655,000
Gross profit		$180,000		$185,000
Operating expenses		126,000		140,000
Net income		$ 54,000		$ 45,000

Maxum uses a periodic inventory system. A detailed review of the accounting records disclosed the following:

1 Because of a clerical error, 60 units of merchandise in the 19X5 ending inventory count were costed at $540 per unit rather than the correct amount of $54 per unit.

2 A $5,000 merchandise purchase on December 31, 19X4, terms F.O.B. destination, was included in the 19X4 ending physical inventory count even though the goods had not yet been received. An investigation revealed that the invoice was recorded when the goods arrived on January 4, 19X5.

3 An examination of 19X4 purchasing activity revealed that a $26,000 acquisition of land had been incorrectly charged to the Purchases account.

Instructions

a Prepare corrected income statements for 19X4 and 19X5.

b Determine the impact of the preceding errors on the December 31, 19X5, owner's equity balance.

P9-B2 *Inventory valuation methods: Computations and concepts* (L.O. 3, 4)

Roller Blade Company began business on January 1 of the current year. Purchases of skates and roller blades were as follows:

1-2-3

Jan.	5	200 units @ $80
Apr.	22	60 units @ $90
June	5	300 units @ $100
July	8	100 units @ $110
Nov.	13	40 units @ $120

Roller Blade sold 440 units at an average price of $175 per unit. The company uses a periodic inventory system.

Instructions

a Calculate cost of goods sold, ending inventory, and gross profit under each of the following inventory valuation methods:
  (1) First-in, first-out
  (2) Last-in, first-out
  (3) Weighted average
b Which of the three methods would be chosen if management's goal is to:
  (1) Minimize the amount of income taxes paid to the federal government?
  (2) Match the oldest inventory costs against current revenues on the income statement?
  (3) Use a method that has been generally accepted by accounting practitioners?

P9-B3 *FIFO; lower of cost or market* (L.O. 3, 5)

On March 2 of the current year, Glen Riley became manager of a newly opened branch store of the Tall Pine Nursery. Riley made the following purchases during the first month of operation:

1-2-3

Spruce trees
Mar.	2	105 trees @ $30
	16	155 trees @ $40

Elm trees
Mar.	2	130 trees @ $10
	18	70 trees @ $15
	29	30 trees @ $18

Maple trees
Mar.	2	40 trees @ $50

An end-of-month physical inventory count revealed that the nursery had 75 spruce trees, 58 elm trees, and 38 maple trees in stock. Total sales for March amounted to $14,500; expenses (excluding cost of goods sold) were $3,100.

The company uses the FIFO inventory valuation method in conjunction with a periodic inventory system.

Instructions

a Compute the nursery's ending inventory, cost of goods sold, and net income for the first month of operation.
b Assume that the grower of the elm trees recently announced a price decrease to $14.50. Determine the impact of the announcement on the nursery's ending inventory valuation.
c Prepare the journal entry necessary to value the company's inventory at the lower of cost or market.

P9-B4 *Gross profit method and insurance from casualties* (L.O. 6)

On October 17, 19X9, an earthquake severely damaged the American Home Video Store. The insurance company has agreed to reimburse the owner on the basis of an inventory estimate derived by using the gross profit method. American's rate of earnings has been relatively stable in recent years, with the 19X8 income statement revealing the following:

Net sales	$320,000
Cost of goods sold	192,000
Net income	48,000
Inventory, Dec. 31	35,000

American's accountant has compiled additional information for 19X9:

Net sales through Oct. 17	$265,000
Net purchases recorded through Oct. 17	168,000
Purchases recorded but not received as of Oct. 17	3,000

Instructions

a Determine the cost of inventory on hand at American Home Video on the date of the earthquake. The gross profit rate is to be based on the company's 19X8 operating experience.

b Assume that the owner decided not to reopen the store and sold all salvageable videos for $2,000. What would be the amount of the loss claimed for insurance?

c How would you treat the proceeds received from the insurance company? Would the proceeds result in the *actual* inventory loss from the earthquake being more or less than the amount computed in part (b)?

P9-B5 *Retail method and inventory shrinkage* (L.O. 6)

Pro Stop, a sporting goods store, uses the retail method of inventory valuation. A review of the company's accounting records disclosed the following information for the year ended December 31:

Inventory, Jan. 1		Purchasing Activity	
Cost	$ 79,300	Purchases	
Retail	128,900	Cost	$296,600
Sales	432,000	Retail	498,100
Sales returns	17,600	Returns	
		Cost	7,200
		Retail	12,500

Instructions

a Using the retail method, estimate the cost of the company's inventory on December 31.

b If the firm's physical count on December 31 revealed an ending inventory at retail of $185,500, compute the cost of inventory shrinkage.

c Pro Stop is located in a fashionable shopping mall. Would you expect that the firm's cost-to-retail ratio is higher or lower than that of a sporting goods department of a locally-owned discount store? Briefly explain.

P9-B6 *Perpetual inventory systems: FIFO* (L.O. 7)

The McGeorge Company carries parts that are in high demand by the automotive industry. Given the competitive nature of its business, McGeorge uses a perpetual inventory system. The following information pertains to a particular exhaust component:

June 1   Beginning inventory: 800 units @ $14

Purchases		Sales	
June 10	1,000 units @ $15.50	June 7	300 units @ $22
17	600 units @ $16.10	12	400 units @ $23
20	1,000 units @ $16.25	14	600 units @ $23
		19	800 units @ $24
		28	900 units @ $24

Instructions

a Using a format similar to that of Exhibit 9-8, prepare a perpetual inventory record for the exhaust component. McGeorge uses the FIFO method of inventory valuation.
b Prepare summary journal entries to record total purchases and sales.
c Why do you think McGeorge implemented a perpetual inventory system rather than a periodic system?

*P9-B7 *Perpetual inventory systems: LIFO and moving average* (L.O. 7)
Refer to the beginning inventory, purchases, and sales data of the McGeorge Company in Problem 9-B6.

Instructions

a Assuming use of a LIFO cost flow assumption, prepare a perpetual inventory record for the exhaust component by using a format similar to that shown in Exhibit 9-8. (*Note:* Keep in mind that the exhibit illustrates the first-in, first-out method.)
b Assuming use of the moving-average method, determine the cost of the June 30 ending inventory and also the cost of goods sold during June.

EDB9-1 *Inventory valuation: The J.M. Smucker Company* (L.O. 3, 4, 5)

ELECTRONIC DATA BASE

The J.M. Smucker Company is involved with the manufacturing and marketing of food products. The firm is probably best known for its preserves, jams, jellies, marmalades, and ice cream toppings.

Instructions

By using the text's Electronic Data Base, access the balance sheet and accompanying notes of The Smucker Company and answer the questions that follow. Unless otherwise indicated, responses should be based on data for the most recent year presented.
a Study the presentation of inventories on the balance sheet.
   (1) Are inventories a sizable portion of the company's total assets? Show calculations to support your answer.
   (2) Does the company disclose different types of inventories? If so, what types are disclosed?
b What cost-flow assumption is used to value the majority of the firm's inventories? What factors may have been considered in adopting this assumption?
c Suppose the company had used another popular cost flow assumption.
   (1) Would reported inventory valuations increase or decrease? By how much?

(2) Would the alternative cost flow assumption result in higher or lower net income for the company?

d Does the firm make any attempt to record unrealized losses related to declines in market values of inventories? Briefly explain.

EDB9-2 *Inventory valuation* (L.O. 3, 4, 5)

This problem is a duplication of Problem EDB9-1. It is based on a company selected by your instructor.

Instructions

By using the text's Electronic Data Base, access the specified company's balance sheet and accompanying notes and focus on data for the most recent year reported. Answer requirements (a)–(d) of Problem EDB9-1.

BEYOND THE BASICS

BB9-1 *An in-depth probe of LIFO* (L.O. 3, 4)

The Biscayne Company, a newly organized Florida corporation, is composed of two divisions: Parts Manufacturing and Motor Car Sales. Both divisions currently use the LIFO method of inventory valuation. Because business is slumping, the controller has begun an in-depth review of operations.

The Parts Manufacturing division has experienced skyrocketing raw materials costs and labor difficulties. Two strikes by machinists and assemblers have been especially severe, causing Biscayne to close its plant for the past three months. Fortunately, existing finished goods inventories have been large enough to fill incoming sales orders.

The Motor Car Sales division has been hit with a sharp decline in sales, and the controller is contemplating a change from LIFO to FIFO. The year-end inventory under the LIFO method is anticipated to be $20 million. If FIFO is used, the ending inventory balance would increase to $28 million.

Instructions

a As the Parts Manufacturing division cuts deeper and deeper into finished goods inventory, which costs (high or low) will be charged to cost of goods sold?

b Given your answer in part (a), determine the effect of the strike on earnings and the related tax payments.

c Assuming the Motor Car Sales division is subject to an income tax rate of 40%, determine the effect on net income of the shift from LIFO to FIFO.

d Present a detailed analysis to Biscayne's president regarding the advantages and disadvantages of making the shift.

BB9-2 *Overview of chapter concepts: Multiple choice* (L.O. 1, 3–7)

The following multiple-choice questions relate to various topics discussed in the chapter. Select the best answer.

1 Which of the following should not be included in Franco's ending inventory?

a Goods sold by Franco and currently in transit to the buyer, terms F.O.B. destination.

b Goods held by Franco, on consignment from Wheeler Corporation.

c Goods purchased by Franco and currently in transit, terms F.O.B. shipping point.

d Goods of Franco, consigned to Lamar Company.

2 Quam Company imports exotic plants. The following purchases occurred during the first year of operation:

Jan.	4	300 units @ $23
Mar.	24	100 units @ $37
June	17	400 units @ $50
Oct.	8	200 units @ $60

At year-end, 475 plants remained in the company's greenhouse. Cost of goods sold under the LIFO method would be:

a $14,350. c $25,750.
b $16,850. d $28,250.

3 Anderson Company had the following purchases during the year: January, 200 units at $35; June, 500 units at $40; and October, 300 units at $45. If 800 units were sold at $50 each, the weighted-average unit cost of inventory would be:

a $40. c $41.
b $40.50. d $45.

4 Laredo Company began operations on January 1, 19X1. At the end of 19X1, the firm reported inventory of $25,000, computed by using LIFO. Had the company employed FIFO, the amount reported would have been $28,000. Which of the following comments about Laredo is false?

a The company's income would have been $3,000 higher had FIFO been used.

b The company's income statement provides a better match of current costs and current revenues than would have resulted had FIFO been used.

c The cost of purchases declined continually throughout 19X1.

d The beginning inventory for 19X2 will be $25,000.

5 The lower-of-cost-or-market adjustments related to inventory:

a must be constructed by comparing an inventory's total cost against total market value.

b define market as the achievable sales price in an arm's-length transaction.

c generally result in higher income for a company when goods are recognized as being spoiled or obsolete.

d can be used to adjust an inventory whose cost is determined under the FIFO cost flow assumption.

6 For the month ended March 31, Clemson Corporation had net sales of $85,000, net purchases of $50,000, and gross profit of 40% of sales. If the March 1 inventory was $10,000, an estimate of the company's ending inventory by using the gross profit method would be:

a $9,000. c $26,000.
b $25,000. d $34,000.

7 Winston Company, which uses the retail inventory method, is concerned about theft losses. The firm's beginning inventory cost $120,000 and had a retail valuation of $200,000. Purchases for the period totaled $480,000 and were marked up to sell for $800,000. Sales were $600,000, and a physical count of ending inventory had a retail value of $200,000. An estimate of the cost of stolen goods would be:

a $20,000. c $120,000.
b $40,000. d $240,000.

8 Charleston Company uses a perpetual inventory system. Which of the following debits and credits would be needed to record a sale of merchandise that cost $500 and retailed for $800?

a Credit Profit, $300. c Debit Sales, $800.
b Debit Inventory, $500. d Debit Cost of Goods Sold, $500.

COMMUNICATION OF ACCOUNTING INFORMATION

CAI9-1 *Communication structure: The Goodyear Tire & Rubber Company* (L.O. 3, 5)

Communication Principle: Most business writing and speaking begin with the main point to be communicated (i.e., a purpose statement). This practice aids the reader or listener, who needs to know the context of a discussion to correctly interpret the information that follows. Transition words are often used as pointers to focus on the facts about to be presented. Examples of such pointers include "The major distinction is . . . ," "The most important point is . . . ," and "The basic principles behind this treatment are . . . ."

The purpose statement should be followed by support such as definitions, comparisons and contrasts, and examples. Typical support phrases are "in contrast," "for instance," "to illustrate," "also," "together with," "in addition to," "therefore," "thus," and "similarly." The support generally closes with conclusion sentences, which help a reader/listener return to and recall the purpose statement. Phrases such as "to rephrase," "in review," "in other words," and "to sum up" help signal that the conclusion is near.

■ ■ ■ ■ ■ ■ ■ ■

The name, Goodyear Tire & Rubber, is certainly familiar. In addition to being one of the world's largest producers of tires and rubber products, the company manufactures and sells various chemicals and plastics as well as other goods and services. As you might imagine, inventory is one of Goodyear's most significant assets, totaling $1.3 billion.

Included in the company's annual report is a note that summarizes significant accounting policies. Within this note is the following description of the firm's inventory valuation methods:

> Inventories are stated at the lower of cost or market. Cost is determined using the last-in, first-out (LIFO) method for a significant portion of domestic inventories and the . . . average cost method for other inventories.

The "Summary of Significant Accounting Policies" note is required disclosure. Goodyear's overall summary, like those of many other companies, assumes users are familiar with certain basic accounting concepts. In this case, for instance, some knowledge of cost flow assumptions and declines in valuation is needed.

Instructions

Rewrite Goodyear's note so that a reader with virtually no accounting background could understand the inventory methods used. Be sure to utilize proper organization by providing an introductory (purpose) statement, an explanation, and a conclusion.

Answers to Chapter Quiz

1 b

2 b

3 c

4 a ($400 for A + $600 for B)

5 a

CHAPTER 10

Property, Plant, and Equipment: Acquisition and Depreciation

LEARNING OBJECTIVES

After studying this chapter, you should be able to:

1

Determine the cost of a long-lived asset.

2

Account for cash and lump-sum purchases
of property, plant, and equipment.

3

Explain the concept of depreciation and recognize
the factors that affect asset service life.

4

Compute depreciation by using the straight-line, units-of-output,
declining-balance, and sum-of-the-years'-digits methods.

5

Identify the financial reporting issues related to the
various depreciation methods.

6

Revise a depreciation rate.

7

Demonstrate a very basic knowledge of depreciation and the tax laws.

Many organizations invest large amounts of money in assets that are used to manufacture products or provide services. Marriott Corporation, for example, recently reported an investment of over $3 billion in such assets, Chrysler reported $13 billion, and Texaco Inc., reported $34 billion. Assets with long lives acquired for use in business operations are termed **property, plant, and equipment** and include land, buildings, vehicles, office equipment, machinery, store equipment, and furniture and fixtures. This asset category is sometimes referred to as plant and equipment, plant assets, or fixed assets. Property, plant, and equipment is the most descriptive of these titles, however, and has gained the widest acceptance among accountants for the presentation of productive and service capacity on the balance sheet.

Assets that appear under the property, plant, and equipment caption may be likened to long-term prepaid expenses, because their acquisition entails an advance payment for years of future service. To explain, a firm that prepays rent for several months into the next accounting period will record a prepaid expense on its balance sheet. If that same firm purchases a building, it has, in essence, prepaid for the future services the building is expected to render.

Like prepaid expenses, items of property, plant, and equipment can provide benefits for only a certain period of time and are said to possess a limited service life. (An exception is land, which provides services indefinitely.) As a result, then, just as prepaid expenses become expenses when consumed, plant and equipment are gradually charged to depreciation as the assets are used in operations.

Our discussion of long-lived assets in this chapter and Chapter 11 will focus on the following key issues, which are depicted in Exhibit 10-1:

1 Measurement of asset cost (Chapter 10)

2 Allocation of asset cost to the accounting periods benefited (Chapter 10)

3 Accounting for expenditures that occur after asset acquisition, such as repairs and improvements (Chapter 11)

4 Recording disposals of plant and equipment in the accounts (Chapter 11)

DETERMINING THE COST OF PROPERTY, PLANT, AND EQUIPMENT

OBJECTIVE

1

Determine the cost of a long-lived asset.

The cost of property, plant, and equipment includes acquisition or construction expenditures (and related amounts) required to ready the assets for business use. For the purchase of equipment, such expenditures include the invoice price of the equipment, freight charges incurred by the buyer, insurance on the equipment while in transit, and installation costs such as special electrical wiring and initial testing. The cost of land includes the purchase price; attorney's fees; commissions to a real estate broker; recording fees with the city or county; surveying costs; costs to clear, drain, and grade the land; and the assumption of any mortgages or delinquent property taxes. Thus, if a company purchased a parcel of land by paying $45,000 cash and assuming $5,000 of delinquent property taxes and a $55,000 mortgage, the land is recorded at a cost of $105,000.

The rationale for the preceding accounting treatment is clear. To charge costs related to asset acquisition as an expense of the acquisition period would result in a mismatch of revenues and expenses. Property, plant, and equipment will serve a business for many years, and incidental expenditures like freight, installation, and broker's fees are necessary for acquisi-

EXHIBIT 10-1
Issues Related to Long-Lived Assets

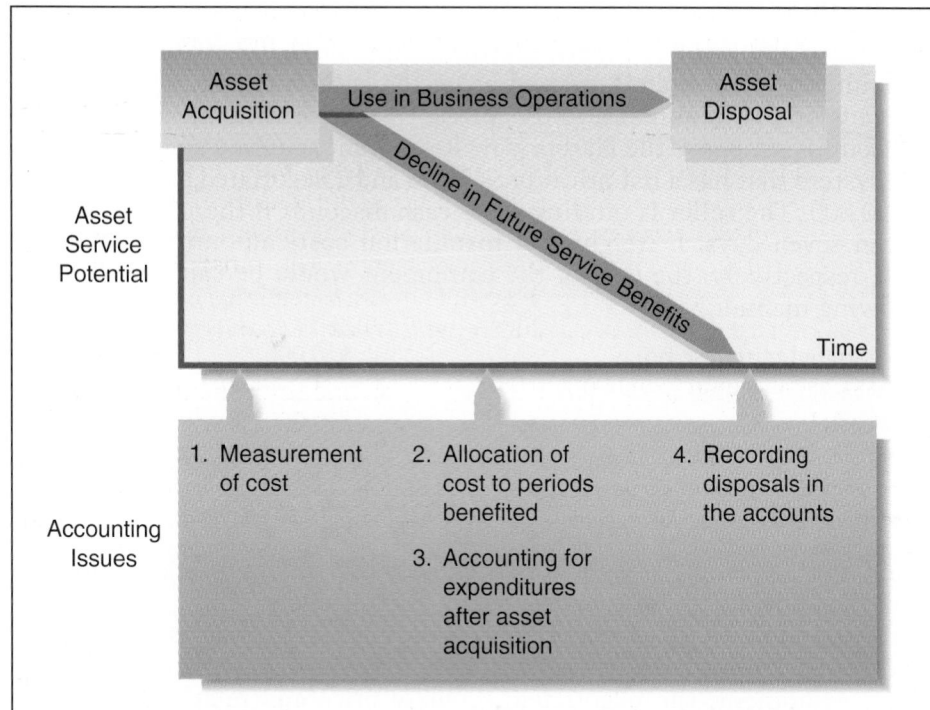

tion and subsequent asset use to occur. In effect, then, these items provide long-run benefits and should be shown on the balance sheet as part of an asset's cost.

Expenditures related to asset acquisition and preparation that fail to provide future economic benefits are expenses. For example, if a piece of equipment was damaged while being installed, the repair costs would not be added to the cost of the equipment. Instead, the repairs are treated as an expense of the current accounting period. Likewise, if a newly purchased machine was being delivered on the buyer's truck and the truck was involved in an accident, the cost of fixing the truck, any damages paid to other parties, and any fines levied on the driver are not charged to the Machinery account. These outlays are not "ordinary and necessary" to place the machine in a position ready to serve the purchaser and are therefore expensed.

A cost that we failed to cite in the preceding discussion is interest. Stated simply, the proper accounting treatment is dependent on the method of asset acquisition. As a general rule, interest costs incurred to finance the *purchase* of property, plant, and equipment are written off as expense. In contrast, interest charges related to financing the *construction* of plant and equipment for a company's own use are often added to the cost of the asset. These latter charges must be incurred during the construction period and be significant in amount to qualify for this special treatment.[1]

---

[1] "Capitalization of Interest Costs," *Statement of Financial Accounting Standards No. 34* (Norwalk, Conn.: Financial Accounting Standards Board, 1979).

Cash Purchase

Property, plant, and equipment may be acquired in a variety of ways, with a commonly encountered method being the **cash purchase.** The recorded asset cost in a cash purchase is the lowest cash price available to the buyer. For example, suppose the Harborview Restaurant acquired a new refrigeration system that has a list price[2] of $25,000 and a negotiated purchase price of $20,000. The seller is offering a 5% cash discount if the invoice is paid within seven days. If freight and installation costs amount to $400 and $900, respectively, the cost of the equipment would be calculated in the following manner:

Negotiated purchase price		$20,000
Less: Cash discount ($20,000 × 0.05)		(1,000)
Net price		$19,000
Add: Freight	$400	
Installation	900	1,300
Acquisition cost		$20,300

The list price is not relevant; it is used only as a guide in establishing the actual amount of the sale by the seller. In a discount store, for instance, you will find that virtually all items can be purchased at a cost well below their stated (and usually crossed out) list price. When determining the cost of the equipment, the negotiated purchase price and related freight and installation charges are relevant. So, too, is the offer of the cash discount.

If Harborview issued a check for $20,300, the refrigeration system would be entered in the Kitchen Equipment account for that amount. If the company could not take advantage of the discount because of a lack of funds, the Kitchen Equipment account would still be debited for $20,300. The $1,000 discount lost is treated as a financing expense (namely, interest) of the current accounting period. The necessary journal entry for the second situation follows:

Kitchen Equipment	20,300	
Interest Expense	1,000	
Cash		21,300
To record acquisition of refrigeration system; discount missed		

Lump-Sum Purchase

Frequently, a business will purchase a number of assets together for a single amount. For example, the acquisition of developed property will often include such assets as land, buildings, parking lots, fences, and lawn sprinkler systems. Transactions of this type are termed **lump-sum purchases.** The cost of a lump-sum purchase must be apportioned among the various assets acquired for reporting and depreciation purposes. These assets generally benefit a business for different periods of time and therefore require different depreciation rates.

Appraisals are often used to aid in the apportionment. To illustrate, assume that Hartley Development Company purchased a building, land

[2] The list price is sometimes referred to as the manufacturer's suggested retail price.

improvements (e.g., parking lots, fences, and lawn sprinkler systems), and land for $40 million cash. The assets' appraisal values along with the necessary cost apportionment follow.

	Appraisal Value	Percentage of Total Appraisal Value	Recorded Cost
Building	$25,000,000	50%	$20,000,000
Land improvements	5,000,000	10	4,000,000
Land	20,000,000	40	16,000,000
Total	$50,000,000	100%	$40,000,000

The acquisition cost is apportioned on the basis of an individual asset's appraised value relative to the appraised value of the entire purchase. For example, because the building is 50% of the property's total value ($25,000,000 ÷ $50,000,000), the cost of the building is established at $20,000,000 ($40,000,000 × 0.50). The recorded amounts for land improvements and land are determined in the same manner. The journal entry to record the purchase is therefore as follows:

Building	20,000,000	
Land Improvements	4,000,000	
Land	16,000,000	
Cash		40,000,000

To record acquisition of developed property

Notice that a distinction is made between land and *land improvements.* It is necessary to establish separate accounts for these assets, because a parcel of land has an indefinite life whereas land improvements do not. As a result, land improvements are depreciated over the number of periods they render benefits or service to a business.

Companies sometimes acquire developed property and subsequently undertake a demolition program, thereby paving the way for new construction. In these instances the entire purchase price is debited to the Land account, along with the costs of removing the old buildings and improvements. Conversely, any proceeds received from selling materials that are salvaged from the demolition process are credited to Land.

Small Items of Property, Plant, and Equipment

Businesses purchase many long-lived items (e.g., tape dispensers, pencil sharpeners, and office clocks) that technically should be classified as property, plant, and equipment. Because of their insignificant purchase price, however, these items are not established as assets in the accounting records. Instead, such amounts are normally written off as expenses in the period of acquisition. This procedure reduces paperwork costs and avoids depreciating small items over long periods of time. Imagine the record keeping associated with depreciating a $5 wastepaper basket over a 10-year life. Virtually all accountants would agree that the $0.50 annual write-off is hardly worth the effort.

In an attempt to avoid an in-depth analysis of its many expenditures, a business will typically make the accounting-treatment decision by using a preestablished minimum dollar cutoff. If, for example, a firm sets a $100 cutoff, all expenditures of $100 or less would automatically be deemed too small to be recorded as part of property, plant, and equipment. Such amounts would therefore be expensed immediately. On the other hand, outlays that exceed $100 would be considered significant and thus treated as assets, to be written off gradually as benefits are received.[3]

Cost/Benefit and Materiality

Whether an outlay should be expensed or carried as an asset is a matter of professional judgment. When evaluating the two possible treatments, the accountant must assess the magnitude and importance of the outlay in question. The proper decision can be made only after careful consideration of the factors of cost/benefit and materiality. More specifically, the expense of developing exact accounting information must be studied relative to the benefits of added precision. If the cost of a company's efforts exceeds the benefits that financial statement users will receive, the extra precision is deemed wasteful and should not be attempted.

This cost/benefit theme is consistent with the concept of **materiality,** which refers to the significance of a particular item or transaction. If judged to be immaterial, an item or transaction would likely have no influence on the decisions made by informed financial statement users. In such cases, theory would take a back seat to practice, and the accountant would handle the item in the most expedient manner possible. Thus, for items of $100 or less in the preceding example, an immediate write-off is preferred rather than a prolonged allocation to the periods of benefit.

DEPRECIATION

OBJECTIVE
3

Explain the concept of depreciation and recognize the factors that affect asset service life.

As we previously noted, all items of property, plant, and equipment (except land) have limited lives and render services over several accounting periods. These services often result in the production of revenues for the firm. Proper accounting therefore requires that a portion of the cost of long-lived assets be written off each year to expense, to be matched against revenues on the income statement. Stated differently, because revenues are generated in each year of asset use, it is only correct that each year's income absorb the costs of producing that revenue.

The process used to allocate the cost of long-lived assets to the accounting periods benefited is known as **depreciation.** Be aware, however, that other definitions of depreciation are commonly encountered. For example, you may have heard new car owners mention the "depreciation" they have suffered since their purchase. To these people depreciation represents a decrease in value, namely, the difference between the amount paid for the car and the vehicle's present resale value. Accountants make no attempt to integrate information into the accounts about the ever-changing market

---

[3] Cutoff limits typically vary from firm to firm and are often dependent on company size. A large expenditure for Joe's Electronics, for instance, could be an insignificant amount to Texas Instruments.

values of property, plant, and equipment. Instead, assets classified in this category are maintained in the accounting records at cost. For depreciable assets this cost is subsequently allocated as expense to the years receiving service or benefits. In accounting, then, *depreciation is a process of allocation, not valuation.*

Determining Service Life

Before an asset's cost is allocated among the periods benefited, a service life must be estimated. **Service life,** sometimes called economic or useful life, is the period of time that depreciable assets provide service to a business. It is important to understand that an asset's service life is frequently different from its physical life. That is, an asset may have physical existence long after the useful life to a business has concluded. Witness, for example, the abandoned equipment behind many manufacturing plants and the numerous railroad tracks that are no longer used by their owners.

When determining an asset's service life, we must consider three factors: physical deterioration, obsolescence, and inadequacy.

Physical Deterioration

The physical deterioration of an asset, sometimes termed "wear and tear," is caused by use in the normal course of business. Repair and maintenance may prolong an asset's service life, but at some point the asset usually requires replacement because it has become worn out. Physical deterioration normally establishes the maximum limit for the estimate of service life.

Obsolescence

Obsolescence is a technological factor relating to being out of date. New technology frequently shortens the service life of assets well before their physical life is over. Businesses that use obsolete machines, for example, cannot compete effectively with companies that use modern, more efficient equipment.

Obsolescence has been a significant factor in shortening the service life of computers. Recent advances in engineering have been dramatic. Businesses that purchased a computer three to five years ago are finding faster, more versatile models are now available, making their equipment out of date and less desirable.

Inadequacy

With business growth, the service capabilities of certain items of depreciable property, plant, and equipment may become inadequate. Plants may no longer be able to keep pace with demand, trucks may be too small, and equipment may be too slow. When assets are inadequate to meet the competitive needs of a company, their service lives have ended. Like obsolescence, inadequacy is an economic (as opposed to physical) determinant of service life.

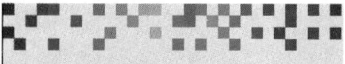

Relative Significance of the Three Factors

All three of the preceding factors should be evaluated when estimating service life. It is conceivable, of course, that one factor may be more important than the others for certain assets. Consider, for example, a small commuter airline that desires to expand and begin service to large metropolitan areas. The airline may find that the service life of its flight equipment is controlled primarily by the factor of inadequacy. On the other hand, a high-precision manufacturer that uses advanced electronics may view obsolescence as the most important determinant of service life for much of its equipment.

In other business situations, all of the factors may be equally important for a particular depreciable asset. In these cases the estimation of service life becomes more difficult. Companies having no experience with a particular type of asset may seek guidance from their accountants, engineers, trade associations, or the asset's seller.

EXECUTIVE BRIEFING
High-Tech Depreciable Lives

Alex Mandl
Chief Financial Officer and Group Executive
AT&T

Estimating the depreciable life for high-tech equipment is not easy. Traditional approaches have relied on historical data for similar equipment or on engineering estimates of how long the equipment can last. These methods just don't work in an environment characterized by ever-shortening life cycles, global competition, and increasingly sophisticated customers.

For example, by 1987, AT&T had almost $25 billion of equipment invested in its analog long distance network. This network was designed to last until the year 2010. In 1988, two things changed those plans—breakthroughs in digital technology along with the software that makes it work, and accelerating customer demand for services that only digital equipment can provide. Suddenly, the analog network would be economically obsolete by the year 1990—20 years ahead of schedule. Since our traditional equipment life estimates never anticipated this change, AT&T took a writedown of $6.3 billion for the underdepreciated equipment.

The bottom line is that using the engineered life for high-tech equipment will generally give the wrong answer. Instead, the economic service life should be employed. This means looking at market trends, competitor strategies, and what's on the drawing board in the laboratories across the globe, *as well as* identifying the engineered life. It's not easy, but it's the only way to accurately portray the profitability of your business.

HIGHLIGHT
Depreciation: Is Nothing Sacred?

At an office of the Roman Catholic diocese in Brooklyn, New York, Monsignor Austin Bennett was going about his spiritual and worldly chores. He was helping minority-group students get room to study at the diocese's 22 schools. He was helping priests take care of their aging parents. And he was helping a custodian from Central America get documents to apply for U.S. citizenship. Then he wrote a nasty letter to the Financial Accounting Standards Board (FASB).

Why was this friendly, pipe-smoking individual launching verbal barbs against the chief rule-making body for accountants? "Because the board is . . . causing more trouble for American churches than all the sinners in their congregations." Msgr. Bennett, accounting practices chairman of the U.S. Catholic Conference, was referring to a then proposed, now enacted ruling that forces churches to depreciate their houses of worship and monuments. The churches, which have always been exempt from this accounting procedure, will naturally find their income reduced because of the added expense.

A reduced level of income could be important since many religious institutions, particularly big ones, issue audited financial statements to substantiate their financial health to suppliers, bank lenders, and parishioners. "Our cathedrals last for centuries and often gain in value with age," Msgr. Bennett asserts. "But they don't last forever," counter[ed] a project manager at the FASB. "The Parthenon may still be there, but its roof has fallen in. Physical assets that are exhaustible should be depreciated."

The period that preceded the FASB's decision brought forth some interesting (and heated) debate. "Depreciating cathedrals and churches is stupid," said a well-known professor emeritus at the Harvard Business School and expert on accounting for non-profit groups. "It would be like trying to compare the cost per soul saved among churches." And a retired Treasury Department official added, "Depreciating churches would be like depreciating the Pyramids and the Sphinx of Egypt, and the Sistine Chapel at the Vatican." Figuring such depreciation would be "the acme of futility."

The ungodly flap over depreciation began several years ago when the accounting profession sought uniformity among nonprofit organizations, as some organizations depreciated their assets whereas others did not. Religious institutions generally argued against depreciation. Notes the FASB's director of accounting standards, "Basically they told us that the structures have been here long before us and would be here long after we're gone. It made sense."

After some debate on the matter, the FASB ruled in favor of depreciation. The board stressed that cathedrals are used up not only by wear and tear but also by the continuous destructive effects of pollutants, vibrations, and so forth. As an FASB spokesman succintly observes, "Church properties can wear out; therefore, they should be depreciated. I can see quibbling about the Pyramids, because their [service] life is so long that the costs per year would be immaterial. But not most churches. Even St. Patrick's Cathedral in Manhattan has parts that must be replaced and other parts that can be salvaged." A "maverick" pastor from Baltimore agrees; he accepts depreciation because he likes challenges. However, as Msgr. Bennett maintains, "[The pastor] is entitled to his opinion, but he speaks only for himself. He has no official accounting status in the Catholic Church."

Methods of Depreciation

OBJECTIVE

4

Compute depreciation by using the straight-line, units-of-output, declining-balance, and sum-of-the-years'-digits methods.

There are several acceptable methods for computing depreciation. The four methods used most often are straight-line, units-of-output, declining-balance, and sum-of-the-years'-digits. Some of these approaches are so common that they are actually built into electronic spreadsheets. Most spreadsheets, for example, employ function commands, which are a series of preprogrammed formulas that accomplish a specific task. To calculate, say, straight-line depreciation, the user need only invoke the proper function command and enter basic data such as asset cost and service life. The rest is done automatically.

Straight-Line Method

Largely because of its simplicity, the **straight-line method** is a very popular way to compute depreciation. Under this approach, the cost of a depreciable asset, minus residual value, is allocated equally over the estimated service life. The **residual value** (sometimes called salvage value) is the amount a business expects to receive upon disposal of an asset at the end of the asset's life. Given the nature of the allocation, the straight-line method is best applied to assets that provide constant, uniform service to an entity.

To illustrate the straight-line method, assume WBBB-TV bought a new television camera for $30,000. The camera has an estimated residual value of $3,000 and an estimated service life of five years. The annual depreciation expense is computed as follows:

$$\frac{\text{Cost} - \text{Residual Value}}{\text{Service Life in Years}} = \text{Annual Depreciation}$$

$$= \frac{\$30,000 - \$3,000}{5 \text{ years}}$$

$$= \$5,400 \text{ annual depreciation}$$

The deduction of the $3,000 residual value from the asset's cost of $30,000 yields a $27,000 **depreciable base**—the total amount that will be written off to depreciation expense over the asset's life.

The following journal entry is used to record depreciation during each year of the camera's life:

Depreciation Expense: Broadcasting Equipment	5,400	
Accumulated Depreciation: Broadcasting Equipment		5,400
To record annual depreciation expense		

This entry reflects a very common practice: the creation of separate accounts for each major group of depreciable assets (e.g., buildings, office equipment, furniture and fixtures, and so forth). Such breakdowns are helpful for internal management analysis as well as for external financial reporting.

In view of the preceding data, WBBB's income statement would reveal annual depreciation expense of $5,400. The firm's balance sheet would disclose the following:

	Year 1	Year 2
Property, plant, & equipment		
Broadcasting equipment	$30,000	$30,000
Less: Accumulated depreciation	5,400	10,800
	$24,600	$19,200

These figures show that accumulated depreciation increases by $5,400 during each year of service life. Recall that the cost of an asset, minus accumulated depreciation, is termed **book value.** As the accompanying schedule illustrates, book value decreases each year and equals the residual value ($3,000) at the end of the camera's life. The asset is said to be fully depreciated at this point and no further depreciation is recorded.

Year	Depreciation Expense	Accumulated Depreciation	Book Value
			$30,000
1	$5,400	$ 5,400	24,600
2	5,400	10,800	19,200
3	5,400	16,200	13,800
4	5,400	21,600	8,400
5	5,400	27,000	3,000

Tips & Techniques

Be aware that a fully depreciated asset may continue to be used in business activities. Put simply, a company will not dispose of dependable equipment and buildings just because the estimated service life has come to an end. The use of such assets beyond their estimated lives may actually boost earnings, as the revenues generated are not decreased by any depreciation expense. Remember, once an asset is fully depreciated, no further write-offs can be taken.

Partial Periods. In the preceding example, we assumed the camera was acquired on January 1. If the purchase was made later in the year, WBBB would record a prorated percentage of the annual depreciation charge. Assuming acquisition on May 1, depreciation for the first year would be $3,600 ($5,400 × $\frac{8}{12}$), because the asset provided services for only eight months. The remaining depreciation expense would then be $5,400 for Years 2, 3, 4, and 5 and $1,800 ($5,400 × $\frac{4}{12}$) for the first four months of Year 6. As before, depreciation totals $27,000 and is recorded over five years of service.

Asset purchases do not always take place on the first day of the month. Most companies have established their own practices for recording depreciation in this situation. For example, when a depreciable asset is acquired during the first 15 days of a month, the purchase is often handled as if it occurred on the first day of the month. If the asset is acquired in the last half of a month, the transaction is treated as occurring on the first day of the following month, and the depreciation computation commences at this time. Other companies record one-half of the first full year's depreciation in the year of acquisition regardless of the date of purchase. Such an approach simplifies the depreciation computation because acquisition dates are ignored. These and other similar practices are acceptable as long as they are followed consistently.

Units-of-Output Method

The **units-of-output method,** sometimes called the units-of-production or activity method, can be employed when an asset's service life is expressible in terms of output (such as miles, hours, or number of times used). Under this approach the asset's cost, minus residual value, is divided by the total estimated output during the service life. This computation generates the depreciation rate. Annual depreciation expense is then calculated by multiplying the depreciation rate by the yearly output. To illustrate, assume a large corporation purchased a business jet for $4 million that has a residual value of $1.5 million. The service life is estimated to be 10,000 flying hours. The depreciation rate is calculated as follows:

$$\frac{\text{Cost} - \text{Residual Value}}{\text{Service Life in Output}} = \text{Annual Depreciation}$$

$$= \frac{\$4,000,000 - \$1,500,000}{10,000 \text{ flying hours}}$$

$$= \$250 \text{ per flying hour}$$

If the jet was used for 500 hours during the year, depreciation expense would total $125,000 ($250 × 500).

The units-of-output method is used when (1) the service capacity of an asset can be reasonably estimated and (2) there is a direct relationship between an asset's use and its decline in service potential. Assets that meet these two criteria include cars, trucks, and machines. In situations where the amount of an asset's output varies considerably from period to period, the units-of-output method achieves a better allocation of cost than do the straight-line or other depreciation approaches. For example, in years of great activity, more of an asset's cost would be depreciated and matched against revenues; in years of low activity, less depreciation expense is recorded. In contrast, the straight-line method produces a constant depreciation charge regardless of the services provided.

Accelerated Depreciation Methods

The two remaining depreciation methods are declining-balance and sum-of-the-years'-digits. Both approaches speed up the recognition of expense and are appropriately termed **accelerated depreciation methods.** As you will soon see, relatively large amounts of depreciation are generated in the early years of asset use and small amounts in later years.

Businesses may prefer to use an accelerated depreciation method for a variety of reasons. First, companies recognize that the services provided by many assets tend to decline over time. For example, consider the transportation services provided by a new car versus those of a less dependable older model. Or note the quality of machining obtained from a new high-precision drill press versus that from an older press with less accurate tolerances. If the services provided are actually greater in the earlier years of asset use, a proper matching of revenues and expenses dictates a gradual reduction in depreciation charges over an asset's lifetime.

Another reason for using an accelerated depreciation method is that repair and maintenance costs normally increase as an asset grows older. When combined with a decreasing amount of depreciation from an accelerated method, the total amount of yearly expense is leveled. The end result for assets that furnish uniform service is a better match of expense against revenue than would be possible by the straight-line technique.

Declining-Balance Method.   The **declining-balance method** involves applying a fixed depreciation rate to the remaining book value of an asset. The rate employed is a multiple of that calculated under the straight-line method. For instance, if a company is computing depreciation by utilizing the popular **double-declining balance** approach, the rate used is twice the straight-line rate. Additionally, any residual value is ignored in the depreciation calculation, thereby permitting even greater expense in the early years of asset use. Consistent with the other approaches presented, however, an asset's book value *cannot* be reduced below the estimated residual value.

Applying the double-declining balance method to the television camera example cited earlier (cost, $30,000; residual value, $3,000; service life, five years), we obtain the accompanying depreciation schedule.

Year	Depreciation Expense	Accumulated Depreciation	Book Value
			$30,000
1	$12,000 ($30,000 × 40%)	$12,000	18,000
2	7,200 ($18,000 × 40%)	19,200	10,800
3	4,320 ($10,800 × 40%)	23,520	6,480
4	2,592 ($6,480 × 40%)	26,112	3,888
5	888 ($3,888 − $3,000)	27,000	3,000

To explain, with the five-year service life, the straight-line depreciation rate is $\frac{1}{5}$, or 20%, per year. The double-declining balance rate, therefore, is 40% (2 × 20%). Depreciation expense in the first year is 40% times the $30,000 book value, or $12,000. The journal entry to record depreciation at the end of the year places $12,000 in the Accumulated Depreciation account, thus reducing the camera's book value to $18,000. Depreciation in the second year falls to $7,200, that is, book value of $18,000 × 40%. Similar computations are performed in Years 3 and 4.

The last year of service life is handled differently. If we had continued with the approach just illustrated, depreciation expense in the fifth year would have been $1,555 ($3,888 × 40%). The camera's book value would therefore be reduced to $2,333 ($3,888 − $1,555), which is below the $3,000 estimated residual value. Thus, depreciation expense in Year 5 amounts to only $888 ($3,888 − $3,000).

If the television camera had been purchased on September 1, depreciation expense would be computed for only four months in Year 1 and would total $4,000 [($30,000 × 40%) × $\frac{4}{12}$]. The necessary procedures for all future periods are similar to those shown in the earlier illustration. For example, because book value at the beginning of Year 2 would be $26,000 ($30,000 − $4,000), depreciation expense for the second year is $10,400 ($26,000 × 40%).

Tips & Techniques

Be extremely careful to ignore residual value in the computation of *yearly* depreciation expense under the double-declining balance method. As the name of this approach implies, annual depreciation is calculated on a declining base (i.e., book value). The residual value is considered *only* when deriving an asset's minimum book value (and, thus, total allowable depreciation write-offs over a service life).

Sum-of-the-Years'-Digits Method. Paralleling the double-declining balance method, the **sum-of-the-years'-digits method** produces more depreciation expense in the early years of asset use. Under this approach, a successively lower depreciation rate is applied each year to a constant depreciable base (cost minus residual value). The rate, which is really a fraction, is derived by setting the numerator equal to the remaining years of life at the beginning of the period. The denominator, in turn, equals the total of the service years. In the case of the television camera, which has a five-year life, the denominator would always equal 15 (5 + 4 + 3 + 2 + 1 = 15). Similarly, for assets having a four-year life, the denominator would be 10 (4 + 3 + 2 + 1 = 10).[4]

Continuing the camera example, the numerator for the first year is 5 because five years of service life remain; then 4 for the second year, and so forth. WBBB's depreciation schedule using the sum-of-the-years'-digits method follows.

Year	Depreciation Expense	Accumulated Depreciation	Book Value
			$30,000
1	$9,000 ($27,000 × $\frac{5}{15}$)	$ 9,000	21,000
2	7,200 ($27,000 × $\frac{4}{15}$)	16,200	13,800
3	5,400 ($27,000 × $\frac{3}{15}$)	21,600	8,400
4	3,600 ($27,000 × $\frac{2}{15}$)	25,200	4,800
5	1,800 ($27,000 × $\frac{1}{15}$)	27,000	3,000

---

[4] The denominator can be easily calculated by the following formula:

$$D = \frac{n(n + 1)}{2}$$

where D equals the denominator and n equals the number of service years. For example, the denominator of an asset having a 10-year service life would be computed as

$$D = \frac{10(10 + 1)}{2} = \frac{110}{2} = 55$$

For assets acquired during the year, the allocation of cost over the service life is more complex. The key to understanding the necessary procedures is to recognize that each fraction ($\frac{5}{15}$, $\frac{4}{15}$, $\frac{3}{15}$, and so on) *must be employed for 12 months no matter when the asset is acquired.* For example, if the camera was purchased on April 1 and used for nine months, the $\frac{5}{15}$ rate would be applied for the remainder of Year 1, producing depreciation expense of $6,750 [($27,000 × $\frac{5}{15}$) × $\frac{9}{12}$]. Depreciation expense for the second year totals $7,650 and is computed by using the $\frac{5}{15}$ rate for three months and the $\frac{4}{15}$ rate for nine months, specifically,

$$\$27,000 \times \tfrac{5}{15} \times \tfrac{3}{12} = \$2,250$$
$$27,000 \times \tfrac{4}{15} \times \tfrac{9}{12} = \underline{5,400}$$
$$\$7,650$$

This process, depicted in the following graphic, is subsequently continued into Year 6.

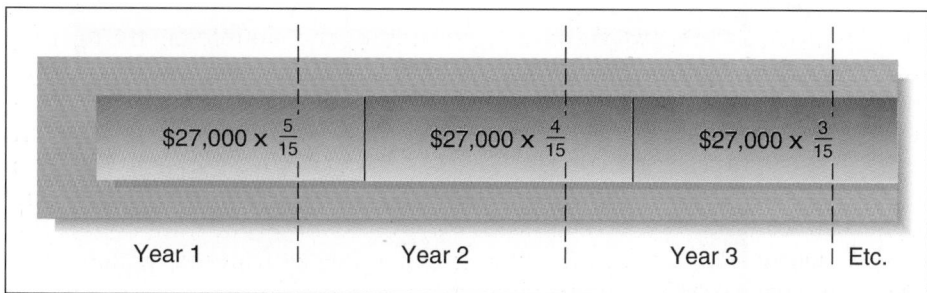

Selection of a Depreciation Method

Exhibit 10-2 shows the annual depreciation expense for the three methods used with the television camera: straight-line, double-declining balance, and sum-of-the-years'-digits. The units-of-output method is disregarded here because the camera's service capacity in units could not be reasonably estimated.

By summing the annual charges from the preceding schedules, you will see that the same total amount is ultimately written off by all of the methods, namely, cost minus residual value. However, as the exhibit so clearly reveals, the amounts and patterns of the yearly allocations differ markedly. The straight-line approach produces lower depreciation expense in the early years of an asset's life than either of the accelerated methods. The gap between straight-line and the other methods tends to decrease as time passes, with a reversal occurring in Year 3. That is, the $5,400 straight-line expense figure actually exceeds the charges obtained with double-declining balance or sum-of-the-years'-digits in later years of use.

Exhibit 10-2 also reveals the movement of book value over time. Although the book value figures under the various approaches decline at differing rates, the end result is the same: the amount ultimately left on the accounting records is residual value ($3,000).

Which method, then, should be selected? The answer to this question depends on a number of factors, including usage patterns, the generation of

OBJECTIVE

5

Identify the financial-reporting issues related to the various depreciation methods.

EXHIBIT 10-2
A Graphical Overview of
Depreciation Methods

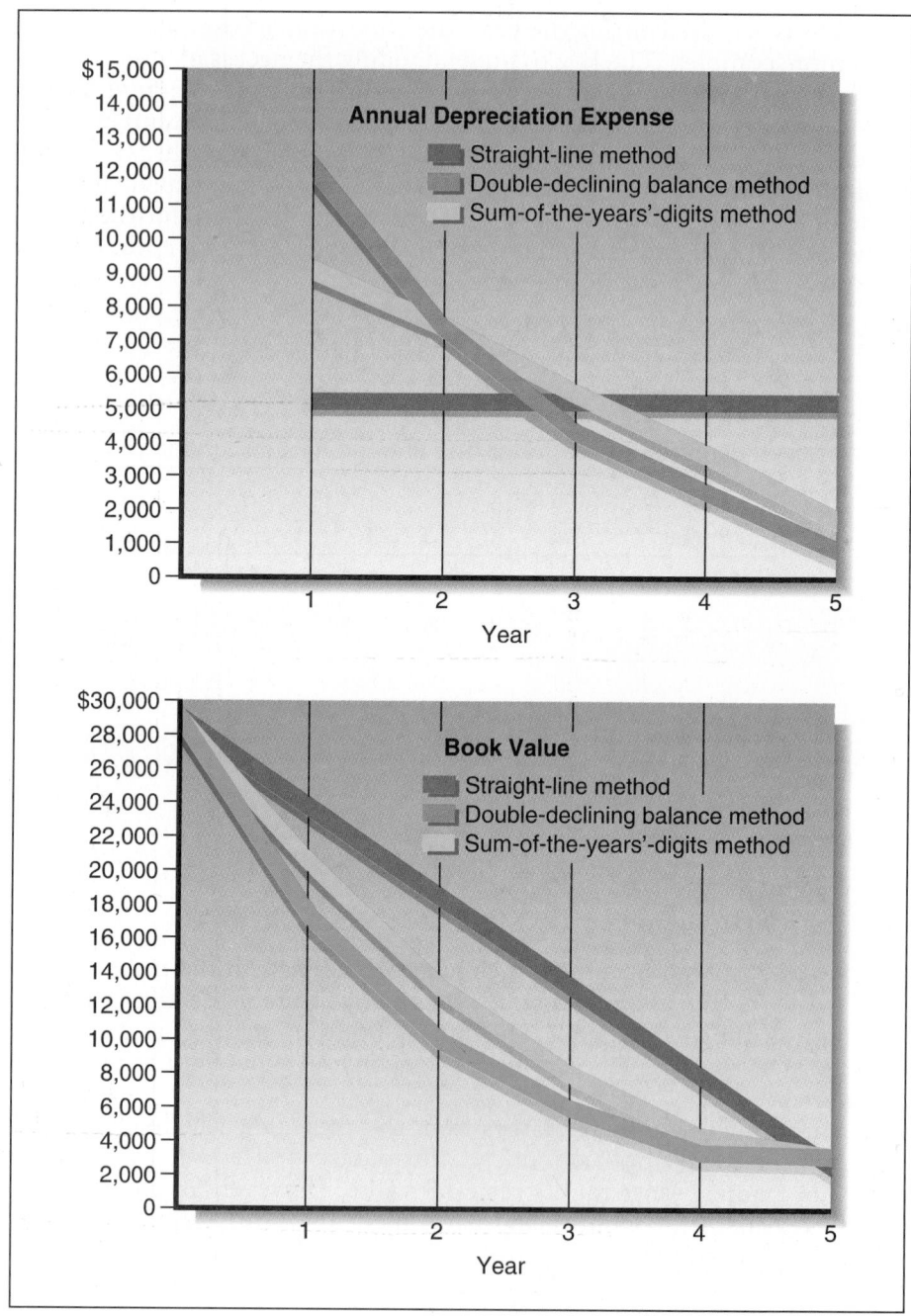

operating efficiencies, obsolescence, and the timing of repair costs. Conceptually, the method chosen should be the one that best parallels the
services delivered (or benefits provided) by an asset. Such a selection is
consistent with proper matching of revenues and expenses. Because the
pattern of service is sometimes difficult to measure, however, practice
often differs from theory. Recent surveys of reporting practices have shown
the straight-line method to be the most popular approach. Companies that

Company	Depreciation Policy
Eastman Kodak Company	Calculated generally by accelerated methods for assets in the United States and by the straight-line method for assets outside the United States.
Mobil Corporation	Computed on a straight-line basis over the useful lives of the various classes of properties or, where appropriate for producing properties, on a unit-of-production basis by individual fields.
Zenith Electronics	Straight-line method for additions of plant and equipment with useful lives of eight years or more; accelerated methods for substantially all other plant and equipment items, including high-technology equipment that may be subject to rapid economic obsolescence.

EXHIBIT 10-3
Comparison of Depreciation Policies

use this method often do so because of the constant nature of the depreciation charge—an element that helps to portray financial stability and smooth earnings over time. Exhibit 10-3 discloses the variation in depreciation policies of several well-known businesses.

Revisions of Depreciation

The calculation of depreciation depends on two estimates: service life and residual value. Estimates, of course, are subject to change and are often incorrect. As an example, unanticipated suburban growth and new developments on the outskirts of town may shorten the service life of buildings located in older, central-city areas. Equipment may be useful for fewer years due to new technology. Or residual values may need revision because of economic developments that take place after an asset has been placed in service. Such occurrences are commonplace.

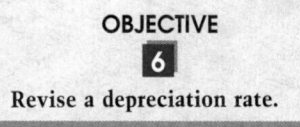

OBJECTIVE
6
Revise a depreciation rate.

When new information alters the estimates used for service life or residual value, the yearly depreciation computation must be changed. This change is achieved by allocating the asset's remaining depreciable base over the remaining service life. Previous years' depreciation amounts are *not* corrected, because the original estimates were based on the best information available at that time.

To illustrate the revision of a depreciation rate, suppose that Patriot Company purchased a building 10 years ago for $5 million. At the time of acquisition the building had an estimated $1 million residual value and a 40-year service life. Assuming Patriot uses the straight-line depreciation method, depreciation of $100,000 [($5,000,000 − $1,000,000) ÷ 40] has been recorded annually for 10 years. The Accumulated Depreciation account as a result presently totals $1 million. Because of altered traffic patterns, management now anticipates a remaining service life of only 20 years. Beginning with the current accounting period, the revised depreciation expense will be $150,000 per year, computed as follows:

Building cost	$5,000,000
Less: Residual value	1,000,000
Original depreciable base	$4,000,000
Less: Depreciation already taken	1,000,000
Remaining depreciable base	$3,000,000
Remaining life	20 years
Revised depreciation per year	$3,000,000 ÷ 20 = $150,000

If the remaining service life had been extended to 50 years, annual depreciation expense would have decreased to $60,000 ($3,000,000 ÷ 50).

Depreciation and the Tax Laws

OBJECTIVE

7

Demonstrate a very basic knowledge of depreciation and the tax laws.

Businesses are entitled to a depreciation deduction when computing the amount of income taxes owed to the federal government. Such a deduction reduces a company's taxable income and associated income tax payments and thus leaves more cash available for purposes of investment.

The tax laws that pertain to depreciation have changed over the years. Not too long ago, for example, the U.S. Congress enacted a new **Accelerated Cost Recovery System (ACRS)** that allowed for a more rapid write-off of asset cost than was previously possible. The system's provisions were later fine-tuned by the Tax Reform Act of 1986, to become what is known as **Modified ACRS** or **MACRS** (pronounced "makers"). More than likely this legislation will change further as our economy, federal deficit, and trade imbalance come under increased scrutiny in Washington.

The Modified Accelerated Cost Recovery System allows companies to depreciate assets over specified predetermined "recovery periods" when computing taxable income. These recovery periods are 3, 5, 7, or 10 years, among others, and depend on the asset in question. For example, automobiles and light-duty trucks have a five-year recovery period (i.e., are said to be "five-year property"), while most machinery, equipment, and furniture are written off over seven years. In general, the recovery period of an asset is shorter than the service life estimate, thereby permitting a business to reap quicker tax savings. MACRS also speeds up the process of cost recovery by using rates that reflect a specialized accelerated depreciation method, namely, a form of declining balance.

MACRS was designed, in part, to spur taxpayer investment in plant and equipment and makes no attempt to correctly match costs and revenues. As such, it is employed in the preparation of income tax returns and should not be used in a company's financial statements.[5]

---

[5] To achieve consistency between a company's tax return and income statement, many small businesses use MACRS for both tax *and* financial reporting. Although theoretically deficient, this practice is followed when cost recovery amounts are relatively insignificant and do not vary greatly from those computed under conventional depreciation methods.

END-OF-CHAPTER REVIEW

1 **Determine the cost of a long-lived asset.** Expenditures that benefit future accounting periods become part of an asset's cost. Such items include acquisition expenditures and related amounts needed to ready the asset for business use (e.g., freight, insurance while in transit, and installation). In contrast, items that fail to provide future economic benefits are expensed when incurred. A typical example is the cost incurred to repair a damaged asset, assuming the damage occurred during installation.

LEARNING OBJECTIVES: THE KEY POINTS

2 **Account for cash and lump-sum purchases of property, plant, and equipment.** Cash purchases of property, plant, and equipment are recorded at the lowest cash price offered to the buyer. Any discounts lost are therefore charged to Interest Expense.

Lump-sum purchases involve the acquisition of several assets for a single price. For reporting and depreciation purposes, the amount paid (or to be paid) must be allocated among the various assets acquired. The necessary apportionment is generally made on the basis of an individual asset's appraised value relative to the appraised value of the entire purchase.

3 **Explain the concept of depreciation and recognize the factors that affect service life.** Accountants define depreciation as the allocation of cost of long-lived assets over an estimated service life. Because depreciation makes no attempt to reflect market values in a company's accounting records, it is said to be a process of allocation, not valuation.

The factors of physical deterioration, obsolescence, and inadequacy must be considered when estimating an asset's service life. Physical deterioration, often called "wear and tear," is caused by asset use and usually sets the maximum limit for the estimate of service life. Obsolescence, a technological factor relating to being out of date, often shortens the service life of an asset to be less than the physical life. Finally, inadequacy relates to an asset's inability to meet expected service needs in a competitive environment.

4 **Compute depreciation by using the straight-line, units-of-output, declining-balance, and sum-of-the-years'-digits methods.** With the popular straight-line method, an equal amount of an asset's depreciable base (cost minus residual value) is allocated to each accounting period. In contrast, with the units-of-output method, the depreciation write-off is based on asset use. A depreciation rate is first calculated by dividing the depreciable base by the total estimated output during the service life. The rate is then multiplied by the yearly usage to arrive at depreciation expense.

The two remaining methods, declining-balance and sum-of-the-years'-digits, are accelerated methods, which generate more depreciation in the early years of an asset's life and less in later years. With declining-balance, a fixed depreciation rate (twice the straight-line rate with double-declining balance) is applied each year to a declining book value. In contrast, the sum-of-the-years'-digits approach uses successively lower rates (fractions) and a constant base (cost minus residual value).

5 **Identify the financial-reporting issues related to the various depreciation methods.** The depreciation method selected affects business income. Conceptually, the method chosen should be the one that best parallels the services delivered or benefits provided by an asset, thereby achieving a proper matching of revenues and

expenses. Practically, however, many firms use the straight-line method to help portray financial stability and smooth earnings over time.

6 Revise a depreciation rate. Companies often find that original estimates of service life and/or residual value are incorrect and need revision. When this situation occurs, the new estimates are used to determine depreciation expense. Such changes require the remaining depreciable base to be spread over the new estimate of remaining service life, with no corrections being made to prior years' depreciation amounts.

7 Demonstrate a very basic knowledge of depreciation and the tax laws. Depreciation is a deductible expense on a company's federal income tax return. Businesses generally employ the Modified Accelerated Cost Recovery System (MACRS) for tax purposes, which gives rise to quicker tax savings from shortened asset recovery periods and a specialized accelerated write-off. Quicker tax savings are attractive to an entity because of available investment opportunities.

KEY TERMS AND CONCEPTS: A QUICK OVERVIEW

accelerated depreciation methods   Methods that yield relatively large amounts of depreciation in the early years of asset use and smaller amounts in later years.

book value   The amount that an asset is carried at in the accounting records—namely, cost minus accumulated depreciation.

cash purchase   A method under which the recorded cost of an asset is the lowest cash price available to the buyer.

declining-balance method   A method of depreciation by which a fixed depreciation rate is applied to the remaining book value each period.

depreciable base   The cost of an item of plant and equipment minus any residual value.

depreciation   The process used to allocate the cost of long-lived items of plant and equipment to the accounting periods benefited.

double-declining balance depreciation   A method of accelerated depreciation in which the straight-line depreciation rate is doubled and applied against the remaining book value (i.e., a declining balance) each period.

inadequacy   The inability of a depreciable asset to meet the competitive needs of a business.

land improvements   Improvements made to land, such as parking lots and lawn sprinkler systems.

lump-sum purchase   The purchase of a number of assets together for a single amount.

materiality   A concept dictating that an accountant must judge the impact and importance of each transaction (or event) to determine its proper handling in the accounting records. Minor items are treated in the most expedient manner possible.

Modified Accelerated Cost Recovery System (MACRS)   A system used to write off (i.e., depreciate) the cost of long-term assets; employed for tax purposes only.

property, plant, and equipment   Assets with long lives acquired for use in business operations and not held for resale to customers.

residual value   The amount that a business expects to receive upon disposal of an asset at the end of the asset's life.

service life   The period of time that depreciable assets provide service to a business; also known as the economic or useful life.

straight-line depreciation   A depreciation method by which the cost of a depreciable asset, minus residual value, is allocated equally over the estimated service life.

sum-of-the-years'-digits depreciation   An accelerated method of depreciation in which a smaller fraction is applied against an asset's cost, minus residual value, each period.

units-of-output depreciation   A depreciation method by which the cost of a depreciable asset, minus residual value, is allocated to the accounting periods benefited based on output (miles, hours, number of times used, and so forth).

The five questions that follow relate to several issues raised in the chapter. Test your knowledge of the issues by selecting the best answer. (The answers appear on p. 416.)

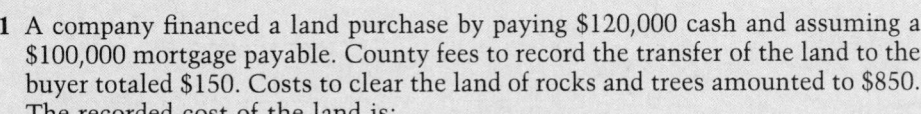

CHAPTER QUIZ

1 A company financed a land purchase by paying $120,000 cash and assuming a $100,000 mortgage payable. County fees to record the transfer of the land to the buyer totaled $150. Costs to clear the land of rocks and trees amounted to $850. The recorded cost of the land is:

a $120,000.	c $220,850.
b $220,000.	d $221,000.

2 Depreciation is:
a a system of cost allocation, not valuation.
b a system of valuation.
c recorded in an effort to reduce assets to their fair market value.
d based on an asset's cost and residual value, but not service life.

3 A machine that was purchased four years ago for $45,000 has an accumulated depreciation balance of $8,000 and a residual value of $5,000. Assuming use of straight-line depreciation, the machine's estimated service life:
a is 4 years.
b is 8 years.
c is 20 years.
d cannot be determined from the above facts.

4 Tiger Lines purchased and began depreciating a new truck on April 1, 19X4. The truck, which cost $60,000, had a five-year service life and a $12,000 residual value. Assuming use of the double-declining balance method, what is the *19X5* depreciation expense?

a $13,440.	c $16,800.
b $14,400.	d $18,000.

5 Revising a depreciation rate because of a change in a service life estimate:
a requires the correction of prior years' financial statements.
b involves allocating the remaining depreciable base over the future years of use.
c requires that sufficient cash be available to replace the asset at the end of the new service life.
d is permitted only if the service life is shortened.

On January 1, 19X1, Hardy Company acquired an automatic can labeler for $63,000, which included shipping charges of $1,000. The machine has an estimated service life of five years (or 30,000 hours of operation) and a residual value of

SUMMARY PROBLEM

$6,000. Insurance on the machine while in transit was $300; insurance against fire and water damage for one year amounted to $500. Finally, installation costs were $2,000 and test runs totaled $700.

During the five years of use (19X1–19X5), the machine was operated for 6,300, 6,000, 5,800, 5,700, and 6,200 hours, respectively.

Instructions

a Compute the machine's cost.
b Rounding final calculations to the nearest dollar, compute yearly depreciation expense by using each of the following methods: (1) straight-line; (2) units-of-output; (3) double-declining balance; and (4) sum-of-the-years'-digits.
c Explain why plant assets are depreciated as opposed to being expensed entirely in the year of acquisition.

Solution

a Purchase price (including shipping) $63,000
   Insurance in transit   300
   Installation   2,000
   Test runs   700
     Total cost $66,000

b (1) Straight-line:

$$\frac{\text{Cost} - \text{Residual Value}}{\text{Service Life in Years}} = \text{Annual Depreciation}$$

$$\frac{\$66,000 - \$6,000}{5 \text{ years}} = \$12,000 \text{ per year}$$

(2) Units-of-output:

$$\frac{\text{Cost} - \text{Residual Value}}{\text{Service Life in Output}} = \text{Depreciation per Unit of Output}$$

$$\frac{\$66,000 - \$6,000}{30,000 \text{ hours}} = \$2.00 \text{ per hour}$$

Year	Hours of Operation	×	Depreciation Per Hour	=	Depreciation Expense
19X1	6,300		$2.00		$12,600
19X2	6,000		2.00		12,000
19X3	5,800		2.00		11,600
19X4	5,700		2.00		11,400
19X5	6,200		2.00		12,400

(3) Double-declining balance:

5-year life = $\frac{1}{5}$ = 20%; 20% × 2 = 40% depreciation rate

Year	Depreciation Expense	Accumulated Depreciation	Book Value
			$66,000
19X1	$26,400 ($66,000 × 40%)	$26,400	39,600
19X2	15,840 ($39,600 × 40%)	42,240	23,760
19X3	9,504 ($23,760 × 40%)	51,744	14,256
19X4	5,702 ($14,256 × 40%)	57,446	8,554
19X5	2,554 ($8,554 − $6,000)*	60,000	6,000

* $8,554 × 40% would reduce the book value below residual value.

(4) Sum-of-the-years'-digits:

Year	Depreciation Expense
19X1	$20,000 ($60,000 × $\frac{5}{15}$)
19X2	16,000 ($60,000 × $\frac{4}{15}$)
19X3	12,000 ($60,000 × $\frac{3}{15}$)
19X4	8,000 ($60,000 × $\frac{2}{15}$)
19X5	4,000 ($60,000 × $\frac{1}{15}$)

c Plant assets have long lives and have years of future service potential. Expensing the entire cost when acquired would result in a mismatch of revenues and expenses on the income statement.

ASSIGNMENT MATERIAL

QUESTIONS

Q10-1 Do all items of property, plant, and equipment have a limited life? Explain.

Q10-2 How is the acquisition cost of a machine determined? Which of the following items are included in the cost of an asset: purchase price, freight charges, cost of installation, medical costs of injured installer, special electrical wiring?

Q10-3 Explain the proper treatment of interest costs related to the purchase of a new automobile.

Q10-4 Which price is used to record the acquisition cost of equipment: list price, negotiated price, or negotiated price minus available cash discount?

Q10-5 How should the cost of property, plant, and equipment acquired in a lump-sum purchase be apportioned to the individual assets? Why is such a division necessary?

Q10-6 Contrast the accounting treatments for land and land improvements.

Q10-7 How are long-lived, low-cost items (e.g., pencil sharpeners and wastebaskets) normally handled in the accounting records?

Q10-8 Briefly discuss the concept of materiality.

Q10-9 What does the term "depreciation" mean in accounting? Is the term used differently by others? Explain.

Q10-10 How is the service life of depreciable plant and equipment determined? Discuss the factors of physical deterioration, obsolescence, and inadequacy in the establishment of service lives.

Q10-11 Define the term "depreciable base."

Q10-12 Is the units-of-output method of depreciation more appropriate to use for some items of plant and equipment than for others? Why?

Q10-13 Briefly explain the concept of accelerated depreciation.

Q10-14 How does a change in the estimated remaining service life of a piece of equipment affect past and future depreciation amounts?

Q10-15 What is the Modified Accelerated Cost Recovery System (MACRS)? Can MACRS be used for financial reporting? Briefly discuss.

Q10-16 What is meant by the term "recovery period," as related to the Modified Accelerated Cost Recovery System?

EXERCISES

E10-1 *Determining acquisition cost* (L.O. 1)

Well-Made Fabricating Company recently purchased a state-of-the-art metal-cutting tool. The invoice price was $300,000, which reflected a 25% trade discount from the $400,000 list price. Other data related to the machine were as follows:

Freight and installation costs	$9,500
Cash discount for prompt payment of invoice	3,000
Materials used during setup and initial testing	800
Finger guards installed around cutting head	2,500
Property taxes paid for first year of ownership	4,500
Advertising brochure to inform customers of new cutting capabilities	1,500

a Determine the cost at which the machine should be recorded.

b Briefly describe and justify the proper treatment of the items that you excluded in part (a).

E10-2 *Lump-sum purchase* (L.O. 2)

You recently purchased the contents of a barber shop for use in a new location of your hair-cutting franchise, Shear Delight. Prior to negotiations for the purchase, you hired a consultant to appraise the shop's assets. The results of the appraisal are as follows:

Reception area furniture	$ 1,000
Product display racks	—
Plumbing and apparatus	16,000
Barber furniture and fixtures	17,000
Equipment	10,000
Linens and supplies	6,000

On the basis of these figures, you offered and paid $45,000 to acquire the assets.

a Allocate the purchase price among the various assets.

b The franchise's chart of accounts revealed the following account titles, among others: Furniture and Fixtures, Plumbing and Apparatus, Other Equipment, and Linens and Supplies. Prepare a journal entry to record the acquisition.

E10-3 *Asset acquisition and straight-line depreciation* (L.O. 1, 4)

A machine was purchased on October 1, 19X1, at a cost of $8,000. Installation charges were $600 and freight was $400. The machine has a residual value of $1,200, a service life of five years, and a physical life of eight years.

a Assuming all expenditures were for cash, record the necessary journal entry to enter the machine in the accounting records.

b Record the entry for straight-line depreciation at the end of 19X1.

c How would the machine and its related depreciation account appear on a balance sheet as of December 31, 19X2? Use proper amounts.

E10-4 *Depreciation methods* (L.O. 4)

1-2-3

Betsy Ross Enterprises purchased a delivery van for $30,000 on January 1, 19X7. The van was estimated to have a service life of five years and a residual value of $6,000. The company is planning to drive the van 20,000 miles annually.

Compute depreciation expense for *19X8* by using each of the following methods:
a Units-of-output, assuming 17,000 miles were driven during 19X8
b Straight-line
c Sum-of-the-years'-digits
d Double-declining balance

E10-5 *Depreciation computations* (L.O. 4)

Alpha Alpha Alpha, a college fraternity, purchased a new heavy-duty washing machine on January 1, 19X3. The machine, which cost $1,000, had an estimated residual value of $100, and an estimated service life of four years (1,800 washing cycles). Calculate the following:
a The machine's book value on December 31, 19X5, assuming use of the straight-line depreciation method.
b Depreciation expense for 19X4, assuming use of the units-of-output depreciation method. Actual washing cycles in 19X4 totaled 500.
c Accumulated depreciation on December 31, 19X5, assuming use of the double-declining balance depreciation method.
d Depreciation expense in 19X4 and 19X5, assuming use of the sum-of-the-years'-digits depreciation method.

E10-6 *Accelerated depreciation; partial periods* (L.O. 4)

Hawn Enterprises purchased a special device on June 1, 19X4, that will be depreciated over a service life of four years. The device cost $42,000 and has a $6,000 estimated residual value.
a Calculate depreciation expense for the year ended December 31, 19X4, by using the sum-of-the-years'-digits and double-declining balance methods.
b Compute the firm's 19X5 depreciation expense by using the sum-of-the-years'-digits and double-declining balance methods.

E10-7 *Depreciation concepts* (L.O. 3, 4, 5)

Evaluate the comments that follow as being True or False. If the comment is false, briefly explain why.
a Depreciation is recorded over the years so that a company's asset valuations are reduced to reflect lower market values.
b A depreciable asset's cost, minus accumulated depreciation, equals book value.
c An asset's depreciable base and book value are identical at the end of the asset's service life.
d A company that uses accelerated depreciation will find that depreciation write-offs speed up, with increased amounts occurring in the later years of an asset's service life.
e Straight-line depreciation is probably the most popular accelerated depreciation method used by businesses.

E10-8 *Revisions of depreciation* (L.O. 6)

1-2-3

MJD, a health care company, holds clinics on how to treat heart attack victims. One year ago the firm bought a $20,000 supply of lifelike rubber bodies for seminar use. At the time of acquisition, the service life and residual value were estimated to be five years and $500, respectively. These estimates now need revision.

Calculate yearly depreciation expense with the straight-line method under the following conditions:

a MJD now estimates that total service life (including earlier years of use) will be eight years and the residual value will be $700.

b MJD now estimates that the remaining time of use will be three years, with a $1,100 residual value.

E10-9 *Financial and tax depreciation methods* (L.O. 5, 7)

At the beginning of the current year, Cook Construction purchased seven pickup trucks for use by job supervisors. Cook's owner has called your accounting firm to ask how these trucks should be depreciated.

a List the possible depreciation methods that the company might consider for use in its financial statements.

b Present several arguments favoring the use of:
  (1) Straight-line depreciation.
  (2) Accelerated depreciation.

c Explain to the owner how the truck depreciation will be handled for tax purposes.

PROBLEMS

Series A

P10-A1 *Cost treatment* (L.O. 1)

Consider the following costs of Shamrock Company:

1 Cost of grading land prior to construction $\textit{0 grade}$
2 Cost of material used during trial runs of new machinery
3 Delinquent property taxes on newly acquired land
4 Damage to equipment, which occurred during installation
5 Fine for fire code violation in building
6 Freight charges on newly acquired equipment
7 Cost of parking lot constructed on property
8 Cost of three wastebaskets purchased for office use
9 Cost of clearing land prior to construction
10 Cost of purchasing used equipment
11 Interest incurred to purchase machinery on credit
12 Current property taxes on land and building
13 Attorney's fees for land and building purchase
14 Construction costs of fence at company headquarters
15 Construction costs of new building
16 Cost of sprinkling system for landscaping

Instructions

a Identify which of the preceding costs should be charged to asset accounts?

b For the costs that you identified in part (a), indicate which asset account(s) should be increased.

P10-A2 *Allocation of costs to asset accounts; lump-sum purchase* (L.O. 1, 2)

Amanda Patterson recently acquired a large Victorian house that she will renovate for use as a bed and breakfast inn. The following transactions occurred during the first five months of the current year:

Jan.   4   Purchased the land, house, and accompanying land improvements for $500,000. The property, which had cost the previous owner $300,000, was appraised recently for $600,000. Forty-five percent of the appraisal value pertained to the land, 40% to the house, and 15% to the improvements.

10 Completed the transaction of January 4; paid $2,800 for legal and title fees. (*Hint:* Allocate this amount among the assets acquired on the basis of appraisal values.)

11 Acquired a one-year fire insurance policy for $3,000 and a policy for miscellaneous liabilities, $2,000.

Feb. 3 Paid a contractor $15,000 for the renovation work, which was scheduled for a two-month completion.

Mar. 3 Hired an interior designer to plan and order the furnishings for the inn. Paid a $20,000 fee for these services.

31 Paid $9,500 as follows: $5,000 for an underground sprinkler system and $4,500 for paving a parking area.

Apr. 14 Paid the contractor $55,000 for completion of the renovation.

20 Purchased office equipment for $14,500, terms 2/10, n/30. Because of confusion created by the construction work, settlement of the invoice was overlooked until May. Also paid a technician $300 to wire and install the equipment.

30 Received the furniture ordered by the decorator. The furniture had a list price of $200,000, but the decorator had negotiated a cash price of $180,000. The trucking company required a $3,000 payment for shipping and handling charges before unloading the goods.

May 25 Paid $1,350 of interest on a bank loan. The loan was used to finance the furniture acquisition.

31 Purchased $125 of stationery to be placed in each guest room.

Instructions

Assign appropriate costs to the Land, Land Improvements, Building, and Furniture & Equipment accounts by using the format that follows. Total each column. If a cost is not charged to one of the preceding accounts, indicate how the expenditure should be treated.

Date	Land	Land Improvements	Building	Furniture & Equipment
	$	$	$	$

P10-A3 *Depreciation computations; change in estimate* (L.O. 1, 4, 6)

Aussie Imports purchased a specialized piece of machinery for $50,000 on January 1, 19X3. At the time of acquisition, the machine was estimated to have a service life of five years (25,000 operating hours) and a residual value of $5,000. During the five years of operations (19X3–19X7), the machine was used for 5,100, 4,800, 3,200, 6,000, and 5,900 hours, respectively.

Instructions

a Compute depreciation for 19X3–19X7 by using the following methods: straight-line; units-of-output; double-declining balance; and sum-of-the-years'-digits.

b On January 1, 19X5, management shortened the remaining service life of the machine to 20 months. Assuming use of the straight-line method, compute the company's depreciation expense for 19X5.

c Briefly describe what you would have done differently in part (a) if

Aussie Imports had paid $47,800 for the machinery rather than $50,000. In addition, assume that the company incurred $800 of freight charges, $1,400 for machine setup and testing, and $300 for insurance during the first year of use.

P10-A4 *Depreciation calculations, partial periods* (L.O. 4)

Empire Treats, Inc., a food wholesaler, operates three delivery vehicles in central Kansas. Data on the vehicles follow.

Vehicle	Date Acquired	Cost	Residual Value	Service Life (Years)	Depreciation Method
2-ton Chevrolet	8/31/X2	$21,000	$ —	7	Straight-line
2-ton Dodge	5/1/X1	15,000	1,000	5	Double-declining balance
2-ton Ford	1/31/X1	22,000	4,000	4	Sum-of-the-years'-digits

Instructions

a Calculate depreciation expense for the 12-month period ended December 31, 19X3.
b Compute the December 31, 19X3, accumulated depreciation and book value of each vehicle.

P10-A5 *Depreciation methods, changes in rates, partial periods* (L.O. 4, 6)

Ridgemar, Inc., purchased a bus for $200,000 on April 1, 19X1. The bus had a residual value of $50,000 and a 10-year (150,000-mile) service life. On January 1, 19X2, the service life was decreased to recognize eight years (or 120,000 miles) of remaining service from that date. Miles driven during 19X1 and the first quarter of 19X2 totaled 16,400 and 4,700, respectively. Accumulated Depreciation accounts based on the straight-line, units-of-output, double-declining balance, and sum-of-the-years'-digits depreciation methods follow.

a

Accumulated Depreciation

| 12/31/X1 | ? |
| 3/31/X2 | 4,336 |

b

Accumulated Depreciation

| 12/31/X1 | ? |
| 3/31/X2 | 10,625 |

c

Accumulated Depreciation

| 12/31/X1 | ? |
| 3/31/X2 | 5,233 |

d

Accumulated Depreciation

| 12/31/X1 | ? |
| 3/31/X2 | 7,197 |

Instructions

Determine which Accumulated Depreciation account corresponds to each of the depreciation methods. Ridgemar rounds final depreciation computations to the nearest dollar.

P10-A6 *Acquisition cost, errors, depreciation* (L.O. 1, 4)

Bubba Clark, a commercial fisherman, bought a used fishing boat for $300,000 at the beginning of 19X1. He estimated that the boat would have a 15-year service life and an $87,000 residual value. Clark made the following additional expenditures before putting the boat in service:

Sales tax	$18,000
Installation of electronic equipment	6,000
Delivery charge	3,000
Annual licenses and registration	2,500
Fuel and supplies	1,500
	$31,000

Clark's business manager has proposed the following disclosure of the boat on the December 31, 19X1, balance sheet:

Boat	$331,000
Less: Depreciation expense	16,267
	$314,733

Depreciation was calculated by using the straight-line method.

Instructions

a The business manager has made several accounting errors. Identify the errors.

b Prepare a journal entry to correct the balance in the Boat account at year-end. Assume that all fuel and supplies have been consumed.

c Present the proper disclosure of the vessel on the December 31, 19X1, balance sheet.

Series B

P10-B1 *Cost treatment* (L.O. 1)

Consider the following costs of the Subway Company:

1 Cost of three antique works of art for the company's new building
2 Purchase price of the land and new building
3 Cost of outside lighting fixtures on the new building's grounds
4 Cost of initial test runs of new equipment
5 Interest incurred to purchase equipment on credit
6 Traffic fines paid by Subway for a driver who was delivering equipment to the new building
7 Cost of grading land prior to construction
8 Current property taxes on the land and building
9 Party costs to celebrate the opening of Subway's new building
10 Installation costs of new machinery
11 Cost of new security fences installed around the parking lot
12 Cost of delinquent property taxes assumed when purchasing land
13 The current month's premium for building fire and liability insurance
14 Significant overhaul costs related to acquisition of used machinery; needed to ready the machinery for its intended use
15 Attorney's fees related to land acquisition
16 Real estate commissions related to land acquisition

Instructions

a Which of the preceding costs should be charged to asset accounts?

b For the costs that you identified in part (a), indicate which asset account(s) should be increased.

P10-B2 *Allocation of costs to plant asset accounts; lump-sum purchase* (L.O. 1, 2)
The following transactions relate to the Post Oak Company for 19X5:

Jan. 10 Purchased new machinery for $12,000 cash. Freight charges amounted to $600, special electrical wiring cost $4,000, and test runs totaled $800.

Feb. 19 Purchased developed property from Baxter Company for $1 million. On the date of acquisition, the appraised value of the property totaled $1.5 million and was subdivided as follows: land, $750,000; land improvements, $60,000; and building, $690,000.

Mar. 21 Acquired a 40-year-old apartment building for $1.3 million. The building had cost the seller only $400,000 several years ago.

Apr. 3 Installed $12,000 of security fencing around the apartment.

May 14 Acquired a one-year fire insurance policy on the apartment building for $7,000.

June 16 Paid $50,000 to the Advance Paving Company to construct a parking lot for the apartment tenants.

July 8 Incurred $11,000 of interest on monies borrowed to finance the apartment building acquisition on March 21.

Aug. 9 Acquired a parcel of land by securing a $290,000 mortgage payable and paying $10,000 of delinquent property taxes to Duval County.

Sept. 15 Purchased several smoke detectors for the apartment from a mail order firm. The detectors cost $64, plus a $6 shipping fee.

Oct. 30 Acquired equipment having a list price of $33,000 and a negotiated price of $27,000. A 4% cash discount was offered if the invoice was settled in 10 days. Because of a clerical oversight, settlement was delayed until December.

Instructions

Assign appropriate costs to the Land, Land Improvements, Building, and Equipment accounts by using the format that follows. Obtain year-end totals. If a cost is not charged to the preceding accounts, indicate how the expenditure should be treated.

Date	Land	Land Improvements	Building	Equipment
	$	$	$	$

P10-B3 *Depreciation computations; change in estimate* (L.O. 1, 4, 6)
Hawkins Company purchased a specialized piece of machinery for $40,000 on January 1, 19X1. At the time of acquisition, the machine was estimated to have a service life of five years (10,000 operating hours) and a residual value of $4,000. During the five years of operation (19X1–19X5), the machine was used for 2,300, 2,100, 1,700, 2,000, and 1,900 hours, respectively.

Instructions

a Compute depreciation for 19X1–19X5 by using the following methods: straight-line; units-of-output; double-declining balance; and sum-of-the-years'-digits.

b On January 1, 19X4, management extended the remaining service life of the machine to four years. Assuming use of the straight-line method, compute the company's depreciation expense for *19X6*.

c Briefly describe what you would have done differently in part (a) if Hawkins, in addition to the $40,000 outlay, had to pay $1,500 for the machine's installation, $800 for freight, and $300 to repair damage that occurred while the machine was being unloaded from the carrier's truck.

P10-B4 *Depreciation calculations, partial periods* (L.O. 4)

1-2-3

Executive Lift, an air shuttle service, has three aircraft. Data on the aircraft follow.

	Cheyenne	Falcon	Cessna
Date acquired	11/2/X4	10/1/X5	2/1/X6
Service life (years)	16	20	25
Depreciation method	SL	SYD	DDB
Cost	$3,000,000	$5,120,000	$6,300,000
Residual value	600,000	500,000	900,000

Instructions

a Calculate depreciation expense for the 12-month period ended December 31, 19X7.

b Compute the December 31, 19X7, accumulated depreciation and book value of each aircraft.

P10-B5 *Depreciation methods, changes in rates, partial periods* (L.O. 4, 6)

1-2-3

Walnut Company purchased a corporate jet for $22.5 million on May 1, 19X1. The jet had an estimated residual value of 30% of cost and a 10-year (50,000-flying-hour) service life. On January 1, 19X2, the service life was extended to recognize 12 years (or 60,000 flying hours) of remaining service from that date. Flying hours during 19X1 and the first quarter of 19X2 totaled 4,200 and 1,600, respectively. Accumulated depreciation accounts based on the straight-line, units-of-output, double-declining balance, and sum-of-the-years'-digits depreciation methods follow.

a

Accumulated Depreciation	
	12/31/X1 ?
	3/31/X2 532,343

b

Accumulated Depreciation	
	12/31/X1 ?
	3/31/X2 384,720

c

Accumulated Depreciation	
	12/31/X1 ?
	3/31/X2 306,250

d

Accumulated Depreciation	
	12/31/X1 ?
	3/31/X2 812,500

Instructions

Determine which Accumulated Depreciation account corresponds to each of the depreciation methods. Walnut rounds final depreciation computations to the nearest dollar.

P10-B6 *Acquisition cost, errors, depreciation* (L.O. 1, 4)

On January 1, 19X3, Mike Miller purchased a used combine for his farm. The combine cost $106,000, which includes $6,000 of sales taxes. As part of the purchase, the dealer agreed to recondition the equipment according to Miller's specifications. The following journal entry was made to record the acquisition:

Farm Equipment	106,000	
Reconditioning Expense	3,000	
Cash		19,000
Loan Payable		90,000

The farm's office manager has calculated depreciation by using the straight-line method, a 10-year service life, and a $19,000 residual value. The following presentation of the combine on the December 31, 19X3, balance sheet was proposed:

Farm equipment	$106,000
Plus: Accumulated depreciation	8,700*
	$114,700

* A review of the general ledger found an $8,700 credit balance in the Accumulated Depreciation account.

Instructions

a Several errors were made when accounting for the combine. Identify the errors.

b Was the farm's 19X3 net income overstated or understated as a result of these errors? By what amount?

c Prepare the journal entries needed to correct and update the accounting records as of December 31, 19X3. Assume that the books have not yet been closed.

ELECTRONIC DATA BASE

EDB10-1 *Analysis of property and equipment investment, depreciation: Rubbermaid Incorporated and The Sherwin-Williams Company* (L.O. 1, 4)

Rubbermaid Incorporated manufactures various plastic and rubber goods for consumer and commercial use. The company's products include desk sets, toys, lawn furniture, and a variety of storage containers. In contrast, Sherwin-Williams manufactures coatings and related items. The firm is perhaps best known among consumers for its paint products.

Instructions

By using the text's Electronic Data Base, access the balance sheets and accompanying notes of both firms and answer the questions that follow. Unless otherwise indicated, responses should be based on data for the most recent year presented.

a Compare the companies' *gross* dollar investment (before any deduction for accumulated depreciation) to the total assets owned. Which of the two firms has a greater percentage of its assets in the form of property, plant, and equipment?

b What are the major categories of property, plant, and equipment disclosed by each firm?

c What method of depreciation is each company using to depreciate its assets?

d Do either of the companies reveal any information on the service lives that are being used to calculate depreciation? Briefly comment on your findings.

e Do either of the firms have any "projects" in process with regard to plant and equipment? Briefly discuss and determine which company is currently more active in this area.

EDB10-2 *Analysis of property and equipment investment, depreciation* (L.O. 1, 4)

This problem is a duplication of Problem EDB10-1. It is based on two companies selected by your instructor.

SEC   **Instructions**

By using the text's Electronic Data Base, access the specified companies' balance sheets and accompanying notes and focus on data for the most recent year reported. Answer requirements (a)–(e) of Problem EDB10-1.

BB10-1 *Acquisition cost, lump-sum purchase, correction of errors* (L.O. 1, 2, 4)

Monrovia Company purchased a small farm on April 1, 19X1, with the intention of converting it to a go-cart track. Monrovia agreed to pay $300,000 over the next six months and to assume the remaining mortgage on the property of $200,000. These costs, together with other transactions related to the conversion, are presented in the Property account.

BEYOND THE BASICS

Property				
4/1	Purchase price	500,000	12/31 Accumulated depreciation (estimate)	6,000
4/10	Land title	1,000		
4/12	Survey costs	4,000		
4/15	Land grading and draining	15,000		
4/30	One-year fire insurance policy on buildings	3,000		
5/1	Material and labor cost to refurbish buildings	20,000		
5/2	Advertising costs for grand opening	3,000		
10/1	Current year's property taxes on land	9,000		

The property acquired included land (appraised value $450,000), buildings (appraised value $90,000), and equipment (appraised value $60,000). The go-cart track opened on May 1, 19X1.

Instructions

a List the errors made by Monrovia in accounting for the purchase and related costs.

b Prepare a schedule that shows how the original lump-sum purchase of property, plant, and equipment should have been handled.

c Prepare a journal entry on December 31, 19X1, that closes out the Property account and allocates the amounts therein to Land, Buildings, Equipment, Accumulated Depreciation, and other appropriate accounts. Assume the buildings and equipment have respective service lives of 20 years and 10 years from the grand opening. The straight-line method of depreciation is used; no residual value is anticipated.

d Present the property, plant, and equipment section of Monrovia's balance sheet as of December 31, 19X1.

BB10-2 *Overview of chapter concepts: Multiple choice* (L.O. 1-4, 6, 7)
The following multiple-choice questions relate to various topics discussed in the chapter. Select the best answer.

1 Brown Company recently acquired an item of equipment having a list price of $30,000 and a negotiated purchase price of $28,000. The firm immediately spent $2,300 to add safety guards and $1,000 to repair damage that occurred during shipment. Later, Brown was offered $32,500 for the asset by another company. Ignoring depreciation, at what amount should the equipment be reported?

a $30,300.   c $32,300.
b $31,300.   d $32,500.

2 The Adelson Institute of Art paid $18 million to acquire an art collection from an estate. The individual pieces had the following appraisal values at the time of acquisition: oil paintings, $15 million; sculptures, $10 million; and watercolors, $5 million. Which of the following computations expresses the correct assignment of cost to the oil paintings?

a $18 million ÷ ($15 million + $10 million + $5 million).
b $15 million ÷ ($15 million + $10 million + $5 million).
c $18 million × (a) above.
d $18 million × (b) above.

3 Maroney's recently purchased a two-line telephone system, a state-of-the-art microcomputer, and a delivery van. Each of these assets was expected to have a five-year service life. The owner reasoned that the van would have 200,000 miles of use within the first five years. In addition, after five years of operation, the volume of phone orders would require more than two lines, and the computer would be regarded as an "antique." Which of the following expresses the factors that likely had the most influence on the service life of the telephone, computer, and van, respectively?

a Inadequacy, obsolescence, physical deterioration.
b Obsolescence, inadequacy, physical deterioration.
c Inadequacy, physical deterioration, obsolescence.
d Physical deterioration, obsolescence, inadequacy.

4 On January 1, 19X4, Flintstone Gravel acquired a truck for $40,000. The truck had a five-year life and $2,000 residual value and will be depreciated by using the double-declining balance method. The accumulated depreciation to report for the year ended December 31, 19X5, would be:

a $9,600.   c $25,120.
b $24,320.   d $25,600.

5 On October 1, 19X3, Rockport Company acquired a new forklift for $22,000. The lift had a four-year life and $2,000 residual value and will be depreciated by the sum-of-the-years'-digits method. The depreciation expense to be reported for the year ended December 31, 19X4, would be:

  a $6,000.   c $8,000.
  b $7,500.   d $8,250.

6 Which of the following statements is incorrect?

  a For an asset having a seven-year life acquired on January 1, 19X3, depreciation expense for the year ended December 31, 19X6, is the same amount under both the straight-line and the sum-of-the-years'-digits methods.

  b An asset having a four-year life and a 50% residual value would be fully depreciated after one year under the double-declining balance method.

  c The beginning-of-year book value, multiplied by twice the straight-line rate, yields the annual double-declining balance depreciation for assets acquired in previous accounting periods.

  d The book value of an asset at the end of the service life is dependent on the depreciation method used.

7 Patterson Company owned equipment that was expected to have a service life of 20 years. The equipment cost $30,000 and had an anticipated residual value of $5,000. After five years of use, the remaining service life was shortened by five years, and the residual value was doubled. The depreciation expense to be recorded in the sixth year, assuming use of the straight-line method, would be:

  a $1,000.   c $1,375.
  b $1,250.   d $2,000.

8 Which of the following observations or comments about the tax treatment of depreciable assets is correct?

  a The "recovery period" is the amount of time it will take a productive asset to generate cash flows sufficient to recoup the asset's cost.

  b MACRS reflects a specialized form of accelerated depreciation.

  c MACRS is theoretically superior to traditional depreciation methods because it achieves a better matching of costs and revenues.

  d Tax laws related to depreciation are relatively stagnant and rarely change.

CAI10-1 *Writing a memo report: General Motors Corporation* (L.O. 4, 5)

**COMMUNICATION
OF ACCOUNTING
INFORMATION**

Communication Principle: A memo report is a short in-house report with limited and specific purposes. In the exercise that follows, you will be writing such a report to your supervisor. Use the memo form and the organizational principle of purpose statements, support, and conclusions (see the communication principles on pp. 297 and 380). The report should be short, consisting of three to four paragraphs that contain all the information requested in the instructions.

    Because you are addressing an expert audience, you may use terminology that most experts would know without definition or explanation. However, do not shortcut by eliminating transition words or pointers that tell the reader where you are and where you are going.

General Motors (GM), the nation's largest domestic producer of automobiles, includes the following description of depreciation policies in its annual report:

> Depreciation is provided based on estimated useful lives of groups of property generally using accelerated methods, which accumulate depreciation of approximately two-thirds of the depreciable cost during the first half of the estimated useful lives.

Instructions

a Your supervisor has just completed a reading of GM's annual report and has asked you to analyze the accelerated write-off of a $100,000 asset having no residual value. Determine the percentage of cost written off during the first half of service life by using both the double-declining balance and sum-of-the-years'-digits methods, assuming (1) a 4-year service life and (2) a 10-year service life. Comment on your findings.

b Briefly explain to your supervisor the rationale that underlies the use of accelerated depreciation methods.

Answers to Chapter Quiz

1 d ($120,000 + $100,000 + $150 + $850)

2 a

3 c [$8,000 ÷ 4 years = $2,000 per year; ($45,000 − $5,000) ÷ $2,000 = 20 years]

4 c [5-year life = 20% per year; 20% × 2 = 40%; $60,000 × 40% × 9/12 = $18,000; ($60,000 − $18,000) × 40% = $16,800]

5 b

CHAPTER
11

Property, Plant, and Equipment/ Natural Resources/Intangibles

LEARNING OBJECTIVES

After studying this chapter, you should be able to:

1

Account for property, plant, and equipment costs incurred after asset acquisition.

2

Prepare journal entries to record discards and sales of property, plant, and equipment.

3

Account for exchanges of similar assets.

4

Calculate natural resource cost and depletion.

5

Recognize the various types of intangible assets and compute amortization.

This chapter continues our discussion of long-lived assets. We will study several additional issues related to property, plant, and equipment and examine two other types of assets that provide long-term benefits to their owners: natural resources and intangibles.

PLANT AND EQUIPMENT COSTS SUBSEQUENT TO ASSET ACQUISITION

OBJECTIVE

Account for property, plant, and equipment costs incurred after asset acquisition.

The costs related to fixed assets often do not stop at acquisition. Many expenditures are made after buildings, machines, and various pieces of equipment have started to serve a business. For example, repairs are performed, new features are added to improve efficiency, major overhauls are undertaken, and parts are replaced.

The accountant must determine how to record these items. Whether they are added to the depreciable base of the asset or written off as expenses may have a significant impact on reported profitability for the period. Generally speaking, such amounts are categorized as either capital expenditures or revenue expenditures.

Capital expenditures are costs that provide future economic benefits to a business. Future economic benefits are said to occur under the following conditions:

1 The service life of an asset is prolonged.

2 The quantity of services expected from an asset has increased.

3 The quality of services provided by an asset has improved.

Given their long-term nature, capital expenditures are debited to property, plant, and equipment accounts. This treatment results in an asset having a larger depreciable base, to be written off gradually in the years to come.

Expenditures that do not fulfill at least one of the three criteria just mentioned are known as **revenue expenditures.** These amounts benefit the current accounting period only and are thus immediately expensed. We will now explore the capital/revenue distinction with several commonly encountered items.

Repairs

Amounts spent to maintain the normal operating condition of an asset are termed **repairs.** Repairs include regular maintenance, minor parts replacement, painting, cleaning, and inspection. Repairs do not increase the future service potential of an asset; rather, such amounts assist in attaining the original service life estimate and anticipated operating efficiency. As a consequence, repair costs are debited to the Repairs Expense account when incurred. *Revenue Expenditure*

Additions

Additions are items that will provide future benefits and be affixed to existing assets. Examples of additions include the installation of air conditioning in a building or vehicle and the construction of a new wing on a building. The cost of an addition is a capital expenditure and is therefore recorded in a property, plant, or equipment account (i.e., capitalized). Generally, the cost is entered in the same account as the original asset to simplify record keeping.

Cap. Exp

Betterments

Betterments, sometimes called improvements or extraordinary repairs, are expenditures that improve or increase the future service potential of an asset. Occasionally, a betterment occurs when a major part of an existing asset is replaced with a similar but superior component, for example, the installation of (1) a new, more efficient heating/cooling system in a building or (2) a new engine in a vehicle. In other cases, the betterment may involve an extraordinary repair such as a major overhaul. Extraordinary repairs normally extend the service life of an asset beyond the original estimate.

Capital Exp.

Often the difference between extraordinary repairs and ordinary repairs and maintenance is not readily evident. The accountant, though, must properly distinguish between these items, because their accounting treatment differs. Ordinary repairs, as we noted earlier, are expenses. In contrast, expenditures that prolong an asset's life are capitalized in the following manner.

An Example

Assume the Simmons Company acquired a freezer on January 1, 19X1, for $20,000. The freezer had an estimated service life of five years, with no residual value. Simmons has depreciated the asset for four years by using the straight-line method, resulting in the following balance sheet disclosure as of December 31, 19X4:

Freezer	$20,000	
Less: Accumulated depreciation	16,000	$4,000

On January 1, 19X5, a new motor costing $1,000 was installed, which extended the freezer's service life by one year. The cost of the new motor is *not* recorded in the Freezer account. Rather $1,000 is debited to Accumulated Depreciation in the manner shown.

Accumulated Depreciation: Freezer	1,000	
Cash		1,000
To record cost of new motor		

This journal entry reduces the balance in the Accumulated Depreciation account to $15,000 ($16,000 − $1,000). The freezer's new book value of $5,000 ($20,000 − $15,000) will be depreciated over the remaining two years of service life at the rate of $2,500 ($5,000 ÷ 2) per year. Upon conclusion of the six-year life, then, depreciation expense will total $21,000, which equals the original cost of the freezer plus the $1,000 motor.

Notice that the debit to Accumulated Depreciation increases the asset's book value, as would a debit to the Freezer account. We follow the former

EXHIBIT 11-1
Summary of Capital and Revenue Expenditures

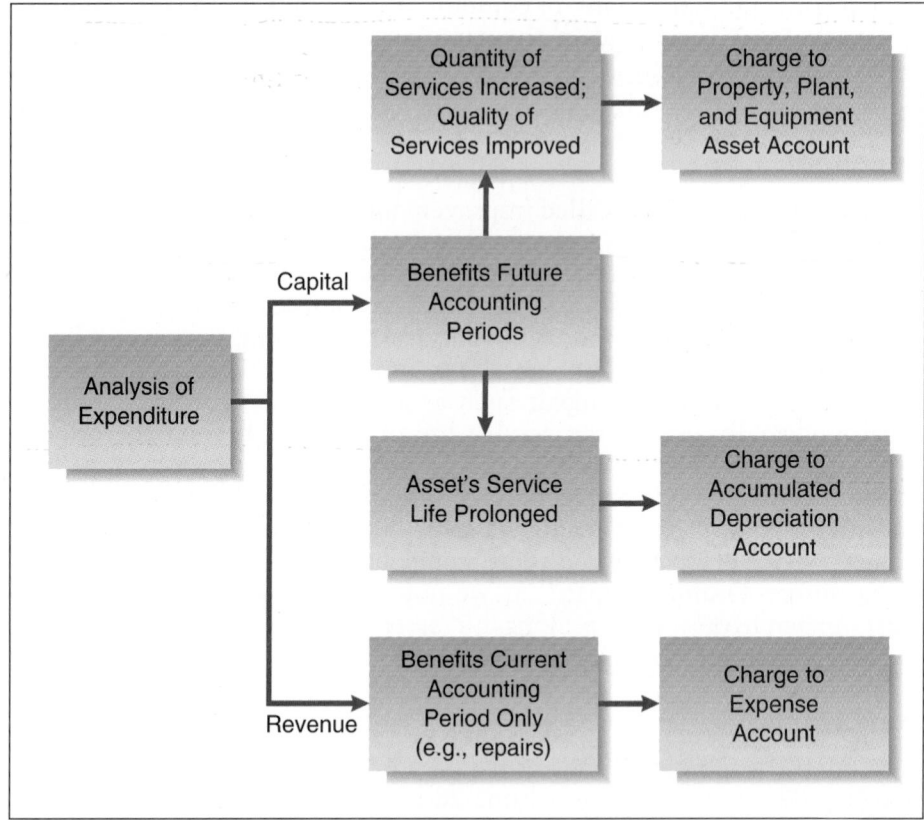

approach for expenditures that prolong an asset's life to, in effect, reclaim (reduce) some past depreciation—an appropriate procedure given the service life extension.

Assessments

Property owners are often assessed for improvements such as new streets, curbs, sidewalks, streetlights, and sewers. These improvements are made for the benefit of the property owners and other residents of the municipality. **Assessments** are normally added to the Land account, because projects such as those just cited are relatively permanent and are maintained and upgraded by the municipality.

The proper treatment of costs incurred after asset acquisition is sometimes confusing. The generalized chart in Exhibit 11-1 may prove helpful when analyzing a transaction and determining its correct handling in the accounting records.

DISPOSALS OF PROPERTY, PLANT, AND EQUIPMENT

Items of property, plant, and equipment are acquired by a firm to render benefits for a number of years. Eventually, these assets will be retired from use by being discarded, sold, or exchanged. When a company disposes of a depreciable asset, depreciation must be taken up to the date of disposal to ensure a proper matching of expenses and revenues.

To illustrate, suppose that Bennigan Company acquired a machine on January 1, 19X1, at a cost of $15,000. The machine has a residual value of $1,000 and is being depreciated over a seven-year life by the straight-line method. As of December 31, 19X2, the machine would appear in the accounting records as follows:

OBJECTIVE
2
Prepare journal entries to record discards and sales of property, plant, and equipment.

Machinery	
1/1/X1 15,000	

Accumulated Depreciation: Machinery	
	12/31/X1 2,000
	12/31/X2 2,000

Assume that Bennigan discarded the machine on October 1, 19X3. Because depreciation was last recorded on December 31, 19X2, nine months of additional depreciation must be taken. Thus, $1,500 ($2,000 $\times \frac{9}{12}$) is entered in the accounts by means of the entry that follows.

Oct. 1   Depreciation Expense: Machinery   1,500
                Accumulated Depreciation: Machinery   1,500
            To record nine months' depreciation

Removal of Assets from the Accounts

Once depreciation is brought up to date, any account balances associated with the machine must be removed from the books. This step is accomplished by debiting the Accumulated Depreciation account for the total depreciation taken to the date of disposal and then crediting the asset account for the asset's original cost. For Bennigan's machine, the necessary journal entry is as follows:

Oct. 1   Loss on Disposal of Property, Plant, & Equipment   9,500
                Accumulated Depreciation: Machinery   5,500
                Machinery   15,000
            To record discarded machine

To explain, recall that an asset's cost, minus accumulated depreciation, represents *book value*, which is the "value" of the asset in the accounting records. Because Bennigan received nothing for a machine having a $9,500 book value ($15,000 − $5,500), a $9,500 loss is incurred.

Sale of Depreciable Assets

In addition to being discarded or abandoned, depreciable assets can also be sold. To properly account for the transaction, the proceeds received upon sale must be compared against book value. If the amount received is greater than the asset's book value, a gain results; if the proceeds are less than book value, a loss arises. For example, assume that an executive desk was acquired for $2,000. Over the years, depreciation in the amount of $1,200 has been recorded. The asset's book value of $800 ($2,000 − $1,200) appears in the accounts as follows:

Office Furniture	
2,000	

Accumulated Depreciation: Office Furniture	
	1,200

If the desk is sold for $500 because of a low demand for used office furniture, a loss occurs. The entry to record this transaction would be as shown:

Cash	500	
Loss on Disposal of Property, Plant, & Equipment	300	
Accumulated Depreciation: Office Furniture	1,200	
Office Furniture		2,000
To record furniture sold at a price below book value		

A loss of $300 is generated because the cash received ($500) is less than the book value of the furniture ($800). The loss would have been reduced (and perhaps eliminated) if the selling price had been greater. On the other hand, the loss could have gone as high as $800 if the asset had been discarded with nothing received in return.

Changing the example, if the furniture is sold for $1,500, a gain arises. The proper journal entry is:

Cash	1,500	
Accumulated Depreciation: Office Furniture	1,200	
Gain on Disposal of Property, Plant, & Equipment		700
Office Furniture		2,000
To record furniture sold at a price above book value		

In this case, a gain of $700 results because the $1,500 sale proceeds exceed the $800 balance sheet valuation.

The preceding examples focused on situations where the amount of cash received differed from the asset's book value. It is possible, of course, that the two amounts could be equal. In such instances, no gain or loss arises. However, a journal entry must still be made to record the sale proceeds and to remove the cost of the asset and any accumulated depreciation from the accounts.

OBJECTIVE

3

Account for exchanges of similar assets.

Exchanges and Trade-ins of Similar Assets

Items of property, plant, and equipment are often exchanged or traded in for newer assets. You may have had some personal experience with trade-ins when purchasing a new car. To acquire the new vehicle, you must surrender the old car, make a cash down payment, and assume an obligation (e.g., a note) for the unpaid balance. The total amount to be paid is dependent on the **trade-in allowance** granted by the dealer for the old vehicle. Often the trade-in allowance is equal to the car's **fair market value** (i.e., the current market price). Sometimes, however, the trade-in allowance varies inversely with the number of cars the dealer has recently sold. If sales are low, trade-in allowances will be high, and vice versa. Because the trade-in allowance can fluctuate for reasons unrelated to the fair value of the asset given or received, it is an unreliable measure to use for accounting purposes.

To properly account for trade-ins, we must attach a value to the old asset. Normally, the asset surrendered is valued at its fair market value, unless the fair value of the asset received is more clearly evident. The fair value of the asset surrendered rarely coincides with the valuation in the accounting records, however, thus giving rise to a gain or loss.

The next few paragraphs focus on the rules related to exchanges of similar or like assets (e.g., the swap of one machine for another). The accounting profession requires that *losses on such transactions be recognized. In contrast, gains are ignored.*[1]

Loss Situation

Assume that Weiss Company has just traded an old delivery truck for a newer model. Data pertaining to the exchange follow.

Delivery Truck Traded In		Delivery Truck Acquired	
Cost	$10,000	Invoice price	$14,000
Accumulated depreciation	8,500	Fair market value of	
Book value on date of		old delivery truck	300
exchange	$ 1,500	Cash paid	$13,700

Weiss has generated a loss on this transaction because the "true" value of the asset surrendered (fair market value of $300) is far less than the asset's value in the accounting records (book value of $1,500). Stated differently, a $1,200 loss has arisen and is recorded as shown.

Delivery Truck (New)	14,000	
Accumulated Depreciation: Delivery Truck	8,500	
Loss on Exchange of Property, Plant, & Equipment	1,200	
Delivery Truck (Old)		10,000
Cash		13,700
To record acquisition of new delivery truck and trade-in of old delivery truck		

Notice that the new vehicle is recorded at its invoice price of $14,000.

Gain Situation

When the fair market value exceeds the book value of the asset relinquished, an apparent gain arises. However, the gain is *not* recognized because an exchange of similar assets does not substantially alter a company's operating capacity or position. In other words, the entity will possess a resource that performs in a manner similar to that surrendered. (One can even think of the transaction as a major refurbishing and upgrade of the original asset.) Any gain recognition at the time of exchange would therefore be premature and not conservative in nature. As a result of this treatment, the cost of the newly acquired asset is the sum of the old asset's book value plus any cash paid or to be paid.

---

[1] The rules stated here are used in the preparation of a company's financial statements. Different procedures are followed when reporting these transactions in the tax returns that are filed with the Internal Revenue Service. As an example, for tax purposes, neither gains *nor* losses on like-for-like exchanges are recognized.

To illustrate, let us assume the same data as in the previous case, with one exception: the fair value of the old delivery truck is now $2,000 rather than $300. The cash paid thus decreases to $12,000 ($14,000 invoice cost − $2,000 fair value), and the following entry becomes necessary:

Delivery Truck (New)	13,500	
Accumulated Depreciation: Delivery Truck	8,500	
Delivery Truck (Old)		10,000
Cash		12,000

To record acquisition of new delivery truck and trade-in of old delivery truck

Because the fair market value of the old vehicle ($2,000) exceeds the $1,500 book value, Weiss has generated a $500 gain on the exchange. As the journal entry shows, however, no gain appears in the accounting records. The new truck is therefore carried at $13,500: the book value of the truck relinquished ($1,500) plus the cash paid ($12,000). Future depreciation of the new asset will be based on the recorded cost of $13,500, not the $14,000 invoice price.

The accounting procedures for exchanges of similar assets, as well as for asset discards and sales, are overviewed in Exhibit 11-2.

EXHIBIT 11-2
Summary of Accounting Rules for Asset Disposals

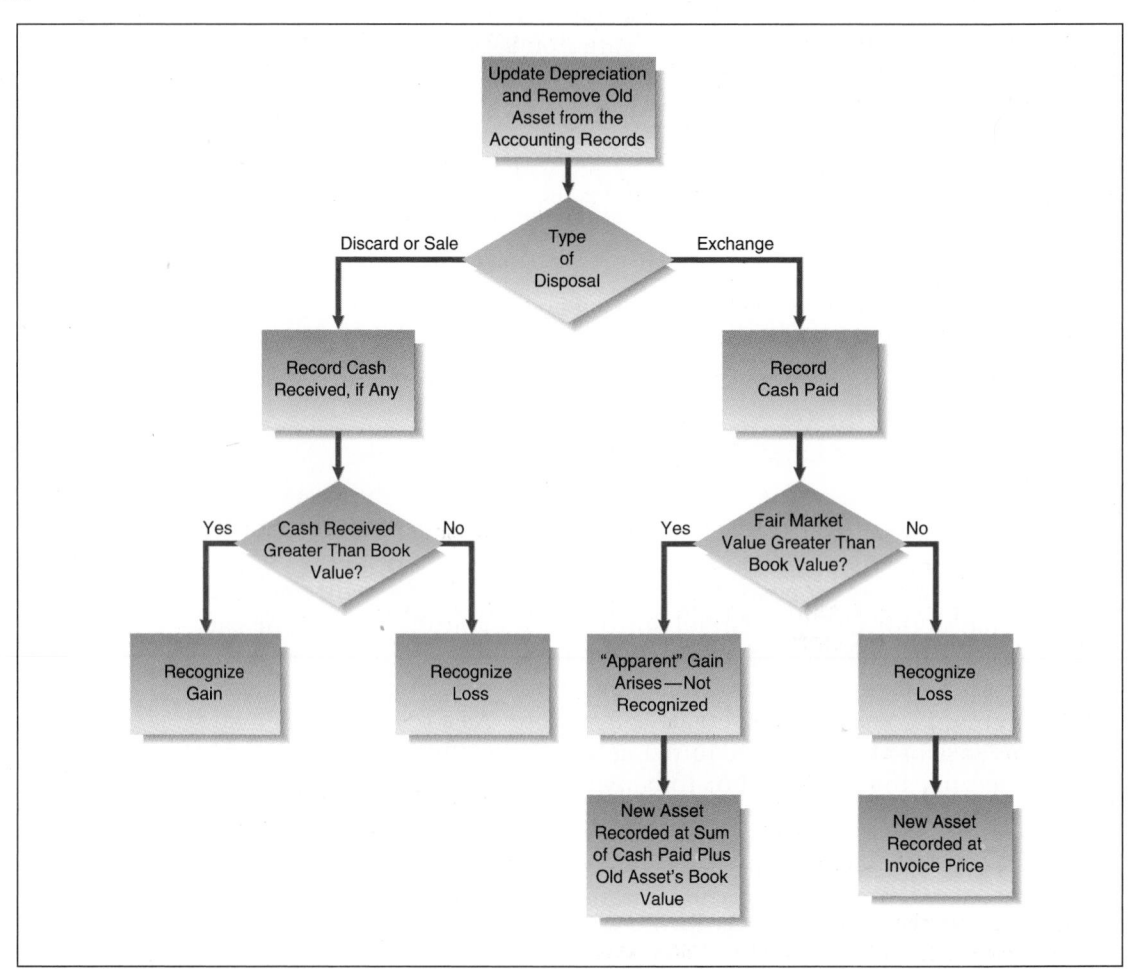

Natural resources represent another major group of assets that provide long-term benefits to their owners. Examples of natural resources include oil and gas wells, mineral deposits, and standing timber. These assets are sometimes called *wasting assets* because they are actually consumed (through removal) and do not maintain their physical presence like property, plant, and equipment.

Natural resources are initially entered in the accounting records at cost. This amount includes cost of the properties, legal fees, surveying costs, and sums expended for exploration and development.

NATURAL RESOURCES

OBJECTIVE
4

Calculate natural resource cost and depletion.

Depletion

As discussed in Chapters 3 and 10, plant and equipment are depreciated. A similar process, known as depletion, is applied to wasting assets. **Depletion** is the allocation of natural resource cost to the resources extracted during an accounting period. The depletion computation is virtually identical to the units-of-output depreciation method. That is, the cost of the natural resource, minus any residual value, is divided by the total estimated units (e.g., tons, barrels) in the resource deposit. The result, depletion per unit of output, is then multiplied by the number of units extracted during the period to determine the depletion charge.

To illustrate the necessary calculations, assume Thompson Oil Company purchased the rights to search for oil in Louisiana. The company spent $150,000 for the rights and another $1,850,000 for exploration costs. After estimated oil reserves of two million barrels were discovered, Thompson incurred costs of $4 million to develop a well. The firm's depletion charge of $3 per barrel is computed in the following manner:

Cost of project
Rights	$ 150,000
Exploration	1,850,000
Well development	4,000,000
Total	$6,000,000

Cost ÷ Estimated Units in Deposit = Depletion Rate

$6,000,000 ÷ 2,000,000 barrels = $3 per barrel

If 300,000 barrels are extracted and sold in the first year of the well's operation, depletion expense would total $900,000 (300,000 barrels × $3). The year-end journal entry to record depletion follows.

Depletion Expense	900,000	
Accumulated Depletion: Oil Property		900,000
To record depletion expense		

The Accumulated Depletion account is a contra asset that is deducted from the cost of the natural resource on the balance sheet. Thompson would therefore disclose its oil properties as follows:

Natural resources
Oil properties	$6,000,000	
Less: Accumulated depletion	900,000	$5,100,000

Companies usually establish separate asset and accumulated depletion accounts for each major category of natural resource owned.

In the example just presented, the entire $900,000 depletion charge was expensed because all extracted oil was sold. The net result was a proper matching of revenues and expenses. If some of the extracted oil was stored for future sale, a portion of the depletion charge must be allocated to an Oil Inventory account (a current asset). For instance, if only 285,000 barrels were sold, depletion expense would total $855,000 (285,000 × $3). Because 15,000 barrels (300,000 − 285,000) remain on hand, Thompson would inventory $45,000 (15,000 × $3) and add this amount to other oil production costs.

Revision of Depletion Rates

Depletion rates are sometimes revised because of changes in the estimation of recoverable resources. The procedure for the revision of depletion rates is identical to that followed for depreciation. As an example, assume that upon conclusion of Thompson's first year of operation, an independent geologist determined another 2.5 million barrels of oil were recoverable. The undepleted book value of the properties is presently $5.1 million ($6,000,000 − $900,000). The remaining book value is spread over the remaining resources, generating a new depletion rate of $2.04 ($5,100,000 ÷ 2,500,000) per barrel.

Depreciable Assets Related to Natural Resources

To develop a natural resource commercially, a company usually must build facilities and acquire equipment. Often the facilities and equipment cannot be moved after the resource deposits are exhausted. It is therefore common practice to depreciate these assets over their own lives or the life of the deposit, whichever is shorter. Many firms use the units-of-output depreciation method for such properties. These entities logically tie depreciation to the resource removal process by basing the depreciation charge on the number of units (e.g., barrels, tons) extracted during the period.

INTANGIBLE ASSETS

OBJECTIVE

5

Recognize the various types of intangible assets and compute amortization.

Long-lived assets that lack physical existence and contribute to the earnings capability of a company are termed **intangible assets.** Examples of intangibles include patents, copyrights, franchises, trademarks and brand names, and goodwill. Intangible assets can provide significant benefits to a business and may be instrumental in a firm's financial success. Yet many financial statement users disagree about placing these assets on the balance sheet. Stated simply, in comparison with the benefits received from other assets such as property, plant, and equipment, the benefits of intangibles are less certain and less determinable.

Intangible assets are entered in the accounting records at cost. Cost includes all expenditures necessary to place the intangible in a service-producing capacity, for example, the purchase price, filing fees, legal fees, and other miscellaneous costs related to acquisition. These expenditures are all capitalized, because they help to provide economic usefulness for extended periods of time. Intangibles are normally presented on the balance sheet in a separate section immediately following property, plant, and equipment.

Patents

A **patent** provides its owner with the exclusive right to use, manufacture, and sell a product or process for a period of 17 years. The federal government issues patents to inventors as a means of encouraging development of new products and technology. Firms may obtain patents by purchasing existing rights from inventors or by formulating their own products and processes through research and development. Although the economic usefulness of a purchased patent and an internally developed patent may be the same, their costs are treated differently.

As we noted, the purchase cost of an intangible is carried as an asset. In contrast, *research and development costs related to the creation of a patent are expensed.* Although expensing costs that result in long-term benefits may seem contrary to the accounting treatment noted in this and other chapters, research and development costs are somewhat unique.

Many organizations spend considerable amounts of money for research projects that culminate in a patent. Large sums are also spent on experimental work that is unsuccessful and leads nowhere. It might seem appropriate to expense the costs of unsuccessful research projects and capitalize the costs of those that result in a favorable outcome. Unfortunately, it is often difficult to assign costs to specific patents. Frequently, for example, patents do not result from one project; instead they are the culmination of knowledge that is obtained from many different undertakings. In addition, some research costs are applicable to more than a single endeavor and thus difficult to trace to specific efforts. As a consequence of these practical problems plus the possibility of a "go nowhere" outcome, businesses are required to expense research and development costs when incurred.[2]

Copyrights

A **copyright** provides its owners, or their heirs, the exclusive right to produce and sell an artistic, musical, or published work. Like patents, these rights are issued by the federal government and can be sold or assigned to others. A copyright is granted for the life of the creator plus 50 years. Normally, however, the useful life to the owner is a much shorter period.

Franchises

A **franchise** gives its owner the right to manufacture or sell certain products or to perform certain services. Although most people associate franchises with fast-food restaurants such as Pizza Hut and Burger King, franchises are established for a variety of activities. Cities, for example, often grant franchises to firms for garbage collection, towing services, and taxi

---

[2] See "Accounting for Research and Development Costs," *Statement of Financial Accounting Standards No. 2* (Norwalk, Conn.: Financial Accounting Standards Board, 1974).

services. A franchise may have an indefinite life (perpetual franchise) or a limited life; some must even be renewed yearly.

The cost of acquiring a franchise is carried in a Franchise account. A few franchises involve no acquisition costs; thus, only legal costs and related fees are capitalized. Other franchises are extremely expensive. Consider what an investor would have to pay to acquire a professional sports club (i.e., a franchise) in today's day and age. A recent study pegged the "value" of eight such operations at $150 million or more. (The New York Yankees led the list at $200 million, followed by the Los Angeles Dodgers.) Factors that were considered in arriving at these numbers included franchise revenues (gate receipts, concessions, parking, and fees from television, radio, and cable broadcasts) and stadium/arena lease agreements (including skybox availability and rentals).[3]

EXECUTIVE BRIEFING
The Significance of Franchising to a Company's Development, Growth, and Earnings

Cary Vollintine
Corporate Controller
Blockbuster Entertainment Corporation

Franchises are a popular organizational form, one that our company has relied on heavily. Here's a little bit of history. By December 1985, the videocassette rental industry had developed into a "mom and pop" format, with over 18,000 specialty rental stores. Blockbuster viewed this situation favorably and visualized a superstore concept—one with sophisticated computer systems to track customers and rental preferences, manage inventory, and provide extensive point-of-sale information.

With a viable idea in place, the key issue was how to develop as many markets as possible while the concept was still innovative. The major strategy was to use all available Blockbuster resources to saturate the major metropolitan areas. Franchising was considered to be the best alternative to simultaneously develop smaller secondary markets as well as to assist the company in the leading population centers.

At the time of this writing, Blockbuster had 1,003 franchise stores (50% of our total outlets), held by 125 franchisees. Revenue from these operations is derived from product sales to franchise owners, initial franchise fees, and royalties and other fees. Royalties range from 3% to 8% of revenue; other fees are primarily for software support provided by the company. Total revenues from franchisees recently amounted to approximately $100 million, a sum that clearly indicates the significance of such operations to the growth and earnings of our firm.

---

[3] For an interesting overview of professional football, baseball, basketball, and hockey franchises, see "Big Leagues, Bad Business," *Financial World*, July 7, 1992, pp. 34–35, 38–39, 42–51.

Trademarks

Each day, as consumers, we encounter trademarks, brand names, and symbols. Consider, for example, our presentation in Exhibit 11-3. These intangible assets are very important to the financial well-being of a business, since a unique product name or recognizable symbol is automatically associated with a specific good and/or service.

The cost of a trademark, brand name, or special symbol includes design fees, market research costs, attorney's fees, and registration fees. Focusing on the last item listed, owners can secure exclusive rights to the use of these intangible assets by registration with the federal government. Trademarks may be registered for a period of 10 years, with renewals possible if certain conditions are met.

Leasehold Improvements

Occasionally, improvements are made on property leased by one party (the lessee) from another party (the lessor). The amounts expended for these assets by the lessee, an intangible called **leasehold improvements,** are re-

**EXHIBIT 11-3
Trademarks and Symbols**

All trademarks and symbols are used with permission of their owners: the National Football League (San Francisco 49ers), Toys "R" Us, Kellogg Company, MasterCard International, Inc., and The National Broadcasting Company. *Tony the Tiger* is a registered trademark of Kellogg Company.

HIGHLIGHT
What's in a Name, Anyway?

Back in 1917, a young fighter named Jack Dempsey stopped in to ask a favor of Jacob Golomb, a retailer and maker of men's bathing suits. The protective headgear Dempsey had been using for training wasn't holding up. Golomb's products had the reputation of outlasting everyone else's. Hence the name, Everlast. Could Golomb make Dempsey some training gear that would last longer than 15 rounds? Why not, said Golomb.

Dempsey went on to flatten Jess Willard in 1919 for the heavyweight title—wearing a pair of Everlast boxing gloves. Suddenly, Golomb had a new market for his distinctive concave logo, which wound up on the headgear, trunks, and boxing gloves of a long line of champions, right down to Muhammad Ali and Joe Frazier. Several years ago the Everlast trademark started appearing on swimsuits again—as well as on jogging suits, T-shirts, pullovers, thermal underwear, mittens, scarves, tank tops, and other sportswear.

Based in New York's tough South Bronx, Everlast Sports Manufacturing Co. doesn't make swimsuits anymore. Or any of the other sportswear products now carrying its name. The firm just licenses the logo. But that logo, it turns out, packs a trademark wallop other marketers can only dream of. "Everlast is in a category by itself. It's [a symbol]," says the executive of a business that tracks trademark recognition for advertisers and consumer-oriented companies.

Since Everlast began licensing, in 1983, the firm has earned at least $2 million in royalties. That may not look like much, but it's crucial to the company, which has seen boxing equipment sales level off in recent years. The family-run business won't disclose figures, but sales of its core products are thought to be in the area of $20 million.

Licensing is helping the firm grow. Riding the crest of the sports boom that's put the logos of baseball, football, and basketball teams on everything from sweatshirts to beer mugs, Everlast's pull is its socko name—one that's not tied to a particular season or one team's success. Think Everlast and you think of washboard stomachs, sweat-matted hair, million-dollar purses—the grit and glory of the ring.

But the closest most buyers of Everlast merchandise have gotten to a smoke-filled gym is a movie ticket to *Raging Bull*. These are the same sorts of folks who buy four-wheel-drive Jeeps to pick up the oat-bran muffins on a Sunday morning. Sort of macho by association. This "macho by association," though, is making big bucks for the company, as customers flock to Bloomingdale's, Macy's, Nordstrom, and the like to purchase their sweats.

Everlast's apparel line gets a lot more exposure than its modest $500,000 advertising budget can buy. Whenever big-time boxers get their pictures in the press, it's usually not hard to spot the large Everlast logo on their gloves or trunks. And there are the ads run by other companies that feature the firm's products. Notes the trademark analyst quoted earlier, "Everlast gets enormous free play, just like Rolls-Royce and Tiffany."

Using the added visibility of its licensing ventures, Everlast is now expanding company manufacturing efforts into a broad range of exercise and weight-lifting equipment for the home. Meanwhile, hardly a week goes by when Golomb doesn't get another request for a license. Everlast men's cologne and Everlast lingerie are among items he's recently rejected. "We never realized how attractive our name was," he says. "Now the goal is to keep it that way."

Source: Adapted from "Swimsuits, Yes; Perfumes, No," *Forbes*, July 23, 1990, pp. 81–82, 86. Excerpted by permission of *Forbes* magazine, © Forbes Inc., 1990.

corded in an account of the same name and may be rather substantial. For example, J.C. Penney recently reported leasehold improvements of $570 million. Leasehold improvements normally become the property of the lessor at the end of the lease period. As such, the amounts expended are written off to expense over the remaining life of the lease or the life of the improvement, whichever is shorter.

Goodwill

The term "goodwill" means different things to different people. A business often refers to the customer goodwill that flows from an excellent reputation, superior products, and prime location. A large corporation may claim it is furthering community goodwill by sponsoring a Little League baseball team and a series of concerts open to the public. Do the foregoing types of goodwill have any value to a business? Of course they do. However, placing a dollar amount on these items is very difficult. Considerable personal opinion is involved, and the items cannot be measured objectively. If the owners and managers of a business were permitted to arbitrarily put a value on such goodwill for entry into the accounting records, the resulting financial statements could seriously misrepresent the entity's financial position.

As a result, generally accepted accounting principles allow only the recording of "purchased" goodwill. For example, suppose that Diamond Computers, owner of a chain of computer stores throughout the country, purchased a local retailer (Valley Computer) on October 1 for $500,000 cash. The current values of Valley's assets and liabilities on the date of acquisition were as follows:

Building	$150,000
Store fixtures	30,000
Inventory	300,000
Prepaid expenses	10,000
Bank loan	(90,000)
	$400,000

Why did Diamond pay $500,000 when the individual assets, minus liabilities, were worth only $400,000? In all likelihood, Diamond's management was impressed with the financial history of Valley and anticipated that Valley's earnings record would continue into the future. To an accountant, the $100,000 difference between the purchase price of the business and the current value of the assets and liabilities acquired is an intangible known as **goodwill.**

The existence of goodwill is normally evidenced by a company's ability to earn a higher rate of income than other businesses in the same field of endeavor. Stated differently, goodwill occurs when the value of the company *as an operating entity* exceeds the value of its individual components (*measurable assets and liabilities*). The entity's resources, including the special attributes of reputation, favorable location, and skillful management, have all been working together to increase the value of the business in the eyes of the purchaser—an increase that is over and above the current value of the resources acquired and liabilities assumed. Generally, the individual impact of each of the preceding factors is not readily identifiable, and the purchaser is paying a lump sum for their collective benefits.

Accounting for Goodwill

The proper accounting for goodwill is demonstrated by continuing the previous example. It is important to recognize that although Valley developed the goodwill, disclosure by management on Valley's financial statements is not appropriate because of the measurement difficulties cited earlier. Diamond, on the other hand, paid $100,000 for this intangible in a valid business transaction and can record the following journal entry:

Building	150,000	
Store Fixtures	30,000	
Inventory	300,000	
Prepaid Expenses	10,000	
Goodwill	100,000	
Loan Payable		90,000
Cash		500,000
Acquired the assets and liabilities		
of Valley Computer		

Observe the manner in which the current value of the assets and liabilities acquired becomes the cost to Diamond. If Valley lacked the ability to achieve above-average earnings because of a marginal location or other factors, Diamond would have probably paid less than $500,000. If, for example, the agreed-upon purchase price was $400,000, Diamond would have bought only the separate assets, minus liabilities. Nothing would have been paid for the unique features of the business.

Guidelines for Determining Goodwill

Calculating the amount *paid* for goodwill in the purchase of a business is fairly straightforward, as was observed in the preceding example. Determining how much a purchaser *should be willing to pay* is another matter. Several techniques have been proposed for estimating goodwill. Among these are the following:

- Multiply sales during the last 12 months by a stipulated percentage.
- Multiply earnings during the last 12 months by a stipulated percentage.
- Multiply the amount by which earnings exceed an industry norm by a stipulated percentage.

Bear in mind that these techniques are merely estimation tools. The exact amount of goodwill is based on the actual selling price of the business, as determined by the buyer and the seller. The preceding tools are just that—tools—and cannot take the place of sound business logic and intelligent financial negotiation.

Amortization of Intangibles

Earlier in the text we discussed the topic of depreciation—a process by which the cost of plant and equipment is allocated to expense over an estimated service life. This same process is applied to intangible assets; the name is changed, however, to **amortization.** The entry to record the periodic amortization of an intangible is a debit to Amortization Expense and a credit to the intangible asset account. This treatment differs slightly from the depreciation entry, where the credit involves the contra asset Accumulated Depreciation. An Accumulated Amortization account is seldom used.

Amortization Procedures

The most troublesome issue in amortization is estimating the intangible's service life. Imagine the difficulty of determining when a food trademark, the unique flavor of a soft drink, or an ice cream franchise would have no future economic value to their owners.

Although many intangibles have specified legal lives, the actual service life may be considerably shorter. For example, the inventor of a new electronic device can obtain exclusive manufacturing and sales rights for 17 years through a patent. Yet the patent may be useful for only five years because of intense competition and rapid technological developments in the electronics industry. Accordingly, the patent should be written off over a five-year period. In general, an intangible should be amortized over the shorter of its legal life or service life; however, in no event should the amortization period exceed 40 years.[4] This latter rule is especially applicable to goodwill and other intangibles that provide seemingly unlimited benefits to their owners.

Because it is difficult to measure changes in the yearly benefits provided by intangibles, most companies use the straight-line method of amortization. As in straight-line depreciation, an equal amount of expense is recorded each period. Several examples of intangible assets and related amortization practices appear in Exhibit 11-4.

ETHICS ISSUE

In an effort to estimate the service life of a soft drink formula, XYZ's accountant contacted the president of the Soft Drink Trade Association. The president is a close relative of XYZ's chief financial officer. Comment.

Company	Intangible	Amortization Policy
A&W Brands, Inc.	Secret flavor formulas	Amortized on a straight-line basis over 37 to 40 years.
The Gillette Company	Dental endorsements	Amortized principally over 13 years by the straight-line method.
The New York Times Company	Amounts paid for subscriber lists	Amortized over the remaining subscription lives.
The Walt Disney Company	Rights to the name, likeness, and portrait of Walt Disney	Amortized over 40 years.

EXHIBIT 11-4
Intangible Assets and Amortization Practices

[4] "Intangible Assets," *Opinions of the Accounting Principles Board No. 17* (New York: American Institute of Certified Public Accountants, 1970), paragraph 29.

An Example

To illustrate the amortization of an intangible asset, assume Kelley Corporation purchased a patent from an inventor for $720,000 on July 1, 19X6. The patent was originally granted to the inventor on January 1, 19X1, will provide benefits to Kelley for $7\frac{1}{2}$ years, and has no residual value. The entries to record the purchase on July 1 and amortization on December 31, 19X6, follow.

July	1	Patents	720,000	
		Cash		720,000
		To record purchase of patent		
Dec.	31	Amortization Expense: Patents	48,000	
		Patents		48,000
		To record six months of amortization expense		

Although the patent has a 17-year legal life, the service life to Kelley is a much shorter period ($7\frac{1}{2}$ years, or 90 months). Because monthly amortization equals $8,000 ($720,000 ÷ 90), amortization of $48,000 is recorded. The Patents account would appear on the firm's December 31, 19X6, balance sheet at $672,000 ($720,000 − $48,000).

Kelley would continue to amortize the patent at the $8,000 monthly rate. Should the service life change, the rate is revised by following procedures similar to those shown for depreciation and depletion. Specifically, the remaining unamortized cost, minus any residual value, is spread over the remaining service life.

END-OF-CHAPTER REVIEW

LEARNING OBJECTIVES: THE KEY POINTS

1 Account for property, plant, and equipment costs incurred after asset acquisition. Expenditures incurred after items of property, plant, and equipment are placed in service often prolong an asset's life, increase the quantity of services provided by an asset, or improve service quality. Such expenditures (e.g., additions and betterments) provide future benefits and should be capitalized in the accounts. If an expenditure does not meet at least one of the preceding criteria, it is known as a revenue expenditure and immediately expensed. A typical expense would be ordinary repairs and maintenance, which are incurred to maintain the normal operating condition of the asset.

2 Prepare journal entries to record discards and sales of property, plant, and equipment. When an asset is discarded or sold, depreciation must be updated to the date of disposal, and the asset's cost and accompanying accumulated depreciation must be removed from the accounting records. Gains and losses are recognized by comparing the asset's book value with the proceeds received. A gain arises when the proceeds received exceed book value; a loss occurs in the opposite situation.

3 Account for exchanges of similar assets. When similar assets are exchanged or traded, gains and losses are figured by comparing book value against the old asset's fair market value. In cases where the fair value of the asset given up is less than the old asset's book value, a loss is recognized and the new asset is recorded at the invoice price. When fair value exceeds book value, an apparent gain results. However, the gain is not recognized, and the new asset is recorded at the book value of the old asset plus any cash paid or to be paid.

4 Calculate natural resource cost and depletion. Natural resources, such as oil and gas and mineral deposits, provide long-term benefits until they are totally consumed through extraction. Such assets are entered in the accounting records at cost, which includes amounts expended for exploration and development. Depletion involves the allocation of this cost to the resources extracted during the period. It is calculated by dividing cost, minus residual value, by the total estimated units in the resource deposit. This computation yields depletion per unit of output, which is multiplied by the number of units extracted to arrive at the depletion charge.

5 Recognize the various types of intangible assets and compute amortization. Long-term assets that lack physical existence and contribute to the earnings capability of a company are called intangibles. Examples of intangibles and accompanying legal lives are patents (17 years), copyrights (life of the creator plus 50 years), franchises, trademarks (10 years, with renewals possible), leasehold improvements, and goodwill. An intangible is gradually expensed via amortization over its legal life or service life, whichever is shorter. In no case may the amortization period exceed 40 years.

KEY TERMS AND CONCEPTS: A QUICK OVERVIEW

additions Items that provide future benefits and are affixed to existing plant and equipment.

amortization The allocation of the cost of intangible assets to the accounting periods benefited.

assessments Amounts charged to property owners by government agencies for improvements such as new streets, sewers, and sidewalks.

betterments Expenditures that improve or increase the future service potential of an item of plant and equipment.

capital expenditures Costs that provide future economic benefits to a business.

copyright An intangible asset that gives its owners or their heirs the exclusive right to produce and sell an artistic, musical, or published work for a stipulated period of time.

depletion The allocation of natural resource cost to the resources extracted during an accounting period.

fair market value The current market price of an asset.

franchise An intangible asset representing rights that authorize the manufacture or sale of certain products and/or the performance of certain services.

goodwill The amount paid by the purchaser of a business in excess of the current value of the assets and liabilities acquired.

intangible assets Long-term assets that lack physical existence—for example, patents, copyrights, and trademarks.

leasehold improvements Improvements made to leased property by the lessee.

patent An exclusive right that permits its owner to use, manufacture, and sell a product or process.

repairs Amounts spent to maintain the normal operating condition of an asset.

revenue expenditures   Costs incurred after asset acquisition that are said to benefit only the current accounting period. Are treated as expenses.

trade-in allowance   The amount a buyer is given for an old asset in an exchange-type transaction.

trademark   An exclusive right to use specific brand names and symbols for a period of 10 years, with renewals possible if certain conditions are met.

CHAPTER QUIZ

The five questions that follow relate to several issues raised in the chapter. Test your knowledge of the issues by selecting the best answer. (The answers appear on p. 452.)

1 Gamble, Inc., installed a heater in one of its earth-moving vehicles at a cost of $1,200. The vehicle did not previously have a heater. Gamble should account for this cost:
   a as an intangible asset.
   b by reducing the Earth-Moving Equipment account.
   c by reducing the Accumulated Depreciation account associated with the vehicle.
   d by increasing the book value of the vehicle.

2 Gains and losses on the sale of a depreciable asset are determined by comparing:
   a book value and the proceeds received.
   b book value and the asset's cost.
   c the proceeds received and the asset's cost.
   d book value and the Accumulated Depreciation account.

3 Solo Company spent $10 million to develop a mine having an estimated four million ounces of silver. During 19X7, 50,000 ounces were mined and processed; 5,000 ounces were sold at $8 per ounce. The 19X7 depletion *expense* is:
   a $2.50.   c $112,500.
   b $12,500.   d $125,000.

4 On January 1, 19X1, Betty Ross purchased a patent for $102,000. The patent had an original legal life of 17 years at the date of issuance; only six of the 17 years remained when acquired. The expected service life to Ross is two years. The 19X1 amortization expense is:
   a $6,000.   c $51,000.
   b $17,000.   d $102,000.

5 Goodwill:
   a is an intangible asset that need not be amortized.
   b is recorded by the seller of a business prior to the sale transaction.
   c is an intangible asset that must be amortized over a period of 40 years or more.
   d may be recorded by the buyer of a business when the acquisition is completed.

SUMMARY PROBLEM

Greystone Granite Company operates a granite quarry. The following schedule shows information about selected assets owned by the firm as of January 1, 19X2:

	Original Cost	Cost Written Off in Prior Periods
Building	$ 50,000	$20,000
Office equipment	18,000	7,200
Granite deposits	100,000	40,000

The following activity occurred during 19X2:

1 At the very beginning of January, Greystone paid a contractor to paint, air condition, and reroof the building. The building previously lacked air conditioning, and the roof was expected to extend the structure's life by five years.
2 On October 1, the company traded its old office equipment for new office equipment that had an invoice price of $28,000. Greystone also had to pay $22,000 cash. Management depreciates all equipment by the straight-line method, assuming a five-year life and no residual value.
3 Geologists originally estimated that the quarry contained 100,000 tons of granite. The company extracted 6,000 tons of granite during the year.
4 On December 31, Marble Enterprises extended an offer to buy all the assets (and assume all the liabilities) of Greystone Granite for $270,000. Fair market value and book value figures for Greystone's assets and liabilities on this date were:

	Fair Market Value	Book Value
Assets	$250,000	$185,000
Liabilities	50,000	50,000

Instructions

a Determine the proper account(s) to debit to record the painting, air conditioning, and reroofing.
b Present the journal entries needed to record the exchange of office equipment.
c Would the substance of the office equipment transaction have changed if the cash payment had amounted to only $17,500? Briefly explain.
d Compute Greystone's depletion charge for 19X2.
e Calculate the amount of goodwill that will be recognized if Marble completes its acquisition of Greystone's assets and liabilities. On whose accounting records will the goodwill be recorded?

Solution

a Painting—Repairs (Painting) Expense
Air conditioning—Building
Reroofing—Accumulated Depreciation: Building

b
Depreciation Expense: Office Equipment	2,700*	
Accumulated Depreciation: Office Equipment		2,700

Office Equipment (New)	28,000	
Accumulated Depreciation: Office Equipment	9,900†	
Loss on Exchange of Property, Plant, & Equipment	2,100‡	
Office Equipment (Old)		18,000
Cash		22,000

* ($18,000 ÷ 5 years) × $\frac{9}{12}$.
† $7,200 + $2,700.
‡ ($18,000 − $9,900) vs. ($28,000 − $22,000).

c A cash payment of $17,500 would indicate a fair market value of $10,500 on the old equipment ($28,000 − $17,500). Thus, the transaction gives rise to an apparent $2,400 gain ($10,500 vs. $8,100 book value). The gain, however, is not recognized because the assets exchanged are similar in nature.

d The depletion charge is $6,000 ($100,000 ÷ 100,000 tons = $1 per ton; 6,000 tons × $1 = $6,000).

e
Amount paid	$270,000
Less: Fair market value of assets acquired and liabilities assumed ($250,000 − $50,000)	200,000
Goodwill	$ 70,000

The goodwill will be entered in the accounting records of Marble Enterprises, the acquiring company.

ASSIGNMENT MATERIAL

QUESTIONS

Q11-1 What factors should be considered in determining whether costs incurred after the acquisition of property, plant, and equipment are treated as capital expenditures or as revenue expenditures?

Q11-2 Discuss the accounting treatment normally given to the following:
a Repairs
b Additions
c Betterments
d Assessments

Q11-3 Why is it necessary to update the depreciation accounts when depreciable assets are sold, discarded, or exchanged?

Q11-4 How is a gain or loss on the sale of an asset calculated?

Q11-5 Assume that an asset exchange is about to occur. Should the asset surrendered be valued at fair market value or the trade-in allowance granted by the dealer? Briefly discuss.

Q11-6 How are gains and losses on the exchange of similar items of property, plant, and equipment handled for financial reporting purposes?

Q11-7 What costs are commonly capitalized in a natural resource account?

Q11-8 Define "depletion."

Q11-9 Explain how a portion of the depletion charge can be included in the current asset section of the balance sheet.

Q11-10 How should a company determine the service life of a company-owned railroad track that is adjacent to a coal mine? Explain which depreciation method may be most appropriate for the railroad track.

Q11-11 Discuss the treatment of research and development costs that are incurred in the development of a patent.

Q11-12 What is a leasehold improvement?

Q11-13 Define "goodwill" and explain how the cost of goodwill is determined.

Q11-14 How is the amortization period of an intangible determined?

EXERCISES

E11-1 *Capital and revenue expenditures* (L.O. 1)
Consider the following transactions and events:
a Installed wind deflectors on three trucks to improve fuel efficiency.
b Replaced the roof on a warehouse.
c Repainted the interior of a restaurant.
d Expanded a company's manufacturing plant by 20,000 square feet.
e Paid a plumber to fix a leak in the hot water heater.
f Removed asbestos insulation in an old building and installed fiberglass insulation.

Determine whether the transactions and events would give rise to a capital expenditure or a revenue expenditure.

E11-2 *Accounting for betterments* (L.O. 1)

Al's Bookstore purchased a building several years ago for $500,000. Straight-line depreciation has been used, assuming a residual value of $50,000 and a service life of 30 years. On June 30, 19XX, the end of Al's fiscal year, the building had a book value of $380,000. On July 1, 19XX, betterments (extraordinary repairs) were made to the building at a cost of $86,000. The betterments were expected to extend the service life of the building by four years, resulting in a remaining service life of 26 years.

a Compute the balance in the Accumulated Depreciation account on June 30, 19XX.

b To what account should the betterments be debited? Why?

c Compute the book value of the building after the betterments have been recorded.

d Calculate depreciation expense for the current and future fiscal years, assuming no change in the estimated residual value.

E11-3 *Journal entries for costs incurred after asset acquisition* (L.O. 1)

Coolidge Company had the following transactions:

a Paid $34,200 for a major overhaul of the firm's overhead conveyor system. The overhaul is expected to extend the system's life by five years.

b Paid $1,000 to install an extra gasoline tank on a heavy-duty truck.

c Paid $105 to have a microcomputer repaired.

d Paid $2,400 to the City of Townsend. The payment covered an assessment to have curbs installed on Coolidge's property.

Prepare the journal entries necessary to record the preceding transactions.

E11-4 *Asset disposals* (L.O. 2)

Lincoln Company purchased a truck on January 1, 19X3. The truck cost $90,000, had a service life of eight years, and had an estimated residual value of $30,000. Lincoln uses the straight-line method of depreciation. Consider the following *independent* cases:

a If Lincoln sold the truck on April 1, 19X6, for $58,000, compute the gain or loss on the sale.

b Assume that Lincoln's driver demolished the truck on July 1, 19X8. The company carries no insurance. If depreciation was last recorded on December 31, 19X7, prepare the necessary entries to (1) update depreciation and (2) remove the truck from the accounts.

E11-5 *Overview of discards, sales, and exchanges* (L.O. 2, 3)

1-2-3

Baubles and Lace purchased four store display units several years ago at a total cost of $35,000. Depreciation to date has amounted to $28,500, and the company has tentatively figured the year's net income at $45,900. Recompute the firm's net income, assuming the occurrence of the following *independent* transactions:

a The units are donated to a charitable organization, with nothing received in return.

b The units are sold to another business for $7,100.

c The units are sold to another business for $3,900.

d The units are exchanged for new store equipment. The fair market value of the old units is $4,200.

e The units are exchanged for new store equipment. The fair market value of the old units is $6,800.

E11-6 *Accounting for exchange of similar assets* (L.O. 3)

Ryan purchased a sorting machine on January 1, 19X1, for $2,400. The machine had an estimated service life of five years and no residual value. On April 1, 19X4, Ryan acquired a new sorter. The invoice price of the new machine was $4,000, service life was estimated to be 10 years, and no residual value was anticipated. Ryan received a $1,200 trade-in allowance, which was equal to the old sorter's fair value, and paid the balance due in cash. Depreciation was last recorded on December 31, 19X3, by use of the straight-line method.

a Prepare Ryan's journal entry(ies) to record the trade-in.

b Repeat part (a), assuming the life of the old sorter was eight years (instead of five years).

E11-7 *Accounting for disposals and exchanges* (L.O. 2, 3)

Evaluate the comments that follow as being True or False. If the comment is false, briefly explain why.

a Losses on the exchange of similar assets are recognized for financial reporting purposes.

b When a depreciable asset is sold, a gain results when the cash received exceeds the asset's book value.

c Both the outright sale of a truck and its exchange for a similar vehicle give rise to identical treatment of gains and losses in the accounting records.

d A dealer's trade-in allowance is normally used for financial accounting purposes when valuing an asset surrendered in an exchange transaction.

e An exchange of similar assets has occurred and must be entered in the accounting records. If the old asset's book value is less than fair market value, the newly acquired asset is recorded at the invoice price.

E11-8 *Depletion* (L.O. 4)

Case Company recently incurred the following costs in developing a mine site:

Mine development	$6,400,000
Rights	300,000
Exploration	1,800,000
	$8,500,000

The mine is expected to contain five million tons of ore. Case extracted and sold 410,000 tons during the first year of operation.

a Present the necessary journal entry to record depletion.

b Show the proper disclosure of the mining property upon conclusion of the first year of operation.

c What would you have done differently in part (a) if Case had extracted 410,000 tons but sold only 360,000? Be specific.

E11-9 *Depletion; revision of rates* (L.O. 4)

American Lumber Corporation purchased a tract of timberland for $1,100,000 in 19X6. An appraiser estimated that the land would be worth $200,000 after 1,500,000 board feet of timber were harvested. Board feet harvested and sold from 19X6 through 19X8 were as follows:

19X6	19X7	19X8
140,000	210,000	230,000

a Calculate depletion expense for 19X6, 19X7, and 19X8.

b Compute the book value of the timberland at the end of 19X8.

c Assume that at the beginning of 19X9, a new study found that only 800,000 board feet remained in the tract. Calculate the new depletion rate for 19X9 and future years.

E11-10 *Amortization of intangibles* **(L.O. 5)**
On October 1, 19X2, Nagato Enterprises paid $97,000 to acquire the following intangible assets from Midland Research Company:

	Amount Paid	Estimated Service Life to Nagato
Patent	$60,000	4 years
Copyrights	10,000	5 years
Trademarks	27,000	9 years

The legal life of the patent expires on September 30, 19X8.

a Compute Nagato's amortization expense for the year ended September 30, 19X3. Briefly explain your calculation with respect to the patent.

b Record the proper journal entry for amortization on September 30, 19X3.

c Assume that in addition to the preceding intangibles, Nagato paid $160,000 to acquire a franchise that has an unlimited service life. Should the franchise be amortized? Briefly explain.

E11-11 *Goodwill* **(L.O. 5)**
Rebecca Sprague is negotiating to buy the Lodi Crushers Football Club. The following information was extracted from the club's recent balance sheet:

Cash	$ —
Accounts receivable	19,000
Prepaid expenses	8,000
Practice field	25,000
Equipment (net)	7,000
Franchise—Nebraska League	10,000
Accounts payable	12,000
Salaries payable	53,000

Current values of the practice field and equipment are $35,000 and $3,000, respectively.

a If Sprague assumed the Crushers' liabilities and purchased the team for $22,000 cash, how much did she pay for goodwill?

b Prepare Sprague's entry to record the purchase of the team.

Series A

PROBLEMS

P11-A1 *Costs incurred after purchase; disposals* **(L.O. 1, 2)**
The records of Portland Equipment Operators revealed the following information about selected assets:

	Date Acquired	Cost	Residual Value	Service Life
Land	8/1/X3	$ 74,500	N/A	N/A
Warehouse	1/1/X4	119,800	$25,000	20 years
Machinery	1/1/X2	700,000	40,000	10 years
Forklifts (4)*	10/1/X4	192,000	48,000	8 years

* The cost and residual value figures are for the four forklifts collectively.

The following transactions and events occurred during the year ended December 31, 19X6:

Jan. 1   Sold one forklift to March Manufacturing for $39,500 cash.
1   Paid $3,690 to add a new loading dock to the warehouse. The new dock will be depreciated over the building's remaining service life and will not affect the facility's estimated residual value.
1   Paid $90,000 for a major overhaul of the machinery. The overhaul was expected to extend the machinery's remaining service life by three years.

Mar. 1   Paid $8,300 for a land assessment to cover the installation of a new water line.

Sept. 3   Paid $250 for miscellaneous repairs to forklift no. 3.

The company uses the straight-line method on all depreciable assets. Depreciation was last recorded on December 31, 19X5.

Instructions

a Prepare journal entries to record the transactions and events that occurred during 19X6.
b Determine Portland's depreciation expense for the year ended December 31, 19X6.

P11-A2 *Journal entries for disposals and exchanges* (L.O. 2, 3)

Ann Arbor Regional Transit (AART) purchased a specialized van on January 1, 19X1, to transport handicapped persons around the city. The van cost $40,000, had an estimated service life of seven years, and had a residual value of $5,000. The company uses the straight-line depreciation method, with depreciation last recorded on December 31, 19X3.

Instructions

a The van was sold for cash on April 1, 19X4. Prepare the required journal entry to update depreciation and then record the sale, assuming a sales price of:
(1) $30,700.
(2) $17,500.
b Independent of part (a), assume the van was exchanged on January 1, 19X4, for a similar van having a $30,000 invoice price. Prepare the required journal entry to record the exchange if the old van had a fair market value of:
(1) $26,000 and AART gave the dealer $4,000 cash.
(2) $22,000 and AART gave the dealer $8,000 cash.
c The rule for gain recognition on exchanges of similar assets is said to stress conservatism in financial reporting. Briefly discuss.

P11-A3 *Disposals and exchanges; analysis* (L.O. 2, 3)

Ocean Enterprises, Inc., disposed of five assets during the 19X7 fiscal year. Information pertaining to these assets follows.

Asset	Cost	Accumulated Depreciation	Cash Received (Paid)	Fair Market Value on Date of Disposal
Freezer	$ 5,000	$ 3,600	$ 1,200	$ 1,200
Furniture	4,000	4,000	—	—
Auto	21,000	9,000	(8,200)	8,100
Building	99,000	38,000	77,000	77,000
Machine	75,000	46,600	(36,000)	30,000

A review of the accounting records revealed the following additional information:

- *Freezer*—The freezer was sold to Romar Manufacturing, one of Ocean's customers.
- *Furniture*—The furniture was donated to an American Veterans group.
- *Auto*—The auto was exchanged for a new auto that had an invoice price of $16,300.
- *Building*—The building was destroyed by an earthquake. Insurance proceeds, which were based on market value, amounted to $77,000.
- *Machine*—The company acquired a new machine having an $84,000 invoice price. The machinery dealer took Ocean's old machine in trade along with $36,000 cash and an $18,000 note payable.

The company's accountant is in the process of computing net income for 19X7. He has determined that income before any gains and losses from asset disposals amounts to $70,000.

Instructions

a Compute Ocean's income after considering gains and losses on the five asset disposals.

b Suppose (1) the auto's fair market value amounted to $13,000 rather than $8,100 and (2) the invoice price of the new auto was $21,200. In view of this new data, will your answer in part (a) increase or decrease? By how much?

P11-A4 *Depletion and natural resources* (L.O. 4)

1-2-3

The Creekside Coal Company purchased a tract of land, together with mineral rights, for $825,000. After incurring exploration costs of $675,000 and legal fees of $150,000, Creekside learned that 2.2 million tons of coal could be extracted from the site. The company estimates that production will be 200,000 tons during the first year and 125,000 tons each year thereafter. The mining site is estimated to have a residual value of $330,000.

Creekside plans to construct the necessary mining structures (buildings, sheds, and so on) on the site for $770,000. According to the contractor, the structures have a life of 20 years, with no residual value. The company does not intend to move the structures when production ceases. Finally, machinery and equipment must be acquired that costs $880,000, has a life of 20 years, and has a residual value of $20,000. The equipment will be moved to other company properties after the mine site is closed.

Instructions

a Determine the company's depletion and depreciation expense for each year the mine is anticipated to operate. Creekside will depreciate the structures by the units-of-output method and the machinery and equipment by the straight-line method.

b Assume that during the first year, 180,000 tons of coal were extracted from the mine. If sales were only 160,000 tons, calculate the total depletion charge and explain how it is treated in the financial statements.

c Assume that the following production has been attained: Year 1, 180,000 tons; Year 2, 170,000 tons; Year 3, 150,000 tons; Year 4, 110,000 tons; and Year 5, 90,000 tons. According to a new report received from the company geologist, one million tons of coal remain in the mine at the start of Year 6. Calculate the depletion charge per ton on future production.

P11-A5 *Intangibles: Acquisition cost and amortization* **(L.O. 5)**

The accounting records of Landmark Company revealed the following information:

- *Patents*—Purchased patent no. 158–12412 for $141,000 on June 1, 19X2. The patent had a seven-year legal life at acquisition and was expected to benefit Landmark for five years. The company incurred $6,000 of legal fees in connection with the purchase and governmental registration.

    At the beginning of January 19X3, Landmark registered an internally developed patent, no. 194–27325. Research and development costs related to the patent amounted to $92,735; legal and filing fees totaled $27,200. Management estimated a service life equal to the legal life granted by the government.

- *Franchise*—On April 1, 19X4, Landmark acquired a fast-food franchise by paying an initial fee of $44,000. (Similar franchises sell for $50,000.) The franchise agreement covered a 10-year period. As part of the agreement, Landmark paid $18,000 on April 1, 19X4, for interior improvements to the facility, which is being leased from a local developer. The lease expires on December 31, 19X7.

Instructions

a Prepare a schedule that shows the acquisition date, cost, service life, and yearly amortization of Landmark's intangibles.

b Compute the book value of the intangibles as of December 31, 19X5.

c Prepare a compound (combined) journal entry to amortize the intangibles for *19X6*.

P11-A6 *Goodwill* **(L.O. 5)**

After two years of negotiating between the owners, Haswell Enterprises agreed to purchase Estronia Company for $200,000. Key balance sheet data of Estronia on November 1, 19XX, the date of acquisition, follow.

Cash	$ 45,000
Accounts receivable	26,400
Inventories	82,000
Prepaid expenses	800
Land	80,000
Building	100,000
Equipment	20,000
Franchise	800
Accounts payable	61,000
Salaries payable	32,000
Mortgage payable	43,000

A probe of Estronia's records revealed the following:

1 The books were last closed on May 1, 19XX, the end of the company's accounting year. No adjustments have been made since that time.

2 The inventories include $18,000 of goods that are obsolete and will be given away to charity.

3 The receivables are overstated by $4,000.

4 Prepaid expenses of $600 have expired.

5 Current market values of property, plant, and equipment are as follows:

Land	$100,000
Building	85,000
Equipment	10,000

6 The franchise will render no future benefits to Haswell.

7 Salaries payable are understated by $5,000 because of a clerical error.

Instructions

a Calculate the amount Haswell paid for goodwill in the acquisition of Estronia.

b Prepare Haswell's journal entry to record the purchase of Estronia. Haswell paid $65,000 cash and issued a short-term note payable for the remaining balance.

c Generally speaking, what gives rise to goodwill?

Series B

P11-B1 *Cost incurred after purchase; disposals* **(L.O. 1, 2)**

Centerline Company had the following transactions and events during the year ended December 31, 19X4:

1 Discarded office furniture on January 1 at the local landfill. Subsidiary records showed that the furniture cost $400 and had accumulated depreciation of $350 at the end of 19X3. The furniture has been fully depreciated down to a residual value of $50 by the double-declining balance method.

2 On January 1, the company paid $46,000 for a new roof on its building. The new roof will extend the building's service life from an original estimate of 25 years to a total life of 30 years. The building originally cost $800,000, has a residual value of $300,000, and had accumulated depreciation at the end of 19X3 of $200,000. Straight-line depreciation is being used.

3 Sold store equipment on January 1 for $4,000 cash. The equipment cost $12,000 and had a book value of $5,000 as of December 31, 19X3.

4 Received a $6,480 land assessment because the city plans to install water and sewer lines to the property. The assessment was paid on March 1.

5 Repaired truck no. 10 on March 1 for $75. The accounting records revealed that the truck initially cost $28,000 and had accumulated depreciation at the beginning of 19X4 of $7,000. Depreciation is based on a four-year service life and zero residual value. The straight-line depreciation method has been used.

6 Added a radio unit to truck no. 10 on July 1. The unit cost $600, has no estimated residual value, and will be depreciated by the straight-line method. The radio will provide benefits to the company over the remaining life of the truck.

Instructions

a Prepare journal entries to record Centerline's transactions and events. Depreciation was last recorded on December 31, 19X3.

b Determine depreciation expense for the year ended December 31, 19X4, for the building and truck no. 10.

P11-B2 *Journal entries for disposals and exchanges* (L.O. 2, 3)

The information that follows relates to printing equipment that was purchased by Graphic Repro on December 1, 19X1:

Acquisition cost	$140,000
Residual value	20,000
Fair market value on:	
January 1, 19X8	45,000
August 1, 19X8	43,000
Estimated service life	8 years

The company depreciates all equipment by the straight-line method. Depreciation was last recorded on December 31, 19X7.

Instructions

Prepare all journal entries needed for the following independent situations:

a The equipment is sold for cash at an amount equal to its fair market value. The sale occurs on:

(1) January 1, 19X8.

(2) August 1, 19X8.

b Assume that the equipment is exchanged for similar equipment having an invoice price of $197,000, with Graphic paying the balance due in cash. The exchange occurs on:

(1) January 1, 19X8.

(2) August 1, 19X8.

c Ignoring any operating efficiencies and depreciation associated with the new equipment, would you expect Graphic to report the same net income in *19X9* under cases (a2) and (b2)? Briefly explain.

P11-B3 *Disposals and exchanges; analysis* (L.O. 2, 3)

Third Avenue Manufacturing disposed of five assets during the 19X2 fiscal year. Information pertaining to these assets follows.

1-2-3

Asset	Cost	Accumulated Depreciation	Cash Received (Paid)	Fair Market Value on Date of Disposal
Furniture	$ 2,800	$ 2,600	$ —	$ —
Computer	10,400	7,100	3,800	3,800
Truck	15,500	6,800	(7,800)	9,300
Building	86,700	15,400	95,000	95,000
Machine	37,500	22,800	(18,000)	14,000

A review of the accounting records revealed the following additional information:

- *Furniture*—The furniture was discarded at a local landfill.
- *Computer*—The computer was sold to Micromatic Systems, one of Third Avenue's suppliers.
- *Truck*—The truck was exchanged for a new truck that had an invoice price of $17,100.

■ *Building*—The building was destroyed by fire. Insurance proceeds, which were based on market value, amounted to $95,000.

■ *Machine*—The company acquired a new machine having a $42,000 invoice price. The machinery dealer took Third Avenue's old machine in trade along with $18,000 cash and a $10,000 note payable.

The company's accountant is in the process of computing net income for 19X2. She has determined that income before any gains and losses from asset disposals amounts to $34,800.

Instructions

a Compute Third Avenue's income after considering gains and losses on the five asset disposals.

b Suppose (1) the machine's fair market value amounted to $15,100 rather than $14,000 and (2) the invoice price of the new machine was $43,100. In view of these new data, will your answer in part (a) increase or decrease? By how much?

P11-B4 *Depletion and natural resources* **(L.O. 4)**

1-2-3

The Aztec Mining Company purchased a tract of land, together with mineral rights, for $155,000. After incurring exploration costs of $125,000 and legal fees of $20,000, Aztec learned that 140,000 tons of high-grade ore could be extracted from the site. The company estimates that production will be 20,000 tons each year. The mining site is anticipated to have a residual value of $20,000 since the land can be used for farming after all mining operations have ceased.

Aztec plans to construct the necessary mining structures (buildings, sheds, and bunkhouses) on the site for $154,000. According to the contractor, the structures will have a life of 20 years, with no residual value; they will be abandoned when production ceases. Finally, machinery and equipment must be acquired that costs $100,000, has a life of 10 years, and has a residual value of $10,000. All equipment will be moved to other company properties after the mine site is closed.

Instructions

a Determine the company's depletion and depreciation expense for each year the mine is anticipated to operate. Aztec will depreciate the structures by the units-of-output method and the machinery and equipment by the straight-line method.

b Assume that during the first year, 18,000 tons of ore were extracted from the mine. If sales were only 12,000 tons, calculate the total depletion charge and explain how it is treated in the financial statements.

c Assume that the following production has been attained: Year 1, 18,000 tons; Year 2, 18,000 tons; Year 3, 25,000 tons; Year 4, 15,000 tons; and Year 5, 30,000 tons. According to a new report received from the company geologist, 100,000 tons of ore remain in the mine at the start of Year 6. Calculate the depletion charge per ton on future production.

P11-B5 *Intangibles: Acquisition cost and amortization* **(L.O. 5)**

Selected 19X3 transactions of the San Jose Company follow.

Jan. 1 Paid $12,000 to purchase the patent rights to a product known as Servo. The patent has a remaining legal life of 10 years and should provide benefits to San Jose for two years.

Apr. 1 Acquired a patent to a new type of boxing glove that was developed in the company's research department. Paid $86,700 of related costs, as follows: legal and filing fees, $1,700; research and development expenditures, $85,000. The patent has an estimated service life equal to its legal life.

July 1   Installed wall partitions in a facility that the company is leasing from Iowa Enterprises. San Jose's lease expires on December 31, 19X6; the partitions cost $14,000.

Aug. 1   Acquired a perpetual franchise to promote sporting events within a 100-mile radius of the city in exchange for a $4,800 note payable. Similar franchises are currently selling for $9,000.

Sept. 1   Acquired the copyright to a play from the estate of the play's author for $3,600 cash. The author died 10 years ago; San Jose should receive benefits from the copyright for a three-year period.

Oct. 1   Registered a new trademark with the federal government; paid legal, filing, and design costs amounting to $10,000.

Instructions

a Prepare journal entries to record the preceding transactions.

b Compute San Jose's amortization expense for the year ended December 31, 19X3.

c Prepare a compound (combined) entry to amortize the intangibles for *19X4.*

P11-B6 *Goodwill* (L.O. 5)

After three years of negotiating between the owners, Michael English agreed to purchase Sports Gear for $40,000. Key balance sheet data of Sports Gear on December 1, 19XX, the date of acquisition, follow.

Cash	$ 3,000
Accounts receivable	38,000
Inventories	10,000
Prepaid expenses	1,000
Building	60,000
Equipment	11,000
Patent	40,000
Accounts payable	17,000
Bank loan payable	55,000

A probe of Sports Gear's records revealed the following:

1 The books were last closed on June 30, 19XX, the end of the company's accounting year. No adjustments have been made since that time.

2 The inventories include $2,000 of products that are defective and must be discarded.

3 Prepaid expenses of $500 have expired.

4 Current market values of the building and equipment are $28,000 and $4,000, respectively.

5 The patent, purchased four years ago, is related to a new type of stop watch. The patent's remaining legal life is 10 years; English believes the patent is worthless.

6 Accounts payable is overstated by $900 because of a clerical error.

Instructions

a Calculate the amount English paid for goodwill in the acquisition of Sports Gear.

b Prepare English's journal entry to record the purchase of Sports Gear. Assume that English paid $10,000 cash and issued a short-term note payable for the remaining balance.

c Should the goodwill be amortized? Why?

EDB11-1 *An overview of intangibles: Mattel, Inc., and Campbell Soup* (L.O. 5)

Mattel, Inc., is a leading manufacturer of toys. The company's main products (Barbie, large dolls, Disney infant and preschool toys, and die-cast vehicles) have accounted for approximately 80% of the firm's total volume over the past few years. Campbell Soup, in contrast, is involved with the manufacture of convenience foods and bakery products. Aside from its well-known Campbell's brand, the company also produces foods that are packaged under the following labels: Franco-American, Godiva, Mrs. Paul's, Pepperidge Farm, Swanson, V8, and Vlasic.

Instructions

By using the text's Electronic Data Base, access the balance sheets and accompanying notes of both firms and answer the questions that follow. Unless otherwise indicated, responses should be based on data for the most recent year presented.

a Both companies disclose property, plant, and equipment and intangibles on their balance sheets. How do the dollar amounts of these two long-term asset categories compare to total assets? Comment on your findings.

b Define the term "net" as used on the balance sheet when referring to a company's intangible assets.

c Review the notes that accompany the financial statements.
   (1) What are the major categories of intangibles disclosed by each firm?
   (2) Is goodwill described in unique terminology by either of the companies? Briefly explain.

d What amortization periods are used by these firms? Does it appear that the firms are following the rules stipulated by the accounting profession? Briefly discuss.

EDB11-2 *An overview of intangibles* (L.O. 5)

This problem is a duplication of Problem EDB11-1. It is based on two companies selected by your instructor.

Instructions

By using the text's Electronic Data Base, access the specified companies' balance sheets and accompanying notes and focus on data for the most recent year reported. Answer requirements (a)–(d) of Problem EDB11-1.

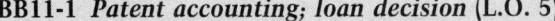

BB11-1 *Patent accounting; loan decision* (L.O. 5)

Dudley Finfrock is the assistant vice-president for commercial lending of the Maplewood National Bank. He has recently been approached by two aggressive companies for business loans. Both companies are engaged in high-technology product development and sales, but each company has used a different approach to achieve its ultimate profit objective.

Linden Electronics is run by two ex-employees of Woodhaven Semiconductor: Judy Brown and Stan Hall. Brown has an orientation toward research; Hall's specialty is sales. With an initial capital of $150,000, the two partners have developed many valuable products. Linden has spent over $80,000 on research and development and has obtained three patents from this effort. (Legal costs and filing fees connected with the patents were negligible because Linden's attorney is a family relative.) Advertising and sales promotion costs have consumed the remaining funds.

Rabway Electronics is also managed by two bright entrepreneurs: Harry Scott and Jack Monroe. Scott and Monroe were finance majors at the local university and possess minimal knowledge of electronics and sales. To establish a viable company, Rabway acquired existing patents from a California firm for $100,000. To generate sales, Scott and Monroe also purchased a franchise for $40,000 to sell a product similar to their own. In this manner the two products could be marketed together. Finally, Rabway spent $10,000 for legal fees related to the patents and franchise.

In the first few years of business, Linden operated at a net loss, while Rabway has generated impressive profits. A comparison of the financial statements and other operating information revealed that sales and production costs of the two companies were virtually identical. In addition, their products were very similar.

Instructions

a Explain the probable cause behind Linden's net losses and Rabway's profits.

b If you were in Dudley's position, would you grant a loan to either of the firms? What factors should be considered?

BB11-2 *Overview of chapter concepts: Multiple choice* (L.O. 1-5)

The following multiple-choice questions relate to various topics discussed in the chapter. Select the best answer.

1 James Company accidentally treated a capital expenditure as a revenue expenditure. Given this error, determine which of the following comments is false.
  a The current period's balance sheet will be in error.
  b The current period's income statement will be in error.
  c Balance sheets of future periods will be in error.
  d Balance sheets of future periods will not be affected.

2 The cost of extraordinary repairs is typically recorded:
  a in the same manner as an assessment or addition.
  b by a charge to an asset account.
  c by a charge to Accumulated Depreciation.
  d by the immediate expensing of the amounts involved.

3 Benson Company, a communications firm, sold for cash an automobile that cost $14,000 and had a book value of $6,500. The sales price was sufficient to produce a $2,000 gain. Which of the following would not be included in the journal entry to record the transaction?
  a A debit to Accumulated Depreciation for $7,500.
  b A credit to Gain on Disposal for $2,000.
  c A debit to Cash for $9,500.
  d A credit to Automobiles for $14,000.

4 Equipment with a book value of $10,000 was exchanged for similiar equipment having an invoice price of $15,000. If no cash was involved, this transaction:
  a gives rise to a $5,000 gain that should be recognized.
  b gives rise to a $5,000 gain that should not be recognized.
  c gives rise to a $5,000 loss that should be recognized.
  d requires that the new equipment be recorded at $15,000.

5 Which of the following comments about depletion and natural resources is incorrect?
  a The depletion computation is similar to the computation for units-of-output depreciation.

b A railroad track built to haul copper from a mine should be depreciated over its 20-year life rather than the anticipated 16-year life of the
mine.

c Depletion related to unsold ore should be reported on the balance
sheet as part of the ore's cost.

d Natural resources are initially entered in the accounting records at
cost.

6 Depreciation is to a truck as:
   a amortization is to a patent.
   b amortization is to an oil well.
   c depletion is to a trademark.
   d depletion is to land.

7 Which of the following comments about goodwill is false?
   a Goodwill may be amortized over a life as long as 40 years.
   b Goodwill is calculated by comparing the purchase price of a business
     to the fair value of the identifiable assets acquired, minus liabilities
     assumed.
   c The amount of goodwill may be influenced by an acquired company's
     business reputation.
   d If managers of Simon Corporation believe that the business has in-
     creased in value due to the opening of a neighboring shopping mall,
     Simon may enter goodwill in its accounting records.

8 Amortization of an intangible should occur over the:
   a service life of the intangible, not to exceed 40 years.
   b legal life of the intangible, not to exceed 40 years.
   c service life of the intangible, unless the service life is less than the
     legal life.
   d legal life of the intangible, unless the legal life exceeds the service life
     by more than 40 years.

CAI11-1 *Preparing a speech: Bristol-Myers Squibb Company* (L.O. 5)

**COMMUNICATION OF
ACCOUNTING
INFORMATION**

Communication Principle: The most important part of any speech is the
introduction. In addition to stating the purpose of the speech, an effective introduction accomplishes these objectives: gains the listeners' attention, relates the subject(s) to the listeners' personal interests,
establishes the credibility of the speaker, and creates a friendly, at-ease
relationship with the audience.

One or more of the following techniques may be used to get the listeners' attention: recite short, dramatic quotations; tell stories or tasteful
jokes; present startling statistics; or use visual aids. Upon completing
this step, the speaker should preview the major points to be covered. The
points should be numbered, and the list should be short—no more than
three or four major issues for a 30-minute presentation. A visual aid is
very useful here.

When "show time" arrives, the introduction should not be read. The
remarks should be memorized and practiced until they sound spontane-
ous. By talking directly to the audience, the speaker will establish a
friendly, warm, and natural relationship—the equivalent of an inviting
style in writing. This approach will dramatically increase the chances of
an effective delivery.

As explained in the body of this chapter, goodwill means different things to different groups of people. In accounting, though, a specific meaning is attached to the term—one that often appears on the balance sheet itself. Consider the case of Bristol-Myers Squibb, which produces many consumer and health-care products (such as Clairol, Windex, and Bufferin). The company uses several descriptive account titles in its financial statements. One of these, Excess of Cost Over Net Tangible Assets Received in Business Acquisitions, is essentially a replacement for goodwill. A related note goes on to say:

> The excess of cost over net tangible assets received in business acquisitions . . . is being amortized on a straight-line basis over periods not exceeding forty years.

Instructions

You are about to prepare a short speech that will be delivered to a group of consumer advocates. The topic is the need for user-friendly annual reports, such as the one published by Bristol-Myers Squibb. (Be sure to cite and thank the company for its efforts.) A small portion of the talk will be devoted to the appropriateness of the firm's amortization policy. Write the introduction to the speech in full and outline the remainder.

Answers to Chapter Quiz

1 d

2 a

3 b ($10 million ÷ 4 million ounces = $2.50 per ounce; 5,000 ounces × $2.50 = $12,500)

4 c ($102,000 ÷ 2 years = $51,000)

5 d

COMPREHENSIVE PROBLEM 2

LaSorda Company's management has always relied on very conservative accounting policies, resulting in the following balance sheet as of December 31, 19X8:

LASORDA COMPANY

LASORDA COMPANY Balance Sheet December 31, 19X8		
Assets		
Current assets		
Cash		$ 15,000
Short-term investments in stock	$ 45,000	
Less: Allowance for decline in market value	5,000	40,000
Accounts receivable	$ 75,000	
Less: Allowance for uncollectibles	7,500	67,500
Inventory		125,000
Total current assets		$247,500
Property, plant, & equipment		
Land	$ 85,000	
Buildings	$289,000	
Less: Accumulated depreciation	78,319	210,681
Equipment	$ 80,000	
Less: Accumulated depreciation	48,000	32,000
Total property, plant, & equipment		327,681
Intangibles		
Patent		28,000
Total assets		$603,181
Liabilities & Owner's Equity		
Current liabilities		
Accounts payable		$ 22,000
Salaries payable		7,000
Taxes payable		8,000
Total current liabilities		$ 37,000
Long-term liabilities		
Bank loans payable		115,000
Total liabilities		$152,000
Owner's equity		
George LaSorda, capital		451,181
Total liabilities & owner's equity		$603,181

George LaSorda, founder of the company, has been approached by a party desiring to buy the firm at a price equal to 200% of owner's equity. George agreed that the price would be fair if owner's equity were revised to reflect the following:

■ *Short-term investments*—The market value of the short-term investments was $85,000 on December 31, 19X8. The reported cost of $45,000 was accurate; however, the $5,000 allowance was established long ago, and investment values have since recovered. This recovery has never been recognized. George desires to report the company's holdings at the market value of $85,000.

■ *Accounts receivable*—The Allowance account is presently equal to 10% of the outstanding receivables balance. LaSorda believes that the company should estimate uncollectible accounts at 2% of the firm's sales ($400,000). The balance in the Allowance account at the begining of the year was $3,000, and customer write-offs during 19X8 totaled $7,000.

■ *Inventory*—Inventory is valued by using the LIFO method. George reports that income for the last three years would have been $45,500 higher had FIFO been employed. (The company is only three years old.) LaSorda desires to use FIFO when calculating the revised owner's equity figure.

■ *Buildings*—The company's three-year-old buildings are being depreciated by the double-declining balance method, based on a 20-year life and $30,000 residual value. George believes the straight-line method would be more appropriate.

■ *Equipment*—The equipment, which is two years old and has no residual value, is being written off by the sum-of-the-years'-digits method over a five-year life. Again, George prefers the straight-line method.

■ *Patent*—The patent was acquired for $28,000 at the beginning of the current year. George believes that this intangible should not be amortized and desires to report the patent at acquisition cost. The original service life of the intangible should have been estimated at 10 years.

Instructions

a Which of George's preferences violate generally accepted accounting procedures? Briefly explain the reason for the violation.

b Why would the accelerated depreciation methods used by this relatively new company be viewed as "more conservative" than the straight-line method?

c Prepare the balance sheet and compute the purchase price that would result if George's preferences were used. Use generally accepted accounting procedures throughout, especially where George's alternatives are technically incorrect. (*Hint:* All changes in the company's income will be reflected by changes in the owner's capital balance.)

d Compare your answer in part (c) with the original balance sheet. Why do you think George wants to eliminate some of the conservatism from the financial statements?

CHAPTER
12

Current Liabilities and Payroll

LEARNING OBJECTIVES

After studying this chapter, you should be able to:

1

Explain the occurrence of and accounting for
typical current liabilities of a business.

2

Account for notes payable when interest is included in the face
value of a note and when interest is recorded separately.

3

Identify typical contingent liabilities and recognize the guidelines that
are used for recording such obligations in the accounts.

4

Prepare journal entries for warranty costs.

5

Calculate and record payroll, including the
employer's tax obligation.

The five preceding chapters have presented various valuation and income determination issues related to current and long-term assets. We now turn our attention to another important element of the fundamental accounting equation: liabilities. **Liabilities** are obligations that (1) have arisen from past transactions or events and (2) are payable in cash, other assets, or services. The measurement and disclosure of liabilities in the financial statements are extremely important because future cash outlays or services are involved. Many suppliers, for example, refuse to grant credit to businesses that have high levels of liabilities for fear of nonpayment. Similarly, most investors shy away from companies heavily burdened by debt because of the risk involved. Substantial debt payments are often accompanied by large outlays for interest, which reduce an investor's chance of receiving dividends. Adding to this problem is the fact that the firm's cash position may be extremely weak in periods of a softening economy.

Be aware that a *commitment* for goods and services is not recognized in the accounting records as a liability. For instance, Whirlpool Corporation, the appliance manufacturer, may sign a three-year labor contract with its hourly personnel. The contract represents a mutual agreement for a future transaction: wages will be paid at the time a service is provided. Note that upon contract signing, Whirlpool's assets have not changed nor does the company owe specific resources for work performed. Consistent with the definition of a liability—an obligation that arises from transactions or events *that have occurred*—the contract is not entered into the accounts.[1]

Earlier in the text we noted that liabilities are classified as either current or long term, depending on the due date (or dates). We will discuss current liabilities in this chapter and long-term obligations in Chapter 17.

CURRENT LIABILITIES

OBJECTIVE

1

Explain the occurrence of and accounting for typical current liabilities of a business.

Current liabilities are debts or obligations that will be paid within one year or the operating cycle, whichever is longer. Payment of current liabilities involves the use of current assets (usually cash) or, on occasion, the creation of another current liability. For example, an account payable could be settled by issuing a short-term interest-bearing note to the creditor.

Current liabilities are reported on the balance sheet at the amount necessary to settle the obligation. Naturally, it is imperative that all debts and obligations be disclosed. The failure to record a current liability not only understates total liabilities but affects assets or expenses as well. Because management may deliberately try to boost net income by hiding unpaid bills, accountants must take great care in their recognition of an entity's short-term debts.

Typical current liabilities include the following:

1 Accounts payable
2 Prepayments (advances) by customers
3 Amounts collected for and payable to third parties
4 The portion of long-term debt due within one year or the operating cycle, whichever is longer

---

[1] Such amounts are sometimes disclosed in the notes that accompany the financial statements.

have happened

5 Accrued liabilities for <u>expenses incurred but not yet paid</u> –

6 Short-term notes payable to banks and other parties

7 Contingent liabilities

Accounts Payable

Accounts payable, sometimes called *trade accounts payable,* represent <u>amounts owed to suppliers for the purchase of goods or services</u>. The creation of these short-term obligations was discussed in Chapter 5.

Most accounting systems are capable of recording trade payables when goods and services are acquired or rendered. More often than not, however, the payable is recorded when an invoice is received from the supplier. Unfortunately, delays, timing differences, and errors frequently permeate the process. For example, the invoice may sit in an in-basket for a few days awaiting processing. Or goods purchased under terms of F.O.B. shipping point may still be in transit at the end of the period. Although the goods legally belong to the purchaser because title has passed, the liability (and inventory) may be erroneously overlooked. After all, there would be no paperwork documenting the goods' arrival at the warehouse, and there is a strong possibility that the purchaser has yet to be invoiced. Because of these and other problems, the accountant must pay particular attention to transactions that occur at the beginning and end of an accounting period. By so doing, the purchases of goods and services (and their associated liabilities) will be correctly entered in the records.

Prepayments (Advances) by Customers

Businesses often receive **prepayments,** or advances, from customers. Insurance companies collect premiums; publishers sell magazine subscriptions; stores issue gift certificates; and transportation firms sell tickets and tokens before their service is delivered. These amounts, frequently termed *unearned revenues* or *deferred revenues,* represent liabilities to the recipient because goods or services are owed in return. You were originally introduced to unearned revenues in Chapter 3 and may find a review of this earlier material helpful.

The balance sheet should report the amount of goods and services owed as of the statement's date. As the obligations are settled, the prepayments are reduced and increased revenues are reported on the income statement. Prepayments for most businesses are relatively modest in amount; however, there are exceptions. In a recent set of financial statements, for instance, Allstate Insurance reported unearned premiums in excess of $5 billion!

Collections for Third Parties

In the normal course of business, organizations often collect money from customers and employees that is payable to others. Retailers, for instance, accumulate sales tax from customers when goods are sold. Subsequently, the monies collected are remitted to the proper governmental authority. Similarly, companies sometimes become involved in United Way or disaster relief activities, receiving funds that are ultimately disbursed to various social service agencies. And, as shown later in this chapter, taxes and other items are customarily deducted from employee wages and forwarded to third parties.

Collections for third parties, such as those just mentioned, are recognized as current liabilities until cash is disbursed to the proper authority. To illustrate the necessary accounting, assume that Yorktown Candle Shoppe sells $1,000 of merchandise on account in a state having a 5% sales tax. The entry to record the sale follows.

Accounts Receivable	1,050	
Sales		1,000
Sales Taxes Payable		50
To record sale and related sales tax		

A liability of $50 ($1,000 × 0.05) is established for the sales tax, which Yorktown now owes to the state treasury. When the tax is remitted, Sales Taxes Payable will be debited and Cash will be credited. The liability is thus eliminated. Other third-party collections are handled in a similar manner.

Current Portion of Long-Term Debt

As we noted, long-term liabilities will be discussed at length in another chapter. At this point, however, it is important to understand that the portion of long-term debt due within one year or the normal operating cycle, whichever is longer, is reported as a current liability. For example, suppose that a company borrowed $200,000 via a long-term loan. If $30,000 is payable within the next 12 months, the appropriate balance sheet disclosure would be as follows:

Current liabilities		
Current portion of long-term debt		$ 30,000
Long-term liabilities		
Loan payable	$200,000	
Less: Balance due currently	30,000	170,000

Treatment as a current liability presumes that the short-term portion will be liquidated by the use of current assets or by the creation of other current liabilities. If not, such amounts remain classified as long-term liabilities until paid or refinanced.

Accrued Liabilities

Accrued liabilities, often called accrued expenses, were also introduced in Chapter 3. Under the accrual basis of accounting, expenses are matched against revenues in the period when incurred. This practice generally results in the recognition of some unpaid expenses and calls for the placement of accrued liabilities on the balance sheet. Examples of accrued liabilities include salaries and wages, vacation pay, income taxes (both federal and state), and interest. To demonstrate the required accounting, we now present illustrations involving salaries and vacation pay.

Accrued Salaries

Accrued salaries and wages result when a reporting period ends in the midst of a payroll period. For example, suppose that Rosenthal Company has a five-day workweek and all employees are paid on Friday. Also assume that the end of the annual accounting period, November 30, falls on Thursday. Although employees will not be compensated until December 1, Rosenthal must accrue payroll expense on November 30 for the work performed from Monday through Thursday. In so doing, revenue and expense for the period just ended will be correctly matched, and current liabilities will be properly recorded. If salaries total $10,500 per day, the adjusting entry is as follows:

Salaries Expense	42,000	
Salaries Payable		42,000
To accrue four days of salaries at $10,500 per day*		

* Payroll taxes should also be accrued at this time.

Accrued Vacation Pay

Many businesses provide paid vacations for their employees. By working 50 weeks throughout the year, for instance, a worker may earn two weeks of paid time-off. From the employer's viewpoint, such fringe benefit plans increase the total cost of employee service—in this particular case by 4% of wage cost $(2 \div 50)$.

Proper accounting treatment requires that the cost of (and obligation for) paid vacations be spread over the entire year so that each reporting period receives an equal share of expense. Imagine the total compensation expense that many companies would experience in July and August if businesses did not follow this practice. The popularity of summer vacations could very well result in depressed earnings for the third calendar quarter. Because employees earn the paid time-off by working *throughout the year,* such amounts should be accrued as services are performed.

To illustrate, assume that Prestonwood Company has a two-week paid vacation plan and monthly salaries of $90,000. In view of personnel turnover, the firm estimates that only 60% of the employees will be entitled to this fringe benefit. Prestonwood's monthly vacation pay accrual will amount to $2,160 ($90,000 × 0.04 × 0.60) and is recorded by the following journal entry:

Vacation Pay Expense	2,160	
Estimated Liability for Vacation Pay		2,160
To record estimated vacation pay expense		

The Estimated Liability for Vacation Pay account is disclosed in the current liability section of the balance sheet and is reduced when actual vacations are taken. For example, assume that Prestonwood now disburses $400 to an employee during her paid time-off. The disbursement is recorded as a debit to the Estimated Liability account and a credit to Cash.

Notes Payable

Short-term notes have many uses in the business world. Notes payable are often employed to finance purchases of merchandise, equipment, real estate, and other similar assets. In addition, notes can be used to secure short-term borrowings from banks. General Mills, for instance, recently reported notes payable to banks of $19.7 million on its year-end balance sheet. Such temporary use of bank credit for periods of less than one year is commonplace and serves as a major source of funds for many businesses.

Notes payable are also issued at the request of creditors when a firm (or individual) is past due in the payment of an account payable. The note is simply substituted for the account payable on the books of the issuing entity. A creditor prefers a note to a delinquent open account: should the issuer fail to pay the debt on schedule, a signed note provides better security if legal remedies are necessary.

Accounting for Notes Payable

To illustrate the proper accounting for notes payable, assume that Corsica Trading Corporation borrowed $80,000 from the Mercantile National Bank on June 3 by signing the obligation shown in Exhibit 12-1. The journal entry to record the receipt of funds and issuance of the note follows.

Cash	80,000	
Notes Payable		80,000
To record note payable to bank;		
180 days at 15%		

Observe that the face value of the note is equal to the amount borrowed and that no interest expense is recorded on the date of issue. Interest will be incurred on a daily basis over the term of the loan.

Next, assume that Corsica's fiscal year ends on October 31. Because the note was issued on June 3 and does not mature until November 30, total interest expense must be apportioned between two accounting periods. As of October 31, the obligation has been outstanding for 150 days, requiring the following adjusting entry:

Interest Expense	5,000	
Interest Payable		5,000
To accrue interest for 150 days:		

$80,000 \times 0.15 \times \frac{150}{360}$

EXHIBIT 12-1
Example of Note Payable

Date <u>June 3, 19XX</u>   New York, New York 10059

For value received, the undersigned promises to pay the Mercantile National Bank in <u>180 days</u> the sum of <u>$80,000</u>, with interest at the rate of <u>15%</u> per year.

R. B. Thompson

Corsica Trading Corporation

Corsica's balance sheet disclosure would therefore appear as shown below.

Current liabilities

:
:

| Notes payable | $80,000 | |
| Interest payable | 5,000 | $85,000 |

When the note is paid on November 30, the following entry is necessary:

Notes Payable	80,000	
Interest Payable	5,000	
Interest Expense	1,000	
Cash		86,000

To record payment to bank for
note payable and interest

The additional $1,000 represents the 30 days of interest incurred in November ($\frac{1}{6}$ of the loan term).

Notes with Interest Included in the Face Value

Many notes, especially those issued to banks and finance companies, do not state interest separately. Instead, interest is included in the obligation's face value. For example, assume that Corsica Trading still needs to raise $80,000. Mercantile National Bank, however, agreed to accept the $86,000 note that appears in Exhibit 12-2.

Corsica's entry to record the proceeds and issue the note follows.

Cash	80,000	
Discount on Notes Payable	6,000	
Notes Payable		86,000

To record note payable to bank;
180 days until maturity

As in the previous case, the obligation is recorded at face value—$86,000 in this instance. Cash received remains at $80,000. The difference between these two figures, $6,000, represents 180 days of future interest, which will be incurred over the term of the note. This amount is entered in an account entitled Discount on Notes Payable, a **contra liability** that is deducted from Notes Payable on the balance sheet. If a balance sheet was prepared

---

Date June 3, 19XX   New York, New York   10059

For value received, the undersigned promises to pay the Mercantile National Bank
the sum of $86,000 in 180 days .

R. B. Thompson

Corsica Trading Corporation

**EXHIBIT 12-2
Note Payable with Interest
Included in the Face Value**

immediately after issuance, Corsica would present the following information:

Current liabilities
Notes payable	$86,000	
Less: Discount on notes payable	6,000	$80,000

The net liability on June 3 is $80,000—the amount borrowed on that day.

Discount Amortization.   Assume it is now October 31, the end of Corsica's fiscal year. Because 150 days have passed since the note's issuance, interest expense must be recognized. As we just stated, the discount's $6,000 balance represents 180 days of future interest charges. Thus, $5,000 ($6,000 × $\frac{150}{180}$) must be removed from the Discount account and transferred to the income statement. The following adjusting entry is needed:

Interest Expense	5,000	
Discount on Notes Payable		5,000
To accrue interest for 150 days and		
amortize the discount		

The process of reducing the discount by recognizing interest expense is frequently referred to as **discount amortization.**

As a result of the adjustment, the Discount on Notes Payable account will have a $1,000 balance ($6,000 − $5,000) and will appear on the balance sheet as shown.

Current liabilities
Notes payable	$86,000	
Less: Discount on notes payable	1,000	$85,000

The net liability is now $85,000: $80,000 borrowed plus accrued interest of $5,000. A separate account for interest payable is *not* established because the interest is already part of the note's face value.

To complete the example, the following entry would be necessary when Corsica pays the note on November 30:

Notes Payable	86,000	
Interest Expense	1,000	
Discount on Notes Payable		1,000
Cash		86,000
To record payment of the note and		
amortize the discount		

This entry recognizes the remaining $1,000 of interest expense that pertains to November and cancels the balance in the Notes Payable account.

Tips & Techniques

A careful observation will reveal that Corsica received $80,000 and ultimately paid $6,000 of interest with *both* notes. Furthermore, both balance sheet presentations at the end of the October 31 fiscal year revealed a total liability of $85,000. To conclude, the notes differed in form only. In the first case, interest was stated separately; in the second case, interest was included in the obligation's face value.

Contingent Liabilities

The liabilities presented thus far have been definite and absolute. Although estimates were sometimes involved (see the vacation pay discussion as an example), there was no uncertainty regarding a company's legal and economic responsibility for the obligation.

Several situations in accounting give rise to a *potential* liability. As we saw in Chapter 8, for instance, the payee of a discounted note receivable was liable to the bank if the maker defaulted and dishonored the note. As another example, businesses are frequently the target of litigation, the outcome of which is sometimes unknown at the time of financial statement preparation. To illustrate this latter situation, consider the following excerpted footnote from a recent annual report of MCI, the giant telecommunications firm:

> The company is a party to a number of lawsuits and other proceedings arising out of the conduct of its business, including certain regulatory proceedings. While the ultimate results of lawsuits or other proceedings cannot be predicted with certainty, the company's management does not expect that these matters will have a material adverse effect on the consolidated financial position or results of operations of the company.
>
> In 1990, certain stockholders of the company filed an action in the United States District Court for the District of Columbia alleging that the company and three of its officers violated securities laws by making material misstatements of, or omitting to state, material facts relating to [the firm's] financial condition and prospects. Although the action is in its early stages, the company believes the claims to be without merit and is defending the action vigorously.

Liabilities of this nature are commonly referred to as **contingent liabilities,** because their outcome hinges on the future. Future events and happenings will convert the contingency into an absolute liability or eliminate it entirely. In addition to discounted notes receivable and lawsuits, other contingent liabilities include obligations related to product warranties and coupon redemptions.

Accounting Rules for Contingencies

Over the years, the treatment of contingent liabilities has been the subject of much debate. Sometimes, contingent liabilities were recorded in the accounts by a journal entry. On other occasions, disclosure was made in the footnotes that accompany the financial statements. On still other occasions, nothing was done for fear of misleading statement users about a liability that might never materialize. This last approach apparently followed the "no news is good news" doctrine.

Because of the wide diversity in treatments, guidelines were eventually issued to "standardize" the accounting for contingent liabilities.[2] The guidelines stipulated that contingent liabilities should be recorded in the accounts when (1) it is *probable* that the future event will occur and (2) the amount of the liability can be *reasonably estimated*. Observe the key words in italics. If only one of these criteria is met, no journal entry is made; a footnote to the financial statements is usually deemed appropriate.

[2] See "Accounting for Contingencies," *Statement of Financial Accounting Standards No. 5* (Norwalk, Conn.: Financial Accounting Standards Board, 1975).

ETHICS ISSUE

S, Inc., is having a bad year financially. To help improve reported performance, management has suggested burying the effects of a significant contingent liability in the notes to the financial statements. A manager was heard saying: ". . . Instead of deriving a reasonable estimate of the financial impact, which we know will be subject to error, simply say that no estimate is possible." Comment.

By their very nature, these criteria are vague and open to interpretation. For example, how does one determine the likelihood of an event's occurrence? What differentiates a *probable* event, as stated in the guidelines, from one that is "reasonably possible"? Also, what is considered a *reasonable* estimate? Because of the subjectivity involved, the accountant cannot work in isolation. Close contact with engineers, lawyers, and other professionals is necessary to implement these rules correctly.

Warranty Costs

To illustrate accounting for a contingent liability that typically meets both guidelines, we will focus on warranty costs. A **warranty** is a promise made by a seller or manufacturer to remedy defects in product quality and performance. Most appliances, for example, are warranted for one year; the major components of automobiles sometimes have a 50,000-mile warranty.

The cost of warranties can normally be estimated, with reasonable accuracy, on the basis of past experience. Because most warranties help to promote the sale of goods and services, such costs should be matched against revenues in the period of sale. At this same time a contingent liability must be entered in the accounts—to recognize that a firm has a potential exposure to warranty work as some of its products become defective.

For example, assume that Drake Electronics began to stock a new camera model late in 19X1. The camera has a two-year warranty; 200 units were sold during the year. Drake estimates that 15% of the cameras will require repair work and that the work will average $40 per unit. The journal entry on December 31 to record the estimated warranty cost of $1,200 (200 units × 0.15 × $40) and establish the liability is as follows:

test

Warranty Expense	1,200	
Estimated Liability for Warranties		1,200
To record warranty costs for 19X1		

As the warranties are honored, Drake will reduce the liability. If 10 cameras are serviced during 19X2, the following journal entry becomes necessary:

Estimated Liability for Warranties	400	
Cash, Salaries Payable, Parts Inventory, and so on		400
To record service cost under warranties: 10 cameras × $40		

The Estimated Liability for Warranties account would be reported on the December 31, 19X2, balance sheet at $800 ($1,200 − $400). This amount represents the estimated warranty cost in 19X3 of servicing units sold in 19X1.

Balance Sheet Disclosure

Current liabilities are normally listed on the balance sheet according to due date (from the earliest to the latest) or maturity value (from the largest to the smallest). Reporting practices vary widely, however. To illustrate a typical disclosure, we present the current liability section from a recent

HIGHLIGHT
Clean It Up!

American Cyanamid is involved in legal proceedings over pollution cleanup at approximately 60 sites. How do we know? Because we searched through the notes tucked away in the back of Cyanamid's latest annual report. A note informs us that the $4.6 billion (revenue) biotechnology and chemical company may face "substantial" cleanup costs. Substantial? What does that mean? Ten million dollars, perhaps? Or several hundred million dollars, enough to wipe out an entire year's earnings? The firm doesn't say.

We're not picking on Cyanamid. It has plenty of company. Such vagueness on the subject of environmental liabilities isn't rare, unfortunately. Most businesses offer some kind of boilerplate in their annual report, but they differ widely on how promptly to reveal a problem, or how much to say about it. In most cases, says an industry analyst, "we don't get very much specific disclosure."

The nation's accounting rulemakers have not provided guidelines on when and how to disclose the mess in your backyard. The applicable accounting rule is an old (1975) standard on the broad subject of contingent liabilities. [As pointed out by your authors,] the standard contains some ambiguous provisions. As partial evidence, a recent survey of 125 industrial companies found that just over a third disclosed their environmental problems to shareholders as soon as federal or state regulators tapped them on the shoulder. Some others disclosed before such notification.

Accounting guidelines say that as soon as a company considers a liability "probable" and reasonably estimable, it must start accruing charges—that is, deducting amounts from today's earnings to cover the future expense. But "reasonably estimated" is vague. Some companies seem to take advantage of this by recognizing the deductions when it's most convenient. Not too long ago, for example, Occidental Petroleum lumped $720 million of environmental charges into a $2.2 billion pretax big bath for "restructuring costs." Others wait for strong earnings before releasing the news.

Not all the blame rests with the companies or their accountants. It sometimes takes the bureaucrats at the Environmental Protection Agency as long as 18 to 30 months to come up with estimates for different cleanup alternatives. There's also uncertainty as to whether a company's insurer will cover some or all of the costs. And lawsuits with suppliers or neighbors have yet to be resolved.

Still, the looming threat is a matter that greatly concerns investors, and they deserve better than they are getting in the way of timely warning. Environmental risks are part of the landscape today, and corporate management will have to face the risks. The chairman of the Financial Accounting Standards Board agrees "there will be a call for more standard setting." He warns, though, that the task is a difficult one. No two oil spills, asbestos hazards, or landfill situations are the same. Nevertheless, he hopes the standard setters will address the issue sometime within the next few years. We'd suggest sooner.

"In the end, it's all judgment," argues a spokesman from an international public accounting firm. True, but investors are entitled to some help in judging the risks.

Source: Adapted from "Messy Accounting," *Forbes*, October 14, 1991, pp. 172, 174. Excerpted by permission of *Forbes* magazine, © Forbes Inc., 1991.

EXHIBIT 12-3
Current Liability Presentation
(in millions)

UNITED TECHNOLOGIES	
Current liabilities	
Short-term borrowings	$ 292
Accounts payable	1,839
Accrued salaries, wages, and employee benefits	943
Accrued restructuring costs	488
Other accrued liabilities	1,758
Long-term debt—currently due	198
Income taxes currently payable	442
Advances on sales contracts	617
Total current liabilities	$6,577

balance sheet of United Technologies, perhaps best known for the manufacture of Pratt & Whitney aircraft engines, Carrier air conditioning systems, Otis elevators, and Sikorsky helicopters (see Exhibit 12-3).

ACCOUNTING FOR PAYROLL

OBJECTIVE

5

Calculate and record payroll, including the employer's tax obligation.

Employees' wages, salaries, related payroll taxes, and fringe benefits are a significant expense for many businesses, particularly those engaged in providing services. For example, Federal Express recently reported employee compensation and benefits amounting to 44.7% of operating revenues. At H&R Block, salaries and related expenses of $559.4 million constituted over 57% of total operating expenses. Accounting for payroll is important not only because large amounts of money are involved but also because various federal and state regulations must be met. By law, businesses must maintain detailed payroll information on individual employees and aggregate information for the entity as a whole.

Computerized Payroll Systems

As a result of the demanding requirements that pertain to payroll record keeping, most companies use computers to process payroll data. Software for in-house microcomputers is readily available at modest prices. Externally, the processing can be done by data processing "service bureaus" (i.e., companies for hire) and even by banks.

Payroll is typically one of the first business functions to be computerized because of the large amount of detailed bookkeeping involved. An overview of the related procedures conveys the impression (and rightly so) that payroll is a labor-intensive chore. Computerization of the payroll function can help a company trim the size of its office staff and/or free up the staff to work on other, more pressing business matters. The computer offers the benefits of processing speed and accuracy, along with the capability of rapid response to system queries. Managers may need weekly data, possibly subdivided by plant or division, to help control operations. Or data may be required to satisfy the requests of governmental agencies when such agencies are studying an entity's compliance (or lack of) with various labor laws. The use of computers assists in meeting these requests and needs on an accurate and timely basis.

Internal Control

Payroll processing systems, whether manual or computerized, must contain strong internal controls to safeguard funds and ensure accurate record keeping. An absence of controls will often lead to a high frequency of errors and, on occasion, fraud. Ingenious embezzlement schemes have involved the issuance of checks to fictitious employees, duplicate paychecks, paychecks to persons who have been terminated or have voluntarily quit, and overpayments to existing personnel. Although several of these schemes may appear to have a low probability of success, keep in mind that in large organizations, communication among departments may often be lacking. Further, payroll is sometimes processed hundreds of miles from a company facility (e.g., manufacturing plant) by personnel who are totally removed from the facility's daily operating activities.

Internal controls must be implemented to guard against such misappropriations. In addition, an entity's payroll system must be sufficiently developed so that records are correctly maintained for new employees, employees who receive promotions, and employees who earn wage and salary increases.

Employees and Independent Contractors

For purposes of payroll accounting, an organization must distinguish between employees and independent contractors. The distinction is important because payroll regulations, whether they pertain to taxes, reporting, or record keeping, apply solely to the employees of an entity. **Employees** are persons who work for a specific business and are directed and closely supervised by that business. **Independent contractors,** on the other hand, frequently perform services for many different organizations at the same time or perhaps finish a project for one firm and then move on to service another. Common examples of independent contractors include certified public accountants, attorneys, management consultants, and architects. Observe that an employer/employee relationship does not exist in these situations. Rather the independent contractor is engaged to provide a service, performs that service without direct supervision from the client, and receives a fee in return.

Employee Earnings

Wages and salaries earned by employees develop either from a negotiated contract between a company and representatives of its employees or from a direct agreement between the company and individual personnel. The former situation is usually encountered for a firm's labor force; the latter relates most often to management.

The wages and salaries earned are paid after the payroll period has concluded. Accurate record keeping is a must, especially for personnel paid by the hour or on the basis of piecework. Time cards, time clocks, and electronic recording systems are commonly used to ensure that each hourly worker is compensated correctly. For employees who receive wages based on productivity, a daily report must be generated that indicates the output and operations performed.

Proper determination of an employee's hours or output is the first step in the calculation of total, or **gross earnings.** Gross earnings are dependent on many factors, including federal regulations and company policy. According to the Federal Fair Labor Standards Act,[3] for example, businesses engaged in interstate commerce must pay overtime of at least one and one-half times the regular rate for hours worked in excess of 40 per week. In addition, many companies establish their own policies and pay premium rates for work on night shifts, split shifts, holidays, and Sundays.

To illustrate the calculation of gross earnings, assume that Paula Hite worked 52 hours during a weekly payroll period at Ajax Fabricators. Paula is paid $10 per hour, and the company compensates for overtime at one and one-half times the regular hourly rate. Paula's gross pay for the week would be $580: [(40 hours × $10) + (12 hours × $15)].

Deductions from Employee Earnings

As many of you know, an employee's **take-home (net) pay** is less than his or her gross pay. And normally it is much less! These two amounts differ because of required tax withholdings by the employer and voluntary deductions that have been authorized by the employee. We will now focus on several common deductions.

Social Security/Medicare Taxes (FICA)

Retirement, financial, and medical benefits are provided to the aged, disabled, survivors, and orphans under the **Federal Insurance Contributions Act (FICA).** Employers are required to withhold a portion of each employee's gross earnings to help fund these government programs. Additionally, the employer must match the employee's contributions. As an example, assume that Kathy Durham earns $24,000 and that all of her earnings are subject to FICA taxes. If the proper FICA computation yields, say, $1,800, this amount will be withheld from Durham's paychecks. A total of $3,600 will ultimately be remitted to the government, composed of Durham's contribution and a matching amount by her employer ($1,800 × 2 = $3,600).

Several significant changes in the accounting for FICA taxes have occurred in recent years. First, both the amount of earnings subject to FICA tax (termed the FICA base) and the tax rate have increased dramatically. Upon inception of the Act in 1937, for example, the first $3,000 of earnings was taxed at a rate of 1%, resulting in a maximum employee contribution of $30. At the time of this writing, the $30 amount had grown to $5,328.90.

Second, more detailed computations and reporting are required. Because

---

[3] This act is sometimes called the Wages and Hours Law.

of variations in rates and bases, employers must now account for FICA as consisting of two separate components: Social Security and Medicare. Illustrations throughout the remainder of this chapter assume the following taxes:

Social Security: 6% on the first $55,000 earned
Medicare: 1.5% on the first $130,000 earned

Federal, State, and City Income Taxes

Employers must also withhold a portion of an employee's gross earnings to satisfy federal income tax laws and the laws of many states and local municipalities. These **income tax withholdings** are later submitted to the appropriate governmental authorities in payment of the employee's tax liability. Because of the nature of the system, income taxes are actually remitted on a pay-as-you-go basis.

The amount withheld for federal income taxes is based on employee earnings, frequency of pay, marital status, and the number of **withholding allowances** claimed. The allowances are reported to an employer at the time of hire on a Form W-4 (Withholding Allowance Certificate) and depend on various factors, including marital status and number of children.

In an effort to secure operating revenues, many state and local governmental units have enacted laws that tax an employee's gross earnings. The amounts withheld for state and local income taxes vary widely but are often a stipulated percentage of gross pay.

Other Deductions

In addition to required Social Security/Medicare and income tax withholdings, many employees voluntarily authorize other deductions from their paychecks. Common examples of such deductions include payments for insurance programs (life, medical, dental) and U.S. savings bonds, contributions to a pension plan, union dues, and charitable contributions.

Calculation of Take-Home Pay

To illustrate the computation of net or take-home pay, we will focus on Tony Disano, a married employee of Trimble Services who earns a weekly salary of $1,200. The information that follows is available.

1 According to his W-4 form, Disano is claiming three withholding allowances.

2 Ohio, the state of employment, has a 2% income tax (assumed).

3 Social Security/Medicare taxes are as noted at the top of this page. Tony's year-to-date earnings before considering the present payroll period amount to $54,000.

4 Disano has authorized a $40 deduction for medical insurance and a $10 contribution to the United Way.

Disano's take-home pay for the current week is calculated as follows:

Gross earnings		$1,200
Less deductions		
Federal income tax	$199	
State income tax ($1,200 × 0.02)	24	
Social Security taxes ($1,000 × 0.06)	60	
Medicare taxes ($1,200 × 0.015)	18	
Medical insurance	40	
United Way contribution	10	351
Net pay		$ 849

The federal income tax withholding amount is based on tables provided by the government. To determine the appropriate withholding, Disano's employer would refer to the table for married persons who are paid on a weekly basis. Trimble would then locate (or in many cases, figure) the amount that corresponds to three allowances and earnings of $1,200. Assume that this process results in income tax withholdings of $199.

Turning to Social Security, employees are subject to a 6% tax computed on a base of $55,000. According to the data presented, Disano has year-to-date earnings of $54,000. Thus, when his current week's salary of $1,200 is considered, the maximum taxable base will be exceeded. For this reason only $1,000 ($55,000 − $54,000) of the current pay is subject to Social Security taxation, and Trimble will deduct $60 ($1,000 × 0.06). Conversely, all of Disano's gross pay will be subject to Medicare taxation ($1,200 × 0.015 = $18) because his cumulative salary is far below the $130,000 base amount.

Payroll Recording and Record Keeping

At the end of each payroll period, the gross earnings, deductions, and net pay of all employees are entered in a **payroll register,** a journal-like device used to record a company's salary and wage data. The top part of Exhibit 12-4 contains the payroll register of Trimble Services (see pp. 472–473).

Observe the manner in which Tony Disano's previously illustrated net pay computation occupies one line of the register. Also note that each employee's gross pay is classified as sales salaries expense or office salaries expense, depending on the type of work performed. Based on data in the register, the following entry is needed to record Trimble's payroll for the last week of the year:

Sales Salaries Expense	1,840.00	
Office Salaries Expense	1,485.00	
Employees' Federal Income Taxes Payable		470.00
Employees' State Income Taxes Payable		66.50
Social Security Taxes Payable		187.50
Medicare Taxes Payable		49.88
Employees' Insurance Program Payable		125.00
Savings Bonds Payable		15.00
United Way Contributions Payable		50.00
Salaries Payable		2,361.12
To record payroll and withholdings		

The credit to Salaries Payable represents the net amount that will be disbursed to personnel on payday. (Generally, several days elapse between the end of the payroll period and payday to allow a company ample time to accumulate information and prepare checks.) Finally, the withholdings are current liabilities because the amounts are owed to various authorities (e.g., the federal government, the United Way, and so forth) and must be paid within a relatively short period of time. At the time of settlement, the proper payable is debited and Cash is credited.

Employee Records

Shortly after the conclusion of a calendar year, an employer must furnish an accounting to each employee of the gross wages and salaries earned and the taxes withheld. Individual employee records are therefore a necessity. These records not only provide the basis for determining the preceding amounts but also assist in the computation of Social Security and other taxes. For example, a cumulative earnings column (see Tony Disano's earnings record in Exhibit 12-4) will signal to Trimble Services that the $55,000 Social Security base is exceeded in the last pay period of the year.

The employer provides the required information to the employee on a **Wage and Tax Statement,** more commonly known as a **W-2** (also shown in Exhibit 12-4). Upon receipt, an employee can proceed with completion of the various tax forms that are filed with the Internal Revenue Service and state and local taxing authorities.

Payroll Taxes of the Employer

Thus far, our discussion of taxes has focused on the employee. Employers are also subject to payroll taxes, specifically, Social Security/Medicare, federal unemployment, and state unemployment.

Social Security/Medicare Tax

The most significant payroll tax levied on the employer is Social Security/Medicare. As we noted earlier, employers must match the contributions of their employees to these programs. Consequently, Social Security and Medicare tax rates on the employee and the employer are identical.

Federal Unemployment Tax

The employer is also required to pay tax under the **Federal Unemployment Tax Act (FUTA).** FUTA is a joint program between the federal government and the various states to financially assist the unemployed. Taxes collected are not distributed directly to those out of work; instead, the funds are used to support the administrative costs of state unemployment programs.

FUTA taxes are levied only on employers. At the time this text was written, the tax was 6.2% of the first $7,000 paid to each employee. Employers, however, can receive a credit of up to 5.4% for amounts remitted to state unemployment funds. Accordingly, many states have set a rate of at least 5.4% for their own programs, resulting in a *net* FUTA cost of 0.8% (6.2% − 5.4%) on a $7,000 earnings base.

Payroll Register

Name	S/O*	Total Hours	Earnings			Federal Income Tax	State Income Tax
			Regular	Overtime	Total		
Al Baker	S	40	320.00		320.00	46.00	6.40
Tony Disano	O	–	1,200.00		1,200.00	199.00	24.00
Sue Kennedy	S	40	720.00		720.00	77.00	14.40
Pete Roe	S	–	800.00		800.00	114.00	16.00
Alice Yurkow	O	45	240.00	45.00	285.00	34.00	5.70
			3,280.00	45.00	3,325.00	470.00	66.50

* S=Sales O=Office

Employee Earnings Record

Name   Tony J. Disano

Address   79 Flora Street

Cleveland, Ohio 44106

Position   Office/Data Processing Manager

Social Security Number   579-89-1111

Single _____   Married __X__

Withholding Allowances __3__

Period Ending	Earnings				Federal Income Tax
	Regular	Overtime	Total	Cumulative	
12/7	1,200.00		1,200.00	51,600.00	199.00
12/14	1,200.00		1,200.00	52,800.00	199.00
12/21	1,200.00		1,200.00	54,000.00	199.00
12/28	1,200.00		1,200.00	55,200.00	199.00
	55,200.00		55,200.00		9,154.00

1 Control number		
QMB No. 1545-0008		
2 Employee's name, address and ZIP code Trimble Services, Inc. 805 Tuck Place Cleveland, Ohio 44108	**6** Statutory employee / Deceased / Pension plan / Legal rep. / 942 emp. / Subtotal / Deferred compensation / Void	
	7 Allocated tips	**8** Advance EIC payment
	9 Federal income tax withheld 9,154.00	**10** Wages, tips, other compensation 55,200.00
3 Employer's identification number 59-1411366	**4** Employer's state I.D. number 35-11486	**11** Social security tax withheld 3,300.00	**12** Social security wages 55,000.00
5 Employee's social security number 579-89-1111		**13** Social security tips	**14** Medicare wages and tips 55,200.00
19 Employee's name, address and ZIP code Tony Disano 79 Flora Street Cleveland, Ohio 44106	**15** Medicare tax withheld 828.00	**16** Nonqualified plans
	17 See instrs. for Box 17	**18** Other Insurance: 1,840.00 United Way: 460.00
20	**21**	**22** Dependent care benefits	**23** Benefits included in Box 10
24 State income tax 1,104.00	**25** State wages, tips, etc. 55,200.00	**26** Name of state Ohio	**27** Local income tax	**28** Local wages, tips, etc.	**29** Name of locality

Copy B To be filed with employee's FEDERAL tax return   Dept. of the Treasury—Internal Revenue Service

Form **W-2 Wage and Tax Statement 19X8**

Deductions					Payment		Distribution	
Social Security Tax	Medicare Tax	Insurance	Other	Total Deductions	Net Earnings	Check No.	Sales Salaries Expense	Office Salaries Expense
19.20	4.80	15.00	SB* 10.00	101.40	218.60	1089	320.00	
60.00	18.00	40.00	UW 10.00	351.00	849.00	1090		1,200.00
43.20	10.80	35.00	UW 20.00	200.40	519.60	1091	720.00	
48.00	12.00	25.00	UW 20.00	235.00	565.00	1092	800.00	
17.10	4.28	10.00	SB 5.00	76.08	208.92	1093		285.00
187.50	49.88	125.00	65.00	963.88	2,361.12		1,840.00	1,485.00

* SB = Savings Bonds   UW = United Way

Pay __$1,200__ per

Hour _____ Week __x__

Two Weeks _____ Month _____

Employee Number __2__

Date of Birth __5/14/XX__

Date Hired __2/10/X8__

Date Terminated _____

Deductions						Payment	
State Income Tax	Social Security Tax	Medicare Tax	Insurance	Other	Total Deductions	Net Earnings	Check No.
24.00	72.00	18.00	40.00	UW 10.00	363.00	837.00	1003
24.00	72.00	18.00	40.00	UW 10.00	363.00	837.00	1030
24.00	72.00	18.00	40.00	UW 10.00	363.00	837.00	1056
24.00	60.00	18.00	40.00	UW 10.00	351.00	849.00	1090
1,104.00	3,300.00	828.00	1,840.00	460.00	16,686.00	38,514.00	

EXHIBIT 12-4
Payroll Record Keeping

State Unemployment Taxes

The various state programs collect **state unemployment taxes** and then disburse these monies to people out of work. As we just noted, many states have implemented a tax rate of at least 5.4%, also computed on an employee's first $7,000 of gross pay. Normally, however, businesses with good labor records receive a merit reduction. This practice makes sense economically because such firms have a low number of layoffs and terminations, thereby saving the state large amounts of unemployment compensation. Employers receiving merit reductions can still obtain a credit for federal purposes of up to 5.4%.

Recording the Employer's Taxes

The entry to record the payroll taxes levied on an employer is made at the same time payroll is recorded. To illustrate the necessary accounting, we will continue the Trimble Services example. Study the payroll register that appears in Exhibit 12-4, along with the following assumptions:

1 Only Tony Disano has exceeded the Social Security base of $55,000. Recall that only $1,000 of Tony's current gross earnings ($1,200) were taxed at the 6% rate.

2 Federal and state unemployment tax rates are 0.8% and 5.4%, respectively, of an employee's first $7,000 of gross earnings. All employees except Pete Roe, a new hire, have earned more than $7,000 for the year.

EXECUTIVE BRIEFING
The Magnitude and Significance of Employee Fringe Benefits

Richard O'Brien
Vice-President, Industrial Relations Staff
General Motors Corporation

Benefits today are no longer considered just "fringe" benefits, but rather are an important element of a total compensation package. In many cases, the level of benefits is a direct result of an employee's pay. For example, a simple raise often increases the amount of life, accident, and disability benefits; income security benefits; and corporate matching contributions to employee savings programs. The benefits portion of the total compensation package thus continues to grow and becomes a significant expense for the company.

To illustrate, in a recent year, a typical U.S. employee's benefits package cost General Motors about $15,900, or 27% of total compensation. (If vacations and holidays are considered, the cost would increase by another $6,000, to 37% of compensation.) The total cost to GM, approximately $6.2 billion for the year or $17 million per day, resulted in roughly $1,450 being added to the cost of each vehicle produced. Considering the requirements in today's business climate, it becomes increasingly important to monitor benefit expenses, making sure that such amounts are competitive, controlled, and meet the changing needs of personnel.

The payroll tax obligation, an expense, is recorded as follows:

Payroll Tax Expense	286.98	
Social Security Taxes Payable		187.50
Medicare Taxes Payable		49.88
Federal Unemployment Taxes Payable		6.40*
State Unemployment Taxes Payable		43.20*
To record employer's payroll taxes		

* Unemployment taxes are calculated only on Roe's salary because all other employees are over the limit. Federal: $800 × 0.008 = $6.40; state: $800 × 0.054 = $43.20.

Observe how Trimble's Social Security and Medicare expenses are identical to the amounts withheld from employee earnings. The liabilities will eventually be removed from the accounting records upon remittance to the proper authority.

END-OF-CHAPTER REVIEW

1 **Explain the occurrence of and accounting for typical current liabilities of a business.** Current liabilities are debts or obligations that will be paid within one year or the operating cycle, whichever is longer. The settlement of current liabilities normally involves the use of current assets (e.g., cash) or the creation of other current liabilities (e.g., a note payable is used to settle an account payable). Examples of current liabilities include accounts payable, notes payable, the current portion of long-term debt, and accrued liabilities for expenses incurred but not yet paid.

2 **Account for notes payable when interest is included in the face value of a note and when interest is recorded separately.** When interest is included in a note's face value, the difference between the note's proceeds and face value is recorded in a contra liability account, Discount on Notes Payable. At the end of each accounting period, this account is amortized (reduced) by the process of recognizing interest expense. In contrast, if interest is stated separately, no Discount account is established. Instead, interest is recorded at the end of the period by a debit to Interest Expense and, if unpaid, a credit to Interest Payable.

3 **Identify typical contingent liabilities and recognize the guidelines that are used for recording such obligations in the accounts.** A contingent liability is a potential liability that may become a definite obligation or be eliminated entirely as the result of a future event. An example is a lawsuit. Contingencies should be recorded in the accounts when it is probable that the future event will occur *and* the amount of the liability can be reasonably estimated. If only one of these guidelines is met, a note to the financial statements is appropriate.

4 **Prepare journal entries for warranty costs.** Warranties are promises made by sellers and manufacturers to correct defects in product quality. Because warranties help to promote the sale of such products, an estimated service cost should be matched against sales revenues when the revenues are generated. This procedure, in turn, establishes a liability in the accounting records. The liability is reduced, perhaps several periods later, when the warranties are honored.

LEARNING OBJECTIVES: THE KEY POINTS

5 Calculate and record payroll, including the employer's tax obligation. Businesses must maintain detailed payroll records on their employees, keeping track of gross earnings and various payroll deductions (e.g., Social Security/Medicare tax, federal and state income tax withholdings, medical insurance, and pension plan contributions). The amounts deducted from employee paychecks are liabilities until paid to the appropriate authorities. A firm must also consider and record the following payroll taxes, which are expenses of the employer: Social Security/Medicare, federal unemployment, and state unemployment.

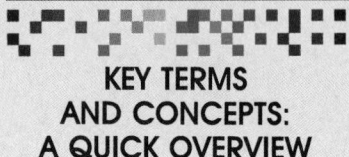

KEY TERMS AND CONCEPTS: A QUICK OVERVIEW

accounts payable   Amounts owed to suppliers for the purchase of goods or services.

accrued liability   The amount owed for an accrued expense.

contingent liability   A potential liability whose outcome hinges on the future.

contra liability   An account used to reduce liability balances in the financial statements.

current liabilities   Debts or obligations that will be paid within one year or the operating cycle, whichever is longer.

discount amortization   The process of reducing a discount on notes payable by recognizing interest expense.

discount on notes payable   A contra-liability account that represents future interest expense.

employee   A person who works for a specific business and is directly and closely supervised by that business.

Federal Insurance Contributions Act (FICA)   A statute, commonly called Social Security, that requires employers to withhold a portion of each employee's gross earnings and to match the employee's contribution.

Federal Unemployment Tax Act (FUTA)   Federal legislation that requires employers to pay taxes to assist the unemployed.

gross earnings   The total earnings of an employee before any deductions are made.

income tax withholdings   The portion of an employee's gross earnings withheld by the employer to satisfy federal (and sometimes state and local) income tax laws.

independent contractor   A person who frequently performs services for many different organizations at the same time, or perhaps finishes a project for one entity and then moves on to service another.

liabilities   Obligations owed by an organization that have arisen from past transactions or events.

notes payable   Written promises to pay a definite amount of money on a specific future date.

payroll register   A journal-like record that summarizes a firm's entire payroll.

prepayments by customers   Monies collected for future goods and services.

state unemployment taxes   Taxes paid by employers to state governments. The taxes are disbursed to the unemployed through the various state programs.

take-home (net) pay   The amount of cash available to an employee after all appropriate payroll deductions are subtracted from gross pay.

Wage and Tax Statement (W-2)   A statement the employer must provide each employee showing gross wages and salaries earned and taxes withheld.

warranty   A promise made by a seller or manufacturer to correct defects in product quality and performance.

withholding allowance   A numerical amount used in computing the amount of federal income taxes withheld from an employee's paycheck.

CHAPTER QUIZ

The five questions that follow relate to several issues raised in the chapter. Test your knowledge of the issues by selecting the best answer. (The answers appear on p. 493.)

1 Which of the following comments is false? Current liabilities:
  a include prepayments (advances) by customers.
  b will be settled within one year or the operating cycle, whichever is longer.
  c must be settled by using cash.
  d arise from past transactions and events.

2 The Discount on Notes Payable account:
  a usually has a credit balance.
  b is associated with a note payable when interest is included in the obligation's face value.
  c represents future interest revenue on the note payable.
  d is used for notes payable when interest is not included in the obligation's face value.

3 A balance in the Estimated Liability for Warranties account at year-end indicates:
  a that the accounting records have not been closed.
  b that the accounting records have not been adjusted.
  c the amount incurred during the year to service outstanding warranty agreements.
  d future amounts expected to be incurred when outstanding warranty agreements are honored.

4 Assume that Robert Conrad, a technical engineer, worked 45 hours last week. He is paid $28 per hour, with hours in excess of 40 being compensated at one and one-half times the regular rate. Income tax withholdings amounted to $270; his medical insurance deduction was $30. The Social Security tax rate is 6% on the first $55,000 earned per employee; Medicare is 1.5% on the first $130,000. Cumulative gross pay before considering the preceding data totaled $54,202. Conrad's take-home pay is:
  a $930.25.
  b $962.17.
  c $982.12.
  d some amount other than those listed above.

5 Social Security and Medicare taxes are levied on:
  a employees only.
  b employers only.
  c both employees and employers.
  d either the employee or the employer depending on the number of withholding allowances claimed by the employee.

SUMMARY PROBLEM

The following transactions took place in July and pertain to Meadowlands Corporation:

1 Two notes were issued during the month to raise needed cash. On July 1, a three-month, 12%, $5,000 note was issued to the First National Bank. The company also executed a 60-day, $3,000 note on July 17 to the Second National Bank. Interest of $80 is included in the face value of the latter obligation.

2 The company recorded its payroll on July 31. Total salaries amounted to $30,000; 80% pertain to the sales staff and 20% to office personnel. Social Security taxes are 6% on a base of $55,000 for each employee; Medicare is 1.5% on a $130,000 base. All employees are under the Social Security base except for Mike Dixon, who earned his normal monthly salary of $10,000. Additional data follow.

Federal income taxes withheld	$3,850
State income taxes withheld	300
Insurance program withholdings	680

Meadowlands has a fiscal year-end of August 31.

Instructions

a Prepare entries on July 1 and July 17 to record issuance of the notes.
b Prepare an entry on July 31 to record the company's payroll.
c Prepare an entry on July 31 to record the company's payroll taxes. Assume the state and federal unemployment tax rates are 5.4% and 0.8%, respectively. Thirty percent of the gross earnings are subject to unemployment taxes.
d Prepare the journal entries required on August 31 to accrue interest on each of the two notes.

Solution

a July 1 Cash   5,000
                 Notes Payable   5,000
              To record note payable to bank; three
              months at 12%

      17 Cash   2,920
            Discount on Notes Payable   80
                 Notes Payable   3,000
              To record note payable to bank; 60 days
              until maturity

b July 31 Sales Salaries Expense   24,000*
            Office Salaries Expense   6,000*
                 Social Security Taxes Payable   1,200†
                 Medicare Taxes Payable   450‡
                 Employees' Federal Income Taxes Payable   3,850
                 Employees' State Income Taxes Payable   300
                 Employees' Insurance Program Payable   680
                 Salaries Payable   23,520
              To record payroll and withholdings

* $30,000 × 0.8 = $24,000; $30,000 × 0.2 = $6,000.
† ($30,000 − $10,000) × 0.06 = $1,200.
‡ $30,000 × 0.015 = $450.

c July 31	Payroll Tax Expense	2,208	
	Social Security Taxes Payable		1,200*
	Medicare Taxes Payable		450†
	State Unemployment Taxes Payable		486‡
	Federal Unemployment Taxes Payable		72*
	To record employer's payroll taxes		

* ($30,000 − $10,000) × 0.06 = $1,200.
† $30,000 × 0.015 = $450.
‡ $30,000 × 0.3 = $9,000; $9,000 × 0.054 = $486.
* $30,000 × 0.3 = $9,000; $9,000 × 0.008 = $72.

d Aug. 31	Interest Expense	100	
	Interest Payable		100
	To accrue interest for two months:		
	$5,000 × 0.12 × $\frac{2}{12}$		
31	Interest Expense	60	
	Discount on Notes Payable		60
	To accrue interest for 45 days and amortize		
	the discount: $80 × $\frac{45}{60}$		

ASSIGNMENT MATERIAL

QUESTIONS

Q12-1 Is a commitment for future goods and services entered in the accounting records as a liability? Explain.

Q12-2 Define the term "current liability" and present six examples.

Q12-3 Why are customer prepayments classified as liabilities?

Q12-4 Present three different situations where a business collects monies from customers and employees and reports such amounts as current liabilities.

Q12-5 Briefly discuss the correct treatment of vacation pay in the accounting records.

Q12-6 Discuss several common uses of notes payable.

Q12-7 What does the Discount on Notes Payable account represent?

Q12-8 Does discount amortization increase or decrease a company's reported interest expense for the year?

Q12-9 How does a contingent liability differ from an absolute liability? Present three examples of contingent liabilities.

Q12-10 What guidelines must be met in order for a contingent liability to be recorded in the accounts?

Q12-11 Why is a warranty considered a contingent liability?

Q12-12 Are internal control procedures important in the area of payroll? Why?

Q12-13 Differentiate between "employees" and "independent contractors." For which group must detailed payroll records be kept?

Q12-14 What is the purpose of requiring businesses to withhold income taxes (federal, state, and local) from employee wages? How are these withholdings treated in the accounting records of the employer?

Q12-15 Discuss the interrelationships between the payroll register, employee earnings record, and Form W-2.

Q12-16 Which payroll taxes are incurred by an employer? How are these taxes treated in the accounting records?

Q12-17 Do most state unemployment programs grant merit reductions to businesses? What is the purpose behind merit reductions?

EXERCISES

E12-1 *Prepayments by customers* (L.O. 1)

Greenland Enterprises began a new magazine in the fourth quarter of 19X2. Annual subscriptions, which cost $18 each, were sold as follows:

	Number of Subscriptions Sold
October	400
November	700
December	1,000

If subscriptions begin (and magazines are sent) in the month of sale:
a Present the necessary journal entry to record the magazine subscriptions sold during the fourth quarter.
b Determine how much subscription revenue Greenland earned by the end of 19X2.
c Compute Greenland's liability to subscribers at the end of 19X2.

E12-2 *Accrued liability; current portion of long-term debt* (L.O. 1)

On July 1, 19X1, Hall Company borrowed $225,000 via a long-term loan. Terms of the loan require that Hall pay interest and $75,000 of principal on July 1, 19X2, 19X3, and 19X4. The unpaid balance of the loan accrues interest at the rate of 10% per year. Hall has a December 31 year-end.
a Compute Hall's accrued interest as of December 31, 19X1.
b Present the appropriate balance sheet disclosure for the accrued interest and the current and long-term portion of the outstanding debt as of December 31, 19X1.
c Repeat parts (a) and (b) using a date of December 31, 19X2, rather than December 31, 19X1. Assume that Hall is in compliance with the terms of the loan agreement.

E12-3 *Accrued vacation pay* (L.O. 1)

Don Pedro Mexican Restaurants, Inc., has a two-week paid vacation plan. Monthly salaries and wages average $400,000. Because of high turnover, the firm estimates that only 30% of the employees will qualify for this fringe benefit.
a Briefly explain the proper accounting treatment for the vacation pay.
b Prepare the journal entry for March that reflects the proper treatment.
c Prepare a journal entry to record the disbursement of $7,500 to employees who took their vacations in August.

E12-4 *Notes payable* (L.O. 2)

1-2-3

Sentry Security Systems purchased $72,000 of office equipment on April 1, 19X3, by signing a three-year, 12% note payable to Sharp, Inc. One-third of the principal, along with interest on the outstanding balance, is payable each April 1 until maturity. (The first payment is due in 19X4.)
a Fill in the following table to reflect Sentry's liabilities, assuming a March 31 year-end.

	March 31		
	19X4	19X5	19X6
Current liabilities			
Current portion of long-term debt	____	____	____
Interest payable	____	____	____
Long-term liabilities			
Long-term debt	____	____	____

b Assuming that interest is properly recorded at the end of each year, present the proper journal entry to record the last payment on April 1, 19X6.

E12-5 *Notes payable; discount amortization* (L.O. 2)
Morgantown Foods purchased four delivery trucks from Metro Truck Sales on October 1, 19X1, for $240,000. Morgantown signed a nine-month note for $261,000; interest is included in the note's face value. Prepare journal entries for Morgantown Foods to record the following:
a The purchase of the trucks on October 1, 19X1
b Discount amortization for the year ended December 31, 19X1
c The note payment and discount amortization on July 1, 19X2

E12-6 *Warranty costs* (L.O. 3, 4)
RJV sells sophisticated scientific instruments to fusion research laboratories. All instruments have a two-year warranty. The company estimates that 5% of the 1,200 units sold during 19X8 will require rework or replacement, at an estimated cost of $150 per unit.
a Is a warranty an example of an absolute liability or a contingent liability? Briefly discuss.
b Prepare the required journal entry to record warranty costs for 19X8.
c Present the necessary balance sheet disclosure on December 31, 19X9, if 35 instruments were returned for servicing during 19X9. Assume that the actual rework cost per unit conformed to original expectations.

E12-7 *Current and contingent liabilities* (L.O. 1, 2, 3, 4)
Evaluate the comments that follow as being True or False. If the comment is false, briefly explain why.
a Collections for third parties normally arise when a business receives prepayments, or advances, from customers.
b The currently maturing portion of a long-term debt should be disclosed as a current liability, with the remaining portion of the debt being shown as a long-term liability.
c Discount amortization procedures are employed when accounting for a note that includes interest in the face amount.
d Because some uncertainty exists, contingent liabilities are never recorded with a journal entry.
e For financial reporting purposes, warranty obligations should be estimated and recorded in the same period that the related sale is made.

E12-8 *Payroll accounting* (L.O. 5)
Assume that the following tax rates and payroll information pertain to Brookhaven Publishing:

Social Security taxes: 6% on the first $55,000 earned
Medicare taxes: 1.5% on the first $130,000 earned
Federal income taxes withheld from wages: $7,500

State income taxes: 5% of gross earnings
Insurance withholdings: 1% of gross earnings
State unemployment taxes: 5.4% on the first $7,000 earned
Federal unemployment taxes: 0.8% on the first $7,000 earned

The company incurred salary expense of $50,000 during February. All employees had earned less than $5,000 by month-end.

a Prepare the necessary entry to record Brookhaven's February payroll, which will be paid on March 1.

b Prepare the journal entry to record Brookhaven's payroll tax expense.

E12-9 *Payroll accounting* (L.O. 5)

The following payroll information relates to Viking Company for the month of July:

Total (gross) employee earnings	$150,000
Earnings in excess of Social Security base earnings	18,000
Earnings in excess of Medicare base earnings	2,000
Earnings in excess of unemployment base earnings	94,000
Federal income taxes withheld	14,500
State income taxes withheld	3,000
Employee deductions for medical insurance	2,200

The Social Security tax rate is 6% on the first $55,000 earned per employee; Medicare is 1.5% on the first $130,000 earned. The state and federal unemployment tax rates are 5.4% and 0.8%, respectively, on the first $7,000 earned per employee.

a Compute the employees' total take-home pay.

b Compute Viking's total payroll-related expenses.

c Assuming a stable work force, is total take-home pay likely to increase, decrease, or remain the same in September? Briefly explain.

E12-10 *Payroll: Computations and analysis* (L.O. 5)

Joe Carey and Ken Wallace work part-time as technical specialists for Alpha, Inc. Carey earns $28 per hour; Wallace is paid a salary of $34,800. Both men worked 1,400 hours during the year. Social Security taxes are 6% of an employee's first $55,000 of gross earnings; Medicare is 1.5% on the first $130,000 earned. Unemployment taxes are computed on each employee's earnings up to $7,000. The state unemployment rate is only 4.6% because of a merit reduction, and the federal unemployment tax rate is 0.8%.

a Calculate the company's annual payroll tax expense for Carey and Wallace.

b What is the total annual cost of having Carey and Wallace on the payroll?

c Would your answer to part (b) be different if Wallace decided to work full-time for $74,000 per year and Carey was laid off? Explain, assuming no change in the unemployment tax rates.

Series A

PROBLEMS

P12-A1 *Current liabilities: Recognition and valuation* (L.O. 1, 2, 3)

The seven transactions and events that follow relate to the 19X2 operations of Blue Giant Products.

1. On February 1, the company signed a one-year contract with the food processors union, agreeing to a 6% wage increase for all employees. The cost of the wage increase is estimated to be $100,000 per month.

2. A customer slipped on a soft drink that he had spilled while walking through a Blue Giant store. The customer injured his back and has filed a $50,000 damage suit against the company. Blue Giant attorneys feel the suit is uncalled for and without merit.

3. Blue Giant purchased merchandise on October 15 for $4,000; terms 5/15, n/60. The company overlooked the discount and intends to pay the supplier in January 19X3.

4. Equipment that cost $12,000 was acquired on November 1 by issuing a three-month, 10%, $12,000 note payable.

5. Office furniture that cost $4,000 was purchased on December 1, with Blue Giant signing a $4,240, 12-month note payable. Interest is included in the note's face value.

6. The company operates in a state where a 6% sales tax has been enacted. Sales of merchandise on account during December amounted to $300,000.

7. On the last day of 19X2, Blue Giant borrowed $1 million from the Monticello Bank. The loan's principal is due in 10 equal annual installments of $100,000 each, with each installment payable on December 31. The loan has a 9% interest rate.

Instructions

a Indicate which of the seven transactions and events would appear in the current liability section of the firm's December 31, 19X2, balance sheet.

b Show how the items in part (a) would be disclosed. Use proper dollar amounts.

c Indicate how the transactions and events that are not current liabilities would be handled for accounting purposes.

P12-A2 *Current liabilities: Entries and disclosure* (L.O. 1, 2, 4)

A review of selected financial activities of Visconti's during 19XX disclosed the following:

Dec. 1 Borrowed $20,000 from the First City Bank by signing a three-month, 15% note payable. Interest and principal are due at maturity.

10 Established a warranty liability for the XY-80, a new product. Sales are expected to total 1,000 units during the month. Past experience with similar products indicates that 2% of the units will require repair, with warranty costs averaging $27 per unit.

22 Purchased $16,000 of merchandise on account from Oregon Company, terms 2/10, n/30.

26 Borrowed $5,000 from the First City Bank; signed a $5,120 note payable due in 60 days.

31 Repaired six XY-80s during the month at a total cost of $162.

31 Accrued three days of salaries at a total cost of $1,400.

31 Accrued vacation pay amounting to 6% of December's $36,000 total wage and salary expense.

Instructions

a Prepare journal entries to record the preceding transactions and events.

b Determine accrued interest as of December 31, 19XX, and prepare the necessary adjusting entry(ies).

c Prepare the current liability section of Visconti's December 31, 19XX, balance sheet.

P12-A3 *Notes payable* (L.O. 2)

Red Bank Enterprises was involved in the following transactions during the fiscal year ended October 31:

Aug.   2   Borrowed $75,000 from the Bank of Kingsville by signing a 120-day note for $79,000.

20   Issued a $40,000 note to Harris Motors for the purchase of a $40,000 delivery truck. The note is due in 180 days and carries a 12% interest rate.

Sept. 10   Purchased merchandise from Paris Enterprises in the amount of $15,000. Issued a 30-day, 12% note in settlement of the balance owed.

11   Issued a $60,000 note to Datatex Equipment in settlement of an overdue account payable of the same amount. The note is due in 30 days and carries a 14% interest rate.

Oct. 10   The note to Paris Enterprises was paid in full.

11   The note to Datatex Equipment was due today, but insufficient funds were available for payment. Management authorized the issuance of a new 20-day, 18% note for $60,700, the maturity value of the original obligation.

31   The new note to Datatex Equipment was paid in full.

Instructions

a Prepare journal entries to record the transactions.
b Prepare adjusting entries on October 31 to record accrued interest.
c Prepare the current liability section of Red Bank's balance sheet as of October 31. Assume the Accounts Payable account totals $203,600 on this date.

P12-A4 *Unearned revenues and warranties* (L.O. 1, 3, 4)

Andress Company, which began business in late 19X3, sells exercise equipment for home use at $250 per unit. The company provides a full warranty on the nonmoving structural parts for two years from the date of customer purchase. It is anticipated that 4% of the units sold will need repair, with repair costs averaging $60 per unit. Andress also offers an introductory, three-hour lesson plan for $24 so that customers can become familiar with the equipment.

Sales (in units) during 19X3 were as follows: exercise equipment, 500; lesson plans, 300. During 19X4, the company serviced 16 units under the warranty agreement; actual unit costs conformed to the original prediction. In addition, 585 hours of lessons were provided.

Instructions

a Prepare year-end journal entries to record the preceding data.
b Assume that 19X4 year-end balances in Accounts Payable and Interest Payable are $28,500 and $1,200, respectively. Compute the firm's total current liabilities as of December 31, 19X4. (*Note:* We are ignoring 19X4 sales for the sake of simplicity.)
c Explain why the cost of product warranties, a contingent liability, can usually be entered in the accounting records prior to the actual repair of equipment.

P12-A5 *Payroll journal entries* (L.O. 5)

The following tax rates and payroll information pertain to the Syracuse operations of IMS Company for November:

Social Security taxes: 6% on the first $55,000 earned
Medicare taxes: 1.5% on the first $130,000 earned
Federal income taxes withheld from wages: $4,400
State income taxes: 6% of gross earnings
Insurance withholdings: 1% of gross earnings
Pension contributions: 2.5% of gross earnings
State unemployment taxes: 5.4% on the first $7,000 earned
Federal unemployment taxes: 0.8% on the first $7,000 earned

Sales staff salaries amounted to $26,000, $3,000 of which is over the unemployment earnings base but subject to all other appropriate taxes. The company's branch manager, Tracy Smith, earned her regular salary of $9,000 during the month. She has been employed by IMS since March 1 and has not missed a single day of work.

Instructions

a Prepare the journal entry to record the November payroll. Smith's salary is classified as an administrative expense by the company.
b IMS matches employees' insurance and pension contributions. Prepare a journal entry to record the firm's payroll taxes and other related payroll costs. Assume that these amounts will be remitted to the proper authorities in December.
c The owner of IMS asked the firm's accountant to reclassify all personnel as independent contractors. The accountant explained that such a reclassification would not be appropriate because, by law, the personnel were considered employees. Briefly comment on the probable reasoning behind the owner's request.

P12-A6 *Payroll register and entries* (L.O. 5)

Sound Stage has three hourly employees and two salaried employees. Payroll data for the month of November follow.

1-2-3

Employee	Hours Reg	OT*	Pay Rate	Gross Pay for Month	Federal Income Tax Withheld	Compensation through Oct. 31
David	160		$5/hr	$ 800	$ 165	$ 1,600
Larimore	160	20	$6/hr	1,140	195	6,200
Markoff	160	10	$4/hr	700	100	7,500
Ramon			$3,500/mo	3,500	380	35,000
Wykovich			$6,000/mo	6,000	1,450	53,000
				$12,140	$2,290	

* Overtime hours are compensated at 150% of the regular hourly rate.

Other information is as follows:

1 Social Security taxes are 6% on a base of $55,000 for each employee; Medicare is 1.5% of the first $130,000 earned.
2 Unemployment taxes are based on the first $7,000 of an employee's earnings. The state and federal rates are 5.4% and 0.8%, respectively.
3 Deductions are made for contributions to the United Way (1% of gross earnings). The company matches employee donations.

4 Ramon and Wykovich perform administrative work; other employees are involved with sales.

Instructions

a Prepare a payroll register for the month of November. Use the column headings that follow and round to the nearest cent.

		Deductions				
Employee	Gross Pay	Federal Income Tax	Social Security Tax	Medicare Tax	United Way	Net Pay

b Prepare the necessary journal entry to record the payroll.
c Record the employer's payroll taxes and United Way contribution. The United Way contribution will be remitted on December 15.

Series B

P12-B1 *Current liabilities: Recognition and valuation* (L.O. 1, 2, 4)

The seven transactions and events that follow relate to the 19X7 operations of American Company.

1 During the Easter season, the company sold 400 $25 gift certificates to customers. By December 31, 275 certificates had been redeemed for merchandise.
2 Equipment that cost $40,000 was acquired on May 1 by signing a 12-month, 12% note payable for $40,000.
3 The company introduced a new product on September 1; sales totaled 500,000 units through the remainder of the year. Each unit carries a 12-month warranty. American estimated that defective units would amount to 2% of sales, with the cost of each unit's replacement averaging $15. No units were replaced during 19X7.
4 A $10,000 computer system was purchased on October 1 by signing a nine-month note payable for $10,900. Interest is included in the note's face value.
5 On November 1, the company signed a contract to purchase $360,000 of spare parts from Central Supply during the next 24 months. The contract called for prices that are 15% below those of Arrow Wholesale, American's present supplier.
6 Accrued salaries payable at year-end total $45,000. This amount was paid on January 3, 19X8.
7 Federal income taxes withheld from employees' paychecks during December totaled $13,000. The withholdings must be remitted to tax authorities by February 1, 19X8.

Instructions

a Indicate which of the seven transactions and events would appear in the current liability section of the firm's December 31, 19X7, balance sheet.
b Show how the items in part (a) would be disclosed. Use proper dollar amounts.
c Indicate how the transactions and events that are not current liabilities would be handled for accounting purposes.

P12-B2 *Current liabilities: Entries and disclosure* (L.O. 1, 2, 4)

A review of selected financial activities of Long Island Company during 19XX disclosed the following:

Mar. 1 Purchased $6,000 of office furniture on account from the Fenton Company, terms 2/10, n/45.

7 Bought $18,000 of store equipment; signed an $18,800 note payable due in 120 days.

10 Established a warranty liability for the Mop-o-Matic, a new product. Sales are expected to total 1,000 units during the month. Past experience with similar products indicates that 3% of the units will require replacement, with warranty costs averaging $8 per unit.

16 Borrowed $20,000 from the Bank of Long Island by signing a 60-day, 12% note payable. Interest and principal are due at maturity.

31 Accrued two days of wage expense; daily payroll amounts to $3,700.

31 Accrued vacation pay amounting to 7% of March's $81,000 wage expense.

31 Replaced 24 Mop-o-Matics during the month at a total cost of $192.

Instructions

a Prepare journal entries to record the preceding transactions and events.
b Determine accrued interest as of March 31, 19XX, and prepare the necessary adjusting entry(ies).
c Prepare the current liability section of Long Island Company's March 31, 19XX, balance sheet.

P12-B3 *Notes payable* (L.O. 2)

The accounting records of Chung, Inc., revealed the following information about notes that had been issued to Hallmark Enterprises and Stateside Marine:

	Hallmark	Stateside
Date of note	May 9	June 27
Face value	$27,000	$18,000
Interest rate	10%	10%
Term of note	120 days	90 days
Maturity date	Sept. 6	Sept. 25
Purpose of note	Purchase of equipment	Settlement of account payable

Chung had also borrowed $32,400 from Union Bank by signing a 120-day note for $33,372. The transaction occurred on May 21.

Instructions

a Prepare the journal entries that Chung would record on May 9, May 21, June 27, and September 6.
b The note to Stateside Marine was due on September 25 but Chung lacked sufficient funds for payment. Management authorized issuance of a new 60-day, 12% note for $18,450, the maturity value of the original obligation. Prepare the necessary journal entry for the issuance.
c Assume now that Chung has a June 30 year-end.
  (1) Prepare the journal entries for accrued interest and discount amortization that would have been necessary on this date.
  (2) Prepare the current liability section of Chung's June 30 balance sheet. The company's Accounts Payable account contains a balance of $45,800.

P12-B4 *Unearned revenues and warranties* (L.O. 1, 3, 4)

Hansen Company, which began business in late 19X5, sells bar code scanners for commercial use at $5,500 per unit. The company provides a full warranty on all parts for two years from the date of customer purchase. Five percent of the units sold are anticipated to need repair, with repair costs averaging $220 per unit. Hansen also provides a professional development course on inventory control to interested users. The course fee is $450 per participant, with advance registration (and payment) being required.

Hansen sold 60 scanning systems during 19X5 and received course fees from 64 people. During 19X6, the company serviced two systems under the warranty agreement; actual unit costs conformed to the original prediction. Course attendees were: 19X5, 0; 19X6, 62.

Instructions

a Prepare year-end journal entries to record the preceding data.

b Assume that 19X6 year-end balances in Accounts Payable and Salaries Payable are $32,600 and $950, respectively. Compute Hansen's total current liabilities as of December 31, 19X6. (*Note:* We are ignoring 19X6 sales for the sake of simplicity.)

c Is the Estimated Liability for Warranties account an example of a contingent liability or an absolute liability? Briefly explain.

P12-B5 *Payroll journal entries* (L.O. 5)

Kitchen Creations incurred wages and salaries of $300,000 during November, 30% of which relate to office personnel and the remainder to sales personnel. Social Security taxes are 6% on a base of $55,000 for each employee; Medicare is 1.5% on the first $130,000 earned. All employees are under the $55,000 base except Susan Hatfield, who earned $7,000 during the month. (Hatfield's annual salary is $84,000.) Federal income taxes withheld amounted to $75,900, and state income taxes withheld totaled $9,000. Other deductions from payroll were authorized for pensions (2% of gross earnings), insurance (1% of gross earnings), and United Way contributions (0.5% of gross earnings).

Instructions

a Prepare the journal entry to record the payroll.

b Prepare a journal entry to record the company's payroll taxes and other related payroll costs. Assume that state unemployment tax is 4.0% because of a merit reduction, and that federal unemployment tax is 0.8%. Twenty percent of the gross earnings are subject to unemployment taxes. Also, the firm matches employee contributions to the United Way and insurance programs. These amounts will be remitted to the proper authorities on December 15.

c Compute total payroll expense for November.

P12-B6 *Payroll register and entries* (L.O. 5)

Santiago Company has three hourly employees (maintenance personnel) and two salaried employees (administrative personnel). Payroll data for the month of November follow.

1-2-3

Employee	Total Earnings through October	Hours Worked	Pay Rate	Federal Withholding
Holmes	$18,600	180*	$10/hr	$ 475
Jax	2,300	100	$8/hr	150
Paige	11,700	170*	$6/hr	250
Freed	52,000		$6,500/mo	1,950
Smythe	58,000		$5,800/mo	2,600

* Hours in excess of 160 are compensated at one and one-half times the regular pay rate.

Santiago deducts 2% from each employee's gross pay for insurance. Social Security taxes are 6% of the first $55,000 earned; Medicare is 1.5% on a base of $130,000. The state unemployment tax rate is 5.4% and the federal unemployment tax rate is 0.8%, both applied to a $7,000 base.

Instructions

a Prepare a payroll register for November similar to that shown in the text. Show the gross pay, federal income tax, Social Security tax, Medicare tax, insurance deduction, and net pay for each employee.

b Prepare the necessary journal entries to record (1) the November payroll and (2) Santiago's payroll tax expense. Deductions for insurance will be remitted to Applegate Career Planners on December 9.

EDB12-1 *Current liabilities and contingencies: Delta Air Lines, Inc., and Boise Cascade Corporation* (L.O. 1, 3)

ELECTRONIC DATA BASE

SEC

Atlanta-based Delta Air Lines is one of our country's largest air carriers. The company provides scheduled air transportation for passengers, freight, and mail throughout the United States and abroad. Boise Cascade, in contrast, is an integrated paper and forest products firm. The company manufactures and distributes paper, office products, and building products and manages timberland to support these operations.

Instructions

By using the text's Electronic Data Base, access the balance sheets and accompanying notes of both firms and answer the questions that follow. Unless otherwise indicated, responses should be based on data for the most recent year presented.

a Review the balance sheets and determine:

  (1) The three largest current liabilities disclosed.

  (2) Whether any of the current liabilities are unique to the operations and activities of the company. List the current liabilities that meet this characteristic.

  (3) Whether current assets are sufficient to cover current obligations. Show calculations.

b Which company has the higher percentage of long-term debt classified as a current liability? Show computations to support your answer.

c Review the footnotes to the financial statements and focus on sections that describe contingencies and/or litigation and legal matters. Comment on the specifics of each company's disclosure, including associated dollar amounts (if any).

EDB12-2 *Current liabilities and contingencies* (L.O. 1, 3)

This problem is a duplication of Problem EDB12-1. It is based on two companies selected by your instructor.

Instructions

By using the text's Electronic Data Base, access the specified companies' balance sheets and accompanying notes and focus on data for the most recent year reported. Answer requirements (a)–(c) of Problem EDB12-1.

BEYOND THE BASICS

BB12-1 *Contingent liabilities* (L.O. 3, 4)

Consider the following independent cases:

1 From January through August of the current year, Western Manufacturing worked on and completed a defense contract for the U.S. Air Force. Western has been reimbursed for its costs plus a profit margin, the costs determined by following Defense Department guidelines. On December 28, government auditors informed Western that the firm had computed its costs incorrectly. The Air Force has requested a $74,000 reimbursement. Conversations with Western's cost accounting department revealed that the Air Force's claim was both accurate and correct.

2 Chase Corporation offers a one-year warranty on its sole product. The probable warranty claims from a given level of sales can be determined on the basis of past experience.

3 On December 15, an explosion occurred at the Vesper Glue Company. Ten people were injured, and five houses located near Vesper's manufacturing facility were severely damaged. Although no lawsuits had been filed by the end of the year, management anticipates future court appearances and several out-of-court settlements. The company was not insured for the casualty.

4 Washington Company has always had an excellent reputation for product quality. Management was therefore shocked to learn that a governmental agency was investigating one of the firm's products for safety violations. Although the investigation has just commenced, Washington's legal counsel said there was "a very remote chance of a product recall."

5 Bonanza, Inc., was sued in February for discriminatory hiring practices. Bonanza's lawyers noted that the plaintiffs had a strong case and would likely win the suit. Although the suit was for $100,000, it would probably be settled for $40,000.

Instructions

a Discuss the accounting treatment for contingent liabilities.

b Indicate and discuss how each of the five cases would be treated in the financial statements. Assume each company's year ends on December 31. Present journal entries when appropriate.

BB12-2 *Overview of chapter concepts: Multiple choice* (L.O. 1, 2, 4, 5)

The following multiple-choice questions relate to various topics discussed in the chapter. Select the best answer.

1 Which of the following statements about current liabilities is true?

a Current liabilities must be settled with cash within one year of the balance sheet date.

b Prepayments to a company's suppliers are not considered current liabilities from the company's viewpoint.

c Current liabilities do not include amounts for items that require estimation, such as warranty obligations.

d Failure to record an accrued liability will cause an understatement of net income.

2 Lexus Corporation recorded salaries expense of $346,000 during 19X3. Cash payments for salaries totaled $372,000, and salaries payable at year-end amounted to $20,000. How much were salaries payable on January 1, 19X3?

a $4,000.   c $26,000.

b $20,000.   d $46,000.

3 On June 1, 19X5, Lipscomb Company financed the purchase of a vehicle by signing a $12,360 note payable. The note had a three-month term and included interest of $360 in its face amount. Which of the following entries should Lipscomb record at the beginning of July?

a Interest Expense   120
    Interest Payable   120
b Interest Expense   120
    Notes Payable   120
c Interest Expense   120
    Discount on Notes Payable   120
d Discount on Notes Payable   120
    Interest Expense   120

4 Compat Company issued a $10,000, one-year note on July 1, 19X7. Accrued interest on the 10% obligation amounted to $500 on December 31, 19X7. A balance sheet prepared on December 31 should reveal:

a interest payable of $500.   c notes payable of $9,500.

b a discount of $500.   d notes payable of $10,500.

5 Jordan sells products that carry a warranty. The company estimates the cost of warranty work at 4% of current sales even though much of the work will not be performed for several years into the future. During 19X3, $45,000 was actually spent on warranty service, and sales totaled $3 million. If the Estimated Liability for Warranties account was disclosed at $52,000 on the 19X2 year-end balance sheet, the respective balances of the Warranty Expense and the Estimated Liability for Warranties accounts at the end of *19X3* should equal:

a $45,000, $120,000.   c $120,000, $75,000.

b $45,000, $127,000.   d $120,000, $127,000.

6 A Wage and Tax Statement (W-2 form) is best prepared by reference to:

a an employee's earnings record.

b the payroll register.

c the most recent W-4 form on file with the company.

d a firm's payroll bank account.

7 Payroll taxes are treated as employee withholdings and/or employer expenses. Which of the following choices contains taxes that are paid only by the employee *and* only by the employer?

a Social Security, Medicare, federal income tax.

b Medicare, state unemployment, state income tax.

c Social Security, Medicare, federal unemployment.

d Federal income tax, state income tax, Social Security.

8 Bill Johnson earned $57,800 from Whitfield Corporation during the year. Federal income taxes of $9,700 were withheld from Johnson's paychecks, along with $2,300 for health insurance. In addition, Whit-

field paid $8,000 for health and workers' compensation insurance on Johnson. The following taxes and earnings bases are in effect:

Social Security: 6% on the first $55,000 earned
Medicare: 1.5% on the first $130,000 earned
State and federal unemployment: 5.4% and 0.8%, respectively, on the first $7,000 earned

Whitfield's total cost of having Johnson on the payroll is:
a $12,601.   c $71,484.
b $70,401.   d $82,401.

COMMUNICATION OF ACCOUNTING INFORMATION

CAI12-1 *Preparing a short report: The Boeing Company* **(L.O. 3)**

Communication Principle: Most reports contain three major sections: introduction, body, and conclusion. The introduction cites some background information and sets forth the major points to be covered. These issues are then discussed one at a time in several paragraphs that constitute the body of the report. Finally, a conclusion reiterates the major points and summarizes the writer's position.

The body of a report should be much longer than the introduction or conclusion and deserves several headings that describe the major issues raised. For instance, if you were writing a report about LIFO and FIFO entitled "A Comparison of LIFO and FIFO," headings that precede several body paragraphs could be "Inventory Valuation and Financial Reporting" and "Income Tax Implications of LIFO." (*Note:* The report's "introduction" and "conclusion" are also labeled.) If properly prepared, a title and body headings should help a reader understand the basic information being presented.

■ ■ ■ ■ ■ ■ ■ ■

The Boeing Company is heavily involved in the development and manufacture of commercial airplanes, aerospace equipment and technology, military equipment, and computer systems and electronics. Much of the company's work is done on a contract basis with the U.S. government.

Exploring new frontiers naturally exposes the firm to a variety of risks and contingencies. A note that accompanies the financial statements includes the following remarks:

> Various legal proceedings, claims and investigations are pending against the Company related to products, contracts and other matters. . . . The Company is also involved in various stages of investigation and cleanup relative to environmental protection matters, some of which relate to waste disposal sites. All costs to date have been expensed, even though the Company is filing claims under existing insurance policies and against other responsible parties. The potential costs related to such matters and the possible impact thereof on future operations are uncertain . . . . In addition, the Company is subject to several U.S. Government investigations of business practices and cost classification from which legal or administrative proceedings could result. Based upon Government procurement regulations, under certain circumstances, a contractor can incur fines and penalties, as well as be suspended or [shut out] from Government contracts.

Boeing goes on to say that based on the information available, the outcome of the preceding matters will not have a significant adverse effect on its financial position. (No dollar amount for these items appears on the balance sheet nor is any dollar amount disclosed in the accompanying notes.)

Instructions

Prepare a short report that addresses the disclosure of contingencies, using Boeing's note as an example. Should Boeing's disclosure raise significant doubts about the company or are such disclosures commonplace? Include as part of the report an argument that businesses should disclose an estimated dollar amount for contingencies, along with several data sources that may be used to derive such estimates.

Answers to Chapter Quiz

1 c

2 b

3 d

4 b [(40 hours × $28) + (5 hours × $42) = $1,330; ($55,000 − $54,202) × 0.06 = $47.88; $1,330 × 0.015 = $19.95; $1,330 − $47.88 − $19.95 − $270 − $30 = $962.17]

5 c

Financial Accounting and Reporting: U.S. and Global Perspectives

LEARNING OBJECTIVES

After studying this chapter, you should be able to:

1

Summarize the objectives of financial reporting.

2

Identify and describe the desirable characteristics of accounting information: relevancy, reliability, comparability, and understandability.

3

Explain the need for generally accepted accounting principles and the roles of various groups in the development process.

4

Define the assumptions, concepts, and modifying conventions that underlie financial accounting and reporting.

5

Describe the revenue realization principle and apply the percentage-of-completion and installment methods.

6

Identify several of the basic issues of international accounting.

A review of almost any newspaper or business periodical over the past few years will surely find stories about our changing financial times. The savings and loan crisis, failed banks, massive fraud cases involving securities dealers, and an ongoing wave of employee layoffs have all made headlines or the nightly news. Some of these problems have been caused by a miserable economy and others by poor management. In some cases, though, the primary culprit has been deficient financial reporting and disclosure by the affected organization. Many shareholders, the courts, and Congress are concerned that the financial-reporting system (and the accounting profession) may not be functioning as originally intended.

We add to these problems the changing nature of doing business in this country. No longer is it safe to adopt an isolationist attitude. Companies are affected greatly by foreign competition and, at the same time, are looking to expand abroad. A recent example that might come to mind is McDonald's successful introduction of burgers, fries, and shakes in Moscow. Partly because business is now conducted in an international accounting arena, a company's efforts to operate profitably and measure that profitability have become more complicated.

Previous chapters of this text have focused on specific practices used to record business transactions and disclose financial affairs. In this chapter we wish to present a broad overview of financial accounting by defining the objectives of financial reporting and the characteristics of accounting information. Our emphasis, however, will be on the assumptions and concepts that serve as the underlying foundation for the balance sheet, income statement, and statement of owner's equity, namely, generally accepted accounting principles. The presentation concludes with a look at the impact of conducting activities with foreign companies and in foreign lands.

OBJECTIVES OF FINANCIAL REPORTING

OBJECTIVE

1

Summarize the objectives of financial reporting.

What are the goals of financial accounting and reporting? How can these goals best be attained? Since the mid-1970s, the accounting profession has devoted considerable effort to a conceptual framework project aimed at discovering the answers to these questions. This project has resulted in a series of pronouncements that are expected to provide the necessary structure for the development of improved measurement and disclosure practices.

The first of these pronouncements identified several objectives of financial reporting.[1] The objectives stipulated that the reporting function should generate information that is helpful:

1 To present and potential investors, creditors, and other users in making various types of decisions.

2 In assessing the amounts, timing, and uncertainty of an organization's cash inflows and outflows.

3 In studying an enterprise's resources, the claims to those resources by

---

[1] See "Objectives of Financial Reporting by Business Enterprises," *Statement of Financial Accounting Concepts No. 1* (Norwalk, Conn.: Financial Accounting Standards Board, November 1978).

creditors and owners, and any related changes in either of the foregoing during an accounting period.

4 In examining an enterprise's financial performance, namely, measures of earnings and its components.

These goals relate to the information needs of various groups of financial statement users. Creditors, stockholders, analysts, and others utilize accounting data for a variety of reasons. Creditors, for example, assess an enterprise's debt-paying ability, while stockholders have an obvious concern about corporate earnings and the probability of future dividend distributions. In view of this variety, financial statements must maintain a *general-purpose* orientation and satisfy different needs of different parties. Unbiased determination and communication of economic information is therefore of utmost importance.

Characteristics of Financial Information

Having established the objectives of financial reporting, the profession then studied desirable characteristics of accounting information.[2] As has been explained throughout the text, firms are often given a choice among various accounting policies. Using specified or unspecified criteria, a business must somehow decide what is the best policy to implement in a specific set of circumstances. Presumably, the selected alternative will be the one that generates the most useful financial information. To judge usefulness, the profession noted that information should possess the following characteristics:

■ Relevancy
■ Reliability
■ Comparability
■ Understandability

> **OBJECTIVE**
> **2**
> Identify and describe the desirable characteristics of accounting information: relevancy, reliability, comparability, and understandability.

Sometimes, as we will now see, these characteristics may conflict with one another.

Relevancy

Information is deemed relevant if it influences the actions of a decision maker. On the surface the concept of relevancy is simple: only produce information that can be actively employed by financial statement users. A deeper probe, however, reveals several practical problems. As noted earlier, different users have different needs. Obviously, a given set of financial statements cannot satisfy *all* needs of *all* interested parties. Thus, some compromise is necessary. In addition, if the relevancy concept were implemented in the strictest sense, businesses would have to abandon the traditional cost basis of accounting. To illustrate, consider a company that purchased a parcel of land for $40,000 many years ago. Although the land is now worth $500,000, the company's balance sheet continues to reveal a

---

[2] See "Qualitative Characteristics of Accounting Information," *Statement of Financial Accounting Concepts No. 2* (Norwalk, Conn.: Financial Accounting Standards Board, May 1980).

valuation of $40,000. Unfortunately, the latter figure (i.e., cost) is totally irrelevant for a decision maker who is attempting to evaluate the current worth of the entity. This particular problem has prompted accountants to study alternative means of asset valuation and is explored further in a later section of this chapter.

Reliability

Financial information must be reliable; specifically, the information must depict the conditions it purports to represent. For net income to be a reliable figure, for instance, it must be a true summary of an enterprise's profit-generating activities. Similarly, the accounts payable figure reported on a balance sheet must depict the trade creditor claims against the entity.

Reliability is influenced by a number of factors, one of which is bias. A measure may represent what it is supposed to, but determination of that measure may be slanted. For example, suppose a company that uses LIFO for valuation of inventory and cost of goods sold is operating in a highly inflationary economy. Assume that management has decided to curtail purchasing activities during the last few months of the accounting period to conserve cash. As a result of this action, inventory levels will decline, and, given the nature of the last-in, first-out system, units that are sold currently will be costed at older (and cheaper) prices. Cost of goods sold will therefore be lower than that computed under the firm's prior (i.e., regular) purchasing program. Overall higher earnings will be reported along with a reliable but possibly biased measure of performance. Cost of goods sold is reliable in that it represents the cost of the units sold. However, the measure may be biased by showing significantly lower costs, caused perhaps by a purposeful manipulation of buying habits and, thus, earnings.

Bias usually benefits certain groups at the expense of others and could erode the public's confidence in financial reporting. Accounting information must be neutral ". . . and report economic activity as faithfully as possible, without coloring the image it communicates for the purpose of influencing behavior in *some particular direction.*"[3] In so doing, accounting and financial reporting are enhanced, thereby increasing their usefulness to parties with widely varying interests.

Comparability

Accounting information is more useful if a company's financial statements are comparable with statements of other enterprises and with those of the same company at different points in time. Comparability among entities is difficult because of the variety of accounting methods found in practice—a situation that is not likely to change.

Comparability of a *single firm's* statements through time is achieved by use of the same accounting methods from one period to the next. This practice offers the advantage of better performance evaluation. Imagine the difficulty, for example, of assessing income trends if a company indiscriminately switched depreciation methods during each financial reporting period. Indeed, an analyst would have trouble determining whether varia-

---

[3] Ibid., paragraph 100.

tions in earnings were caused by changes in the entity's activities and efficiency or by changes in its accounting methods. Our discussion here has been intentionally brief; the topic is discussed further in this chapter under the heading of "Consistency Principle."

Understandability

To achieve any degree of usefulness, financial information must be understandable. Often, as is true in many technical disciplines, terminology and jargon can be extremely troublesome. Consider, for instance, the following satirical interaction between Leonard (a stockholder) and President Jones at an annual stockholders' meeting:

> Leonard motioned for the floor and stood up. "You commented previously that total sales increased. Will you comment on our apparent decrease in earnings?"
>
> "Perhaps I should have pointed out," replied President Jones, "that our figures from year to year reflect changes in accounting. For example, we have used LIFO and FIFO. Our depreciation policy is flexible. There is the question of reporting [earnings] per share on the total amount of shares outstanding, the average amount, or the fully converted amount. Our figures also take into account pooling of interest of our latest acquisition. This is a company making a patented banana slicer suitable for any household. Thus it fits nicely into our banana sales. Let me also point out that our final bottom-line figures are reduced by some write-offs. In addition, we have written off some prepaid costs that we know we will incur in coming years. As a result, we had no taxable income this year. We were fortunate in being able to fund some of our short-term borrowings but at an increased interest cost. These and other such adjustments are included in the footnotes to our annual report."[4]

Many people feel that this parody, written over 20 years ago, accurately reflects the present state of affairs in financial reporting. Economic activities have become so complex that down-to-earth explanations in everyday terms are a near impossibility.

The accounting profession services individuals with varied business and educational backgrounds. Contrary to the impression one may receive when reviewing a firm's financial statements or a company's annual report, accountants do not strive to produce a presentation geared especially for bankers, financial analysts, and other long-term veterans of the business world. Our goal is to produce information that is "comprehensible to those who have a *reasonable* understanding of business and economic activities and are willing to study the information with *reasonable* diligence"[5] (emphasis added).

ETHICS ISSUE

A company has had a bad year and is fearful of reporting the results. An accountant has agreed to prepare the financial statements and accompanying notes in an acceptable (although somewhat confusing) manner. Comment.

Suppose you are pursuing the study of accounting at a university located in the heart of a major metropolitan area. You are living at home in a nice suburb and must drive 12 miles twice each week to attend class. Assume it is common knowledge that the local police department is lax in its enforcement of driving regulations. Speeding, running red lights, tailgating,

THE FOUNDATION OF ACCOUNTING

---

[4] Gerald M. Loeb, "Peter and Leonard Attend an Annual Meeting," *Financial Analysts Journal*, May–June 1971, p. 30. Reprinted with permission of *Financial Analysts Journal*.
[5] "Objectives of Financial Reporting by Business Enterprises," op. cit., paragraph 34.

and other offenses are common occurrences. Given the goings-on around you, your trip to campus would surely be an "exciting" experience. Different drivers all doing their own thing results in a hectic, if not chaotic, commuting environment.

Much of the same would undoubtedly be said about financial reporting if each company could summarize business activity in its own unique way. Picture the plight of an investor who is attempting to evaluate the performance of two different entities whose profitability is measured by two widely divergent sets of rules. The investor's task would be formidable, to say the least.

Generally Accepted Accounting Principles (GAAP)

To bring order to the accounting and reporting process, the accounting profession has developed an underlying foundation for measuring and disclosing the results of business transactions and events. The foundation consists of a set of assumptions, concepts, standards, and procedures collectively known as **generally accepted accounting principles (GAAP).** The establishment of GAAP does not mean that all organizations report and measure financial activity in the same manner. Witness, for example, the accounting alternatives available for uncollectible account estimates, depreciation computations, and inventory valuation. Each business is unique in some way, and thus a rigid set of measurement and reporting techniques is not feasible. In view of this fact, the accounting profession has formulated a generalized framework (i.e., ground rules) within which some diversity is possible.

The Development of GAAP

For the most part, generally accepted accounting principles are an outgrowth of the profession's efforts over the past 60 years. The accounting profession made very little progress toward the establishment of principles and practices until the late 1920s and early 1930s. As with many developments in this country, a disaster provided the stimulus for change. Both the stock market crash of 1929 and the accompanying depression dictated a need for improvements in financial measurement and reporting. In many cases the financial statements of this period failed to disclose the correct financial position and profitability of an entity. Numerous businesses overstated net income along with their financial well-being. Because of this situation, efforts were made to protect investors and establish a generalized set of accounting principles.

The Securities and Exchange Commission.   Given a widespread belief in the 1930s that government should play an increased role in the regulation of business, Congress passed several acts pertaining to the preparation of financial statements for publicly held corporations. The **Securities and Exchange Commission (SEC)** was given the power to administer these acts and to prescribe accounting principles and reporting practices for companies that issue publicly traded securities. Although the SEC has the ultimate authority for determining what constitutes GAAP, most of the commission's power has been informally delegated to other rule-making bodies of the accounting profession. The SEC has primarily served in an advisory role in the development of proposed accounting standards and has been active in promoting the disclosure of added information for financial statement users.

The American Institute of Certified Public Accountants and the Accounting Principles Board.   Several years after the SEC came into existence, the **American Institute of Certified Public Accountants (AICPA)**, a national association of licensed CPAs, began to publish bulletins on suggested accounting practices and rules through its newly organized Committee on Accounting Procedure (CAP). CAP had no authority to enforce its pronouncements and met with some criticism over the years.

In 1959, the AICPA formed a new policymaking body called the **Accounting Principles Board (APB)** to advance the development of generally accepted financial-reporting practices. The APB studied different problem areas and issued rulings (termed *Opinions of the Accounting Principles Board*) on suggested treatment of various topics. Unlike CAP, which could advise but not enforce, the AICPA and the APB collectively declared that departures from the *Opinions* (i.e., GAAP) must be detailed and explained in a company's published financial statements. In view of this ruling, most companies follow GAAP when measuring and disclosing business activity. This practice avoids negative criticism of the firm by creditors and stockholders and, at the same time, reduces the possibility of lawsuits that sometimes arise from ill-advised reporting techniques.

In the late 1960s and early 1970s, disagreement once again arose concerning the development of accounting principles. The work of the APB was branded as ineffective, primarily because of the following factors:

1 Members of the Accounting Principles Board were part-time, unpaid volunteers. Thus, policies were formulated by professionals who could not devote their full attention to the issues at hand.

2 Board members maintained relationships with their accounting firms and clients and may have inadvertently compromised their position and vote for fear of injuring clientele.

The AICPA reacted to these criticisms by performing a thorough study of the APB's operation and policymaking procedures. In the early 1970s, the APB was abolished and replaced by the Financial Accounting Standards Board, a body independent of the AICPA. Although the APB and the Committee on Accounting Procedure are no longer in operation, their pronouncements are still in force and considered GAAP unless specifically amended or superseded by newer rulings.

The Financial Accounting Standards Board.   Currently, standards of financial reporting in the United States are formulated by the **Financial Accounting Standards Board (FASB)**, a private-sector organization. Rulings of the board are GAAP and are called *Statements of Financial Accounting Standards* as opposed to *Opinions*.

Aside from its independence from the AICPA, the FASB differs from the APB in three major respects. First, members of the FASB serve on a full-time basis and must sever all ties with their previous employers. Member independence is therefore increased since the chance for employer or client influence is reduced (and probably eliminated). Second, FASB members are well paid for their efforts. At the time of this writing, their annual salaries were as follows: chair, $370,000; board members, $300,000. The final difference between the FASB and APB involves representation. Recognizing that accounting has far-reaching effects, the FASB has a broader-based membership, with backgrounds in public accounting as well as industry, government, academia, and the securities markets. This last characteristic enables the board to better serve the public interest.

During its existence the FASB has been relatively active. However, there have been complaints that the board moves too slowly on certain critical financial-reporting issues, fails to field test its proposals, and overlooks the cost of policy implementation. Some of this criticism is coming from the SEC. On the development of a new reporting standard for financial institutions, for instance, *The Wall Street Journal* reported:

> In the past few weeks, the SEC's mission has taken on a new urgency. Accounting rule makers who pride themselves on the stately pace of the standard-setting process are shocked by what they see as a government-inspired stampede. SEC staffers are calling up the standard setters, who are accustomed to taking months and years to deliberate on a single issue, and demanding results now. And in a striking departure, the SEC is not only dictating the timetable but also letting rule makers know what answers it wants.[6]

Whether the SEC will continue this aggressive behavior into the future is uncertain. One fact is known, however: some powerful individuals in the financial community believe that the FASB should be overhauled.

Other Influential Bodies. In addition to the SEC and the FASB, many other groups influence the establishment of generally accepted accounting principles. Among them are various accounting organizations, such as the *American Accounting Association (AAA)* and the *Institute of Management Accountants (IMA)*. The AAA is comprised primarily of educators; in contrast, most of the IMA's members are employed in business and assist in furnishing information for planning, control, and decision making. These organizations play no official role in the development of accounting standards; however, they regularly communicate their position on numerous matters to the profession's policymaking bodies. The *Internal Revenue Service (IRS)*, which administers the tax laws passed by Congress, also has some impact on the development process. Although most tax regulations do not directly affect financial reporting, businesses often simplify matters by using specified tax practices for both the filing of tax returns with the government *and* the preparation of financial statements.

Add to the preceding organizations various professional and trade associations; public accounting and business firms; and bankers, analysts, and other financial statement users. The net result is the formula for how generally accepted accounting principles (standards) are developed in this country. The overall process is depicted in Exhibit 13-1.

---

[6] See "Tackling Accounting, SEC Pushes Changes with Broad Impact," *The Wall Street Journal*, September 27, 1990, pp. A1, A8.

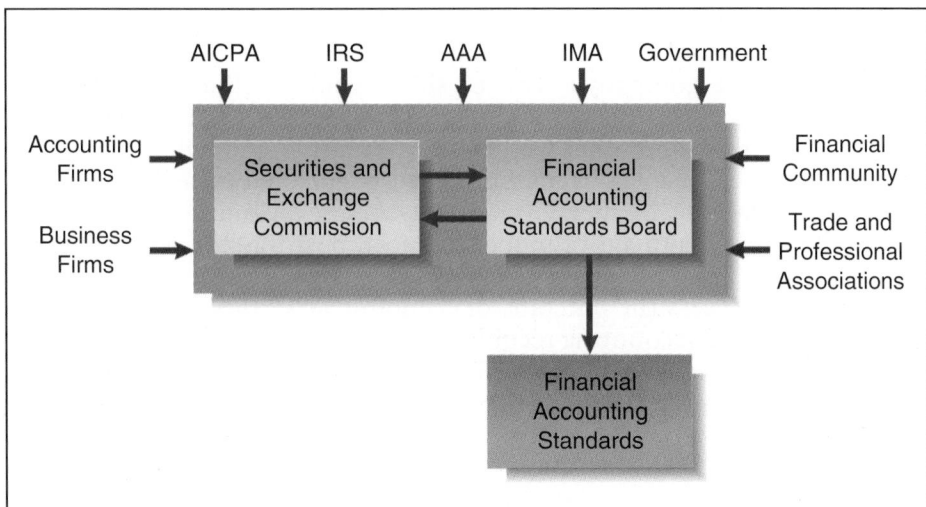

EXHIBIT 13-1
The Development of Financial Accounting Standards

Specific Principles and Assumptions

APB *Opinions* and FASB *Statements* stipulate the proper accounting treatments that are afforded to a number of different topical areas. Throughout the first 12 chapters of this text, you were exposed to the following pronouncements, among others:

Pronouncement	Topic
APB Opinion No. 17	Intangible assets
FASB Statement No. 2	Accounting for research and development costs
FASB Statement No. 5	Accounting for contingencies
FASB Statement No. 12	Short-term investments
FASB Statement No. 34	Capitalization of interest cost

OBJECTIVE

4

Define the assumptions, concepts, and modifying conventions that underlie financial accounting and reporting.

Although the *Opinions* and *Statements* are considered GAAP by the accounting profession and the financial community, these pronouncements are not, in a true sense, "principles." Instead, they are rulings that pertain to accounting practice. Underlying accounting practice is a set of assumptions, concepts, and modifying conventions that form the basis for the FASB's work. These items will be discussed in the following sections.

Entity Assumption

Recall from Chapter 1 that financial reporting is based on the entity assumption. An **entity** is an economic unit organized to pursue business activity. Examples of entities include corporations, individuals, clubs, governmental units, and a host of other organizations. It is important to note that each entity has its own assets, liabilities, revenues, and expenses and must be accounted for accordingly. In effect, the entity is a boundary for reporting, namely, a unit that is separate and distinct both from its owners and from other operations.

The absence of the entity assumption would make a mockery of the accounting process. To illustrate, assume that Jeremy Carson, a well-to-do engineer, organized a small company to conduct research in the solar energy field. If Carson's individual transactions were merged with those of the business, the company's balance sheet would include Carson's own clothing, his residence, his automobile, and other assets and liabilities that pertain solely to his personal well-being. Similarly, the income statement would combine business transactions with personal revenues and expenses. In sum, the financial statements of the business would fail to reflect the energy company's proper financial position and operating performance.

To correctly assess the outcome of economic activity, each entity must maintain separate accounting records and prepare separate sets of financial statements. That is, owner and business transactions must be segregated, along with the transactions of other independent economic units.

Going-Concern Assumption

A key assumption in accounting is that a business will continue to operate for an indefinite period of time unless there is substantial evidence to the contrary. Stated differently, the business is presumed to be a **going concern.** Even though all entities do not survive, the going-concern assumption is valid in the majority of cases and forms the basis for many accounting practices. For example, if we expected a business to terminate in the near future, items such as land and equipment would be expensed upon acquisition because of a low probability of receiving benefits beyond the current period. These resources, of course, are treated as assets.

The going-concern assumption also provides some justification for the use of an accounting system based on historical cost. Should a company plan to cease operations in the near term, asset valuation on the balance sheet could properly take the form of liquidation (sale) prices in view of the assets' impending disposal.

Periodicity Assumption

Although a business is assumed to conduct operations for long periods of time, investors, creditors, governmental authorities, and other financial statement users cannot wait forever to analyze performance. Initially introduced in Chapter 3, the **periodicity assumption** holds that for reporting purposes, an entity's life can be divided into discrete time periods such as months, quarters, or years. As a result of this assumption, the accountant must assign business transactions to specific reporting periods. In many cases this task presents no special problems. For example, a check written on March 1 in payment of March rent is easily traced to March.

Difficulty arises, however, when dealing with expenditures that span several periods. To illustrate, consider a long-lived machine. If a company wants to produce a yearly income statement, the machine's cost must be allocated to the period in question via depreciation expense. As you saw in Chapter 10, depreciation can be computed (and cost allocated) by several acceptable methods, each producing different results. Most accountants recognize that cost allocations normally result in arbitrary figures, thus diminishing the usefulness of financial statements. Aside from depreciation, the periodicity assumption also forms the basis for amortization and the adjusting process at the conclusion of an accounting period.

Monetary Unit Assumption

All countries have a unit of exchange. The United States uses the dollar; Mexico, the peso; and Japan, the yen. Business organizations adopt the national currency of their home country to quantify financial activity. Accounting therefore assumes that an entity's transactions can be expressed in terms of a common measuring unit, namely, money. If all organizations in a given country use the same measure, or **monetary unit,** extensive comparative analysis by financial statement users is possible.

Financial reporting in the United States is based on the premise that the dollar is a stable evaluation unit, thereby permitting dollars of different years to be combined in the financial statements. When computing the balance in a company's Land account, for instance, land transactions of the 1990s are mixed with transactions that occurred in prior years. This calculation is reasonable provided that the dollar is, in fact, stable. Historically, accounting policymakers have taken the position that fluctuations in the value of the dollar are small and can be ignored.

Is this a valid position, however? Consider the dollar in comparison with other units of measure, say, square feet. If you were to measure the area of the room you are presently in today, next year, and five years from now, an accurate measurement would undoubtedly yield the same result each time. In contrast, consider the amount of goods and services you could purchase for $50 over the same time period. In all likelihood the goods and services acquired would decline each year due to rising prices and a reduction in the dollar's purchasing power. Because of this behavior (i.e., instability), especially in periods of high inflation, some accountants contend that transactions occurring today cannot be combined with those of earlier periods. The net result would be the combination of dollars of different purchasing powers and, hence, misleading financial statements.

Historical-Cost Principle

Accountants have been faced with many problems over the years. One of the most troublesome (and debated) issues has been the financial statement valuation of goods, services, and resources acquired in business transactions. As noted in Chapter 1, accounting is based on the **historical-cost principle.** That is, acquisitions of the preceding items are recorded in the accounts at cost, with cost defined as the exchange or transaction price.

The use of historical cost has received mixed reviews. In its favor, historical cost is objective and definite. To explain, the use of cost and exchange prices gives rise to objective valuations created by negotiation between two *independent* parties—a buyer and a seller. Also on the favorable end of the spectrum, cost can be verified by inspecting canceled checks, contracts, invoices, and other similar documents.

Critics of historical cost note that employment of the cost basis *after asset acquisition* produces out-of-date asset valuations and distorted income figures. The latter arise because of cost-based depreciation and amortization computations. Critics therefore contend that fair market values should be integrated in the financial statements. This practice, while having obvious benefits, does have an inherent problem. Assume, for instance, that five accountants are trying to compute the fair market value ("current worth") of an old manufacturing plant. The "current worth" would probably be influenced by a number of factors that are difficult to quantify, such as the plant's physical condition, its location, and the general state of the real-estate market. Even competent appraisal services that specialize in this type of work would have differing ideas, culminating in dissimilar (and subjective) estimates. Subjectivity, of course, would erode the public's confidence in a company's financial statements.

An Experiment by the FASB.   Fluctuating purchasing powers of the dollar, out-of-date asset valuations, and distorted income figures have prompted the study of financial-reporting models other than historical cost. These models, which have most relevance in periods of moderate-to-excessive rising prices, come under the caption of *inflation accounting*. The more popular models focus on (1) adjustment of historical-cost figures by use of a general price level index[7] and (2) detailed examinations and revaluations of the individual assets owned to recognize "current worth."

The mechanical details of these approaches are beyond the scope of this text. Be aware, though, that during the early 1980s, the Financial Accounting Standards Board experimented and actually required large corporations to disclose certain inflation-adjusted information. The disclosures were not to be made in the financial statements themselves but rather in the accompanying notes.[8] Shortly thereafter, in 1986, the FASB made such disclosures voluntary. This decision was brought about by several factors, including business complaints that the required information was too expensive to produce and could be misinterpreted, a lowering of inflation rates, and a diminished interest in the topic by the SEC.

Objectivity Principle

The thrust of the objectivity principle has been discussed in preceding sections of this chapter. Simply stated, the **objectivity principle** requires that accounting information be free from bias and verifiable by an independent party (such as an external auditor). The resulting financial statements will therefore reflect a fair and neutral view of an organization's business affairs.

Although a high degree of objectivity is desirable, it is difficult to eliminate all personal opinion and judgment from accounting measurement. Consider the accounting procedures related to depreciable assets, for example. Although the cost of a long-lived asset can be determined objectively, estimates are needed when computing service life and residual value, and personal opinion is used when selecting a depreciation method. Naturally, variations in any of the preceding factors will produce different effects on

---

[7] The consumer price index (CPI) is an example of such an index. This popular statistic measures retail price changes of a variety of items (food, clothing, transportation, and so forth) throughout the country.

[8] See "Financial Reporting and Changing Prices," *Statement of Financial Accounting Standards No. 33* (Norwalk, Conn.: Financial Accounting Standards Board, 1979); and "Financial Reporting and Changing Prices: Elimination of Certain Disclosures," *Statement of Financial Accounting Standards No. 82* (Norwalk, Conn.: Financial Accounting Standards Board, 1984).

net income and asset valuations. As long as the estimates and related decisions are reasonable, made by a competent party, and verifiable, the objectivity principle is considered to have been implemented to the greatest extent possible.

Revenue Realization Principle

The generation of revenue in our economy takes many different forms. Hospitals, for instance, earn revenues by rendering health-care services; professional sports clubs sell tickets and broadcasting rights; department stores sell merchandise; and construction companies build roads, homes, office complexes, and a host of other facilities. Although our list of revenue-generating activities is far from complete, a question arises as to when these enterprises should recognize revenue in their accounting records. Theoretically, revenue generation is a continuous process for most firms. Practically, however, revenue is said to be *realized* (earned) when both of the following conditions are satisfied:

1 The earnings process is complete or virtually complete.
2 The amount of revenue can be objectively measured.

For most businesses these two tests are met when merchandise is sold or when services are rendered. In either case the transaction and earnings process is complete at this point, and the revenue is measurable on the basis of the exchange price between the buyer and the seller.

  Although the time of sale (or rendering of services) is the general rule for recognizing revenue, realization is sometimes advanced or delayed, as depicted in the time line shown in Exhibit 13-2.

Revenue Recognized During Production.   Many companies engage in construction projects that take several years to complete, such as ships, shopping malls, and dams. Because these firms generate revenues over long periods, it may be more appropriate to enter revenue in the accounting records throughout a project's life instead of waiting until the venture is completed (i.e., the point of sale). Accordingly, a method of revenue recognition termed **percentage of completion (POC)** may be used. Under the POC method, profit is allocated to each accounting period on the basis of progress toward project completion. Completion is usually judged by comparing the current period's construction costs with the total expected costs over the project's life.

  As an example, assume that Brennan Construction signed a $44 million contract to build a shopping mall over the next three years. Brennan's

OBJECTIVE

5

Describe the revenue realization principle and apply the percentage-of-completion and installment methods.

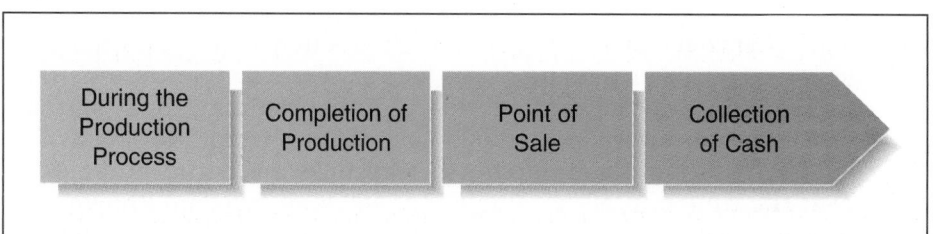

**EXHIBIT 13-2
Revenue Recognition
Time Line**

accounting department has estimated total construction costs at $40 million, resulting in a $4 million profit for the company. The following schedule shows the actual costs incurred by the firm along with the annual profit recognized:

Year	(A) Actual Costs Incurred	(B) Percentage of Work Completed (A ÷ $40,000,000)	(C) Profit Recognized ($4,000,000 × B)
1	$10,000,000	25%	$1,000,000
2	24,000,000	60	2,400,000
3	6,300,000	Remainder	300,000*
	$40,300,000		$3,700,000

* Remaining amount needed to yield total income of $3.7 million.

For the first two years, the percentage of work completed is derived by dividing the actual costs incurred by the $40 million total project cost. The resulting percentage is then multiplied by the $4 million estimated profit to compute annual income. Year 3, the last year of construction, is handled in a different fashion. Total construction costs amount to $40.3 million, generating an overall contract profit of $3.7 million ($44,000,000 − $40,300,000). Since profit of $3.4 million has already been recognized ($1,000,000 + $2,400,000), Brennan can realize only $300,000 in Year 3.

Because of the objectivity principle, the POC method is used only when a business has the ability to make reasonably dependable estimates of contract revenues, contract costs, and the extent of progress toward completion. In those instances where substantial uncertainty surrounds the estimation process, other procedures are followed.

Tips & Techniques

Percentage of completion can be employed for either all or part of a company's operation. Westinghouse Electric, for instance, noted the following in a recent annual report:

Sales are recorded primarily as products are shipped and services are rendered. The percentage-of-completion method of accounting is used for nuclear steam supply system orders with delivery schedules generally in excess of five years, major power generation systems with a cycle time in excess of one year, and certain construction projects where this method of accounting is consistent with industry practice.

Revenue Recognized Upon Completion of Production. In some situations revenue is recognized at the end of production. For example, assume that Brennan Construction had great difficulty in determining total contract costs. Because the related percentage calculations would be somewhat questionable, it is more appropriate to recognize the entire profit ($3.7 million) at the time of project completion, when all facts are known.

Recognition also occurs upon completion of production in selected, well-developed markets such as those for certain farm products and precious metals. For instance, farmers may face a situation in which the sale and price of their crops are reasonably assured and no significant delivery costs are involved. Revenue in this case can be recognized upon harvest, as the earnings process is complete and the amount of revenue can be objectively measured.

Revenue Recognized at the Time of Receipt.   As we noted in Chapter 3, many professionals (e.g., lawyers, dentists, and architects) use a form of cash-basis accounting for their practices. Under the cash basis, revenue is realized at the time cash is collected from customers and clients. Probably because the method is simple and accepted by the Internal Revenue Service, cash-basis accounting is widely used by individuals and small businesses. The cash basis is not in accord with GAAP, however, because revenue realization is delayed beyond the point where the earnings process is complete.[9] The cash basis is appropriate in those few instances when revenues cannot be correctly determined at the time of sale, specifically, when collectibility of customer accounts is in serious doubt. This situation sometimes arises with installment sales made to individuals who have no (or poor) credit histories.

Installment sales occur in the retail field, especially home furnishings and appliances, where payments are spread over several years. Revenues can be recognized by using a variation of the cash basis called the **installment method.** Sellers that use the installment method allocate a sale's profit to different accounting periods based on the amount of cash received from customers. For example, suppose that on September 1, Beachwood Kitchens sold $1,500 of new appliances to Joyce Chambers, who has no credit history and has been employed for only two weeks. Chambers paid $300 down and agreed to remit the balance owed via 24 end-of-month installments of $50 each.[10] If the appliances cost Beachwood $900, the company has generated a $600 profit, or a 40% return on sales ($600 ÷ $1,500 = 40%). Because each dollar collected from Chambers represents a 40% profit, the company's recognition schedule would appear as follows:

Year	Cash Collected		Profit Percentage		Profit Recognized
1	$ 500*	×	40%	=	$200
2	600†	×	40	=	240
3	400‡	×	40	=	160
	$1,500				$600

* $300 down payment + four monthly installments of
  $50 each.
† Twelve monthly installments of $50 each.
‡ Eight monthly installments of $50 each.

---

[9] Most professional practices do not issue "published financial statements," or statements to owners (i.e., stockholders) that have been audited by a CPA. "Unpublished" statements need not be prepared in accordance with GAAP.

[10] To simplify matters, we will ignore interest.

Similar to the cash basis, the installment method does not conform to GAAP unless, as noted earlier, considerable uncertainty surrounds collectibility of the receivable. If certain conditions are satisfied, the installment method is acceptable to the IRS and affords users the advantage of postponing income taxes. Postponement arises because revenues are not taxed until cash is received.

Matching Principle

Like revenue realization, the **matching principle** is another important consideration in the calculation of accounting income. Originally discussed in Chapter 3, this principle holds that all costs and expenses associated with the production of revenue should be recognized when the revenue is recognized. Stated differently, expenses should be matched against and deducted from the revenues they helped to create.

The matching principle is the underlying reason behind the adjusting process. Consider, for example, the accounting treatment for depreciable assets. At the end of a reporting period, depreciation expense is recorded in the accounts via an adjustment. Why? Long-term assets such as plant and equipment generate revenues (or benefits) for prolonged periods of time. Thus, a *portion* of the assets' cost (i.e., depreciation expense) is written off each period and matched against the revenues created by the assets' use. Notice that only part of the cost is currently expensed; the remainder will be written off in future periods against the future revenues generated.

Consistency Principle

Financial statements are frequently compared over periods of time to examine trends, assess growth patterns, and so forth. To enhance these studies, accountants have implemented the principle of **consistency,** which holds that entities employ the same accounting practices in each reporting period. Picture the difficulties that would result if a company switched back and forth between LIFO and FIFO and other measurement techniques at will. Indeed, such a practice would create havoc for financial statement users who, in many cases, would be forced to compare the noncomparable.

It is important to note that consistency does not prohibit all change. Changes in the methods of recording and reporting business transactions are allowable whenever the end result is a better or more fair presentation of economic activity. When such changes occur, the reason for the change and the impact on net income must be disclosed in the financial statements.

Principle of Full Disclosure

So that investors, creditors, and analysts are not misled, a set of financial statements includes much more than just account balances. An entity must provide a complete reporting (**full disclosure**) of all facts important enough to influence the judgment of an informed user of financial information. Just what an "informed user" really means is, itself, open to debate. Accountants, however, have agreed that full disclosure should include the following items as a minimum:

1 A summary of the significant accounting policies used in statement preparation.

2 Principles and practices peculiar to the industry in which the entity operates, along with departures from GAAP.

3 Changes in accounting policies and the impact on net income.

4 Impending lawsuits and contingencies.

5 Significant events that occurred after the accounting period being reported but prior to issuance of the financial statements, for example, major casualties such as fires and tornadoes.

6 Significant transactions that took place during the period, such as business acquisitions and mergers.

Full disclosure often takes the form of parenthetical comments within the body of the statements and a separate set of footnotes. The notes that accompany the financial statements of Alberto Culver Company appear in Appendix C at the end of the text.

Materiality

There are many instances in accounting where theory gives way to expediency, especially when dealing with very small amounts or transactions. To illustrate, suppose a company recently acquired five pencil sharpeners for $75. If the principles and practices introduced in the preceding pages were followed to the letter, the sharpeners would be entered in the accounts as long-term assets and depreciated over their lifetime. Assuming a 10-year life, annual straight-line depreciation would amount to $7.50, a pittance for almost any organization. To avoid the administrative problems and costs of keeping track of these items over the next 10 years, most companies would expense the entire $75 immediately at the time of acquisition.

This accounting treatment is justified for two reasons. First, the transaction is very small; and second, it will probably have a minimal impact on the financial statements. This example has focused on the concept of materiality. **Materiality** dictates that the accountant must judge the impact and importance of each transaction (or event) to determine the proper treatment in the accounting records and the resultant financial statements. In general, an amount is said to be material if knowledge of it would influence the decisions of an informed financial statement user.

Materiality is a relative concept and is often judged by using comparative analysis. For example, a potential expense item could be compared against some type of dollar limit. If the item exceeds the limit, it is deemed material; if under the limit, the item is considered immaterial and would be expensed. The dollar limit and exactly what is material varies from company to company: what is immaterial for Shell Oil might be very significant to Joe's Garage. There is no guideline stating that 10% is always material or that any expenditure over $500 is always significant. Again, materiality is a relative concept.

Conservatism

An accountant is faced with a number of different decisions in attempting to measure and report the financial affairs of an enterprise. Frequently, the "proper" decision is difficult to determine. After exercising sound judgment and considering the objectives of financial reporting, other accounting principles, and industry practices, the accountant often turns to the doctrine of conservatism. **Conservatism** holds that when alternative accounting valuations and measurements are possible, the alternative selected should be the one least likely to overstate assets and/or net income.

Over the years, conservative financial statements have found favor with statement users. Conservatism allows users to downplay the impact of overly optimistic company managements who may be inclined to record revenue in the accounts before the revenue is earned, capitalize items that should be expensed, and follow other similar practices, many of which tend to improve reported financial position and profitability. Overly optimistic financial statements could mask impending losses and mislead users.

The application of conservatism in accounting becomes evident when studying the lower-of-cost-or-market method for valuing short-term investments. For instance, suppose Remy Company purchased $15,000 of stock on October 1, to be held as a short-term investment. Assume that on December 31, the end of the firm's accounting period, the investment was worth $22,000. If this is the only security held by Remy, the $7,000 increase in value would be ignored when preparing the financial statements. Conservatism says to disregard increases in value while holding the stock. Consistent with the guidelines established for revenue realization, such gains (i.e., profits) will be recognized upon sale. Interestingly, if the value of the securities had fallen by $7,000, a write down below cost and the recording of a loss are justified. Why? The result is a lower, more conservative asset valuation and a reduced net income.

INTERNATIONAL ACCOUNTING

OBJECTIVE
6

Identify several of the basic issues of international accounting.

Globalization is a hot topic these days at many companies and business schools. Modern communications systems, transportation technology, and a basic desire to survive have prompted numerous entities to become multinational concerns. Foreign operations are now a key factor in the business plans of most major U.S.-based corporations. These operations make a significant contribution to an entity's total revenues and profit, having a much greater impact than the average "person on the street" may realize. As evidence, we present Exhibit 13-3.

Given the magnitude of world markets, American corporations have a strong desire to develop foreign trade. As these firms are well aware, however, international trade is a two-way street. Witness popular consumer items in this country such as Nestlé chocolate, Mercedes-Benz automobiles, and Seiko watches, all of which are products of companies headquartered in foreign lands.

An increased attention to the accounting aspects of international trade is accompanying this globalization of trade. U.S. firms, for example, maintain their records in dollars and settle their transactions in dollars. Companies of other countries, of course, do not. Businesses in the United States produce financial statements that are in accord with generally accepted accounting principles. Foreign entities, in contrast, are often subject to a totally different reporting framework. The last few pages of this chapter address several basic issues related to doing business in foreign markets: uniformity of international accounting standards, accounting for foreign currency transactions, and disclosure of international financial affairs.

HIGHLIGHT
I'll Take a Large with Pepperoni and Corn

The expansion of business into foreign lands can be an interesting experience. Just ask Domino's, which gave Japan its first taste of take-out pizza in 1985. That pizza came from a tiny Domino's outlet, the chain's first in Asia. From the beginning, the outlet faced stiff competition—not only from the American eat-in chains that had opened but also from a Japanese diet heavy on raw fish, rice, and seaweed. Still, in a decade when Japanese exports to the United States have soared, Domino's has proven there are some American products that the Japanese can't get enough of. This situation has developed in spite of early market research.

Initial market studies were discouraging. Experts said that home delivery of pizza simply couldn't be done in Japan. The country's consumers were known to dislike both tomatoes and cheese—they thought the latter looked and tasted like soap. And pizza wasn't considered a meal. The Japanese viewed it as a snack food, which made it hard to justify the hefty prices necessary to make the business profitable.

In addition, there was concern that Domino's take-out concept wouldn't be much of a draw for Japanese consumers. Home delivery, known in Japan as *demae*, was nothing new. Neighborhood shops routinely deliver the likes of raw fish and noodles. Further, the research showed, since Japanese families generally live in tiny apartments, those spending a little more for a meal preferred to go out to spacious coffee shops and restaurants.

Finally, Domino's vaunted guarantee of delivery within 30 minutes seemed impossible in Tokyo, a sprawling, snarled web of nameless streets where sequential addresses don't exist. (Buildings are numbered not by location, but by the order in which they were built.)

As management noted, "When you bring over a concept from the U.S., you have to decide what you have to change to make it acceptable for the Japanese market. But what's most important is what not to change, because you might lose the very factor that made [the concept] successful."

In Japan, Domino's made three procedural modifications. It made the pizzas smaller, reducing the U.S. sizes—12 and 16 inches—to 10 and 14 inches. The firm added two optional toppings that U.S. pizza lovers might consider almost sacrilegious (if not stomach-curdling): corn and tuna. And, to help drivers cope with Tokyo's horrendous traffic and narrow streets, the company used souped-up, streamlined Honda motor scooters rather than cars.

An additional problem was discovered just before the first Japanese Domino's was scheduled to open. "Nobody knew how to make a pizza," recalls high-level executive J. B. Sassano. "I was the only one." Sassano spent weeks reorganizing the new store, making it look and work exactly like a Domino's in the States. Then he set to work teaching a group of college students raised on sushi and smoked eel the art of pizza preparation. Four weeks later, Sassano put his stamp of approval on the product, and Domino's opened for business.

The shop began deliveries in the fall of 1985, charging between $7 and $21 per pizza and promising customers they'd have their food in 30 minutes or get a refund of 700 yen, about $5. Within a few months, the store had to double and then triple the number of delivery scooters. Six months after that, a second Domino's opened.

Domino's has kept its lead, management says, by maintaining product integrity. But the firm may have other advantages as well. In a country increasingly fascinated with things American, Domino's has not only the taste of the States but also the look. Just like its American stores, Domino's Japanese outlets are decorated in red, white, and blue. Additionally, at the top of every menu are three words that carry the exotic odor of pepperoni rising off a circular pie: "From the U.S.A."

Source: Adapted from "Slicing the Japanese Pie," *American Way*, November 1, 1989, pp. 40, 42–43. Reprinted by permission of Thomas J. Meyer, the author, and *American Way*, the inflight magazine of American Airlines. Copyright 1989 by American Airlines.

EXHIBIT 13-3
Large U.S. Multinational Firms

Rank*	Company	Foreign Revenue as a % of Total Revenue	Foreign Operating Profit as a % of Total Operating Profit
1	Exxon	74.9%	83.5%
2	IBM	60.7	75.5
3	General Motors	30.3	†
4	Ford Motor	36.7	27.0
5	Mobil	55.3	83.7
22	Coca-Cola	61.2	72.1
25	Johnson & Johnson	51.7	50.1
36	FW Woolworth	43.6	42.6
49	Sara Lee	28.6	52.3
81	Borden	28.4	24.5

* Companies are ranked in terms of foreign revenue.
† General Motors had profitable foreign operations but, overall, produced a net loss for the period under study.
Source: Adapted from "U.S. Corporations With the Biggest Foreign Revenues," *Forbes,* July 22, 1991, pp. 286–288.

Uniformity of International Accounting Standards

As noted several times in this text, a desirable characteristic of financial information is comparability among firms. We observed that differences in accounting methods sometimes make such comparisons difficult. These difficulties are compounded at the international level because of significant variations in political systems, economic systems, and fundamental principles of measurement. Consider, for instance, the *small* sampling of differences that appears in Exhibit 13-4. (We emphasize the word "small," given the number of variations that actually exist.) In view of this situation, a valid question arises: Can a user rely on and correctly analyze a

EXHIBIT 13-4
A Sampling of Differences in Financial Reporting

Accounting/Reporting Topic	U.S. Practice	Foreign Practice
Inventory valuation	Lower of cost or market	Japan: Cost
Depreciation	Straight-line, units-of-output, declining balance, sum-of-the-years'-digits	Italy: Straight-line
Financial statement disclosure of accounting policies	Full disclosure	Switzerland: Optional disclosure
Goodwill amortization	Written off over 40 years to expense	Great Britain: Charged to owners' (stockholders') equity, thus boosting income
Effects of inflation	Voluntary disclosure in the notes to the financial statements	Brazil: Impact integrated directly in the financial statements

foreign entity's financial statements when making credit-extension, investment, and other common business decisions?

The IASC and the IFAC

As global activities have expanded, the need and demand for uniform international accounting standards have increased. To meet this need, several private-sector and governmental standard-setting organizations have been established. Foremost among these groups are the International Accounting Standards Committee (IASC) and the International Federation of Accountants (IFAC).

The IASC membership consists of representatives from professional accounting societies of numerous countries. The U.S. representative to this organization is the American Institute of Certified Public Accountants. The IASC operates in a manner very similar to the Financial Accounting Standards Board (FASB) and issues standards that relate to specific financial reporting topics. Unlike the FASB, however, the IASC lacks authority to prescribe accounting rules, relying instead on members' attempts to have the standards adopted in their respective countries.

The IFAC is also comprised of representatives from professional accounting organizations throughout the world. Like the IASC, the IFAC's authority is self-imposed by the voluntary efforts of its membership. This body is primarily concerned with auditing and other professional matters, such as ethics and education.

The major goals of these organizations are to bring a degree of uniformity to international accounting standards and to develop and enhance a coordinated worldwide accounting profession. Realistically, achievement of these goals will be a long and difficult process. One should remember that the development of generally accepted accounting principles within even a single country (e.g., the United States) usually has required decades of evolution and debate.

Accounting for Foreign Currency Transactions

International trade is complicated by the various currencies that are used in the world's marketplace. Whenever an entity buys goods from a foreign supplier or sells goods to a foreign customer, the parties involved must agree on the currency to be used in settling the transaction. From the perspective of a U.S. company, if settlement will be made in U.S. dollars, then no unique measurement and reporting problems arise. In contrast, if settlement requires the use of a foreign currency, special accounting considerations are introduced. To appreciate these considerations, it is necessary to have a basic understanding of *currency exchange rates.*

At any point in time, the currency of one country may be exchanged into the currency of another. The conversion is based on the **spot rate** in effect at the time of exchange. For example, the spot rate might indicate that a U.S. firm could purchase one Swiss franc for $0.70. Spot rates tend to fluctuate throughout a reporting period in response to changes in inflation, interest rates, and political climate. These rates are eventually used to record a host of foreign currency transactions.

Purchase Transactions

To illustrate the necessary accounting for purchases that occur in a foreign currency, assume that Jewelry Import (JI) of New York acquired watches from Alps Exporting of Switzerland. According to terms of the transaction, JI must pay 20,000 Swiss francs to the foreign firm in 60 days. If the spot rate at the time of purchase was $0.70 per franc, how should Jewelry Import enter the transaction in its accounts? Recording the transaction in francs would result in financial records that contain a hodgepodge of different currencies, making data summarization and financial statement preparation impossible. It is therefore necessary to enter the transaction in U.S. dollars even though ultimate settlement will be made in the Swiss currency. The entry needed on the date of purchase is as follows:

Purchases	14,000	
Accounts Payable		14,000
Purchased merchandise on account		

Notice that the account payable is established at the number of U.S. dollars required to purchase 20,000 francs at $0.70 each. The computation is generalized in the following manner:

$$\frac{\text{Transaction Amount in}}{\text{Foreign Currency Units}} \times \text{Spot Rate} = \frac{\text{Transaction Amount}}{\text{in U.S. Dollars}}$$

Sixty days later, Jewelry Import will acquire the francs from a commercial bank at the spot rate in effect on that date. These francs will then be delivered to Alps Exporting in settlement of the transaction. Because exchange rates fluctuate daily, the spot rate will likely differ from the $0.70 rate that existed on the date of purchase. Suppose, for example, that the spot rate has changed and stands at $0.68 on the date of settlement. When Jewelry Import purchases the Swiss currency, the firm will be required to pay only $13,600 (20,000 francs × $0.68). A journal entry to reflect the purchase of francs and the payment to Alps Exporting would be

Accounts Payable	14,000	
Exchange Gain		400
Cash		13,600
Acquired Swiss francs and paid		
related foreign currency payable		

This entry indicates that a liability originally established at $14,000 was settled by a cash outlay of only $13,600. The difference constitutes a foreign currency transaction exchange gain. Conversely, Jewelry Import would have suffered an exchange loss had the spot rate risen between the date of purchase and the date of payment.

Sale Transactions

Similar accounting treatment applies to sales on account that will be settled in a foreign currency. Suppose, for example, that American Export sells goods to a British company. The terms of sale require the foreign firm to pay 1,000 British pounds in 90 days. If the spot rate on the date of sale is $1.80 per pound, the transaction would be recorded as follows:

Accounts Receivable	1,800	
Sales		1,800
Sold merchandise on account		

Ninety days later, assume the spot rate stands at $1.75 and the purchaser delivers the British currency to American Export. If American Export immediately sells the pounds at a commercial bank for $1,750 (1,000 pounds × $1.75), the appropriate journal entry would be as shown.

Cash	1,750	
Exchange Loss	50	
Accounts Receivable		1,800
Collected British pounds on account		
and converted to U.S. dollars		

The exchange loss reflects the fact that American Export agreed to accept 1,000 pounds and that the value of those pounds declined by $0.05 each. If the exchange rate had risen, a gain would have resulted.

End-of-Period Adjustments

In each of the preceding illustrations, the exchange gains and losses were recorded upon settlement of the payable or receivable. Because financial statements are often prepared between the date of a transaction and the time of settlement, an end-of-period adjustment is required. Specifically, foreign currency payables and receivables must be adjusted to reflect their U.S. dollar amount as of the financial statement date. For instance, suppose that a U.S. company having a December 31 year-end purchased goods on December 1 and agreed to pay 1 million Japanese yen in 60 days. The spot rate was $0.0074 per yen on December 1, $0.0077 on December 31, and $0.0076 near the end of January when the payable was settled. The entries that follow would be needed.

Dec.	1	Purchases	7,400	
		Accounts Payable		7,400
		Purchased merchandise on account		
	31	Exchange Loss	300	
		Accounts Payable		300
		Adjusted foreign currency payable to		
		reflect spot rate		
Jan.	30	Accounts Payable	7,700	
		Exchange Gain		100
		Cash		7,600
		Acquired yen and paid related		
		foreign currency payable		

Notice that on December 31 the payable is adjusted upward by $300 [($0.0077 − $0.0074) × 1,000,000 yen] and the related loss is recorded. On January 30, however, the firm needs only $7,600 to settle its debt. The $100 change from year-end is therefore reported as a gain. This accounting treatment reflects the impact of rate changes on income as the changes occur and also results in proper valuation of foreign currency payables and receivables.

EXECUTIVE BRIEFING
Doing Business in Foreign Lands

Susan Quigley
Director, Finance
Toronto Blue Jays Baseball Club

More than likely, the mention of "international business" creates a picture of American firms engaged in
transactions with Asian, South American, or European
entities. We can naturally take an opposite view: a for-
eign company having significant activities in the United States. That is our
situation at the Toronto Blue Jays Baseball Club in Canada.

We receive revenues from several U.S. sources: Major League Baseball's
Central Fund (which includes television revenue); corporate licensing royalties and rights fees; and gate receipts from visiting other teams' stadiums.
Approximately 20% of our total revenue is in U.S. dollars. In contrast, about
70% of expenses are in U.S. funds. Such expenses include players' salaries,
minor league clubs' costs (we have nine such clubs), and scouting and ama-
teur draft outlays.

When our budgets are prepared, Canadian and U.S. currencies are segregated to determine the net requirement in U.S. dollars for the upcoming period. As part of this process, we estimate a spot rate and use techniques that
allow us to "lock in" rates, thus removing some of the uncertainty from the
foreign exchange process. We are not experts in the foreign exchange game,
though: sometimes we win and sometimes we lose. Fortunately, there are
companies that specialize in U.S. dollar trading. Considering the rapid escala-
tion in players' salaries in recent years, we may soon be using more of their
services.

Disclosure of International Financial Affairs

The internationalization of business has led to increased financial statement disclosures, generally in the accompanying notes. Companies that
meet certain guidelines must reveal specified information relative to their
international operations. Such information is useful to investors and creditors who are sensitive to the unique risks associated with conducting business in foreign lands. For example, if an entity generates a large percentage
of its sales and earnings in a country that has a past history of governmental takeovers, a potential (and somewhat pessimistic) investor might shy
away from a long-term commitment of funds.

Typical corporate disclosures include sales, income, and identifiable assets, all categorized by major geographic area of operation. A sample presentation is shown in note 8 of Appendix C at the conclusion of the text.

END-OF-CHAPTER REVIEW

1 Summarize the objectives of financial reporting. The financial-reporting function should generate information that is helpful (1) to a wide variety of users who must make various types of decisions, (2) in assessing future cash flows, (3) in studying a firm's financial position and any related changes during the accounting period, and (4) in examining an entity's financial performance (i.e., earnings). Above all, the information conveyed should be general purpose and unbiased in its orientation.

2 Identify and describe the desirable characteristics of accounting information: relevancy, reliability, comparability, and understandability. Relevancy relates to the influence of information on the actions of a decision maker. That is, information would be deemed relevant if it influences the actions of an investor, creditor, or other financial statement user. Reliability, on the other hand, refers to the ability of information to accurately depict the conditions it is supposed to represent. To be reliable and to instill public confidence in the information being reported, an entity's disclosures must be free from bias. Comparability refers to making a company's financial statements comparable with the statements of other firms and with those of the same firm at different points in time. Finally, understandability involves making a company's financial statements comprehensible to those who have a reasonable understanding of business activities and are willing to study the information with reasonable diligence.

3 Explain the need for generally accepted accounting principles and the roles of various groups in the development process. The foundation that brings order to accounting and reporting is a set of assumptions, concepts, standards, and procedures known as generally accepted accounting principles (GAAP). In the 1930s, the Securities and Exchange Commission was given the power to prescribe accounting principles and practices for publicly held corporations. Since its beginning, however, the SEC has elected to delegate authority to rule-making bodies of the accounting profession. The current private-sector group in charge of formulating GAAP is the Financial Accounting Standards Board. Although other groups influence the development of GAAP, financial reporting is largely the result of FASB and SEC interaction.

4 Define the assumptions, concepts, and modifying conventions that underlie financial accounting and reporting. Twelve fundamental concepts form the basis for financial accounting. A short description of each follows.

■ *Entity assumption*—an assumption that a business is viewed as a unit separate and apart from its owners and other firms.

■ *Going-concern assumption*—the belief that a business will continue to operate for an indefinite period of time unless there is substantial evidence to the contrary.

■ *Periodicity assumption*—a financial-reporting assumption that an entity's life can be divided into discrete time periods.

■ *Monetary unit assumption*—the ideas that (1) an entity's transactions and events can be expressed in terms of a common measuring unit (i.e., the dollar) and (2) the dollar's purchasing power is stable.

■ *Historical-cost principle*—the principle of recording goods, resources, and services at cost, with cost defined as the exchange or transaction price.

■ *Objectivity principle*—the requirement that accounting information be definite, verifiable, and free from bias.

**LEARNING OBJECTIVES:
THE KEY POINTS**

- *Revenue realization*—the basis that allows companies to enter revenue in the accounting records when earned, which is generally when goods are sold or when services are rendered.
- *Matching principle*—the principle that expenses should be recognized in the same period as the revenues that they helped to produce.
- *Consistency principle*—the idea that businesses should employ the same accounting practices in each reporting period to improve comparability of financial statements.
- *Full disclosure principle*—the requirement that an entity must provide a complete reporting of all facts important enough to influence the judgment of an informed user of financial information.
- *Materiality*—a concept dictating that an accountant should judge the impact and importance of each transaction and event to determine its proper handling in the accounting records. Minor items are treated in the most expedient manner possible.
- *Conservatism*—a doctrine that when alternative valuations and measurements are possible, the alternative selected should be the one that is least likely to overstate assets and/or net income.

5 Describe the revenue realization principle and apply the percentage-of-completion and installment methods. Revenue is said to be realized when (1) the earnings process is complete or virtually complete and (2) the amount of revenue can be objectively measured. Most revenues are realized when merchandise is sold or services are rendered. However, when the earnings process is spread over several accounting periods, the percentage-of-completion (POC) and installment methods may be used.

POC is often employed to account for long-term construction contracts. Profit is recognized on the basis of progress toward project completion, which is frequently determined by relating the amount of cost incurred to the total cost to be incurred. Another approach, the installment method, is used in retail environments when collectibility of receivables is in doubt. With this method, profit is allocated to different accounting periods on the basis of cash received from customers.

6 Identify several of the basic issues of international accounting. The text presents three basic issues related to international accounting. First, because of variations in economic systems and accounting principles, comparability and compatibility of financial information prepared in different countries are impaired. Several groups, however, are working to bring a degree of uniformity to international accounting standards. Foreign currency transactions are a second area of concern to accountants, as international trade occurs in various currencies. If settlement is to be made in a foreign currency, a gain or loss must be recorded if the spot rate fluctuates between the transaction date and the date of settlement (or the end of the period). A third issue that must be addressed involves the disclosure of foreign operations. Sales, income, and identifiable assets, all categorized by geographic area of operation, are normally shown in the notes that accompany the financial statements.

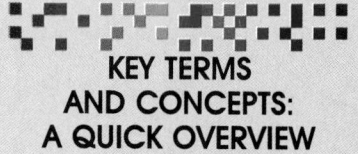

**KEY TERMS
AND CONCEPTS:
A QUICK OVERVIEW**

Accounting Principles Board (APB) A former policymaking body of the AICPA charged with the responsibility of developing generally accepted accounting principles.

American Institute of Certified Public Accountants (AICPA) A national organization of licensed CPAs.

comparability   A characteristic of financial information that allows users to make comparative evaluations among firms and with the same firm at different points in time.

conservatism   A concept holding that when different valuations and measurements are possible, the alternative selected should be the one that is least likely to overstate assets and/or net income.

consistency principle   A principle stipulating that entities should employ the same accounting practices in each reporting period.

entity assumption   An assumption that a company is considered a unit separate from its owner and from other firms.

Financial Accounting Standards Board (FASB)   The private-sector organization currently in charge of formulating standards of financial reporting in the United States.

full disclosure principle   A principle holding that an entity must provide a complete reporting of the facts important enough to influence the judgment of an informed financial statement user.

generally accepted accounting principles (GAAP)   A set of assumptions, concepts, and practices that provides a foundation for measuring and disclosing the results of business transactions and events.

going-concern assumption   An assumption that a business will continue to operate for an indefinite time period unless there is substantial evidence to the contrary.

historical-cost principle   The principle of recording goods, resources, and services acquired at cost (i.e., the exchange or transaction price).

installment method   A method of revenue recognition by which a sale's profit is allocated to different accounting periods. The allocation is based on the amount of cash received from customers.

matching principle   The principle that all costs and expenses associated with the production of revenue are recognized when the revenue is recognized.

materiality   A concept dictating that an accountant must judge the impact of each transaction (or event) to determine its proper handling in the accounting records.

monetary unit assumption   An assumption that an entity's transactions can be expressed in terms of a common measuring unit, such as the U.S. dollar.

objectivity principle   A principle requiring that accounting information be free from bias and verifiable by an independent party.

percentage-of-completion method   A method of revenue recognition by which profit is allocated to different accounting periods based on the percentage of the total project completed.

periodicity assumption   An assumption stipulating that for reporting purposes, an entity's life can be divided into discrete time periods such as months, quarters, or years.

relevancy   A characteristic of financial information. Information is deemed relevant if it influences the actions of a decision maker.

reliability   A characteristic of financial information. Information is deemed reliable if it accurately depicts the conditions it purports to represent.

revenue realization principle   The principle that revenue is earned when (1) the earnings process is complete or virtually complete and (2) the amount of revenue can be objectively measured.

Securities and Exchange Commission (SEC)   An agency of the federal government that administers several securities acts and prescribes accounting principles and reporting practices for companies that issue publicly traded securities.

spot rate   The rate that is used to convert one currency into another.

understandability   A characteristic of financial information. Information is considered understandable if it is comprehensible to those who (1) have a reasonable understanding of economic activities and (2) are willing to study the information with reasonable diligence.

CHAPTER QUIZ

The five questions that follow relate to several issues raised in the chapter. Test your knowledge of the issues by selecting the best answer. (The answers appear on p. 541.)

1 If financial statements are prepared so that creditors benefit at the expense of other user groups, the financial statements are not:

a understandable.   c relevant.

b reliable.   d comparable.

2 Generally accepted accounting principles:

a vary from state to state.

b dictate that all large companies use precisely the same accounting practices.

c are currently established by the Accounting Principles Society of America.

d are established by the Financial Accounting Standards Board.

3 Which assumption or principle holds that financial statements should be verifiable by an independent party?

a Periodicity.   c Consistency.

b Matching.   d Objectivity.

4 Kent signed a $20 million contract to construct a four-mile road over a two-year period. It is estimated that total costs for the road will be $18 million, producing a $2 million profit. Three miles of the road were completed during Year 1 at a cost of $13.5 million. Kent recognized $1.5 million in profit by following the percentage-of-completion method. If the road was finished in Year 2 at an additional cost of $4.2 million, how much profit should be recognized in Year 2?

a $0.   c $800,000.

b $500,000.   d $2,300,000.

5 Tyson (USA) sold merchandise to a Hong Kong company for 100,000 Hong Kong dollars when the spot rate was $0.13 per U.S. dollar. At year-end, the spot rate was $0.15; by the date of settlement, it had risen to $0.16. Tyson would record the sale in its accounting records at:

a $13,000.   c $16,000.

b $15,000.   d some amount other than those above.

SUMMARY PROBLEM

John Lyle and Amy Greenspan are both enrolled in an introductory accounting course at Western University. A recent assignment involved a classroom presentation concerning accounting theory and generally accepted accounting principles. An excerpt from a preliminary draft of Lyle's presentation follows.

> . . . And consistent with the power given to it by Congress, the Securities and Exchange Commission is the major policymaker when it comes to setting present-day accounting standards.

. . . In view of the first part of my presentation, let us now focus on the construction industry as an example. According to the matching concept, revenue should be recognized in the accounting records when the earnings process is complete or virtually complete. This guideline is the sole criterion that companies must follow in this regard. Accordingly, most construction firms use the percentage-of-completion method, which, as its name implies, allows a business to recognize a contract's total profit upon completion of a project.

. . . On a somewhat related issue, these entities are also required to recognize gains that arise from inflation, with the gains being disclosed on the historical-cost income statement. Such a recognition policy is conservative because it makes the accounting records of construction companies consistent with those of other businesses in this country.

John has asked Amy to evaluate his preliminary draft so that any erroneous statements can be corrected before the presentation is given in class.

Instructions

Assume the role of Amy Greenspan and prepare a list of errors, if any, that John Lyle has made.

Solution

John has made a number of errors in his preliminar draft. The errors are detailed as follows:

a The Financial Accounting Standards Board is the major policymaker when it comes to setting present-day accounting standards. The SEC serves primarily in an advisory role.

b The matching principle is used incorrectly; it focuses on the recognition of expense, not revenue. Revenue realization is the proper principle to cite.

c Two criteria must be satisfied to recognize revenue in the accounting records, so Lyle is only partly correct. In addition to the earnings process being complete or virtually complete, the amount of revenue must be able to be measured objectively.

d Under the percentage-of-completion method, profit is recognized during the term of the construction project, not totally upon project completion.

e Companies in this country are no longer required to report inflation-adjusted information. The disclosures are now voluntary. Such information is not integrated in the historical-cost financial statements; it is disclosed on a supplementary basis only.

f Conservatism means that businesses select accounting practices that are least likely to overstate asset valuations and/or net income. This doctrine has nothing to do with making financial statements comparable with those of other firms. Furthermore, if a gain has arisen from inflation, its recognition could easily be deemed nonconservative.

ASSIGNMENT MATERIAL

Q13-1 Financial reporting attempts to generate information that is helpful in assessing the amounts, timing, and uncertainty of an organization's cash inflows and outflows. Briefly discuss why creditors would be interested in this information.

QUESTIONS

Q13-2   Briefly explain why accountants prepare general-purpose financial statements.

Q13-3   Bearing in mind that accounting information should be relevant, discuss a possible problem of using financial statements that are based on historical cost.

Q13-4   Accountants strive to produce comparable financial statements. Briefly discuss.

Q13-5   Briefly discuss the need for an underlying foundation of financial reporting, namely, generally accepted accounting principles.

Q13-6   Which organization has ultimate authority over the reporting practices of most large corporations? Explain.

Q13-7   Discuss the basic differences between the APB and the FASB.

Q13-8   Define the entity assumption and discuss its need in financial reporting.

Q13-9   The going-concern assumption forms the basis for many of the accounting practices illustrated in this text. Define the going-concern assumption and list several of these practices.

Q13-10   Briefly define the historical-cost principle. Why is cost preferred for asset valuations?

Q13-11   Is the disclosure of inflation-adjusted financial information mandatory or voluntary?

Q13-12   Revenue is said to be realized when two tests are met. What are these two tests and when are they met by most businesses?

Q13-13   Present an example of when it is permissible to recognize revenue during the production process.

Q13-14   Warner Developers has extreme difficulty in estimating future construction costs. When would the company likely recognize revenues related to a three-year highway project?

Q13-15   Present an example of when it is permissible to recognize revenue at the time of receipt.

Q13-16   Metro Delivery was founded in 19X1 and implemented a straight-line depreciation policy for its truck fleet.
     a   Should Metro use straight-line depreciation in 19X2 and 19X3? Why? Discuss from the viewpoint of a statement user.
     b   *Must* Metro use straight-line depreciation in 19X2 and 19X3? Explain.

Q13-17   Discuss materiality. How is the materiality of a particular item often determined?

Q13-18   Have strides been made toward the uniformity of international accounting standards? Briefly discuss.

Q13-19   How can companies experience gains and losses from foreign currency transactions?

EXERCISES

E13-1   *Characteristics of accounting information* (L.O. 2)
The accounting profession has identified relevancy, reliability, comparability, and understandability as desirable characteristics of accounting information. Consider the following data concerning buildings that are owned by Company A and Company B:

Company	Cost of Building	Accumulated Depreciation	Fair Market Value
A	$500,000	$200,000	$750,000
B	500,000	150,000	750,000

A uses sum-of-the-years'-digits depreciation; B uses straight-line.

a At what figure would Company A's building appear on a balance sheet? Comment on the relevancy of this figure to an investor who is attempting to evaluate the current worth of the entity.

b By studying the book value of the buildings, comment on a barrier to achieving comparability of the two firms' financial statements.

c Considering the knowledge level of many potential investors and the use of elaborate accounting methods such as accelerated depreciation, what characteristic of accounting information becomes difficult to satisfy? Briefly explain.

E13-2 *Knowledge of GAAP* (L.O. 4)

Evaluate the comments that follow as being True or False. If the comment is false, briefly explain why.

a The entity assumption holds that a business unit may not arbitrarily change its accounting practices from one year to the next.

b Expenses incurred in the generation of revenue should be recognized in the same accounting period that the revenue is recognized.

c According to conservatism, small expenditures for assets are expensed as incurred rather than capitalized.

d The going-concern assumption dictates that financial statements be prepared both quarterly and annually to report financial position and profitability.

e Increases in the value of assets above cost are ignored in a company's accounting records.

E13-3 *Analysis of GAAP* (L.O. 2, 4)

Twenty years ago, the president of Samson Company began a policy of investing excess company funds in classic cars. Total investments over the years have amounted to $102,000. The company is now in need of a bank loan to finance an equipment modernization program. To impress the banker, the president proposed valuing the cars on the company's balance sheet at $157,500—the current fair market value.

a According to GAAP, at what amount should the cars be valued? Why?

b Which of the two preceding amounts is consistent with the principle of objectivity and the doctrine of conservatism? Explain.

c Which of the two amounts is more relevant to the banker? Explain.

E13-4 *Revenue realization; percentage of completion* (L.O. 5)

In 19X3, DeHaven & Associates signed a contract to build a bridge for $8.9 million. The company anticipates total costs of $8 million and an August 19X5 project completion date. The following schedule shows the costs incurred during each year of construction. Complete the remainder of the schedule, assuming that DeHaven uses the percentage-of-completion method of revenue realization.

	19X3	19X4	19X5
Actual costs incurred	$1,600,000	$4,400,000	$2,150,000
Percentage of work completed during the year	_____	_____	_____
Profit to be recognized	_____	_____	_____

E13-5 *Revenue recognition; installment method* (L.O. 5)

Lovely Cove Development Company sells lakefront property. The firm uses the installment method of revenue (and profit) recognition because of a high uncertainty of collections from clientele.

On July 1, 19X1, Lovely Cove sold a lot that had originally cost the firm $21,000. The terms of sale were as follows:

Payment Due Date	Amount Due
July 1, 19X1	$ 4,000
December 1, 19X1	4,000
August 5, 19X2	10,000
December 1, 19X2	2,000
October 9, 19X3	10,000

The purchaser made all payments according to the original schedule. Ignoring interest costs, calculate the amount of profit Lovely Cove should recognize in 19X1, 19X2, and 19X3.

E13-6 *Revenue realization* (L.O. 5)

Consider the following transactions and events, which occurred during 19X3:

1 Eagle Corporation rendered services on account amounting to $34,600. Of this total, clients had paid $27,900 by year-end.

2 Johnson Publishing received $72 on May 5 for a two-year subscription to *The Modern Accountant*, a monthly publication. The subscription began with the magazine's June issue.

3 Crown Construction uses the percentage-of-completion method to recognize revenue. On January 2, the company signed a $70 million long-term contract to build a new manufacturing plant. Total costs were expected to be $64 million. Crown incurred $16 million of construction expenditures during 19X3 related to this project.

4 Ontario Furnishings sold $350,000 of goods on installment contracts at an average gross profit rate of 30%. Outstanding customer balances on these contracts by year-end amounted to $305,000.

All four companies follow generally accepted accounting principles and have a December 31 year-end. In the case of Ontario Furnishings, assume that the installment method is permissible because collectibility of customer receivables is in doubt.

a Determine the amount of revenue that Eagle Corporation and Johnson Publishing would recognize during 19X3.

b Determine the amount of profit that Crown Construction and Ontario Furnishings would recognize during 19X3.

E13-7 *Analysis of GAAP* (L.O. 4)

Jody Vogel and Kaye Lewis are accountants for Bright Beverage and Bottling Corporation. Bright recently completed a special promotion in which customers won cash prizes based on amounts printed on the underside of bottle caps. Vogel believes that the cost of the promotional activities should be recorded as an asset. He feels that the campaign attracted new customers who will continue to buy Bright products long into the future. Lewis, on the other hand, feels that future benefits are uncertain; therefore the promotional costs should be expensed immediately. Robert Williams, chief financial officer for Bright, was asked to express an opinion on the matter. He said that either method would be acceptable because of the dollar amounts involved.

Briefly discuss the positions of Vogel, Lewis, and Williams. Be sure to introduce the appropriate assumptions, principles, and modifying conventions that form the basis of each employee's suggested treatment.

E13-8   *Conservatism* (L.O. 4)

The following information relates to Trapnell Company, a new business that began operation in 19X7:

1 A $19,200 advertising program was expensed in December 19X7. The program was expected to generate increased sales from December 19X7 through February 19X8.

2 Net income of 19X7 reflected a $13,400 loss related to unsalable inventories. (Trapnell sells high-fashion women's clothing in an outlet mall south of St. Louis.)

3 The company rejected a $70,000 offer for a parcel of land purchased earlier in the year for $52,000. No entry was made in the accounting records to reflect the increased valuation.

4 Straight-line depreciation of $11,000 on newly acquired store fixtures was deducted from revenues when computing 19X7 net income. Management rejected use of the double-declining balance depreciation method.

a Briefly discuss the doctrine of conservatism as it is used in accounting.
b Analyze each of the preceding items and determine:
  (1) Whether the company took a conservative approach in its accounting treatment of the item and
  (2) Whether the treatment is in accord with generally accepted accounting principles.

E13-9   *International accounting* (L.O. 6)

Dapore Industries has decided to expand operations abroad by doing business with companies located in Hong Kong, Japan, and China. All business will be conducted from Dapore's corporate headquarters in Seattle. Briefly identify the accounting implications of Dapore's decision and the probable impact on the firm's financial statements.

E13-10   *International accounting* (L.O. 6)

Midland Trading Corporation is a U.S. company that engages in numerous transactions involving foreign currencies. Three of the firm's transactions follow.

■ *Transaction no. 1*—Purchased merchandise on account from Mizu Company of Japan, agreeing to pay $4,000 in 30 days. On the date of purchase, the spot rate was $0.0070 per Japanese yen. On the settlement date, the spot rate was $0.0066 per yen.

■ *Transaction no. 2*—Purchased merchandise on account from Luxar Company of Switzerland, agreeing to pay 30,000 Swiss francs in 60 days. The spot rate was $0.73 per franc on the date of purchase and increased to $0.79 by the settlement date.

■ *Transaction no. 3*—Sold merchandise on account to Downing Clothing Corporation of London, agreeing to accept 9,000 British pounds in 90 days. The spot rate was $1.90 per pound at the time of settlement, up from $1.80 on the sale date.

Prepare journal entries for Midland Trading Corporation to record each of these transactions and their related settlement. Disregard year-end financial statement adjustments.

E13-11 *International accounting* (L.O. 6)

On December 1, 19X1, a U.S. company having a December 31 year-end purchased goods on account from a French supplier. Terms of the purchase required the U.S. company to deliver 80,000 French francs to the supplier on January 11, 19X2. The spot rate for a French franc fluctuated as follows:

Date	Spot Rate
Dec. 1, 19X1	$0.20
Dec. 31, 19X1	0.23
Jan. 11, 19X2	0.22

Prepare the three journal entries required by this transaction.

PROBLEMS

Series A

P13-A1 *Analysis of GAAP and transactions* (L.O. 4, 5)

You are the chief accountant of Westside Tool & Die, Inc. The president of the firm, Jim Norton, having graduated from college over 20 years ago, has decided to update himself in the area of financial reporting. After completing several weeks of an accounting course at a local university, Norton became involved in a heated debate with Joan Mencer, one of your staff members. The following topics were discussed:

a Three years ago the company acquired a patent from an inventor for $52,000. The current book value is $40,000 as a result of amortization. A recent appraisal indicated that the patent is worth $115,000. Norton believes that the balance sheet should contain the current valuation of $115,000; Mencer, in contrast, favors $40,000.

b Westside recently acquired a sophisticated computer system for $240,000. Following Norton's suggestion, all system expenditures costing less than $100 were expensed. Such expenditures totaled $4,000. Mencer felt that these outlays should be capitalized in the Computer Equipment account because they render long-term benefits.

c Norton had company personnel design and build a security gate for his vacation home. He claimed that no entry is needed on the company's books because the personnel didn't have to work overtime on the project. Mencer believes that the $11,000 cost should be recorded as follows:

Miscellaneous Expense	11,000	
Cash, Supplies, and so on		11,000

d The company was having an exceptionally poor fourth quarter. Norton instructed the plant's accountant to omit the quarterly adjusting entry for truck depreciation in an effort to boost net income. Mencer was opposed to this treatment for reasons not stated.

e Westside sold a large machine on the installment basis to the Brazilian Air Force at a profit of $4 million. Norton wants to recognize the profit in the year of sale, even though no cash has yet been received. Mencer prefers to recognize profit as the Air Force settles its obligation, because Brazil has had great difficulty in paying its international debt.

f The company has been sued for $1 million on a sex discrimination charge by a former secretary. Consultation with Westside's attorney indicates that the secretary has a very strong case. Norton wants to indicate the possibility of a lawsuit in the notes to the financial statements. Mencer claims that a note is unnecessary because the case has not yet been decided.

Assume that prior to considering any of these items, Westside had tentatively figured 19XX net income at $800,000.

Instructions

Decide who, if anyone, is correct in each of the disagreements and state the logic for your answer. Cite GAAP when appropriate. In some cases more than one principle may apply.

P13-A2 *Analysis of GAAP and transactions; financial statement impact* (L.O. 4, 5)

You are reviewing the accounting records of Novachek Industries for the current year ended December 31. The following information has come to your attention:

1 The company, which uses the accrual basis of accounting, failed to record $8,000 of interest revenue. Collection will take place in the next reporting period.

2 Short-term stock investments purchased by the firm for $22,700 had a year-end market value of $17,600. Feeling that the market would soon rebound, management refused to authorize a December 31 adjustment to properly value the securities.

3 Freight charges of $2,500 relating to the purchase of equipment on December 28 were expensed when incurred.

4 Inventories that cost $9,000 had a year-end fair market value of $10,100. Accordingly, the company's accountant made the following entry:

Inventories	1,100	
Gain from Appreciation		1,100

5 Short-term loans payable of $35,000, recently secured to finance equipment purchases, were accidentally entered in the accounting records at $53,000.

6 Novachek's financial statements for the current year revealed the following information:

Net income	$ 32,400
Assets	100,000
Liabilities	60,000
Owner's equity	40,000

Instructions

a Set up a four-column schedule with the following headings: net income, assets, liabilities, and owner's equity. By adjusting Novachek's reported balances, compute corrected financial statement totals using the information presented in items (1)–(5).

b For items (1)–(4) only, determine if any generally accepted accounting principles have been violated. Briefly explain your answer.

P13-A3 *Understanding revenue recognition* (L.O. 4, 5)

I Love Yogurt (ILY) is a franchisor/management company that helps private investors open and operate yogurt shops. The firm provides continuing advice and guidance for a fee. In addition, ILY sells yogurt, cups and spoons, and kitchen equipment, and licenses the use of its name and advertising. The following transactions and events occurred during 19X2, the first year of operation:

- The company received franchise fees of $2 million. Forty percent of the consulting services related to these fees were performed by the end of 19X2 at a cost of $200,000.
- Late in 19X2, ILY ran a regional advertising campaign that cost $280,000. The company plans to bill its franchisees $500,000 in early 19X3 for this service.
- Actual sales of cups, spoons, yogurt, and other products to franchisees totaled $7.2 million. Of this amount, 90% has been billed. Of the amount already billed, 80% has been collected. The cost of products sold totaled $4.1 million.
- ILY sold equipment to new franchisees in the amount of $6 million. By year-end, $2.5 million of the balances due had been collected. This equipment cost ILY $4.2 million; sales will be accounted for by using the installment method.
- Late in 19X2, the company created a construction department to build new stores. By year-end, projects were in progress that had a contract price of $5.8 million and total expected costs of $5 million. Costs incurred to date amounted to $1 million. ILY will use the percentage-of-completion method to account for construction activities.

Instructions

Prepare a schedule that indicates the amount of profit I Love Yogurt earned during 19X2.

P13-A4 *Revenue realization: Percentage-of-completion and installment methods* (L.O. 5)

San Diego Shipyards recently won a $35 million bid to build two ships for the Navy. Management anticipates the $32 million total project cost will be incurred over a three-year period (19X2–19X4), and delivery of the ships will occur in late 19X4. The company received $5 million when the contract was signed in January 19X2 and another $10 million at the end of each year. The actual costs were as follows: 19X2, $7,040,000; 19X3, $20,160,000; and 19X4, $4,980,000. San Diego uses the percentage-of-completion method to account for its contracts.

In an unrelated transaction, the firm sold property to a local developer for $2,125,000. (The property had originally cost the company $850,000 when acquired 12 years ago.) San Diego received 30% of the sales price as a down payment in 19X2; the remaining balance will be received in equal amounts during 19X3 and 19X4. Management will use the installment method to account for this transaction.

Instructions

a For the Navy contract, prepare a schedule that shows the profit to be recognized during 19X2, 19X3, and 19X4.
b For the property sale, prepare a schedule that shows the profit to be recognized during 19X2, 19X3, and 19X4.

P13-A5 *Matching principle, income statement construction* (L.O. 4, 5)

On January 1 of the current year, Ron Tracy opened a furniture repair business. The first year's income statement, prepared by using the cash basis of accounting, follows.

TRACY'S REPAIR SHOP
Income Statement
For the Year Ended December 31, 19XX

Cash receipts		
Cash sales	$30,000	
Receipts from customers on account	3,500	
Interest on savings account	300	
Total receipts		$33,800
Cash disbursements		
Owner withdrawals	$ 3,600	
Employee wages	13,000	
Supplies	4,200	
Delivery van	12,400	
Insurance	200	
Utilities	700	
Rent	2,500	
Total disbursements		36,600
Net income (loss)		$ (2,800)

The following information was obtained from a review of the company's records:

1 Customers still owe $2,900 for repair services performed. Tracy believes that uncollectible accounts will total 3% of credit sales; to date, however, no accounts have been written off the books.

2 Tracy owes his sole employee $570 for services rendered during the last two weeks of the year.

3 As of December 31, Tracy owed various vendors $1,500 for purchases of supplies. An inventory count on this date revealed $1,100 of supplies remained on hand.

4 The delivery van was acquired on March 1 and was expected to have a service life of five years. The $12,400 figure on the income statement includes $400 of minor repairs performed on various dates subsequent to acquisition.

5 Insurance outlays include prepayments of $75.

6 On December 31, Tracy owed DCI, Inc., $100 for 19XX shop rental charges.

Tracy recently learned from one of his customers, a CPA, that the cash basis improperly matches expenses against related revenues.

Instructions

a Using the matching principle along with other generally accepted accounting principles, prepare an income statement that better reflects financial performance. Assume use of straight-line depreciation for the van.

b As shown in the income statement, Tracy deducted the entire cost of the delivery van in the year of acquisition. Explain how this accounting treatment violates the matching principle.

P13-A6 *International accounting* (L.O. 6)

Polaris Enterprises is a U.S. company engaged in international trade. The business activity that follows occurred in 19XX.

Jan. 9   Sold merchandise on account to Peking Company of China, agreeing to accept 1 million renminbi in 60 days. The current spot rate is $0.19 per renminbi.

Feb. 2   Purchased merchandise on account from the TYT Company of Austria, agreeing to pay 100,000 schillings in 60 days. The spot rate is currently $0.094 per schilling.

Mar. 10 Settled the transaction of January 9. The spot rate was $0.182 per renminbi.

Apr. 2   Settled the purchase of February 2. The spot rate was $0.101 per schilling.

18   Purchased merchandise on account from Paris Products, agreeing to pay 500,000 French francs in 90 days. The spot rate on this date stood at $0.20 per franc.

May 14   Sold merchandise on account to Spanish Imports, agreeing to accept 3 million pesetas in 60 days. The current spot rate is $0.009 per peseta.

Instructions

a Prepare journal entries to record the preceding transactions.

b Polaris Enterprises ends its fiscal year on May 31. Prepare any adjusting entries that may be necessary to update the accounting records for exchange gains and losses. The spot rates for foreign currencies on this date are as follows:

Austrian schilling	$0.11
Chinese renminbi	0.20
French franc	0.18
Spanish peseta	0.011

Series B

P13-B1 *Analysis of GAAP and transactions* (L.O. 4, 5)

You are the chief accountant of Atlanta Stereo & TV. The owner of the firm, Gene Cummings, having graduated from college several years ago, has decided to update himself in the area of financial reporting. After completing several weeks of accounting at a local university, Cummings became involved in a heated debate with Al Warren, one of your staff members. The following topics were discussed:

a In reviewing the inventory records, Warren found that LIFO was used to account for stereos and FIFO was used for all other merchandise. Warren maintains that this procedure violates generally accepted accounting principles. Cummings, on the other hand, has no objections to the firm's inventory costing techniques.

b In December 19X1, the company spent $50,000 for 25 vacation tours to Hawaii. The tours will be awarded to employees who produce the highest first quarter sales in 19X2. The following entry was made:

Marketing Expense	50,000	
Cash		50,000

Warren claims the entry is satisfactory. Cummings disagrees, claiming there is no justification for reducing 19X1 income.

c On May 13, Atlanta sold $3,200 of merchandise on account to Jerry

Burns, a valued customer. Warren favors a journal entry on May 13 that reflects $3,200 of sales. In contrast, Cummings feels the sale should be recorded when cash is received by the firm.

d Atlanta recently completed and occupied a new office building. Following Warren's suggestion, all items of office equipment having a unit cost of less than $100 were expensed. The equipment had an average life of five years and a total cost of $34,000. Cummings is opposed to this accounting treatment for reasons not stated.

e Two years ago Atlanta acquired a building complex (including land) for $550,000. The current book value is $470,000. A recent appraisal indicated that the land and building are worth $120,000 and $600,000, respectively. Cummings favored the following balance sheet presentation:

Building and land $470,000

The presentation favored by Warren was: Land, $120,000; Building, $600,000.

f A bid was received to build a loading platform for $4,700. Feeling that the amount was too high, warehouse employees built their own platform for $3,000. Warren feels the platform should be recorded in the accounts at $3,000; Cummings favors the following entry:

Loading Platform	4,700	
Cash, Supplies, and so on		3,000
Construction Gain		1,700

Assume that prior to considering any of these items, Atlanta had tentatively figured 19X1 net income at $234,000.

Instructions

Decide who, if anyone, is correct in each of the disagreements and state the logic for your answer. Cite GAAP when appropriate. In some cases more than one principle may apply.

P13-B2 *Analysis of GAAP and transactions; financial statement impact* (L.O. 4, 5)

You are reviewing the accounting records of Reno Enterprises for the current year ended December 31. The information that follows has come to your attention.

1 On December 9, the company determined that a $5,000 uninsured theft of cash had occurred. The accounts have yet to be adjusted for the amount of the theft.

2 The company, which uses the accrual basis of accounting, failed to record $1,400 of wage expense. Payment will take place in the next reporting period.

3 Inventories costing $15,600 had a year-end fair market value of $21,700. Accordingly, Reno's bookkeeper made the following adjustment in the accounting records:

| Inventories | 6,100 | |
| Income from Appreciation | | 6,100 |

4 Import duties of $1,200 relating to the purchase of equipment on December 29 were improperly expensed when incurred.

5 On October 1, Reno purchased $120,000 of equipment at a going-out-of-business sale. The equipment, which normally sold for $150,000, was recorded as follows:

Equipment	150,000	
Cash		120,000
Gain on Bargain Purchase		30,000

Reno expects to use the equipment for 10 years and employs the straight-line method of depreciation.

6 The company's financial statements for the current year revealed the following information:

Net income (loss)	$ (2,000)
Assets	195,000
Liabilities	120,000
Owner's equity	75,000

Instructions

a Set up a four-column schedule with the following headings: net income (loss), assets, liabilities, and owner's equity. By adjusting the company's reported balances, compute corrected financial statement totals using the information presented in items (1)–(5).

b For items (2)–(5) only, determine if any generally accepted accounting principles have been violated. Briefly explain your answer.

P13-B3 *Understanding revenue recognition* (L.O. 4, 5)

1-2-3

Jim's Gym is a franchisor/management company that helps investors open and operate private health clubs. The firm provides continuing advice and guidance for a fee. In addition, it sells athletic gear and weight-lifting equipment and licenses the use of its name and advertising. The following transactions and events occurred during 19X4, the first year of operation:

■ The company received franchise fees of $3 million. Sixty percent of the consulting services related to these fees were performed by the end of 19X4 at a cost of $350,000.

■ Actual sales of athletic gear totaled $1.3 million. Of this amount, 80% has been billed. Of the amount already billed, franchisees still owe $347,000. The cost of products sold totaled $940,000.

■ The company ran a nationwide promotion campaign in November at a cost of $645,000. Each of the firm's 96 franchisees will be billed $10,000 in early 19X5 for this service. Although not yet invoiced, the proper amounts due from the Columbus and Albany franchisees were received by December 31, 19X4.

■ Late in 19X4, a new gym construction division was created. On December 31, projects were in progress that had a contract price of $7 million and total expected costs of $4.9 million. These jobs were 10% complete. The firm will use the percentage-of-completion method to account for construction activities.

■ The company sold weight machines to new franchisees in the amount of $2.8 million. By year-end, $1.1 million of the balances due were still outstanding. This equipment cost Jim's Gym $2.1 million; sales will be accounted for by using the installment method.

Instructions

Prepare a schedule that indicates the amount of profit Jim's Gym earned during 19X4.

P13-B4 *Revenue realization: Percentage-of-completion and installment methods*

(L.O. 5)

1-2-3

Bennett Developers recently signed a long-term contract for the construction of apartments throughout New Mexico for $40 million. Bennett's accounting department has estimated total construction costs of $38 million. The contract stipulated a $900,000 payment to Bennett upon contract signing and periodic payments throughout the project's three-year life. Additional information follows.

	19X1	19X2	19X3
Cash collected	$12,000,000*	$18,000,000	$10,000,000
Actual costs incurred	9,500,000	22,800,000	5,900,000

* Includes the $900,000 payment upon signing.

The project was completed on December 28, 19X3.

In a separate transaction, the company sold a parcel of land to Recreational Housing for $5 million. Bennett originally paid $4.2 million for the parcel. Terms of sale required a 30% down payment on December 1, 19X1, by Recreational Housing and 20 equal monthly payments beginning on January 1, 19X2.

Instructions

a Calculate the total profit that Bennett has earned on the apartment project.

b Bennett will use the percentage-of-completion method to account for the apartment project. Prepare a schedule that reveals the profit earned in 19X1, 19X2, and 19X3.

c Bennett will use the installment method to account for the land sale. Prepare a schedule that reveals the profit earned in 19X1, 19X2, and 19X3.

P13-B5 *Matching principle, income statement construction* **(L.O. 4, 5)**

The trial balance of Jiffy Chefs as of December 31, 19X8, the end of the first year of operation, follows.

Cash	$ 6,000	
Accounts receivable	14,400	
Equipment	18,500	
Accounts payable		$ 2,200
Note payable		9,800
A. Markwalder, capital		7,600
A. Markwalder, drawing	4,000	
Service revenue		52,000
Salaries expense	14,800	
Insurance expense	1,200	
Utilities expense	1,700	
Rent expense	11,000	
	$71,600	$71,600

Additional information was obtained from a review of the company's accounting records.

1 The bookkeeper expensed a $1,200 insurance policy that covers a one-year period beginning on October 1, 19X8.

2 The equipment was acquired on January 1, 19X8, and is expected to have an eight-year service life and a $500 residual value.

3 The Service Revenue account includes a $1,500 client deposit for work that will be performed in January 19X9. Further, the company earned $2,700 of revenue in 19X8 that has not yet been entered in the accounting records nor billed to clients.

4 As of December 31, 19X8, Jiffy Chefs owed Office Wholesale $700 for supplies, $500 of which were used during December.

5 The note payable, due in three years, was issued on March 1 and carried an annual interest rate of 12%.

6 Uncollectible accounts are estimated to be 4% of year-end accounts receivable.

Instructions

a Prepare an income statement for Jiffy Chefs that properly reflects financial performance for the first year of operation. Use the straight-line depreciation method for the equipment.

b Prepare a brief explanation of the matching principle. Also, explain why the company's adjusting entries for items no. 5 (interest on the note) and no. 6 (uncollectible accounts) are consistent with this principle.

P13-B6 *International accounting* **(L.O. 6)**

Canyon Enterprises is a U.S. company engaged in international trade. The following business activity occurred in 19XX:

Jan. 15   Purchased merchandise on account from the Toronto Company of Canada, agreeing to pay 15,000 Canadian dollars in 60 days. The spot rate is currently $0.84 per Canadian dollar.

Feb. 22   Sold merchandise on account to an Israeli company, agreeing to accept 6 million shekels in 60 days. The current spot rate is $0.50 per shekel.

Mar. 16   Settled the purchase of January 15. The spot rate was $0.82 per Canadian dollar.

Apr. 10   Purchased merchandise on account from a Pakistani firm, agreeing to pay 1 million rupees in 90 days. The spot rate on this date stood at $0.047 per rupee.

     17   Settled the transaction of February 22. The spot rate was $0.54.

May   1   Sold merchandise on account to Swedish Imports, agreeing to accept 50,000 krona in 50 days. The current spot rate is $0.175 per krona.

Instructions

a Prepare journal entries to record the preceding transactions.

b Canyon Enterprises ends its fiscal year on May 31. Prepare any adjusting entries that may be necessary to update the accounting records for exchange gains and losses. The spot rates for foreign currencies on this date are as follows:

Canadian dollar	$0.92
Israeli shekel	0.57
Pakistani rupee	0.056
Swedish krona	0.19

ELECTRONIC DATA BASE

EDB13-1 *Accounting principles; foreign operations: Apple Computer, Inc.* (L.O. 4, 6)

Apple Computer develops, manufactures, and markets personal computer systems. The company is a leader in systems for business, education, government, and the home—both in this country and abroad.

Instructions

By using the text's Electronic Data Base, access the income statement and accompanying notes of Apple Computer, Inc., and answer the questions that follow. Unless otherwise indicated, responses should be based on data for the most recent year presented.

a Review the summary of significant accounting policies that has been prepared by the company.

(1) The summary is the result of applying a significant principle of accounting. What principle is it?

(2) What policy or valuation method does the company use with respect to revenue recognition? Inventory valuation? Depreciation of plant and equipment?

b Does the income statement reveal that any "unusual" transactions or events occurred during the period? Briefly explain.

c Do the notes to the financial statements describe any "unusual" transactions or events that occurred during the period? Briefly discuss.

d The company has operations in other parts of the world.

(1) What percentage of the firm's sales are made in the United States? Has this percentage changed over, say, the past two years?

(2) Comment on the trend in domestic and foreign operating income over the past few years.

EDB13-2 *Accounting principles; foreign operations* (L.O. 4, 6)

This problem is a duplication of Problem EDB13-1. It is based on a company selected by your instructor.

Instructions

By using the text's Electronic Data Base, access the specified company's income statement and accompanying notes and focus on data for the most recent year reported. Answer requirements (a)–(d) of Problem EDB13-1.

BEYOND THE BASICS

BB13-1 *Analysis of GAAP* (L.O. 2, 4, 5)

Lambert Corporation, a manufacturer of mobile homes, has experienced substantial operating losses in recent years and is in dire financial trouble. As a result, the firm's creditors have become concerned and are now refusing to lend additional funds. To help determine what corrective actions are necessary, management has retained the services of an independent consultant. The consultant's report follows.

To the Directors of Lambert Corporation:

I have reviewed the financial position of Lambert Corporation. In short, Lambert qualifies as the typical going concern, as it may soon go out of business. I feel that the changes described in the following paragraphs are needed.

First, the firm must adopt different accounting procedures. For example, I strongly believe that revenue realization should occur at the start of production when the earnings process is complete. I was shocked to learn that your accountants wait until the point of sale; this clearly explains the recent operating losses. My recommendation will bring your policies in line with those of other companies for which I do consulting work. The change to a comparable reporting practice will mean that the firm is following GAAP, specifically, the principle of consistency.

Next, management needs to borrow funds to meet current operating expenses. These funds can be obtained by borrowing against certain assets. Before approaching another banker, however, I would recommend that you first increase the carrying amount of specified assets (e.g., land and buildings) on the balance sheet to reflect current market values. This practice is acceptable because costs have risen over the years. Also, I suggest that you list on the balance sheet certain personal assets of the corporation's directors.

Finally, the fears of your creditors are well understood. Bear in mind, however, that the creditors are not accounting experts and, as such, are not expected to read and understand financial statements. Perhaps they think you are burying something in the accompanying notes. Henceforth, I would recommend that Lambert comply with disclosure rules. These rules require that a firm fully reveal all pertinent financial facts directly on the face of the balance sheet and the income statement.

In review, your problems are accounting related. I trust my recommendations will assist the company and will help it return to profitable operations. If I may be of further assistance, please do not hesitate to call.

Very truly,

Arthur Cannon
Consultant

Instructions

a Identify the various accounting assumptions, principles, concepts, and conventions that Arthur Cannon alluded to in his report.

b Discuss how Cannon misused each of the items identified in part (a).

BB13-2 *Overview of chapter concepts: Multiple choice* (L.O. 2-6)
The following multiple-choice questions relate to various topics discussed in the chapter. Select the best answer.

1 Which of the following pairings of information characteristics and accounting principles/assumptions is the most illogical?
a Understandability/full disclosure.
b Comparability/consistency.
c Reliability/objectivity.
d Relevancy/historical cost.

2 Generally accepted accounting principles:
a are approved by managing partners of large public accounting firms.
b underlie *Statements of Financial Accounting Standards*, which are issued by the Securities and Exchange Commission.
c are the result of interaction between the Securities and Exchange Commission and the Financial Accounting Standards Board.
d are adopted if approved by 25% of the voting CPAs.

3 Which of the following is an application of conservatism in accounting?

a Use of the lower-of-cost-or-market method for inventory valuation.

b Overestimation of revenues when constructing a budgeted income statement.

c Use of FIFO to determine cost of goods sold in a period of rising prices.

d Ignoring a potential liability for product warranties when preparing the financial statements.

4 Although challenged frequently, the historical-cost principle is still widely supported for financial reporting because historical cost:

a is an objectively determinable amount.

b is a good measure of current value for a going concern.

c facilitates the calculation of economic income.

d results in the lowest income tax accruals.

5 Howard Corporation recently recorded the following entry to reflect increased values of its real estate holdings:

Land	70,000	
Buildings	340,000	
Income from Appreciation		410,000

Howard Corporation:

a has violated the historical-cost principle.

b has violated the revenue realization principle.

c has followed conservative accounting practices.

d has done more than one of the above, namely, _____, _____.

6 Which of the following statements regarding revenue realization is false?

a The installment method of revenue recognition is normally in accord with GAAP.

b Revenue should be recognized when the earnings process is complete or virtually complete.

c The percentage-of-completion method postpones revenue recognition on a construction project until title to the property passes to the buyer.

d More than one of the above is false, namely, _____, _____.

7 Farmer Corporation, with total assets of $175,000, has a policy of immediately expensing all items of plant and equipment that cost less than $75. In view of this policy, we can say that Farmer:

a is correctly following the doctrine of materiality.

b is technically in violation of the matching principle.

c is not in violation of the matching principle.

d is doing more than one of the above, namely, _____, _____.

8 Hewlett Corporation (a U.S. company) owes Packard Corporation 5,000 units of a foreign currency. This payable was created at a time when the spot rate was $0.50 per foreign currency unit. Hewlett now desires to prepare a balance sheet. The spot rate is currently $0.45 but is expected to climb to $0.56 by the time the payable is settled. The account payable should be reported on Hewlett's balance sheet:

a at $2,250.

b at $2,500.

c at $2,800.

d in foreign currency units.

**COMMUNICATION
OF ACCOUNTING
INFORMATION**

CAI13-1 *A checklist for reports: The Black & Decker Corporation* (L.O. 4)
Communication Principle: How do we evaluate the success of reports? A report succeeds when it can easily be used to find information or to help make decisions. These qualities help make a report useful:

1 An impartial tone that reassures the reader that the report is a credible, fair, and objective source.
2 A clear organizational scheme reflected in the order of the headings. One such scheme is the movement from general principles to specific illustrations.
3 A traditional format and professional appearance.

In contrast, a report is not effective if it is marked by the following characteristics:

1 The assumption of only one kind of reader—expert or general—and a lapse either into jargon and too many details or into generalities with too few specifics.
2 The lack of a purpose statement that directs the reader and focuses attention.
3 The creation of more questions than answers on the part of the reader. The reader is left with the impression of incompleteness, vagueness, and confusion.

■ ■ ■ ■ ■ ■ ■ ■ ■

Black & Decker is a manufacturer of quality tools/appliances used in and around the home and for commercial applications. Power saws, hedge trimmers, irons, and toaster ovens are just a few of the company's many products.

A review of a recent Black & Decker annual report found the following:

■ Sales, operating income, and identifiable assets are subdivided and reported by geographic regions of activity.
■ Inventories are reported at the lower of cost or market.
■ Property, plant, and equipment are reported at cost. Appropriate assets are being depreciated by use of the straight-line method.
■ Individual amounts owed to the company's many suppliers do not appear in the notes that accompany the financial statements.

Instructions

Assume that Karen Sawyer, a Black & Decker employee, was having a bad day. A high-ranking executive heard her say: "Nobody does anything by the book around here." To make the point that the company does do things by the book, the executive has asked Karen to review the firm's financial statements and the accompanying notes. She is to construct a report that (1) discusses the use of generally accepted accounting principles (GAAP) in financial reporting and (2) cites instances where Black & Decker has followed GAAP.

Assume the role of Karen Sawyer and prepare the report, being sure to observe the guidelines set forth in the communication principle. When discussing the use of GAAP at Black & Decker, indicate and briefly explain the specific concept or principle that is being followed.

Answers to Chapter Quiz

1 b

2 d

3 d

4 c ($20.0 million − $13.5 million − $4.2 million = $2.3 million total profit; $2.3 million − $1.5 million = $800,000)

5 a

CHAPTER 14

Partnerships

LEARNING OBJECTIVES
After studying this chapter, you should be able to:

1

Explain the unique characteristics of a partnership.

2

Account for partnership formation and income distribution, including situations that give rise to an earnings deficiency.

3

Account for partner admissions and withdrawals.

4

Perform the procedures related to partnership liquidations.

Through the first thirteen chapters of this text we have focused on the sole proprietorship to illustrate financial reporting and measurement practices. We now turn our attention to another popular entity form: the partnership. The Uniform Partnership Act, adopted by most states to govern this form of organization, defines a **partnership** as "an association of two or more persons to carry on, as co-owners, a business for profit." Partnerships are an attractive type of entity for small emerging companies, which often need more talent, experience, and capital than a single owner can provide.

Most partnerships have fewer than five owners; others, however, are quite large. Arthur Andersen & Co., for example, an international public accounting firm, recently reported having 2,393 partners throughout its worldwide operation in 67 countries. The partnership form of organization is encountered in professional practices such as accounting, law, medicine, and dentistry. Furthermore, it is used by small retail establishments, manufacturers, home builders, and service businesses.

Def & characteristic

adv. & disadv.

CHARACTERISTICS OF A PARTNERSHIP

OBJECTIVE

1

Explain the unique characteristics of a partnership.

Partnerships possess several distinctive features that have important implications for accountants. These features are discussed in the following sections.

Ease of Formation

A partnership is easily created by a voluntary agreement between two or more people. Although the agreement may be oral and finalized by a handshake, good business practice dictates the creation of a formal written "contract" between the parties involved.

This document is commonly known as the **articles of partnership.** Generally speaking, the articles detail the rights, responsibilities, and duties of the partners. In addition, specific policies are normally stated with regard to partner investments and withdrawals, the division of net income (and net loss), the admission of new partners, the withdrawal of partners, and procedures to be followed in the event of partner disputes or a partner's death.

Unlimited Liability

Consistent with the financial reporting principles discussed in the previous chapter, a partnership is viewed as an *accounting entity* that is separate and distinct from its owners. Consequently, the personal economic activities of the partners (e.g., the acquisition of household furniture, the payment of a weekly grocery bill) are not combined with the transactions of the business. In contrast, the partnership is not a separate *legal entity* and as such, has no legal status under common law.

Because of this latter feature, each owner is held personally liable (i.e., has **unlimited liability**) for the debts of the enterprise. Thus, if a partnership experiences cash flow problems and becomes unable to pay its bills, the partners are required to surrender personal assets to help settle the firm's obligations.

HIGHLIGHT
A Need for Business "Partners"

When listening to the Beatles sing "Help," you probably did not apply the song or its namesake movie to business entities. The Beatles, though, were right on target when it comes to partnerships. John, Paul, Ringo, and George's tune pinpoints a major reason why businesspeople often forge an alliance and work together as partners.

Consider the case of Debbi Fields, an internationally acclaimed business phenomenon while still in her 20s. Fields is the founder of Mrs. Fields Inc., probably the world's best-known maker of chocolate chip cookies. She got into the business entirely by accident: Her husband, Randy, was a financial consultant whose clients could not resist the batches of cookies that Debbi set out in his office. When Debbi decided to turn her baking skill into a business, a banker who liked her chocolate chip cookies lent her $50,000, and she opened her first store, in Palo Alto, California. She was 20 at the time.

By 1986, Randy Fields had quit consulting and joined his wife's business. One year later, after opening 173 stores, they were running a total of 543 owned-and-operated stores in six countries, including Japan and Australia. The company earned $18 million on sales of $104 million. The couple even bought La Petite Boulangerie, a nationwide bakery chain, from PepsiCo. There was nothing that Debbi couldn't do.

But just when everything looked so terrific, it was actually falling apart. Among other things, many new stores were too close to existing ones; others were simply not in the right neighborhoods. In 1988, Mrs. Fields closed 97 stores and took a $20 million real-estate writedown. Net loss for the year: $19 million.

A mark of the most successful people is that they can learn while suffering through difficult setbacks. "I really believe that one of my roles is to grow and

learn," says Fields, recalling the retrenchment period. Specifically, she learned to delegate the daily running of the business to professional managers. "I have," she says, "worked very hard on removing myself from the day-to-day details that do not allow me to keep the company focused on where it's going."

In 1988, Fields began bringing in executives as "partners." These executives were not partners in the true sense of owners/partners—Mrs. Fields is organized as a corporation—but they were professionals who had the expertise to get the job done. A chief financial officer was hired along with a head of operations. Together they formed a team and allowed Debbi to assume her managerial duties.

Shortly after the hiring, the company signed a licensing agreement with a division of Marriott Corp., allowing the latter to open at least 60 Mrs. Fields shops, mainly in highway plazas and airports. Other deals are in the works with several supermarket chains to create in-store bakeries that will make and sell Fields' products. In addition, Debbi hopes to extend her product line by developing Mrs. Fields Bakeries. The bakeries, which offer muffins, bread, sandwiches, and soups, are being sited in larger but typically less expensive space.

In the new role she has created for herself, Debbi Fields has more time to read every comment sent in by customers—several hundred a month—and spends two-thirds of the year visiting her stores and meeting with local managers. She has learned a valuable lesson: A successful entrepreneur cannot, and should not, try to do everything herself. "Partners" are needed to run a business. These individuals should be team players who bring expertise, a willingness to work, and peace of mind to the entire operation.

Source: Adapted from "Succeeding by Failing," *Forbes*, June 25, 1990, p. 160. Excerpted by permission of *Forbes* magazine, © Forbes Inc., 1990.

Mutual Agency

Partnerships have **mutual agency**; that is, each partner acts as an agent of the partnership in business transactions. As a result, the partnership is bound to the commitments and obligations made by any partner on behalf of the firm. For this reason partners must be selected with great care, as irresponsible personnel could create a difficult working environment and spell financial disaster.

Co-ownership of Property and Income

According to the Uniform Partnership Act, partners are really the co-owners of an enterprise. Thus, a partner who invests a building in the firm retains no personal rights to the building. (The asset becomes jointly owned by all partners.) Similarly, the partnership's net income belongs to all of the partners and can be divided among them in any agreed-upon manner.

Limited Life

Unless there is an agreement to the contrary, the death, bankruptcy, retirement, incapacity, or withdrawal of a partner ends the partnership. Other events that call for termination of the firm (sometimes known as **dissolution**) include accomplishment of the firm's objective and the admission of new partners. Dissolution does not necessarily mean that operations cease and the remaining assets are sold. Rather, if the surviving partners agree, a new entity can be formed, and activities can continue uninterrupted.

An Overview: Advantages and Disadvantages of Partnerships

ETHICS ISSUE

Two of your clients, Big and Small, want to form a partnership. Your independent review of the partnership agreement finds several biases in favor of Big, making Big a much bigger and better client. What would you do?

The partnership form of organization offers several advantages. Initially, there is the obvious opportunity to combine persons who possess capital and/or specialized skills to start and operate a business. Furthermore, in comparison with corporations, partnerships are subject to fewer reporting requirements and less governmental regulation and therefore have more operating flexibility. Decisions that require formal, time-consuming actions by stockholders and corporate management can often be settled quickly among the partnership's members.

As for disadvantages, the features of mutual agency, limited life, and unlimited liability sometimes present problems. Unlimited liability is especially an obstacle when trying to raise substantial amounts of additional capital. Most people who invest in stocks and other alternatives (e.g., stamps, coins, art, or gold) are willing to incur a loss. However, because personal assets such as a home and a car may be exposed to a partnership's creditors, many investors tend to shy away from this entity form. The risk is simply too great.

Income taxes are another factor that should be considered when evaluating the partnership. A business that operates as a partnership does not pay income taxes. Instead, the firm's net income (or net loss) is allocated to the partners, and the partners pay income taxes personally on their share. This treatment is in contrast to that afforded corporations. Not only is a corporation a taxable entity, but the shareholders are also taxed on the amount of dividends received.[1] These facts, coupled with differences in corporate and individual tax rates, create a need for effective planning when selecting the entity form for a new business.

PARTNERSHIP ACCOUNTING

Partnership accounting does not differ significantly from that described earlier in the text for sole proprietorships. Transactions unique to partnerships arise only in the area of owner's equity and relate to business formation, income distribution, admittance and withdrawal of partners, and liquidation. To handle the necessary record keeping, separate capital and drawing accounts are maintained for each owner.

Partnership Formation and Owner Investments

fair market value

Accounting for a partnership begins when owners (i.e., partners) invest their personal assets into the firm. Investments in a partnership may take the form of cash, noncash assets such as land or buildings, and even an entire operating business. To illustrate the proper record keeping, suppose that Steve Leake and Dotty Mueller, both CPAs, decided to form a partnership on January 2, 19X1. Leake invested $15,000 cash; Mueller invested her existing accounting practice. According to the balance sheet from the preceding year, the practice had the following assets and liabilities:

> **OBJECTIVE**
>
> **2**
>
> Account for partnership formation and income distribution, including situations that give rise to an earnings deficiency.

Assets		
Cash		$ 3,000
Accounts receivable	$4,000	
Less: Allowance for uncollectible accounts	500	3,500
Supplies		1,000
Equipment	$5,000	
Less: Accumulated depreciation	1,200	3,800
Total assets		$11,300
Liabilities		
Accounts payable		$ 2,500

As of January 2, 19X1, the equipment had a fair market value of $6,000. The necessary journal entries to record the partners' investments follow.

Cash	15,000	
Leake, Capital		15,000

To record investment by Leake in the partnership of Leake and Mueller

Cash	3,000	
Accounts Receivable	4,000	
Supplies	1,000	
Equipment	6,000	
Allowance for Uncollectible Accounts		500
Accounts Payable		2,500
Mueller, Capital		11,000*

To record investment by Mueller in the partnership of Leake and Mueller

* The capital account is credited for the net assets (total assets minus total liabilities) contributed by Mueller.

---

[1] Should the shareholders sell their stock, income tax is levied on any gains that arise.

Observe that the Equipment account is debited for $6,000 and *not* the book value of $3,800. Noncash assets are entered in the new records at fair market value—the actual acquisition cost to the partnership. A failure to use fair market value would improperly ignore prior increases in asset valuation. To explain, suppose the equipment was recorded at its $3,800 book value and immediately sold by the partnership for $6,000. The $2,200 gain would be shared by both partners, which is unfair to Mueller. The increase in valuation occurred while the asset was in her possession; therefore she should receive full and proper credit for her investment. The use of book value in this case would significantly understate Mueller's capital account on the books of the new entity.

Partnership Earnings: Nature and Distribution

Paralleling the role of a sole proprietor, partners are considered owners of a firm and *not* employees. Thus, any amounts distributed as remuneration for services rendered are generally treated as withdrawals of capital as opposed to business expenses. Treatment as an expense would destroy net income as a measure of the enterprise's earnings ability, because an owner could set his or her own compensation level and greatly influence the reported profit. Further, unlike sales, office, and administrative personnel, the partner is not just working to earn a weekly paycheck. He or she is striving to improve the overall financial well-being of the business.

In view of this ownership role, partners are "rewarded" at the end of the period by being allocated a share of the company's earnings.[2] Earnings (or losses) can be split in many different ways. Most partnership contracts are quite specific on this matter and are structured to recognize variations in time, talent, and/or money provided. If no provisions are stated, profits and losses are divided equally.

Recognition of Services

A study of many partnerships will often reveal considerable differences among the partners in terms of service. Some partners have been with the business for many years; others are relative newcomers. One partner may have an outstanding reputation for some type of specialty interest, say, open-heart surgery; others, possibly, do not. Variations in these factors, business contacts, and effort devoted to the firm are often recognized in the form of salary differentials. Assume, for example, that Leake and Mueller's articles of partnership provide for monthly salary allowances of $1,000 and $1,200, respectively, with any remaining net income to be divided equally. If 19X1 net income amounted to $38,000, the following division would be made:

---

[2] This procedure is really the same as that illustrated earlier in the text for sole proprietorships. Recall that part of the closing process involves an increase to the owner's capital account for the firm's net income.

	Leake	Mueller	Total
Division of net income			
Salary			
Leake ($1,000 × 12 months)	$12,000		
Mueller ($1,200 × 12 months)		$14,400	$26,400
Remainder of $11,600 ($38,000 − $26,400)			
divided equally	5,800	5,800	11,600
	$17,800	$20,200	$38,000

Once determined, net income is transferred to the capital accounts by the following closing entry:

Income Summary	38,000	
Leake, Capital		17,800
Mueller, Capital		20,200
To record the division of net income		

We again stress that partners are owners and *not* employees. Thus, **salary allowances** are not business expenses. Rather, these amounts are considered only in the division of net income.

Partners often withdraw their salaries throughout the year, requiring that entries be made in the drawing accounts. To illustrate the proper accounting, assume that Leake and Mueller have each withdrawn their salary allowances along with an additional $800. End-of-period balances in the partners' drawing accounts will total $12,800 ($12,000 + $800) and $15,200 ($14,400 + $800), respectively. The impact of these events is shown on the firm's statement of partners' (i.e., owners') equity, which appears in Exhibit 14-1.

The statement's bottom line is eventually carried forward to the prac-

LEAKE AND MUELLER, CPAs
Statement of Partners' Equity
For the Year Ended December 31, 19X1

	Leake	Mueller	Total
Beginning balance, Jan. 1	$ —	$ —	$ —
Increases			
Partner investments	$15,000	$11,000	$26,000
Net income	17,800	20,200	38,000
Subtotal	$32,800	$31,200	$64,000
Decreases			
Drawings: salary	$12,000	$14,400	$26,400
Drawings: other	800	800	1,600
Total	$12,800	$15,200	$28,000
Ending balance, Dec. 31	$20,000	$16,000	$36,000

EXHIBIT 14-1
Statement of Partners' Equity

tice's December 31 balance sheet in the following manner (liability total is assumed):

Total liabilities		$58,500
Partners' equity		
Steve Leake, capital	$20,000	
Dotty Mueller, capital	16,000	36,000
Total liabilities & partners' equity		$94,500

As a final step, the drawing accounts would be closed to the partners' capital accounts:

Leake, Capital	12,800	
Mueller, Capital	15,200	
Leake, Drawing		12,800
Mueller, Drawing		15,200
To close partners' drawing accounts		

By tracing through the entries presented, observe that the capital accounts were credited for the initial investment at the time of formation and later for each partner's share of net income. The entry to close the drawing accounts will therefore reduce Leake, Capital, and Mueller, Capital, to the balances reported on the partners' equity statement.

Recognition of Invested Capital

Total invested capital is a major factor in the success of businesses that carry inventory or have substantial equipment needs. Thus, partnership agreements often consider differences in the amount of capital contributed by individual partners. Recognition is particularly prevalent for firms that have "silent" partners, or partners who provide substantial financial support but do not become involved in daily management activities.

Several methods that are commonly employed focus on the amount of a partner's capital contribution. For example, an entity's income (or loss) may be distributed by using a ratio of the beginning-of-period capital balances. If partner A's capital account contains, say, $120,000 on January 1 and B's contains $80,000, the total owners' equity of the firm, $200,000, forms the basis for the proper allocation. In this particular case, any earnings (or losses) generated would be divided in a 60 : 40 ratio (A: $120,000 ÷ $200,000 = 60%; B: $80,000 ÷ $200,000 = 40%).

A careful study of this procedure could prompt a partner to withdraw vast sums of cash for personal use shortly after the period begins and then to make reinvestments late in the year, just prior to computing the next period's allocation base. Although the partner might personally benefit from this practice, the business could experience a capital shortage. To discourage large withdrawals and at the same time promote capital retention, partnership agreements sometimes call for the ratio to be calculated on the basis of *average* account balances. This latter approach relies on a month-by-month analysis of a partner's invested capital and results in the computation of a weighted-average balance for use in the allocation procedure.

The amount of a partner's invested capital can also be recognized by use of an **interest allowance,** computed on either the beginning or average balance in the capital account. The interest allowance is similar to the salary allowance discussed earlier: it is employed only in the division of net income (or loss) and is not an expense of the partnership.

To illustrate the accounting that accompanies an interest allowance, we will continue the Leake and Mueller example. Assume that the partnership agreement now contains the following provisions:

1 Monthly salaries of $1,000 and $1,200 to Leake and Mueller, respectively

2 Interest of 15% to both partners, computed on the basis of their beginning capital balances

3 Any remaining income (or loss) to be divided equally

It is one year later and 19X2 net income totals $42,000. The proper division between Leake and Mueller follows.

	Leake	Mueller	Total
Division of net income			
Salary			
Leake ($1,000 × 12 months)	$12,000		$26,400
Mueller ($1,200 × 12 months)		$14,400	
Interest*			
Leake ($20,000 × 0.15)	3,000		5,400
Mueller ($16,000 × 0.15)		2,400	
	$15,000	$16,800	$31,800
Remainder of $10,200 ($42,000 − $31,800)			
divided equally	5,100	5,100	10,200
	$20,100	$21,900	$42,000

* Interest is computed on the January 1, 19X2 (i.e., December 31, 19X1), capital balances. These balances are taken from the statement of partners' equity that appears in Exhibit 14-1.

The journal entry to close the accounting records requires a debit to Income Summary for $42,000 and a credit to Leake, Capital, and Mueller, Capital, for $20,100 and $21,900, respectively.

Earnings Deficiency

In the previous examples, salary and interest allowances were less than the total earnings of the firm. Naturally, it is possible for a partnership to incur a net loss or have insufficient income to cover the allowances. In these cases an **earnings deficiency** arises. Unless provisions are made to the contrary, the partnership agreement is still followed; that is, authorized salary and interest allowances continue to be recognized. Because of insufficient earnings, however, a deficiency is allocated to the partners, normally in the same ratio as that for profits and losses. Leake and Mueller, for example, would share the deficiency equally.

To focus on the related procedures, suppose that Leake and Mueller's partnership agreement continues to stipulate respective monthly salaries of $1,000 and $1,200 and interest allowances of 15%. Now, however, assume that 19X2 net income amounted to only $20,000. The proper allocation follows.

	Leake	Mueller	Total
Division of net income			
Salary	$12,000	$14,400	$ 26,400
Interest	3,000	2,400	5,400
	$15,000	$16,800	$ 31,800
Deficiency of $11,800 ($31,800 − $20,000)			
divided equally	(5,900)	(5,900)	(11,800)
	$ 9,100	$10,900	$ 20,000

The required closing entry is similar to those shown previously: Income Summary is debited for $20,000, with corresponding credits of $9,100 to Leake, Capital, and $10,900 to Mueller, Capital.

EXECUTIVE BRIEFING
Features That We Consider When Dividing Firm Income Among the Partners

James Brocksmith, Jr.
Deputy Chairman and Chief Operating Officer
KPMG Peat Marwick, Certified Public Accountants

Since quality client service is the centerpiece of KPMG's strategy, it is the most important determinant of partner compensation. But you have to have some way of measuring service. First, we survey all of our clients every year to determine their level of satisfaction, so we have objective information *by partner.* Second, we measure profitability by client—because there is a direct relationship between client satisfaction with our services and the fees we can charge. Third, we measure the technical quality of work performed for clients, with the work of every partner being evaluated every year. We also consider participation in firm-wide strategic initiatives, to reward investments in future client satisfaction. In addition, each partner sets short- and long-term goals that are agreed to with his or her managing partner yearly, and we measure progress toward the achievement of those goals.

The objectives of the process are to create incentives to deliver quality services, to encourage partners' sense of collegiality and satisfaction with the firm, and to reinforce confidence in long-term ownership. Thus, we recognize sustained performance as well as specific accomplishments, and teamwork as well as individual initiative. The process involves a lot of give and take—between and among the partners—but the final proof of the equity of the income division is that it must (and does!) survive a secret ballot of all partners. The vote symbolizes that the process serves more than the equitable division of income; it serves our common dedication to the firm and to our clients as well.

Admission of a New Partner

multiple choice

OBJECTIVE

3

Account for partner admissions and withdrawals.

The Leake and Mueller partnership was a new entity formed with investments from both Steve Leake and Dotty Mueller. Observe that Leake did not invest in Mueller's accounting practice; instead, a new business was established. Frequently, individuals are admitted to existing partnerships either by (1) purchasing an interest from one or more of the present partners or (2) making an investment directly in the firm. The method of entry depends on several factors. For example, interests are often purchased when existing partners wish to decrease their involvement in daily activities because of changing goals, illness, or retirement. Investments directly in the business, on the other hand, sometimes occur when firms are growing and have a need for additional capital.

Purchase of an Interest

When an entering partner purchases an interest from a current partner, the assets and liabilities of the firm do not change. To illustrate, assume that Leake and Mueller have capital balances of $20,000 and $16,000, respectively. After lengthy negotiation both partners have agreed to sell 40% of their respective interests in the business to Ann Colby, a CPA. Colby will pay Leake and Mueller $15,000 each. The effect of the transaction, shown pictorially in Exhibit 14-2, gives rise to the journal entry that follows.

Leake, Capital	8,000	
Mueller, Capital	6,400	
Colby, Capital		14,400
To record the transfer of 40% of present		
capital balances to Colby		

Notice that the price paid by Colby is in excess of the interest acquired from each partner. This situation arises from the negotiation process and is a personal matter among the parties involved. The cash goes to Leake and Mueller personally, and all that is needed on the firm's records is a transfer of ownership (i.e., capital balances).

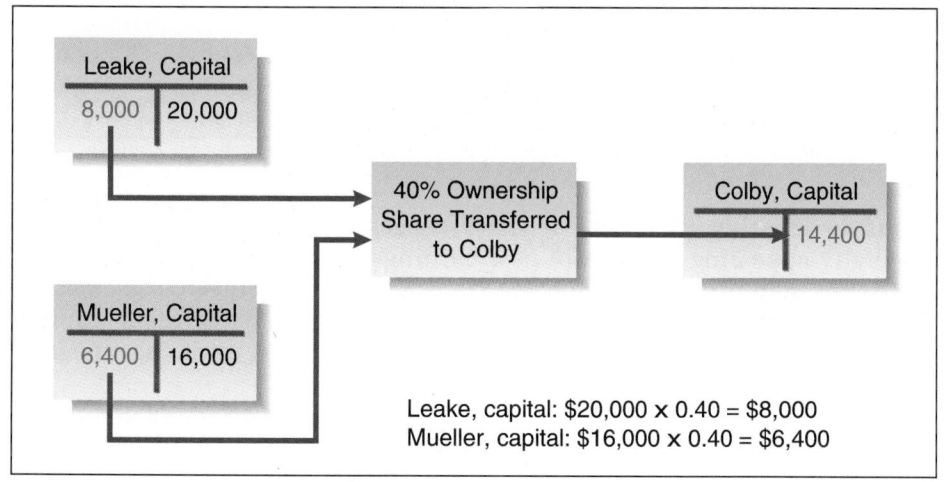

EXHIBIT 14-2
Purchase of a Partner's Interest

Investment in the Firm

In addition to purchasing an interest from existing partners, an incoming partner may invest directly in the business. In this case the new partner makes payment to the partnership, and total firm assets increase. If the partnership assets and liabilities are valued correctly, the entering partner's investment will be equal to the negotiated percentage of the new entity's total capital. To explain, we will again assume Leake and Mueller have respective capital balances of $20,000 and $16,000. Suppose that both partners have agreed to grant Colby a one-third interest in the business for a cash investment of $18,000. Colby's investment will bring total firm capital to $54,000:

Leake, capital	$20,000
Mueller, capital	16,000
Investment by Colby	18,000
Total	$54,000

Observe that the $18,000 investment represents one-third of the owners' equity of the new partnership ($54,000 $\times \frac{1}{3}$ = $18,000). Colby paid nothing extra to gain a one-third interest; nothing extra was given to her to provide the cash inflow. The necessary journal entry to update the accounting records is as follows:

Cash	18,000	
Colby, Capital		18,000
To record the admission of Colby		
to the partnership		

Tips & Techniques

Many students mistakenly believe that a new partner who acquires a specified partnership interest, say, one-third, is automatically entitled to the same share of the entity's earnings. As noted earlier, income-sharing agreements often contain interest and salary allowances that consider unique attributes of the partners. The division of net income (or loss) is subject to negotiation among the owners and may therefore be quite different from the partners' percentage ownership interests.

Bonus to Existing Partners. If the prospect of joining a partnership is especially appealing because of past earnings records and other favorable factors, an incoming partner may be required to pay a bonus to the existing owners. Any bonuses paid are allocated to the present partners' capital accounts according to the profit- and loss-sharing ratio in the partnership agreement.

For instance, assume that Colby was required to invest $24,000 for a one-third interest in the firm. The entity's total capital would now amount to $60,000:

Leake, capital	$20,000
Mueller, capital	16,000
Investment by Colby	24,000
Total	$60,000

Colby's interest would therefore be $20,000 ($60,000 × $\frac{1}{3}$). Apparently, then, she is paying a $4,000 bonus ($24,000 − $20,000) to Leake and Mueller for admission. If profits and losses are shared equally, the bonus is split 50 : 50 and the required journal entry is as follows:

Cash	24,000	
Leake, Capital		2,000
Mueller, Capital		2,000
Colby, Capital		20,000

To record the investment of Colby and
bonus to existing partners

Bonus to New Partner.   Occasionally, an organization is anxious to attract a new partner who possesses specialized skills, significant capital, or unique managerial ability. In these instances the existing owners may grant the incoming partner a larger business interest than is justified by the amount of the investment. In essence, a bonus is being given to the newcomer.

For example, assume that Colby was required to invest only $9,000 for her one-third interest. As the following figures show, total capital after admission would amount to $45,000:

Leake, capital	$20,000
Mueller, capital	16,000
Investment by Colby	9,000
Total	$45,000

Because a one-third interest has been granted, Colby, Capital, must contain a balance of $15,000 ($45,000 × $\frac{1}{3}$) after the transaction. She has there—fore received a $6,000 bonus over and above her $9,000 investment—namely, a bonus provided by Leake and Mueller. Given the source of the bonus and the fact that profits and losses are shared equally, $3,000 reductions in each of the existing capital accounts are needed to properly reflect Colby's equity interest:

Cash	9,000	
Leake, Capital	3,000	
Mueller, Capital	3,000	
Colby, Capital		15,000

To record the investment of Colby and
bonus to new partner

Withdrawal of a Partner ← *A major problem*

Aside from admission, the composition of a partnership will also change when an owner withdraws or retires from the firm. The exiting owner's business interest may be purchased by the remaining partners or even an outsider (if the other partners approve). In both cases the assets and liabilities of the firm remain unchanged because the exchange of interests is strictly a personal matter among the parties involved. However, a journal entry is needed to eliminate the withdrawing partner's capital balance and to record an increase in the capital account(s) of the purchaser(s). The required entry parallels that shown on page 553 for the admission of a new partner who purchases an interest from a present owner.

Purchase by the Partnership

Rather than sell to other individuals, the withdrawing party may agree to sell his or her interest to the partnership. In this situation, company assets will be used for payment. Quite often, the articles of partnership will specify the procedures to follow and the price to be paid for a withdrawing owner's interest. The price can vary widely and may be equal to, less than, or greater than the partner's capital balance. The first case is the simplest and requires a debit to the appropriate partner's capital account and a credit to Cash. The other situations are more complex and are discussed in the following sections.

Payment Less Than the Capital Balance.   A partnership may pay less than the capital balance of the exiting owner if past operations have been relatively unsuccessful or if the firm has an extremely weak cash position. In addition, this situation sometimes arises if friction has developed between the partner leaving and those remaining in the business. Because the exiting partner is willing to accept an amount less than that appearing in the accounting records, a bonus is actually being paid to the remaining owners. The bonus is split among these individuals according to the firm's profit-and loss-sharing ratio.

To illustrate, we will continue the Leake-Mueller-Colby partnership example. Assume that (1) the partners have present capital balances of $20,000, $16,000, and $18,000, respectively, and (2) all profits and losses are divided equally. Mueller has decided to withdraw from the firm and has agreed to accept $10,000 for her interest. The following entry is necessary:

Mueller, Capital	16,000	
Leake, Capital		3,000
Colby, Capital		3,000
Cash		10,000

To record the purchase of Mueller's
interest by the partnership

Observe that Leake and Colby have "profited" from Mueller's settlement. The elimination of a $16,000 capital balance for only $10,000 benefits the business by $6,000, which is split equally among the ongoing owners.

Payment Greater Than the Capital Balance.   Negotiations between the firm and an exiting partner sometimes result in a settlement price in excess of the partner's capital balance. Frequently, the agreed-upon price is considerably greater. Keep in mind that accounting records are based on historical cost; thus, increases in the market values of company assets have been ignored. Historical-cost valuations, coupled with the fact that the partnership may have substantial earnings potential, could result in a somewhat unrealistic (i.e., low) capital balance. If the outcome of negotiation involves a payment in excess of the withdrawing partner's equity, the capital balances of the ongoing partners are reduced according to the profit- and loss-sharing ratio. In this situation, a bonus is being paid to the exiting owner.

For example, assume the present respective capital balances of Leake, Mueller, and Colby are $20,000, $16,000, and $18,000. Mueller has decided to leave the business and the firm has agreed to pay $30,000 for her interest. If net income is divided equally, Mueller's withdrawal and payment of her $14,000 bonus ($30,000 − $16,000) would be recorded as follows:

Mueller, Capital	16,000	
Leake, Capital	7,000	
Colby, Capital	7,000	
Cash		30,000

To record the purchase of Mueller's interest by the partnership

In this case the bonus is charged against the capital accounts of Leake and Colby. Stated differently, the firm (i.e., the remaining owners) must "foot the bill" for the payout to Mueller over and above her capital interest.

The preceding discussion is summarized in Exhibit 14-3. By following the color coding scheme, you can clearly see that accounting for partner withdrawals closely parallels that for partner admissions.

EXHIBIT 14-3
Accounting for Partner Admissions and Withdrawals

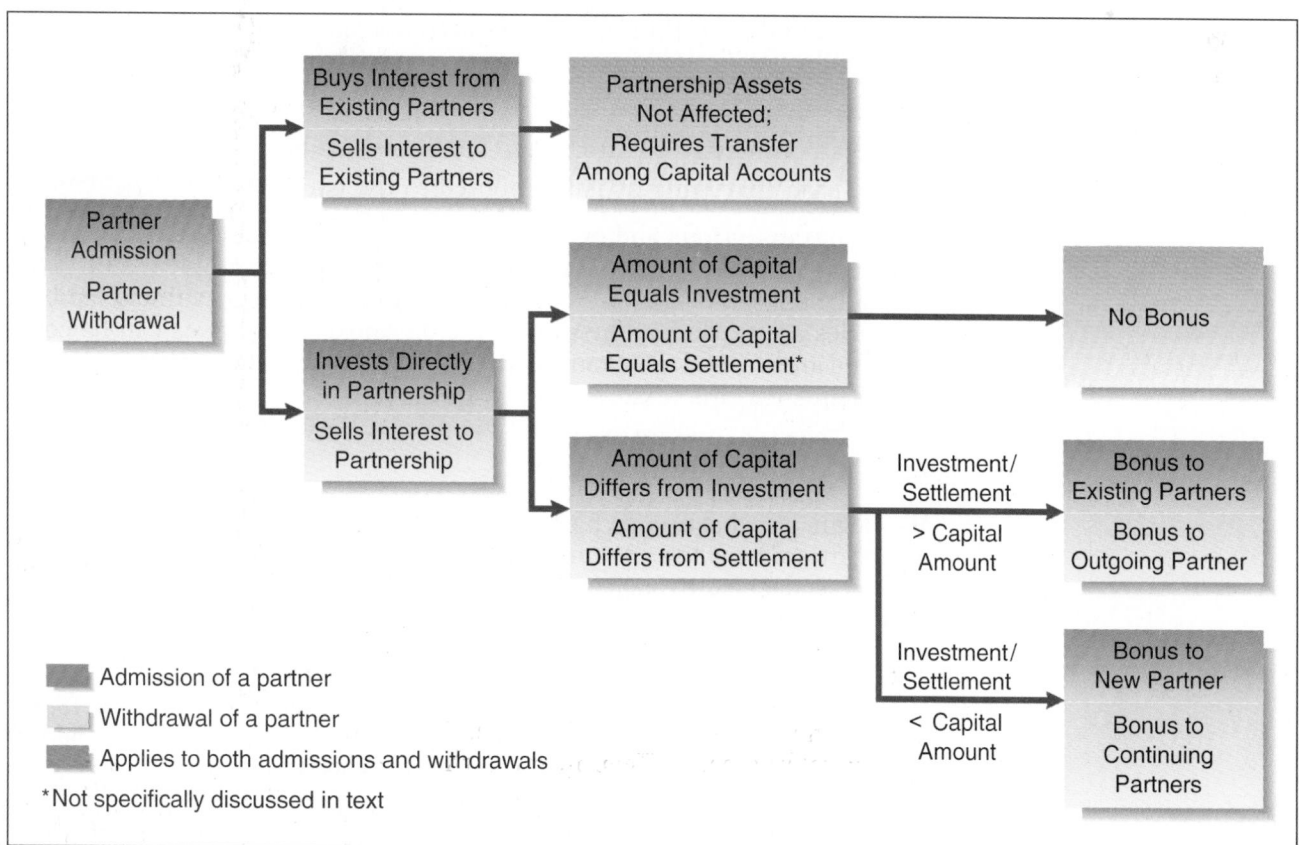

Death of a Partner

The death of a partnership member automatically ends the legal life of a partnership. At this point, the firm's obligation to the estate of the deceased owner must be determined. It is therefore necessary to compute income (or loss) from the beginning of the current accounting period to the date of death so that a proper share can be included in the deceased partner's capital account.

The articles of partnership typically state the procedures to be followed in the event of an owner's death, including how assets are to be valued and when payment should be made to the estate. Often, insurance policies are carried on all partners, with the firm named as beneficiary. This practice ensures that adequate cash is available at the time of death and that the business can satisfy requirements of the partnership agreement.

Liquidation of a Partnership

OBJECTIVE 4

Perform the procedures related to partnership liquidations.

Earlier in the chapter we noted that a partnership is dissolved when a new partner is admitted to the firm or an existing partner withdraws from the business. Although dissolution has occurred, the partnership's activities may continue if the remaining partners agree to form a new entity.

If this course of action is undesirable or if the entity has experienced significant financial problems (e.g., sizable losses), it may be in the partners' best interests to cease operations. The process of terminating a partnership and discontinuing business activities is known as **liquidation.** In the usual case, liquidation involves three steps:

1 The noncash assets are sold for cash.
2 The amounts due creditors (i.e., liabilities) are paid.
3 Any cash that remains is distributed to the partners.

These transactions and events normally occur over a period of time and in piecemeal fashion. For simplicity, our illustrative example will assume that all noncash assets are sold for a single, lump-sum amount and all liabilities are settled at the same time. Because liquidations can be complex and are covered in advanced accounting courses, only a basic overview is presented in this text.

Sale of Noncash Assets at a Loss

We begin our discussion by focusing on a situation where the noncash assets are sold at a loss. Assume that the partnership of Leake, Mueller, and Colby has decided to suspend operations. The firm's balance sheet prior to liquidation follows.

Assets		Liabilities & partners' equity	
Cash	$ 60,000	Accounts payable	$ 15,000
Noncash assets	50,000	Leake, capital	43,000
	$110,000	Mueller, capital	40,000
		Colby, capital	12,000
			$110,000

Suppose the noncash assets are sold for $32,000, which results in an $18,000 loss ($50,000 − $32,000) for the firm. The partners absorb such gains and losses in the profit- and loss-sharing ratio as stipulated in the articles of partnership. If the ratio calls for an equal division, the journal entry to record the asset sale would be as follows:

Cash	32,000	
Leake, Capital	6,000	
Mueller, Capital	6,000	
Colby, Capital	6,000	
Noncash Assets		50,000
To record the sale of noncash assets		

Notice that the loss is charged directly to the owners' capital accounts, resulting in the following balances:[3]

	Cash	+ Noncash Assets	= Accounts Payable	+ Leake, Capital	+ Mueller, Capital	+ Colby, Capital
Prior to asset sale	$60,000	$50,000	$15,000	$43,000	$40,000	$12,000
Asset sale	+32,000	−50,000		−6,000	−6,000	−6,000
	$92,000	$ —	$15,000	$37,000	$34,000	$ 6,000

Once the assets are sold, the liabilities are paid. Any cash that remains is then distributed to Leake, Mueller, and Colby *in an amount equal to their capital balances.* The necessary journal entries are:

Accounts Payable	15,000	
Cash		15,000
To record payment of liabilities		

Leake, Capital	37,000	
Mueller, Capital	34,000	
Colby, Capital	6,000	
Cash		77,000
To record cash distributions to partners		

Tips & Techniques

Notice that the profit- and loss-sharing ratio is used in the division of liquidation gains and losses, *not* in the allocation of assets among the owners. The ratio's name indicates its purpose. The distribution of assets at liquidation is really the opposite of what occurs when partners invest directly into the firm at the time of business formation. These latter two situations are neither dependent on nor influenced by the income-sharing agreement.

---

[3] An alternative treatment calls for an $18,000 debit to a separate Loss on Sale of Assets account. The Loss account's balance is then allocated equally to the partners, producing the same $6,000 reductions as those just shown.

Creation of a Capital Deficiency. In the previous example, each partner's capital account was of sufficient size to absorb the $6,000 share of the loss. Suppose, however, that the noncash assets are sold for only $8,000. In this case a $42,000 loss arises ($50,000 − $8,000), which reduces each of the capital balances by $14,000 ($42,000 ÷ 3). After the liabilities are paid, $53,000 cash remains in the business, and Colby's capital account contains a $2,000 debit balance. These figures are shown in the accompanying chart.

	Cash	+	Noncash Assets	=	Accounts Payable	+	Leake, Capital	+	Mueller, Capital	+	Colby, Capital
Prior to asset sale	$60,000		$50,000		$15,000		$43,000		$40,000		$12,000
Asset sale	+8,000		−50,000				−14,000		−14,000		−14,000
	$68,000		$ —		$15,000		$29,000		$26,000		$ (2,000)
Payment of liabilities	−15,000				−15,000						
	$53,000		$ —		$ —		$29,000		$26,000		$ (2,000)

The $2,000 debit balance is commonly referred to as a **capital deficiency.** Just as Leake and Mueller have respective claims against the partnership of $29,000 and $26,000, the partnership has a $2,000 claim against Colby. Notice that until the deficiency is settled, insufficient cash is available for disbursement to the owners who possess credit balances. Colby would therefore be requested to remit $2,000 to the firm.

Removal of a Capital Deficiency. If Colby settles her $2,000 obligation, the deficiency is removed from the accounting records. As a result of this receipt, the partnership's cash would increase to $55,000 and thus allow a distribution of $29,000 to Leake and $26,000 to Mueller. The required journal entries follow.

Cash	2,000	
Colby, Capital		2,000

To record receipt of cash from Colby to settle deficiency

Leake, Capital	29,000	
Mueller, Capital	26,000	
Cash		55,000

To record cash distributions to partners

On the other hand, if Colby is unable or unwilling to pay, the $2,000 deficiency is charged against the other partners according to the profit- and loss-sharing ratio. Leake and Mueller would therefore absorb $1,000 each to allow the closing of the partnership's books, producing the balances shown.[4]

---

[4] In the event of an unequal profit- and loss-sharing ratio, similar procedures would continue to be followed. Suppose, for example, that partners A, B, and C share income in a ratio of 50 : 40 : 10, respectively. If C has an $18,000 capital deficiency, the deficiency would be split between A and B in the following manner: A, 50/90 × $18,000 = $10,000; B, 40/90 × $18,000 = $8,000.

	Cash	=	Leake, Capital	+	Mueller, Capital	+	Colby, Capital
After payment of liabilities	$53,000		$29,000		$26,000		$(2,000)
Allocation of Colby deficiency			−1,000		−1,000		+2,000
	$53,000		$28,000		$25,000		$ —

The following entry is needed to record the allocation in the accounts:

Leake, Capital	1,000	
Mueller, Capital	1,000	
Colby, Capital		2,000
To distribute capital deficiency and close Colby's capital account		

The cash balance of $53,000 would then be distributed, with $28,000 going to Leake and $25,000 to Mueller.

Leake, Capital	28,000	
Mueller, Capital	25,000	
Cash		53,000
To record cash distributions to partners		

Colby's inability to pay the $2,000 capital deficiency does not relieve her liability to Leake and Mueller. If the latter two individuals desire, legal action could be initiated to obtain the amount due. Bear in mind that with unlimited liability, a deficient partner's personal assets can be taken and sold by the court to raise the necessary funds.

Sale of Noncash Assets at a Gain

The focus in our liquidation example has been the sale of assets at a loss, primarily because of the unique accounting problems associated with a capital deficiency. Noncash assets can, of course, be sold at a gain. If, for example, the partnership's noncash assets of $50,000 were sold for $71,000, a $21,000 gain would arise. Assuming that profits and losses continue to be shared equally, Leake, Mueller, and Colby would each pick up $7,000 ($21,000 ÷ 3) of gain. The required journal entry would thus contain credits of $7,000 to each partner's capital account to reflect the increase in equity from the transaction. The remaining journal entries for settlement of liabilities and the partners' cash distributions parallel those shown earlier.

END-OF-CHAPTER REVIEW

1 Explain the unique characteristics of a partnership. A partnership is a business owned by two or more persons. This popular organizational form is a separate accounting entity but not a separate legal and tax entity. Partnerships are easy to establish, with any property invested in the business (and subsequent income

LEARNING OBJECTIVES: THE KEY POINTS

earned) being jointly owned by the partners. Partners have unlimited liability for the debts of the firm and are bound by the commitments and obligations made by the other owners (i.e., mutual agency). Further, unless otherwise agreed on, a partnership is dissolved by the withdrawal of a partner or the admission of new partners.

2 Account for partnership formation and income distribution, including situations that give rise to an earnings deficiency. Accounting for partnerships begins when the owners invest their personal assets into the firm. Noncash investments are recorded at fair market value, and both noncash and cash investments are entered in the proper partner's capital account.

Any net income or net loss of the business is divided among the partners according to the partnership agreement. If no provisions are stated, profits and losses are shared equally. In the income allocation process, recognition may be given for services provided to the business (via salary allowances) and/or for capital provided (via interest allowances). Such allowances must be considered regardless of the firm's earnings. If insufficient income is available to cover the allowances, an earnings deficiency arises, with the deficiency being allocated to the partners in the profit- and loss-sharing ratio.

3 Account for partner admissions and withdrawals. When an entering partner purchases an interest from an existing partner, no change in partnership assets occurs. However, the capital accounts must be updated to reflect the transfer of equity interests among the owners. In another type of transaction, an entering partner may make an investment directly in the firm. Company assets increase and the new partner must be given credit in the accounting records for the amount invested (or some multiple thereof). If the amount invested is greater than the capital balance awarded, the existing partners are receiving a bonus. Should the situation be reversed, the current partners are providing a bonus to the incoming owner. Bonuses are divided among the partners according to the firm's profit- and loss-sharing ratio.

Partner withdrawals are accounted for in a manner similar to that of partner admittances. The withdrawing partner may sell his or her interest to the continuing partners or to the partnership itself. In the latter case, the exiting owner's capital balance is compared against the amount of cash settlement to determine whether any bonuses are involved. Once again, bonuses may be provided either by or to the ongoing partners.

4 Perform the procedures related to partnership liquidations. The liquidation of a partnership involves three steps: sale of noncash assets, payment of creditors, and distribution of remaining cash to the partners in the amount of the partners' capital balances. When selling the noncash assets, a gain or loss may arise. Such gains and losses are allocated among the partners according to the profit- and loss-sharing ratio.

The allocation of losses may cause a capital deficiency (i.e., debit balance) in a partner's capital account. When the deficiency is settled, adequate cash will then exist to pay partners who possess credit balances. If the deficiency is not settled, it is allocated among the "nondeficient" partners consistent with the profit- and loss-sharing ratio.

**KEY TERMS
AND CONCEPTS:
A QUICK OVERVIEW**

articles of partnership The agreement in a partnership that details the rights, responsibilities, and duties of each of the partners.

capital deficiency A debit balance in a partner's capital account.

dissolution The termination of a partnership's life.

earnings deficiency   The condition that exists when a partnership incurs a net loss or has insufficient earnings to cover salary and interest allowances.

interest allowances   A consideration used in the division of net income of many partnerships. The allowances recognize differences in capital provided to the firm by the partners.

liquidation   The process of terminating a partnership and discontinuing operations.

mutual agency   A feature of partnerships whereby each partner acts as an agent of the partnership in business transactions.

partnership   A company formed by two or more persons to carry on, as co-owners, profitable business activity.

salary allowances   A consideration used in the division of net income in many partnerships. The allowances recognize differences in seniority, reputation, business contacts, and time devoted to the firm by the partners.

unlimited liability   The fact that each partner is held personally liable for the debts of the enterprise.

The five questions that follow relate to several issues raised in the chapter. Test your knowledge of the issues by selecting the best answer. (The answers appear on p. 580.)

CHAPTER QUIZ

1 Which of the following statements about partnerships is true?
   a A partnership has an unlimited life.
   b A partnership pays income taxes on its earnings.
   c Partners have unlimited liability for the debts of the firm.
   d Partners who invest assets in a partnership retain sole ownership rights to the assets until it is evident that the business will be successful.

2 Land invested in a partnership by a partner should be recorded in the partnership's accounting records at:
   a the investing partner's acquisition cost.
   b the book value on the investing partner's accounting records.
   c the land's fair market value at the time of investment.
   d the land's expected selling price on the date of disposal.

3 Rome and Athens formed a partnership by investing $30,000 and $60,000, respectively. The following terms regarding the division of income were agreed on: (1) Rome is to receive a salary allowance of $10,000; (2) both partners are entitled to a 10% interest allowance, computed on the original capital investments. Any remaining amounts are to be split equally. How would net income of $15,000 be divided?
   a Rome, $6,000; Athens, $9,000.   c Rome, $11,000; Athens, $4,000.
   b Rome, $7,500; Athens, $7,500.   d Rome, $13,000; Athens, $6,000.

4 The law firm of Lincoln, Stein, and Dyke is organized as a partnership. The partners' capital balances are $100,000, $200,000, and $150,000, respectively. Lincoln is leaving the firm for health reasons and is being paid $127,000 by the partnership for her interest. Assume that all profits and losses are divided equally. As a result of this withdrawal, Stein's capital balance will:
   a remain at $200,000.   c decrease to $191,000.
   b increase to $213,500.   d decrease to $186,500.

5 The Uncle Otto partnership is being liquidated. The firm's balance sheet follows.

Assets
Noncash assets $108,000

Partners' equity
Allen, capital $ 60,000
Tyler, capital   41,000
Flynn, capital   7,000
                         $108,000

If the noncash assets are sold for $38,000 and profits and losses are divided in a 4:2:1 ratio, how much cash will be distributed to Allen? Assume that any capital deficiencies are not paid by the deficient partner.
a $18,000.   c $20,000.
b $18,500.   d $60,000.

SUMMARY PROBLEM

Warren Smithson is a designer of custom jewelry. His firm, organized as a sole proprietorship, has grown over the years and has the following balance sheet data as of December 31, 19X1:

Assets
Cash		$ 3,500
Accounts receivable	$8,700	
Less: Allowance for uncollectibles	300	8,400
Inventory		19,700
Equipment	$5,000	
Less: Accumulated depreciation	2,100	2,900
Total assets		$34,500

Liabilities
Accounts payable $ 6,800

On January 1, 19X2, Smithson and Lisa Anderson formed a partnership known as S & A Associates. Anderson invested $10,000 cash and inventory having a fair market value of $5,800; Smithson relinquished control of the proprietorship's assets and liabilities to the new entity. The proprietorship's inventory and equipment were estimated to have a fair market value of $24,200 and $2,200, respectively, on the date of partnership formation. The partnership agreement called for monthly salaries of $2,000 to Smithson and $1,500 to Anderson, with remaining profits and losses to be shared in a 7:3 ratio.

Instructions

a Prepare the required journal entries on January 1, 19X2, to record formation of the new partnership.
b If 19X2 partnership income amounted to $48,000, determine the proper allocation of earnings to Smithson and Anderson.
c If the salary allowances were the only amounts withdrawn during the year, prepare the December 31, 19X2, statement of partners' equity for the firm.
d Assume that the partnership sells all of its assets and pays all liabilities on January 2, 19X3, as part of a liquidation. If a loss of $50,000 is incurred on the

sale of noncash assets, how much cash would Smithson receive in final settlement of his partnership interest?

Solution

a
Cash	10,000	
Inventory	5,800	
Anderson, Capital		15,800

To record investment by Anderson in S & A Associates

Cash	3,500	
Accounts Receivable	8,700	
Inventory	24,200	
Equipment	2,200	
Allowance for Uncollectibles		300
Accounts Payable		6,800
Smithson, Capital		31,500*

To record investment by Smithson in S & A Associates

*Calculated as the difference between the jewelry firm's total assets and total liabilities.

b
	Smithson	Anderson	Total
Division of net income			
Salary			
Smithson ($2,000 × 12 months)	$24,000		
Anderson ($1,500 × 12 months)		$18,000	$42,000
Remainder of $6,000 ($48,000 −			
$42,000) divided 7 : 3	4,200	1,800	6,000
	$28,200	$19,800	$48,000

c

S & A ASSOCIATES Statement of Partners' Equity For the Year Ended December 31, 19X2			
	Smithson	Anderson	Total
Beginning balance, Jan. 1	$ —	$ —	$ —
Increases			
Partner investments	$31,500	$15,800	$47,300
Net income	28,200	19,800	48,000
Subtotal	$59,700	$35,600	$95,300
Decreases			
Withdrawals	24,000	18,000	42,000
Ending balance, Dec. 31	$35,700	$17,600	$53,300

d
Smithson's capital balance, Dec. 31, 19X2	$35,700
Less: Share of liquidation loss ($50,000 × 0.70)	35,000
Smithson's cash distribution	$ 700

ASSIGNMENT MATERIAL

QUESTIONS

Q14-1 What are the articles of partnership?

Q14-2 Describe "mutual agency" and "unlimited liability" as related to partnerships. How do these features influence the selection of partners?

Q14-3 A partnership is said to have a limited life. Does the death of a partner terminate business operations? Explain.

Q14-4 Briefly discuss the advantages and disadvantages of the partnership form of organization.

Q14-5 Akers and Howard are discussing the formation of a partnership. Howard will invest a computer system that originally cost $24,000. If the system has a $15,000 fair market value at the time of investment, what amount will be recorded in Howard's capital account? Why?

Q14-6 Discuss the accounting treatment of salary allowances that are provided to partners. Are the allowances considered an expense? Why?

Q14-7 What problem could arise if a partnership's earnings are allocated to partners by using a ratio computed on the basis of beginning-of-period capital balances? How can this problem be resolved?

Q14-8 What is an earnings deficiency? How is such a deficiency resolved?

Q14-9 Generally speaking, an incoming partner can acquire an interest in a partnership in two ways. What are these two approaches?

Q14-10 Baker has a $24,000 capital interest in the ABC partnership and is entitled to one-third of all profits and losses. Assume that Baker sells her entire interest to Doane for $60,000.
   a What amount will be recorded in Doane's account on the partnership's books?
   b How much cash will be received by the business?

Q14-11 Suppose that James is withdrawing from the JKL partnership. Why might James be willing to settle for less than the balance in her capital account? How would this difference be recorded?

Q14-12 Briefly distinguish between partnership dissolution and partnership liquidation.

Q14-13 Name the three steps that are performed in a partnership liquidation.

Q14-14 How are liquidation gains and losses divided among a firm's partners? Assuming no capital deficiency, how is any remaining cash divided among the partners?

Q14-15 Capital deficiencies sometimes occur during the liquidation of a partnership. What is a "capital deficiency" and how is it treated for accounting purposes?

EXERCISES

E14-1 *Partner investments; journal entries* (L.O. 2)
The LP partnership was formed on January 1, 19X7, by investments from Bill Levy and Marv Parcells. Levy contributed $30,000 cash and $80,000 of land. Parcells contributed various assets from a business that he had oper-

ated over the past five years. A balance sheet from that business disclosed the following:

Accounts receivable	$ 27,000
Allowance for uncollectibles	(3,200)
Equipment	68,000
Accumulated depreciation	(24,000)

The partners confirmed that the allowance for uncollectible accounts should be decreased by $600. In addition, an independent appraisal determined that fair market values of the land and equipment on January 1 were $125,000 and $35,000, respectively.

Prepare the journal entires needed to record the investments of Levy and Parcells.

E14-2 *Income distribution: Different arrangements* **(L.O. 2)**

1-2-3

Frank, Gatti, and Hogan recently invested $30,000 each and formed the Apex partnership. During the first year of operation, the business generated a net income of $39,000. Determine the proper division of income among the partners for the following independent cases:

a Income is divided on the basis of a ratio of the beginning capital investments.

b Partners are allowed 12% interest on their investments; the remaining profits and losses are allocated on a 6 : 1 : 3 basis.

c Frank and Hogan each receive salary allowances of $24,000 per year; the remaining profits and losses are shared equally.

E14-3 *Income distribution among partners* **(L.O. 2)**

1-2-3

The beginning capital balances in the partnership of Kell, Reardon, and Talbot are $20,000, $40,000, and $30,000, respectively. The partnership agreement contains the following provisions for the division of net income:

1 Partners are allowed 10% interest on their beginning capital balances.

2 Reardon and Talbot each have salary allowances of $10,000.

3 Remaining profits and losses are shared equally among the three partners.

Determine the appropriate division of net income (or net loss) among the partners for the independent cases that follow.

a Net income is $47,000.

b Net income is $14,000.

c Net loss is $7,000.

E14-4 *Statement of partners' equity* **(L.O. 2)**

Patrick Newton and Debbie Stevens are partners in Soup & Such, a small restaurant. Terms of the partnership agreement call for respective monthly salaries of $900 and $1,200, with any remaining profits and losses to be divided equally. The restaurant generated net income of $26,800 during the year. Other information follows.

	Newton	Stevens
Beginning capital balance	$24,300	$36,800
Withdrawals during the year	15,600	20,400

Prepare a statement of partners' equity for the year ended December 31.

E14-5   Partner admission; journal entries (L.O. 3)

Rhodes and Smith are partners in a toy business and have capital balances of $126,000 and $144,000, respectively. Net income (or net loss) is shared equally. Prepare journal entries to record the admission of a new partner, West, assuming each of the following independent situations:

a West invests $67,500 and receives a 20% interest in the new partnership.

b West invests $100,000 in the partnership for a 25% interest. Is a bonus being awarded to Rhodes and Smith or to West?

c West purchases 60% of Smith's interest for $95,000.

E14-6   Partner withdrawal; journal entries (L.O. 3)

Ahmed, Odom, and Zwicker operate a management consulting practice and share profits and losses equally. Capital balances at the end of 19X3 are $70,000, $80,000, and $100,000, respectively. Zwicker is retiring and is considering two options for withdrawal from the partnership:

■ Selling his interest to Odom (with Ahmed's approval) for $120,000.

■ Selling his interest to the partnership for $120,000.

a Prepare journal entries that the partnership would record for each option.

b Ignoring income tax considerations, do you think it matters to Zwicker which option is selected? Briefly discuss.

c Repeat part (a), assuming that Zwicker will receive $92,000 rather than $120,000.

E14-7   Partnership liquidation; no capital deficiency (L.O. 4)

Assume that the partnership of Keith Baker and Mary Middleton had the following post-closing trial balance when the partners decided to liquidate:

Cash	$ 2,000	
Noncash assets	78,000	
Liabilities		$15,000
Baker, capital		40,000
Middleton, capital		25,000
	$80,000	$80,000

Profits and losses are divided equally. Consider the following independent situations:

Case 1: The noncash assets are sold for $90,000.
Case 2: The noncash assets are sold for $36,000.

For each of the preceding cases, prepare journal entries to record (a) sale of the noncash assets, (b) payment of the liabilities, and (c) cash distributions to the partners.

E14-8   Partnership liquidation (L.O. 4)

The JKL partnership is about to liquidate. The company's accountant has prepared the following tabulation:

Cash	+	Noncash Assets	=	Accounts Payable	+	Jacobs, Capital	+	Key, Capital	+	Landon, Capital
$60,000		$250,000		$25,000		$80,000		$170,000		$35,000

Assume the partners share profits and losses equally and if a capital deficiency arises, none of it is paid by the deficient partner. The noncash assets will be sold for $100,000.

a Determine whether the JKL partnership will experience a gain or a loss on the sale of noncash assets. How much of this gain or loss is allocated to each partner?

b Does a capital deficiency arise in this situation? Explain.

c By using the preceding tabulation, show the asset sale, the payment of accounts payable, and the final cash distribution to the partners.

E14-9 *Analysis of partnership liquidation* (L.O. 4)
The Davis-Edwards-Felix partnership recently liquidated. Noncash assets were sold for $96,000, and all creditors have been paid. Partners shared profits and losses as follows: Davis, 20%; Edwards, 30%; Felix, 50%. Balances in each partner's capital account before and after the asset sale follow.

	Davis	Edwards	Felix
Before assets were sold	$30,000	$ 2,000	$27,000
After assets were sold	22,400	(9,400)	8,000

a Determine the book value of the assets that were sold.

b Calculate the amount of cash on hand at the present time. Assume that Edwards has not yet settled his capital deficiency.

E14-10 *Partnership concepts* (L.O. 2, 3, 4)
Evaluate the comments that follow as being True or False. If the comment is false, briefly explain why.

a In the absence of a formal profit- and loss-sharing agreement, all profits and losses are divided equally among the partners.

b Salary and interest allowances are normal expenses of a partnership.

c An earnings deficiency is allocated to a firm's partners in accordance with the profit- and loss-sharing agreement.

d In partnership liquidations, cash is distributed to partners in accordance with the profit- and loss-sharing agreement.

e Jones invested $50,000 in the Smith/Sampson/Black partnership and was given a $42,000 capital interest in return. As a result of this transaction, the balance in Smith's capital account will increase because a bonus is being given to the existing partners.

Series A

PROBLEMS

P14-A1 *Investment by partners; financial statements* (L.O. 2)
Abram, Haas, and Tidwell formed a partnership to practice law by combining their respective sole proprietorships. The assets and liabilities contributed to the firm on January 2, 19X4, the date of formation, follow.

	Book Value	Fair Market Value
Abram		
Land	$40,000	$115,000
Mortgage payable	38,000	38,000
Haas		
Office supplies	42,000	30,000
Office equipment	64,000	48,000
Tidwell		
Cash	50,000	50,000
Accounts receivable	20,000	18,000
Short-term investments	4,000	7,000

Instructions

a Prepare journal entries to record the investments of Abram, Haas, and Tidwell in the new partnership.

b Prepare a classified balance sheet for the partnership immediately after the investments are recorded.

c The partners share profits and losses equally, and the first year's net income was $66,000. Cash withdrawals of $5,000 were made by Abram, $22,000 by Haas, and $17,000 by Tidwell. Prepare the December 31, 19X4, statement of partners' equity for the firm.

P14-A2 *Income distribution; statement of partners' equity* (L.O. 2)

Johnson, Kenyon, and Rambo are partners in a bookkeeping service. The partners' beginning and average capital balances for 19XX follow.

	Beginning	Average
Johnson	$85,000	$90,000
Kenyon	40,000	40,000
Rambo	65,000	75,000

Investments during the year amounted to $10,000 for Johnson and $20,000 for Rambo. Net income totaled $36,000.

Instructions

a Prepare a schedule to show the distribution of net income among the partners for each of the following independent cases:

(1) The partners are granted a 12% interest allowance on beginning capital and share any remaining income equally.

(2) Johnson, Kenyon, and Rambo are granted a 12% interest allowance on average capital and share any remaining income on a 5:3:2 basis, respectively.

(3) Each partner is granted both a 10% interest allowance on average capital and a monthly salary allowance of $1,100. Johnson, Kenyon, and Rambo share remaining profits or losses on a 4:4:2 basis, respectively.

b Focusing on case (1) in part (a), assume that the interest allowances were withdrawn during the year along with other amounts as follows: Johnson, $4,000; Kenyon, $3,500; and Rambo, $7,800. All withdrawals were recorded in the partners' drawing accounts. Prepare the statement of partners' equity for the year ended December 31, 19XX.

P14-A3 *Income distribution; journal entries* (L.O. 2)

Lemont, Whittaker, and Wiley invested $20,000 each on January 1, 19X4, and formed a partnership to operate a car dealership. The articles of partnership contained the following provisions:

1 Partners are granted 10% interest on their beginning investments.

2 Lemont will receive a monthly salary allowance of $1,000.

3 Remaining profits and losses are shared on a 5:3:2 basis among the partners.

Whittaker and Wiley withdrew their interest allowances during 19X4 along with an additional $3,000 and $15,000, respectively. Lemont withdrew 80% of her salary allowance.

Instructions

a Determine the proper division of 19X4 net income (or net loss) among Lemont, Whittaker, and Wiley for the following independent cases:

(1) Net income of $50,000.
(2) Net income of $5,000.
(3) Net loss of $20,000.

b For part (a2), prepare journal entries to record (1) the transfer of net income to the capital accounts and (2) the closing of the drawing accounts.

c For part (a2), present the proper disclosure of partners' equity on the firm's December 31, 19X4, balance sheet.

P14-A4 *Admission to a partnership* (L.O. 3)

Barden, Larkins, and Winter operate a tax practice that is organized as a partnership. The accounting records disclosed the following information at the end of 19X7:

	Barden	Larkins	Winter
Capital balance	$30,000	$80,000	$40,000
Share of profits and losses	10%	60%	30%

Assume that the existing partnership will be dissolved on January 1, 19X8, when Engle is admitted as a new partner. The options that follow have been considered for Engle's admission:

1 Barden, who is interested in pursuing other opportunities, has offered to give his entire interest to Engle, his niece.
2 Engle agrees to invest $37,500 in the partnership for a 20% interest in the firm.
3 Winter agrees to sell 40% of his interest to Engle for $16,000.
4 Engle is willing to invest $20,000 in the partnership for a 25% interest in the firm.
5 The existing partners agree to give Engle a 10% interest in the firm for an investment of $30,000 in the partnership.
6 Larkins and Winter offer to sell 60% of their interests to Engle for $55,000 and $25,000, respectively.

Instructions

a Prepare journal entries that the partnership would record for each of the preceding independent situations.

b Focus on option no. 5 for a moment. Briefly discuss several possible reasons that might explain why Engle was willing to invest $30,000 in exchange for a 10% interest in the firm.

P14-A5 *Partner withdrawal; journal entries* (L.O. 3)

The Chen family has operated a business called Dockside Imports for many years. The capital balances of the partners on December 31, 19X8, were: Dorothy Chen, $320,000; Robert Chen, $400,000; and Tina Chen, $180,000.

The first eight months of 19X9 generated favorable financial results, with the following figures being reported: sales, $5 million; cost of goods sold, $3.64 million; and operating expenses, $860,000. On the basis of these results, the partners anticipated that the business would be profitable for the tenth straight year. The partnership agreement stipulates that Dorothy, Robert, and Tina share profits (and losses) on a 3:6:1 basis, respectively.

On September 1, 19X9, because of serious health problems, Tina requested permission for an immediate withdrawal from the partnership. Because the Chens are a very close-knit family, Dorothy and Robert approved the request with absolutely no hesitation.

Instructions

a Update the partners' capital accounts through August 31 for the appropriate share of income or loss and then prepare journal entries to record the withdrawal of Tina under the following independent cases:
  (1) Per stipulations in the articles of partnership, Tina sells her interest to the partnership at an amount equal to the balance in her capital account.
  (2) Tina sells her interest to the partnership for $120,000 cash and a $20,000 note.
  (3) Tina sells 40% of her interest to each of the two remaining partners for $125,000 (for a total of $250,000).
  (4) Tina sells her interest to a new partner, Louise Wong, for $600,000.
  (5) Tina sells her interest to the partnership in exchange for a $500,000 note, to be paid in 10 annual installments of $50,000 each.

b Compute the total partners' equity of the firm after Tina sells her interest in case (2) of part (a).

c Considering all facts presented in the problem's narrative, is case (2) of part (a) likely to occur? Briefly explain.

P14-A6 *Partnership liquidation* (L.O. 4)

Manny, Moe, and Abe operate a delivery business as a partnership and share net income (and net losses) in a 5 : 3 : 2 ratio, respectively. Because the business was not as successful as planned, the partners decided to liquidate. A post-closing trial balance disclosed the following account balances as of December 31, 19X3:

MANNY, MOE, AND ABE		
Post-Closing Trial Balance		
December 31, 19X3		
Cash	$ 38,000	
Short-term investments	3,000	
Delivery equipment (net)	64,000	
Accounts payable		$ 1,800
Utilities payable		200
Manny, capital		35,000
Moe, capital		60,000
Abe, capital		8,000
	$105,000	$105,000

Instructions

a Prepare journal entries to record the sale of the noncash assets and payment of the liabilities assuming the noncash assets are sold for:
  (1) $14,000.
  (2) $98,000.

b Assume that case (1) of part (a) actually occurred.
  (1) Determine the partnership's cash balance after the liabilities are settled.
  (2) Assume that any partner with a capital deficiency is unable to pay the balance due the partnership. Prepare journal entries to allocate the deficiency to the remaining partners and distribute the firm's ending cash balance.

(3) Assume that any partner with a capital deficiency is able to pay the balance due the partnership. Present journal entries to record the receipt of cash from the deficient partner and distribute the firm's ending cash balance.

Series B

P14-B1 *Investment by partners; financial statements* (L.O. 2)

On August 8, 19XX, Lancer, Mix, and Norton formed a partnership to distribute computer supplies. Lancer invested cash of $85,000 and a delivery van that originally cost $7,500. The vehicle's fair market value at the time of investment was $5,000. Mix contributed short-term marketable securities consisting of 1,000 shares of U.S. Paper capital stock (cost per share, $40; market value per share, $70). Finally, Norton contributed the following items from his existing business:

	Recorded Value	Fair Market Value
Accounts receivable	$32,000	$32,000
Allowance for uncollectibles	(2,000)	(6,000)
Computer supplies inventory	51,000	57,000
Warehouse equipment (net)	0*	7,000
Accounts payable	10,500	10,500

* Fully depreciated.

Instructions

a Prepare journal entries to record the investments of Lancer, Mix, and Norton in the partnership.
b Prepare a classified balance sheet for the partnership immediately after the investments.
c Assume that net income of $72,600 was generated through the end of 19XX. Cash withdrawals of $25,000 were made by Lancer, $30,000 by Mix, and $45,000 by Norton. If the partners divide all profits and losses equally, prepare the December 31, 19XX, statement of partners' equity for the firm.

P14-B2 *Income distribution; statement of partners' equity* (L.O. 2)

1-2-3

Kates, Nixon, and Petty formed a partnership at the beginning of 19X1, with equal investments of $10,000. The partners agreed that Kates and Petty would receive salary allowances of $6,000 each and that remaining profits and losses would be divided 1 : 6 : 3. The partnership earned $17,000 during the first year of operation, and no partner made any withdrawals.

In January 19X2, the partners renegotiated and agreed to salary allowances of $6,000 each and 10% interest on the year's beginning capital balances. Any remaining income (or loss) was to be divided equally. Kates and Nixon withdrew $7,000 each during the year; Petty withdrew $16,000. Net income for 19X2 was $23,750.

Still seeking a more equitable distribution of net income, the partners amended their agreement again at the beginning of 19X3. The partners each agreed to salary allowances of $7,000 and interest allowances of 15%, the latter computed on average capital balances. Remaining profits and losses would be shared equally. Net income for 19X3 was $18,000; additional data for each partner follow.

	Average Capital Balance	Withdrawals Made During the Year
Kates	$18,000	$14,000
Nixon	14,000	13,500
Petty	12,000	10,750

Instructions

a Prepare schedules that show the distribution of net income among the partners for 19X1, 19X2, and 19X3.

b Prepare the statement of partners' equity for the year ended December 31, 19X2.

P14-B3 *Income distribution; journal entries* (L.O. 2)

Jackson, Hudson, and Rice invested $70,000 each at the beginning of 19X2 and formed a partnership to operate a restaurant. The articles of partnership contained the following provisions:

1 Partners are granted 20% interest on their beginning investments.

2 Hudson will receive an annual salary allowance of $10,000; Rice's annual salary allowance is $40,000.

3 Remaining profits and losses are shared on a 4 : 4 : 2 basis among the partners.

Jackson and Rice withdrew their interest allowances during 19X2 along with an additional $12,000 and $20,000, respectively. Hudson had no withdrawals.

Instructions

a Determine the proper division of net income (or net loss) among Jackson, Hudson, and Rice for the following independent cases:
   (1) Net income of $100,000.
   (2) Net income of $70,000.
   (3) Net loss of $60,000.

b For part (a1), prepare journal entries to record (1) the transfer of net income to the capital accounts and (2) the closing of the drawing accounts.

c For part (a1), present the proper disclosure of partners' equity on the firm's December 31, 19X2, balance sheet.

P14-B4 *Admission to a partnership* (L.O. 3)

Mantle, Maris, and Berra operate a partnership to render financial planning services. A review of the firm's articles of partnership found no provisions for interest and salary allowances. Further study of this document and the accounting records disclosed the following information:

	Capital Balance, December 31, 19X3	Share of Profits and Losses
Henry Mantle	$90,000	30%
Cheryl Maris	70,000	45
Thomas Berra	40,000	25

Assume that Terri Richardson will be admitted to the partnership on January 1, 19X4, and the partnership agreement will be redrawn.

Instructions

a Prepare journal entries to record the admittance of Richardson under each of the following independent cases:

(1) Richardson invests $100,000 in the partnership and receives a one-third interest in the firm.

(2) Because of increasing friction between Maris and Berra, Maris sells 80% of her interest to Richardson for $30,000.

(3) Richardson invests $80,000 in the partnership and receives a 40% interest in the firm.

(4) Mantle gives 20% of his capital interest to Richardson, who is his niece.

(5) Richardson invests $50,000 in the partnership and receives a 15% interest in the firm.

(6) Richardson purchases 60% of Berra's interest directly from Berra for $24,000.

b Focus on part (a3) for a moment. Briefly discuss several possible reasons that might explain why Richardson received a 40% interest in the firm for her $80,000 investment.

P14-B5 *Partner withdrawal; journal entries* (L.O. 3)

Fertig, Marino, and Piper have operated a business called the Pike Street Market for many years. The capital balances of the partners on December 31, 19X1, were: Fertig, $250,000; Marino, $300,000; and Piper, $75,000.

The first nine months of 19X2 generated favorable financial results, with the following figures being reported: sales, $1 million; cost of goods sold, $575,000; and operating expenses, $325,000. The partners were hopeful that the year's final quarter would be profitable, so that a net income would be reported for the fifteenth straight year. The partnership agreement stipulates that Fertig, Marino, and Piper share profits (and losses) on a 4 : 4 : 2 basis, respectively.

On October 1, 19X2, because of marital problems and an impending divorce settlement, Marino requested permission for an immediate withdrawal from the partnership. Although they were sorry to see him go, Fertig and Piper approved Marino's request.

Instructions

a Update the partners' capital accounts through September 30 for the appropriate share of income or loss and then prepare journal entries to record the withdrawal of Marino under the following independent cases:
(1) Marino sells his interest to a new partner, Diaz, for $760,000.
(2) Marino sells 50% of his interest to each of the two remaining partners for $300,000 (for a total of $600,000).
(3) Per stipulations in the articles of partnership, Marino sells his interest to the partnership at an amount equal to the balance in his capital account.
(4) Marino sells his interest to the partnership for $460,000.
(5) Marino sells his interest to the partnership in exchange for a $190,000 note due in 10 months.

b Compute the total partners' equity of the firm after Marino sells his interest in case (4) of part (a).

c Why is a bonus sometimes paid to a withdrawing partner?

P14-B6 *Partnership liquidation* (L.O. 4)

Coe, Dodd, and Eaton operate a repair business as a partnership and share net income (and net losses) in a 3 : 4 : 3 ratio, respectively. Because the business was not as successful as planned, the partners decided to liquidate. A post-closing trial balance disclosed the following account balances as of December 31, 19X1:

COE, DODD, AND EATON Post-Closing Trial Balance December 31, 19X1		
Cash	$ 40,000	
Inventory	31,000	
Equipment (net)	60,000	
Accounts payable		$ 11,000
Salaries payable		1,000
Coe, capital		23,100
Dodd, capital		58,000
Eaton, capital		37,900
	$131,000	$131,000

Instructions

a Prepare journal entries to record the sale of the noncash assets and payment of the liabilities assuming the noncash assets are sold for:
(1) $141,000.
(2) $7,000.

b Assume that case (2) of part (a) actually occurred.
(1) Determine the partnership's cash balance after the liabilities are settled.
(2) Assume that any partner with a capital deficiency is able to pay the balance due the partnership. Present journal entries to record the receipt of cash from the deficient partner and distribute the firm's ending cash balance.
(3) Assume that any partner with a capital deficiency is unable to pay the balance due the partnership. Prepare journal entries to allocate the deficiency to the remaining partners and distribute the firm's ending cash balance.

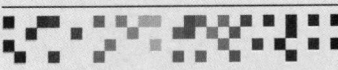

BEYOND THE BASICS

BB14-1 *Partnership features* (L.O. 1, 2)

Knapp, Shingler, and Smith, three dentists from Indianapolis, recently attended a convention of the National Dental Association. There they heard a speaker who talked about the formation of successful dental partnerships. An excerpt from the speaker's presentation follows.

> Several guidelines should be considered when entering this entity form. First, prospective partners must be compatible; they need the ability to exchange and discuss business and/or professional viewpoints freely. Second, the partnership should provide the anticipated return (i.e., profit) on investment for all parties. Third, prospective partners should be willing to share in the decision making. Finally, all partners must contribute with equal capacity, unless differences are known and accepted in advance. Quite simply, effort and commitment that differ from that originally anticipated are the biggest disrupters of partnerships.

Smith came away impressed and approached Knapp and Shingler about merging their respective practices, forming a partnership, and building suitable professional space.

Knapp is 57 years old, married, with two grown children. Shingler is 33, married, with four young children. Smith is 29, twice divorced, and has no offspring. Knapp and Shingler have conservative life-styles; Smith could be characterized as a jet-setter. The three dentists are respected by their patients. Knapp and Shingler are active in community affairs and the local dental society.

Selected data from the three practices during the past 12 months follow.

	Knapp	Shingler	Smith	
Billings for services	$240,000	$180,000	$100,000	520000
Collections	235,000	160,000	75,000	470 000
Office expenses	90,000	130,000	50,000	270 000
Dental assistants	4	6	1	11
Hours worked per week	40	50	28	118

In forming the partnership, each dentist would contribute $50,000. Knapp would write a check for the entire amount, while Shingler would invest $25,000 cash and sign a note for the remaining balance. Smith, on the other hand, is currently strapped for cash and would have to borrow his total contribution from a local bank.

Instructions

a Analyze the data presented and discuss the possible reasons why Knapp, Shingler, and Smith are considering a partnership.

b Are the guidelines for a successful partnership present in this proposed merger? Briefly explain.

c Should written articles of partnership be prepared for the practice? If "yes," list several items to be included in the agreement.

d Recommend a method to divide the practice's profit (or loss).

e Briefly assess the likelihood that the proposed partnership will survive on a long-term basis.

BB14-2 *Overview of chapter concepts: Multiple choice* (L.O. 1, 2, 3, 4)
The following multiple-choice questions relate to various topics discussed in the chapter. Select the best answer.

1 Which of the following is neither an advantage nor a disadvantage of the partnership form of organization?
a Unlimited liability of partners.
b Ease of formation.
c Use of interest and salary allowances in the distribution of company income.
d Mutual agency.

2 Noll and Jackson formed a partnership to practice law. Noll invested his personal library in the firm. The law books cost Noll $21,000 and were estimated to have a fair market value of $18,000. The publisher is still owed $5,000; the partnership will assume this obligation. In addition, Noll contributed other books that were given to him by a retiring attorney. The estimated current worth of these books is $6,000. For what amount should Noll, Capital, be increased?
a $13,000.   c $22,000.
b $19,000.   d $24,000.

3 Harold Lane has operated a small accounting practice for many years and has built a rather significant client base. Knowing that he would be retiring in 19X5, Lane formed a partnership in 19X3 with Tom Brogato,

a young CPA. Brogato contributed few clients to the firm but agreed to take on the bulk of the workload. Six months after formation, Lane would assume fewer and fewer responsibilities for daily operations. In view of this arrangement, the partners would likely:

a share profits and losses equally and not use salary and interest allowances.

b use differing amounts of salary allowances.

c use differing amounts of interest allowances.

d use differing amounts of salary allowances and interest allowances.

4 The partnership of Clanton, Berry, and Konowski generated net income of $51,000. Clanton and Berry each receive a salary allowance of $15,000. In addition, all partners are entitled to 10% interest on their $100,000 beginning capital balances. Any remaining amounts are to be divided equally. If Berry withdrew $4,000 for personal use during the year, how much of the net income will be credited to Berry's capital account?

a $18,000.

b $22,000.

c $25,000.

d $28,000.

5 Lyle Nelson was interested in joining the highly successful partnership of Casey and Maxwell. Casey and Maxwell had individual capital balances of $80,000 each and shared profits and losses equally. Nelson was willing to invest $140,000 for a one-third interest in the firm. If this investment occurred, how much would be credited to Casey's capital account?

a $0.

b $20,000.

c $70,000.

d $140,000.

6 Sally Ryan saw that added expertise was needed to turn around the marginal partnership of Garcia and Hicks. Garcia and Hicks had individual capital balances of $40,000 each and shared profits and losses equally. Ryan was willing to invest $20,000 for a one-fourth interest in the business. If Ryan joins the firm, how much would be credited to Garcia's capital account?

a $0.

b $2,500.

c $5,000.

d $25,000.

7 Clancy Furniture is quitting business. The accounting records revealed the following balances: cash, $20,000; inventory, $100,000; accounts payable, $30,000; Cleary, capital, $40,000; and Lance, capital, $50,000. Cleary and Lance share all profits and losses equally. If the company's inventory is to be sold at 50% below cost, how much cash will be distributed to the partners upon liquidation of the firm?

a Cleary, $15,000; Lance, $25,000.

b Cleary, $40,000; Lance, $50,000.

c Cleary, $35,000; Lance, $35,000.

d Cleary, $20,000; Lance, $20,000.

8 McClancy Furniture is quitting business. The accounting records revealed the following balances: cash, $20,000; inventory, $100,000; accounts payable, $30,000; Mac, capital, $10,000; Cleary, capital, $30,000; and Lance, capital, $50,000. Profits and losses are shared equally, and any resulting negative capital balances in liquidation are absorbed by the other partners. If the company's inventory is to be sold for $40,000, how much cash will be distributed to Cleary and Lance upon liquidation of the firm?

a Cleary, $10,000; Lance, $30,000.
b Cleary, $30,000; Lance, $50,000.
c Cleary, $5,000; Lance, $25,000.
d Cleary, $15,000; Lance, $15,000.

CAI14-1 *The follow-up letter: Harrison, O'Brien, and Weinstein* (L.O. 2)

COMMUNICATION OF ACCOUNTING INFORMATION

Communication Principle: After an important business meeting where a verbal understanding has been reached, a follow-up letter is appropriate. The follow-up letter serves several purposes:

1 The letter documents the agreement, giving everyone involved the opportunity to confirm or deny the stated terms.

2 The written contents serve as an important refresher when memories fade, thus reducing the possibility of future disputes.

3 The letter, once acknowledged by the recipient, may be the only tangible evidence of the agreement and may be useful if arbitration or legal remedies are necessary.

4 Documentation will help ensure that planned actions occur, as it is easier to overlook a verbal commitment than a written one.

The letter should detail the responsibilities of each affected party and clearly identify any financial terms and conditions. If the subject matter is very important, the sender should request that the recipient acknowledge the contents by some specific action. Such actions might include signing and returning a copy of the letter, confirming the agreement with a telephone call, or sending a written reply.

It is important that the letter be written in a concise style so that significant terms are not obscured. Above all, the letter should take a positive tone (e.g., I look forward to a long and prosperous association . . .). The goal is to build a positive future working relationship, not insult, create distrust, or taint the progress that was made in the original meeting.

■ ■ ■ ■ ■ ■ ■ ■

Mary Ann Harrison, senior managing partner in the law firm of Harrison, O'Brien, and Weinstein, has just informed Peter Woodside of his admission into the firm as a junior partner. This is an important day for Peter, who has worked many years for this recognition. His enthusiasm, though, is somewhat tempered by the terms of the offer.

The company's financial performance has declined somewhat in recent years, although Mary Ann believes this situation is temporary. Terms of partnership admittance require that Peter contribute $100,000 to the firm's capital. He will receive a 15% interest allowance, computed on the beginning-of-period balance in his capital account. In addition, a salary allowance will be calculated at $75 per hour, based on hours of work performed that can be billed to clients. (Mary Ann noted that there will be a minimum of 1,000 hours annually.) Finally, the other partners have agreed that both the $75 hourly rate and billable time will double during the next five years. A specified timetable has not yet been agreed to, however.

The firm's income distribution plan is a closely guarded secret, and only senior partners receive written contracts. Although Peter fully trusts Mary Ann, he is uncomfortable with the informal nature of the arrangement. He has agreed to join the firm as a junior partner but wishes to enclose a letter of understanding with his $100,000 capital contribution.

Instructions

Assume the role of Peter Woodside and draft a letter to the firm of Harrison, O'Brien, and Weinstein.

Answers to Chapter Quiz

1 c

2 c

3 c [Rome: $10,000 + ($30,000 × 0.10) = $13,000; Athens: $60,000 × 0.10 = $6,000; deficiency of $4,000 (($13,000 + $6,000) − $15,000) shared equally). Thus, Rome: $13,000 − $2,000 = $11,000; Athens: $6,000 − $2,000 = $4,000.]

4 d ($127,000 − $100,000 = $27,000 bonus paid by the continuing partners, to be shared equally; $200,000 − $13,500 = $186,500)

5 a [$108,000 − $38,000 = $70,000 loss; Allen's share: $70,000 × $\frac{4}{7}$ = $40,000; Flynn's share: $70,000 × $\frac{1}{7}$ = $10,000, causing a $3,000 capital deficiency ($7,000 − $10,000); Allen's share of deficiency: $3,000 × $\frac{4}{6}$ = $2,000; cash distribution: $60,000 − $40,000 − $2,000 = $18,000]

CHAPTER 15

Introduction to Corporations

LEARNING OBJECTIVES

After studying this chapter, you should be able to:

Identify the features, advantages, and disadvantages
of a corporate entity.

Summarize the distinctions between common and preferred stock.

Calculate the dividends associated with preferred stock.

Explain the concepts of and demonstrate the accounting treatments for
par, no-par, and stated-value stock, and stock subscriptions.

Prepare and interpret the stockholders' equity
section of a corporate balance sheet.

Define, explain, and calculate book value per share.

Economic activity in the United States is conducted via three forms of business organization: sole proprietorships, partnerships, and corporations. Although the vast majority of companies operate as either proprietorships or partnerships, the bulk of private-sector receipts and earnings are generated by corporations. These facts become apparent after studying the data that appear in Exhibit 15-1.

Perhaps the most obvious conclusion to be drawn from these figures is that corporations engage in financial activities on a much larger scale than the other entity types. Given that 19.7% of the firms produce 90% of this country's business receipts, the corporate form of organization clearly dominates our economy in monetary terms.

This chapter introduces accounting considerations unique to corporations and expands upon the material presented earlier in the text. Our focus will be on issues that relate to owners' (in this case, *stockholders'*) equity—the major area of difference among the three popular enterprise alternatives.

THE NATURE OF CORPORATIONS

OBJECTIVE
1

Identify the features, advantages, and disadvantages of a corporate entity.

In the early 1800s, Supreme Court Justice Marshall defined a **corporation** as "an artificial being, invisible, intangible, and existing only in contemplation of the law." Consistent with this definition, the corporation is viewed as a legal entity having an existence separate and distinct from its owners. Corporations may therefore buy and sell property in their own names. Additionally, corporations can enter into contracts, defend themselves in court, and transact business in the same manner as a person would.

Corporate Form of Organization: Advantages

The corporate form of organization is often considered preferable to both a sole proprietorship and a partnership for conducting business affairs. This preference arises for the following reasons.

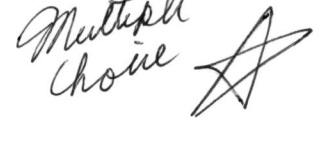

EXHIBIT 15-1
A Comparison of Alternative Forms of Business Organization

Entity Form	Number of Firms	Percent of Total	Business Receipts* $	Business Receipts* Percent of Total	Net Income* $	Net Income* Percent of Total
Sole proprie-torship†	13,091,000	71.3%	$ 611	6.0%	$106	24.7%
Partnership	1,648,000	9.0	411	4.0	(5)	(1.2)
Corporation	3,612,000	19.7	9,186	90.0	328	76.5
	18,351,000	100.0%	$10,208	100.0%	$429	100.0%

* Dollar amounts are in billions.
† Figures are for nonfarm proprietorships only.

Source: U.S. Bureau of the Census, *Statistical Abstract of the United States, 1991* (Washington, D.C.: Government Printing Office, 1991), p. 525.

Transferability of Ownership

Recall from our previous discussions that a corporation is divided into transferable units of ownership called **shares of stock.** These shares are readily transferable from one investor to another without affecting corporate operations. Frequently, the transfer occurs in an organized market such as the New York Stock Exchange, a mechanism where the stocks of roughly 2,000 businesses can be bought or sold. With the possible exception of family-owned entities or corporations owned by a few persons (termed **closely held corporations**), the acquisition and sale of stock are routine matters and do not require the approval of other owners.[1]

Perpetual Existence

Because a transfer of ownership does not affect business operations, a corporation is said to have a continuous, or perpetual, existence. Contrast this feature with that of a partnership where, unless the partnership agreement states otherwise, a change in ownership terminates the entity's life. Since it is not unusual for larger firms to have more than a million shares traded on a single day, perpetual existence is needed to ensure continuity of financial activities.

Limited Liability of Stockholders

The owners of a corporation are termed its **stockholders.** Because of the corporation's separate legal existence, stockholders have *limited liability*; that is, the most they can lose is the amount of their investment. Creditors of the firm have a claim against the entity's assets only; the personal assets of the owners cannot be used to satisfy corporate debts. Recall that this feature does not apply to partnerships (and sole proprietorships also), where each owner may be held liable for the debts of the business.

Ease of Raising Capital

Limited liability tends to make the corporation an attractive alternative for investors. This feature, coupled with the fact that ownership is divided into many units, provides a corporation with ready access to additional capital funds. The need for and the ability to raise substantial amounts of capital have prompted virtually all large businesses to adopt the corporate form of organization.

Corporate Form of Organization: Disadvantages

Multiple Choice

Although the corporation offers many advantages, several disadvantages must be considered.

---

[1] As an aside, do not liken the closely held corporation to a "mom-and-pop-type" business. *Forbes* magazine prepares an annual list of the 400 largest private companies in the United States (i.e., companies that have too few stockholders to be required to file certain reports with the Securities and Exchange Commission or companies whose stock is not available to the general public). The following firms were included in a recent compilation: United Parcel Service, Mars, Montgomery Ward, Levi Strauss, Hallmark Cards, Polo Ralph Lauren, Del Monte Foods, E&J Gallo Winery, Budget Rent a Car, and United Van Lines.

Double Taxation

As noted in Chapter 14, partnerships are not taxable entities; instead, an owner is taxed personally on his or her share of the earnings. This same feature also applies to proprietorships. Corporations, on the other hand, are required to pay income taxes. The taxes are heavy and often amount to about 40% of taxable income when both federal and state obligations are considered. In addition, any earnings distributed as dividends are income to the recipient stockholders and are subject to personal income tax. Thus, the same earnings can be taxed twice. The taxing of income to the corporation and the subsequent taxing of dividends to the stockholder is commonly termed **double taxation.**

Heavy Regulation

In comparison with sole proprietorships and partnerships, corporations are subject to greater governmental regulation. Most corporations that sell their stock to the general public (termed **publicly held corporations**) must follow the financial reporting directives of the Securities and Exchange Commission (SEC). Corporate entities are also subject to widely varying state laws. Furthermore, depending on the activities in which it is involved, a corporation may come under the scrutiny of specialized agencies. Examples of such agencies include the Interstate Commerce Commission, the Nuclear Regulatory Commission, and the Federal Deposit Insurance Corporation.

Organization of a Corporation

A corporation is created by obtaining a **charter** from one of the states. The charter is granted after the appropriate state department reviews and approves an application for incorporation. The application spells out, among other things, the firm's business purpose and the organizational structure.

After the entity is created, a stockholders' meeting is usually held to adopt the bylaws that govern the conduct of business activities and also to elect the *board of directors*. The board of directors is entrusted with wide-ranging powers and serves to protect the basic interests of stockholders. In fulfilling its duties and obligations, the board will usually meet several times each year to discuss and evaluate various matters, for example, corporate policy, general business affairs, the declaration of dividends, major contract decisions, and the hiring and remuneration of officers.

Corporate officers manage the company and oversee daily activities. Executives typically included in this select group are a president, several vice-presidents, a secretary, and a treasurer. The president is the chief executive of the company and has final authority (subject to review by the board of directors) for most major decisions. Numerous vice-presidents normally assist the president, often specializing in a functional area such as marketing, finance, production, personnel, and so on. The secretary is charged with maintaining minutes for meetings of the directors and stockholders. The secretary may also become involved in various other legal and contractual matters that affect the corporation.

EXECUTIVE BRIEFING
The Advantages and Disadvantages of Being a Privately Held Company: The Mary Kay Experience

Richard Rogers
Chairman, Mary Kay Corporation

In 1985, Mary Kay went from being a publicly held corporation to one of private ownership. The traditional reasons for becoming (or remaining) private were important: (1) managing for long-term instead of quarter-to-quarter results; (2) achieving greater cost efficiency by avoiding the reporting costs of public ownership; and (3) focusing top management's full attention on the core business rather than shareholder relations issues.

But one other reason was even more important: private ownership provided a more stable, less volatile base for day-to-day operations and sales force performance. In our experience, members of the sales force tend to get caught up in the ebb and flow of financial information that is reported in newspapers and business periodicals. When an industry downturn hit during 1984–85, the company's public status negatively affected employee motivation and made it more difficult to recruit new sales force members. Our ranks decreased by more than 30%.

Going private provided the solution. Outside the daily gaze of the business pages, we quietly accepted a slight decline in operating income for one more year while deploying new programs to bring performance back on track. The result: a compounded annual growth rate of 21% in sales and 29% in operating cash flow from 1986 to 1989. Although public ownership is fine for many firms, life "outside of the fishbowl" has helped us immensely.

The treasurer is the custodian of corporate funds and must oversee cash position, monitor cash inflows and outflows, and review major financing activities. Given the nature of their duties, the treasurer and the controller often report to the vice-president of finance. The **controller** is the chief accounting officer of the firm and is responsible for internal and external reporting. More specifically, the controller oversees the company's internal control system; supplies management with information needed for planning, control, and decision making; and is held accountable for generating financial statements and the various reports that are filed with regulatory agencies (such as the Securities and Exchange Commission). Exhibit 15-2 illustrates the typical upper-level organizational structure of a medium-size corporate entity.

Naturally, in smaller corporations, several of these functions may be combined. For instance, the treasurer and the vice-president of finance may be the same individual. Furthermore, in many family-run businesses, it is not uncommon for a husband/wife team to comprise both top management *and* the board of directors.

EXHIBIT 15-2
Corporate Organizational
Structure

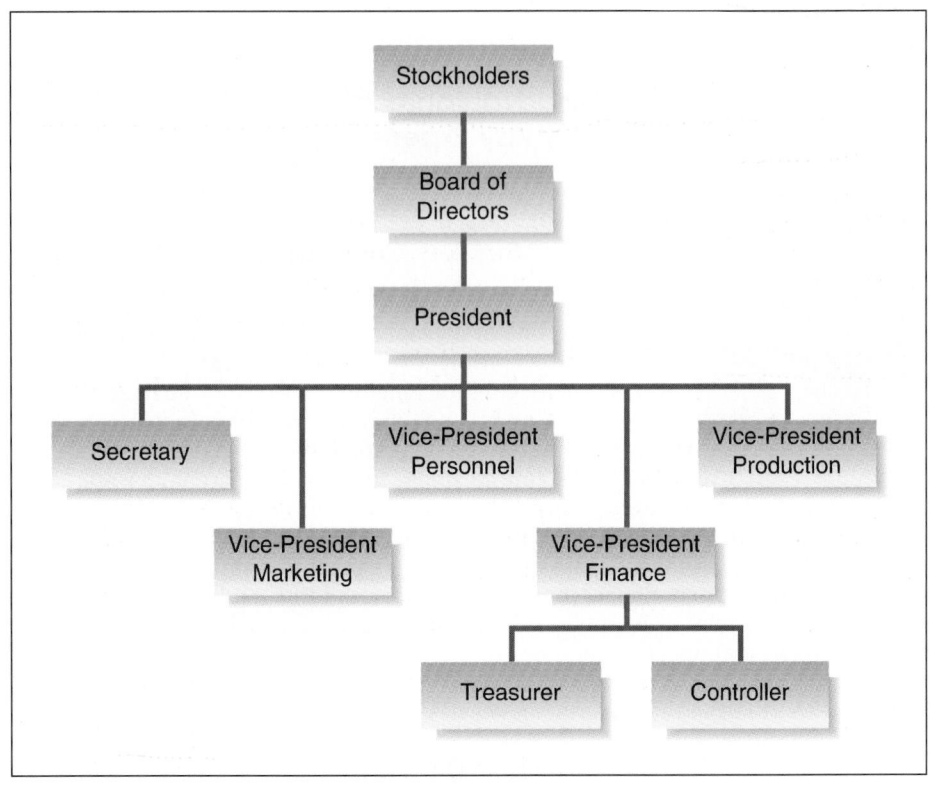

Organization Costs

Forming a corporation is more involved and costly than forming a sole proprietorship or partnership. In addition to state incorporation fees, there are legal costs connected with preparing the application for incorporation, expenses incurred by the founders, and numerous other outlays.[2] These one-time expenditures are debited to an account entitled Organization Costs, which is disclosed on the balance sheet as either an intangible asset or an "other asset."

Treatment as an asset is justified because such costs contribute to corporate formation; thus, the benefits derived extend over a number of years. Normally, however, the number of years is unknown, since most corporations have an indefinite life. Recall from Chapter 11 that intangible assets with seemingly unlimited lives are amortized over a period not to exceed 40 years. Most firms amortize organization costs over five years, which is the minimum period allowable under existing income tax regulations. Businesses are permitted to follow this practice because organization costs are small in relation to total assets, and the effect of the associated amortization charges on net income is typically insignificant.

---

[2] A study of small businesses found that the typical cost of a $10 million initial public stock offering amounted to $1,182,000. See "Special Report: Small Business," *The Wall Street Journal*, May 15, 1987, p. 13D.

Common Stock

The corporate charter specifies the types and number of shares of capital stock that a corporation is permitted to issue. Normally, the charter allows for the issuance of more shares than are currently needed. This practice saves the time and expense of seeking repeated approvals from stockholders and state authorities for additional stock issues at a later date. The number of shares allowed by the charter is termed the **authorized stock.**

Many corporations issue different classes of stock to provide flexibility in raising capital and to appeal to various types of investors. The stock classes usually have distinctive rights and privileges. All corporations issue **common stock**—an ownership interest that controls the board of directors (and thus corporate management) by exercising voting rights. Common stockholders are often rewarded with increased stock values when net income rises and, conversely, with decreased values when profitability falls. Overall, then, it is the common stockholder who reaps the benefits of corporate success and pays the price of business failure.

Evidence of corporate ownership is provided by a legal document known as a *stock certificate.* An example of such a certificate for the common shares of American Telephone and Telegraph (AT&T) is shown in Exhibit 15-3.

Rights of Common Stockholders

The owners of common stock typically have the following rights:

1 To share in any dividend distributions that may be declared by the board of directors.

> **OBJECTIVE**
> **2**
>
> **Summarize the distinctions between common and preferred stock.**

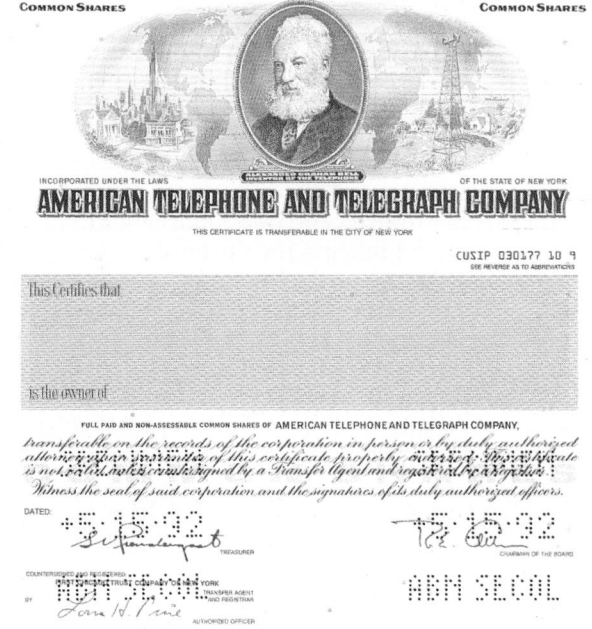
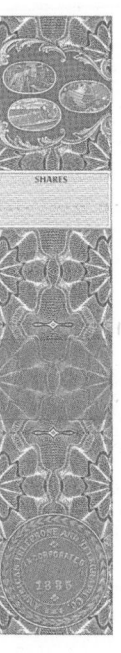

EXHIBIT 15-3
Stock Certificate

HIGHLIGHT

Stock Certificates: Cash, History, and Electronic Blips

When Florence Richards bought 300 shares in the North European Oil Company during the 1930s, it was to cheer up her boyfriend, an unhappy stockbroker, and not to get rich. Shares in the New Jersey firm, established to look for oil in Germany, never sold for more than 25 cents each. In 1937, after Hitler's rise to power, the company closed its doors.

Richards thought her $75 investment was lost—until she contacted stock detective Micheline Masse 50 years after the original purchase. Masse found out that when oil was discovered in the North Sea in 1957, the North European Oil Company paid its back taxes and changed its name to Northern European Royalty Trust. The value of Richards's stock? $54,550. Masse says that she has helped clients recover some $3 million from supposedly worthless stock certificates. "Billions of dollars are still out there waiting to be claimed."

According to Masse, there's a 40% chance that an old stock certificate can draw cool, clean cash (a 10% chance that it has intrinsic value now, a 10% chance that it will have intrinsic value in the future, and a 20% chance that it has value as a collectible). Collectibles? Yes—old stock certificates can be sold to scripophilists, or stock certificate collectors. Values usually range from $5 to $1,000, although much higher amounts have been paid. [1]

Consider, for instance, a Standard Oil certificate signed by founder John D. Rockefeller in the 1870s and you've got values that have been multiplying by as much as 43% a year. A decade ago the Rockefeller Standards were going for as little as $275 apiece; a recent asking price was around $10,000. The Standards are top-of-the-line stuff, in brisk demand because of the Rockefeller signature. There are probably no more than 300 of the old certificates currently in existence. Certificates signed by other industrial giants are likewise in demand: Thomas Edison on his Edison Storage Battery Company; Henry Ford on the certificates of the Highland Park

State Bank he set up for his employees; founders Henry Wells and William Fargo on shares of the old American Express Company. [2]

Interestingly, the old, respected stock certificate may soon become a thing of the past. An international group of bankers and stock executives known as the Group of Thirty is pushing to speed up the way securities trades are processed. And stock certificates are a major obstacle to any acceleration effort. The Group says that replacing stock certificates with a paperless "electronic book-entry system" would enable the U.S. securities markets to reduce the period needed to settle stock trades, thus becoming more efficient and globally competitive.

Wall Street generally likes the idea, in part because it would save money and eliminate a lot of processing headaches. But critics worry that the Street may scare off small investors by doing away with stock certificates—at a time when it needs all the customers it can keep. In a recent survey of 750 investors, for example, 81% opposed eliminating stock certificates. A large majority of those surveyed cited the potential for computer error or the collapse of a brokerage firm as reasons for wanting to hold on to their certificates. [3]

These findings somewhat contradict those of Merrill Lynch, which claims that only 2.1% of its clients actually ask for certificates these days. Certificates are "now the unusual request, as opposed to the usual request," says a spokesman. In fact, to somewhat discourage the practice, the giant brokerage firm recently announced a $15 client service fee just to process the document. [4]

As time marches on, it appears once again that America's love for paper may soon give way to electronic blips. Those pieces of paper, though, may have value and should not be taken lightly. The situation could be described by the old saying: "Beauty is in the eyes of the beholder" . . . or is it stockholder . . . or is it collector . . . or is it . . . ?

Sources: Adapted from "Days May Be Numbered for Stock Certificates: 'Paperless' Trades Would Speed up Settlements," *The Wall Street Journal,* November 27, 1990, p. C1 [3]; "Stalking Stocks," *Alaska Airlines Magazine,* September 1989, pp. 10–12 [1]; "Stock Certificates Move a Step Closer to the Scrap Pile," *The Wall Street Journal,* July 10, 1991, pp. C1, C8 [4]; and "Taking Stock," *Forbes Personal Affairs,* October 23, 1989, pp. 16, 18 [2]. The first article is reprinted by permission of *The Wall Street Journal,* © Dow Jones & Company, Inc., 1990 (all rights reserved worldwide). The second article is reprinted by permission of *Alaska Airlines Magazine.*

2 To subscribe to any additional common stock issued by the corporation (known as the **preemptive right**). Existing stockholders are given the opportunity to maintain their respective interests in a corporate entity by acquiring additional shares on a pro rata basis. A stockholder who owns 15% of a corporation's common stock is therefore allowed to purchase 15% of any new shares issued before those shares are offered to other investors.

The preemptive right is not a hard-and-fast rule. For example, stockholders have sometimes waived the preemptive right, thereby permitting the issuance of large blocks of stock to be used in acquiring other businesses. In other situations, certain states have allowed the issuance of shares with no preemptive rights attached.

3 To share in the final disposition of assets if the corporation is liquidated. At the end of a corporation's life its assets are sold, and the cash generated is used to settle the claims of creditors. Any remaining cash (or assets) is shared proportionately by the common stockholders on the basis of the number of shares owned.

4 To elect the board of directors and to vote on other important corporate issues. Common stockholders are frequently asked to consider such matters as proposed mergers; the selection of independent auditors; changes in corporate bylaws and management pension programs; and the types and amounts of stock that can be issued.

The preceding rights apply to most common stockholders, not all. Sometimes, different classes of common stock are issued with rights other than those described. The Adolph Coors Company, for instance, perhaps best known for its brewing operation, has Class A and Class B common stock. Class A stock has voting rights and is retained by the Coors family; Class B stock is nonvoting and has been issued to the general public.

Preferred Stock: Nature and Characteristics

Rather than have multiple classes of common stock, some corporations have achieved differentiation by issuing **preferred stock.** As its name implies, preferred stock has several preferential rights; in comparison with common stock, however, other rights are given up in return.[3] Normally, preferred stock appeals to investors who want a safe investment with a steady dividend. Why? The reasons become apparent in the upcoming sections where we discuss characteristics of most preferred stocks.

No Voting Rights

Preferred stockholders generally have no vote in corporate affairs. Exceptions are made, however, by special contracts or by state law. In some cases voting privileges are awarded after certain conditions have been met, such as the absence of dividends for a specified period of time.

---

[3] As in the case of common shares, corporations may issue various classes of preferred stock. In what might be an extreme example, Pacific Gas & Electric (a San Francisco–based public utility) has 20 different types of preferred shares, each with its own features and rights.

OBJECTIVE

3

Calculate the dividends associated with preferred stock.

Dividend Preference

Voting rights are often forfeited in exchange for a preference in dividend distributions. Specifically, preferred stockholders are entitled to receive dividends before any distributions are made to common stockholders. In most instances, however, the owners of preferred shares receive only a stipulated amount per share regardless of the profitability of the firm. This situation arises because preferred dividends are expressed either on a per-year basis or as a percentage of par value. (Par value refers to the face value of a share of stock and is discussed later in the chapter.) A 10% preferred stock with a $25 par value, for example, has a dividend of $2.50 per year.

Although many businesses take pride in their dividend records, keep in mind that dividend distributions are not mandatory but are subject to the discretion of the board of directors. Consequently, when a company's cash position is weak or when earnings are marginal, dividends may not be disbursed. For this reason most preferred stocks are **cumulative.** That is, the rights to preferred dividends that are omitted in a given year accumulate, with the amounts said to be **in arrears.** Dividends in arrears must be paid before any subsequent dividends can be declared and paid on a corporation's common stock.

An Example.   To illustrate these features, suppose Flora, Inc., has 20,000 shares of 10%, $5 par, cumulative preferred stock and 50,000 shares of $1 par common. Dividend distributions for the past four years are listed in the second column of the following table. Because the annual preferred dividend requirement is $10,000 (20,000 shares × $5 × 0.10), the dividends would be divided between preferred and common shareholders as shown.

Year	Total Dividends Distributed	Annual Preferred Requirement	Dividends in Arrears	Dividends Distributed Preferred	Dividends Distributed Common
1	$27,000	$10,000	$ —	$10,000	$17,000
2	6,000	10,000	4,000	6,000	—
3	3,000	10,000	11,000	3,000	—
4	25,000	10,000	—	21,000	4,000

Observe that distributions in Year 2 amounted to only $6,000. Since preferred stockholders are entitled to receive $10,000, dividends are $4,000 in arrears. All $6,000 thus goes to the preferred stockholders because of their right to receive dividends before any distributions to common. In Year 3, Flora failed to cover the annual preferred requirement by $7,000 ($10,000 − $3,000), raising arrearages to $11,000. Preferred again gets the entire distribution, in this instance $3,000. Finally, the dividends in Year 4 were sufficient to meet not only the arrearage but also the annual requirement. Common stockholders therefore receive the remaining $4,000 ($25,000 − $11,000 − $10,000).

Dividends in arrears are not a liability because they have never been declared by the board of directors. Such amounts are typically disclosed in the notes to the financial statements. Although we have emphasized the cumulative feature, realize that some preferred stock is noncumulative; that is, unpaid dividends do not accumulate and are lost. Because noncumulative preferred stock lacks investor appeal, it is not frequently encountered in practice.

Asset Preference upon Liquidation

Most preferred stock has a preference over common stock in the event of corporate liquidation. After creditor claims are settled, preferred stockholders are entitled to their share of the remaining assets prior to any distributions to the holders of common (i.e., the residual owners).

Callable

Many preferred stock issues are **callable,** which means the issuing corporation retains the right to reacquire (call) the stock at a preset price. To make this feature somewhat attractive to investors, the call price is generally set slightly above the original issue price.

The call feature allows a corporation to raise capital from a stock issuance and then cancel the stock and return the investors' funds. Such actions may be desirable when the cash is no longer needed or the stock becomes financially burdensome. The latter situation will arise if the preferred stock is issued when interest (and dividend) rates are high. Should the rates drop suddenly, the stock can be called and replaced with cheaper financing.

Convertible

Some preferred stock is **convertible** into common stock at the option of the stockholder. Conversion normally occurs in a stipulated exchange ratio; for example, one share of preferred may be convertible into five shares of common. Convertible preferred is appealing to both investors and the issuing company. From the investors' viewpoint, there is a strong likelihood of a regular, assured dividend on the preferred stock. Furthermore, should the corporation's common stock rise in value, investors have the privilege of conversion and can thereby increase the worth of their holdings. From the company's point of view, a smaller dividend can usually be paid because investors find the conversion feature attractive.

Par-Value Stock

The common and preferred classifications are based on the rights afforded to the respective groups of stockholders. Stocks can also be categorized as par value or no-par value. **Par-value stock** has a fixed dollar amount per share specified by the corporate charter. The amount varies among businesses and is sometimes influenced by state laws that tax the par value of shares issued.

The significance of par value is that it represents the **legal capital** per share of stock. Total legal capital, obtained by multiplying the par value per share times the number of shares issued, denotes the minimum amount of owners' equity that must be maintained for protection of the creditors. To explain, recall that stockholders have limited liability and cannot be held personally liable for corporate obligations. In an effort to provide some protection to the creditors, state laws thus require a minimum permanent investment from the owners to help settle claims on company assets. Dividend declarations that reduce total stockholders' equity below legal capital are therefore not permitted.

OBJECTIVE

4

Explain the concepts of and demonstrate the accounting treatments for par, no-par, and stated-value stock, and stock subscriptions.

Issuing Par-Value Stock

If a corporation is large or is attempting to sell a substantial amount of stock, the services of an investment banking firm will normally be used. Typical investment bankers include Shearson Lehman Brothers Inc., and Merrill Lynch, Pierce, Fenner & Smith Inc. The investment banker, often referred to as an *underwriter*, has the responsibility of selling the stock, at a set price, to the public. Underwriters charge a commission for their services and often advertise stock issuances in newspapers and business periodicals. The sale of stock is typically made on the basis of a **prospectus,** a document required by the SEC that contains information about the corporation's products, management, and financial affairs.

Issue Price

Stocks may be issued at, above, or below par value, given the arbitrary manner in which par is determined. The latter issuances are seldom encountered and are actually illegal in many states. Why? Although the sale proceeds are less than par, the stock is still considered fully paid. However, the stockholder is held contingently liable to the corporation's creditors for the difference between the sale price and the par amount specified in the firm's charter. Should corporate assets be insufficient to settle creditor claims if operations cease, the original stockholders may be called upon to furnish additional cash. To avoid this situation, virtually all corporations issue stock at or above par.

The issue price for new stock is determined by the corporation along with an underwriter or financial advisers. The following factors are considered: past, present, and future corporate earnings; financial position; expected dividend rates; market position of the company's products and services; current state of the investment market; and recent prices of competitors' stock.

Once stock is issued, its **market price** (the price at which a share can be bought or sold) continually changes. The changes reflect investor evaluation of the corporation's progress and prospects. If growth prospects are evident, the price of the shares should rise; if the future looks bleak, the price should fall. As a typical example we cite the case of a Kansas City–based telecommunications company. The firm announced a big drop in earnings, layoffs of 1,000 employees, and a delay in completing its acquisition of the U.S. Sprint long-distance service. Investors reacted negatively to the news, and in one day the company's stock lost nearly 23% of its value.

It is important to note that market fluctuations do *not* affect the corporation's financial position. If, for instance, a company issues stock at $50 per share and the market price later plummets to $10 per share, the firm does not suffer directly from the decrease in valuation. The decrease is absorbed by the stockholders. Of course, if more investment capital is needed, the entity may be unable to attract the investors and funds it once did at the original $50 price.

Accounting for Par-Value Stock

The issuance of par-value stock may require entries in more than one owners' equity account. Specifically, an amount equal to the par value of the shares issued is placed in a capital stock account, either Common

Stock or Preferred Stock. Then, if the stock is issued at a price greater than par, the difference between the issue price and par is recorded in an account entitled Paid-in Capital in Excess of Par Value. To state this important allocation differently, the funds received from investors are recorded as legal capital (the par value) and as additional paid-in capital (amounts received in excess of par).

To illustrate the proper accounting, assume McCord Corporation is authorized to issue 50,000 shares of $5 par, 8% cumulative preferred stock and 20,000 shares of $10 par common. Further assume that the corporation has issued 30,000 shares of preferred at par and 10,000 shares of common at $18. The required journal entries follow.

Cash	150,000	
Preferred Stock		150,000

To record issuance of 30,000 shares of $5 par, 8% preferred at $5 per share

Cash	180,000	
Common Stock		100,000
Paid-in Capital in Excess of Par Value		80,000

To record issuance of 10,000 shares of $10 par common at $18 per share

Observe that in both cases the par value of the issued shares was placed in a capital stock account. In addition, note that the $80,000 paid in excess of par was recorded separately.

Tips & Techniques

Realize that the preceding entries are made *only* at the time of stock issuance. Daily stock transactions of investors (e.g., purchases and sales) normally involve shares that have been previously issued, with no additional cash being received by the corporation. In these instances the corporation does not record a formal journal entry—all that is needed is an updating of the list of stockholders.

Balance Sheet Presentation

The owners' (stockholders') equity section of McCord's balance sheet would appear as shown in Exhibit 15-4. Notice how the balance sheet discloses the two major sources of corporate equity: stockholder investments (**paid-in capital**) and **retained earnings.** Retained earnings represents capital generated from profitable operations that is kept in the business; an in-depth discussion will be presented in Chapter 16. At this point assume the account's $240,000 balance was obtained from McCord's general ledger.

Exhibit 15-4 reveals two other important points. First, considerable detail is required in terms of disclosure. The features of the various stock issues are described along with the number of shares authorized by the corporate charter, issued by the firm, and held by the stockholders (termed

OBJECTIVE

Prepare and interpret the stockholders' equity section of a corporate balance sheet.

EXHIBIT 15-4
Stockholders' Equity of McCord Corporation

Stockholders' Equity		
Capital stock		
Cumulative 8% preferred stock, $5 par, 50,000 shares authorized, 30,000 shares issued and outstanding	$150,000	
Common stock, $10 par, 20,000 shares authorized, 10,000 shares issued and outstanding	100,000	$250,000
Paid-in capital in excess of par value: common		80,000
Total paid-in capital		$330,000
Retained earnings		240,000
Total stockholders' equity		$570,000

outstanding shares).[4] Second, note that the $80,000 paid by stockholders in excess of par value is considered neither revenue nor profit. It is merely additional invested capital that is shown separately from the capital stock accounts.

Our illustration has focused on the issuance of stock at par and in excess of par. Should stock be issued below par, the difference between par and the issue price (i.e., a *discount*) is debited to an account entitled Discount on Capital Stock. The discount account is subtracted from the capital stock accounts when determining total paid-in capital.

No-Par Stock

In the early days of corporations, the issuance of par-value stock sometimes misled investors. Par value was occasionally equated with the "true" worth of the stock, that is, market value. This factor, coupled with the contingent liability problem should issuance take place at a discount, prompted many corporations to consider **no-par stock.**

Because the par-value concept is absent, the entire proceeds must be credited to a capital stock account. For instance, assume Canton Corporation is authorized to issue 20,000 shares of no-par common stock. If 10,000 shares are issued at $18 per share, the required journal entry would be as follows:

Cash	180,000	
Common Stock		180,000
To record issuance of 10,000 shares of no-par common at $18 per share		

This example has deliberately used the same numbers as the McCord Corporation illustration on page 593. Notice that both issues of common stock generated identical proceeds: $180,000. With no-par stock, however, total invested capital is recorded in one equity account rather than two.

---

[4] The number of shares issued and the number of shares outstanding can differ. This situation will also be discussed in Chapter 16.

Stated-Value Stock

Although most states permit the issuance of no-par stock, some states require corporations to set a minimum issue price. This price, known as the stock's **stated value,** allows for protection of the creditors in terms of legal capital. In essence, then, stated value can be likened to par value.

Because of the similarity, accounting for stated-value stock closely parallels that for par-value stock. To illustrate, we will continue the Canton Corporation example. Assume that to comply with state law, Canton's board of directors has assigned a $10 stated value to each share. The issuance of 10,000 shares at $18 per share would now be recorded as follows:

Cash	180,000	
Common Stock		100,000
Paid-in Capital in Excess of Stated Value		80,000
To record issuance of 10,000 shares of no-par		
common (stated value, $10) at $18 per share		

The stated value of the issued stock is entered in the Common Stock account. Any added amount is then recorded as Paid-in Capital in Excess of Stated Value, which is similar to additional paid-in capital received on par-value shares.

Issuing Stock for Assets Other Than Cash

Thus far we have concentrated on stock issues that generate cash. The cash, in turn, was used for the purchase of assets, payment of expenses, and other similar purposes. Frequently, corporations issue stock in direct exchange for land, buildings, and even other businesses. In addition, stock is sometimes used to settle claims of attorneys and other professionals for services rendered, particularly at the time of corporate formation when cash balances may be low.

The issuance of shares for noncash assets or services creates a valuation problem. Namely, what value should be used to record the transaction? The general rule is that the assets or services acquired are recorded at their fair market value or the fair market value of the stock, whichever is more clearly discernible. If the corporation's shares are actively traded on one of the stock exchanges, determination of the stock's market value is a relatively simple matter. *The Wall Street Journal* and the financial pages of most metropolitan newspapers will provide the necessary information. When stock is not actively traded, as in a closely held corporation, an appraisal of the asset's (or service's) market value may be more appropriate.

ETHICS ISSUE

You have the opportunity to audit the financial statements of a cash-poor, publicly held corporation. You would be given a sizable number of common shares for your services. How would you respond, knowing the results of your audit may affect the stock's market price?

To illustrate the proper accounting treatment, assume Fuqua Industries is a small family-run business located in Wyoming. Fuqua's attorney has agreed to accept 40 shares of $5 par common for $850 of legal work performed in organizing the corporation. The required journal entry follows.

Organization Costs	850	
Common Stock		200
Paid-in Capital in Excess of Par Value		650
To record issuance of common stock in exchange		
for legal services		

Because Fuqua's stock is not actively traded, the $850 billing is more clearly determinable as the market value of the transaction.

Stock Subscriptions

Rather than use the services of an underwriter, small corporations occasionally sell stock directly to investors on a **subscription** basis. Investors agree to purchase the stock at a given price, with payment taking place on a specific future date or via installments. After the subscriber pays in full, the shares of stock are issued.

For example, assume investors subscribed to 1,000 shares of Glover Corporation $5 par common stock at $22 per share. The journal entry that follows would be made.

Subscriptions Receivable: Common Stock	22,000	
Common Stock Subscribed		5,000
Paid-in Capital in Excess of Par Value		17,000
To record subscriptions to 1,000 shares of $5 par common at $22 per share		

Subscriptions Receivable is established to indicate that $22,000 will be forthcoming from investors. This account is similar to other receivables and normally appears as a current asset on the balance sheet. Common Stock Subscribed is a temporary paid-in capital account that is credited for the par value of the shares subscribed (1,000 shares × $5). Observe that at this point it would be incorrect to credit Common Stock because the shares have not yet been issued. Finally, the $17,000 difference is placed in the Paid-in Capital in Excess of Par Value account.

Next, assume investors subscribing to 750 shares paid in full. Glover would therefore issue the stock and record the following entries:

Cash	16,500	
Subscriptions Receivable: Common Stock		16,500
To record collections from subscribers of 750 shares (750 shares × $22 = $16,500)		
Common Stock Subscribed	3,750	
Common Stock		3,750
To record issuance of 750 shares under subscription agreements		

The first entry is similar to that made to record other receipts of cash on account. The second entry removes $3,750 (750 shares × $5 par) from Common Stock Subscribed and recognizes the issuance of common shares. Consistent with previous illustrations, the capital stock account is again carried at par value.

Should subscribers to the remaining 250 shares now pay 40% of their balances due, no additional shares would be issued. Issuances occur only when full payment is made; thus, the required journal entry would be:

Cash	2,200	
Subscriptions Receivable: Common Stock		2,200
To record partial payment on subscriptions for 250 shares (250 shares × $22 × 0.40)		

Corporate Equity: A Comprehensive Illustration

The stockholders' equity section in Exhibit 15-5 brings together several of the concepts discussed in the chapter. Notice that preferred stock is presented first, followed by common stock. Next, additional paid-in capital is

Stockholders' Equity		
Capital stock		
Cumulative 9% preferred stock, $10 par, 30,000 shares authorized, 20,000 shares issued and outstanding		$200,000
Common stock, no-par, $5 stated value, 15,000 shares authorized, 10,000 shares issued and outstanding	$ 50,000	
Common stock subscribed, no-par, $5 stated value, 2,000 shares	10,000	60,000
Total capital stock		$260,000
Additional paid-in capital		
Paid-in capital in excess of par value: preferred	$120,000	
Paid-in capital in excess of stated value: common	48,000	168,000
Total paid-in capital		$428,000
Retained earnings		150,000
Total stockholders' equity		$578,000

EXHIBIT 15-5
Corporate Equity

disclosed to complete total equity contributed by stockholders. The final element is retained earnings. Although variations in terminology and presentation exist in practice, the exhibit is representative and should convey the message that corporate equity is more complex than equity of both sole proprietorships and partnerships.

Owners, creditors, and analysts use a variety of measures to assess corporate performance and financial position. One of these measures is **book value per share,** or the amount of stockholders' equity allocable to an individual share of stock. Stated differently, book value represents a corporation's net assets (total assets minus total liabilities) expressed on a per-share basis.

The calculation of book value depends on the classes of stock outstanding. If a corporation has only common stock, book value is computed by dividing total stockholders' equity by the number of common shares outstanding at the end of the accounting period. For example, assume Ranger Corporation has the following stockholders' equity on August 31, the end of the firm's fiscal year:

BOOK VALUE PER SHARE

OBJECTIVE
6

Define, explain, and calculate book value per share.

Stockholders' Equity	
Common stock, $1 par value, 100,000 shares authorized, 50,000 shares issued and outstanding	$ 50,000
Paid-in capital in excess of par value	350,000
Retained earnings	600,000
Total stockholders' equity	$1,000,000

The book value per share is therefore $20 ($1,000,000 ÷ 50,000 shares).

An Example with Two Classes of Stock

If a corporation has two classes of stock (e.g., common and preferred), total stockholders' equity must be allocated between the respective ownership interests. The first step in this allocation involves assigning the call value (sometimes referred to as the *redemption or liquidating value*) of the preferred stock plus any dividends in arrears[5] as preferred equity. Next, the sum of these two items is subtracted from total stockholders' equity to generate equity attributable to the common shareholders. The book value per common and preferred shares can then be determined by dividing the equity relating to the two stock classes by their respective outstanding shares.

To illustrate the necessary accounting, we will focus on the stockholders' equity section of Orleans, Inc. (see Exhibit 15-6). Further information reveals that dividends on the preferred stock are $4,000 in arrears at year-end.

EXHIBIT 15-6
Stockholders' Equity of Orleans, Inc.

Stockholders' Equity		
Preferred stock, $100 par value, 5% cumulative, callable at $110, 1,000 shares authorized, 400 shares issued and outstanding	$ 40,000	
Common stock, $1 par value, 100,000 shares authorized, 30,000 shares issued and outstanding	30,000	$ 70,000
Additional paid-in capital		
Paid-in capital in excess of par: preferred	$ 5,000	
Paid-in capital in excess of par: common	200,000	205,000
Total paid-in capital		$275,000
Retained earnings		595,000
Total stockholders' equity		$870,000

The allocation of Orleans' stockholders' equity follows.

Total stockholders' equity		$870,000
Allocated to preferred stock		
Call value: 400 shares × $110	$44,000	
Dividends in arrears	4,000	48,000
Allocated to common stock		$822,000

Observe that the $5,000 paid-in capital in excess of par on the preferred stock is not allocated to preferred equity. This amount will not be returned to the preferred shareholders should their stock be called.

---

[5] Dividends in arrears apply solely to cumulative preferred stock.

The book value per share for each class of stock can now be calculated in the following manner:

Preferred stock: $48,000 ÷ 400 shares = $120.00 per share
Common stock: $822,000 ÷ 30,000 shares = $27.40 per share

Meaning of Book Value

Book value is equivalent to a corporation's net assets per share of stock. Some stockholders therefore believe that should the corporation terminate operations and liquidate, they would receive an amount equal to the book value per share. Rarely, however, does this belief become reality. When an entity liquidates, the assets are usually sold at a price far different from their valuation on a balance sheet. Remember, the balance sheet is cost-based and ignores increases in valuation that arise from inflation. Furthermore, because the corporation is selling out, the amounts received for certain assets may be only a small percentage of their original cost. Added to this is the fact that liabilities are often settled at less than the amount owed. These events alter corporate equity and the amounts disbursed to stockholders upon liquidation.

The importance of book value arises from its inclusion in many legal contracts. In a small corporation, for instance, stockholders may agree to sell their holdings to the other owners at the book value per share existing on specified future dates. Or banks may lend funds to a corporation, subject to the maintenance of a minimum book value. Under no circumstances should book value per share be equated with a stock's market value, as these two measures normally differ. Consider, for example, the following figures, which were in existence at the time this text was written:

Corporation	Book Value per Share	Market Value per Share
Aetna Life & Casualty	$ 64.33	$ 44.00
Aluminum Co. of America (Alcoa)	54.55	64.38
Atlantic Richfield	42.85	106.75
Caterpillar, Inc.	38.89	43.88
McDonnell Douglas	100.96	73.25
Xerox Corp.	36.93	68.50

Book value, a measure based on historical cost, is just one of the many factors investors use in studying the appropriateness of a stock's market price.

END-OF-CHAPTER REVIEW

1 Identify the features, advantages, and disadvantages of a corporate entity. The corporate form of organization has several key features, which often make it preferable for conducting business affairs. Shares of ownership are easily transferred, and regardless of any change in ownership, the corporation has a continuous existence.

LEARNING OBJECTIVES: THE KEY POINTS

In addition, the stockholders have limited liability, which serves to protect the assets of the owners from being used to satisfy corporate obligations. Finally, because liability is limited and ownership is divided into many shares, capital is more easily raised by corporations than by the other forms of business organization.

Two disadvantages of corporations are double taxation and heavy regulation. Double taxation is the taxing of income to the corporation and the subsequent taxing of dividends to stockholders.

2 Summarize the distinctions between common and preferred stock. Common stock represents an ownership interest that controls the board of directors via the voting process. In addition, common stockholders have the rights to (1) share in dividend distributions, (2) subscribe to any additional common stock that is issued by the company (i.e., the preemptive right), and (3) share in the final disposition of assets in the event of liquidation.

In contrast, preferred stock is an ownership interest that has certain preferential rights over those associated with common stock. However, to obtain these rights, others (e.g., voting) are given up in return. Preferred stockholders are entitled to receive dividends before any distributions are made to common stockholders. Furthermore, most preferred stock has preference over common stock in asset distributions should corporate liquidation occur.

3 Calculate the dividends associated with preferred stock. Preferred stockholders are entitled to receive dividends each period. If the stock is cumulative, any preferred dividends omitted in a given year accumulate and must be paid before future dividends are declared and paid on common shares. Such accumulated amounts are said to be in arrears and are disclosed in the notes to the financial statements.

4 Explain the concepts of and demonstrate the accounting treatments for par, no-par, and stated-value stock, and stock subscriptions. A corporation's stock may be characterized as having a par value or no par value. Par value is an amount specified in the corporate charter; it represents the firm's legal capital (a minimum permanent investment) per share. When par-value stock is sold, an amount equal to the par value of the issuance is placed in a capital stock account. Any receipts in excess of par are recorded in Paid-in Capital in Excess of Par Value. When no-par stock is issued, the entire proceeds are credited to a capital stock account. No-par stock may have a stated value assigned by the board of directors, which, in effect, serves to establish a minimum issue price. Accounting for stated-value stock is similar to that for par-value stock.

Small corporations sometimes sell stock directly to investors on a subscription basis. When subscriptions are received, credit entries are made to the Common Stock Subscribed account for the par or stated value of the shares and to Paid-in Capital in Excess of Par (or Stated) Value for any excess. When the stock is issued to investors, the Common Stock Subscribed account is debited and Common Stock is credited.

5 Prepare and interpret the stockholders' equity section of a corporate balance sheet. Stockholders' equity has three sections. The first, called capital stock, discloses the Preferred Stock, Common Stock, and Stock Subscribed accounts. The additional paid-in capital section appears next and contains the accounts for any amounts paid in excess of par or stated value. The final section is for retained earnings.

6 Define, explain, and calculate book value per share. Book value per share is the amount of stockholders' equity allocable to an individual share of stock. If a corporation has both preferred and common stock, book value is computed for both classes. To calculate book value for preferred shares, the total of the shares' call (i.e., redemption) value, plus any dividends in arrears if the stock is cumulative, is divided by preferred shares outstanding. The book value of common stock is total stockholders' equity, minus the preferred equity just described, divided by the common shares outstanding. Although book value is not equivalent to the value of stock in the marketplace, it is nonetheless an important element in many legal contracts.

authorized stock   The number of shares of stock a corporation is permitted to issue as specified in its charter.

book value per share   The amount of stockholders' equity allocable to an individual share of stock.

callable preferred stock   Preferred stock that can be reacquired by the issuing corporation at a preset price.

charter   A state-issued document that provides evidence of business incorporation.

closely held corporation   A corporation owned by only a few persons.

common stock   A corporate ownership interest that controls management by exercising voting rights.

controller   The chief accounting officer of a company.

convertible preferred stock   Preferred stock that can be converted into common stock at the option of the stockholder.

corporation   A form of business organization that is a separate legal entity from its owners. Ownership is in the hands of investors who have acquired shares of the corporation's stock.

cumulative preferred stock   Preferred stock where the rights to dividends omitted in a given year accumulate. These dividends must be paid before any subsequent dividends are distributed to common stockholders.

dividends in arrears   Dividends that have been omitted on cumulative preferred stock.

double taxation   The taxing of income to both a corporation and the corporation's stockholders.

legal capital   The minimum amount of owners' equity that must be maintained for the protection of creditors; obtained by multiplying the par value per share times the number of shares issued.

market value   The price at which a share of stock can be bought or sold.

no-par stock   A share of stock that lacks a par value.

organization costs   Costs incurred to organize a corporation, such as state incorporation fees and legal costs.

outstanding shares   Shares issued by a firm and held by the stockholders.

paid-in capital   The amount of stockholder investments in a corporation.

par-value stock   Stock that has an arbitrary fixed amount per share specified in the corporate charter.

preemptive right   The right of existing stockholders to maintain their respective interests in a corporation by acquiring additional shares of new stock issues on a pro rata basis.

preferred stock   Stock that gives its holders preference over common stockholders in dividend distributions and distributions of assets upon liquidation.

prospectus   A document related to new stock issues that is required by the SEC; contains information about the corporation's products, management, and financial affairs.

publicly held corporation   A corporation that sells its stock to the general public.

retained earnings   The portion of stockholders' equity that has been generated by profitable operations and retained in the business.

shares of stock   Transferable units of ownership in a corporation.

stated-value stock   No-par stock that has a minimum issue price established to allow for protection of the creditors in terms of legal capital.

stock subscriptions   Agreements with investors to purchase stock at a given price, with payment taking place on a future date or via installments.

stockholders   The owners of a corporation.

stockholders' equity   The summation of a corporate entity's capital stock and retained earnings.

CHAPTER QUIZ

The five questions that follow relate to several issues raised in the chapter. Test your knowledge of the issues by selecting the best answer. (The answers appear on p. 618.)

1 Which of the following statements is false?
  a All corporations issue preferred stock.
  b Stockholders have limited liability.
  c Corporate earnings are subject to double taxation.
  d Corporations face heavier governmental regulation than sole proprietorships.

2 Which of the following rights do not apply to common stockholders?
  a The right to share in dividends if declared by the board of directors.
  b The preemptive right.
  c The right to vote on changes in a corporation's bylaws.
  d The right to receive dividends that are in arrears.

3 Fenton Corporation is authorized to issue 10,000 shares of $5 par-value common stock. If 60% of these shares are issued at $20, what amount should be credited to the Common Stock account?
  a $30,000.   c $90,000.
  b $50,000.   d $120,000.

4 Equador's balance sheet revealed the following accounts:

Notes payable	$150,000
Preferred stock	100,000
Common stock	200,000
Paid-in capital in excess of par: preferred	10,000
Paid-in capital in excess of par: common	95,000
Retained earnings	400,000

The total amount invested by stockholders and the total stockholders' equity are:

	Invested by Stockholders	Total Stockholders' Equity
a	$105,000	$955,000
b	305,000	805,000
c	405,000	805,000
d	555,000	955,000

5 Bright Eyes, Inc., has outstanding 100,000 shares of $5 par-value common stock and 10,000 shares of $100 par-value preferred stock. The preferred stock is cumulative and has a call price of $115 per share. If there are no dividends in arrears and total stockholders' equity amounts to $4,000,000, what is the book value per share of the common stock?

a $2.85.
b $5.00.

c $28.50.
d $30.00.

SUMMARY PROBLEM

A review of the accounting records of Paragon Corporation as of December 31, 19X5, found the following information:

Preferred stock, 10% cumulative, $2 par, callable at $9, 60,000 shares authorized, 50,000 shares issued and outstanding	$100,000
Common stock, no-par, $5 stated value, 25,000 shares authorized, 15,000 shares issued and outstanding	75,000
Common stock subscribed, no-par, $5 stated value, 3,000 shares	15,000
Paid-in capital in excess of par value: preferred	250,000
Paid-in capital in excess of stated value: common	134,000
Retained earnings	380,000

The company has $24,000 of dividends in arrears at year-end.

Instructions

a Compute Paragon's total legal capital, total paid-in capital, and total stockholders' equity. (*Hint:* Common stock subscribed is part of legal capital.)
b If all of the preferred stock was sold in a single transaction, what journal entry would have been made? What was the issue price per share?
c Assume that $30,000 is collected as final payment for the subscription of 3,000 shares. What journal entries will be necessary?
d Ignoring part (c), determine the book value per common share.
e How would the dividends in arrears be disclosed in Paragon's financial statements?

Solution

a Preferred stock, $2 par	$100,000
Common stock, no-par, $5 stated value	75,000
Common stock subscribed, no-par, $5 stated value	15,000
Total legal capital	$190,000
Total legal capital	$190,000
Paid-in capital in excess of par value	250,000
Paid-in capital in excess of stated value	134,000
Total paid-in capital	$574,000
Total paid-in capital	$574,000
Retained earnings	380,000
Total stockholders' equity	$954,000

b Cash   350,000
    Preferred Stock   100,000
    Paid-in Capital in Excess of Par Value   250,000
    To record issuance of 50,000 shares of preferred stock

The issue price per share of preferred stock was $7 ($350,000 ÷ 50,000 shares).

c Cash   30,000
    Subscriptions Receivable: Common Stock   30,000
    To record collections from subscribers

Common Stock Subscribed   15,000
    Common Stock   15,000
    To record issuance of 3,000 shares under subscription agreements

d Total stockholders' equity $954,000
    Allocated to preferred stock
        Call value: 50,000 shares × $9 $450,000
        Dividends in arrears   24,000   474,000
    Allocated to common stock $480,000

The book value per common share is $32 ($480,000 ÷ 15,000 shares).

e The dividends in arrears would be disclosed in the notes to the financial statements.

ASSIGNMENT MATERIAL

QUESTIONS

Q15-1 What is a corporation? Discuss the advantages of the corporate form of organization.

Q15-2 Briefly explain the disadvantages of the corporate form of organization.

Q15-3 Discuss the duties and responsibilities of the directors of a corporation. How do directors gain their authority?

Q15-4 Describe a typical corporation's leadership structure.

Q15-5 Distinguish between authorized stock and outstanding stock.

Q15-6 List the rights typically possessed by common stockholders.

Q15-7 Briefly explain the dividend preference associated with preferred stock.

Q15-8 How does cumulative preferred stock differ from noncumulative preferred stock?

Q15-9 Are dividends in arrears on cumulative preferred stock a liability? Explain.

Q15-10 What is "callable preferred stock"? Why do corporations issue such stock?

Q15-11 Discuss the meaning of "legal capital."

Q15-12 Why is stock rarely issued below par value?

Q15-13 Discuss the impact of par value in determining the market price of a new stock issue.

Q15-14 Do changes in a stock's market value influence a company's financial position? Briefly discuss.

Q15-15 Briefly distinguish between total paid-in capital and total stockholders' equity.

Q15-16 When stock is issued in exchange for services or noncash assets, at what amount should the transaction be recorded?

Q15-17 Discuss the process of selling par-value stock on a subscription basis.

Q15-18 Define book value per share. Describe how book value per common share is calculated when a corporation has both common and preferred stock outstanding.

Q15-19 Integrity Machining's common stock has a book value per share of $20. Will the stock's market price be less than, equal to, or greater than $20 per share? Briefly discuss.

EXERCISES

E15-1 *Stockholders' equity concepts* (L.O. 1, 2, 3, 4)

Evaluate the comments that follow as being True or False. If the comment is false, briefly explain why.
a Corporations are subject to double taxation. Thus, a 40% tax rate on income becomes an effective tax rate of 80% to the corporation.
b Common stockholders are likely to be rewarded with increases in the market value of their shares as a corporation becomes more profitable.
c Most preferred stockholders are entitled to receive dividends that are cumulative in nature.
d Par value virtually always coincides with a stock's original issue price.
e Par-value stock is generally worth more than no-par stock.

E15-2 *Preferred stock dividends* (L.O. 3)

1-2-3

Johnson Brothers, Inc., has two classes of stock: $50 par-value, 12% cumulative preferred and $1 par-value common. One thousand shares of preferred and 80,000 shares of common stock have been outstanding since the beginning of 19X3. No dividends were in arrears at the beginning of 19X3.
a Complete the following table:

Year	Dividends Paid	Dividends in Arrears	Preferred Dividends	Common Dividends
19X3	$4,000	_____	_____	_____
19X4	6,500	_____	_____	_____
19X5	7,500	_____	_____	_____
19X6	9,000	_____	_____	_____

b Calculate the dividends that would have been paid to the common stockholders in 19X4 and 19X5 if the preferred stock had been noncumulative.

E15-3 *Issuance of stock* (L.O. 4)

Prepare journal entries to record the issuance of 100,000 shares of common stock at $20 per share for each of the following independent cases:
a Jackson Corporation has common stock with a par value of $1 per share.

b Royal Corporation has no-par common with a stated value of $5 per share.

c French Corporation has no-par common; no stated value has been assigned.

E15-4 *Issuance of stock; organization costs* **(L.O. 1, 4)**
The Snowbound Corporation was incorporated in July. The firm's charter authorized the sale of 200,000 shares of $10 par-value common stock. The following transactions occurred during the year:

July   1   Sold 45,000 shares of common stock to investors for $18 per share. Cash was collected and the shares were issued.

        7   Issued 600 shares to Sharon Dale, attorney-at-law, for services rendered during the corporation's organizational phase. Dale charged $12,600 for her work.

Aug. 11   Sold 20,000 shares to investors for $22 per share. Cash was collected and the shares were issued.

Dec. 14   Issued 30,000 shares to the MJB Company for land valued at $900,000.

Prepare journal entries to record each of the transactions.

E15-5 *Stock subscriptions; journal entries* **(L.O. 4)**
Investors recently subscribed to 5,000 shares of B&J Travel's $1 par-value common stock at $10 per share. During the year, the company received 80% of the balances due, which resulted in the issuance of 4,000 shares of stock.
a Prepare journal entries to record:
  (1) The subscriptions to investors.
  (2) The receipt of cash from subscribers.
  (3) The issuance of shares.
b Determine the year-end balance in the Common Stock Subscribed account.
c Determine the year-end balance in the Common Stock Subscriptions Receivable account.

E15-6 *Stock subscriptions; analysis* **(L.O. 4)**
During 19X1, investors subscribed to 5,000 shares of Gates Corporation $1 par-value common stock at $4 per share. The firm's December 31, 19X1, balance sheet revealed the following accounts:

Common stock subscriptions receivable $9,000
Common stock subscribed   2,600

a Present the journal entry recorded by Gates when the original subscriptions were made.
b Determine the amount of cash received from subscribers.
c Determine the number of subscribed shares issued by the company.

E15-7 *Analysis of stockholders' equity* **(L.O. 4, 5)**
Star Corporation issued both common and preferred stock during 19X6. The stockholders' equity sections of the company's balance sheets at the end of 19X6 and 19X5 follow.

	19X6	19X5
Preferred stock, $100 par value, 10%	$ 580,000	$ 500,000
Common stock, $10 par value	2,350,000	1,750,000
Paid-in capital in excess of par value		
Preferred	24,000	—
Common	4,620,000	3,600,000
Retained earnings	8,470,000	6,920,000
Total stockholders' equity	$16,044,000	$12,770,000

800 new shares issued

a Compute the number of preferred shares that were issued during 19X6.

b Calculate the average issue price of the common stock sold in 19X6.

c By what amount did the company's paid-in capital increase during 19X6?

d Did Star's total legal capital increase or decrease during 19X6? By what amount?

E15-8 *Preparation of stockholders' equity section* **(L.O. 5)**

The accounts and balances that follow were extracted from the adjusted trial balance of Grove Park Enterprises:

Common stock, $5 par value	$?
Paid-in capital in excess of par value: common	90,000
Common stock subscribed	6,000
Preferred stock, $2 par value	?
Paid-in capital in excess of par value: preferred	66,000
Retained earnings	74,000

A review of the corporate charter revealed that Grove Park was authorized to issue 100,000 shares of common stock and 80,000 shares of 10% cumulative preferred stock. The number of shares issued and outstanding were: common, 10,000; preferred, 15,000.

Prepare Grove Park's stockholders' equity section in good form.

E15-9 *Preparation of stockholders' equity section* **(L.O. 4, 5)**

The following data relate to LeMaster Corporation as of December 31, 19XX, the close of the current accounting period:

■ *Preferred stock*—The company has 1,000 shares of $50 par-value cumulative preferred stock authorized. The stock pays a 10% dividend; to date, 400 shares have been issued at $55 per share.

■ *Common stock*—A total of 25,000 shares of $1 stated-value common stock is authorized. To date, 10,000 shares have been issued at $10 per share, and an additional 3,000 shares have been subscribed to at $15 per share.

Assuming a retained earnings balance of $177,000, prepare the stockholders' equity section of LeMaster's December 31, 19XX, balance sheet.

E15-10 *Identification of errors* **(L.O. 1, 4, 5)**

Assume that a review of the accounting records of several different corporations disclosed the following:

■ *Corporation A*—Expenditures of $34,600 related to corporate start-up and formation were debited to Organization Expense and credited to Cash.

■ *Corporation B*—A 1,000-share issuance of $5 par-value preferred stock at $18 per share was recorded in the following manner:

Cash	18,000	
Preferred Stock		5,000
Gain on Stock Issuance		13,000

■ *Corporation C*—Cash and Common Stock were respectively debited and credited for the $25,000 proceeds from a 3,000-share issuance of no-par common stock.
■ *Corporation D*—The $100,000 proceeds from a 10,000-share issuance of $2 stated-value common stock were recorded as follows:

Cash	100,000	
Stated-Value Stock		100,000

■ *Corporation E*—The end-of-period balance sheet had the following captions under stockholders' equity: capital stock, paid-in capital, and retained earnings. All three subsections were combined to compute the total paid-in capital for the firm.

Briefly describe any errors that were made by these companies. *Note:* Corrected journal entries and financial statements are not required.

E15-11 *Book value per share* **(L.O. 6)**

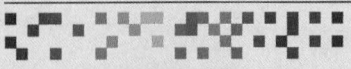

The Blackford Corporation had the following stockholders' equity for 19X2 and 19X1:

	19X2	19X1
Preferred stock, $100 par, 8% cumulative, callable at $105, 10,000 shares authorized, 3,000 shares outstanding	$ 300,000	$ —
Common stock, $1 par, 1,000,000 shares authorized, 600,000 shares outstanding	600,000	600,000
Additional paid-in capital		
Preferred	30,000	—
Common	14,400,000	14,400,000
Retained earnings	13,809,000	12,000,000
Total stockholders' equity	$29,139,000	$27,000,000

a Determine Blackford's book value per share for 19X1.
b Compute Blackford's book value per share of both the preferred and the common stock in 19X2. There are no dividends in arrears.

PROBLEMS

Series A

P15-A1 *Preferred stock dividends* **(L.O. 2, 3)**

Furlow Industries was organized at the beginning of 19X1. Information about the company's stock follows.

Preferred stock
    Class A—$50 par, 8% cumulative, 10,000 shares issued and outstanding

Class B—$10 par, 10% noncumulative, 6,000 shares issued and out-standing

Common stock—$5 par, 100,000 shares authorized, 80,000 issued and outstanding

Class A preferred has preference over class B, and both have preference over common.

No dividends were distributed in 19X1. Distributions in 19X2, 19X3, and 19X4 amounted to $55,000, $75,000, and $90,000, respectively.

Instructions

a Would Furlow have any dividends in arrears at the end of 19X1? If "yes," how would such amounts be treated in the financial statements?

b Determine the dividends distributed in 19X2, 19X3, and 19X4 to class A stockholders, class B stockholders, and common stockholders.

c Suppose Kenneth Sanchez is considering a purchase of Furlow's stock at the beginning of 19X5, primarily because of the accompanying dividend. What factor(s) should Sanchez consider in deciding whether to acquire class A stock, class B stock, or common stock?

P15-A2 *Issuance of stock* (L.O. 1, 4, 5)

Ventures, Inc., was formed on January 1 to invest in artwork. The company is authorized to issue 10,000 shares of $1 par-value common stock and 1,000 shares of 10%, $50 par-value cumulative preferred stock. The following selected transactions occurred during the first quarter of operation:

Jan. 3 Sold 5,000 shares of common stock to the corporation's founders at $30 per share.

19 Sold 600 shares of preferred stock at $58 per share.

Feb. 4 Issued 100 common shares to an attorney for $3,300 of legal work related to corporate start-up and formation.

11 Issued 2,000 shares of common stock to Pierre LaTour in exchange for a painting appraised at $75,000. The art originally cost LaTour $30,000.

Instructions

a Prepare journal entries to record the company's transactions.

b Prepare the stockholders' equity section of the firm's March 31 balance sheet. The Retained Earnings balance on this date totals $41,000.

c The president of Ventures believes that organization costs should be expensed immediately. Briefly explain why the president's view is incorrect.

P15-A3 *Preparation of stockholders' equity section* (L.O. 3, 4, 5)

Barney's corporate charter authorized the issuance of 100,000 shares of $100 par, 12%, cumulative, nonparticipating preferred stock and 1 million shares of no-par common. The board of directors has assigned a $5-per-share stated value to the common stock. Through December 31 of the current year, the firm has issued 25,000 of the preferred shares, generating $3 million cash. In addition, common shares were issued as follows:

■ Five hundred thousand shares were sold to investors at $8 per share.

■ Four hundred thousand shares were exchanged for buildings and equipment having a fair market value of $3.1 million and $450,000, respectively.

Dividends on the preferred stock were $150,000 in arrears at the beginning of the current year. Dividend distributions in the past 12 months have amounted to $500,000.

On December 17, Barney's finance department learned that one of the initial corporate investors had sold his entire holding of 3,900 common shares to Harold Lundgen for $22 per share. The investor originally paid $8 per share.

Instructions

Prepare Barney's stockholders' equity section as of December 31 of the current year along with any appropriate footnotes. Assume the Retained Earnings balance on this date totals $1,430,000.

P15-A4 *Stock subscriptions* (L.O. 4, 5)

Casey, Inc., was formed in January 19X3 when John Casey invested $1,000 for 100 shares of $2 par-value common stock. Shortly thereafter, the company received subscription agreements for 10,000 shares that totaled $150,000. Investors are required to pay 40% of amounts due at the time of subscription, with remaining balances due within one year. Casey is authorized to issue 100,000 shares of stock and issues shares to subscribers when full payment is received.

Instructions

a Prepare journal entries to record:
  (1) The issuance of stock to John Casey.
  (2) The subscription agreements from investors.
  (3) The initial receipts from subscribers.
b During 19X3, subscribers to 30% of the shares paid the remaining amounts due on their agreements. If all the shares were originally subscribed to at the same price:
  (1) Prepare the required journal entries for Casey, Inc.
  (2) Compute the balance in the Subscriptions Receivable account as of December 31, 19X3.
c Prepare the stockholders' equity section of the firm's December 31, 19X3, balance sheet. Retained earnings on this date amounted to $45,900.

P15-A5 *Analysis of stockholders' equity accounts* (L.O. 4, 5)

1-2-3

The following selected information relates to the Luoma Corporation:

Preferred stock, 11% cumulative, $7.50 par, 100,000 shares authorized, ? shares issued and outstanding	$ 600,000
Paid-in capital in excess of par: preferred	?
Common stock, $5 stated value, 700,000 shares authorized, 500,000 shares issued and outstanding	2,500,000
Paid-in capital in excess of stated value: common	7,500,000
Common stock subscribed (? shares)	11,000
Subscriptions receivable: common stock	?
Dividends payable	66,000
Retained earnings	?
Total stockholders' equity	12,072,000
Total legal capital	?

The preferred stock was issued at an average price per share of $7.90. The subscriptions occurred at a price of $21 per share. Subscribers made down payments of $36,000; to date, however, none of these shares have been issued.

Instructions

Determine the six unknowns of the Luoma Corporation. (*Hint:* Consider common stock subscribed as part of legal capital.)

P15-A6 *Book value per share* (L.O. 6)

The stockholders' equity section of Camping Haven, Inc., revealed the following information on January 1, 19XX:

Preferred stock, $100 par value, 10% cumulative, callable at $105	$ 200,000
Common stock, $2 par value	600,000
Paid-in capital in excess of par value: preferred	10,000
Paid-in capital in excess of par value: common	1,400,000
Retained earnings	990,000
Total stockholders' equity	$3,200,000

Dividends in arrears on the preferred stock totaled $20,000 at the beginning of 19XX.

Instructions

a Calculate the book value per share of both the preferred stock and the common stock on January 1.
b Calculate the book value per common share immediately after each of the following transactions and events. Consider each item independently.
   (1) An additional 20,000 shares of common stock were sold to the public at $10.70 per share.
   (2) The Retained Earnings account contained a balance of $1,055,000 on December 31, 19XX; preferred dividends totaling $15,000 had been paid during the year.
c Does book value per share indicate the amount that stockholders would receive if a corporation sold its assets, paid its bills, and liquidated? Explain.

Series B

P15-B1 *Preferred stock dividends* (L.O. 2, 3)

The information that follows pertains to Hendricks Corporation, which has three types of stock outstanding.

	Class A Preferred	Class B Preferred	Common
Shares outstanding	5,000	3,000	100,000
Par value	$10	$5	$1
Dividend information			
Fixed rate	4%	10%	
Cumulative?	Yes	No	

Class A preferred has preference over class B, and both have preference over common.

At the end of 19X2, Hendricks had $3,000 of dividends in arrears. Distributions in 19X3, 19X4, and 19X5 totaled $4,300, $3,500, and $5,800, respectively.

Instructions

a Class A and class B preferred stockholders have a preference over common stockholders in dividend distributions.
 (1) Explain what this comment means.
 (2) Is it possible for common stockholders to receive more dividends than preferred stockholders despite this preference? Briefly explain.
b Determine the dividends distributed in 19X3, 19X4, and 19X5 to class A stockholders, class B stockholders, and common stockholders.
c Where would the $3,000 arrearage be disclosed in the 19X2 financial statements?

P15-B2 *Issuance of stock* (L.O. 4, 5)
The bookkeeper of Porter Furniture prepared the following stockholders' equity section for inclusion in the December 31 balance sheet:

Preferred stock, $100 par, 10% cumulative, 2,500 shares authorized, 2,000 shares issued and outstanding	$200,000
Common stock, $5 par, 50,000 shares authorized, 20,000 shares issued and outstanding	100,000
Additional paid-in capital	
Preferred	30,000
Common	160,000
Retained earnings	45,000
Total stockholders' equity	$535,000

Both the preferred and common stock issuances occurred on February 2 of the current year and are reflected in the bookkeeper's figures. Unfortunately, though, two transactions were overlooked:

Feb. 19   The company issued 500 shares of common stock to its attorney for $7,500 of legal work related to corporate formation.
Aug. 23   Porter issued 100 shares of preferred stock to the Atlantic Railway in exchange for a parcel of land appraised at $15,000. The land was carried on Atlantic's balance sheet at a cost of $7,000.

Instructions

a Prepare journal entries to record the transactions of February 2, February 19, and August 23.
b Prepare the corrected stockholders' equity section of the December 31 balance sheet in good form.
c Do you see any potential problems for the company if it wishes to have a sizable preferred stock issuance in the not-too-distant future? Briefly explain.

P15-B3 *Preparation of stockholders' equity section* (L.O. 3, 4, 5)
Gordon's corporate charter authorized the issuance of 5,000 shares of $100 par, 10%, cumulative, nonparticipating preferred stock and 100,000 shares of no-par common. The board of directors has assigned a $2-per-share stated value to the common stock. Through December 31 of the current year, the firm has issued 2,000 of the preferred shares, generating $206,000 cash. In addition, common shares were issued as follows:

■ Three thousand shares were sold to investors at $30 per share.
■ One thousand shares were exchanged for land and buildings having a fair market value of $20,000 and $28,000, respectively.

Dividends on the preferred stock were $22,000 in arrears at the beginning of the current year. Dividend distributions in the past 12 months have amounted to $67,500.

On December 6, Gordon's finance department learned that one of the initial investors in the corporation had sold his entire holding of 600 common shares to Vernon Lewis for $54 per share. The investor originally paid $30 per share.

Instructions

Prepare Gordon's stockholders' equity section as of December 31 of the current year along with any appropriate footnotes. Assume the Retained Earnings balance on this date totals $217,300.

P15-B4 *Stock subscriptions* (L.O. 4, 5)

Wesson, Inc., was formed in January 19X6 when Al Wesson invested $5,000 for 500 shares of $1 par-value common stock. Shortly thereafter, the company received subscription agreements for 30,000 shares that totaled $450,000. Investors are required to pay 30% of amounts due at the time of subscription, with remaining balances due within one year. Wesson is authorized to issue 75,000 shares of stock and issues shares to subscribers when full payment is received.

Instructions

a Prepare journal entries to record:
   (1) The issuance of stock to Al Wesson.
   (2) The subscription agreements from investors.
   (3) The initial receipts from subscribers.
b During 19X6, subscribers to 60% of the shares paid the remaining amounts due on their agreements. If all the shares were originally subscribed to at the same price:
   (1) Prepare the required journal entries for Wesson, Inc.
   (2) Compute the balance in the Common Stock Subscribed account as of December 31, 19X6.
c Prepare the stockholders' equity section of the firm's December 31, 19X6, balance sheet. Retained earnings on this date amounted to $35,400.

P15-B5 *Analysis of stockholders' equity accounts* (L.O. 4, 5)

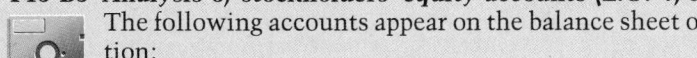

The following accounts appear on the balance sheet of the Austin Corporation:

Preferred stock, $5 par value	$105,000
Paid-in capital in excess of par value: preferred	189,000
Common stock, $10 par value	270,000
Paid-in capital in excess of par value: common	216,000
Common stock subscribed	3,500
Retained earnings	576,800
Notes payable	59,600
Subscriptions receivable: common stock	7,400

Instructions

a How many shares of preferred stock and common stock have been issued?
b What was the average issue price of the preferred stock?
c How many shares of common stock have been subscribed but not yet issued?

d How much remains to be paid on the common stock subscriptions?
e Compute the total amount of legal capital. *Note:* Consider common stock subscribed as part of legal capital.
f Compute the total paid-in capital.
g Compute the total stockholders' equity.

P15-B6 *Book value per share* (L.O. 6)
The stockholders' equity section of Quarry, Inc., revealed the following information on January 1, 19XX:

Preferred stock, $100 par value, 9% cumulative, callable at $108	$ 100,000
Common stock, $3 par value	300,000
Paid-in capital in excess of par value: preferred	12,000
Paid-in capital in excess of par value: common	1,200,000
Retained earnings	188,000
Total stockholders' equity	$1,800,000

Dividends in arrears on the preferred stock totaled $18,000 at the beginning of 19XX.

Instructions

a Calculate the book value per share of both the preferred stock and the common stock on January 1.
b Calculate the book value per common share immediately after each of the following transactions and events. Consider each item independently.
   (1) An additional 10,000 shares of common stock were sold to the public for $24 per share.
   (2) The Retained Earnings account contained a balance of $1,138,000 on December 31, 19XX; no preferred dividends had been paid during the year.
c Explain the meaning of book value per share to one of Quarry's stockholders. Assume the stockholder has a weak accounting background.

ELECTRONIC DATA BASE

SEC

EDB15-1 *Understanding corporate equity: Compaq Computer Corporation and Capital Cities/ABC, Inc.* (L.O. 1, 5)
Compaq Computer is a world leader in desk-top, portable, laptop, and notebook personal computers as well as PC systems. Capital Cities, in contrast, is actively involved in broadcasting (through its ABC television and radio networks) and the publishing of newspapers and magazines.

Instructions

By using the text's Electronic Data Base, access the balance sheets and accompanying notes of both firms and answer the questions that follow. Unless otherwise indicated, responses should be based on data for the most recent year presented.
a Review the balance sheets and determine:
   (1) The funds provided to the company from preferred stock issuances.
   (2) The par value of a share of common stock.
   (3) The number of common shares issued.

b Locate information in the financial statement notes relative to each firm's issuances of common stock.
  (1) Determine the swing in market value (from low to high) of a share of common stock during the year. What are some general factors that may have caused this swing?
  (2) How many stockholders does each company have?
c Many corporations have established stock option programs as a fringe benefit for certain personnel. Employees may exercise their options to purchase shares of stock in the firm or the options may lapse (i.e., expire) without being exercised.
  Locate each company's disclosure in the financial statement notes, and review the options exercised versus the options lapsed for the three years presented. Have there been any interesting "changes in attitude" over this period for employees of either corporation? If "yes," briefly discuss and include possible reasons for the change.

EDB15-2 *Understanding corporate equity* **(L.O. 1, 5)**

This problem is a duplication of Problem EDB15-1. It is based on two companies selected by your instructor.

Instructions

By using the text's Electronic Data Base, access the specified companies' balance sheets and accompanying notes and focus on data for the most recent year reported. Answer requirements (a)–(c) of Problem EDB15-1.

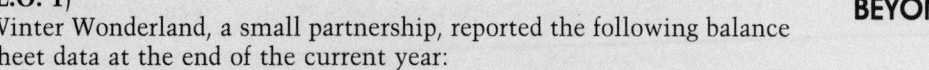

BB15-1 *Unlimited and limited liability; owner and creditor perspectives* **(L.O. 1)**

BEYOND THE BASICS

Winter Wonderland, a small partnership, reported the following balance sheet data at the end of the current year:

Assets		$80,000
Liabilities	$25,000	
Owners' equity	55,000	$80,000

Instructions

a Briefly discuss the meaning of unlimited liability from a partner's point of view.
b Assume that the partners plan to withdraw $54,500 of assets. What would be your reaction as a creditor if the firm was in serious financial difficulty and, prior to settling creditor obligations, expected to sell remaining assets for only 60% of book (carrying) value? Consider the unlimited liability characteristic in drafting your response.
c Briefly discuss the meaning of limited liability from a stockholder's point of view. Is limited liability an advantage or disadvantage of being a stockholder?
d Given the same facts as in part (b), namely, withdrawals of $54,500 and a 60% liquidation value, would your response as a creditor change if Winter Wonderland was a small, closely held corporation rather than a partnership? Explain.

BB15-2 *Overview of chapter concepts: Multiple choice* (L.O. 1-4, 6)

The following multiple-choice questions relate to various topics discussed in the chapter. Select the best answer.

1 Jim Hoover and his accountant recently met to discuss various business and accounting matters related to incorporation of Hoover Oil and Gas. Which of the following statements would not have been made by the accountant?

  a For control purposes, outside investors will likely buy shares of the new entity's preferred stock.

  b It will be necessary to obtain a charter to create the corporation.

  c The company's executive officers will be accountable to the board of directors.

  d It would probably be advantageous for the company if any preferred stock issuances are callable.

2 Rights of common stockholders generally include which of the following?

  a A return of par value in the event of corporate liquidation or bankruptcy.

  b The right to vote on important matters.

  c The right to convert the common shares into preferred stock or notes.

  d The right to dividends in every profitable year.

3 Rapid Corporation had 2,000 shares of cumulative 5%, $100 par-value preferred stock outstanding. Dividends in arrears at the start of 19X4 totaled $30,000. If $60,000 of dividends were paid in December 19X4, how would the company have divided the distribution between preferred and common shares?

  a Preferred, $30,000; common, $30,000.

  b Preferred, $40,000; common, $20,000.

  c Preferred, $10,000; common, $50,000.

  d Preferred, $60,000; common, $0.

4 Paid-in capital in excess of par value is ignored:

  a when computing total legal capital.

  b when computing total stockholders' equity.

  c when computing the amount that a corporation received from the original issuance of shares.

  d when dealing with preferred stock transactions.

5 Assume that 1,000 shares of stock are issued for $10 per share. What is the impact on total paid-in capital if the shares have (a) a $1 par value or (b) no par value?

	$1 Par	No Par Value
a	Increase by $1,000	Increase by $0
b	Increase by $1,000	Increase by $1,000
c	Increase by $0	Increase by $1,000
d	Increase by $10,000	Increase by $10,000

6 Meredith issued 1,000 shares of $1 par-value common in exchange for 10 acres of land. The land originally cost the seller $1,000 per acre and is estimated to be worth $5,000 per acre on the date of exchange. How much should be credited to Paid-in Capital in Excess of Par as a result of this stock issuance?

  a $0.   c $49,000.

  b $1,000.   d $50,000.

7 The balance in the Common Stock Subscribed account:
 a will always equal the balance in the Subscriptions Receivable account.
 b may be greater than or less than the balance in the Subscriptions Receivable account.
 c is typically disclosed in the current asset section of the balance sheet.
 d is deducted from the Common Stock account in the stockholders' equity section of the balance sheet.

8 The following information relates to King Corporation:

Preferred stock, 7% cumulative, $10 par, callable at $11 per share, 25,000 shares issued and outstanding	$250,000
Common stock, $1 par, 400,000 shares issued and outstanding	400,000
Paid-in capital in excess of par: preferred	100,000
Paid-in capital in excess of par: common	350,000
Retained earnings	250,000

If there are no dividends in arrears, the book value per common share (rounded to the nearest cent) would be:
 a $1.00. c $2.50.
 b $2.44. d $2.69.

CAI15-1 *Visual aid preparation: American Brands, Inc.* (L.O. 2, 3, 4)

COMMUNICATION OF ACCOUNTING INFORMATION

Communication Principle: Most modern business presentations include slides or overhead transparencies. These visual aids help gain the listener's attention, provide a sense of organization, and emphasize major points. Further, visual aids accompanied by handouts increase the likelihood that important points will be remembered.

The preparation of visual aids for an oral presentation is a special communication challenge. Every word should count and there should be very few of them. Handouts may simply be copies of the transparencies, unless more detailed written material is needed.

Here are some principles of good visual aids:

1 Keep visuals simple and short. Never crowd a transparency with too much information or too many words. A definition may be put in the form of an equation, for instance. Use phrases instead of sentences, and words instead of phrases wherever possible.
2 Include a list of no more than five major points, all of them brief and about the same length and importance.
3 Use legible, large type—much larger than normal typewriting or word processing. Do not create transparencies freehand. Nothing looks more unprofessional than sloppy, handmade transparencies.
4 Check spelling and math very carefully. These errors are glaring when enlarged and copied; they are very embarrassing.
5 Use color and different type styles for emphasis.
6 "Show" with exhibits, pictures, graphs, pie charts, and brief tables, instead of trying to "tell" exclusively in words.
7 Use a few good visual aids that support major points instead of many that support every point. Audiences groan when they see a hefty stack of transparencies or a full tray of slides.

■ ■ ■ ■ ■ ■ ■ ■

American Brands, Inc., is a highly diversified corporation, engaged in businesses that range in scope from tobacco production to life insurance. In addition, the company manufactures such recognizable goods as Master locks and Titleist golf balls, among others. The firm's balance sheet is rather involved, including a variety of stockholders' equity components. Among these are redeemable (callable) preferred stock of $130.1 million. The stock is without par value but has been assigned a $30.50 stated value. Further examination of the company's annual report indicates that holders of these shares are entitled to a $2.75 cumulative dividend. In addition, the holders have preference over common stockholders in the event of asset liquidation.

Instructions

You are employed in the company's public relations department. In an effort to address various questions that may arise at an upcoming meeting of the corporation's board of directors, management has asked you to prepare appropriate overhead transparency masters for a presentation. The transparency masters should briefly illustrate the nature of the callable preferred stock issue and disclose the following:

■ The reason stock "without par value" has been assigned a stated value.
■ The approximate number of shares in the hands of stockholders.
■ The nature of a cumulative dividend.
■ The preference feature should liquidation occur.

Answers to Chapter Quiz

1 a

2 d

3 a (6,000 shares × $5 per share)

4 c (Invested by stockholders: $100,000 + $200,000 + $10,000 + $95,000 = $405,000; Total stockholders' equity: $405,000 + $400,000 = $805,000)

5 c (10,000 shares × $115 = $1,150,000; $4,000,000 − $1,150,000 = $2,850,000; $2,850,000 ÷ 100,000 shares = $28.50)

CHAPTER

16

Corporations: Additional Equity Issues and Income Reporting

LEARNING OBJECTIVES

After studying this chapter, you should be able to:

1

Define treasury stock and account for its acquisition and reissuance.

2

Handle cash dividends, stock dividends, and stock splits in the accounting records.

3

Explain the proper treatment of prior period adjustments and restrictions that may be imposed on retained earnings.

4

Apply the disclosure rules for discontinued operations, extraordinary items, accounting changes, and intraperiod tax allocation.

5

Explain the meaning of and compute earnings per share.

In the preceding chapter we discussed various topics that pertain to the corporate form of business organization. The discussion included the advantages and disadvantages of this popular entity form, the computation of book value per share, and the proper accounting treatment for preferred and common stock issuances. This chapter continues our presentation of corporate equity. Specifically, we will focus on the reacquisition of stock by corporations, retained earnings, dividends and stock splits, and corporate reporting of income and earnings per share.

Much of the material contained within these pages is particularly important to present and potential investors—some of the key users of financial statements. Newspapers, for example, regularly publish articles with headlines similar to the following:

- General United's Earnings per Share Falls 15%
- Largent Corporation Has 3-for-2 Stock Split
- Garrett, Inc., Declares 10% Stock Dividend

The investing public must have a fundamental understanding of these events to correctly determine the impact on both corporate financial affairs and, more important, investment holdings. Although your present financial position may not permit "wheeling and dealing" in the stock market, the future often brings change. Our goal is to provide you with an introduction to the topics noted in the first paragraph so that some analysis of corporate equity and profitability is possible.

TREASURY STOCK

OBJECTIVE
1

Define treasury stock and account for its acquisition and reissuance.

Corporations frequently find it advantageous to reacquire shares of their own stock. These shares, which are commonly reissued at a later date, are termed **treasury stock.** Treasury stock is purchased for a variety of reasons. Some corporations have reacquired their own shares for use in company retirement and employee stock purchase programs. Other companies have purchased treasury stock to rid themselves of a particular stockholder or group of stockholders. For instance, large corporate entities sometimes purchase the interests of very small investors (e.g., those owning 10 shares or less) to save the costs of mailing annual reports, processing minute dividend checks, and so forth.[1] Treasury stock is also acquired for use in future acquisitions of other companies and to guard against hostile takeovers by other firms. Finally, some businesses have secured treasury holdings in an attempt to boost the *earnings per share of common stock*—a measure widely used to judge the operating success of an entity.

Whatever the purpose, the acquisition of treasury stock is commonplace. A review of recent annual reports disclosed the treasury stock holdings that appear in Exhibit 16-1.

Corporate action to purchase treasury stock reduces the number of shares outstanding; however, the number of shares issued is unaffected. Issued shares can be reduced only if they are formally retired and canceled by the corporation. Because treasury stock is no longer outstanding, it is

---

[1] Kmart extended such an offer not too long ago, using 100 shares as the cutoff point. Approximately 13,200 stockholders took advantage of the proposal, and the discounter was able to buy back 366,285 shares.

EXHIBIT 16-1
Treasury Stock Holdings

Corporation	Number of Treasury Shares	Percentage of Total Shares Issued	Acquisition Cost of Treasury Shares
Alberto Culver	5,967,692	17.4%	$ 32,479,840
Bassett Furniture	1,894,944	19.8	51,551,707
H.J. Heinz	27,966,044	9.7	692,547,000
Liz Claiborne	2,986,737	3.4	83,116,000
Lotus Development	19,033,779	31.1	261,984,000

Note: All citations refer to common stock only.

not entitled to voting privileges nor to any cash dividends declared by the board of directors.

Acquisitions of Treasury Stock

The most common treatment for treasury stock acquisitions requires a debit to a Treasury Stock account. Thus, if Hunt Corporation purchased 5,000 shares of its $10 par-value common stock at $70 per share, the journal entry would be as follows:

Treasury Stock	350,000	
Cash		350,000
To record the purchase of 5,000 shares of treasury stock at $70 per share		

Treasury stock is *not* regarded as an asset, since a corporation cannot own part of itself. The acquisition of treasury stock really involves a reduction in stockholders' equity because funds are being returned to the selling stockholders. To illustrate, assume Hunt had authorization to issue 15,000 shares of $10 par-value common stock. Further, assume that all of the shares were issued at $90 per share and that retained earnings amounts to $440,000. After the acquisition of the 5,000 treasury shares, the firm's stockholders' equity section would appear as follows:

Stockholders' Equity	
Common stock, $10 par value, 15,000 shares authorized and issued, 10,000 shares outstanding	$ 150,000
Paid-in capital in excess of par value	1,200,000
Total paid-in capital	$1,350,000
Retained earnings	440,000
	$1,790,000
Deduct: Treasury stock (5,000 shares) at cost	350,000
Total stockholders' equity	$1,440,000

Observe that the Common Stock and Paid-in Capital in Excess of Par Value accounts are not reduced by the treasury stock purchase. However, the cost of the 5,000 shares is deducted later in the stockholders' equity section. Finally, note that the number of shares issued and the number outstanding now differ because of the shares held "in the treasury."

Reissuance of Treasury Stock

At the time of reissuance, the Treasury Stock account is credited for the acquisition cost of the reissued shares. If the reissue price exceeds the acquisition cost, the difference is recorded as additional paid-in capital. For example, assume Hunt now sells 1,000 of the treasury shares for $79 per share. The necessary journal entry follows.

Cash	79,000	
Treasury Stock		70,000
Paid-in Capital from Treasury Stock		9,000
To record sale of 1,000 shares of treasury stock at $79 per share		

The $70,000 credit to the Treasury Stock account is based on the $70-per-share acquisition cost. It is important to note that the $9,000 excess over cost is not a gain to be reported on the income statement. As shown throughout the text, gains and losses arise from the sale of goods and services and from other earnings activities. Conversely, transactions that involve the issuance (or reissuance) of capital stock are equity transactions and affect paid-in capital. In Hunt's case, investors were willing to pay $79,000 for shares that had an original acquisition cost of $70,000; thus, paid-in capital must increase by $9,000. The increase is recorded in a separate account entitled Paid-in Capital from Treasury Stock.

The stockholders' equity section immediately after the reissuance would appear as follows:

Stockholders' Equity		
Capital stock		
Common stock, $10 par value, 15,000 shares authorized and issued, 11,000 shares outstanding		$ 150,000
Additional paid-in capital		
Paid-in capital in excess of par value	$1,200,000	
Paid-in capital from treasury stock	9,000	1,209,000
Total paid-in capital		$1,359,000
Retained earnings		440,000
		$1,799,000
Deduct: Treasury stock (4,000 shares) at cost		280,000
Total stockholders' equity		$1,519,000

Total stockholders' equity has increased by $79,000 ($1,519,000 versus $1,440,000), reflecting the amount of funds generated from the treasury stock sale.

Reissuance Below Cost

Treasury shares can also be reissued at or below cost. We will now illustrate the latter case because of the complexities involved. Just as reissuance above cost gave rise to additional paid-in capital, reissuance below cost calls for a reduction of paid-in capital. For example, assume Hunt sells an additional 2,000 treasury shares. This time, however, the selling price is only $66 per share. The journal entry to record the sale is:

Cash	132,000	
Paid-in Capital from Treasury Stock	8,000	
Treasury Stock		140,000
To record sale of 2,000 shares of treasury stock at $66 per share		

As before, Treasury Stock is credited for the cost of the reissued shares, in this case $140,000 (2,000 shares × $70). Because the sale has generated proceeds of only $132,000, paid-in capital must be reduced by $8,000 ($140,000 − $132,000). In effect, the reduction is a cancellation of paid-in capital from earlier treasury stock sales, thereby requiring a debit to the Paid-in Capital from Treasury Stock account for $8,000.

If this account's balance is insufficient to absorb the entire (or any of the) reduction, the remaining debit is entered in the Retained Earnings account. To illustrate, if the 2,000 shares were sold for $128,000, paid-in capital should be reduced by $12,000 ($140,000 − $128,000). As shown in the stockholders' equity section from the previous illustration, however, Paid-in Capital from Treasury Stock has a balance of only $9,000. Consequently, the required journal entry would debit this account for $9,000 and charge the remaining $3,000 against Retained Earnings.

RETAINED EARNINGS

We now turn our attention to the last major element of stockholders' equity: retained earnings. As defined in Chapter 15, **retained earnings** represents the portion of stockholders' equity that has been generated by profitable operations and kept in the business. At the conclusion of the reporting period, a corporation's net income is transferred to the Retained Earnings account as part of the closing process. More specifically, the following journal entry is needed (amount is assumed):

Income Summary	150,000	
Retained Earnings		150,000
To close net income to Retained Earnings		

Because of this treatment, the Retained Earnings account will normally possess a credit balance. On occasion, though, a debit ("negative") balance may arise, which is commonly referred to as a **deficit.** Deficits are usually caused when firms operate at a loss for a number of years or have a sizable loss in one period that wipes out years of profitability.

Dividends

A number of items affect the retained earnings balance throughout the year, including dividends. **Dividends** represent a distribution of corporate

OBJECTIVE

2

Handle cash dividends, stock dividends, and stock splits in the accounting records.

earnings to stockholders and may be in the form of cash, assets other than cash, or additional shares of stock.

Many corporate entities attempt to attract investors by establishing a consistent dividend policy. In contrast, numerous businesses pay no dividends or severely restrict distributions. Many of these latter firms are referred to as *growth companies* because they continually reinvest profits in expansionary projects to achieve even greater income levels. Investors in growth companies expect to realize a return on investment by selling their shares at a substantial gain.

Dividend Dates

Three important dates are connected with dividend distributions:

1 **Date of declaration**—All dividends must be declared (approved) by the board of directors. The declaration date is the date when the dividend is formally approved and the corporation becomes legally liable for payment.

2 **Date of record**—The stockholders of a corporate entity change constantly. To determine who will receive the dividend, the corporation establishes a record date. All stockholders as of the date of record are entitled to the declared dividend even if they dispose of their holdings prior to the dividend's distribution. As a result, stock sold between the record date and the date of distribution is sold without the current dividend rights attached, that is, *ex-dividend*. The record date follows the date of declaration by a few weeks, thereby allowing any stock transactions that may be in process to be completed.

3 **Date of payment**—As specified in the dividend declaration, the date of payment is the date when the dividend will be issued to the stockholders. Generally, the date of payment is several weeks after the record date.

Cash Dividends

Most dividends are paid in cash. To distribute a cash dividend, companies must satisfy two conditions. First, an entity must have an adequate cash balance. A lack of funds or an extremely tight cash position can force a corporation's board of directors to reduce or omit a payout. Such distribution decisions must be made with great care, however, because dividends are often a key element in an investor's expected return from holding stock. The market price of stock has been known to drop dramatically when a dividend declaration was less than anticipated.

The second condition for a dividend is an adequate balance in the Retained Earnings account. Given that dividends are distributions of earnings, total corporate profits must be sufficient to *support* amounts given to stockholders. Remember, though, that dividends are *paid* not with earnings, but with cash.

It is, of course, entirely possible for a company to be both profit-rich and cash-poor. As an example, consider recent data extracted from the financial statements of Hershey Foods, perhaps best known for its chocolate products. The company had an ending retained earnings balance of $1.2 billion and a cash balance of only $71 million. Although the firm has been profitable over the years and has generated sizable earnings, its cash balance would permit only a much smaller distribution of funds to stockholders.

Accounting for Cash Dividends.   To illustrate the necessary accounting for cash dividends, assume Dale Corporation has 100,000 shares of common stock outstanding. On July 15, the board of directors declared a $0.25 quarterly dividend to stockholders of record on August 7. The dividend will be distributed on September 1. The proper journal entries follow.

July	15	Retained Earnings	25,000
		Dividends Payable	25,000
		To record declaration of cash dividend of $0.25 per share	
Aug.	7	No entry required	
Sept.	1	Dividends Payable	25,000
		Cash	25,000
		To record payment of dividend declared on July 15	

Observe that the cash dividend is based on the number of shares outstanding. If Dale had originally issued 100,000 shares and then reacquired 10,000 as treasury stock, the board of directors would have declared a quarterly dividend of $22,500 (90,000 shares × $0.25). Should a balance sheet be prepared after the date of declaration but prior to the date of payment, Dividends Payable would be disclosed as a current liability.

Some corporations follow an alternative recording practice on the declaration date. Rather than reduce Retained Earnings directly, the debit is recorded in a temporary account called Dividends. The Dividends account is then closed to Retained Earnings at the end of the accounting period.

Stock Dividends

Many corporations distribute additional shares of their own stock as dividends. The distribution, referred to as a **stock dividend,** most frequently involves the issuance of common shares to existing common stockholders. Additional shares are issued in proportion to stockholders' present ownership in the firm. For example, suppose Ellen Bagley owns 20,000 shares of a cosmetics company that she founded several years ago. Assuming a total of 100,000 shares are outstanding, Bagley has a 20% ownership interest. If the board of directors declares a 10% stock dividend, an additional 10,000 shares (100,000 shares × 0.10) will be issued to stockholders. Bagley is entitled to 20% of the distribution, which results in the following figures:

	Before Stock Dividend	10% Stock Dividend	After Stock Dividend
Corporate shares	100,000	10,000	110,000
Ellen Bagley's shares	20,000	2,000	22,000
Ownership interest	20%	20%	20%

As you can see, a stockholder's percentage ownership remains the same. Furthermore, the corporation's assets and liabilities are unaffected because they are not involved in the distribution. Why, then, are stock dividends issued and what is the effect, if any, on corporate equity? The answers to these questions become apparent in the following sections.

Reasons for Issuing Stock Dividends. Several reasons have been advanced for the issuance of stock dividends. First, stock dividends enable a corporation to make a distribution to shareholders while, at the same time, conserving cash. The cash can then be invested in expanding operations, new projects, and other similar undertakings.

Second, stock dividends result in a nontaxable distribution to the stockholder. Cash dividends are taxable when received. Stock dividends, on the other hand, are not income and therefore no taxes are involved. Income taxes are often assessed, however, when and if the shares are sold.

Finally, stock dividends are said to improve a stock's attractiveness by decreasing the market value per share (to be discussed shortly) and expanding the ownership base. To explain the latter, stock dividends increase the number of shares outstanding. As investors sell all or part of their holdings, the number of stockholders is likely to grow.

Accounting for Stock Dividends. The accounting treatment for stock dividends depends on the size of the distribution. Most stock dividends are small, involving issuances of less than 20–25% of the existing shares outstanding. For small stock dividends the accounting profession recommends a reduction in retained earnings equal to the market value of the additional shares to be issued. Market value is used because stockholders view the dividend's "true worth" as being equivalent to the fair market value of the shares received.

As an example of the proper accounting, assume Mastercraft Corporation had the following stockholders' equity section on June 1:

Stockholders' Equity	
Common stock, $20 par value, 800,000 shares authorized, 300,000 shares issued and outstanding	$ 6,000,000
Paid-in capital in excess of par value	1,000,000
Retained earnings	12,000,000
Total stockholders' equity	$19,000,000

On June 15, the board of directors declared a 10% stock dividend that will be distributed on July 15. The closing market price of Mastercraft's common stock on June 15 was $33 per share, giving rise to the following journal entry:

June 15	Retained Earnings	990,000	
	Stock Dividend Distributable		600,000
	Paid-in Capital in Excess of Par Value		390,000
	To record declaration of 10% stock dividend		

The declaration involves the future issuance of 30,000 shares (300,000 shares × 0.10); thus, Retained Earnings must be debited for $990,000 (30,000 shares × $33). Next, an account entitled Stock Dividend Distributable is established for the par value of the dividend (30,000 shares × $20 = $600,000). This account is *not* a liability because Mastercraft has no obligation to distribute cash or any other asset. If a balance sheet is prepared between the declaration date and ultimate distribution of the shares, Stock Dividend Distributable would be presented in the stockholders' equity section as an addition to (i.e., a separate component of) the Common Stock account. Finally, consistent with the material presented in Chapter 15, the difference between the "issue price" ($990,000) and par value ($600,000) is credited to Paid-in Capital in Excess of Par Value.

The following entry is made on July 15 to record issuance of the common shares:

```
July 15   Stock Dividend Distributable          600,000
               Common Stock                                600,000
          To record issuance of stock dividend of
          30,000 shares
```

Stock Dividends and Corporate Equity.   The net effect of the stock dividend is to transfer $990,000 of retained earnings to Common Stock and other paid-in capital accounts. The accompanying schedule, constructed from the entries on June 15 and July 15, shows that total stockholders' equity remains unchanged.

Account	Before Stock Dividend	Declaration and Issuance*	After Stock Dividend
Common stock	$ 6,000,000	$ +600,000 (I)	$ 6,600,000
Paid-in capital in excess of par value	1,000,000	+390,000 (D)	1,390,000
Stock dividend distributable	—	{ +600,000 (D) −600,000 (I)	—
Retained earnings	12,000,000	−990,000 (D)	11,010,000
	$19,000,000	$ —	$19,000,000

* D = declaration on June 15; I = issuance on July 15.

Overall, a stock dividend is merely a shifting of amounts within the stockholders' equity section. The end result is that (1) $990,000 of retained earnings is no longer available for future dividend distributions and (2) additional shares of common stock are outstanding.

Stock Dividends and Market Value.   Stock dividends usually affect the per-share market price of a corporation's stock. To illustrate, we will continue the previous example. Observe that the total fair market value of Mastercraft's common shares on the date of declaration amounted to $9.9 million (300,000 shares × $33). Since an additional 30,000 shares will soon be outstanding, the unit market price should drop to $30 ($9,900,000 ÷ 330,000 shares). However, as noted in the previous chapter, a stock's market price is dependent on a variety of factors. Thus, when a stock dividend is very small, there is a strong likelihood that other market influences could obscure the decrease in price.

Large stock dividends, namely, those in excess of 20–25%, are a different matter. Because of a substantial increase in the number of shares outstanding, the market price per share will drop significantly. For example, if a firm doubles the outstanding shares by a 100% stock dividend, the market price should fall by about 50%. Large stock dividends are therefore afforded different accounting treatment from that of small stock dividends. Rather than value the distribution at fair market value, the Retained Earnings account is debited for the par or stated value of the dividend, with a corresponding credit to Stock Dividend Distributable. This treatment is a logical outgrowth of accounting for stock splits, the next topic for discussion. As we will now see, large stock dividends are similar to stock splits.

Stock Splits

Most publicly held corporations are interested in maintaining the marketability of their stock. Frequently, when a share's market price rises substantially, many small investors look for other investment alternatives. Stated simply, investors prefer to purchase round lots of stock (i.e., 100-share multiples) to take advantage of lower commission rates from brokers. Because a round lot of a high-priced stock is beyond the reach of individuals with limited funds, corporations often attempt to reduce the market price per share.

One way to accomplish a reduction in market price is to issue a large stock dividend; another way is a stock split. A **stock split** involves increasing the number of shares outstanding and, at the same time, reducing the stock's par or stated value per share. For example, assume a corporation has 200,000 shares of $10 par-value stock outstanding, which is currently selling for $80 per share. The company wants to reduce the market price to $20 per share and, accordingly, the board of directors approves a 4-for-1 stock split.

This action results in a reduction of par value from $10 to $2.50 ($10 ÷ 4) and an increase in the number of outstanding shares from 200,000 to 800,000 (200,000 × 4). Total corporate equity thus remains unchanged. A stockholder who owned 200 shares prior to the split will possess 800 shares after the split. Observe that the stockholder is no better off, since the total market value of his or her shares remains at $16,000: (200 shares × $80) versus (800 shares × $20). The stockholder's position is improved only if the market value of the stock later increases.

Because a stock split does not change the balance in any of the corporation's accounts, no formal entry is required. However, a memorandum should be recorded in the journal to note that a stock split has occurred. The memorandum should reveal that (1) the number of shares issued and outstanding has increased and (2) the par or stated value per share has been reduced. The accounting treatment for stock splits therefore differs from that of large stock dividends, the latter of which requires a dollar transfer from Retained Earnings to the capital stock accounts. The reason for the differing treatments is that although both splits and dividends increase the number of shares, stock dividends do not affect a share's par or stated value. An entry is therefore needed to record the increased amount of legal capital caused by the distribution.

Other Items That Affect Retained Earnings

Although our presentation has concentrated on dividends, other items affect retained earnings as well. As we noted earlier in the chapter, for example, the reissuance of treasury stock at a price below cost may give rise to a reduction in retained earnings. Retained earnings are also influenced by prior period adjustments and restrictions.

Prior Period Adjustments

Accountants, like other professionals, are not perfect. Even with a strong system of internal control, significant errors sometimes enter the financial records. Most are detected soon after occurrence; some, however, may go unnoticed for several years. Examples of such errors include mathematical mistakes, oversights, and the use of unacceptable principles and methods.

Errors that affect the net income of previous periods are corrected by the use of **prior period adjustments.** To illustrate the proper accounting treatment, assume Mercer Corporation overlooked several pieces of equipment in 19X1 and thereby understated depreciation expense by $10,000. If the error is not discovered until a subsequent reporting period, say, 19X2, the prior period adjustment to correct the records would be as follows:

Retained Earnings	10,000	
Accumulated Depreciation: Equipment		10,000
To correct the 19X1 understatement of depreciation expense		

Correcting 19X1 depreciation expense directly is not possible because the year's revenue and expense accounts have been closed. The understated expense overstated net income, which in turn overstated the balance in the Retained Earnings account at the end of the period. Retained Earnings is therefore debited to record the necessary reduction.

Prior period adjustments are reported as an adjustment to the beginning retained earnings balance in the year that the correction is made—19X2 in Mercer's case. The adjustment is shown on a net-of-tax basis and is disclosed on the statement of retained earnings. (Both net-of-tax reporting and the appropriate method of disclosure will be discussed shortly.)

OBJECTIVE

3

Explain the proper treatment of prior period adjustments and restrictions that may be imposed on retained earnings.

Restrictions on Retained Earnings

Corporate business dealings often restrict the amount of retained earnings available for dividend distributions. Some of these restrictions arise from provisions that are contained in debt agreements. The provisions help to protect the lender until the debt is settled. In other cases state law may be a factor, as many states require restrictions on retained earnings equal to the cost of any treasury stock held by the entity. Still other restrictions may be self-imposed. For example, the board of directors may change a company's dividend policy because of needed plant expansion or a probable loss of assets from an impending lawsuit.

Although several different methods are available to handle such restrictions, the most popular approach is to use a note to the financial statements. A typical disclosure would appear as follows:

Note 11: Retained earnings restrictions
   The Company has a retained earnings balance of $356 million as of December 31, 19X6. Under the most restrictive terms of existing borrowing agreements, amounts free for use in dividend distributions total $125.9 million at the end of the current year.

Reporting Changes in Retained Earnings

Changes in the Retained Earnings account are often disclosed on a separate financial report known as the **statement of retained earnings.** A representative example appears in Exhibit 16-2.

EXHIBIT 16-2
Statement of Retained Earnings

DONLEY CORPORATION Statement of Retained Earnings For the Year Ended December 31, 19X2		
Retained earnings, 12/31/X1 (as reported)		$ 80,000
Less: Correction of prior period inventory error (net of $6,000 tax)		9,000
Retained earnings, 12/31/X1 (restated)		$ 71,000
Add: Net income		100,000
		$171,000
Less: Cash dividends on preferred stock	$15,000	
Stock dividends on common stock	45,000	60,000
Retained earnings, 12/31/X2		$111,000

Several other options are available to corporations to report this information. For instance, some companies construct a combined statement of income and retained earnings, thereby doing away with a separately prepared income statement. Yet another approach, and one that appears to be gaining in popularity, is the use of a comprehensive **statement of stockholders' equity.** This report discloses changes that occurred during the period in each of the stockholders' equity components (including retained earnings). The statement reveals beginning balances and summarizes the transactions and events that affected the various accounts. Ending account balances are reported, and these amounts correspond to the amounts presented on the balance sheet.

Exhibit 16-3 contains a statement of stockholders' equity for Donley Corporation. All numbers in this illustration are assumed except for those in the Retained Earnings column. Careful examination of this shaded column will indicate that the data reported are identical to those shown in the "stand-alone" statement in Exhibit 16-2.

CORPORATE INCOME REPORTING

Investors are extremely interested in the periodic net income earned by corporations. Net income provides the basis for dividend distributions and greatly influences the market price of a corporation's common stock. Because of these factors, the income statement must provide adequate disclosure of earnings activities and be constructed in a format that is informative for investors and other users.

To achieve these goals, the accounting profession has stipulated that ordinary business income should be segregated from income caused by unusual and uncommon transactions and events. Why? Imagine the difficulty in evaluating corporate earnings if ordinary business transactions—such as buying and selling merchandise, renting equipment, and paying wages—were mixed together with the results of major catastrophes and other nonrecurring events. A high or low net income figure could be interpreted as being typical, even though it was caused by one-time and unusual happenings.

DONLEY CORPORATION Statement of Stockholders' Equity For the Year Ended December 31, 19X2						
	Preferred Stock, $10 Par Value	Common Stock, $5 Par Value	Paid-in Capital in Excess of Par Value	Retained Earnings	Treasury Stock	Total
Balance, 12/31/X1	$150,000	$50,000	$110,000	$ 80,000	$(16,000)	$374,000
Prior period adjustment (net of $6,000 tax)				(9,000)		(9,000)
Issued 5,000 shares of common at $30		25,000	125,000			150,000
Purchased 2,000 shares of treasury stock at $22					(44,000)	(44,000)
Net income				100,000		100,000
Cash dividends:						
Preferred				(15,000)		(15,000)
Common				(45,000)		(45,000)
Balance, 12/31/X2	$150,000	$75,000	$235,000	$111,000	$(60,000)	$511,000

EXHIBIT 16-3
Statement of Stockholders'
Equity

Current accounting practice dictates separate disclosure for the results of continuing operations (a very useful figure for prediction of future earnings), followed by the results of discontinued operations, extraordinary items, and the financial effects of changes in accounting principle. Because of their unique nature, we will now explore the latter three topical areas.

Discontinued Operations

Many corporations are involved in diverse types of business activities. Consider Loews Corporation, for instance, which is involved with insurance (CNA Financial), tobacco products (Lorillard, Inc.), hotels, watches (Bulova), and oil drilling. It is apparent that Loews, like many other entities, conducts operations in several distinct business segments. A **segment** is defined as a component of a company whose activities represent a major line of business or class of customer.[2] Normally, the assets and operating results of a given segment are clearly distinguishable from the other assets and operations of the firm.

OBJECTIVE

4

Apply the disclosure rules for discontinued operations, extraordinary items, accounting changes, and intraperiod tax allocation.

---

[2] "Reporting the Results of Operations," *Opinions of the Accounting Principles Board No. 30* (New York: American Institute of Certified Public Accountants, 1973), paragraph 13.

ETHICS ISSUE

Your client, a fast-food operator, sold three marginal restaurants and wants to report the transaction under "discontinued operations." You disagree and promptly get fired. If the client then gives you one day to reconsider your position, what would you do?

Often, after an in-depth review of corporate activity and profitability, an entity will decide to dispose of one or more of its segments. A disposal usually results from inadequate earnings or disappointing expectations about the segment's future. Sometimes, however, a segment is sold not because its financial performance has been weak but because the company desires to concentrate in other activities.

When a segment is sold, abandoned, or otherwise disposed of, its operations are said to be **discontinued.** The results of discontinued operations are disclosed in a separate category on the income statement immediately after income from continuing operations. Specifically, the operating results of the disposed segment (i.e., revenues minus cost of goods sold and expenses) along with any gain or loss on the disposal must be shown net-of-tax.

To illustrate the proper accounting treatment, we will focus on Quality Products, Inc., a company that produces bakery goods and soft drinks. In addition, the firm operates a chain of movie theaters and golf courses throughout the country. Recently, in a downsizing effort, Quality sold its beverage segment (Hi-Pro Fruit Drinks) and generated a substantial profit on the transaction. A condensed income statement is presented in Exhibit 16-4.

As you can see by analyzing the data, the disposed segment significantly boosted Quality's "bottom-line" earnings. Note also that the bulk of the increase came from the sale of assets and facilities, not from Hi-Pro's daily activities. It should now be apparent that separate disclosure of discontinued operations helps financial statement users better assess the future of an entity's ongoing business affairs.

EXHIBIT 16-4
Disclosure of Discontinued Operations

QUALITY PRODUCTS, INC. Income Statement For the Year Ended December 31, 19X2		
Sales		$920,000
Cost of goods sold		640,000
Gross profit		$280,000
Operating expenses		170,000
Income from continuing operations before tax		$110,000
Income tax on continuing operations		35,000
Income from continuing operations		$ 65,000
Discontinued operations		
Income from discontinued operations, net-of-tax	$ 1,500	
Gain on disposal of Hi-Pro Division, net-of-tax	35,500	37,000
Net income		$102,000

Extraordinary Items

Corporate income statements disclose earnings from all types of business endeavors. Occasionally, sizable gains and losses arise from transactions and events that are clearly different from the usual affairs of the firm. Such occurrences, known as **extraordinary items,** are afforded special accounting treatment.

To achieve uniformity in reporting, the accounting profession has stipulated that extraordinary items must be *unusual in nature* and *occur infrequently*.[3] Note that *both* criteria must be satisfied. A transaction or event is considered unusual if it has a high degree of abnormality and is unrelated to the ordinary and typical activities of the entity. To judge whether the "unusual" criterion is met, one must consider a company's scope of operation, lines of business, operating policies, geographical location of facilities and activities, and extent of governmental regulation. The second test, that of "infrequency," is satisfied when a transaction or event is not reasonably expected to recur in the foreseeable future.

Applying the Guidelines

Happenings that meet the two criteria (and that give rise to extraordinary gains and losses) are rare. Examples *may* include major casualties such as earthquakes, floods, and hurricanes; a seizure of assets by a foreign government; and newly enacted laws and regulations. From a practical point of view, it is difficult to generalize whether a particular event is always extraordinary. As the following illustration shows, each case must be evaluated on its own merits.

Suppose a business is located in a low-lying area that is prone to flooding once every four or five years. If a heavy rainstorm and its flood waters cause considerable damage to the firm's inventory, the loss is not considered extraordinary because it fails the infrequency-of-occurrence criterion. That is, on the basis of past history, another flood will probably occur in the foreseeable future. Changing the example slightly, suppose the flood loss is caused by a dam that breaks in a nearby valley. The break is highly unusual and, once repaired, is not likely to happen again. Because both tests are met, this flood loss is labeled extraordinary.

As another example, this one from real life, we cite recent disclosures of Carter Hawley Hale Stores, Inc. The company's Emporium division, which operates 22 department stores in and around San Francisco, suffered extensive damage from the major earthquake that affected that area in October 1989. Eleven of the firm's facilities were closed for short periods of time, and one remained closed until August 1990. Interestingly, losses incurred in excess of insurance reimbursements were classified as extraordinary even though the northern California area is prone to tremors. Management followed this reporting procedure because of the disaster's *magnitude,* which it claimed satisfied both guidelines.

The following specific items are not considered extraordinary by the accounting profession:[4]

---

[3] Ibid., paragraph 20.
[4] Ibid., paragraph 23.

1 Write-down or write-off of receivables, inventories, and intangible assets.

2 Gains and losses from the sale or abandonment of property, plant, and equipment used in a business.

3 Effects of a strike, including those against competitors and major suppliers.

Such items, if material, are normally presented among nonoperating (other) revenues and expenses.

Disclosure of Extraordinary Items

Extraordinary items are disclosed in a separate section of the income statement immediately following discontinued operations. If a company has no discontinued operations, extraordinary items are presented after earnings from continuing activities. Again, a net-of-tax amount must be shown.

Changes in Accounting Principle

Recall that accountants follow the consistency principle when preparing financial statements. Consistency requires that the same valuation methods be employed from one period to the next. Occasionally, a company may decide an alternative reporting practice is more appropriate than the method currently in use. For example, in view of changing business conditions, an entity may now find an accelerated depreciation method (e.g., double-declining balance) to be preferable to the straight-line approach, or the weighted-average inventory valuation technique to be more proper than FIFO. The preceding examples illustrate a **change in accounting principle,** namely, a switch from one generally accepted accounting principle to another. To prevent the comparability of financial statements from deteriorating over time, such changes should be made infrequently and only when the newly implemented practice will result in improved financial reporting.

When a company changes its reporting methods and practices, it must compute the cumulative effect of such changes. The **cumulative effect** is the difference between the total net income reported in prior years and the income that would have been reported over the same period had the new practice been in use. For example, assume that Addison Corporation has decided to switch depreciation methods, from straight-line to double-declining balance. A review of the accounting records reveals that total aftertax income would have been $50,000 lower had the accelerated method been employed in earlier years. The $50,000 figure (i.e., the cumulative effect of the change in accounting principle) is reported on the income statement of the period of change as a reduction in earnings. The reduction is presented at the bottom of the statement, after any discontinued operations and extraordinary items, and is labeled as follows: "Cumulative effect on prior years of a change in accounting principle, net-of-tax."

A corporation's annual report to shareholders normally includes financial statements from prior periods, thereby allowing the shareholder to perform various types of comparative studies. These statements typically *are not recast* to reflect the change in principle; however, additional supplemental disclosure is required to show recomputed amounts for selected items "as if" the new principle had been in use.[5] Details of this supplemental disclosure (and the accompanying note) are usually covered in advanced accounting courses.

EXECUTIVE BRIEFING
The Need for Separate Disclosure of Unusual Events

Thomas Plaskett
Former Chairman and Chief Executive Officer
Pan American World Airways, Inc.

Most business transactions and events are "normal and ongoing." Some, however, are not and deserve special treatment in the financial statements. Consider the unfortunate circumstances faced by our firm: Pan American World Airways. Despite our best planning and managerial skill, external events were so financially devastating that they eradicated months and years of progress. Such was the case with the terrorist bombing of flight 103 over Lockerbie, Scotland, in December of 1988. With continual reminders of the tragedy being broadcast and printed by the media, customers were reluctant to fly to Europe with us, or with other U.S. flag carriers.

We experienced an immediate and irreversible decline in passengers, and revenue was off by nearly 40% in the six months after the attack. Overall, the revenue loss was in excess of $400 million, and there was nothing we could have done to have prevented it. This disaster was followed shortly thereafter by the Gulf War and an even greater decline in revenues—in excess of 60% from the prior year. As a result, all of our financial flexibility and limited resources were wiped out. The rest, unfortunately, is history, as the company was eventually forced to file for bankruptcy.

Net-of-Tax Reporting

Examine the income statement of Bridgeport Corporation, which is presented in Exhibit 16-5. Observe how the statement is consistent with the special income reporting categories discussed earlier in the chapter. In addition, notice the treatment of Bridgeport's tax expense as it relates to these elements. The company is following a practice known as **intraperiod tax allocation,** which relates (i.e., matches) income taxes to the various elements that contribute to the firm's tax bill. Such items include continuing operations, discontinued operations, extraordinary items, changes in accounting principle, and prior period adjustments.[6]

---

[5]A few accounting changes have been pinpointed by the profession as requiring a restatement of the financial statements of prior periods.

[6] Prior period adjustments and the related tax impact are shown on the statement of retained earnings (or the statement of stockholders' equity). See Exhibits 16-2 and 16-3.

EXHIBIT 16-5
Intraperiod Tax Allocation and
Corporate Income Reporting

BRIDGEPORT CORPORATION
Income Statement
For the Year Ended December 31, 19XX

Sales			$2,000,000
Cost of goods sold			1,200,000
Gross profit			$ 800,000
Operating expenses			
Selling		$ 280,000	
Administrative		170,000	450,000
Income from operations			$ 350,000
① Other revenue (expense)			
Loss on sale of machinery			(50,000)
② Income from continuing operations before tax			$ 300,000
Income tax on continuing operations			120,000
Income from continuing operations			$ 180,000
③ Discontinued operations			
Earnings from Sunrise Division operations,			
less applicable taxes ($110,000 – $44,000)		$ 66,000	
Loss on disposal of Sunrise facilities, less			
tax savings ($250,000 – $100,000)		(150,000)	(84,000)
Income before extraordinary item			$ 96,000
④ Extraordinary item			
Flood loss, less tax savings ($60,000 – $24,000)			(36,000)
⑤ Cumulative effect on prior years of a change			
in accounting principle, less applicable			
taxes ($25,000 – $10,000)			15,000
Net income			$ 75,000

KEY

① *Other revenue (expense):* Beforetax gains, losses, revenues, and expenses that arise from transactions and events not directly related to ordinary business activities (see Chapter 5).

② *Income from continuing operations:* Net-of-tax reporting for the income generated from ongoing activities of the entity.

③ *Discontinued operations:* Net-of-tax reporting for a discontinued segment of the business. The segment's operating results and any gains or losses on the disposal of the segment are disclosed separately.

④ *Extraordinary items:* Net-of-tax reporting for gains/losses that arise from unusual and infrequent transactions and events.

⑤ *Cumulative effect of a change in accounting principle:* Net-of-tax reporting for the impact on prior years' income of a change in reporting practices.

To expand, a careful review of Bridgeport's disclosures will find the company is subject to a 40% income tax rate. Items that raise net income result in a 40% tax expense; items that reduce net income generate a 40% tax savings. From the information presented in Exhibit 16-5, Bridgeport's net tax expense totals $50,000:

Tax on continuing operations	$ 120,000
Tax on Sunrise Division operations	44,000
Tax savings on disposal of Sunrise facilities	(100,000)
Tax savings on flood loss	(24,000)
Tax on change in accounting principle	10,000
Net tax expense	$ 50,000

Without intraperiod allocation, the tax expense would appear as a single line item on the income statement, as shown below.

Income tax expense $50,000

Such a presentation is deficient, especially for the uninformed financial statement user. The presentation fails to show that the company had two significant tax-saving items during the period: the loss on the disposal of Sunrise facilities and the flood loss. Further, the $50,000 expense amount could be construed as being "typical," even though only one of the contributing factors (the continuing operations) is likely to recur in the future. Most accountants agree that intraperiod tax allocation results in improved disclosure, which is less apt to mislead statement readers.

Tips & Techniques

Students often have trouble remembering the proper sequence of disclosures on the bottom portion of a comprehensive income statement. The acronym O-DEC may help overcome the problem. *O* stands for *other revenue and expense,* which is really part of income from continuing operations. Thus, a hyphen separates it from the other three components. *D* represents *discontinued operations; E* stands for *extraordinary items;* and *C* symbolizes a *change in accounting principle.*

The income statement provides considerable insight into the profitability of corporate activities. Rather than take the time to study all of the statement's intricacies, investors frequently rely on a single computation called **earnings per share (EPS)** of common stock. Earnings per share is similar to the won-loss percentage of a sports club at the end of the season. Specifically, it represents a summary of all items that affect profitability. Earnings-per-share data are widely disseminated in the financial press and also are disclosed on the face of the income statement. No other ratio is afforded such prominence.

Earnings per share is often analyzed to assess future prospects for corporate income and dividends. If current earnings are favorable and the financial outlook is bright, investors are usually willing to pay a higher price to acquire shares of the corporation's common stock. Generally speaking, a higher EPS will result in a higher market price.

Because of the widespread use of the earnings-per-share measure, numerous computational and disclosure rules have been established to achieve

EARNINGS PER SHARE

OBJECTIVE

5

Explain the meaning of and compute earnings per share.

HIGHLIGHT
The Misleading "Bottom Line"

You have just received the news that a $100,000 inheritance will soon be coming your way. Now, what to do with the money? Given a fascination with the stock market, you have decided to acquire common shares of several well-known corporations. Your broker has provided information about recent net income (i.e., "bottom-line") figures, but has cautioned there's more to the figures than meets the eye. To what is the broker referring? In plain and simple terms, the "bottom line" is a mixture of results from normal recurring activities and those from unique, one-time events and transactions. Indeed, a closer look is needed to see just how a company is doing. Two recent cases in point: General Motors (GM) and Eastman Kodak.

Not too long ago, General Motors reported a third-quarter net loss of *2 billion,* compared with earnings of $517 million a year earlier. A real downer, you say. Not necessarily. A closer inspection showed that GM actually had a profit from operations of $109 million—a small sum for this firm but, nevertheless, a profit as opposed to a loss. What did the firm in was a special charge (i.e., write-off) of $2.1 billion to cover plant closings.

The charge covers the costs of closing at least 7 of the company's 38 assembly plants in the United States and Canada and of closing related parts factories as well, affecting more than 20,000 workers. (Many of these workers, however, will get up to three years' pay.) The auto maker, which eliminated 40,000 white-collar jobs, some 25% of its North American total, in 1987 and 1988, now plans to reduce its salaried work force by 25% by the middle of the decade. By the time the shutdowns end, GM estimates it will have cut roughly $1 billion from yearly operating costs.

In effect, GM has accepted a financial walloping to clear the way for greater profits in the future. The huge write-off, the chief financial officer notes, "covers all foreseeable circumstances," including plant closings that won't actually occur for two to three years. Adds the company's chairman, the fiscal surgery is "a major element in GM's long-term strategic plan to improve the competitiveness and profitability of its North American operations." [1]

Turning to Kodak, the corporation recently posted a quarterly net loss of $206 million—obviously bad news. However, the firm also posted a 22% rise in operating earnings as it continued to benefit from restructuring moves that began a year earlier. What happened to create this "bottom-line" misery? During the quarter a federal judge ordered Kodak to pay $909.5 million for infringing on patents held by Polaroid Corporation. The net loss reflected this charge, which was offset against operating profits of $835 million (up from $486 million one year earlier).

The Rochester, New York, concern had solid gains in its health and chemicals segments. Overall, the operating results were in line with analysts' expectations. These results mark the second consecutive quarter in which Kodak has seen improvements from a cost-cutting program that eliminated 7,500 jobs, or 5% of the firm's worldwide work force. [2]

These two examples clearly show that the "bottom line" may be somewhat misleading. This overall summary figure, which is often quoted in the financial press, can be likened to the kitchen sink. In other words, it contains a little bit of this and a little bit of that. Indeed, a closer look at the components is needed to get a better idea of where a company has been and where it is headed.

Authors' update: These companies again took large, "one-time" write-offs in late 1991.

Sources: Adapted from "Eastman Kodak Posts Net Loss for 3rd Quarter," *The Wall Street Journal,* November 1, 1990, p. A3 [2]; and "Huge GM Write-off Positions Auto Maker to Show New Growth," *The Wall Street Journal,* November 1, 1990, pp. A1, A6 [1]. The second article listed is reprinted by permission of *The Wall Street Journal,* © Dow Jones & Company, Inc., 1990. All rights reserved worldwide.

reporting uniformity.[7] Our discussion will concentrate on the basics only, because the specific rules are technical and complex. Like several other topics presented in this chapter, earnings per share is typically covered more thoroughly in an advanced accounting course.

Two preliminary steps are needed to figure the earnings per share of common stock: (1) determine the weighted-average number of shares outstanding and (2) compute the earnings available to common stockholders.

Weighted-Average Shares Outstanding

The computation of earnings per share begins with an assessment of the number of common shares outstanding. In some firms the number of common shares remains constant during the accounting period. For many corporations, however, outstanding shares will change because of new stock issues, the purchase of treasury stock, and other similar transactions. In these situations earnings per share is based on a weighted average. The weighted average is calculated by multiplying the number of common shares outstanding by the fraction of the year the shares are in the hands of stockholders.

To illustrate, assume that Briarwood Manufacturing had 60,000 common shares outstanding at the beginning of the year. On September 1, an additional 15,000 shares were issued. The weighted-average number of shares would be computed as follows:

Outstanding Shares		Fraction of Year Outstanding		Weighted Average
60,000	×	$\frac{8}{12}$	=	40,000
75,000	×	$\frac{4}{12}$	=	25,000
				65,000

The weighted average represents the number of equivalent shares that have been outstanding for the entire year. That is, the initial 60,000 shares were outstanding for 12 months. In contrast, the 15,000-share issuance has been outstanding for only 4 months, which is equivalent to 5,000 shares for the entire year ($15,000 \times \frac{4}{12} = 5,000$). Thus, Briarwood's weighted-average total is 65,000 (60,000 + 5,000). The weighting procedure is necessary because the capital provided by the new stock has helped generate earnings for only a fraction of the accounting period.

Earnings Available to Common Stockholders

Keep in mind that our goal is to derive the earnings per share of *common stock*. For corporations that have only common shares outstanding, all reported earnings are allocated to the common stockholders. If some preferred stock is outstanding, however, a different procedure is followed. Preferred stock is a *senior security*, so called because of its preferential

---

[7] See "Earnings Per Share," *Opinions of the Accounting Principles Board No. 15* (New York: American Institute of Certified Public Accountants, 1969).

treatment in dividend distributions and corporate liquidations. As a result, dividend claims of preferred stockholders must be deducted from net income to arrive at the earnings allocable to common shares.

For example, assume that Briarwood had issued 5,000 shares of $100 par-value, 10% preferred stock in addition to the common shares described earlier. If net income for the year amounted to $180,000, the earnings available to common stockholders would total $130,000:

Net income	$180,000
Less: Dividends on preferred stock (5,000 shares × $100 × 0.10)	50,000
Earnings available to common stockholders	$130,000

Earnings per share of common stock can now be computed as follows:

$$\text{Earnings Per Share} = \frac{\text{Earnings Available to Common Stockholders}}{\text{Weighted-Average Common Shares Outstanding}}$$

$$\text{EPS} = \frac{\$130,000}{65,000}$$

$$\text{EPS} = \$2.00$$

Primary Versus Fully Diluted Earnings Per Share

As we noted in the previous chapter, some preferred stocks are convertible into common shares. If these or other types of convertible securities are ultimately exchanged for common stock, the number of common shares will increase and earnings per share will be reduced (i.e., *diluted*). To inform common stockholders of the potential dilution, businesses must disclose additional EPS information. Specifically, corporations with potentially dilutive securities must report both **primary earnings per share** and **fully diluted earnings per share.**

Primary earnings per share is calculated by ignoring the dilutive effect of convertible securities.[8] Fully diluted EPS, on the other hand, is based on the *assumption* that all dilutive securities were converted into common shares at the beginning of the accounting period. If the securities were issued during the current reporting period, conversion is assumed as of the date of issuance. Note that the conversion is merely an assumption. The intention is to show how earnings per share would be affected *if* common stock was issued to satisfy all existing dilutive commitments.

To illustrate the required computations, we will continue the Briarwood Manufacturing example, with one modification. Assume that each of the firm's preferred shares is convertible into seven common shares at the option of the preferred stockholder. If we assume conversion at the beginning of the current period, then:

---

[8] If convertible securities (and others) meet certain tests, the securities are considered to be equivalent to common stock and enter into primary-earnings-per-share calculations. These tests are beyond the scope of this text and will be ignored.

■ No dividends would have been paid on the preferred stock.
■ An additional 35,000 shares of common stock (5,000 preferred shares ×
  7) would be outstanding.

Briarwood's required earnings-per-share calculations are as follows:

	Primary*	Fully Diluted
Net income	$180,000	$180,000
Less: Dividends on convertible preferred stock (5,000 shares × $100 × 0.10)	50,000	—
Earnings available to common stockholders	$130,000 ÷	$180,000 ÷
Weighted-average common shares outstanding		
For primary earnings per share	65,000	
For fully diluted earnings per share (65,000 shares + 35,000 shares from assumed conversion)		100,000
Earnings per share	$2.00	$1.80

* This is the same computation that appeared on page 640.

EPS Disclosure

The reporting of earnings per share normally parallels the information
shown on the income statement. Thus, if a corporation has discontinued
operations, extraordinary items, or a cumulative effect from a change in
accounting principle, per-share data for these elements are disclosed. Most
financial analysts feel that by presenting such disclosures, a clearer picture
of financial performance is made available for evaluation purposes. A sample presentation of per-share data for Midway Corporation, which has
100,000 weighted-average common shares outstanding and no potentially
dilutive securities, appears in Exhibit 16-6.

Income from continuing operations	$100,000
Income from discontinued operations (net-of-tax)	50,000
Income before extraordinary item	$150,000
Extraordinary loss (net-of-tax)	(10,000)
Net income	$140,000
Earnings per share	
Income from continuing operations	$ 1.00
Income from discontinued operations	0.50
Income before extraordinary item	$ 1.50
Extraordinary loss	(0.10)
Net income	$ 1.40

EXHIBIT 16-6
Disclosure of
Earnings-Per-Share Data

END-OF-CHAPTER REVIEW

LEARNING OBJECTIVES: THE KEY POINTS

1 Define treasury stock and account for its acquisition and reissuance. Shares of stock that have been reacquired by the issuing corporation are termed treasury stock. The shares' cost is charged to the Treasury Stock account at the time of acquisition, with the account's balance subsequently disclosed on the balance sheet as a reduction in stockholders' equity. Upon reissuance, the cost of shares sold is removed from the Treasury Stock account. Furthermore, any difference between the cost and proceeds per share is treated as either an addition to or a deduction from Paid-in Capital from Treasury Stock. In some cases, a charge against the Retained Earnings account may be necessary.

2 Handle cash dividends, stock dividends, and stock splits in the accounting records. Dividends represent a distribution by a corporation to its stockholders and may be in the form of cash, noncash assets, or additional shares of stock. Such distributions are declared by the board of directors and issued to stockholders who own shares as of the record date. The ultimate impact of cash and stock dividends is a reduction in the firm's retained earnings balance.

With stock dividends, Retained Earnings is debited for either the market value (in the case of small stock dividends) or the par or stated value (with large stock dividends) of the shares to be distributed. The impact of a stock dividend is to shift amounts from Retained Earnings to Capital Stock and Paid-in Capital accounts, thereby producing no increase or decrease in total stockholders' equity.

A stock split is used to reduce the market value per share. The underlying procedures involve increasing the number of shares outstanding and simultaneously decreasing the par or stated value. Total stockholders' equity remains unchanged, and no formal journal entry is required. A memo notation in the journal is appropriate.

3 Explain the proper treatment of prior period adjustments and restrictions that may be imposed on retained earnings. A prior period adjustment (i.e., a journal entry) corrects the Retained Earnings account for errors that affect the net income of previous accounting periods. Such items are reported as an adjustment to the retained earnings balance at the beginning of the year in which the correction is made.

Restrictions on retained earnings inform statement users that a portion of the retained earnings balance is unavailable for dividend declarations. Such restrictions, which may be voluntary, contractual, or imposed by state law, are generally handled by a note to the financial statements.

4 Apply the disclosure rules for discontinued operations, extraordinary items, accounting changes, and intraperiod tax allocation. Financial statement users are extremely interested in the net income generated by corporations. To help users assess future cash flows, the financial results of ordinary business activities are segregated from income that arises because of "unusual" transactions and events. Thus, the results from segments sold, abandoned, or otherwise disposed of during the year are separately disclosed as discontinued operations, after any income from continuing operations. In a similar fashion, gains and losses from occurrences that are both unusual and infrequent are labeled as extraordinary items and disclosed accordingly.

Another item that requires separate disclosure is a change in accounting principle, such as the change from one depreciation method to another. Such a shift requires presentation of the cumulative effect of the change, which is the difference between total net income of previous years and the income that would have been reported had the new practice been in use.

By following intraperiod tax allocation procedures, which relate income tax to the items that give rise to the tax, income from continuing operations and the preceding major income statement components, along with prior period adjustments, are shown on a net-of-tax basis.

5 Explain the meaning of and compute earnings per share. Earnings per share represents the per-share earnings available to common stockholders. In one of its simplest forms, earnings per share is calculated as net income, minus preferred dividends, divided by the weighted-average common shares outstanding. The computation of weighted-average shares involves multiplying the number of common shares outstanding by the fraction of the year the shares were in the hands of stockholders. Those corporations that have potentially dilutive securities, such as convertible preferred stock, must disclose two figures: primary earnings per share and fully diluted earnings per share.

**KEY TERMS
AND CONCEPTS:
A QUICK OVERVIEW**

cash dividend   A dividend that involves a distribution of cash and reduces retained earnings.

change in accounting principle   A change from one generally accepted accounting principle to another.

cumulative effect   The difference between the net income reported in prior years and the income that would have been reported using a new accounting principle.

date of declaration   The date when a dividend is formally declared (approved) by the board of directors.

date of payment   The date when a dividend will be distributed to stockholders.

date of record   The date used to determine the stockholders entitled to receive a declared dividend.

deficit   A debit (negative) balance in the Retained Earnings account.

discontinued operations   A segment of a business that is sold, abandoned, or otherwise disposed of.

dividends   A distribution of income by a corporation to its stockholders.

earnings per share (EPS)   A widely used profitability ratio; computed as earnings available to common stockholders (net income minus any preferred dividend requirements) divided by the weighted-average common shares outstanding.

extraordinary gains and losses   Gains and losses that are both unusual in character and infrequent in occurrence.

fully diluted earnings per share   A calculation of earnings per share based on the assumption that potentially dilutive securities were converted into common shares at the beginning of the accounting period.

intraperiod tax allocation   The practice of relating income tax expense to the items that give rise to the tax.

primary earnings per share   A calculation of earnings per share for firms with potential dilution. The calculation ignores the dilutive effect of convertible securities.

prior period adjustments   Corrections of errors that affect the net income of previous accounting periods.

restrictions on retained earnings   Restrictions that reduce the amount of retained earnings available for dividend distributions.

retained earnings   The portion of stockholders' equity that has been generated by profitable operations and retained in the business.

segment   A component of a company whose activities represent a major line of business or class of customer.

statement of retained earnings   A financial statement that discloses the changes in the Retained Earnings account during an accounting period.

statement of stockholders' equity   A financial statement that discloses the changes in all stockholders' equity accounts maintained by a business.

stock dividend   A dividend that involves a distribution of a company's own shares of stock.

stock split   An increase in the number of outstanding shares and an accompanying reduction of the stock's par or stated value per share.

treasury stock   Shares of stock reacquired by the issuing corporation.

CHAPTER QUIZ

The five questions that follow relate to several issues raised in the chapter. Test your knowledge of the issues by selecting the best answer. (The answers appear on p. 661.)

1 Which of the following statements about treasury stock is false?
  a The excess of the sales price of treasury stock over the stock's cost is considered paid-in capital.
  b When treasury stock is reissued at a price in excess of cost, "gains" occur that increase the Retained Earnings account.
  c When treasury stock is reissued at a price that is less than cost, the transaction may result in a reduction of the Retained Earnings account.
  d The acquisition of treasury stock causes stockholders' equity to decrease.

2 The declaration of a cash dividend on common stock:
  a decreases Retained Earnings.
  b increases Retained Earnings.
  c decreases total liabilities.
  d generally occurs shortly after the date of record.

3 Sampson Corporation declared a 4% stock dividend on 20,000 shares of $5 par-value common stock. The stock's market value on the date of declaration was $20 per share. What is the impact of the declaration-date journal entry on total stockholders' equity?
  a $4,000 increase.   c $16,000 decrease.
  b $4,000 decrease.   d No effect.

4 Extraordinary items:
  a are disclosed on the statement of retained earnings and statement of stockholders' equity.
  b are disclosed as part of income from continuing operations.
  c are unusual or infrequent in nature.
  d are unusual and infrequent in nature.

5 Earnings per share is determined by dividing the weighted-average number of common shares outstanding into:
  a net income.
  b net income minus preferred stock dividends.

c net income minus both preferred and common stock dividends.
d ending retained earnings.

Lisbon Corporation began 19X2 with the following stockholders' equity:

SUMMARY PROBLEM

Stockholders' Equity		
Preferred stock, $100 par value, 12% nonconvertible, cumulative, 1,000 shares authorized, 500 shares issued and outstanding	$50,000	
Common stock, $2 par value, 10,000 shares authorized, 7,000 shares issued and outstanding	14,000	$ 64,000
Additional paid-in capital		
Paid-in capital in excess of par: common		87,000
Total paid-in capital		$151,000
Retained earnings		99,000
Total stockholders' equity		$250,000

During 19X2, Lisbon had beforetax income from continuing operations of $100,000. A $30,000 uninsured fire loss occurred in March; the loss will be classified as extraordinary. A 40% income tax rate is in effect.

On July 1, the company purchased 2,000 shares of its own common stock at $30 per share. This treasury stock was later reissued on December 31 at $36 per share. No dividends were paid during the year on common shares; however, the preferred stock's regular dividend requirement was satisfied.

In October, Lisbon's accountant discovered that he had incorrectly calculated 19X1 depreciation expense by $7,000. This error resulted in a $4,200 aftertax overstatement of 19X1 net income.

Instructions

a Prepare the lower portion of Lisbon's 19X2 income statement, beginning with income from continuing operations before tax. Include primary-earnings-per-share data. *Hint:* In performing the EPS calculations, the company reduces income from continuing operations by the preferred dividend requirement.
b Prepare Lisbon's 19X2 statement of retained earnings.
c Prepare the stockholders' equity section of Lisbon's December 31, 19X2, balance sheet.

Solution

a Income from continuing operations before tax	$100,000
Income tax on continuing operations, 40%	40,000
Income from continuing operations	$ 60,000
Deduct: Extraordinary loss (net of $12,000 tax)	18,000
Net income	$ 42,000

Earnings per share*
   Income from continuing operations $ 9.00
   Extraordinary loss   (3.00)
   Net income $ 6.00

* Weighted-average common shares outstanding:

$$7,000 \times \tfrac{6}{12} = 3,500$$
$$5,000 \times \tfrac{6}{12} = 2,500$$
$$6,000$$

Earnings available to the common stockholders:

Income from continuing operations	$60,000
Less: Dividends on preferred stock (500 shares × $100 × 0.12)	6,000
Income from continuing operations available to common stockholders	$54,000

Income from continuing operations per share:

$$\frac{\$54,000}{6,000 \text{ shares}} = \$9.00 \text{ per share}$$

Extraordinary item per share:

$$\frac{\$18,000}{6,000 \text{ shares}} = \$3.00 \text{ per share}$$

b

LISBON CORPORATION
Statement of Retained Earnings
For the Year Ended December 31, 19X2

Retained earnings, 12/31/X1 (as reported)	$ 99,000
Less: Correction of prior period error (net of $2,800 tax*)	4,200
Retained earnings, 12/31/X1 (restated)	$ 94,800
Add: Net income	42,000
	$136,800
Less: Cash dividends on preferred stock	6,000
Retained earnings, 12/31/X2	$130,800

* $7,000 – $4,200.

c

Stockholders' Equity

Preferred stock, $100 par value, 12% nonconvertible, cumulative, 1,000 shares authorized, 500 shares issued and outstanding	$50,000	
Common stock, $2 par value, 10,000 shares authorized, 7,000 shares issued and outstanding	14,000	$ 64,000
Additional paid-in capital		
Paid-in capital in excess of par: common	$87,000	
Paid-in capital from treasury stock	12,000*	99,000
Total paid-in capital		$163,000
Retained earnings		130,800
Total stockholders' equity		$293,800

* 2,000 shares × ($36 − $30).

ASSIGNMENT MATERIAL

QUESTIONS

Q16-1 What is treasury stock? Why do corporations purchase treasury stock?

Q16-2 Should purchased treasury stock be disclosed as an asset? Why?

Q16-3 Explain how the Retained Earnings account can have a debit balance.

Q16-4 Does a corporation become legally liable for dividend distributions on the date of declaration or the date of record?

Q16-5 What two conditions must be satisfied to declare and distribute a cash dividend?

Q16-6 Discuss the effect of a stock dividend on (1) a stockholder's percentage ownership position and (2) total stockholders' equity of the issuing corporation.

Q16-7 Differentiate between a small and a large stock dividend. Are both of these dividends accounted for in the same manner? Explain.

Q16-8 Differentiate between a large stock dividend and a stock split.

Q16-9 What is a prior period adjustment? Explain the proper accounting and reporting treatment for prior period adjustments.

Q16-10 What is the purpose of a restriction on retained earnings? What are some possible causes of restrictions?

Q16-11 Explain the relationship, if any, between the statement of retained earnings and the statement of stockholders' equity.

Q16-12 Why should a corporation segregate ordinary business income from income caused by unusual and infrequent transactions and events?

Q16-13 How are the financial results of discontinued operations disclosed on the income statement?

Q16-14 What two criteria must be satisfied for an event or transaction to be classifed as an extraordinary item? Discuss each of the criteria and present three examples of possible extraordinary items.

Q16-15 Explain the proper treatment for a change in accounting principle.

Q16-16 Briefly discuss the practice of intraperiod tax allocation. Explain what the practice is and why it is used.

Q16-17 Why do stockholders closely monitor an entity's earnings per share?

Q16-18 Is the earnings-per-share calculation based on shares outstanding at the beginning of the year or the end of the year, or on a weighted average of the shares outstanding during the year?

Q16-19 Differentiate between primary and fully diluted earnings per share.

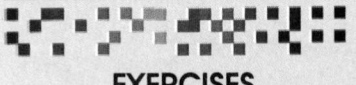

EXERCISES

E16-1 *Treasury stock transactions* (L.O. 1)
FedEx Corporation reacquired 20,000 shares of its common stock ($10 par value) on February 2 for $28 per share. These shares were subsequently sold as follows:

Apr. 9   6,000 shares at $35 per share
June 13   4,000 shares at $28 per share
Oct. 18   5,500 shares at $22 per share

Prepare all necessary journal entries for FedEx Corporation.

E16-2 *Dividends and stock splits* (L.O. 2)
Consider the following transactions and events of Companies X, Y, and Z:

- Company X—Declared a $20,000 cash dividend.
- Company Y—Declared a 10% stock dividend on 50,000 shares of $2 par-value common stock. Market value at the time of declaration was $8 per share.
- Company Z—Authorized a 3-for-1 stock split.

a Prepare journal entries, if needed, for Companies X, Y, and Z.
b Set up a chart as follows to show the effects of the transactions and events for the three firms. Use the notation: I = increase, D = decrease, and NE = no effect.

	Number of Shares Outstanding	Total Paid-in Capital	Retained Earnings	Total Stockholders' Equity
X				
Y				
Z				

E16-3 *Preparation of stockholders' equity section* (L.O. 1, 2)
MBM Corporation had the following equity accounts at the beginning of the year:

Common stock, $10 par	$200,000
Paid-in capital in excess of par value	100,000
Retained earnings	500,000
Total stockholders' equity	$800,000

The following events took place during the current year:

Feb. 24 Declared a $2 dividend per share.
May 10 Announced a 2-for-1 stock split.
Sept. 18 Declared and issued a 10% stock dividend; market value at
the time of declaration was $12 per share.
Dec. 30 Reacquired 500 shares of common (treasury) stock at $18 per
share.

Assuming net income of $92,000, prepare an updated stockholders' equity
section for MBM at the end of the year, after the accounting records have
been closed.

E16-4 *Statement of retained earnings* **(L.O. 2, 3)**
Cary Corporation had an ending retained earnings balance on December
31, 19X2, of $4.8 million. The following information pertains to 19X3:
a Cash dividends of $300,000 were declared and paid to common stock-
holders.
b A 3% stock dividend was declared and distributed on December 31. The
stock's fair market value at the time of declaration was $20 per share;
150,000 shares were outstanding.
c Income was $600,000 before tax.
d An error was discovered on March 17 that occurred in 19X1 and understated beforetax income of that year by $40,000.
e Cary is subject to a 40% income tax rate.

Prepare the corporation's 19X3 statement of retained earnings.

E16-5 *Statement of stockholders' equity* **(L.O. 2, 3)**
Fischer Corporation, a manufacturer of locks and security devices, began
19X4 with the following stockholders' equity balances:

Preferred stock, $50 par value	$200,000
Common stock, $2 par value	600,000
Paid-in capital in excess of par: common	450,000
Retained earnings	430,000

The following selected transactions and events occurred during the year:

■ Issued 5,000 shares of common stock for $70,000.
■ Declared and paid $12,000 of preferred dividends and $30,000 of com-
mon dividends.
■ Generated net income of $47,000.
■ Recorded a $24,000 prior period adjustment (net of $16,000 tax) related
to an overstatement of 19X2 net income.

Prepare Fischer Corporation's statement of stockholders' equity for the
year ended December 31, 19X4.

E16-6 *Corporate income reporting* **(L.O. 3, 4)**
Consider the five cases that follow.
1 Patrick's foreign assembly plant was heavily damaged during a violent
government takeover in a normally stable country. The company's insurance policy does not cover such losses.
2 United Corporation switched from straight-line depreciation to sum-of-
the-years'-digits depreciation for all assets currently in use.
3 AMV, Inc., sold a vacant tract of land next to the firm's warehouse and
generated a substantial gain. The company has other tracts of land, some
of which may be sold in the future.

4 Commerce, Inc., manufactures recreational and military vehicles. Recently, all military equipment facilities and assets were sold at a large loss.

5 Allstate discovered a mathematical error in 19X7 that related to the computation of 19X6 depreciation expense.

a Analyze the cases individually and determine which of the following reporting classifications is most appropriate: other revenue and expense, discontinued operations, change in accounting principle, extraordinary item, or prior period adjustment.

b Which of the cases would be disclosed on the income statement?

E16-7   *Discontinued operations* (L.O. 4)
The following information pertains to Stovall Corporation for the year ended December 31, 19XX:

Sales	$1,000,000
Cost of goods sold	600,000
Selling expenses	150,000
Administrative expenses	200,000

In 19XX, Stovall disposed of its retail division. The retail division generated 20% of the firm's total sales and accounted for 25% and 30% of total cost of goods sold and operating expenses, respectively. The division was sold at a beforetax gain of $25,000. Prepare Stovall's 19XX income statement, assuming a 40% tax rate.

E16-8   *Abbreviated income statement* (L.O. 2, 3, 4)
LBO, Inc., had income from operations of $180,000 for the year ended December 31, 19X5. A review of the accounting records disclosed the following:

Gain on sale of building	$60,000
Dividends	10,000
Extraordinary loss	40,000
Prior period adjustment from an understatement of advertising expense	25,000

LBO is subject to a 40% income tax rate.

a Which of the preceding items would not appear on the company's income statement? Where would these items be disclosed?

b Prepare an abbreviated income statement for LBO, beginning with income from operations. Use good form; disregard earnings-per-share data.

E16-9   *Equity issues and income reporting* (L.O. 1, 2, 3, 4)
Evaluate the comments that follow as being True or False. If the comment is false, briefly explain why.

a A purchase of treasury stock reduces the stockholders' equity of the acquiring company.

b A restriction on retained earnings reduces a company's total retained earnings balance.

c The issuance of a previously declared 3,000-share stock dividend causes a reduction in the Retained Earnings account.

d If certain criteria are met, extraordinary gains and losses may be disclosed on the statement of retained earnings.

e Gains and losses from discontinued operations should be disclosed on the income statement on a net-of-tax basis.

E16-10 *Weighted-average shares outstanding* (L.O. 5)
Autorama, Inc., began the year with 80,000 common shares outstanding. On April 1, 28,000 newly issued shares were sold to the public for $45 per share. On August 1, the company reacquired 6,000 shares (i.e., treasury stock), which were subsequently reissued two months later. Calculate the weighted-average shares outstanding during the year.

E16-11 *Primary and fully diluted earnings per share* (L.O. 5)
Truman, Inc., had the following stock outstanding throughout the year:

Common stock, $1 par, 500,000 shares	$ 500,000
8% preferred stock, $100 par, 10,000 shares	1,000,000

Each share of preferred is convertible into 30 shares of common stock. Net income for the year totaled $400,000.
a Compute primary earnings per share.
b Compute fully diluted earnings per share.

E16-12 *Corporate income reporting* (L.O. 5)
The following item appeared under the heading of Business Briefs in a recent edition of the *California Tribune:*

> **SEA BREEZE REPORTS 152% RISE IN EARNINGS PER SHARE**
> Los Angeles—David Anthony, chairman and chief executive officer of Sea Breeze, a nationwide retailer of swimwear, today announced a 152% rise in earnings per share. The company reported earnings per share of $2.90 for the year ended September 30, 19X2, which compares favorably with $1.15 per share for 19X1.

Assume that you attended the stockholders' meeting where the announcement was made. The data that follow were distributed to all attendees.

	Fiscal Year Ended	
	9/30/X2	9/30/X1
Earnings per common share		
Continuing retail operations	$ 2.84	$ 2.42
Discontinued operations	0.14	(1.27)
Extraordinary item	(0.08)	—
Net income	$ 2.90	$ 1.15

Evaluate the *Tribune's* reporting of Sea Breeze's earnings.

PROBLEMS

Series A

P16-A1 *Accounting for treasury stock, cash dividends, and stock splits* (L.O. 1, 2)
Beachfront Properties, Inc., had the following stockholders' equity on January 1, 19X5:

Common stock, $6 par value, 600,000 shares authorized, 100,000 shares issued and outstanding	$ 600,000
Paid-in capital in excess of par value	1,035,000
Retained earnings	570,000
Total stockholders' equity	$2,205,000

Selected transactions and events from 19X5 follow.

Jan. 16   Authorized a 2-for-1 stock split.
Feb. 10   Reacquired 32,000 common shares at a cost of $256,000, to be held as treasury stock.
June 14   Sold 8,000 of the treasury shares for $80,000.
Aug. 23   Sold 5,000 of the treasury shares for $30,000.
Nov. 16   Declared a cash dividend of $0.20 on each share outstanding.
Dec. 16   Paid the dividend that was declared on November 16.

Instructions

a Set up a table similar to the following that shows the total number of shares outstanding *after* each transaction and event.

Date	Shares Outstanding
Jan. 1	100,000
Jan. 16	
Feb. 10	
Etc.	

b Prepare the journal entries needed to record the company's transactions and events.
c Prepare the stockholders' equity section as of December 31, 19X5. Net income for the year amounted to $257,100.

P16-A2 *Equity transactions: Journal entries and stockholders' equity section* (L.O. 1, 2)

An examination of the ledger of Goodrich Metals revealed the following accounts on January 1:

Common stock, $1 par, 50,000 shares authorized, 30,000 shares issued, 29,500 shares outstanding	$ 30,000
Paid-in capital in excess of par value	270,000
Retained earnings	370,500*
Treasury stock, 500 shares at cost	6,000

* Goodrich is required by state law to restrict retained earnings at an amount equal to the cost of any treasury shares held by the firm.

The following transactions and events occurred during the year:

Jan. 7   Declared a $0.20 dividend per share to stockholders of record on January 23. The dividend will be distributed on February 8.
Feb. 8   Paid the dividend declared on January 7.
Apr. 15   Sold 300 shares of treasury stock for $4,500.
June 30   Declared a 10% stock dividend on the shares outstanding, to stockholders of record on July 15. The dividend will be distributed on August 15. Fair market value on the date of declaration was $14 per share.
Aug. 15   Issued the stock dividend declared on June 30.
Dec. 31   Net income for the year amounted to $98,000. Closed the Income Summary account to Retained Earnings.

Instructions

a Prepare journal entries to record Goodrich's transactions and events.
b Prepare the stockholders' equity section of Goodrich's December 31 balance sheet, along with any appropriate notes to the financial statements.

P16-A3 *Statement of retained earnings and stockholders' equity section* (L.O. 1, 2, 3)

Mansfield Merchants, Inc., had the following stockholders' equity on January 1, 19X9:

Common stock, $1 par, 1,000,000 shares authorized,
800,000 shares issued and outstanding $ 800,000
Paid-in capital in excess of par value   3,200,000
Retained earnings   1,950,000
Total stockholders' equity $5,950,000

Selected transactions and events from 19X9 follow. The transactions and events occurred in the sequence presented.

Declared (and later issued) a 5% stock dividend. Market value at the time of declaration was $10 per share.	$400,000
Acquired 20,000 treasury shares at $8 per share	160,000
Declared (and later paid) a cash dividend	24,600
Sold 12,000 treasury shares at $9 per share	108,000
Detected an error that took place in 19X8. The company failed to record a $70,000 gain on a land sale, which affected taxes by $21,000.	49,000

Instructions

a Prepare a statement of retained earnings for the year ended December 31, 19X9. Net income for the year was $736,800.

b Prepare the stockholders' equity section for the corporation's December 31, 19X9, balance sheet.

P16-A4 *Corporate financial reporting* (L.O. 4, 5)

Fidelity Corporation has requested your advice concerning the proper accounting treatment for each of the following events and transactions, which occurred during 19XX:

1 One of the company's distribution centers suffered $400,000 of damage in July when a satellite fell from outer space and crashed into the building. Fidelity's insurance does not cover the damage, and the foreign government that owned the satellite refuses to accept responsibility.

2 The company disposed of its leisure goods segment in October. The sale of the division resulted in a $1.3 million gain. From January 1, 19XX, through the date of sale, however, the segment lost $500,000 from operations.

3 On March 3, Fidelity sold stock of Simon Corporation at a $50,000 gain. The Simon stock was acquired as an investment several years earlier. Fidelity regularly engages in such investment activity.

4 The company has used the straight-line depreciation method on all items of plant and equipment. At the beginning of 19XX, management decided to change to the sum-of-the-years'-digits approach and calculated that prior years' depreciation expense would have been $200,000 greater had the accelerated method been employed.

Fidelity Corporation is subject to a 40% income tax rate and had 100,000 shares of common stock outstanding throughout 19XX. The firm's accountant has correctly computed 19XX income from operations at $6.5 million. Assume that all dollar amounts cited in items (1)–(4) are before tax.

Instructions

a Discuss the proper accounting treatment for the transactions and events described in items (1)–(4).
b Prepare the lower portion of the company's income statement (starting with income from operations of $6.5 million) for the year ended December 31, 19XX. Include appropriate earnings-per-share information.

P16-A5 *Corporate income reporting* (L.O. 4, 5)

Astro, Inc., operates a chain of bodybuilding centers and driving schools. The driving schools have been marginally profitable and were discontinued in May 19X3. The data that follow pertain to the 19X3 fiscal year.

	Bodybuilding Centers	Driving Schools
Sales	$5,000,000	$3,400,000
Operating expenses	3,200,000	3,150,000
Loss on disposal of driving school assets		(400,000)
Gain on sale of building	300,000	
Extraordinary flood loss	(100,000)	
Change in accounting principle	70,000	

The change in accounting principle resulted from a switch in depreciation methods for the bodybuilding centers. The cumulative effect of the switch will cause a $70,000 hike in earnings.

Astro had 100,000 shares of no-par common stock outstanding throughout 19X3. Dividends of $20,000 were declared and paid on these shares in October. The company is subject to a 40% income tax rate; all amounts presented in the problem are expressed on a beforetax basis.

Instructions

Prepare Astro's 19X3 income statement for the year ended November 30. Use good form and be sure to disclose the company's earnings per share.

Series B

P16-B1 *Accounting for treasury stock, cash dividends, and stock splits* (L.O. 1, 2)

You Fix It, Inc., had the following stockholders' equity on January 1, 19X8:

Common stock, $5 par value, 400,000 shares authorized, 70,000 shares issued and outstanding	$350,000
Paid-in capital in excess of par value	185,000
Retained earnings	360,000
Total stockholders' equity	$895,000

The following transactions and events occurred during the year:

Jan. 11 Approved a 2-for-1 stock split.
Feb. 23 Reacquired 10,000 common shares for $220,000, to be held as treasury stock.
July 6 Declared a cash dividend of $0.80 per share.
  13 Sold 3,000 of the treasury shares for $87,000.
Aug. 5 Distributed the dividend that was declared on July 6.
Nov. 22 Declared a cash dividend of $1 per share.
Dec. 15 Sold 6,000 of the treasury shares for $114,000.

Instructions

a Prepare the journal entries needed to record You Fix It's transactions and events.

b Prepare the company's stockholders' equity section as of December 31, 19X8. Net income for the year amounted to $112,800.

P16-B2 *Equity transactions: Journal entries and stockholders' equity section* **(L.O. 1, 2)**
An examination of the ledger of Home Cooking, Inc., revealed the following accounts on January 1:

Common stock, $10 par, 50,000 shares authorized, 30,000 shares issued, 28,000 shares outstanding	$300,000
Paid-in capital in excess of par value	90,000
Retained earnings	240,000*
Treasury stock, 2,000 shares at cost	25,000

* Home Cooking's board of directors has placed a $70,000 restriction on retained earnings to allow for future equipment acquisitions.

The following transactions and events occurred during the year:

Mar. 14 Declared a 4% stock dividend on the shares outstanding, to stockholders of record on March 28. The dividend will be distributed on April 14. Fair market value on the date of declaration was $15 per share.

Apr. 3 Sold 1,500 shares of treasury stock for $21,000.

14 Issued the stock dividend declared on March 14.

Oct. 9 Declared a $0.65 dividend per share to stockholders of record on October 23. The dividend will be distributed on November 9.

Nov. 9 Paid the dividend declared on October 9.

Dec. 31 Net income for the year amounted to $105,000. Closed the Income Summary account to Retained Earnings.

Instructions

a Prepare journal entries to record Home Cooking's transactions and events.

b Assume that the company's board met on December 30 and increased the restriction for equipment acquisitions by 20% of the original amount. Prepare the stockholders' equity section of Home Cooking's December 31 balance sheet, along with any appropriate notes to the financial statements.

P16-B3 *Statement of retained earnings and stockholders' equity section* **(L.O. 1, 2, 3)**
Roadside Equipment had the following paid-in capital on January 1, 19X2:

Common stock, $5 par, 150,000 shares authorized, 20,000 shares issued and outstanding	$100,000
Paid-in capital in excess of par value	370,000

On December 31, 19X2, prior to the accounting records being closed, the Retained Earnings account contained the following entries:

Retained Earnings			
2/18 Stock dividend	120,000	1/1 Balance	290,000
5/14 Correction of error	48,000		
12/31 Cash dividend	52,000		

A review of the accounting records disclosed that:

1 A 15% stock dividend was declared on February 18 when the market price was $40 per share. The dividend was distributed one month later.

2 The $48,000 error correction is net of $32,000 of tax and relates to 19X1 sales revenue.

3 Four thousand treasury shares were reacquired beginning in May at a total cost of $140,000. Seventy percent of these shares were subsequently sold for $120,400.

4 19X2 net income amounted to $110,700.

Instructions

a Prepare a statement of retained earnings for the year ended December 31, 19X2.

b Prepare the stockholders' equity section of the company's December 31, 19X2, balance sheet.

P16-B4 *Corporate financial reporting* (L.O. 4, 5)

Champion, Inc., has requested your advice concerning the proper accounting treatment for each of the following events and transactions, which occurred during 19XX:

1 On October 15, Champion sold stock of Wiser Corporation at a $30,000 loss. The Wiser stock was acquired as an investment several years earlier. Champion regularly engages in such investment activity.

2 The company has utilized the double-declining balance depreciation method on all items of plant and equipment. At the beginning of 19XX, management decided to change to the straight-line approach and calculated that prior years' depreciation expense would have been $150,000 lower had the new method been employed.

3 The company disposed of its oil drilling segment in July. The sale of the division resulted in a $750,000 loss. From January 1, 19XX, through the date of sale, however, the segment had generated $200,000 of income from operations.

4 One of the company's warehouses suffered $300,000 of damage in April when a truck hauling nuclear waste crashed into the structure. Champion's insurance does not cover this type of damage, and the trucking company responsible has filed for bankruptcy.

Champion, Inc., is subject to a 40% income tax rate and had 10,000 shares of common stock outstanding throughout the year. The firm's accountant has correctly computed 19XX income from operations at $880,000. Assume that all dollar amounts cited in items (1)–(4) are before tax.

Instructions

a Discuss the proper accounting treatment for the transactions and events described in items (1)–(4).

b Prepare the lower portion of the company's income statement (starting with income from operations of $880,000) for the year ended December 31, 19XX. Include appropriate earnings-per-share information.

P16-B5 *Corporate income reporting* (L.O. 2, 4, 5)

African Importers, Inc., had the following activity during 19X5. (All amounts presented are before consideration of related tax effects.)

Cost of goods sold	$ 7,068,000
Decrease in earnings from cumulative effect of change in accounting principle	20,000
Dividends declared	64,000
Extraordinary loss from earthquake	36,000
Gain on sale of assets from discontinued segment	240,000
Loss on sale of land	14,000
Net sales	11,400,000
Operating expenses	2,832,000
Operating loss on discontinued segment	50,000

The company is subject to a 30% income tax rate. African Importers had 100,000 weighted-average shares of common stock outstanding during 19X5.

Instructions

Prepare the corporation's income statement for the year ended December 31, 19X5, in good form. Include any necessary earnings-per-share information.

EDB16-1 *Corporate equity and income reporting: The Quaker Oats Company and The Home Depot* (L.O. 1-5)

ELECTRONIC DATA BASE

SEC

Quaker Oats is a world-wide marketer of consumer grocery products. The company is well known for its cereals, Aunt Jemima mixes and syrups, Ken-L Ration and Gaines dog food, Rice-A-Roni, and Gatorade. Home Depot, in contrast, is America's largest home center retailer. The firm is especially popular with do-it-yourselfers and home remodeling contractors.

Instructions

By using the text's Electronic Data Base, access the financial statements and accompanying notes of both firms and answer the questions that follow. Unless otherwise indicated, responses should be based on data for the most recent year presented.

a Analyze the financial statements and determine each company's earnings per share and dividends per common share for the three years reported. In general, have changes in earnings per share been reflected in the dividends distributed to stockholders? Briefly comment.

b Did either of the companies have any discontinued operations? If "yes,"
  (1) How much of an impact did the discontinued operations have on current net income?
  (2) What is the nature of the discontinued operations, as described in the notes that accompany the financial statements?

c By reviewing the statement of stockholders' equity, determine for each firm:
  (1) The nature of any issuances of new common shares during the year.
  (2) The nature of any treasury stock transactions during the year.

d Did either company report a prior period adjustment? If so, briefly describe.

EDB16-2 *Corporate equity and income reporting* (L.O. 1-5)

This problem is a duplication of Problem EDB16-1. It is based on two companies selected by your instructor.

Instructions

By using the text's Electronic Data Base, access the specified companies' financial statements and accompanying notes and focus on data for the most recent year reported. Answer requirements (a)–(d) of Problem EDB16-1.

BEYOND THE BASICS

BB16-1 *Analysis of stock dividends and splits* (L.O. 2)

This problem consists of two unrelated questions that pertain to stock dividends and stock splits.

Part I

Evaluate the following statements for the management of Dakota, Inc., and decide whether the statements apply to:

1 Stock dividends only
2 Stock splits only
3 Both stock dividends and stock splits
4 Neither stock dividends nor stock splits

_____ a The par or stated value of the stock is changed.
_____ b Total stockholders' equity remains unchanged.
_____ c The distribution is considered an expense of the issuing corporation.
_____ d There is a transfer from Retained Earnings to capital stock accounts.
_____ e The distribution results in income upon receipt by the stockholder.
_____ f The distribution results in a larger percentage of corporate ownership for an individual stockholder.

Part II

On December 31, 19X1, Dakota, Inc., had the following stockholders' equity section:

Common stock, $100 par	$2,000,000
Paid-in capital in excess of par value	400,000
Retained earnings	1,900,000
Total stockholders' equity	$4,300,000

Net income of $340,000 was generated during 19X2. Four independent stockholders' equity sections for Dakota as of December 31, 19X2, follow. The sections differ because of various transactions that occurred during the year. Fair market value of the common stock when each transaction took place was $120 per share. By using the following code, indicate the type of transaction that occurred.

1 Small stock dividend
2 Large stock dividend
3 Stock split
4 None of the above

	A	B	C	D
Shares oustanding	21,000	40,000	26,000	20,000
Common stock	$2,100,000	$2,000,000	$2,600,000	$2,000,000
Paid-in capital in excess of par value	420,000	400,000	400,000	400,000
Retained earnings	2,120,000	2,240,000	1,640,000	2,240,000
Transaction type				

BB16-2 *Overview of chapter concepts: Multiple choice* (L.O. 1-5)

The following multiple-choice questions relate to various topics discussed in the chapter. Select the best answer.

1 America Corporation purchased 1,000 shares of its $5 par-value common stock for $25 per share. The stock was originally issued at $20. Subsequently, 500 of the treasury shares were sold at $22 per share. As a result of these transactions:

   a a loss of $5,000 would be reported on the income statement.

   b America's retained earnings balance would increase.

   c the balance in the Treasury Stock account would be $14,000.

   d total stockholders' equity decreases.

2 Cash dividends on preferred stock would be reported as a liability at year-end if the amounts:

   a are declared but unpaid.

   b are not declared but are in arrears.

   c are declared and paid.

   d will be declared during the upcoming period.

3 Which of the following would cause a reduction in retained earnings equal to the fair market value of the shares distributed to stockholders?

   a A 10% stock dividend.   c A 6-for-5 stock split.

   b A 40% stock dividend.   d A 2-for-1 stock split.

4 Which of the following statements is true?

   a A stock split will reduce a company's total assets.

   b A stock dividend, because of its effect on retained earnings, reduces total stockholders' equity.

   c A retained earnings restriction has no impact on the total retained earnings balance reported on a balance sheet.

   d The financial impact of a labor strike is normally classified as an extraordinary item.

5 A prior period adjustment requires:

   a a change in a period's beginning retained earnings balance.

   b a change in the current period's operating income.

   c the reporting of a cumulative effect.

   d the reporting of an extraordinary item.

6 The statement of stockholders' equity:

   a discloses transaction details that would otherwise appear on the balance sheet.

   b is generally issued along with a company's balance sheet, income statement, and statement of retained earnings in an effort to disclose economic activity.

   c would not disclose the period's net income.

   d would reveal the details of any treasury stock transactions that occurred during the period along with the amounts of dividends declared.

7 Which of the following items need not be reported on a net-of-tax basis?
  a Infrequent gains and losses that are "normal" in nature.
  b Discontinued operations.
  c The cumulative effect of a change in accounting principle.
  d Prior period adjustments.

8 Ethco Consulting had 50,000 common shares outstanding for the first half of the year and 70,000 common shares outstanding for the last half of the year. The company had net income of $100,000, paid $40,000 of preferred dividends, and paid $20,000 of common dividends. (The preferred stock is not convertible.) How much is Ethco's earnings per share (rounded to the nearest cent)?
  a $0.33.   c $1.00.
  b $0.67.   d $1.67.

COMMUNICATION OF ACCOUNTING INFORMATION

CAI16-1 *The personal touch: Maytag Corporation (L.O. 4)*
Communication Principle: Personalizing a piece of writing for a reader is one way that abstract concepts can be made more comprehensible. Personalizing can be achieved by following several simple procedures:

1 Use personal pronouns such as "you," "I," or "we." In other words, write directly to an individual reader rather than indirectly and generally to just *any* reader. For instance, the phrase "You can look at the company's continuing operations to see . . ." involves the reader directly, whereas "The company's continuing operations can be seen . . ." does not.
2 Use active voice instead of passive. In an active sentence, "actors" or people come first; in a passive sentence, objects or things come first. To illustrate, "The accountant wrote an excellent report" is active. "An excellent report was written by the accountant" is passive. Experts agree that the more personalized nature of active voice makes writing more effective.
3 Use concrete examples that a reader can understand. In the situation that follows, for instance, examples of discontinued operations may be introduced to help a reader comprehend how such events affect earnings.
4 Write in a style and vocabulary appropriate to the reader's age, educational level, occupation, and culture.

Personalized documents are generally more persuasive than impersonal ones. Because letters are written to one person, they are, by definition, personal. Use this opportunity to communicate information clearly and, at the same time, respond to a client and make a friend.

■ ■ ■ ■ ■ ■ ■ ■

Maytag Corporation is well known for its washers and dryers. In addition, the company manufactures other recognizable products that are sold under the names of Admiral, Hoover, Jenn-Air, Magic Chef, and Norge. All told, the company has 22 manufacturing operations in seven different countries.

In two recent successive years, Maytag reported the following amounts (in thousands of dollars):

	19X8	19X7
Income from continuing operations	$135,522	$147,678
Income after discontinued operations (i.e., net income)	158,562	152,703

Instructions

Assume that a biology professor desires to invest in a company that has reasonable growth in net income and is considering Maytag on the basis of this criterion. Write a letter that explains, in a nontechnical way, the nature of and reporting for discontinued operations. Be sure to show the amount of gain or loss attributable to discontinued activities for each year. Also include an evaluation of Maytag's earnings trend as it relates to the professor's investment standard.

Answers to Chapter Quiz

1 b

2 a

3 d (The $16,000 decrease to Retained Earnings is offset by a $4,000 increase to Stock Dividend Distributable and a $12,000 increase to Paid-in Capital in Excess of Par Value.)

4 d

5 b

CHAPTER 17

Long-Term Liabilities

LEARNING OBJECTIVES

After studying this chapter, you should be able to:

1

Describe the basic differences between bondholders and stockholders, and identify the various types of bonds that may be issued.

2

Account for bond issues, including those issued between interest dates.

3

Distinguish between contract and effective interest rates, and premiums and discounts.

4

Explain the concept of present value.

5

Calculate amortization under both the straight-line and effective-interest methods.

6

Account for bond retirements and convertible bonds.

7

Recognize the accounting issues related to mortgage notes and leases.

8

Explain the fundamentals of accounting for income taxes and employee benefit plans.

Businesses constantly need funds to finance their diverse activities. As we have shown in earlier chapters, funds may be obtained from different sources. For example, short-term projects and investments in current assets (e.g., inventory buildups) are typically financed by short-term credit such as accounts payable and by the cash generated from profitable operations. These funding sources are not always adequate or satisfactory, however. Long-term projects such as an expansion of facilities or the addition of a new product line dictate the need for a more permanent source of capital. Imagine the difficulty of financing a new office complex with liabilities that would have to be renewed every three months. Indeed, the prospect of resecuring the necessary credit four times a year for the next 30 or 40 years is unappealing.

Generally speaking, long-term investments are financed by long-term capital. Examples of long-term capital include capital stock and numerous types of debt, such as bonds and notes. Bonds and notes are commonly encountered in practice and can vary in importance as a source of asset funding (see Exhibit 17-1).

This chapter explores long-term liabilities, with a concentration on bonds. Other long-term liabilities, specifically, mortgages, leases, deferred taxes, pensions, and post-retirement health-care benefits, will be considered as well.

BONDS: GENERAL FEATURES

OBJECTIVE

Describe the basic differences between bondholders and stockholders, and identify the various types of bonds that may be issued.

Suppose an automobile manufacturer has decided to build a new plant to produce subcompacts. The plant's construction cost might be more than a single lender is capable of supplying. The manufacturer therefore has two basic financing alternatives available: the issuance of additional shares of stock or the issuance of bonds. **Bonds** enable a borrower to split a large loan into many small divisible units. Each of these units (known as a bond) is essentially a note payable, that is, a written promise to pay a sum of money on a specified future date. Like capital stock, bonds are issued through an underwriter to the investing public. Once outstanding, such obligations can be bought and sold on organized securities exchanges and are thus easily transferable.

Although stocks and bonds may seem somewhat similar, their holders have distinctly different rights. Stockholders are the owners of a corporation; bondholders, on the other hand, are creditors whose claims are classified as long-term debt on the balance sheet. To protect the bondholders' interests, the issuing firm usually appoints a *trustee*. The trustee, often a large bank, plays the role of a third party to monitor the issuer's adherence to stated terms of the bonds. For example, bond issues frequently permit dividends to be paid to stockholders only if certain working capital levels are maintained. If bond provisions are violated, the trustee may initiate appropriate action, such as lawsuits or perhaps the seizure and foreclosure of any property pledged as collateral on the bond issue. The provisions of a bond issue are normally stipulated in an accompanying document called a **bond indenture.**

Exhibit 17-2 summarizes two further differences between bondholders and stockholders based on the creditor/owner relationship.

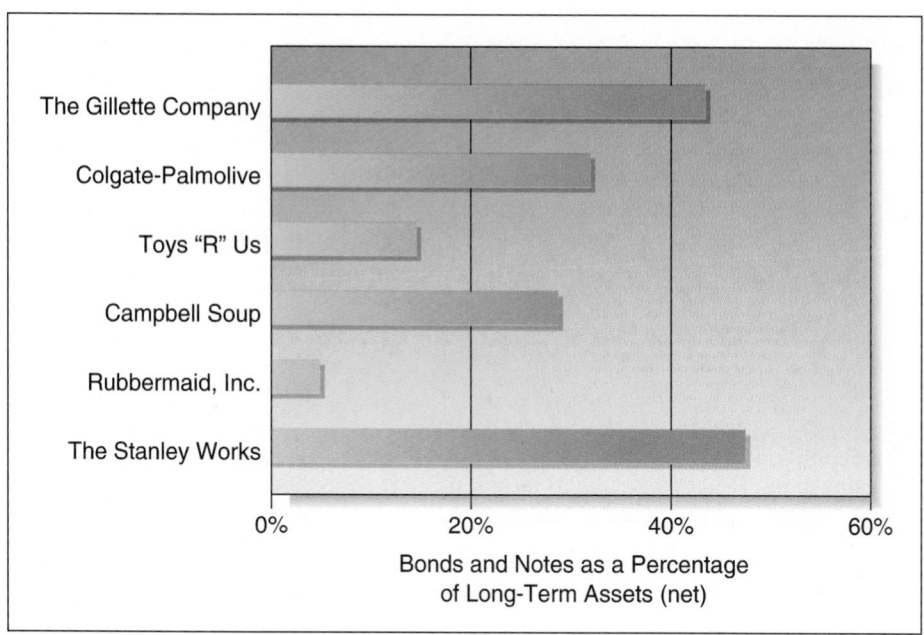

EXHIBIT 17-1
Bonds and Notes as a Source of Funding

Types of Bonds

Bonds are issued by corporations, the federal government, states, school districts, and local municipalities. These entities have varying financial needs, and the bonds they issue appeal to different types of investors. As a result, many types of bonds are used in the fund-raising process. Consider, for example, the recent long-term liability disclosure of Texaco, Inc. (see Exhibit 17-3).

Although this illustration is somewhat technical, the following discussion should help to clarify the firm's balance sheet presentation.

EXHIBIT 17-2
Differences Between Bondholders and Stockholders

	Bondholders (Creditors)	Stockholders (Owners)
Claim on income	Bondholders receive interest and have a yearly fixed claim on income. Interest must be paid regardless of the level of earnings.	Stockholders are paid dividends, subject to income levels and the discretion of the corporate directors.
Claim in liquidation	Bondholders have a prior claim on assets in the event of bankruptcy.	Stockholders have a residual claim on business assets. Should bankruptcy occur, the owners receive proceeds from asset liquidation only after the amounts due creditors have been settled.

EXHIBIT 17-3
Long-Term Liability
Disclosure of Texaco, Inc.
(in millions)

Long-term debt*	
$7\frac{1}{4}$% serial debentures, due through 1998	$ 175
$7\frac{3}{4}$%–$8\frac{7}{8}$% debentures, with sinking fund payments through 2005	505
$7\frac{7}{8}$%–10% guaranteed notes, due 1994–2003	1,897
$8\frac{1}{4}$%–$9\frac{3}{4}$% guaranteed debentures, due 2006–2031	898
7.6% medium-term notes, maturing 1993–2021	450
Pollution Control Revenue Bonds, variable rate, due 2012	166
Other	847
	$4,938
Less current portion	77
Total long-term debt	$4,861

* Various details have been omitted by the authors for the sake of brevity. Companies ordinarily disclose considerable information about long-term obligations, including maturities forthcoming in each of the next five years.

Secured and Debenture Bonds

Many bonds are **secured;** that is, assets have been pledged as security for the bondholders should the issuing company fail to meet its obligations under the indenture agreement. Virtually any type of property can be pledged. As an example, mortgage bonds are generally backed by property, plant, and equipment; collateral trust bonds by negotiable securities; and so forth.

In contrast to secured bonds, **debenture bonds** have no assets pledged as security. The marketability of debenture bonds is therefore based on the general credit of the issuing company. To sell debentures, the issuer must have a long period of substantial earnings as well as favorable prospects for future income and solvency. Many corporations have issued *subordinated* debentures. Should liquidation occur, the holders of subordinated bonds are paid only if sufficient assets remain after settling the claims of other designated creditors (as specified in the indenture agreement).

Registered and Coupon Bonds

Bonds can also be classified by the manner in which the related interest is disbursed. Most of the bonds issued in recent years have been **registered bonds;** that is, the issuing firm maintains a record of the purchaser's name and address. At the time interest is paid, the disbursing company simply mails a check to the bond's registered owner. Naturally, when a change in ownership occurs, the issuing company must be notified so that interest can be paid to the proper party.

Interest payments on **coupon bonds** are handled in a different fashion. Coupon bonds have small detachable coupons that correspond to each interest period and are payable to the bearer. The bondholder detaches the coupon as it falls due and deposits it at a bank for collection. By shifting the responsibility for collection to the bondholder and the bank, the issuing company avoids the need to maintain an up-to-date list of bond owners.

Other Bond Classifications

Many bond issues have a single maturity date for the entire issue. With **serial bonds,** however, bondholders are repaid in periodic installments over a number of years. For example, in 19X1 a company could issue $20 million of bonds that begin to mature in 19X6 at the rate of $4 million per year. This staggering of maturity dates allows investors (i.e., lenders) to select bonds that satisfy their cash flow needs.

Companies often create a special fund to repay a bond issue. Cash is set aside each year and invested in income-producing securities. The periodic cash deposits plus the investment income are then used for repayment. Funds of this type are commonly termed **sinking funds** and, appropriately, the bonds are sometimes called **sinking-fund debentures.** Sinking funds will be discussed later in this chapter.

Some bonds are **convertible** into shares of common stock at the option of the bondholder. The conversion feature allows a creditor to exchange a security with fixed interest receipts for one whose increase in value will be substantial should the issuing company enjoy high levels of profitability. Convertible bonds are also discussed later in the chapter.

Many bonds are **callable** at the option of the issuing firm. Callable bonds permit the issuer to repay bondholders prior to the specified maturity date, a feature that is often exercised if funds become available at lower interest rates. In return for this feature, the issuer compensates the bondholder by setting a call price that normally exceeds the bonds' face value.

Finally, in the mid-1970s and throughout the 1980s, corporations raised billions of dollars by using so-called **junk bonds.** Such bonds are less than "investment grade" (i.e., somewhat risky) and, thus, speculative in nature. These bonds are sometimes issued by new firms with no track records or by established companies that are in poor financial health.

Accounting for bonds can be quite complex; no doubt you will see why as we proceed through the chapter. For this reason we will start with a very basic illustration, with modifications (and realism) being added along the way. Before doing so, however, two simple facts regarding bonds must be explained. First, all bonds have a *face value*—a set amount to be repaid on the bond's maturity date. The face value is usually $1,000 or some multiple thereof. Second, bonds can be issued at any price, with the price normally expressed as a percentage of face value. For example, a $1,000 bond issued at 97 will cost the buyer $970.

Given this information, assume that on January 1, Tyler Corporation issued $500,000 of 10-year, 12% bonds at 100. Interest is payable semiannually on January 1 and July 1. The entry to record the issuance follows.

ACCOUNTING FOR BOND ISSUES: THE BASICS

OBJECTIVE

2

Account for bond issues, including those issued between interest dates.

Jan. 1	Cash	500,000	
	Bonds Payable		500,000
	To record issuance of 10-year, 12% bonds		

The Bonds Payable account is classified in the long-term liability section of the balance sheet until one year prior to the maturity date. At that time the bonds become a current liability and are disclosed accordingly. An exception to this treatment occurs when bonds will be retired by using a sinking

HIGHLIGHT

Bonds: A Little Bit of This and a Little Bit of That

Most bond issues are pretty much run of the mill. Corporations borrow money, pay interest, adhere to directives in the indenture agreement, and repay investors at maturity. Consider, though, the following somewhat unusual cases.

■ *Read the fine print*—In 1987, Continental Airlines issued $350 million of aircraft bonds. These bonds were originally secured with a huge pool of planes and engines, allowing all the bondholders to sleep at night. Now, the value of those assets has eroded, and entire planes have disappeared. Unnoticed by some investors, Continental's agreement allowed the carrier to remove several planes from the collateral pool and sell them to raise cash. The remaining planes, analysts say, are mostly gas guzzlers that cost a lot to maintain—20-year-old narrow-bodied aircraft. A consultant notes that sale prices for such aircraft "are being eroded fairly sharply. A lot of older planes just need to be scrapped."

Who's to blame for this unfortunate situation? Wall Street professionals say that the details in bond indentures are negotiated by securities firms and investors. Bond buyers sometimes waive restrictions on an issuer in exchange for a higher interest rate on the bonds that are being sold. And in good times, when investors are in a buying mood, the power shifts to the issuer, and investors sign off on permissive covenants. [1]

■ *Light bulbs and gaskets*—Not too long ago, Trans World Airlines (TWA) issued bonds that were secured mainly by a grab bag of assets. These assets included some durable spare parts, but also a lot of disposable items such as light bulbs and gaskets. Further collateral was provided by the company's take-off and landing privileges at airports (i.e., slots) that, strictly speaking, don't legally belong to TWA. (Airport slots are granted by the Federal Aviation Administration and are often sold or swapped by carriers.)

The spare-parts financing, devised by Merrill Lynch, received high marks for imagination. "You've got to admit that some security is better than none," says one investment banker. The problem was that the airline's traditional collateral (aircraft and engines) had already been pledged to lenders in existing debt agreements. So TWA had to scramble to find other collateral for new loans. "They're digging pretty far down in the barrel," noted a financial analyst. [2]

■ *Center Court, please*—Most bonds are interest bearing, with cash payments taking place on a periodic basis. Here's an interesting exception. The Ground Company holds the deed on the 42 acres of grass that are the heart of the Wimbledon tennis tradition. Every five years the firm issues 2,100 debentures; in place of interest, each bond entitles holders to one Center Court ticket for each of the 13 days that Wimbledon is played. In effect, the bonds are season tickets good for five years. So far, they have been renewable at the option of the bearer for each successive five-year period.

So what's a ticket worth? Just ask John Cook, who serves as a middleman between Wimbledon bondholders who want to sell their tickets and corporate entertainment types who are hungry to treat important clients. Cook recently figured that the value of a ticket from the bondholders' view is £96, about four times the box office price. Yet so scarce are tickets that Cook has no trouble selling any that come his way. Recently, he was offered about £5,500 for a bondholder's seat—an average of over £400 per ticket. [3]

The Continental, TWA, and Wimbledon debt issues, especially the latter two, add a bit of spice to the otherwise routine world of bond financing. Gaskets and seats are definite exceptions to the rule. In the meantime, advantage company. Or is it advantage bondholder? Or is it . . . ?

Sources: Adapted from "Continental Air Bonds' Terms Spur Turbulence," *The Wall Street Journal,* December 14, 1990, pp. C1, C2 [1]; "Power Tennis on the Tea Lawn," *Forbes,* June 11, 1990, pp. 72, 74–76 [3]; and "TWA to Sell $300 Million Notes Secured in Part by Light Bulbs," *The Wall Street Journal,* June 2, 1989, pp. C1, C2 [2]. The first and third articles are reprinted by permission of *The Wall Street Journal,* © Dow Jones & Company, Inc., 1990 and 1989. All rights reserved worldwide. The second article is excerpted by permission of *Forbes* magazine, © Forbes Inc., 1990.

fund, which is a noncurrent asset. Bonds retired by the use of noncurrent assets continue to be classified as long-term liabilities until the date of maturity.

The first semiannual interest date is July 1. Interest of $30,000 ($500,000 $\times$ 0.12 $\times \frac{6}{12}$) will be disbursed to bondholders and is recorded as follows:

July 1	Bond Interest Expense	30,000	
	Cash		30,000
	To record semiannual interest on bonds		

Upon the bonds' maturity, Tyler must repay the $500,000 it has borrowed. The entry to record the cash outlay and bond retirement is:

(Year of Retirement)

Jan. 1	Bonds Payable	500,000	
	Cash		500,000
	To record retirement of bonds		

Bonds Issued Between Interest Payment Dates

The interest payment dates associated with a bond are printed on the face of the bond certificate. Bonds, however, can be issued at any time, and issuance between interest dates occurs quite often. To simplify record keeping, it is common practice to collect from the bond's purchaser any interest that has accumulated since the last interest date. The issuing firm can then pay a full period's interest to the bondholder on the next semiannual disbursement date without having to keep track of the date of sale. As we will now show, the interest that has been collected is eventually returned to the investor.

Continuing the Tyler Corporation example, we assume the same facts as before except that the bonds are issued on May 1, four months after the printed interest date. The entry to record the issuance follows.

May 1	Cash	520,000	
	Bonds Payable		500,000
	Bond Interest Payable		20,000
	To record issuance of bonds plus collection		
	of 4 months' accrued interest		

Tyler has received $520,000: the $500,000 issue price plus $20,000 of interest, the latter of which has accumulated from January 1 through April 30 ($500,000 $\times$ 0.12 $\times \frac{4}{12}$). The interest is recorded as a current liability because it is owed to the bondholders and will be returned on the next interest date.

When semiannual interest is paid two months later on July 1, Tyler will record the following entry:

July 1	Bond Interest Payable	20,000	
	Bond Interest Expense	10,000	
	Cash		30,000
	To record semiannual interest payment		

Although six months' interest is being paid, remember that the company received four months' accrued interest on May 1. Thus, Tyler's actual

EXHIBIT 17-4
Accounting for Interest on Bonds Issued Between Payment Dates

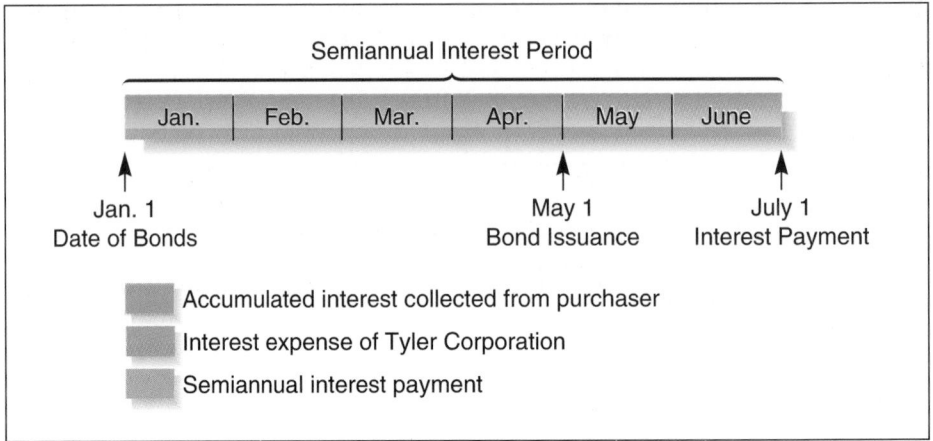

Semiannual Interest Period

| Jan. | Feb. | Mar. | Apr. | May | June |

Jan. 1
Date of Bonds

May 1
Bond Issuance

July 1
Interest Payment

■ Accumulated interest collected from purchaser
■ Interest expense of Tyler Corporation
■ Semiannual interest payment

expense is for May and June only and amounts to $10,000 ($500,000 × 0.12 × $\frac{2}{12}$). The entire process is shown graphically in Exhibit 17-4.

FACTORS THAT AFFECT BOND ISSUE PRICES

OBJECTIVE

Distinguish between contract and effective interest rates, and premiums and discounts.

Suppose a large corporation is in the process of issuing bonds that bear a 10% interest rate. In addition to receiving approval from the firm's directors, the corporation must (1) obtain permission from the SEC, (2) have the bond certificates printed, and (3) have the bond issue publicized. All of these procedures take time. Given the dynamic nature of our economy, the original 10% interest rate may or may not be attractive to investors by the time the bonds are actually issued. Investors may therefore be willing to pay more or less than face value to secure a particular holding.

To illustrate, assume the going rate of interest is currently 11%. The corporation attempting to market the 10% bond issue mentioned previously may encounter some difficulty, because investors can obtain higher yields elsewhere. To make the bonds more attractive, the corporation could sell the issue for less than face value. In this manner a bondholder would still receive 10% interest as printed on the certificate (often called the nominal or **contract interest rate**); however, by lending the corporation a smaller amount, the investor's actual yield is increased. For example, if a $1,000 bond is issued at 91, the corporation cited would pay $100 of interest ($1,000 × 0.10) for the use of $910. The actual or **effective interest rate** is therefore greater than 10%. In conclusion, bonds are often issued below face value when their contract interest rate is less than the interest rate prevailing at the time of sale.

Interest rates are but one factor affecting the issue price. Consider, for instance, bond issues of companies with poor earnings records. Suppose that an entity with a history of losses issued 11% bonds at a time when the going rate of interest was 11%. Many investors might possibly be reluctant to purchase these bonds because of the firm's financial difficulties. Bondholders, of course, are concerned about timely interest receipts and the retirement of debt on the scheduled maturity date. As in the previous example, a drop in the issue price may be needed to make the bonds an attractive investment. When bonds are sold at less than face value, the difference between the issue price and face value is commonly referred to as a **discount.**

Naturally, the opposite situation can occur, with issuance at a price in excess of face value. If, for example, a company attempted to sell a 13% bond issue when the prevailing interest rate was 11%, demand could be overwhelming. Investors might be willing to pay more than face value to obtain the 13% receipts, thus depressing the actual, or yield, rate. In this particular case, the difference between the issue price and face value is called a **premium.**

Present Value

The amount an investor is willing to pay for a bond is determined by three items: (1) the cash inflows connected with the bond issue, (2) the timing of the cash inflows, and (3) the rate of return acceptable to the investor. To explain, a bond investment involves two cash inflows: periodic interest receipts and the return of principal on the maturity date. Interest, of course, is a primary consideration. If the receipts are unattractive, the investor will turn elsewhere to find more profitable opportunities.

The timing of these cash flows is also important. After an initial outlay, investors prefer a rapid inflow of funds so that reinvestment and other projects can be pursued. Dollars received soon after an investment is made are therefore regarded more favorably than inflows that occur in later periods. Finally, all investors seek a return on their precious funds. The return they desire is dependent on a number of factors, one of which is risk. Different investments have different risk levels. Consider, for example, the purchase of an insured certificate of deposit at a bank (a safe investment) versus the acquisition of a racehorse, which could produce large profits or large losses. Investors generally require higher rates of return as their exposure to risk increases.

A tool known as **present value** integrates cash flows, their timing, and the rate of return to determine the amount an investor is willing to pay for a bond—or any investment for that matter. An introduction to present value appears in the appendix to this chapter; a more detailed discussion is contained in Chapter 28.

> **OBJECTIVE**
>
> **4**
>
> Explain the concept of present value.

Bonds Issued at a Discount

To illustrate the necessary accounting for bonds issued at a discount, assume Homestead Corporation sold $200,000 of 4-year, 9% bonds on January 1. The company received only $193,537 because the going rate of interest in the marketplace was in excess of 9%. The entry that follows is needed to record the bond issue.

Jan. 1	Cash	193,537	
	Discount on Bonds Payable	6,463	
	Bonds Payable		200,000
	To record issuance of 4-year, 9% bonds		

The bonds would appear on Homestead's balance sheet as follows:

Long-term liabilities
Bonds payable $200,000
Less: Discount on bonds payable 6,463 $193,537

By deducting the Discount on Bonds Payable account from the bonds' face value, Homestead's net liability becomes $193,537—the amount borrowed on January 1. Stated differently, the bonds are shown at their **carrying value,** or face value minus the unamortized discount.[1]

Meaning of a Bond Discount

As we discussed in Chapter 12, a discount represents future interest expense. This idea is best understood by examining the cash flows related to the bond issue:

Cash to be paid
Interest payments over 4 years
($200,000 × 0.09 × 4) $ 72,000
Face value at maturity 200,000
Total $272,000
Less: Cash received 193,537
Cost of borrowing $ 78,463

Although Homestead is required to pay $72,000 of interest per the bond indenture, issuance at a discount has raised the cost of borrowing by $6,463 ($78,463 − $72,000). Not by accident, this increase corresponds with the balance in the Discount account as of January 1.

To reflect the higher borrowing cost, the discount must be periodically transferred to interest expense over the bond issue's life. This process, commonly known as *discount amortization,* is performed by using the straight-line method or the effective-interest method.

Discount Amortization: Straight-Line Method

Under **straight-line amortization,** an equal amount of discount is allocated to each interest period via the following formula:

$$\text{Periodic Straight-Line Amortization} = \frac{\text{Total Discount or Premium}}{\text{Number of Interest Periods}}$$

If we assume Homestead pays interest semiannually on June 30 and December 31, the discount will be amortized over eight installments (4 years × 2 interest periods per year) of $808 each ($6,463 ÷ 8). The following entries are therefore necessary on each interest date:

---

[1] Carrying value is defined differently for bonds issued in excess of face value. This definition will be presented shortly.

OBJECTIVE

5

Calculate amortization under both the straight-line and effective-interest methods.

Bond Interest Expense	9,000	
Cash		9,000

To record semiannual interest payment:
$200,000 \times 0.09 \times \frac{6}{12}$

Bond Interest Expense	808	
Discount on Bonds Payable		808

To record semiannual discount amortization

The two entries show that Homestead's interest expense is determined by the semiannual contractual payment of $9,000 and by amortization of the discount. Interest therefore amounts to $9,808 and grows to $78,464 ($9,808 \times 8 periods) over the life of the bond issue. Notice that aside from a $1 rounding error, this figure agrees with the total borrowing cost computed in the preceding discussion.

In addition to affecting Interest Expense, the amortization entry also reduces the Discount account and forces an increase in bond carrying value. For example, Homestead's balance sheet disclosure on June 30 (six months after issuance) would be as follows:

Long-term liabilities		
Bonds payable	$200,000	
Less: Discount on bonds payable	5,655*	$194,345

* $6,463 − $808.

By the time the maturity date is reached, the balance in Discount on Bonds Payable will be zero, which results in a $200,000 net liability.

A Compound-Entry Approach. Amortization procedures vary somewhat in practice. Many companies record amortization at the end of the accounting period rather than on each interest payment date. Furthermore, rather than have separate journal entries to record discount amortization and the payment of interest, some businesses use a compound (combined) entry. Homestead's entries on June 30, for instance, could have been recorded as follows:

Bond Interest Expense	9,808	
Discount on Bonds Payable		808
Cash		9,000

To record semiannual interest payment
and discount amortization

Discount Amortization: Effective-Interest Method

Despite its widespread use and popularity, the straight-line amortization of bond discount has a conceptual flaw. Straight-line amortization recognizes an equal amount of interest expense each period. At the same time, however, the bond carrying value (i.e., the net amount owed) is growing. Many accountants object to the straight-line method because of this apparent inconsistency. That is, if increasing amounts are owed, the amount of interest expense recorded each period should increase throughout the bond issue's life.

The preceding problem can be overcome by using the **effective-interest method** of amortization. With this approach, interest expense is calculated as a constant *percentage* of bond carrying value; thus, increasing carrying values are matched by increasing amounts of expense. Consistent with the method's name, the related computations are derived by using a bond's effective interest rate, not the contract rate. According to a ruling issued by the accounting profession, the effective-interest method must be utilized when it produces results that differ significantly from the straight-line approach.[2] Often, however, the two methods generate similar outcomes within a given reporting period.

An Example.   To illustrate bond discount amortization with the effective-interest method, we will use the same facts we employed in the previous example. Our initial approach, however, will be from a slightly different perspective. The facts are as follows:

- A $200,000, 4-year, 9% bond issue.
- Semiannual interest payments on June 30 and December 31.
- Proceeds amounting to $193,537, resulting in a 10% effective interest rate.[3]

Recall that (1) the amount an individual or firm is willing to pay for an investment is termed present value and (2) *present value is in part dependent on the rate of return acceptable to the investor* (10% in this case). Now, assume that you recently inherited $193,537 from a wealthy relative. After lengthy negotiation you have agreed to open a savings account at a local bank and leave the money on deposit for the next four years. The bank will pay you $9,000 at the end of each six-month period and will return $200,000 upon conclusion of the fourth year. Assuming the $9,000 is withdrawn semiannually, the savings account would appear as follows for the first year:

	First 6-Month Period		Second 6-Month Period	
Beginning balance	$193,537		$194,214	
Add: Interest at 5% *	9,677		9,711	
	$203,214	+$677	$203,925	+$711
Less: Semiannual cash withdrawal	9,000		9,000	
Ending balance	$194,214		$194,925	

* 10% annual rate ÷ 2 semiannual interest periods.

Observe that the account's balance is rising each period. Furthermore, notice that the increase is equal to the difference between the semiannual

---

[2] See "Interest on Receivables and Payables," *Opinions of the Accounting Principles Board No. 21* (New York: American Institute of Certified Public Accountants, 1971).
[3] The relationship between bond prices and the effective interest rate becomes apparent after studying the appendix to this chapter.

Semiannual Interest Period	(A) Effective Semiannual Interest Expense (5% × Carrying Value)	(B) Semiannual Interest Payment (4½% × Face Value)	(C) Discount Amortization (A − B)	(D) Bond Discount Balance	(E) End-of-Period Bond Carrying Value (Face Value − D)
Issue date				$6,463	$193,537
1	$ 9,677	$ 9,000	$ 677	5,786	194,214
2	9,711	9,000	711	5,075	194,925
3	9,746	9,000	746	4,329	195,671
4	9,784	9,000	784	3,545	196,455
5	9,823	9,000	823	2,722	197,278
6	9,864	9,000	864	1,858	198,142
7	9,907	9,000	907	951	199,049
8	9,951*	9,000	951	—	200,000
	$78,463	$72,000	$6,463		

* Difference due to rounding.

EXHIBIT 17-5
Discount Amortization Schedule

interest of 5% and the cash withdrawal. By changing our perspective, we could say that the balance in the savings account corresponds to the carrying value of the bond issue. The increase in carrying value is caused by discount amortization, which, during the first six months outstanding, amounted to $677. These facts are reflected in the discount amortization schedule that appears in Exhibit 17-5. A review of the exhibit reveals that interest expense and discount amortization rise each period, a direct result of applying a constant interest rate against a growing bond carrying value.

The journal entries for the effective-interest method are the same as those noted earlier for straight-line amortization. Naturally, however, the amounts differ. Using information presented in the amortization table, the entries at the end of the first semiannual interest period would be as follows:

Bond Interest Expense	9,000	
Cash		9,000
To record semiannual interest payment		
Bond Interest Expense	677	
Discount on Bonds Payable		677
To record semiannual discount amortization		

Bonds Issued at a Premium

Bonds are sold at a premium when their contract interest rate exceeds the prevailing market rate for bonds of a similar grade. In this particular case, investors are willing to pay more than face value to obtain the higher interest receipts. To illustrate the proper accounting, we will again use the Homestead Corporation example, with one modification. Assume the

$200,000, 9% bond issue is now sold for $206,733. The entry to record the bond issue is:

Jan. 1	Cash	206,733	
	Premium on Bonds Payable		6,733
	Bonds Payable		200,000
	To record issuance of 4-year, 9% bonds		

If Homestead were to prepare a balance sheet on January 1, the bonds would be disclosed as follows:

Long-term liabilities
    Bonds payable $200,000
    Add: Premium on bonds payable   6,733 $206,733

The bond carrying value of $206,733 is Homestead's net liability and is calculated by adding the premium to the bonds' face value. Since only $200,000 will be repaid at maturity (per the bond indenture), the carrying value must be reduced over the life of the issue. The necessary reduction is achieved through the amortization process discussed earlier.

Tips & Techniques

The thrust of premium and discount amortization is perhaps best explained by means of the following diagram:

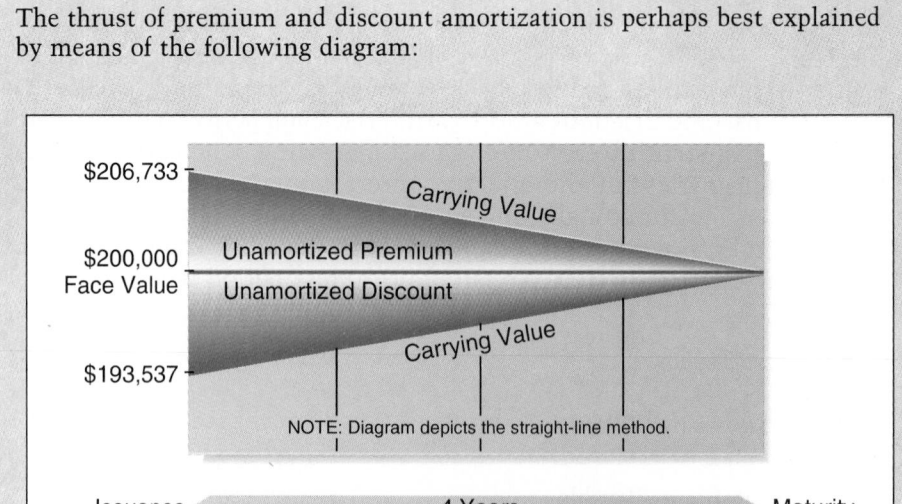

Each year, a selected amount of premium or discount is written off to interest expense. The write-off of discount raises bond carrying value; in contrast, premium amortization produces a carrying-value reduction. In both cases, by the end of four years, carrying value reaches $200,000—the bonds' face value and the company's payoff at maturity.

Meaning of a Bond Premium

The meaning of a bond premium is best explained by examining the cash inflows and outflows related to the company's issue.

Cash to be paid		
Interest payments over 4 years		
($200,000 × 0.09 × 4)	$ 72,000	
Face value at maturity	200,000	
Total	$272,000	
Less: Cash received	206,733	
Cost of borrowing	$ 65,267	

Notice that Homestead's cash payments for interest amount to $72,000; however, the total cost of borrowing is only $65,267. It is apparent, then, that a premium represents a payment by bondholders that reduces the issuing firm's interest expense, in this instance by $6,733 ($72,000 − $65,267). Observe that the reduction equals the balance in the Premium account on January 1. At this point we can conclude that a premium is the opposite of a discount, given the premium's effect on interest expense and its disclosure on the balance sheet (i.e., an addition to Bonds Payable as opposed to a reduction).

Premium Amortization

A premium can also be amortized by either the straight-line or effective-interest methods. If straight-line amortization is used, $842 of premium ($6,733 ÷ 8) will be written off during each semiannual interest period. The entries that follow are therefore required on June 30 and each subsequent interest date.

Bond Interest Expense	9,000	
Cash		9,000
To record semiannual interest payment:		
$200,000 × 0.09 × $\frac{6}{12}$		

Premium on Bonds Payable	842	
Bond Interest Expense		842
To record semiannual premium amortization		

The amortization entry reduces both the Premium and the Bond Interest Expense accounts, the latter resulting in a six-month borrowing cost of $8,158 ($9,000 − $842). Over the life of the bond issue, total expense will amount to $65,264 ($8,158 × 8 periods), which, except for a small rounding error, agrees with the borrowing cost calculated earlier. Finally, observe that as the premium becomes smaller, the bond carrying value decreases and will eventually become $200,000—the amount Homestead owes as of the maturity date. As partial evidence, compare Homestead's January 1 balance sheet disclosure with that of June 30:

	Jan. 1	June 30
Long-term liabilities		
Bonds payable	$200,000	$200,000
Add: Premium on bonds payable	6,733	5,891*
	$206,733	$205,891

* $6,733 − $842.

Effective-Interest Amortization. We turn now to the effective-interest method. Applying a constant percentage against a declining carrying value yields decreasing amounts of interest expense each period. For instance, suppose the bond issue's proceeds of $206,733 came about because investors were willing to accept an 8% effective interest rate. Returning to our earlier method of explanation, assume that you have agreed to open a $206,733 savings account in exchange for a $9,000 payment at the end of each six-month period. The savings account would appear as follows for the first year:

	First 6-Month Period		Second 6-Month Period	
Beginning balance	$206,733		$206,002	
Add: Interest at 4%*	8,269		8,240	
	$215,002	−$731	$214,242	−$760
Less: Semiannual cash withdrawal	9,000		9,000	
Ending balance	$206,002		$205,242	

* 8% annual rate ÷ 2 semiannual interest periods.

The savings account's balance, which corresponds to the bond carrying value, declines each period because the 4% interest is less than the $9,000 cash withdrawal. The difference between these two amounts is equivalent to the premium amortization of the bond issuer. Homestead's premium amortization schedule is shown in Exhibit 17-6.

Amortization Schedules and Spreadsheets. A careful study of this schedule (as well as that shown on p. 675) should convey the impression that significant procedure is involved. This characteristic makes preparation of amortization schedules very adaptable to computers, especially in conjunction with spreadsheet software. Special spreadsheet functions exist that allow automatic calculation of both present value and payment amounts on long-term debt. Once again, the user can minimize computational efforts and concentrate instead on an analysis of the resulting numbers.

Year-End Interest Accruals

In previous examples we assumed that one of the semiannual interest dates coincided with the company's year-end. When this situation does not

Semiannual Interest Period	(A) Effective Semiannual Interest Expense (4% × Carrying Value)	(B) Semiannual Interest Payment (4½% × Face Value)	(C) Premium Amortization (B − A)	(D) Bond Premium Balance	(E) End-of-Period Bond Carrying Value (Face Value + D)
Issue date				$6,733	$206,733
1	$ 8,269	$ 9,000	$ 731	6,002	206,002
2	8,240	9,000	760	5,242	205,242
3	8,210	9,000	790	4,452	204,452
4	8,178	9,000	822	3,630	203,630
5	8,145	9,000	855	2,775	202,775
6	8,111	9,000	889	1,886	201,886
7	8,075	9,000	925	961	200,961
8	8,039*	9,000	961	—	200,000
	$65,267	$72,000	$6,733		

* Difference due to rounding.

EXHIBIT 17-6
Premium Amortization Schedule

occur, it is necessary to accrue interest from the last payment date until the end of the reporting period. Because premiums and discounts affect interest expense, amortization must be recorded as well.

To illustrate the required procedures, we will use data from the preceding example in which Homestead issued its bonds at a premium. Recalling that the interest payment dates were June 30 and December 31, assume the company's fiscal year now ends on August 31. Prior to preparing the financial statements, the following adjusting entries are needed:

Aug. 31	Bond Interest Expense	3,000	
	Bond Interest Payable		3,000
	To accrue interest expense for 2 months		

		Straight-Line	Effective-Interest
Aug. 31	Premium on Bonds Payable	281	253
	Bond Interest Expense	281	253
	To amortize bond premium for 2 months		

The first entry recognizes the company's contractual obligation to disburse $9,000 of interest for each six-month period the bonds are outstanding. Because bondholders were last paid on June 30, Homestead has incurred and owes interest of $3,000 ($9,000 × $\frac{2}{6}$). Turning to the second entry, the Bond Interest Expense account must be credited to reduce Homestead's borrowing cost for the months of July and August. Semiannual amortization under the straight-line method amounted to $842 (see p. 677); thus, $281 ($842 × $\frac{2}{6}$) of amortization is needed to update the records. If the effective-interest method is used, the computation is slightly more complex. According to information that appears in Exhibit 17-6, Homestead would have recorded $731 of premium amortization upon conclusion of the first semiannual interest period and $760 at the end of the second period. Because two months of the second period have now passed, year-end amortization amounts to $253 ($760 × $\frac{2}{6}$).

On December 31, the next interest payment date, two entries are again necessary:

Dec. 31	Bond Interest Payable	3,000	
	Bond Interest Expense	6,000	
	Cash		9,000
	To record semiannual interest payment		

		Straight-Line	Effective-Interest
Dec. 31	Premium on Bonds Payable	561	507
	Bond Interest Expense	561	507
	To amortize bond premium		
	for 4 months		

The first entry records the semiannual interest payment and another four months of interest expense (September 1–December 31). The Bond Interest Payable account is debited to eliminate the two months of interest owed as of August 31. The second entry records premium amortization as follows: straight-line, $561 ($842 × $\frac{4}{6}$); effective-interest, $507 ($760 × $\frac{4}{6}$). Similar procedures are then followed in later reporting periods. Had the bonds been issued at a discount, the amortization entry would have required a debit to Bond Interest Expense and a credit to Discount on Bonds Payable.

Bond Retirement

OBJECTIVE

6

Account for bond retirements and convertible bonds.

Bonds are sold under the money and credit conditions that prevail at the time of issue. Frequently, in order to raise the necessary funds, the issuing company must incur high effective interest rates and make promises to bondholders that inhibit future financing flexibility. Examples of such promises include restrictions on dividend payments and the maintenance of a certain working capital position (current assets minus current liabilities).

Most companies protect themselves and take advantage of changing market conditions (and possible lower interest rates) by including a call provision on bond issues. Such a provision allows issuers to reacquire the bonds at a stipulated percentage of face value. Bonds may be called and be replaced by an issue that carries a lower interest rate (known as **bond refunding**) or be retired and canceled (known as **bond retirement**). In either case, any difference between the bond carrying value and the call price is treated as a gain or a loss in the year when the call occurs.[4]

To illustrate the proper accounting, assume Troup Manufacturing retired a $400,000, 8% bond issue that had an unamortized premium balance

---

[4] Sizable gains and losses that result from the extinguishment of debt are reported on the income statement as an extraordinary item. This special disclosure treatment arose from market conditions that existed in the early 1970s, allowing companies to realize significant gains (sometimes amounting to millions of dollars) on the early retirement of debt.

of $16,000. If the bonds were called at 106 on one of the semiannual interest dates,[5] Troup would record the following entry:

Bonds Payable	400,000	
Premium on Bonds Payable	16,000	
Loss on Bond Retirement	8,000	
Cash		424,000

To record retirement of bond issue at 106

The retirement calls for the removal of the bonds from the accounting records at their current carrying value ($416,000). Thus, Bonds Payable and Premium on Bonds Payable are both debited. The loss arose because the amount paid was greater than the carrying value; had the opposite situation occurred, a gain would have been generated. Overall, the required accounting treatment is similar to that for the retirement and sale of a depreciable asset. Recall that depreciation expense is first updated. Next, the asset's book value is removed from the records via both the asset and accumulated depreciation accounts. As a final step, a gain or loss on disposal is computed by comparing book value with the sale proceeds.

Convertible Bonds

Earlier in the chapter we noted that some bonds can be converted into shares of common stock at the option of the bondholder. Because of the conversion feature, the value of the bond will usually rise as the market value (i.e., price) of the issuing company's stock increases. Even if the market price of the stock remains static or drops, the bondholder will continue to receive periodic interest payments, as well as the bond's face value on the maturity date. Conversion is therefore a desirable feature for an investor—and also for the issuing company. The company benefits because investors are willing to accept lower interest rates in exchange for the conversion privilege. Furthermore, upon conversion, the company issues shares at a preset exchange price—a price per share that is typically higher than the stock's market price at the time the bond was issued.

If bonds are converted, the carrying value of the bonds must be transferred to the common stock accounts. For example, assume Maynard Corporation has the following convertible bond issue outstanding:

Long-term liabilities		
Bonds payable	$80,000	
Less: Discount on bonds payable	4,000	$76,000

Each $1,000 bond may be converted into 40 shares of $20 par-value common stock. If all of the bonds are converted, the following entry is needed:

Bonds Payable	80,000	
Discount on Bonds Payable		4,000
Common Stock		64,000
Paid-in Capital in Excess of Par Value		12,000

To record bond conversion into 3,200 shares of common stock (80 bonds × 40 shares per bond)

---

[5] Prior to recording the retirement, journal entries are needed to update related interest payments and premium (or discount) amortization.

In accordance with proper equity accounting, the Common Stock account is credited for the par value of the shares issued (3,200 shares × $20 par = $64,000). Given this treatment, the $12,000 difference between the carrying value ($76,000) and par value ($64,000) is recorded as paid-in capital in excess of par value. Observe that no gain or loss is recognized because no earnings activity has occurred. The transaction is a simple exchange of long-term debt for shares of common stock.

Bond Sinking Funds

In an effort to further protect the bondholders, companies are sometimes required to make periodic deposits to a special fund that is used for retiring the bonds at maturity. The fund, commonly called a **bond sinking fund**, is normally under the supervision of a trustee. The trustee is permitted to invest the company's deposits in income-producing securities. If all goes according to plan, the cash deposits plus the investment income should be sufficient to pay the bondholders the proper amount due. Any cash deficiencies would be supplemented by additional deposits; in contrast, excess cash is returned by the trustee to the contributing company.

The cash and securities in a sinking fund are restricted solely for use in bond retirement and cannot be used to meet current expenses or pay current liabilities. Sinking funds, therefore, are not current assets. Instead, such amounts are disclosed in the long-term investments section of the balance sheet.

OTHER LONG-TERM OBLIGATIONS

In addition to bonds, other types of long-term obligations are frequently encountered in practice. These obligations include mortgage notes, leases, deferred income taxes, and liabilities for employee benefit plans.

Mortgage Notes

Mortgage notes are often used to finance the purchase of real estate. To secure the necessary funding, borrowers agree to pledge certain assets as collateral (security) for the note. Should the borrower fail to meet required payments or other specified conditions, the lender may foreclose on the assets pledged.

Mortgage notes are normally paid in monthly installments, with each installment representing both interest and partial payment on the note's principal. Although the total monthly payment usually remains constant, the allocation between interest and principal will differ each period. Virtually all mortgage obligations, as well as other long-term loans, require that interest be computed on the basis of the unpaid principal. Thus, each successive monthly payment contains a declining interest charge because of the decreasing note balance. For example, assume that an entity secured a 12%, $200,000 mortgage on August 1. Based on monthly payments of $3,500, the allocation between interest and principal for payments of September through December would be as follows:

ETHICS ISSUE

T, Inc., recently experienced a cash shortage and arranged to "borrow" $4 million from a $14 million sinking fund. The fund's trustee is Amy Thomas, an employee of the First National Bank and also the sister of T's president. T returned the monies (with interest) well before the cash was needed for bond retirement. Comment.

OBJECTIVE

7

Recognize the accounting issues related to mortgage notes and leases.

Payment Date	(A) Monthly Payment	(B) Monthly Interest (1% of Unpaid Note Balance)*	(C) Reduction in Principal (A − B)	(D) Unpaid Note Balance (Previous Balance − C)
Issuance date				$200,000
Sept. 1	$3,500	$2,000	$1,500	198,500
Oct. 1	3,500	1,985	1,515	196,985
Nov. 1	3,500	1,970	1,530	195,455
Dec. 1	3,500	1,955	1,545	193,910

* 12% annual rate ÷ 12 one-month interest periods. All figures are rounded to the nearest dollar.

These data are then entered in the accounting records by formal journal entries. To illustrate, the entry needed on September 1 is:

Sept. 1	Interest Expense	2,000	
	Mortgage Note Payable	1,500	
	Cash		3,500
	To record monthly payment of interest and reduction in principal of note		

Leases

Businesses are faced with several options when acquiring the services of long-term assets. There is, of course, the outright purchase. Another possibility that has become extremely popular in recent years is some form of lease agreement. Recent statistics have shown, for example, that 80% of large American businesses employ leasing as a financial tool. Items that may be acquired through this means include automobiles, airplanes, office equipment, and machinery.

A **lease** is an arrangement that allows one party, the *lessee*, to use the assets of another party, the *lessor*, for a stated period of time. Leasing has grown in significance even though in the long run it is usually more expensive than purchasing. From the lessee's viewpoint, leasing offers several advantages:

1 Lease payments are generally 100% tax deductible in the year the amounts are paid.

2 A lease arrangement often permits 100% financing. That is, no down payment may be necessary.

3 The risk of obsolescence on the leased asset rests with the lessor.

Operating Leases Versus Capital Leases

There are two general categories of leases: operating and capital. Under an **operating lease,** the lessee obtains the right to use leased property for a limited period of time and treats amounts paid under the agreement as expense. The lessor, in turn, recognizes amounts received as revenue and retains the leased asset on its balance sheet. The contract signed by a person who rents a car for a day, a week, or some other short period of time is an example of an operating lease.

In contrast, many lease agreements provide usage rights for nearly the entire service life of the leased asset. Such agreements frequently contain a provision for the lessee to acquire the property at a bargain purchase price upon conclusion of the contract term. Leases that meet these or other specific criteria are known as **capital leases.**[6] A careful study of a capital lease reveals the lessee is really acquiring an asset through an installment purchase plan. Yet prior to the mid-1970s, long-term lessees were not required to disclose the asset and obligation for future lease payments (a liability) on their balance sheets. This practice gave rise to the term *off balance-sheet financing*. Under current regulations, however, the lessee must now record both the assets leased under a capital lease agreement and the liability to the lessor.

Accounting for Capital Leases

Although the details of accounting for capital leases are quite complex, you already have a frame of reference to understand the necessary fundamentals. We have indicated that a capital lease is similar to an installment purchase, with the lessee recording the asset leased (i.e., "purchased"), along with the related obligation to the lessor. A typical journal entry would be as follows (the amount is assumed):

Equipment	650,000	
Lease Obligation		650,000
To record long-term capital lease		

After the initial recording, the lessee will depreciate the asset by using one of the depreciation methods discussed earlier in the text (straight-line, sum-of-the-years'-digits, and so forth).

Turning to the liability, the required accounting is essentially the same as the accounting for a mortgage note. Each lease payment is allocated between principal and interest, and interest is calculated as a percentage of the outstanding balance due the lessor. Payments would be recorded in the following manner (again, the amounts are assumed):

Interest Expense	5,500	
Lease Obligation	4,800	
Cash		10,300
To record monthly lease payment, including interest		

The following excerpt from a recent annual report of Scott Paper Company provides a representative example of the disclosure that is typically given to capital leases:

A capital lease transfers substantially all of the benefits and risks of ownership of the leased property to the Company. On the Company's consolidated balance sheet, the following amounts of capitalized leases are included in plant assets and the related obligations are included in debt:

---

[6] See "Accounting for Leases," *Statement of Financial Accounting Standards No. 13* (Norwalk, Conn.: Financial Accounting Standards Board, 1976).

	(Millions)
Plant assets under capital leases	$ 65.9
Accumulated depreciation	(30.3)
Net capital leases	$ 35.6
Current lease obligations	$ 9.8
Long-term lease obligations	18.5
Capital lease obligations	$ 28.3

All other leases are accounted for as operating expenses. . . .

EXECUTIVE BRIEFING
Leasing: What It Means to an International Airline

Holly Nelson
Director, Financial Accounting
Northwest Airlines, Inc.

The methods of financing equipment acquisitions have changed in recent years. Consider that our company, prior to the 1980s, not only owned all of its aircraft but had little in outstanding loans. As of December 31, 1979, Northwest owned 110 aircraft worth $1.1 billion and had only $100 million in long-term debt—a remarkable achievement.

The 1980s, though, saw industry deregulation and the need to grow quickly to keep pace with competition. In evaluating financing alternatives, leasing was found to provide the lowest cost of capital for the company. The latter part of the decade saw an increase in the complexity of leases, requiring one to decipher considerable legal jargon just to determine the proper accounting.

At a recent year-end, Northwest reported 363 aircraft in its fleet, of which 41% were financed under either capital or long- or short-term operating agreements. It is apparent from these figures that leasing is now a fact of life with the firm. The complexity of the agreements, though, continues to grow. The Gulf War, the recession, industry consolidation, and competitor bank-ruptcies have made equipment financing very challenging for the industry. Airline treasury personnel will no doubt overcome this obstacle and become more creative in their quest to fund aircraft deliveries. We accountants, natu-rally, can hardly wait.

Liabilities for Federal Income Taxes

Corporations in this country are subject to the federal income tax laws enacted by Congress. As a result, these businesses must report the amount of income subject to taxation, along with the related tax obligation, to the Internal Revenue Service. Taxes must also be disclosed on the income statement because such amounts affect profitability. In the attempt to satisfy the government and, at the same time, stockholders, creditors, and

OBJECTIVE
8

Explain the fundamentals of accounting for income taxes and employee benefit plans.

managers, a reporting problem typically arises—one that has an impact on the liability section of corporate balance sheets.

Financial statements are not governed by tax law; rather, they are based on generally accepted accounting principles (GAAP). Because of differences between GAAP and income tax regulations, there is often a variance between pretax income as reported in the financial statements (called **pretax financial income**) and income reportable to the IRS (known as **taxable income**). In view of this situation, the *taxes paid to* (or *due*) the government may not be an appropriate measure of a company's *tax expense* for a given accounting period.

Differences Between Taxable Income and Financial Income

Variations between taxable income and pretax financial income arise from several factors, including so-called **temporary differences.**[7] These items result when given revenues and expenses are recognized in different periods for income tax and financial reporting purposes. As an example, property management companies often receive advance rental payments from tenants. For tax purposes, these amounts are generally included in taxable income immediately upon receipt. In contrast, for accounting purposes, the rentals are reported on the balance sheet as a liability, with revenues recognized in future periods as the facilities are occupied (and services provided). Focusing on another situation, businesses are required to estimate product warranty liabilities and to expense such amounts in the year of sale when computing financial income. For tax purposes, however, a company must wait until such time as the liability is settled, which often occurs in a period after the sale transaction.

Deferred Income Taxes

The temporary differences just discussed (and others) cause financial income and taxable income to differ in given years. To illustrate the reporting issues, assume the following figures for Hardy Enterprises, a service business that was formed at the beginning of 19X3:

	19X3 Income Statement		19X3 Tax Return	
Service revenue		$100,000		$100,000
Less operating expenses				
Salaries	$30,000		$30,000	
Advertising	12,000		12,000	
Depreciation	15,000	57,000	20,000	62,000
Pretax financial income		$ 43,000		
Taxable income				$ 38,000
Income taxes due government at 30%				$ 11,400

---

[7] See "Accounting for Income Taxes," *Statement of Financial Accounting Standards No. 96* (Norwalk, Conn.: Financial Accounting Standards Board, 1987).

A close examination of the data will reveal that the variance between pretax financial income and taxable income is caused solely by the company's depreciation expense. This example assumes that Hardy uses the straight-line method for financial reporting and the Modified Accelerated Cost Recovery System (MACRS) for tax purposes.

The company is subject to a 30% income tax rate, which gives rise to the following journal entry:

Income Tax Expense	12,900	
Income Taxes Payable		11,400
Deferred Income Taxes		1,500
To record 19X3 income taxes		

The entry shows that the taxes currently due the government ($11,400) are derived from revenues and expenses (i.e., deductions) on the tax return. The $1,500 deferral and $12,900 expense amounts are slightly more difficult to understand.

Generally, the straight-line and MACRS methods will produce the same *total* depreciation expense over an asset's life and, thus, the same total income and taxes. Given that 19X3 pretax financial income is $5,000 greater than 19X3 taxable income, it stands to reason that the situation will be reversed in *future* years. In other words, Hardy will eventually report an additional $5,000 of taxable income to the government, which will result in a further tax liability of $1,500 ($5,000 × 0.30). The use of temporary differences in 19X3 has effectively allowed the company to postpone (defer) tax payments into upcoming periods. The outcome of this procedure is that the firm's tax expense ($12,900) is really a summation of the taxes due currently ($11,400) plus the increase in the deferred tax liability ($1,500).

Deferred taxes are a very significant amount for most large corporate entities. For example, Marriott recently reported income tax expense of $63 million, of which only $16 million was currently due the government. The substantial growth in the firm's long-term deferred tax liability has made considerable funds available to cover operating expenses or for reinvestment.

Employee Benefit Plans

We conclude our study of long-term obligations by taking a brief look at two popular employee benefit plans: pensions and postretirement health care. A **pension plan** is an agreement between a company and its employees that provides for retirement benefits. Once highly discretionary, such plans are now commonplace and are viewed as an important element of virtually all wage and fringe benefit packages. By instituting a pension plan, an entity assumes a very significant (and costly) obligation.

Pensions give rise to several unique issues. For instance, measuring the magnitude of the obligation is often troublesome because numerous uncertainties are involved. Employee life expectancies and turnover rates, company retirement policies, interest rates that are generated on monies set aside in pension funds, and other factors must all be studied very carefully. To deal with these issues, accountants rely on certain assumptions that are made by *actuaries*, or persons who specialize in reviewing such matters for insurance firms and other similar entities.

In addition to determining the amount of the pension obligation, an entity must also provide funds to satisfy its pension commitment. Employers typically finance retirement plans by making periodic cash payments directly to a *pension fund*. The fund is a separate legal and accounting entity responsible for investing firm contributions, administering the plan, and making disbursements to retired personnel or their beneficiaries. Not surprisingly, the contributions of large firms and the earnings thereon have resulted in the accumulation of sizable amounts of pension fund assets. The fair market value, for example, of the net assets in General Electric's principal pension funds recently totaled $23.2 billion, or about $48,000 for each of the 485,000 people covered.

The details of pension plan accounting are complex and clearly beyond the scope of this text.[8] What you should gain from this discussion, though, is some understanding of the amounts that are shown on a company's (i.e., the employer's) financial statements. Because a pension obligation is created during the term of employment, it is charged to expense during this period in accord with the matching principle. In all likelihood, during this same period, the employer is also transferring cash to the pension fund. If the transfers fail to cover the amount of reported expense, a liability is created for the "unfunded" portion.[9] It is important to understand that the liability reported on the employer's balance sheet generally relates to the payment deficiencies and does *not* reflect the actual sum owed to employees. This latter amount is much, much larger and is an obligation of the separate pension fund.

Pronouncements currently in effect require a substantial amount of disclosure, including the fair value of plan assets and the projected pension benefit obligations. A comparison of these two items can be quite revealing. Consider, for example, that the fair value of The Reader's Digest Association pension assets was 127% of the company's estimated future benefit obligations. In contrast, Procter & Gamble (known for such products as Crest toothpaste, Tide detergent, and Old Spice cologne) reported only a 65% figure. Such disclosures and comparisons assist statement users in assessing the future cash flows necessary to fulfill the various plan requirements.

Postretirement Health-Care Benefits

Until just recently, one of the biggest liabilities for many businesses did not appear on the balance sheet. Many full-time employees are covered by health-care plans whose benefits continue after retirement, thereby obligating individual companies to millions (in some cases, billions) of dollars of *future* costs. Under accounting rules in effect as late as 1990, businesses did not have to report these liabilities nor set aside any money for them. (Health insurance benefits were typically expensed when paid.)

Although in somewhat the same realm as pension plans, accounting for

---

[8] See "Employers' Accounting for Pensions," *Statement of Financial Accounting Standards No. 87* (Norwalk, Conn.: Financial Accounting Standards Board, 1985).

[9] Additional liability amounts may need to be reported under certain conditions.

postretirement health-care benefits introduces added measurement problems. Health-care benefits in many instances are not capped by stipulated dollar limits, so the calculation of an entity's maximum dollar exposure is extremely difficult. Further, the use of such plans by participants is hard to predict, and "health-care inflation" fluctuates dramatically over time. Of course, there is the added complication that new diseases (such as AIDS) will arise.

The Financial Accounting Standards Board now requires that retiree health-care costs be entered on the employer's books as a liability.[10] Not only does a company have to record obligations for its current retiree population, but postretirement benefits for the present-day work force must be recorded as well.

**APPENDIX:
PRESENT VALUE**

As we noted in the body of this chapter, investors use the concept of present value to determine the amount they are willing to pay for a bond issue. To illustrate present value, assume that today is January 1 and you have $1,000 to invest. After studying various alternatives, you have narrowed the field to investments A and B. The investments each promise a $100 cash inflow during the next 12 months. However, as the following schedule shows, the timing differs.

	A	B
Cash outlay required on Jan. 1	$1,000	$1,000
Forecasted cash inflows		
Mar. 31	$ 25	
June 30	25	
Sept. 30	25	
Dec. 31	25	$ 100
	$ 100	$ 100

Although A and B both yield a 10% rate of return ($100 ÷ $1,000), most people would select investment A for two reasons. First, the future is generally unpredictable and full of uncertainty. Thus, all other things being equal, a more rapid recovery of investment dollars helps to reduce the risk associated with an outlay. The dollars are in hand, and the investor becomes less concerned about events that may stop or inhibit the generation of returns. Investment A is also preferred for another reason. Money has a *time value;* specifically, a dollar today is worth more than a dollar in the future. Dollars received early in the year or in the early years of a long-lived project can be reinvested to generate additional earnings. The inflows associated with investment A can, therefore, be put to work. Nothing, however, can be done with the $100 from investment B until December 31.

Present value recognizes the time value of money and weights cash flows occurring in earlier periods more heavily than those that take place

---

[10] See "Employers' Accounting for Postretirement Benefits Other than Pensions," *Statement of Financial Accounting Standards No. 106* (Norwalk, Conn.: Financial Accounting Standards Board, 1990).

further in the future. Before we proceed, we must first examine a concept with which most of you are familiar—compound interest.

Compound Interest and Present Value

Earlier in the text we introduced the computation of simple interest with the following formula:

Interest = Principal × Rate × Time

Notice that interest is calculated on principal only. In contrast, **compound interest** is computed on principal *and* on previously computed interest as well. To illustrate the related calculations, assume you deposited $100 in a savings account that pays 10% interest. If interest is compounded annually, the deposit will grow to $121 by the end of two years.

	Year 1	Year 2
Beginning of year	$100	$110
Add: 10% interest	10	11*
End of year	$110	$121

* $110 × 0.10.

The preceding concept is sometimes referred to as **future value,** because it reflects the amount to which an outlay will grow by the end of a designated time period.

Approaching the same example from a slightly different perspective, suppose you are willing to accept a 10% return on your money. If an investment opportunity is available that promises a $110 cash inflow at the end of one year, how much would you be willing to invest today to obtain that inflow? We hope you answered $100. Why? If you invest $100 today at a 10% interest rate, the investment will grow to the $110 you can receive. The $100 is termed the investment's **present value,** or the amount an investor is willing to pay to obtain a specified cash flow ($110) on a future date (one year from now) at a given rate of return (10%).

Observe that the preceding question could have been phrased as follows: Given a 10% rate of return, how much would you be willing to invest today to receive $121 at the end of two years? As before, the answer is $100.

Relationship Between Compound Interest and Present Value

By using a factor of $(1 + r)^n$, where r is equal to the interest rate per period and n equals the number of periods, we can illustrate the relationship between present value and compound interest (i.e., future value). For compound interest the calculations are as follows:

Original Amount	→	End of Year 1	→	End of Year 2
$100 × $(1.10)^1$ =		$110 × $(1.10)^1$ =		$121

Alternatively, the same results could have been achieved by the following computation:

$$\$100 \times (1.10)^2 = \$121$$

In either case a present amount is compounded at a 10% interest rate and extended two years into the future.

For present value the situation is reversed—a future amount is *discounted* and brought back to today. This process is diagrammed below.

End of Year 2		End of Year 1		Original Amount
$\$121 \quad \times \quad \dfrac{1}{(1.10)^1}$	=	$\$110 \quad \times \quad \dfrac{1}{(1.10)^1}$	=	$\$100$

In a manner similar to compound interest, discounting could have been illustrated as follows:

$$\$121 \times \frac{1}{(1.10)^2} = \$100$$

Fortunately, tables are available to simplify present value calculations. See Table 1 in Appendix D at the end of the text, which is the present value of $1 at various interest rates and for various time periods. The use of the table may be shown with the example just cited. Observe that the 10% column and 2-period row reveal a factor of 0.82645, which is the present value of $1 received in two years at a 10% interest rate. Because we desire to find the present value of $121 and not $1, the following multiplication is necessary:

Cash Flow	Present Value Factor		Present Value
$121	× 0.82645	=	$100

Present Value and Annuities

Most investment opportunities are accompanied by cash flows that occur over a time span of several years. Consider, for instance, the following schedule of discounted cash flows that has been constructed for a planned investment of Westcott Enterprises. The schedule is based on a 10% interest rate.

Year	Cash Flow		Present Value Factor		Present Value
1	$2,000	×	0.90909	=	$1,818
2	2,000	×	0.82645	=	1,653
3	2,000	×	0.75132	=	1,503
4	2,000	×	0.68301	=	1,366
5	2,000	×	0.62092	=	1,242
Total present value					$7,582

Although more cash flows are involved, we continue to multiply monetary amounts by present value factors extracted from Table 1. These factors reveal the time value of money, with the $2,000 inflow that occurs in

Year 1 having a greater present value (i.e., "worth") to Westcott than the inflow that occurs in Year 5 ($1,818 versus $1,242). The figures indicate a total present value of $7,582—the maximum amount the firm can afford to pay to acquire this investment and still generate a 10% return on its funds.

As you may have gathered, present value computations can become rather tedious. The Westcott illustration dealt with five cash flows. The calculations would be considerably more burdensome in a longer term, more realistic investment, say, 10 years, with different inflows and out-flows occurring within a single period. Fortunately, two shortcuts are available to minimize the procedural difficulties.

Notice that in each year the present value factor is multiplied by a $2,000 monetary amount. The calculations would have required less work had the annual cash flow been multiplied by the summation of the individual factors (0.90909 + 0.82645 + 0.75132 + 0.68301 + 0.62092 = 3.79079). As the following figures show, the same result is achieved: $2,000 × 3.79079 = $7,582.

Another possibility is to recognize that this example has focused on the concept of an **annuity**—a series of equal cash receipts or disbursements over a number of years. To further simplify the process, the individual present value factors from Table 1 are often combined to produce an annuity table (see Table 2 in Appendix D). The factor in Table 2 for a $1 annuity to be received over the next five years, discounted at 10%, is 3.79079. Thus, the following calculation becomes appropriate:

Cash Flow		Present Value Factor		Present Value
$2,000	×	3.79079	=	$7,582

Periods of Less Than One Year

Virtually all of our illustrations have focused on annual cash flows. Cash flows may occur more frequently; for example, bond interest is often paid on a semiannual basis, quarterly interest is added to savings accounts, and so forth. The tables included at the end of the text can still be used when this situation arises; however, a slight modification is needed.

The time that elapses between the cash flows under evaluation is termed the **interest period.** It is imperative that *the percentage rate employed correspond with the interest period in question.* For instance, consider a company that desires a 12% return via $50,000 annual cash flows in each of the next eight years. In this particular case, the tables may be used as illustrated in earlier examples, giving rise to a factor from the 12% column and the 8-period row. Suppose, however, that the cash flows will now be $25,000 on a semiannual basis. The semiannual flows occur every six months, giving rise to two interest periods per year and a total of 16 over the project's life. The 12% annual rate must be halved to 6% to become aligned with the six-month period. Thus, the proper factor is found at the intersection of the 6% column and the 16-period row.

The procedures just shown may be used not only with more frequent cash flows but also with more frequent compounding. For instance, if 8% interest is compounded quarterly over the next three years, there would be 12 interest periods (4 periods × 3 years) of 2% each.

Present Value and Bond Prices

The present value concepts discussed in this appendix are often used to determine bond issue prices. The issue price is calculated by figuring the present value of the cash flows related to the bonds, namely, interest payments and the return of principal to investors. As an example, assume Franklin Corporation plans to issue $500,000 of 10-year, 10% bonds. Interest of $25,000 will be payable semiannually on June 30 and December 31 ($500,000 \times 0.10 \times \frac{6}{12} = $25,000$). If the going rate of interest in the economy is also 10%, the issuance price would be computed as follows:

Present value of interest payments: $25,000 \times 12.46221^*$	$311,555
Present value of principal payment: $500,000 \times 0.37689$†	188,445
Total present value (anticipated issue price)	$500,000

* Table 2, 5%, 20 periods.
† Table 1, 5%, 20 periods.

Notice how the present value coincides with the face value of the bonds. The reason is because Franklin's bonds pay interest equal to the prevailing market rate; thus, investors are willing to pay 100% of face value for bond acquisitions.

Modifying the illustration, suppose the annual interest rate for other similar bond issues is now 12%. Franklin's bonds, however, continue to pay 10% (i.e., $25,000 interest for each six-month period). By using factors for the prevailing 12% rate,[11] the present value becomes $442,648:

Present value of interest payments: $25,000 \times 11.46992^*$	$286,748
Present value of principal payment: $500,000 \times 0.31180$†	155,900
Total present value (anticipated issue price)	$442,648

* Table 2, 6%, 20 periods.
† Table 1, 6%, 20 periods.

The bonds will be issued at a discount because investors can obtain a 12% return elsewhere. By receiving less than face value and still paying the same 10% contract interest, the company has increased the effective yield. Franklin's bonds have now become competitive for the limited funds of the investing public.

END-OF-CHAPTER REVIEW

1 Describe the basic differences between bondholders and stockholders, and identify the various types of bonds that may be issued.   Stockholders are the owners of a corporation. As such, they may receive dividends, subject to the availability of funds and the discretion of corporate directors. In the event of liquidation, stock-

LEARNING OBJECTIVES:
THE KEY POINTS

---

[11] The prevailing rate is used in present value calculations because it is the lowest rate of return an investor is willing to accept.

holders are entitled to asset proceeds only if monies are available after paying all other claims. Bondholders, on the other hand, are creditors who are entitled to regular interest payments regardless of income levels. Furthermore, creditors have a claim against assets (before stockholders) if a business were to liquidate.

The chart that follows summarizes key characteristics of the bonds discussed in this chapter.

Type of Bond	Distinguishing Characteristics
Secured	Has assets pledged as security for the bondholders.
Debenture	Issued on the general credit of the corporation.
Registered	Issuing company maintains a record of bond purchasers and mails interest directly to bond owners.
Coupon	Has small detachable coupons that are used for interest collection.
Serial	Issue has staggered maturity dates.
Sinking-fund debenture	Is repaid by using proceeds from a special fund called a sinking fund.
Convertible	Can be converted into common stock at the option of the bondholder.
Callable	Can be reacquired by the issuing firm prior to maturity.
Junk	Securities that are lower quality and speculative in nature.

2 Account for bond issues, including those issued between interest dates.   Bonds are recorded at their original issue price, along with any interest that has accrued since the last interest payment date. The first interest disbursement will include interest expense from the issue date to the payment date, plus a return of any accrued interest received when the obligations were sold. Periodic interest expense should be increased for amortization of discount and decreased for amortization of premium.

3 Distinguish between contract and effective interest rates, and premiums and discounts.   The issue price of a bond is affected by the interest rate printed on the bond (the contract interest rate) relative to the going market rate for obligations of a similar grade. In general, if a bond has a contract rate that is less than the market rate, it will sell below face value (i.e., at a discount). The opposite case will give rise to a premium. The discount or premium causes the actual interest rate, known as the effective rate, to differ from the contract rate. Discounts raise the actual yield rate above the contract rate, and premiums have the opposite impact. Bond prices are also affected by the issuer's financial condition.

4 Explain the concept of present value.   Present value represents the amount an investor is willing to pay to secure a stream of future cash flows at a given rate of return. The cash flows related to a bond issue are the periodic interest receipts and the return of principal. These amounts are multiplied by the appropriate factors, which are available in table form and based on the number of periods and the effective interest rate, to derive the issue price. The periodic receipts of interest often represent an annuity, or a series of equal cash flows.

5 Calculate amortization under both the straight-line and effective-interest methods.   Discounts and premiums must be amortized over a bond issue's life to reflect differences between the contract interest cost and the effective interest cost. The straight-line method assigns an equal amount of amortization to each period. In contrast, the theoretically preferred effective-interest method assigns sufficient amortization to each period so that interest expense is a constant percentage of bond carrying value.

6 Account for bond retirements and convertible bonds. When bonds are retired, interest and amortization should be updated and the related unamortized premium or discount removed from the accounting records. The difference between the bond carrying value and the amount paid to retire the bonds results in a gain or a loss. Convertible bond accounting involves removing the bonds and any related premium or discount from the books. Furthermore, common stock and additional paid-in capital equal to the bond carrying value are recorded, and no gain or loss is recognized.

7 Recognize the accounting issues related to mortgage notes and leases. Mortgage notes are long-term liabilities used to purchase real estate. Mortgages are typically paid in equal monthly installments, with each payment representing both interest and a reduction of the note's principal. Interest is computed on the basis of the unpaid note balance, a declining amount each month. Therefore, each successive payment consists of a decreasing interest component and a greater amount to apply toward principal

A lease is an agreement that allows one party, the lessee, to use the assets of another party, the lessor, for a stated period of time. With an operating lease, the lessee obtains the right to use leased property for a limited time period and treats amounts paid to the lessor as an expense. The lessor recognizes the monies received as revenue and retains the leased asset on its balance sheet. Alternatively, capital leases are structured so that the lessee is really acquiring an asset through an installment purchase. In this case the lessee records the leased asset in its accounting records, along with the accompanying liability to the lessor.

8 Explain the fundamentals of accounting for income taxes and employee benefit plans. Income reported in the financial statements is based on generally accepted accounting principles, whereas income reported to the government (namely, the Internal Revenue Service) is based on tax regulations. Differences between pretax financial income and taxable income are common, often arising from so-called temporary differences. These items result when given revenues and expenses are recognized in different periods for income tax and financial reporting purposes. When temporary differences have occurred and cause taxable income to be less than financial income, a Deferred Income Tax liability account is established to reflect the future taxes due the government.

A pension plan is an agreement between a company and its employees that provides for retirement benefits. Monies are remitted to a separate pension fund, which later disburses benefits to retirees and/or their beneficiaries. Following the accrual basis of accounting and the matching concept, pension costs are expensed and the pension obligation is created during the term of employment. This practice is followed even though the pension is not paid until retirement.

Turning to postretirement health-care benefits, these costs for many years have been recorded on a pay-as-you-go basis. The end result has been a very substantial unrecorded liability for businesses. The Financial Accounting Standards Board now requires that such liabilities be entered in the accounting records and disclosed in a company's financial statements.

---

annuity A series of equal cash flows over a number of years.

bond A formal written document that provides evidence of long-term indebtedness.

bond discount The difference between the face value of bonds and the issue price, when issuance occurs below face value.

bond indenture A document that stipulates the provisions of a bond issue.

**KEY TERMS
AND CONCEPTS:
A QUICK OVERVIEW**

bond premium   The difference between the face value of bonds and the issue price, when issuance occurs above face value.

bond refunding   The replacement of a bond issue with other bonds that carry a lower interest rate.

bond retirement   The cancellation of bonds that have been called.

callable bond   A bond that can be reacquired by the issuing firm prior to the maturity date.

capital lease   A lease under which the lessee is actually acquiring an asset via an installment purchase plan.

carrying value of a bond   The face value of a bond minus the unamortized bond discount (or plus the unamortized bond premium).

compound interest   Interest that is calculated on both principal and previously accumulated interest.

contract interest rate   The interest rate printed on the face of a bond certificate.

convertible bond   A bond that can be converted into common stock at the option of the bondholder.

coupon bonds   Bonds having small detachable coupons that correspond to each interest period and are payable to the bearer.

debenture bond   A bond that has no assets pledged as security and is issued on the general credit of the corporation.

deferred taxes   A postponement of income taxes that arises from temporary differences.

effective-interest amortization   A method of bond discount and premium amortization by which interest expense is calculated as a constant percentage of bond carrying value.

effective interest rate   The actual interest rate on a bond, which may be different than the contract interest rate.

future value   The amount an original sum will increase to, given an interest rate and a designated time period.

interest period   The time that elapses between cash flows in future value and present value computations.

junk bonds   Bonds that are less than investment grade and speculative in nature.

lease   An agreement that allows the lessee to use the assets of the lessor for a stated period of time.

mortgage note   A long-term note issued to finance the purchase of real estate.

operating lease   A lease under which the lessee obtains the right to use leased property for a very limited period of time.

pension plan   An agreement between a company and its employees that deals with retirement benefits.

postretirement health-care benefits   Health-care benefits for retirees that are treated as a liability by the employer/company.

present value   The amount an investor is willing to pay to secure a specified cash flow on a future date at a given rate of return.

pretax financial income   Pretax income reported in the financial statements.

registered bond   A bond for which the issuing company maintains a record of the purchaser's name and address and mails interest to the registered bond owner.

secured bond   A bond for which assets are pledged as security for the bondholders.

serial bond   A bond issue in which bonds mature at different dates.

sinking fund   A fund established to ensure that sufficient funds are available to pay bondholders at maturity.

sinking-fund debentures   Bonds that are retired by using the proceeds from a sinking fund.

straight-line amortization   A method by which an equal amount of bond discount or premium is allocated to each interest period.

taxable income   Income reported in a tax return to the Internal Revenue Service.

temporary differences   Differences in the timing of revenues and expenses for tax and accounting purposes. That is, revenues and expenses are recognized in different accounting periods for income tax and financial-reporting purposes.

The five questions that follow relate to several issues raised in the chapter. Test your knowledge of the issues by selecting the best answer. (The answers appear on p. 713.)

CHAPTER QUIZ

1 When the interest payment dates of a bond are June 1 and December 1, and a bond issue is sold on August 1, the amount of cash received by the issuer upon sale will be:
   a increased by the accrued interest from August 1 to December 1.
   b increased by the accrued interest from June 1 to August 1.
   c decreased by the accrued interest from August 1 to December 1.
   d decreased by the accrued interest from June 1 to August 1.

2 Bonds payable are sold at 98 when there is a difference between the:
   a issue date and maturity date.
   b contract interest rate and effective interest rate.
   c carrying value and maturity value.
   d face value and maturity value.

3 Bonds payable sold at 104 should be disclosed on the balance sheet at their face value:
   a plus any unamortized discount.   c minus any unamortized discount.
   b plus any unamortized premium.   d minus any unamortized premium.

4 On June 1, 19X7, Denver, Inc., issued $100,000 of 10%, 5-year debenture bonds at 105. The bonds were dated June 1, 19X7; the company uses the straight-line amortization method. If the bonds are called and retired at 105 on June 1, 19X9, the company would experience:
   a a loss of $2,000.   c a loss of $3,000.
   b a gain of $2,000.   d neither a gain nor a loss.

5 Sampson recently purchased land secured by an interest-bearing mortgage note that requires 120 monthly payments of $500, for a total of $60,000. Which of the following best describes the note's principal?
   a Less than $60,000.
   b More than $60,000.
   c Exactly $60,000.
   d Cannot be determined from the above facts.

SUMMARY PROBLEM

On January 1, 19X1, Kristopher Corporation issued $100,000 of 8%, 10-year bonds for $87,538. The bonds were priced to generate an effective yield of 10% to investors, are dated January 1, 19X1, and pay semiannual interest on June 30 and December 31. On April 1, 19X2, the entire bond issue was called at 103, plus accrued interest. Kristopher uses the straight-line method of amortization and rounds all computations to the nearest dollar.

Instructions

a Prepare journal entries to record (1) the bond issuance on January 1, 19X1, and (2) the semiannual interest payment and discount amortization on June 30, 19X1, and December 31, 19X1. *Note:* Combine the interest payment and amortization into a single entry (see p. 673).
b Compute total bond interest expense for 19X1.
c Present the proper disclosure of the bond issue on Kristopher's December 31, 19X1, balance sheet.
d Prepare journal entries to record the bond retirement on April 1, 19X2. *Hint:* Examine when amortization was last recorded.
e Compute the discount amortization that would have been recorded on June 30, 19X1, and December 31, 19X1, if Kristopher had used the effective-interest method rather than the straight-line method.

Solution

a Jan.   1   Cash   87,538
            Discount on Bonds Payable   12,462
              Bonds Payable   100,000
            To record issuance of bonds

   June 30   Bond Interest Expense   4,623
              Discount on Bonds Payable   623
              Cash   4,000
            To record semiannual interest payment
            and amortization

   Dec. 31   Bond Interest Expense   4,623
              Discount on Bonds Payable   623
              Cash   4,000
            To record semiannual interest payment
            and amortization

            Calculations: See part (b)

b Cash payment for interest each six months
     ($100,000 × 0.08 × $\frac{6}{12}$) $4,000
  Straight-line discount amortization each six months
     [($12,462 ÷ 10 years) × $\frac{6}{12}$]   623

  Total bond interest expense $4,623
  Number of six-month periods   ×2
  Bond interest expense for 19X1 $9,246

c Long-term liabilities
    Bonds payable $100,000
    Less: Discount on bonds payable   11,216* $88,784

    * $12,462 − $623 − $623.

d Apr. 1 Bond Interest Expense ... 312
 Discount on Bonds Payable ... 312
 To amortize bond discount for three
 months: ($12,462 ÷ 10 years) × $\frac{3}{12}$

 Bonds Payable ... 100,000
 Bond Interest Expense ... 2,000
 Loss on Bond Retirement ... 13,904
  Discount on Bonds Payable ... 10,904
  Cash ... 105,000
 To record retirement of bond issue at 103,
 plus accrued interest

 Calculations:
  Cash payment
   Accrued interest ($100,000 × 0.08 × $\frac{3}{12}$) ... $ 2,000
   Bond acquisition ($100,000 × 1.03) ... 103,000
   ... $105,000

  Loss on retirement
   Bonds payable ... $100,000
   Less: Unamortized discount on 4/1/X2
    ($11,216 − $312) ... 10,904
   Bond carrying value ... $ 89,096
   Less: Call price ($100,000 × 1.03) ... 103,000
   Loss on bond retirement ... $ 13,904

e

Semiannual Interest Period	(A) Effective Semiannual Interest Expense (5% × Carrying Value)	(B) Semiannual Interest Payment (4% × Face Value)	(C) Discount Amortization (A − B)	(D) Bond Discount Balance	(E) End-of-Period Bond Carrying Value (Face Value − D)
Issue date				$12,462	$87,538
6/30/X1	$4,377	$4,000	$377	12,085	87,915
12/31/X1	4,396	4,000	396	11,689	88,311

ASSIGNMENT MATERIAL

QUESTIONS

Q17-1 Are bonds normally used to meet current obligations and pay operating expenses? Explain.

Q17-2 Differentiate between the rights of stockholders and those of bondholders.

Q17-3 Differentiate between registered and coupon bonds.

Q17-4 What are junk bonds?

Q17-5 Jupiter Corporation is issuing bonds that have an individual face value of $500. If the bonds are sold at 104, will Jupiter receive $104 for each bond? Explain.

Q17-6 How is interest handled on bonds that are issued between interest payment dates? Explain the purpose behind this accounting treatment.

Q17-7 Bates, Inc., recently issued $400,000 of 10% bonds at 102.
a Were the bonds sold at a discount or at a premium?
b In all likelihood, was the prevailing rate of interest in the marketplace for similar bonds equal to, greater than, or less than 10%?
c Is the effective interest rate equal to, greater than, or less than the contract interest rate?

Q17-8 What is meant by the term "bond carrying value"? Will carrying value increase or decrease over the life of a bond issue when bonds are issued at a discount?

Q17-9 Differentiate between a bond discount and a bond premium.

Q17-10 Differentiate between straight-line and effective-interest amortization. Which method is preferred? Why?

Q17-11 How does bond retirement differ from bond refunding?

Q17-12 What is a bond sinking fund? Where is a sinking fund disclosed on the balance sheet?

Q17-13 Explain how a typical mortgage note payment is allocated between principal and interest.

Q17-14 A student once commented, "All leases are fundamentally alike, with amounts paid by the lessee recorded as an expense of the period." Evaluate the student's remark.

Q17-15 Pretax financial income and taxable income often differ because of so-called temporary differences. Briefly explain the meaning of "temporary differences."

Q17-16 A student once commented: "Pension plan costs are normally expensed in the period that disbursements are made to retired employees." Is the student's comment correct? Briefly explain.

Q17-17 Explain several of the problems associated with trying to measure a company's postretirement health-care liability.

*__Q17-18__ What is meant by the term "future value"?

*__Q17-19__ Explain the concept of present value to someone with a limited business background.

*__Q17-20__ Explain the relationship between compound interest and present value.

*__Q17-21__ What is an annuity?

*__Q17-22__ Briefly explain how present value is used to determine bond issue prices.

EXERCISES

E17-1 *Bonds issued between interest dates* (L.O. 2)
Sage Corporation issued $500,000 of 12% bonds on May 1, 19X1, at 100 plus accrued interest. The bonds are dated January 1, 19X1, and pay interest each June 30 and December 31.

---

* An asterisk preceding an item indicates that the material is covered in an appendix to this chapter.

a Prepare journal entries to record (1) the bond issuance on May 1, 19X1; (2) the first interest payment on June 30, 19X1; and (3) the second interest payment on December 31, 19X1.

b Compute Sage's 19X1 bond interest expense.

E17-2 *Overview of bonds* **(L.O. 2, 3, 5)**

Evaluate the comments that follow as being True or False. If the comment is false, briefly explain why.

a When bonds are issued at a discount, the proceeds received exceed the bonds' face value.

b The effective interest rate is lower than the contract interest rate for bonds that are issued at a premium.

c For bonds that are sold at a discount, carrying value is lower than face value.

d Premium amortization results in a company's interest expense being less than interest paid.

e The journal entry to amortize a discount involves a debit to Discount on Bonds Payable.

E17-3 *Bond discount; straight-line amortization* **(L.O. 2, 5)**

Triangle Company issued $800,000 of 12% bonds on January 1, 19X3, for $767,600. The bonds are due on December 31, 19X8, and pay interest semiannually on June 30 and December 31.

a Prepare the required journal entry to record the bond issuance on January 1, 19X3.

b Prepare entries to record the interest payment and discount amortization on June 30 and December 31, 19X3. Triangle uses the straight-line method of amortization.

c Compute 19X3 bond interest expense.

d Present the proper disclosure of the bond issue on Triangle's December 31, 19X3, balance sheet.

E17-4 *Bond premium; straight-line amortization* **(L.O. 2, 5)**

Castillo Company issued $200,000 of 10%, 4-year bonds on January 1, 19X1, for $216,000. The bonds pay interest semiannually on June 30 and December 31.

a Prepare the required journal entry to record the bond issuance on January 1, 19X1.

b Prepare entries to record the interest payment and premium amortization on June 30 and December 31, 19X1. Castillo uses the straight-line method of amortization.

c Compute 19X1 bond interest expense.

d Present the proper disclosure of the bond issue on Castillo's December 31, 19X1, balance sheet.

E17-5 *Bond discount; effective-interest amortization* **(L.O. 2, 5)**

1-2-3

The Eagle Corporation issued $400,000 of 8% bonds for $382,056 on January 1, 19X1. The bonds pay interest semiannually on June 30 and December 31 and were priced to yield an effective interest rate of 9%.

a Prepare the required journal entry to record the bond issuance on January 1.

b Prepare entries to record the interest payment and discount amortization on June 30 and December 31, 19X1. Eagle utilizes the effective-interest method of amortization; round to the nearest dollar.

c Compute 19X1 bond interest expense.

d Present the proper disclosure of the bond issue on Eagle's December 31, 19X1, balance sheet.

E17-6 *Using an amortization table* (L.O. 2, 3, 5)
Several years ago Garza Corporation issued bonds having a maturity value of $100,000. A partial amortization table revealed the following:

Date	Interest Expense	Interest Paid	Amount Unamortized	Carrying Value
6/30/X8	$4,912	$4,500	$1,361	$98,639
12/31/X8	4,932	4,500	929	99,071

a Prepare the balance sheet disclosure for the bonds as of December 31, 19X8.
b Compute the amount of amortization for the six-month period ended December 31, 19X8.
c What is the effective interest rate for these bonds?

E17-7 *Bond premium; effective-interest amortization* (L.O. 2, 5)
The Arctic Corporation issued $600,000 of 11%, 8-year bonds for $632,512 on January 1, 19X4. The bonds pay interest semiannually on June 30 and December 31 and were priced to yield an effective interest rate of 10%.
a Prepare the required journal entry to record the bond issuance on January 1.
b Prepare entries to record the interest payment and premium amortization on June 30 and December 31, 19X4. Arctic uses the effective-interest method of amortization; round to the nearest dollar.
c Compute 19X4 bond interest expense.
d Present the proper disclosure of the bond issue on Arctic's December 31, 19X4, balance sheet.

E17-8 *Bond retirement* (L.O. 5, 6)
Hackberry Corporation issued $400,000 of 12% bonds at 97 on January 1, 19X2. Interest is paid semiannually on June 30 and December 31. The bonds have a 10-year life from the date of issuance; Hackberry uses the straight-line method of amortization. On July 1, 19X8, the bonds were called at 105 and retired.
a Compute the amount of unamortized discount as of the call date.
b Present the entry necessary on July 1, 19X8.
c Discuss possible reasons why Hackberry exercised the call provision.

E17-9 *Convertible bonds* (L.O. 6)
On January 1, Howard Corporation issued $500,000 of convertible bonds. Each $1,000 bond is convertible into 20 shares of Howard's $2 par-value common stock. All of the bonds were converted exactly four years after issue, when the unamortized bond discount stood at $7,400.
a Prepare the journal entry necessary to record the bond conversion.
b Explain why convertible bonds are attractive for (1) an investor and (2) the issuing company.

E17-10 *Mortgage notes* (L.O. 7)
On June 1 of the current year, Leonard Company acquired a building complex for $2 million, which included $500,000 of land. Leonard paid $400,000 down and secured a long-term mortgage note for the remaining balance. The note carried a 12% interest rate, which is computed on the unpaid balance at the beginning of each month. Leonard will repay the note in monthly installments of $19,000, with the first installment due on July 1.

a Prepare the journal entry to record Leonard's purchase on June 1.
b Prepare the journal entry to record Leonard's first payment on July 1.
c Compute the company's interest expense for the current fiscal year ended August 31. Round to the nearest dollar.

E17-11 Leases and lease accounting (L.O. 7)
Henry Company, a small family-owned corporation, is studying the possibility of signing a long-term lease for two new delivery vehicles. Walter Henry, the company's president, is skeptical of leasing and has always believed in the outright purchase of needed property, plant, and equipment.
a Discuss the advantages of leasing from the firm's viewpoint.
b Discuss the basic difference between an operating lease and a capital lease.
c Would Henry's lease probably be accounted for as an operating lease or as a capital lease? Why?
d Discuss the balance sheet impact, if any, of Henry's lease.

E17-12 Lease accounting issues (L.O. 7)
Grid Network Corporation recently entered into two separate lease agreements. One of these agreements was for occupancy of office space at $800 per month; the other was for use of a copy machine at $200 per month. Grid's accountant evaluated details of the lease agreements and determined that the office space lease should be accounted for as an operating lease. The copy machine agreement, in contrast, was a capital lease, with the following entry being made in the accounting records:

Copy Machine	6,000	
Lease Obligation		6,000
To record long-term capital lease		

The interest rate on the capital lease obligation was 1% per month, computed on the unpaid balance at the beginning of the month.
a Prepare Grid's journal entry for the first month's rent of the office space.
b Prepare the journal entry to record the first payment on the capital lease.
c Given that the copy machine will provide benefits over time, how should the $6,000 asset cost be handled in the accounting records?

E17-13 Income taxes; temporary differences (L.O. 8)
Jarvis & Jarvis Backhoe Service began operations at the beginning of 19X2 by acquiring a $60,000 tractor. The only difference between the company's 19X2 income statement and tax return is caused by depreciation of $2,000 and $10,000, respectively. Income before considering depreciation is $75,000; Jarvis & Jarvis is subject to a 25% tax rate.
a Compute the taxes currently due the government.
b Prepare the journal entry for 19X2 income taxes.
c In what section of the balance sheet will the company's Deferred Income Taxes account be disclosed?

*E17-14 Understanding future and present value concepts (L.O. 4)
The appendix covered the following topics, among others:

1—Future value
2—Present value of a single sum
3—Present value of an annuity

Determine the concept(s) most appropriate to compute the following amounts:

_____ a The amount that must be invested today to purchase a $25,000 automobile 10 years from now.

_____ b The amount that a savings account will contain in six years because of additional interest that will be earned.

_____ c The amount that a company should be willing to pay for a machine that promises $10,000 cash savings in each of the next five years.

_____ d The issue price of bonds that have semiannual interest payments.

*E17-15 **Time value of money and present value** (L.O. 4)
Stephanie Rogers requires a 14% rate of return on all investments. She is considering an investment that will provide the following cash inflows:

At the End of Year	Cash Inflow
1	$15,000 ⎫ $30,000
2	15,000 ⎭
3	16,000 ⎫ $30,000
4	14,000 ⎭
	$60,000

a Observe how the investment results in two cash inflows of $30,000, each of which is spread over two years. Which of the $30,000 inflows would be more attractive to Rogers? Explain your answer.

b By using present value, compute the maximum amount that Rogers should be willing to pay for this investment. Round to the nearest dollar.

*E17-16 **Present value computations** (L.O. 4)

Rounding to the nearest dollar, determine the present value of the following cash flows:

a Annual receipts of $24,000 for the next six years, discounted at a rate of 14%.

b Receipts of $3,000 every six months for five years, discounted at a rate of 12%.

c Payments of $60,000 for the next eight years, followed by payments of $40,000 for two years. All cash flows are discounted at a rate of 10%.

*E17-17 **Bond pricing** (L.O. 3, 4)
Austin Manufacturing is considering the issuance of $600,000 of 8-year bonds that have a 10% contract interest rate. The bonds pay interest semiannually on June 30 and December 31. Assume a prevailing interest rate of 12% for similar bonds.

a Determine whether the bonds will be issued at a premium or a discount. Explain your answer. *Hint:* No computations are necessary.

b Determine the anticipated proceeds (i.e., present value) of the bond issue. Round your calculations to the nearest dollar.

PROBLEMS

Series A

P17-A1 Bonds: Balance sheet presentation and analysis (L.O. 1, 2, 3, 5)
The following account balances were extracted from the general ledger of Richmond Corporation on January 1, 19X7:

12% secured bonds	$200,000
9% debenture bonds	100,000
Premium on secured bonds	1,000
Discount on debenture bonds	3,000

Monthly amortization of premium and discount amounts to $20 and $50, respectively.

Instructions

a A study of the company's accounts reveals the presence of both secured bonds and debenture bonds. All other things being equal, would an investor prefer secured bonds or debenture bonds? Briefly explain.

b Determine the company's net bond liability to investors on January 1, 19X7.

c Prepare the proper balance sheet disclosure for the bond issues outstanding as of December 31, 19X7.

d Explain the need for discount and premium amortization.

e Which of the two bond issues (secured or debenture) has a contract interest rate that is less than the effective rate? Briefly explain.

P17-A2 Bond computations: Straight-line amortization (L.O. 2, 5)

Southlake Corporation issued $900,000 of 8% bonds on March 1, 19X1. The bonds pay interest on March 1 and September 1 and mature in 10 years. Assume the independent cases that follow.

1-2-3
■ *Case A*—The bonds are issued at 100.
■ *Case B*—The bonds are issued at 96.
■ *Case C*—The bonds are issued at 105.

Southlake uses the straight-line method of amortization.

Instructions

Complete the following table:

	Case A	Case B	Case C
a Cash inflow on the issuance date	_____	_____	_____
b Total cash outflow through maturity	_____	_____	_____
c Total borrowing cost over the life of the bond issue	_____	_____	_____
d Interest expense for the year ended December 31, 19X1	_____	_____	_____
e Amortization for the year ended December 31, 19X1	_____	_____	_____
f Unamortized premium as of December 31, 19X1	_____	_____	_____
g Unamortized discount as of December 31, 19X1	_____	_____	_____
h Bond carrying value as of December 31, 19X1	_____	_____	_____

P17-A3 *Bonds: Journal entries, issuance through retirement* (L.O. 2, 5, 6)

The following information relates to a bond issue of Transamerican, Inc.:

Date of bonds	May 31, 19X4
Issue date	June 30, 19X4
Maturity date	May 31, 19X7
Face amount	$800,000
Proceeds from issuance	$814,000, plus accrued interest
Interest payment dates	May 31, November 30
Contract (nominal) interest rate	12%
Amortization method	Straight-line

Transamerican will amortize the premium over the 35 months that the bonds are expected to be outstanding.

Instructions

a Prepare journal entries to record (1) the bond issuance on June 30, 19X4; (2) the semiannual interest payment and premium amortization on November 30, 19X4; and (3) accrued interest and premium amortization on December 31, 19X4.

b Compute total bond interest expense for 19X4.

c What is the net carrying value of Transamerican's bonds on December 31, 19X4? Show how this amount would be disclosed on the company's year-end balance sheet.

d Prepare journal entries to record the semiannual interest payment and premium amortization on May 31, 19X5.

e Assume that the entire bond issue was called at 103, plus accrued interest, on September 30, 19X5. Prepare journal entries to record the bond retirement. *Hint:* Examine when amortization was last recorded.

P17-A4 *Amortization analysis and journal entries* (L.O. 2, 3, 5)

The following schedule reflects Zeta Corporation's issuance of 3-year bonds on January 1, 19X5, and the subsequent interest amounts:

Date	Interest Expense	Interest Paid	Amount Unamortized	Carrying Value
1/1/X5			$10,152	$210,152
6/30/X5	$10,508	$12,000	8,660	208,660
12/31/X5	10,433	12,000	7,093	207,093
6/30/X6	10,355	12,000	5,448	205,448
12/31/X6	10,272	12,000	3,720	203,720
6/30/X7	10,186	12,000	1,906	201,906
12/31/X7	10,094*	12,000	—	200,000

* Difference due to rounding.

Instructions

a Did Zeta Corporation use the straight-line or effective-interest amortization method? Explain your answer.

b Determine whether the bonds were issued at a premium or at a discount. Explain your answer.

c What is the annual contract interest rate on the bonds?

d Present the journal entry to record the bond issuance on January 1, 19X5. The bonds are dated January 1, 19X5.

e Present the journal entries required on June 30, 19X6.

P17-A5 Bonds: Effective-interest discount amortization (L.O. 2, 5)
Morris Manufacturing issued $100,000 of 4-year, 11% bonds on January 1, 19X2. The bonds pay interest semiannually on June 30 and December 31 and were priced to generate an effective yield of 12% to investors. The bonds were sold for $96,895.

Instructions
a Prepare the journal entry necessary on January 1 to record issuance of the bonds.
b Assuming that Morris uses the effective-interest method of amortization, prepare the following:
   (1) A discount amortization schedule similar in format to Exhibit 17-5. Round calculations to the nearest dollar.
   (2) Compound journal entries to record semiannual interest payments and discount amortization for the first year the bonds are outstanding.
c Present the proper disclosure of the company's bonds on the December 31, *19X3*, balance sheet.

P17-A6 Deferred income taxes (L.O. 8)
At the beginning of 19X5, Channel 5 News purchased a helicopter having a 20-year service life and no residual value. The helicopter, which cost $890,000, is being depreciated more rapidly for tax purposes than for financial-reporting purposes. Taxes payable based on the firm's 19X5 tax return totaled $180,000; tax expense disclosed on the income statement was $206,700. There are no differences between taxable income and financial accounting income other than depreciation. Assume a 30% income tax rate.

Instructions
a Calculate the deferred income taxes arising during 19X5 from the helicopter.
b Prepare the journal entry necessary to record tax expense, taxes payable, and the deferred income tax liability.
c If Channel 5 uses straight-line depreciation for financial-reporting purposes, determine the amount of helicopter depreciation on the firm's 19X5 tax return.
d Explain the nature of deferred taxes. Why are such amounts reported as a liability?

Series B

P17-B1 Bonds: Balance sheet presentation and analysis (L.O. 1, 2, 3, 5)
The following information relates to a $1,200,000 bond issue of Metro Media, Inc.:

Contract (nominal) interest rate	10%
Issue date	March 1, 19X3
Interest payment dates	February 28, August 31
Maturity date	March 1, 19X7
Amortization method	Straight-line

Instructions
a If Metro Media were in marginal financial health, would it likely have more success in issuing these bonds if the obligations were secured bonds or debenture bonds? Briefly discuss, assuming the interest rates would not differ.

b How much cash will Metro Media pay to bondholders on each interest date?

c If the market rate of interest for similar obligations is more than 10% on March 1, 19X3, will the bonds be issued at, above, or below face value? Briefly explain.

d Did the company collect any interest from the purchasers when the bonds were issued? Explain.

e Assume that the bonds were issued at 98. Calculate monthly amortization and show how the bonds would be presented on Metro Media's December 31, 19X4, balance sheet.

P17-B2 *Bond computations: Straight-line amortization* (L.O. 2, 5)

The Pardee Corporation issued $600,000 of 10% bonds on May 1, 19X3. The bonds pay interest on May 1 and November 1 and mature in eight years. Assume the following independent cases:

1-2-3
- *Case A*—The bonds are issued at 100.
- *Case B*—The bonds are issued at 104.
- *Case C*—The bonds are issued at 98.

Pardee uses the straight-line method of amortization.

Instructions

Complete the table that follows.

	Case A	Case B	Case C
a Cash inflow on the issuance date	____	____	____
b Total cash outflow through maturity	____	____	____
c Total borrowing cost over the life of the bond issue	____	____	____
d Amortization for the year ended December 31, 19X3	____	____	____
e Interest expense for the year ended December 31, 19X3	____	____	____
f Unamortized discount as of December 31, 19X3	____	____	____
g Unamortized premium as of December 31, 19X3	____	____	____
h Bond carrying value as of December 31, 19X3	____	____	____

P17-B3 *Bonds: Journal entries, issuance through retirement* (L.O. 2, 5, 6)

On May 1, 19X1, American Housing Corporation issued $300,000 of 12%, 5-year bonds for $294,200 plus accrued interest. The bonds are dated March 1, 19X1, and pay semiannual interest on March 1 and September 1. American uses the straight-line method of amortization and will amortize the discount over the 58 months that the bonds are expected to be outstanding.

Instructions

a Prepare journal entries to record (1) the bond issuance on May 1, 19X1; (2) the semiannual interest payment and discount amortization on September 1, 19X1; and (3) accrued interest and discount amortization on December 31, 19X1.

b Compute total bond interest expense for 19X1.

c Present the proper disclosure of the bond issue on American's December 31, 19X1, balance sheet.

d Prepare journal entries to record the semiannual interest payment and discount amortization on March 1, 19X2.

e Assume that the entire bond issue was called at 101, plus accrued interest, on July 1, 19X2. Prepare journal entries to record the bond retirement. *Hint:* Examine when amortization was last recorded.

P17-B4 *Amortization analysis and journal entries* (L.O. 2, 3, 5)

The schedule that follows reflects Burk Corporation's issuance of 3-year bonds on January 1, 19X1, and the subsequent interest amounts:

Date	Interest Expense	Interest Paid	Amount Unamortized	Carrying Value
1/1/X1			$6,000	$ 94,000
6/30/X1	$6,500	$5,500	5,000	95,000
12/31/X1	6,500	5,500	4,000	96,000
6/30/X2	6,500	5,500	3,000	97,000
12/31/X2	6,500	5,500	2,000	98,000
6/30/X3	6,500	5,500	1,000	99,000
12/31/X3	6,500	5,500	—	100,000

Instructions

a Determine whether the bonds were issued at a premium or at a discount. Explain your answer.

b Did Burk Corporation use the straight-line or effective-interest amortization method? Explain your answer.

c What is the annual contract interest rate on the bonds?

d Present the journal entry to record the bond issuance on January 1, 19X1. The bonds are dated January 1, 19X1.

e Present the journal entries required on June 30, 19X1.

P17-B5 *Bonds: Effective-interest premium amortization* (L.O. 2, 5)

Hilo Electronics issued $600,000 of 9%, 5-year bonds on January 1, 19X3. The bonds pay interest semiannually on June 30 and December 31 and were priced to generate an effective yield of 8% to investors. The bonds were sold for $624,330.

Instructions

a Prepare the journal entry necessary on January 1 to record issuance of the bonds.

b Assuming that Hilo uses the effective-interest method of amortization, prepare the following:

(1) A premium amortization schedule similar in format to Exhibit 17-6. Round calculations to the nearest dollar.

(2) Compound journal entries to record semiannual interest payments and premium amortization for the first year the bonds are outstanding.

c Present the proper disclosure of the company's bonds on the December 31, *19X5*, balance sheet.

P17-B6 *Deferred income taxes* (L.O. 8)

At the beginning of 19X7, See-Saw Protective Eyewear purchased a new lens grinder having a 10-year service life and no residual value. The grinder, which cost $150,000, is being depreciated more rapidly for tax purposes than for financial-reporting purposes. Taxes payable based on the firm's 19X7 tax return totaled $230,000; tax expense disclosed on the income statement was $232,500. There are no differences between taxable income and financial accounting income other than depreciation. Assume a 20% income tax rate.

Instructions

a Calculate the deferred income taxes arising during 19X7 from the lens grinder.
b Prepare the journal entry necessary to record tax expense, taxes payable, and the deferred income tax liability.
c If See-Saw uses straight-line depreciation for financial-reporting purposes, determine the amount of lens grinder depreciation on the firm's 19X7 tax return.
d Briefly describe the process of tax deferral. Is tax deferral a desirable practice from a company's viewpoint? Why?

ELECTRONIC DATA BASE

EDB17-1 *An overview of debt and lease disclosures: Reebok International and Wendy's International* (L.O. 1, 7)

Reebok International creates consumer products for people with active lifestyles in sports, physical fitness, and recreation. Reebok, Rockport, and Avia are a few of the company's well-known brands. Wendy's, on the other hand, operates fast-food restaurants throughout the world. The firm currently has franchises in 24 countries, with contracts signed or negotiated to develop in 20 more.

Instructions

By using the text's Electronic Data Base, access the balance sheets and accompanying notes of both firms and answer the questions that follow. Unless otherwise indicated, responses should be based on data for the most recent year presented.

a Comment on the amount of detail presented on the balance sheet that relates to each company's long-term debt obligations.
b Review the notes that accompany the financial statements, specifically, the long-term debt disclosure. Have either of the companies used debentures or subordinated debentures as a means of financing? If so,
    (1) What interest rate is being paid and when are the obligations due?
    (2) How significant are these obligations as a source of long-term funding?
c Have either of the companies obtained financing from a foreign source? If "yes," briefly describe.
d Access the disclosure of lease information in the accompanying notes to the financial statements.
    (1) What types of assets does each company lease?
    (2) What types of leases are being used by these firms?
    (3) Have the companies obligated themselves to substantial future payments under the lease agreements presently in force? Briefly explain.

EDB17-2 *An overview of debt and lease disclosures* (L.O. 1, 7)

This problem is a duplication of Problem EDB17-1. It is based on two companies selected by your instructor.

Instructions

By using the text's Electronic Data Base, access the specified companies' balance sheets and accompanying notes and focus on data for the most recent year reported. Answer requirements (a)–(d) of Problem EDB17-1.

BEYOND THE BASICS

BB17-1 *Bond financing versus stock financing* (L.O. 1)

Europa Fashion operates a chain of upscale clothing stores throughout the country. A recent balance sheet of the firm revealed $200,000 of 8% bonds payable and $400,000 of common stock. A proposed modernization program requires that the company raise $300,000 of new financing. Two alternatives are being considered: (1) issue 10% bonds or (2) issue 10,000 additional shares of common stock, increasing the total number of shares in the hands of stockholders to 30,000.

Europa has been marginally profitable over the last few years, generating income significantly below that of other firms in the same line of business. Fortunately, the company has been able to avoid operating at a loss. Inventories, receivables, and payables balances are at all-time highs; cash balances, on the other hand, are at dangerously low levels.

Instructions

a Suppose you are a stockholder of Europa. Do you see any possible problems of financing the modernization program with bonds? Explain.

b Suppose the current date is January 10, 19X2. The company can issue $300,000 of bonds that mature on January 10, 19X6, or a serial issue that is due at the beginning of 19X3, 19X4, 19X5, and 19X6 in $75,000 increments. If interest rates are the same for both issues, would Europa likely opt for the serial bonds? Why?

c Assume that Europa is subject to a 40% income tax rate. Calculate earnings-per-share figures for the two alternatives if management expects earnings of $50,000 before interest and taxes.

BB17-2 *Overview of chapter concepts: Multiple choice* (L.O. 1, 3, 5, 7, 8)

The following multiple-choice questions relate to various topics discussed in the chapter. Select the best answer.

1 Which of the following statements is incorrect?

a Junk bonds are somewhat speculative in nature.

b Most recent bond issuances have been registered bonds rather than coupon bonds.

c A sinking-fund bond is accompanied by the creation of a special fund in which cash payments are set aside for eventual bond retirement.

d A company with a marginal earnings record would probably have more trouble issuing secured bonds than debenture bonds.

2 Montgomery Company plans to issue bonds that have a contract interest rate of 9%. If the prevailing interest rate for bonds of a similar grade is 10%, one could expect that:

a the bonds are not an attractive investment.

b the bonds will be sold at face value.

c the bonds will be sold at a discount.

d the bonds will be sold at a premium.

3 McNeil Corporation neglected to amortize $900 of bond premium during the current year. This error would:

a understate total liabilities at the end of the current year.
b overstate total liabilities at the end of the current year.
c understate the current year's net income.
d result in more than one of the above, namely, _____ , _____ .

4 Which of the following would produce increasing amounts of interest expense over a bond issue's life?
a Effective-interest amortization of bond discount.
b Effective-interest amortization of bond premium.
c Straight-line amortization of bond discount.
d Straight-line amortization of bond premium.

5 Coastal Marina reported interest expense of $41,015 and $40,866 in two successive six-month periods. The semiannual interest payment in each period amounted to $45,000. From this information one can conclude that Coastal:
a uses the straight-line method of amortization.
b is amortizing a bond discount.
c is computing interest expense by using the effective yield rate to investors rather than the contract interest rate.
d will be reporting an increasing carrying value over the bond issue's life.

6 Blevins Company financed the purchase of a new building by signing a 12%, $300,000 mortgage note. Terms of the note stipulate that interest is to be computed on the unpaid balance at the beginning of each month. After making two monthly payments of $4,000 each, the firm decides to pay the note's outstanding balance. The outstanding principal is:
a $297,990.   c $300,000.
b $298,000.   d $306,000.

7 Which of the following statements about lease accounting is correct?
a Operating leases typically give rise to a long-term liability on the accounting records of the lessee.
b Interest expense is recorded by the lessee with a capital lease but not with an operating lease.
c Interest expense is recorded by the lessee with an operating lease but not with a capital lease.
d Interest expense is recorded by the lessee with both operating and capital leases.

8 Deferred tax considerations have an effect on:
a the balance sheet and the income statement.
b the balance sheet but not the income statement.
c neither the income statement nor the balance sheet.
d the income statement but not the balance sheet.

**COMMUNICATION OF
ACCOUNTING
INFORMATION**

CAI17-1 *Writing a recommendation report: AT&T* (L.O. 2, 6)
Communication Principle: One of the many types of reports in business is the recommendation report. The report's objective is to present an opinion that will lead to decisions or action. Like other types of formal communication, the recommendation report is divided into distinct sections that are set off by headings (see p. 492).

Given the nature of the report, the major conclusions are usually placed near the beginning. This practice allows the reader to quickly review the suggested alternatives, with perhaps only a quick scanning of the report's remaining sections. The recommendation report is geared to the requirements of busy executives who are pressed for time; it is direct and efficient.

After an introduction that contains a brief description of the problem or assignment, the report has a section entitled "Recommendations." This section should be no more than two paragraphs long and should contain the writer's major recommendations—often numbered and set off for easy reading. A follow-up section, typically the longest in the report, may have a heading such as "Presentation of Supporting Information." Here, the criteria for judgment and the reasons for the recommendations are presented. Graphic and tabular information (and related explanations) are introduced if appropriate.

Finally, the report ends with a conclusion. The recommendations are recapped in a brief paragraph that spells out what ought to be done. In a properly organized report, no new information is introduced at this point.

■ ■ ■ ■ ■ ■ ■ ■

AT&T's business is moving and managing information, domestically and globally. This includes providing long-distance telecommunications services along with systems and products that combine communications and computers. The corporation is huge; it has debenture bonds outstanding of approximately $6.4 billion. The interest rates, due dates, and maturities are as follows:

$4\frac{3}{8}$% to $4\frac{3}{4}$%, due 1992–1999	$1.3 billion
$5\frac{1}{8}$% to $7\frac{1}{8}$%, due 1995–2003	1.9 billion
$7\frac{1}{2}$% to 9%, due 1992–2031	3.2 billion

Instructions

You are a member of AT&T's corporate staff and have been asked to write a report. The report should present a recommendation concerning the use of $1 billion of cash on hand. Possible uses of the funds are the retirement of outstanding debt (be sure to specify which of the three bond issues should be selected), investment in various expansion and cost-saving programs that return 9%–11%, or the acquisition of government securities that yield approximately 7%. Assume that (1) the bonds were issued at face value and (2) indentures require that obligations be retired at face value (i.e., no gain or loss).

Answers to Chapter Quiz

1 b

2 b

3 b

4 a (Carrying value on June 1, 19X9, is $103,000: $100,000 + $3,000 unamortized premium; $105,000 payment − $103,000 carrying value = $2,000 loss)

5 a

COMPREHENSIVE PROBLEM 3

HOUSTON CONSULTING

Houston Consulting renders financial services to a variety of small businesses. Each business has its own accounting staff to record routine transactions but relies on Houston's guidance in preparing selected complex journal entries and financial statements and in analyzing financing alternatives.

The company is in the process of completing engagements with five firms that are involved with computers and information-processing systems. A summary of the issues at hand and the tasks to be performed follows.

- *F&S Systems Design*—Management is considering a change from the partnership form to the corporate form of business organization. Gary Franklin, one of the partners, desires a checklist of the advantages and disadvantages of corporations. He also wants to know how a corporation is organized and what par value should be used.

- *Interstate Processing*—The January 1, 19X8, stockholders' equity section for Interstate Processing follows.

Common stock, $4 par value, 800,000 shares authorized, 50,000 shares issued and outstanding	$ 200,000
Paid-in capital in excess of par value	4,000,000
Retained earnings	3,800,000
Total	$8,000,000

Selected transactions and events for the year are:

Jan.	4	Declared a cash dividend of $0.25 per share on the common stock.
Feb.	4	Distributed the January 4 dividend.
Mar.	30	Authorized a 4-for-1 stock split to lower the price on the common stock.
Aug.	7	Declared a 5% stock dividend on all shares outstanding; the market price per share is $20.
Sept.	7	Distributed the August 7 stock dividend.

Interstate's accountant has just resigned from the firm. Management has requested that Houston prepare journal entries to record the preceding transactions and events. In addition, an end-of-year stockholders' equity section is needed. Net income for 19X8 amounted to $300,000.

- *Security Computers, Inc.*—In mid-August, Houston received the income statement of Security Computers, as prepared by Security's accountant. The income statement follows.

SECURITY COMPUTERS, INC.
Income Statement
For the Year Ended June 30, 19X8

Sales		$11,060,000
Cost of goods sold		6,000,000
Gross profit		$ 5,060,000
Less:		
Selling expenses	$2,000,000	
Administrative expenses	1,930,000	3,930,000
Income from operations		$ 1,130,000
Income taxes		452,000
Income from operations after taxes		$ 678,000
Other revenue (expense)		
Gain on sale of division		36,000
Net income		$ 714,000

Security disposed of its office furnishings division on June 29, 19X8. The division had generated 30% of the firm's sales and accounted for 20% of cost of goods sold and 30% of selling and administrative expenses. The division's assets and facilities were sold at a beforetax gain of $60,000. The company is subject to a 40% income tax rate.

Security's accountant did not separate the results of the office furnishings division from those of continuing operations because, as the accountant noted, "we helped that division become profitable and we want to receive credit on our income statement." Some additional information from Security indicates that:

- On January 15, Security experienced a $50,000 gain from the results of a flood. A building was destroyed in this extraordinary event, and insurance proceeds exceeded the book value by $50,000. Security's accountant recorded the gain as a credit to Sales.

- On May 4, one of the company's trucks was sold for $10,000 more than its book value. This gain was also placed in the Sales account.

- Traditionally, Security has used the double-declining balance depreciation method on all items of plant and equipment. At the beginning of the fiscal year, management agreed to change to the straight-line method and calculated that prior years' depreciation expense would have been $70,000 lower had the new method been used. To correct for the overstatement, Security's accountant recorded this amount as a reduction of the current year's depreciation (split equally between selling and administrative expenses).

The president of Security Computers is aware that several accounting errors have been made. She is in need of:

1 A corrected income statement (disregard earnings-per-share amounts).
2 An analysis of the business operations of the office furnishings division relative to the results of continuing corporate operations. Did the company err in selling the office furnishings division?

■ *CompuTech, Inc.*—CompuTech is considering the issuance of bonds to raise some much needed long-term capital. The company has no experience in such matters and therefore desires a short report that details the general characteristics of bonds along with the different types of bonds that could be issued.

■ *Data Services*—On July 1, 19X8, Data Services issued $2 million of 12%, 5-year bonds for $1,859,530. The bonds pay interest semiannually on June 30 and December 31 and were priced to yield an effective rate of 14%. The firm has requested the following:

1 The journal entry to record the bond issuance.
2 The 19X8 entry to record interest expense and effective-interest amortization. Data Services has a December 31 year-end and rounds all computations to the nearest dollar.
3 The proper disclosure of the bond issue on the December 31, 19X8, balance sheet.

Instructions

You are an employee of Houston Consulting. Respond to the specific requests of the five companies.

CHAPTER
18

Long-Term Investments

LEARNING OBJECTIVES

After studying this chapter, you should be able to:

1

Account for investments in bonds.

2

Contrast and use the lower-of-cost-or-market and equity methods of accounting for stock investments.

3

Identify parent/subsidiary relationships.

4

Explain the reason for consolidated financial statements and the related concepts of intercompany transactions and elimination entries.

5

Prepare consolidated financial statements immediately after acquisition.

6

Calculate and record a company's minority interest.

7

Account for subsidiaries acquired at a cost in excess of book value.

Investments in assets are a fact of life for all businesses. Companies that sell merchandise or render services must invest vast sums of money for needed inventories, machinery, equipment, and facilities. Frequently, when sufficient funds are available, a business will purchase the securities of other entities. As we saw in Chapter 7, for example, excess funds are commonly used to acquire various short-term investments. Recall that short-term investments are both *readily salable* and *intended to be converted into cash* within the current operating cycle or one year, whichever is longer.

Investments in securities that do not meet these criteria are classified as noncurrent (long-term) assets on the balance sheet. Long-term securities investments are made for a variety of reasons. Many companies desire the dividend or interest income associated with the securities. Furthermore, businesses often seek to obtain a sufficient number of shares to substantially influence or control the operations of other entities. This practice is followed by firms that want to expand activities in existing markets, diversify by adding new product lines, or ensure a steady source of raw materials and supplies. The preceding points are illustrated in Exhibit 18-1, which lists several corporations along with selected controlled subsidiaries.

This chapter focuses on long-term investments in corporate securities—both bonds and stocks. As you will see, accounting for stock acquisitions can become quite complicated because proper record keeping depends on the percentage of shares owned.

INVESTMENTS IN BONDS

OBJECTIVE
1
Account for investments in bonds.

In Chapter 17 we discussed bonds from the viewpoint of the issuing corporation. We now turn our attention to bond accounting by investors. The primary issues involved are recording the initial investment, treatment of interest and the related amortization of bond discount or premium, and the sale of bonds before maturity. The following sections will show that bond accounting for the investor is very similar to that practiced by the issuer.

Recording the Initial Investment

Bond investments are initially entered in the accounts at cost, that is, the purchase price plus brokerage fees and any other costs related to acquisition. The amount paid for a bond depends on the market price that exists on the date of purchase. A bond's market price is influenced by a number of different factors, including the cash flows associated with the bond issue, the timing of the cash flows, and the rate of return acceptable to the investor.

In addition to the purchase price and other incidental costs, bond investors may be required to pay accrued interest. Recall that the issuing corporation disburses a full period's interest on each interest payment date, regardless of the period of time a bond is held by an investor. As a result of this practice, the purchaser must pay for any interest that has accumulated up to the date of acquisition. To illustrate, assume Foxmire Corporation purchased $300,000 of Harkness Corporation 10-year bonds on March 1, 19X1. Additional facts that relate to Foxmire's investment follow.

EXHIBIT 18-1
Corporations and Selected
Subsidiaries

Corporation	Primary Area of Identity	Subsidiaries
Anheuser-Busch Companies	Beer	Eagle Snack Foods Metal Container Corporation Manufacturers Railway Company
The Dial Corp.	Personal care products	Dobbs House Restaurants Greyhound Lines of Canada Motor Coach Industries (bus manufacturer)
Paramount Communications	Filmed entertainment	USA Cable Network Madison Square Garden New York Knickerbockers
Ralston Purina	Food products	Eveready Battery Company

- Date of bonds: January 1, 19X1
- Contract interest rate: 8%
- Interest payment dates: June 30 and December 31
- Purchase price: $262,991 plus accrued interest

The journal entry to record the bond purchase is:

Mar. 1	Investment in Bonds	262,991	
	Bond Interest Receivable	4,000	
	Cash		266,991
	To record investment in Harkness bonds		

Consistent with the proper accounting treatment for all assets, the Investment in Bonds account is established at cost. Although the bonds were acquired at an amount different from their face value, a separate discount (or premium) account is not used. Instead, the discount (or premium) is commingled with the investment and will be amortized over the remaining life of the bond issue. Finally, observe that Foxmire paid $4,000 for accrued interest for the two months that have passed since January 1 ($300,000 \times 0.08 \times \frac{2}{12} = $4,000$). The Bond Interest Receivable account is debited, because Foxmire expects to collect the interest from Harkness at a later date.

Bond Interest Revenue

The periodic interest receipts normally represent the primary source of revenue related to a bond investment. Continuing our previous example, suppose it is now June 30 and Foxmire receives the first semiannual interest payment of $12,000 ($300,000 \times 0.08 \times \frac{6}{12}$). Because two months of this interest ($4,000) was recorded as Bond Interest Receivable on March 1, the following entry is necessary:

June 30	Cash	12,000	
	Bond Interest Receivable		4,000
	Bond Interest Revenue		8,000
	To record the receipt of semiannual interest		

The $8,000 credit shows that Foxmire has earned interest for only four months (March 1–June 30)—the length of time the company has owned the securities. Assuming a calendar year reporting period, future interest receipts would be recorded in their entirety in the Bond Interest Revenue account.

Bond Discounts

As we illustrated in Chapter 17, bond discounts and premiums respectively increase and decrease the interest expense incurred by the issuing corporation. Similarly, discounts and premiums also affect the interest earned by the investor. In Foxmire's case, for example, the bonds were acquired below their $300,000 face value, thus giving rise to a $37,009 discount ($300,000 − $262,991). As the following computations show, the discount raises the firm's investment income above the total interest collected during the life of the bond issue:

Cash to be received		
Interest receipts over 10 years ($300,000 × 0.08 × 10 years)		$240,000
Face value at maturity		300,000
Total		$540,000
Cash paid for investment		
Purchase price	$262,991	
Accrued interest	4,000	266,991
Income from investment		$273,009

The $273,009 of investment income is deemed interest because it is generated on money that has been lent to Harkness.

Discount Amortization. In addition to the cash interest received, Foxmire must gradually recognize income from the discount. This income can be derived by using the effective-interest amortization process described earlier in the text.[1] The proper accounting procedures are slightly different, however, because of the manner in which the discount was initially recorded.

   Under the effective-interest method, the amount of amortization to recognize each period is determined by a two-step process:

1 Multiply the bonds' carrying value by the effective interest rate to figure total interest revenue.

2 Compute amortization as the difference between the amount of interest revenue calculated in Step 1 and the cash received for interest.

   In the Foxmire illustration, for instance, the bonds have an initial carrying value of $262,991. Although this amount was given as part of the example's original data on page 719, it would actually be derived by dis-

---

[1] The straight-line amortization method is also acceptable if the results obtained do not differ significantly from those achieved with the effective-interest method. The latter approach is conceptually superior and will be utilized throughout the chapter.

counting the future cash flows related to the bond issue. Assume for the sake of simplicity that the discounting process generated an effective yield to investors of 10%. In view of this new information, we can now compute the amortization to be recorded on June 30—the first semiannual interest date.

Observe that four months have passed since Foxmire's acquisition on March 1. Total interest revenue for this period, Step 1 of the process, is $8,766 ($262,991 \times 0.10 \times \frac{4}{12}$). During this same period, the company's *net* cash flow from interest amounted to $8,000:

Receipts on June 30	$12,000
Less: Accrued interest paid to Harkness on March 1	4,000
Net cash flow from interest	$ 8,000

As described in Step 2, the amortization to be recorded is thus $766 ($8,766 − $8,000), giving rise to the following journal entry:

June 30	Investment in Bonds	766	
	Bond Interest Revenue		766
	To record discount amortization		

The entry's credit is logical because, as shown earlier, a discount increases investment income above the cash amounts received for interest. The debit to Investment in Bonds is not as easily understood. Keep in mind that Foxmire's discount is included in the Investment account. *For illustrative purposes only*, assume that the discount had been recorded separately. The amortization entry on June 30 would therefore have had the following impact:

Account	As of Acquisition	Amortization	As of June 30
Investment in bonds	$300,000	$ —	$300,000
Less: Discount on bond investment	37,009	766	36,243
	$262,991	$766	$263,757

The net result is a $766 rise in the investment's carrying value. To enter this increase in the accounting records, the amortization entry must appropriately debit the Investment in Bonds account.

Continuing the example, the interest revenue to recognize on December 31, the next semiannual interest date, will be $13,188 ($263,757 × 0.10 × $\frac{6}{12}$). Because the semiannual cash receipt from Harkness will again amount to $12,000 ($300,000 × 0.08 × $\frac{6}{12}$), the proper amortization figure is $1,188 ($13,188 − $12,000). The amortization process will continue over the life of the bond issue, with the carrying value increasing to $300,000 on the bonds' scheduled maturity date. More detailed illustrations of effective-interest amortization (as related to bonds payable) can be found in Chapter 17.

Premium Amortization

Although our example has focused on the acquisition of bonds at a discount, similar procedures are followed for bonds purchased at a price in excess of face value, that is, at a premium. The investment is still entered in the accounting records at cost. However, a premium has the opposite effect of a discount and reduces interest income over the life of the issue. The premium must therefore be amortized by means of this entry:

Bond Interest Revenue	XXX	
Investment in Bonds		XXX
To record premium amortization		

The debit records the reduction in interest revenue, while the credit lowers the Investment in Bonds account. Eventually, the Investment account will equal the face value of the bonds acquired.

The amortization computations are obtained by using the two-step process described earlier for bonds acquired at a discount. In Step 2, however, the cash received from interest will now exceed the interest revenue figure. In view of this situation, the difference between these two amounts (i.e., the period's amortization) is subtracted from bond carrying value rather than added.

Sale of Bonds Before Maturity

Because of other investment opportunities or perhaps favorable conditions in the bond market, long-term bond investments are often sold prior to their scheduled maturity date. When the sale occurs, it is necessary to update amortization to the date of disposal. This procedure is required to ensure that the correct amount of interest revenue has been recorded and also to determine the investment's carrying value as of the sale date.

To focus on the required accounting, let us return to the Foxmire Corporation example. Suppose that Foxmire sold its investment in Harkness bonds on August 31, 19X3. Recall that the company amortizes the discount on each semiannual interest date, resulting in a carrying value of $268,877 on June 30, 19X3. We will assume that all journal entries through June 30 have been properly prepared.

Because two months have passed since amortization was last recorded, Foxmire must update the accounts in the following manner:

Aug. 31	Investment in Bonds	481	
	Bond Interest Revenue		481
	To record two months of discount amortization		
	$[(\$268,877 \times 0.10 \times \frac{2}{12}) - (\$300,000 \times 0.08 \times \frac{2}{12})]$		

The entry causes an increase in the investment's carrying value to $269,358 ($268,877 + $481).

If the bonds were sold at 102 plus accrued interest, the following entry would be needed to record the sale and eliminate the investment from the books:

Aug. 31	Cash	310,000	
	Investment in Bonds		269,358
	Bond Interest Revenue		4,000
	Gain on Sale of Bonds		36,642
	To record sale of bond investment		

Foxmire has generated $310,000 of cash from the transaction, composed of a $306,000 sale price ($300,000 × 1.02) and $4,000 of accrued interest

($300,000 $\times$ 0.08 $\times$ $\frac{2}{12}$). The gain arises because the bonds' selling price exceeds the investment's carrying value ($269,358); had the situation been reversed, a loss would have been recorded.

INVESTMENTS IN STOCK

In addition to purchasing bonds, companies can also invest in the capital stock of other entities. Like bonds, stock investments are initially entered in the accounts at cost, namely, the purchase price plus any other necessary expenditures related to acquisition (e.g., brokers' fees). Subsequent to the initial recording, the accounting treatment to be used depends on the degree of control that can be exerted over the company whose shares were acquired (known as the **investee**). Generally speaking, the degree of control is influenced by the percentage of the investee's common stock owned by the investor.

Three accounting/reporting methods have been developed: (1) lower of cost or market, (2) equity, and (3) consolidated financial statements. The use of these methods is summarized in Exhibit 18-2.[2] The underlying details of the exhibit, along with the meaning of influence and control, will become apparent in the upcoming presentation.

OBJECTIVE

2

Contrast and use the lower-of-cost-or-market and the equity methods of accounting for stock investments.

Lower-of-Cost-or-Market Method

The **lower-of-cost-or-market method** is used to account for long-term stock acquisitions of investors who are unable to exercise significant influence over the investee corporation. The ability to exert influence over an entity may take several different forms, including ownership of a sizable percentage of the investee's outstanding common shares, representation on the investee's board of directors, participation in policymaking processes, interchange of managerial personnel, and technological dependency. In many instances the determination of whether an investor can influence an investee is not always clear. To provide some uniformity in practice, the accounting profession has recommended that "an investment of less than 20% of the voting stock of an investee should lead to a presumption that an investor does not have the ability to exercise significant influence unless such ability can be demonstrated."[3]

Percentage of Investee Corporation Owned	Presumed Degree of Influence Over Investee	Accounting/Reporting Method
Less than 20%	No significant influence	Lower of cost or market
From 20% to 50%	Significant influence	Equity
Greater than 50%	Controlling interest	Consolidated statements

EXHIBIT 18-2
Use of Accounting/
Reporting Methods

[2] See "The Equity Method of Accounting for Investments in Common Stock," *Opinions of the Accounting Principles Board No. 18* (New York: American Institute of Certified Public Accountants, 1971).
[3] Ibid., paragraph 17.

Under the lower-of-cost-or-market method, stock investments are initially entered in the accounting records at cost. Any dividends received from the investment during the reporting period are recorded as revenue. Furthermore, changes in the value of the securities (subject to certain limits) are recognized and recorded in the accounts by comparing an investment portfolio's aggregate market value against its cost. If this cost-versus-market comparison sounds familiar, the technique is similar to that discussed earlier in the text for short-term investments. Should you need a refresher, refer to Chapter 7.

An Example

To illustrate the lower-of-cost-or-market method, assume the following information relates to Savko Company:

- On January 1, Savko purchased 15,000 common shares of Fresno Manufacturing Corporation at $30 per share. Fresno has 150,000 shares of common stock outstanding.
- During the year Fresno reported net income of $290,000 and paid $120,000 of dividends.
- On December 31, the close of Savko's accounting period, Fresno's common stock had a market value of $27 per share.

Given that Savko owns 10% of Fresno (15,000 shares ÷ 150,000 shares), the following entries are necessary to record the previously mentioned transactions and events:

Investment by Savko

Investment in Fresno Manufacturing	450,000	
Cash		450,000
To record the acquisition of 15,000 shares of		
Fresno at $30 per share		

Announcement of Fresno's Earnings of $290,000

No entry required

Receipt of Cash Dividends

Cash	12,000	
Dividend Revenue		12,000
To record the receipt of 10% of Fresno's dividends		

Valuation at Lower of Cost or Market on December 31*

Unrealized Loss on Long-Term Investments†	45,000	
Allowance for Decline in Market Value of		
Long-Term Investments		45,000
To reduce the investment in Fresno to market		
value: ($30 − $27) × 15,000 shares		

* For simplicity we will assume that Fresno is the only long-term investment owned by Savko.

† According to a ruling of the Financial Accounting Standards Board, unrealized gains and losses on *long-term* investments are not included in the current year's net income. Unrealized losses related to such investments are shown on the balance sheet as a reduction of stockholders' equity.

On the basis of these entries, Savko's investment would appear as follows on the year-end balance sheet:

Long-term investments
    Investment in Fresno Manufacturing $450,000
    Less: Allowance for decline in market value of
            long-term investments   45,000 $405,000

Equity Method

When a company acquires a substantial percentage (20% or more) of the voting shares of a corporation, the acquiring firm normally gains the ability to significantly influence both the financial and the operating policies of the investee. In such instances, unless there is evidence to the contrary, a material economic relationship is formed between the investor and investee, and the **equity method** of accounting must be used.

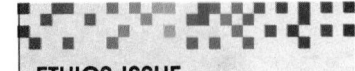

Under the equity method, long-term investments in common stock are initially recorded at acquisition cost. The Investment account is then increased or decreased to reflect changes in the retained earnings of the investee. Specifically, the Investment account is increased for the investor's share of reported investee net income and decreased for the investor's share of any investee net losses or dividends. The "investor's share" is based on the percentage of voting stock owned; the income, loss, and dividend amounts relate strictly to periods after the stock is acquired. Realize that *the equity method focuses principally on changes in the investee's retained earnings, not changes in the market value of the investee's shares.*

To illustrate the equity method, we will use the same facts as in the previous example. Assume, however, that Savko purchased 45,000 shares of Fresno, resulting in a 30% ownership interest (45,000 shares ÷ 150,000 shares). Savko will use the equity method, which requires the following entries:

Investment by Savko
    Investment in Fresno Manufacturing   1,350,000
        Cash   1,350,000
    To record the acquisition of 45,000 shares of
    Fresno at $30 per share

Announcement of Fresno's Earnings of $290,000
    Investment in Fresno Manufacturing   87,000
        Investment Revenue   87,000
    To record 30% share of Fresno's earnings:
    $290,000 × 0.30 = $87,000

Receipt of Cash Dividends
    Cash   36,000
        Investment in Fresno Manufacturing   36,000
    To record the receipt of cash dividends:
    $120,000 × 0.30 = $36,000

Valuation at Lower of Cost or Market on December 31
    No entry required

On the basis of these entries, Savko's investment would be reported on the year-end balance sheet at $1,401,000, as shown by the following T-account:

Investment in Fresno Manufacturing			
Initial investment	1,350,000	Share of dividends	36,000
Share of income	87,000		
	(1,401,000) 1,437,000		

Observe that the $51,000 increase in the investment's carrying value (after the initial acquisition) corresponds to 30% of the increase in Fresno's Retained Earnings account [($290,000 net income − $120,000 dividends) × 0.30 = $51,000]. Also notice that Savko did not recognize any revenue at the time the dividend was received. Although this procedure may seem illogical, bear in mind that (1) dividends represent a distribution of earnings and (2) Savko has already recognized $87,000 of Fresno's net income. If the dividends were recorded as additional revenue, they would be double-counted. Appropriately, then, the Investment account is reduced because the dividend has decreased Savko's share of Fresno's net worth (i.e., retained earnings).

Rationale for the Equity Method

As we have shown on numerous occasions throughout this text, financial statements are used by a number of different parties (e.g., owners, managers, and creditors, to name just a few). To meet the varied needs of these groups, the statements must be objective and neutral. Should bias be present, some users may benefit at the expense of others. For example, if management can manipulate revenue recognition to show higher earnings, creditors and investors may make incorrect decisions regarding the financial health and well-being of the enterprise. It is in this light that the equity method was developed.

Suppose for a moment that a company owned 40% of an investee corporation. Also assume that the investor company was experiencing abnormally low earnings, while the investee was extremely profitable. The investor, with significant influence over operations because of its ownership position, could convince the investee to distribute unusually large amounts of dividends. Had the equity method not been developed, the investor would report the dividends as revenue and thereby manipulate (i.e., control) its own profit. In situations where the ownership interest is 20% or more, the equity method presents a better picture of financial performance because such distributions do not affect investor earnings. Instead, these amounts are treated as a reduction in the Investment account.

Controlling Investments

OBJECTIVE

3

Identify parent/subsidiary relationships.

Thus far we have studied the prescribed accounting practices for companies that have minimal effect (i.e., less than 20% ownership) and those that have significant influence (i.e., from 20% to 50% ownership) on their investee corporations. We now turn our attention to a control type of relationship, that is, possession of more than 50% of the common shares outstanding. By exercising the voting rights connected with these shares, the investor can elect the board of directors of the investee corporation and thereby control the latter's policies and activities.

HIGHLIGHT

Mergers and Change—"Let's Do It Our Way"

With a slew of monopoly routes and a fortress hub in Pittsburgh, USAir appeared to have a license to make money in the 1980s. It didn't do much marketing. It didn't buy jumbo jets. It didn't offer first class service. It wouldn't even give customers an extra bag of peanuts. While other carriers were mired in red ink, USAir earned a profit in every year except one following deregulation.

So confident were the company's executives that they undertook one of the biggest airline combinations in history in 1987, acquiring both Pacific Southwest Airlines (PSA) and Piedmont Aviation, Inc. The two mergers made USAir the nation's sixth largest airline and left it with dominant market shares in Pittsburgh, Charlotte, and other cities.

The mergers, however, also meant that USAir no longer had things quite so soft. Forced out into the rough-and-tumble arena of national competition, it suddenly had to worry a whole lot about the industry's really tough players. Moreover, in absorbing two successful carriers into its system, USAir adopted what it called a "Mirror Image" strategy of making them do everything exactly its way. In this, USAir gave up some of the very elements that made the target airlines successful. In part, as a result, costs have jumped and profits have fallen.

Consider some of the "minor" things. Both PSA and Piedmont had already shown their profitability and customer appeal. Piedmont, headquartered in Winston-Salem, North Carolina, had attracted a loyal following with its Southern hospitality and outstanding service. PSA had wooed West Coast fliers with a playful style, allowing the crew to begin safety briefings with lines like, "In case you haven't been in [a car] since 1962, this is a seat belt."

Piedmont had what many in the industry believed was a more sophisticated ticket pricing system, which balanced full-fare and discount tickets more profitably. USAir scrapped the Piedmont system and still uses only its own. "The revenue differential was astounding"—and lower—on many flights, says one former Piedmont executive.

Industry analysts say USAir needed more sensitivity when it came to marketing trends and customer preferences. When the company cut the old Piedmont practice of serving passengers whole cans of soda, instead of just a cupful, Piedmont frequent fliers put their foot down. Cost-cutting was one thing, but this was downright stingy, they wrote to the *Charlotte Observer*. Scolded, USAir started handing out the cans again.

Passengers on Piedmont had also come to love the baskets of granola bars, cookies, and crackers handed around in first class and the snacks served on flights of less than two hours. When USAir cut that admittedly minor service, complaints again flowed in. Back came the baskets, but minus the cookies.

USAir's experience with PSA also taught it that adhering to a not-invented-here philosophy can cost you in the end. PSA used to hand out cold snacks—a quick and easy service—on its short-haul California routes. USAir changed those to hot meals. But, burdened with trays and the need to heat meals, attendants couldn't keep up with the schedule. Several flights wound up circling airports while the crew frantically tried to collect trays and stow away carts.

So USAir is back to cold snacks on those flights. It still, however, hasn't reinstituted PSA's practice of letting passengers buy tickets on board or in coupon books. And gone now are the smiling faces PSA had painted on the noses of its planes. PSA's former chief financial officer says that was a big marketing mistake. "That was one of the most recognized trademarks in California," he notes. The chairman of USAir says the company had to take the smile off because it wanted all planes to look alike. "It's very difficult to have a smile on everywhere," he says.

To complicate matters, the airline had to wrestle with major problems such as fleet, personnel, and schedule integration—a real nightmare to say the least. The point? Mergers bring change, some for the good and some for the bad. Unfortunately, in USAir's case, the carrier imposed its own way of doing business rather than following the practice of "don't fix what isn't broke."

EXHIBIT 18-3
Legal Versus Economic Entity

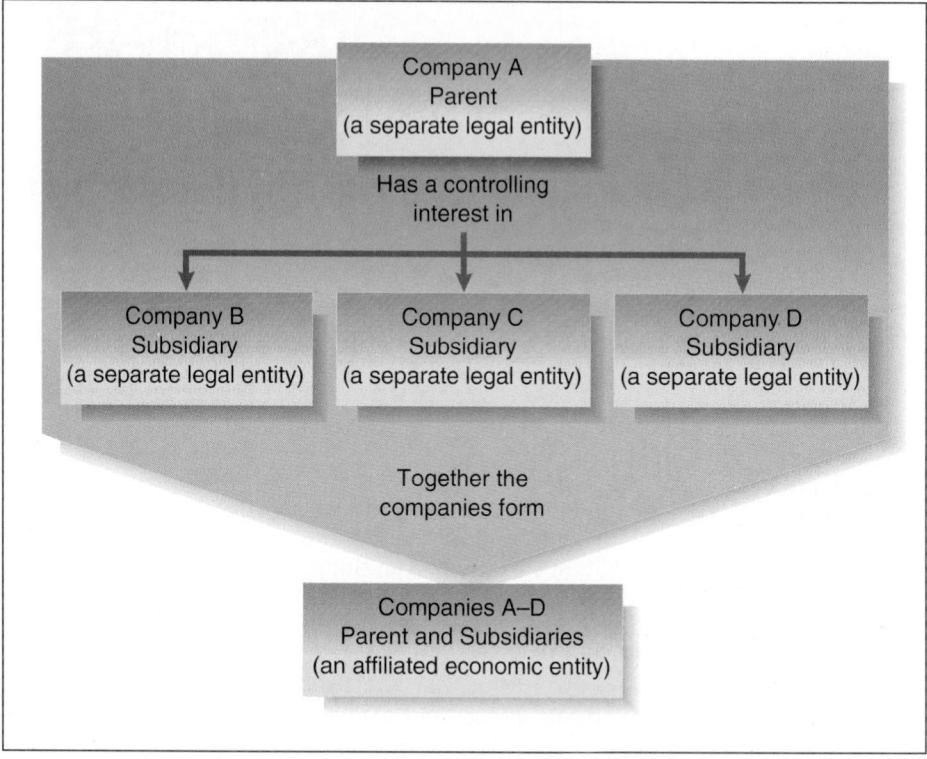

Legal Versus Economic Entities

Given the relationship between the majority owner (termed the **parent**) and its majority-owned companies (termed **subsidiaries**), a question arises concerning definition of the entity. For instance, if Company A owns more than 50% of Companies B, C, and D, are four separate business units involved or is there just one large interwoven operation? To explore this issue more fully, we must become more specific. In our example we have four separate companies that operate as individual **legal entities**—units authorized by the relevant governmental authorities to conduct business. These firms engage in their own activities and prepare separate sets of financial statements. In reality, however, Companies B, C, and D are affiliated with Company A, and together the four companies form a single **economic entity.** The relationship between the legal entities and the economic unit is shown in Exhibit 18-3.

The economic entity is assembled to pursue the objectives of operational efficiency and profit. For example, as we noted earlier in the chapter, many companies have controlling interests in other corporations to ensure themselves of a steady source of raw materials and supplies. As a typical illustration, auto manufacturers often have separate subsidiaries that provide financing and other services to customers and dealers.

Corporate structures that maintain individual "unit" (i.e., subsidiary) operations, rather than merge all activities into a single massive legal entity, are popular for several reasons. The reasons frequently include a savings in income taxes, conformity with governmental regulation, and a reduction of risk. To explain the risk factor, should a particular subsidiary encounter financial difficulties, the separate entity could be sold or liquidated without having a significant impact on the other companies in the affiliated group.

EXECUTIVE BRIEFING
Why Corporate Diversification Is a Plus Financially

Hans Storr
Executive Vice-President and
    Chief Financial Officer
Philip Morris Companies Inc.

Some people think of diversification as a way to reduce risk; they want to put their eggs in more than one basket. At Philip Morris, we have diversified to get a larger number of bigger and better eggs.

Since the beginning of the 1980s, we have been focused on agriculturally based consumer brands that we understand from our experience in tobacco. We have applied our global finance, purchasing, production, and marketing skills to buy Miller and build it into the world's third largest beer company, and to combine Kraft, General Foods, and Jacobs Suchard into the world's second largest food company. Supported by our financial position and credit rating, these companies are realizing economies and business-building opportunities that they would not have had as separate businesses. For instance, our food companies now benefit from each other's access to international markets and are sharing ways of developing fat-free and other new health-oriented products. One result: By 1991, annual net income from our General Foods brands was more than twice the amount, and was growing much faster, than in 1985, when we acquired the company. Overall, then, we're getting a greater number of bigger and better eggs. The end result is that Philip Morris's firms can compete more effectively in global consumer markets.

Consolidated Financial Statements

Because of their separate legal status, a parent and its subsidiaries maintain individual accounting records and prepare separate sets of financial statements. Normally, however, the operating performance and financial position of the single economic entity are collectively reported to stockholders and other user groups via consolidated financial statements.

Consolidated financial statements present a combined picture of the parent and its controlled subsidiaries, as if only one company existed. On a consolidated balance sheet, for instance, the Cash account shows the total cash owned by the entire affiliated group; Accounts Payable reveals the total amounts owed to suppliers, and so forth. This same collective process applies to a consolidated income statement. For example, the balance in

OBJECTIVE
4

Explain the reason for consolidated financial statements and the related concepts of intercompany transactions and elimination entries.

the Sales account represents the total sales revenues earned by a parent and its subsidiary firms.

Consolidated statements disclose the financial activities of the total enterprise, namely, the activities that are under the parent's control. Furthermore, the statements provide more insight than could be gained by examining the separate statements of the various individual legal entities. Representative consolidated statements appear at the end of this text in Appendix C.

Intercompany Transactions

Companies within an affiliated group frequently have transactions with one another. Parent firms often purchase materials and supplies from their subsidiaries. In addition, a parent will commonly lend money to a subsidiary to help finance operations or capital improvement programs. Such transactions, referred to as **intercompany transactions,** present no special accounting problems for the individual entities involved. When consolidated financial statements are prepared, however, it is an entirely different story.

As an example, assume Parent Company owns a controlling interest of Sub Company. Sub is in need of funds and borrows $100,000 from Parent by signing a note payable. The transaction would appear on the balance sheets of both enterprises in the following manner:

PARENT COMPANY Balance Sheet		SUB COMPANY Balance Sheet	
Assets		Liabilities	
Notes receivable	$100,000	Notes payable	$100,000

Suppose that a consolidated balance sheet of the two companies is now desired. If the two balance sheets were merely added together to reflect the financial position of the combined entity, the results would be misleading. Put simply, the combined entity would report that it expects to both receive and pay $100,000 in the near future. Actually, this disclosure is incorrect because the $100,000 represents an expected transfer of cash from Sub to Parent, both of which are in the same economic unit.

Tips & Techniques

Expanding further on our illustration, we emphasize that the combined unit does not have a claim on an outside party, nor does the unit owe an outsider. To properly reflect the impact of this transaction on the Parent/Sub affiliation, neither the note receivable nor the note payable should appear on the companies' consolidated balance sheet.

Work Sheet and Eliminations

When constructing the consolidated financial statements, the accountant first prepares a formal work sheet to combine the account balances of the parent and its subsidiary companies. Although the amounts are merged on the work sheet, combined accounting records are *not* established in a ledger.

As we will soon illustrate, most work sheets have two columns that are used for eliminations. **Eliminations** are required for intercompany items contained in the records of the parent and subsidiaries that do not appear in the consolidated financial statements, for example, the note receivable and note payable cited earlier. The elimination is performed by making an entry on the work sheet that debits intercompany credit balances and credits intercompany debit balances. To illustrate, the elimination entry that follows is needed for the $100,000 note.

Notes Payable (Sub)	100,000	
Notes Receivable (Parent)		100,000
To eliminate intercompany receivable and payable		

We stress that eliminations are made on the work sheet only; *they are never entered in the accounts of either a parent or its subsidiaries*. Entries into the accounts would formally (and erroneously) cancel transactions between the companies.

Consolidation upon Acquisition

To demonstrate the consolidation process, consider the balance sheets of Engle Corporation and Grant, Inc., that appear in Exhibit 18-4. On January 1, 19X2, Engle acquired 100% of Grant's outstanding stock from existing shareholders for $175,000—the stock's book value. Engle will record the acquisition as shown on page 732.

OBJECTIVE

5

Prepare consolidated financial statements immediately after acquisition.

	Engle	Grant
Cash	$ 400,000	$ 25,000
Accounts receivable (net)	600,000	30,000
Inventories	800,000	40,000
Property, plant, & equipment (net)	1,500,000	230,000
Total assets	$3,300,000	$325,000
Accounts payable	$ 300,000	$ 60,000
Bonds payable	1,300,000	90,000
Common stock	1,000,000	100,000
Retained earnings	700,000	75,000
Total liabilities & stockholders' equity	$3,300,000	$325,000

EXHIBIT 18-4
Balance Sheets of Engle Corporation and Grant, Inc. (as of December 31, 19X1)

Jan. 1   Investment in Grant   175,000
        Cash   175,000
        To record the acquisition of 100%
        of Grant, Inc.

The only effect of this transaction on Engle's accounting records is the exchange of one asset, Cash, for another (Investment in Grant). The Investment account is established in Engle's ledger and will be maintained under the equity method of accounting, as described in an earlier section of this chapter.[4] Grant's books are unaffected because the exchange of outstanding shares among stockholders has no impact on the issuing firm. The balance sheets of the two companies immediately after the acquisition appear in the first two columns of the work sheet contained in Exhibit 18-5.

The Investment Elimination.   As Exhibit 18-5 reveals, an intercompany transaction must be eliminated in order to prepare the consolidated balance sheet. The color numbers in the first two columns show that the

EXHIBIT 18-5
Consolidated Balance Sheet
Work Sheet of Engle
Corporation and Grant, Inc.

			Intercompany Eliminations		Consolidated Balance Sheet
ENGLE AND GRANT Consolidated Balance Sheet Work Sheet January 1, 19X2					
Account	Engle	Grant	Debit	Credit	
Cash	225,000*	25,000			250,000
Accounts receivable (net)	600,000	30,000			630,000
Inventories	800,000	40,000			840,000
Investment in Grant	175,000			(a) 175,000	
Property, plant, & equipment (net)	1,500,000	230,000			1,730,000
	3,300,000	325,000			3,450,000
Accounts payable	300,000	60,000			360,000
Bonds payable	1,300,000	90,000			1,390,000
Common stock: Engle	1,000,000				1,000,000
Common stock: Grant		100,000	(a) 100,000		
Retained earnings: Engle	700,000				700,000
Retained earnings: Grant		75,000	(a) 75,000		
	3,300,000	325,000	175,000	175,000	3,450,000

* $400,000 original balance minus $175,000 acquisition cost.

---

[4] When consolidated financial statements are prepared, the parent may employ an alternative practice (called the cost method) to maintain the Investment in Subsidiary Company account. Because the same consolidated results can be derived from either approach, we will assume use of the equity method to simplify our discussion.

$175,000 investment by Engle (a 100% ownership interest) is represented by Grant's stockholders' equity of common stock ($100,000) and retained earnings ($75,000). Stated differently, since Engle owns 100% of Grant, all common stock financing of the combined entity is provided by Engle's shareholders. Thus, if the stockholders' equity accounts of the parent and subsidiary were simply combined on a consolidated statement, the financing provided by Engle's investors and operations (i.e., retained earnings) would be overstated. For these reasons the Investment account must be eliminated (via a credit because it has a debit balance), along with Grant's Common Stock and Retained Earnings accounts (via debits because they possess credit balances).

The result is a consolidated balance sheet—the combination of Engle and Grant's individual balance sheets minus the elimination. The information that appears in the right-hand column of the work sheet is recast as shown in Exhibit 18-6. The consolidated financial statement reveals that the combined entity has $3.45 million of assets, owes $1.75 million to outside creditors, and has $1.7 million of stockholders' equity, the last amount being provided solely by Engle Corporation.

ENGLE AND GRANT Consolidated Balance Sheet January 1, 19X2		
Assets		
Current assets		
Cash		$ 250,000
Accounts receivable (net)		630,000
Inventories		840,000
Total current assets		$1,720,000
Property, plant, & equipment (net)		1,730,000
Total assets		$3,450,000
Liabilities & Stockholders' Equity		
Current liabilities		
Accounts payable		$ 360,000
Long-term liabilities		
Bonds payable		1,390,000
Total liabilities		$1,750,000
Stockholders' equity		
Common stock	$1,000,000	
Retained earnings	700,000	
Total stockholders' equity		1,700,000
Total liabilities & stockholders' equity		$3,450,000

EXHIBIT 18-6
Consolidated Balance Sheet of Engle Corporation and Grant, Inc.

Minority Interest

To obtain control of a subsidiary, the parent need not acquire a 100% ownership interest as in the previous example. Acquisitions of more than 50% but less than 100% of the outstanding voting stock of other corporations occur frequently. In such cases the parent company is said to obtain a majority interest, while the other owners of the subsidiary have a **minority interest.**

To illustrate the proper accounting for a minority interest, we will modify the Engle/Grant example. Recall that Grant had $100,000 of common stock and $75,000 of retained earnings as of December 31, 19X1. Assume now that Engle purchases an 80% interest in Grant for $140,000, the purchase price corresponding to the book value of Grant's stock ($175,000 × 0.80 = $140,000). Engle will record the acquisition by the following entry:

Jan. 1	Investment in Grant	140,000	
	Cash		140,000
	To record the acquisition of 80% of Grant, Inc.		

The companies' ownership position is shown in Exhibit 18-7. Since Engle owns 80% of Grant, 80% of the subsidiary's common stock and retained earnings balances are eliminated when consolidated financial statements are prepared. The remaining 20% of Grant's ownership represents the minority interest and is listed as such on the consolidated balance sheet (see Exhibit 18-8).

The work sheet contains two elimination entries. Entry (a) eliminates Engle's Investment account along with 80% of Grant's stockholders' equity, thus avoiding the possible overstatement as described in the original example. Entry (b) transfers the remaining 20% of Grant's common stock and retained earnings into a new account entitled Minority Interest in Grant. A typical balance sheet presentation of the minority interest is shown immediately below the exhibit on the next page.

EXHIBIT 18-7
Illustration of Minority Interest

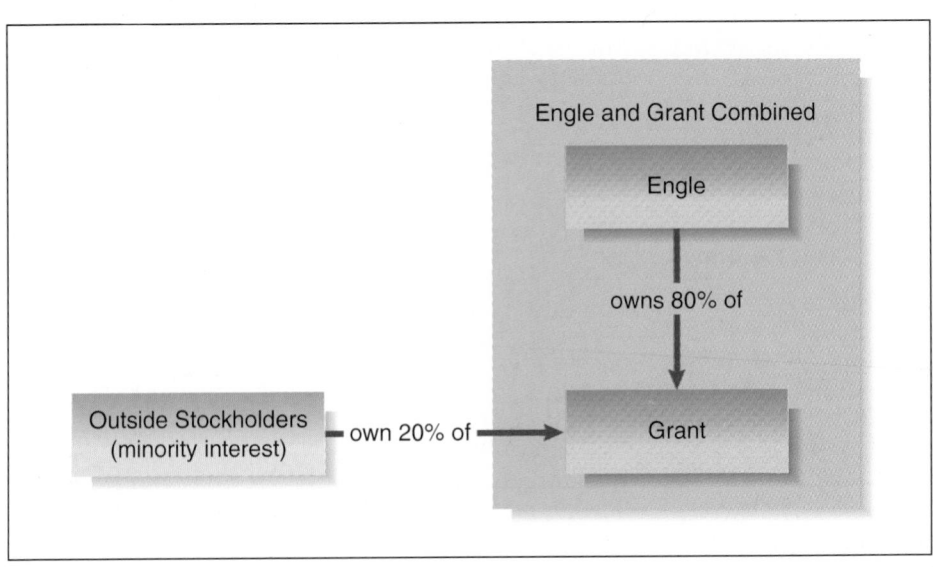

Engle and Grant Combined

Engle

owns 80% of

Grant

Outside Stockholders (minority interest) — own 20% of →

			Intercompany Eliminations		Consolidated Balance
Account	Engle	Grant	Debit	Credit	Sheet
Cash	260,000*	25,000			285,000
Accounts receivable (net)	600,000	30,000			630,000
Inventories	800,000	40,000			840,000
Investment in Grant	140,000			(a) 140,000	
Property, plant, & equipment (net)	1,500,000	230,000			1,730,000
	3,300,000	325,000			3,485,000
Accounts payable	300,000	60,000			360,000
Bonds payable	1,300,000	90,000			1,390,000
Common stock: Engle	1,000,000				1,000,000
Common stock: Grant		100,000	(a) 80,000		
			(b) 20,000		
Retained earnings: Engle	700,000				700,000
Retained earnings: Grant		75,000	(a) 60,000		
			(b) 15,000		
Minority interest in Grant				(b) 35,000	35,000
	3,300,000	325,000	175,000	175,000	3,485,000

ENGLE AND GRANT
Consolidated Balance Sheet Work Sheet
January 1, 19X2

* $400,000 original balance minus $140,000 acquisition cost.

Stockholders' equity
   Minority interest in Grant $ 35,000
   Common stock   1,000,000
   Retained earnings   700,000
                    $1,735,000

EXHIBIT 18-8
Consolidated Balance Sheet Work Sheet with Minority Interest

Accounting for minority interests in this manner provides added disclosure in the financial statements. The statement reader can now see that the controlling stockholders of the Engle/Grant combined entity have equity of $1.7 million, while outside stockholders of the Grant subsidiary have equity (i.e., claims against Grant) of only $35,000.

Alternatively, the consolidated balance sheets of some corporations report the minority interest between the liability and stockholders' equity sections. Companies that follow this practice are stressing the limited role of the minority interest in ownership affairs.

Acquisition of Subsidiary at More or Less Than Book Value

In all of our illustrations thus far, we have assumed the amount paid by the parent was equal to the book value of the ownership interest acquired. In the preceding example, for instance, Engle paid $140,000 to purchase 80% of Grant's $175,000 stockholders' equity ($175,000 × 0.80 = $140,000). Normally, the acquisition cost of a subsidiary does not coincide with the subsidiary's book value.

OBJECTIVE
7
Account for subsidiaries acquired at a cost in excess of book value.

Remember from Chapter 15 that book value represents a company's net assets (assets minus liabilities) and is calculated by using figures extracted from the balance sheet—a cost-based financial statement. Given the impact of inflation in our economy, asset valuations and book value are frequently understated and do not reflect current market values. Adding to this problem, an ongoing business often has a number of "unrecorded assets" that a purchaser is willing to pay for and acquire. As an example, a corporation's established reputation among clientele, its ability to earn greater-than-normal profits, and the company's top management team all enable a buyer to begin operations in a favorable position. Finally, a business may have something of vital interest to a purchaser such as valuable patents or established product markets. Collectively, the preceding factors all contribute to the fact that subsidiaries are often acquired at a price in excess of book value. Sometimes, the difference between cost and book value is substantial. Caesars World, for example, reports a cost nearly $53 million in excess of book amounts on the purchase of its hotel operations in Las Vegas and Atlantic City.

An Example.   To illustrate the necessary accounting in this type of situation, assume Stafford Corporation acquired a 100% controlling interest in Trout, Inc., for $260,000 on December 31, 19XX. The balance sheets of both companies immediately *after* the acquisition are shown in Exhibit 18-9.

Stafford has paid $260,000 for a company having a book value (i.e., stockholders' equity) of $200,000. Why? Assume that during negotiations for the acquisition, Stafford's management found that Trout's property, plant, and equipment was undervalued by $35,000. In addition, Stafford was willing to pay an extra $25,000 because of favorable forecasts of Trout's future earnings and Trout's leadership position in its field of operation. To summarize, the $260,000 investment is represented by the following:

100% ownership interest	
Common stock: Trout	$160,000
Retained earnings: Trout	40,000
Increase in property, plant, & equipment (net)	35,000
Favorable earnings prospects, reputation, and so on	25,000
	$260,000

EXHIBIT 18-9
Balance Sheets of Stafford Corporation and Trout, Inc. (as of December 31, 19XX)

	Stafford	Trout
Cash & other assets	$ 90,000	$ 70,000
Property, plant, & equipment (net)	140,000	180,000
Investment in Trout	260,000	—
Total assets	$490,000	$250,000
Accounts payable	$ 60,000	$ 50,000
Common stock	250,000	160,000
Retained earnings	180,000	40,000
Total liabilities & stockholders' equity	$490,000	$250,000

In the preparation of a consolidated balance sheet, the following work sheet elimination entry is needed:

Common Stock: Trout	160,000	
Retained Earnings: Trout	40,000	
Property, Plant, & Equipment	35,000	
Goodwill	25,000	
Investment in Trout		260,000

To eliminate Trout's stockholders' equity accounts against the Investment account and to revalue the assets acquired

The entry first offsets Trout's stockholders' equity accounts against Stafford's $260,000 investment. Furthermore, since Stafford paid an additional $35,000 to acquire the subsidiary's plant and equipment, the Property, Plant, & Equipment account is debited to reflect the increased cost. Finally, favorable earnings prospects, reputation, good management, and other similar factors collectively give rise to the intangible asset *goodwill*, requiring a $25,000 debit to that account. The preceding treatment is in accordance with a ruling of the accounting profession, which states that "the excess of the cost of the acquired company over the sum of the amounts assigned to identifiable assets acquired less liabilities assumed should be recorded as goodwill."[5] Rather than debit Goodwill, a firm will sometimes use a more descriptive account title such as Excess of Cost over Book Value in Subsidiary.

The net result of the elimination is the consolidated balance sheet that appears in Exhibit 18-10.

Book Value in Excess of Cost. Our example has focused on the case in which a parent pays more than the book value of the subsidiary acquired. The opposite situation, book value greater than cost, is not encountered as frequently in practice. The necessary accounting treatment is somewhat similar to that just illustrated. Because of added complexities, however, discussion of the associated procedures is postponed to advanced-level courses.

Consolidated Income Statement

A consolidated income statement is prepared in much the same fashion as a consolidated balance sheet. Revenue and expense accounts of the parent and subsidiaries are combined, and intercompany transactions are eliminated. The eliminations allow statement users to analyze figures that reflect activities with external parties, as opposed to transactions that have occurred entirely within the affiliated company network.

As an example, consider a corporation that is engaged in the manufacture and sale of motion picture films. The corporation has established two separate entities: production and marketing. Production sells its entire output to marketing, which, in turn, distributes the films to movie theaters and other outside establishments. It is apparent that marketing is the

---

[5] "Accounting for Business Combinations," *Opinions of the Accounting Principles Board No. 16* (New York: American Institute of Certified Public Accountants, 1970), paragraph 87.

EXHIBIT 18-10
Consolidated Balance Sheet of Stafford Corporation and Trout, Inc.

STAFFORD AND TROUT Consolidated Balance Sheet December 31, 19XX		
Assets		
Cash & other assets		$160,000
Property, plant, & equipment (net)		355,000*
Goodwill		25,000
Total assets		$540,000
Liabilities & Stockholders' Equity		
Current liabilities		
Accounts payable		$110,000
Stockholders' equity		
Common stock	$250,000	
Retained earnings	180,000	
Total stockholders' equity		430,000
Total liabilities & stockholders' equity		$540,000

* $140,000 + $180,000 + $35,000 = $355,000.

true generator of sales revenues for the corporation, with production's revenues being strictly intercompany. Unless an elimination entry is made in the preparation of the consolidated income statement, the combination of the two Sales accounts would present an incorrect picture of corporate revenues and net income.

Two typical transactions that require an elimination entry are intercompany sales and interest on loans (or other obligations) between the parent and the subsidiary. When analyzing these transactions, keep in mind that a sale by one affiliate is represented by a purchase or, if the merchandise is sold, by cost of goods sold on another affiliate's records. Similarly, interest revenue for one member of the economic entity is interest expense for another. The necessary eliminations that underlie the preparation of a consolidated income statement can become quite complicated and are clearly beyond the scope of this text.

END-OF-CHAPTER REVIEW

LEARNING OBJECTIVES: THE KEY POINTS

1 Account for investments in bonds. Bond investments are recorded at their purchase price plus any costs incidental to the acquisition (e.g., brokerage fees). Additionally, a bond investor will pay for any accrued interest as of the date of purchase, with such amounts being recorded in the Bond Interest Receivable account. On the next interest payment date, the investor will receive a full period's interest regardless of how long the investment has been held.

The amount of bond interest revenue is increased or decreased by the periodic amortization of discounts and premiums, respectively. This discount or premium should be amortized by the effective-interest method, which basically involves two steps. Interest revenue is first calculated by multiplying the carrying value by the effective interest rate. The amortization amount is then computed as the difference between interest revenue and the cash received for interest.

When bond investments are sold, the amortization process is updated to the date of disposal. The bonds are removed from the accounts, and the sale proceeds and any accrued interest are recorded. Finally, the difference between the updated carrying value and the selling price is recognized as a gain or a loss on the transaction.

2 Contrast and use the lower-of-cost-or-market and equity methods of accounting for stock investments. Stock investments are accounted for by either the lower-of-cost-or-market method or the equity method. The lower-of-cost-or-market approach is used when the investor lacks the ability to exercise significant influence over the investee (typically less than 20% ownership). Under this method, the investment is recorded in the accounts at cost, and any dividends received are recognized as revenue. Should the market value of the shares fall below cost, an unrealized loss is entered in the accounting records.

The equity method is used when the investor has the ability to exercise significant influence over an investee (typically 20% or more ownership). With this approach, the Investment account is increased for the investor's pro rata share of investee net income and decreased for any dividends received and net losses incurred. The Investment account therefore increases and decreases with changes in the retained earnings of the investee corporation.

3 Identify parent/subsidiary relationships. When one company acquires a controlling interest (over 50% ownership) in another business, a parent/subsidiary relationship is created. The acquiring company becomes the parent, and the acquired company is the subsidiary. Although the companies remain separate legal entities and maintain separate accounting records, the firms have (in substance) become a single affiliated economic unit.

4 Explain the reason for consolidated financial statements and the related concepts of intercompany transactions and elimination entries. Consolidated financial statements are prepared because the parent and subsidiary represent a single economic unit. As such, transactions among the affiliated firms (i.e., intercompany transactions) must be eliminated on the work sheet when consolidated statements are constructed. A failure to do so would result in misleading reports of financial position and profitability, because the entity would be reporting transactions it has both with outside businesses and with itself.

5 Prepare consolidated financial statements immediately after acquisition. Consolidated financial statements are often prepared by first constructing a work sheet. The work sheet is used to combine assets, liabilities, and stockholders' equity of the parent and its subsidiaries. Prior to these amounts being merged, a set of columns is used to record the elimination of intercompany transactions (e.g., intercompany investments/equity, payables/receivables, and so forth). After all appropriate eliminations are made, the columns are summed across the work sheet to arrive at the amounts to be disclosed in the consolidated financial statements.

6 Calculate and record a company's minority interest. A minority interest is created in the consolidation process when a parent owns less than 100% of a controlled subsidiary. The portion of subsidiary equity owned by outsiders is not eliminated against the parent's investment but instead is transferred to a Minority

Interest account. Such amounts appear on the consolidated balance sheet, often being disclosed in the stockholders' equity section.

7 Account for subsidiaries acquired at a cost in excess of book value. When a subsidiary is acquired at more than book value, the excess is attributable to undervalued assets and/or goodwill. To consolidate, the elimination entry involves a credit to the Investment account and debits to the equity accounts of the subsidiary. Because the credit is greater than the debits, additional debits must be recorded on the books. These amounts will increase specific assets that are undervalued and, when appropriate, will recognize goodwill.

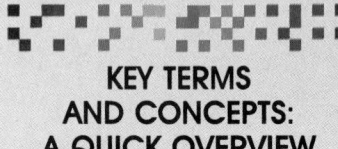

KEY TERMS AND CONCEPTS: A QUICK OVERVIEW

consolidated financial statements A set of financial statements that combines the activities of the parent and controlled subsidiaries as if only one company existed.

controlling interest A greater-than-50% ownership interest in a subsidiary company.

economic entity A group of companies that function as a single entity to pursue the objectives of operational efficiency and profit.

elimination entry An entry made on the consolidated work sheet to eliminate intercompany transactions from consolidated financial statements.

equity method A method of accounting for long-term investments in common stock, where the Investment account includes the acquisition cost and a share of the investee's net income, net losses, and dividends.

intercompany transaction A transaction between two affiliated companies such as a parent and a subsidiary.

investee A company whose shares have been acquired by an investor.

legal entity A unit authorized by the relevant government authority to conduct business.

lower-of-cost-or-market method A method of accounting for long-term investments in stock. The method is used when a company owns less than 20% of an investee's common shares.

minority interest The portion of a subsidiary entity owned by parties other than the parent (controlling) company.

parent A company that is the majority owner of another company.

subsidiary A company that has another company as its majority stockholder.

CHAPTER QUIZ

The five questions that follow relate to several issues raised in the chapter. Test your knowledge of the issues by selecting the best answer. (The answers appear on p. 757.)

1 Tobias purchased $400,000 of Sanborn Co., bonds at 104, plus accrued interest of $8,000. Brokerage fees amounted to $2,000. As a result of this purchase, Tobias should increase the Investment in Bonds account by:

a $402,000.   c $418,000.
b $410,000.   d $426,000.

2 When the percentage ownership of an investee corporation is less than 20% of the outstanding voting stock and no significant investor influence is present, the accounting method to be used is:

a consolidated financial statements.   c equity.

b lower of cost or market.   d pooling of interests.

3 On January 1, 19X2, Hansen paid $2 million to acquire 40% of TYG Corporation's common stock. Hansen exercises significant influence over TYG via membership on the latter firm's board of directors. During 19X2, TYG distributed total dividends of $125,000 and reported $600,000 of net income. The carrying value of Hansen's investment on December 31, 19X2, should be:

a $2,000,000.   c $2,475,000.

b $2,190,000.   d $2,600,000.

4 Which of the following statements concerning consolidated financial statements is true?

a Elimination entries should be recorded in the accounting records of the parent.

b Elimination entries should be recorded in the accounting records of subsidiary companies.

c Elimination entries should be recorded in the accounting records of both the parent and its subsidiary companies.

d Elimination entries should be recorded only on the consolidated work sheet.

5 On a consolidated balance sheet for a parent company and a 60% owned subsidiary, the total stockholders' equity will typically equal:

a the parent's stockholders' equity.

b the parent's stockholders' equity plus the minority interest.

c the parent's stockholders' equity minus the minority interest.

d the subsidiary's stockholders' equity.

SUMMARY PROBLEM

Polaris Oil Corporation was formed on January 1 of the current year and acquired various long-term investments throughout its first 12 months of operation. Details of the investments are described in the following paragraphs.

On July 1, Polaris acquired 1,000 shares of Lindel Corporation's common stock at $7 per share. Lindel has 100,000 shares of common stock outstanding; Polaris is unable to exercise significant influence over Lindel's management. Lindel paid dividends of $0.10 per share on December 1; its common stock was selling for $4.75 per share at year-end.

On October 1, Polaris purchased 2,000 shares of Miller Corporation's common stock for $36,000. Miller has 5,000 shares of common stock outstanding, and Polaris is able to exercise significant influence over the acquired firm's management. Miller earned $9,000 during the last quarter of the year and paid dividends of $1 per share on November 1. The fair market value of the stock on December 31 totaled $36,400.

On December 31, Polaris acquired 100% of the outstanding common shares of Shawnee Oil for $85,000. At the time of purchase, Shawnee's equity accounts consisted of Common Stock ($30,000) and Retained Earnings ($55,000).

Instructions

a Identify the proper method that Polaris should use to account for its investment in Lindel Corporation and prepare journal entries to record the following:

(1) The initial investment on July 1.

(2) The receipt of dividends on December 1.

(3) Any necessary year-end adjustments.

b Identify the proper method that Polaris should use to account for its investment in Miller Corporation and prepare journal entries to record the following:
  (1) The initial investment on October 1.
  (2) The receipt of dividends on November 1.
  (3) Any necessary year-end adjustments.
c Identify the proper method that Polaris should use to account for its investment in Shawnee Oil and prepare the following:
  (1) The journal entry to record the initial investment on December 31.
  (2) The work sheet elimination entry that is necessary to prepare a consolidated balance sheet as of December 31.

Solution

a The investment in Lindel Corporation common stock should be accounted for by employing the lower-of-cost-or-market method. Polaris owns 1% (1,000 ÷ 100,000) of the common shares and does not have the ability to exercise significant influence.

(1) July 1	Investment in Lindel		7,000	
	Cash			7,000
	To record the acquisition of 1,000 shares of Lindel at $7 per share			
(2) Dec. 1	Cash		100	
	Dividend Revenue			100
	To record the receipt of Lindel dividends: 1,000 shares × $0.10 = $100			
(3) Dec. 31	Unrealized Loss on Long-Term Investments		2,250	
	Allowance for Decline in Market Value of Long-Term Investments			2,250
	To reduce the investment in Lindel to market value: 1,000 shares × ($7.00 − $4.75)			

b The investment in Miller Corporation common stock should be accounted for by using the equity method. Polaris has the ability to exercise significant influence and owns 40% (2,000 ÷ 5,000) of the outstanding common shares.

(1) Oct. 1	Investment in Miller		36,000	
	Cash			36,000
	To record the acquisition of 2,000 shares of Miller			
(2) Nov. 1	Cash		2,000	
	Investment in Miller			2,000
	To record the receipt of cash dividends of $1 per share			
(3) Dec. 31	Investment in Miller		3,600	
	Investment Revenue			3,600
	To record 40% share of Miller's earnings: $9,000 × 0.40 = $3,600			

c Polaris and Shawnee should be consolidated because Polaris controls the firm through a 100% ownership position.

(1) Dec. 31	Investment in Shawnee Oil		85,000	
	Cash			85,000
	To record the acquisition of 100% of Shawnee Oil			

(2) Dec. 31 Common Stock: Shawnee Oil   30,000
               Retained Earnings: Shawnee Oil   55,000
                 Investment in Shawnee Oil   85,000
               To eliminate Shawnee's stockholders'
               equity accounts against the Investment
               account

ASSIGNMENT MATERIAL

QUESTIONS

Q18-1 Why do companies make long-term securities investments?

Q18-2 What is the proper accounting treatment for brokers' fees incurred on the purchase of corporate securities?

Q18-3 Putnam Company must pay $6,000 of accrued interest to acquire $100,000 of Zimmer Corporation bonds. If the bonds are purchased at 98, should Putnam debit the Investment in Bonds account for $104,000 ($98,000 + $6,000)? Explain.

Q18-4 Explain when the straight-line amortization method is an acceptable substitute for effective-interest amortization.

Q18-5 What steps are performed when computing effective-interest amortization?

Q18-6 Garcia Corporation recently amortized $3,000 of discount on a bond investment. Determine the impact of the amortization entry on the following:
a Interest revenue for the year.
b Interest received from the bond issuer.
c The bond investment's carrying value.

Q18-7 Should accrued interest be considered when computing the gain or loss on the sale of a bond investment? Briefly discuss.

Q18-8 Discuss the differences between the lower-of-cost-or-market and equity methods when accounting for an investor's share of investee dividends and net income.

Q18-9 Benjamin, Inc., owns 30% of Baugh Corporation. During the current year, Baugh paid dividends totaling $40,000. Discuss (a) the proper treatment of the dividends on Benjamin's records and (b) the underlying reason behind that treatment.

Q18-10 Discuss the rationale that underlies the equity method of accounting.

Q18-11 Distinguish between a legal entity and an economic entity.

Q18-12 Why are elimination entries needed in the preparation of consolidated financial statements? Where are the eliminations recorded?

Q18-13 Explain why the acquisition cost of a subsidiary seldom agrees with the subsidiary's book value.

EXERCISES

E18-1 Straightforward bond investment; no amortization (L.O. 1)

Titan Manufacturing acquired $600,000 of 10% bonds on March 1 at 100% of face value, plus accrued interest. The bonds are dated January 1 and pay interest each June 30 and December 31.

a Prepare journal entries to record (1) the bond acquisition on March 1; (2) the receipt of interest on June 30; and (3) the receipt of interest on December 31.

b Compute Titan's total interest revenue for the year ended December 31.

E18-2 Bond investments; effective-interest amortization (L.O. 1)

Windsor Devices, Inc., purchased $500,000 of 8% bonds on January 1, 19XX, for $437,689. The bonds have a 10-year life, pay seminannual interest each June 30 and December 31, and were priced to generate a 10% effective interest rate.

a Prepare Windsor's journal entry to record the bond purchase on January 1.

b Prepare entries to record the interest receipt and discount amortization on June 30 and December 31, 19XX. Windsor uses the effective-interest method of amortization; round calculations to the nearest dollar.

c Compute total interest revenue for 19XX.

d Present the proper disclosure of the bond investment on Windsor's December 31, 19XX, balance sheet.

E18-3 Effective-interest amortization of bond discount and premium (L.O. 1)

On January 1, 19X2, Hopkins Company purchased two different bond issues to be held as long-term investments. The following information is available:

1-2-3

Bond Issue	Face Value	Contract Interest Rate (%)	Effective Interest Rate (%)	Purchase Price
1	$100,000	8%	10%	$ 87,538
2	100,000	7	6	107,439

All bonds pay interest on June 30 and December 31. Hopkins uses the effective-interest method of amortization.

a Compute the total interest *received* during 19X2.

b Compute amortization to be recorded during 19X2. Round calculations to the nearest dollar.

c Determine the amount of bond interest revenue to be reported on the firm's 19X2 income statement.

E18-4 Sale of bond investment (L.O. 1)

The Wizard Corporation purchased $500,000 of 9% bonds for $470,776 on January 1, 19X1. The bonds were dated January 1, 19X1, were scheduled to mature on December 31, 19X9, and had an effective yield to investors of 10%. Interest is paid semiannually on June 30 and December 31. On October 1, 19X3, Wizard sold the bonds at 103 plus accrued interest.

a Assume that the investment's carrying value stands at $476,516 as of June 30, 19X3. Using effective-interest amortization and rounding computations to the nearest dollar, determine the carrying value as of October 1, 19X3.

b Prepare the journal entries necessary on October 1, 19X3.

E18-5 *Basic accounting for stock investment* **(L.O. 2)**

On January 1 of the current year, Hagan Company acquired 10,000 shares of Atlantic Corporation's common stock at $10 per share. The following information has come to your attention:

1 During the current year, Atlantic generated net income of $240,000 and paid dividends totaling $72,000.
2 The year-end market price of Atlantic's common stock was $9.25 per share.
3 Hagan has no other long-term investments.

Assume that Atlantic has 100,000 shares of common stock outstanding.

a Determine which method (lower-of-cost-or-market or equity) should be used to account for Hagan's investment.
b Present all appropriate journal entries for Hagan Company.
c Compute the year-end carrying value of Hagan's investment.

E18-6 *Basic accounting for stock investment* **(L.O. 2)**

On January 1, 19X4, Emerson Services purchased 8,000 common shares of Affiliated Enterprises for $8 per share. Information pertaining to Affiliated follows.

Common stock outstanding ($1 par, 25,000 shares), Dec. 31, 19X4	$25,000
Net income, 19X4	80,000
Dividends paid, 19X4	10,000

Affiliated's year-end market price was $7 per share.

a What method should Emerson use to account for its investment in Affiliated? Why?
b Prepare the journal entries that Emerson would record in 19X4 pertaining to the investment.
c Show the proper presentation of the Investment in Affiliated account on Emerson's 19X4 year-end balance sheet.

E18-7 *Lower-of-cost-or-market and equity methods* **(L.O. 2)**

On January 1, 19X3, Davidson Enterprises purchased 10,000 common shares of Keystone, Inc., and 30,000 common shares of Software, Inc. The acquisitions cost $57,500 and $240,000, respectively. Information about these two firms follows.

	Keystone, Inc.	Software, Inc.
Common shares outstanding	40,000	300,000
19X3 net income	$72,000	$190,000
19X3 dividends	$20,000	$ 60,000
19X3 year-end market value per share	$5	$7

a Determine whether the investments in Keystone and Software should be accounted for by using the lower-of-cost-or-market method or the equity method. Explain the rationale behind your answer.
b Present the proper disclosure of Davidson's long-term stock investments on the December 31, 19X3, balance sheet.
c Compute the total investment revenue and dividend revenue that Davidson would report on its 19X3 income statement.

E18-8   *Straightforward consolidation; minority interest* (L.O. 4, 5, 6)

On April 1, Palmer Corporation acquired 75% of the outstanding common shares of Snee, Inc., for $1,200,000. The condensed balance sheets of each company immediately after the acquisition follow.

	Palmer	Snee	Consolidated
Cash	$ 500,000	$ 10,000	$_____
Other assets	900,000	1,890,000	_____
Investment in Snee	1,200,000	—	_____
	$2,600,000	$1,900,000	$
Liabilities	$ 80,000	$ 300,000	$_____
Minority interest in Snee	—	—	_____
Common stock	1,500,000	1,000,000	_____
Retained earnings	1,020,000	600,000	_____
	$2,600,000	$1,900,000	$

a   Prepare any necessary elimination entries.

b   Determine the amounts that would be presented on a consolidated balance sheet.

E18-9   *Overview of consolidation concepts* (L.O. 4, 6, 7)

On December 31, NBA Company acquired a key competitor by purchasing 90% of CBA Corporation's outstanding common stock for $2,700,000. CBA's year-end balance sheet disclosed the following information:

Assets	$3,300,000
Liabilities	300,000
Common stock ($10 par)	2,250,000
Retained earnings	750,000

In negotiating the acquisition, management determined that the amounts appearing on CBA's balance sheet approximated current market values.

a   Should consolidated financial statements be prepared in this situation? Why?

b   Calculate the difference, if any, between acquisition cost and the book value of the subsidiary interest purchased.

c   Calculate the minority interest and explain what the minority interest represents.

E18-10   *Elimination entries* (L.O. 4, 7)

A summary of Maverick Corporation's balance sheet at the close of business on January 2, 19X4, appeared as follows:

Cash & other current assets	$ 400,000
Property, plant, & equipment	630,000
	$1,030,000
Liabilities	$ 540,000
Common stock	100,000
Retained earnings	390,000
	$1,030,000

Early on January 3, Opportunity Corporation acquired all of Maverick's outstanding common stock for $1,200,000. Management was willing to pay this price because it believed the property, plant, and equipment was actually worth $820,000. Opportunity has also attached a significant value to Maverick's outstanding business reputation and customer base.

a Calculate the amount of goodwill associated with this business acquisition.

b Prepare the elimination entry that is necessary to consolidate the two companies on January 3, 19X4.

c If, in 19X3, Maverick had issued a $25,000 note payable to Opportunity, what additional elimination entry would be needed in the consolidation process?

E18-11 *Overview of stock investments* (L.O. 2, 6, 7)

Evaluate the comments that follow as being True or False. If the comment is false, briefly explain why.

a When an investment is accounted for by using the equity method, an allowance account is needed to reduce the investment to market value.

b Dividends received are treated as revenue under the equity method.

c When financial statements of a parent are consolidated with those of a 60% owned subsidiary, the Investment account is offset against the minority interest of the investee.

d CyberTech has 50,000 common shares outstanding. If Ross owns 4,500 of these shares, Ross should use the lower-of-cost-or-market method to account for its investment.

e Only in rare cases are subsidiaries acquired at a cost in excess of book value.

Series A

PROBLEMS

P18-A1 *Bond investment computations* (L.O. 1)

1-2-3

Productivity, Inc., purchased $600,000 of 12% bonds on March 1, 19X2. The bonds pay interest on March 1 and September 1 and mature in four years. Assume the following independent cases:

Case A—The bonds are purchased for $638,780, representing a 10% yield to investors.

Case B—The bonds are purchased for $531,041, representing a 16% yield to investors.

Productivity uses the effective-interest method of amortization and has an accounting period that ends on December 31.

Instructions

Complete the following table, rounding all computations to the nearest dollar.

	Case A	Case B
a Cash outflow for acquisition on March 1, 19X2	_____	_____
b Total cash inflow through maturity (interest plus principal)	_____	_____
c Total investment income over the life of the bond issue	_____	_____
d Interest received in 19X2	_____	_____
e Amortization to be recorded in 19X2	_____	_____
f Total interest revenue for 19X2	_____	_____
g Investment carrying value as of December 31, 19X2	_____	_____

P18-A2 *Bond entries: Acquisition through sale, bond discounts* **(L.O. 1)**

On January 1, 19X1, Wilson Corporation purchased $900,000 of 9%, 10-year bonds for $843,921. The bonds are dated January 1, 19X1, and pay semiannual interest on June 30 and December 31. On March 1, 19X2, Wilson sold 70% of the bonds at 102 plus accrued interest. The company uses effective-interest amortization and rounds all computations to the nearest dollar. The effective interest rate is 10%.

Instructions

a Prepare journal entries to record the following:
  (1) The bond investment on January 1, 19X1.
  (2) The semiannual interest receipt and discount amortization on June 30, 19X1, and December 31, 19X1.
b Compute total bond interest revenue for 19X1.
c Present the proper disclosure of the bond investment on Wilson's December 31, 19X1, balance sheet.
d Prepare entries to record the bond sale on March 1, 19X2. *Hint:* Examine when amortization was last recorded.

P18-A3 *Lower-of-cost-or-market and equity methods* **(L.O. 2)**

Dale Pest Control invested $70,000 at the beginning of 19X2 by purchasing common stock of Arctic, Inc., and Pacific, Inc. Information about the two investments follows.

	Arctic, Inc.	Pacific, Inc.
Dale's percentage of ownership	10%	35%
Number of shares acquired	3,500	35,000
Acquisition cost	$35,000	$35,000
19X2 year-end market price	$8 per share	$0.75 per share

Assume that 19X2 net income and total dividend payments of each investee amounted to $50,000 and $10,000, respectively.

Instructions

a Determine the method(s) that Dale should use to account for its investments.
b Focusing on the investment in Arctic, Inc., prepare any journal entries that Dale would record for:
  (1) Acquisition of the common shares.
  (2) Dividends received.

(3) Net income earned by the investee.

(4) Year-end market valuation.

c Repeat part (b) for the investment in Pacific, Inc.

d Present the proper disclosure of the two investments on Dale's 19X2 year-end balance sheet.

P18-A4 *Long-term stock investment concepts* (L.O. 2, 3, 6)

Presley Corporation, a distributor of music memorabilia, has long-term investments in several companies. The companies and percentages of voting stock owned are: A, 60%; B, 5%; C, 40%; and D, 100%. To prepare for the annual stockholders' meeting, Presley's president has asked for a "crash course" in accounting for such investments.

Instructions

a Complete the following table:

	Company			
	A	B	C	D
(1) Does Presley have a controlling interest in the company?	___	___	___	___
(2) What method should Presley use to account for the investment (lower-of-cost-or-market or equity)?	___	___	___	___
(3) Are declines in the company's market value per share recognized in Presley's financial statements?	___	___	___	___
(4) Would a share of the company's earnings be reflected in Presley's financial statements?	___	___	___	___
(5) Would Presley recognize a portion of the company's dividends as revenue?	___	___	___	___
(6) Should the company's financial statements be consolidated with those of Presley?	___	___	___	___
(7) For those companies that are consolidated, does a minority interest appear in the consolidated financial statements?	___	___	___	___

b Explain to Presley's president the basic differences between a parent, a subsidiary, and an investee.

P18-A5 *Basic consolidation; minority interest* (L.O. 5, 6)

Polk Corporation purchased 70% of the outstanding common stock of Swift, Inc., on December 31 of the current year. The companies' individual balance sheets immediately after the acquisition follow.

	Polk	Swift
Cash	$ 10,000	$?
Receivable from Swift	5,200	—
Investment in Swift	51,800	?
Other assets	350,000	200,000
	$417,000	$?
Liabilities	$ 16,000	$?
Payable to Polk	—	5,200
Common stock	350,000	70,000
Retained earnings	51,000	4,000
	$417,000	$?

The companies have combined cash resources of $13,000 and collectively owe outsiders $139,800.

Instructions

a Present Polk's journal entry to record the acquisition of Swift.
b Prepare a consolidated balance sheet work sheet similar in form to that illustrated in the chapter.
c Prepare a formal consolidated balance sheet for the combined entity.

P18-A6 ***Straightforward consolidation; cost in excess of book value*** **(L.O. 5, 7)**
On December 31, 19X4, Sharp Oil Corporation acquired 100% of the outstanding stock of Val Verde Drilling Company for $650,000. Balance sheet information for the two companies immediately after the acquisition follows.

	Sharp	Val Verde
Cash	$ 98,300	$ 41,500
Accounts receivable (net)	112,500	57,600
Inventories	317,600	191,400
Investment in Val Verde	650,000	—
Land	60,000	12,750
Property, plant, & equipment (net)	566,100	306,950
Receivable from Val Verde	20,000	—
	$1,824,500	$610,200
Accounts payable	$ 142,000	$ 49,400
Taxes payable	39,700	13,800
Bonds payable	500,000	—
Payable to Sharp Oil	—	20,000
Common stock ($5 par)	800,000	—
Common stock ($10 par)	—	400,000
Retained earnings	342,800	127,000
	$1,824,500	$610,200

With the exception of land, the fair market value of Val Verde's assets and liabilities corresponded to the book value amounts as of the acquisition date. A recent appraisal indicated Val Verde's land was worth $65,000.

Instructions

a Prepare a consolidated work sheet similar in format to that illustrated in the chapter.

b Prepare a formal consolidated balance sheet.

Series B

P18-B1 **Bond investment computations (L.O. 1)**

Boston Graphics purchased $400,000 of 9% bonds on June 1, 19X1. The bonds pay interest on June 1 and December 1 and mature in five years. Assume the following independent cases:

1-2-3 ▪ *Case A*—The bonds are purchased for $355,838, representing a 12% effective yield to investors.

▪ *Case B*—The bonds are purchased for $416,220, representing an 8% effective yield to investors.

Boston uses the effective-interest method of amortization and has an accounting period that ends on December 31.

Instructions

Complete the following table, rounding all computations to the nearest dollar.

	Case A	Case B
a Cash outflow for acquisition on June 1, 19X1	_____	_____
b Total cash inflow through maturity (interest plus principal)	_____	_____
c Total investment income over the life of the bond issue	_____	_____
d Interest received in 19X1	_____	_____
e Amortization to be recorded in 19X1	_____	_____
f Total interest revenue for 19X1	_____	_____
g Investment carrying value as of December 31, 19X1	_____	_____

P18-B2 **Bond entries: Acquisition through sale, bond premiums (L.O. 1)**

On January 1, 19X5, Deerfield Corporation purchased $800,000 of 10%, 12-year bonds for $921,974. The bonds are dated January 1, 19X5, and pay semiannual interest on June 30 and December 31. On May 1, 19X6, Deerfield sold 60% of the bonds at 103 plus accrued interest. The company uses effective-interest amortization and rounds all computations to the nearest dollar. The effective interest rate is 8%.

Instructions

a Prepare journal entries to record the following:
   (1) The bond investment on January 1, 19X5.
   (2) The semiannual interest receipt and premium amortization on June 30, 19X5, and December 31, 19X5.

b Compute total bond interest revenue for 19X5.

c Present the proper disclosure of the bond investment on Deerfield's December 31, 19X5, balance sheet.

d Prepare entries to record the bond sale on May 1, 19X6. *Hint:* Examine when amortization was last recorded.

P18-B3 *Lower-of-cost-or-market and equity methods* (L.O. 2)

Birmingham Corporation recently acquired a long-term investment in Ambrose, Inc. Ambrose has 40,000 shares of $2 par-value common stock outstanding. The following information is available:

Jan.   1   Purchased 10,000 shares of Ambrose common stock at $20 per share.

Dec. 31   Ambrose declared and paid a cash dividend of $0.60 per share.

     31   Received a copy of Ambrose's income statement that disclosed net income of $42,000.

     31   The market price of Ambrose's stock was $17 per share.

Instructions

a Which accounting method should Birmingham use for its long-term investment in Ambrose, Inc.? Why should this method be used?

b Present Birmingham's required journal entries.

c Present the proper disclosure of the Investment account on Birmingham's December 31 balance sheet.

d Repeat requirements (a), (b), and (c), assuming that Birmingham had purchased 3,000 shares of Ambrose's stock at $20 per share.

P18-B4 *Long-term stock investment concepts* (L.O. 2, 3, 6)

Surf Corporation, a manufacturer of automotive equipment, has long-term investments in several companies. The companies and percentages of voting stock owned are: A, 80%; B, 30%; C, 100%; and D, 10%. To prepare for the annual stockholders' meeting, Surf's president has asked for a "crash course" in accounting for such investments.

Instructions

a Complete the table that follows.

	Company			
	A	B	C	D
(1) Does Surf have a controlling interest in the company?	____	____	____	____
(2) What method should Surf use to account for the investment (equity or lower-of-cost-or-market)?	____	____	____	____
(3) Should the company's financial statements be consolidated with those of Surf?	____	____	____	____
(4) For those companies that are consolidated, does a minority interest appear in the consolidated financial statements?	____	____	____	____
(5) Are declines in the company's market value per share recognized in Surf's financial statements?	____	____	____	____
(6) Would a share of the company's earnings be reflected in Surf's financial statements?	____	____	____	____

	Company			
	A	B	C	D

(7) Would Surf recognize a share
of the company's dividends
as revenue?   ____   ____   ____   ____

b Explain to Surf's president the basic differences between the lower-of-
cost-or-market method and the equity method.

P18-B5 *Basic consolidation; minority interest* (L.O. 5, 6)
For the past few years, Lincoln Company and Summit, Inc., have been
friendly business rivals. Although the companies are not affiliated, Lincoln has borrowed money from Summit and vice versa. Part of this friend-
liness stems from the fact that the presidents of the two firms are brothers.
    On December 31 of the current year, Lincoln acquired a 75% interest in
Summit for $180,000 cash. The balance sheets of the two companies *prior
to the acquisition* follow.

LINCOLN COMPANY	
Cash	$370,000
Note receivable from Summit	40,000
Other assets	290,000
Total assets	$700,000
Current liabilities	$ 80,000
Note payable to Summit	50,000
Common stock	250,000
Retained earnings	320,000
Total liabilities & stockholders' equity	$700,000

SUMMIT, INC.	
Cash	$ 65,000
Note receivable from Lincoln	50,000
Other assets	190,000
Total assets	$305,000
Current liabilities	$ 25,000
Note payable to Lincoln	40,000
Common stock	70,000
Retained earnings	170,000
Total liabilities & stockholders' equity	$305,000

Instructions

a Present Lincoln's journal entry to record the acquisition of Summit.

b Prepare a consolidated work sheet similar in form to that illustrated in the chapter.

c Prepare a formal consolidated balance sheet for the combined entity.

P18-B6 *Straightforward consolidation; cost in excess of book value (L.O. 5, 7)*
On December 31, 19X3, Warner Industries acquired 100% of the outstanding stock of Sperry Company for $600,000. The separate balance sheets of Warner and Sperry immediately after the acquisition follow.

	Warner	Sperry
Cash	$ 220,000	$140,000
Accounts receivable (net)	64,000	16,000
Inventories	780,000	182,000
Investment in Sperry	600,000	—
Land	265,000	100,000
Building (net)	438,000	—
Receivable from Sperry	33,000	—
	$2,400,000	$438,000
Accounts payable	$ 77,000	$ 43,000
Salaries payable	260,000	2,000
Loan payable	550,000	—
Payable to Warner	—	33,000
Common stock, $10 par	1,000,000	—
Common stock, $1 par	—	100,000
Retained earnings	513,000	260,000
	$2,400,000	$438,000

The fair value of Sperry's assets and liabilities equaled their book values as of the acquisition date, with the exception of inventory. An independent appraiser indicated that Sperry's inventory was worth $300,000.

Instructions

a Prepare a consolidated work sheet similar in format to that illustrated in the chapter.

b Prepare a formal consolidated balance sheet.

BEYOND THE BASICS

BB18-1 *Understanding consolidated statements (L.O. 4–7)*
Payton, Inc., has two subsidiaries, Atlas Manufacturing and Miami Glass Corporation, and possesses 80% and 100% of the respective firms' outstanding voting shares. A review of the companies' consolidated balance sheet revealed the following selected information:

Assets	
Investment in Atlas Manufacturing	$ —
Investment in Miami Glass	—
Excess of cost over book value in subsidiary investment	45,000

Liabilities	
Loans payable	85,000
Stockholders' equity	
Minority interest	65,000
Common stock	150,000
Paid-in capital in excess of par value	50,000
Retained earnings	215,000

Instructions

One of Payton's stockholders has been reviewing the consolidated statements and has come to you with the following questions. Prepare appropriate answers, explaining any necessary assumptions.

a Payton has two long-term investments. Why do both Investment accounts contain zero balances?

b What gives rise to an excess of cost over book value?

c What is meant by the Minority Interest account and to which subsidiary does it relate?

d A recent article in a leading financial publication mentioned a $750,000 loan from Payton to Atlas; yet the loan was not disclosed on the consolidated balance sheet? Why?

BB18-2 *Overview of chapter concepts: Multiple choice* (L.O. 1–4, 6, 7)
The following multiple-choice questions relate to various topics discussed in the chapter. Select the best answer.

1 If a bond is purchased at a discount and the effective-interest amortization method is used, the annual bond interest revenue:
 a will increase over the life of the bond.
 b will decrease over the life of the bond.
 c will remain constant over the life of the bond.
 d will never differ significantly from that calculated by using the straight-line method.

2 On January 1, 19X4, Harper Corporation purchased $100,000 of Hoover Corporation bonds. The 12%, 5-year bonds are dated January 1, 19X4, and pay interest on June 30 and December 31. Harper paid $107,721, resulting in an effective yield of 10%. If interest revenue and effective-interest amortization are recorded every six months, how much is the total bond interest revenue for 19X4?
 a $10,741.   c $12,838.
 b $10,772.   d $12,927.

3 Garrett Corporation sold a bond investment for $103,000, which included $2,000 of accrued interest. Amortization was recorded just prior to the sale, resulting in a carrying value of $103,000. Which of the following would not be part of the journal entry to record the sale?
 a A credit to Investment in Bonds for $103,000.
 b A credit to Gain on Sale of Bonds for $2,000.
 c A debit to Cash for $103,000.
 d A debit to Loss on Sale of Bonds for $2,000.

4 On January 1, 19X2, Milton Corporation purchased 5,000 shares of Lawrence Corporation common stock at $20 per share. Lawrence had 50,000 shares outstanding, 19X2 net income of $80,000, and 19X2 dividends of $30,000. At the end of 19X2, Lawrence's common stock price had declined to $18. As a result of this investment, Milton:

a will report total investment revenue of $8,000.

b will prepare end-of-period elimination entries.

c will have a $10,000 unrealized loss.

d will use the equity method of accounting.

5 On January 1, 19X5, Wilson Corporation bought 50,000 shares of Kincade Corporation common stock at $15 per share. Kincade had 125,000 shares outstanding, 19X5 net income of $220,000, and 19X5 dividends of $100,000. At the end of 19X5, Kincade's common stock price had increased to $18. As a result of this investment, Wilson:

a will report $40,000 of dividend revenue.

b will disclose the Investment in Kincade account at $900,000 on the 19X5 year-end balance sheet.

c will use consolidated financial statements.

d will disclose the Investment in Kincade account at $798,000 on the 19X5 year-end balance sheet.

6 Illinois Corporation acquired a portion of St. Louis Corporation's outstanding common stock. In the resulting consolidated financial statements, the minority interest is reported at $400,000. If the total stockholders' equity of St. Louis was $2,000,000, what percentage of the outstanding stock was acquired by Illinois?

a Cannot be determined from the facts given.

b 20%.

c 50%.

d 80%.

7 Rainbow Corporation acquired 100% of Pot of Gold's outstanding common stock for $500,000. If Pot of Gold had total stockholders' equity of $300,000, which of the following statements is definitely true?

a This transaction will result in the recording of goodwill in the consolidated financial statements.

b A minority interest disclosure will appear in the consolidated financial statements.

c The carrying value of selected tangible assets will be increased in Pot of Gold's accounting records.

d The account, Investment in Pot of Gold, will not appear in the consolidated financial statements.

8 When one corporation has a controlling interest in the stock of another company:

a a parent/subsidiary relationship is said to exist.

b the parent corporation may own 20% of the other firm's stock.

c minority interests cease to exist.

d the subsidiary will lose its legal identity.

COMMUNICATION OF ACCOUNTING INFORMATION

CAI18-1 *Preparing an oral presentation: Sara Lee Corporation* (L.O. 3, 4, 6)

Communication Principle: Preparing an oral presentation requires imagination and organization. The first challenge is to gain the audience's attention through a dynamic introduction. By using the principles cited in CAI11-1 on page 451, the speaker must focus the audience on the subjects to be discussed. Like the introduction to a report, a presentation's opening introduces and clearly outlines the speaker's main points. In contrast, the conclusion should summarize the major ideas discussed and remind the audience of what they now know or understand.

When preparing a speech, the author should write out the introduction and then the conclusion—word for word. Once these two sections are completed, the remainder of the presentation is developed through a detailed outline. Standard principles of outline organization include the following:

1 Every main point should have two or more subpoints.
2 Main points and subpoints should be of comparable importance and weighted relatively equally in terms of coverage.
3 The organization should be kept as simple as possible. Outlines for oral presentations should contain no more than five main points and preferably only three. Two or three subpoints, including illustrations, are more than enough for an audience to remember.

Above all, be brief. No matter how long the presentation actually is, if you continually tell yourself that the material must be covered in 5 or 10 minutes, you will find it easier to keep the speech to a manageable length. Remember that with a simpler, clearer, and shorter presentation, the audience is sure to be more appreciative.

■ ■ ■ ■ ■ ■ ■ ■

Sara Lee Corporation is a leading brand-name food and consumer packaged goods company. Familiar products of the firm include Jimmy Dean Sausage, Sara Lee baked goods, Hanes underwear, Champion activewear, and Kiwi shoe polish. Sara Lee's consolidated balance sheet recently disclosed an account entitled Minority Interest in Subsidiaries, with a balance of approximately $347 million. The company also reported year-end cash of $125 million.

Instructions

Assume that you are an accountant at one of Sara Lee's manufacturing facilities. The local chapter of the Rotary Club has asked you to deliver a 30-minute presentation, providing an overview of the company's consolidated financial statements. The presentation should address the following points:

■ The basic purpose of the consolidation process.
■ The difference in accounting between "control" and "total ownership."
■ The nature of the Minority Interests account.
■ An indication of whether the reported consolidated asset amounts (e.g., the cash balance) are totally owned by Sara Lee or merely "controlled" by the company.

Prepare the speech's introduction, an outline of the major points to be covered, and an appropriate conclusion.

Answers to Chapter Quiz

1 c [($400,000 × 1.04) + $2,000]
2 b
3 b [$2,000,000 + ($600,000 × 0.40) − ($125,000 × 0.40)]
4 d
5 b

CHAPTER 19

Statement of Cash Flows

LEARNING OBJECTIVES

After studying this chapter, you should be able to:

Explain the purpose of the statement of cash flows.

Classify and analyze operating, investing, and financing activities.

Demonstrate the proper accounting treatment for significant noncash investing/financing transactions.

Use both the direct and indirect methods of computing cash flows from operating activities.

Prepare and interpret a statement of cash flows.

Most accountants agree that the income statement and the balance sheet disclose valuable information to investors, creditors, managers, and a host of other parties. The income statement, for example, focuses on the results of operations and reveals an entity's revenues and expenses for a given accounting period. The balance sheet, on the other hand, discloses information concerning a company's economic resources, financial obligations, and owners' equity at a specific point in time.

One of the purposes of financial statements is to assist users in making predictions about an entity's future cash inflows and outflows. Users can predict the future only if they have a sufficient information base; unfortunately, the income statement and balance sheet alone are not capable of providing this base. The accounting profession therefore requires another report to improve financial disclosures of business enterprises. This report is the **statement of cash flows,** which reveals the cash flows generated or consumed by a firm's operating, investing, and financing activities. The information contained on the statement is helpful in answering questions such as the following:

- Did an entity fund its activities from operations? From bank loans? From stockholder investments?
- Were the funds obtained by an organization used to expand facilities? Reduce outstanding debt? Replace aging plant and equipment?
- Were the dividends paid greater than the funds provided by business operations?
- Why did net income differ from the firm's cash receipts and disbursements?

These and similar questions are routinely asked by creditors, stockholders, and financial analysts. By collecting information on how funds are generated and used in an organization, the statement of cash flows provides insight that is not afforded by other financial disclosures and reports.

STATEMENT FORMAT AND CLASSIFICATIONS

The statement of cash flows has undergone considerable change in recent years. For a long time, companies revealed inflows and outflows of funds on a report known as the *statement of changes in financial position.* Businesses could employ differing definitions of funds and had few set rules to follow when presenting such information to external statement users. Because of this situation, analysts found it very difficult to compare the reports of different companies.

The Financial Accounting Standards Board studied the problem and decided that clearer definitional and presentation guidelines were necessary.[1] The outcome of the Board's work is the statement shown in Exhibit 19-1. As you can see, businesses must disclose the cash flows that arise from three broad categories: operating activities, investing activities, and financing activities. In addition, organizations are required to reveal significant *noncash* investing/financing transactions. Matrix Corporation was able to

---

[1] See "Statement of Cash Flows," *Statement of Financial Accounting Standards No. 95* (Norwalk, Conn.: Financial Accounting Standards Board, 1987).

EXECUTIVE BRIEFING
The Statement of Cash Flows: A Banker's Perspective

Linda Woodside
Senior Vice-President, NationsBank

Good collateral, a significant net worth, and a strong revenue stream—doesn't this sound like a winning combination for a company that desires to obtain a loan? The answer is "not necessarily," although it is a good start. The key missing element is cash flow.

Consider an individual who approached our institution with a loan request for his real estate development company. Earlier projects of the firm had been successful, having displayed consistent profitability. The company's rapid growth, however, had required some short-term borrowings. A review of the statement of cash flows indicated a serious cash deficiency problem caused by principal payments on existing bank notes. Because these payments do not directly affect profitability, a focus on the balance sheet and income statement alone would not have revealed the shortfall.

A clear understanding of a borrower's cash flow is one of the most important components of financial statement analysis in banking. This measure presents the lender with a moving picture of a company's financial health by focusing on receipts and disbursements. Stated simply, a business that cannot generate sufficient cash to cover its operating needs has a dismal future and does not represent a good credit risk.

MATRIX CORPORATION Statement of Cash Flows For the Year Ended December 31, 19XX	
Cash flows from operating activities	
Details	
Net cash provided (used) by operating activities	$ 70,000
Cash flows from investing activities	
Details	
Net cash provided (used) by investing activities	(15,000)
Cash flows from financing activities	
Details	
Net cash provided (used) by financing activities	4,000
Net increase (decrease) in cash	$ 59,000
Cash balance, January 1, 19XX	31,000
Cash balance, December 31, 19XX	$ 90,000
Schedule of noncash investing/financing activities	
Details	$ 12,000

EXHIBIT 19-1
Example of a Statement of Cash Flows

produce net cash inflows from operating activities and financing activities of $70,000 and $4,000, respectively. Investing transactions, on the other hand, were a cash drain, resulting in a $15,000 excess of disbursements over receipts. We will now discuss each of the statement's major sections in detail.

Operating Activities

Generally speaking, **operating activities** give rise to transactions and events that enter into net income computations. Picture, for instance, the production and sale of goods and services—the major source of earnings for most large businesses. The cash flows related to these activities, such as receipts from customers, and payments for inventory, employee salaries and wages, taxes, interest, and other normal business expenses are classified as operating cash flows. Receipts of both loan interest and dividends also qualify for inclusion in this category. A review of *Statement No. 95* will find that the FASB defined operating activities in a "catchall" sense, namely, to include all cash transactions and events not otherwise classified as investing or financing items.

Investing Activities

Investing activities, or those that involve investment of an entity's resources, constitute the next major type of activity for a business. Companies acquire the securities (e.g., bonds and shares of stock) of other firms and purchase long-term assets such as property, plant, and equipment. In addition, an entity (e.g., a financial institution) may make a loan to another organization. All of these transactions arise from a company's investing activities and result in a cash outflow during the period.

In a similar but opposite manner, these activities frequently generate cash inflows. The stock and bond investments and long-term resources may be sold, and outstanding loan principal may be collected. Needless to say, investing activities may take many different forms and consume and generate substantial amounts of cash.

Financing Activities

Companies need funds for a variety of business purposes. These funds are often obtained from different sources such as the issuance of capital stock, bonds, and mortgage notes, and various types of loan agreements. **Financing activities** are those activities that supply a firm with funds from either the firm's owners or creditors. The items just cited (stock, bonds, and so forth) all provide an entity with cash inflows and normally commit the entity to specific cash outflows (e.g., dividends and the repayment of principal). These latter items are also considered to arise from financing activities, as are cash outflows for treasury stock acquisitions. Two exceptions to financing cash flows are trade payables and interest, both of which are related to the operating activities of the business.

Exhibit 19-2 summarizes an entity's various cash flow activities and presents examples of typical inflows and outflows for the operating, investing, and financing categories.

EXHIBIT 19-2
An Overview of Operating,
Investing, and Financing
Activities

Operating Activities

- *General thrust*—Activities that are primarily related to the production and sale of goods and services, and that enter into the determination of income for the firm
- *Typical cash inflows*—Receipts from customers, loan interest, dividends
- *Typical cash outflows*—Payments for inventory, employee salaries and wages, taxes, interest, and other normal business expenses

Investing Activities

- *General thrust*—Activities that involve investment of a company's resources
- *Typical cash inflows*—Receipts from the sale of stocks and bonds of other firms and from the disposal of long-term resources such as land, buildings, and equipment; the receipt of loan principal from borrowers
- *Typical cash outflows*—Payments made to acquire long-term assets or the securities of other firms; loans made by the entity to other businesses

Financing Activities

- *General thrust*—Activities that provide a business with resources from either its owners or creditors
- *Typical cash inflows*—Receipts from stock and bond issuances, proceeds from mortgage notes and loans
- *Typical cash outflows*—Payments of loan principal to creditors, acquisitions of treasury stock, and dividend distributions

Investing and Financing Transactions That Do Not Affect Cash

Several significant investing and financing transactions affect the financial position of a business but do not affect cash. For example, a building may be acquired by securing a long-term loan such as a mortgage payable. Or land may be obtained in exchange for preferred stock. Neither transaction involves an immediate receipt or disbursement of cash; nonetheless, the financial position of the enterprise has changed through the increases in assets, liabilities, and stockholders' equity. Because a statement of cash flows would be incomplete if significant investing and financing transactions were omitted, the accounting profession requires that such transactions be reported even though no receipts and payments are involved.

Noncash transactions are disclosed on the statement as a separate noncash investing/financing activity. To illustrate, assume $10 million of common stock is exchanged for a building of the same value. The event would be separately reported as a $10 million noncash transaction, appropriately labeled as Common Stock Issued for Building. In essence, one could visualize that common stock is issued for cash (a financing inflow), and the cash is simultaneously disbursed to acquire the asset (an investing outflow). We emphasize that this scenario is mentioned merely to assist your understanding of the exchange. Keep in mind that no cash was ever involved.

OBJECTIVE

3

Demonstrate the proper accounting treatment for significant noncash investing/financing transactions.

Cash and Cash Equivalents

When preparing the statement of cash flows, companies broadly define "cash" to consist of both cash *and* cash equivalents. **Cash equivalents** are short-term, highly liquid investments that mature in 90 days or less. Examples include money market accounts, certain Treasury bills, and other financial instruments that firms may use to generate returns (e.g., interest) on excess funds.

It is important to note that cash equivalents are not the same as short-term investments in marketable securities, as discussed in Chapter 7. The latter securities, which include stocks and bonds of other corporations, are often held by a business beyond the stipulated 90-day time frame. Given this situation, sales and purchases of short-term investments are disclosed on the statement of cash flows in the investing activities section. In contrast, transfers of funds between the Cash account and various cash equivalents are *not* reported because cash and cash equivalents are viewed as being identical. Stated differently, "cash is cash" no matter what the form.

A FURTHER PROBE OF OPERATING ACTIVITIES

Before we can illustrate the procedures needed to prepare the statement of cash flows, further study of operating activities is necessary. Recall that transactions and events related to operating activities affect a firm's net income. Also recall from earlier chapters that most large companies, to be in accord with generally accepted accounting principles, compute net income by using the accrual basis of accounting. Under the accrual basis, revenues are recognized when goods and services are sold or rendered, and expenses are recognized when incurred.

Because of the focus on amounts *earned* and *incurred*, the resulting net income figure likely includes revenues not yet collected from customers and expenses not yet paid to creditors. Sales, of course, may be made in one period and collected in another. In addition, expenses such as taxes, salaries, and interest are often accrued at the end of one period, with payment occurring in the future. As a consequence of these "timing" differences, the accrual-based net income figure must be adjusted in the statement-preparation process to achieve our objective: a focus on the entity's operating cash flows. The required adjustments basically involve a conversion to the cash basis of accounting, thereby allowing a business to report the revenues *received* and the expenses *paid*. This process is depicted pictorially in Exhibit 19-3.

The conversion may be accomplished by two different approaches: the direct method and the indirect method. Both approaches are acceptable for purposes of external financial reporting; however, use of the direct method is encouraged by the FASB. The Board feels that the detailed disclosures of the direct method provide more useful information for investors and other financial statement readers.

The Direct Method

Under the **direct method,** individual items on the income statement are translated from the accrual basis to the cash basis of accounting. Sales, for example, is adjusted to reflect the actual cash inflows remitted by cus-

OBJECTIVE

4

Use both the direct and indirect methods of computing cash flows from operating activities.

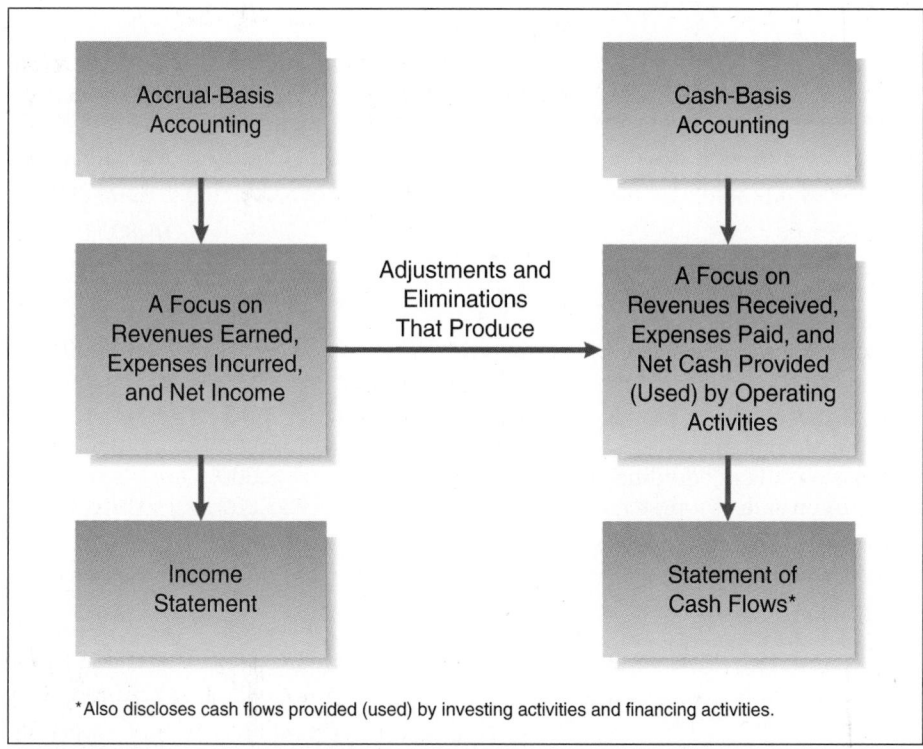

EXHIBIT 19-3
The Relationship Between Income and Net Cash Provided (Used) by Operating Activities

tomers, while cost of goods sold and expenses are converted to show the amounts disbursed to suppliers, employees, and so forth. The result of this translation follows.

Cash received from customers		$XX,XXX
Less cash payments for:		
Purchases of merchandise	$XX,XXX	
Selling & administrative expenses	XX,XXX	
Interest	XX,XXX	
Income taxes	XX,XXX	XX,XXX
Net cash provided (used) by operating activities		$XX,XXX

To illustrate the necessary procedures, we will use selected data of the Powell Corporation (see Exhibit 19-4).

Cash Received from Customers

Most companies extend credit to their customers. Because of both credit sales and the accompanying possibility of uncollectible accounts, accrual-based sales revenues generally do not coincide with cash collections. In Powell's case, for instance, Accounts Receivable rose by $25,000 during the year. This increase indicates that revenues have been earned; however, certain customers have yet to settle their balances with the firm.

The T-account shown on page 766 is based on figures in the preceding exhibit.

EXHIBIT 19-4
Powell Corporation Data

POWELL CORPORATION Income Statement For the Year Ended December 31, 19X2		
Sales		$3,000,000
Cost of goods sold		1,200,000
Gross profit		$1,800,000
Expenses		
Selling & administrative	$1,455,000	
Building depreciation	25,000	
Equipment depreciation	70,000	1,550,000
		$ 250,000
Other revenue (expense)		
Interest expense	$ (200,000)	
Loss on sale of equipment	(5,000)	
Gain on sale of long-term investments	15,000	(190,000)
Income before income taxes		$ 60,000
Income taxes		20,000
Net income		$ 40,000

Account	Dec. 31, 19X2	Dec. 31, 19X1	Increase (Decrease)
Accounts receivable (net)	$400,000	$375,000	$ 25,000
Merchandise inventory	425,000	450,000	(25,000)
Prepaid selling expenses	5,000	4,000	1,000
Accounts payable	470,000	340,000	130,000
Income taxes payable	40,000	39,000	1,000

Accounts Receivable			
12/31/X1	375,000	Collections	?
Sales	3,000,000		
	3,375,000		
	400,000		

To derive the ending balance of $400,000, it is apparent that Powell collected $2,975,000 ($3,375,000 − $400,000) from clientele. Accrual-based sales revenues may therefore be converted to cash collections via the following formula:

$$\text{Cash Received from Customers} = \text{Sales} \begin{cases} + \text{ Decrease in Accounts Receivable} \\ - \text{ Increase in Accounts Receivable} \end{cases}$$

$$\$2{,}975{,}000 = \$3{,}000{,}000 - \$25{,}000$$

Cash Payments for Merchandise

The computation of cash outlays for merchandise is slightly more complex than the calculation just illustrated. The starting point is the cost-of-goods-sold figure on the income statement. Complications arise, however, since goods acquired during the period may still be in inventory or, conversely, goods purchased in previous periods may have been sold during 19X2. Furthermore, it is likely that cash payments to suppliers will differ from the total cost of merchandise acquired because of purchases made on credit. In view of this situation, changes in *both* the Merchandise Inventory and Accounts Payable accounts must be taken into consideration.

Data for Powell Corporation reveal a $25,000 decrease in inventory, meaning the company disposed of merchandise that was acquired prior to 19X2. The firm's cost of goods sold will therefore exceed the cost of goods purchased during the year. As the figures that follow indicate, 19X2 purchases amounted to $1,175,000.

Merchandise Inventory			
12/31/X1	450,000	Cost of goods sold	1,200,000
Purchases	?		
(425,000)			

$$\text{Let X} = \text{purchases}$$
$$\$450,000 + X - \$1,200,000 = \$425,000$$
$$X = \$1,175,000$$

The next issue is: Did Powell pay for all of these goods during the period? This question can be answered by examining the amounts owed to suppliers.[2]

Accounts Payable			
Payments	?	12/31/X1	340,000
		Purchases	1,175,000
			1,515,000
		(470,000)	

The T-account shows that the $470,000 owed as of December 31, 19X2, arises only if 19X2 payments totaled $1,045,000 ($1,515,000 − $470,000). Alternatively, we can arrive at the same conclusion by analyzing the change in Accounts Payable. For example, the $130,000 rise in the account ($470,000 − $340,000) means that some goods acquired in 19X2 were not paid for by year-end. Cash payments to suppliers were therefore less than the cost of merchandise purchased, with total disbursements amounting to $1,045,000 ($1,175,000 − $130,000).

---

[2] We are assuming that all accounts payable are related to purchases of merchandise.

The preceding computations are summarized in the formula that follows.

$$\text{Cash Payments for Merchandise} = \text{Cost of Goods Sold} \begin{cases} + \text{Increase in Inventory} \\ - \text{Decrease in Inventory} \end{cases} \begin{cases} + \text{Decrease in Accounts Payable} \\ - \text{Increase in Accounts Payable} \end{cases}$$

$$\$1,045,000 = \$1,200,000 - \$25,000 - \$130,000$$

Cash Payments for Selling and Administrative Expenses

There is a strong likelihood that selling and administrative expenses as reported on the income statement will not equal cash payments for services acquired. Several factors, including prepaid expenses, cause these two amounts to differ. Recall that companies often pay for items in advance (e.g., insurance, rent, and advertising), with the amounts spent being written off to expense upon consumption. As a result of this accounting treatment, a rising balance of prepaid expenses indicates that the cost of prepaid items acquired during the year exceeded the cost of those consumed. Thus, cash outflows would exceed the amounts expensed.

An examination of Powell's prepaid expenses revealed a $1,000 increase during 19X2. Given that the company reported $1,455,000 of selling and administrative expenses on its accrual-based income statement, cash payments must have amounted to $1,456,000 ($1,455,000 + $1,000). The following formula may be used in the conversion process:[3]

$$\text{Cash Payments for Selling \& Administrative Expenses} = \text{Selling \& Administrative Expenses} \begin{cases} + \text{Increases in Prepaid Expenses} \\ - \text{Decreases in Prepaid Expenses} \end{cases}$$

Cash Payments for Interest and Income Taxes

The final items to consider are interest and income taxes. For most businesses, the related cash outflows seldom coincide with the amount of expense incurred. Interest and taxes are often accrued at the end of one period, with payment taking place on some future date. For example, a review of Powell's data reveals a $1,000 increase in the Income Taxes Payable account, meaning that some reported expense has yet to be paid to taxing authorities. Cash payments for taxes will therefore be less than the accrual-based expense figure. An appropriate formula to use is:

$$\text{Cash Payments for Income Taxes} = \text{Income Tax Expense} \begin{cases} + \text{Decrease in Income Taxes Payable} \\ - \text{Increase in Income Taxes Payable} \end{cases}$$

---

[3] This formula and the next one are sometimes modified. See the upcoming discussion entitled "The Need for Flexibility."

The computation for Powell reveals that $19,000 was disbursed during the period:

$$\$19,000 = \$20,000 - \$1,000$$

A similar procedure is followed to derive interest payments. Because of the absence of an Interest Payable account, the company's expense as disclosed on the income statement ($200,000) equaled the funds remitted to lenders.

The Need for Flexibility

Our examples of prepaid expenses and accruals dealt with selling and administrative items and income taxes, respectively. Be aware that businesses often accrue amounts in the selling and administrative category (e.g., wages), and those same businesses may prepay income taxes and/or interest. The proper accounting treatment in such cases parallels that illustrated earlier. That is, the appropriate prepaid items would be handled with income tax and interest computations (increases being added and decreases subtracted). Also, relevant accruals such as Wages Payable would be merged with selling and administrative expenses, resulting in the following formula:

Cash Payments for Selling & Administrative Expenses	=	Selling & Administrative Expenses	$\Big\{$	+ Increases in Prepaid Expenses − Decreases in Prepaid Expenses	$\Big\{$	+ Decreases in Accrued Liabilities − Increases in Accrued Liabilities

An Overview

The calculations in the preceding sections can be summarized to show that operating activities generated a net cash inflow of $255,000:

Cash received from customers		$2,975,000
Less cash payments for:		
Purchases of merchandise	$1,045,000	
Selling & administrative expenses	1,456,000	
Interest	200,000	
Income taxes	19,000	2,720,000
Net cash provided by operating activities		$ 255,000

This information is eventually combined with the results of financing and investing activities to form the statement of cash flows.

Income Statement Items That Were Disregarded

A review of the data in Exhibit 19-4 will show that we failed to consider several income statement items when computing cash flows from operating activities. Depreciation, for instance, was ignored because it is a *non-cash* expense. Picturing the typical year-end adjustment for this cost (i.e., a debit to Depreciation Expense and a credit to Accumulated Depreciation), it is apparent that cash is not affected. Amortization is a similar expense that also falls into this category.

We also ignored the loss on the sale of equipment and the gain from the sale of long-term investments. These items are examples of **nonoperating gains and losses,** or gains and losses that arise from investing and financing activities. Given the emphasis on *operating* transactions, such amounts are not used in the conversion process. (The cash flow effects of nonoperating gains and losses are reflected in a company's investing and financing disclosures, as we will show shortly.)

The Indirect Method

A company's cash flow from operating activities may be computed by using an alternative approach to that just presented. Under the **indirect method,** operating cash flows are calculated by starting with accrual-basis net income as reported on the income statement. This figure is then converted to the cash basis by adding and subtracting certain amounts. Stated differently, rather than adjust the *individual* income statement items (sales, cost of goods sold, interest expense, and so forth) to reflect receipts and disbursements, the conversion is done indirectly through bottom-line income. The conversion process requires the accountant to address the issues of noncash expenses, gains and losses on nonoperating transactions, and changes in the balances of selected accounts (e.g., Accounts Receivable and Merchandise Inventory).

Noncash Expenses; Nonoperating Gains and Losses

Under the direct method, noncash expenses such as depreciation and amortization were ignored when deriving cash flows from operating activities. Keep in mind that with the *indirect* method, the starting point is net income. Depreciation and amortization, of course, are deducted from revenues when computing this figure. Because these expenses cause a decrease in profitability without an accompanying reduction in cash, they must be added back to net income to arrive at an entity's operating cash flows. In Powell's case, the $40,000 net income figure would be increased by the depreciation write-offs of $25,000 and $70,000 as the first step in computing the proper cash flow number.

Similar procedures are followed for gains and losses from nonoperating activities, which are also considered in the calculation of net income. The computation of net cash flows from *operating* activities requires that such amounts be "backed out" of accrual income when performing the conversion process. To the extent that net income includes nonoperating gains, these gains must be subtracted to arrive at cash flows from operating activities. Conversely, losses must be added.

Current Assets and Current Liabilities

As a final step, changes in certain account balances must be studied to determine uncollected revenues, unpaid purchases, interest and income taxes incurred but not yet disbursed, and so forth. The accounts are the same as those utilized with the direct method: the current assets and current liabilities of Powell Corporation that appear in Exhibit 19-4.

When using the indirect method, the accountant is making additions to and subtractions from net income rather than adjusting individual income statement components. With one exception, the rules concerning the treatment of increases and decreases in account balances are identical to those shown on the preceding pages. Powell, for instance, subtracted its $25,000 increase in Accounts Receivable from sales when converting the accrual-based figure to cash received from customers (see p. 766). The same effect is achieved under the indirect method, but now the increase is subtracted from net income. Had there been a decrease in the accounts receivable balance, the decrease would have been added to net income.

The exception just noted relates to components that are deducted from revenues in the determination of net income, namely, cost of goods sold, selling and administrative expenses, interest expense, and income tax expense. Rules for the addition and subtraction of current assets and current liabilities connected with these items are the opposite of those presented earlier. For example, Powell's $1,000 increase in the Income Taxes Payable account means reported expense exceeded disbursements to taxing authorities. A larger expense amount translates into less income than cash flow, calling for an *addition* to net income when converting to the cash basis. Generally stated, decreases in current assets and increases in current liabilities are added to accrual-based net income in the conversion process, whereas increases in current assets and decreases in current liabilities are subtracted.

These addition and subtraction rules apply only to current assets and current liabilities that are related to operations. Consider that certain short-term obligations (e.g., notes payable and notes receivable) are often created in borrowing transactions, which are *financing* activities. Placement of such items in the operating section of the cash flows statement is therefore not appropriate.

The procedures required by the indirect method are summarized in Exhibit 19-5. Application of these rules to the Powell Corporation data yields a net cash flow from operating activities of $255,000—the same as the result achieved under the direct approach. The outcome is identical; only the methodology differs.

The information needed to construct the statement of cash flows comes from a variety of sources: the income statement, statement of retained earnings, comparative balance sheets, and ledger accounts. To illustrate the necessary procedures, we will continue the Powell Corporation example (see Exhibit 19-6 for additional data). As you study this material, proceed slowly and keep the previous discussion in mind.

PREPARATION OF A STATEMENT OF CASH FLOWS

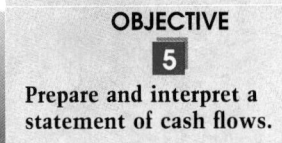

OBJECTIVE

5

Prepare and interpret a statement of cash flows.

Step 1: Analyze the Cash Account

Because the statement will concentrate on the inflows and outflows of cash, the first step is to determine the change in Powell's Cash account. According to the comparative balance sheets, the company's cash increased by $50,000 during 19X2. The increase, which represents the bottom-line amount to be explained on the statement of cash flows, is caused by the firm's operating, investing, and financing activities.

EXHIBIT 19-5
Computing the Cash Flow from Operating Activities: Indirect Approach

	Adjustment Needed to Accrual-Basis Income
Net income, accrual basis	$XX,XXX
Add (deduct) items to convert net income to a cash basis	
Noncash expenses (e.g., depreciation, amortization)	Add
Gains/losses related to nonoperating activities	
Gains	Deduct
Losses	Add
Current assets related to operating activities	
Increase in account balance	Deduct
Decrease in account balance	Add
Current liabilities related to operating activities	
Increase in account balance	Add
Decrease in account balance	Deduct
Net cash provided (used) by operating activities	$XX,XXX

For Powell Corporation

Cash flows from operating activities		
Net income		$ 40,000
Add (deduct) items to convert net income to a cash basis		
Building depreciation expense	$ 25,000	
Equipment depreciation expense	70,000	
Loss on sale of equipment	5,000	
Gain on sale of long-term investments	(15,000)	
Increase in accounts receivable (net)	(25,000)	
Decrease in merchandise inventory	25,000	
Increase in prepaid selling expenses	(1,000)	
Increase in accounts payable	130,000	
Increase in income taxes payable	1,000	215,000
Net cash provided by operating activities		$255,000

Step 2: Determine Net Cash Flow from Operating Activities

Step 2, which is the focal point of the direct and indirect methods, has already been performed. Observe that the account balance changes introduced earlier for current assets and current liabilities (Accounts Receivable, Merchandise Inventory, Prepaid Selling Expenses, Accounts Payable, and Income Taxes Payable) are now reflected in the firm's comparative balance sheets.

A careful study of the balance sheets will find two current accounts—Cash and Notes Payable—that were ignored in the initial presentation (Exhibit 19-4). Cash was omitted because our objective was to show how changes in other current accounts affected the cash generated from operations. Similarly, Notes Payable was disregarded because the obligations

HIGHLIGHT
Let the Cash Flow

The statement of cash flows has evolved from a supplementary academic exercise into a report that is considered to be a primary financial statement. As recently as 30 years ago, few companies monitored cash flows very closely even though accounting educators urged them to do so. Why the fuss over inflows and outflows? In plain and simple terms, all companies move on cash, not income. You can't pay creditors with profits; they accept cash. You can't pay employees with earnings, only cash. And when someone asks if a firm has been making money, all they probably want to know is whether the company has any cash left over to show for its efforts.

A finance professor at the University of Southern California notes that the preceding comments may sound extreme. However, he observes that time and time again managers complain, "If I'm making such big profits, why don't I have any money?" It doesn't matter whether the industry is high tech or low, smokestack or service. In the end an entity must have enough money to pay its obligations or its survival will be threatened. [1] Although they have since reorganized and continue to operate, many companies (including Chrysler) have learned this lesson the hard way.

To the surprise of many, businesses can have cash flow problems not only when sales are low but also when demand is strong. To illustrate the phenomenon of going broke while making a profit, we will focus on the Pure Spring Water Co., which began operations in May with $30,000 cash. [2] The firm expects to find customers who are willing to pay $25 per month for its bottled water products. Customers are billed when serviced and settle their accounts in the following month. Pure Spring pays its supplier $15 per customer upon pickup of the bottled goods.

The company serviced 400 customers in May. Customer billings totaled $10,000 (400 × $25); the supplier was paid $6,000 (400 × $15). No receivables were collected.

May 31: Cash, $24,000   Receivables, $10,000
Net income, $4,000

Sales tripled during June, with the firm servicing 1,200 customers. Pure Spring paid its supplier $18,000 (1,200 × $15) and billed customers $30,000 (1,200 × $25) for water sold. The company collected May's receivables of $10,000.

June 30: Cash, $16,000   Receivables, $30,000
Net income, $12,000

During July, sales once again skyrocketed. Sales and billings amounting to $75,000 were made to 3,000 customers (3,000 × $25 = $75,000). Pure Spring paid the supplier $45,000 (3,000 × $15) and collected $30,000 from June's receivables.

July 31: Cash, $1,000   Receivables, $75,000
Net income, $30,000

A heat wave struck and temperatures soared in August. The firm serviced 6,000 customers and billed $150,000 for water sold. July's receivables of $75,000 were collected, and Pure Spring wrote a $90,000 check (6,000 × $15) to cover the cost of its purchases. The bank paid the check, but only after the bank president was assured that the rapidly growing water company would "clean up its act."

Aug. 31: Cash, $(14,000)   Receivables, $150,000
Net income, $60,000

Pure Spring's dilemma (along with those of much less successful entities) would have been highlighted in the operating activities section of the statement of cash flows. In general, the statement of cash flows signals effective implementation of a company's cash management strategies or, conversely, forthcoming problems.

Sources: Adapted from "How to Go Broke . . . While Making a Profit," *Business Week,* April 28, 1956, pp. 46–47 [2]; and "When is There Cash in Cash Flow?" *Harvard Business Review,* March/April 1987, pp. 38–39, 42–43, 46, 48–49 [1].

EXHIBIT 19-6
Powell Corporation Financial Information

POWELL CORPORATION
Comparative Balance Sheets
December 31, 19X2 and 19X1

	19X2	19X1	Increase (Decrease)
Assets			
Current assets			
Cash	$ 100,000	$ 50,000	$ 50,000
Accounts receivable (net)	400,000	375,000	25,000
Merchandise inventory	425,000	450,000	(25,000)
Prepaid selling expenses	5,000	4,000	1,000
Total current assets	$ 930,000	$ 879,000	$ 51,000
Property, plant, & equipment			
Land	$ 200,000	$ 115,000	$ 85,000
Buildings	1,450,000	1,250,000	200,000
Accumulated depreciation: buildings	(50,000)	(25,000)	(25,000)
Equipment	725,000	800,000	(75,000)
Accumulated depreciation: equipment	(250,000)	(260,000)	10,000
Total property, plant, & equipment	$2,075,000	$1,880,000	$ 195,000
Other assets			
Long-term investments	$ 880,000	$1,000,000	$(120,000)
Total assets	$3,885,000	$3,759,000	$ 126,000
Liabilities & Stockholders' Equity			
Current liabilities			
Accounts payable	$ 470,000	$ 340,000	$ 130,000
Notes payable*	—	300,000	(300,000)
Income taxes payable	40,000	39,000	1,000
Total current liabilities	$ 510,000	$ 679,000	$(169,000)
Long-term liabilities			
Bonds payable	$2,070,000	$2,000,000	$ 70,000
Stockholders' equity			
Common stock, par value $1	$ 195,000	$ 130,000	$ 65,000
Paid-in capital in excess of par	635,000	500,000	135,000
Retained earnings	475,000	450,000	25,000
Total stockholders' equity	$1,305,000	$1,080,000	$ 225,000
Total liabilities & stockholders' equity	$3,885,000	$3,759,000	$ 126,000

* Owed to First Pacific Trust for monies borrowed in late 19X1.

EXHIBIT 19-6
(continued)

POWELL CORPORATION
Statement of Retained Earnings
For the Year Ended December 31, 19X2

Retained earnings, 1/1/X2	$450,000
Add: Net income	40,000
	$490,000
Less: Cash dividend	15,000
Retained earnings, 12/31/X2	$475,000

arose from borrowing transactions (i.e., *financing* activities) conducted with First Pacific Trust. Remember, the current assets and current liabilities used with the direct and indirect conversion methods must pertain to operations.

Step 3: Analyze Remaining Balance Sheet Accounts

The third step is to analyze the remaining balance sheet accounts to determine the effect, if any, of a company's investing and financing activities. We begin with an evaluation of Land.

Land

The Land account increased by $85,000 during the year. An analysis of the ledger account revealed that land was purchased for cash on October 19.

	Land	
1/1/X2	Balance	115,000
10/19/X2	Purchased land for cash	85,000
		200,000

The increase in this asset results from an $85,000 use of cash and would be reported in the statement of cash flows as an investing activity, as follows:

Cash flows from investing activities	
Purchase of land	$(85,000)

Buildings

Continuing down the balance sheet, the next account, Buildings, increased $200,000, from $1.25 million to $1.45 million. An examination of the ledger account revealed that a building was acquired on the last day of the year in exchange for 65,000 shares of the company's $1 par-value common stock.

Buildings		
1/1/X2 Balance	1,250,000	
12/31/X2 Acquired		
building; issued		
common stock	200,000	
	1,450,000	

Although the acquisition does not involve cash, the financial position of Powell Corporation has been significantly affected. Recall from our earlier discussion that such exchange transactions are reported on the statement of cash flows as a noncash investing/financing activity. Therefore, the building acquisition is disclosed in a separate schedule in the manner shown.

Schedule of noncash investing/financing activities
Common stock issued for building $200,000

Accumulated Depreciation: Buildings

The Accumulated Depreciation: Buildings account increased by $25,000 during 19X2 because of annual depreciation expense (see the income statement in Exhibit 19-4).

Accumulated Depreciation: Buildings		
	1/1/X2 Balance	25,000
	12/31/X2 Adjusting entry:	
	annual	
	depreciation	25,000
		50,000

The proper treatment of this expense was considered previously in the computation of net cash flows from operating activities and need not be addressed again.

Equipment and Accumulated Depreciation: Equipment

Powell's Equipment balance decreased by $75,000 during the year, perhaps because of a discard or a sale. A probe of the general ledger revealed that two transactions actually occurred.

May 1   Sold $100,000 of equipment for cash.
Nov. 1   Purchased $25,000 of equipment for cash.

Equipment					
1/1/X2	Balance	800,000	5/1/X2	Disposal for cash	100,000
11/1/X2	Purchase for cash	25,000			
	⟨725,000⟩	**825,000**			

As you can see, overreliance on ending account balances could result in a failure to detect all changes in cash. In this case, for instance, Powell had a receipt and a disbursement of cash that require separate disclosure. Offsetting or netting is really inappropriate.

Continuing our examination of these two transactions, the Accumulated Depreciation: Equipment account reveals that (1) depreciation associated with the disposal totaled $80,000 and (2) 19X2 depreciation expense amounted to $70,000.

Accumulated Depreciation: Equipment				
5/1/X2 Disposal	80,000	1/1/X2	Balance	260,000
		12/31/X2	Adjusting entry: annual depreciation	70,000
			⟨250,000⟩	**330,000**

From an analysis of both ledger accounts, we can determine that the equipment sold on May 1 had a $20,000 book value (cost of $100,000 minus accumulated depreciation of $80,000). Furthermore, the income statement reported a $5,000 loss from equipment sales, meaning that Powell must have received cash proceeds of $15,000 on the disposal. The necessary calculations are:

Equipment cost	$100,000
Accumulated depreciation	80,000
Book value	$ 20,000
Proceeds from disposal	15,000
Loss	$ 5,000

The purchase and sale of equipment arose from investment-related activities and are disclosed on the statement of cash flows as follows:

Cash flows from investing activities	
Purchase of equipment	$(25,000)
Proceeds from disposal of equipment	15,000

Regardless of whether a loss (or gain) is generated, the proceeds received would be the amount reported on the statement. This procedure is logical because the statement is prepared to explain the change in a company's cash balance, and the proceeds would be the amount debited to the Cash account in the transaction's journal entry.

Long-Term Investments

The comparative balance sheets indicate that the Long-Term Investments account decreased from $1 million to $880,000 during the year. The ledger account appears as shown:

Long-Term Investments			
1/1/X2 Balance	1,000,000	4/15/X2 Sold securities for cash	120,000
(880,000)			

Powell's management reports that the securities were sold for $135,000, thus generating the $15,000 gain that appears on the income statement (see Exhibit 19-4). The gain was handled previously when computing the net cash flow from operating activities. The $135,000 inflow, on the other hand, would be disclosed in the investing activities section as follows:

> Cash flows from investing activities
>   Proceeds from sale of long-term investments $135,000

Notes Payable

The next balance sheet account to be considered is Notes Payable.

Notes Payable		
8/15/X2 Paid to First Pacific Trust 300,000	1/1/X2 Balance	300,000
	(-0-)	

As stated in Exhibit 19-6, the balance in this account arose from a borrowing transaction with First Pacific Trust. The $300,000 debt reduction during 19X2 was caused by repayment of the note's principal and is therefore considered a financing activity of the firm. The proper presentation on the statement of cash flows follows.

> Cash flows from financing activities
>   Payment to settle short-term note $(300,000)

Bonds Payable

A review of the ledger showed that Powell had issued $70,000 of bonds on February 14.

Bonds Payable			
	1/1/X2	Balance	2,000,000
	2/14/X2	Issued bonds at face value for cash	70,000
			2,070,000

The issuance is disclosed in the financing activities section of the statement of cash flows in the following manner:

Cash flows from financing activities
    Proceeds from bond issue $70,000

Common Stock and Paid-in Capital in Excess of Par

During 19X2, the Common Stock and Paid-in Capital in Excess of Par accounts increased by $65,000 and $135,000, respectively. These hikes were caused by the issuance of 65,000 shares of $1 par-value stock in exchange for a $200,000 building (see p. 775) and appear in the ledger as shown:

Common Stock, Par Value $1			
	1/1/X2	Balance	130,000
	12/31/X2	Issued 65,000 shares for building	65,000
			195,000

Paid-in Capital in Excess of Par			
	1/1/X2	Balance	500,000
	12/31/X2	Issued 65,000 shares for building	135,000
			635,000

Proper disclosure of the December 31 issuance on the statement of cash flows was illustrated earlier when the Buildings account was discussed. Observe that *for statement presentation purposes,* it is not necessary to subdivide the $200,000 into the individual amounts that were credited to Common Stock and Paid-in Capital in Excess of Par. Such a breakdown would have minimal value to financial statement users.

Retained Earnings

The final account on Powell's comparative balance sheet is Retained Earnings, which increased by $25,000 during 19X2. As reported on the statement of retained earnings (see Exhibit 19-6), this increase was the result of $40,000 of net income and a $15,000 cash dividend. The Retained Earnings account therefore appears as follows:

Retained Earnings				
4/30/X2 Cash dividend	15,000	1/1/X2	Balance	450,000
		12/31/X2	Net income (via closing)	40,000
			⟨475,000⟩	490,000

Net income was previously considered when computing cash flow from operating activities. The dividend distribution, a financing transaction, is reported in the following manner:

> Cash flows from financing activities
>   Dividend paid $(15,000)

Step 4: Financial Statement Preparation

Once the changes in all balance sheet accounts have been determined and analyzed, the formal financial statement is prepared. The statement of cash flows for Powell Corporation appears in Exhibit 19-7 (direct method) and Exhibit 19-8 (indirect method). Observe that the statement is merely the summation of the operating activities discussion (direct, p. 000; indirect, Exhibit 19-5) and the individual investing, financing, and noncash investing/financing activities (noted in shaded blocks) from Step 3. The combined inflows and outflows under both methods produce a $50,000 increase in cash, which agrees with the company's comparative balance sheet presentation.

Tips & Techniques

A review of Exhibits 19-7 and 19-8 will reveal identical investing and financing disclosures; only the operating sections differ. The direct approach is said to be more useful to lenders, who desire information on specific inflows and outflows when judging a company's ability to repay debt. However, many people find the indirect approach easier to understand because most businesses have used this means of disclosure in the past. In sum, neither method is clearly superior, and the method selected for reporting is a matter of personal preference.

POWELL CORPORATION Statement of Cash Flows—Direct Approach For the Year Ended December 31, 19X2		
Cash flows from operating activities		
Cash received from customers		$2,975,000
Less cash payments for:		
Purchases of merchandise	$1,045,000	
Selling & administrative expenses	1,456,000	
Interest	200,000	
Income taxes	19,000	2,720,000
Net cash provided by operating activities		$ 255,000
Cash flows from investing activities		
Purchase of land	$ (85,000)	
Purchase of equipment	(25,000)	
Proceeds from disposal of equipment	15,000	
Proceeds from sale of long-term investments	135,000	
Net cash provided by investing activities		40,000
Cash flows from financing activities		
Payment to settle short-term note	$ (300,000)	
Proceeds from bond issue	70,000	
Dividend paid	(15,000)	
Net cash used by financing activities		(245,000)
Net increase (decrease) in cash		$ 50,000
Cash balance, January 1, 19X2		50,000
Cash balance, December 31, 19X2		$ 100,000
Schedule of noncash investing/financing activities		
Common stock issued for building		$ 200,000

EXHIBIT 19-7
Statement of Cash Flows: Direct Approach

ETHICS ISSUE

A statement of cash flows reveals a large cash increase because of one-time, unusual inflows. The accountant wants to add a special explanatory note for unsophisticated statement users, but management objects. What should happen?

Some Thoughts on Interpretation

Although not specifically emphasized in the statement-preparation process, the *relationship* among operating, investing, and financing cash flows is important. This relationship is especially significant when analyzing managerial and business performance. Consider, for example, the following data of three different companies ($000 omitted):

	Brown	Green	Purple
Net cash provided (used) by			
Operating activities	$ (500)	$ 900	$ 1,600
Investing activities	(2,600)	(1,500)	(1,100)
Financing activities	3,100	600	(500)
	$ —	$ —	$ —

Each of the firms has the same net cash flow ($0); however, the individual patterns differ.

EXHIBIT 19-8
Statement of Cash Flows:
Indirect Approach

POWELL CORPORATION Statement of Cash Flows—Indirect Approach For the Year Ended December 31, 19X2		
Cash flows from operating activities		
Net income		$ 40,000
Add (deduct) items to convert net income to a cash basis		
Building depreciation expense	$ 25,000	
Equipment depreciation expense	70,000	
Loss on sale of equipment	5,000	
Gain on sale of long-term investments	(15,000)	
Increase in accounts receivable (net)	(25,000)	
Decrease in merchandise inventory	25,000	
Increase in prepaid selling expenses	(1,000)	
Increase in accounts payable	130,000	
Increase in income taxes payable	1,000	215,000
Net cash provided by operating activities		$ 255,000
Cash flows from investing activities		
Purchase of land	$ (85,000)	
Purchase of equipment	(25,000)	
Proceeds from disposal of equipment	15,000	
Proceeds from sale of long-term investments	135,000	
Net cash provided by investing activities		40,000
Cash flows from financing activities		
Payment to settle short-term note	$(300,000)	
Proceeds from bond issue	70,000	
Dividend paid	(15,000)	
Net cash used by financing activities		(245,000)
Net increase (decrease) in cash		$ 50,000
Cash balance, January 1, 19X2		50,000
Cash balance, December 31, 19X2		$ 100,000
Schedule of noncash investing/financing activities		
Common stock issued for building		$ 200,000

Brown, for instance, is probably a young, growth-oriented firm. Initial cash flows from daily operating activities are negative, perhaps because of start-up losses. Additionally, the company may be experiencing sizable outlays to build inventories, and receivables may be growing as the customer base expands. During this same period, major investments are being made in various long-lived assets such as buildings and equipment. The net outflows from operating and investing activities dictate a need for external financing so that business endeavors may continue.

Green appears to be a more mature firm than Brown. Daily operations have grown to the point where a positive cash flow is being generated. The company is investing in needed plant and equipment, and though outside financing is necessary, operating activities are playing a major role in funding the acquisitions.

Finally, Purple seems to be a well-established entity in its field. Operating activities produce significant cash inflows that are more than enough to cover needed investment. In addition, the $500 excess cash flow ($1,600 − $1,100) is being used to reduce outstanding debt that was generated during earlier life-cycle stages or perhaps for dividend distributions to stockholders.

These three scenarios illustrate cash flow relationships for different types of entities.[4] Be aware that these relationships will vary among industries depending on their maturity. The important point is that you, as an accounting student, should not become totally consumed with statement-preparation procedures as shown on the previous pages. Knowledge of the information being conveyed by the numbers is equally if not more significant.

Some accountants use a work sheet when constructing the statement of cash flows. A work sheet provides more structure and helps to ensure that no accounts are accidentally overlooked in the statement-preparation process. Whether or not a work sheet is generated, the end result is the same: a financial report that reveals an entity's operating, investing, and financing activities.

To illustrate a work sheet for the indirect method of statement presentation, we will utilize data relating to Powell Corporation that were introduced earlier in the chapter. It is helpful to review Exhibits 19-4 and 19-6 at this time.

Construction of a work sheet requires performance of the five steps that follow.

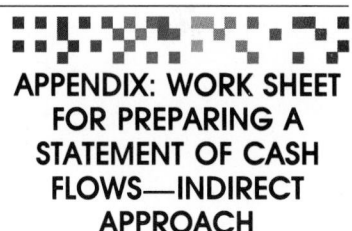

APPENDIX: WORK SHEET FOR PREPARING A STATEMENT OF CASH FLOWS—INDIRECT APPROACH

- ■ *Step 1*—Enter the beginning and ending account balances of all balance sheet items (see Exhibit 19-9). All accounts with debit balances are listed first, followed by those with credit balances. This procedure results in the accumulated depreciation accounts being listed together with liabilities and the components of stockholders' equity.
- ■ *Step 2*—Obtain the total of the debits and credits, both at the beginning and end of the year, to assure that the required equality is maintained on the two dates.
- ■ *Step 3*—Insert the headings "Operating Activities," "Investing Activities," "Financing Activities," and "Noncash Activities" on the work sheet where shown. Leave sufficient space so that a number of items may eventually be recorded.
- ■ *Step 4*—Make entries in the Analysis columns of the work sheet to account for (1) changes in the noncash accounts during the reporting period *and* (2) the accompanying inflows and outflows of cash. These

---

[4] Be cautioned that the three cases are generalized. Brown, for instance, may be a mature company that has had to rely on external financing to undertake a dramatic, costly expansion. A classic example might be a successful regional airline that begins to offer service on a national and international scale. Negative operating cash flows will be generated until passenger loads increase to a profitable level.

EXHIBIT 19-9
Cash Flow Work Sheet—Indirect Approach

POWELL CORPORATION
Work Sheet for Statement of Cash Flows—Indirect Approach
For the Year Ended December 31, 19X2

	Account Balances, 12/31/X1	Analysis of Transactions for 19X2 — Debit		Analysis of Transactions for 19X2 — Credit		Account Balances, 12/31/X2
Debits						
Cash	50,000	(x)	50,000			100,000
Accounts receivable (net)	375,000	(d)	25,000			400,000
Merchandise inventory	450,000			(e)	25,000	425,000
Prepaid selling expenses	4,000	(f)	1,000			5,000
Land	115,000	(i)	85,000			200,000
Buildings	1,250,000	(i*)	200,000			1,450,000
Equipment	800,000	(k)	25,000	(l)	100,000	725,000
Long-term investments	1,000,000			(m)	120,000	880,000
	4,044,000					4,185,000
Credits						
Accumulated depreciation: buildings	25,000			(b)	25,000	50,000
Accumulated depreciation: equipment	260,000	(l)	80,000	(c)	70,000	250,000
Accounts payable	340,000			(g)	130,000	470,000
Notes payable	300,000	(n)	300,000			—
Income taxes payable	39,000			(h)	1,000	40,000
Bonds payable	2,000,000			(o)	70,000	2,070,000
Common stock	130,000			(i)	65,000	195,000
Paid-in capital in excess of par	500,000			(j)	135,000	635,000
Retained earnings	450,000	(p)	15,000	(a)	40,000	475,000
	4,044,000					4,185,000

Operating activities				
Net income	(a)	40,000		
Building depreciation expense	(b)	25,000		
Equipment depreciation expense	(c)	70,000		
Increase in accounts receivable			(d)	25,000
Decrease in merchandise inventory	(e)	25,000		
Increase in prepaid selling expenses			(f)	1,000
Increase in accounts payable	(g)	130,000		
Increase in income taxes payable	(h)	1,000		
Loss on sale of equipment	(l)	5,000		
Gain on sale of long-term investments			(m)	15,000
Investing activities				
Purchase of land	(l)	15,000		
Purchase of equipment	(m)	135,000		
Proceeds from disposal of equipment			(i)	85,000
Proceeds from sale of long-term investments			(k)	25,000
Financing activities				
Payment to settle short-term note	(o)	70,000		
Proceeds from bond issue			(n)	300,000
Dividends paid			(p)	15,000
Noncash activities				
Common stock issued for building	(j)	200,000	(j*)	200,000
		1,497,000		1,447,000
			(x)	50,000
		1,497,000		1,497,000
Increase in cash				

entries are used for work sheet preparation purposes only; they are never recorded in the general journal. The entries may be made in any order; our sequence will parallel Exhibit 19-5 and the discussion on pages 775–780.

(a) *Generated net income of $40,000 during the year.* Profitable operations represent a source of cash for a firm. The analysis entry recognizes this fact by establishing a line entitled "Net Income" in the Operating Activities section. In addition, Retained Earnings is increased (credited) by $40,000 to reflect that income is closed to this account at the end of the reporting period.

(b) *Building depreciation expense of $25,000.* Depreciation must be added back to net income to arrive at cash flows from operating activities. Recall that although depreciation is deducted from revenues to determine an entity's earnings, no cash is consumed. The required entry in the Analysis columns involves a credit to Accumulated Depreciation: Buildings and an offsetting debit to Building Depreciation Expense, immediately below Powell's net income figure.

(c) *Equipment depreciation expense of $70,000.* This amount is treated in similar fashion to the expense in item (b).

(d) *Increase in accounts receivable, $25,000.* As noted earlier in the chapter, changes in both current assets and current liabilities related to operations must be considered when deriving the cash flow from operating activities. Decreases in current assets and increases in current liabilities are added to net income to convert to a cash-basis figure, whereas increases in current assets and decreases in current liabilities are subtracted. The analysis entry reflects the rise in accounts receivable via a $25,000 debit to that account. Further, a credit appears in the Operating Activities section to produce a subtraction from net income, the net income amount having been entered earlier as a debit.

The following require similar entries on the work sheet to compute the net cash flow from operating activities:

(e) *Decrease in merchandise inventory, $25,000.*
(f) *Increase in prepaid selling expenses, $1,000.*
(g) *Increase in accounts payable, $130,000.*
(h) *Increase in income taxes payable, $1,000.*

As shown in Exhibit 19-5, two additional items were considered in the operating cash flow computation: a $5,000 loss on the sale of equipment and a $15,000 gain from the sale of long-term investments. These items will be discussed shortly.

(i) *Purchased land for $85,000 cash.* This transaction required the use of cash and also resulted in an $85,000 increase to the Land account. The necessary entry is therefore a debit to Land, with an offsetting credit to establish a line for Purchase of Land in the Investing Activities section.

(j) *Acquired a $200,000 building in exchange for 65,000 shares of $1 par-value common stock.* This exchange transaction involves three accounts and is disclosed as a noncash activity. First, the Common Stock and Paid-in Capital in Excess of Par Value accounts are credited for $65,000 and $135,000, respectively, to reflect the issuance of additional shares, with a $200,000 debit then being made to the line "Common Stock Issued for Building." Next, the Buildings account is debited (see j *) to record the acquisition, and a credit is entered on the same line as that just noted: "Common Stock Issued for Building."

(k) *Purchased $25,000 of equipment for cash.* This acquisition resulted in a cash outflow and also a $25,000 increase in the Equipment account. The analysis entry requires a debit to Equipment. In addition, a corresponding credit is needed in the Investing Activities section to establish the Purchase of Equipment line item.

(l) *Disposed of $100,000 of equipment for cash; incurred a $5,000 loss.* The underlying details of this transaction are shown on page 777. The required work sheet entry involves recognition of $15,000 cash proceeds, along with reductions in Equipment ($100,000) and Accumulated Depreciation: Equipment ($80,000). The $5,000 loss is recorded by a debit and is added to net income to arrive at cash flows from operations.

(m) *Sold $120,000 of long-term investments for $135,000; generated a $15,000 gain.* This transaction requires a reduction (i.e., credit) in the Long-Term Investments account for $120,000 and the establishment of a $135,000 receipt of cash in the Investing Activities section (via a corresponding debit). Furthermore, because the $15,000 gain is (1) included in net income and (2) "investing" in nature, it must be subtracted when computing cash flows from *operating* activities. The gain is therefore set out (by means of a credit) in the Operating Activities section to yield the desired result.

(n) *Paid a short-term note payable, $300,000.* This financing activity resulted in a cash outflow during the period. The necessary entry is reflected by a debit to the Notes Payable account and a credit to the line entitled "Payment to Settle Short-Term Note."

(o) *Issued $70,000 of bonds payable at face value.* The issuance increases cash via a financing activity. The work sheet entry recognizes this fact and also increases (credits) the Bonds Payable account to reflect the rise in Powell's liabilities.

(p) *Paid cash dividends, $15,000.* Powell paid $15,000 of dividends during 19X2. The analysis entry therefore involves a $15,000 debit to Retained Earnings to record the appropriate reduction. In addition, a $15,000 credit is made in the Financing Activities section to establish a line item for the payment.

■ *Step 5*—Compute the difference between the beginning and ending cash balances, and place the difference (labeled x) on the Cash line in the Analysis columns. Increases are entered in the debit column and decreases in the credit column. Next, total the Analysis columns and place the difference, which should correspond to the increase or decrease, at the bottom of the work sheet for balancing purposes. The document is now complete and can be used to prepare the formal statement of cash flows. (Compare the bottom of the work sheet with the statement that appears in Exhibit 19-8.)

END-OF-CHAPTER REVIEW

**LEARNING OBJECTIVES:
THE KEY POINTS**

1 Explain the purpose of the statement of cash flows. The statement of cash flows is designed to provide information about the nature and sources of an entity's cash inflows and outflows. These items are categorized into operating, investing, and financing classifications. Overall, this important report lends insight into a company's need for external financing and the firm's ability to generate future cash flows, meet obligations, and pay dividends.

2 Classify and analyze operating, investing, and financing activities. Operating activities give rise to transactions and events that enter into the determination of net income. The Financial Accounting Standards Board defines these activities to include all cash transactions and events that are not otherwise considered in the investing or financing categories. Examples include receipts from customers, normal business expenses, and receipts of dividends and loan interest. In contrast, investing activities involve the investment of a firm's resources. Typical examples of such transactions are the acquisition and sale of both productive assets (e.g., property, plant, and equipment) and securities of other firms. Finally, financing activities provide a business with resources from either its owners or its creditors. Common financing transactions include the issuance and retirement of stock and debt.

3 Demonstrate the proper accounting treatment for significant noncash investing/financing transactions. Noncash investing and financing transactions (e.g., the issuance of stock for land) are reported separately on the statement of cash flows. The purpose of this disclosure is to reveal the impact of such transactions on a company's financial position, even though no direct receipt or disbursement of cash has occurred.

4 Use both the direct and indirect methods of computing cash flows from operating activities. Under the direct method, individual income statement items are converted from the accrual basis of accounting to the cash basis of accounting. For instance, to translate sales revenues into the amount of cash received from customers, decreases in accounts receivable are added to sales, and increases are subtracted. To determine cash payments for merchandise, an entity's cost of goods sold is adjusted for changes in merchandise inventory (increases are added and decreases are subtracted) and accounts payable (decreases are added and increases are subtracted).

The indirect method, on the other hand, begins with the net income figure, adds back noncash expenses (e.g., depreciation and amortization), and adjusts for gains and losses on nonoperating transactions. In addition, changes in current assets and current liabilities related to operations are added to or subtracted from net income. Decreases in current assets and increases in current liabilities are added to net income, whereas increases in current assets and decreases in current liabilities are subtracted.

5 Prepare and interpret a statement of cash flows. The statement of cash flows may be prepared by using either the direct method or the indirect method, although the former approach is encouraged by the FASB. The direct method begins with a presentation of cash receipts and disbursements for specific operating items (including interest and taxes) to arrive at cash flows from operating activities. Cash flows from investing and financing activities are reported next, followed by a schedule of noncash investing/financing transactions.

The indirect method begins with a reconciliation of net income to cash flows from operations and then presents cash flows from investing and financing activities. The statement concludes with the same schedule of noncash investing/financing transactions.

The relationship among cash flows from operating, investing, and financing activities varies from company to company and from industry to industry. New, emerging companies often have negative operating cash flows and need considerable external financing. In contrast, mature firms frequently produce enough cash flow from operating activities to both cover new investment and reduce outstanding debt.

**KEY TERMS
AND CONCEPTS:
A QUICK OVERVIEW**

cash equivalents   Short-term, highly liquid investments that mature in 90 days or less.

direct method of statement construction   An approach whereby individual income statement items are converted from the accrual basis to the cash basis of accounting.

financing activities   Those activities that supply a company with funds from the company's owners or creditors.

indirect method of statement construction   An approach whereby cash flow from operations is derived by making certain adjustments to accrual-basis net income.

investing activities   Those activities that involve investment of an entity's resources.

nonoperating gains and losses   Gains and losses that arise from investing and financing activities.

operating activities   Company activities primarily related to the production and sale of goods and services, and that enter into the calculation of net income.

statement of cash flows   A financial statement that reveals the operating, investing, and financing cash flows of a company.

CHAPTER QUIZ

The five questions that follow relate to several issues raised in the chapter. Test your knowledge of the issues by selecting the best answer. (The answers appear on p. 815.)

1 Which of the following is a financing activity?
  a Purchase of office equipment.   c Receipt of dividends.
  b Payment of dividends.   d Sale of merchandise on account.

2 When preparing a statement of cash flows, the direct method is often used in calculating the cash flows from:
  a operating, investing, and financing activities.
  b investing and financing activities.
  c operating and investing activities.
  d operating activities only.

3 When converting accrual-based net income to the cash basis with the indirect method, which of the following items is added in the operating activities section of the cash flow statement?
  a Dividends paid.   c Loss on the sale of land.
  b Cash dividends received.   d Gain on the sale of land.

4 Phillips Corporation's net cash flow provided by investing activities totaled $100,000 for the year. Dividends paid amounted to $5,000, payments to retire outstanding loans were $40,000, depreciation expense on buildings was $15,000, and new equipment acquired cost $30,000. If the company sold land for cash, the proceeds from the sale must have been:

a $10,000.   c $100,000.

b $25,000.   d $130,000.

5 The balance of Ebony's Machinery account increased by $50,000 during the year. Machinery that cost $80,000 was discarded at a local landfill; additional equipment of $130,000 was purchased via the issuance of common stock. In view of these transactions, an examination of the company's cash flows from investing activities will show:

a a $130,000 outflow for the machinery purchase.

b a $130,000 outflow for the machinery purchase and an $80,000 inflow from disposal.

c a $130,000 outflow for the machinery purchase and an $80,00 loss.

d nothing.

SUMMARY PROBLEM

Colwell Corporation had the following balance sheets:

	Dec. 31, 19X2	Dec. 31, 19X1
Assets		
Cash	$ 59,000	$ 87,000
Accounts receivable (net)	189,000	223,000
Inventory	65,000	45,000
Prepaid selling expenses	15,000	12,000
Land	150,000	120,000
Equipment	125,000	150,000
Accumulated depreciation: equipment	(85,000)	(75,000)
Buildings	280,000	200,000
Accumulated depreciation: buildings	(85,000)	(70,000)
Patents (net of amortization)	24,000	27,000
Total assets	$737,000	$719,000
Liabilities & Stockholders' Equity		
Accounts payable	$ 88,000	$120,000
Notes payable	160,000	90,000
Income taxes payable	60,000	70,000
Bonds payable	100,000	150,000
Common stock, $10 par	210,000	180,000
Additional paid-in capital	50,000	50,000
Retained earnings	69,000	59,000
Total liabilities & stockholders' equity	$737,000	$719,000

The following additional information was extracted from the accounting records:

1 Three thousand shares of common stock were issued for land having a fair market value of $30,000.

2 Equipment having a book value of $13,000 (cost, $25,000; accumulated depreciation, $12,000) was sold for $20,000 cash, producing a $7,000 gain.

3 A building was constructed for $80,000 cash.

4 The notes payable relate to various borrowing agreements signed with Fairfax
Savings Bank.

5 Long-term bonds of $50,000 were retired; no gain or loss was incurred.

6 Cash dividends of $10,000 were declared and paid during 19X2.

7 The 19X2 income statement revealed the data shown:

Sales	$1,450,000
Cost of goods sold	835,000
Selling & administrative expenses	510,000
Equipment depreciation expense	22,000
Building depreciation expense	15,000
Patent amortization expense	3,000
Interest expense	32,000
Income tax expense	20,000
Net income	20,000

Instructions

a Prepare a statement of cash flows for the year ended December 31, 19X2. Use the
direct method.

b Prepare a statement of cash flows for the year ended December 31, 19X2. Use the
indirect method.

Solution

a

COLWELL CORPORATION Statement of Cash Flows For the Year Ended December 31, 19X2		
Cash flows from operating activities		
Cash received from customers		$1,484,000*
Less cash payments for:		
Purchases of merchandise	$887,000†	
Selling & administrative expenses	513,000‡	
Interest	32,000	
Income taxes	30,000‡	1,462,000
Net cash provided by operating activities		$ 22,000
Cash flows from investing activities		
Proceeds from sale of equipment	$ 20,000	
Payment for building construction	(80,000)	
Net cash used by investing activities		(60,000)
Cash flows from financing activities		
Proceeds from issuance of notes payable	$ 70,000	
Payment to retire bonds payable	(50,000)	
Payment of cash dividends	(10,000)	
Net cash provided by financing activities		10,000
Net increase (decrease) in cash		$ (28,000)
Cash balance, January 1, 19X2		87,000
Cash balance, December 31, 19X2		$ 59,000
Schedule of noncash investing/financing activities		
Common stock issued for land		$ 30,000

*Sales ($1,450,000) + decrease in accounts receivable ($34,000).
†Cost of goods sold ($835,000) + increase in inventory ($20,000) + decrease in accounts payable ($32,000).
‡Selling and administrative expenses ($510,000) + increase in prepaid selling expenses ($3,000).
‡Income tax expense ($20,000) + decrease in income taxes payable ($10,000).

b

COLWELL CORPORATION Statement of Cash Flows For the Year Ended December 31, 19X2		
Cash flows from operating activities		
Net income		$ 20,000
Add (deduct) items to convert net income to a cash basis		
Equipment depreciation expense	$ 22,000	
Building depreciation expense	15,000	
Patent amortization expense	3,000	
Gain on sale of equipment	(7,000)	
Decrease in accounts receivable (net)	34,000	
Increase in inventory	(20,000)	
Increase in prepaid selling expenses	(3,000)	
Decrease in accounts payable	(32,000)	
Decrease in income taxes payable	(10,000)	2,000
Net cash provided by operating activities		$ 22,000
Cash flows from investing activities		
Proceeds from sale of equipment	$ 20,000	
Payment for building construction	(80,000)	
Net cash used by investing activities		(60,000)
Cash flows from financing activities		
Proceeds from issuance of notes payable	$ 70,000	
Payment to retire bonds payable	(50,000)	
Payment of cash dividends	(10,000)	
Net cash provided by financing activities		10,000
Net increase (decrease) in cash		$(28,000)
Cash balance, January 1, 19X2		87,000
Cash balance, December 31, 19X2		$ 59,000
Schedule of noncash investing/financing activities		
Common stock issued for land		$ 30,000

ASSIGNMENT MATERIAL

QUESTIONS

Q19-1 What information does the statement of cash flows disclose? Give several examples.

Q19-2 Describe the nature of operating activities, including specific examples of operating cash inflows and outflows.

Q19-3 Define investing activities, citing several examples of typical investing inflows and outflows.

Q19-4 List five examples of financing activities. Which of these cause cash inflows and which cause cash outflows?

Q19-5 Why are noncash transactions, such as the exchange of common stock for a building, included on a statement of cash flows? How are these noncash transactions disclosed?

Q19-6 What is a cash equivalent? What is the basic difference between a cash equivalent and most short-term marketable securities?

Q19-7 Differentiate between the direct and indirect methods of preparing the statement of cash flows.

Q19-8 Both the direct and indirect methods of reporting are permitted when preparing the statement of cash flows. Which of the two approaches is encouraged by the Financial Accounting Standards Board?

Q19-9 Is net income normally equal to cash provided by operating activities? Why?

Q19-10 Items such as depreciation expense reduce net income without an accompanying decrease in cash. Under the indirect method, how are these and similar items treated when determining the cash provided from operating activities?

Q19-11 Meridian Corporation recently sold some equipment, generating a $6,000 loss on one transaction and a $5,000 gain on another. How are these items treated when computing the net cash flow from operating activities? Assume use of the indirect method.

Q19-12 Briefly discuss the relationship among operating, investing, and financing cash flows for many new, growing companies.

EXERCISES

E19-1 *Classification of activities* **(L.O. 2)**
Classify each of the following transactions as arising from an operating (O), investing (I), financing (F), or noncash investing/financing (N) activity.
_____ a Received $80,000 from the sale of land.
_____ b Received $3,200 from cash sales.
_____ c Paid a $5,000 dividend.
_____ d Purchased $8,800 of merchandise for cash.
_____ e Received $100,000 from the issuance of common stock.
_____ f Paid $1,200 of interest on a note payable.
_____ g Acquired a new laser printer by paying $650.
_____ h Acquired a $400,000 building by signing a $400,000 mortgage note.

E19-2 *Direct calculation of operating cash flows* **(L.O. 4)**
Selected balance sheet accounts of HMS Electronics at the end of 19X5 and 19X6 follow.

1-2-3

	Dec. 31, 19X6	Dec. 31, 19X5
Accounts receivable	$ 73,000	$ 79,000
Inventory	134,000	121,000
Accounts payable (suppliers of merchandise)	164,000	179,000
Interest payable	33,000	28,500

HMS makes all sales and purchases on account and employs the accrual basis of accounting. The firm's 19X6 income statement revealed sales, cost of goods sold, and interest expense of $425,000, $310,000, and $45,000, respectively.

Determine the following, assuming the company plans to prepare a statement of cash flows by using the direct method:

a Cash collections from customers.
b Merchandise purchases for the year.
c Cash paid to suppliers of merchandise.
d Interest paid during the year.

E19-3 *Indirect calculation of operating cash flows* **(L.O. 4)**

Video Corporation's balance sheet revealed the following account balance information:

Account	Dec. 31, 19X6	Dec. 31, 19X5
Accounts receivable	$52,000	$57,000
Merchandise inventory	75,000	68,000
Accounts payable	21,000	19,500

The accrual-basis net income was $107,000. In computing net income, the company recorded $12,600 of depreciation expense; there were no gains or losses from investing and financing activities.

On the basis of the preceding information, calculate Video's cash flows from operating activities by using the indirect method.

E19-4 *Indirect calculation of operating cash flows* **(L.O. 4)**

1-2-3

Specialty Services, Inc., reported a net income of $110,000 for the year just ended, which includes an $18,000 gain on the sale of long-term investments. The following data were obtained from comparative balance sheets:

	Oct. 31, 19X2	Oct. 31, 19X1
Trade accounts receivable	$245,000	$203,000
Merchandise inventory	230,000	308,000
Accumulated depreciation: equipment	120,000	65,000
Accounts payable	190,000	124,000
Accrued liabilities	38,000	73,000

There were no purchases or disposals of equipment during the year. The long-term investment had a carrying (book) value of $77,000 and was sold for cash on June 15.

On the basis of the preceding information, determine the cash provided by operating activities from November 1, 19X1, through October 31, 19X2. The firm uses the indirect method of statement preparation.

E19-5 *Overview of direct and indirect methods* **(L.O. 4)**

Evaluate the comments that follow as being True or False. If the comment is false, briefly explain why.

a Both the direct and indirect methods will produce the same cash flow from operating activities.
b Depreciation expense is added back to net income when the indirect method is used.
c One of the advantages of using the direct method rather than the indirect method is that larger cash flows from financing activities will be reported.

d The cash paid to suppliers is normally disclosed on the statement of cash flows when the indirect method of statement preparation is employed.

e The dollar change in the Merchandise Inventory account appears on the statement of cash flows only when the direct method of statement preparation is used.

E19-6 ***Statement preparation from cash flow listing: Direct method*** **(L.O. 5)**
In response to a banker's request, Baxter Corporation's accountant has compiled the following cash flow information for the year ended December 31, 19X7:

Beginning cash balance		$ 173,000
Add: Cash receipts		
Receipts from customers	$945,000	
Proceeds from sale of land	30,000	
Proceeds from stock issuance	600,000	
Proceeds from long-term bank loan	83,000	1,658,000
		$1,831,000
Deduct: Cash disbursements		
Payments to suppliers*	$345,000	
Payments to employees	231,000	
Payments for interest	24,000	
Payments for dividends	50,000	
Repayment of mortgage note	100,000	
Purchase of building	700,000	1,450,000
Ending cash balance		$ 381,000

* For merchandise acquisitions.

A review of the company's accounting records revealed that Baxter had also purchased equipment in exchange for a $35,000 note payable.

Prepare a statement of cash flows in good form by using the direct method.

E19-7 ***Statement preparation: Direct method*** **(L.O. 5)**
The comparative balance sheets of Village Company follow.

VILLAGE COMPANY Comparative Balance Sheets December 31, 19X2 and 19X1		
	Dec. 31, 19X2	Dec. 31, 19X1
Cash	$ 5,000	$ 7,000
Accounts receivable (net)	12,000	18,000
Merchandise inventory	35,000	28,000
Property, plant, & equipment	40,000	30,000
Less: Accumulated depreciation	(17,000)	(10,000)
Total assets	$ 75,000	$ 73,000
Accounts payable*	$ 25,000	$ 21,000
Income taxes payable	4,000	1,000
Common stock	24,000	24,000
Retained earnings	22,000	27,000
Total liabilities & stock. equity	$ 75,000	$ 73,000

* Relate to purchases of merchandise.

The firm's accrual-basis income statement revealed the following data: sales, $120,000; cost of goods sold, $80,000; selling and administrative expenses, $25,000; depreciation expense, $7,000; and income taxes, $3,000. (There was no interest expense.) Dividends declared and paid during 19X2 totaled $10,000. Finally, Village purchased $10,000 of equipment for cash on August 14.

a Determine the increase or decrease in cash during 19X2.
b Prepare a statement of cash flows by using the direct method.

E19-8 **Statement preparation: Indirect method (L.O. 5)**
Refer to the data pertaining to Village Company in Exercise 19-7.
a Determine the increase or decrease in cash during 19X2.
b Prepare a statement of cash flows by using the indirect method.

E19-9 **Equipment transaction and cash flow reporting (L.O. 5)**
The property, plant, and equipment section of ProComp, Inc.'s comparative balance sheet follows.

	Dec. 31, 19X4	Dec. 31, 19X3
Property, plant, & equipment		
Land	$ 94,000	$ 94,000
Equipment	652,000	527,000
Less: Accumulated depreciation	(316,000)	(341,000)

New equipment purchased during 19X4 totaled $280,000. The 19X4 income statement disclosed equipment depreciation expense of $41,000 and a $9,000 loss on the sale of equipment.

a Determine the cost and accumulated depreciation of the equipment sold during 19X4.
b Determine the selling price of the equipment sold.

c Show how the sale of equipment would appear on a statement of cash flows prepared by using the indirect method.

E19-10 *Evaluation of cash flows* (L.O. 5)

The following statement of cash flows was prepared for Yellowstone Company:

YELLOWSTONE COMPANY Statement of Cash Flows For the Year Ended December 31, 19X2		
Cash flows from operating activities		
Cash received from customers		$240,000
Less cash payments for:		
Purchases of merchandise	$180,000	
Selling & administrative expenses	75,000	
Interest	20,000	275,000
Net cash used by operating activities		$ (35,000)
Cash flows from investing activities		
Sale of equipment	$ 20,000	
Sale of vehicles	10,000	
Sale of long-term investments	40,000	
Net cash provided by investing act.		70,000
Cash flows from financing activities		
Retirement of long-term debt		(50,000)
Net increase (decrease) in cash		$ (15,000)
Cash balance, January 1, 19X2		54,000
Cash balance, December 31, 19X2		$ 39,000

Evaluate the nature of the decrease in cash. Does your analysis indicate any potential problems for Yellowstone?

E19-11 *Evaluation of cash flows* (L.O. 5)

Summaries of the cash flow statements issued by Halper, Porter, and Bryan follow.

	Halper	Porter	Bryan
Cash flows provided by operating activities	$ 9,000	$63,000	$ 6,700
Cash flows provided by investing activities	2,200	4,900	56,200
Cash flows provided by financing activities	67,300	10,600	15,600
Total	$78,500	$78,500	$78,500

A review of the companies' statements found that Halper issued $70,000 of bonds during the period. Bryan, on the other hand, sold a parcel of land for $65,000.

Focusing solely on the facts presented, assume that Halper, Porter, and Bryan have approached you for a line of credit to buy merchandise from your store. Which of the three companies would you likely favor? Briefly explain.

Series A

PROBLEMS

P19-A1 *Transaction analysis: Operating, investing, and financing activities* (L.O. 2, 3)

The management of Maui Corporation desires to know the nature of each of the following transactions and events:

1 Collected cash from customers for cash sales.
2 Purchased a short-term investment for cash.
3 Secured a mortgage note to finance the acquisition of a building.
4 Issued 10-year bonds for cash.
5 Paid a short-term nonoperating note.
6 Sold equipment having a book value of $30,000 for $30,000 cash.
7 Sold a parcel of land at cost; received a long-term note.
8 Received dividends on a long-term stock investment.
9 Paid income taxes.
10 Issued preferred stock in exchange for a valuable patent.
11 Reacquired treasury stock for cash.
12 Paid previously declared cash dividends.

Instructions

a Briefly explain the difference between investing and financing activities and noncash investing/financing activities.

b Design a table with the following columnar headings: operating activity, investing activity, financing activity, and noncash investing/financing activity. Classify the 12 transactions listed by using these headings. For all classifications except noncash investing/financing, indicate whether the transaction causes a cash inflow (+) or a cash outflow (−).

P19-A2 *Operating activities: Direct and indirect methods* (L.O. 4)

The 19X5 income statement of Office Products, Inc., follows.

1-2-3

OFFICE PRODUCTS, INC. Income Statement For the Year Ended December 31, 19X5		
Net sales		$980,000
Cost of goods sold		
Beginning inventory	$235,000	
Net purchases	720,000	
Goods available for sale	$955,000	
Less: Ending inventory	260,000	
Cost of goods sold		695,000
Gross profit		$285,000
Expenses		
Selling & administrative	$149,000	
Depreciation	54,000	203,000
		$ 82,000
Other revenue (expense)		
Interest expense	$ (18,000)	
Gain on sale of equipment	26,000	8,000
Income before income taxes		$ 90,000
Income taxes		27,000
Net income		$ 63,000

The following additional information was obtained from the general ledger and management personnel:

1 Accounts payable related to the purchases of merchandise decreased during 19X5 by $32,800. In contrast, accounts receivable increased by $23,700.

2 Prepaid expenses and wages payable increased throughout 19X5 by $2,400 and $5,600, respectively.

3 The balance in the Income Taxes Payable account on January 1 was $4,900; the December 31 balance was $4,100.

4 The company financed a $78,000 equipment purchase by signing a note payable that is due in 19X8.

Instructions

a Prepare the operating activities section of the statement of cash flows by using the direct method.

b Prepare the operating activities section of the statement of cash flows by using the indirect method.

P19-A3 *Statement of cash flows: Direct method* (L.O. 5)

The Tulsa Bulldogs, a minor league baseball team, is having great difficulty paying its bills. Management cannot understand how the firm can generate net income and continually be short of cash. The balance sheet accounts of the Bulldogs follow.

	Sept. 30, 19X2	Oct. 1, 19X1
Cash	$ —	$ 25,000
Receivable from major league affiliate	400,000	634,000
Concessions inventory	134,000	79,000
Prepaid selling expenses	25,700	19,000
Ball park & other fixed assets	922,600	857,000
Accumulated depreciation	527,000	480,000
Accounts payable (for concessions)	29,000	50,800
Salaries & bonuses payable	97,200	230,500
Accrued taxes payable	16,000	14,000
Federal income taxes payable	—	129,000
Common stock	600,000	580,000
Retained earnings	213,100	129,700

Other data are as follows:

1 Net income was $100,000. Dividends declared and paid totaled $16,600.
2 Tulsa's accrual-basis income statement revealed revenues from admissions, concessions, and the major league affiliate that totaled $4,350,000. Other key figures are cost of concessions sold, $950,000; selling and administrative expenses, $3,179,000; depreciation expense, $47,000; income tax expense, $74,000; and interest expense, $0.
3 The Accrued Taxes Payable account is used for various taxes that are treated as selling and administrative expenses.
4 No disposals of fixed assets occurred during the year. In February, the Bulldogs acquired a new scoreboard for cash.
5 Additional common stock was sold on May 15 for $20,000 cash.

Instructions

a Prepare a statement of cash flows for the year ended September 30, 19X2, by using the direct method.
b Prepare a brief evaluation of the Bulldogs' existing cash problem.

P19-A4 Cash flow information: Direct and indirect methods (L.O. 5)
The comparative year-end balance sheets of Sign Graphics, Inc., revealed the following activity in the company's current accounts:

	19X5	19X4	Increase (Decrease)
Current assets			
Cash	$ 55,400	$ 35,200	$ 20,200
Accounts receivable (net)	83,800	88,000	(4,200)
Inventory	243,400	233,800	9,600
Prepaid expenses	25,400	24,200	1,200
Current liabilities			
Accounts payable	$123,600	$140,600	$(17,000)
Taxes payable	43,600	49,200	(5,600)
Interest payable	9,000	6,400	2,600
Accrued liabilities	38,800	60,400	(21,600)
Note payable	44,000	—	44,000

The accounts payable were for the purchase of merchandise. Prepaid expenses and accrued liabilities relate to the firm's selling and administrative expenses. The company's condensed income statement follows.

| SIGN GRAPHICS, INC. |
| Income Statement |
| For the Year Ended December 31, 19X5 |

Sales		$713,800
Less: Cost of goods sold		323,000
Gross profit		$390,800
Less: Selling & administrative expenses	$186,000	
Depreciation expense	17,000	
Interest expense	27,000	230,000
		$160,800
Add: Gain on sale of land		21,800
Income before taxes		$182,600
Income taxes		36,800
Net income		$145,800

Other data:
1 Long-term investments were purchased for cash at a cost of $74,600.
2 Cash proceeds from the sale of land totaled $76,200.
3 Store equipment of $44,000 was purchased by signing a short-term note payable. Also, a $150,000 telecommunications system was acquired by issuing 3,000 shares of preferred stock.
4 A long-term note of $49,400 was repaid.
5 Twenty thousand shares of common stock were issued at $5.19 per share.
6 The company paid cash dividends amounting to $128,600.

Instructions

a Prepare the operating activities section of the company's statement of cash flows, assuming use of:
(1) The direct method.
(2) The indirect method.
b Prepare the investing and financing activities sections of the statement of cash flows.

P19-A5 *Statement of cash flows: Indirect method* (L.O. 5)
Comparative balance sheets of Micro Supply, Inc., appear as follows:

MICRO SUPPLY, INC.
Comparative Balance Sheets
October 31, 19X5 and 19X4

	19X5		19X4	
Assets				
Current assets				
Cash		$ 427,000		$ 130,000
Short-term investments		105,000		205,000
Accounts receivable (net)		195,000		377,000
Merchandise inventory		1,100,000		918,000
Total current assets		$1,827,000		$1,630,000
Property, plant, & equipment				
Land		$ 17,000		$ 20,000
Equipment	$500,000		$300,000	
Less: Accumulated depreciation	97,000	403,000	80,000	220,000
Total property, plant, & equipment		$ 420,000		$ 240,000
Intangible assets				
Copyrights (cost of $19,000 less amortization)		7,000		8,000
Total assets		$2,254,000		$1,878,000
Liabilities & Stockholders' Equity				
Current liabilities				
Accounts payable (for merchandise)		$ 900,000		$ 732,000
Accrued liabilities		50,000		15,000
Income taxes payable		80,000		120,000
Total current liabilities		$1,030,000		$ 867,000
Long-term liabilities				
Bonds payable		650,000		900,000
Stockholders' equity				
Common stock	$300,000		$100,000	
Retained earnings	274,000	574,000	11,000	111,000
Total liabilities & stockholders' equity		$2,254,000		$1,878,000

Additional information:
a The company retired $250,000 of bonds during the year and sold $100,000 of short-term investments. No gain or loss was incurred on either transaction.
b Common stock of $200,000 was issued at par value to acquire equipment.
c The 19X5 accrual-basis income statement revealed net income of $263,000, along with the following: sales, $946,000; cost of goods sold,

$419,700; selling and administrative expenses, $97,800; depreciation and amortization expense, $18,000; interest expense, $74,000; gain on the sale of land, $5,000; and income tax expense, $78,500.

d No dividends were paid during the year.

Instructions

Prepare a statement of cash flows by using the indirect method.

P19-A6 *Analysis of a statement of cash flows* (L.O. 5)

The statements of cash flow for Computer World, Inc., for 19X6 and 19X7 follow.

	19X7	19X6
Cash flows from operating activities		
Net income (loss)	$ 63,600	$ (29,800)
Add (deduct) items to convert net income to a cash basis		
Depreciation expense	61,300	56,000
Write-off of worthless patent	—	94,900
Gain on sale of equipment	(9,000)	(39,200)
Decrease in accounts receivable	11,700	200
Increase in inventories	(200)	(5,400)
Decrease in accounts payable	(17,300)	—
Increase in accrued liabilities	8,000	4,100
Decrease in income taxes payable	(22,100)	(27,300)
Net cash provided (used) by operating activities	$ 96,000	$ 53,500
Cash flows from investing activities		
Proceeds from sale of equipment	$ 50,300	$ 146,900
Acquisition of property, plant, & equipment	(52,000)	(64,500)
Purchase of long-term investments	(2,900)	(261,600)
Net cash provided (used) by investing activities	$ (4,600)	$(179,200)
Cash flows from financing activities		
Proceeds from short-term notes payable	$ 7,800	$ 1,800
Proceeds from long-term debt	67,500	316,900
Repayment of long-term debt	(148,700)	(181,700)
Purchase of treasury stock	—	(9,100)
Payment of cash dividends	(19,900)	(18,800)
Net cash provided (used) by financing activities	$ (93,300)	$ 109,100
Net increase (decrease) in cash	$ (1,900)	$ (16,600)

Instructions

As part of the training to become a stockbroker, you have been asked to analyze the preceding statements of cash flow. Answer the questions that follow.

a Operating activities provided (as opposed to used) cash in 19X6. Briefly explain how this is possible when the company actually generated a net loss for the year.

b Depreciation is treated as a "positive number" when computing net cash provided by operating activities. Does this treatment mean that depreciation is a source of cash for the company? Briefly discuss.

c Briefly discuss the major differences in investing activities during the two years.

d Study the relationship among operating, investing, and financing cash flows and activities for 19X6. Would the relationship parallel that of a young firm, a middle-aged firm, or a mature firm? Why?

e Repeat part (d), using the data of 19X7.

*P19-A7 **Work sheet: Statement of cash flows** (L.O. 5)
Refer to the data pertaining to Micro Supply, Inc., in Problem 19-A5.

Instructions

a Prepare a work sheet similar in format to that shown in Exhibit 19-9.

b Prepare a formal statement of cash flows by using the indirect method.

Series B

P19-B1 **Transaction analysis: Operating, investing, and financing activities** (L.O. 2, 3)
The management of St. Thomas Corporation desires to know the nature of each of the following transactions and events:

1 Issued common stock for cash.

2 Issued preferred stock in exchange for a parcel of land and a building.

3 Paid employee salaries.

4 Called and retired $200,000 of bonds.

5 Borrowed money by signing a note payable due in three years.

6 Purchased merchandise for cash.

7 Received interest on an outstanding loan.

8 Purchased new equipment for cash.

9 Reduced the balance of a long-term nonoperating note payable by issuing common stock.

10 Sold land for cash.

11 Paid dividends to stockholders.

12 Received cash from customers on account.

Instructions

a Briefly distinguish among operating, investing, and financing activities.

b Design a table with the following columnar headings: operating activity, investing activity, financing activity, and noncash investing/financing activity. Classify the 12 transactions listed by using these headings. For all classifications except noncash investing/financing, indicate whether the transaction causes a cash inflow (+) or a cash outflow (−).

P19-B2 **Operating activities: Direct and indirect methods** (L.O. 4)

1-2-3

The information that follows was taken from the financial statements of Weaver Optical, Inc.

---

* An asterisk preceding an item indicates that the material is covered in an appendix to this chapter.

	Dec. 31, 19X2	Dec. 31, 19X1
Balance sheet accounts		
Accounts receivable (net)	$ 49,700	$ 54,300
Inventory	88,500	68,600
Prepaid selling expenses	4,600	3,900
Accounts payable (relate to merchandise purchases)	61,800	59,700
Interest payable	6,200	7,300
Mortgage payable (long-term)	158,000	168,000
19X2 income statement data		
Sales	$1,200,000	
Sales returns & allowances	15,000	
Cost of goods sold	800,000	
Selling & administrative expenses	60,000	
Depreciation expense	40,000	
Interest expense	20,000	
Loss on sale of equipment	45,000	
Income tax expense	75,000	

Instructions

a Prepare the operating activities section of the statement of cash flows by using the direct method.

b Prepare the operating activities section of the statement of cash flows by using the indirect method.

P19-B3 *Statement of cash flows: Direct method* (L.O. 5)

David Green, M.D., is disturbed that his practice, The Hair Transplant Center, has only $50 cash as of March 31, 19X5. He believes that the Center experienced a very profitable quarter of activity. In an effort to analyze what happened, you have determined the following account balance changes from January 1 through March 31:

	Increase (Decrease)
Cash	$(23,950)
Accounts receivable	91,000
Prepaid rent	1,580
Equipment	7,000
Accumulated depreciation: equipment	10,500
Patent	(1,000)
Accounts payable (for operating expenses)	12,000
Federal income taxes payable	(500)
Long-term debt (advance payment)	(4,000)
Common stock	7,000
Retained earnings	49,630

Other data are:

1 The accrual-basis income statement revealed net income of $60,000, composed of the following: service revenues, $172,000; operating expenses, $80,000; depreciation expense, $10,500; amortization expense, $1,000; income tax expense, $18,900; and interest expense, $1,600.

2 Cash dividends were declared and paid before the end of the quarter.

3 No disposals or sales of equipment took place. The Center purchased new equipment in March from a family friend, who accepted 200 shares of common stock for payment.

Instructions

a Prepare a statement of cash flows for the quarter ended March 31, 19X5, by using the direct method.
b Prepare a brief explanation for Dr. Green concerning his current cash dilemma. Suggest ways that he might be able to improve his cash flow.

P19-B4 *Cash flow information: Direct and indirect methods* (L.O. 5)
The 19X2 accrual-basis income statement of Restaurant Outfitters, Inc., follows.

RESTAURANT OUTFITTERS, INC. Income Statement For the Year Ended December 31, 19X2		
Sales		$490,000
Less: Cost of goods sold		210,000
Gross profit		$280,000
Less: Selling & administrative expenses	$195,000	
Depreciation expense	15,000	
Interest expense	1,000	211,000
		$ 69,000
Less: Loss on sale of machinery		3,000
Income before taxes		$ 66,000
Less: Income tax expense		22,000
Net income		$ 44,000

Balance sheets for 19X1 and 19X2 contained the following accounts:

	Dec. 31, 19X2	Dec. 31, 19X1
Assets		
Cash	$ 5,000	$ 45,000
Accounts receivable (net)	52,000	37,000
Inventory	41,000	25,000
Machinery (net)	60,000	60,000
Total assets	$158,000	$167,000
Liabilities & Stockholders' Equity		
Accounts payable	$ 27,000	$ 64,000
Long-term note payable	5,000	20,000
Common stock, $5 par value	5,000	4,000
Paid-in capital in excess of par value	20,000	16,000
Retained earnings	101,000	63,000
Total liabilities & stockholders' equity	$158,000	$167,000

Other data are:
1 Common stock (200 shares) was sold for $25 per share in the middle of 19X2.
2 Dividends of $6 per share were declared and paid in late 19X2.
3 Machinery that cost $20,000 and having a book value of $13,000 was sold for $10,000 cash. New machinery was purchased for $28,000 cash.
4 Changes in the Accounts Receivable and Accounts Payable accounts were caused by sales and purchases of merchandise, respectively.
5 The note payable relates to a borrowing transaction.

Instructions

a Prepare the operating activities section of the company's statement of cash flows, assuming use of:
(1) The direct method.
(2) The indirect method.
b Prepare the investing activities and financing activities sections of the statement of cash flows.

P19-B5 *Statement of cash flows: Indirect method* (L.O. 5)
Comparative balance sheets of Goodrich Company appear as follows:

GOODRICH COMPANY
Comparative Balance Sheets
December 31, 19X2 and 19X1

	19X2		19X1	
Assets				
Current assets				
Cash		$ 15,000		$ 45,000
Accounts receivable (net)		100,000		115,000
Inventory		485,000		400,000
Total current assets		$600,000		$560,000
Property, plant, & equipment				
Land		$ 12,000		$ 9,000
Machinery	$ 90,000		$ 70,000	
Less: Accumulated depreciation	24,000	66,000	14,000	56,000
Total property, plant, & equipment		$ 78,000		$ 65,000
Intangible assets				
Patents (cost of $10,000 less amortization)		3,000		4,000
Total assets		$681,000		$629,000
Liabilities & Stockholders' Equity				
Current liabilities				
Accounts payable (for merchandise)		$390,000		$370,000
Income taxes payable		10,000		8,000
Total current liabilities		$400,000		$378,000
Long-term liabilities				
Mortgage payable		6,000		7,000
Stockholders' equity				
Common stock	$200,000		$180,000	
Retained earnings	75,000	275,000	64,000	244,000
Total liabilities & stockholders' equity		$681,000		$629,000

Additional information:
a No dividends were declared or paid during 19X2.
b The 19X2 accrual-basis income statement revealed net income of $11,000, along with the following: sales, $647,000; cost of goods sold, $579,000; selling and administrative expenses, $40,300; depreciation and amortization expense, $11,000; interest expense, $700; and income tax expense, $5,000.
c Common stock of $20,000 was issued at par value to acquire machinery on February 4.

d Land was purchased for cash on May 10.

e Goodrich paid $1,000 on the mortgage note during the year.

Instructions

Prepare a statement of cash flows by using the indirect method.

P19-B6 *Analysis of a statement of cash flows* (L.O. 5)

The statements of cash flow for High Flyers, Inc., for 19X8 and 19X9 follow.

	19X9	19X8
Cash flows from operating activities		
Net income (loss)	$ 129,800	$ 126,100
Add (deduct) items to convert net income to a cash basis		
Depreciation expense	130,900	123,800
Gain on sale of building	(2,600)	(19,600)
(Increase) decrease in accounts receivable	(33,700)	21,200
Increase in inventories	(5,000)	(3,700)
Increase (decrease) in accounts payable	3,800	(24,800)
Increase (decrease) in accrued liabilities	(2,400)	8,400
Decrease in taxes payable	(40,400)	(39,600)
Net cash provided (used) by operating activities	$ 180,400	$ 191,800
Cash flows from investing activities		
Proceeds from sale of building	$ 60,000	$ 142,800
Purchase of long-term investments	(68,400)	(45,400)
Acquisition of property, plant, & equipment	(113,000)	(44,500)
Net cash provided (used) by investing activities	$(121,400)	$ 52,900
Cash flows from financing activities		
Proceeds from short-term notes payable	$ 80,800	$ 70,300
Proceeds from bond issuance	65,100	130,000
Repayment of long-term debt	(104,700)	(261,200)
Payment of cash dividends	(85,400)	(82,500)
Purchase of treasury stock	(83,700)	(81,400)
Net cash provided (used) by financing activities	$(127,900)	$(224,800)
Net increase (decrease) in cash	$ (68,900)	$ 19,900

Instructions

As part of the training to become an investment analyst, you have been asked to evaluate the preceding statements of cash flow. Answer the questions that follow.

a Net income improved from 19X8 to 19X9; yet cash provided by operating activities declined. Briefly explain how this happened.

b Explain why the gains that arise from building sales are subtracted when computing the cash flows from operating activities.

c Briefly discuss the major difference(s) in financing activities during the two years. What appears to have caused the difference(s)?

d Study the relationship among operating, investing, and financing cash flows and activities for 19X8. Would the relationship parallel that of a middle-aged firm, a mature firm, or perhaps even an aging firm? Why?

e Repeat part (d), using the data of 19X9.

*P19-B7 Work sheet: Statement of cash flows (L.O. 5)

Refer to the data pertaining to Goodrich Company in Problem 19-B5.

Instructions

a Prepare a work sheet similar in format to that shown in Exhibit 19-9.

b Prepare a formal statement of cash flows by using the indirect method.

ELECTRONIC DATA BASE

EDB19-1 A look at the statement of cash flows: NIKE, Inc., and A&W Brands, Inc. (L.O. 5)

NIKE is involved with the design and production of athletic and casual footwear, apparel, and accessories. A&W Brands, in contrast, is a marketer of soft drinks and a manufacturer of soft drink concentrates. The company is perhaps best known among consumers for its root beer and Country Time Lemonade products.

Instructions

By using the text's Electronic Data Base, access the income statements and cash flow statements of both firms and answer the questions that follow. Unless otherwise indicated, responses should be based on data for the most recent year presented.

a Do these companies use the direct or indirect methods of reporting cash flows from operating activities?

b Did either of the firms experience an extremely significant change in cash flows from operating activities over the past two years? If "yes,"
   (1) Briefly explain the major cause(s) of the change.
   (2) Determine whether the change is expected, given the information reported on the income statement.

c What are the three largest uses of cash for each company?

d Study the *relationship* of the cash flows from operating, investing, and financing activities for the two corporations.
   (1) Determine how each company is funding its investing activities.
   (2) Suppose the current year's relationship of cash flows from operating, investing, and financing activities repeated itself for the next two years. Which of the two firms might fare better if the economy then became buried in a deep recession? Briefly explain.

EDB19-2 A look at the statement of cash flows (L.O. 5)

This problem is a duplication of Problem EDB19-1. It is based on two companies selected by your instructor.

Instructions

By using the text's Electronic Data Base, access the specified companies' income statements and statements of cash flow and focus on data for the most recent year reported. Answer requirements (a)–(d) of Problem EDB19-1.

BEYOND THE BASICS

BB19-1 *Balance sheet preparation from cash flow information* (L.O. 5)

Anderson Corporation reported the following balance sheet information as of January 1, 19X1:

Cash	$ 10,000	Accounts payable	$12,000
Accounts receivable	24,000	Interest payable	5,000
Inventory	37,000	Bonds payable	70,000
Equipment	119,000	Common stock	50,000
Accumulated depreciation	(39,000)	Retained earnings	14,000

The company's statement of cash flows for the year ended December 31, 19X1, follows.

ANDERSON CORPORATION
Statement of Cash Flows
For the Year Ended December 31, 19X1

Cash flows from operating activities		
Cash received from customers		$174,000
Less cash payments for:		
Purchases of merchandise	$ 57,000	
Selling & administrative expenses	41,000	
Interest	9,000	
Income taxes	18,000	125,000
Net cash provided by operating activities		$ 49,000
Cash flows from investing activities		
Purchase of land		(20,000)
Cash flows from financing activities		
Payment to retire bonds	$(20,000)	
Dividends paid	(7,000)	
Net cash used by financing activities		(27,000)
Net increase (decrease) in cash		$ 2,000
Cash balance, January 1, 19X1		10,000
Cash balance, December 31, 19X1		$ 12,000

The company's income statement disclosed that $45,000 of net income had been generated during 19X1. Depreciation expense amounted to $6,000. A review of the general ledger revealed the following changes in account balances during the year:

Accounts receivable, increase	$10,000
Inventory, decrease	7,000
Accounts payable,* increase	4,000
Interest payable, decrease	3,000

* Relate to purchases of merchandise.

Instructions

Prepare a balance sheet for Anderson Corporation as of December 31, 19X1.

BB19-2 *Overview of chapter concepts: Multiple choice* (L.O. 2, 3, 4, 5)

The following multiple-choice questions relate to various topics discussed in the chapter. Select the best answer.

1 Which of the following would not be classified in the operating activities section of the statement of cash flows?
a Interest paid.   c Dividends paid.
b Interest received.   d Dividends received.

2 When preparing the statement of cash flows, "cash" is defined to consist of cash and cash equivalents. Cash equivalents include:
a all readily marketable securities.
b marketable securities that are likely to be sold within a company's normal operating cycle.
c short-term liquid investments that will mature within 90 days.
d certificates of deposit from approved banks, without regard to maturity.

3 Which of the following statements is true regarding the direct and indirect approaches to computing cash flows from operating activities?
a The FASB prefers the direct approach.
b The FASB requires the direct approach.
c The FASB prefers the indirect approach.
d The FASB requires the indirect approach.

4 Which of the following typically need not be "adjusted" to compute cash flows from operating activities when using the direct approach?
a Rent expense.   c Depreciation expense.
b Service revenue.   d Tax expense.

5 If a company prepares a statement of cash flows by using the direct approach, information about cash payments for merchandise must be calculated. If one attempts to adjust cost of goods sold to yield cash paid for merchandise purchases, then:
a any increase in inventory must be subtracted.
b any decrease in inventory must be added.
c any decrease in accounts payable must be added.
d any increase in accounts receivable must be subtracted.

6 A review of Mercy Corporation's Land account found that the beginning account balance equaled the ending account balance. There were, however, a number of debits and credits to Land during the year. Which of the following statements best describes this situation?
a The accountant need not examine the account any further when preparing the statement of cash flows.
b The investing activities section of the statement of cash flows will likely be affected.
c The financing activities section of the statement of cash flows will be affected.
d Mercy will disclose a noncash investing/financing transaction.

7 Gratis Corporation's general ledger revealed the following balances:

	Equipment	Accumulated Depreciation: Equipment
January 1	$275,000	$ 75,000
December 31	300,000	100,000

During the year, equipment having an original cost of $50,000 was sold for $27,000, producing a $7,000 gain. The amount of depreciation expense that should be added to accrual-basis net income to compute cash flows from operating activities is:

a $0.   c $25,000.
b $5,000.   d $55,000.

8 If the indirect method of calculating cash flows from operating activities is used, each of the following items would be added to net income except for:

a depreciation.
b a loss on the sale of a building.
c a decrease in accounts receivable.
d an increase in mortgages payable.

**COMMUNICATION OF
ACCOUNTING
INFORMATION**

CAI19-1 *Constructing a group report: The Coca-Cola Company* (L.O. 4)

Communication Principle: Many reports are written by groups (teams) rather than individuals. Individuals are likely to be responsible for certain parts of the report, and then one or more team members assemble the parts into a coherent whole. The greatest challenge in writing a group report often involves combining dissimilar segments to achieve a "common voice." In other words, the final product should sound and look as though it was written by one person. This is often an editing nightmare of the highest order—just ask the authors of your textbook! The first challenge, though, is for a writer to complete his or her assigned part so it can be merged with the others.

Let us consider what is involved. Each writer must directly answer the specific questions assigned in a clear and complete way. Look at the needed response in the context of the entire report. How important is the response to the whole? How long will it be? What will be the main headings and subheadings? What is needed in terms of illustrations, graphics, calculations, and tables?

Eventually, the parts will be combined, and an introduction and conclusion will be added. To help make this process more efficient, each team member (when possible) should use the same style and format. For example, place a heading before the discussion of each main idea. Then begin each section with a brief statement that explains the subject. Use short, complete sentences and short paragraphs, with each paragraph addressing one question or concern at a time. Do anything that will help the compilation of the final product. A team effort and spirit of cooperation are needed. If every group member thinks only of him- or herself, the project will consume additional hours and generate considerable ill will.

■ ■ ■ ■ ■ ■ ■ ■

Coca-Cola is a global soft drink company, serving over 200 billion drinks in a single year. The firm also has a sizable foods division that manufactures and markets citrus products under the Minute Maid name.

Coca-Cola's statement of cash flows is prepared by using the indirect approach. A highly summarized presentation of the statement's operating activities section follows (amounts in thousands):

Net income		$1,044,703
Adjustments		
Depreciation	$169,768	
Loss on exchange	27,945	
Other items	8,157	
Decrease in receivables	33,887	
Increase in inventories	(25,744)	
Increase in prepaid expenses	(35,496)	
Decrease in accounts payable	(36,139)	
Decrease in other current liabilities	(20,244)	122,134
Net cash provided by operating activities		$1,166,837

Assume that Howard Goetz, Amy Lawson, and Larry Wong are enrolled in an introductory accounting course at State University. The professor has assigned a class project that involves a written overview of Coca-Cola's disclosure. In addition to a basic discussion of the nature of cash flows from operating activities, the students must address the following questions:

- Why is depreciation, a noncash expense, needed to compute the net cash provided by operating activities?
- How could the company release an erroneous statement, given that one decrease (receivables) is added to net income whereas others (accounts payable, other current liabilities) are subtracted?
- What, if anything, constrains Coca-Cola from making its presentation more user friendly? (A clearer presentation would disclose cash received from customers, minus a detailed listing of individual cash payments for purchases and normal business expenses.) Also, how would such a presentation affect cash flows from investing and financing activities?

Instructions

a Form a team with two other students in your class to assume the roles of Goetz, Lawson, and Wong. Divide the issues to be addressed among the team members and prepare written responses. Be sure that one team member is given the responsibility of combining and editing the individual responses into a coherent, polished product. The final report to the professor should include a brief introduction and conclusion.

b Have the class member who performed the final edit briefly describe his or her experience. Are there any suggestions for improvement?

Answers to Chapter Quiz

1 b

2 d

3 c

4 d (Proceeds − $30,000 = $100,000; proceeds = $130,000)

5 d

CHAPTER

20

Financial Statement Analysis: An Annual Report Focus

LEARNING OBJECTIVES

After studying this chapter, you should be able to:

1

Construct a horizontal analysis of comparative financial statements.

2

Prepare a vertical analysis and explain the associated benefits of common-size statements.

3

Compute and interpret liquidity, activity, profitability, and coverage ratios.

4

Recognize why statement analysis is improved by the use of comparative standards and segment reporting.

5

Explain the concept of earnings quality as it relates to a company's reported income.

6

Recognize the purpose and content of notes that accompany the financial statements.

7

Review an audit report and understand the type of audit opinion that a company has received.

Throughout this text we have introduced various real-world illustrations to help enliven the material being presented. Most of the illustrations were extracted from information that is made available to the public via an **annual report,** a corporate publication used to keep stockholders informed about the company's business affairs and economic well-being. The typical annual report includes information about the entity's products and accomplishments, the financial statements and accompanying notes, management reports, and an auditor's report. Also included is a letter from the president and/or chairman of the board that describes the company's plans for the future. In short, annual reports are the main communication link between management and the stockholders.

The purpose of this chapter is to help sharpen your skills in using and interpreting externally available financial information. Our presentation will focus on the major content of an annual report and various tools that may be used for analysis.[1]

TOOLS OF ANALYSIS

Three tools are frequently used to evaluate financial statements: horizontal analysis, vertical analysis, and ratio analysis. To illustrate these tools, we will focus on a set of two-year comparative financial statements of the Handy Corporation. In addition, we will integrate other analyses that are of special interest to particular statement users.

Horizontal Analysis

OBJECTIVE

1

Construct a horizontal analysis of comparative financial statements.

The calculation of dollar and percentage changes for corresponding items in comparative financial statements is termed **horizontal analysis.** In such an analysis, the earlier period is established as a base against which the later period is compared. As an example, the percentage change in the Cash account is computed by dividing the account's change between the two periods (say, 19X2 and 19X1) by the Cash balance of the base period (19X1). A complete horizontal analysis of the financial statements of Handy Corporation is presented in Exhibit 20-1 on pages 820–821.

Focusing on the income statement, the horizontal analysis reveals that the sizable increase in net income was mainly due to a $4 million rise in sales (11.1%) coupled with reductions in cost of goods sold ($2 million; 8.3%), administrative expenses ($650,000; 16.3%), and interest expense ($150,000; 18.8%). These reductions, however, were partially offset by increases in selling expenses and income taxes, the former causing an overall hike in operating expenses of $550,000, or 6.3%.

Overall, horizontal analysis provides information about the magnitude, direction, and relative importance of changes in individual and aggregate financial statement items. Such information is useful in assessing whether an enterprise has become stronger or weaker over a period of time and whether improvements are needed in particular areas.

---

[1] Annual report data are often studied by using a computerized data base—a massive compilation of facts and statistics on literally thousands of companies. (An example is *SEC-ONLINE*, a small portion of which has been reproduced on diskettes that accompany this text.) The data base's files are accessed electronically through use of a microcomputer, long distance telephone lines, and a modem. Although no two data bases are exactly alike, typical content includes a firm's current financial disclosures as well as disclosures from preceding accounting periods.

Vertical Analysis

Important changes and trends can also be studied by using vertical analysis. With **vertical analysis,** each figure on a financial statement is related to a relevant total and stated as a percentage of that total. Examine Exhibit 20-2 on page 822, which contains a vertical analysis of Handy's income statements. Observe how each item is expressed as a percentage of net sales. The analysis reveals that 12¢ of every sales dollar remained as profit in 19X2, up from 4¢ in 19X1.

Switching to the balance sheet, individual assets are stated as a percentage of total assets, and each of the liability and stockholders' equity accounts is expressed in relation to the total of liabilities plus stockholders' equity. As an example, a vertical analysis of Handy's assets follows.

| | 19X2 | | 19X1 | |
	$	Percent	$	Percent
Assets				
Current assets	$ 8,000,000	37.0%	$ 7,000,000	34.6%
Plant & equipment (net)	12,200,000	56.5	11,500,000	56.8
Intangibles (net)	1,000,000	4.6	1,200,000	5.9
Other assets	410,000	1.9	550,000	2.7
Total assets	$21,610,000	100.0%	$20,250,000	100.0%

OBJECTIVE

2

Prepare a vertical analysis and explain the associated benefits of common-size statements.

The figures show that despite a $1.36 million increase in total assets, the individual components remained relatively stable. The largest change is for current assets, which, in terms of total assets, increased by 2.4% (37.0% − 34.6%).

Common-Size Financial Statements

One of the basic benefits of vertical analysis is the final product: **common-size financial statements.** That is, with all items stated on some common ground (e.g., percentages), users can evaluate financial statements in relative terms and not be concerned about differences in absolute size. This benefit becomes especially helpful when comparing one company against another company or industry averages. Consider, for example, recent abbreviated income statements (in thousands) of two specialty retailers: The Gap, Inc., and The Limited, Inc.:

| | The Gap, Inc. | | The Limited, Inc. | |
	$	Percent	$	Percent
Net sales	$2,518,893	100.0%	$6,149,218	100.0%
Cost of goods sold	1,568,921	62.3	4,355,675	70.8
Gross profit	$ 949,972	37.7%	$1,793,543	29.2%
Expenses & income taxes	720,099	28.6	1,390,241	22.6
Net income	$ 229,873	9.1%	$ 403,302	6.6%

EXHIBIT 20-1
Horizontal Analysis of
Comparative Financial
Statements

HANDY CORPORATION
Comparative Income Statements
For the Years Ended December 31, 19X2 and 19X1

	19X2	19X1	Increase (Decrease)	Percentage Change from 19X1
Net sales	$40,000,000	$36,000,000	$ 4,000,000	11.1%
Cost of goods sold	22,000,000	24,000,000	(2,000,000)	(8.3)
Gross profit	$18,000,000	$12,000,000	$ 6,000,000	50.0
Operating expenses				
Selling	$ 6,000,000	$ 4,800,000	$ 1,200,000	25.0
Administrative	3,350,000	4,000,000	(650,000)	(16.3)
Total operating expenses	$ 9,350,000	$ 8,800,000	$ 550,000	6.3
Operating income	$ 8,650,000	$ 3,200,000	$ 5,450,000	170.3
Interest expense	650,000	800,000	(150,000)	(18.8)
Income before income taxes	$ 8,000,000	$ 2,400,000	$ 5,600,000	233.3
Income taxes, 40%	3,200,000	960,000	2,240,000	233.3
Net income	$ 4,800,000	$ 1,440,000	$ 3,360,000	233.3
Earnings per share*	$2.38	$0.70	$1.68	240.0

* Calculated as $\dfrac{\text{Net Income} - \text{Preferred Dividends}}{\text{Common Shares Outstanding}}$

HANDY CORPORATION
Comparative Statements of Retained Earnings
For the Years Ended December 31, 19X2 and 19X1

	19X2	19X1	Increase (Decrease)	Percentage Change from 19X1
Balance, Jan. 1	$ 5,900,000	$5,500,000	$ 400,000	7.3%
Net income	4,800,000	1,440,000	3,360,000	233.3
Total	$10,700,000	$6,940,000	$3,760,000	54.2
Less: Dividends				
Common	$ 2,000,000	$1,000,000	$1,000,000	100.0
Preferred	40,000	40,000	—	—
Total dividends	$ 2,040,000	$1,040,000	$1,000,000	96.2
Balance, Dec. 31	$ 8,660,000	$5,900,000	$2,760,000	46.8

HANDY CORPORATION Comparative Balance Sheets December 31, 19X2 and 19X1				
	19X2	19X1	Increase (Decrease)	Percentage Change from 19X1
Assets				
Current assets	$ 8,000,000	$ 7,000,000	$ 1,000,000	14.3%
Plant & equipment (net)	12,200,000	11,500,000	700,000	6.1
Intangibles (net)	1,000,000	1,200,000	(200,000)	(16.7)
Other assets	410,000	550,000	(140,000)	(25.5)
Total assets	$21,610,000	$20,250,000	$ 1,360,000	6.7
Liabilities & Stockholders' Equity				
Liabilities				
Current liabilities	$ 3,500,000	$ 3,400,000	$ 100,000	2.9
Long-term liabilities	6,500,000	8,000,000	(1,500,000)	(18.8)
Total liabilities	$10,000,000	$11,400,000	$(1,400,000)	(12.3)
Stockholders' equity				
10% preferred stock, $10 par value	$ 400,000	$ 400,000	$ —	—
Common stock, $1 par value	2,000,000	2,000,000	—	—
Paid-in capital, common stock	550,000	550,000	—	—
Retained earnings	8,660,000	5,900,000	2,760,000	46.8
Total stockholders' equity	$11,610,000	$ 8,850,000	$ 2,760,000	31.2
Total liabilities & stockholders' equity	$21,610,000	$20,250,000	$ 1,360,000	6.7

EXHIBIT 20-1
(continued)

The Limited's net sales were 2.4 times greater than those of The Gap, thus producing larger dollar figures for both cost of goods sold and expenses and income taxes. In addition, a substantially higher profit was generated. However, when percentages are considered, The Gap was actually more profitable, having 9.1¢ of every sales dollar left as income (in comparison with 6.6¢ for its competitor).

Ratio Analysis

A third method of financial statement evaluation is **ratio analysis.** Ratios are employed to study liquidity, activity, profitability, and coverage of obligations. Although any number of ratios can be constructed and presented, our discussion will focus only on those that are commonly encountered and widely used by statement analysts.

It is important to note that a ratio is merely a mathematical expression of relationships. In essence, one could view a ratio as being similar to a

OBJECTIVE

3

Compute and interpret liquidity, activity, profitability, and coverage ratios.

EXHIBIT 20-2
Vertical Analysis of Income Statements

	HANDY CORPORATION Comparative Income Statements For the Years Ended December 31, 19X2 and 19X1			
	19X2		19X1	
	$	Percent	$	Percent
Net sales	$40,000,000	100.0%	$36,000,000	100.0%
Cost of goods sold	22,000,000	55.0	24,000,000	66.7
Gross profit	$18,000,000	45.0	$12,000,000	33.3
Operating expenses				
Selling	$ 6,000,000	15.0	$ 4,800,000	13.3
Administrative	3,350,000	8.4	4,000,000	11.1
Total operating expenses	$ 9,350,000	23.4	$ 8,800,000	24.4
Operating income	$ 8,650,000	21.6	$ 3,200,000	8.9
Interest expense	650,000	1.6	800,000	2.2
Income before income taxes	$ 8,000,000	20.0	$ 2,400,000	6.7
Income taxes, 40%	3,200,000	8.0	960,000	2.7
Net income	$ 4,800,000	12.0%	$ 1,440,000	4.0%

thermometer, that is, a gauge of performance. For example, suppose you feel ill, you take your temperature, and the thermometer reads 102.6 degrees. The obvious conclusion? Something is wrong with your body. In no way, however, can the thermometer indicate whether you have the flu, an infected ear, or mononucleosis. The thermometer simply indicates that something is amiss and serves as a starting point for further investigation. Similarly, a ratio presents information regarding a single financial relationship; it cannot tell the complete story.

Liquidity Ratios

The ability of a business to meet current debts as the obligations come due can be measured with **liquidity ratios.** Appropriately, short-term creditors have great interest in the liquidity ratios of their clients and customers, both present and potential. Weak ratios sometimes indicate a high probability of nonpayment. In addition to short-term creditors, management and stockholders are also interested in liquidity ratios, especially those of their own firm. The inability to meet current obligations taints a company's reputation, reduces its credit rating, and generally means an increase in future borrowing costs.

Current Ratio. The most widely used measure of liquidity is the **current ratio,** which relates total current assets to total current liabilities. The computation of the current ratio for Handy Corporation, based on figures presented in Exhibit 20-1, follows.

$$\text{Current Ratio} = \frac{\text{Current Assets}}{\text{Current Liabilities}}$$

19X2	**19X1**
$\dfrac{\$8,000,000}{\$3,500,000} = 2.29$	$\dfrac{\$7,000,000}{\$3,400,000} = 2.06$

Handy's ratios show that at the end of 19X2 the company had $2.29 of current assets for every $1.00 of current liabilities. Thus, the firm's position has improved since the end of 19X1.

Although the ratio has increased, is Handy really "better off"? This is actually a difficult question to answer, especially when the following factors are considered. Observe that the current ratio uses a numerator of *total* current assets. Given the nature of the computation, all current assets are therefore treated equally, with no consideration given to composition and individual component liquidities. One hundred dollars of cash, for example, is obviously more useful in satisfying existing obligations than $100 of unsold inventory. Because both amounts are treated in the same manner when deriving the ratio, knowledge of Handy's asset composition is needed to determine whether debt-paying ability has really improved.

To further complicate the picture, the current ratio can be manipulated by management. A business can deliberately improve its current ratio by paying short-term obligations at or near the end of the accounting period. Although current assets and current liabilities will both decline by the same amount, the ratio actually increases. For example, if a firm with current assets of $100,000 and current liabilities of $50,000 voluntarily paid a $10,000 account payable, the current ratio would improve from 2 to 2.25 ($90,000 ÷ $40,000). The practice of intentionally increasing a ratio to improve financial appearance is commonly known as *window dressing*.

Given these problems, the current ratio (and others) must be used with great care. The general rule employed by bankers and other creditors is that the current ratio should be at least 2. Be aware, however, that ratios tend to vary by type of business. For instance, the median current ratio is 0.7 for restaurants, 1.2 for wholesalers of dairy products, and 2.1 for manufacturers of cutlery and handtools.[2] Such variations are caused by differences in operating practices. Companies in some industries carry high levels of inventories and receivables to serve their customers. Also, certain industries tend to rely more heavily on trade accounts payable than others. Consequently, the general rule of 2 is just as its name implies—general. There are, as always, many exceptions.

Quick Ratio. Another measure of short-term, debt-paying ability is the **quick ratio.** Rather than compare total current assets with current liabilities, the quick ratio excludes merchandise inventory and prepaid expenses from the asset base. Inventory is not an immediate source of cash because months may pass until the time of sale, and prepaid expenses are consumed in operations. Thus, the current assets that remain—cash, short-

---

[2] The industry figures used in this chapter are taken from *Annual Statement Studies: 1991* (Philadelphia: Robert Morris Associates, 1991).

term investments, and accounts receivable—represent a ready or "nearly ready" source of cash to satisfy the claims of creditors. In comparison with the current ratio, the quick ratio is a more stringent test of a company's ability to settle short-term obligations.

Handy's individual current assets appear below.

	19X2	19X1
Current assets		
Cash	$1,000,000	$ 400,000
Short-term investments	1,000,000	1,000,000
Accounts receivable (net)	2,000,000	1,500,000
Merchandise inventory	3,900,000	4,000,000
Prepaid expenses	100,000	100,000
	$8,000,000	$7,000,000

The company's quick ratio is therefore computed as follows:

$$\text{Quick Ratio} = \frac{\text{Cash + Short-Term Investments + Accounts Receivable}}{\text{Current Liabilities}}$$

19X2

$$\frac{\$1,000,000 + \$1,000,000 + \$2,000,000}{\$3,500,000} = 1.14$$

19X1

$$\frac{\$400,000 + \$1,000,000 + \$1,500,000}{\$3,400,000} = 0.85$$

Many analysts feel that a quick ratio of 1 is satisfactory, with each dollar of short-term debt being backed by $1 of cash or near-cash assets. Handy's ratio improved to meet this standard by the end of 19X2. Note that the quick ratio will vary among industries; thus, the standard guideline of 1 should be used with caution.

Activity Ratios

A firm's effectiveness in using specific resources can be analyzed by employing **activity ratios,** often termed *turnover ratios.* Managers, and to a lesser extent stockholders and short-term creditors, have a keen interest in these performance measures. The two most popular activity ratios are accounts receivable turnover and inventory turnover.

Accounts Receivable Turnover.   The number of times a company's receivables turn into cash each year is shown by **accounts receivable turnover.** As a result, this ratio provides some indication of the quality of both the receivables and the firm's collection efforts.

Accounts receivable turnover is computed by dividing net credit sales by the average accounts receivable during the year. Average receivables are calculated by summing the beginning and ending receivables and dividing by 2. Assuming that Handy Corporation's sales are all on account, the 19X2 turnover ratio would be computed as follows:

$$\text{Accounts Receivable Turnover} = \frac{\text{Net Credit Sales}}{\text{Average Accounts Receivable}}$$

$$= \frac{\$40,000,000}{\dfrac{\$1,500,000 + \$2,000,000}{2}}$$

$$= 22.86 \text{ times}$$

The fact that receivables turned over 22.86 times indicates an average collection period of about 16 days (365 days ÷ 22.86 times). To assess whether this result is satisfactory, additional information about Handy's credit terms is needed. If the terms are n/30, then the company is doing an excellent job in granting credit and collecting the resulting accounts. If the terms are n/10, however, questions may surface concerning receivables management. Perhaps sales are being made to marginal customers, or perhaps the company's collection efforts have been lax.

Like other ratios, receivables turnover and collection periods vary among businesses. This fact becomes apparent when studying the following figures:

Type of Business	Median Collection Period (Days)
Radio and TV retailers	10
Grocery wholesalers	20
Sports and recreation clubs	33
Knitted goods manufacturers	38
Optical goods manufacturers	48

The longer the collection period, the more funds are tied up in receivables, thereby restricting the funds available for other investment opportunities.

Inventory Turnover.   The number of times a firm's inventory investment is turned into sales can be determined with the **inventory turnover ratio.** Normally, high turnovers are indicative of sound inventory management, at least in terms of generating cash. To explain, inventory turnover is calculated by dividing cost of goods sold by the average inventory. Average inventory, in turn, is computed by adding the beginning and ending inventories and dividing by 2. As the average inventory grows, turnover will decrease unless there is a corresponding increase in sales and the accompanying cost of goods sold. Thus, a company that stocks a larger-than-normal inventory will have a lower turnover than another business that can generate the same sales with a lower merchandise investment.

As a result, it appears that organizations should maintain low inventories to achieve high turnovers. By doing so, firms minimize funds invested in excessive (and sometimes slow-moving) goods and reduce associated carrying costs (e.g., storage, insurance, taxes, obsolescence, and deterioration). This strategy may backfire, however, as low inventories frequently lead to stockouts, lost sales, and lost customers. Furthermore, quantity discounts and reduced freight rates may be unavailable because of insufficient purchasing activity. Inventory management is, indeed, a double-edged sword that requires close attention.

The 19X2 inventory turnover ratio for Handy Corporation is calculated as follows:

$$\text{Inventory Turnover Ratio} = \frac{\text{Cost of Goods Sold}}{\text{Average Inventory}}$$

$$= \frac{\$22,000,000}{\dfrac{\$4,000,000 + \$3,900,000}{2}}$$

$$= 5.57 \text{ times}$$

The ratio shows that the inventory turned 5.57 times, or approximately once every 66 days (365 days ÷ 5.57 times). To improve turnover, management could purchase more conservatively or stimulate sales from existing stock.

Profitability Ratios

Ratios are also used to examine an organization's operating success (or lack thereof) during an accounting period. These measures, known as **profitability ratios,** are computed on the basis of sales or investment and are of special interest to management, stockholders, union officials and employees, and creditors.

Profit Margin on Sales.   The ratio of net income to net sales, commonly known as the **profit margin on sales,** is a popular measure of profitability. Significant decreases in this ratio from year to year should be investigated; consistent deterioration may indicate a need for stringent cost control programs. As noted below, Handy's profit margin for 19X2 showed a great improvement over 19X1.

$$\text{Profit Margin on Sales} = \frac{\text{Net Income}}{\text{Net Sales}}$$

19X2	19X1
$\dfrac{\$4,800,000}{\$40,000,000} = 12.0\%$	$\dfrac{\$1,440,000}{\$36,000,000} = 4.0\%$

Profit margins can be computed separately, as shown, or be considered an outgrowth of vertical analysis (see Exhibit 20-2).

Return on Assets.   The **return on assets,** often termed *return on investment* or *ROI,* measures profitability from a given level of asset investment. This ratio focuses on operations, specifically, the effectiveness of resources used in generating profit. Return on investment is typically calculated by dividing net income plus interest expense by the average total assets employed in business activity. The addition of interest expense produces a figure that represents earnings from operations, prior to any financing costs. Stated differently, we wish to focus on how well the asset investment was *used*, not on the related methods and costs of securing an entity's resources. The 19X2 return on assets for Handy Corporation is computed as follows:

$$\text{Return on Assets} = \frac{\text{Net Income} + \text{Interest Expense}}{\text{Average Assets}}$$

$$= \frac{\$4,800,000 + \$650,000}{\dfrac{\$20,250,000 + \$21,610,000}{2}}$$

$$= \frac{\$5,450,000}{\$20,930,000}$$

$$= 26.0\%$$

Handy's rate of return is quite high. For every $1.00 of assets employed, the company has generated $0.26 of income.

Return on Common Stockholders' Equity.   Many corporations are heavily financed from investments made by common stockholders. A widely used ratio, called **return on common stockholders' equity,** measures the profit generated on funds provided by these investors. This ratio is often calculated by dividing net income, minus preferred dividends, by the average common stockholders' equity. By subtracting preferred dividends, we derive the income that belongs to the common shareholders—the true residual owners of a corporation. Handy's 19X2 ratio is computed as follows:

$$\frac{\text{Return on Common}}{\text{Stockholders' Equity}} = \frac{\text{Net Income} - \text{Preferred Dividends}}{\text{Average Common Stockholders' Equity}}$$

$$= \frac{\$4,800,000 - \$40,000}{\dfrac{\$8,450,000 + \$11,210,000}{2}}$$

$$= \frac{\$4,760,000}{\$9,830,000}$$

$$= 48.4\%$$

The common stockholders' equity figures are obtained from Exhibit 20-1 by taking total stockholders' equity and subtracting the $400,000 of preferred stock outstanding.

Handy has earned over 48¢ for each dollar invested by common shareholders, which, like the return on assets discussed earlier, is quite impressive. Notice, however, that the return on common equity is much higher than the return on assets. The difference is caused by trading on the equity.

Trading on the Equity.   In the process known as **trading on the equity,** sometimes called *leverage,* a company secures funds at fixed interest and preferred dividend rates and then invests the funds to earn a return greater than their cost. To explain, Handy is earning 26.0% on its assets. Yet a careful review of Exhibit 20-1 will find that the company is paying only 10% before tax for funds obtained via long-term debt ($650,000 interest expense ÷ $6,500,000 of long-term liabilities)[3] and a 10% dividend on outstanding preferred stock ($40,000 ÷ $400,000). The difference between the amounts earned and the amounts paid on such funds benefits the common stockholders and is reflected by the 48.4% return on their equity.

The company is said to be trading on the equity at a gain; that is, it has positive financial leverage. Naturally, the opposite case is possible. For instance, if the firm obtained funding at 10% but earned only 7% on investments, Handy would be trading on the equity at a loss. Net income suffers along with the payoff to the common stockholders.

Other Profitability Ratios.   Other profitability ratios include **earnings per share,** which was discussed in Chapter 16, and the **price-earnings (P/E) ratio.** This latter measure, computed by dividing the market price of a share of common stock by the annual earnings per share, is used to examine investor attitudes. As an example, at the time this text is being written, the P/E ratios of Southwest Airlines and Hewlett-Packard are 38 and 18, respectively. By showing a willingness to pay 2.1 times more for each dollar of reported earnings, investors must feel the air carrier's financial future will be more prosperous than that of the massive electronics manufacturer.

Another profitability measure is the **dividend payout ratio,** which is used to study the percentage of earnings distributed to stockholders. The necessary computations involve dividing the annual cash dividend per share by earnings per share. A related ratio, the **dividend yield,** is the annual cash dividend per share divided by the current market price of the stock. This ratio provides insight to investors about the short-term rate of return (from dividends) on their invested funds.

Tips & Techniques

A company's dividend yield must be interpreted with great care. Many investors prefer to acquire stocks that have attractive yields because of the cash flow involved. Be cautioned, however, that the company now has less cash to invest in its own projects, perhaps restricting growth. Some investors will therefore focus on businesses that pay few, if any, dividends but that have high expansion potential accompanied by steadily rising stock prices.

Coverage Ratios

The solvency of an entity can be judged by computing **coverage ratios.** These ratios are of primary importance to long-term creditors, who have an obvious concern about the receipt of interest and the repayment of amounts borrowed.

---

[3] For purposes of simplicity, we are assuming the interest pertains strictly to long-term obligations.

Debt to Total Assets. The percentage of total capital provided by the creditors of a business is shown by the **debt to total assets ratio.** Debt includes all obligations, both current and long term. The debt to total assets ratios for Handy at the end of 19X2 and 19X1 follow.

$$\text{Debt to Total Assets} = \frac{\text{Total Debt}}{\text{Total Assets}}$$

19X2	19X1
$\dfrac{\$10,000,000}{\$21,610,000} = 46.3\%$	$\dfrac{\$11,400,000}{\$20,250,000} = 56.3\%$

As you can see, total liabilities outstanding declined by $1.4 million during 19X2. Furthermore, observe that debt declined in percentage terms as a means of financing Handy's asset investment. Apparently, the creditors are playing a reduced role (when compared with the owners) in terms of providing investment funds. This fact becomes evident when focusing on a *ratio of total debt to total stockholders' equity.* The debt to equity ratio for Handy at the end of 19X2 was 0.86 ($10,000,000 ÷ $11,610,000), down from 1.29 ($11,400,000 ÷ $8,850,000) upon conclusion of 19X1. A ratio of 1 signifies that the creditors and owners are furnishing equal amounts of funds for business activity.

The debt to total assets ratio is of interest to both creditors and stockholders. Creditors generally prefer a low ratio, indicating that a large percentage of asset financing is provided by the owners and/or operations. Low debt means low monthly outlays for principal and interest and, thus, a reduced risk of nonpayment should sales and earnings fall.

Stockholders, in contrast, sometimes desire a high debt to total assets ratio. As shown earlier, the presence of debt in the capital structure can give rise to positive leverage and benefit the common stockholders. Increased debt normally increases leverage. However, too much debt may actually cause common stock dividends to be reduced or eliminated in periods of slow business activity. Remember, interest payments must be met; conversely, dividends to common stockholders are paid at the discretion of the board of directors. What we have are conflicting views. Generally, debt is acceptable if it is used in moderation. However, the "right" amount of debt varies among industries and is extremely difficult to determine.

Times Interest Earned. Although a company may be heavily financed by debt, it is possible that earnings are more than adequate to cover the required interest charges. If, however, interest coverage is marginal, the creditors' position may be threatened. Insight into the amount of protection that is afforded the long-term creditors is provided by a ratio called **times interest earned.**

The times interest earned ratio is computed by dividing income before taxes and interest by the interest charges themselves. Observe that income *before* taxes is used because interest, in part, determines tax expense. For Handy the number of times interest was earned improved significantly

from 19X1 to 19X2. As the following calculations show, the more than threefold increase was caused by a combination of lower interest charges and higher earnings.

$$\text{Times Interest Earned} = \frac{\text{Income Before Income Taxes and Interest}}{\text{Interest Charges}}$$

19X2	19X1
$\frac{\$8,650,000}{\$650,000} = 13.3$	$\frac{\$3,200,000}{\$800,000} = 4$

EXECUTIVE BRIEFING
Debt Can Be Dangerous

James Preston
Chairman and Chief Executive Officer
Avon Products, Inc.

Avon found itself with more than $1.1 billion of liabilities a few years ago due to a disastrous diversification effort. That's a monstrous burden for a company with annual sales of just over $3 billion. Interest payments were more than $100 million a year. The company's survival depended on reducing obligations, which meant a total focus on generating cash. Investing in tomorrow was delayed. Research expenses were cut to a minimum. Capital spending for new equipment was limited. Training was virtually eliminated. New market entries were delayed. The banks imposed restrictions to ensure that payment would be forthcoming.

All of these actions would have been bad enough, but Avon's weakened financial position attracted a series of raiders. We were forced to fight a war on two fronts—our competitors in the marketplace and the raiders on Wall Street. In the end, we won both battles. In just two years, we slashed our debt by more than 50%. We're still cutting, which will give us the flexibility to further increase dividends, to enter more new markets, to further modernize, and to develop more state-of-the-art beauty products. We're doing a lot of these things again, but with earnings. We borrowed to diversify and almost didn't survive.

Further Insights into Statement Analysis

Horizontal analysis, vertical analysis, and ratios are extremely useful tools for assessing financial performance. Recognize, though, that *these tools are not ends in themselves and cannot convey all the details behind financial success or failure.* They are merely a starting point for further evaluation and questioning. As part of this investigative process, it is not uncommon for analysts to use comparative standards and to look behind the numbers that are being reported.

Comparative Standards

Accountants, creditors, and stockholders continually employ comparative standards when judging an entity's financial relationships. Popular standards include past performance of the business and performance of other firms in the same industry. Relating the current data of a company with data of preceding years (i.e., horizontal analysis) helps in determining whether relationships are improving or deteriorating. Unfortunately, single-company analyses do not provide a sufficiently broad basis for comparison. For example, if a candy manufacturer incurred a net loss of $200,000 in 19X1 and a net loss of only $50,000 in 19X2, the firm has shown considerable improvement. However, if the manufacturer remains the only unprofitable candy producer in the country, the earnings records of both years can be viewed as being unfavorable.

The use of an external standard (or yardstick) often overcomes the limitation of single-company studies. That is, an entity's performance can be compared with the performance of a similar company or perhaps with averages of several companies in the same industry, so-called **industry norms.** (Examples of the latter can be found on pages 823 and 825.) Similar-company comparisons, although logical, frequently create problems for the analyst.

Consider that many businesses operate in diverse markets with distinctly different product lines. An example might be a corporation that is involved primarily in soft drink bottling but that also engages in the manufacture of small appliances, the operation of movie theaters, and trucking. An analyst studying this organization would definitely err by comparing the firm's financial statements against those of another entity that has only bottling activities. The diversified company's statements, of course, would present a combined picture of overall corporate endeavors.

To help overcome the problem, companies that are engaged in distinctly different business activities and meet certain criteria must follow a practice known as **segment reporting.** This practice involves the disclosure of selected information to supplement that shown in the financial statements. Per *Statement of Financial Accounting Standards No. 14,* the sales, income, and identifiable assets of the individual segments would be shown as a note to the statements. Segment reporting thus provides an analyst with more detailed information, allowing improved (i.e., "like-for-like") comparisons to be made. Further, the practice makes it more difficult for firms to "hide" segments (winners and losers alike) within the realm of *total* sales, income, and asset figures on the income statement and the balance sheet.

An Example.   As an illustration of segment reporting, we will focus on the activities of The Black & Decker Corporation.   The company's recent annual report revealed the following segment data (in thousands):

Segment	(A) Sales	(B) Operating Income	(C) Identifiable Assets
Consumer & home improvement products	$3,224,372	$254,143	$4,605,945
Commercial & industrial products	728,206	95,580	1,574,051
Information systems & services	684,376	32,307	380,563

The disclosure shows some interesting results. The largest segment, Consumer and Home Improvement Products, generated the greatest amount of operating income. However, when income is considered in relation to sales and the asset investment identified with this segment, Black & Decker's other activities were more "profitable." Commercial and Industrial Products yielded a higher return from each sales dollar, and Information Systems and Services produced greater profits per dollar invested. These facts become more evident in the chart that follows, which reveals the operating income on sales ratios (B ÷ A) and the return on assets (B ÷ C).

Segment	Operating Income on Sales Ratio		Return on Assets	
	Percent	Rank	Percent	Rank
Consumer & home improvement products	7.88%	2	5.51%	3
Commercial & industrial products	13.13	1	6.07	2
Information systems & services	4.72	3	8.49	1

A Look Behind the Numbers

OBJECTIVE 5

Explain the concept of earnings quality as it relates to a company's reported income.

Whether performing a comparison or studying a company in isolation, an analyst should look behind the numbers. As shown in earlier chapters, a company's financial health and well-being are a function of the estimates and accounting policies used by management. Let us consider earnings to illustrate this point, specifically, the *nature* of earnings.

Picture two companies that have identical asset investments and the same net income. Suppose further that both businesses employ straight-line depreciation. If firm A writes its assets off over a 10-year life while firm B uses an 8-year life, we could say that B is employing more conservative accounting practices. That is, B's choice of service life produces greater annual depreciation expense and a bigger impact (i.e., decrease) on income. Other favorable factors must therefore be attributed to firm B, given that total earnings are the same for the two entities.

Additionally, bottom-line income is influenced by both one-time transactions and those that arise from normal business activity. Consider the performance of X Company, which reported $150,000 of income from operations, versus that of Y Company. Assume that Y had $50,000 of income from operations for the period just ended along with a $100,000 gain on the sale of real estate. Although the total earnings figures for the two entities are identical, financial analysts would view X's situation more favorably than Y's. Put simply, income from ongoing activities is typically more attractive than income from a one-time (and possibly irregular) source.

The two preceding examples focus on an organization's **quality of earnings.** In other words, an assessment is made of both the methods used to determine income and the source from which the income arose. "Quality" earnings are said to result from steady, continuous sources and the use of conservative accounting practices. Notes to the financial statements (to be discussed next) and various disclosures within a statement's body help an analyst study the nature of the figures reported by management.

In sum, it should now be evident that financial statement analysis in-

HIGHLIGHT
When Is A Segment Not A Segment?

Jessica Reif, a securities analyst, explains what she does for a living: "I spend a good part of my time trying to get numbers that aren't reported." In this day of information overload, aren't people like Reif drowning in numbers? In numbers, yes. But in useful numbers, not necessarily—especially when analysts and other investors try to disaggregate a large corporation to see how each of its important segments is doing.

Consider IBM. As befits its size, the computer company is in several lines of business, including personal computers, mainframes, electronic mail systems, and semiconductors. (IBM's semiconductor facilities rank among the world's largest.) How is each of these segments doing? That's hard to say. IBM reports figures for a grand total of one segment, called "information-processing systems, software, communications systems, and other products and services."

CBS, whose operating profits dropped by $173 million between 1984 and 1988, is another example. Analysts want to know just how badly the company's television network—traditionally CBS's bread and butter—is doing. But CBS, which operates the television network, 6 television stations, 5 radio networks, and 19 radio stations, currently reports only one segment. All the networks and stations are lumped together under broadcasting.

"We know that the network has done badly," says a media analyst, "but we don't know how badly." Instead, the analyst and his peers must deduce what they can from such annual report phrases as "Network sales declined slightly" and "Television stations sales rose modestly," plus management's hints and industry research. Will CBS consider increasing the number of segments it reports? "Historically, we have always reported this way," observes a CBS spokeswoman. "We are an integrated company, and we don't plan to start doing it any other way."

Typically, companies voice two objections to providing information on their separate lines of business. First, they say, it would give an advantage to their competitors. Second, it would cost too much. But neither objection holds much water. "I'm not aware of anyone who ever lost a nickel giving this kind of information to their competitors," notes a finance executive at General Electric. "Nevertheless, there's an innate fear of disclosure."

How should a company determine how many segments to report? A partner from a large accounting firm has a sound idea: If a company has businesses that respond differently to changes in the economy, face different kinds of competitors, or earn different levels of profits, then the company should probably report the businesses separately. "It really comes down to the risks and the rewards," he says. "Ask yourself: Are the risks different? Are the rewards different? If either answer is a significant yes, then you've got two segments."

Securities and Exchange Commission officials say their agency is certainly interested in good segment reporting. The SEC has required several companies to split their segments more narrowly. "It's a key component of financial reports," observes the SEC chief accountant. "Auditors ought to challenge the companies, and if investors believe a company is doing inappropriate segment reporting, they ought to write to us." The SEC's address: 450 Fifth St. N.W., Washington, D.C. 20549.

Source: Adapted from "An Innate Fear of Disclosure," *Forbes,* February 5, 1990, pp. 126, 128. Excerpted by permission of *Forbes* magazine, © Forbes Inc., 1990.

volves much more than the calculation of simple percentages and ratios. Diverse business activities and the use of different accounting practices complicate what many novices initially feel is a relatively straightforward task. If the job is to be done properly, the analyst must assume the role of a detective and perform in-depth investigative work prior to reaching any conclusions.

ADDITIONAL ANNUAL REPORT DISCLOSURES

Our focus thus far has been on the financial statement component of annual reports, both analysis and interpretation. As noted on the first page of this chapter, annual reports contain numerous other corporate disclosures. Three of the more significant items are the notes that accompany the financial statements, management reports, and the auditor's report. We will now examine these elements and, where appropriate, reference the disclosures of Kmart Corporation.[4]

Notes to the Financial Statements

OBJECTIVE

Recognize the purpose and content of notes that accompany the financial statements.

To help users understand the information being reported, corporations prepare a series of **notes to the financial statements.** The notes are viewed as an integral part of the statements, being essential for a full disclosure of business and economic affairs. Over the past several decades, notes have grown in both number and length to where they now occupy more room in the annual report than the financial statements themselves. Kmart's financial statements, for example, were presented on four pages of a recent annual report; the accompanying notes occupied 16 pages. There are several reasons for this situation, including an increase in the complexity of business transactions, added disclosure requirements by the accounting profession, a greater demand for details by statement users, and an increased tendency on the part of U.S. citizens and businesses to file lawsuits.

Notes to the financial statements are quite varied, as each company has its own unique set of transactions, contracts, and circumstances. Normally, however, notes serve one of three basic functions by (1) summarizing significant accounting policies, (2) disclosing supplementary information, or (3) providing explanatory information.

Summary of Significant Accounting Policies

Corporations that issue financial statements in accordance with GAAP must include a summary of significant accounting policies. Statement users need to be aware of the accounting practices employed by a business so that a sound evaluation can be made.

The summary is typically presented as the first note to the financial statements or in a separate section just before the notes. Within this section companies generally describe those principles and methods that have been selected for use from the available alternatives. In addition, the sum-

---

[4] Financial data pertaining to Kmart are excerpted from the company's 1991 annual report, portions of which are reprinted by permission.

mary discloses both unusual applications of generally accepted accounting principles and practices that are peculiar to the industry in which the business operates.

Excerpts from the summary of significant accounting policies for Kmart Corporation appear in Exhibit 20-3. Here we learn, among other things, that the company uses the retail method of inventory valuation in conjunction with (primarily) a LIFO cost flow assumption. Furthermore, straight-line depreciation is employed for financial statement purposes, whereas accelerated methods are used when reporting income taxes to the government. In addition, store operating costs incurred prior to the opening of a new facility are expensed when incurred.

Supplementary Information

An increasing number of notes are devoted to fulfilling the requirements of the SEC and FASB for supplemental (additional) financial information. Two examples of supplemental disclosure involve segment reporting (as just discussed) and **interim** (quarterly) financial data. The latter data allow users to compare quarterly results and gain insights regarding the pattern of sales and earnings over the year. Such disclosures are especially helpful in the evaluation of seasonal businesses, or those firms that generate the majority of their revenues in a relatively short period of time. A classic example of such a business would be a natural gas utility, whose peak activity occurs during the winter months. Although not reproduced here,

EXHIBIT 20-3
Notes to Consolidated Financial Statements

A—Summary of Significant Accounting Policies

Fiscal Year: The company's fiscal year ends on the last Wednesday in January. Fiscal years 1991 and 1990 each consisted of 52 weeks and ended on January 29, 1992, and January 30, 1991, respectively. The 1989 fiscal year consisted of 53 weeks and ended on January 31, 1990.

Inventories: Merchandise inventories are valued at the lower of cost or market, primarily using the retail method, on the last-in, first-out basis for substantially all domestic inventories and the first-in, first-out basis for the remainder.

Depreciation: The company computes depreciation on owned property principally on the straight-line method for financial statement purposes and on accelerated methods for income tax purposes. Most store properties are leased and improvements are amortized over the term of the lease but not more than 25 years. Other annual rates used in computing depreciation for financial statement purposes are 2% to 4% for buildings, 10% to 14% for store fixtures, and 5% to 33% for other fixtures and equipment.

Pre-Opening and Closing Costs: The company includes store operating costs incurred prior to opening a new retail unit in current period expenses. When the decision to close a retail unit is made, the company provides for future net lease obligations, nonrecoverable investments in fixed assets, other expenses directly related to discontinuance of operations, and estimated operating losses through expected closing dates.

recent interim data of Kmart revealed that approximately 31% of revenues were traceable to the company's fourth quarter, which includes the Christmas season. The quarter was extremely profitable, producing nearly 56% of the year's net income.

Explanatory Information

Notes may also be used to expand on the information presented in the body of the financial statements. For example, the property, plant, and equipment owned by a firm is often disclosed via a single line-item on the balance sheet. To provide further information, a note may reveal the individual components (land, land improvements, buildings, machinery and equipment) and their related cost. Long-term liabilities are often treated in this manner, with a note used to furnish details on the types and amounts of debt owed by the business (e.g., installment obligations, mortgage notes, bonds, and so forth).

Management and Audit Reports

The annual report typically includes several accounting-related reports prepared by management. One, called *Management's Discussion and Analysis*, explains the differences between the current year's financial statements and those of preceding periods. In essence, the discussion provides an overview, from management's perspective, of what went right and what went wrong during the year. Trends are highlighted, and changes in such items as profitability, financial position, and cash flow are explained.

Another report that is sometimes included is the *Report of Management's Responsibility for Financial Statements*. This narrative informs users that management shoulders the burden for the estimates and accounting principles used in the financial statements. The report also notes the steps that have been taken to help safeguard company resources and assure compliance with sound business and reporting practices. Such steps include the maintenance of an internal audit department and a strong system of internal control, and a review of company accounting records by an independent CPA firm. Furthermore, most large corporations have established an **audit commitee** that typically consists of outside directors (e.g., executives from other businesses, university administrators, consultants, and so forth). The committee meets with management, the internal auditors, and the independent accountants to determine whether each group has carried out its assigned responsibilities.

The Audit Report

OBJECTIVE

7

Review an audit report and understand the type of audit opinion that a company has received.

As just noted, the financial statements of a business are the representations and responsibility of management. An **audit report,** prepared by independent certified public accountants, presents the auditor's opinion concerning whether the statements are free of material errors and irregularities. Such a report increases the credibility of both the financial statements and the accompanying notes.

The auditor's report is the end result of an audit, a process that involves the examination of a company's transactions, documents, and internal

To the Shareholders and Board of Directors of Kmart Corporation

In our opinion, the accompanying consolidated balance sheets and the related consolidated statements of income, shareholders' equity and of cash flows present fairly, in all material respects, the financial position of Kmart Corporation and its subsidiaries at January 29, 1992 and January 30, 1991, and the results of their operations and their cash flows for each of the three years in the period ended January 29, 1992, in conformity with generally accepted accounting principles. These financial statements are the responsibility of the company's management; our responsibility is to express an opinion on these financial statements based on our audits. We conducted our audits of these statements in accordance with generally accepted auditing standards which require that we plan and perform the audit to obtain reasonable assurance about whether the financial statements are free of material misstatement. An audit includes examining, on a test basis, evidence supporting the amounts and disclosures in the financial statements, assessing the accounting principles used and significant estimates made by management, and evaluating the overall financial statement presentation. We believe that our audits provide a reasonable basis for the opinion expressed above.

As discussed in Note (G) to the financial statements, the company changed its method of determining retail price indices used in the valuation of LIFO inventories in 1990.

Price Waterhouse

200 Renaissance Center, Detroit, Michigan
March 4, 1992, except as to Subsequent Event (Note B) which is as of March 24, 1992.

EXHIBIT 20-4
Audit Report

control structure. This examination plays a very critical role in our society. By rendering an objective, unbiased opinion on a firm's financial statements and underlying accounting system, the auditor helps to instill public confidence in management's disclosures. As history so vividly shows, a reliance on financial statements that have not been subjected to such an examination can be extremely hazardous to a user's financial welfare. An example of an audit report is shown in Exhibit 20-4.

Observe that this report begins with the phrase "in our opinion." The auditor is not guaranteeing the financial statements nor certifying that they are 100% correct. To do so would be impossible, given that estimates (such as uncollectible accounts expense and asset service life) are inherent in the accounting process. Further, an audit is conducted by using sampling techniques and not by checking every transaction that occurred. An opinion, then, merely reflects the auditor's best judgment as to whether the statements are a "fair" representation of a company's economic transactions and events.

Kmart's audit report is *unqualified,* indicating the auditor (Price Waterhouse) has no significant reservations about the fairness of the statements. If major concerns did arise during the examination process, a *qualified* opinion would be issued. For example, if the scope of the auditor's work was restricted because of incomplete or poorly kept client records, or if the accounting principles used were improper, such facts would be disclosed in the report. A qualified audit report will include the phrase "except for" to indicate the nature of the qualification.

A Final Thought on Annual Reports

The annual report of Alberto Culver Company appears in Appendix C at the end of the text. (Because of space limitations, we have omitted nine pages of photographs and marketing revelations.) Take a few minutes to examine the firm's financial statements and accompanying notes, the management reports, and the auditor's report. No doubt, many of the disclosures will be familiar to you. The majority, however, will likely seem foreign. The financial affairs of corporations are quite complex and often deal with topics that are reserved for study in advanced accounting courses. In view of this situation, you are advised to concentrate on the presentation in general, *not* the intimate details.

Our overview of annual reports was written to acquaint you with this important disclosure mechanism. Although they serve as a primary link between corporations and stockholders, many people argue that annual reports fall far short of their goal. In support of this point, we conclude this chapter with the following comments from *The Wall Street Journal:*

> Companies have long sought to look their best in annual reports. But consultants and financial analysts say that in recent years, as economic pressures and foreign and domestic competition have mounted, the reports are going much further than ever in hiding bad news, leaving out embarrassing events, and blowing the corporation's own horn. . . .
>
> Because many managements prefer to slough over problems rather than face them, most annual reports excel more in communications than in disclosure, says [a consultant who advises companies on how to construct reports that are more forthright. He] adds: "This makes many reports read like Truman Capote novels—truth in fiction.[5]

On the basis of this chapter, it is difficult to judge the validity of these comments. We suggest, however, that you obtain a "live" annual report from your library or by writing to a company's director of shareholder relations.[6] You may find it particularly interesting to review the report of a corporation that you know from newspaper accounts has had a very bad year. Is the presentation upbeat and optimistic in an attempt to downplay the past or is the mood relatively somber? Hopefully, our discussion has given you the ability to both analyze the firm and, at the same time, make more informed investment decisions.

END-OF-CHAPTER REVIEW

LEARNING OBJECTIVES: THE KEY POINTS

1 Construct a horizontal analysis of comparative financial statements. Horizontal analysis provides information about the magnitude, direction, and relative importance of changes in individual and aggregate financial statement items. The process involves the calculation of dollar and percentage changes by establishing earlier period dollar amounts as a base against which later period amounts are compared.

---

[5] See "Firms' Annual Reports Are Short on Candor and May Get Shorter," *The Wall Street Journal,* September 9, 1987, pp 1, 24.
[6] Publicly held corporations are usually more than willing to distribute their annual report to virtually anyone who asks.

2 Prepare a vertical analysis and explain the associated benefits of common-size financial statements. With vertical analysis, each figure on a financial statement is related to a relevant total and stated as a percentage of that total. On an income statement, for instance, each amount is expressed as a percentage of net sales. This type of analysis helps users interpret performance and is the basis for the preparation of common-size financial statements. Such statements focus on percentages, thereby allowing a valid comparison of companies that are vastly different in terms of size.

3 Compute and interpret liquidity, activity, profitability, and coverage ratios. Ratio analysis involves the mathematical expression of selected financial relationships. Liquidity ratios, for example, measure the ability of a business to meet current debts as the obligations come due. In contrast, activity ratios measure a firm's effectiveness in using specific resources (e.g., inventory). Profitability ratios are employed to assess an organization's operating success (or lack thereof) during an accounting period, and coverage ratios, such as times interest earned, are computed to measure the solvency of an entity. Thirteen ratios used daily in American business are discussed in the chapter and summarized in the table that follows.

Ratio	Method of Computation	Significance
(1) Liquidity ratios		
(a) Current ratio	$\dfrac{\text{Current assets}}{\text{Current liabilities}}$	Measures ability to meet short-term debts
(b) Quick ratio	$\dfrac{\text{Cash + short-term investments + accounts receivable}}{\text{Current liabilities}}$	Measures very short-term debt-paying ability
(2) Activity ratios		
(a) Accounts receivable turnover	$\dfrac{\text{Net credit sales}}{\text{Average accounts receivable}}$	Provides insight into credit and collection policies
(b) Inventory turnover	$\dfrac{\text{Cost of goods sold}}{\text{Average inventory}}$	Provides insight into inventory management policies
(3) Profitability ratios		
(a) Profit margin on sales	$\dfrac{\text{Net income}}{\text{Net sales}}$	Shows the net income generated from each sales dollar
(b) Return on assets	$\dfrac{\text{Net income + interest expense}}{\text{Average assets}}$	Indicates effectiveness of resources used in generating profit
(c) Return on common stockholders' equity	$\dfrac{\text{Net income - preferred dividends}}{\text{Average common stockholders' equity}}$	Reveals the earnings rate on capital provided by common shareholders
(d) Earnings per share	See Chapter 16	Measures the earnings applicable to a share of common stock
(e) Price-earnings ratio	$\dfrac{\text{Market price per share}}{\text{Earnings per share}}$	Shows the amount investors are willing to pay for each dollar of corporate earnings
(f) Dividend payout ratio	$\dfrac{\text{Cash dividend per share}}{\text{Earnings per share}}$	Reveals corporate policy regarding retention or distribution of earnings

Ratio	Method of Computation	Significance
(g) Dividend yield	$\dfrac{\text{Cash dividend per share}}{\text{Market price per share}}$	Indicates the investor's short-term rate of return from dividends
(4) Coverage ratios		
(a) Debt to total assets	$\dfrac{\text{Total debt}}{\text{Total assets}}$	Shows the percentage of assets financed by long- and short-term borrowings
(b) Times interest earned	$\dfrac{\text{Income before income taxes and interest}}{\text{Interest charges}}$	Measures a firm's ability to cover and meet fixed interest charges

4 Recognize why statement analysis is improved by the use of comparative standards and segment reporting. Comparative standards allow an analyst to study how a firm is performing in relation to either other companies or industry averages. When a given entity is studied in isolation, one can determine whether relationships are improving or deteriorating for that business and only that business. Comparisons therefore permit broader evaluations and provide additional operational insight.

Segment reporting requirements allow such comparisons to be made for companies that operate in diverse industries. Sales, income, and identifiable assets for a firm's major operating units are disclosed in the notes to the financial statements. Users can thus better assess the profitability and importance of each segment to the overall entity.

5 Explain the concept of earnings quality as it relates to a company's reported income. Earnings quality refers to the nature of earnings, as determined by looking behind the numbers that comprise a company's reported income figure. Quality earnings are said to result from steady ongoing sources (i.e., activities) and the use of conservative accounting practices.

6 Recognize the purpose and content of notes that accompany the financial statements. Notes are used to improve disclosure for the financial statement user. Companies prepare notes to summarize accounting policies, disclose supplemental data consistent with rulings of the SEC and the FASB, and present underlying details of financial statement items (e.g., the composition of plant and equipment). Disclosures that fall in the second (supplemental) category include those for interim and segment data.

7 Review an audit report and understand the type of audit opinion that a company has received. An audit report discloses the auditor's opinion of whether the financial statements are free of material errors and irregularities. It is important to note that the report is an opinion, not a guarantee. Companies strive to secure an unqualified opinion, meaning the auditor has no significant reservations about the statements' fairness. In contrast, a qualified opinion indicates the presence of a problem such as the use of improper accounting principles or poorly kept client records.

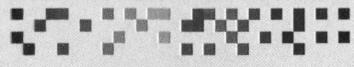

**KEY TERMS
AND CONCEPTS:
A QUICK OVERVIEW**

Note: The meaning and underlying calculations of specific ratios discussed in this chapter can be found in the chart that begins on page 839.

activity ratios Ratios that provide insight about a firm's effectiveness in using specific resources; often called turnover ratios.

annual report   A publication prepared by a company for distribution to stockholders and others; contains the firm's financial statements and other information.

audit committee   A committee of outside directors that meets with management, internal auditors, and external auditors to evaluate each group's work.

audit report   A report that presents the auditor's opinion regarding the fairness of the financial statements.

common-size financial statements   Statements that reveal account balances in both dollars and percentages, thereby facilitating different types of comparative analysis.

coverage ratios   Ratios used to judge the solvency of an entity.

horizontal analysis   The calculation of dollar and percentage changes for corresponding items in comparative financial statements.

industry norms   Averages of several companies in the same industry.

interim financial data   Data that are prepared for reporting periods other than a company's year-end.

liquidity ratios   Ratios that measure the ability of a business to meet current debts as the obligations come due.

notes to the financial statements   A supplemental, yet integral, part of the financial statements that expands on the information contained in the body of the statements.

profitability ratios   Ratios that examine an organization's operating success (or lack of success) during an accounting period.

quality of earnings   An assessment of (1) the methods used to determine income and (2) the sources from which the income arose.

ratio analysis   The use of mathematical relationships to study a firm's liquidity, activity, profitability, and coverage of obligations.

segment reporting   The disclosure of selected information when a company is involved in several distinct business activities.

trading on the equity   The process of securing funds at fixed interest and preferred dividend rates and investing the funds to earn a return greater than their cost; also called leverage.

vertical analysis   An analysis in which each figure on a financial statement is related to a relevant total and stated as a percentage of that total.

The five questions that follow relate to several issues raised in the chapter. Test your knowledge of the issues by selecting the best answer. (The answers appear on p. 865.)

CHAPTER QUIZ

1 Vertical analysis:
   a cannot be used to compare companies of different size.
   b provides information about the magnitude, direction, and relative importance of changes in individual financial statement items.
   c is needed to assess the coverage of obligations.
   d results in common-size financial statements.

2 London Corporation paid $1,000 of accounts payable with cash on the last day of the month. The company had a current ratio of 4 before the disbursement. As a result of this payment, the current ratio will:

a increase.

b decrease.

c remain unchanged.

d fluctuate, but the direction of the change depends on unstated facts.

3 Jedd, Inc., has obtained long-term debt at a 14% interest rate and is achieving a return on assets of 42%. These figures indicate that Jedd will have:

a a 28% increase in earnings per share.

b a 28% increase in the profit margin on sales.

c a return on common stockholders' equity of less than 14%.

d a return on common stockholders' equity of more than 14%.

4 The following information relates to the North Airlines, Pencil, and Aluminum Siding Company:

	Sales	Operating Income	Identifiable Assets
Airline	$4,000	$ 20	$2,000
Pencils	1,000	80	1,600
Aluminum siding	2,000	400	4,000

Which of the segments was least profitable in terms of dollar profit, profit margin on sales, and return on assets, respectively?

a Pencils, airline, aluminum siding.   c Airline, airline, airline.

b Airline, pencils, aluminum siding.   d Airline, airline, pencils.

5 Annual reports:

a are issued to corporate managers but not to stockholders.

b contain a corporation's financial statements, accompanying notes, and various other management disclosures.

c contain a corporation's financial statements but not the auditor's report.

d focus more on marketing the corporation's products than on disclosing financial information.

SUMMARY PROBLEM

Eagle Point Enterprises is a large corporation that has business activities in such diverse areas as building maintenance services, real-estate investment, truck leasing, and auto parts distribution. The following selected data were obtained from the company's comparative income statements and balance sheets:

Income Statement Data
(In Thousands)

	For the Year Ended	
	12/31/X2	12/31/X1
Net sales	$19,400	$16,400
Cost of goods sold	11,500	9,500
Selling expenses	2,800	2,400
Administrative expenses	3,300	3,000
Interest expense on long-term debt	300	420

Balance Sheet Data
(In Thousands)

	As of	
	12/31/X2	12/31/X1
Cash	$25,400	$23,900
Short-term investments	10,500	13,600
Accounts receivable (net)	3,600	2,800
Inventories	15,800	13,100
Prepaid expenses	700	1,000
Total current liabilities	22,400	21,500
Long-term debt	3,000	4,300

At the beginning of 19X2, top management implemented a firmwide cost control program aimed at selling and administrative expenses. The company rounds all computations to one decimal place and has no cash sales.

Instructions

a Determine the 19X2 percentage increase in selling expenses and administrative expenses over the amounts incurred in 19X1.
b By performing a vertical analysis of selling expenses and administrative expenses, determine whether the cost control programs are working. Comment on your findings.
c Compute the following ratios for 19X2:
  (1) Current ratio
  (2) Quick ratio
  (3) Accounts receivable turnover
  (4) Times interest earned
d Which of the preceding ratios would probably most interest a short-term creditor? Why?
e Given the diverse nature of Eagle Point's activities, what practice might the firm be required to follow when reporting to stockholders and other external parties?

Solution

a Selling expenses increased by $400 ($2,800 − $2,400), or 16.7% of the 19X1 amounts ($400 ÷ $2,400). Similarly, administrative expenses incurred were $300 higher in 19X2 than in 19X1 ($3,300 − $3,000), or 10% greater than 19X1 levels ($300 ÷ $3,000).
b A vertical analysis would express the expense figures as a percentage of net sales, as follows:

	19X2		19X1	
Net sales	$19,400	100.0%	$16,400	100.0%
Expenses				
Selling	$ 2,800	14.4%	$ 2,400	14.6%
Administrative	3,300	17.0	3,000	18.3

The vertical analysis shows a decline in the percentage of both selling expenses and administrative expenses to net sales. It therefore appears that the cost control programs are taking hold.

c (1) Current ratio = current assets ÷ current liabilities

   Current assets = $25,400 + $10,500 + $3,600 + $15,800 + $700
             = $56,000
   Current ratio = $56,000 ÷ $22,400 = 2.5

(2) Quick ratio = (cash + short-term investments + accounts receivable) ÷ current liabilities

Appropriate assets = $25,400 + $10,500 + $3,600 = $39,500
Quick ratio = $39,500 ÷ $22,400 = 1.8

(3) Accounts receivable turnover = net credit sales ÷ average accounts receivable

Average accounts receivable = [($2,800 + $3,600) ÷ 2] = $3,200
Turnover = $19,400 ÷ $3,200 = 6.1

(4) Times interest earned = income before income taxes and interest ÷ interest charges

Income before income taxes and interest
= $19,400 − $11,500 − $2,800 − $3,300 = $1,800
Times interest earned = $1,800 ÷ $300 = 6.0

d A short-term creditor would be most interested in liquidity ratios to assess the probability of payment on a timely basis. The two liquidity ratios presented are the current ratio and the quick ratio, with the latter being a more severe test of debt-paying ability.

e Eagle Point may have to follow the guidelines of segment reporting. Such disclosures, which typically occur in the notes to the financial statements, will allow a user to better study the widely varying activities of the firm.

ASSIGNMENT MATERIAL

QUESTIONS

Q20-1 What is an annual report?

Q20-2 Distinguish between horizontal analysis and vertical analysis. Which type of analysis results in common-size financial statements?

Q20-3 What is one of the basic benefits associated with the use of common-size financial statements?

Q20-4 A student once noted: "This ratio stuff is great. It's unbelievable how ratios can tell the complete story behind the problems of a business." Comment on the student's observation.

Q20-5 Briefly describe the following types of ratios and identify the financial statement users most interested in each type.
a Liquidity ratios
b Activity ratios
c Profitability ratios
d Coverage ratios

Q20-6 What is the current ratio? Present a short critique of this widely used financial measure.

Q20-7 Why do many analysts prefer the quick ratio over the current ratio for judging debt-paying ability?

Q20-8 What insight can be provided by the accounts receivable turnover ratio? The inventory turnover ratio?

Q20-9 Discuss the differences between the return on assets and the return on common stockholders' equity.

Q20-10 What does it mean to "trade on the equity"? How can such trading be successful? Unsuccessful?

Q20-11 Briefly explain how the price-earnings ratio gives insights about investor attitudes.

Q20-12 Why is financial information of a business often compared with the past performance of the same company and the performance of other companies? What difficulties do comparisons with other firms entail?

Q20-13 How do users of financial information benefit from segment reporting?

Q20-14 An analyst claims that Morton Corporation has a low quality of earnings. Briefly discuss what is meant by this comment.

Q20-15 Briefly·explain the types of information typically disclosed by notes to the financial statements.

Q20-16 Why are interim data useful to readers of financial statements?

Q20-17 Does a "clean" audit report serve to guarantee the fairness of the financial statements? Briefly discuss.

Q20-18 Would a company rather obtain a qualified opinion or an unqualified opinion from its auditor? Why?

EXERCISES

E20-1 *Horizontal analysis* (L.O. 1)
The Mary Lynn Corporation has been operating for several years. Selected data from the 19X1 and 19X2 financial statements follow.

	19X2	19X1
Current assets	$ 76,000	$ 80,000
Property, plant, & equipment (net)	99,000	90,000
Intangibles	25,000	50,000
Current liabilities	40,800	48,000
Long-term liabilities	143,000	160,000
Stockholders' equity	16,200	12,000
Net sales	500,000	500,000
Cost of goods sold	332,500	350,000
Operating expenses	93,500	85,000

Prepare a horizontal analysis for 19X1 and 19X2. Briefly comment on the results of your work.

E20-2 *Vertical analysis* (L.O. 2)
Study the data pertaining to the Mary Lynn Corporation that appear in Exercise 20-1. Prepare a vertical analysis for 19X1 and 19X2, and briefly evaluate the results of your work.

E20-3 *Liquidity ratios* (L.O. 3)
Edison, Stagg, and Thornton have the following financial information at the close of business on July 10:

	Edison	Stagg	Thornton
Cash	$4,000	$2,500	$1,000
Short-term investments	3,000	2,500	2,000
Accounts receivable	2,000	2,500	3,000
Inventory	1,000	2,500	4,000
Prepaid expenses	800	800	800
Accounts payable	200	200	200
Notes payable: short-term	3,100	3,100	3,100
Accrued payables	300	300	300
Long-term liabilities	3,800	3,800	3,800

a Compute the current and quick ratios for each of the three companies. (Round calculations to two decimal places.) Which firm is the most liquid? Why?

b Suppose Thornton is using FIFO for inventory valuation and Edison is using LIFO. Comment on the comparability of information between these two companies.

c If all short-term notes payable are due on July 11 at 8 A.M., comment on each company's ability to settle its obligation in a timely manner.

E20-4 **Liquidity and activity ratios** (L.O. 3)
Evaluate the comments that follow as being True or False. If the comment is false, briefly explain why.

a The current ratio can be deliberately improved by performing a process known as window dressing.

b All other things being equal, a company normally prefers to have a high inventory turnover rather than a low inventory turnover.

c The basic difference between the current ratio and the quick ratio lies in the treatment of accounts receivable and prepaid expenses.

d The current ratio treats all current assets as being equally liquid.

e The sale of merchandise to businesses that have marginal credit ratings tends to improve a firm's accounts receivable turnover.

E20-5 **Computation and evaluation of activity ratios** (L.O. 3)
The following data relate to Alaska Products, Inc:

	19X5	19X4
Net credit sales	$832,000	$760,000
Cost of goods sold	440,000	350,000
Cash, Dec. 31	125,000	110,000
Accounts receivable, Dec. 31	180,000	140,000
Inventory, Dec. 31	70,000	50,000
Accounts payable, Dec. 31	115,000	108,000

The company is planning to borrow $300,000 via a 90-day bank loan to cover short-term operating needs.

a Compute the accounts receivable and inventory turnover ratios for 19X5. Alaska rounds all calculations to two decimal places.

b Study the ratios from part (a) and comment on the company's ability to repay a bank loan in 90 days.

c Suppose that Alaska's major line of business involves the processing and distribution of fresh and frozen fish throughout the United States. Do you have any concerns about the company's inventory turnover ratio? Briefly discuss.

E20-6 Activity ratios (L.O. 3)

The following information pertains to the Rockville Corporation:

1-2-3

Ending accounts receivable	$ 340,000
Ending inventory	265,000
Total sales	2,000,000
Customer collections on account	1,560,000
Purchases	1,250,000
Gross profit rate	40%
Percentage of credit sales to total sales	80%

a Compute the firm's accounts receivable turnover ratio.
b Compute the firm's inventory turnover ratio.

E20-7 Profitability ratios, trading on the equity (L.O. 3)

Digital Relay has both preferred and common stock outstanding. The company reported the following information for 19X7:

1-2-3

Net sales	$1,500,000
Interest expense	120,000
Income tax expense	80,000
Preferred dividends	25,000
Net income	130,000
Average assets	1,100,000
Average common stockholders' equity	400,000

a Compute the profit margin on sales and the rates of return on assets and common stockholders' equity, rounding calculations to two decimal places.
b Does the firm have positive or negative financial leverage? Briefly explain.

E20-8 Coverage ratios (L.O. 3)

Dresser, Inc., has the following financial information:

	19X6	19X5
Current liabilities	$ 800,000	$1,000,000
Long-term liabilities	2,000,000	1,800,000
Common stock	1,000,000	1,000,000
Retained earnings	4,200,000	3,200,000
Total liabilities & stockholders' equity	$8,000,000	$7,000,000

During 19X6, Dresser incurred interest expense and income taxes of $200,000 and $500,000, respectively. No dividends were paid during the year.

Compute the following ratios for 19X6, rounding calculations to two decimal places:
a Debt to total assets
b Debt to total ending stockholders' equity
c Times interest earned

E20-9 Evaluation of selected ratios (L.O. 3, 4)

Selected ratios of the Glenwood Power Equipment Company and averages for the power equipment industry follow.

	Glenwood	Industry
Current ratio	2.21	1.63
Average collection period of receivables	39 days	21 days
Inventory turnover	4.1	1.9
Profit margin on sales	7.0%	8.8%
Return on assets	10.0%	9.5%
Debt to total assets	31.7%	39.8%

Evaluate these ratios and determine whether you Agree or Disagree with the following statements:

a Glenwood has better debt-paying ability than the "average" company in the power equipment industry.

b Glenwood is performing below average in managing its inventories.

c The amount of income generated, given the company's resources, exceeds that produced by the industry.

d Glenwood may need to improve its management of credit and customer collections.

e In view of the company's revenues, Glenwood's ability to produce earnings is significantly below the industry norm.

E20-10 Use of ratios to predict bankruptcy (L.O. 3)

The annual report of Tennyson, Inc., disclosed profitable operations just months before the company declared bankruptcy. A close analysis of the financial statements revealed significant one-time gains, none of which were improper.

a Comment on the use of profitability ratios in this case as being a likely predictor of the company's financial problems.

b Briefly discuss how, collectively, the quick ratio, the debt to total assets ratio, and the times interest earned ratio might have presented some hint of Tennyson's impending bankruptcy.

E20-11 Segment reporting and analysis (L.O. 4)

The Walt Disney Company is a large Los Angeles–based entertainment corporation. The firm has three operating segments: theme parks and resorts, filmed entertainment, and consumer products. The following segment information (in millions) was obtained from a recent annual report:

Segment	Revenues	Operating Income	Identifiable Assets
Theme parks and resorts	$2,864.7	$617.0	$5,165.7
Filmed entertainment	2,593.7	318.1	1,878.2
Consumer products	724.0	229.8	351.4

a Relate operating income to identifiable assets and determine which segment was the least effective in terms of generating income from each dollar of asset investment.

b Relate operating income to revenues and determine which segment was least successful in terms of generating income from a given dollar of sales.

c Which of the segments was most successful in terms of generating revenues from each dollar of asset investment? Briefly explain and show related computations.

E20-12 Quality of earnings (L.O. 5)

Clifton Corporation and Norton, Inc., are large, publicly held companies whose shares are traded on a national stock exchange. In recent years,

Clifton has become the "darling of Wall Street" because of extremely high earnings. Norton's stock, on the other hand, has gone nowhere, somewhat paralleling trends in the firm's bottom-line income. A review of each corporation's annual report revealing the following information:

	Clifton	Norton
Sales	$25 million	$25 million
Inventory method	FIFO	LIFO
Depreciation method	Straight-line	Accelerated
Service life of buildings	50 years	40 years
Extraordinary gains	Yes	No

Assume that both companies have been operating in an inflationary economy in recent years.
a What is meant by the phrase "quality of earnings"?
b Which company appears to have the higher quality of earnings? Explain your answer.

E20-13 *Assessment of management's discussion* (L.O. 6)
The management discussion and analysis of Crownover Suites, an Arizona-based hotel operator, follows.

The company is pleased to report a 20% rise in earnings per share, to $3.60 for the year ended December 31, 19X8. This result compares favorably with earnings of $3 per share for the previous year. On a different note, we are obviously concerned and grieved about the August bomb explosion at the Indianapolis facility. The bomb was detonated by a crazed extortionist upon our refusal to meet his demands for a $5 million payment. Because we carry insurance on the replacement cost of assets (as opposed to original acquisition cost), the bombing netted the firm a $50,000 aftertax gain.

Assuming that Crownover had 50,000 shares of common stock outstanding, evaluate management's discussion of 19X8 operations and earnings.

Series A

PROBLEMS

P20-A1 *Horizontal and vertical analysis* (L.O. 1, 2)
The following financial statements pertain to Waterloo Corporation:

WATERLOO CORPORATION
Comparative Balance Sheets
December 31, 19X5 and 19X4

	19X5	19X4
Assets		
Current assets		
Cash	$ 11,250	$ 12,500
Accounts receivable (net)	18,500	25,000
Inventories	38,500	35,000
Prepaid expenses	3,750	3,750
Total current assets	$ 72,000	$ 76,250
Property, plant, & equipment		
Buildings (net)	$102,750	$101,250
Equipment (net)	28,500	30,000
Vehicles (net)	32,000	40,000
Total property, plant, & equipment	$163,250	$171,250
Trademarks (net)	$ 14,750	$ 2,500
Total assets	$250,000	$250,000
Liabilities & Stockholders' Equity		
Current liabilities		
Accounts payable	$ 49,000	$ 70,000
Notes payable	13,500	40,000
Federal taxes payable	2,500	25,000
Total current liabilities	$ 65,000	$135,000
Long-term debt	$ 50,000	$ 25,000
Total liabilities	$115,000	$160,000
Stockholders' equity		
Common stock, $10 par	$ 25,000	$ 25,000
Retained earnings	110,000	65,000
Total stockholders' equity	$135,000	$ 90,000
Total liabilities & stockholders' equity	$250,000	$250,000

WATERLOO CORPORATION Comparative Income Statements For the Years Ended December 31, 19X5 and 19X4		
	19X5	19X4
Net sales	$550,000	$500,000
Cost of goods sold	330,000	250,000
Gross profit	$220,000	$250,000
Operating expenses	132,500	100,000
Income before interest & taxes	$ 87,500	$150,000
Interest expense	12,500	3,000
Income before taxes	$ 75,000	$147,000
Income taxes	30,000	58,800
Net income	$ 45,000	$ 88,200

Instructions

a Prepare a horizontal analysis of the balance sheet, showing dollar and percentage changes. Round all calculations in instructions (a) and (b) to two decimal places.

b Prepare a vertical analysis of the income statement by relating each item to net sales.

c Briefly comment on the results of your analysis.

P20-A2 *Ratio computation* (L.O. 3)

1-2-3

The financial statements of the Lone Pine Company follow.

LONE PINE COMPANY
Comparative Balance Sheets
December 31, 19X2 and 19X1
($000 Omitted)

	19X2	19X1
Assets		
Current assets		
Cash & short-term investments	$ 400	$ 600
Accounts receivable (net)	3,000	2,400
Inventories	2,000	2,200
Total current assets	$5,400	$5,200
Property, plant, & equipment		
Land	$1,700	$ 600
Buildings & equipment (net)	1,500	1,000
Total property, plant, & equipment	$3,200	$1,600
Total assets	$8,600	$6,800
Liabilities & Stockholders' Equity		
Current liabilities		
Accounts payable	$1,800	$1,700
Notes payable	1,100	1,900
Total current liabilities	$2,900	$3,600
Long-term liabilities		
Bonds payable	4,100	2,100
Total liabilities	$7,000	$5,700
Stockholders' equity		
Common stock	$ 200	$ 200
Retained earnings	1,400	900
Total stockholders' equity	$1,600	$1,100
Total liabilities & stockholders' equity	$8,600	$6,800

LONE PINE COMPANY
Statement of Income and Retained Earnings
For the Year Ended December 31, 19X2
($000 Omitted)

Net sales*		$36,000
Less: Cost of goods sold	$20,000	
Selling expenses	6,000	
Administrative expenses	4,000	
Interest expense	400	
Income taxes	2,000	32,400
Net income		$ 3,600
Retained earnings, Jan. 1		900
		$ 4,500
Cash dividends declared and paid		3,100
Retained earnings, Dec. 31		$ 1,400

* All sales are on account.

Instructions

Compute the following items for the Lone Pine Company for 19X2, rounding all calculations to two decimal places when necessary:
a Quick ratio
b Current ratio
c Inventory turnover ratio
d Accounts receivable turnover ratio
e Return on assets
f Profit margin on sales
g Return on common stockholders' equity
h Debt to total assets
i Number of times interest is earned
j Dividend payout ratio

P20-A3 *Financial statement construction via ratios* (L.O. 3)
Incomplete financial statements of Lock Box, Inc., are presented below.

1-2-3

LOCK BOX, INC.
Income Statement
For the Year Ended December 31, 19X3

Sales	$	?
Cost of goods sold		?
Gross profit		$15,000,000
Operating expenses & interest		?
Income before tax	$	?
Income taxes, 40%		?
Net income	$	?

```
┌─────────────────────────────────────────────────────────────┐
│                        LOCK BOX, INC.                         │
│                       Balance Sheet                           │
│                     December 31, 19X3                         │
├─────────────────────────────────────────────────────────────┤
│                                                               │
│                           Assets                              │
│                                                               │
│  Cash                                            $      ?      │
│  Accounts receivable                                    ?      │
│  Inventory                                              ?      │
│  Property, plant, & equipment                   8,000,000     │
│    Total assets                               $24,000,000     │
│                                                               │
│             Liabilities & Stockholders' Equity                │
│                                                               │
│  Accounts payable                                $      ?      │
│  Notes payable (short-term)                        600,000    │
│  Bonds payable                                   4,600,000    │
│  Common stock                                    2,000,000    │
│  Retained earnings                                      ?      │
│    Total liabilities & stockholders' equity   $24,000,000     │
│                                                               │
└─────────────────────────────────────────────────────────────┘
```

Further information:
1 Cost of goods sold is 60% of sales. All sales are on account.
2 The company's beginning inventory is $5 million; inventory turnover is 4.
3 The debt to total assets ratio is 70%.
4 The profit margin on sales is 6%.
5 The firm's accounts receivable turnover is 5. Receivables increased by $400,000 during the year.

Instructions

Using the preceding data, complete the income statement and the balance sheet.

P20-A4 *Effect of transactions on ratios* (L.O. 3)
The transactions and events in the following table pertain to Allied Products for 19X5. Opposite each transaction is a ratio that the company plans to disclose in its annual report.

	Transaction/Event	Ratio
a	Purchased equipment for cash.	Current ratio
b	Sold an office building at a gain.	Profit margin on sales
c	Declared a cash dividend.	Quick ratio
d	Paid an account payable.	Return on assets
e	Sold merchandise on account.	Times interest earned
f	Wrote off an uncollectible account against the Allowance account	Debt to total assets
g	Recorded accrued salaries expense.	Debt to total assets
h	Purchased treasury stock.	Dividend payout ratio
i	Tightened credit terms to customers.	Accounts receivable turnover

j	Reported a 2% rise in earnings per share.	Price-earnings ratio
k	Issued additional shares of common stock.	Return on common stockholders' equity
l	Paid semiannual interest on bonds.	Earnings per share
m	Granted a sales discount to a customer.	Profit margin on sales
n	Had a 2-for-1 common stock split.	Return on common stockholders' equity
o	Eliminated slow-moving merchandise from inventory.	Inventory turnover

Prior to each transaction, Allied's ratios all met or exceeded industry standards. None of the ratios equaled 1.0.

Instructions

Indicate whether the transaction or event increased, decreased, or had no effect on the ratio listed.

P20-A5 *Reading a corporate annual report* **(L.O. 3, 6, 7)**

Larry Wilson was recently asked to analyze the annual report of Alberto Culver Company as part of a class project in accounting principles. Larry's professor furnished the following list of questions to be answered, all of which pertain to the 1991 fiscal year:

a What is the company's largest cost or expense?

b What is the ratio of gross profit to sales?

c What effective income tax rate is the company experiencing?

d What is the firm's largest current asset?

e Under present agreements, how much long-term debt is due and payable within the next fiscal year?

f What were the four largest consumers of cash during the year?

g How much depreciation and amortization expense was recorded during the year?

h How many shares of common stock were issued and sold during the year?

i Does Alberto Culver use the first-in, first-out inventory valuation method?

j What service life estimate does the company use for goodwill and trade names?

k Does the company lease some of its facilities? How do you know?

l Did Alberto Culver have a "good" year?

m Did the company expand its Sally beauty supply operation? Explain.

n Which accounting firm audited the company's financial statements?

o Was the accounting firm satisfied with the integrity and fairness of Alberto Culver's financial statements? Briefly explain.

Instructions

Disclosures from Alberto Culver's annual report are presented in Appendix C at the end of the text. Assume the role of Larry Wilson and answer his professor's questions. Be sure to list the data source (notes to the financial statements, balance sheet, and so forth) for each answer.

Series B

P20-B1 *Horizontal and vertical analysis* (L.O. 1, 2)

The financial statements that follow pertain to Roseville Corporation.

ROSEVILLE CORPORATION
Comparative Balance Sheets
December 31, 19X2 and 19X1

	19X2	19X1
Assets		
Current assets		
Cash	$ 5,000	$ 20,000
Short-term investments	—	35,000
Accounts receivable (net)	250,000	50,000
Inventories	370,000	115,000
Prepaid expenses	15,000	10,000
Total current assets	$ 640,000	$ 230,000
Property, plant, & equipment		
Land	$ 45,000	$ 15,000
Buildings (net)	440,000	450,000
Equipment (net)	250,000	200,000
Vehicles (net)	121,000	100,000
Total property, plant, & equipment	$ 856,000	$ 765,000
Copyright (net)	$ 4,000	$ 5,000
Total assets	$1,500,000	$1,000,000
Liabilities & Stockholders' Equity		
Current liabilities		
Accounts payable	$ 300,000	$ 140,000
Salaries payable	10,000	10,000
Income taxes payable	190,000	150,000
Total current liabilities	$ 500,000	$ 300,000
Long-term debt	$ 400,000	$ 400,000
Total liabilities	$ 900,000	$ 700,000
Stockholders' equity		
Common stock, $5 par	$ 200,000	$ 50,000
Retained earnings	400,000	250,000
Total stockholders' equity	$ 600,000	$ 300,000
Total liabilities & stockholders' equity	$1,500,000	$1,000,000

ROSEVILLE CORPORATION		
Comparative Income Statements		
For the Years Ended December 31, 19X2 and 19X1		
	19X2	19X1
Net sales	$8,000,000	$4,000,000
Cost of goods sold	4,500,000	2,500,000
Gross profit	$3,500,000	$1,500,000
Operating expenses	2,500,000	750,000
Income before interest & taxes	$1,000,000	$ 750,000
Interest expense	35,000	40,000
Income before taxes	$ 965,000	$ 710,000
Income taxes	386,000	284,000
Net income	$ 579,000	$ 426,000

Instructions

a Prepare a horizontal analysis of the income statement, showing dollar and percentage changes. Round all calculations in instructions (a) and (b) to two decimal places.

b Prepare a vertical analysis of the balance sheet, relating each asset to total assets and each liability and stockholders' equity account to the total of liabilities plus stockholders' equity.

c Briefly comment on the results of your analysis.

P20-B2 *Ratio computation* (L.O. 3)

1-2-3

Selected financial information for Solar Thermal, Inc., follows.

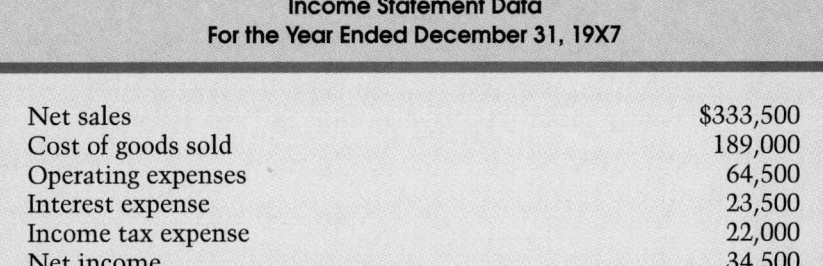

Income Statement Data	
For the Year Ended December 31, 19X7	
Net sales	$333,500
Cost of goods sold	189,000
Operating expenses	64,500
Interest expense	23,500
Income tax expense	22,000
Net income	34,500

Balance Sheet Data **As of December 31, 19X7 and 19X6**		
	19X7	**19X6**
Cash	$ 18,500	$ 15,000
Accounts receivable (net)	94,000	75,500
Inventories	186,000	153,000
Prepaid expenses	2,500	5,000
Property, plant, & equipment (net)	343,500	288,000
Total assets	644,500	536,500
Total current liabilities	143,000	133,500
Long-term liabilities	122,500	117,500
Common stock, $1 par	29,500	10,000
Additional paid-in capital	169,000	125,500
Retained earnings	180,500	150,000

All sales are on account, and cash dividends declared and paid during 19X7 amounted to $4,000.

Instructions

Compute the following items for 19X7, rounding all calculations to two decimal places:
a Current ratio
b Quick ratio
c Accounts receivable turnover ratio
d Inventory turnover ratio
e Profit margin on sales
f Return on assets
g Debt to total assets
h Return on common stockholders' equity
i Dividend payout ratio
j Number of times interest is earned

P20-B3 *Financial statement construction via ratios* **(L.O. 3)**

Incomplete financial statements of Image, Inc., follow.

1-2-3

IMAGE, INC. Balance Sheet December 31, 19X7	
Assets	
Cash	$ 1,000,000
Accounts receivable	?
Inventory	?
Property, plant, & equipment	?
Total assets	$16,000,000
Liabilities & Stockholders' Equity	
Accounts payable	$ 700,000
Notes payable (short-term)	?
Bonds payable	?
Common stock	?
Retained earnings	1,500,000
Total liabilities & stockholders' equity	$16,000,000

IMAGE, INC. Income Statement For the Year Ended December 31, 19X7	
Sales	$?
Cost of goods sold	12,000,000
Gross profit	$?
Operating expenses & interest	?
Income before tax	$?
Income taxes, 35%	?
Net income	$?

Further information:
1 Image's accounts receivable turnover ratio is 10. Credit sales, which amount to 80% of total sales, are $20 million. The accounts receivable balance doubled during the year.
2 The inventory turnover ratio is 5. The beginning inventory was $3 million.
3 The current ratio is 2.
4 The debt to total assets ratio is 75%
5 Operating expenses and interest total 40% of sales.

Instructions

Using the preceding data, complete the balance sheet and the income statement. Round computations to the nearest dollar.

P20-B4 *Effect of transactions on ratios* (L.O. 3)

The transactions and events in the following table pertain to Eller Services for 19X9. Opposite each transaction is a ratio that the company plans to disclose in its annual report.

	Transaction/Event	Ratio
a	Paid off a long-term bank loan.	Current ratio
b	Declared and paid an extra dividend to preferred stockholders.	Return on common stockholders' equity
c	Experienced a $3-per-share jump in the common stock market price.	Price-earnings ratio
d	Sold merchandise for cash.	Debt to total assets
e	Invested excess cash in short-term securities.	Quick ratio
f	Converted bonds payable into common stock.	Debt to total assets
g	Changed from FIFO to LIFO during a period of rising prices.	Inventory turnover
h	Purchased inventory for cash from a competitor who was going out of business.	Current ratio
i	Recorded depreciation for the year.	Times interest earned
j	Sold a truck at a loss.	Profit margin on sales
k	Issued bonds payable.	Dividend yield
l	Acquired store equipment on account.	Quick ratio
m	Sold treasury stock at cost.	Return on assets
n	Took advantage of several substantial purchases discounts.	Profit margin on sales
o	Adjusted the Prepaid Insurance account to recognize policies expiring during the period.	Earnings per share

Prior to each transaction, Eller's ratios all met or exceeded industry standards. None of the ratios equaled 1.0.

Instructions

Indicate whether the transaction or event increased, decreased, or had no effect on the ratio listed.

P20-B5 *Reading a corporate annual report* (L.O. 3, 6, 7)

Sharon McDonald was recently asked to analyze the annual report of Alberto Culver Company as part of a class project in accounting principles. Sharon's professor furnished the following list of questions, all of which pertain to the 1991 fiscal year:

a Did the company declare any dividends during the year? If so, what type(s) were declared?

b What types of stock has Alberto Culver issued?

c In relation to the data of previous years, what is true about the firm's earnings per share?

d What amount of accounts receivable does the company anticipate will be uncollectible?

e What depreciation method does Alberto Culver use for most of its long-term assets?

f On the basis of the data presented, in which quarter does the firm typically generate most of its sales revenue?

g How much cash was generated from operating activities, long-term debt issuances, and asset disposals, respectively?

h Does Alberto Culver operate in different business segments? Explain.

i What financial statements of the company were audited by KPMG Peat Marwick?

j Did Peat Marwick find significant violations of generally accepted accounting principles by Alberto Culver? Briefly discuss.

k Was the company affected by the 1990 Gulf War? If so, how?

l What is Alberto Culver's profit margin on sales?

m In what quarter of the year did the market price of the Class A common stock peak?

n The firm completed a new manufacturing facility during the year. Where is it located?

o Alberto Culver leases a number of its assets. Are the majority of its lease payments attributable to operating leases or to capital leases?

Instructions

Disclosures from Alberto Culver's annual report are presented in Appendix C at the end of the text. Assume the role of Sharon McDonald and answer the professor's questions. Be sure to list the data source (notes to the financial statements, balance sheet, and so forth) for each answer.

ELECTRONIC DATA BASE

SEC

EDB20-1 *A brief look at statement analysis: Nordstrom, Inc., and The Neiman Marcus Group, Inc.* (L.O. 3, 4, 6, 7)

Nordstrom, Inc., is a fashion retailer offering a wide selection of apparel, shoes, and accessories. The company operates through department and specialty stores, primarily in the western U.S. Neiman Marcus is involved in essentially the same business, selling goods through its Neiman Marcus, Bergdorf Goodman, and Contempo Casuals stores.

Instructions

By using the text's Electronic Data Base, access the balance sheets, financial statement notes, management's discussion and analysis, and audit reports of both firms and answer the questions that follow. Unless otherwise indicated, responses should be based on data for the most recent year presented.

a Compute the current ratios of the two companies.

  (1) Which of the two companies is in a better position to settle its short-term obligations? Briefly discuss.

  (2) By reviewing the summary of significant accounting policies, do you have any reservations about the comparative analysis that you just performed? Briefly explain.

b Which quarter produces the highest revenues for each firm? (*Hint:* These companies disclose such information in management's discussion and analysis as opposed to the financial statement notes.) Comment on any differences that you find.

c Review the audit reports of the two firms. Is there anything different about the reports? Briefly discuss.

d Does either company report segment information in the notes that accompany the financial statements? Comment on your findings.

EDB20-2 *A brief look at statement analysis* (L.O. 3, 4, 6, 7)

This problem is a duplication of Problem EDB20-1. It is based on two companies selected by your instructor.

Instructions

By using the text's Electronic Data Base, access the specified companies' balance sheets, financial statement notes, and audit reports and focus on data for the most recent year reported. Answer requirements (a)–(d) of Problem EDB20-1.

BEYOND THE BASICS

BB20-1 *Corporate annual reports; other data sources* (L.O. 6, 7)

Obtain an annual report from a large, publicly held corporation and a current copy of a metropolitan newspaper that contains stock price information. (*The Wall Street Journal* may be substituted for the metropolitan newspaper.) Your instructor will provide suggestions on where to obtain these items.

Instructions

After reviewing the annual report and the stock price listings in the newspaper, determine the following:

a Name of corporation
b Key products and/or services
c Location of corporate headquarters
d Number of members on the board of directors
e Most recent calendar or fiscal year reported. *Note:* Items that follow should be answered for the most recent year reported or, if appropriate, the end of that year.
f Total revenues
g Net income
h Earnings per share
i Total assets, liabilities, and stockholders' equity
j Current ratio
k Retained earnings balance
l Dividends declared on common stock
m Largest source of cash from financing activities
n Largest use of cash in investing activities
o Net change in cash and cash equivalents
p Inventory method(s) used by the firm
q Depreciation method(s) used by the firm
r Were there any discontinued operations? If so, briefly describe.
s Number of business segments in which the company operates
t Name of company's certified public accountants
u Type of audit opinion received (qualified or unqualified)
v Name of stock exchange where common stock is traded
w Current per-share market price of common stock (see newspaper)
x Number of common shares bought and sold during the trading day (see newspaper)
y The increase or decrease in the common stock price during the trading day (see newspaper)

BB20-2 *Overview of chapter concepts: Multiple choice* (L.O. 1–4, 6, 7)

The following multiple-choice questions relate to various topics discussed in the chapter. Select the best answer.

1 Lansing Corporation had the following data for 19X4 and 19X5:

	19X5	19X4
Net sales	$1,000,000	$ 750,000
Cost of goods sold	900,000	650,000
Year-end assets	5,000,000	2,000,000

A horizontal analysis would reveal that gross profit:
a was 10% of sales in 19X5.
b was 5% of 19X4 year-end assets.
c was $0 for the two-year period.
d changed 0% from 19X4 to 19X5.

2 Which of the following is often considered to be an outgrowth of vertical analysis?
a Horizontal analysis.
b Business segment analysis.
c Common-size financial statements.
d Liquidity analysis via the current and quick ratios.

3 Train Whistle Corporation reported $57,000 of current assets and $28,000 of current liabilities on its year-end balance sheet. Included in these amounts were the following selected accounts:

Short-term investments	$15,000
Inventories	20,000
Prepaid expenses	7,000
Taxes payable	9,500

Which of the following sets of numbers would be used to compute the numerator and denominator of the current ratio (CR) and quick ratio (QR), respectively?

	CR Numerator	CR Denominator	QR Numerator	QR Denominator
a	$57,000	$28,000	$57,000	$18,500
b	57,000	28,000	30,000	28,000
c	42,000	28,000	30,000	28,000
d	57,000	28,000	15,000	28,000

4 Linda Sue Garment Company had net income of $100,000, income taxes of $40,000, and interest expense of $20,000. The times interest earned ratio is:
a 5.   c 7.
b 6.   d 8.

The following data of Horatio Company are to be used in answering Questions 5 and 6.

Assets	
Cash	$ 50,000
Accounts receivable	?
Inventory	?
Property, plant, & equipment	592,000
Total	$864,000

Liabilities & stockholders' equity

Current liabilities	$?
Long-term debt	?
Common stock	600,000
Retained earnings	?
Total	$?

The company's current ratio is 4, and the inventory turnover ratio is 10.5. The firm's average inventory equals the ending inventory, and cost of goods sold amounts to $1,470,000.

5 Horatio's ending inventory is:
a $42,000.   c $140,000.
b $60,000.   d $270,000.

6 Horatio's total current liabilities are:
a $68,000.   c $264,000.
b $184,000.   d $1,088,000.

7 Which of the following would not customarily be reported for a business segment?
a Revenues.   c Identifiable assets.
b Operating income.   d Common stock.

8 Which of the following would not be found in the notes that accompany the financial statements?
a The inventory method used by the company.
b Quarterly revenues and earnings, assuming the business is highly seasonal.
c A comment by the company's auditors concerning whether the financial statements are prepared in accord with generally accepted accounting principles.
d The underlying details (e.g., interest rates and maturity dates) of any bonds that have been issued by the company.

COMMUNICATION OF ACCOUNTING INFORMATION

CAI20-1 *The use of illustrations: Texas Instruments* (L.O. 3)

Communication Principle: At the heart of any report or presentation are illustrations. Many reports fail because writers do not sufficiently illustrate their points or because illustrations are used ineffectively.

Illustrations, including calculations, must be introduced carefully so the reader grasps their significance. These items must be set off with indentations and white space, be large and clear, be labeled, and contain only the most necessary details. When an illustration appears, it should be mentioned in the report's text, and important aspects should be explained to help the reader understand the material.

With the proper use of illustrations, we come face to face with a primary communication principle: strategic repetition. Preview, present, and review, or say the same thing in several different ways to ensure comprehension.

■ ■ ■ ■ ■ ■ ■ ■

Texas Instruments is a company actively involved in technology development and implementation. Much of its work revolves around electronics and semiconductors, both with the Department of Defense and with many commercial businesses. Selected data (in thousands) from a recent year-end annual report of the firm follow.

Net sales	$6,294,800
Cost of goods sold	4,817,600
Interest expense	33,400
Net income	366,300
Preferred dividends	30,400
Income tax expense	150,100
Cash	541,300
Accounts receivable, beginning	848,200
Accounts receivable, ending	942,100
Short-term investments	239,100
Inventories, ending	769,700
Inventories, beginning	738,700
Current assets	2,548,600
Current liabilities	1,199,400
Total assets	4,427,500
Total liabilities	2,183,900

Instructions

You have been asked to prepare a financial evaluation of Texas Instruments. Construct the portion of the evaluation that pertains to liquidity and activity relationships of the company, assuming your readers have limited knowledge of ratio analysis. In addition to the appropriate calculations, be sure to explain what each of these relationships and accompanying ratios shows.

Answers to Chapter Quiz

1 d

2 a

3 d

4 c

Segment	Profit	Profit Margin on Sales	Return on Assets
Airline	$ 20	$20 ÷ $4,000 = 0.5%	$20 ÷ $2,000 = 1%
Pencils	80	$80 ÷ $1,000 = 8.0%	$80 ÷ $1,600 = 5%
Aluminum siding	400	$400 ÷ $2,000 = 20.0%	$400 ÷ $4,000 = 10%

5 b

CHAPTER

21

Introduction to Managerial and Cost Accounting

LEARNING OBJECTIVES

After studying this chapter, you should be able to:

1

Distinguish between financial and managerial accounting.

2

Describe the planning, control, and decision-making components of managerial accounting.

3

Define cost accounting and identify several of its recent changes.

4

Explain the composition of the three fundamental manufacturing costs: direct materials, direct labor, and factory overhead.

5

Differentiate between product costs and period costs.

6

Identify the unique features of the manufacturing balance sheet and income statement.

7

Explain variable and fixed cost behavior.

As we move into Chapter 21, a look back at previous discussions reveals that many diverse topics have been presented. These topics have ranged in scope from earnings per share, to the valuation of inventory on the balance sheet, to the statement of cash flows. Although diversity appears to have been the theme, a substantial amount of this material does have some common ground. This common ground is known as financial accounting. A brief overview of financial accounting is helpful at this point because of the differences between it and the focus of most of the text's remaining chapters—managerial accounting.

FINANCIAL ACCOUNTING

OBJECTIVE

1

Distinguish between financial and managerial accounting.

Financial accounting is concerned primarily with external reporting, that is, reporting the results of economic activities to parties outside the firm. Interested recipients of financial accounting information include present and potential owners, suppliers, bankers, and bondholders. Owners and investors use this information in determining whether to buy, hold, or sell ownership interests (i.e., shares of stock). Suppliers, bankers, and bondholders will conduct business with an entity if repayment will be forthcoming. As a result, these latter groups find financial accounting information useful in deciding whether or not to extend credit. In general, by communicating such information as earnings (income statement) and financial position (balance sheet), financial accounting strives to present a fair picture of the business in which the preceding parties have an interest.

A review of our earlier presentations will find several other distinguishing characteristics of financial accounting. For example, the financial statements that are constructed for external distribution tend to be highly aggregated, with a focus on disclosures for the company as a whole. Segmented reportings, although required in some instances, normally present minimal detail on "parts" of the firm.

Further, the financial statements serve to summarize transactions and events that have already occurred. In other words, the focus is on past, historical data. The data are summarized and reported in conformity with generally accepted accounting principles (GAAP), which facilitates the comparison of widely varying businesses by analysts. In addition, the use of GAAP assures outsiders that an entity's financial disclosures are based on a set of common rules that have been accepted by the accounting profession. Thus, users do not have to rely on an organization's unique measurement methods that may have been "created" to inflate economic well-being.

Finally, much of financial accounting is mandatory, with a business having little or no say in the matter. The underlying reason is regulation—a fact of life in our society. Ranging in scope from the powerful Securities and Exchange Commission (SEC) to the departments that handle state sales tax collections, various agencies must determine whether a business has complied with the laws and mandates to which it is subject. Financial accounting and an historical record-keeping system are the information source for satisfying the demands of these agencies (e.g., the issuance of financial statements to investors, the filing of a tax return with the Internal Revenue Service, and so forth).

Exhibit 21-1 summarizes the key issues just raised and shows that financial accounting can be contrasted with managerial accounting. As its name implies, **managerial accounting** is oriented toward reporting the results of operations to managers and other interested parties within a business. Much of this information, unlike that produced via financial accounting, is often concerned with small segments of activity. For example, a company may construct a quarterly income statement for stockholders as part of its financial-reporting requirements. Managers, however, generally need more detail to properly perform their duties. Thus, for internal use, profitability reports are often generated on a monthly basis and subdivided by divisions, departments, and products.

Given that many managers are involved with planning activities (to be discussed shortly), reports that are issued to executives frequently have a strong future orientation. Historical data are accumulated and reported, but only to the extent that such figures help to assess (1) conformity with current plans or (2) what the future will bring. In view of this situation, it is not uncommon for managerial reports to focus on *forthcoming* costs, revenues, cash flows, and resource needs—items that are ignored in financial accounting because of the historical emphasis.

It is important to note that internal reports may be prepared by using an "anything goes" philosophy. GAAP, which apply to financial accounting only, need not be followed, thereby allowing a company to do whatever it pleases when reporting to in-house personnel (i.e., management). For example, if a business wanted to ignore depreciation on internally distributed financial statements, it could do so. Or if a company desired to write up

Issue	Financial Accounting	Managerial Accounting
Users of information	External parties: stockholders, creditors, analysts, regulatory agencies	Internal parties: managers of the firm
Scope of reports	Highly aggregated	Focus on a firm's segments (e.g., products and departments); often cover a short period of time
Information reported	Past transactions and events	Both past and future items (e.g., costs, cash flows, and so forth)
Reporting standards	Based on generally accepted accounting principles (GAAP)	No constraining factors
Nature of reporting	Mandatory: reports must be filed consistent with regulatory agency requirements	Highly discretionary; considerable diversity among businesses and managers

EXHIBIT 21-1
Differences Between Financial and Managerial Accounting

EXHIBIT 21-2
Examples of Information
Generated for Internal Use

Company	Information Reported
Hyatt Hotels	Construction cost per room at a planned facility
Kellogg Company	Cash outlay necessary to manufacture and introduce a new type of breakfast cereal
Toys "R" Us	Profit per square foot of selling space
Time Warner	Subscriber renewal rates on *Time, People,* and *Money* magazines
MCI Communications	Uncollectible accounts experience with residential and commercial users

inventory and short-term investments to reflect market values in excess of cost, that, too, would be permissible.[1]

A Cost/Benefit Theme

Accounting systems produce a wide assortment of information so that executives can manage a business. As an example, see Exhibit 21-2. Given the absence of preestablished rules, much of the information generated for use within a firm is discretionary (optional). The information is produced because it is helpful to a manager when performing his or her duties. Varying responsibilities among managers, of course, create different information needs, and some of the needs are more important than others.

Because of limited resources, an organization normally cannot satisfy all the desires of its executives. As a result, a guideline must be established for the generation of discretionary information. A suggested approach employs **cost-benefit analysis,** where a manager compares the cost of producing information against the benefits to be derived from the information's use. If the benefits exceed the costs, generation of the needed facts and figures is appropriate; if not, rejection is in order.

Managerial Accounting Applications

OBJECTIVE
2
Describe the planning, control, and decision-making components of managerial accounting.

Managerial accounting plays an important role in three basic functions of management: planning, control, and decision making.

Planning

Virtually every company is formed to achieve certain goals and objectives. The owners, for example, expect the firm to earn a profit and an adequate return on investment, while management strives to produce goods and services that are characterized by quality and dependability. Marketing and the sales force attempt to achieve a reasonable share of the market by attracting loyal customers.

An organization attains its objectives by planning. **Planning** involves the formulation of methods and strategies that implement a company's objec-

---

[1] Although diversity is the rule, most firms have not strayed too far from the norm.

tives in definite terms. As an example, consider the common business practice of establishing specified credit policies. These policies permit the generation of profitable sales volume without an abnormally high rate of uncollectible accounts, thereby providing a return to the owners. At the same time, if the entity's credit policies are consistent with the terms offered by competitors, an acceptable market share can be attained.[2]

Sometimes, the objectives of a business will conflict with one another. For instance, suppose a company decided to enlarge its market share. To attract new customers, the firm might loosen its credit policy. Conceivably, an excessive concentration on obtaining market share could result in high levels of uncollectible accounts, thus undermining the objective of profitability. A business must continually evaluate its objectives and the policies implemented for their attainment. Although eliminating all conflict is extremely difficult, harmony and consistency (achieved by intensive planning) help an organization improve overall results.

Planning takes place in all facets of an organization. Often, plans are expressed quantitatively in formal reports known as **budgets,** which are prepared for areas that management deems critical and in need of close monitoring and evaluation. Such areas include sales, production, capital expenditures, and cash flow. Even entire financial statements can be forecast. Although budgeting and forecasting are readily associated with managerial accounting, managerial accounting assists in other planning activities as well. These activities are examined in higher-level courses and in the study of other business disciplines such as quantitative methods, marketing, and finance.

Control

The control function is an outgrowth of planning. No matter how extensively and effectively a business plans, unexpected events can occur. Furthermore, because plans merely reflect an organization's best guess about the future, prediction errors are common.

If management is to have insight regarding a company's progress toward its objectives, feedback is a necessity. Frequently, the feedback is in the form of a performance report (see Exhibit 21-3). The performance report pinpoints **variances,** or deviations from the budget. The individual in charge of Western Territory operations, for example, analyzes the variances, explains to management why August net income was $6,700 less than budget, and takes corrective action. Such action may entail generating additional sales, cutting costs, or changing personnel.

Whatever the form, the common feature is **control,** which helps bring an organization back on target in terms of achieving the original plan. Control not only assists in eliminating deviations from budgets, but it also renders valuable perspectives for the next round of planning. By closely monitoring operations, managers generally obtain a better "feel" for the business, which, in turn, leads to more effective budgeting and policy formation. The relationship between planning and control is shown in Exhibit 21-4.

---

[2] Many other factors influence market share, such as price, advertising policies, and product quality.

**EXHIBIT 21-3
Performance Report**

THORNDIKE ENTERPRISES Western Territory Performance Report For the Month Ended August 31, 19XX				
	Budget	Actual	Variance	Explanation
Sales	$68,000	$62,100	$5,900U	
Cost of goods sold	42,500	42,700	200U	
Gross profit	$25,500	$19,400	$6,100U	
Operating expenses				
Salaries	$ 6,400	$ 6,600	$ 200U	
Fuel	3,100	3,800	700U	
Advertising	4,500	4,200	300F	
Rent	2,000	2,000	—	
Total expenses	$16,000	$16,600	$ 600U	
Net income	$ 9,500	$ 2,800	$6,700U	

U = unfavorable; F = favorable.

Decision Making

Managerial accounting also plays an important role in **decision making.** Decision making can be viewed as an integral part of planning and control rather than as a separate, independent management function. The implementation of a successful planning program, for example, requires that managers choose from among alternative objectives and policies. Similarly, the fine-tuning and control of operations dictate that appropriate corrective action be selected and implemented.

The decision process has far-reaching effects and normally involves much more than just "number crunching." Many managers, especially those involved with accounting and finance, place considerable emphasis on net income, cash flow, and other quantitative measures of performance. Often, important qualitative factors such as business ethics, corporate image, and employee morale are mistakenly disregarded.

To illustrate the importance of qualitative factors in decision making, assume that Frank Rosa is employed as a foreman by the Nicholson Manufacturing Company. Management has decided to install some new machinery in Rosa's department. Although Rosa and his workers will be using the

**EXHIBIT 21-4
Planning and Control**

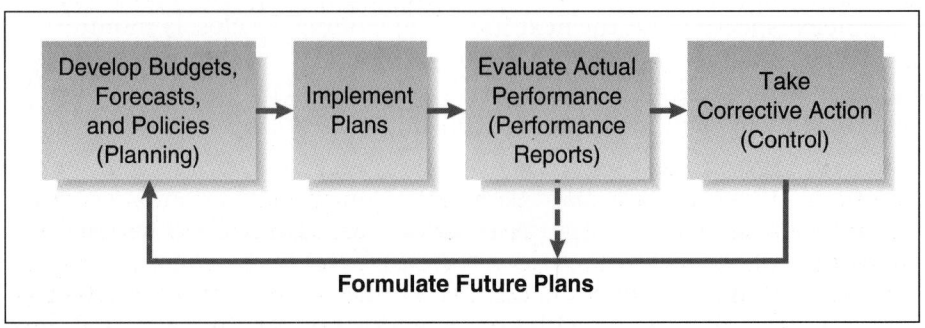

Develop Budgets, Forecasts, and Policies (Planning) → Implement Plans → Evaluate Actual Performance (Performance Reports) → Take Corrective Action (Control)

Formulate Future Plans

machines, they were not consulted in the selection process. Rosa has received minimal pay increases over the past few years, and with this latest incident, he has an extremely negative attitude about the company. His "I don't give a darn," or "who cares," outlook is reflected in his work and possibly in the work of his subordinates. Because negativism at the top of an enterprise tends to permeate lower levels of the organizational structure, Rosa's workers may be disenchanted and could have low morale. Low morale often affects productivity, which, in turn, impacts profitability. In Nicholson's case it is apparent that employee morale and the involvement of users in the decision process (both qualitative considerations) are indeed important. Effective decision making requires an evaluation of qualitative factors in conjunction with the quantitative outcome.

EXECUTIVE BRIEFING
The Blackout Decision: It's a Balancing Act

Dick Maxwell
Director of Broadcasting Services
National Football League

Most business decisions involve an analysis of revenues and costs. This one is no exception. The National Football League's (NFL's) position as the nation's most popular sport is directly related to two annual barometers—attendance and television viewership. A delicate balance is needed in order to maximize each. The so-called Blackout Rule (no local TV if the game is not sold out 72 hours in advance of kickoff) is an integral part of the equation.

The League's four-year contracts, with rights fees reported to be $3.6 billion, account for over 60% of revenues. So why not show a home game locally? The answer is a bit of the "chicken and egg" theory. If non-sold-out home games are televised locally over a period of time, fans will simply stay home to watch games, thus hindering attendance. Poorly attended games damage the NFL's TV product, as packed stadiums set the stage for exciting television. If the NFL continues to provide attractive programming, then viewership will remain solid. It is, indeed, a philosophical balancing act.

All businesses need an intimate knowledge of their costs to help ensure successful performance. As we progress through the study of managerial accounting, you will find that cost analysis can be somewhat troublesome. Some costs vary as activity changes, while other costs remain constant. Certain costs are relevant when evaluating a decision alternative; others can be ignored. Because of management's dependence on cost information, a brief introduction to cost accounting is a logical starting point for understanding the planning, control, and decision-making processes.

Cost accounting deals with the collection, assignment, and interpretation of cost. Cost data are captured by an organization's information system and then assigned to various business segments and activities. Examples of such segments include territories, departments, and products. Activities, in contrast, may encompass the design of a new advertising campaign, the operation of a summer recreation program by a city, and the

COST ACCOUNTING

OBJECTIVE
3

Define cost accounting and identify several of its recent changes.

implementation of a new all-day ticket plan by an amusement park. The purpose of the assignment process is to answer the age-old question, "How much does it cost?" Once cost is determined, management can proceed with an analysis of the following:

- Anticipated cost for various planning needs.
- Budgeted versus actual cost for control and evaluation.
- Relevant costs of different alternatives for use in decision making.
- Costs of producing goods and services for use in pricing and inventory valuation.

A Changing Face

For many years, the field of cost accounting could be characterized as rather stagnant. The methods and practices that were employed in the 1930s seemed appropriate for the 1960s and even the 1970s—at least in their users' eyes. Recently, though, companies have begun to modify their systems and thinking. These modifications are discussed in the next four sections.

Increased Focus on Managerial Accounting

Historically, cost accounting has had a heavy financial accounting orientation because of its use by manufacturers to determine production costs. The cost of goods produced influences inventory valuation on the balance sheet and cost of goods sold on the income statement. As we have just shown, cost accounting also provides information to management for planning, controlling, and decision making. Thus, cost accounting is now viewed as an integral part of both financial *and* managerial accounting. In many companies the managerial emphasis is growing because of business restructurings and mergers, expansion into international markets, and changing operating environments.

Expanded Use by Service Businesses

The service sector is probably the fastest growing segment of our economy. Firms that specialize in medical, legal, financial, transportation, and communication services all need some knowledge of their costs so that they can set and attain profit targets. As this sector explores new endeavors and continues to expand, its managers will undoubtedly have an increased demand for cost information.

Integration with New Manufacturing Technologies and Philosophies

Production processes in recent years have shifted away from labor-intensive methods in favor of automation. It is not uncommon today for state-of-the-art facilities to employ **computer integrated manufacturing (CIM).** With such a system, product design, testing, and production are fully automated through the use of computers, computer-controlled machines, and robots. One aspect of CIM is a *flexible manufacturing system*—a group of machines that can make a family of goods (e.g., different models of engines, VCRs, and so forth). Upon completing a batch of one product, the machines and robots are quickly reprogrammed so that they can promptly begin manufacturing another.

Manufacturers have also implemented **just-in-time (JIT)** production techniques. These techniques require that inventories be reduced to bare minimum levels, in some cases close to zero, to eliminate waste and to save carrying costs. (The costs of insurance, storage, obsolescence, taxes, spoilage, and financing all fall into this category.) With JIT, materials ideally arrive at the plant just in time to enter manufacturing, and goods are produced just in time for delivery to the customer.

The impact on cost accounting of computer integrated manufacturing and just-in-time techniques is significant. As you will see in Chapters 22–24, these innovations change the types of and relationships among the various manufacturing costs incurred.

Growing Emphasis on Product Quality and Globalization

In today's competitive business climate, companies are striving more than ever to turn out quality services and products. Many managements have learned the hard way that dissatisfied customers and flawed products can spell financial disaster for an entity. Quality, though, costs money, requiring the accountant to measure the related outlays for inspections, defective units, rework, and warranties. Yet quality is necessary to compete in a global economy.

The world is changing. Products from Japan, Taiwan, Hong Kong, and China are creating havoc for many American manufacturers. Third World countries are emerging, and Russia and other countries in Eastern Europe are adapting to a free-market system. Stated simply, U.S. businesses need sound cost information so that proper decisions can be made. Antiquated costing procedures or a lack of adequate data will place a firm at a competitive disadvantage, allowing other companies to excel at the deficient firm's expense.

MANUFACTURING ORGANIZATIONS

Given this introduction to cost accounting, we now turn our attention to manufacturers. Unlike the merchandising company, which purchases goods for resale, a manufacturer acquires raw materials and uses its plant, equipment, and employees to produce a finished product. Because of these production activities, accounting for manufacturers is more complex than accounting for service businesses and merchandisers. Realize, however, that like the other two types of organizations, the manufacturer also has sales, administrative, and financial-reporting responsibilities. Thus, manufacturers face many of the same measurement problems and use many of the same accounting practices as service and merchandising concerns.

Manufacturing Costs

In order to produce finished goods from raw materials, a manufacturer incurs three types of costs: direct materials, direct labor, and factory overhead.

HIGHLIGHT
When Is A Factory Not A Factory?

Answer: When it's a Red Lobster or Olive Garden restaurant, two immensely popular chains owned by General Mills. Average sales per location are $2.8 million a year at Olive Garden and $3 million for Red Lobster, both high for the industry. Same-store sales are growing by 3% a year—this when other restaurants are struggling to stay afloat.

Behind all this success is a food factory where economies of scale and automation are applied to bringing down costs, thus making bargain prices possible. It is a bona fide example of productivity gains, so impressive in manufacturing, but so hard to come by in the service sector. This restaurant operation disproves the rule.

For General Mills, a restaurant is simply the end of a long assembly line. At the beginning of the line, raw material goes in. Each year Red Lobster serves 60 million pounds of seafood, which it buys from all over the world. At General Mills' processing plant in St. Petersburg, Florida, shrimp arrive frozen in boxes from Ecuador and Thailand and are loaded onto a conveyor belt to be peeled, de-veined, cooked, quick frozen, and packed. Other seafood, like swordfish, arrives at warehouses around the country, where it is inspected and flown fresh daily to Red Lobster restaurants. This processing and supply system saves about 25 cents per pound over the average restaurant's seafood cost and ensures consistent quality.

At the Olive Garden, raw materials are even simpler. Each restaurant makes its own pasta daily from semolina, water, and salt. It costs Olive Garden less than 40 cents a pound—including labor—compared with 55 cents if the noodles were purchased already prepared.

Every night, each restaurant's computer tells the manager what to expect the next day, based on what was served the same day the previous week and the same day the previous year. "The computer will tell you if you serve 516 people the next day, you will

serve these items in these quantities," says the president of Red Lobster USA. " 'So before you go home,' it says, 'I want you to pull 30 pounds of shrimp, 40 pounds of pollack, and 40 pounds of crab out of the freezer. Then tomorrow morning I want your production people to make 85 scampi dishes, 6 stuffed flounders,' and so on. You know what people are going to eat." The president figures waste has been cut by $5 million a year. Because the system also uses history to predict busy periods, improved scheduling has cut labor costs to 16% of revenues, down nearly one full percentage point in a year—a savings of more than $10 million. In the low-margin restaurant trade, even small savings help.

In the kitchen, meals are prepared to precise specifications. Swordfish is cooked no more than four to five minutes per side on a grill set to blast at 450 degrees. A one-pound Maine lobster is steamed for 10 minutes, no more, no less. Cooks place food on plates according to an illustrated diagram that specifies how many sprigs of parsley should be on the plate, and where. Apart from ensuring consistency and controlling costs, clever food placement can make an ordinary portion appear enormous.

Quality control is important. Managers carry thermometers in their shirt pockets to run spot checks of food temperatures. Clam chowder must be no cooler than 150 degrees when it hits the table, coffee at least 180 degrees, and salads no warmer than 40 degrees. If temperatures are off, it means something is wrong—a server may be slow, soup may be steaming away on a stove that's too hot, or air filters may be clogged, subtly altering air flow in and out of the kitchen.

In a steel, chemical, or cement plant, process controls like these would be second nature. By adapting them to a service business, General Mills has been able to deliver good value to the customer and superior profits to shareholders.

Source: Adapted from "Dinnerhouse Technology," *Forbes,* July 8, 1991, pp. 98–99. Excerpted by permission of *Forbes* magazine, © Forbes Inc., 1991.

Direct Materials

Direct materials include all materials that (1) form an integral part of the finished product and (2) are easily traced to the finished product. Several examples of direct materials are major subassemblies such as the seat, back, and frame of a chair; the wheels of a bicycle; the electronic components of a computer; and the sheet metal and glass in an automobile. Direct materials do not include minor items like glue, varnish, and nails. Although no one would dispute the importance of these latter items to a finished product, determining and tracing their cost to the units manufactured is troublesome (and expensive). Imagine, for example, the difficulty of calculating the cost of glue consumed in producing a single piece of wooden furniture. As a result of these problems and for purposes of expediency, minor materials are normally accounted for as **indirect materials** and treated as part of factory overhead.

OBJECTIVE

4

Explain the composition of the three fundamental manufacturing costs: direct materials, direct labor, and factory overhead.

Direct Labor

Direct labor represents the gross wages of personnel who work directly on the goods being produced. The wages of assembly-line workers and machine operators are included in this cost classification.

A manufacturer employs many other personnel who indirectly contribute to the production of finished goods. Examples include maintenance workers, supervisors, plant guards, and storeroom personnel. As with indirect materials, tracing the cost of these latter personnel to specific units manufactured can be difficult. Wages of the factory employees just mentioned are therefore treated as **indirect labor** and accounted for as part of factory overhead.

Factory Overhead

Factory overhead, sometimes called manufacturing burden, consists of all factory-related costs other than direct materials and direct labor. Included in this classification are indirect materials, indirect labor, factory and equipment depreciation, utilities, taxes, repairs, and maintenance. Observe that *factory overhead costs pertain solely to manufacturing activity.* For example, depreciation on machinery used in production is properly considered part of overhead, whereas depreciation on cars used by the sales staff is not. The latter cost is a selling expense. Similarly, insurance on the factory facilities is overhead. Insurance on the corporate offices, however, is treated as an administrative expense. Frequently, costs incurred by an entity as a whole (e.g., utilities and general maintenance) must be allocated among factory overhead, selling expense, and administrative expense to ensure proper accounting. This allocation is necessary because, as we will soon illustrate, the accounting treatment of selling and administrative expenses is considerably different from that for overhead.

Like indirect materials and indirect labor, the other elements of factory overhead are extremely difficult to trace to specific units of production. Thus, accountants normally estimate the overhead that goes into each product as opposed to determining the actual cost incurred. Overhead is discussed in more detail in Chapter 22.

Accountants sometimes combine the three production cost elements.

Prime cost consists of costs easily traced to the finished product, that is, direct materials plus direct labor. **Conversion cost** is the cost to convert raw material into finished product, namely, direct labor plus factory overhead.

Financial Statements of a Manufacturer

Direct materials, direct labor, and factory overhead eventually find their way to the financial statements. This process is easily understood if we first review the accounting practices of a merchandising concern. As a merchandising business acquires goods for resale, the costs incurred are inventoried on the balance sheet as an asset. Later, when sales are made, the inventory is taken off the balance sheet and transferred to the income statement in the form of cost of goods sold. The reason for this procedure is to match the cost of the items sold against related sales revenues.

Essentially the same practice is performed by the manufacturer. Rather than pay significant sums of money to acquire merchandise for resale, the manufacturer purchases direct materials, hires and compensates a labor force, and incurs factory overhead. These costs are all put "in process" and eventually result in the manufacture of finished product. At the end of the accounting period, the finished goods still owned appear as inventory on the balance sheet, whereas the units sold are written off via cost of goods sold. This process is illustrated in Exhibit 21-5.

Product and Period Costs

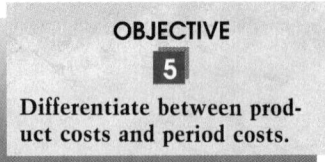

OBJECTIVE

5

Differentiate between product costs and period costs.

The costs that go into inventory—direct materials, direct labor, and factory overhead—are termed **product costs.** These costs are attached to the units they helped to produce and are inventoried until the time of sale. This accounting treatment can be contrasted with that of **period costs**—noninventoriable costs that are deducted as expenses of the current reporting period. Such treatment is justified because no future benefits are said to

**EXHIBIT 21-5
The Manufacturing Process**

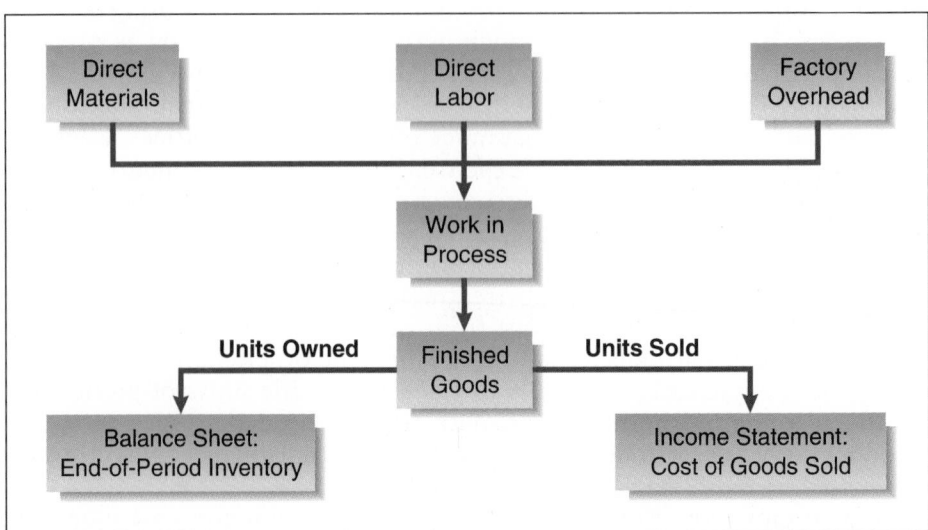

result from the related expenditure. Period costs consist of selling and administrative expenses and include sales commissions, advertising, and management salaries.

To illustrate the difference between product and period costs, assume that Conant Manufacturing Corporation began operations in 19X1. Building depreciation for the year amounted to $50,000, with 50% relating to sales and administrative facilities and 50% to the factory. Of the total units produced, 80% were sold in 19X1 and 20% in 19X2. Assuming no ending work in process, Exhibit 21-6 depicts the timing of the 19X1 building depreciation on the related income statements.

To explain, the selling and administrative costs are expensed when incurred. In contrast, the factory (product) cost is attached to inventory. Because only 80% of the production is sold in 19X1, $20,000 ($25,000 × 0.80) of depreciation is initially written off through cost of goods sold. The $5,000 balance is included in the cost of inventory. When these units are sold in 19X2, the remaining factory depreciation is released to the income

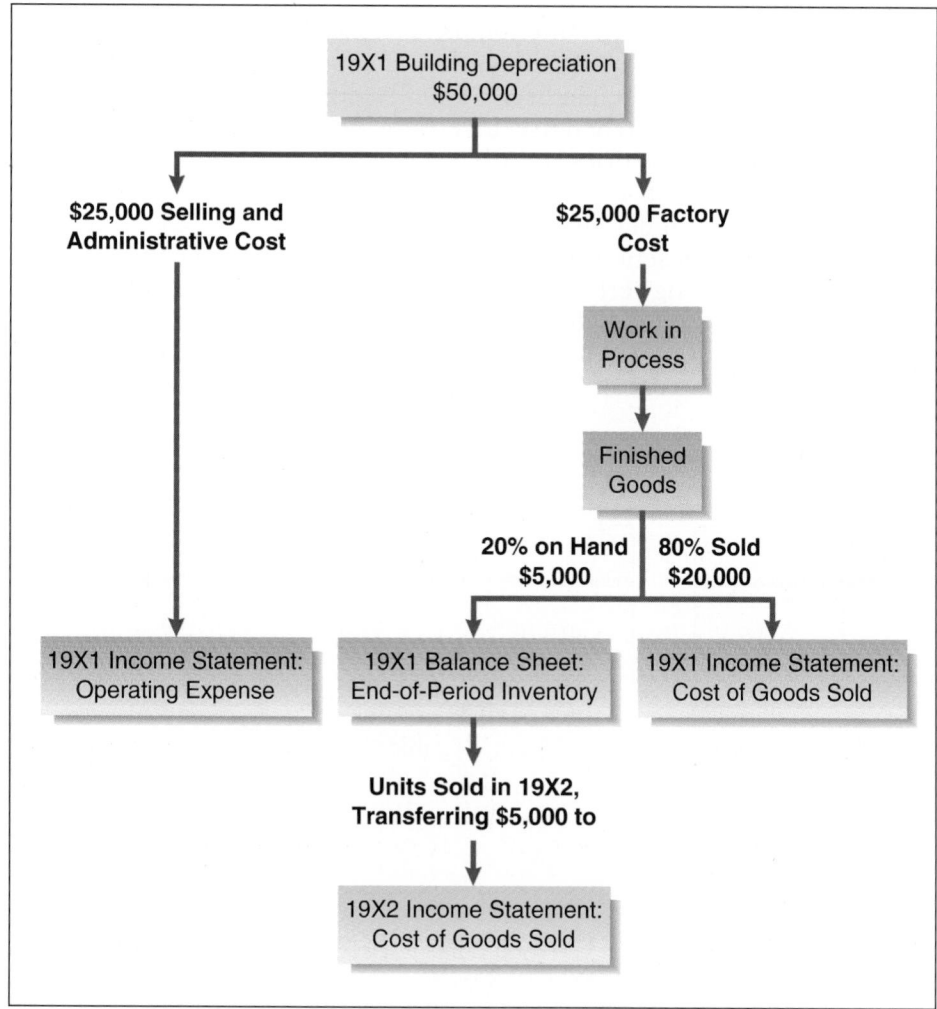

EXHIBIT 21-6
Timing of Product Costs and Period Costs

statement. Overall it is a matter of timing. Period costs are expensed upon incurrence; product costs are written off when the related inventory is sold.

The correct determination of product and period costs is important since errors will likely affect net income and the reported inventory valuation. Unfortunately, however, the distinction between these two costs is not always clear. Consider, for example, the salary of the manufacturing vice-president. This individual spends considerable time overseeing production policies and problems. Should the salary be treated as part of factory overhead or as an administrative operating expense? Perhaps the salary should be allocated between the two cost classifications on some equitable basis. If so, what basis should be used? Although most companies would treat the salary of the manufacturing vice-president as an administrative expense, issues like these are difficult to resolve. Businesses must therefore analyze each cost in depth, make an informed decision, and be consistent in their accounting treatment.

Balance Sheet

OBJECTIVE

6

Identify the unique features of the manufacturing balance sheet and income statement.

Now that you have a better grasp of production cost flows, we can examine the manufacturer's financial statements. The balance sheet of a manufacturer is identical to that of a merchandising concern, with one exception (see Exhibit 21-7). A merchandiser normally discloses one inventory account: Inventory or Merchandise Inventory. In contrast, businesses engaged in production activities usually establish three inventory accounts: Raw Materials, Work in Process, and Finished Goods.

Raw Materials includes the items to be processed into salable goods. **Work in Process** represents the cost of goods started but not completed by the end of the reporting period. The balance in this account is computed by totaling the direct material, direct labor, and factory overhead charges that pertain to the production in progress. Finally, as its name implies, **Finished Goods** contains the cost of completed production that is owned by the firm.

EXHIBIT 21-7
Merchandising and Manufacturing Balance Sheets

MERCHANDISING FIRM		
Current assets		
Cash		$ 15,000
Accounts receivable	$64,000	
Less: Allowance for uncollectibles	4,000	60,000
Inventory		190,000
Prepaid expenses		6,000
Total current assets		$271,000

MANUFACTURER		
Current assets		
Cash		$ 10,000
Accounts receivable	$ 43,000	
Less: Allowance for uncollectibles	3,000	40,000
Inventories		
Finished goods	$115,000	
Work in process	51,000	
Raw materials	24,000	190,000
Prepaid expenses		11,000
Total current assets		$251,000

EXHIBIT 21-8
Inventory Disclosures

Pacific Gas and Electric

Inventories
  Fuel oil
  Nuclear fuel
  Gas stored underground
  Materials and supplies

Quaker State Corporation

Inventories
  Crude oil
  Finished and in-process petroleum
    products
  Coal
  Other

H.J. Heinz Company

Inventories
  Finished goods and work in
    process
  Packaging material and
    ingredients

Quaker Oats Company

Inventories
  Finished goods
  Grain and raw materials
  Packaging materials and supplies

These three accounts represent the traditional split of inventory, with variations frequently found in practice. Consider the disclosures in Exhibit 21-8, which appeared in recent corporate annual reports. These businesses have adapted the general model to meet their own needs. This practice is acceptable providing that it results in adequate disclosure and a fair measure of financial position.

Income Statement

To illustrate the computation of net income for a manufacturer, assume that Golden, Inc., produces paint and various decorating supplies. Exhibit 21-9 contrasts Golden's income statement with that of Meadow Paint and Wallpaper, a retailer.

Notice that the two income statements are very similar. Meadow's cost of goods sold is computed on the basis of the firm's beginning and ending inventories and net purchases. Golden, on the other hand, does not acquire goods for resale; it makes them. Thus, the cost of goods manufactured replaces net purchases.

Tips & Techniques

Observe that of the three inventory accounts carried by a manufacturer, only Finished Goods is used in the cost-of-goods-sold calculation. The logic is that a manufacturer's finished goods correspond to the merchandise inventory of a retailer (or wholesaler), with both inventory types being offered for sale. Raw Materials and Work in Process, of course, are not resold.

Cost of goods manufactured (see the supporting schedule in Exhibit 21-9) is derived by examining the three cost elements of a manufactured product. Direct materials used, direct labor, and factory overhead are summed to arrive at the total production costs for the period. Next, the beginning

MEADOW PAINT AND WALLPAPER (Merchandiser) Income Statement		
Sales		$224,000
Cost of goods sold		
Beginning inventory	$ 36,000	
Net purchases	161,000	
Goods available for sale	$197,000	
Less: Ending inventory	55,000	
Cost of goods sold		142,000
Gross profit		$ 82,000
Operating expenses		
Selling	$ 46,000	
Administrative	24,000	70,000
Net income		$ 12,000

GOLDEN, INC. (Manufacturer) Income Statement		
Sales		$356,000
Cost of goods sold		
Beginning finished goods inventory	$ 45,000	
Cost of goods manufactured	277,000	
Goods available for sale	$322,000	
Less: Ending finished goods inventory	61,000	
Cost of goods sold		261,000
Gross profit		$ 95,000
Operating expenses		
Selling	$ 58,000	
Administrative	29,000	87,000
Net income		$ 8,000

GOLDEN, INC. Schedule of Cost of Goods Manufactured		
Direct materials used		
Beginning raw materials inventory	$ 21,000	
Net purchases	109,000	
Direct materials available	$130,000	
Less: Ending raw materials inventory	28,000	
Direct materials used		$102,000
Direct labor		79,000
Factory overhead		
Indirect materials used	$ 6,000	
Indirect labor	36,000	
Utilities	15,000	
Depreciation: factory	23,000	
Taxes	17,000	
Insurance	4,000	101,000
Total manufacturing costs		$282,000
Add: Beginning work in process inventory		7,000
		$289,000
Less: Ending work in process inventory		12,000
Cost of goods manufactured		$277,000

Note: This example assumes that the Raw Materials account contains direct materials only, with indirect materials being housed in a separate Factory Supplies account. Under an alternative procedure that is shown in the next chapter, the cost of both material types may be entered in the same account.

EXHIBIT 21-9
Income Statements of a Merchandising Firm and a Manufacturer

and ending work in process inventories are added and subtracted, respectively, to generate cost of goods manufactured. The reason for involving work in process can be described as follows. At the beginning of the accounting period, Golden had $7,000 of goods in production. During the period $282,000 of manufacturing costs were incurred, yielding $289,000 ($7,000 + $282,000) of costs "in process." If $12,000 of production remains in progress at year-end, $277,000 ($289,000 − $12,000) of goods must have been completed. Stated differently, $277,000 represents the cost of goods manufactured. This amount is later transferred to the income statement to compute cost of goods sold.

The manufacturing, selling, and administrative costs of an organization are not always presented in the traditional financial statement formats for purposes of planning and control. Frequently, costs are subdivided and studied in terms of their behavior. As noted earlier, some costs vary with changes in activity, whereas others remain constant. We will now overview variable and fixed cost behavior to help you understand the subject matter that follows. An in-depth study of this topic appears in Chapter 24.

COST BEHAVIOR

OBJECTIVE

7

Explain variable and fixed cost behavior

Variable Costs

Variable costs vary in direct proportion to a change in an activity base. The activity base may be sales, production, miles driven, students in a university, hours of machine operation, or any other measure of volume. To illustrate the concept of a variable cost, assume the Green Company is a manufacturer of ballpoint pens. The firm's top selling model, the Smoothwriter, requires $0.30 of direct materials. Green markets the Smoothwriter for $1.20 and pays its sales force a 5% commission. Two activity bases are involved in this example. The cost of direct materials used varies with production, and total commissions vary with the number of pens sold. This distinction is shown in the table that follows. Observe that a variable cost changes in total, but the cost per unit remains the same.

Direct Materials			Sales Commissions		
Number of Pens Produced	Material Cost Per Pen	Total Material Cost	Number of Pens Sold	Commission Per Pen*	Sales Commissions
50,000	$0.30	$15,000	45,000	$0.06	$2,700
60,000	0.30	18,000	55,000	0.06	3,300
70,000	0.30	21,000	65,000	0.06	3,900
80,000	0.30	24,000	75,000	0.06	4,500

* $1.20 × 0.05 = $0.06.

In addition to direct materials and sales commissions, other common examples of variable costs include direct labor, supplies, and fuel.

Fixed Costs

Unlike variable costs, **fixed costs** remain constant in total when changes occur in the activity base. As a result of this behavior, the fixed cost *per unit* fluctuates. That is, an increase in activity will cause a given sum of dollars to be spread over a greater volume level, thereby causing a decrease in the per-unit figure. Naturally, opposite results will occur if activity falls. Typical fixed costs include management salaries, advertising, straight-line depreciation, rent, property taxes, and insurance.

Continuing the Green Company example, assume that the firm uses an $85,000 machine in its manufacturing activities. The machine has a $5,000 residual value and a five-year service life, generating annual straight-line depreciation of $16,000 [($85,000 − $5,000) ÷ 5]. On the basis of different production levels, the depreciation per pen will be as follows:

Annual Depreciation	Number of Pens Produced	Depreciation Per Pen
$16,000	50,000	$0.32
16,000	60,000	0.267
16,000	70,000	0.229
16,000	80,000	0.20

From the preceding figures, it is apparent that the fixed cost per unit (i.e., depreciation per pen) is relevant at one and *only* one activity level. Multiplying a $0.20-per-pen depreciation rate, for example, by production levels other than 80,000 fails to yield the total depreciation charge of $16,000. When working with fixed costs, it is usually safer to deal in terms of total costs rather than unit costs.

END-OF-CHAPTER REVIEW

LEARNING OBJECTIVES: THE KEY POINTS

1 Distinguish between financial and managerial accounting. Financial accounting focuses on reporting financial position and the results of operations to external parties (i.e., those outside the organization). The information presented is highly aggregated and is really a summary of an entity's past transactions and events. Financial accounting disclosures are based on generally accepted accounting principles (GAAP) and, for the most part, are mandatory.

In contrast, managerial accounting is concerned with reporting to managers within a business. Both past and future data items are reported, normally for selected "parts" of the firm (e.g., divisions, products, and so forth). There are no rules and regulations that must be followed for internal reporting, with the result being a wide variety of reports and disclosures among businesses and managers. The decision to produce internal information is usually made on a cost-benefit basis.

2 Describe the planning, control, and decision-making components of managerial accounting. Planning involves the study of an organization's objectives and the translation of those objectives into various methods, strategies, and programs. One form of planning is the creation of budgets. Control involves the monitoring of actual results in comparison with an entity's original plan. Feedback is provided by performance reports and variances, allowing a manager to focus on areas where corrective action may be needed. Finally, decision making requires the selection of a given alternative from a set of alternatives. If good decisions are to be made, a manager must consider both the quantitative outcome and the related qualitative factors.

3 Define cost accounting and identify several of its recent changes. Cost accounting involves the collection, assignment, and interpretation of cost to answer an age-old question, "How much does it cost?" Costs may be compiled for anything from a product, to a department, to a program run by a city. Recently, several changes have occurred in this field. Cost accounting is assisting more in the planning, control, and decision-making (i.e., managerial) activities of companies. Further, with the growth of the service sector, it has seen an expanded use by service businesses. The rising popularity of computer integrated manufacturing and just-in-time production methods has affected cost accounting in terms of the nature of and relationship among the various manufacturing costs incurred. Finally, the growing emphasis on product quality and international trade has led to increased use of cost information to measure the costs of quality and to help secure global markets.

4 Explain the composition of the three fundamental manufacturing costs: direct materials, direct labor, and factory overhead. Direct materials, direct labor, and factory overhead are the three cost components of manufactured goods. Direct materials are those materials that form an integral part of the finished product and, at the same time, are easily traced to the product. Direct labor consists of the wages of those employees who work directly on the product (e.g., assembly-line workers). Finally, factory overhead comprises all other factory costs such as indirect materials, indirect labor, and equipment depreciation. Unlike direct materials and direct labor, factory overhead is not easily traced to a manufactured good.

5 Differentiate between product costs and period costs. Product costs are the costs incurred in manufacturing operations, namely, direct materials, direct labor, and factory overhead. These costs are inventoried until the manufactured good is sold, at which time the costs are transferred to cost of goods sold on the income statement. In contrast, period costs are unrelated to production operations. Such costs are expensed as incurred and include those generated by selling and administrative activities.

6 Identify the unique features of the manufacturing balance sheet and income statement. The balance sheet of a manufacturer typically reveals three inventory accounts: Raw Materials, Work in Process, and Finished Goods. The manufacturing income statement is the same as that for a merchandising firm, with one exception: net purchases is replaced by an entity's cost of goods manufactured. Cost of goods manufactured is computed by summing the costs of direct materials used, direct labor, and factory overhead, and then adding the beginning work in process balance and subtracting the ending work in process.

7 Explain variable and fixed cost behavior. Variable costs are those that change in direct proportion to a change in an activity base (sales, production, and so on). Fixed costs, on the other hand, remain constant. Because of these behavior patterns, variable costs per unit remain constant and per-unit fixed costs fluctuate.

---

budget A formal management plan that is expressed in quantitative terms.

computer integrated manufacturing A fully automated system that involves product design, testing, and production.

**KEY TERMS
AND CONCEPTS:
A QUICK OVERVIEW**

control An activity that helps bring an organization back on target in terms of achieving its original plans.

conversion cost The cost of converting raw material into finished product—namely, direct labor plus factory overhead.

cost accounting An area of accounting that deals with the collection, assignment, control, and evaluation of costs.

cost-benefit analysis An approach to decision making in which an alternative's costs are compared against the accompanying benefits.

cost of goods manufactured The total of direct materials used, direct labor, and factory overhead, plus the beginning work in process inventory, minus the ending work in process inventory.

decision making An integral part of the planning and control process that requires managers to choose from among alternative courses of action.

direct labor The gross wages of personnel who work directly on the goods being produced.

direct materials All materials that form an integral part of and are easily traceable to the finished product.

factory overhead All factory-related costs other than direct materials used and direct labor.

financial accounting An area of accounting concerned primarily with external reporting.

finished goods The inventory of completed production that is owned by a firm.

fixed cost A cost that remains constant in total when changes occur in an activity base.

indirect labor The wages of factory employees who do not work directly on the product; treated as part of factory overhead.

indirect materials Minor materials (such as glue, varnish, and nails) used in manufacturing a product; treated as part of factory overhead.

just-in-time production A production method in which inventories are reduced to bare minimum levels, sometimes close to zero.

managerial accounting An area of accounting oriented toward reporting the results of operations to managers and other interested parties within an organization.

period cost A cost unrelated to the acquisition or manufacture of inventory. It is expensed when incurred.

planning The development of methods and strategies that implement a company's objectives in definite terms.

prime cost Those costs easily traced to the finished product—namely, direct materials used plus direct labor.

product cost A cost that goes into inventory—specifically, direct materials, direct labor, and factory overhead.

raw materials The items to be processed into salable goods (i.e., the direct and indirect materials owned).

variable cost A cost that varies directly with a change in an activity base.

variance Deviations from a budgeted amount.

work in process The inventory of goods started but not completed during the period.

CHAPTER QUIZ

The five questions that follow relate to several issues raised in the chapter. Test your knowledge of the issues by selecting the best answer. (The answers appear on p. 901.)

1 Managerial accounting:
  a focuses primarily on reporting to regulatory agencies.
  b is governed by generally accepted accounting principles.
  c is highly discretionary and varies greatly from business to business.
  d should be considered as a substitute for financial accounting.

2 Which of the following items is properly classified as factory overhead?
  a Wages of a carpenter who builds fine wooden furniture.
  b The cost of sandpaper used in the production of furniture.
  c The cost of the plastic keys on a microcomputer's keyboard.
  d Depreciation on office equipment used at a company's corporate headquarters.

3 Which of the following statements is correct?
  a Period costs are properly inventoried on the balance sheet.
  b Direct labor is a typical example of a period cost.
  c Product costs are expensed as incurred.
  d Direct material is a typical product cost.

4 Cost of goods manufactured:
  a is added to the cost of the beginning finished goods inventory on the income statement.
  b includes selling and administrative expenses.
  c ignores the beginning and ending balances of the Work in Process account.
  d is normally disclosed on a company's balance sheet.

5 Which of the following is an example of a variable cost?
  a Salary of a plant supervisor.
  b Advertising costs.
  c Direct materials.
  d Straight-line depreciation on a factory machine.

SUMMARY PROBLEM

The following data were extracted from the accounting records of Bradley Plumbing Fixtures for the year ended December 31, 19X7:

Purchases of direct material	$235,700
Direct labor	458,900
Factory utilities	18,700
Work in process, Jan. 1	24,400
Advertising costs	6,000
Finished goods, Dec. 31	124,400
Factory depreciation*	11,600
Indirect labor	43,500
Raw materials inventory, Jan. 1	55,600
Finished goods, Jan. 1	112,000
Raw materials inventory, Dec. 31	45,000
Indirect materials used	11,300
Plant insurance	3,200
Work in process, Dec. 31	26,600

* Computed by the straight-line method.

Instructions

a Calculate the company's cost of goods manufactured and cost of goods sold for the year ended December 31, 19X7.
b Whose wages did Bradley likely classify as indirect labor?
c Assume that Bradley has been experiencing steadily rising costs in recent years. Briefly describe a report that management probably receives in its efforts to control operations.
d Three of Bradley's costs are plant insurance, indirect materials used, and factory depreciation. Classify these costs as being either variable or fixed in terms of behavior.

Solution

a Cost of goods manufactured

Direct materials used		
Beginning raw materials inventory	$ 55,600	
Net purchases	235,700	
Direct materials available	$291,300	
Less: Ending raw materials inventory	45,000	
Direct materials used		$246,300
Direct labor		458,900
Factory overhead		
Factory utilities	$ 18,700	
Factory depreciation	11,600	
Indirect labor	43,500	
Indirect materials used	11,300	
Plant insurance	3,200	88,300
Total manufacturing costs		$793,500
Add: Beginning work in process inventory		24,400
		$817,900
Less: Ending work in process inventory		26,600
Cost of goods manufactured		$791,300
Cost of goods sold		
Beginning finished goods inventory		$112,000
Cost of goods manufactured		791,300
Goods available for sale		$903,300
Less: Ending finished goods inventory		124,400
Cost of goods sold		$778,900

Note: Advertising costs are selling expenses and are therefore excluded from these calculations.

b Indirect labor includes wages of factory personnel who do not work directly on the product. Typical examples are factory supervisors, maintenance people, plant guards, and storeroom employees.
c Management likely receives a performance report that details actual and budgeted amounts for all costs incurred. The differences, or variances, between the amounts are studied to see if any corrective action is necessary.
d Plant insurance, fixed; indirect materials used, variable; factory depreciation, fixed.

ASSIGNMENT MATERIAL

Q21-1 Briefly discuss several of the major features associated with financial accounting.

Q21-2 Is managerial accounting concerned solely with the reporting of past transactions and events? Why?

Q21-3 What agency, if any, establishes the "ground rules" for managerial accounting practices?

Q21-4 How does a company ultimately decide whether to produce a discretionary report for a manager?

Q21-5 The sales manager of Snyder Company desires to maximize the firm's market share and has proposed a loosening of credit terms. Discuss the conflict that might arise between the sales manager and the vice-president of finance.

Q21-6 What is the purpose of issuing performance reports?

Q21-7 In addition to the quantitative outcome, what other factors should be considered in the decision process? Why?

Q21-8 Briefly define the terms "computer integrated manufacturing" and "flexible manufacturing system."

Q21-9 What types of cost information might interest a company that is greatly concerned about product quality?

Q21-10 What are the three cost elements of a manufactured product?

Q21-11 Why are indirect materials and indirect labor treated as part of factory overhead?

Q21-12 Differentiate among direct materials, direct labor, and factory overhead in terms of cost traceability to the finished product.

Q21-13 Dave Malloy, an engineer at Lexton Manufacturing, has just spent an exhausting weekend analyzing utility costs. Management wished to know the approximate percentage of electricity consumed by the company's (1) sales and administrative offices and (2) manufacturing plant. Dave mumbled under his breath, "Who cares? Utility cost is utility cost." Explain to Malloy why his analysis is needed.

Q21-14 When does a product cost appear on a balance sheet? On an income statement?

Q21-15 Discuss the balance sheet differences between a merchandiser and a manufacturer.

Q21-16 Blakely Manufacturing and Diaz Wholesalers both employ a sales manager. Discuss the differences, if any, in the accounting treatment of the salaries of the two sales managers.

E21-1 *Product costs and period costs* (L.O. 5)
The costs that follow were extracted from the accounting records of several different manufacturers:

1 Weekly wages of an equipment maintenance worker
2 Marketing costs of a soft drink bottler
3 Cost of sheet metal in a Honda automobile
4 Cost of president's subscription to *Fortune* magazine
5 Monthly operating costs of pollution control equipment used in a steel mill
6 Weekly wages of a seamstress employed by a jeans maker
7 Cost of compact discs (CDs) for newly recorded releases of Rush, Billy Joel, and Bryan Adams

a Determine which of these costs are product costs and which are period costs.
b For the product costs only, determine those that are easily traced to the finished product and those that are not.

E21-2   Overview of manufacturing costs (L.O. 4, 5, 6)
Evaluate the comments that follow as being True or False. If the comment is false, briefly explain why.
a The cost of cement in a road-building project would typically be classified as direct material.
b Normally, conversion costs are easily traced to a finished product.
c The Finished Goods inventory account contains the period costs of a manufacturer.
d Direct materials used + direct labor + beginning work in process inventory − ending work in process inventory = cost of goods manufactured.
e Product costs appear as inventory on a balance sheet until such time as the related units are sold.

E21-3   Definitions of manufacturing concepts (L.O. 4)

Interstate Manufacturing produces brass fasteners and incurred the following costs for the year just ended:

Materials and supplies used	
Brass	$ 75,000
Repair parts	16,000
Machine lubricants	9,000
Wages and salaries	
Machine operators	128,000
Production supervisors	64,000
Maintenance personnel	41,000
Other factory overhead	
Variable	35,000
Fixed	46,000
Sales commissions	20,000

Compute:
a Total direct materials consumed
b Total direct labor
c Total prime cost
d Total conversion cost

E21-4   Understanding cost flows (L.O. 6)
Executive Wares, which began business on January 1, 19X4, sells high-priced office accessories to executives. One of the company's products, catalog item no. 12, consists of a leather appointment book and a matching pen and pencil set—all assembled and packaged in a gift box by Executive Wares.

During 19X4, the firm purchased 8,000 19X5 appointment books from its supplier at $14 each. The following data are available as of June 30:

Appointment books issued to the Packaging Department from the storeroom	6,500
Gift sets completed	5,400
Completed gift sets in the warehouse	2,200
Completed gift sets given to customers as samples	20

If no errors or theft occurred during the period, determine the cost of the appointment books that would appear:

a In the company's (1) raw materials, (2) work in process, and (3) finished goods inventories as of June 30.

b As cost of goods sold for the period ended June 30.

c As an operating expense for the period ended June 30.

E21-5 *Understanding financial statements* (L.O. 5, 6)
Consider the following elements of financial statements:

A—Inventories on the balance sheet
B—Cost of goods sold on the income statement
C—Operating expenses on the income statement
D—Schedule of cost of goods manufactured

Identify where the following items would be found in the financial statements:

_____ a The newspaper advertising of the Buffalo Bills football team

_____ b The wages of refinery personnel employed by Shell Oil

_____ c The cost of Whoppers eaten by customers of Burger King (from Burger King's viewpoint)

_____ d The year-end incompleted production of Goodyear Tire

_____ e Depreciation on a passenger jet owned by British Airways

_____ f Utilities incurred by Whirlpool Corporation in assembling washers and dryers

_____ g The products held for sale by Macy's department store

_____ h The compensation paid to the president and vice-presidents of Dow Chemical

_____ i The fabric acquired during the period by Levi Strauss for use in its Dockers product line

E21-6 *Basic manufacturing computations* (L.O. 6)
Lyon Manufacturing reported total manufacturing costs (direct materials used, direct labor, and factory overhead) of $549,000 for 19X3. Sales and operating expenses were $759,200 and $142,500, respectively. The following information appeared on company balance sheets:

	For the Year Ended	
	12/31/X3	12/31/X2
Finished goods	$150,000	$153,700
Work in process	86,400	74,100

Compute cost of goods manufactured, cost of goods sold, and net income for 19X3.

E21-7 *Schedule of cost of goods manufactured, income statement* (L.O. 6)
The following information was taken from the ledger of Jefferson Industries, Inc.:

Direct labor	$ 85,000	Administrative expenses	$59,000
Selling expenses	34,000	Work in process	
Sales	300,000	Jan. 1	29,000
Finished goods		Dec. 31	21,000
Jan. 1	115,000	Direct material purchases	88,000
Dec. 31	131,000	Depreciation: factory	18,000
Raw (direct) materials		Indirect materials used	10,000
on hand		Indirect labor	24,000
Jan. 1	31,000	Factory taxes	8,000
Dec. 31	40,000	Factory utilities	11,000

Prepare the following:

a A schedule of cost of goods manufactured for the year ended December 31.

b An income statement for the year ended December 31.

E21-8 *Basic cost behavior patterns* (L.O. 7)

Indianapolis Precision manufactures selected parts for jet skis. The accounting records revealed the following behavior for two component costs of factory overhead in May and August when production totaled 10,000 units and 12,500 units, respectively:

Cost A: $22,500   Cost B: $3.20 per unit

On the basis of this information, determine:

a The fixed cost per unit in May and August.

b The variable cost per unit in May and August.

c The total cost of A and B incurred during August.

d The total expected cost for A and B of producing 11,600 units, assuming that present cost behavior patterns continue.

E21-9 *Understanding cost behavior* (L.O. 7)

The planning department of Herzog Company has prepared budgets for three probable levels of operation for the upcoming year. Because of their significance, the following costs have been selected for study:

| | Level of Activity (Units) | | | | | |
| | 10,000 | | 12,000 | | 15,000 | |
	Total	Per Unit	Total	Per Unit	Total	Per Unit
Direct materials	$ 90,000	$ 9.00	$108,000	$ 9.00	$135,000	$ 9.00
Direct labor	120,000	12.00	144,000	12.00	180,000	12.00
Advertising	300,000	30.00	300,000	25.00	300,000	20.00
Management salaries	180,000	18.00	180,000	15.00	180,000	12.00
	$690,000	$69.00	$732,000	$61.00	$795,000	$53.00

Addressing his executive staff, Herzog's president commented: "It's imperative that we implement cost-cutting programs to reduce advertising and management salaries. As shown by the per-unit costs, these variable expenditures are destroying our profit margins. Our fixed outlays of direct materials and direct labor (constant at $9.00 and $12.00 per unit, respectively) also need some improvement. I know our competitors are paying approximately $19.25 for these same two production factors."

Comment on the president's remarks.

E21-10 *Variable and fixed cost calculations* (L.O. 7)

Frontier Industries began operations on January 1 of the current year to produce a single product. Sales far exceeded expectations, with the firm disposing of all 50,000 units manufactured. The following unit costs were incurred:

Direct material	$36
Direct labor	14
Variable factory overhead	6
Fixed factory overhead	20
Variable selling costs	4
Fixed selling costs	8

Management expects to produce and sell 58,000 units and 54,000 units, respectively, in the upcoming accounting period.

Compute the company's total expected production and selling costs. Assume that unit variable costs and total fixed costs are unchanged from the previous period.

Series A

PROBLEMS

P21-A1 *Cost classification* (L.O. 4, 5, 7)

E. Turner & Sons manufactures barbecue grills. For each of the following costs, determine cost behavior (variable or fixed) and whether the cost is a product or a period cost. If a product cost, identify the cost as direct materials (DM), direct labor (DL), or factory overhead (FOH). Item (a) is presented as an example.

Cost	Variable/Fixed	Product/Period	DM/DL/FOH
a Property taxes on the factory	Fixed	Product	FOH
b Salary of the production supervisor			
c Freight costs on shipments to out-of-state customers			
d Wages of assembly personnel			
e Grill tops and frames			
f Straight-line depreciation on factory equipment			
g Paint used to touch up production scratches			
h Customer rebate offered on grill no. 301			
i Heating costs for manufacturing facilities			
j Wheels attached to portable models			
k Fees paid for plant security			
l Advertising costs for new product line			

P21-A2 *Straightforward manufacturing statements* (L.O. 6)

The following information was extracted from the accounting records of Olympic Company for the year just ended:

Sales	$628,000
Work in process, Jan. 1	56,700
Advertising expense	23,500
Direct material purchases	231,500
Finished goods, Dec. 31	67,800
Indirect materials used	12,300
Direct labor	85,600
Direct materials, Jan. 1	45,500
Finished goods, Jan. 1	55,900
Direct materials, Dec. 31	38,200
Sales staff salaries	33,300
Work in process, Dec. 31	47,400
Indirect labor	50,700

Utilities, taxes, insurance, and depreciation are incurred jointly by Olympic's manufacturing, sales, and administrative facilities. The costs were as follows:

Utilities	$40,000
Taxes	25,000
Insurance	10,000
Depreciation	36,000

The first three costs are allocated proportionately on the basis of square feet occupied by the three functional areas. A review of the company's facilities revealed the following percentages would be appropriate: manufacturing, 50%; sales, 30%; and administrative, 20%. Depreciation is allocated 70%, 20%, and 10%, respectively.

Instructions

a Prepare a schedule of cost of goods manufactured in good form.
b Prepare an income statement in good form.

P21-A3 *Manufacturing accounting computations* (L.O. 6)

1-2-3

The following information was obtained from the records of Metropolitan Corporation for the current year ended December 31:

Direct materials
Beginning inventory	500 units @ $6.20
Purchase no. 1	1,100 units @ $6.20
Purchase no. 2	1,400 units @ $6.20

Payroll costs
Direct labor	$40,500
Indirect labor	18,600
Administrative salaries	83,600
Sales salaries	38,200

Other costs
Building depreciation (70% of the building is devoted to production activities, with the remainder split equally between sales and administration)	$30,000
Other factory costs	5,900
Other selling expenses	16,100
Other administrative expenses	18,800

Metropolitan's beginning work in process inventory totaled $10,500; the ending work in process was $6,000. During the accounting period, the finished goods inventory rose from 300 units (cost: $21,250) to 1,000 units (cost: $68,700). The company produced 1,500 completed units, sold 800 completed units at $280 each, and consumed 2,000 units of direct materials.

Instructions

a Calculate the cost of direct materials used during the accounting period.
b Compute Metropolitan's cost of goods manufactured.
c Compute the company's cost of goods sold.
d Determine net income for the year just ended.

P21-A4 Estimate of ending inventories (L.O. 4, 6)
On May 23, the Oklahoma branch of Freeport Chemicals suffered extensive damage from a tornado. The building that housed the raw material and work in process inventories was totally destroyed. Management has gathered the following information in an attempt to estimate the company's loss:

Direct labor averages 40% of conversion cost.
Gross profit averages 30% of sales.
Total manufacturing costs (direct materials used, direct labor, and factory overhead) through May 23 amounted to $726,000. Operating expenses were $187,000.
Sales generated, direct material purchased, and factory overhead incurred through May 23 totaled $1,200,000, $233,000, and $300,000, respectively.

Inventory data are:

	January 1	May 23
Raw materials	$142,000	$?
Work in process	310,000	?
Finished goods	408,000	370,000

Instructions

Estimate the raw materials and work in process inventories destroyed. *Hint:* Prepare a detailed schedule of cost of goods manufactured and an income statement for the period ended May 23.

P21-A5 Manufacturing statements and cost behavior (L.O. 6, 7)
Tampa Foundry began operations during the current year, manufacturing various products for industrial use. One such product is light-gauge aluminum, which the company sells for $36 per roll. Cost information for the year just ended follows.

	Variable Cost Per Unit	Fixed Cost
Direct materials	$4.50	$ —
Direct labor	6.50	—
Factory overhead	9.00	50,000
Selling	—	70,000
Administrative	—	135,000

Production and sales totaled 20,000 rolls and 17,000 rolls, respectively. There is no work in process. Tampa carries its finished goods inventory at the average unit cost of production.

Instructions

a Determine the cost of the finished goods inventory of light-gauge aluminum.

b Prepare an income statement for the current year ended December 31.

c On the basis of the information presented:
  (1) Does it appear that the company pays commissions to its sales staff? Explain.
  (2) What is the likely effect on the $4.50 unit cost of direct materials if next year's production increases? Why?

Series B

P21-B1 *Cost classification* (L.O. 4, 5, 7)

The Robin Hill Company manufactures corrugated cardboard boxes for industrial use. For each of the following costs, determine cost behavior (variable or fixed) and whether the cost is a product or a period cost. If a product cost, identify the cost as direct materials (DM), direct labor (DL), or factory overhead (FOH). Item (a) is presented as an example.

Cost	Variable/Fixed	Product/Period	DM/DL/FOH
a Fire insurance on the factory	Fixed	Product	FOH
b Rolls of paper used in production			
c Ink consumed in printing operations			
d Salary of the sales manager			
e Wages paid to folding machine operators			
f Auditor's fees			
g Monthly salaries of inspection personnel			
h Units-of-output depreciation on cutting machine			
i Air-conditioning costs of executive offices			
j Machine lubricant			
k Machine repair costs			
l Freight-out			

P21-B2 *Straightforward manufacturing statements* (L.O. 6)

The information that follows pertains to Hampton Manufacturing for the year ended December 31:

Direct material purchases	$ 297,000
Sales commissions	80,000
Direct labor	270,000
Indirect labor	162,000
Sales	1,050,000

Advertising expense	25,000
Indirect materials used	35,000
Insurance	20,000
Utilities	90,000
Taxes	30,000
Depreciation	50,000

Insurance, utilities, taxes, and depreciation are incurred by the company as a whole and must be allocated proportionately among manufacturing, selling, and administrative activities. The proper allocations are:

	Manufacturing	Selling	Administrative
Insurance, utilities, and taxes	60%	30%	10%
Depreciation	80	10	10

Inventory data follow.

	January 1	December 31
Raw materials	$ 35,000	$ 40,000
Work in process	115,000	160,000
Finished goods	421,000	400,000

Instructions

a Prepare a schedule of cost of goods manufactured in good form.
b Prepare an income statement in good form.

P21-B3 *Manufacturing accounting computations* (L.O. 6)

1-2-3

The following information was obtained from the records of Post Corporation for the current year ended December 31:

Direct materials
Beginning inventory	1,600 units @ $8.30
Purchase no. 1	2,300 units @ $8.30
Purchase no. 2	1,000 units @ $8.30

Payroll costs
Direct labor	$59,700
Indirect labor	30,000
Administrative salaries	24,600
Sales salaries	29,500

Other costs
Building depreciation (80% of the building is devoted to production activities, with the remainder split equally between sales and administration)	$35,000
Other factory costs	22,700
Other selling expenses	9,100
Other administrative expenses	15,800

Post's beginning work in process inventory totaled $8,900; the ending work in process was $10,100. During the accounting period, the finished goods inventory declined from 2,100 units (cost: $206,400) to 1,650 units (cost: $178,800). The company produced 750 completed units, sold 1,200 completed units at $320 each, and consumed 3,500 units of direct materials.

Instructions

a Calculate the cost of the ending direct materials inventory.
b Compute Post's cost of goods manufactured.
c Compute the company's cost of goods sold.
d Determine net income for the year just ended.

P21-B4 *Estimate of ending inventories* (L.O. 4, 6)

Midway Products, a manufacturer of painting equipment, suffered extensive damage at its main manufacturing plant on March 31 as a result of a fire. Fortunately, all raw materials inventories were stored in an adjacent warehouse. The following information has been gathered in an attempt to estimate the cost of the work in process and finished goods inventories destroyed:

Goods available for sale on Mar. 31	$220,000
Direct labor	70,000
Sales through Mar. 31	280,000
Work in process, Jan. 1	13,000
Finished goods, Jan. 1	29,000
Net income through Mar. 31	25,000

The company's accounting staff indicated that sales are usually made at a gross profit rate of 40%. Furthermore, the cost of direct materials consumed averages 30% of prime cost, and factory overhead amounts to 50% of total manufacturing costs incurred. Midway expects full reimbursement from its insurance company for any losses suffered.

Instructions

Estimate the work in process and finished goods inventories destroyed. *Hint:* Prepare a detailed schedule of cost of goods manufactured and an income statement for the quarter ended March 31.

P21-B5 *Manufacturing statements and cost behavior* (L.O. 6, 7)

The Willow Creek Company, a manufacturer of specialized calculators, began operations on January 1 of the current year. Each calculator requires the following variable costs:

Direct materials	$12
Direct labor	5
Variable factory overhead	14
	$31

The fixed costs incurred during the year are shown below.

Factory overhead	$ 80,000
Selling	40,000
Administrative	120,000
	$240,000

Production totaled 40,000 calculators, of which 38,000 were sold at $40 each. Assume no work in process. Willow Creek carries its finished goods inventory at the average unit cost of production.

Instructions

a Determine the cost of Willow Creek's ending finished goods inventory.

b Prepare Willow Creek's income statement for the current year ended December 31.

c Suppose Willow Creek reduced production to meet decreased demand. If the present cost behavior patterns continue, determine the effect of the new production policy on the manufactured cost per calculator. Explain the reasoning behind your answer.

BEYOND THE BASICS

BB21-1 *Analysis of product cost error* (L.O. 5, 6)

Mansfield, Inc., began to manufacture a new product in January 19X1. The following costs were incurred in the production of 15,000 units:

Direct materials	$ 51,000
Direct labor	90,000
Factory overhead	31,500
	$172,500

Demand was below expectations, and by the end of 19X1 production was stopped. Mansfield sold 11,000 units in 19X1 and 3,000 units in 19X2. The firm's accountant recently discovered that Sales Salaries Expense was accidentally debited in 19X1 for $19,500 of wages paid to assembly-line workers.

Instructions

Assuming no work in process at the end of 19X1, determine the impact and amount of the error on the following:

a 19X1 ending finished goods inventory and net income.

b 19X2 ending finished goods inventory and net income.

BB21-2 *Overview of chapter concepts: Multiple choice* (L.O. 1–7)

The following multiple-choice questions relate to various topics discussed in the chapter. Select the best answer.

1 Which of the following statements about cost/managerial accounting is correct?

a Managerial accounting principles (MAP) are defined in rulings issued by the MAP Board.

b Planning, control, and decision making are facilitated by the generation of managerial accounting information.

c "Managerial accounting" and "cost accounting" are terms that describe the same accounting function.

d In some selected cases, factory overhead is *not* treated as a manufacturing cost.

2 Which of the following costs is not a component of factory overhead?

a Indirect labor.

b Factory equipment.

c Maintenance costs of folding machines.

d Air-conditioning costs of the machine shop.

3 Which cost is considered to be both a prime cost and a conversion cost?

a Direct material.

b Direct labor.

c Factory overhead.

d Sales commissions.

4 Jorgenson Manufacturing began operations in 19X4. The company's 19X4 depreciation charge is properly allocated as follows:

Sales activities	25%
Administrative activities	35%
Manufacturing activities	40%

Of the total inventory produced, only 75% was sold during the year. What percentage of the depreciation charge would appear on the 19X4 income statement?

a 60%.

b 90%.

c 100%.

d Some other amount.

5 Consider the following information:

Cost of goods manufactured	$150,000
Direct material purchases	70,000
Factory overhead	20,000
Beginning work in process	60,000
Ending work in process	30,000
Ending direct materials	20,000
Ending finished goods	120,000
Net income	30,000
Sales	200,000
Direct materials used	60,000
Cost of goods sold	110,000

Total manufacturing costs incurred during the period were:

a $20,000.

b $60,000.

c $120,000.

d $180,000.

6 The 19X5 work in process inventories of Parkhurst, Inc., totaled $20,000 on January 1 and $15,000 on December 31. If total manufacturing cost was 90% of cost of goods sold, how much was cost of goods sold?

a Cannot be determined from the information presented.

b 110% of total manufacturing cost.

c ($20,000 − $15,000) ÷ 0.90.

d ($20,000 − $15,000) + 110% of total manufacturing cost.

7 Machine lubricant used on processing equipment in a manufacturing plant would be classified as a:

a variable, period cost.

b fixed, period cost.

c variable, product cost.

d fixed, product cost.

8 A newly hired accountant made four observations about costs:

The fixed cost per unit is constant at all activity levels.

The variable cost per unit is constant at all activity levels.

Variable costs are always product costs.

Fixed costs are virtually always paid uniformly throughout an accounting period.

Which of the following statements is true?

a Only one of the accountant's observations is correct.

b Two of the observations are false.

c Three of the observations are true.

d The observations are either all true or all false.

CAI21-1 *The executive summary* (L.O. 3)

Communication Principle: Daily business activities require that managers absorb large amounts of information quickly, often without the benefit of significant study time. Detailed written reports, prepared by key staff members, are an important element of this process. Such reports customarily include an executive summary (or cover letter) that:

- Identifies the critical issues requiring attention.
- Highlights potential solutions and their possible outcomes (and shortcomings).
- Includes a recommendation, if appropriate.
- Concludes by noting that staff members are waiting for a decision and specifies any deadlines that must be met.

The executive summary should always be brief and to the point and should be consistent with the content of the accompanying report. The summary's writer must assume that the executive lacks the time for an in-depth study of the key issues despite being held accountable for the eventual results.

■ ■ ■ ■ ■ ■ ■ ■

Zeos Machine Tools, Inc., is a large manufacturer located in Indianapolis. The company's profit has been deteriorating over the years because of inefficient facilities, antiquated production policies, and increased pressures from foreign competition. Joe Baker, an assistant to the manufacturing vice-president, has completed a detailed study that proposes several major changes for Zeos. These changes include the installation of a computer integrated manufacturing (CIM) system, just-in-time (JIT) production techniques, and the calculation and monitoring of quality costs.

Joe believes that once authorization is received, the first phase of CIM and JIT could be fully operational in 18 months at a cost of $5.8 million. In contrast, quality reports could be produced in 6 months, after necessary computer programs are developed. Related costs and data-gathering procedures are expected to total $85,000. Combined, these improvements will lead to overall, nonquantifiable increases in long-term profitability.

Instructions

Assume the role of Joe Baker and write the report's executive summary.

Answers to Chapter Quiz

1 c

2 b

3 d

4 a

5 c

CHAPTER 22

Job Order Costing Systems

As shown in the previous chapter, cost accounting generates information that both meets the needs of management and satisfies external-reporting requirements. Specifically, cost information assists in planning, control, and decision making while, at the same time, providing a basis for inventory valuation and income measurement. In order to accomplish these tasks, an organization must be able to calculate (i.e., accumulate) the cost of its goods, services, and activities. This chapter introduces the topic of cost accumulation by focusing on job order costing systems, which are used by both manufacturing and service businesses.

COST DETERMINATION

OBJECTIVE

Explain the problems encountered in computing the actual cost of a product or service.

The determination of the "actual" cost of a good or service is extremely difficult. Several topics presented in earlier chapters of the text attest to this fact. In the area of inventory, for example, many people feel that the specific identification method is the most precise method of inventory costing. Recall that under specific identification the cost of the units is attached to the units themselves, leaving little doubt regarding the cost of goods on hand, used, or sold. Nevertheless, relatively few businesses use this costing method because of the many practical problems it presents. Instead, most firms turn to a cost flow *assumption* such as LIFO, FIFO, or weighted average. Although these assumptions are acceptable accounting alternatives, the inability to determine actual cost introduces imprecision into the costing process.

Further complicating matters, many costs are not easily traced to the finished product. As we noted in Chapter 21, factory overhead possesses this characteristic. Factory depreciation, utilities, plant security, and other comparable production costs are incurred by manufacturing activities as a whole, and identification with specific goods is very troublesome.

A similar tracing problem exists in many divisionalized organizations, where a given cost benefits several segments of activity. Picture Sears, Roebuck and Co., which owns and operates the following subsidiaries:

Subsidiary	Area of Identity
Allstate Insurance	Insurance
Dean Witter	Financial services
Coldwell Banker	Real estate
Discover Credit Corp.	Credit cards

The president and others in the high-level corporate staff of Sears make decisions and handle operating matters that serve the entity as a whole. Significant difficulties arise, however, when attempting to trace the cost of broad corporate activities back to smaller segments, such as a new insurance program from Allstate or a real-estate promotion from Coldwell Banker. The program and promotion have probably benefited from the actions of top management and should therefore absorb a portion of corporate cost. Yet, determining the proper cost that should be charged is a guess, at best.

Because a clear relationship between inputs (costs) and outputs (products and activities) is often lacking, cost determination frequently relies on estimates. Estimates, of course, are subjective and arbitrary. In sum, although the material presented in the following pages may appear very precise, realize that the calculation of the actual cost of a process, good, or service on a timely basis is a near impossibility.

Several different types of systems are available to an entity to accumulate costs. We now turn our attention to job order costing. Another popular system, process cost accounting, is discussed in Chapter 23.

With a **job order system,** costs are gathered by job or order. Such systems are commonly used when cost accumulation by job is a fairly easy task, a situation that often arises when goods are made (1) upon the receipt of a customer order, (2) according to customer specifications, or (3) in separate batches. Custom-home builders, for example, frequently employ job systems because of the ease in tracing costs to specific building sites. Similarly, print shops use job systems to cost individual customer orders.

The costs of each job are accumulated on a separate **job cost sheet** (see Exhibit 22-1). Direct materials used and direct labor are identified with and charged to the specific job on which they were incurred. Since factory overhead is not easily traced to a manufactured product, individual jobs are charged with an estimated overhead cost.

The operation of a job cost system follows the flow of costs illustrated in Chapter 21. The three cost elements of direct materials, direct labor, and

JOB ORDER SYSTEMS

OBJECTIVE

2

Explain the nature and use of a job order costing system.

JOB COST SHEET

Manufactured for:

Stock _____

Customer _____

Job No. _____

Date:

Needed _____

Started _____

Completed _____

Product _____

No. of Units _____

Direct Materials			Direct Labor				Factory Overhead	
Date	Requisition No.	Amount	Date	Ticket No.	Hours	Amount	Date	Amount

Overhead Rate: _____

COST SUMMARY

Direct materials $ _____

Direct labor   _____

Factory overhead   _____

Total cost $ _____

EXHIBIT 22-1
Job Cost Sheet

factory overhead are combined and put "in process" to manufacture products. Eventually, the work in process is completed. The completed goods that are sold are reported as cost of goods sold on the income statement; the unsold units are carried in the Finished Goods inventory account on the balance sheet. This process is shown in the top half of Exhibit 22-2.

Perpetual Inventories

To handle the necessary record keeping, a manufacturing firm establishes various accounts and procedures that parallel the general cost flow (see the

EXHIBIT 22-2
Manufacturing Cost Flows

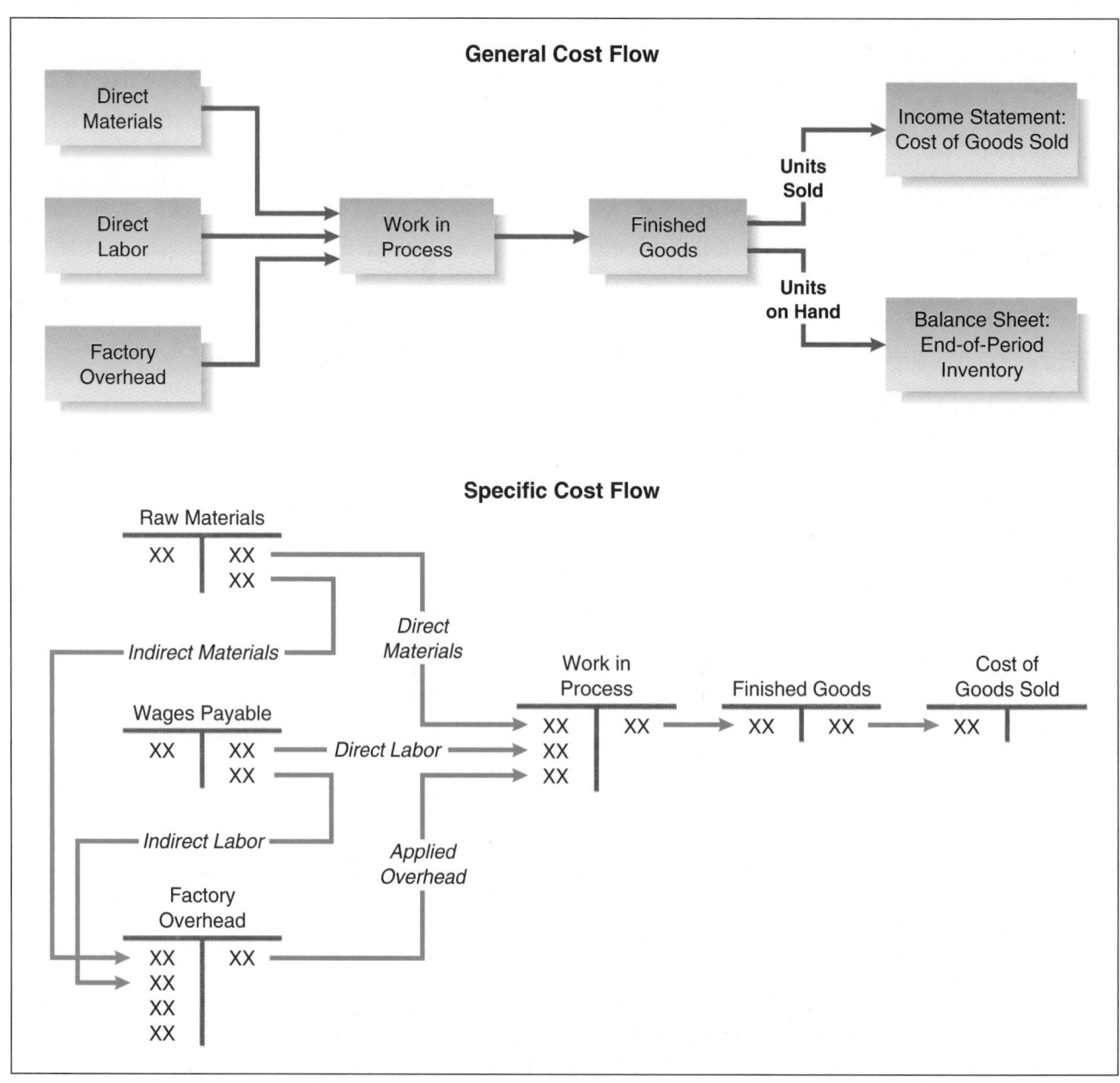

specific cost flow in the bottom half of Exhibit 22-2). Many manufacturers use perpetual inventory systems in which the Raw Materials, Work in Process, and Finished Goods accounts are continually updated during the period to reflect increases and decreases. Especially popular with companies that have computerized their accounting records, perpetual systems improve managerial control and allow for more timely reporting of operating results and financial position. To illustrate use of a perpetual inventory system in conjunction with job order costing, we will explore the August transactions of Valley Manufacturing Corporation.

Accounting for Materials

As noted in the previous chapter, the costs of direct and indirect materials owned may be housed together in a single Raw Materials inventory account. We will assume that this procedure is followed by Valley Manufacturing and all companies in our end-of-chapter exercises and problems. The following entry was therefore made when Valley purchased $80,000 of materials and factory supplies (i.e., indirect materials) on account:

Raw Materials	80,000	
Accounts Payable		80,000
Purchased direct materials and factory supplies		

Materials are kept in a storeroom or warehouse and issued upon receipt of a **materials requisition.** As shown in Exhibit 22-3, $4,000 of materials have been issued for use on job no. 864, and the requisition has been posted to the related cost sheet. These materials are *direct materials* because they can be identified with a given job. The entry to record the issuance is shown below.

Work in Process	4,000	
Raw Materials		4,000
Issued direct materials for job no. 864		

Indirect materials (e.g., sandpaper, lubricants, and so on) are not easily (or economically) traced to individual jobs; thus, no attempt is made to charge specific cost sheets. Instead, indirect materials consumed are treated as part of factory overhead. During August, Valley used $2,800 of miscellaneous factory supplies in manufacturing operations. The following entry is needed:

Factory Overhead	2,800	
Raw Materials		2,800
Issued indirect materials		

The Factory Overhead account is debited to record *actual* overhead charges. The manner in which each job is charged with an *estimated (applied)* share of overhead will be illustrated shortly.

Accounting for Labor

The accounting treatment for labor is very similar to that of materials. Factory labor costs are classified as either direct or indirect. Recall that direct labor, like direct materials, is easily identified with given jobs. Indi-

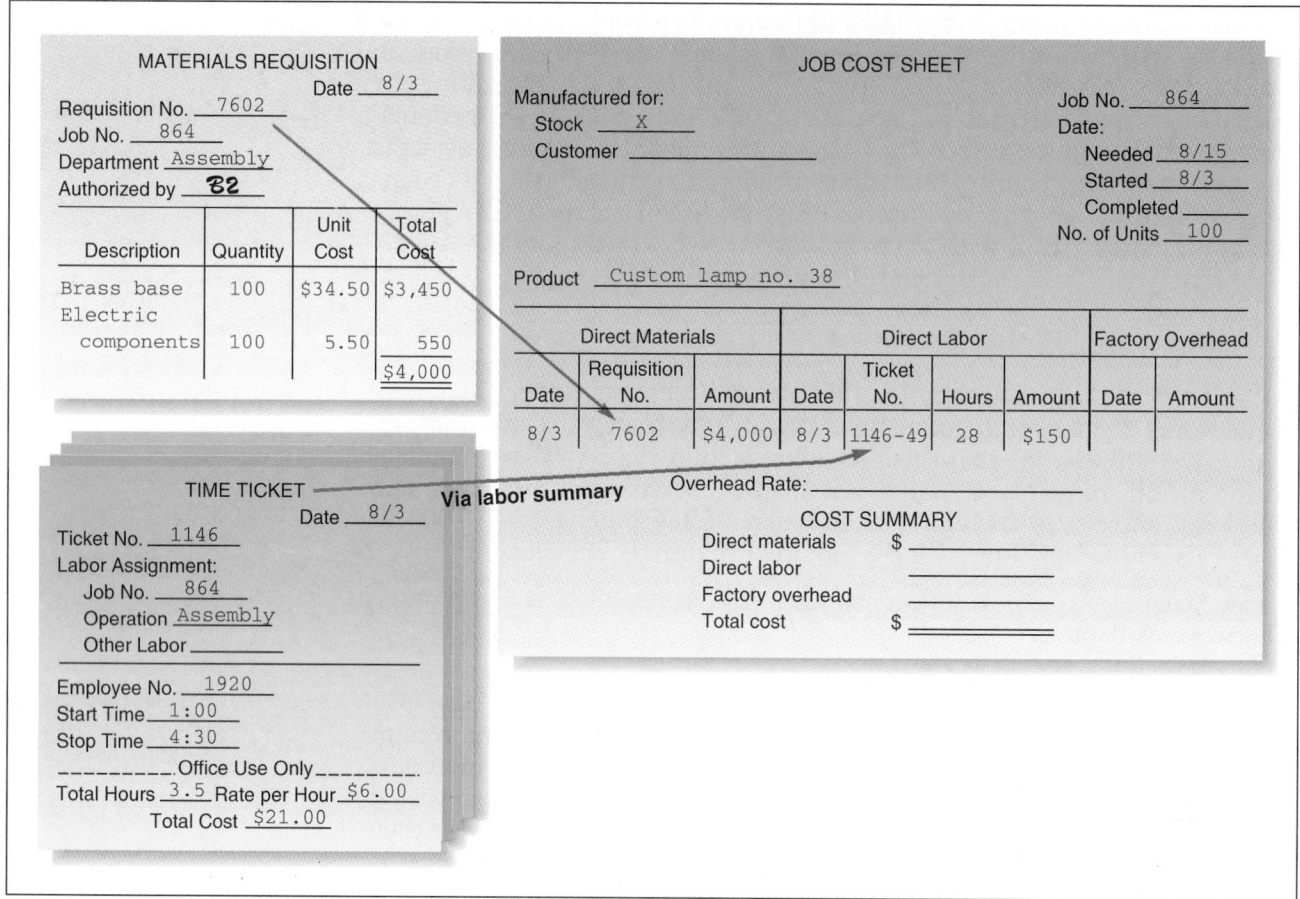

EXHIBIT 22-3
Document Interrelationships in a Job Order System

rect labor, on the other hand, is not and is considered part of factory overhead.

Labor costs are accumulated by means of time tickets and labor summaries. Each day, each factory employee completes a **time ticket.** As shown in Exhibit 22-3, the time ticket gathers daily labor information and shows the specific job to which the employee was assigned. If the employee was not working on a job, the type of indirect labor activity performed would be noted as "Other Labor." At the end of the day the time tickets are collected, sorted, and summarized in the form of a *labor summary*, which shows the total direct and indirect labor costs incurred. Direct labor costs are subdivided by job and then posted to job cost sheets.

The proper entry to record the direct labor on job no. 864 and the incurrence of $200 of indirect labor follows.[1]

Work in Process	150	
Factory Overhead	200	
Wages Payable		350
To record direct and indirect labor		

---

[1] We are ignoring employee withholdings in this example.

Like the cost of direct materials, direct labor is charged to Work in Process to accumulate the cost of jobs in production. When the employees are paid, Wages Payable will be debited and Cash will be credited.

Accounting for Overhead

Up to this point the computation of job cost has not been difficult, primarily because direct materials and direct labor could easily be traced to individual jobs. We now turn our attention to the third and most complicated element of product cost: factory overhead.

Because of tracing and record-keeping problems, jobs are charged with an estimated (as opposed to actual) overhead cost. The use of estimated overhead charges is not only practical but also has two side benefits. First, total job cost can be figured at the time of job completion. Timely cost information is beneficial in setting prices for customers and in other routine operating decisions that are made by management.

Second, estimated overhead charges tend to smooth product costs over a period of time. Actual costs change each month, and in addition, volume fluctuates. The cost of production is therefore dependent on when manufacturing takes place. As an example, picture the highly seasonal business of a soft drink manufacturer. Suppose the company's *fixed* production costs each month are relatively stable. In light of this situation, when volume peaks in the hot summer months, the actual manufacturing cost per bottle will decrease. This decrease results from spreading constant dollar amounts over increased activity levels. In winter when production is lower, the cost per bottle will rise. Thus, in an effort to avoid fluctuating overhead charges, estimated rates are set and implemented for a certain period of time, often one year. This practice removes the cost "penalties" and "bonuses" of producing in December and July, respectively, because inventory is costed at the same amount no matter when manufacturing occurs.

Overhead Application Rates. The estimated overhead cost of a job or product is determined by using an **overhead application rate.** The application rate relates overhead to a specific application base and is computed as follows:

$$\frac{\text{Estimated Factory Overhead}}{\text{Estimated Application Base}} = \text{Overhead Application Rate}$$

To explain, product costs must be calculated as accurately as possible. Therefore at the beginning of a reporting period, the accountant performs an in-depth study of factory overhead. The accountant is interested in learning how overhead behaves in relation to changes in various factors of production (e.g., direct labor hours, direct labor cost, or machine hours). If a strong correlation exists between factory overhead and, say, direct labor cost, overhead on a given job is best determined by selecting direct labor as the application base. In a heavily automated situation where much of the overhead is caused by the operation of machines, machine hours may be more appropriate.

OBJECTIVE

3

Compute an overhead application rate and apply overhead to production.

In general, we select an application base that (1) is inexpensive to compute, (2) is easily traced to the job or product, and (3) has a strong cause and effect relationship with overhead. The last guideline means that the base should have a significant influence on the amount of overhead incurred, thereby helping to improve the accuracy of the costing process.

Use of the Overhead Application Rate. Once the application base is chosen, the overhead rate can be developed and used in product costing. The amount of overhead charged to an individual job is determined by multiplying the application rate by the amount of application base associated with that job. This process is best understood by using a numerical example.

Assume that Valley Manufacturing has chosen direct labor hours as an application base because of the company's heavy emphasis on manual assembly work. After a review of operations, Valley's accountant anticipates 40,000 direct labor hours of activity for the year. In addition, the following factory overhead estimates have been derived:

Indirect materials used	$ 20,000
Indirect labor	140,000
Utilities	15,000
Taxes	30,000
Insurance	10,000
Building depreciation	40,000
Equipment depreciation	25,000
Total estimated overhead	$280,000

The firm's overhead application rate of $7 per direct labor hour is computed as follows:

$$\frac{\text{Estimated Factory Overhead}}{\text{Estimated Application Base}} = \text{Overhead Application Rate}$$

$$\frac{\$280,000}{40,000 \text{ direct labor hours}} = \$7 \text{ per direct labor hour}$$

The $7 rate can now be applied to individual jobs to determine the estimated overhead cost. Examine Exhibit 22-4, which contains the completed cost sheet for job no. 864. Compare this exhibit with Exhibit 22-3, and notice that additional material costs (requisition no. 7638) and additional labor costs (tickets no. 1187–89 and no. 2010–11) have been incurred. On the basis of 58 total direct labor hours, Valley has applied or determined an overhead cost of $406 (58 hours × $7).[2] The proper entry to record the applied overhead is:

Work in Process	406	
Factory Overhead		406
To record applied overhead		

---

[2] If desired, overhead could be applied daily as the number of direct labor hours becomes known. If a job is not completed by the end of the accounting period, overhead should be applied on the basis of the work performed to date to properly value the production in process.

EXHIBIT 22-4
Completed Job Cost Sheet

JOB COST SHEET

Manufactured for: Job No. _____864_____

Stock ____X____   Date:

Customer _____   Needed ___8/15___

                              Started ___8/3___

                              Completed ___8/5___

Product ___Custom lamp no. 38___   No. of Units ___100___

Direct Materials			Direct Labor				Factory Overhead	
Date	Requisition No.	Amount	Date	Ticket No.	Hours	Amount	Date	Amount
8/3	7602	$4,000	8/3	1146-49	28	$150	8/5	$406
8/5	7638	1,050	8/4	1187-89	20	120		
		$5,050	8/5	2010-11	10	54		
					58	$324		

Overhead Rate: ___$7 per direct labor hour___

COST SUMMARY

Direct materials	$	5,050
Direct labor		324
Factory overhead		406
Total cost	$	5,780

The Work in Process account is debited to add factory overhead to the other two costs of production: direct materials used and direct labor. As a result of the preceding entry, Work in Process now contains all the costs that pertain to job no. 864. The credit to the Factory Overhead account takes an estimated portion of Valley's total overhead and applies it to specific jobs—a process that will become clearer after the next two sections.

Tips & Techniques

Students sometimes reverse the computation of the application rate, dividing the estimated application base by estimated factory overhead. An easy way to remember the proper calculation is to picture the definition of the word "base," namely, the lowest layer or foundation. Translating, the *bottom* number in the formula serves as the *basis* on which a company desires to apply overhead to production.

HIGHLIGHT
Cost Accounting At Its Finest: The $7 Aspirin

In an Ann Landers column not too long ago, a former patient of a California hospital complained about being charged $7 for a single aspirin tablet that he received during his stay. Rather than write an angry commentary on the rising cost of American medical care, Landers offered a logical argument justifying the $7 aspirin. (She received her information from a highly respected insurance company executive.)

According to the executive, the price of the aspirin included several elements that together made up the cost of the tablet:

- The prescribing physician's time. All medications in a hospital must be controlled and prescribed by physicians.
- The dispensing pharmacist's time. This involves interpreting the prescription, accessing the product, and dispensing the aspirin tablets, usually into a tiny paper cup. The cup is also a cost.
- The administering nurse's time in ensuring that the patient takes the prescribed aspirin.
- The medical records department's efforts in keeping records, indicating that medication was prescribed, dispensed, and administered.
- A surcharge for the hospital's unreimbursed Medicare patients. Because Medicare pays only a stipulated percentage of what is charged to the patient, the hospital passes along any unreimbursed costs (and most likely the profit element, too) to other areas of patient care, such as the aspirin tablet.

Although Landers's column did not mention them, one could logically argue that the following costs are shifted to the tablet as well: the cost of care provided to impoverished patients who have no insurance and cannot pay for medical treatment; uncollectible accounts receivable; the cost of mal-practice insurance; the cost of new high-tech equipment; and hospital administrative and operating costs. If that's not enough, the hospital will add on an amount for profit—it can't sell its products at cost.

The end result of all these additions? The aspirin, which may have cost the hospital as little as $0.006 each from a supplier, now goes for $7. As one professional observes, the $7 aspirin tablet is the single most significant item in the medical profession. It has more cost elements than any other product, more hidden labor charges, more overhead and administration, and one of the highest gross margins per unit of any medical product or service sold.

Trivial? Not really. Consider that patients spend more than 240 million days in hospitals every year. Based on the fact that 5% of all aspirin production is sold to institutions, the average patient winds up consuming 4.785 aspirin each day during his or her stay. The end result adds $33.50 a day to the bill, or a total of $8.04 billion to the cost of hospital care in the United States each year. This is nothing to sneeze at. You say your local hospital charges only $4 per dose? You're lucky, but that still adds almost $2.3 billion in medical costs, or about 1% of the annual tab.

The moral of the story? Cost accounting is a tool that can be adapted to figure the cost of most anything—including the acquisition and dispensing of the seemingly gold-plated aspirin tablet. Whether the cost-shifting practices described in the preceding paragraphs are "correct" is a matter of debate. Shifting the cost of a hospital employee's lunch break or a patient's personal bankruptcy to the tablet may be going a bit too far. If such practices continue in medical care and elsewhere, they will make the $600 toilet seat purchased by the federal government a few years back seem like a real bargain.

Source: Adapted from "The Legacy of the $7 Aspirin," *Management Accounting*, April 1990, pp. 38–41.

Actual Overhead. The Factory Overhead account is used to accumulate both actual and applied overhead. As was shown earlier, for example, Factory Overhead is debited to record indirect materials used and indirect labor. Other actual overhead items are recorded in this account as well. To illustrate, assume that Valley Manufacturing experienced the following factory costs during August:

Utilities	$ 1,300
Taxes	2,500
Insurance	900
Building depreciation	3,500
Equipment depreciation	2,200
Total	$10,400

Further assume that payments for utilities and taxes are not due until September and that the insurance figure represents the expiration of a prepaid policy. Valley's required journal entry to record these overhead costs is:

Factory Overhead	10,400	
Accounts Payable		1,300
Taxes Payable		2,500
Prepaid Insurance		900
Accumulated Depreciation: Building		3,500
Accumulated Depreciation: Equipment		2,200
To record actual overhead costs		

The entry's credits should be familiar: they are identical to those shown in the first part of the text. The expiration of a prepaid expense calls for a reduction in an asset account; recording depreciation generates a credit to Accumulated Depreciation; and so forth. The debit, however, is different. In earlier chapters all these costs were charged to expense accounts. Now, no expenses are involved and the costs are debited to Factory Overhead. Why? The change in procedure is caused by a change in business purpose. These costs are not expenses for a manufacturing entity; rather they are product costs, which must be attached to the units produced. This attachment takes place through the application of factory overhead discussed earlier.

Only *factory* costs are recorded in the overhead account. Selling and administrative costs such as advertising, managerial salaries, and sales commissions continue to be written off as expenses. Remember, these costs are period costs and, as such, never inventoried.

Applied Overhead. The accumulation of actual overhead throughout the period and the application of overhead to jobs force the Factory Overhead account to assume the following status:

Factory Overhead			
Actual overhead \	XXX	XXX	Overhead is
costs are recorded \	XXX	XXX	applied to
by debits as /	XXX	XXX	jobs during the
incurred /			period via credits

It should now be apparent that the application process simply takes a "chunk" of overhead and attaches it to production. By the end of the reporting period, if all goes according to plan, overhead applied will equal total overhead incurred. This situation rarely occurs, however, and a later section of the chapter will show the proper accounting treatment for such cases.

Accounting for the Completion and Sale of Manufactured Products

By viewing Exhibit 22-5, you can see the interrelationships among the journal entries illustrated in the preceding sections, the job cost sheet, and Valley's Work in Process account. In practice, separate entries would be made on August 3, 4, and 5 to record the individual transactions.

Upon completion, jobs are transferred to the finished goods warehouse to await sale. Paralleling this physical transfer, Valley would record the following entry to recognize the completion of production:

Finished Goods   5,780
   Work in Process   5,780
Completed job no. 864

Eventually, the finished goods inventory will be sold. Suppose, for example, that 25 of the 100 lamps manufactured on job no. 864 are sold on account at $80 apiece. From information found on the job cost sheet, the cost per lamp is $57.80 ($5,780 ÷ 100 lamps). Thus, two entries are needed:

EXHIBIT 22-5
Interrelationships Among Manufacturing Journal Entries, the Job Cost Sheet, and the Work in Process Account

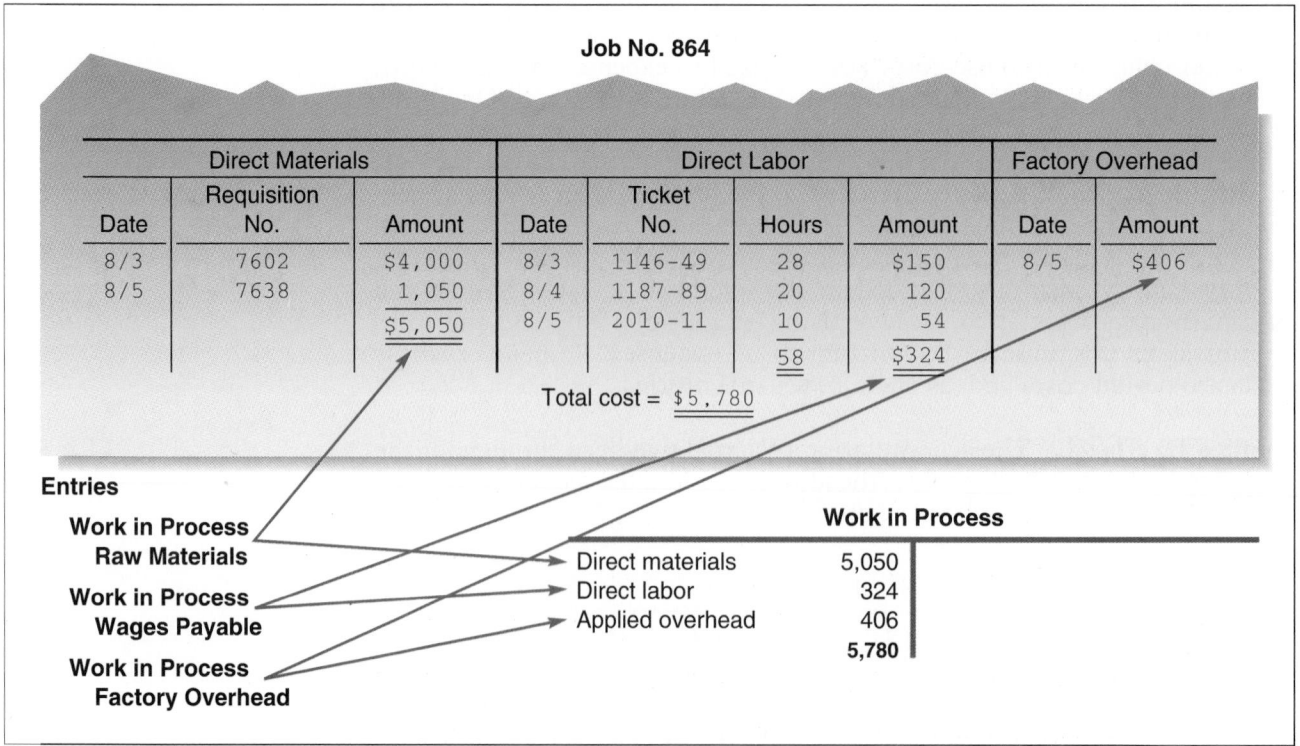

Cost of Goods Sold	1,445	
Finished Goods		1,445
To record the cost of lamps sold		

Accounts Receivable	2,000	
Sales		2,000
To record sale on account		

The first entry transfers the production cost of the 25 lamps sold ($57.80 × 25 = $1,445) from Finished Goods to the Cost of Goods Sold account. The second entry places the sales revenues generated ($80 × 25 = $2,000) in the accounting records. As noted at the beginning of this example, Valley Manufacturing uses a perpetual inventory system. Should you need a review of inventory systems, we refer you to Chapter 9.

EXECUTIVE BRIEFING
Job Order Costing

W. G. Loeken
Vice-President Finance, Boeing Commercial
Airplane Group, The Boeing Company

Job order cost collection is the foundation of The Boeing Company's accounting system. A valid assignment of product and period outlays by program is essential because of the high unit cost and the inherent complexity of manufacturing our 737, 747, 757, 767, and 777 family of airliners. For instance, the annual cost of producing jets is approaching $20 billion, and an innumerable volume of transactions are associated with each aircraft. The cost of one airplane rolling out of our factory represents not only the efforts of Boeing's engineering, manufacturing, and administrative organizations, but also the significant contributions from our subcontractor network that spans the globe. Job order costing allows our accounting function to summarize and assign to individual programs the costs that are generated from these varied sources.

Job cost data are essential for the preparation of financial statements, tax returns, and internal performance reporting. Another important role involves establishing new airplane program viability. Airlines order aircraft for delivery as far as 10 years into the future. Current job data along with extensive program cost history form the basis for forecasting future production expenditures.

Boeing's survival depends on our ability to accurately predict aircraft pricing, markets, and cost performance, given the billions of dollars at stake. Accounting and accurate job data play a key role in this process.

A Recap

The sale of finished production completes the flow of manufacturing costs through the accounting system. Please reexamine the bottom half of Exhibit 22-2. Notice that material, labor, and overhead costs all begin in their own accounts. Indirect materials used and indirect labor are transferred to Factory Overhead to join other miscellaneous production costs. Direct materials used, direct labor, and overhead *applied* are then charged to Work in Process. As production is completed, manufacturing costs are debited to the Finished Goods account. Finally, the sale of inventory requires a transfer of cost from Finished Goods to Cost of Goods Sold. Although variations of this flow are found in practice because of manufacturing complexities (e.g., multiple processing departments), Exhibit 22-2 accurately depicts the movement of costs for both small manufacturing firms and industrial giants.

Work in Process: A Control Account

The Work in Process account in the previous example contained the costs of job no. 864 until the job was completed. Normally, a business manufactures many jobs simultaneously and is unable to finish all production by the end of the accounting period. To handle the necessary record keeping, Work in Process assumes the role of a control account and is supported by individual job cost sheets.

To illustrate, assume that Avanti Corporation had job no. 614 in process on January 1. Information relating to job no. 614 follows.

Direct materials used	$ 5,500
Direct labor	8,000
Factory overhead applied, 150% of direct labor	12,000
	$25,500

Manufacturing activity that took place during the year is shown in Exhibit 22-6.

Avanti's Work in Process account and summary journal entries appear in Exhibit 22-7. Observe that the cost of completed jobs (no. 614 and no. 615) has been removed from Work in Process and transferred to Finished Goods. Jobs no. 616 and no. 617 are still in production; thus, the $89,000 ending Work in Process balance coincides with the total of these two jobs' cost

EXHIBIT 22-6
Avanti Corporation
Manufacturing Activity

	Job No. 614	Job No. 615	Job No. 616	Job No. 617	Total
Direct materials used	$ —	$ 9,000	$20,000	$ 4,000	$ 33,000
Direct labor	5,000	10,000	18,000	8,000	41,000
Factory overhead applied, 150% of direct labor	7,500	15,000	27,000	12,000	61,500
Total	$12,500	$34,000	$65,000	$24,000	$135,500
Job status, 12/31	Completed	Completed and sold	In process	In process	

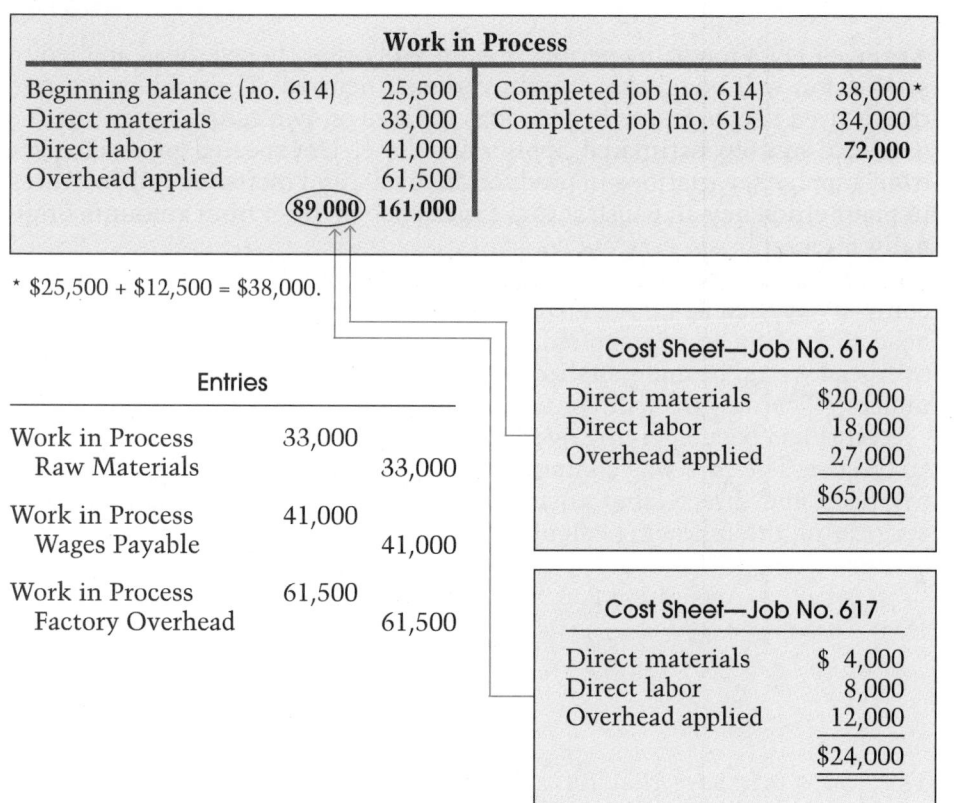

EXHIBIT 22-7
Work in Process Control
Account of Avanti Corporation

sheets ($65,000 + $24,000 = $89,000). The Work in Process and job cost sheet relationship is an example of the control account/subsidiary ledger arrangement discussed in Chapter 6. Recall that a control account (Work in Process) appears in the general ledger and is composed of various lower-level accounts. The lower-level accounts (in this case, job cost sheets) that support a control account are collectively known as a subsidiary ledger.

Computerized Job Costing Systems

As you may have concluded, the record keeping associated with a job costing system is burdensome, especially if manual accounting procedures are used. Thankfully, computerized systems are available that electronically capture the needed data and make the amount of bookkeeping bearable. For example, bar codes and scanners are often used to track the materials issued to production. Management may gather direct labor data by requiring employees to insert their magnetically encoded identification cards into a terminal. Also, machines may be linked on-line to computers, with software capturing the equipment's start and stop times. (Such information is important if machine hours are used as the overhead application base.) Indeed, without computerized systems, product costing (a prime objective) would likely take a back seat to paper shuffling and record keeping.

A FURTHER PROBE OF OVERHEAD

OBJECTIVE

Account for over- or under-applied overhead at the end of the reporting period.

At the end of a reporting period, it is unlikely that the overhead applied to production will equal the actual overhead incurred. The application rate that is used to charge overhead to jobs is based on two estimates: estimated overhead and an estimated application base. Unexpected price changes from suppliers, variations in production levels, and increases and decreases in plant efficiency all cause actual experience to differ from amounts originally forecast.

Overhead can be either overapplied or underapplied. If, for example, a company applied $74,000 of overhead but actually incurred $68,000, overhead is said to be **overapplied** by $6,000. If the situation was reversed, overhead would be **underapplied.** To examine the implications of over- and underapplication, we will continue the Avanti Corporation example.

Avanti has been applying overhead to jobs at the rate of 150% of direct labor cost. The rate was computed by taking the year's forecasted factory overhead and direct labor costs, $60,000 and $40,000, respectively, and performing the following calculation:

$$\text{Application Rate} = \frac{\text{Estimated Factory Overhead}}{\text{Estimated Application Base}}$$

$$= \frac{\$60,000}{\$40,000}$$

$$= 150\%$$

The 150% rate says that for every $1.00 of direct labor expected to be incurred, the firm anticipates $1.50 of factory overhead.

Throughout the accounting period Avanti applied $61,500 of overhead to jobs no. 614–617 (see Exhibit 22-6). If we assume that actual overhead incurred amounted to $65,000, overhead would be underapplied by $3,500:

EXHIBIT 22-8
Application of Factory Overhead for Avanti Corporation

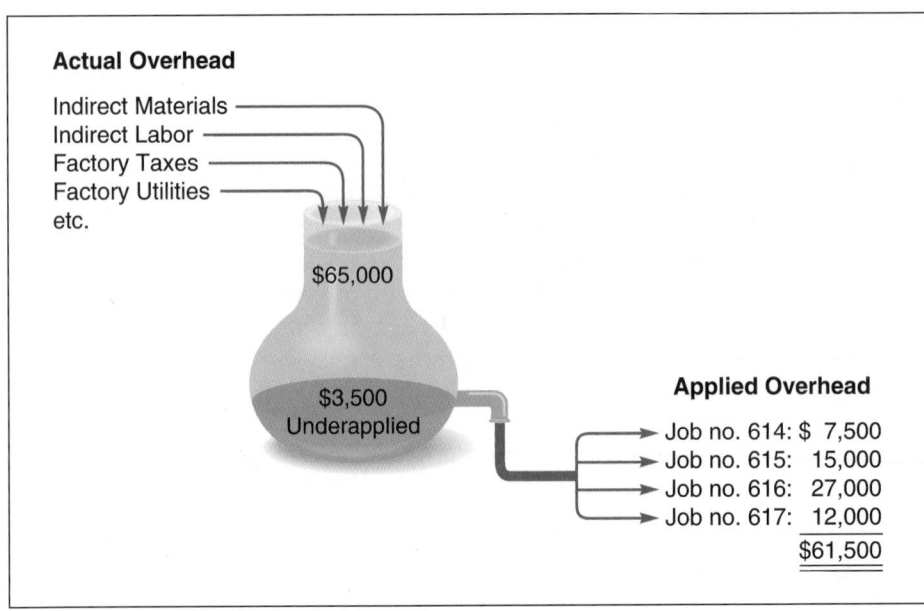

Actual overhead	$65,000
Applied overhead	
Direct labor cost × 150% ($41,000 × 150%)	61,500
Underapplied overhead	$ 3,500

Exhibit 22-8 depicts the entire process in pictorial form.

Effects of Over- and Underapplied Overhead

Avanti's underapplication means that insufficient overhead has been charged to the Work in Process account. Unfortunately, the problem does not stop here, because each job produced during the period has been costed incorrectly. From the job status that appears in Exhibit 22-6, jobs no. 616 and no. 617 are still in process (Work in Process), job no. 614 has been completed but is still on hand (Finished Goods), and job no. 615 has been sold (Cost of Goods Sold). Because of the understated application rate, the ending balances in these three accounts are understated as well. Thus, an adjusting entry is needed upon conclusion of the reporting period.

The adjusting entry first considers the status of the Factory Overhead account. In Avanti's case the account appears as follows:

Factory Overhead	
Actual	Applied
65,000	61,500

The overhead account must be closed so the company can start anew, accumulating costs for the next period's production activities. Thus, Factory Overhead is credited for $3,500. The $3,500 debit can either be (1) allocated to Work in Process, Finished Goods, and Cost of Goods Sold on some equitable basis or (2) charged entirely to Cost of Goods Sold.

The first approach, which raises each account's balance to counteract the understatement, is theoretically correct. However, because the balances in the three accounts cited consist of the costs of individual jobs, each job cost sheet must be adjusted as well. Avanti had only four jobs; in a more realistic environment, the amount of bookkeeping required could be overwhelming. Consequently, the allocation approach is only used when the amount of over- or underapplied overhead is so great that a lack of proration will result in misleading financial statements.

The second method, charging the entire $3,500 to Cost of Goods Sold, is the more popular approach. The necessary journal entry follows.

Cost of Goods Sold	3,500	
Factory Overhead		3,500
To adjust cost of goods sold for underapplied overhead		

The entry raises Cost of Goods Sold to $37,500 ($34,000 from job no. 615 + $3,500), and this amount is reported on Avanti's income statement.

The procedures illustrated are reversed for overapplied overhead.

The New Manufacturing Environment

OBJECTIVE

5

Recognize the impact of automation on overhead application rates.

Earlier in the chapter we noted that the application base selected should have a strong cause and effect relationship with overhead. Labor hours or labor cost may be appropriate in a setting where considerable manual assembly work is required to complete a product; hospital beds occupied may explain a large portion of the overhead incurred at a health-care facility; a company's building maintenance costs may be tied to square footage; and so forth. These application bases are said to be **cost drivers,** or factors that cause specific costs to be incurred within an organization.

Companies naturally have a wide selection of application bases to choose from, with some bases being better than others. If an improper base is selected—one that fails to cause (i.e., drive) overhead costs—the outcome will be questionable overhead application rates. Such rates typically result in distorted product costs, inventory valuations, and income measurements, perhaps leading to erroneous decisions on the part of management.

Surveys of manufacturers' accounting practices have found (and continue to find) that direct labor is one of the most popular, if not *the* most popular, application base for factory overhead. This finding is interesting, especially when one considers the dramatic change in cost drivers over the years. Factory workers are continually being replaced by robots and computer-controlled machines, as companies strive to trim costs and improve product quality. In heavily automated facilities, it is not uncommon for overhead (which includes equipment depreciation and operating costs) to account for more than half of all production costs. Direct labor, on the other hand, which may have comprised 40% of manufacturing costs as recently as 25 years ago, frequently amounts to no more than 5% today.[3] The declining labor component, coupled with increasing overhead charges, has led some businesses to experience application rates in excess of 1,000% of direct labor!

Robots Versus People

To present a very clear (and perhaps frightening) picture of the trade-off between factory overhead and direct labor, we cite two examples from Japan.[4] Matsushita Electric has a factory where Panasonic VCRs are produced. Here, 530 robots wind wire slightly thinner than a human hair 16 times through a pinhole in the video head. This operation goes on 24 hours a day. The outcome? The robots work five times faster and more reliably than the *3,000* part-time workers they replaced. (The employees did the work for Matsushita on a subcontract basis.) These computer-driven marvels also inspect their own output.

The Yokohama camcorder factory of The Victor Co. of Japan (JVC) is another interesting example. Automated vehicles deliver components to 64 robots that perform 150 assembly and inspection tasks for eight different models—all on a single production line. The entire process is controlled by *2* workers, down from 150 in pre-robot days.

---

[3] For an enlightening article on the new manufacturing technology, see "Accounting Bores You? Wake Up," *Fortune,* October 12, 1987, pp. 43–44, 48, 52–53.

[4] These illustrations are taken from "Why Japan Loves Robots and We Don't," *Forbes,* April 16, 1990, pp. 148, 150–53.

Cases such as these are becoming more commonplace. Although direct labor may be an appropriate cost driver in some situations, it certainly is not in all. To conclude, many firms' cost accounting systems are obsolete and in need of change, especially in light of automation and the new manufacturing environment. Ask many professionals and they will say that accurate cost information is often the deciding factor in gaining the strongly pursued competitive advantage, foreign or otherwise.

Thus far, most of our discussion has dealt with production-type settings, perhaps leaving you with the impression that job costing systems are used exclusively by manufacturing organizations. This is not the case, as cost accumulation by job is popular in the service sector of our economy as well. Such systems are used to determine the cost of:

JOB COSTING: SERVICE APPLICATIONS

OBJECTIVE

6

Apply job costing systems to service organizations.

- Servicing clients by accountants, financial planners, management consultants, architects, and lawyers.
- Providing patient care by hospitals.
- Implementing drug abuse programs by social service agencies.
- Beginning new flights to vacation resort areas by airlines.

In the preceding examples, the ''job'' becomes the client, patient, program, and flight segment, respectively.

Job cost information is used in several of these cases for setting prices, which, of course, affect profitability. Even for those organizations that operate without a profit motive (e.g., colleges and universities, charitable organizations, and so forth), job cost input assists managers when planning, controlling operations, and allocating resources.

Direct and Indirect Costs

Job costing in service entities revolves around the proper handling of direct and indirect costs. **Direct costs,** or those easily traced to a job, are charged to the individual jobs that are worked on during the accounting period. In contrast, **indirect costs** (those not easily traced) are treated as general overhead and applied in the same manner as factory overhead for a manufacturer.[5]

A review of job costing systems and procedures over the years will find an increased attempt by businesses to have more of their costs fall in the direct category. This practice, which is now more easily accomplished because of computers and available software, helps satisfy client inquiries concerning fee composition and leads to improved costing of services.

An Illustration

Given the distinction between direct and indirect costs, we now focus on the operations of InfoNet, a consulting firm that specializes in the design of management information systems. A portion of InfoNet's budget for 19X3 follows.

---

[5] These definitions will be expanded somewhat in Chapter 27.

Revenue from billings		$10,500,000
Less direct costs		
Professional staff time	$4,000,000	
Computer charges	2,600,000	
Long-distance charges	350,000	
Overnight delivery	50,000	7,000,000
		$ 3,500,000
Less indirect costs (rent, utilities, other nontraceable items)		2,100,000
Operating income		$ 1,400,000

The company's accountants and management feel that total direct costs is the most appropriate base to charge overhead (i.e., indirect costs) to client jobs. Accordingly, a 30% application rate was developed:

$$\text{Application Rate} = \frac{\text{Estimated Overhead}}{\text{Estimated Application Base}}$$

$$= \frac{\$2,100,000}{\$7,000,000}$$

$$= 30\%$$

In March, InfoNet completed a consulting job for Oregon Department Stores. The job cost sheet for this project is shown in Exhibit 22-9. Directly traceable costs total $30,000 and are charged to the Oregon project. In addition, $9,000 ($30,000 × 0.30) of overhead is applied to the job, bringing the total cost to $39,000.

EXHIBIT 22-9
Job Cost Sheet for a Service Business

JOB COST SHEET

Client <u>Oregon Department Stores</u> Job No. <u>165</u>
<u>Portland, Oregon</u>

Engagement <u>Design of marketing</u> Date:
<u>retrieval system</u> Started <u>1/10/X3</u>
Completed <u>3/29/X3</u>

Direct costs:	
Professional staff time	$ 19,000
Computer charges	10,500
Long-distance charges	400
Overnight delivery	100
Total	$ 30,000
General overhead (<u>30</u> % of total direct costs)	9,000
Total cost of engagement	$ 39,000
Target income (___ % of total direct costs)	$ ___
Client billing	$ ___

Client Billings

Notice that the last two lines of the client's cost sheet are left blank. If desired, InfoNet could compute a target income amount to be earned on each job—a target so the company can proceed toward attaining its overall income goal of $1,400,000. The job's income and costs are eventually combined to yield the amount that InfoNet must bill the client.

For example, InfoNet's original budget reveals estimated operating income and direct costs of $1,400,000 and $7,000,000, respectively. If each job is anticipated to produce the same rate of profit for the firm, an income computation rate could be developed in a manner similar to that shown for an overhead application rate, namely:

$$\text{Income Computation Rate} = \frac{\text{Estimated Income}}{\text{Estimated Application Base}}$$

$$= \frac{\$1,400,000}{\$7,000,000}$$

$$= 20\%$$

InfoNet wants to earn $6,000 ($30,000 × 0.20) from the Oregon job, meaning that the amount billed must equal $45,000 ($39,000 + $6,000). Stated differently, if revenues from the job are $45,000 and costs amount to $39,000, the Oregon project will contribute $6,000 toward InfoNet's 19X3 total operating income.

END-OF-CHAPTER REVIEW

LEARNING OBJECTIVES: THE KEY POINTS

1 Explain the problems encountered in computing the actual cost of a product or service. The actual cost of a good or service is usually very difficult to calculate. Various estimates and assumptions are used in accounting, which introduces imprecision into the costing process. Further, many costs (e.g., factory overhead, corporate administration, and so forth) are not easily traced to finished products, departments, and divisions.

2 Explain the nature and use of a job order costing system. Job costing systems are used in environments where it is relatively easy to classify costs by job or order. This situation often arises when goods are manufactured upon receipt of a customer's order, according to customer specifications, or in separate batches. The costs of direct materials used, direct labor, and factory overhead applied are all accumulated on a job cost sheet. These costs are charged to the Work in Process account. Upon job completion the costs are transferred to Finished Goods inventory and, at the time of sale, to Cost of Goods Sold.

3 Compute an overhead application rate and apply overhead to production. Because of the difficulty and/or cost of tracing factory overhead to a manufactured product, it becomes necessary to apply (i.e., estimate) overhead for inventory costing purposes. An application rate is developed by dividing a company's estimated factory overhead by an estimated application base. The rate is then multiplied by the amount of the application base associated with the job in question. Overhead bases should be relatively inexpensive to compute, easily traced to the product, and have a strong bearing on the amount of overhead actually incurred.

4 Account for over- or underapplied overhead at the end of the reporting period. Overhead is applied in the manner just described under learning objective 3. The required journal entry involves a debit to the Work in Process account and a credit to Factory Overhead. The Factory Overhead account is also used to accumulate (on the debit side) the actual overhead incurred by the company. At the end of the reporting period, the amount of over- or underapplication is calculated as the difference between actual overhead and applied overhead. Over- or underapplied amounts are most commonly adjusted against the Cost of Goods Sold account or, if significant, allocated among Work in Process, Finished Goods, and Cost of Goods Sold.

5 Recognize the impact of automation on overhead application rates. Automation has resulted in people being replaced by robots and computer-controlled machines. Thus, for many companies, direct labor as a percentage of product cost is shrinking while factory overhead is increasing. The rise in factory overhead is attributed to equipment operating costs, including lease payments and depreciation. The outcome for those firms that continue to use direct labor as an application base is an increase in overhead rates.

6 Apply job costing systems to service organizations. Job costing systems can be used by service enterprises to accumulate the costs of rendering a service. The "job" may consist of providing consulting services to a client, repair services to a customer, health-care services to a patient, and so forth. Direct costs (those easily traced to a client job) are charged to the job cost sheet. Indirect costs, or those not easily traced, are treated as overhead and applied in a manner similar to that used for factory overhead.

**KEY TERMS
AND CONCEPTS:
A QUICK OVERVIEW**

cost driver   A factor that causes given costs to be incurred within an organization.

direct cost   A cost that is easily traced to a job.

indirect cost   A cost that is not easily traced to a job; treated as overhead.

job cost sheet   A document that is used to accumulate costs in a job order system.

job order system   A system of cost accumulation that gathers costs by job or order.

materials requisition   An order for materials to be issued from the storeroom.

overapplied overhead   A situation arising when the factory overhead applied to production is greater than the amount of factory overhead actually incurred.

overhead application rate   The rate used to apply factory overhead to jobs or products. Computed as estimated factory overhead divided by the estimated application base.

time ticket   A ticket used to gather labor time. Shows the specific job or jobs to which an employee was assigned.

underapplied overhead   A situation arising when the factory overhead applied to production is less than the amount of factory overhead actually incurred.

The five questions that follow relate to several issues raised in the chapter. Test your knowledge of the issues by selecting the best answer. (The answers appear on p. 942.)

1 Which of the following businesses would be least likely to use a job costing system?

a Automobile repair shop.   c Crude oil refinery.

b Custom-home builder.   d Motion picture producer.

2 The journal entry to record the use of indirect materials in production activities is:

a debit Work in Process; credit Raw Materials.

b debit Factory Overhead; credit Raw Materials.

c debit Raw Materials; credit Work in Process.

d debit Work in Process; credit Factory Overhead.

3 Direct materials, direct labor, and factory overhead applied are initially brought together in which of the following accounts?

a Work in Process.   c Cost of Goods Sold.

b Finished Goods.   d Income Summary.

4 SRT, Inc., applies factory overhead on the basis of direct labor cost. The company's accountant has forecast $180,000 of factory overhead and $200,000 of direct labor for 19X5. Actual factory overhead and direct labor for 19X5 amounted to $185,000 and $210,000, respectively. Overhead for 19X5 is:

a underapplied by $4,000.   c overapplied by $4,000.

b underapplied by $9,000.   d overapplied by $9,000.

5 In today's modern manufacturing environment, many companies:

a are experiencing a decrease in overhead application rates.

b are experiencing a decrease in factory overhead and an increase in direct labor cost.

c can ignore cost drivers because of a recent pronouncement from the Financial Accounting Standards Board.

d have a labor component that may be as low as 5% of total product cost.

Riverdale Manufacturing Company uses a job order system to accumulate production costs. The firm, which applies overhead on the basis of direct labor hours, derived the following estimates for 19X3 manufacturing activity: direct labor hours: 45,000; factory overhead: $180,000. Selected data applicable to January 19X3 follow.

January 1 balance of work in process: $19,000
Direct materials used: $60,000
Direct labor incurred (3,500 hours): $28,000
Indirect materials used: $3,900
Indirect labor incurred: $7,600
Factory utilities: $1,000
Equipment depreciation: $2,000
Cost of goods completed: $94,500

Instructions

a Determine Riverdale's overhead application rate.

b Calculate the amount of overhead applied to production during January.

c Present entries to record (1) direct materials used, (2) direct labor incurred, (3) factory overhead incurred, (4) factory overhead applied to production, and (5) cost of goods completed during the month.

d Determine the cost of the company's work in process inventory on January 31.

e Determine the amount of over- or underapplied overhead during January.

Solution

a Overhead Application Rate $= \dfrac{\text{Estimated Factory Overhead}}{\text{Estimated Application Base}}$

$= \dfrac{\$180,000}{45,000 \text{ hours}}$

$= \$4$ per direct labor hour

b Overhead applied: 3,500 hours $\times$ \$4 = $\underline{\$14,000}$

c (1) Work in Process 60,000
      Raw Materials 60,000
      Issued direct materials to production

  (2) Work in Process 28,000
      Wages Payable 28,000
      To record direct labor incurred

  (3) Factory Overhead 14,500
      Raw Materials 3,900
      Wages Payable 7,600
      Accounts Payable 1,000
      Accumulated Depreciation: Equipment 2,000
      To record actual factory overhead costs

  (4) Work in Process 14,000
      Factory Overhead 14,000
      To record applied overhead [see part (b)]

  (5) Finished Goods 94,500
      Work in Process 94,500
      To transfer completed units to finished goods

d Riverdale's ending work in process inventory is $26,500, as shown by the following T-account:

Work in Process			
Balance	19,000	(5)	94,500
(1)	60,000		
(2)	28,000		
(4)	14,000		
	121,000		
	(26,500)		

e Overhead is underapplied by $500.

Overhead incurred	$14,500
Overhead applied	14,000
Underapplied overhead	$ 500

ASSIGNMENT MATERIAL

Q22-1 Briefly explain several of the problems encountered when trying to compute the actual cost of a good or service.

Q22-2 Discuss the general features associated with a job order costing system. In what types of applications are job order systems used?

Q22-3 Explain how the flow of costs through an accounting system parallels the flow of goods and materials through a manufacturing plant.

Q22-4 Contrast the proper accounting treatments of direct materials and indirect materials.

Q22-5 How does the use of a predetermined overhead rate smooth product costs over a period of time?

Q22-6 Explain how an overhead application rate is developed and used to apply overhead to specific jobs.

Q22-7 List the characteristics of a good overhead application base.

Q22-8 Ritten Company's factory depreciation for the year just ended totaled $40,000 and was recorded as follows:

Depreciation Expense	40,000	
Accumulated Depreciation: Factory		40,000

Comment on the appropriateness of Ritten's journal entry.

Q22-9 Discuss the relationship between the Work in Process account and individual job cost sheets.

Q22-10 If overhead is underapplied, will the Factory Overhead account contain a debit or credit balance? What is the probable effect of the underapplication on the Work in Process balance (before adjustment) at the end of the accounting period?

Q22-11 What is probably the most popular application base for overhead? Can this base be criticized in light of today's manufacturing environment? Briefly explain.

Q22-12 List several possible applications of job costing systems by service enterprises.

Q22-13 Distinguish between a direct cost and an indirect cost.

E22-1 *Manufacturing journal entries* (L.O. 2, 3)

The following selected transactions and events occurred at Pipeline Manufacturing during March:

Mar. 3 Purchased $10,000 of direct materials and $7,300 of indirect materials on account from Sunbelt Distributors.

  7 Issued $3,100 of direct materials and $700 of indirect materials from the storeroom.

  14 Incurred $5,600 of direct labor and $3,400 of indirect labor.

  17 Recorded $1,300 of overhead incurred on account.

Mar. 20 Applied $2,800 of overhead to production.

23 Noted that $6,200 of production had been completed.

26 Sold goods on account at a profit of 30% of cost. The goods cost $5,000.

Prepare journal entries to record the preceding transactions and events.

E22-2 *Analysis of job cost sheet* (L.O. 2, 3)

Sumpter Manufacturing began job no. 587 in December 19X6 and recorded material, labor, and overhead charges of $38,800 through year-end. The bottom portion of page 2 of the job's cost sheet is reproduced below.

Summary of January charges	
Direct materials used	$12,600
Direct labor (580 hours)	4,350
Factory overhead applied	6,728
Total	$23,678

Job no. 587 was completed on January 30, 19X7.

a Determine Sumpter's overhead application rate, assuming the company uses direct labor hours for an application base.

b What is the total cost of job no. 587?

c Prepare the journal entries recorded in January related to job no. 587.

E22-3 *Cost flows and overhead application* (L.O. 2, 3)

Cleveland Metals uses a job cost system and applies factory overhead to production at a predetermined rate of 180% of direct labor cost. Data pertaining to recent operations follow.

1-2-3 ■ Job no. 636 was the only job in process on January 1 of the current year. The Work in Process account contained a $24,600 balance on this date.

■ Jobs no. 637, 638, and 639 were started during January.

■ Total direct material requisitions and direct labor incurred during January amounted to $89,200 and $114,500, respectively.

■ The only job that remained in process on January 31 was job no. 638, with costs of $15,000 for direct materials and $20,000 for direct labor.

a Compute the total cost of the work in process inventory on January 31.

b Compute the cost of jobs completed during January, and present the proper journal entry to reflect job completion.

E22-4 *Job costing and overhead application* (L.O. 2, 3, 4)

Uniflex applies overhead on the basis of direct labor cost. In December 19X4, the company's cost accountant made the following predictions for 19X5 operations: direct labor cost, $620,000; factory overhead, $961,000.

Uniflex worked on jobs no. 241 and no. 242 in January. The costs incurred and production status of these two jobs appear in the table that follows.

	Job No. 241	Job No. 242
Direct materials	$26,000	$47,000
Direct labor	18,000	24,000
Production status	In process	In process

By the end of 19X5, actual direct labor cost amounted to $612,500, and factory overhead incurred totaled $967,500. There was no work in process on January 1, 19X5.

Compute the following:

a Uniflex's overhead application rate.

b The balance of the Work in Process account on January 31, 19X5.

c The amount of over- or underapplied overhead for 19X5. Be sure to indicate whether overhead was overapplied or underapplied.

E22-5 *Job costing and overhead application* (L.O. 2, 3)

1-2-3

Oxford Enterprises uses a job costing system to accumulate manufacturing costs. Overhead is applied to products on the basis of machine hours in the machining department and direct labor cost in the assembly department. The following estimates pertain to 19X4:

	Machining	Assembly
Machine hours	40,000	5,000
Direct labor cost	$270,000	$800,000
Factory overhead	810,000	960,000

Job no. 328 was the only job in process at the end of 19X4. Its cost sheet revealed the data that follow.

	Machining	Assembly
Machine hours	100	10
Direct labor cost	$1,100	$3,500
Direct materials cost	1,900	3,400

a Compute Oxford's overhead application rates in the machining department and the assembly department.

b Calculate the total amount of overhead applied to job no. 328.

c Determine the total cost of job no. 328.

E22-6 *Overview of job costing and overhead application* (L.O. 2, 3, 4, 5)

Evaluate the comments that follow as being True or False. If the comment is false, briefly explain why.

a A materials requisition forms the basis for the following journal entry: debit Work in Process; credit Raw Materials.

b The Work in Process account normally contains the following costs for the jobs in production at year-end: direct materials used, direct labor, and actual factory overhead.

c Direct labor cost is a good overhead application base to use if a company is highly automated.

d The amount of over- or underapplied overhead at year-end is normally closed to the Work in Process account.

e An overhead application rate is derived by the following computation: estimated factory overhead divided by an estimated application base.

E22-7 *Overhead application: Working backward* (L.O. 3)

The Towson Manufacturing Corporation applies overhead on the basis of machine hours. The following divisional information is presented for your review:

	Division A	Division B
Actual machine hours	22,500	?
Estimated machine hours	20,000	?
Overhead application rate	$4.50	$5.00
Actual overhead	$110,000	?
Estimated overhead	?	$90,000
Applied overhead	?	$86,000
Over- (under-) applied overhead	?	$6,500

Find the unknowns for each of the divisions.

E22-8 *Direct costs and indirect costs* (L.O. 6)

Executive Airlines is studying whether to begin flight service from Chicago to St. Louis. Identify the following costs as a direct cost or an indirect cost of the Chicago/St. Louis flight segment, assuming the route would be serviced by aircraft that would continue to be flown throughout Executive's extensive route system:

a Passenger beverage service

b Airport landing fees

c Monthly engine maintenance service

d Fuel consumed

e Commissions paid to travel agents on tickets sold

f Salary of Executive's director of route planning

E22-9 *Cost drivers, service business* (L.O. 6)

Don't Bug Me treats insect-infested homes and trees in Omaha, Nebraska. The company utilizes many liquid pesticides that are purchased in 55-gallon drums and later divided into 10-gallon containers for crew use. The pesticides are accounted for as indirect materials (i.e., supplies) in the firm's job cost system.

a Why do you think the company treats pesticides as indirect materials (as opposed to direct costs) of servicing a client?

b What is a cost driver?

c Management insists that crews estimate square footage and tree height, respectively, for homes and trees serviced. Why is this procedure necessary?

PROBLEMS

Series A

P22-A1 *Preparation of job cost sheet and journal entries* (L.O. 2, 3)

Nycom, Inc., manufactures items that are used in the electronics industry. The company, which uses a job costing system, has two departments: machining and finishing. The machining department applies overhead to products at the rate of $15 per machine hour. Finishing, in contrast, uses an application rate of 250% of direct labor cost.

On March 19, 19X3, Nycom received an order from Sensormatic for 225 photons, model no. 116. Production began immediately, and the order (known as job no. 4155) was completed on March 31. Paperwork supporting the order revealed the following:

Document*	Date	Department	Hours	Amount
MR 1165	3/19	Machining	—	$5,600
MR 1169	3/21	Machining	—	3,500
TT 1450-52	3/23	Machining	45	400
MUR 46	3/23	Machining	105	—
MR 4330	3/27	Finishing	—	700
TT 1475-76	3/31	Machining	30	300
MUR 47	3/31	Machining	50	—
TT 6608-13	3/31	Finishing	200	2,000

* MR = materials requisition; TT = time ticket; MUR = machine usage report.

Instructions

a Prepare a job cost sheet for the Sensormatic order as of March 31. Use the following column headings:

Direct Materials			Direct Labor			Machine Usage		Factory Overhead
Date	Requisition	Amount	Ticket	Hours	Amount	Report	Hours	Amount

b Prepare journal entries to record (1) the issuance of direct materials, (2) direct labor incurred on the order, and (3) the application of factory overhead. All materials requisitions should be combined in one entry, all time tickets in another, and so forth.

c If company policy is to sell goods at a profit of 80% of total job cost, present the journal entries necessary to recognize completion and sale of the photons.

P22-A2 *Basic job costing with journal entries* (L.O. 2, 3)

Santos Manufacturing, which uses a job cost system, applies overhead to production at the rate of $8 per labor hour. The company reported a work in process inventory of $86,900 on December 1 of the current year, consisting of job no. 362. The following activity took place during December:

1 Issued direct materials from the storeroom and incurred direct labor charges on various jobs as shown.

Job No.	Direct Materials	Direct Labor Cost	Direct Labor Hours
362	$10,500	$ 4,500	450
365	20,700	3,000	280
366	16,900	8,400	830
367	5,400	2,200	240
368	9,600	6,300	600
	$63,100	$24,400	2,400

2 Incurred miscellaneous factory charges: indirect materials used, $3,500; indirect labor, $5,900; and equipment depreciation, $4,000.

3 Completed jobs no. 362 and no. 366.

4 Sold job no. 366 on account for $43,100.

Instructions

a Prepare journal entries for December to record the following. (*Note:* Use summary entries where appropriate by combining individual job data.)

(1) The issuance of direct materials, the direct labor incurred, and the application of factory overhead to production.
(2) The indirect materials used, the indirect labor charges, and equipment depreciation.
(3) The completion of jobs no. 362 and no. 366.
(4) The sale of job no. 366.

b Establish a T-account for Work in Process and determine the account's ending balance on December 31.

c Prepare a schedule of the jobs still in process (and the related costs) as of December 31.

P22-A3 *Computations using a job order system* (L.O. 2, 3)

General Corporation employs a job order cost system. On May 1, the following balances were extracted from the general ledger:

Work in process	$ 35,200
Finished goods	86,900
Cost of goods sold	128,700

Work in Process consisted of two jobs, no. 101 ($20,400) and no. 103 ($14,800). During May, direct materials requisitioned from the storeroom amounted to $96,500, and direct labor incurred totaled $114,500. These figures are subdivided as follows:

Direct Materials		Direct Labor	
Job No.	Amount	Job No.	Amount
101	$ 5,000	101	$ 7,800
115	19,500	103	20,800
116	36,200	115	42,000
Other	35,800	116	18,000
	$96,500	Other	25,900
			$114,500

Job no. 115 was the only job in process at the end of the month. Job no. 101 and three "other" jobs were sold during May at a profit of 20% of cost. The "other" jobs contained material and labor charges of $21,000 and $17,400, respectively.

General applies overhead daily at the rate of 150% of direct labor cost as labor summaries are posted to job orders. The firm's fiscal year ends on May 31.

Instructions

a Compute the total overhead applied to production during May.
b Compute the cost of the ending work in process inventory.
c Compute the cost of jobs completed during May.
d Compute the cost of goods sold for the year ended May 31.

P22-A4 *Job order costing, overhead emphasis* (L.O. 2, 3, 4)

Toledo Company uses a job order system to accumulate manufacturing costs. On December 31, 19X1, the work in process inventory consisted of job no. 764, costed as follows:

Direct materials	$ 4,800
Direct labor	12,500
Applied overhead	10,000
	$27,300

Because of changing plant conditions and labor markets, the cost accounting department calculated a new overhead application rate for use throughout 19X2. Estimated totals for direct labor cost and factory overhead for 19X2 amounted to $300,000 and $270,000, respectively. Actual results follow.

Direct materials used	$259,600
Direct labor	316,000
Indirect materials	23,700
Indirect labor	144,900
Factory depreciation	55,300
Factory taxes	12,700
Factory utilities	55,200
	$867,400

All jobs were completed and sold by December 31, 19X2, except for job no. 821, which contained direct material costs of $10,900 and direct labor charges of $22,500. This job was still in production and was anticipated to be completed in early January. The company charges any under- or overapplied overhead to Cost of Goods Sold.

Instructions

a Determine the 19X2 overhead application rate, using direct labor cost as the application base.

b Determine the total cost of the company's work in process inventory as of December 31, 19X2.

c Determine the amount of under- or overapplied overhead for the year. Be sure to indicate whether overhead was underapplied or overapplied.

d Compute the company's cost of goods sold. Toledo had no finished goods inventory on January 1, 19X2.

P22-A5 *Flow of costs: Finding unknowns* (L.O. 2, 3)

Selected ledger accounts for Ruffin Manufacturing for the year ended December 31, 19X4, follow.

Raw Materials		
Balance, 1/1	19,000	89,000
	?	

Wages Payable	
	58,000

Factory Overhead		
Indirect materials	7,000	?
All other	97,000	

Work in Process		
Balance, 1/1	?	240,000
Direct materials	?	
Direct labor	51,000	
Applied overhead	?	

Finished Goods		
Balance, 1/1	114,000	?

Cost of Goods Sold	
296,000	

A year-end count revealed ending raw materials and work in process inventories of $25,000 and $14,000, respectively. Ruffin uses an overhead application rate of 200% of direct labor cost.

Instructions

a Compute the amount of indirect labor incurred in operations.
b Compute total direct materials used.
c Determine Ruffin's purchases of raw materials during the year.
d Calculate the amount of overhead that was applied to production.
e Determine the cost of the ending finished goods inventory.
f Compute the cost of the beginning work in process inventory.

P22-A6 *Job costing in a service business* (L.O. 6)
Diego, Hyatt, and Stevens, a prestigious law firm located in San Antonio, uses a job order system to monitor the cost of servicing clientele. The office manager has prepared the following budget for 19X7:

Client billings		$11,520,000
Less: Professional staff costs (85%)	$6,000,000	
Administrative staff costs (75%)	2,000,000	
Computer time (80%)	500,000	
Photocopying (70%)	200,000	
Other office costs (20%)	300,000	9,000,000
Net income		$ 2,520,000

The numbers in parentheses indicate the percentage of cost that is directly traceable to client jobs. The remaining, nontraceable portion is charged to clients by using a predetermined overhead application rate. The office manager feels that total direct cost is the most appropriate overhead application base.

In March, the firm completed work on a suit for Picante Foods. The following costs were directly chargeable to Picante:

Professional staff	$25,000
Administrative staff	6,400
Computer time	2,500
Photocopying	3,700
Other office costs	400

Instructions

a Determine the firm's total budgeted traceable and nontraceable costs and the overhead application rate.
b Calculate the firm's estimated income for the year as a percentage of traceable costs.
c Compute the total cost of the Picante job and the amount that Diego, Hyatt, and Stevens would bill the client.

d The office manager can acquire new software that would allow the firm to increase the percentage of direct (as opposed to indirect) costs. Briefly explain why Diego, Hyatt, and Stevens would be interested in this software.

Series B

P22-B1 *Preparation of job cost sheet and journal entries* (L.O. 2, 3)

Durable Goods manufactures items that are used in the plastics industry. The company, which uses a job costing system, has two departments: cutting and finishing. The cutting department applies overhead to products at the rate of $20 per machine hour. Finishing, in contrast, uses an application rate of 300% of direct labor cost.

On August 12, 19X4, Durable received an order from Arriva, Inc., for 450 wedge forms, model no. 19. Production began immediately, and the order (known as job no. 3434) was completed on August 31. Paperwork supporting the order revealed the following:

Document*	Date	Department	Hours	Amount
MR 2298	8/12	Cutting	—	$1,500
MR 2317	8/15	Cutting	—	6,400
MUR 59	8/17	Cutting	80	—
TT 1190-92	8/17	Cutting	30	300
MR 6680	8/19	Finishing	—	800
MUR 62	8/31	Cutting	140	—
TT 1235-38	8/31	Cutting	50	500
TT 6608-14	8/31	Finishing	200	1,800

* MR = materials requisition; TT = time ticket; MUR = machine usage report.

Instructions

a Prepare a job cost sheet for the Arriva order as of August 31. Use the following column headings:

	Direct Materials		Direct Labor			Machine Usage		Factory Overhead
Date	Requisition	Amount	Ticket	Hours	Amount	Report	Hours	Amount

b Prepare journal entries to record (1) the issuance of direct materials, (2) direct labor incurred on the order, and (3) the application of factory overhead. All materials requisitions should be combined in one entry, all time tickets in another, and so forth.

c If company policy is to sell goods at a profit of 60% of total job cost, present the journal entries necessary to recognize completion and sale of the wedge forms.

P22-B2 *Basic job costing with journal entries* (L.O. 2, 3)

Academy Entertainment makes music videos. The company had two productions in process at the start of 19X3: Barry James ($78,500) and Amy Murphy LIVE ($42,700). The following activity occurred during the first quarter:

1 Costs that are directly traceable to the videos produced amounted to $387,700, subdivided as shown.

Production	Film and Costumes	Actors and Directors	Costume and Set Designers
Barry James	$15,000	$ 35,600	$ 2,900
Amy Murphy LIVE	6,300	20,000	5,700
Malibu Troupe	32,000	75,000	57,300
A Kiss in Time	21,900	54,000	62,000
	$75,200	$184,600	$127,900

2 Overhead included charges for indirect materials used ($5,000), indirect labor ($42,000), and utilities ($14,000).
3 Video production times totaled 450 hours, allocated as follows: Barry James, 40 hours; Amy Murphy LIVE, 65 hours; Malibu Troupe, 150 hours; and A Kiss in Time, 195 hours. Overhead is applied to each production at the rate of $26 per hour.
4 Academy completed Barry James and Malibu Troupe. Barry James was sold on account to a distribution syndicate for $175,000.

A review of the firm's general ledger found accounts entitled Film, Props, and Supplies (i.e., Raw Materials); Videos in Process; Completed Videos; Cost of Videos Sold; and Studio Overhead.

Instructions

a Prepare journal entries as of March 31 to record the following. (*Note:* Use summary entries where appropriate by combining individual video data.)
   (1) The issuance of film and costumes, and the direct labor incurred.
   (2) The studio overhead incurred during the quarter.
   (3) The application of studio overhead to video production.
   (4) The completion of Barry James and Malibu Troupe, and the sale of Barry James.
b Determine the videos still in production as of March 31 and calculate the costs incurred to date on the individual projects.
c Establish a T-account for Videos in Process and determine the account's balance on March 31.

P22-B3 *Computations using a job order system* (L.O. 2, 3)

1-2-3

Fresno Corporation employs a job order cost system. On July 1, the following balances were extracted from the general ledger:

Work in process	$ 50,900
Finished goods	118,700
Cost of goods sold	185,400

Work in Process consisted of two jobs, no. 421 ($31,700) and no. 423 ($19,200). During July, direct materials requisitioned from the storeroom amounted to $73,700, and direct labor incurred totaled $87,500. These figures are subdivided as follows:

Direct Materials		Direct Labor	
Job No.	Amount	Job No.	Amount
421	$10,100	421	$15,000
425	22,400	423	19,600
426	29,300	425	24,300
Other	11,900	426	11,100
	$73,700	Other	17,500
			$87,500

Job no. 425 was the only job in process by the end of the month. Job no. 421 and three "other" jobs were sold during July at a profit of 40% of cost. The "other" jobs contained material and labor charges of $9,400 and $14,500, respectively.

Fresno applies overhead daily at the rate of 180% of direct labor cost as labor summaries are posted to job orders. The firm's fiscal year ends on July 31.

Instructions

a Compute the total overhead applied to production during July.
b Compute the cost of the ending work in process inventory.
c Compute the cost of jobs completed during July.
d Compute the cost of goods sold for the year ended July 31.

P22-B4 *Job order costing, overhead emphasis* (L.O. 2, 3, 4)

1-2-3

Madison Brothers uses a job order system to accumulate manufacturing costs. On December 31, 19X4, the work in process inventory consisted of job no. 176, costed as follows:

Direct materials	$ 39,800
Direct labor	50,000
Applied overhead	60,000
	$149,800

Because of changing plant conditions and labor markets, the cost accounting department calculated a new overhead application rate for use throughout 19X5. Estimated totals for direct labor cost and factory overhead for 19X5 amounted to $700,000 and $910,000, respectively. Actual results follow.

Direct materials used	$ 822,500
Direct labor	710,000
Indirect materials	64,500
Indirect labor	461,900
Factory depreciation	122,700
Factory insurance	10,900
Factory utilities	238,600
	$2,431,100

All jobs were completed and sold by December 31, 19X5, except for job no. 229, which contained direct material costs of $31,400 and direct labor charges of $42,800. This job was still in production and was anticipated to be completed in early January. The company charges any under- or overapplied overhead to Cost of Goods Sold.

Instructions

a Determine the 19X5 overhead application rate, using direct labor cost as the application base.

b Determine the total cost of the company's work in process inventory as of December 31, 19X5.

c Determine the amount of under- or overapplied overhead for the year. Be sure to indicate whether overhead was underapplied or overapplied.

d Compute the company's cost of goods sold. Madison Brothers had no finished goods inventory on January 1, 19X5.

P22-B5 *Flow of costs: Finding unknowns* **(L.O. 2, 3, 4)**

Selected ledger accounts for Ormsby Manufacturing for the year ended December 31, 19X3, follow.

Raw Materials		
Balance, 1/1	17,000	84,000
	92,000	

Wages Payable	
	104,000

Factory Overhead		
Indirect labor	16,000	132,000
Other	120,000	

Work in Process		
Balance, 1/1	26,000	?
Direct materials	72,000	
Direct labor	?	
Applied overhead	?	

Finished Goods		
Balance, 1/1	37,000	?
	286,000	

Cost of Goods Sold	
?	

The year-end count of completed goods on hand revealed the following:

Item No.	Quantity (Units)	Unit Cost
118	4,500	$5.20
124	6,400	8.40
131	10,100	6.50

Ormsby applies overhead on the basis of direct labor cost.

Instructions

a Compute the amount of indirect materials used in operations.
b Compute total direct labor for the period.
c Determine Ormsby's overhead application rate.
d Compute the ending work in process balance.
e Determine total credits to the Finished Goods account.
f Compute the over- or underapplied overhead.

P22-B6 *Job costing in a service business* (L.O. 6)

Hartwell and Associates renders consulting services to a number of medical practices. To determine the cost of each consulting engagement, Hartwell uses a job order cost system. All costs traceable to specific clients are charged to individual client jobs. Other costs incurred by the firm, but not identifiable with specific clients, are charged to jobs via a predetermined overhead application rate. Clients pay Hartwell for directly chargeable costs, overhead, and a markup. The markup is sufficient to enable the firm to earn its budgeted operating income for the year.

On the basis of past experience, Hartwell has prepared the following budget for the upcoming year:

Cost	Total	Directly Traceable to Specific Jobs	Not Traceable to Specific Jobs
Consulting staff	$200,000	$180,000	$20,000
Office staff	30,000	12,000	18,000
Travel	20,000	15,000	5,000
Other office costs	10,000	1,000	9,000
	$260,000	$208,000	$52,000

The budget also revealed expected revenues and operating income of $364,000 and $104,000, respectively.

Instructions

a Determine the company's overhead application rate. The rate is based on total costs traceable to client jobs.
b Compute Hartwell's estimated income for the year as a percentage of costs traceable to client jobs.
c In January, Hartwell completed a project for the Ohio Medical Group (OMG). The following costs were directly chargeable to OMG:

Consulting staff	$4,500
Office staff	300
Travel	1,100
Other office costs	100

Compute the total billing to OMG.
d Observe that part of the consulting staff's time is not directly traceable to specific jobs. List several possible underlying reasons.

BEYOND THE BASICS

BB22-1 *Overhead application and cost drivers* (L.O. 3, 5)

Overhead allocation (i.e., application) is a fact of life in business. Overhead may be allocated to products, departments, divisions, and so forth by an application base, and the selection of that base is a crucial issue in accounting. Consider the five cases that follow.

- *Case A*—The Drury Manufacturing Company has extensive automated facilities, with many machines and robots controlled by computers. The firm applies factory overhead to products on the basis of direct labor cost.

- *Case B*—Amber Company's corporate headquarters is occupied by five divisions. The firm's building maintenance cost is allocated (charged) to the five divisions on the basis of the square footage occupied by each division.

- *Case C*—Rent All rents a wide variety of equipment, including bulldozers, servingware for parties, small garden and workshop tools, and so forth. The servingware and small tools divisions generate a large number of rentals for short periods of time (e.g., a few days and/or hours). In contrast, the construction equipment division has fewer rentals, but the rentals produce more revenue and cover a longer period of time. The divisions vary greatly in terms of profitability and operating problems. Rent All allocates company administrative cost on the basis of the number of rental invoices written in each division.

- *Case D*—Rent All (from Case C) has a maintenance and repair department that furnishes repair services to the company's divisions. Periodically, the department totals all maintenance costs, including major parts, and divides by the total service calls made. The result is the cost per service call. Each division is then charged on the basis of the number of service calls requested during the period.

- *Case E*—Crossroads Company operates a cafeteria for the convenience of its personnel. The cafeteria offers meals at extremely low prices and generates a loss. The loss is allocated to the firm's six departments on the basis of the number of employees in each department.

Instructions

Recall that in overhead allocation, the application base selected should have a strong bearing on the amount of overhead incurred. Consider the allocation bases and procedures used in the five cases presented and briefly evaluate whether the allocation described is acceptable or could be improved.

BB22-2 *Overview of chapter concepts: Multiple choice* (L.O. 2, 3, 4, 5)

The following multiple-choice questions relate to various topics discussed in the chapter. Select the best answer.

1 Which of the following businesses would be least likely to use a job cost system?
a Law firm.
b Hospital.
c Custom-home builder.
d Canned soup manufacturer.

2 The document used in a job cost system to accumulate production costs is known as a:
a purchase order.
b production cost report.
c job cost sheet.
d manufacturing requisition.

3 The Work in Process account will ordinarily include:
a only prime costs.
b amounts related to direct materials and conversion costs.
c only conversion costs.
d manufacturing and administrative costs.

4 Classic Boat Manufacturing uses a job cost system. On January 28, the company recorded direct labor of $5,000 and indirect labor of $2,000. The proper journal entry to record these amounts would include:
a a credit to Factory Overhead for $2,000.
b a credit to Work in Process for $7,000.
c a debit to Work in Process for $3,000.
d a debit to Factory Overhead for $2,000.

5 An overhead application rate is calculated by:
a dividing the estimated factory overhead by the estimated application base.
b dividing the estimated application base by the estimated factory overhead.
c dividing the actual factory overhead by the estimated application base.
d dividing the actual application base by the estimated factory overhead.

6 AeroCopter manufactures helicopters and uses a job cost system. The current year's business activity has decreased significantly because of unexpected cancellations of government contracts. The Factory Overhead account may therefore contain a debit balance at the end of the period, indicating:
a an operating loss.
b underapplied amounts to Work in Process.
c overapplied amounts to Work in Process.
d the dollar value of lost business.

7 Gregg Company had $3,000 of overapplied factory overhead at the end of 19X7. A year-end journal entry for this amount would include:
a a debit to Factory Overhead.
b a credit to Factory Overhead.
c a debit to Cost of Goods Sold.
d a credit to Cost of Goods Manufactured.

8 A "cost driver" is the term used to describe:
a any situation that involves under- or overapplied overhead.
b a cost that significantly exceeds the amount originally budgeted.
c factors that cause specific costs to be incurred within an organization.
d direct material and direct labor.

CAI22-1 *The employee evaluation* (L.O. 2)

Communication Principle: Many companies use written employee evaluations to provide feedback about on-the-job performance. These evaluations identify problem areas and clearly instruct the employee as to what is expected.

Depending on the circumstances, it is generally better to enhance (but not dilute or confuse) the communication with something positive. For example, managers may note an employee's strengths, point out the contribution of the employee's actions to the overall organization, and so forth before focusing on the problem areas.

COMMUNICATION OF ACCOUNTING INFORMATION

Generally speaking, a manager's remarks should be carefully packaged, as the goal is to move the organization forward, not backward. Managers who are successful and well respected by their peers have learned that everyone responds differently to criticism. These managers also know that "it's not what you say but how you say it."

■ ■ ■ ■ ■ ■ ■ ■

Richard Weglin acquired a medium-size manufacturing business several years ago. The company produces a quality product but has never been very profitable. Weglin's goal in buying the business was to institute cost controls, which have always been lacking, and to guide the company toward becoming a leader in its field. Thus far, things are going according to plan, and a job cost system is working well.

Weglin's best employee is Randall Hughes, a machinist who makes a critical precision part used in the company's product. Hughes is a model employee in almost every way. His workmanship is unsurpassed, and other employees respect and treat him as their role model. Unfortunately, though, there is a problem. Hughes has been with the firm for many years, long before the present job cost system was implemented. Despite being reminded over the years, he continually forgets to record the time spent on each job. In discussing this problem, Hughes has said:

- "Did I do that again? I guess old habits are hard to break."
- "These procedures are for the young guys. I know exactly how long it should take me to make each part."
- "You know I stay busy—what are you worried about?"
- "Just write something down for me; it will all work out in the end."

Weglin, in complete frustration, has decided to approach Hughes about this problem through a written employee evaluation.

Instructions

Assume the role of Weglin and prepare the evaluation. Assume that Hughes does not understand the operation and importance of a sound job cost system.

Answers to Chapter Quiz

1 c

2 b

3 a

4 c [Application rate = 90% ($180,000 ÷ $200,000); applied overhead = $210,000 × 0.90 = $189,000; $189,000 − $185,000 = $4,000 overapplied]

5 d

CHAPTER 23

Process Costing, Activity-Based Costing, and Just-in-Time Production

LEARNING OBJECTIVES

After studying this chapter, you should be able to:

1

Explain the basic features that are associated with
a process cost accounting system.

2

Define and calculate equivalent units of production.

3

Identify the factors that affect the computation of equivalent units.

4

Prepare a production cost report.

5

Distinguish between conventional and activity-based costing systems,
and use the latter to compute product costs.

6

Describe the basic features associated with a
just-in-time production system.

7

(Appendix) Use the weighted-average process costing method to calculate
the cost of goods completed and ending work in process inventory.

As you saw in Chapter 22, many companies accumulate production costs (and service costs as well) by use of a job order system. These systems are often employed by businesses such as custom-home builders, furniture manufacturers, and print shops, all of which typically operate in an environment that is subdivided into specific jobs or orders.

There are, as you can well imagine, numerous manufacturing applications that lack the job order "orientation." Picture the manufacture of paint, for example, where finished goods (e.g., one-gallon cans) continually roll off a production line. The manufacturing plant does not produce a batch of paint for the Decorating Den (say, job no. 376), then stop, and later resume operation to process the goods needed by Discount City (job no. 377). Manufacturing is ongoing and continuous; thus, product costing by job or order becomes difficult, if not impossible.

In such situations, accountants turn to a **process costing system** to accumulate costs. Process costing systems are often employed in steel, petroleum, chemical, and flour production as well as in many assembly types of industries (e.g., appliances and bicycles). Chapter 23 explores these systems along with two recent innovations in accounting and manufacturing: activity-based costing and just-in-time production.

PROCESS COSTING VERSUS JOB ORDER COSTING

OBJECTIVE

Explain the basic features that are associated with a process cost accounting system.

To a great extent, process costing systems operate in much the same manner as job order systems. Both systems are established to accumulate costs for a business and both use the same accounts. These accounts include Raw Materials, Work in Process, Finished Goods, Cost of Goods Sold, and Factory Overhead—all introduced earlier in the text. Furthermore, the flow of costs through these accounts is essentially the same no matter what system is used. The issuance of direct materials to production, for instance, would be recorded under process costing by a debit to Work in Process and a credit to Raw Materials; the cost of completed units is debited to Finished Goods and credited to Work in Process; and so forth. Should you need a refresher of production cost flows, we refer you to pages 907 through 915.

How the Systems Differ

There are three basic differences between job order and process cost accounting, all of which arise because of the nature of a continuous manufacturing environment. Such environments normally result in the manufacture of mass-produced, homogeneous goods. In other words, the units are virtually identical, all having received the same amounts of direct material, direct labor, and factory overhead through the process.

Since activities cannot be subdivided by job and there is really no need to do so, costs under a process system are accumulated by *process or department* for a specified period of time (e.g., one month). Often a process and department are synonymous—the blending process takes place in the blending department, the assembly process in the assembly department, and so on. Then, since all units are identical, equal costs are assigned to each unit produced during the period.

A second difference between the systems arises because in many manufacturing applications, several steps (i.e., processes) are required to complete a product. In our earlier paint illustration, for instance, various chemicals and colorings are combined in the mixing department. Next, the filling department pours the paint into cans, adds lids, and passes the cans along to a subsequent packaging operation. Here, labels are attached and the containers packed four to a case. As a final step, the cases are transferred to a finished goods warehouse.

This sequence of events is depicted in the middle of Exhibit 23-1, which shows the basic differences between job order costing and process cost accounting. Notice that the separate operation and departmental orientation requires a separate Work in Process account for each major manufacturing activity. Direct materials and direct labor, costs easily traced to production, are charged to the department where consumed or incurred. Factory overhead is then applied by using an overhead application rate.

The lack of cost accumulation by job or order does away with the use of job cost sheets. The sheets are replaced by *production cost reports*—the third basic difference between the two systems. These reports, which document the units and costs that flow through a manufacturing department, will be shown later in the chapter.

Earlier in the discussion we noted that process costing systems accumulate departmental costs *for a period of time.* Most businesses do not complete all production by the period's end; some units typically remain in process. As the following example reveals, in-process inventories create a measurement problem when calculating the costs assignable to manufactured goods.

The Paige Corporation, which uses a process cost system, began operations on January 2 of the current year. The following information pertains to the first month of activity:

MEASURING PRODUCTION VOLUME IN A PROCESS COSTING SYSTEM

Manufacturing Costs		Production	
Direct materials used	$ 90,000	Units completed	80,000
Direct labor	50,000	Units in process,	
Applied factory overhead*	60,000	¼ complete	80,000
Total manufacturing costs	$200,000		

* 120% of direct labor cost.

Paige has a $200,000 cost pool that must be split between 80,000 completed units and 80,000 units in process, as shown in the accompanying diagram:

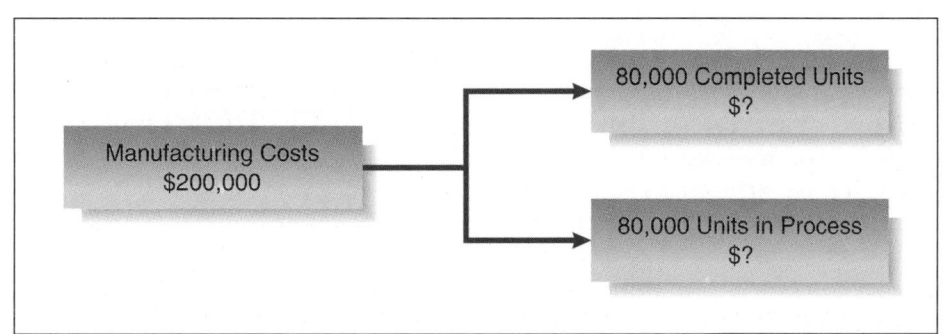

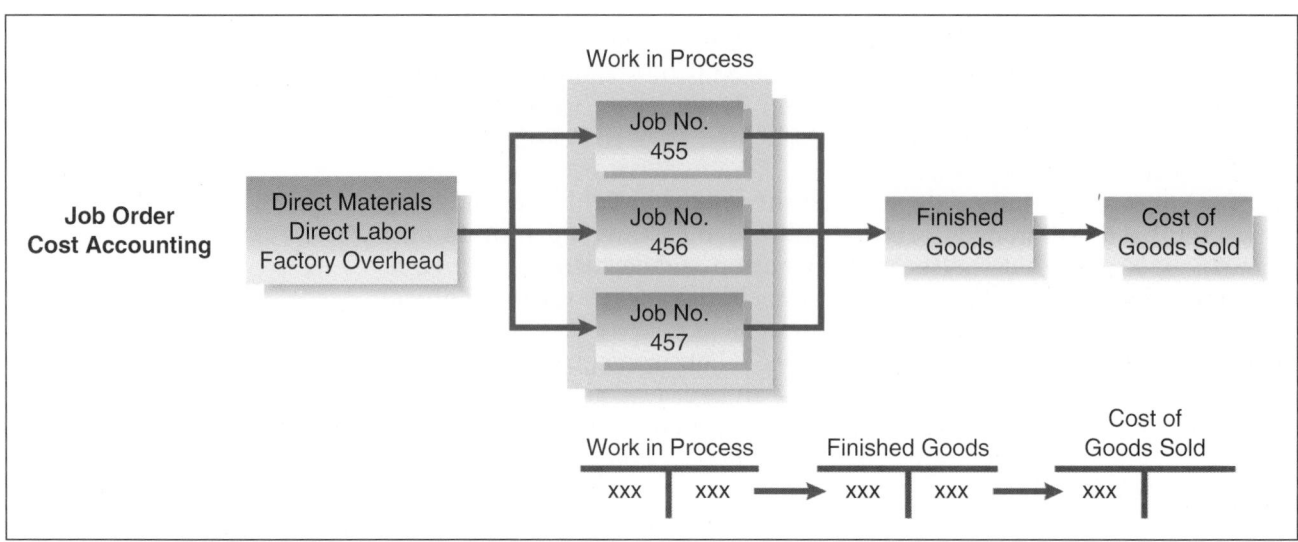

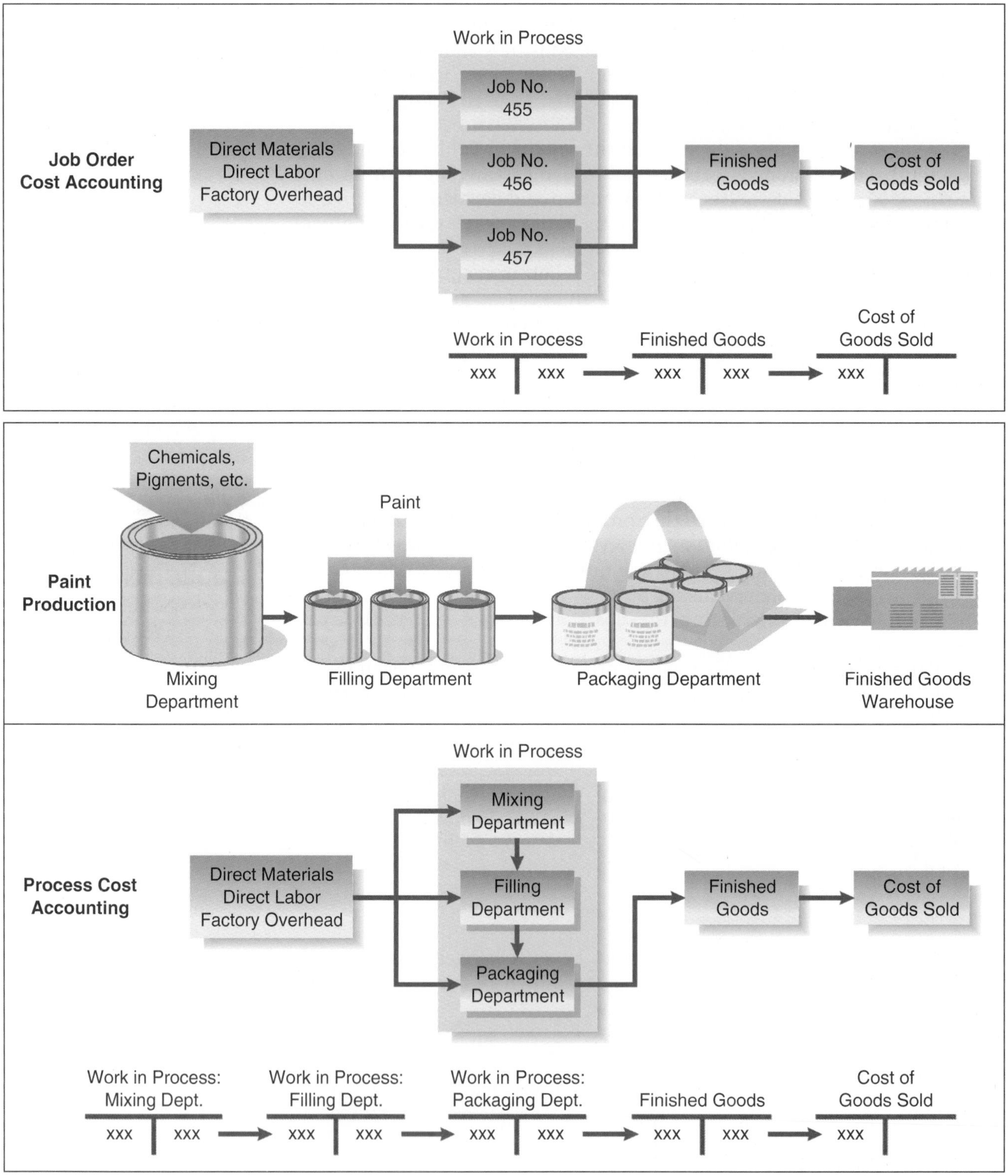

Job Order Cost Accounting

Direct Materials
Direct Labor
Factory Overhead

Work in Process

Job No. 455

Job No. 456

Job No. 457

Finished Goods

Cost of Goods Sold

Work in Process		Finished Goods		Cost of Goods Sold
xxx	xxx	xxx	xxx	xxx

Paint Production

Chemicals, Pigments, etc.

Paint

Mixing Department

Filling Department

Packaging Department

Finished Goods Warehouse

Process Cost Accounting

Direct Materials
Direct Labor
Factory Overhead

Work in Process

Mixing Department

Filling Department

Packaging Department

Finished Goods

Cost of Goods Sold

Work in Process: Mixing Dept.		Work in Process: Filling Dept.		Work in Process: Packaging Dept.		Finished Goods		Cost of Goods Sold
xxx	xxx	xxx	xxx	xxx	xxx	xxx	xxx	xxx

EXHIBIT 23-1
Job Order Costing Versus
Process Cost Accounting

In more familiar terms, the cost pool is located in the Work in Process account at the end of January. To ensure that direct materials, direct labor, and factory overhead follow the flow of production, a portion of the $200,000 must be removed from this account and transferred to Finished Goods.

Some individuals would say that Work in Process should be credited for $100,000 (i.e., one-half of the cost pool) because 50% of Paige's total production is completed. Stated differently, since the average cost per unit is $1.25 ($200,000 ÷ 160,000 units), $100,000 (80,000 completed units × $1.25) should be transferred to the Finished Goods account. Although the preceding computation is straightforward, it is, at the same time, logically unsound. We cannot add 80,000 completed units to 80,000 units in process. It's like adding apples and oranges—a meaningless total is generated.

Equivalent Units

To arrive at a proper measure of performance, accountants use a base known as equivalent units. An **equivalent unit** is a physical unit stated in terms of a finished unit. For example, if a company started work on 12 physical units (e.g., cars, tons, gallons) and the units are 75% complete at the end of the period,[1] 9 equivalent units (12 × 0.75) have been produced. It is important to note that *none* of these units are currently completed—all are still in process. The company has simply done the work *equivalent* to manufacturing nine finished goods (see Exhibit 23-2).

OBJECTIVE 2

Define and calculate equivalent units of production.

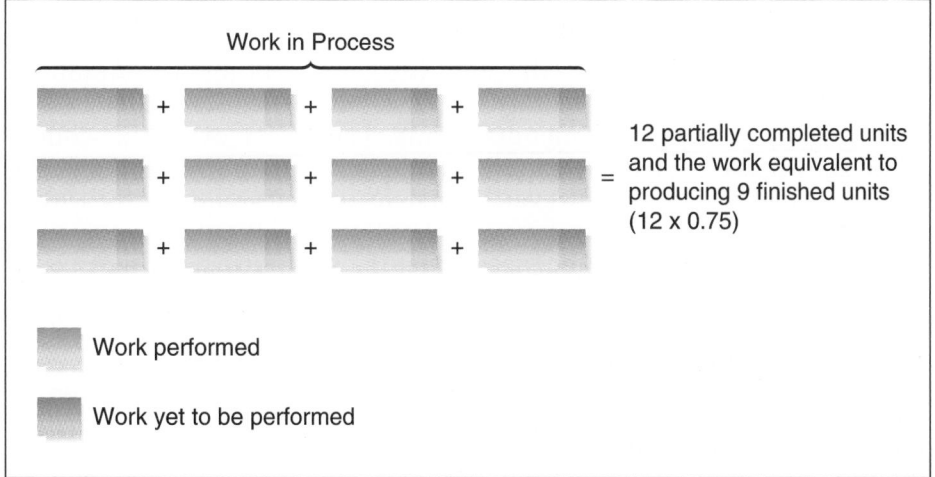

**EXHIBIT 23-2
The Concept of Equivalent Units**

Returning to the Paige Corporation example, 100,000 equivalent units of production took place in January:

	Physical Units		% of Work Completed During January		Equivalent Units
Units completed	80,000	×	100%	=	80,000
Units in process, ¼ complete	80,000	×	25%	=	20,000
					100,000

[1] The 75% figure refers to an average stage of completion in a continuous process.

Because operations commenced at the beginning of the year, the 80,000 units completed were all started in January. Consequently, 100% of the work on these goods occurred during the month.

Factors That Affect Equivalent Production

Having introduced the concept of equivalent units, we must now become a bit more detailed. Three factors must be considered in all equivalent-unit computations:

- The presence of a beginning work in process inventory
- The introduction of production costs at different points in the manufacturing process
- The method of process costing used

Beginning Work in Process Inventory

If a firm has a beginning work in process inventory, the goods must be studied to determine the work performed in prior periods. Assume, for instance, that at the start of May a company has 500 units in process that are three-fifths complete. To finish the goods during the current accounting period (i.e., May), 200 equivalent units of production are needed (500 × $\frac{2}{5}$ = 200). Equivalent-unit calculations focus on the work performed during the *present* period because of the need to figure the current unit cost of manufacturing.

Cost Incurrence in the Manufacturing Process

A second point to consider is that the three factors of production (direct materials, direct labor, and factory overhead) are generally introduced in different ways throughout manufacturing. Labor and overhead, collectively known as *conversion cost*, are often incurred uniformly through the process. Direct materials, however, can be introduced at different stages of production. In some products, for example, all materials enter manufacturing at the beginning. With other goods, materials are introduced at specific points after manufacturing has commenced (e.g., a part may be added at the 50% stage of completion, the product may be encased in protective packaging at the end of the process, and so forth).

The uniform introduction of conversion cost and the introduction of materials at specified points require the calculation of separate equivalent-unit figures. For example, assume that Sparks Company uses a process cost system. At the beginning of July, the firm had a work in process inventory of 3,000 units, 30% complete. During July, the beginning work in process was completed along with 7,500 other units that had entered production. Finally, on July 31 the factory foreman determined that the ending work in process totaled 5,000 units, 20% complete. All materials are introduced at the start of manufacturing, and labor and overhead are incurred uniformly throughout the process. The equivalent units for July are calculated as follows:

	Physical Units	Equivalent Units	
		Materials	Conversion
Completed			
Beginning work in process	3,000	—	2,100
Units started and completed	7,500	7,500	7,500
Ending work in process	5,000	5,000	1,000
	15,500	12,500	10,600

To explain, the beginning work in process inventory received no additional material. Remember, these units were begun last period, and all material is introduced at the start of production. To complete the beginning inventory, 70% of the work was performed in July, resulting in 2,100 (3,000 × 0.70) equivalent conversion units. Next, observe that 7,500 units were started and completed. Thus, all material for these units was introduced during the current month along with 100% of the processing, giving rise to 7,500 equivalent units of materials and conversion. Finally, we assume that the ending work in process was started in July, resulting in the introduction of 5,000 equivalent units of material. Because the ending inventory is only 20% complete, Sparks did 1,000 (5,000 × 0.20) equivalent units of conversion. These facts are depicted graphically in Exhibit 23-3.

EXHIBIT 23-3
Computation of Equivalent Units

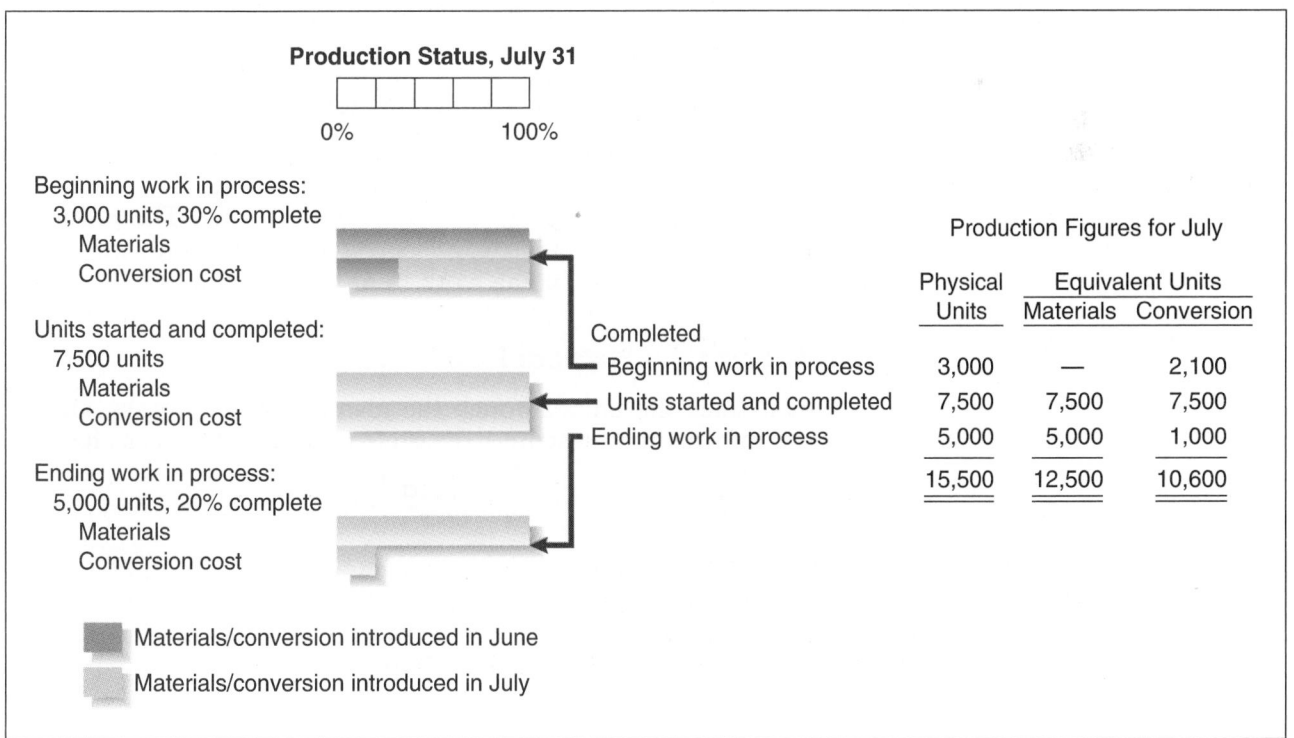

Process Costing Method

The third issue to address in the computation of equivalent units is the process costing method used by the firm. Two approaches are available: FIFO and weighted average.

Under the **FIFO method,** the beginning work in process inventory is assumed to be the first batch of goods completed (i.e., the first-in are the first-out). This batch is therefore treated as being separate and distinct from those units that are started and completed during the period. In addition, under the FIFO method, any work performed on the beginning work in process inventory in the previous accounting period must be considered when calculating the current period's equivalent units. These features are not new; they were both discussed and illustrated in the just-concluded Sparks Company example.

The remainder of our presentation will use the FIFO process costing approach. The weighted-average method, which typically results in different equivalent-unit figures, is introduced in an appendix to this chapter.

COMPREHENSIVE EXAMPLE

OBJECTIVE
4

Prepare a production cost report.

To bring together a number of the concepts discussed thus far, we will study the manufacturing operations of Berloff, Inc. The following information pertains to September:

- Beginning work in process inventory: 4,000 units, 75% complete; cost, $21,900
- Number of units started during September: 13,000
- Total units completed: 11,000
- Ending work in process inventory: 6,000 units, 40% complete
- September manufacturing costs: direct materials used, $32,500; conversion cost, $48,880

All materials are introduced at the start of the process, and conversion costs are incurred uniformly throughout manufacturing. The following approach is suggested to calculate the cost of goods completed during September and the cost of the ending work in process inventory.

Step 1: Analyze the Physical Flow

Berloff must trace the units through the manufacturing process. On the basis of the information presented, the proper physical flow is as follows:

	Physical Units	
Beginning work in process	4,000	
Units started	13,000	
Units to account for	17,000	←
Completed		
Beginning work in process	4,000	Must be equal
Units started and completed	7,000	
Ending work in process	6,000	
Units accounted for	17,000	←

The production manager has 17,000 units to account for during the month: the beginning work in process and the units started in September.

Assuming no spoilage, these units have either been completed by the company's manufacturing activities or are still in production at month-end. As you can see, the completed goods are really composed of two separate batches: the units in process on September 1 and an additional 7,000 units that were started and completed during the period. The latter batch is obtained by subtracting the beginning work in process from the total finished units manufactured (11,000 − 4,000 = 7,000).

Step 2: Compute Equivalent Units

Once the physical flow is determined, current production is then translated into equivalent units. Because materials are introduced at the start of the process and labor and overhead are incurred evenly, the figures presented in Exhibit 23-4 are obtained (see the numbers in color type).

Step 3: Compute Equivalent-Unit Costs

The cost per equivalent unit is calculated by dividing production costs by the equivalent units computed in Step 2. Just as the equivalent production figures are calculated for current activity, so, too, are the unit costs. The necessary procedures appear at the top of the next page.

EXHIBIT 23-4
Equivalent Production Figures for Berloff, Inc.

	Physical Units		
Beginning work in process	4,000		
Units started	13,000		
Units to account for	17,000		

		Equivalent Units	
	Physical Units	Materials	Conversion
Completed			
Beginning work in process*	4,000	—	1,000
Units started and completed†	7,000	7,000	7,000
Ending work in process‡	6,000	6,000	2,400
Units accounted for	17,000	13,000	10,400

* All materials were added last period; 25% of the conversion was performed in this period.
† All materials and conversion were introduced in this period.
‡ Units were started in this period; all materials were introduced plus 40% of the conversion.

Costs	Total	Materials	Conversion
Beginning work in process	$ 21,900	$ —	$ —
Current	81,380	32,500	48,880
Total cost to account for	$103,280	$32,500 ÷	$48,880 ÷
Equivalent units*		13,000	10,400
Cost per equivalent unit		$2.50	$4.70

* From Step 2.

ETHICS ISSUE

The controller of Webcore, Inc., does not want to take the time to study the stage of completion of the ending work in process inventory. "It's a trivial exercise for our company because production is steady. Let's forget about equivalent-unit calculations; who cares if the work in process valuation is slightly in error? Just assume the goods are 50% complete." Comment.

Note that the cost of the beginning work in process inventory ($21,900) is disregarded in unit-cost computations—a logical procedure because this amount represents work performed in the previous period. The production manager, however, is still held accountable for the related expenditures, requiring that the $21,900 figure be reflected in the $103,280 total.

Step 4: Cost Assignment

Berloff's cost pool of $103,280 must now be assigned to the goods completed during the period and the ending work in process inventory. This assignment is accomplished by multiplying the cost per equivalent unit by the proper number of equivalent units. As shown in Exhibit 23-5, the cost of goods completed is $77,000, and the ending work in process is $26,280.

Because the prior period cost of $21,900 was not considered when computing equivalent-unit figures, it is attached entirely to the beginning work in process inventory. That is, no prior period cost is allocated to either the units started and completed or the partially completed production at the end of the period. Observe that the total cost accounted for ($103,280) agrees with the total cost to account for (as shown in Step 3).

Production Cost Report

Companies that use a process costing system document the period's manufacturing activity on a **production cost report.** The report is a summary of the units and costs that have passed through a department. In actuality, it

EXHIBIT 23-5
Cost Assignment of Berloff, Inc.

	Equivalent Units				
	Materials	Conversion	**Completed**		
			Beginning work in process		
			Prior period cost	$21,900	
			Conversion cost: 1,000 × $4.70	4,700	$ 26,600
Completed			Units started and completed		
Beginning work in process	—	1,000	Materials: 7,000 × $2.50	$17,500	
Units started and completed	7,000	7,000	Conversion cost: 7,000 × $4.70	32,900	50,400
Ending work in process	6,000	2,400	Total cost of completed goods		$ 77,000
Units accounted for	13,000	10,400	Ending work in process		
			Materials: 6,000 × $2.50	$15,000	
			Conversion cost: 2,400 × $4.70	11,280	26,280
			Total cost accounted for		$103,280

is the combined result of Steps 1–4 just discussed. Briefly review these steps and then focus on Exhibit 23-6—the end product of the entire process.

BERLOFF, INC.
Production Cost Report
For the Month Ended September 30, 19XX

	Physical Units		
Beginning work in process	4,000		
Units started	13,000		
Units to account for	17,000		

		Equivalent Units	
		Materials	Conversion
Completed			
Beginning work in process	4,000	—	1,000
Units started and completed	7,000	7,000	7,000
Ending work in process	6,000	6,000	2,400
Units accounted for	17,000	13,000	10,400

Costs	Total		
Beginning work in process	$ 21,900	$ —	$ —
Current	81,380	32,500	48,880
Total cost to account for	$103,280	$32,500 ÷	$48,880 ÷
Equivalent units		13,000	10,400
Cost per equivalent unit		$2.50	$4.70

Cost Assignment		
Completed		
Beginning work in process		
Prior period cost	$21,900	
Conversion cost: 1,000 × $4.70	4,700	$ 26,600
Units started and completed		
Materials: 7,000 × $2.50	$17,500	
Conversion cost: 7,000 × $4.70	32,900	50,400
Total cost of completed goods		$ 77,000
Ending work in process		
Materials: 6,000 × $2.50	$15,000	
Conversion cost: 2,400 × $4.70	11,280	26,280
Total cost accounted for		$103,280

STEP 1 STEP 2 STEP 3 STEP 4

EXHIBIT 23-6
Production Cost Report: FIFO

The Work in Process Account

The production cost report is really a disclosure mechanism for various amounts contained in the general ledger. As evidence, we present Berloff's Work in Process account:

Work in Process		
Beginning balance	21,900	
Materials	32,500	
Conversion	48,880	
	103,280	

The balance of $103,280 coincides with the costs that Berloff's production manager had to account for during the period. Because the cost of completed units totals $77,000, the following journal entry is needed on September 30:

Finished Goods	77,000	
Work in Process		77,000
To transfer the cost of completed units to finished goods		

This entry, identical to that shown in Chapter 22 for a job order system, makes the Work in Process account consistent with the figures presented on the production cost report.

A Subsequent Processing Department

Our example assumes that Berloff's goods do not require any further work. As noted earlier in the chapter, items manufactured in a continuous process must often pass through several departments. For example, goods may be started in the assembly department and then transferred to the finishing department for final processing.

In Berloff's case, suppose that our illustration focused on the operations of Department A. If, say, the 11,000 units completed were transferred to Department B for additional work, the proper journal entry would have been:

Work in Process: Dept. B	77,000	
Work in Process: Dept. A		77,000
To transfer 11,000 completed units to Department B		

Recall that each department maintains its own Work in Process account. The accounting in Department B would parallel that shown for Department A, with several minor modifications. These modifications are typically discussed in advanced accounting courses.

In recent years, several significant changes have occurred in the ways that companies determine the cost of their products. These changes are due, in part, to increased competition and a feeling that the costs derived by using conventional procedures were highly inaccurate. Products that consumed few manufacturing resources were often charged with a high amount of cost, and vice versa. Unfortunately, incorrect costs may have significant ramifications for a firm when it comes to price setting and decision making. Because prices are often based on cost, product overcosting may result in a loss of sales since the affected firm cannot compete against companies that sell cheaper goods. Undercosting, in contrast, may mislead a business into boosting volume of what is actually an unprofitable product. The greater the activity, the bigger the negative impact on bottom-line income.

ACTIVITY-BASED COSTING

OBJECTIVE

Distinguish between conventional and activity-based costing systems, and use the latter to compute product costs.

The Problem of Averaging

The problem of over- and undercosted products often arises because of the averaging that occurs in many accounting procedures. To illustrate, let us focus on a straightforward nonmanufacturing example. Assume that the Gibsons, Hartleys, Mortons, and Weavers have developed close ties over the years through various social gatherings. On a weekly basis, each couple has paid $10 into a "pool" that will be used for a dream vacation in Hawaii. The total contributions now stand at $14,000. Suppose the couples take the vacation and their expenditures total exactly $14,000, subdivided as follows:

	Gibsons	Hartleys	Mortons	Weavers
Airfare	$1,400	$1,400	$1,400	$1,400
Condominium*	600	800	900	700
Rental car	100	200	150	100
Meals	300	500	600	400
Tours	200	400	500	300
Miscellaneous	300	400	550	400
Total	$2,900	$3,700	$4,100	$3,300

* Varies with the number of bedrooms and view.

Friendships aside, when the pool is used to pay the preceding outlays, the Gibsons and Weavers would no doubt object. Each of these couples put in $3,500 ($14,000 ÷ 4) and spent less than they contributed. If we assume the pool's funds are divided equally, the Gibsons and Weavers would have subsidized the "good times" of the Hartleys and Mortons. The end result of the averaging procedure follows.

	Gibsons	Hartleys	Mortons	Weavers
Actual cost (i.e., amount paid)	$3,500	$3,500	$3,500	$3,500
Trip expenditures	2,900	3,700	4,100	3,300
Over-/undercosted	Over	Under	Under	Over

As these figures indicate, the use of averages will over- or undercost each couple's trip. The Gibsons, for example, *actually paid* $3,500, but their expenditures totaled only $2,900. Their true cost will exceed their outlays in Hawaii by $600, resulting in an "overcosted" vacation. The situation is reversed for the Hartleys and Mortons, whose pool contributions (i.e., costs) were less than the total they paid for food, lodging, airfare, and other items.

Extending the Concept to a Business

This simplified example has shown the problems encountered when costs are averaged. These same problems occur in business organizations, particularly in entities that have widely varying departments and activities. Consider the graphic that appears in Exhibit 23-7. Here we depict a manufacturing company that is composed of four departments: painting, machining, assembly, and finishing. Each department, in turn, performs various activities. The machining department, for instance, is involved with production run setups, material handling, processing, inspection, and rework of defective units.

Suppose our focus is on factory overhead. To improve accuracy, overhead costs are accumulated in each department rather than tallied for the company as a whole and spread (i.e., averaged) among the four units. This procedure would be akin to the Gibsons, Hartleys, Mortons, and Weavers abandoning the pool concept and paying solely for their own expenditures. When the time comes to figure product costs, each department is now free to select an application base that best drives the department's overhead incurrence. Machining might use machine hours, assembly might use labor hours, and so forth.

Although this procedure seems logical, it may contain an inherent deficiency. Just as work performed and overhead incurrence vary widely among departments, activities may vary widely *within* a department. The use of machine hours by the machining operation appears reasonable at first glance. Consider, however, that some of the department's activities

EXHIBIT 23-7
Organization of a Manufacturing Company

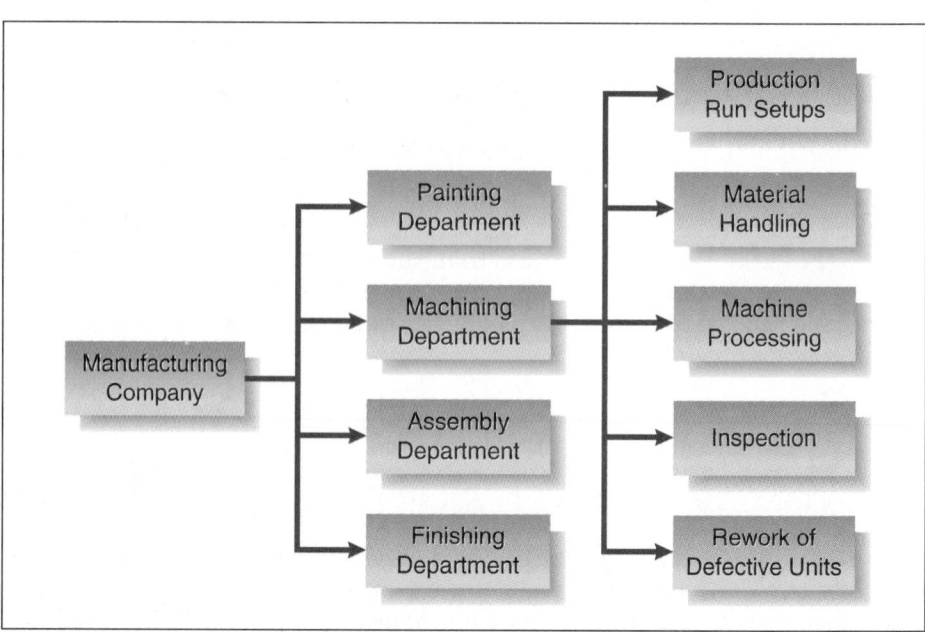

(e.g., setup and inspection) bear little relation to the number of hours processed. Also, some products may be manufactured in long production runs of many units and require few setups and inspections. Others may have the opposite attributes: small production runs and constant testing. The use of machine hours in this case (1) is an inappropriate cost driver and (2) fails to discriminate between the high-cost/low-cost good. To solve these problems, many companies are turning to a technique known as activity-based costing (ABC).

The Nature of ABC

Activity-based costing (ABC) involves dividing a department into specific activities and then selecting an application base (cost driver) for each activity. By following such a procedure, costing accuracy is dramatically improved. Subdividing a department in this manner produces another benefit as well—for both manufacturers *and* service entities. Studying an activity gives managers insights about the activity, in particular, the efficiency with which the activity is being performed and its contribution to the organization. Through this process, cost savings may be identified, and the activity may be restructured (or perhaps even eliminated). The purpose is to identify those activities that add value to the product or business and those that do not.

An Example

To illustrate the procedures related to an activity-based system, we will focus on the machining department of Superior Metal Works. The firm, which uses a conventional accounting system, applies overhead to its two products (Standard and Deluxe) on the basis of machine hours. The following data are available:

- Estimated departmental overhead for the period: $500,000
- Machine processing time per unit: 8 hours
- Expected production volume of each product: 625 units

Superior calculated an overhead application rate of $50 per machine hour in the manner shown.

$$\text{Overhead Application Rate} = \frac{\text{Estimated Machining Overhead}}{\text{Estimated Machine Hours}}$$

$$= \frac{\$500,000}{10,000 \text{ hours}^*}$$

$$= \$50 \text{ per machine hour}$$

* (625 units of Standard × 8 hours) + (625 units of Deluxe × 8 hours).

On the basis of the information presented, Superior would charge $400 of overhead ($50 per hour × 8 hours) to both Standard and Deluxe.

Suppose a closer look at the company's machining department found three different activities being performed: setup, machine processing, and inspection. In addition, we now learn that the Standard model is produced in several large runs and requires minimal inspection to achieve quality standards. With the Deluxe model, manufacturing runs are small and quality is assured through a series of detailed performance tests. If Superior decides to use ABC, the company would identify cost drivers for its activities and then develop individual activity application rates. The necessary procedures follow.

	Setup	Machine Processing	Inspection
Cost driver	Number of setups	Machine hours (MH)	Inspection hours (IH)
Activity cost	$150,000	$300,000	$50,000
Driver volume	10	10,000	2,000
Application rate	$15,000 per setup	$30 per MH	$25 per IH

The amounts used in these calculations are yearly estimates, with the result being an estimated cost divided by an estimated application base (cost driver). The volume figures for each base are obtained by summing the individual activity of both Standard and Deluxe. The accompanying table shows the costs computed for both products.

	Standard		Deluxe	
	Driver Volume	Cost	Driver Volume	Cost
Setups at $15,000	2	$ 30,000	8	$120,000
Machine processing at $30 per machine hour	5,000	150,000	5,000	150,000
Inspection at $25 per inspection hour	500	12,500	1,500	37,500
Total		$192,500		$307,500

When each of these figures is expressed on a per-unit basis, the results are rather startling when compared with those obtained by using conventional accounting:

	Standard	Deluxe
Conventional accounting	$400	$400
Activity-based costing*	308	492

* $192,500 ÷ 625 units = $308; $307,500 ÷ 625 units = $492.

You can see that by averaging all departmental activities together and using a base that failed to discriminate between the activities performed, the Standard model was penalized. That is, it was charged with $400 of cost when a better estimate would have been only $308. The situation is reversed for the Deluxe model.

As noted earlier in the discussion, incorrect cost figures can lead to incorrect decisions on the part of management. Suppose, for example, that direct material and direct labor costs on the Deluxe model were $200, raising total conventional product costs to $600 ($200 + $400). Assume further that the Deluxe selling price had been set at $660. ABC would reveal that instead of making $60 profit on every unit sold, Superior was really losing $32 [$660 − ($200 + $492)]. It is evident that any attempts to boost sales would actually have been detrimental to the firm.

To conclude, the procedures related to ABC are definitely more involved than those followed with conventional systems. Rather than just one cost driver, the system requires use of multiple cost drivers. Multiple cost drivers give rise to additional computations and record-keeping chores. Fortunately, computer-controlled machines and scanning systems accumulate much of the needed information automatically, thus eliminating potential drudgery for the accountant. Many companies that are using ABC find that the system's benefits far exceed the costs and headaches associated with implementation.

On several occasions throughout the text, we have noted that manufacturers have three types of inventories: raw materials, work in process, and finished goods. Until recently, you could walk into most any factory and warehouse facility and see stockpiles of goods awaiting, in, or through production. In the 1980s, though, many companies adopted procedures used by Japanese firms—procedures that strive for minimal (and sometimes zero) inventories on hand.

Let us stop and think about why companies, especially manufacturers, carry inventories. In the simplest case, finished goods are held to satisfy customer demand, and raw materials are stored to keep production running smoothly. Some writers have suggested that American manufacturers operate with a *just-in-case (JIC)* mind-set. In other words, finished goods are needed because the firm is unable to accurately predict product demand. Raw materials are held to offset any defects that may be discovered during manufacturing or just in case a supplier cannot meet agreed-on delivery dates. Thus, keeping extra units on hand is really a means of compensating for fluctuating customer demand, defective parts, and late shipments.

Unfortunately, this "insurance" is costly. Inventories must be stored and moved through the production facility. The goods are taxed by local governments and are subject to obsolescence and deterioration. Further, a considerable amount of money is tied up and gathering dust in warehouses and on plant floors. The company could likely use these funds elsewhere for more profitable endeavors or perhaps to reduce outstanding debt. Stated simply, in many situations, the acquisition or manufacture of goods for inventory is viewed as wasteful. To help eliminate these problems and regain a competitive edge, many American businesses have begun to use just-in-time (JIT) production systems.

JUST-IN-TIME PRODUCTION

OBJECTIVE
6

Describe the basic features associated with a just-in-time production system.

Characteristics of JIT Production

Under a **just-in-time (JIT)** system, goods are manufactured just in time to fill customer orders. This philosophy extends backward through the system, with manufactured parts (such as subassemblies) being produced just prior to being used in making the finished good. In addition, raw materials are acquired only when they are ready to enter production. In theory, the goal is to cut inventory levels to zero. Normally, however, management is more than satisfied if inventories are reduced to bare minimum levels after JIT procedures are instituted. These bare minimum levels are often amounts that will satisfy demand or usage for only a few days and, in some cases, a few *hours*!

Just-in-time systems are characterized by a "demand-pull" philosophy. That is, the sale of a finished unit triggers the whole process. The sale dictates the need to produce a finished good and for various preceding workstations to perform the necessary manufacturing tasks. These workstations need raw materials and thus activate the request to a supplier for shipment. Under a JIT system, nothing is produced until the sales order is in hand. The "pull" system may be contrasted with a "push" system, which has been and is still used by many companies. Here, raw materials are put into production and pushed through various fabrication activities, perhaps accumulating on the shop floor in the form of work in progress. Eventually these goods will be completed, but the lack of a sales order contributes to stockpiling in warehouses. As noted earlier, inventory accumulation becomes a very expensive proposition.

A number of factors must be satisfied if a company is to be successful at JIT production. Two elements worthy of mention at this point are supplier reliability and a commitment to total quality control.

Supplier Reliability

Because a company has drastically reduced or abandoned raw material inventories, JIT production gives rise to changes in purchasing patterns. Where a company would have acquired a month's supply of parts and stored them in a warehouse, JIT dictates that many small purchases be made. Several shipments per day from a given supplier are not uncommon. Suppliers must be willing to work under these terms and, most important, must be reliable. Since materials basically enter production shortly after arrival, late deliveries and partially filled orders cannot be tolerated. To streamline the entire process, the manufacturer and suppliers' computers often communicate with each other when it comes time to order and ship goods.

Further complicating matters, the materials received must be of top quality. The quality standards sought are often much higher than normal, given the lack of backup to cover defects. Many suppliers have been able to meet JIT manufacturers' rigid standards; however, some have not. This inability to upgrade quality, the reliability problem just discussed, and a desire for stronger buyer/seller relations have created an interesting trend: large manufacturing firms are slashing the number of suppliers used. The manufacturers are demanding higher levels of service and are willing to pay a price to get the job done. As an example, Xerox found that its cheapest suppliers were sometimes lax in pulling substandard goods out of the company's purchases. Partly in response to this situation, Xerox has reduced suppliers from 5,000 to about 500 and, at the same time, cut the reject rates on parts by a factor of 13.[2]

---

[2] For an interesting discussion of suppliers and quality, see "Suppliers Struggle to Improve Quality As Big Firms Slash Their Vendor Rolls," *The Wall Street Journal*, August 16, 1991, pp. B1, B2.

HIGHLIGHT

J–I–T Spells Effective Inventory Management

Skill in managing inventories can have a significant impact on a business. Let us focus on Chrysler Corporation and Corning Inc., to illustrate the point. In the late 1970s, when auto demand seemed to escalate forever, Chrysler's management decided that, rather than build cars at dealer or customer request, it would stockpile vehicles to keep factories running smoothly despite swings in orders. When demand suddenly slowed, Chrysler got sandbagged. All around Detroit, thousands of its cars sat unsold on company lots.

"It was a big joke around town," recalls a former manager. "Everywhere you looked you saw Chrysler vehicles." He and others say the decision to stockpile inventory was the single biggest cause of the company's near-collapse in 1979. Since then, Chrysler has made significant improvements. At its Belvidere, Illinois plant, for example, parts inventories are used up every 2.5 working days—a performance matching the best Japanese standards.

Another big advocate of effective inventory management is Corning Inc. The firm installed a just-in-time production system at its ceramics plant in Erwin, New York. Prior to adopting the JIT system, Corning warehoused large supplies of everything it needed, even the cardboard boxes that package the finished ceramic parts. Now, every night, its one cardboard supplier delivers what it thinks Corning will need the next day.

Surveying the two eye-level stacks near the factory's loading dock, a Corning purchasing agent gestures to the pallets, which once occupied yards and yards of space. "This is it," he says. "Moreover, Corning pays just for what it uses, and it does so through one contract rather than, as before, through 40 separate orders." The savings are enormous. Carrying each $1 of inventory typically costs manufacturers 20 to 25 cents. Corning says that so far its program has saved as much as $10 million at the Erwin plant and some $180 million throughout the company.

The program began with a companywide campaign. "Inventory is evil, and we sought to eradicate it," notes an executive who oversees manufacturing at Erwin and 10 other factories. A study at the New York facility found that just 6% of inventory was "live"—in use—at any moment. Total space devoted to storage, though, was 185,000 square feet, equalling six football fields. Today, two leased warehouses have been eliminated. Gone too are about two-thirds of the stocks formerly warehoused at the factory. And because Corning now supplies its customers only as needed, it is better able to notice a drop in demand and adjust its output gradually.

Coupled with the JIT system are speedier service and closer contacts with customers. Thanks to a new electronic order-processing system, the company typically manufactures and delivers ceramic parts in less time than it used to take just to *confirm* an order. To illustrate system capabilities, the manager of materials control pulled out an invoice that he had saved from several years ago. According to one line on the printout, Erwin would deliver 22,000 pieces of a certain type of ceramic in the week ending October 30, 1988. Now, the invoices specify not just the week but the day and even the minute. How successful is this system? In a five-month period, the company had only one service blemish. (A driver misread an order's paperwork and hauled a load of ceramic to Alabama instead of Philadelphia.) In 1987, 30% of Erwin's shipments weren't delivered on time. Now, the manager says, "We send it today, and the customer uses it tomorrow."

The JIT system isn't perfect, though, especially when a firm's customers are using the same philosophy. Because most Corning clientele also carry leaner inventories, on-time delivery is crucial. At Corning and countless other companies, serious interruptions due to a strike anywhere along the chain of supply, bad weather, or any other mishaps could seriously affect a firm's production. "We're more vulnerable to supply disruptions," concedes an Erwin customer.

Total Quality Control (TQC)

Some spoilage and defective units are common in almost all manufacturing operations. Given the lack of inventories in a JIT system, spoilage and defects can bring an entire manufacturing process to a grinding halt. Consistent with JIT is a commitment to **total quality control (TQC),** a concept that strives for perfection in both materials acquisition and the manufacturing process.

EXECUTIVE BRIEFING
Quality: A Major Concern to Automobile Manufacturers

Robert Weil
Vice-President and Controller
American Honda Motor Company, Inc.

In the U.S. automobile industry, consumer buying power is strong and competition is fierce. Manufacturers for many years have offered varying-length warranty packages as a means of gaining a competitive marketing advantage. Obviously, this can be very expensive, depending on the quality of the product and the extent of coverage. It is an especially important issue when an all-new, redesigned model is introduced.

Take, for example, the introduction of the 1990 Honda Accord, a vehicle accompanied by a three-year, 36,000-mile warranty. Honda's financial staff had to evaluate the accounting issues of estimating and recording the related liability and expense. Perhaps more important, though, operations people had to address several new challenges in the effort to successfully launch this redesigned model. As a result, significant steps were taken to ensure conformity with quality standards in design, manufacture, distribution, and customer delivery. In response to this "total quality effort," the Accord has become the best-selling car in the United States for the past few years.

Honda and the other automakers realize that a product's reputation is not earned on warranty coverage. Rather, it is based on the standards used in design and the ability of manufacturing to achieve those standards. Factors such as these collectively contribute to a high-quality product, which, in turn, leads to a high level of customer satisfaction.

Manufacturing excellence is of such concern in today's business climate that many companies are now computing and monitoring so-called **quality costs.** These are costs related to dealing with or eliminating the acquisition or manufacture of marginal goods. Examples include expenditures for:

Quality engineering	Production stoppages
Product design changes	Rework of bad units
Equipment maintenance	Lost sales and lost customers
Inspection	Warranties
Field testing	Product liability suits

Given the wide diversity of quality costs, TQC advocates feel it is cheaper in the long run to operate in a zero-defect environment. This fact is made very clear by the general manager of Hewlett-Packard's Computer Systems Division, who stated:

The earlier you detect and prevent a defect, the more you can save. If you throw away a defective 2-cent resistor before you use it, you lose 2 cents. If you don't find it until it has been soldered into a computer component, it may cost $10 to repair the part. If you don't catch the component until it is in the user's hands, the repair will cost hundreds of dollars. Indeed, if a $5,000 computer has to be repaired in the field, the expense may exceed the manufacturing cost.[3]

The physical flow of goods in many continuous manufacturing processes is on a first-in, first-out basis, with units in process at the beginning of a period being the first ones completed. As we explained in Chapter 9, the costing method used to account for inventory may be entirely different from the actual flow of goods through a warehouse (or in this case, a manufacturing facility). Accordingly, many companies have adopted weighted-average process costing.

APPENDIX: PROCESS COSTING AND THE WEIGHTED-AVERAGE METHOD

OBJECTIVE

7

Use the weighted-average process costing method to calculate the cost of goods completed and ending work in process inventory.

Features of Weighted-Average Costing

The focus of **weighted-average costing** is that all goods completed during the period are carried at the same unit cost. This cost, a weighted average, is derived by combining costs that are present in the beginning work in process inventory with those that arise from current manufacturing activities. On a per-unit basis, such amounts could differ because of recent wage increases, changes in supplier prices for materials, and other factors. Nevertheless, any differences are downplayed in favor of the weighted-average method's primary advantages: simplicity and reduced record-keeping requirements.

Given the preceding cost treatment, there is no need to account for the units completed as two separate batches of goods: those from the beginning work in process and those actually begun during the period (see p. 950). These batches are lumped together in the weighted-average approach, and it is assumed that *all* units completed are started and completed during the period. As an outgrowth of this assumption, any work performed previously on the beginning work in process inventory is ignored when computing equivalent units.

An Example

To illustrate these features we will use data from Berloff, Inc., which appear in the body of the chapter. Key data from page 950 are reproduced here for your convenience.

■ Beginning work in process inventory: 4,000 units, 75% complete; cost $21,900 (materials, $8,470; conversion, $13,430)[4]

---

[3] See "Product Quality: Profitable at Any Cost," *The New York Times*, March 3, 1985, Section 3, p. 3.

[4] The material and conversion cost figures ($8,470 and $13,430, respectively) are new here. The weighted-average method requires these amounts for the calculation of average cost figures.

- Number of units started during September: 13,000
- Total units completed: 11,000
- Ending work in process inventory: 6,000 units, 40% complete
- September manufacturing costs: direct materials used, $32,500; conversion cost, $48,880

All materials are introduced at the start of the process, and conversion costs are incurred uniformly throughout manufacturing.

The four steps that follow are required to figure the cost of finished goods manufactured and the cost of ending work in process inventory.

Step 1: Analyze the Physical Flow

To ensure that all units are properly accounted for, the company must trace its goods through production activities. As shown by the following tabulation, the 17,000 units charged to the department (beginning work in process plus units started) have either been completed or are still in process:

	Physical Units
Beginning work in process	4,000
Units started	13,000
Units to account for	17,000
Completed	11,000
Ending work in process	6,000
Units accounted for	17,000

(Units to account for 17,000 and Units accounted for 17,000 — Must be equal)

Step 2: Compute Equivalent Units

Next, the preceding figures are converted into equivalent units, as shown in Exhibit 23-8. Because the 11,000 finished units are assumed to be *started and completed* during the month, these units have 100% of the materials and conversion introduced in September (and, thus, 11,000 equivalent units each). The fact that the beginning work in process inventory actually had the materials added and 75% of the conversion work performed in August is ignored under the weighted-average method. Finally, the ending work in process inventory was started in September and progressed through 40% of the manufacturing operation, giving rise to 6,000 and 2,400 equivalent units for materials and conversion cost, respectively.

Step 3: Compute Equivalent-Unit Costs

The computation of the cost per equivalent unit, shown immediately below the exhibit, is very straightforward: production costs are divided by equivalent-unit totals.

EXHIBIT 23-8
Equivalent Production Figures:
Weighted-Average Method

	Physical Units		
Beginning work in process	4,000		
Units started	13,000		
Units to account for	17,000		

		Equivalent Units	
		Materials	Conversion
Completed	11,000	11,000	11,000
Ending work in process	6,000	6,000	2,400
Units accounted for	17,000	17,000	13,400

Costs	Total	Materials	Conversion
Beginning work in process	$ 21,900	$ 8,470	$13,430
Current	81,380	32,500	48,880
Total cost to account for	$103,280	$40,970 ÷	$62,310 ÷
Equivalent units*		17,000	13,400
Cost per equivalent unit		$2.41	$4.65

* From Step 2.

The combination of previous period and current costs and the related division procedure result in the calculation of *average* costs. These figures are now allocated to the month's total manufacturing output.

Step 4: Cost Assignment

Berloff incurred $103,280 of production costs to complete 11,000 units and partially manufacture 6,000 units. The cost of these goods is determined by multiplying the amount of material consumed and work performed (i.e., the equivalent-unit figures) by the unit costs just computed. Step 4, the cost assignment process, appears at the bottom of the company's production cost report in Exhibit 23-9.

BERLOFF, INC.
Production Cost Report
For the Month Ended September 30, 19XX

STEP 1

	Physical Units
Beginning work in process	4,000
Units started	13,000
Units to account for	17,000

STEP 2

		Equivalent Units	
		Materials	Conversion
Completed	11,000	11,000	11,000
Ending work in process	6,000	6,000	2,400
Units accounted for	17,000	17,000	13,400

STEP 3

Costs	Total		
Beginning work in process	$ 21,900	$ 8,470	$13,430
Current	81,380	32,500	48,880
Total cost to account for	$103,280	$40,970 ÷	$62,310 ÷
Equivalent units		17,000	13,400
Cost per equivalent unit		$2.41	$4.65

STEP 4

Cost Assignment

Completed		
Materials: 11,000 × $2.41	$26,510	
Conversion cost: 11,000 × $4.65	51,150	$ 77,660
Ending work in process		
Materials: 6,000 × $2.41	$14,460	
Conversion cost: 2,400 × $4.65	11,160	25,620
Total cost accounted for		$103,280

EXHIBIT 23-9
Production Cost Report:
Weighted-Average Method

END-OF-CHAPTER-REVIEW

LEARNING OBJECTIVES:
THE KEY POINTS

1 **Explain the basic features that are associated with a process cost accounting system.** Process costing systems are used in continuous process and assembly-line types of industries. With such systems, the manufacturing costs incurred flow through the Raw Materials, Work in Process, Finished Goods, and Cost of Goods

Sold accounts—the same as those established for a job order firm. In contrast, however, the cost accumulation method is significantly different, with costs being accumulated by department (or process) for a given time period. Furthermore, each department maintains its own Work in Process account and reports manufacturing activity on a production cost report.

2 Define and calculate equivalent units of production. Equivalent units are the basis for assigning inventoriable costs under a process costing system. On conclusion of a typical accounting period, many units have been fully manufactured whereas others are still in production. Because fully completed units cannot be combined with in-process units (i.e., the two batches are not the same), some common measurement base must be found. This base is equivalent units, or physical units that are stated in terms of finished units. If, for example, a company started 1,000 units into production and these goods are 70% complete at the end of the period, the firm has done the work equivalent to manufacturing 700 finished units. None of these goods are finished, however; they are all still in process.

3 Identify the factors that affect the computation of equivalent units. Three factors must be considered in the calculation of equivalent units: the presence of a beginning work in process inventory, the introduction of various production factors at different points in the manufacturing process, and the method of process costing used by the firm. If a company has a beginning work in process inventory, then some manufacturing work occurred on these units in the previous accounting period. Should the FIFO method of costing be in use, as illustrated in the body of the chapter, the work performed last period must be considered when determining equivalent-unit totals. In addition, because materials tend to be introduced at specific points in a manufacturing operation and conversion costs are incurred uniformly throughout a process, separate equivalent-unit figures must be computed for these costs.

The final factor to consider is whether the firm is using FIFO or weighted-average costing. As just noted, previous period manufacturing activity affects equivalent-unit calculations under FIFO. With weighted average, however, as explained in the chapter appendix, such work is ignored.

4 Prepare a production cost report. A production cost report summarizes both units manufactured and production costs for a given accounting period. The physical flow of goods through the production process is reported as are the equivalent units of materials added and work performed. Further, equivalent-unit costs are disclosed, and manufacturing costs are assigned to goods completed and the ending work in process inventory. The latter two amounts are obtained by multiplying the equivalent-unit figures by the per-unit costs.

5 Distinguish between conventional and activity-based costing systems, and use the latter to compute product costs. Under a conventional accounting system, the costs of various activities are merged together and averaged over the units produced. With activity-based costing (ABC), a cost driver is selected for each activity to compute an application rate. The rate is then used to apply an activity's cost to the product. The use of ABC normally results in improved costing and decision making.

6 Describe the basic features associated with a just-in-time production system. In a just-in-time (JIT) production system, inventories are reduced to bare minimum levels (ideally, zero). The system operates with a "demand-pull" philosophy, meaning that the manufacture of a finished good is triggered by the receipt of a sales order. JIT systems reduce inventory carrying costs and are highly dependent on supplier reliability and the user's commitment to total quality control (TQC).

7 (Appendix) Use the weighted-average process costing method to calculate the cost of goods completed and ending work in process inventory. The weighted-average method is employed by many businesses to simplify costing and reduce record keeping. Under this approach, all goods completed during a period are assumed to be started and completed during that period. Any previous manufacturing activity on the beginning work in process inventory is therefore ignored in the computation of equivalent units. This method is known as the weighted-average approach because the previous period costs in the beginning work in process are averaged together with current manufacturing costs, and all units produced during the period are carried at the same unit-cost figure.

KEY TERMS AND CONCEPTS: A QUICK OVERVIEW

activity-based costing (ABC)   A costing method under which departments are divided into activities, and the cost of individual activities is applied to manufactured products.

equivalent unit   A physical unit stated in terms of a finished unit.

FIFO process costing   A method whereby the beginning work in process inventory is assumed to be the first batch of goods completed.

just-in-time (JIT) production   A production system in which inventories are deemed to be wasteful and the manufacturing process is "pulled" by the receipt of a sales order.

process costing system   A system of cost accumulation that gathers costs by process or department.

production cost report   A report that is used in a process costing system; shows costs and units, classified by department.

quality costs   The costs of dealing with or eliminating the acquisition or manufacture of marginal goods.

total quality control (TQC)   A concept that focuses on zero defects in both raw materials acquisitions and the manufacturing process.

weighted-average process costing   A process costing method under which all goods manufactured during a period are carried at the same unit cost.

CHAPTER QUIZ

The five questions that follow relate to several issues raised in the chapter. Test your knowledge of the issues by selecting the best answer. (The answers appear on p. 984.)

1 Process cost accounting systems:
   a use distinctly different general ledger accounts than job order systems.
   b frequently accumulate costs by department.
   c are seldom found in assembly-line manufacturing plants.
   d may, in selected cases, use job order cost sheets.

2 Equivalent units:
   a are normally computed separately for direct materials and conversion cost.
   b are finished units stated in terms of physical units.
   c cannot be used to calculate the *cost* of the ending work in process inventory.
   d are generally equal (in total) for both completed goods and the ending work in process inventory.

3 Harris Company introduces direct material at the beginning of its manufacturing operation. The following data pertain to July:

   Beginning work in process: 4,000 units, 20% complete
   Units started and completed: 7,000
   Ending work in process: 3,000 units, 60% complete

Assuming the use of FIFO process costing, the total equivalent units for direct materials amounted to:

a 8,800.   c 12,000.
b 10,000.   d 14,000.

4 A production cost report:

a documents manufacturing costs of companies that use process costing systems and job order systems.
b discloses equivalent units but not the cost per equivalent unit.
c discloses the cost of completed goods but not the cost of the ending work in process inventory.
d summarizes equivalent-unit calculations, unit-cost calculations, and the assignment of manufacturing costs to goods completed and the ending work in process inventory.

5 A just-in-time production system:

a relies on the use of activity-based costing.
b can be brought to a halt by defective units acquired from suppliers.
c normally has minimal impact on the inventory levels that are carried by a company.
d is characterized as being "demand-push" in nature.

Santa Fe Manufacturing uses a FIFO process costing system to accumulate production costs. Selected data applicable to January of the current year follow.

SUMMARY PROBLEM

Beginning work in process inventory: 8,000 units, $\frac{1}{4}$ complete; cost, $17,500
Number of units started in January: 20,000
Total units completed: 22,000
Ending work in process inventory: 6,000 units, $\frac{2}{3}$ complete
Direct materials used in January: $60,000
January conversion cost: $42,000

Instructions

a Compute January's equivalent production figures for materials and conversion cost. Materials are added at the start of the process; conversion costs are incurred evenly throughout manufacturing.
b Compute the equivalent-unit costs for materials and conversion costs.
c Determine the cost of goods completed during January and the ending work in process inventory.
d Present the journal entry to transfer completed production to finished goods.

Solution

a

	Physical Units
Beginning work in process	8,000
Units started	20,000
Units to account for	28,000

	Physical Units	Equivalent Units Materials	Equivalent Units Conversion
Completed			
Beginning work in process*	8,000	—	6,000
Units started and completed†	14,000	14,000	14,000
Ending work in process‡	6,000	6,000	4,000
Units accounted for	28,000	20,000	24,000

* All materials added last period; three-fourths of the conversion performed in this period.
† All materials and conversion introduced in this period; 14,000 units derived by subtracting the beginning work in process inventory from the total units completed (22,000).
‡ Units were started in this period; all materials were introduced plus two-thirds of the conversion.

b	Costs	Total	Materials	Conversion
	Beginning work in process	$ 17,500	$ —	$ —
	Current	102,000	60,000	42,000
	Total cost to account for	$119,500	$60,000 ÷	$42,000 ÷
	Equivalent units		20,000	24,000
	Cost per equivalent unit		$3.00	$1.75

c Completed

Beginning work in process			
Prior period cost		$17,500	
Conversion cost: 6,000 units × $1.75		10,500	$ 28,000
Units started and completed			
Materials: 14,000 units × $3.00		$42,000	
Conversion cost: 14,000 units × $1.75		24,500	66,500
Total cost of completed units			$ 94,500
Ending work in process			
Materials: 6,000 units × $3.00		$18,000	
Conversion cost: 4,000 units × $1.75		7,000	25,000
Total cost accounted for			$119,500

d	Finished Goods	94,500	
	Work in Process		94,500
	To transfer the cost of completed units to finished goods		

ASSIGNMENT MATERIAL

Q23-1 In what type of production setting is a process cost accounting system often found?

Q23-2 How are job order systems and process costing systems similar?

Q23-3 How are costs accumulated under a process costing system?

Q23-4 Explain the concept of equivalent units to someone who has no background in cost accounting.

Q23-5 The Gateway Company uses a process costing system. An examination of goods in production at the end of the accounting period revealed 6,000 units, two-thirds complete. Would it be correct to say that 4,000 finished units were manufactured? Why?

Q23-6 Why is it usually necessary to compute separate equivalent-unit totals for direct materials and conversion cost?

Q23-7 Explain the basic features that are associated with a FIFO process costing system.

Q23-8 List the four steps that are required when preparing a production cost report.

Q23-9 What journal entry is needed to record the transfer of completed goods from one processing department to another?

Q23-10 Briefly explain why costing accuracy generally improves when a company adopts activity-based costing.

Q23-11 How might activity-based costing lead to the elimination of a company's non-value-adding activities?

Q23-12 What normally happens to inventories after a just-in-time production system is installed?

Q23-13 List several of the conditions that must exist for a company to use just-in-time production successfully.

Q23-14 Maxell Company is striving for significant improvements in product quality. List several of the quality costs the firm will likely incur in its quest for zero defects.

*Q23-15 What basic features are associated with weighted-average process costing?

*Q23-16 What benefits does the use of weighted-average process costing offer in comparison with FIFO?

E23-1 *Industry characteristics and costing systems* (L.O. 1)
Consider the activities of the following businesses. Determine whether each business would be more likely to use a job order system or a process costing system.

---

* An asterisk preceding an item indicates that the material is covered in an appendix to this chapter.

a Shipbuilder
b Petroleum refiner
c Candy manufacturer
d Trophy shop
e Brick manufacturer
f Shopping mall developer
g Book publisher
h Manufacturer of nuts and bolts
i Brewery
j Motion picture studio
k Frozen orange juice producer
l Manufacturer of jet aircraft
m Manufacturer of washers and dryers
n Nuclear power plant

E23-2 *Overview of process costing* (L.O. 1, 2, 3, 4)
Evaluate the comments that follow as being True or False. If the comment is false, briefly explain why.
a The basic objective of a process costing system is to determine the cost of goods completed during the period and the cost of the ending work in process inventory.
b Under a FIFO process costing system, all goods completed during May are assumed to be started and completed in May.
c Unit manufacturing costs are the result of dividing the period's production costs by the number of physical units (e.g., tons, gallons, and so forth) manufactured.
d Each manufacturing department that uses a process costing system will maintain its own Work in Process account.
e Process costing systems are normally found in continuous manufacturing environments.

E23-3 *Calculation of equivalent units* (L.O. 2, 3)
Consider the following independent cases:

■ *Case A* Beginning work in process: 1,200 units, $\frac{2}{3}$ complete
Units started and completed: 4,000
Ending work in process: 1,600 units, $\frac{1}{4}$ complete
■ *Case B* Beginning work in process: 6,000 units, $\frac{1}{3}$ complete
Total units completed during the period: 15,000
Ending work in process: 3,000 units, $\frac{1}{6}$ complete

All materials are added at the start of the process, and conversion costs are incurred uniformly throughout manufacturing. Assuming use of FIFO, compute total equivalent units for materials and conversion costs for each of the preceding cases.

E23-4 *Computation of physical and equivalent units* (L.O. 2, 3)
Baylor Manufacturing produces industrial chemicals and uses a FIFO process costing system. The data that follow relate to September operations.

| | | Percentage Complete | |
	Pounds	Materials	Conversion
Work in process, 9/1	17,500	70%	60%
Work in process, 9/30	15,000	20	10

Sixty thousand pounds were started into production during the month.
a Compute the number of pounds completed in September.
b Calculate Baylor's equivalent units for materials and conversion cost.

E23-5 *Understanding a process costing system* (L.O. 2, 3, 4)
Entek Manufacturing uses a FIFO process costing system. The following figures pertain to June:

	Physical Units	Equivalent Units	
		Materials	Conversion
Completed production			
Beginning work in process	1,100	—	715
Units started and completed	3,700	3,700	3,700
Ending work in process	1,900	1,900	380
	6,700	5,600	4,795

All materials are introduced at the start of the process; conversion cost is incurred uniformly throughout production. Current costs per equivalent unit are: materials, $4.40; conversion cost, $12.
a Why are no equivalent units computed for materials with respect to the beginning work in process inventory?
b What percentage of the conversion work was performed on the beginning work in process during May?
c What is the total cost of direct materials used during June?
d How many units will be transferred to the finished goods warehouse in June?

E23-6 *Cost of goods completed and ending work in process* (L.O. 4)

1-2-3

Accutech Manufacturing's cost accounting department has calculated the following equivalent production figures for August:

	Physical Units	Equivalent Units	
		Materials	Conversion
Completed production			
Beginning work in process	900	—	600
Units started and completed	2,600	2,600	2,600
Ending work in process	1,500	1,500	1,000
	5,000	4,100	4,200

Prior period costs pertaining to the August 1 work in process inventory amounted to $4,500. Current costs per equivalent unit are: materials, $3.50; conversion, $5.00.
a Determine the cost of production completed in August.
b Determine the cost of the ending work in process inventory.

E23-7 *Cost of goods completed and ending work in process* (L.O. 2, 3, 4)
Ozark Manufacturing uses a FIFO process costing system to accumulate production costs. The following information pertains to April:

- Beginning work in process: 4,000 units, ¼ complete; cost, $42,000
- Units started into production: 7,000
- Total units completed during the period: 8,000
- Ending work in process: 3,000 units, ⅔ complete

All materials are introduced in the initial processing stages, and conversion cost is incurred evenly through production. Materials used during April amounted to $70,000; conversion cost totaled $36,000.

a Compute equivalent-unit figures for materials and conversion cost.

b Compute the cost of production completed during April and the ending work in process inventory.

E23-8 *Activity-based costing* (L.O. 5)

Allied Fabricating uses machine hours to apply factory overhead to units that are processed in the machining department. The company's accountant has computed the following estimates for the current period: machine hours, 25,000; factory overhead, $350,000.

The firm is considering a switch to an activity-based costing system and has derived the data that follow for the machining department's various activities:

Activity	Cost Driver	Application Rate
Production setup	Number of setups	$700 per setup
Machine processing	Machine hours	$8 per machine hour
Inspection	Inspection hours	$3 per inspection hour

Allied recently manufactured 2,500 units of part no. A431 for use in auto transmissions. Each part took 15 minutes of machine time to produce. Four machine setups were involved, and inspection time totaled 85 hours.

a Compute the amount of overhead that would be applied to the A431 production if Allied's existing accounting procedures are used.

b Compute the cost of A431 production, assuming the use of activity-based costing.

c Suppose the company is in a very competitive market, where cost is a big factor in determining a product's selling price. With part A431, would Allied's existing accounting procedures or activity-based costing seem more appropriate? Briefly explain.

E23-9 *Just-in-time production* (L.O. 6)

Del Mar Manufacturing is considering the installation of a just-in-time production system. The company expects the following items will change if the new system is implemented:

Warehousing costs	Number of suppliers used
Lost sales to customers	Inventory obsolescence costs
Quality of raw materials purchased	Funds available for investment

a Briefly discuss the meaning of a just-in-time production system.

b Evaluate the six items that are expected to change, and determine whether each item would likely increase or decrease. No explanations are needed.

*E23-10 *Equivalent units and unit cost computations* (L.O. 7)

Fittings Unlimited uses a weighted-average process costing system. The data that follow pertain to May.

Units started into production	19,000
Units in process, May 31 (40% complete)	7,000
Units in process, May 1 (30% complete)	6,000
Units completed	18,000

The beginning work in process contained material and conversion costs of $10,000 and $22,000, respectively. The firm's current manufacturing costs amounted to: materials, $40,000; conversion, $264,000.

a Determine the company's equivalent units for May.

b Calculate the cost per equivalent unit for materials and conversion cost.

*E23-11 *Cost of goods completed and ending work in process* (L.O. 7)

Cobblestone Corporation has a two-stage production operation. Goods pass from cleaning to milling to finished goods. The following information pertains to the cleaning department for October:

Total goods completed	6,000 units
Ending work in process (40% complete)	1,200 units
Beginning work in process (30% complete)	1,500 units

All materials are added at the beginning of production; conversion costs are incurred uniformly throughout manufacturing. The weighted-average costs per equivalent unit are: materials, $3.20; conversion, $12.00.

a Calculate the cost of goods completed and prepare the journal entry to record the transfer of goods from the cleaning department.

b Calculate the cost of the ending work in process.

Series A

PROBLEMS

P23-A1 *Straightforward process costing* (L.O. 2, 3, 4)

Chief Manufacturing uses a FIFO process costing system to accumulate production costs. The following information pertains to August:

- Beginning work in process inventory: 6,000 units, 70% complete; cost, $34,650
- Costs incurred in August: direct materials used, $28,500; conversion cost, $22,800
- Total units completed: 9,000
- Ending work in process inventory: 7,000 units, 40% complete
- Number of units started during August: 10,000

All materials are introduced at the start of the process, and conversion costs are incurred uniformly throughout manufacturing. Units pass directly from Chief's sole production department to the finished goods warehouse.

Instructions

a Prepare a production cost report in good form.

b Prepare the necessary journal entry to record the completed production for August.

P23-A2 *Production cost report; partial computations for second month* (L.O. 2, 3, 4)

MicroMatic uses a FIFO process costing system. The following data pertain to July of the current year:

1-2-3

	Units	Cost
July 1 work in process, 30% complete	6,000	$ 42,750
July 31 work in process, 20% complete	3,000	?
Total units completed	18,000	?
Units started during July	15,000	
July manufacturing costs		
Direct materials used		69,000
Conversion cost		147,840

A review of the next month's accounting records found that 22,000 units were started into production during August. Completed units totaled 17,500, and the August 31 work in process was 40% complete.

All materials are introduced at the start of manufacturing; conversion costs are incurred uniformly throughout the process.

Instructions

a Prepare a production cost report for July.

b Compute the equivalent units for materials and conversion cost in August.

P23-A3 *Production cost computations* (L.O. 2, 3, 4)

Consumer Health Foods produces a variety of health food items that are available at retail stores throughout the country. One of the company's products is Fruit & Grain, a popular breakfast cereal. The cereal is a combination of grain, bananas, and raisins, all of which are introduced at the beginning of the blending process. During June, the company used the following: grain, $19,200; bananas, $20,000; and raisins, $16,900. Other data for June are:

- Conversion cost
  - Direct labor: Five employees worked 160 hours each and were paid $12 per hour.
  - Overhead: Overhead is applied at the rate of $29 per labor hour.
- Beginning work in process: 20,000 pounds, 30% complete; cost, $7,900
- Ending work in process: 25,000 pounds, 40% complete
- Total production completed during the month: 160,000 pounds

Conversion cost (i.e., direct labor and overhead) is incurred uniformly throughout manufacturing; a FIFO process costing system is used.

Instructions

Compute:

a Total production costs for June.

b Cost of goods completed during the month.

c Cost of the work in process inventory on June 30.

P23-A4 *Process costing and cost flow* (L.O. 2, 3, 4)

Stillwater Corporation uses a FIFO process costing system. All materials are introduced at the start of the process, and conversion costs are incurred uniformly throughout manufacturing. The following T-accounts were extracted from the company's records as of March 31:

Work in Process

3/1 Balance 1,800 units,		To finished goods:	
$\frac{1}{3}$ complete	14,720	1,800 units from 3/1	
Started 6,000 units		inventory	?
Materials	9,000	4,000 units started and	
Conversion	37,700	completed in March	?

Finished Goods

3/1 Balance 4,000 units	30,800	To cost of goods sold:	
From work in process:		? units	65,580
5,800 units	?		

The ending work in process inventory is 30% complete.

Instructions

a Compute the following:
   (1) Total equivalent units and the cost per equivalent unit for both materials and conversion cost.
   (2) The cost of units started in February and completed in March.
   (3) The cost of units started and completed in March.
   (4) The cost of units transferred to finished goods.
   (5) The cost of Stillwater's ending work in process inventory.
b If 2,100 finished units were on hand on March 31, determine (1) the ending balance in the Finished Goods account and (2) the number of units sold during March.

P23-A5 *Activity-based costing* (L.O. 5)

Telcom Manufacturing applies factory overhead to its two products (L23 and L24) on the basis of direct labor hours. Estimated factory overhead and direct labor time for the current accounting period are $400,000 and 10,000 hours, respectively. Information about the products follows.

	L23	L24
Estimated production volume	1,000	1,400
Direct materials per unit	$30	$19
Direct labor per unit		
3 hours at $8	24	
5 hours at $8		40

The company, which installed a considerable amount of automated equipment several years ago, has seen a significant decline in profit. Management believes that incorrect and "outdated" calculations of product cost are a major contributor to the problem.

Telcom's overhead can be identified with three major activities. These activities and other relevant data are summarized as shown.

	Cost	Volume of Cost Driver*		
		L23	L24	Total
Purchase order processing	$ 40,000	300	100	400
Machine processing	220,000	4,500	3,500	8,000
Inspection	140,000	250	750	1,000
	$400,000			

* Number of purchase orders processed, machine hours worked, and inspection hours, respectively.

Instructions

a Assuming use of direct labor hours to apply overhead to production, compute the total costs of L23 and L24 if the expected manufacturing volume is attained.

b Compute activity application rates for purchase order processing, machine processing, and inspection.

c Assuming use of activity-based costing, compute the total costs of L23 and L24 if the expected manufacturing volume is attained.

d Telcom's selling prices are based heavily on cost. Use the data presented and the results from parts (a) and (c) to determine why the firm is experiencing a significant decline in profit.

*P23-A6 *Straightforward process costing: Weighted average* (L.O. 7)

Red River, Inc., uses a weighted-average process costing system. The following information relates to operations for October:

- Work in process
    October 1: 10,000 units, 40% complete; cost, $41,600 (materials, $18,000; conversion, $23,600)
    October 31: 4,000 units, 75% complete
- October manufacturing costs
    Direct materials used: $46,600
    Conversion cost: $174,400
- Units started into production: 24,000
- Total units completed: 30,000

All materials are introduced at the start of manufacturing; conversion cost is incurred uniformly throughout the process. Units pass directly from Red River's sole production department to the finished goods warehouse.

Instructions

a Prepare a production cost report for October.

b Prepare the journal entry necessary to record the month's completed goods.

Series B

P23-B1 *Straightforward process costing* (L.O. 2, 3, 4)

University Company uses a FIFO process costing system to accumulate production costs. The following information pertains to department no. 1 for July:

- Number of units started during July: 12,000
- Total units completed: 9,000
- Ending work in process inventory: 5,000 units, 40% complete

■ Beginning work in process inventory: 2,000 units, 25% complete; cost, $8,600
■ Costs incurred in July: direct materials used, $38,400; conversion cost, $47,250

All materials are introduced at the start of the process, and conversion costs are incurred uniformly throughout manufacturing. Units pass directly from department no. 1 to department no. 2 and then to finished goods.

Instructions

a Prepare a production cost report in good form.
b Prepare the necessary journal entry to record the completed production for July.

P23-B2 *Production cost report; partial computations for second month* **(L.O. 2, 3, 4)**

HRS Assembly, Inc., operates a FIFO process costing system. All materials enter production at the beginning of the process; conversion costs are incurred evenly throughout manufacturing. The data that follow pertain to November of the current year.

■ Work in process, 11/1: 20,000 units, 70% complete; cost, $81,500
■ Units started into production: 70,000
■ Total units completed: 85,000
■ Direct materials consumed: $140,000
■ Conversion costs: $240,500
■ Work in process, 11/30: 5,000 units, 60% complete

Instructions

a Prepare a production cost report for November.
b The following data relate to December: new production started, 78,000 units; total units completed, 76,000. If the ending work in process is 20% complete, calculate December's equivalent units for materials and conversion cost.

P23-B3 *Production cost computations* **(L.O. 2, 3, 4)**

Singapore Electronics assembles various components that are used in the aircraft industry. The company's major product, a pressure gauge, is the result of assembling three parts: DR532, HB4-786, and 429GY. All parts are introduced at the beginning of Singapore's manufacturing process; labor and overhead (i.e., conversion costs) are incurred uniformly throughout production. During March, the following costs were incurred:

■ Direct materials used: DR532, $100,500; HB4-786, $207,300; 429GY, $32,400
■ Direct labor: 2,500 hours at $8

The overhead application rate is 260% of direct labor cost.

The beginning work in process inventory (8,000 units, 80% complete) was carried in the accounting records at a cost of $85,000. The ending work in process amounted to 4,000 units, 60% complete. Singapore finished a total of 40,000 gauges during the period.

Instructions

Assuming use of a FIFO process costing system, determine:
a Total production costs for March.
b Cost of goods completed during the month.
c Cost of the work in process inventory on March 31.

P23-B4 *Process costing and cost flow* (L.O. 2, 3, 4)

1-2-3

Spare Parts, Inc., uses a FIFO process costing system. All materials are introduced at the start of the process, and conversion costs are incurred uniformly throughout manufacturing. The following T-accounts were extracted from the company's records as of December 31:

Work in Process				
12/1	Balance 4,000 units,		To finished goods:	
	¾ complete	33,500	4,000 units from 12/1	
	Started 9,000 units		inventory	?
	Materials	32,400	6,000 units started and	
	Conversion	43,450	completed in December	?

Finished Goods				
12/1	Balance 7,000 units	63,000	To cost of goods sold:	
	From work in process:		? units	134,136
	10,000 units	?		

The ending work in process inventory is 30% complete.

Instructions

a Compute the following:
  (1) Total equivalent units and the cost per equivalent unit for both materials and conversion cost.
  (2) The cost of units started in November and completed in December.
  (3) The cost of units started and completed in December.
  (4) The cost of units transferred to finished goods.
  (5) The cost of the company's ending work in process inventory.
b If 2,400 finished units were on hand on December 31, determine (1) the ending balance in the Finished Goods account and (2) the number of units sold during December.

P23-B5 *Activity-based costing* (L.O. 5)

Pratt Manufacturing applies factory overhead to its products on the basis of machine hours. The rate in effect for the current accounting period is $100 per hour. The company's two products, Superior and Regular, require the same amount of direct labor ($65) but differing amounts of direct material ($75 and $40, respectively). Pratt anticipates that it will produce 5,000 units of Superior and 4,000 units of Regular.

Suzanne Batzer, the company's controller, is studying the use of activity-based costing for the firm. She has determined that overhead can be identified with three major activities and has gathered the following data:

Activity	Cost Driver	Cost
Production setups	Number of setups	$ 60,000
Machine processing	Number of machine hours	340,000
Packing and shipping	Number of shipments	100,000
		$500,000

Estimated cost-driver data for the two products and the company as a whole are:

	Total	Superior	Regular
Number of setups	40	11	29
Number of machine hours	5,000	3,000	2,000
Number of shipments	125	30	95

Instructions

a Assuming use of the present $100-per-hour application rate, compute the total costs of Superior and Regular production if the expected manufacturing volume is attained.

b Compute activity application rates for production setup, machine processing, and packing and shipping.

c Assuming use of activity-based costing, compute the total costs of Superior and Regular if the expected manufacturing volume is attained.

d The company currently sells a unit of Regular for $162. If Pratt's marketing manager suggested a campaign to promote sales of Regular, how would Batzer likely respond?

*P23-B6 *Straightforward process costing: Weighted average* (L.O. 7)

Surfing Equipment uses a weighted-average process costing system. The following information relates to department A for March:

- Units started into production: 34,000
- Total units completed: 29,000
- March manufacturing costs
  Direct materials used: $299,250
  Conversion cost: $379,350
- Work in process
  March 1: 7,000 units, 70% complete; cost, $114,400 (materials, $59,500; conversion, $54,900)
  March 31: 12,000 units, 80% complete

All materials are introduced at the start of manufacturing; conversion cost is incurred uniformly throughout the process. Units pass directly from department A to department B and then to finished goods.

Instructions

a Prepare a production cost report for March.

b Prepare the journal entry necessary to record the month's completed goods.

BB23-1 *Process costing calculations: Partial data* (L.O. 2, 3, 4)

Dr. Jeffrey Hough, an accounting professor, has just finished writing an examination that covers FIFO process costing. Unfortunately, while Jeff was attending a birthday dinner with his spouse, the family dog became hungry and ate selected parts of problem no. 3.

Problem no. 3 deals with Kent Industries. Material A is added at the beginning of Kent's process; packaging material is added at the end. Conversion costs are incurred uniformly throughout production. Consider the following fragmented data:

BEYOND THE BASICS

	Physical Units	Material A	Packaging	Conversion
Completed				
Beginning work in process	14,000	—		12,600
Units started and completed	32,000	32,000	32,000	32,000
Ending work in process	10,000	10,000		3,000
Units accounted for	56,000	42,000		47,600

Costs	Total	Material A	Packaging	Conversion
Beginning work in process	$90,800	—		
Current costs		$252,000		
Cost per equivalent unit		$6	$0.20	$5.50

Dr. Hough has given the fragments to his student assistant to determine whether the examination questions can still be answered. The professor is considering using the fragments alone as a new test problem.

Instructions

Assume the role of the student assistant and determine answers to the following:

a How many units were started into production during the period?

b What percentage of the conversion work was performed on the beginning work in process in the last accounting period?

c How far into the process is the ending work in process inventory?

d Why has the company established equivalent-unit columns for both material A and packaging?

e Calculate the total equivalent units for packaging.

f Determine the total conversion cost for the period.

g Calculate the cost of goods completed during the period.

BB23-2 *Overview of chapter concepts: Multiple choice* (L.O. 1–6)
The following multiple-choice questions relate to various topics discussed in the chapter. Select the best answer.

1 Process costing systems:
   a are normally used when goods are manufactured in small discrete batches.
   b require the use of separate Work in Process accounts by each manufacturing department.
   c can accurately cost the goods completed during a period but not the ending work in process inventory.
   d rely on equivalent units to account for direct materials and physical units to account for conversion cost.

2 Juicy Jams Manufacturing employs a FIFO process costing system. The following information is available for 19X1:

Work in process, Jan. 1	200,000 units
Production started and completed	1,000,000 units
Work in process, Dec. 31	150,000 units
Materials used	$1,150,000
Conversion cost	$1,710,000

The January 1 work in process was 75% complete at the start of the year; the December 31 work in process was 60% complete at year-end. All materials are introduced at the start of production, and conversion cost is incurred evenly throughout manufacturing. The respective equivalent-unit costs for materials and conversion are:

a $1.00, $1.38.   c $1.35, $1.38.
b $1.00, $1.50.   d $1.35, $1.50.

3 Harvest Manufacturing uses a FIFO process costing system. The company had a January 1 work in process inventory of 40,000 units, 30% complete (cost: $127,000). The company finished a total of 200,000 units during the month and had the following equivalent-unit costs: materials, $2; conversion, $4.50. If all materials are introduced at the start of manufacturing and conversion cost is incurred evenly throughout, the cost of completed goods would be:

a $1,221,000.   c $1,300,000.
b $1,293,000.   d $1,373,000.

4 The journal entry to record the transfer of goods from Department A to Department B for additional manufacturing would include:

a a debit to Work in Process: Department A.
b a debit to Work in Process: Department B.
c a debit to Finished Goods: Department B.
d a credit to Finished Goods: Department A.

5 Activity-based costing:

a results in averaging the costs of highly diversified activities.
b generally improves costing accuracy.
c uses fewer cost drivers than conventional accounting systems.
d usually increases the number of non-value-adding activities in a company.

6 Morgan uses an industrial oven to mold plastic products. Historically, the company has applied factory overhead on the basis of oven hours. Estimated overhead is $125,000, and 5,000 oven hours are expected during a typical year. Plastic products related to job no. 256 required 40 oven hours to manufacture. A recent study found that starting the oven for each job required $300 of electricity. In addition, hourly charges of $2 for electricity and $14 for repair time were incurred for each hour of oven operation. If inspectors closely monitored 13 hours of baking at a cost of $15 per hour, the difference in job cost of using activity-based costing rather than conventional techniques would be:

a $0.   c $135.
b $60.   d $165.

7 Just-in-time concepts suggest that a company maintain minimum inventory levels of:

a raw materials.   c finished goods.
b work in process.   d all of the above.

8 Total quality control recognizes that:

a the repair of defective goods may cost more than the original manufactured cost of a product.

b an ample supply of raw material should be maintained to accommodate rework needs.

c profitability may improve by tolerating a reasonable defect rate for finished goods.

d a firm should take pride when all categories of quality costs are increasing.

COMMUNICATION OF ACCOUNTING INFORMATION

CAI23-1 *Documentation of procedures* **(L.O. 2, 3, 4)**

Communication Principle: Businesses spend considerable sums to design and install reporting systems and procedures. Generally, these efforts are successful, and the monies invested produce the intended results. Occasionally, though, things don't work out as planned. If key personnel leave and the details of system operations are sketchy, the company may be in for troubled times.

To avoid this situation, employees are often asked to document business procedures—accounting and otherwise. In drafting such documentation, the following goals and considerations should be kept in mind:

1 Although an employee may have a clear understanding today, memories frequently fail. Recalling the past is easier if extra effort is taken initially to develop good explanatory material.

2 Other employees are unaware of the "fine points" stored in current users' brains. Incomplete documentation can create as many problems for later users as the documentation is supposed to solve. Detailed, logically organized instructions are therefore a must.

3 Writing should be concise. Extraneous thoughts or comments are apt to confuse the reader.

4 Information should be filed in an accessible manner and updated as necessary. Lost or out-of-date supporting materials have marginal, if any, value.

5 The documentation should be reviewed by an employee who is unfamiliar with the system and/or procedure. What may seem clear to one individual may not be as clear to others.

■ ■ ■ ■ ■ ■ ■ ■

Tyson Manufacturing has recently installed a FIFO process costing system identical to that described in the text. Materials are introduced at the start of production; conversion cost is incurred uniformly throughout manufacturing.

Instructions

Document the procedures that underlie the preparation of a production cost report for Tyson's system. Your documentation should be sufficiently detailed and aimed at an employee who has a limited accounting background. After reviewing the documentation, the employee should be able to apply the appropriate calculations to various fact situations.

Answers to Chapter Quiz

1 b

2 a

3 b (Beginning work in process, 0; units started and completed, 7,000; ending work in process, 3,000)

4 d

5 b

COMPREHENSIVE PROBLEM 4

Durham Manufacturing produces furniture in North Carolina. The firm uses a job costing system to account for its Russell wooden furniture line, which is produced upon receipt of a customer's order. The company is also involved with the manufacture and assembly of Easton office partitions, a brand noted for its durability and economical price. Durham uses a process costing system to account for these goods.

A review of the accounting records found that five "Russell jobs" were in inventory on January 1, 19X7. Data on these jobs follow.

Job Number	Work in Process	Finished Goods
457		$36,700
459	$12,200	
461	21,500	
462		57,300
463	18,300	

The January 1 work in process for the Easton line cost $26,500 and consisted of 1,200 units, $\frac{1}{4}$ complete. In the manufacture of these goods, all materials are introduced at the start of the process, and conversion costs are incurred evenly throughout production.

The company must calculate an overhead application rate for use during the next 12 months. Durham employs direct labor hours as an application base, and the firm's accountant has derived the following estimates for 19X7:

Direct labor (52,000 hours)	$420,000	Utilities	$33,000
Indirect materials used	18,000	Taxes	40,000
Indirect labor	49,600	Insurance	11,000
Factory depreciation	30,400		

The following data relate to operations for January:

- All direct and indirect materials are charged to the Raw Materials account when acquired. January purchases on account amounted to: direct materials, $58,000; indirect materials, $3,700.
- Materials requisitioned for production during the month are shown in the accompanying chart.

	Direct Materials	Indirect Materials	Total
Job no. 459	$ 4,100		$ 4,100
Job no. 463	5,800		5,800
Job no. 464	13,700		13,700
Job no. 465	17,500		17,500
Russell production		$ 800	800
Easton production	54,600	1,100	55,700

Easton production started during January totaled 2,600 physical units.
- January payroll was distributed in the following manner:

	Hours	Cost
Job no. 459	300	$ 2,350
Job no. 461	150	1,200
Job no. 463	550	4,500
Job no. 464	200	1,700
Job no. 465	750	5,900
Easton production	2,500	20,000
Indirect labor—Russell	210	2,000
Indirect labor—Easton	250	2,200
Selling & administrative	—	6,000

- Other factory costs related to January were: depreciation, $2,400; utilities, $2,800; taxes, $4,000; and insurance, $900. The amount for insurance represents the expiration of a prepaid policy. Other amounts, except for depreciation, were paid as incurred.
- Durham completed job nos. 459, 461, and 464 during the month, along with a total of 2,000 units related to the Easton product line. Easton work in process on January 31 amounted to 1,800 units, $\frac{1}{3}$ complete.
- The company prices its job orders at 150% of cost; in contrast, Easton goods are priced to sell at 130% of cost. Job nos. 457 and 459 were shipped and invoiced to customers. In addition, the firm sold Easton products on account that had a total manufacturing cost of $17,300.

Instructions

You have just been hired as a managerial accountant by Durham Manufacturing. Prepare answers to the following:

a What functions would you expect to perform for the firm as a newly hired managerial accountant?

b Distinguish between product and period costs and specify the proper accounting treatment for each.

c Easton production is expected to become heavily automated by the beginning of next year. Would the use of labor hours as an overhead application base continue to be appropriate for these goods? Explain.

d Determine the overhead application rate for 19X7.

e Determine the amount of under- or overapplied overhead as of January 31, 19X7. Be sure to label your answer as underapplied or overapplied.

f Compute the cost of jobs completed during January.

g Prepare a production cost report for January for the Easton product line. The report should reveal equivalent units of production, cost per equivalent unit, the cost of goods completed during the period, and the cost of the ending work in process inventory. Durham uses the FIFO method of process costing.

h Analyze all data presented along with your answers to requirements (d)–(g) and present the necessary journal entries for January. Durham charges under- or overapplied overhead to Cost of Goods Sold at the end of each month. (*Note:* Prepare summary entries by combining individual job data.)

CHAPTER 24

Cost-Volume-Profit Analysis

LEARNING OBJECTIVES

After studying this chapter, you should be able to:

1

Identify the characteristics of variable, step, fixed, and mixed (semivariable) cost functions.

2

Use the scattergraph and high-low method for examining cost behavior.

3

Compute and explain the meaning of a company's break-even point and contribution margin.

4

Calculate the sales needed to generate a particular target income figure.

5

Use sales price, cost, and volume data to determine the impact of various operating changes on profitability.

6

Apply cost-volume-profit analysis to multiproduct firms.

7

State the limiting assumptions on which cost-volume-profit analysis is based.

During the past decade, many firms have felt the effects of increased operating costs and sharp competition. In an effort to maintain adequate earnings growth and cash flow generation, companies have been forced to alter existing business practices. Retailers have extended store hours and occasionally changed their image to appear more "lean and mean." Manufacturers have increased the use of "high-tech" production methods to improve efficiency and product quality. And, in an example that may be very close to home, consider something as basic as the menu of your favorite fast-food restaurant. No doubt that menu has undergone considerable expansion, with the addition of breakfasts, salad bars, specialty sandwiches, and desserts to the standard fare.

Operating changes such as those just cited can be implemented only after extensive analysis. Businesses must determine how increases and decreases in revenue, cost, and volume affect net income. As you learned in an earlier chapter, certain costs fluctuate with changes in activity, while other costs remain constant. The study of interrelationships among the preceding factors is often termed **cost-volume-profit (CVP) analysis.** You will soon see that CVP analysis is a useful planning tool for managers.

COST BEHAVIOR

OBJECTIVE

Identify the characteristics of variable, step, fixed, and mixed (semivariable) cost functions.

Effective CVP analysis requires a thorough understanding of cost behavior and calls for an expansion of the material presented in Chapter 21. Before we do so, however, a word of caution is necessary. It is important to understand that costs often exhibit different behavior patterns under differing sets of circumstances. For instance, many costs do not change when small fluctuations in volume occur. Those same costs, however, may increase (or decrease) greatly when the activity change is more pronounced. Also, certain costs may follow a definite behavior pattern when closely monitored and controlled by management. Remove the controls and the predictable pattern may vary significantly from what was originally observed.

In sum, it is frequently difficult to generalize about the behavior of a given cost. An accounting educator once likened costs to people: they both have unique personalities and behave as individuals. Given this introduction, we will now explore four types of costs: variable, step, fixed, and mixed.

Variable Costs

Recall that a **variable cost** varies in direct proportion to a change in an activity base (e.g., sales, production, miles driven, and so forth). As a result, if an activity base triples, a true variable cost should triple; if the base is halved, the cost should decrease by 50%. Common examples of variable costs include direct materials, direct labor, supplies, sales commissions, and fuel.

To determine whether a cost possesses variable characteristics, one should observe the cost's behavior over wide ranges of volume. Consider, for instance, the wear and tear on automobile tires. Short daily trips and even total monthly mileage will have little effect on tire wear and tread depth. Over time—say, several years—daily driving will take its toll. Eventually, after a substantial number of miles have been traveled, the tires will have to be replaced.

Because variable costs change in direct proportion to fluctuations in an activity base, the variable cost *per unit* is constant. To illustrate, assume that Yellowstone Manufacturing normally produces 10,000 to 12,000 units each month. On the basis of the data in columns A and B, the accounting department has calculated labor cost at $8 per unit:

(A) Units Produced	(B) Total Labor Cost	(B) ÷ (A) Cost Per Unit
10,000	$80,000	$80,000 ÷ 10,000 = $8
10,500	84,000	$84,000 ÷ 10,500 = $8
11,000	88,000	$88,000 ÷ 11,000 = $8
11,500	92,000	$92,000 ÷ 11,500 = $8
12,000	96,000	$96,000 ÷ 12,000 = $8

Notice that the $8 figure holds true at all volume levels.

The Economist's View

Those readers who have taken an economics course may have noticed an apparent conflict between the economist's and accountant's views of variable cost behavior. Economic models generally assume that per-unit variable cost does not remain stable; rather, it changes with increases in activity. For example, picture a company that produces trucks by an assembly-line process. If the firm employed only two laborers, the number of trucks manufactured would surely be low. Furthermore, the process would be inefficient, because each employee would have to perform a multitude of tasks. As demand increases, the firm could raise its output by hiring more personnel. Instead of being a "jack of all trades," a worker could specialize, improve capital utilization, and become more efficient. The net result is a decreasing variable cost per unit. Naturally, a business can improve operations only so far. At some point production problems are encountered because of capacity constraints, lack of activity and departmental coordination, bottlenecks, and other factors. The culmination is a decrease in productivity and an accompanying rise in the variable cost per unit.

The accounting and economic views of variable cost behavior are graphed in Exhibit 24-1. The accountant's variable cost is graphed as a straight-line, linear function. The economist's curve, in contrast, first depicts a decreasing cost per unit and later an increasing unit cost. The gradual upward slope to the right still indicates, however, that *total* variable cost increases with additional activity.

Both of the preceding views are correct. The accountant, however, normally studies costs over a smaller range of activity than does the economist. Examine Exhibit 24-2, which shows the behavior of a curvilinear cost function. Notice that within the narrow shaded band, linear behavior (i.e., a constant per-unit amount) is realistic. The band depicts the **relevant range,** or the area of activity where a specified cost relationship is expected to hold true. Normally, the relevant range is an area in which the entity has had some recent operating experience. Generally stated, the assump-

EXHIBIT 24-1
Differing Views of Variable Cost

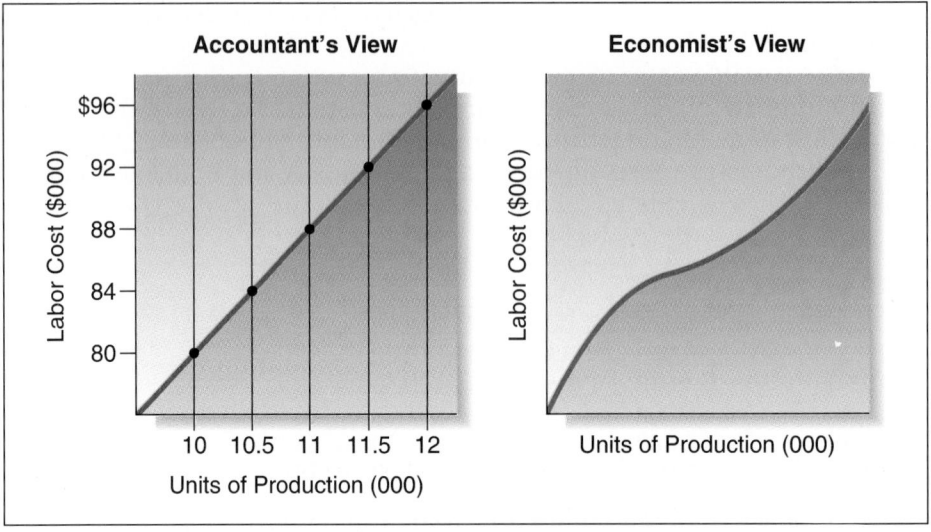

tion of linearity within this narrow band is acceptable and not likely to result in substantial inaccuracies when analyzing costs.

Step Cost

A careful inspection of specific variable cost functions will often reveal different behavior patterns. Although direct materials and sales commissions change in response to small changes in production and sales, respectively, other variable costs vary only when substantial increases or decreases occur in the activity base. For example, consider the clerical staff needed to process customer orders in a mail-order firm. By working at different paces, employees can usually handle a range of orders. The number of orders processed will be low if the office staff is working at a relaxed pace or high if efforts intensify. Thus, when small fluctuations in activity (i.e., orders) occur, the total cost of office personnel remains constant. If orders dramatically increase, however, additional staff will be hired, and the total office costs will rise.

Because the personnel cost increases in proportion to the number of sales orders, the cost is classified as variable. In this case, though, the cost

EXHIBIT 24-2
Curvilinear Variable Cost and the Relevant Range

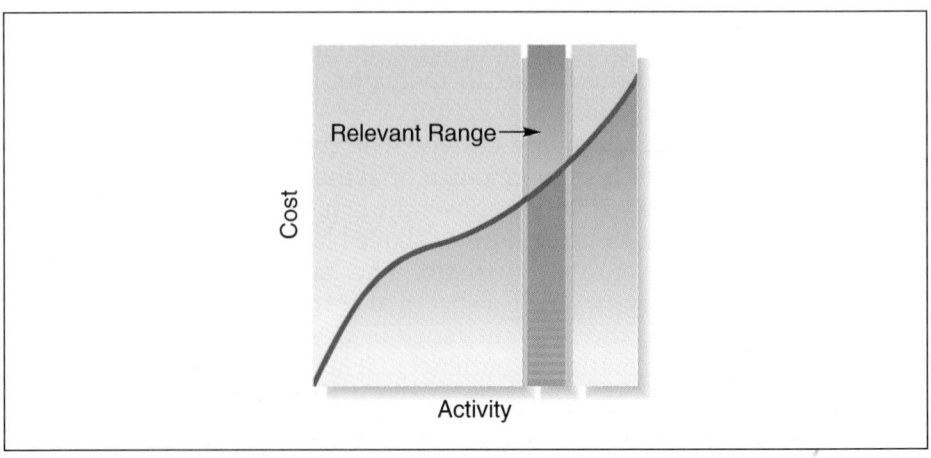

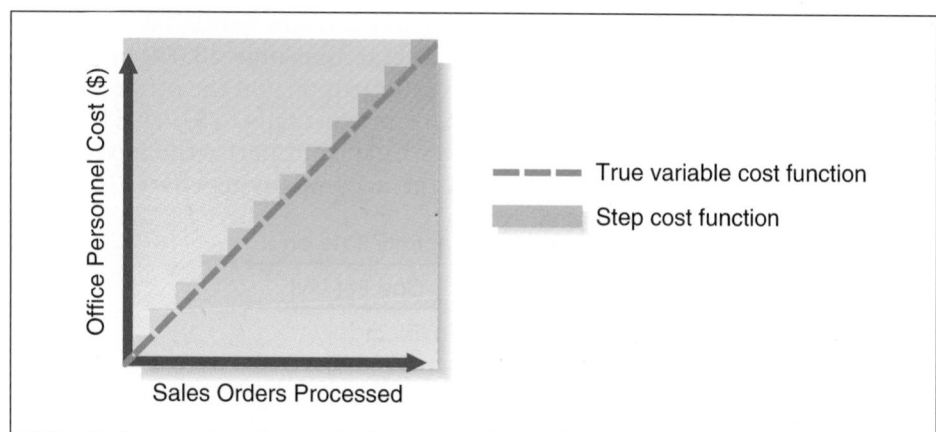

EXHIBIT 24-3
Step Cost Function

function changes only when sizable changes are experienced in the activity base. Specifically, the office cost will rise in "chunks" as new workers are added to the payroll. Cost functions that behave in this manner are frequently termed **step costs** and tend to approximate the behavior of a "true" variable cost (see Exhibit 24-3).[1]

A careful review of the step cost function provides the underlying explanation of a popular business practice: operating at the rightmost portion of a step. By so doing, an organization gets the most for its money, that is, maximum activity just prior to a cost increase.

Fixed Costs

Fixed costs are costs that do not change when the activity base fluctuates. To illustrate a fixed cost, assume Yellowstone Manufacturing leased machinery for $100,000 that is capable of producing from 40,000 to 60,000 units per year depending on utilization. Because the lease payment remains the same no matter how many units are produced, the following graph is appropriate.

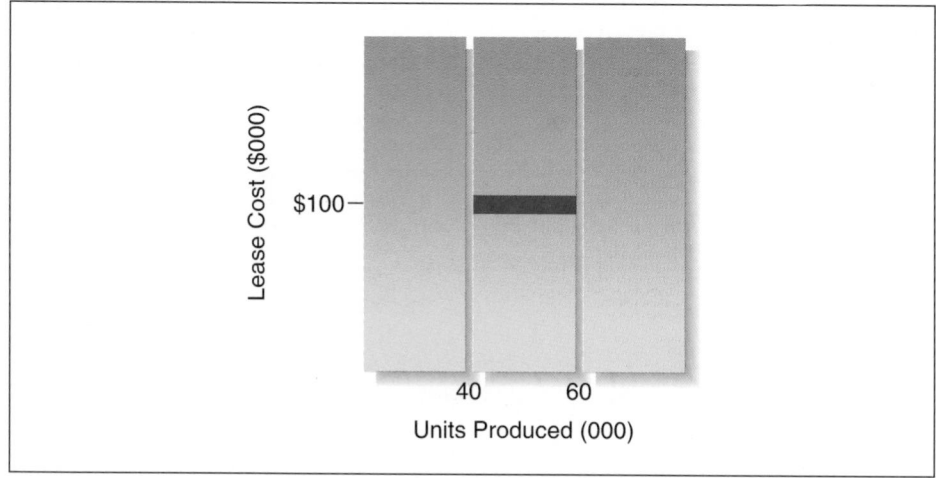

---

[1] Although our example has depicted a step cost as a type of variable cost, be aware that the step function may also resemble a fixed cost. This situation occurs when the steps become very wide or, in other words, when an extremely large activity change is needed to force an increase (or decrease) in cost. An explanation is provided on page 992.

Constant dollars combined with changing activity cause variations in the fixed cost *per unit*. If Yellowstone manufactures only 40,000 units, the lease cost is $2.50 per unit ($100,000 ÷ 40,000 units). On the other hand, if production climbs to 60,000 units, the per-unit cost falls to $1.67 ($100,000 ÷ 60,000 units). In view of this behavior, we can summarize the movement of fixed and variable costs as shown in the accompanying chart.

Type of Cost	Effect of Changes in the Activity Base on	
	Total Cost	Cost Per Unit
Variable	Increase or decrease	No effect
Fixed	No effect*	Increase or decrease

*This is a general rule, as further explained in the next section.

Total Fixed Costs Can Change

Although total fixed costs remain static, they can, in fact, vary. Both time and other ranges of activity will readily cause increases or decreases in this significant cost element. To explain, virtually all costs change over the years because of inflation and variations in business practices. In the previous illustration, for example, Yellowstone might have leased the same equipment in future years at an increased cost or perhaps have turned to another lessor to obtain newer technology. Whether a cost is, indeed, fixed depends on the time period under study. In the long run, most costs change to match increases and decreases in manufacturing and sales activities.

Ranges of activity also affect fixed cost behavior. Notice that Yellowstone's equipment can manufacture up to 60,000 units per year. If production increases beyond this point, additional machinery must be leased, which forces fixed costs to rise. The additional machinery will allow the firm to handle a new range of activity, say, 60,001 to 80,000 units. If production increases once again, then even more machinery must be acquired. Costs that behave in this manner can be graphed as shown in Exhibit 24-4. The graph reveals that fixed costs will change with wide

EXHIBIT 24-4
Fixed Cost Behavior

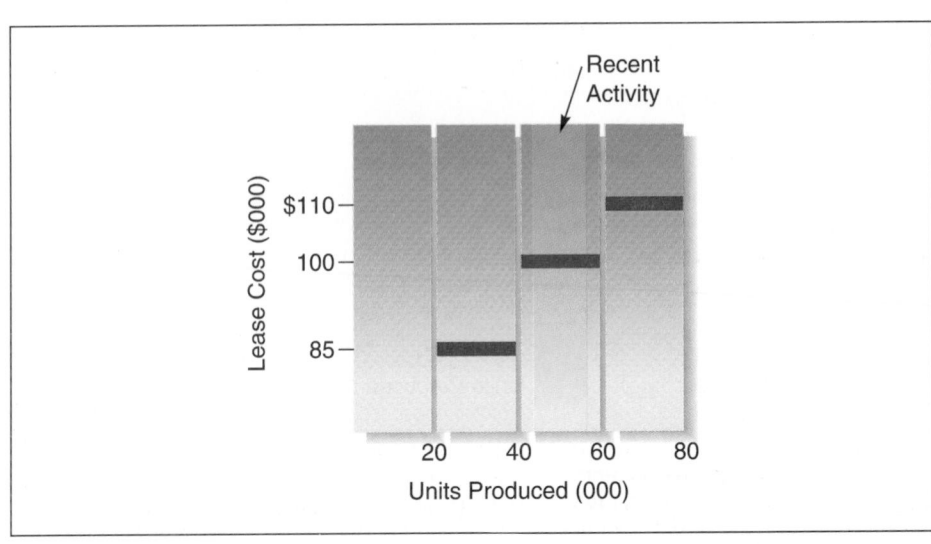

fluctuations in activity. The shaded band represents Yellowstone's most recent manufacturing experience—in essence, the relevant range. If the relevant range has been properly defined, normal operations should produce fixed costs that can be graphed as a single horizontal line.

Committed and Discretionary Fixed Costs

Fixed costs are substantial for many companies, especially those engaged in manufacturing. Heavy capital equipment and inventory requirements generate sizable depreciation write-offs, lease costs, and various related outlays. For purposes of planning, fixed costs are often subdivided into two types: committed and discretionary.

Committed fixed costs arise from an organization's commitment to engage in operations. By opening its doors and commencing activities, a firm must secure a plant, equipment, and management team. Immediately, as a result, an obligation is made to incur such costs as depreciation, rent, insurance, property taxes, and executive salaries.

By their very nature, most committed costs are not easily changed by daily business activities and decisions. Even if activity slows because of a depressed economy, many of these costs will still be incurred. Obviously, executives can vote to take salary cuts, layoffs can be instituted, and certain operations may be sold or perhaps temporarily closed. However, significant cutbacks in committed costs normally prevent a company from achieving its long-run goals and objectives.

Discretionary fixed costs are those that originate from top management's yearly spending decisions. That is, in preparing the annual operating budget, management will decide the amount it wishes to allocate to certain forthcoming activities. Fixed costs typically determined in this fashion include advertising, research and development, employee training, and contributions.

The Underlying Differences. Aside from the manner in which they originate, committed and discretionary fixed costs differ in two important ways. First, when a business decides to engage in or expand operations, it conducts a careful study of both its current *and* future economic position. Buildings will not be built and equipment will not be acquired unless *long-run* profitability is anticipated. In view of their nature, it is apparent that committed costs are geared heavily to the future. Discretionary fixed costs, conversely, are short term in orientation and are based on management's expectations for the forthcoming accounting period.

The second distinction between committed and discretionary costs concerns cost elimination. As noted, committed costs are not easily changed. Once the decision to incur them is made, an organization becomes locked-in and must live with its obligation for a number of years. Because of this relative stranglehold, companies strive for effective facility utilization as a means of coping with committed costs. Such a strategy is very logical: the associated inflexibility dictates an uphill battle if cost reduction is attempted to improve earnings. In contrast, discretionary costs also lock in an organization; however, the period of obligation is normally much shorter. Frequently, for example, discretionary costs are set by yearly contracts. Should financial difficulties arise, cost cutbacks can be achieved more rapidly, possibly without significant damage to long-run objectives.

Increased Fixed Costs

Over the years there has been a shift by businesses toward higher levels of fixed cost incurrence (relative to variable cost). Consider, for example, that labor unions have fought long and hard for guaranteed annual wages and workweeks, both of which have transformed direct labor (a variable cost) into a cost that is not totally responsive to changes in production. Another factor is an increased use of automated facilities and robots, as discussed earlier in the text. Automation and its accompanying charges for depreciation, property taxes, leasing, and maintenance have added to a company's fixed costs while often, at the same time, reducing the labor force.

Although guaranteed wages and workweeks may be attractive from a social viewpoint, and automation may lead to improved efficiency and product quality, operating flexibility will frequently suffer. A manager will normally have more decision-making alternatives available in a variable cost environment—one where costs are readily changed and/or eliminated should the need arise.

Mixed (Semivariable) Costs

Many cost functions contain both variable and fixed cost elements. Companies, for instance, often pay their salespeople a weekly salary plus a commission. The commission, generally a stipulated percentage of sales, varies with the revenues generated. As another example, electric utilities frequently bill their customers a fixed amount each month, plus a certain number of cents per kilowatt-hour used. Both of these cost functions are termed **mixed,** or **semivariable, costs.** Like a variable cost, a mixed cost changes in response to fluctuations in the activity base. Mixed cost movement, however, is not directly proportional because of the presence of a constant fixed charge. The elements of a mixed cost are shown graphically in Exhibit 24-5.

Observe that the variable and fixed cost elements are combined to generate the total mixed cost. To illustrate, assume that New England Products pays Howard Polk a $200 weekly salary plus a 10% sales commission. If Polk's sales for the week just ended total $2,450, New England's compensation cost of $445 would be computed in the manner shown on the next page.

EXHIBIT 24-5
Mixed Cost

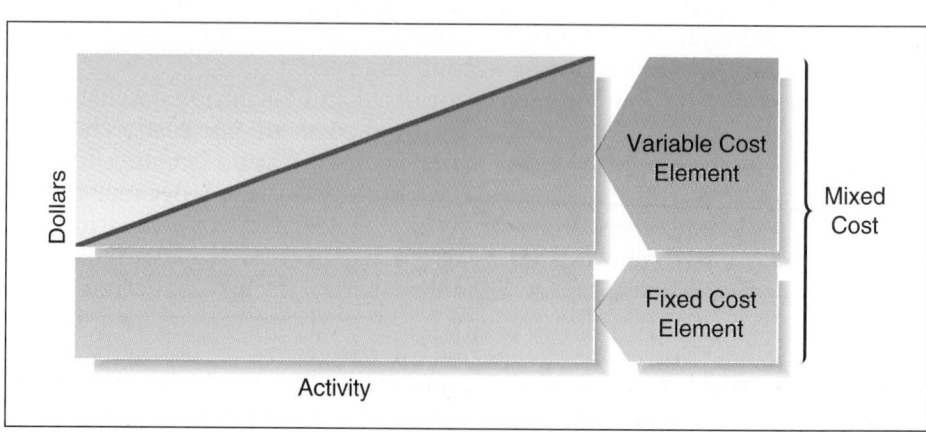

Fixed salary cost	$200
Variable cost: $2,450 \times 0.10$	245
Total (mixed) cost	$445

Most accountants and cost analysts have little difficulty understanding the differences among variable, step, fixed, and mixed costs. The determination of how specific costs behave, however, is another matter. Recall our earlier warning—the same costs can behave differently in different situations. To further complicate the picture, many costs are influenced by more than one factor at a given time. Direct materials used, for example, is normally classified as a variable cost. Use varies with production but is also influenced by material quality and worker efficiency. Turning to another area, gasoline consumption increases with the number of miles driven. However, consumption is also affected by the vehicle involved, wind conditions, the type of driving (city or highway), and other factors.

COST ANALYSIS

You are probably beginning to realize that cost analysis is an extremely difficult task. In practice, many companies assume that cost behavior can be sufficiently explained by concentrating on only one key factor rather than the many variables that may actually affect expenditure levels. Management, as a result, must exercise judgment when examining cost functions. Cost analysis in most organizations is heavily dependent on assumptions and estimates, with perfection being the exception rather than the rule.

Several techniques have been developed to study cost behavior. These techniques include the scattergraph, the method of least squares, and the high-low method.

Scattergraph

A **scattergraph** is a graphical representation of observed relationships between costs and activity levels. Using operating data, one plots the costs incurred at various levels of activity. On the basis of the observed relationships, the costs are then identified as being fixed, variable, or mixed. To illustrate use of a scattergraph, assume that Zephyr Bus Lines wants to analyze the maintenance costs incurred to service its bus fleet. An examination of maintenance records for a recent six-month period revealed the following information:

OBJECTIVE

2

Use the scattergraph and high-low method for examining cost behavior.

Month	Maintenance Labor Hours	Maintenance Cost
January	1,400	$25,000
February	1,200	22,400
March	1,600	24,500
April	1,800	24,700
May	1,900	28,000
June	2,000	30,000

A casual inspection of the data reveals that some variable cost is present, since higher levels of activity (labor hours) generate higher costs. This

EXHIBIT 24-6
Scattergraph

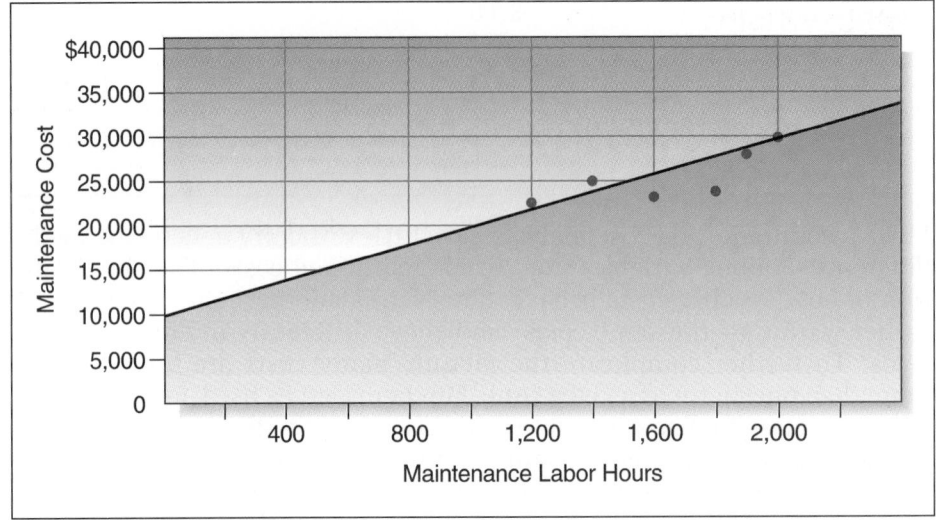

observation is confirmed by examining the scattergraph in Exhibit 24-6. The line through the data points, drawn by visual approximation, intersects the cost axis at $10,000—the fixed cost of Zephyr's maintenance operation. The variable cost per hour can now be found by studying the total cost of any point that falls on the line.[2] The computations that follow show the proper approach.

Total cost at 2,000 hours	$30,000
Less fixed cost	10,000
Variable cost	$20,000

Variable cost per hour: $20,000 ÷ 2,000 hours = $10 per hour

The scattergraph is somewhat imprecise because of the manner in which the cost line is determined. Nevertheless it is a starting point for analyzing cost behavior.

Method of Least Squares

The **method of least squares** is a statistical technique that overcomes the imprecision of the scattergraph. Rather than determine the cost line by approximation, the least-squares method relies on mathematical formulas to minimize the sum of the squares of the distances from the data points to the line. With this approach the best possible line fit is obtained, and higher accuracy is achieved. The details of the least-squares method are normally presented in most statistics courses and many advanced managerial accounting courses.

---

[2] The hourly variable cost is equal to the slope of the line.

High-Low Method

Unlike the scattergraph and the method of least squares, the **high-low method** focuses on only two data points when analyzing costs: those at the highest and lowest levels of activity within the relevant range. From these two points a generalization about variable and fixed cost behavior is made.

To illustrate the related procedures, we will continue the Zephyr Bus Lines example. Observe that the highest and lowest activity occurred during June and February, respectively. By studying these two months, we see that an 800-hour increase in labor time caused maintenance cost to rise by $7,600. These figures are obtained from the following computations:

	Maintenance Labor Hours	Maintenance Cost
Highest activity (June)	2,000	$30,000
Lowest activity (February)	1,200	22,400
Difference	800	$ 7,600

The increase in total cost represents variable cost. Thus, the variable maintenance cost per hour amounts to $9.50 ($7,600 ÷ 800 hours).

Once the variable portion is known, fixed cost can be determined by returning to either of the two months under study. Because total cost equals variable cost plus fixed cost, the latter amount is found by subtraction:

	High Point (2,000 Hours)	Low Point (1,200 Hours)
Total cost	$30,000	$22,400
Less variable cost @ $9.50 per hour	19,000*	11,400†
Fixed cost	$11,000	$11,000

* 2,000 hours × $9.50 = $19,000.
† 1,200 hours × $9.50 = $11,400.

As the calculations show, fixed costs are the same at both volume levels—an expected finding since we are working within one range of activity. Observe, though, that the fixed costs (and the variable costs as well) differ from the amounts obtained by using the scattergraph. This result is expected because the two techniques use different approaches when dealing with historical cost/activity relationships.

The high-low method is a straightforward approach to cost analysis; yet the method has been criticized because it relies on only two data observations and ignores all others. Given this situation, it is important that the points selected for evaluation be representative of normal behavior and not reflect unusual happenings. Selecting nonrepresentative points will taint the results obtained.[3]

ETHICS ISSUE

United, Inc., will be closing 2 of its 11 factories. A major deciding factor is a factory's variable and fixed cost structure. Your plant regularly uses the high-low method of analysis, but you know that the scattergraph will give a more accurate (and unfavorable) picture of the plant's actual cost behavior. Which method should be used? Why?

---

[3] A scattergraph is helpful in spotting such points. So-called *outliers* will fall far away from the other data.

COST-VOLUME-PROFIT ANALYSIS

OBJECTIVE

Compute and explain the meaning of a company's break-even point and contribution margin.

Once variable and fixed costs are determined, cost-volume-profit analysis can begin. Managers utilize CVP analysis in many different ways. Various cost strategies can be explored, such as trade-offs between incurring fixed salary costs or variable sales commissions. CVP can also be used to examine pricing policies and their impact on market share; profit strategies such as purposely incurring a loss on a product to generate additional customer traffic in a retail store; and other similar issues.

An important and highly publicized facet of cost-volume-profit analysis is break-even analysis. This popular management tool concentrates on finding the **break-even point**—the level of activity where revenues and expenses are equal. Net income, as a result, is zero.

The break-even point can be calculated by employing either an equation or a contribution approach. To illustrate both methods, we will assume that the University Bookstore is studying whether to add a collection of mugs to its product line. Each mug costs $7 and will be sold for $10. The following additional monthly costs will be incurred:

Rental cost of display case	$300
Salary of part-time salesperson	600
	$900

Equation Approach

As its name implies, the equation approach relies on a mathematical equation to compute the break-even point. The equation is based on the calculation of net income, that is:

Sales		$XXX
Less: Variable costs	$XXX	
Fixed costs	XXX	XXX
Net income		$XXX

Because net income equals zero at the break-even point, the following expression is constructed:

$$\text{Sales} - \text{Variable Costs} - \text{Fixed Costs} = 0$$

Transforming, we have

$$\text{Sales} = \text{Variable Costs} + \text{Fixed Costs}$$

The equation requires that variable costs be expressed as a percentage of sales. An examination of the University Bookstore data reveals that the $300 display case rental and the $600 salary are both fixed since neither amount changes with volume. The $7 mug cost, on the other hand, is variable, making variable cost in our example 70% of sales ($7 ÷ $10 selling price).

The break-even point can now be found in the following manner:

$$Sales = Variable\ Costs + Fixed\ Costs$$
$$S = VC + FC$$
$$S = 0.7S + \$900$$
$$0.3S = \$900$$
$$S = \$3,000$$

The calculations show that monthly sales must total $3,000 to break even. Stated differently, sales in excess of 300 mugs ($3,000 ÷ $10 selling price) will generate net income; in contrast, sales of less than 300 mugs will produce a net loss.

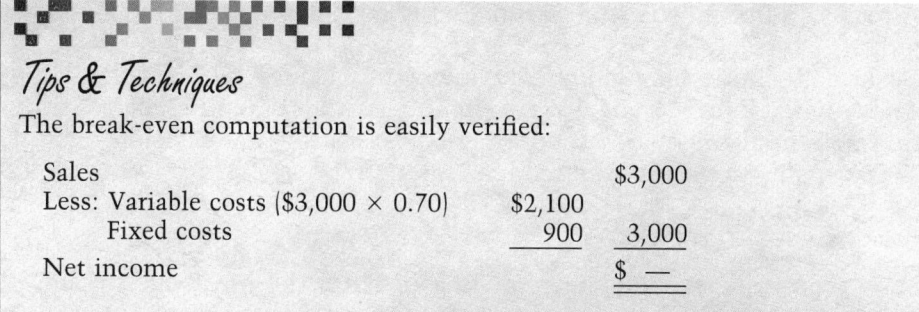

Tips & Techniques

The break-even computation is easily verified:

Sales		$3,000
Less: Variable costs ($3,000 × 0.70)	$2,100	
Fixed costs	900	3,000
Net income		$ —

This calculation shows that the variable cost element must, as its name implies, "be free" to vary with dollar sales. By expressing the mug's cost as a *percentage* of sales rather than as a flat dollar amount (i.e., $7), the proper cost behavior pattern is achieved.

Contribution Approach

The contribution approach focuses on unit profitability. Because mugs are purchased for $7 and later sold for $10, the bookstore is better off by $3 for each mug sold. The $3 figure is termed the **contribution margin,** namely, selling price minus variable cost per unit. Stated simply, the contribution margin represents the amount that each mug contributes toward covering fixed costs and generating net income.

To illustrate, examine the data in the following chart.

Mugs Sold	Revenue	Total Variable Cost	Fixed Cost	Total Cost	Net Income
0	$ 0	$ 0	$900	$ 900	$(900)
1	10	7	900	907	(897) >$3
2	20	14	900	914	(894) >$3
⋮	⋮	⋮	⋮	⋮	⋮
300	3,000	2,100	900	3,000	0
301	3,010	2,107	900	3,007	3 >$3
302	3,020	2,114	900	3,014	6 >$3

The first line shows product-line profitability immediately after the decision to carry the mugs. Specifically, the salesperson has been hired and the display case has been rented; however, no merchandise has been sold. Each sale then contributes $3 toward covering the fixed costs and decreases the overall loss. Although the decision to stock the goods will eventually prove profitable, the bookstore must first generate sufficient volume to completely offset the fixed costs and break even. The break-even point is computed in the following manner:

$$\frac{\text{Fixed Costs}}{\text{Unit Contribution Margin}} = \text{Break-Even Point in Units}$$

$$\frac{\$900}{\$3} = 300 \text{ mugs}$$

After the 300th mug is sold, income will be produced at the rate of $3 per unit.

The contribution margin is a very powerful business tool and should not be dismissed lightly. In addition to its use in profit planning, the contribution margin also assists in performance evaluation and decision making. These applications are explored in Chapter 27.

Break-Even Analysis: Was It Ever Used?

Now that you have an understanding of what the break-even point is, consider the real-life example that follows. *Forbes* recently presented some data about the Grand Hyatt Wailea, a newly opened luxury hotel on Maui, Hawaii. The facility cost $600 million to build, or approximately $800,000 per room, and comes complete with a $2 million statue and 800 tons of imported granite from Japan. Financing costs alone run close to $100,000 per day. Combining all the variable and fixed costs of operation, the Grand Hyatt will have to charge an average room rate of $500 a day to break even—and that assumes a 100% occupancy rate!

These figures are obviously quite ambitious, especially considering that recent occupancy rates in the surrounding area ran about 52%. Also, the average room rate was about $130. As the *Forbes* reporter noted, the project likely never made economic sense.[4]

A Graphical Representation

The break-even point and CVP relationships are frequently presented in a graphical format known as a **break-even chart.** The graph is useful because it allows managers to (1) review earnings over a wide range of activity and (2) examine the effects on profitability of changes in sales and costs.

The break-even chart for our mug example appears in Exhibit 24-7. With sales volume graphed on the horizontal axis and dollars on the vertical axis, the chart is constructed in the following manner:

1 Fixed costs are depicted by drawing a line parallel to the horizontal axis.

2 Total costs are represented by first computing the total cost of an arbitrarily selected volume level. The calculations for a selected volume of 500 mugs follow (see p. 1002).

---

[4] See "Banzai Loans," *Forbes*, November 11, 1991, p. 40.

EXECUTIVE BRIEFING
The Meaning of Cost-Volume-Profit Analysis to a Business

R. David Thomas
Senior Chairman and Founder
Wendy's International, Inc.

In 1988 and 1989, consumer research indicated that
Wendy's was perceived as relatively high cost and, therefore, not as good a "value" as some of our quick-service
restaurant competitors. We didn't feel this was true,
since value is not just a low price, but "quality received for money spent."
However, to a certain extent, perception is reality, so we developed a strategy
to enhance our value image. The concept involved packaging a core menu of
seven items, all priced at $0.99, which we call the Super Value Menu (SVM).

The products were primarily existing offerings; they were not modified in
quantity or quality to offset the reduced $0.99 selling price and accompany-
ing drop in per-unit profit (contribution) margin. The SVM proved to be popular, and *total* sales and contribution margin per store increased significantly.
Since many restaurant operating costs are essentially fixed in nature, unlike
food costs, which tend to vary directly with sales, the higher sales provided a
greater overall profit. In addition, consumer perception of the "value" of
Wendy's products has improved markedly since the Super Value Menu introduction.

EXHIBIT 24-7
Break-Even Chart

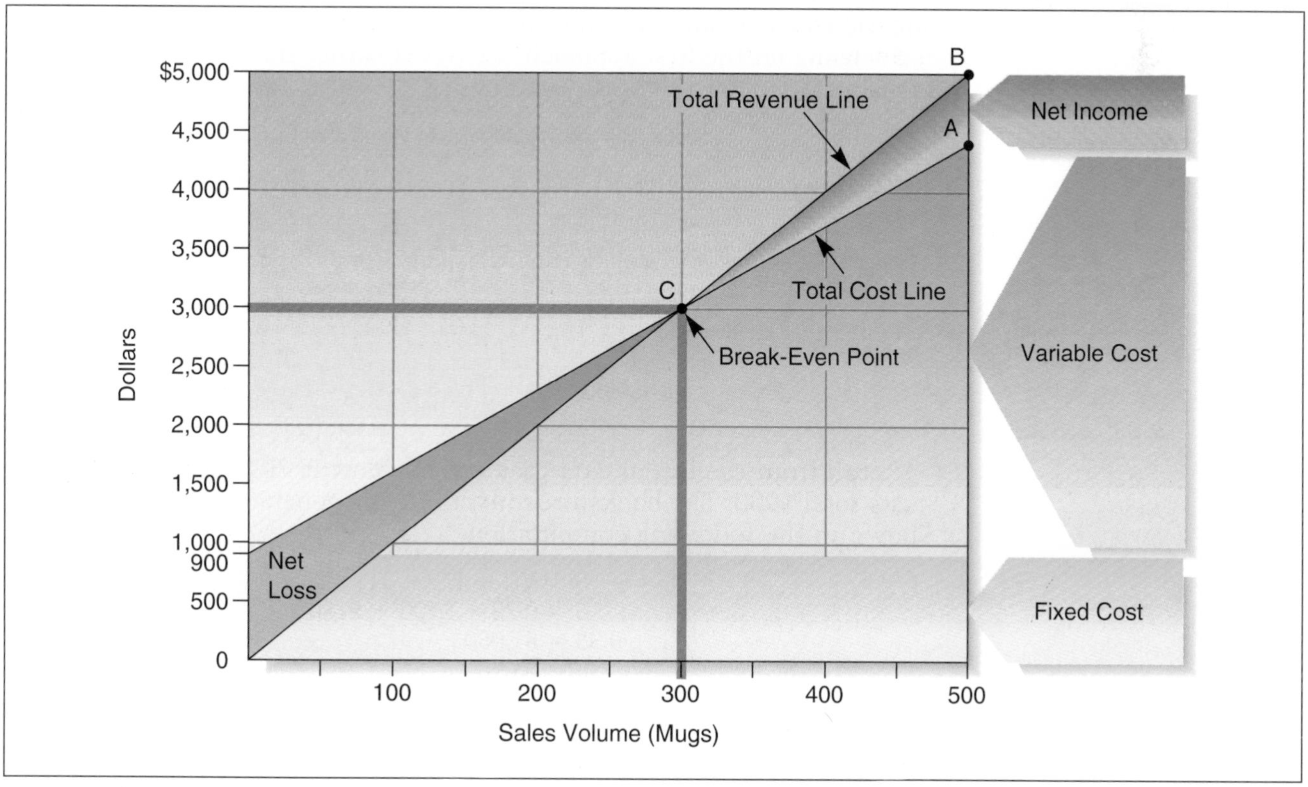

Variable cost (500 mugs × $7)	$3,500
Fixed cost	900
Total cost	$4,400

The total cost line is then extended from the intersection of the fixed cost line and the vertical axis to $4,400 (point A).

3 Sales revenues are plotted in a manner similar to that described in Step 2. A diagonal line is extended from the graph's origin through a point that represents the total revenues of an arbitrarily selected activity level. If we again choose 500 mugs, the line would be extended through point B, or $5,000 (500 mugs × $10).

Point C represents break-even operations: $3,000 of sales (300 mugs). The graph readily discloses that sales in excess of 300 mugs will be profitable, because total revenues will exceed total costs. In contrast, should volume drop below this figure, the University Bookstore will generate a loss from its new product line.

Target Income

OBJECTIVE

4

Calculate the sales needed to generate a particular target income figure.

In addition to finding the break-even point, CVP analysis can be used to identify the sales necessary to produce a particular level of income (often called the **target income**). To illustrate the related procedures, we will continue the University Bookstore example. Assume that the mugs will be carried in stock only if they generate a monthly income of $150. The sales required to achieve this level of profitability can be calculated by modifying the equation and contribution approaches to break-even analysis.

Focusing on the first approach, we noted earlier that the following relationship is true at the break-even point:

$$\text{Sales} - \text{Variable Costs} - \text{Fixed Costs} = 0$$

Because we now desire to earn a given income figure, the equation becomes

$$\text{Sales} - \text{Variable Costs} - \text{Fixed Costs} = \text{Target Income}$$

or

$$\boxed{\text{Sales} = \text{Variable Costs} + \text{Fixed Costs} + \text{Target Income}}$$

Recall from the initial data that variable cost is 70% of sales and fixed costs total $900. The bookstore must therefore generate sales of $3,500, as shown in the following computation:

$$
\begin{aligned}
S &= VC + FC + TI \\
S &= 0.7S + \$900 + \$150 \\
0.3S &= \$1,050 \\
S &= \$3,500
\end{aligned}
$$

On the basis of the $10 selling price, volume must total 350 mugs ($3,500 ÷ $10).

Turning to the contribution method, the bookstore previously calculated that each mug contributes $3 ($10 selling price − $7 variable cost) toward covering fixed costs and producing a profit. As shown on page 1000, 300 mugs must be sold just to break even. Now, to achieve the $150 target figure, volume must increase by 50 units per month ($150 ÷ $3). In view of this fact, the break-even formula is modified as follows:

$$\frac{\text{Fixed Costs + Target Income}}{\text{Unit Contribution Margin}} = \text{Required Sales in Units}$$

$$\frac{\$900 + \$150}{\$3} = 350 \text{ mugs}$$

Operating Changes

New technology, shifts in management, and variations in efficiency are commonplace for most businesses. These events and others are usually accompanied by changes in costs and revenues and thus affect an organization's CVP relationships. Consider, for example, the following break-even load factors[5] for several of this country's airlines:

OBJECTIVE

5

Use sales price, cost, and volume data to determine the impact of various operating changes on profitability.

	1991	1990	1989	1988	1987
American Airlines	61.6%	61.8%	57.9%	56.0%	58.5%
Delta Air Lines	62.6	58.0	56.1	52.7	51.1
USAir	62.7	64.5	60.6	56.0	57.3
United Airlines	69.5	66.5	63.0	62.2	63.0

Observe the variation over the years and among different carriers within the same year. Although there are a number of underlying causes, several of the more significant include fleet composition in terms of size, age, and fuel efficiency; route systems and structures (e.g., long haul versus short haul, business versus vacation); fleet financing methods; passenger fare composition (i.e., full-fare versus discount traffic); and labor and jet fuel contracts.

Airlines must respond to changes in these factors to stay in the black. Some have done so successfully, whereas others have not. Those in the latter category have incurred significant operating losses (occasionally leading to bankruptcy) or, in some cases, been absorbed by another carrier. Airlines are not alone—all businesses are faced with variations in their cost and revenue patterns.

Because management's ability to analyze operating changes often spells the difference between prosperity or failure, it is desirable to focus on the impact of changes in CVP relationships. To do so, we will continue the University Bookstore example. As a refresher, recall the following data:

Selling price per mug	$10	Fixed costs	
Variable cost per mug	7	Display case rental	$300
Contribution margin	$ 3	Salary of salesperson	600
			$900

Sales necessary to reach break-even point: 300 mugs
Sales necessary to generate a target income of $150: 350 mugs

---

[5] The break-even load factor is the percentage of seats that must be filled on scheduled flights to break even.

Change in Fixed Costs

Assume the bookstore is considering hiring a more experienced salesperson who requires a $720 monthly salary. Management wants to know the effect on the break-even point of this $120 increase in fixed cost. The desired information can be obtained in several different ways. Employing the contribution approach, we see the new break-even volume is 340 mugs:

$$\frac{\text{Fixed Costs}}{\text{Unit Contribution Margin}} = \frac{\$1,020}{\$3} = 340 \text{ mugs}$$

Or, since each mug contributes $3 toward fixed obligations, an additional 40 mugs must be sold to cover the $120 cost increase ($120 ÷ $3 = 40 mugs). Thus, the break-even point will jump from 300 to 340 units.

Changes in Fixed Costs and Variable Costs

Returning to the original data, assume the bookstore is exploring different compensation methods. Rather than a $600 monthly salary, a plan is being considered that calls for a base salary of $200 plus a $1-per-mug sales commission. Specifically, management wants to learn the sales volume required to yield the target monthly income of $150. In this case, total fixed costs fall to $500 ($200 + $300 display case rental). Furthermore, because variable costs rise by $1 from the commission, the mug's contribution margin decreases to $2 ($10 − $8). These two changes are combined to generate the following results:

$$\frac{\text{Fixed Costs + Target Income}}{\text{Unit Contribution Margin}} = \text{Required Sales in Units}$$

$$\frac{\$500 + \$150}{\$2} = 325 \text{ mugs}$$

The computation shows that with the change in salary structure, the bookstore can suffer a drop in monthly sales of 25 mugs (350 − 325) and still produce the target income figure. The plan is therefore advantageous and should be implemented. Not only do the numbers support the change, but an important qualitative consideration is present as well. The compensation plan under study (i.e., reward via commission) often increases employee motivation. Higher motivational levels, in turn, frequently lead to improved sales performance.

Changes in Fixed Costs and Sales Volume

Again returning to the original data, assume that operations have been quite profitable, with monthly sales averaging 400 mugs. Management is now considering a larger display case at an increased rental cost of $75 per month. The added space will allow the bookstore to carry a greater selection of merchandise, and sales are expected to total 440 units. Should the new display case be acquired?

Because both revenues and costs will change, management should compare the additional revenues that arise from the new display case against the additional costs. If additional revenues exceed additional costs, the proposal should be accepted; if not, rejection is in order. The following analysis reveals a net benefit in favor of the larger display case:

Additional revenues: 40 mugs × $10		$400
Less additional costs		
Variable: 40 mugs × $7	$280	
Increased rental	75	355
Net monthly benefit		$ 45

Observe that we have ignored the current volume of 400 mugs in our analysis. No matter which alternative is selected (i.e., maintain the present situation or acquire the larger case), these goods will continue to be sold. The analysis should concentrate on those items that change as a result of the decision, namely, the 40-unit increase in sales and the higher rental charge. Decisions of this nature are explored further in Chapter 27.

Changes in Sales Price and Sales Volume

Independent of the previous example that focused on a change in fixed costs and sales volume, assume that monthly sales have averaged 550 mugs. The bookstore is considering an increase in selling price from $10 to $12 despite a possible drop in the number of units sold. Before the final decision is made, management wishes to know how much sales can decline before there is a detrimental effect on profitability.

Because current sales total 550 mugs, the present product-line net income is $750 per month:

Sales (550 mugs × $10)	$5,500
Less variable cost (550 mugs × $7)	3,850
Contribution margin	$1,650
Less fixed cost	900
Net income	$ 750

With a new selling price of $12, the unit contribution margin becomes $5 ($12 − $7). Using the following technique, which was illustrated earlier in the chapter, we find that 330 mugs must be sold to maintain current profit levels.

$$\frac{\text{Fixed Costs + Target Income}}{\text{Unit Contribution Margin}} = \text{Required Sales in Units}$$

$$\frac{\$900 + \$750}{\$5} = 330 \text{ mugs}$$

Thus, the bookstore can suffer a monthly sales loss of 220 units (550 − 330) without any impact on net income.

Tips & Techniques

The preceding illustrations have shown several different methods of examining and solving business problems. As you gain more experience, you will find that the correct answer can be obtained by using alternative approaches. As long as your logic is sound and the text or your instructor does not specify a particular method, feel free to use any of the approaches presented.

CVP Analysis for Multiproduct Firms

OBJECTIVE

6

Apply cost-volume-profit analysis to multiproduct firms.

Most businesses engaged in retailing, wholesaling, and manufacturing activities sell more than one product, normally in differing volumes and at different markups. Although the University Bookstore example focused on the use of CVP analysis for a single item only, the procedures illustrated can, with minor modification, be employed when multiple goods are involved. As an example, assume that Stewart Distributors sells toasters, food processors, and mixers. The following data are anticipated for the upcoming year:

Product	Forecasted Sales (Units)	Selling Price	Variable Cost
Toaster	40,000	$20	$16
Food processor	100,000	44	37
Mixer	60,000	34	26
	200,000		

Fixed costs: $335,000

As before, the break-even point can be found by dividing fixed costs by the unit contribution margin. Rather than dealing with the contribution margin of one product, however, Stewart has three margins to consider. Adding a further complication, the margins are not expected to occur with the same frequency. For every toaster sold, for example, the firm anticipates selling $2\frac{1}{2}$ food processors and $1\frac{1}{2}$ mixers. In view of this situation, Stewart must weight the unit contribution margins by the **sales mix,** or the relative proportion of individual product sales to total sales. The computations that follow reveal a weighted "unit" contribution margin of $6.70:

Product	Forecasted Sales (Units)	Sales Mix*		Unit Contribution Margin†		Weighted Contribution Margin
Toaster	40,000	20%	×	$4	=	$0.80
Food processor	100,000	50%	×	7	=	3.50
Mixer	60,000	30%	×	8	=	2.40
	200,000					$6.70

* Forecasted individual product sales ÷ 200,000 units.
† Selling price minus variable cost for each product.

HIGHLIGHT

Charge Less and Earn More: Cost-Volume-Profit in Action

Alamo Rent A Car was born hustling. The name, for example, has nothing to do with the site of the San Antonio battle for Texas independence (Alamo is headquartered in Fort Lauderdale). The name was picked because it began with an "A" and would come first in the Yellow Pages' rent-a-car listings. But as a relative latecomer to the business, Alamo needed more than just a listings gimmick. It decided to become a price-cutter, advertising daily rental prices as much as 20% lower than its bigger competitors, and with no extra charge for mileage.

Just 18 years later, Alamo has revenues of more than $740 million a year, with over 10% of the $6.5 billion airport rental car market. The company now ranks fifth behind the big four (Hertz, Avis, National, and Budget). How profitable is it? The president of this privately held entity noted that profit margins have ranged between 3% and 5%—better than Hertz's rental car operation and second only to Avis's.

Renting cars is a competitive business. Are the Alamo people so smart that they can undercut their big competitors and still earn more per revenue dollar than most of them? On selected cars and under certain conditions, the answer is yes. Rent a Chevy Beretta from Alamo with no extras in Los Angeles on Wednesday through Friday, for example, and you pay $31.99 a day, with free mileage. A comparable vehicle from Hertz runs $38.99.

How do you beat the competition like that and still make good money? Management has succeeded in keeping costs among the lowest in the industry. For one thing, the company picks its spots very carefully, running only 110,000 cars at 118 of the most highly trafficked locations in the United States and United Kingdom. Hertz, by contrast, runs 420,000 cars at 5,000+ locations in 120 countries. Half of Alamo's rental counters are not in airport terminals where rents are sky-high; the firm prefers cheaper locations nearby.

But to be consistently more profitable than Hertz, Alamo clearly has to have more going for it than low overhead and cheap cars. Alamo used to prod its telephone and counter agents to get customers to trade up to more expensive cars and sign on for collision insurance, at what were the highest rates in the industry—$11.99 a day for a mid-size car. The insurance surcharge yielded a nice profit, earning net margins of around 20%. Because of some recent changes, customers can now choose among three policies, ranging from $4 to $10 a day, depending on coverage.

Insurance aside, a look back in time finds that Alamo really took off in the early 1980s. Management figured that airline deregulation would mean more travelers could afford to fly on their vacations and would need a cheap rental car once they got to their destinations. It was right: The leisure rent-a-car market has grown 10% to 15% a year, versus 5% for the commercial market.

Now that the other rental car companies have begun chasing Alamo's vacation travel customers, Alamo has begun chasing the budget-minded business traveler. The firm now has 45 primarily business locations, which produce nearly 35% of revenues.

The company, though, needs both the business traveler and the convenience of airport counter space to keep up its 20%-a-year average growth rate. Many of Alamo's locations are still outside the airport gates, so customers must ride a bus that carries them to a rental office, where they sign the papers and get the cars. In the last five years Alamo has opened airport desks in nearly half of its locations, including Atlanta, Philadelphia, and Boston. This airport counter space is expensive—about 10% of daily gross revenues—and could squeeze margins. If past history holds true, however, this shouldn't be a problem. Management has shown a real flair for defending Alamo's cut-rate niche in this highly competitive business.

Note: Certain facts in this article were updated by the text's authors.

Source: Adapted from "Born to Hustle," *Forbes,* May 28, 1990, pp. 190, 194. Excerpted by permission of *Forbes* magazine, © Forbes Inc., 1990.

Stewart's break-even point is therefore 50,000 "units" ($335,000 ÷ $6.70). Because each "unit" is really a combination of the three products in the same proportions as the predicted mix, the following product-line sales are necessary:

Product	Sales Mix		Break-Even "Units"		Break-Even Sales by Product (Units)
Toaster	20%	×	50,000	=	10,000
Food processor	50%	×	50,000	=	25,000
Mixer	30%	×	50,000	=	15,000

On the basis of the calculations presented, it is evident that if the sales mix varies, the "unit" contribution margin will differ. Thus, the break-even volume will change.

Limiting Assumptions of CVP Analysis

OBJECTIVE

7

State the limiting assumptions on which cost-volume-profit analysis is based.

The CVP model that we have presented is used to analyze the financial relationships within an organization. Businesses continually change their operating practices, and many of the changes affect the relationships expressed in the model. CVP studies are therefore based on several limiting assumptions, a few of which have been touched upon in the preceding pages:

1 All costs can be classified as fixed or variable.
2 Fixed costs remain constant through the range of analysis (i.e., the relevant range).
3 The behavior of costs and revenues is linear through the range of analysis.
4 Technology, efficiency, costs, and selling prices remain as predicted.
5 The sales mix remains as predicted (i.e., constant).
6 Inventory levels remain fairly stable.

Management must be fully aware of the preceding assumptions if CVP analysis is to be used properly. Given the dynamic nature of business, a failure to recognize the model's restrictive features could lead to serious deficiencies in the planning and decision processes.

END-OF-CHAPTER REVIEW

LEARNING OBJECTIVES: THE KEY POINTS

1 Identify the characteristics of variable, step, fixed, and mixed (semivariable) cost functions. A variable cost is one that varies in direct proportion to a change in an activity base (e.g., sales, production, and so forth). As a result of this behavior, the total cost incurred increases or decreases, and the per-unit amount remains constant. Sometimes, a sizable movement is needed in the activity base for a cost to change. A function that behaves in this manner is known as a step cost because the cost fluctuations really occur in "chunks."

Step functions are often viewed as a specialized type of variable cost. However, when an extremely large activity change is needed to force a change in the dollar amount incurred, the function's behavior tends to approximate that of a fixed cost. A fixed cost remains constant in total over a range of activity; in contrast, the cost per unit fluctuates. Finally, a mixed (semivariable) cost fluctuates with a change in the activity base but does not move in direct proportion to the base. The mixed cost contains both variable and fixed elements.

2 Use the scattergraph and high-low method for examining cost behavior. The scattergraph is a graph of past observations between an activity base and the level of cost incurred. Points are plotted and a straight line is then fit through the points by visual approximation. The line's intersection with the cost axis is the amount of fixed cost incurred; the line's slope is the unit variable cost.

In contrast, the high-low method focuses only on the highest and lowest data observations. The variable cost per unit (or hour) is calculated by studying the cost change between the two points in question relative to the activity base change. Fixed cost is then determined by subtracting the variable cost incurred at the highest (or lowest) point from that point's total cost.

3 Compute and explain the meaning of a company's break-even point and contribution margin. The break-even point is the level of activity where total revenues and total costs are equal. Net income is therefore zero. Break-even sales may be computed in both dollars and units, as follows:

Dollars (equation method): Sales = Variable Costs + Fixed Costs
Units (contribution approach): Fixed Costs ÷ Unit Contribution Margin

The contribution margin is the mathematical difference between selling price and variable cost. This figure is the amount that each unit contributes toward covering fixed costs and generating income. That is, if the contribution margin is $8 per unit, overall income will rise by $8 for each unit that is sold by the firm.

4 Calculate the sales needed to generate a particular target income figure. The break-even model can be modified to find the sales required to produce a target income level. In both the equation approach and the contribution approach, the desired income is added to the fixed cost figure and treated as a "dollar obligation" that must be covered by sales.

5 Use sales price, cost, and volume data to determine the impact of various operating changes on profitability. The formulas to find the break-even point, whether modified for the target income figure or not, are helpful in studying the impact of various operating changes on the entity. Such changes include increases and decreases in sales prices, variable costs, and fixed costs; the addition of new product lines; and so forth. All that a user need do is adjust the variable under study, perform the necessary computations, and analyze the results.

6 Apply cost-volume-profit analysis to multiproduct firms. CVP analysis can be used in single- or multiple-product settings. To compute the break-even point, fixed costs are once again divided by the contribution margin per unit. A "unit" in this case is really a combination of a company's various products in preset proportions known as a sales mix (i.e., the percentage of individual product sales to total unit sales). A weighted contribution margin is found by weighting (multiplying) individual product margins with the sales mix percentages, the result then being divided into total fixed costs.

7 State the limiting assumptions on which cost-volume-profit analysis is based. The CVP model assumes that all costs can be classified as variable or fixed, with costs falling in the latter category being constant through the range of analysis. Further, costs and revenues have linear, straight-line relationships. The components used in the model (e.g., costs, revenues, and sales mix) must remain as predicted, and inventory levels must remain fairly stable during the accounting period.

**KEY TERMS
AND CONCEPTS:
A QUICK OVERVIEW**

break-even chart   A presentation of the break-even point and other CVP relationships in a graphic format.

break-even point   The level of activity where revenues and expenses are equal and net income is zero.

committed fixed cost   A cost that arises from an organization's commitment to engage in operations—for example, property taxes, rent, and depreciation.

contribution margin   Selling price minus variable cost per unit.

cost-volume-profit analysis   The study of price, cost, volume, and profit interrelationships.

discretionary fixed cost   A fixed cost that originates from top management's yearly appropriation decisions—for example, advertising expense and research and development expense.

fixed cost   A cost that remains constant in total when changes occur in an activity base.

high-low method   A method of cost analysis that uses two data observations (the highest and lowest) to make generalizations about variable and fixed cost behavior.

method of least squares   A statistical technique for determining cost behavior.

mixed (semivariable) cost   A cost that contains both fixed and variable elements.

relevant range   The area of activity where a cost relationship is expected to hold true.

sales mix   The relative proportion of individual product sales to total sales.

scattergraph   A graphic representation of observed relationships between costs and activity levels.

step cost   A cost function that increases or decreases in "chunks," namely, when substantial changes occur in the activity base.

target income   A particular level of income that a company strives to attain.

variable cost   A cost that varies in direct proportion to a change in an activity base.

CHAPTER QUIZ

The five questions that follow relate to several issues raised in the chapter. Test your knowledge of the issues by selecting the best answer. (The answers appear on p. 1024.)

1 Variable costs (from the accountant's viewpoint):
   a are graphed by means of a curvilinear line.
   b remain constant in total through the relevant range.
   c are constant on a per-unit basis through the relevant range.
   d are commonly divided into committed and discretionary classifications.

2 The high-low method of analyzing cost behavior:
   a can be used to determine the variable and fixed components of a mixed cost function.
   b uses the same number of data observations as a scattergraph.
   c relies on the following computation to figure the variable cost per unit (or hour): Change in activity between the high and low points ÷ change in cost between the high and low points.
   d results in different amounts of fixed cost at the high and low data points.

3 Foster Company has sales of $800,000, variable costs that total 60% of sales, and fixed costs of $180,000. The firm's break-even point is:

a $140,000.

b $300,000.

c $450,000.

d $560,000.

4 The contribution margin:

a is the amount that each unit contributes toward covering variable costs and producing income.

b is the result of subtracting both the variable and fixed costs per unit from the selling price.

c may, in selected cases, be less than net income.

d is the difference between a unit's selling price and variable cost and, when divided into fixed costs, will produce the unit sales required to break even.

5 The cost-volume-profit model:

a can be used only by single-product companies.

b assumes that the sales mix will remain as predicted.

c assumes that technology, efficiency, and costs can change.

d cannot be used to study operating changes of the firm.

Kennett Company manufactures and sells a single product. Sales peak in March and generally bottom out in October. The following cost and volume information was extracted from the accounting records:

SUMMARY PROBLEM

	March	July*	October
Production and sales (units)	25,000	19,000	14,000
Total cost incurred	$195,300	$176,200	$156,800

* An average month.

The company's product sells for $9 per unit.

Instructions

a Using the high-low method, compute Kennett's variable cost per unit and total monthly fixed cost.

b Compute the firm's contribution margin per unit.

c Determine the break-even point in both units and dollar sales.

d Determine the sales volume (in units) required to generate a target income of $29,150 per month.

e Assume that Kennett wants to add a second product (known as product no. 2). Data related to this product follow.

Selling price per unit	$7.00
Variable cost per unit	$4.20
Additional fixed costs	$65,800

Management anticipates that product no. 2 will initially account for 20% of the company's total sales volume; the remaining 80% will be generated by the existing product (known as product no. 1). If Kennett adds the new product to its merchandise line, compute the new monthly break-even point (in units).

Solution

a

	Units	Total Cost
Highest activity (March)	25,000	$195,300
Lowest activity (October)	14,000	156,800
Difference	11,000	$ 38,500

Variable cost per unit = $38,500 ÷ 11,000 units = $3.50

	High Point (25,000 Units)	Low Point (14,000 Units)
Total cost	$195,300	$156,800
Less variable cost @ $3.50 per unit	87,500*	49,000†
Fixed cost	$107,800	$107,800

* 25,000 units × $3.50 = $87,500.
† 14,000 units × $3.50 = $49,000.

b

Selling price	$9.00
Less variable cost per unit	3.50
Contribution margin	$5.50

c
$$\frac{\text{Fixed Costs}}{\text{Unit Contribution Margin}} = \text{Break-Even Point in Units}$$

$$\frac{\$107,800}{\$5.50} = 19,600 \text{ units}$$

A break-even point of 19,600 units produces a sales level of $176,400 (19,600 units × $9).

d
$$\frac{\text{Fixed Costs + Target Income}}{\text{Unit Contribution Margin}} = \text{Required Sales in Units}$$

$$\frac{\$107,800 + \$29,150}{\$5.50} = 24,900 \text{ units}$$

e

Product	Selling Price		Variable Cost		Contribution Margin		Sales Mix		Weighted Contribution Margin
1	$9.00	−	$3.50	=	$5.50	×	80%	=	$4.40
2	7.00	−	4.20	=	2.80	×	20%	=	0.56
									$4.96

Fixed costs now total $173,600 ($107,800 from product no. 1 + $65,800 from product no. 2). Therefore:

$$\frac{\text{Fixed Costs}}{\text{''Unit'' Contribution Margin}} = \text{Break-Even Point in ''Units''}$$

$$\frac{\$173,600}{\$4.96} = 35,000 \text{ ''units''}$$

Each "unit" is a mixture of product no. 1 and product no. 2 in the 80:20 sales mix. The break-even point is thus computed as follows:

Product	Sales Mix		Break-Even "Units"		Break-Even Sales by Product (Units)
1	80%	×	35,000	=	28,000
2	20%	×	35,000	=	7,000

ASSIGNMENT MATERIAL

QUESTIONS

Q24-1 In evaluating the cost of operating his automobile, a professor once commented: "Fuel is a fixed cost and insurance is a variable cost. I always pay the same amount per gallon and my mileage is fairly constant. On the other hand, the cost per mile for insurance varies with the distance that I drive." Comment on the professor's observations.

Q24-2 Differentiate between the accountant's and economist's views of variable cost behavior.

Q24-3 What is meant by the relevant range of activity?

Q24-4 Discuss the characteristics of a step cost function. In general, where is the best place to operate on a step?

Q24-5 An accounting professor once commented: "In the long run even fixed costs are variable." Evaluate the professor's comment.

Q24-6 Distinguish between committed and discretionary fixed costs. Which type can be cut back more easily without doing significant long-run harm to the organization? Explain.

Q24-7 Briefly comment on the trend toward increased fixed cost incurrence by businesses during the past decade. How does this trend affect operating flexibility?

Q24-8 Identify the inherent problems of the scattergraph and the high-low method.

Q24-9 Define the break-even point.

Q24-10 Define the contribution margin. What does the contribution margin represent, and how is it used in finding the break-even point?

Q24-11 Product A has a negative contribution margin. Explain how a negative contribution margin can arise, and determine whether product A should continue to be sold.

Q24-12 Discuss the benefits associated with using a break-even chart.

Q24-13 Determine the effect, if any, on the break-even point that each of the following events would have:
a An increase in sales price
b A decrease in fixed cost
c An increase in the number of units sold

Q24-14 Will a change in a company's sales mix likely affect the break-even point? Briefly explain.

Q24-15 What are the limiting assumptions of CVP analysis?

EXERCISES

E24-1   *Cost behavior* (L.O. 1)
Melinda and Arthur Cooley own a fast-food restaurant in Salt Lake City. The following costs are under evaluation:
a Property taxes paid.
b Franchise fees paid ($10,000 per year plus 15% of gross sales).
c Food costs.
d Straight-line depreciation on restaurant equipment.
e Donations of food and supplies to charitable organizations.
f Local advertising.
g Paper supplies (napkins, cups, and so on).

Classify each of these costs as variable, committed fixed, discretionary fixed, or mixed.

E24-2   *Cost behavior patterns* (L.O. 1)
Consider the graphs that follow, each of which represents a different cost or expense of Society Jewelers, an operator of 22 jewelry stores throughout Illinois.

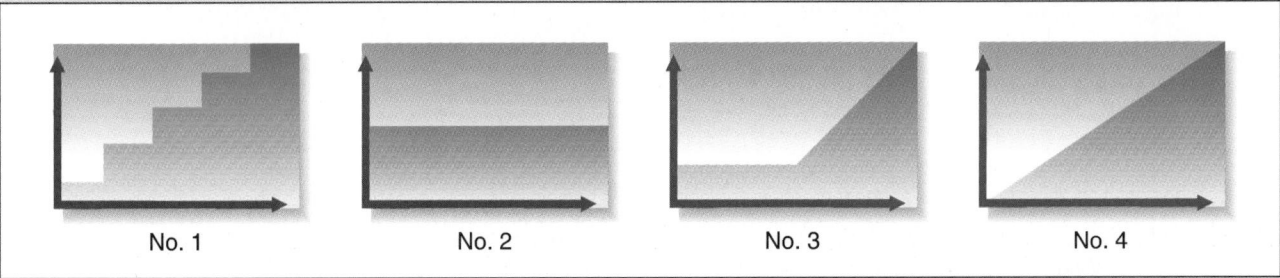

No. 1   No. 2   No. 3   No. 4

The vertical axis measures dollars and the horizontal axis represents an activity base (number of sales, clerks, and so forth). Select the graph that best describes the following items:
a Straight-line depreciation on store equipment.
b Store manager compensation. Each store manager is paid a monthly salary, plus a commission after a certain level of sales is reached.
c Cost of jewelry sold during the period.
d Weekly wages of store clerks who work a 40-hour week. One clerk is hired for every 100 sales made during the month.
e Rental charges on the firm's warehouse and distribution center.

E24-3   *High-low method* (L.O. 2)

1-2-3

The following cost data pertain to 19X6 operations of Heritage Products:

	Quarter 1	Quarter 2	Quarter 3	Quarter 4
Shipping costs	$58,200	$58,620	$60,125	$59,400
Orders shipped	120	140	175	150

The company uses the high-low method to analyze costs.
a Determine the variable cost per order shipped.
b Determine the fixed shipping costs per quarter.
c If present cost behavior patterns continue, determine total shipping costs for 19X7 if activity amounts to 570 orders.

E24-4 *High-low method; cost determination* (L.O. 2)

1-2-3

Dempsey and Associates experienced the following costs when manufacturing 800 and 900 units, respectively:

	800 Units	900 Units
Direct material	$ 9,200	$10,350
Property taxes	1,100	1,100
Maintenance	6,200	6,850
	$16,500	$18,300

Determine the anticipated outlays for direct material, property taxes, and maintenance cost if 880 units are produced. Dempsey uses the high-low method to analyze cost behavior.

E24-5 *Break-even and other CVP relationships* (L.O. 3, 4, 5)

Delta Gamma Upsilon sorority is in the process of planning its annual homecoming dinner and dance. The treasurer anticipates the following costs for the event, which will be held at the Regency Hotel:

Room rental	$300
Dinner cost (per person)	25
Chartered buses	500
Favors and souvenirs (per person)	5
Band	900

Each person would pay $40 to attend; 200 attendees are expected.
a Will the event be profitable for the sorority? Show computations.
b How many people must attend for the sorority to break even?
c Suppose the sorority encouraged its members to drive to the hotel and did not charter the buses. Further, a planned menu change will reduce the cost per meal by $2. If each member will still be charged $40, compute the contribution margin per person.

E24-6 *Break-even and other CVP relationships* (L.O. 3, 4, 5)

Cedars Hospital has average revenue of $180 per patient day. Variable costs are $45 per patient day; fixed costs total $4,320,00 per year.
a How many patient days does the hospital need to break even?
b What level of revenue is needed to earn a target income of $540,000?
c If variable costs drop to $36 per patient day, what increase in fixed costs can be tolerated without changing the break-even point as determined in part (a)?

E24-7 *Break-even and other CVP relationships* (L.O. 3, 4, 5)

In 19X4, Century Manufacturing produced and sold 70,000 pressure gauges at $32 each. This level of activity amounted to 70% of the firm's total productive capacity. The costs related to the pressure-gauge line were as follows:

	Variable	Fixed
Manufacturing	$770,000	$240,000
Selling	210,000	180,000
Administrative	—	390,000
Total	$980,000	$810,000

a Compute the income or loss generated from sales of pressure gauges in 19X4.

b How many gauges must be sold to break even?

c Considering your answer in part (b), at what percentage of total productive capacity must Century operate to achieve a break-even operation?

d Suppose that management wants to lower the break-even point. Should it attempt to increase or decrease fixed administrative costs?

E24-8 *CVP relationships: Working backward* (L.O. 3, 4)
Determine the missing amounts in each of the independent cases that follow.

Case	Units Sold	Sales	Variable Costs	Contribution Margin Per Unit	Fixed Costs	Net Income
A	?	$70,000	$?	$6	$14,000	$10,000
B	7,000	?	42,000	5	?	8,000
C	4,000	53,000	?	?	21,000	(2,000)
D	8,000	92,000	40,000	?	24,000	?

E24-9 *Overview of CVP relationships* (L.O. 3, 4, 6)
Evaluate the comments that follow as being True or False. If the comment is false, briefly explain why.

a The contribution margin is computed by subtracting the fixed cost per unit from the selling price.

b The sales required to produce a certain target income figure will exceed a firm's break-even sales.

c An automobile dealer has a negative contribution margin on each auto sold. The owner nonetheless claims that the dealership can be profitable by selling more cars than the competition. (*Note:* Ignore leasing, body shop, and service department considerations.)

d An increase in selling price will decrease a company's break-even point.

e The sales mix is an important consideration when figuring the break-even point in a multiproduct company.

E24-10 *Break even with multiple products* (L.O. 6)
Infant Products sells three different models of car seats: Economy, Standard, and Superior. Projected information on the three models follows.

	Economy	Standard	Superior
Sales (units)	5,000	30,000	15,000
Selling price	$30	$40	$55
Variable cost	16	23	35

Total fixed costs are anticipated to be $739,200.

a Determine the company's sales mix.

b Calculate the number of Economy, Standard, and Superior models that must be sold to break even.

c Analyze your calculations from parts (a) and (b). If Infant Products wishes to improve overall profitability, should it attempt to increase or decrease sales of the Superior car seat relative to the other two models? Why?

Series A

P24-A1 *Scattergraph and high-low method* (L.O. 2)

P. Thurmond has a highly automated machine-shop. The firm is studying maintenance cost behavior and has gathered the following data for a recent six-month period:

Month	Machine Hours	Maintenance Cost
July	18,000	$36,000
August	20,000	39,600
September	18,500	37,000
October	19,000	38,200
November	22,000	36,400
December	17,000	35,400

Instructions

a Prepare a scattergraph by plotting machine hours on the horizontal axis and maintenance cost on the vertical axis.

b By fitting a line through the plotted points, determine Thurmond's monthly fixed cost and the variable cost per machine hour.

c Determine the variable and fixed costs by using the high-low method.

d In view of Thurmond's cost behavior, which of the two methods (scattergraph or high-low) appears more appropriate? Explain your answer.

P24-A2 *Cost behavior and analysis* (L.O. 1, 2)

The chief accountant of Stevenson Corporation is studying certain costs (direct labor, plant security, utilities, and maintenance) in an effort to better control operations. Normal production activity ranges from 7,500 to 8,000 units per month. In the past three months the following cost behavior has been observed:

	Month 1	Month 2	Month 3
Production (units)	7,540	7,950	7,680
Direct labor	$18,850	$19,875	$19,200
Plant security	14,600	14,600	14,600
Utilities	28,044	29,520	28,548

In addition, maintenance costs have displayed the following step behavior:

Activity Range (Units)	Cost
Up to 7,600	$ 8,000
7,601–7,800	9,500
7,801–8,000	11,000

Stevenson uses the high-low method to analyze cost behavior.

Instructions

a Production for next month is expected to total 7,850 units. Calculate the cost of direct labor, plant security, utilities, and maintenance for this level of activity.

b Comment on the cost-effectiveness of producing at a 7,850-unit level of activity with respect to maintenance costs. If you feel this is an ineffective production level, describe how effectiveness could be improved.

c There is a high probability that Stevenson's production volume will nearly double in forthcoming months because of a new customer. Can the data and methods used in part (a) for predicting the cost of 7,850 units be employed to estimate total costs for, say, 17,500 units? Why?

P24-A3 *Straightforward CVP analysis* (L.O. 3, 4, 5)

The following information pertains to 19X6 operations of Downey Enterprises:

1-2-3

Sales (11,100 units at $50)	$555,000
Variable costs	
Cost of goods sold	233,100
Sales commissions	77,700
Fixed costs	
Salaries	180,000
Rent	60,000
Other	13,000

The company sells a single product through a series of retail outlets; no manufacturing activities are involved.

Instructions

a Compute the 19X6 break-even point in both dollar and unit sales.

b What sales level is needed to achieve a target income of $9,900?

c Assume that management wants to cut salaries by $30,000 and increase sales commissions to $10 per unit. Determine the effect of these changes on the unit contribution margin, and explain the meaning of the contribution margin to Downey's president, who has a manufacturing background.

d Returning to the original data, assume that management is willing to pay an extra $3 commission on all units sold in excess of the company's break-even point. If 19X7 sales are expected to be 11,850 units, calculate the year's net income (or loss).

P24-A4 *Break-even and other CVP analysis* (L.O. 3, 4, 5)

Hodge and Best manufactures a single product. The information that follows relates to current operations.

1-2-3

Sales (80,000 units @ $15)		$1,200,000
Less: Variable cost	$720,000	
Fixed cost	360,000	1,080,000
Net income		$ 120,000

Instructions

a The sales outlook for next year is bleak. Calculate the number of units that must be sold to break even if current revenue and cost behavior patterns continue.

b If Hodge and Best wishes to earn a target income of $90,000 during the next accounting period, what level of dollar sales must be generated?

c Management is studying an increase in the selling price to $18 per unit. If consumers balk and volume drops, calculate the number of units that must be sold to earn the target income of $90,000. Should the change be implemented? Why?

d Hodge and Best's projected break-even point and target income are the result of interactions of numerous financial events and transactions. Determine the impact of the following operating changes by filling in the blanks below with "increase," "decrease," or "not affect."

(1) An increase in direct labor cost will _____ total variable costs, _____ the contribution margin, and _____ the break-even point.

(2) An increase in plant insurance will _____ the break-even point and _____ the dollar sales level calculated in part (b).

P24-A5 *CVP and analysis of operations* (L.O. 3, 4, 5)

Oceanic, Inc., is performing some basic computations related to automating its Michigan plant. Two different proposals are under study: basic and extensive. The following manufacturing cost information is available:

	Variable Cost Per Unit	Annual Fixed Costs
Basic	$8.00	$460,000
Extensive	6.40	612,000

Other data are:

Selling price per unit	$ 32
Fixed selling and administrative costs	60,000

The company pays a 10% sales commission on all units sold.

Instructions

a If annual sales are expected to average 120,000 units, would Oceanic be better off with basic automation or extensive automation? Show computations.

b How many units must the company sell to break even if the basic proposal is selected?

c Suppose that the basic proposal requires that Oceanic purchase additional equipment that is not reflected in the preceding figures. The equipment will cost $83,200 and will be depreciated over a five-year life by the straight-line method. In light of this new information, what would you have done differently in part (b) when computing the break-even point?

d Ignoring part (c), at what sales level (in units) will Oceanic be indifferent between the basic and extensive automation proposals?

Series B

P24-B1 *Scattergraph and high-low method* (L.O. 2)

Velez Manufacturing has a highly automated machine shop. The firm is studying utilities cost behavior and has gathered the following data for a recent six-month period:

Month	Machine Hours	Utilities Cost
January	22,000	$26,100
February	24,000	28,500
March	25,000	29,000
April	27,000	31,200
May	26,000	29,900
June	28,000	32,100

Instructions

a Prepare a scattergraph by plotting machine hours on the horizontal axis and utilities cost on the vertical axis.

b By fitting a line through the plotted points, determine Velez's monthly fixed cost and the variable cost per machine hour.

c Determine the variable and fixed costs by using the high-low method.

d In general, will the scattergraph and the high-low method yield identical results? Why?

P24-B2 *Cost behavior and analysis* (L.O. 1, 2)

Recent cost and activity data from the machining department of Eastbay Manufacturing follow.

Month	Machine Hours	Factory Overhead
August	35,000	$484,000
September	42,000	547,000
October	46,000	616,000
November	38,000	529,500

Conversations with the company's accountant revealed that October's costs consisted of machine supplies ($138,000), plant insurance ($13,000), and maintenance ($465,000). These costs are characterized as being variable, fixed, and mixed, respectively. Not included in the $616,000 total for October were supervision costs, which display the following step behavior:

Activity Range (Machine Hours)	Cost
Up to 20,000	$ 47,000
20,001–35,000	77,000
35,001–50,000	107,000

Instructions

a Determine the amount of maintenance cost incurred in August.

b Analyze the department's maintenance cost by using the high-low method. Determine the monthly fixed portion and the variable cost per machine hour.

c If present cost behavior patterns continue, estimate the total amount of factory overhead the company can expect in December if 43,000 machine hours are worked.

d Suppose that the department worked only 22,000 machine hours in July because new equipment was being installed. Would you have any reservations about using the July data in the high-low method? Briefly explain.

P24-B3 *Straightforward CVP analysis* (L.O. 3, 4, 5)

FRB, Inc., sells a single product for $40. The following costs and expenses were incurred at store no. 504:

1-2-3

Variable Costs Per Unit		Annual Fixed Costs	
Invoice cost	$24	Salaries	$60,000
Sales commission	4	Advertising	14,000
		Other	16,000

The company sold 8,200 units during 19X4.

Instructions

a Compute the 19X4 break-even point in both dollar and unit sales.

b By how much will sales have to increase in 19X5 over 19X4 levels if management wishes to earn a target income of $14,400?

c At present, how much does each unit provide toward covering FRB's fixed costs and generating income? Assume that management feels this amount is too low. What alternatives are available to FRB?

d What would be the effect on the break-even point if management reduced salary costs by $11,600 and increased the $4 sales commission by 20%?

P24-B4 *Break-even and other CVP analysis* (L.O. 3, 4, 5)

Quebec, Inc., manufactures and sells a single product. The information that follows relates to the year just ended, when 230,000 units were sold:

1-2-3

Sales price per unit	$	10
Variable cost per unit		4
Fixed costs		930,000

Instructions

a Determine the number of units that Quebec sold in excess of its break-even point.

b If current revenue and cost patterns continue, compute the dollar sales needed next year to produce a target income of $492,000.

c Assume that a different compensation plan was in effect during the current year. Rather than pay six salespeople an average salary of $36,000 each, management has proposed that the salespeople receive a $10,000 base salary and a 6% commission based on gross sales.

   (1) Would the company have been better off financially if the new plan had been adopted for the year just ended? By how much?

   (2) What effect might paying a commission have on gross sales? Briefly explain.

d In addition to the compensation plan described in part (c), Quebec is studying the impact of other operating changes as well. State whether you agree or disagree with the following findings of a newly hired staff accountant:

   (1) A rise in property taxes will increase the break-even point.

   (2) A decrease in raw material cost will increase the contribution margin and decrease total fixed costs.

P24-B5 *CVP and analysis of operations* (L.O. 3, 4, 5)

The Ditmar Company is exploring two possible manufacturing methods to produce a short-lived, fad product. The following unit-cost data have been generated by the firm's accounting department:

	Process A	Process B
Direct materials	$ 3.00	$ 4.50
Direct labor	4.00	5.00
Variable overhead	10.00	12.50

The fixed manufacturing costs associated with processes A and B total $760,000 and $541,000, respectively. Management anticipates that regardless of which process is selected, the fad product will require the following selling and administrative expenses: advertising, $80,000; sales commissions, 10%. The marketing department has tentatively set a selling price of $50. Ditmar will manufacture sufficient units to meet demand; no inventory will be carried.

Instructions

a Compute the number of units that Ditmar must sell to break even if process A is selected.

b Which of the two processes will be more profitable for the company if sales total 35,000 units?

c Compute the dollar sales level necessary to generate a target income of $69,000 if process B is selected.

d At what volume level (in units) will management be indifferent between process A and process B?

BEYOND THE BASICS

BB24-1 *Sales mix evaluation* (L.O. 5, 6, 7)

Michelle Williams operates the concession stand at the Roxy Theater. On the basis of last year's operating results, she has established the following budget for 19X2:

	Food	Beverage	Total
Expected number of sales	80,000	120,000	200,000
Sales revenue	$100,000	$96,000	$196,000
Less: Variable costs	72,000	12,000	84,000
Contribution margin	$ 28,000	$84,000	$112,000
Less: 20% of gross sales paid to theater		$39,200	
Fixed costs		60,000	99,200
Net income			$ 12,800

Patrons changed their buying habits during 19X2, and Williams had 120,000 food sales and 80,000 beverage sales. The average sale amount and contribution margin per sale remained as budgeted.

Instructions

a Williams achieved her budget of 200,000 sales and believes that 19X2 net income will approximate $12,800. Prepare an income statement to determine the concession stand's operating performance. Explain any significant variations from the budget.

b Refer to the original budget. Assume the fixed costs can be subdivided as follows: food, $16,000; beverage, $8,000; and general, $36,000. Williams is considering the elimination of food sales because, as she notes, "The food operation is more trouble than it's worth." Determine the budgeted net income for 19X2 if the food service is dropped and the associated fixed costs are eliminated.

c What other factors should be considered when evaluating the possible elimination of the food operation?

BB24-2 *Overview of chapter concepts: Multiple choice* (L.O. 1, 2, 3, 4, 7)

The following multiple-choice questions relate to various topics discussed in the chapter. Select the best answer.

1 JWA, Inc., has prepared a graph of its factory rent for 19X5. If the horizontal axis represents units of production and the vertical axis is production cost per unit, the graph would show:

a a line sloping up to the right.   c a vertical line.

b a line sloping down to the right.   d a horizontal line.

2 Ideally, when dealing with a step cost, one should operate:
a on the top step.
b at the leftmost portion of a step.
c in the middle of a step.
d at the rightmost portion of a step.

3 Which of the following items does not logically belong with the other three?
a Method of least squares. c Scattergraph.
b Break-even chart.   d High-low method.

4 Gouche Company uses the high-low method to analyze cost behavior. The following information is available:

Month	Hours of Activity	Repair Cost
March	2,000	$185,000
June	1,100	131,000
October	1,400	152,000

A labor strike occurred in June, the first in the firm's history. On the basis of Gouche's data, a reasonable estimate of total variable cost for 1,800 hours of activity would be:
a $99,000.   c $166,500.
b $108,000.   d $174,000.

5 Butler Company produced and sold 1,000 units of its sole product during a recent accounting period. The following information is known:

Direct materials used	$16,000
Direct labor	15,000
Variable factory overhead	8,000
Fixed factory overhead	5,000
Selling & administrative expense	
Variable	11,000
Fixed	10,000

If the selling price was $80, how many units must Butler sell to break even?
a 417.   c 583.
b 500.   d 1,000.

6 Foster reported sales of $400,000, a contribution margin of $10 per unit, fixed costs of $160,000, and a net income of $48,000. How many units did Foster sell?
a 19,200.   c 24,000.
b 20,800.   d 40,000.

7 Which of the following statements about the contribution margin is false?
a The contribution margin is the mathematical difference between selling price and the variable cost per unit.
b The contribution margin may be used to find the sales needed to earn a particular target income figure.
c The contribution margin is the amount by which profit will increase for each unit sold beyond the break-even point.
d The contribution margin may be increased by a reduction in fixed costs.

8 Cost-volume-profit analysis depends on certain underlying assumptions. Which of the following is not included among these assumptions?

a Costs and revenues are predictable and linear over the relevant range.

b The sales mix will change as fixed costs increase beyond the relevant range.

c Variable costs fluctuate proportionately with volume.

d Any increases or decreases in inventory levels throughout the period are insignificant in amount.

COMMUNICATION OF ACCOUNTING INFORMATION

CAI24-1 *Presentation visuals* (L.O. 3, 4)

Communication Principle: Accountants (and employees in general) must often communicate information to persons who have little or no understanding of the relevant subject matter. Given that "one picture is worth a thousand words," communication can frequently be enhanced by the use of graphs and pictures.

Fortunately, many computer software packages are available to aid in this process. Basic graphics can be prepared on most electronic spreadsheets. In addition, other packages are available that assist in the development of sophisticated artistic presentations.

You should plan to become familiar with these tools. Reading levels are declining, managers are busier than ever, and preparing graphics is as easy as pressing a few keys on a computer's keyboard. Effective communication in today's electronic age is not only written but is visual as well.

■ ■ ■ ■ ■ ■ ■ ■

Hiotech, Inc., manufactures an expensive piece of equipment that is inserted into blood vessels to remove blockages and other obstructions from the heart area. (The associated technology involves a laser beam that is attached to a very thin fiber optic cord.) The equipment has variable manufacturing and distribution costs of $2,460,000 and sells for $3,460,000. Related fixed manufacturing costs are $15,000,000 per year.

Because of such a high cost, the market for the product is very limited. Annual sales are expected to total only 12 units. Hiotech's directors, mostly doctors, are nevertheless very excited about the medical advances associated with the equipment. They are also delighted that each unit makes $1,000,000 for the company.

Instructions

a Calculate the number of units that must be sold to break even.

b Comment on the economic viability of this particular product.

c Prepare one or more pie charts (i.e., circle graphs) that could be used in a presentation to the doctors. The charts should demonstrate the concept of break even and show that the product is not profitable for the company. (*Note:* If available, computer software should be used for this part of the solution.)

Answers to Chapter Quiz

1 c

2 a

3 c (S = VC + FC; S = 0.6S + $180,000; S = $450,000)

4 d

5 b

CHAPTER
25

Budgeting

Businesses in this country continually strive to increase profitability. In an effort to boost net income, companies construct new facilities, undertake research programs, hire employees with needed skills, and introduce new product lines. These actions are usually not haphazard; rather, they are part of a carefully defined plan to achieve a certain objective.

Business planning may assume several different forms. When dealing with the long run, companies formulate generalized goals along with strategies and policies to achieve those goals. For example, suppose a manufacturer of household cleaning products wants to enter the car care market. Accordingly, the company could establish a strategy to acquire an existing manufacturer of car care products or perhaps engage in an extensive research program to develop new products internally. Planning of this nature is essential, because it helps chart an entity's operation over many future periods.

Another facet of planning involves budgets. A **budget** is a formal quantitative expression of management expectations. Unlike strategies and policies, budgets contain considerable detail. In effect, a budget can be likened to a blueprint, that is, an intricate plan that serves as a framework for future action.

BENEFITS OF BUDGETING

OBJECTIVE

1

State the benefits of budgeting.

If done correctly, budgeting is a time-consuming, arduous process. It goes without saying that an in-depth look at the future involves numerous assumptions, much uncertainty, and often considerable employee input. Furthermore, managers must frequently turn away from current, pressing problems to devote full attention to the budget effort. With all these unattractive features, the question arises, "Why budget?" Normally, the benefits of budgeting outweigh the associated problems. Budgets formalize planning, serve as a basis for performance evaluation, and assist in communication and coordination within an entity.

Formalize Planning

Budgets are an outgrowth of the planning process. Because budgets force managers to look ahead and study the future, a formal "plan of attack" can be prepared. To picture the related benefits, imagine building a home without the previously mentioned blueprint. The contractor might encase the walls in plasterboard, only to discover that electrical outlets and heating vents were forgotten. Or the foundation might be laid and then found to be over the property line. Indeed, the building process would be chaotic at best. Similarly, without a formal plan, management will have to spend considerable time "fighting fires" rather than concentrating on the attainment of long-run goals and objectives.

The implementation of a budget enables companies (and individuals) to pinpoint potential problems before the problems occur. Operating distractions are thus greatly reduced, since anticipation often leads to the introduction of preliminary corrective action. The eventual outcome of planning is a direction-oriented entity—one that knows where it wants to go and how it wants to get there.

Serve as a Basis for Performance Evaluation

Although best known for its role in planning, a budget also assists management in the appraisal of performance and control of operations. As explained in Chapter 21, organizations often prepare reports that compare actual results against a predetermined plan. The budget therefore serves as a yardstick in judging whether performance has been up to par. Should deficiencies arise, corrective action can be taken to bring the organization back on target.

Some businesses attempt to evaluate performance by comparing current results against the actual results of previous accounting periods. Unfortunately, this type of evaluation has an inherent deficiency. To illustrate, assume that a company's total operating expenses last year amounted to $200,000. If the company was subjected to a 10% inflation rate and current expenses total only $210,000, the immediate conclusion might be that management has done a creditable job in controlling costs. However, if last year's expenses were excessive because of significant inefficiencies, the entire evaluative picture could change. For instance, suppose that last year's expenses would have been $180,000 under reasonably efficient operating conditions. Allowing for an $18,000 increase from inflation, current expenses would exceed the $198,000 target by $12,000 ($210,000 − $198,000).

Comparisons with past data simply do not reveal whether current performance is acceptable. Bear in mind that past data bring all that was bad about the past into the evaluation. Furthermore, if a company's operating environment has changed significantly because of new technology, a new management team, or other factors, studies of past versus present very quickly approach the meaningless level. Current performance is best judged against a budget for the same period.

Assist in Communication and Coordination

Business operations dictate the performance of many diverse activities. These activities include the production and sale of goods and services, purchasing, credit extension and the collection of accounts, data processing, and the financing of operations. In very small enterprises these functions are often supervised by the same person. In larger organizations, however, operations are normally divided and are the responsibility of different managers.

To achieve company objectives, close coordination of activities is a necessity. Imagine the problems that could arise if coordination was lacking. The marketing department could undertake a large advertising campaign for a new product and then find that production was halted by a shortage of needed raw materials. Or at a time when marketing was attempting to expand the company's market share, the credit department might be tightening credit standards because of recent problems with uncollectible accounts. In both of these cases, embarrassment is sure to result.

Where do budgets fit in? When a budget for the overall organization is being prepared, individual managers must communicate their plans. The plans are then examined to determine whether they are feasible and consistent with the plans of other operating units. The budget process therefore serves as a gigantic blender that integrates and coordinates diverse activities to help attain company goals.

EXECUTIVE BRIEFING
Learning to Live Within a Budget

Phil Gramm
United States Senator (Texas)

As your authors have stressed, a budget is a plan of action—one that takes goals and objectives and expresses them in monetary terms. Once the plan is established, actual results can be evaluated and, if necessary, corrections made. I have seen the benefits of this process from different perspectives, first as a professor of economics at Texas A&M University and now as a U.S. senator. (I am a coauthor of the Gramm-Rudman Act, which limits the amount of the federal budget deficit.)

Be sure to keep the following comments in mind no matter what your career path might be. Although the comments may seem philosophical, their underlying message conveys a strong sense of practicality that can bestow large rewards:

> Life imposes economic constraints on nations, on states and cities, on businesses, and on families. Those who learn to operate within a budget, to make rational decisions, and to set out financial plans for the future, prosper. Those who do not grasp the lessons of simple budgetary constraints and of the economic, political, and social implications of double-entry bookkeeping, inevitably suffer from lower living standards. The lesson? Creating and abiding by a budget are key in the management of life, success, and financial well-being.

BUDGET CONSTRUCTION

The construction of a budget varies dramatically from one business to the next. Many companies establish formal procedures that are followed to the letter. In contrast, other enterprises employ "seat of the pants" management and merely scribble some hastily derived projections on the back of an envelope. Because of the wide variety of approaches found in practice, any attempt at a detailed discussion on how to budget or "The Ten Easy Steps to Budgeting" is fruitless. There are, however, several general concepts with which you should be familiar. A short discussion of these concepts follows.

Construction Flows

Most medium- and large-size entities are composed of several management levels. See Exhibit 25-1, for example, which depicts a typical organizational hierarchy. The budget-building process generally follows the organizational structure, with construction proceeding from higher- to lower-management levels, or vice versa.

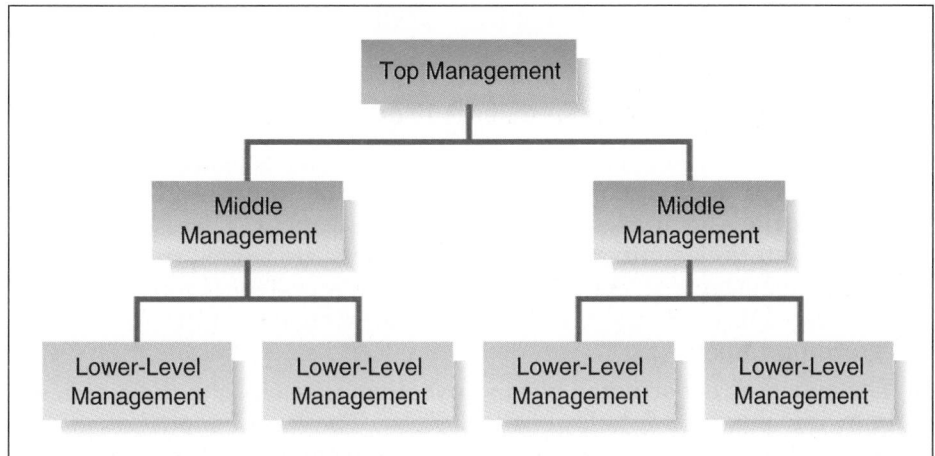

EXHIBIT 25-1
Organizational Hierarchy

Top-Down Approach

With the **top-down approach,** virtually all budget development takes place at the upper echelons of management. The budget is imposed on lower-level personnel, who rarely become involved in the construction process. On paper, the top-down approach offers the advantage of producing a document that reflects overall organizational goals. Preparation is carried out by those who have the best view of companywide operations, namely, top management. Upper-level executives can study the interactions of the lower units and determine the consistency of the units' plans and expectations.

In most cases this apparent advantage gives rise to a significant problem. When the budget is imposed from above, lower-level managers often feel that their opinions and operating perspectives are not important. Although lower-level employees will be evaluated against the budget, they have done little to assist in its development. Consequently, they often resent this "dictatorial" approach and adopt a "who cares" attitude, both of which result in a negative outlook toward budget achievement.

> **OBJECTIVE**
> **2**
> Distinguish between top-down and bottom-up budgeting.

Bottom-Up Approach

Unlike the top-down approach, **bottom-up budgeting** emphasizes lower-level employee participation in the development process. The bottom-up approach usually begins with the issuance of general budget guidelines by top management or perhaps by a budget committee. The budget committee normally consists of company executives along with representatives from functional areas such as sales, production, and finance. The guidelines often include yearly goals, anticipated inflation rates, available resources, and other similar data.

Once this information is communicated, the employees responsible for achieving the desired results assemble appropriate budgets. The process begins at the lower levels of the organizational structure and works its way upward. Individual budgets are grouped by major operating units, such as divisions and territories, and eventually reach top management or the budget committee. The budgets are reviewed, and suggestions for improvement are offered. Lower-level managers then make the necessary revisions, and ultimately, a compromise is reached.

The bottom-up approach offers several distinct advantages over a budget that is handed down from top management:

1   Bottom-up (i.e., *participative*) budgets are really self-imposed. By consulting with and incorporating the goals of lower-level employees, greater strides are made toward budget achievement. That is, individuals throughout the organization know their views are valued and considered by top management. As a result, employee morale and job satisfaction generally increase, and employees make extensive efforts to meet the agreed-on targets.

2   The budget is constructed by employees who are close to the action and know the intricate details of daily activity. The same cannot be said for a budget that is prepared solely by top management with no lower-level input. Consequently, the bottom-up approach usually results in a more realistic performance target.

On the negative side, the increased employee involvement makes the bottom-up method time-consuming and expensive to administer. Nevertheless, it is a popular tool among progressive companies. Because the broad perspectives of top management are combined with the detailed operating knowledge of lower-level personnel, a powerful budget document is created—one that encompasses the views of all ranges of the organizational hierarchy.

Budget Estimation

By its nature, a budget is a series of future estimates. These estimates should not be arrived at haphazardly; instead, significant care should be exercised in their determination.

Normally, budget estimates are based on both the past and the future. Although historical information is often a good starting point for prediction, modification of past trends may be necessary because of changing conditions. As an example, suppose that a company is attempting to budget sales for a particular product. The company currently has a 26% market share and has increased its share by 1% in each of the past five years. Should business conditions remain relatively stable, the firm would be correct in anticipating a 27% share of total sales for the upcoming period. If, however, new competition or technological innovations are present, these factors must be considered if the sales estimate is to have much meaning.

Estimation and Slack

As noted earlier, budgets are frequently used in performance evaluation. Well aware of this fact, many managers build **slack,** or padding, into their budgets to avoid unfavorable appraisals. For instance, sales and operating capabilities may be underestimated and expenses may be overestimated. Thus, when the actual results are tabulated and sales are "down" and expenses are "up," the manager is still deemed to have met his or her

OBJECTIVE

3

Explain the concept of slack as it relates to the estimation process.

budget (and company objectives). In essence, slack has given the manager some leeway in the performance of daily activities.

Slack permeates the entire budget process and sometimes tends to perpetuate itself. As an example, in many not-for-profit entities, operating units are given a maximum spending limit for specific types of expenditures. A governmental entity, for instance, may be authorized to spend $5,000 for new equipment acquisitions during the fiscal year. If the yearend is rapidly approaching and considerable funds have yet to be used, the unit may go on a buying spree. Why? If funds remain, administrators might take the position that the current equipment budget was apparently in excess of amounts really needed. Consequently, there could be a strong tendency for cutbacks in the next budget period. This "use it or lose it" philosophy often gives rise to status-quo or larger (i.e., slack-filled) budgets in future years and may result in questionable operating practices that conflict with an entity's goals.

Slack is a significant problem for many budget makers and is extremely difficult to eliminate. Although it is easier said than done, budget estimates should be realistic and should shy away from excessive optimism and pessimism. Unrealistic estimates defeat the entire purpose of the budgeting effort. The net result is aptly described by the acronym GIGO: garbage in, garbage out.

> **ETHICS ISSUE**
>
> In your position as a department manager, you must submit a budget for next year. You know that other managers "pad" their budgets by at least 10%. Would you follow this same procedure?

The Budget Period

Budgets normally cover differing periods of time. Those prepared for acquisitions of property, plant, and equipment (i.e., capital expenditures), for example, often involve substantial dollar outlays and extend five to ten years into the future. Such a long time horizon is necessary so that costly mistakes can be avoided. To illustrate, a company would likely study longterm sales forecasts before deciding whether to undertake a multistore expansion into new retail markets. Although the coming year's forecast may appear favorable, long-run prospects may be bleak. By relying on too short a time period for evaluation, the firm could be making a bad investment from which it would be unable to recover.

> **OBJECTIVE**
>
> **4**
>
> Recognize the variations in budget periods.

In contrast, budgets that pertain to *operations* are generally prepared for a one-year time frame and usually coincide with the period employed for external financial reporting. For purposes of control and evaluation these budgets are often subdivided into quarters and months. The benefit of following this latter procedure is evident after studying Exhibit 25-2.

The exhibit depicts the budgeted monthly cash balances of a seasonal business. Notice that if the budget is viewed over a one-year period, we see a favorable cash position—the balance increases by $20,000 (from $80,000 in January to $100,000 in December). A breakdown by months, however, shows the need for short-term financing from the end of May through July because of seasonal cash needs and a drop below the $50,000 minimum. Generally speaking, shorter budget periods usually enable a closer monitoring of operations.

In actuality, many businesses use a combination of monthly, yearly, and long-term budgets. In recent years a number of organizations have turned to continuous budgets. A **continuous budget** covers a one-year period, with a new month being added as the current month is completed. For example,

EXHIBIT 25-2
Cash Balances of a Seasonal Business

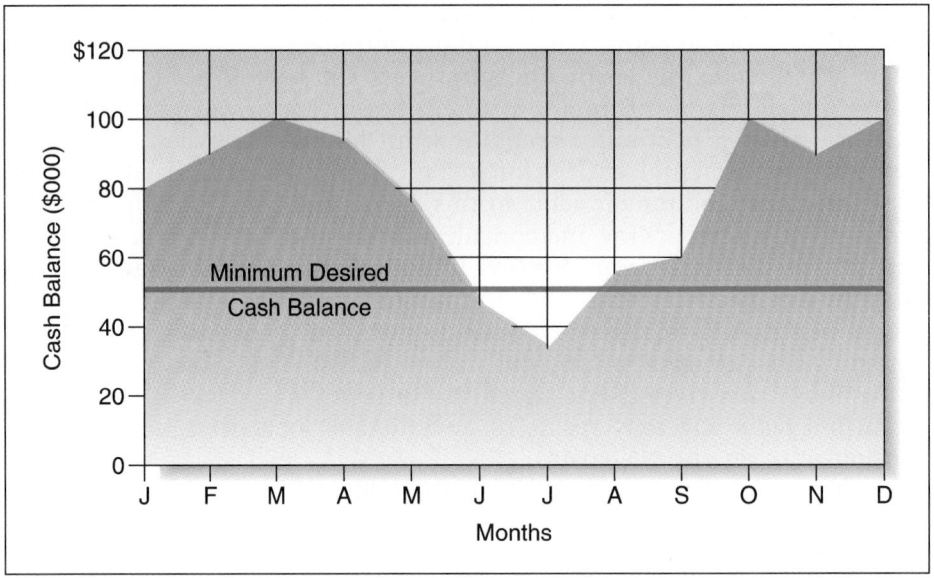

assume that a budget for 19X1 operations is prepared. As soon as January 19X1 ends, a budget is added for January 19X2. Continuous budgets offer the advantage of forcing management to continually think about the future. The planning process is not confined to only a few months of each year but becomes an ongoing, stabilized activity.

Budget Limitations and Human Relations

OBJECTIVE
5
Discuss the limitations of budgeting, especially in the human relations area.

Critics contend that several limitations are associated with budgeting. First, a budget is only as good as the effort that goes into its preparation. Top management must thoroughly support the budget process, or the entire exercise will be a lesson in futility. Second, budgeting cannot replace effective day-to-day management. That is, the budget is a tool to be used by managers; it is not an end in itself and will not automatically improve a faltering operation. Although the critics' observations are correct, the preceding comments really apply to all tools of management.

Perhaps the most significant limitation of budgeting lies in the human relations and administration area. Many organizations overemphasize the use of budgets in control—and they often do so in an incorrect manner. To explain, employees are frequently disenchanted with methods used to evaluate performance. Budgets disclose weaknesses and are often studied by upper management when finding who's to blame in unfavorable times. To avoid possible employee negativism, management should emphasize that budgeting is a positive tool that assists in achieving company goals, monitoring progress toward those goals, and setting standards of performance.

The administration of a budget program is a difficult task. Executives often become overly involved with the numerical aspects of budget construction and lose sight of the fact that employees are people. Employees have feelings and are sensitive to management looking over their shoulders to appraise performance. Unless the budget process considers human relations, even the best efforts will go for naught and be met with resistance.

Earlier in the chapter we noted that budget preparation often follows a company's organizational structure. Budgets for the company's individual operating units (e.g., departments, divisions, territories, and so forth) are generated and later combined. This process culminates in the **master budget,** a comprehensive set of integrated budgets that serves as the financial plan for the entire organization. Although variations are found in practice, the master budget generally consists of the following:

1 Sales budget
2 Production budget
3 Direct material purchases budget
4 Direct labor budget
5 Factory overhead budget
6 Selling and administrative expense budget
7 Capital expenditures budget
8 Cash budget
9 Budgeted income statement
10 Budgeted balance sheet
11 Budgeted statement of cash flows

COMPREHENSIVE BUDGETING

OBJECTIVE
6

Prepare a master budget.

These budgets cannot be prepared independently. Sales levels, for example, influence production plans. The number of units manufactured affects direct material, direct labor, and overhead costs, and all of these items have a bearing on an entity's cash budget and financial statements. The relationships within a master budget are shown in Exhibit 25-3.

These relationships will become more apparent in the example that follows. At this point, observe how the sales budget is the starting point in the budgeting process. In addition, note how the cash budget and the budgeted financial statements summarize the entire planning effort.

Master Budget Illustration

To illustrate the preparation of a master budget, we will focus on Hillcroft Corporation. The company wants to study first-quarter activity for 19X2 by constructing a master budget similar to that just discussed.[1] The firm's December 31, 19X1, balance sheet appears in Exhibit 25-4.

Sales Budget

The sales budget is probably the most important element of the master budget. Production, cash flow, the financial statements, and a number of other items all depend on sales, in terms of both units sold and revenues generated. A grossly incorrect sales budget will therefore be reflected throughout the entire budgeting process.

The sales budget is based on a forecast of sales volume. Forecasted volume is influenced by such factors as previous sales patterns, current and expected economic conditions, actions of competitors, and advertising and

---

[1] We will omit the capital expenditures budget and the statement of cash flows to simplify the presentation.

**EXHIBIT 25-3
Relationships Within the
Master Budget**

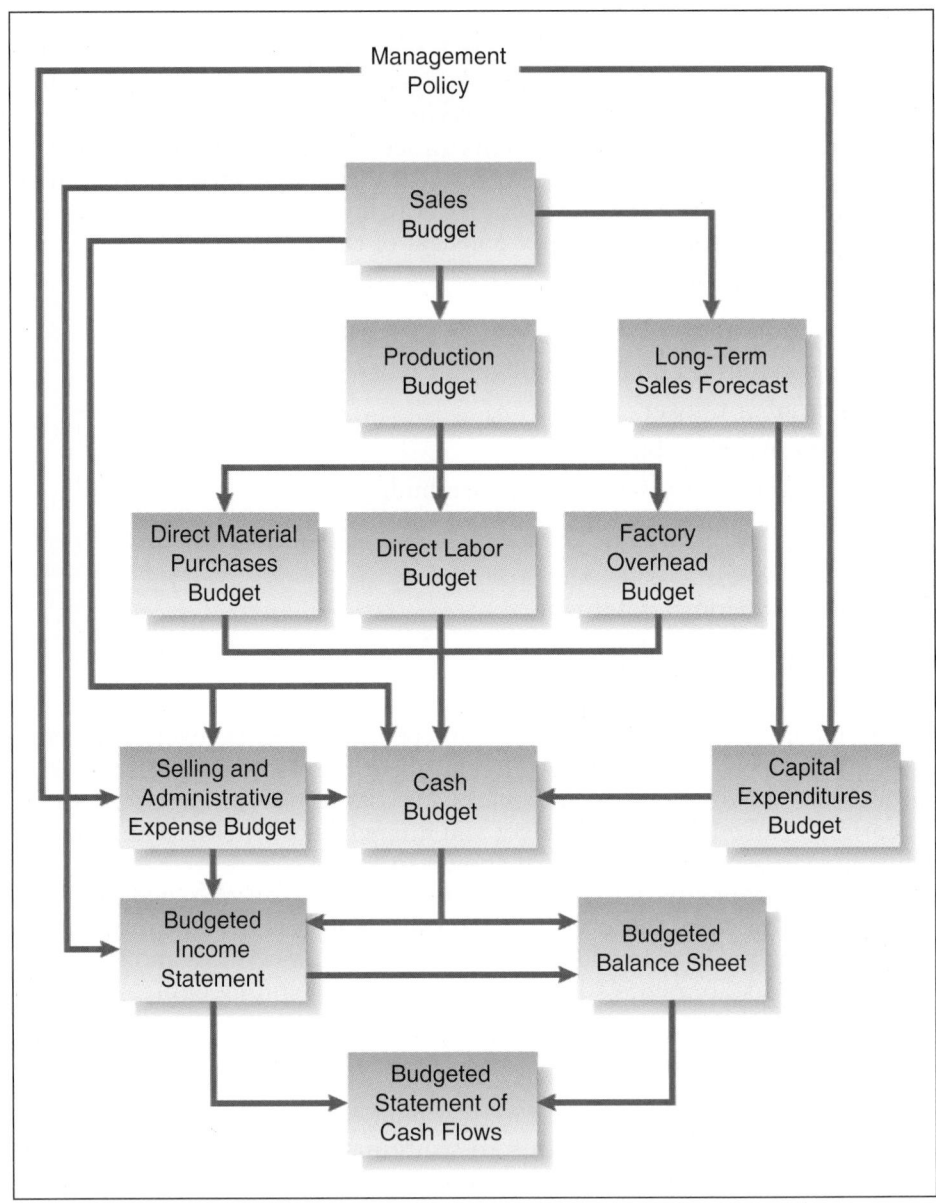

marketing strategies. Estimates of volume can be calculated by using several different techniques. For example, a company can (1) study the relationship of sales to various economic indicators (such as interest rates and disposable income), (2) use various statistical forecasting methods, or (3) quiz its sales staff regarding customer purchase plans for the upcoming period.

Once the forecast is derived, the sales budget is prepared by multiplying the expected volume by the estimated selling price per unit. Hillcroft's sales budget is shown in Exhibit 25-5.

Schedule of Cash Collections. Although not part of the formal sales budget, a schedule of expected cash collections is easily generated at this

```
                    HILLCROFT CORPORATION
                        Balance Sheet
                      December 31, 19X1

                           Assets

Current assets
   Cash                                        $ 7,000
   Accounts receivable                          10,000
   Finished goods (1,500 units × $7.00)         10,500
   Direct materials (6,900 units × $1.50)       10,350    $ 37,850

Property, plant, & equipment
   Plant & equipment                           $70,000
   Less: Accumulated depreciation                5,000      65,000
      Total assets                                        $102,850

               Liabilities & Stockholders' Equity

Current liabilities
   Accounts payable                                        $  8,000
Stockholders' equity
   Common stock                                $40,000
   Retained earnings                            54,850      94,850
      Total liabilities & stockholders' equity            $102,850
```

EXHIBIT 25-4
Opening Balance Sheet of
Hillcroft Corporation

time. The schedule provides information that will be needed when preparing the cash budget. To illustrate the necessary procedures, assume Hillcroft's sales are all on account. Seventy percent of the sales are collected in the month of sale; the remaining 30% are collected in the following month. The corporation's cash collection schedule appears in Exhibit 25-6.

Production Budget

Once the sales budget is completed, a company's production requirements can be determined. Aside from sales, the number of units scheduled for manufacturing depends on raw material and facilities availability and desired finished goods inventory levels. Finished goods are often budgeted in

```
                    HILLCROFT CORPORATION
                        Sales Budget
                For the Quarter Ended March 31, 19X2

                        January  February  March    Total

Expected sales (units)    4,500    5,500    7,000   17,000
Selling price per unit   × $10    × $10    × $10    × $10
Budgeted sales revenues $45,000  $55,000  $70,000 $170,000
```

EXHIBIT 25-5
Sales Budget of Hillcroft
Corporation

EXHIBIT 25-6
Schedule of Cash Collections
for Hillcroft Corporation

HILLCROFT CORPORATION
Schedule of Cash Collections
For the Quarter Ended March 31, 19X2

	January	February	March	Total
Accounts receivable, 12/31/X1	$10,000*			$ 10,000
January sales ($45,000)	31,500	$13,500		45,000
February sales ($55,000)		38,500	$16,500	55,000
March sales ($70,000)			49,000	49,000
Total budgeted cash collections	$41,500	$52,000	$65,500	$159,000

* From Exhibit 25-4.

Note: Because only $49,000 of March sales are collected in March, the remaining $21,000 ($70,000 − $49,000) will appear on Hillcroft's end-of-quarter balance sheet as accounts receivable.

advance so that adequate stock levels can be maintained. As explained in Chapter 23, businesses try to avoid carrying excessive goods because of associated storage, insurance, taxes, and interest costs, and the possibility of deterioration and obsolescence. Further, these same entities resist precariously low inventories that could lead to stockouts, lost sales, and even lost customers.

The budgeted units of production in any given period can be calculated as follows:

Number of units to be produced	
Number of units sold	XXX
Add: Desired ending finished goods inventory (units)	XXX
Total finished units needed	XXX
Less: Beginning finished goods inventory (units)	XXX
Number of units to be produced	XXX

By adding budgeted sales to the units desired for the ending finished goods inventory, we obtain the total units needed during the period. Because some of these units are already on hand in the form of beginning finished goods inventory, the remainder will have to be manufactured.

Hillcroft wants to maintain an ending finished goods inventory that covers 50% of the following month's sales. This inventory policy gives rise to the production budget shown in Exhibit 25-7.

Direct Material Purchases Budget

Now that production requirements are known, the direct material purchases budget can be prepared. Budgeted purchases are based on anticipated manufacturing schedules and a firm's desired ending raw material inventories. The latter amounts are sometimes influenced by supplier de-

EXHIBIT 25-7
Production Budget of Hillcroft
Corporation

HILLCROFT CORPORATION
Production Budget
For the Quarter Ended March 31, 19X2

	January	February	March	Total
Number of units sold (Exhibit 25-5)	4,500	5,500	7,000	17,000
Add: Desired ending finished goods inventory (50% × following month's sales)	2,750	3,500	3,800[†]	3,800[‡]
Total finished units needed	7,250	9,000	10,800	20,800
Less: Beginning finished goods inventory*	1,500	2,750	3,500	1,500[‡]
Number of units to be produced	5,750	6,250	7,300	19,300

* The beginning finished goods inventory is the ending finished goods inventory from the preceding month. January's beginning inventory of 1,500 units appears on the balance sheet presented in Exhibit 25-4.

[†] April's sales are assumed to be 7,600 units. Thus, the desired ending finished goods inventory in March is 3,800 units (7,600 units × 50%).

[‡] The ending and beginning inventories are used here, not the total of the inventories. Insertion of totals will result in incorrect calculations. As an example, summation of the ending inventory figures yields 10,050 units (2,750 + 3,500 + 3,800), which, when added to sales, produces total finished units needed of 27,050 (10,050 + 17,000). The result is misleading because Hillcroft needs only 20,800 units during the quarter: 17,000 units to cover sales and 3,800 units to generate the desired March 31 finished goods inventory.

livery schedules, the availability of "specials" and quantity discounts, and management's purchasing strategy for heading off price increases.

The amount of materials to purchase can be computed in a manner similar to that for finding the budgeted units of production, namely:

Direct materials to be purchased	
Direct materials used in production (units)	XXX
Add: Desired ending direct materials inventory (units)	XXX
Total direct materials needed	XXX
Less: Beginning direct materials inventory (units)	XXX
Direct materials to be purchased (units)	XXX

Assume that Hillcroft uses two units of direct material in each completed product and that each direct material unit costs $1.50. Management desires to maintain an ending materials inventory equal to 60% of the direct materials needed in the following month's production. The company's direct material purchases budget is shown in Exhibit 25-8.

Schedule of Cash Disbursements for Material Purchases. Given Hillcroft's purchasing program, we can now construct a schedule of the required cash disbursements. This schedule, like the schedule of cash collec-

EXHIBIT 25-8
Direct Material Purchases
Budget of Hillcroft Corporation

HILLCROFT CORPORATION
Direct Material Purchases Budget
For the Quarter Ended March 31, 19X2

	January	February	March	Total
Planned production in units (Exhibit 25-7)	5,750	6,250	7,300	19,300
Units of direct material per finished unit	× 2	× 2	× 2	× 2
Direct materials used in production (units)	11,500	12,500	14,600	38,600
Add: Desired ending direct materials inventory (units)*	7,500	8,760	9,960	9,960
Total direct materials needed	19,000	21,260	24,560	48,560
Less: Beginning direct materials inventory (units)†	6,900	7,500	8,760	6,900
Direct materials to be purchased (units)	12,100	13,760	15,800	41,660
Cost per unit	× $1.50	× $1.50	× $1.50	× $1.50
Cost of direct material purchases	$18,150	$20,640	$23,700	$62,490

* The desired ending inventory equals 60% of the direct materials used in the following month's production. Ending inventories are computed as follows:

January: 60% × 12,500 = 7,500
February: 60% × 14,600 = 8,760
March: 60% × 16,600 (assumed) = 9,960

† The beginning direct materials inventory is the ending direct materials inventory from the preceding month. January's beginning inventory of 6,900 units appears on the balance sheet presented in Exhibit 25-4.

tions, is useful when preparing the cash budget. To illustrate the necessary procedures, assume that Hillcroft expects to pay 60% of its purchases during the month of purchase and the remaining 40% in the following month. The schedule of cash disbursements for materials appears in Exhibit 25-9.

Direct Labor Budget

The direct labor budget is also based on the production schedule. Direct labor must be budgeted so that management can determine if sufficient personnel are available to manufacture the company's product. Lack of proper planning could lead to labor shortages or overstaffing, both of which result in production inefficiencies. Furthermore, employee morale could suffer because of possible layoffs or extensive overtime to meet manufacturing schedules.

Direct labor requirements are determined by multiplying the number of direct labor hours per finished unit by the number of units to be produced. The result is then multiplied by the estimated direct labor cost per hour to

EXHIBIT 25-9
Schedule of Cash Disbursements for Material Purchases
of Hillcroft Corporation

HILLCROFT CORPORATION
Schedule of Cash Disbursements for Material Purchases
For the Quarter Ended March 31, 19X2

	January	February	March	Total
Accounts payable, 12/31/X1	$ 8,000*			$ 8,000
January purchases ($18,150)	10,890	$ 7,260		18,150
February purchases ($20,640)		12,384	$ 8,256	20,640
March purchases ($23,700)			14,220	14,220
Total disbursements for purchases	$18,890	$19,644	$22,476	$61,010

* From Exhibit 25-4.

Note: Because only $14,220 of March purchases are paid in March, the remaining $9,480 ($23,700 − $14,220) will appear on Hillcroft's end-of-quarter balance sheet as accounts payable.

generate total budgeted labor costs. For example, assume Hillcroft Corporation pays its workers $6 per hour and that each finished unit requires 0.5 hours of direct labor time. The necessary computations appear in Hillcroft's direct labor budget, which is shown in Exhibit 25-10.

Factory Overhead Budget

The factory overhead budget incorporates all production costs other than direct materials and direct labor. Such costs include indirect materials, indirect labor, depreciation, maintenance, and utilities. The first step in constructing a realistic overhead budget is to study the behavior of individual overhead costs. Observe, for example, that several of the preceding costs vary with changes in production volume, whereas others remain static. Once cost behavior is determined, we then compute overhead application rates similar to those described in Chapter 22.

Assume that Hillcroft's variable overhead application rate is $1.40 per

EXHIBIT 25-10
Direct Labor Budget of Hillcroft
Corporation

HILLCROFT CORPORATION
Direct Labor Budget
For the Quarter Ended March 31, 19X2

	January	February	March	Total
Planned production in units (Exhibit 25-7)	5,750	6,250	7,300	19,300
Labor time per unit (hours)	× 0.5	× 0.5	× 0.5	× 0.5
Total labor hours needed	2,875	3,125	3,650	9,650
Direct labor cost per hour	× $6	× $6	× $6	× $6
Total budgeted direct labor cost	$17,250	$18,750	$21,900	$57,900

EXHIBIT 25-11
Factory Overhead Budget of
Hillcroft Corporation

HILLCROFT CORPORATION
Factory Overhead Budget
For the Quarter Ended March 31, 19X2

	January	February	March	Total
Budgeted direct labor hours (Exhibit 25-10)	2,875	3,125	3,650	9,650
Variable overhead rate	× $1.40	× $1.40	× $1.40	× $1.40
Budgeted variable overhead	$4,025	$4,375	$5,110	$13,510
Budgeted fixed overhead	1,930	1,930	1,930	5,790
Budgeted total overhead	$5,955	$6,305	$7,040	$19,300
Less: Depreciation	700	700	700	2,100
Cash disbursements for factory overhead	$5,255	$5,605	$6,340	$17,200

direct labor hour. Fixed overhead charges are anticipated to be $1,930 per month, which includes $700 of straight-line depreciation. Exhibit 25-11 contains the company's factory overhead budget.

Tips & Techniques

As the exhibit indicates, the overhead budget contains *total* fixed factory overhead costs of $1,930—*not* a fixed application rate multiplied by the number of labor hours. The reason for this treatment is that fixed costs are, indeed, fixed and do not vary with activity. Whether Hillcroft anticipates 2,875, 3,125, or 3,650 labor hours makes no difference because the same fixed charges will be incurred each month.

The overhead budget reveals that total estimated overhead for the quarter amounts to $19,300—a figure that is needed to cost Hillcroft's single product. Assuming the use of direct labor hours as an application base, the overhead application rate will equal $2.00 per hour ($19,300 ÷ 9,650 budgeted labor hours). Further, notice there is a difference between total budgeted overhead and the firm's required cash disbursements for overhead. Depreciation, although a factory cost, does not entail a cash outlay and is therefore subtracted to generate monthly cash payments. We are assuming that all other overhead is paid when incurred.

Selling and Administrative Expense Budget

All manufacturing organizations incur costs unrelated to production activities, namely, selling and administrative (S&A) expenses. Like factory overhead, S&A expenses have variable and fixed components and require an in-depth review (in terms of cost behavior) prior to budget preparation.

Hillcroft's variable selling and administrative costs are freight-out and

HILLCROFT CORPORATION Selling and Administrative Expense Budget For the Quarter Ended March 31, 19X2				
	January	February	March	Total
Expected sales, in units (Exhibit 25-5)	4,500	5,500	7,000	17,000
Variable S&A expense per unit	× $0.80	× $0.80	× $0.80	× $0.80
Budgeted variable expenses	$3,600	$4,400	$5,600	$13,600
Fixed S&A expenses				
Salaries	$2,000	$2,000	$2,000	$ 6,000
Advertising	600	600	600	1,800
Insurance	1,900	—	—	1,900
Miscellaneous	500	1,500	500	2,500
Total fixed expenses	$5,000	$4,100	$3,100	$12,200
Total budgeted S&A expenses	$8,600	$8,500	$8,700	$25,800

sales commissions, which total $0.80 per unit. Fixed costs include salaries, advertising, insurance, and other miscellaneous items. The firm's S&A expense budget appears in Exhibit 25-12. It is important to note that a new activity base is employed because these expenses vary with *sales*, not production.

Cash Budget

The cash budget, which is based on many of the budgets previously discussed, serves to summarize a considerable portion of the budgeting process. This important document provides management with assistance in assessing a company's future cash needs. The cash budget is typically composed of four major sections:

- Cash receipts
- Cash disbursements
- Analysis
- Financing

The *receipts section* discloses the total cash available during the period before considering any disbursements. Total cash available is computed by adding an entity's beginning cash balance to total cash receipts. For most businesses the major sources of receipts are cash sales and collections from customers on account.

The cash *disbursements section* details expected cash payments during the budget period. Such payments include outlays for materials, labor, overhead, selling and administrative expenses, dividends, taxes, and capital improvements.

The *analysis section* combines the information presented in the receipts and disbursements sections and discloses whether an organization has excess cash or a cash deficiency. Excessive cash balances should be used to retire outstanding loans or be invested in safe short-term securities such as certificates of deposit and government notes. If the latter course of action is followed, a firm can generate a return on its investment and can reacquire the cash (if needed) in a short period of time. Should a deficiency arise, the need for additional cash is dictated. Because the deficiency is disclosed before it actually occurs, management can take corrective action to prevent possible loan defaults, past-due bills, and other undesirable outcomes.

Finally, the *financing section* provides a schedule of expected borrowings and repayments and also shows the related interest payments on borrowed funds. Overall, this section enables companies to determine financing requirements and thereby give banks and other lending institutions advance notice of funding amounts.

Cash Budget Illustration. To illustrate the cash budget, we will continue the Hillcroft Corporation example. Assume that Hillcroft requires a minimum cash balance of $6,000, with bank loans available in $1,000 multiples at a 15% interest rate. For simplicity we assume that loans are obtained at the beginning of a month and are repaid at the end of the month of repayment. Interest is paid at the time the principal is repaid. Finally, the company will have a $3,000 quarterly tax payment in March and expects to

EXHIBIT 25-13
Cash Budget of Hillcroft Corporation

HILLCROFT CORPORATION Cash Budget For the Quarter Ended March 31, 19X2			
	January	February	March
Beginning cash balance*	$ 7,000	$ 6,505	$ 6,006
Add receipts: customer collections (Exhibit 25-6)	41,500	52,000	65,500
Cash available before disbursements	$48,500	$58,505	$71,506
Less disbursements			
Material purchases (Exhibit 25-9)	$18,890	$19,644	$22,476
Direct labor (Exhibit 25-10)	17,250	18,750	21,900
Factory overhead (Exhibit 25-11)	5,255	5,605	6,340
S&A expenses (Exhibit 25-12)	8,600	8,500	8,700
Income taxes	—	—	3,000
Dividends	—	—	500
Total disbursements	$49,995	$52,499	$62,916
Cash excess (deficiency) before financing	$ (1,495)	$ 6,006	$ 8,590
Financing			
Borrowing to maintain $6,000 minimum balance (at beginning of period)	$ 8,000	$ —	$ —
Repayment (at end of period)	—	—	(2,000)
Interest at 15% per annum	—	—	(75)
Ending cash balance	$ 6,505	$ 6,006	$ 6,515

* January's beginning cash balance of $7,000 is obtained from Exhibit 25-4. Subsequent beginning balances are the ending cash balances of the preceding period.

distribute a $500 cash dividend on March 31. Hillcroft's cash budget appears in Exhibit 25-13.

To explain the financing section, management requires a $6,000 minimum cash balance. Because borrowings are in $1,000 multiples, $8,000 of funding is needed in January ($8,000 − $1,495 = $6,505). All borrowings are assumed to be repaid as soon as possible, also in $1,000 increments. In view of this situation, $2,000 of debt can be retired in March without reducing the cash balance below the desired minimum. Interest is figured for three months, because the obligation was outstanding from January 1 through March 31 ($2,000 × 0.15 × $\frac{3}{12}$ = $75).[2]

Budgeted Income Statement

The preparation of budgeted financial statements, often called **pro forma statements,** is the final step in budget construction. The first of these statements, the income statement, projects the forecasted results of operations and serves as a useful tool against which actual performance can be measured. Information needed for its construction is taken from the various budgets discussed in preceding sections of the chapter. Hillcroft's budgeted income statement is shown in Exhibit 25-14.

EXHIBIT 25-14
Budgeted Income Statement
of Hillcroft Corporation

HILLCROFT CORPORATION
Budgeted Income Statement
For the Quarter Ended March 31, 19X2

Sales (Exhibit 25-5)		$170,000
Cost of goods sold		
Beginning finished goods inventory (Exhibit 25-4)	$ 10,500	
Cost of goods manufactured (19,300 units × $7)	135,100	
Goods available for sale	$145,600	
Less ending finished goods inventory		
(3,800 units × $7)	26,600	
Cost of goods sold		119,000
Gross profit		$ 51,000
Less S&A expenses (Exhibit 25-12)		25,800
Income before interest and taxes		$ 25,200
Less interest expense		300*
Income before taxes		$ 24,900
Income taxes (Exhibit 25-13)		3,000
Net income		$ 21,900

* Interest expense is calculated as follows:

From Exhibit 25-13	$ 75
Accrued interest on remaining loan balance ($6,000 × 0.15 × $\frac{3}{12}$)	225
	$300

---

[2] This example assumes that the interest payment pertains solely to the amount of principal being repaid.

The most difficult part of the statement is the computation of cost of goods manufactured and the ending finished goods inventory. As noted in Hillcroft's production budget (see Exhibit 25-7), the firm produced 19,300 units during the quarter. The cost per unit of $7 is computed in the following manner:

Direct material (2 units of direct material at $1.50 per unit; see Exhibit 25-8)	$3.00
Direct labor (0.5 hours per unit at $6 per hour; see Exhibit 25-10)	3.00
Variable factory overhead (0.5 hours per unit at $1.40 per hour; see Exhibit 25-11)	0.70
Fixed factory overhead (see Exhibit 25-11 and the following discussion)	0.30
Manufactured cost per unit	$7.00

The fixed factory overhead is calculated on the basis of estimated direct labor hours. Because Hillcroft anticipates $5,790 of fixed overhead and 9,650 labor hours (both figures taken from Exhibit 25-11), the rate per hour is $0.60 ($5,790 ÷ 9,650 hours). As a result, each finished unit is charged with $0.30 (0.5 labor hours × $0.60) of fixed production cost.

Once the $7-per-unit manufacturing cost is computed, the ending finished goods inventory can be determined. From information that appears in Exhibit 25-7, the company has estimated finished goods at 3,800 units as of March 31. The inventory is therefore costed at $26,600 (3,800 units × $7).

Budgeted Balance Sheet

The budgeted balance sheet as of March 31 is derived by combining the beginning balance sheet (see Exhibit 25-4) with the information presented in the other budgets. Hillcroft's end-of-quarter balance sheet is shown in Exhibit 25-15.

BUDGETING AND COMPUTERS

OBJECTIVE

7

Recognize the adaptability of budgets to computers.

No doubt you have gotten the impression that budget construction is extremely tedious and procedural. Furthermore, as discussed earlier in the chapter, the budget process usually consists of several rounds, with changes and refinements being added along the way. These characteristics make budgeting very adaptable to computers. Computers speed up the process and eliminate much of the drudgery for the accountant, thereby allowing more time for analysis and evaluation.

Computerized budgeting applications have expanded greatly in recent years, primarily because of the increased use of microcomputers and the availability of software packages known as *electronic spreadsheets* (see p. 239). The spreadsheet (i.e., work sheet) configures the memory of a computer to resemble an accountant's columnar pad, actually, a pad that is much larger than could be printed on a piece of paper. For instance, a popular spreadsheet at the time of this writing has in excess of 8,100 rows and 250 columns. This vast working area is employed to perform mathematical operations (e.g., the multiplication of data in cell D15 by that

EXHIBIT 25-15
Budgeted Balance Sheet of
Hillcroft Corporation

HILLCROFT CORPORATION
Budgeted Balance Sheet
March 31, 19X2

Assets

Current assets		
Cash (Exhibit 25-13)	$ 6,515	
Accounts receivable (Exhibit 25-6)	21,000	
Finished goods (Exhibit 25-14)	26,600	
Direct materials (Exhibit 25-8)	14,940*	$ 69,055
Property, plant, & equipment		
Plant & equipment (Exhibit 25-4)	$70,000	
Less: Accumulated depreciation	7,100[†]	62,900
Total assets		$131,955

Liabilities & Stockholders' Equity

Current liabilities		
Accounts payable (Exhibit 25-9)	$ 9,480	
Loan payable (Exhibit 25-13)	6,000[‡]	
Interest payable (Exhibit 25-14)	225	$ 15,705
Stockholders' equity		
Common stock (Exhibit 25-4)	$40,000	
Retained earnings	76,250[§]	116,250
Total liabilities & stockholders' equity		$131,955

*9,960 units × $1.50 per unit = $14,940.

[†]Accumulated depreciation, Jan. 1 (Exhibit 25-4)	$ 5,000
Straight-line depreciation, Jan.–Mar. (Exhibit 25-11)	2,100
Accumulated depreciation, Mar. 31	$ 7,100

[‡]Original loan – repayment ($8,000 – $2,000 = $6,000).

[§]Retained earnings, Jan. 1 (Exhibit 25-4)		$54,850
Add: Net income (Exhibit 25-14)	$21,900	
Deduct: Dividends (Exhibit 25-13)	500	21,400
Retained earnings, Mar. 31		$76,250

contained in cell D19, with the result being stored in cell E24) and to format various schedules and reports.[3]

Use of a Spreadsheet

To prepare a budget with a spreadsheet, the user must enter mathematical formulas into the computer. The formulas express the financial relation-

---

[3] A cell is a spreadsheet component that stores data. Each cell is referenced by its address, as determined by a column and row location. Cell G37, for instance, is found at the intersection of column G and row 37.

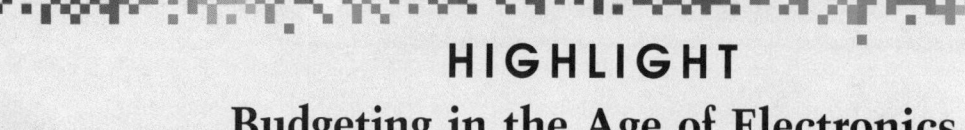

HIGHLIGHT
Budgeting in the Age of Electronics

How would you spend $15.7 billion? The 49 senators and 98 representatives in the Washington State legislature answered that question not too long ago, with a little help from a custom application created by using the popular Lotus 1-2-3 spreadsheet package. The budget process combined many opinions from dozens of state agencies, the governor, the Republican-controlled Senate, and the Democrat-controlled House of Representatives. A huge 1-2-3 application called the Legislative Analyst Work Station (LAWS) helped keep the inputs sorted by tracking who recommended what, and it also showed the effects of changes on the bottom line.

LAWS created a structure for debate and helped legislative discussions rise above procedural nit-picking to the policy level. "We argue over minuscule detail ad nauseam," acknowledges a Democrat senator from the Second District. "In years past, we had terrible fights over what set of [budget] numbers were accurate. This system has started to erase that." With LAWS, the senator says, "everyone agrees on the same set of numbers. We argue over the policy that drove those numbers, but not over somebody's forgetting to multiply by five."

How does it work? The Washington State legislature passes a major budget in odd-numbered years, and the quantity of information involved is staggering. The master file of a major budget contains 17,000 to 20,000 records. The data for state agency requests plus the governor's proposed budget form a stack of paper seven feet high!

Paper height aside, the process begins when the governor's staff in the Office of Financial Management (OFM) receives spending requests from more than a hundred state agencies. The OFM uses that data to prepare a budget proposal on a large IBM (i.e., mainframe) computer system. House and Senate analysts hook into the mainframe and then electron-ically transfer selected data to microcomputers. It is on the micros that LAWS converts the data into a common spreadsheet format.

Guided by the legislature, the analysts massage the budget figures agency by agency, trying to match available dollars with political priorities. Budget requests bounce back and forth as fiscal committees, both legislative chambers, and a host of special-interest groups battle to influence the process. At each step, LAWS lets everyone involved see the effects of suggested changes quickly, in summary form.

It wasn't always this way, however, recalls an administrator. Although the governor's office had a mainframe computer for many years, the legislature lacked in-house data-processing capabilities. Adding machines and calculators were the rule rather than the exception.

"Washington State is definitely a leader in the area of budget development . . . ," says an official at the National Conference of State Legislatures. "In terms of legislative use of automation in the budget process, it's certainly one of the best." Michigan, Kentucky, Vermont, and Florida have all expressed interest in LAWS. Communication is one of the system's strongest features, especially when the mainframe-to-microcomputer link is considered.

In summary, LAWS frees budget analysts from data-entry chores and leaves them more time for analysis. The system has also dramatically improved communication between the House and the Senate. The senator quoted earlier notes that it used to take two or three weeks just to get preliminary budget numbers. "Now you can get them almost over-night," he says. Adds another official, "This system has helped demystify the budget process. It's given the Legislature a lot more control over [this huge dollar allocation exercise]."

Source: Adapted from "A Better Way to Build a Budget," *Lotus,* October 1991, pp. 56–59. Copyright © 1991, Lotus Publishing Corp. Used with permission. All rights reserved.

ships of the entity, for example, the fact that the ending cash balance is equal to the beginning cash balance + receipts − disbursements. Or that 70% of a firm's sales are on account, with the following collection pattern: 60% collected in the month after sale, 38% collected in the second month after sale, and 2% uncollectible. The company's data (e.g., expected monthly sales) are then keyed into the computer, and the computer performs the necessary calculations as instructed by the formulas.

Once the formulas are developed, spreadsheets allow managers to perform "what if" testing. That is, a manager can study the financial impact of changes in specified budget variables. As an example, refer to Exhibit 25-16, which contains a simplified spreadsheet prepared by an executive of the Drake Company. The first half of the exhibit depicts quarterly sales, cost of goods sold, and gross profit—all computed by assuming an opening sales level of 90,000 units, a 4% growth rate, a selling price of $9, and a 55% cost of goods sold. The second half shows the resulting calculations if three of the underlying budget assumptions are changed.

If these calculations were part of the company's master budget and had to be computed manually, the related mathematics would easily take hours to perform. And even then, Drake might not be satisfied with the results and might want to study a different set of assumptions. With a spreadsheet, the three variables can be changed by depressing a few keys; electronics does the rest. Newly generated reports and pro forma statements are produced in a matter of seconds, thereby giving the manager additional insights in a cost-effective and timely manner.

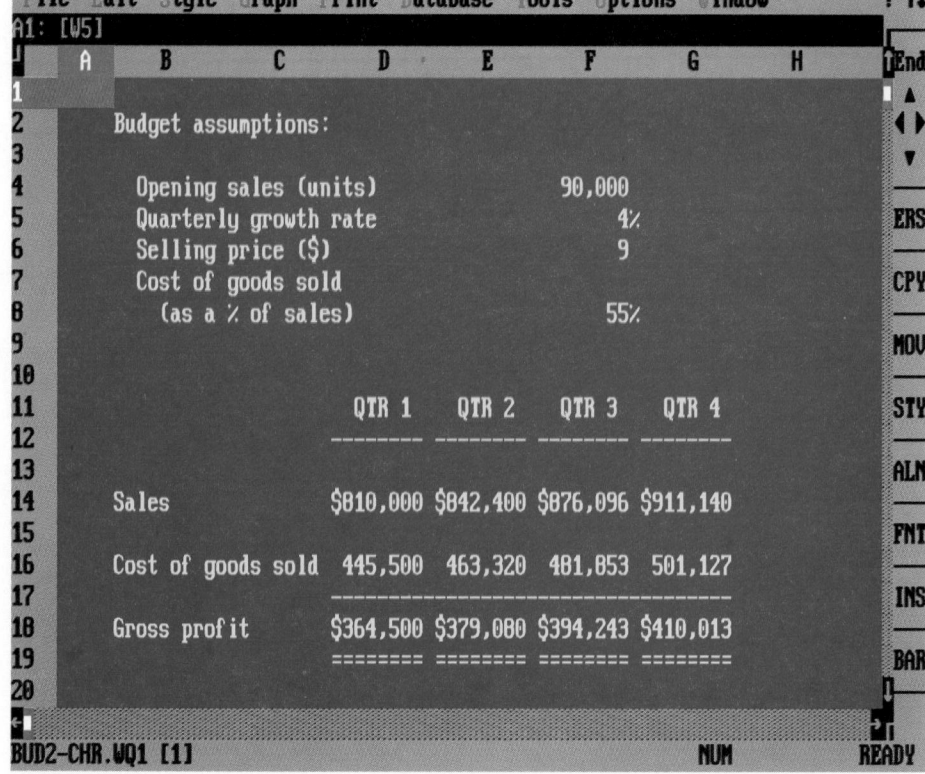

EXHIBIT 25-16
Spreadsheets and Financial Planning

EXHIBIT 25-16
(continued)

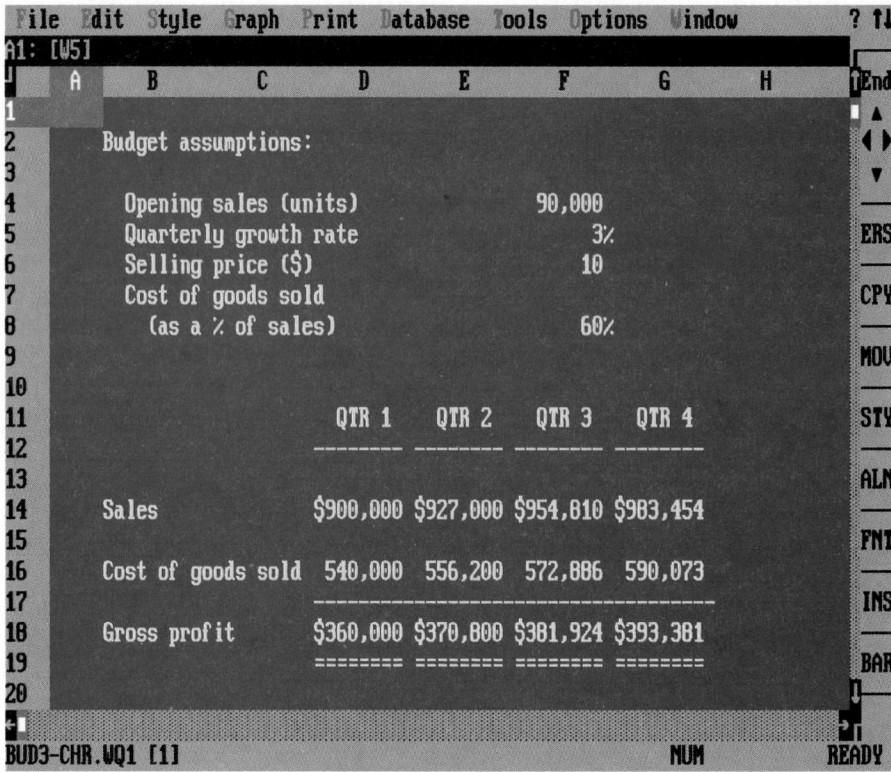

```
 File  Edit  Style  Graph  Print  Database  Tools  Options  Window        ? ↑↓
A1: [W5]
     A      B       C       D       E       F       G       H          End
1                                                                       ▲
2        Budget assumptions:                                           ◄ ►
3                                                                       ▼
4          Opening sales (units)                90,000
5          Quarterly growth rate                   3%                  ERS
6          Selling price ($)                       10
7          Cost of goods sold                                          CPY
8           (as a % of sales)                      60%
9                                                                      MOU
10
11                              QTR 1    QTR 2    QTR 3    QTR 4        STY
12                             —————    —————    —————    —————
13                                                                     ALN
14       Sales               $900,000 $927,000 $954,810 $983,454
15                                                                     FNT
16       Cost of goods sold   540,000  556,200  572,886  590,073
17                             ———————  ———————  ———————  ———————      INS
18       Gross profit        $360,000 $370,800 $381,924 $393,381
19                           ========  ========  ========  ========    BAR
20
BUD3-CHR.WQ1 [1]                                            NUM         READY
```

END-OF-CHAPTER REVIEW

**LEARNING OBJECTIVES:
THE KEY POINTS**

1 State the benefits of budgeting. Budgets provide three basic benefits for an organization. First, a formal plan of attack is created, allowing managers to pinpoint problems before the problems actually occur. Daily operating distractions are therefore reduced, because a look at the future often leads to adoption of corrective actions. A second benefit is that budgets serve as a basis for performance evaluation. Actual performance is compared against budgeted amounts, giving management insight into whether operations have been up to par. Finally, budgets assist in communicating and coordinating the goals of different operating units (e.g., divisions, departments, and so forth). The budgets of these units are examined and integrated when developing a plan for attaining overall company objectives.

2 Distinguish between top-down and bottom-up budgeting. With top-down budgeting, virtually all budget development takes place at the higher levels of the entity. This approach tends to reflect the goals of the entire firm as opposed to those of individual subunits (e.g., divisions). However, because of their lack of involvement, lower-level employees often resent the budget effort and do little toward budget achievement.

In contrast, the bottom-up approach stresses active participation of lower-level employees in the budget construction process. Given their involvement, these employees usually make greater strides toward attaining budgetary goals. Further, budgets are more realistic because people who best know the operation are providing valuable input.

3 Explain the concept of slack as it relates to the estimation process. Slack refers to the use of padding in budget estimates to avoid unfavorable performance appraisals. As an example, a manager may underestimate sales and overestimate expenses when preparing a budget. Later, when actual sales are "down" and expenses are "up" and both amounts are compared against budgeted figures, the manager is deemed to have met his or her target for the period.

4 Recognize the variations in budget periods. Different types of budgets tend to cover differing time periods. Budgets for capital expenditures are long term in nature, often extending five to ten years into the future. Operations budgets are typically prepared for a one-year period. Finally, budgets used to assess actual performance are frequently subdivided into quarters and months.

5 Discuss the limitations of budgeting, especially in the human relations area. Several limitations are associated with budgets. Like other management tools, a budget is only as good as the effort that goes into its preparation. The degree of support by top management is a key factor in the success (or failure) of any budget program. In addition, budgets are not ends in themselves; they cannot replace effective day-to-day operating decisions.

Because budgets are used in performance appraisals, employees often become disenchanted with the budgetary effort and its end product. Employees should be educated that budgets are helpful tools that assist in the attainment of company goals, not a means to fix blame when evaluating personnel.

6 Prepare a master budget. A master budget is a series of integrated budgets that serves as a financial plan for an organization. The starting point in the budget process is the sales budget, which logically flows into the production budget. Production levels, in turn, affect the direct material purchases budget, the direct labor budget, and the factory overhead budget. Other elements of the master budget include the selling and administrative expense budget, a capital expenditures budget, a cash budget, and pro forma (i.e., forecasted) financial statements.

7 Recognize the adaptability of budgets to computers. Because of the heavy computational emphasis, budgets are extremely adaptable to computers. Computers eliminate much of the procedural drudgery for the accountant, thereby allowing more time for analysis and evaluation. An electronic spreadsheet is a helpful tool that allows different scenarios to be explored by changing only a few key input variables.

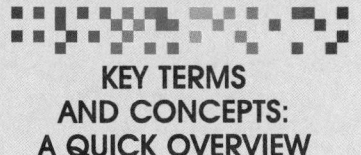

**KEY TERMS
AND CONCEPTS:
A QUICK OVERVIEW**

bottom-up budgeting An approach that emphasizes lower-level employee participation in the development of a budget.

budget A formal quantitative expression of management expectations generated for any area that management deems critical.

continuous budget A budget that covers a one-year period. A new month is added when the current month is completed.

master budget A comprehensive set of integrated budgets that serves as an entity's financial plan.

pro forma financial statements Forecasted financial statements that are prepared as the final step of the budgeting process.

slack The use of padding in budgets to avoid unfavorable appraisals.

top-down budgeting A budgeting approach in which a large portion of the development takes place at the upper echelons of management and the budget is imposed on lower-level personnel.

CHAPTER QUIZ

The five questions that follow relate to several issues raised in the chapter. Test your knowledge of the issues by selecting the best answer. (The answers appear on p. 1069.)

1 Which of the following statements is false?
   a Budgets are used in both the planning and control of daily operations.
   b Budgets assist in coordinating the diverse goals of a company's different sub-units (e.g., divisions, departments, and so forth).
   c Top-down budgeting is sometimes known as participative budgeting.
   d Budgets help to formalize a company's planning process.

2 Bottom-up budgeting:
   a generally results in increased efforts toward budget attainment by lower-level employees.
   b often results in less realistic budgets than top-down budgeting.
   c is used solely by manufacturing companies.
   d is another name for top-down budgeting.

3 The first budget to be prepared is normally the:
   a cash budget.   c pro forma balance sheet.
   b production budget.   d sales budget.

4 Which of the following listings is the most logical sequence of budget preparation?
   a Production budget, sales budget, cash budget, pro forma income statement.
   b Sales budget, cash budget, production budget, pro forma balance sheet.
   c Sales budget, production budget, direct labor budget, cash budget.
   d Production budget, direct material purchases budget, pro forma balance sheet, cash budget.

5 The cash budget:
   a assists management in predicting both cash shortages and cash deficiencies.
   b is dependent on the figures that are generated in other, previously prepared budgets.
   c discloses any borrowings and loan repayments that are expected to occur.
   d possesses the characteristics noted in (a), (b), and (c) above.

SUMMARY PROBLEM

Rochester Manufacturing sells a single product. Last year's sales (19X7) totaled 60,000 units, but volume is expected to increase by 10% in 19X8 because of a strong economy. In view of this situation, Rochester will raise its selling price to $22.

Each unit requires four square feet of direct material at $1.75 per square foot. The following selected inventory information for 19X8 is available:

Finished goods inventory, Jan. 1	5,600 units
Desired finished goods inventory, Dec. 31	4,200 units
Direct materials inventory, Jan. 1	18,700 square feet
Desired direct materials inventory, Dec. 31	21,300 square feet

The January 1 accounts receivable balance is $63,000. All sales are on account and are spread evenly throughout the year. Rochester's collection pattern is: 35% collected in the month of sale; 60% collected in the month following sale; and 5% uncollectible.

Instructions

a Determine the amount of cash the company would expect to collect in January and February.

b Compute the number of units that Rochester expects to produce in 19X8.

c Compute the cost of direct material purchases for 19X8.

d Suppose that morale is low because of recent layoffs. If management wants to improve employee relations, would it likely use the top-down or the bottom-up approach to budget preparation? Briefly explain.

e Rochester's management wants to examine the financial impact of several different selling prices and advertising programs. What should management consider doing to its budget preparation procedures to avoid overwhelming office personnel with paperwork?

Solution

a Sales in 19X8 will total 66,000 units (60,000 units × 1.10). Transactions are spread evenly through the year at the rate of 5,500 units per month (66,000 units ÷ 12 months). Collections are 35% in the month of sale and 60% in the month following sale.

	January	February
Accounts receivable, Jan. 1	$ 63,000	
January sales ($121,000)*	42,350	$ 72,600
February sales ($121,000)*		42,350
Total cash collections	$105,350	$114,950

* 5,500 units × $22 per unit.

b
Number of units to be sold	66,000
Add: Desired ending finished goods inventory	4,200
Total finished units needed	70,200
Less: Beginning finished goods inventory	5,600
Number of units to be produced	64,600

c
Planned production	64,600
Direct materials (square feet) per finished unit	× 4
Direct materials used in production	258,400
Add: Desired ending direct materials inventory	21,300
Total direct materials needed	279,700
Less: Beginning direct materials inventory	18,700
Direct materials to be purchased	261,000
Cost per square foot	× $1.75
Cost of direct material purchases	$456,750

d The company should use bottom-up, or participative, budgeting. By becoming involved in the budget process, the employees will likely view their knowledge and insight as being important to top management. What the employees do not need at this point is a top-down ("dictatorial") approach.

e Management should consider the use of electronic spreadsheets. "What if" analysis is simplified by pressing only a few keys on the computer as opposed to generating mounds of time-consuming paperwork.

ASSIGNMENT MATERIAL

QUESTIONS

Q25-1   Briefly discuss the advantages of budgeting.

Q25-2   Is a budget a planning tool, a control tool, or both? Explain.

Q25-3   When evaluating performance, many organizations compare current results with the actual results of previous accounting periods. Is an organization that follows this approach likely to encounter any problems? Explain.

Q25-4   Explain how a budget assists in coordinating the plans of an organization's various subunits (divisions, departments, and so forth).

Q25-5   Define and fully explain the top-down approach to budgeting.

Q25-6   Briefly explain the bottom-up approach to budgeting.

Q25-7   Should budget data be based on the past, the future, or both? Explain.

Q25-8   Briefly discuss the concept of slack as it pertains to budgeting.

Q25-9   Calabro Corporation, a manufacturer with annual sales approaching $75 million, is beginning the budget process for the upcoming year. Should Calabro use long-term budgets, yearly budgets, or monthly budgets? Explain your answer.

Q25-10   What is a continuous budget?

Q25-11   Aside from the work involved in the preparation process, why do some employees resent budgets?

Q25-12   Why is an accurate sales forecast so important in the preparation of a master budget?

Q25-13   What factors influence a company's expected direct material purchases?

Q25-14   Why is it necessary to carefully budget direct labor requirements for an upcoming period?

Q25-15   Explain how a cash budget leads to effective management of an organization's cash balances.

Q25-16   Explain the concept of "what if" testing and how the computer can be of assistance.

EXERCISES

E25-1   *Overview of the budgeting process* (L.O. 1, 2, 4, 6)

Evaluate the comments that follow as being True or False. If the comment is false, briefly explain why.

a   When assessing current performance, a comparison of actual results against a predetermined budget is generally preferred over a comparison of the current period's actual results with those of the preceding period.

b   Lower-level managers are inclined to work harder to achieve budgeted targets if the top-down (rather than the bottom-up) budget approach is used.

c   Virtually all budgets are one year in duration.

d Land & Sea plans to sell 36,700 units of its single product during the coming year. If the beginning and ending finished goods inventories are 15,900 and 17,700 units, respectively, the company's production budget will reveal that 38,500 units should be manufactured.

e The last step in the construction of a master budget is the preparation of a cash budget.

E25-2 *Participative budgeting; slack* (L.O. 2, 3)

Mark Jacobs is the newly hired marketing manager of Electronics, Etc., a retail chain of 68 stores located in the northeast. The company recently adopted a participative approach to budgeting and uses performance reports to compare actual and budgeted results.

Mark has been asked to prepare the 19X8 advertising budget. Business has been relatively stable over the past few years, with annual advertising outlays averaging $6.5 million. Top management does not expect any new marketing programs during 19X8 nor are any hikes in media rates anticipated. Mark's budget called for outlays totaling $6.8 million.

a Does Electronics, Etc., use a top-down or a bottom-up approach to budgeting? Briefly explain.

b Did Mark appear to understand the concept of slack when he prepared the advertising budget? Briefly discuss, being sure to explain why the budget reflected a $300,000 increase in expenditures.

E25-3 *Schedule of cash collections* (L.O. 6)

Sugarland Company sells a single product and anticipates opening a new facility in Charlotte on May 1 of the current year. Expected sales during the first three months of activity are: May, $60,000; June, $80,000; and July, $85,000.

Thirty percent of all sales are for cash; the remaining 70% are on account. Credit sales have the following collection pattern:

Collected in the month of sale	60%
Collected in the month following sale	35
Uncollectible	5

a Prepare a schedule of cash collections for May through July.

b Compute the expected balance in Accounts Receivable as of July 31.

E25-4 *Production budget* (L.O. 6)

Paste Products anticipates the following unit sales during the first four months of the upcoming year:

January	30,000
February	35,000
March	38,000
April	40,000

The company wants to maintain its finished goods inventory at 40% of the following month's sales. The January 1 finished goods inventory will be 11,500 units.

Prepare a production budget for January through March.

E25-5 *Direct material purchases budget* (L.O. 6)

Bass Corporation manufactures a home video recorder that requires four no. S1326 circuit boards. Anticipated production of recorders for the upcoming year follows.

Quarter	Production (Units)
First	8,000
Second	10,000
Third	12,000
Fourth	16,000

Bass wants to stock enough circuit boards to meet 30% of the following quarter's production needs. Circuit boards cost $2.50 each; the cost has been fairly stable over the past six months.

Assuming a beginning circuit board inventory of $23,750, prepare a direct material purchases budget for the first three quarters of the year.

E25-6 *Production and cash-outlay computations* (L.O. 6)

RPR, Inc., anticipates that 120,000 units of product K will be sold during May. Each unit of product K requires four units of raw material A. Actual inventories as of May 1 and budgeted inventories as of May 31 follow.

	May 1	May 31
Product K (units)	55,000	60,000
Raw material A (units)	40,000	37,000

Each unit of raw material A costs $8; RPR pays for all purchases in the month of acquisition. Invoices that account for 80% of the cost of materials acquired will be paid within 10 days of receipt, entitling the company to a 2% cash discount.

a Determine the number of units of product K to be manufactured in May.
b Compute the May cash outlay for purchases of raw material A.

E25-7 *Analysis of operations: Cash emphasis* (L.O. 6)

Lexington Wood Products manufactures and distributes wooden baseball bats. Business is seasonal, with a large portion of the sales occurring in late winter and early spring. Production is heavy during the last quarter of the year to meet demand, and Lexington experiences a temporary cash strain during this period. Payroll costs rise because considerable overtime is scheduled. Furthermore, customer collections are low because the fall season produces only modest sales. This year there are added problems because of high inflation rates and declining sales, the latter caused by the increased popularity of aluminum bats. Also, only 25% of the customers are paying their balances in the month of sale. The average collection period is approximately 62 days.

Fortunately, the cash strain arises only during the last quarter. The Cash account builds up during the first two quarters as sales exceed production. Excess cash is invested in U.S. Treasury bills and certificates of deposit.

Assume that Lexington regularly experiences the preceding cash strain. What actions could the firm take to "ease the squeeze" on cash? Consider possible changes in operations when preparing your answer.

E25-8 *Abbreviated cash budget; financing emphasis* (L.O. 6)

An abbreviated cash budget for Big Chuck Enterprises follows.

1-2-3

	July	August	September
Beginning cash balance	$ 10,000	$?	$?
Add: Cash receipts	50,000	63,000	71,000
Deduct: Cash payments	(64,000)	(58,000)	(64,000)
Cash excess (deficiency) before financing	$ (4,000)	$?	$?
Financing			
Borrowing to maintain minimum balance	?	?	?
Principal repayment	?	?	?
Interest payment	?	?	?
Ending cash balance	$?	$?	$?

Big Chuck wishes to maintain a $10,000 minimum cash balance at all times. Additional financing is available (and retired) in $1,000 multiples at a 12% interest rate. Assume that borrowings take place at the beginning of the month; retirements, in contrast, occur at the end of the month. Interest is paid at the time of repaying principal and computed on the portion of principal repaid.

a Find the unknowns in Big Chuck's abbreviated cash budget.

b Determine the outstanding loan balance as of September 30, after any repayments have been made.

E25-9 *Cash budget* (L.O. 6)

Tennessee Merchandising has had continual problems with cash flow. The following information has come to your attention:

a The company has an opening cash balance of $10,000 on January 1. Management wishes to maintain a minimum cash balance of $8,000 at all times.

b Budgeted sales for January total $200,000. Sales are expected to increase at the rate of 5% per month over the next six months. Sales from the preceding November and December amounted to $170,000 and $180,000, respectively.

c All sales are on credit and subject to the following collection pattern:

- Sixty percent collected in the month of sale.
- Thirty percent collected in the month following sale.
- Ten percent collected in the second month following sale.

d All merchandise purchases are paid for in the month of purchase. The cost of acquisitions is expected to average 70% of the month's sales revenues.

e Operating expenses are budgeted as follows:

	January	February	March
Selling (excluding depreciation)	$16,000	$20,000	$25,000
Administrative (excluding depreciation)	12,000	12,000	12,000
Depreciation	6,000	6,000	7,000

f The company will acquire $28,000 of new equipment in March for cash.

g Additional financing is available (and retired) in $1,000 multiples at a 16% interest rate. Assume that all borrowings take place at the beginning of the month; retirements occur at the end of the month. Interest is paid at the time of repaying principal and computed on the portion of principal repaid.

Analyze Tennessee's cash position by preparing a cash budget for January through March. Has the company solved its cash flow problems or will additional financing be necessary?

PROBLEMS

Series A

P25-A1 *Production and purchases budgets; purchasing policy* (L.O. 6)

Mason, Inc., manufactures and distributes various parts for lawn mowers. The company's main product, a bilateral assembly, requires five units of direct material at a cost of $0.60 per unit. To keep production moving smoothly, the firm must maintain a direct materials inventory equal to 70% of the following month's production needs.

Sales projections in units for the last six months of 19X6 follow.

Month	Estimated Sales
July	9,000
August	12,000
September	16,000
October	22,000
November	29,000
December	26,000

Management wants to carry a finished goods inventory equal to 40% of the following month's sales. On June 30, 19X6, the finished goods inventory totaled 3,200 assemblies. On the same date, 30,000 units of direct material were in the warehouse.

Instructions

a Prepare a production budget for July through September.
b Prepare a direct material purchases budget for July through September.
c List several factors that could cause a change in the company's present direct material inventory policy.

P25-A2 *Cash budget covering three months* (L.O. 6)

Riverside Corporation is a distributor of medical supplies. Management is studying the company's cash needs for October through December and has assembled the following information:

	October	November	December
Sales	$60,000	$54,000	$50,000
Purchases of merchandise	26,000	21,000	19,000
Cash operating costs	33,000	31,000	25,000
Depreciation expense	2,000	2,200	2,500
Equipment acquisitions	8,000	5,000	—

The pro forma balance sheet on September 30 revealed the following account balances:

Cash	$ 6,500
Accounts receivable	21,000
Accounts payable	18,000

Seventy percent of all customer accounts are collected in the month of sale; 25% are collected in the following month. Because of a liberal credit policy, uncollectibles amounting to 5% of sales are anticipated. Management feels that only $20,000 of the accounts outstanding on September 30 will be received.

Forty percent of the merchandise purchases are paid for in the month of purchase to take advantage of a 2% discount. The remaining 60% are paid in the month following purchase.

Riverside maintains a $6,000 minimum cash balance at all times. Should borrowing be necessary, financing is available (and retired) in $1,000 multiples at a 16% interest rate. Assume all borrowings take place at the beginning of the month; retirements occur at the end of the month. Interest is paid at the time of repaying principal and computed on the portion of principal repaid.

Instructions

a Prepare a schedule of cash collections for October through December.
b Prepare a schedule of cash disbursements for merchandise purchases for October through December.
c Prepare a cash budget similar to that shown in Exhibit 25-13.

P25-A3 *Cash budget for service enterprise; analysis of operations* (L.O. 6)
The Eastside Tennis Club frequently experiences cash flow difficulties, with its checking account often below a desired minimum balance of $12,000. The following information pertains to club operations for the upcoming year (19X2):

1 The directors anticipate that 400 memberships will be sold. Family memberships ($150) will comprise 60% of this total; the remainder are individual memberships ($50).
2 Members are assessed hourly fees for court time; the rate depends on whether usage occurs during "prime" time or "regular" time. The following hours and rates are expected:

	Prime Time	Regular Time
Rate per hour	$10	$7
Hours of use	4,300	6,500

3 With the exception of accounts that total $2,500, all billings for memberships and court fees are expected to be collected during the year.
4 John Connors, club pro, is paid a salary of $20,000 plus 20% of all court fee revenues. Connors gives private lessons and expects to earn an additional $3,500. Lesson fees are paid directly to Connors by the participating members.
5 Expenses incurred during 19X1 were: maintenance, $34,000; utilities, $13,500; and taxes, $6,200. Maintenance and utilities are expected to increase by 10% during 19X2; taxes should amount to $6,800. All expenses will be paid when incurred.
6 An examination of the club's records revealed outstanding accounts payable of $1,000 on January 1, 19X2. These amounts will be paid by the end of February.
7 The addition of one new court and improved lighting will cost $45,000. The club will pay $20,000 down, with the remaining balance financed by a short-term note. Interest and principal payments during 19X2 will amount to $3,600.
8 The cash balance on January 1, 19X2, amounts to $5,000.

Instructions

a Prepare a cash budget for 19X2 for the Eastside Tennis Club. Disregard financing [except for that noted in item (7)] to meet minimum balance requirements.

b Assume that the budget revealed an ending cash balance of $4,400. In light of the club's target minimum of $12,000, what actions could the directors take to improve the ending cash position?

P25-A4 *Pro forma statements* (L.O. 6)

1-2-3

The Traxton Company's balance sheet as of December 31, 19X1, follows.

TRAXTON COMPANY Balance Sheet December 31, 19X1		
Assets		
Cash		$ 17,500
Accounts receivable		98,000
Merchandise inventory		51,800
Plant & equipment	$96,000	
Less: Accumulated depreciation	29,000	67,000
Total assets		$234,300
Liabilities & Stockholders' Equity		
Accounts payable		$ 68,200
Common stock, $10 par	$70,000	
Retained earnings	96,100	166,100
Total liabilities & stockholders' equity		$234,300

Traxton has gathered the following information relating to January 19X2:

1 Budgeted sales total $450,000. Historically, cash sales have averaged 30% of total sales. Sixty percent of the firm's credit sales are collected in the month of sale; the remainder are collected in the following month.

2 Merchandise purchases are expected to total $370,000. Obligations to suppliers are settled as follows:

- Forty percent are paid in the month of purchase, subject to a 2% discount.
- Twenty percent are paid in the month of purchase after the discount period has lapsed.
- Forty percent are paid in the month following purchase.

Management has budgeted the January 31 inventory at $74,900.

3 Monthly operating expenses are paid as incurred and subdivided as follows:

Variable	15% of sales
Fixed (includes depreciation)	$62,400

4 The plant and equipment have a 10-year service life. Traxton uses the straight-line method of depreciation.

5 The company plans to acquire $20,000 of land on January 31 by paying $9,000 down and signing a short-term note for the remaining balance.

6 Traxton will declare a $0.30-per-share cash dividend on January 21. The dividend will be distributed on February 21.

Instructions

a Determine Traxton's January 31 cash balance.

b Prepare a pro forma income statement for January. Disregard income taxes and earnings-per-share computations.

c Prepare a pro forma balance sheet as of January 31.

P25-A5 *Comprehensive budgeting* (L.O. 6)

The balance sheet of Watson Company as of December 31, 19X1, follows.

WATSON COMPANY
Balance Sheet
December 31, 19X1

Assets

Cash		$ 4,595
Accounts receivable		10,000
Finished goods (575 units × $7.00)		4,025
Direct materials (2,760 units × $0.50)		1,380
Plant & equipment	$50,000	
Less: Accumulated depreciation	10,000	40,000
Total assets		$60,000

Liabilities & Stockholders' Equity

Accounts payable to suppliers		$14,000
Common stock	$25,000	
Retained earnings	21,000	46,000
Total liabilities & stockholders' equity		$60,000

The following information has been extracted from the firm's accounting records:

1 All sales are made on account at $20 per unit. Sixty percent of the sales are collected in the month of sale; the remaining 40% are collected in the following month. Forecasted sales for the first five months of 19X2 are: January, 1,500 units; February, 1,600 units; March, 1,800 units; April, 2,000 units; May, 2,100 units.

2 Management wants to maintain the finished goods inventory at 30% of the following month's sales.

3 Watson uses four units of direct material in each finished unit. The direct material price has been stable and is expected to remain so over the next six months. Management wants to maintain the ending direct materials inventory at 60% of the following month's production needs.

4 Seventy percent of all purchases are paid in the month of purchase; the remaining 30% are paid in the subsequent month.

5 Watson's product requires 30 minutes of direct labor time. Each hour of direct labor costs $7.

Instructions

a Rounding computations to the nearest dollar, prepare the following for January through March:
   (1) Sales budget
   (2) Schedule of cash collections
   (3) Production budget
   (4) Direct material purchases budget
   (5) Schedule of cash disbursements for material purchases
   (6) Direct labor budget

b Determine the balances in the following accounts as of March 31:
   (1) Accounts Receivable
   (2) Direct Materials
   (3) Accounts Payable

P25-A6 *Budgeting and spreadsheets* (L.O. 6, 7)

Fashion Sense is in the process of preparing a budgeted income statement for the first quarter of 19X8. The information that follows is known.

January sales	$150,000
Cost of goods sold	60% of sales
Operating expenses	
Variable	20% of sales
Fixed	$10,000 per month
Sales growth rate	2% per month

Management wants the budget to be established in the following format:

Budget assumptions			
Sales growth rate			1.02
Cost of goods sold			0.60
Variable expenses			0.20
Fixed expenses per month			10,000

	January	February	March
Sales	150,000		
Cost of goods sold			
Gross profit			
Operating expenses			
Variable			
Fixed			
Total			
Net income			

Instructions

a Manually prepare the budgeted income statement as requested by management.

b Prepare a spreadsheet model for the income statement and print the desired budget.

c Repeat part (b), assuming January sales of $180,000 and a variable expense percentage of 15% rather than 20%.

d On the basis of your answer to part (c), what benefits would a company experience by using a spreadsheet model in the budgeting process?

Series B

P25-B1 *Production and purchases budgets; inventory policy* (L.O. 6)
Procraft, Inc., manufactures and distributes various parts for videocassette recorders. The company's main product, a switching device, requires two units of direct material at a cost of $1.50 per unit. To keep production moving smoothly, the company must maintain a direct materials inventory equal to 40% of the following month's production needs.

Sales projections in units for the first six months of 19X2 follow.

Month	Estimated Sales of Switching Devices
January	40,000
February	44,000
March	46,000
April	50,000
May	48,000
June	45,000

Management wants to carry a finished goods inventory equal to 30% of the following month's sales. On December 31, 19X1, the finished goods inventory totaled 11,000 switches. On the same date, 25,000 units of direct material were in the warehouse.

Instructions

a Prepare a production budget for January through March.
b Prepare a direct material purchases budget for January through March.
c List several factors that could cause a change in the company's present finished goods inventory policy.

P25-B2 *Cash budget covering three months* (L.O. 6)
Atra Corporation is a distributor of recording equipment. Management is studying the company's cash needs for July through September and has assembled the following information:

	July	August	September
Sales	$60,000	$70,000	$85,000
Purchases of merchandise	40,000	46,000	48,000
Cash operating costs	37,500	35,500	39,000
Depreciation expense	3,000	3,300	3,300
Equipment acquisitions	11,000	—	—
Sale of delivery trucks	—	—	20,000

The pro forma balance sheet on June 30 revealed the following account balances:

Cash	$23,000
Accounts receivable	22,800
Accounts payable	15,900

Sixty percent of all customer accounts are collected in the month of sale; 35% are collected in the following month. Because of a liberal credit policy, uncollectibles amounting to 5% of sales are anticipated. Management feels that only $19,000 of the accounts outstanding on June 30 will be received.

Sixty percent of the merchandise purchases are paid for in the month of purchase to take advantage of a 2% discount. The remaining 40% are paid in the month following purchase.

Atra maintains a $5,000 minimum cash balance at all times. Should borrowing be necessary, financing is available (and retired) in $1,000 multiples at a 16% interest rate. Assume all borrowings take place at the beginning of the month; retirements occur at the end of the month. Interest is paid at the time of repaying principal and computed on the portion of principal repaid.

Instructions

a Prepare a schedule of cash collections for July through September.

b Prepare a schedule of cash disbursements for merchandise purchases for July through September.

c Prepare a cash budget similar to that shown in Exhibit 25-13.

P25-B3 *Cash budget for service enterprise; analysis of operations* (L.O. 6)

Pat Mallory operates Green Up, a year-round lawn service and landscape business in Florida. The following information has been assembled to prepare a cash budget for 19X5:

1 Green Up has two types of clients (commercial and residential) and offers two types of services (regular and enhanced). The number of clients and weekly billing rates are:

	Total Number of Clients	Weekly Billing Rate	
		Regular	Enhanced
Commercial	60	$30	$50
Residential	40	25	35

Sixty-five percent of the clients use the regular service; the remaining 35% use the enhanced service.

2 The firm will provide 50 shrub planting jobs throughout the year. Each job averages six hours, and the billing rate is $25 per hour.

3 With the exception of $17,000 of uncollectibles, all amounts billed are expected to be received during 19X5.

4 Trees, shrubs, and supplies acquired from wholesalers will cost $28,000. Green Up adds 30% to cost for a profit and then bills clients.

5 Operating expenses incurred during 19X4 were: labor, $95,000; gasoline, $4,000; other, $5,000; and depreciation, $1,400. A 5% increase in labor, gasoline, and other is expected; depreciation will remain constant.

6 In 19X4, Green Up purchased an office refrigerator, fax machine, mobile telephone, microcomputer, new mowers, and a pickup truck. Total cost was $20,500, of which $4,300 will be paid during 19X5.

7 Green Up is organized as a sole proprietorship, and Mallory expects to withdraw $5,000 per month from the business.

8 The beginning cash balance on January 1, 19X5, is $4,500.

Instructions

a Prepare the 19X5 cash budget for Green Up. Disregard the financing section.

b Assume that the budget revealed an ending cash balance of $6,200. If Mallory wants to adopt a new policy of maintaining a $10,000 minimum balance throughout the year, what changes in operations would you recommend?

P25-B4 *Pro forma statements* (L.O. 6)

Aircon Company's balance sheet as of December 31, 19X6, follows.

AIRCON COMPANY
Balance Sheet
December 31, 19X6

Assets

Cash		$ 10,900
Accounts receivable		31,200
Merchandise inventory		64,500
Plant & equipment	$84,000	
Less: Accumulated depreciation	16,000	68,000
Total assets		$174,600

Liabilities & Stockholders' Equity

Accounts payable		$ 56,000
Common stock, $1 par	$30,000	
Retained earnings	88,600	118,600
Total liabilities & stockholders' equity		$174,600

Management has gathered the following information relating to January 19X7:

1 Budgeted sales total $200,000. Historically, cash sales have averaged 10% of total sales. Seventy percent of the firm's credit sales are collected in the month generated; the remainder are collected in the following month.

2 Merchandise purchases are expected to total $120,000. Obligations to suppliers are settled as follows:

- Sixty percent are paid in the month of purchase, subject to a 1% discount.
- Five percent are paid in the month of purchase after the discount period has lapsed.
- Thirty-five percent are paid in the month following purchase.

Management has budgeted the January 31 inventory at $47,800.

3 Monthly operating expenses are paid as incurred and subdivided as follows:

Variable	7% of sales
Fixed (includes depreciation)	$17,900

4 The plant and equipment have a 20-year service life. Aircon uses the straight-line method of depreciation.

5 The company plans to acquire $16,000 of land on January 31 by paying $3,000 down and signing a short-term note for the remaining balance.

6 Aircon will declare a $0.15-per-share cash dividend on January 24. The dividend will be distributed on February 24.

Instructions

a Determine Aircon's January 31 cash balance.

b Prepare a pro forma income statement for January. Disregard income taxes and earnings-per-share computations.

c Prepare a pro forma balance sheet as of January 31.

P25-B5 *Comprehensive budgeting* (L.O. 6)

The balance sheet of Mid-America Company as of December 31, 19X8, follows.

MID-AMERICA COMPANY Balance Sheet December 31, 19X8		
Assets		
Cash		$ 14,800
Accounts receivable		26,000
Finished goods (1,200 units × $8.00)		9,600
Direct materials (6,000 units × $1.50)		9,000
Plant & equipment	$115,000	
Less: Accumulated depreciation	12,000	103,000
Total assets		$162,400
Liabilities & Stockholders' Equity		
Accounts payable to suppliers		$ 12,000
Common stock	$ 50,000	
Retained earnings	100,400	150,400
Total liabilities & stockholders' equity		$162,400

The following information has been extracted from the company's records:

1 All sales are made on account at $15 per unit. Forty percent of the sales are collected in the month of sale; the remaining 60% are collected in the following month. Forecasted sales for the first five months of 19X9 are: January, 2,600 units; February, 2,900 units; March, 3,100 units; April, 3,500 units; May, 3,200 units.

2 Management wants to maintain the finished goods inventory at 20% of the following month's sales.

3 Mid-America uses three units of direct material in each finished unit. The direct material price has been stable and is expected to remain so over the next six months. Management wants to maintain the ending direct materials inventory at 70% of the following month's production needs.

4 Eighty percent of all purchases are paid in the month of purchase; the remaining 20% are paid in the subsequent month.

5 Mid-America's product requires 20 minutes of direct labor time. Each hour of direct labor costs $9.

Instructions

a Rounding computations to the nearest dollar, prepare the following for January through March:
   (1) Sales budget
   (2) Schedule of cash collections
   (3) Production budget
   (4) Direct material purchases budget
   (5) Schedule of cash disbursements for material purchases
   (6) Direct labor budget
b Determine the balances in the following accounts as of March 31:
   (1) Accounts Receivable
   (2) Direct Materials
   (3) Accounts Payable

P25-B6 *Budgeting and spreadsheets* (L.O. 6, 7)

Harbor Wear is in the process of preparing its 19X4 budget. The following facts are known.

1 Sales for the last quarter of the year will be: October, $80,000; November, $95,000; and December, $120,000.
2 Twenty percent of the firm's sales are for cash; the remainder are on account. Sixty percent of the credit sales are collected in the month of sale; 36% are collected in the month following sale; and 4% are uncollectible.
3 October collections from September credit sales are expected to total $18,800.

Management has requested that the following budget report be prepared:

Budget assumptions			
Cash sales			0.20
Credit sales collected in the:			
Month of sale			0.60
Month following sale			0.36
	October	November	December
Total sales	80,000	95,000	120,000
Cash sales			
Credit collections:			
Previous sales			
Current sales			
Total			
Total collections			

Instructions

a Manually prepare the budget report as requested by management.
b Prepare a spreadsheet model for the cash collections and print the desired budget.
c Repeat part (b), assuming October sales of $70,000 and a cash sales percentage of 25% rather than 20%.
d On the basis of your answer to part (c), comment on the number of alternatives that a spreadsheet user can effectively explore when preparing a budget.

BEYOND THE BASICS

BB25-1 *Master budget relationships* (L.O. 6)

The data that follow pertain to Trinity Enterprises, which manufactures a single product.

1 All sales are on account, with 60% collected in the month of sale and 40% in the following month. The selling price is $20 per unit.

2 The schedule of cash collections for January through March of 19X5 revealed the following receipts for the period:

	Cash Receipts		
	January	February	March
December receivables	$32,000		
January sales	54,000	$36,000	
February sales		66,000	$44,000
March sales			72,000

3 Finished goods inventories are maintained at 30% of the following month's sales.

4 Each finished product contains five units of direct material, with each unit being purchased from a local supplier for $2. Delivery is within hours of placing an order; thus, Trinity stocks no direct material inventories.

5 Seventy percent of all direct material purchases are paid in the month of purchase, subject to a 2% discount. Ten percent are paid in the month of purchase but after the discount period has lapsed, and the remaining 20% are settled in the month following purchase.

6 Trinity wants to maintain a minimum cash balance of $15,000. Total payments in January are expected to be $106,500.

7 The December 31, 19X4, balance sheet revealed the following selected figures:

Cash	$24,900
Accounts receivable	32,000
Finished goods (? units)	22,950

Instructions

Determine:

a Sales revenues earned in December 19X4.

b Total sales revenues to be reported on Trinity's pro forma income statement for the first quarter of 19X5.

c Accounts receivable to be reported on the March 31, 19X5, pro forma balance sheet.

d Number of units in the December 31, 19X4, finished goods inventory.

e Units of finished goods to be manufactured in January 19X5.

f Units of finished goods to be manufactured in February 19X5.

g February 19X5 payments for direct material purchases.

h Financing required in January, if any, to maintain the firm's minimum cash balance.

BB25-2 *Overview of chapter concepts: Multiple choice* (L.O. 1–7)

The following multiple-choice questions relate to various topics discussed in the chapter. Select the best answer.

1 One of the basic benefits associated with an extensive budgeting effort is:

a an increase in sales.

b a decrease in operating expenses.

c the development of an objective basis for performance evaluation.

d an improvement of cash flow.

2 Which of the following features is associated with the bottom-up approach to budgeting?

a The budget is imposed on lower-level personnel, who rarely become involved with budget construction.

b Initial drafts of the budget have a very high likelihood of reflecting goals of the overall organization (as opposed to goals of individual subunits).

c Initial budget guidelines are issued by top management, with subsequent budget development occurring at lower levels of the firm.

d Job satisfaction and employee morale tend to be lower than with top-down budgeting.

3 The use of padding to avoid unfavorable appraisals is known as budgetary:

a variance.　　　　　　　　　　c cushion.

b slack.　　　　　　　　　　　　d burden.

4 A budget that covers a one-year period, with a new month being added as the current month is completed, is known as a

a master budget.　　　　　　　c continuous budget.

b capital budget.　　　　　　　d revised budget.

5 Which of the following is a frequently cited limitation and/or criticism of budgeting?

a The encouragement of suboptimal resource allocation.

b The discouragement of effective day-to-day management.

c An overemphasis on control, with detrimental effects on employee relations.

d A definite lack of organizational support and employee enthusiasm.

6 Shale Corporation is in the process of estimating its cash receipts for June. Twenty percent of the company's sales are for cash; the remaining 80% are on account. Of the credit sales, 30% are collected in the month of sale; 65% are collected in the month following sale; and 5% are uncollectible. The following information is known:

Estimated cash receipts in June from sales prior to June	$56,000
Total June sales	80,000
Accounts written off in June	6,000
June cost of goods sold	45,000

Total anticipated cash receipts in June are:

a $40,200.　　　　　　　　　　c $85,200.

b $75,200.　　　　　　　　　　d $91,200.

7 The following information relates to Gray Company:

June sales: 10,000 units

Finished goods inventories: June 1, 1,000 units; June 30, 1,500 units

Direct materials inventories: June 1, 1,700 pounds; June 30, 1,200 pounds

Manufacturing costs: Direct materials, $6 per pound; direct labor, $9 per hour; and factory overhead, $7 per hour

Every unit of finished goods requires two pounds of direct materials and one hour of direct labor. If there is no work in process, June direct material purchases and cost of goods manufactured will respectively be:

a $123,000 and $231,000. c $126,000 and $231,000.

b $123,000 and $294,000. d $126,000 and $294,000.

8 Which of the following statements about computerized budgeting is most correct?

a Budgeting is improved because of the ease with which variables can be revised and corresponding new budgets prepared.

b Budget integrity is undermined because of the ease with which managers can massage variables to produce the desired budget effect.

c Computers add little to the budget effort, because budgets are still based on subjective evaluations that must be made by humans.

d When prepared on a computer, the budget will not be meaningful because the people who must adhere to the budget will not have given it sufficient personal attention.

COMMUNICATION OF ACCOUNTING INFORMATION

CAI25-1 *The justification memo* **(L.O. 1, 2, 3)**

Communication Principle: The business environment is often characterized as a world in which scarce resources must be allocated among alternative courses of action. Not only is this statement true for our entire economy, but it is also valid within a single organization.

In view of this situation, individuals (and departments) are frequently called upon to defend their resource requests—especially at budget time. Keep the following points in mind when developing memorandum or verbal presentations for this purpose:

- *Be truthful.* Honesty with superiors is a fundamental obligation. Managers who exaggerate their budgetary needs in order to provide a "cushion" may soon find that their requests are subjected to arbitrary cuts, as superiors assume that padding is the rule rather than the exception.

- *Be consistent.* Provide clear descriptions of the consequences of alternative budgetary actions and show how prior projections have been fulfilled. Upper-level managers are more likely to take heed of budget requests if there is consistency between past forecasts and actual results.

- *Be concise.* Don't ramble on and on. Cases should be stated simply and precisely, leaving the ultimate decision to those responsible. If a manager's presentation is perceived as "whining," it will likely do more harm than good.

- *Focus on organizational goals.* Resource requests should show how the overall organization will benefit. Upper-level managers normally favor team players who take a corporate rather than an individual division or department perspective.

■ ■ ■ ■ ■ ■ ■ ■

Mill Road Products recently adopted a zero-defect policy for its manufactured goods. In addition, management wants to reduce the firm's overall inventory investment and avoid hiring any new employees.

Frank Barnett heads Department 109, which produces an electrical component requiring minimal manufacturing time and lengthy, detailed inspections. Previously, inspectors randomly tested finished goods. In light of Mill Road's new policy, however, they must now check every unit produced. As a result, the inventory of completed but uninspected goods is rising rapidly.

Barnett's corrective options include occasional reassignment of production personnel to inspection. This action will reduce long-run output but will remedy the inventory buildup problem. Another possibility is to hire additional inspectors, increasing the annual payroll by $90,000.

Instructions

Draft a persuasive memo to upper management that defines Barnett's problem and requests management to consider additional funds to hire more inspectors. Barnett is well respected by his superiors but senses that they have minimal interest in eliminating the department's problem. You may assume that sufficient customer demand exists to absorb all the units that can be manufactured.

Answers to Chapter Quiz

1 c

2 a

3 d

4 c

5 d

ing on variances, managers can avoid spending countless hours in a review of what is going right. Their efforts instead can be devoted to areas that need attention, a process frequently known as **management by exception.**

To illustrate the fundamentals of variance analysis, we will begin by concentrating on direct materials and direct labor. Suppose that a company reported the following results on conclusion of a recent month's activity:

Cost	Actual	Standard	Variance
Direct materials used	$36,500	$33,000	$3,500U
Direct labor	59,400	62,700	3,300F

Notice that both direct material consumption and direct labor incurrence failed to conform to the original plan. The company spent $3,500 more than anticipated for materials, giving rise to an *unfavorable variance.* In contrast, direct labor cost was $3,300 less than planned and created a *favorable variance.*

Management now wants to know why the variances arose. Material and labor costs will stray from standard because of deviations in the following factors:

1 Direct materials:
   a The per-unit acquisition cost of materials
   b The quantity of materials consumed
2 Direct labor:
   a The hourly wage rate
   b The number of hours worked

Variance Calculation

The impact of these price and quantity factors on the total variances can be determined by several relatively simple calculations. The calculations are perhaps best illustrated by the model that appears in Exhibit 26-7.

Careful study of the model reveals that the price variance is really the difference between the actual and standard prices, multiplied by the actual quantity of material or labor put into production. For direct materials the price variance is commonly known as the **materials price variance.** With labor, however, the name changes slightly to the **labor rate variance** to be more attuned to the area of study.

The quantity variance is slightly more difficult to understand. Exhibit 26-7 shows the quantity variance is calculated by comparing (Aq × Sp) and (Sq × Sp). If we take the difference between these two expressions, the following formula is derived:

$$\text{Quantity Variance} = Sp\,(Aq - Sq)$$

The formula shows that by weighting the difference in quantities by the standard price, the quantity variance is measured in dollars.

Additionally, it is important to note that the standard quantity is subtracted from the actual quantity. The actual quantity represents the actual input (pounds, gallons, hours, and so on) placed in production. In contrast, *the standard quantity is the amount of input that should have been used in manufacturing activities during the period.* As an example, assume that a company manufactures a single product that requires three pounds of

OBJECTIVE

5

Calculate direct material, direct labor, and factory overhead variances.

EXHIBIT 26-7
General Model for Variance Analysis of Direct Materials and Direct Labor

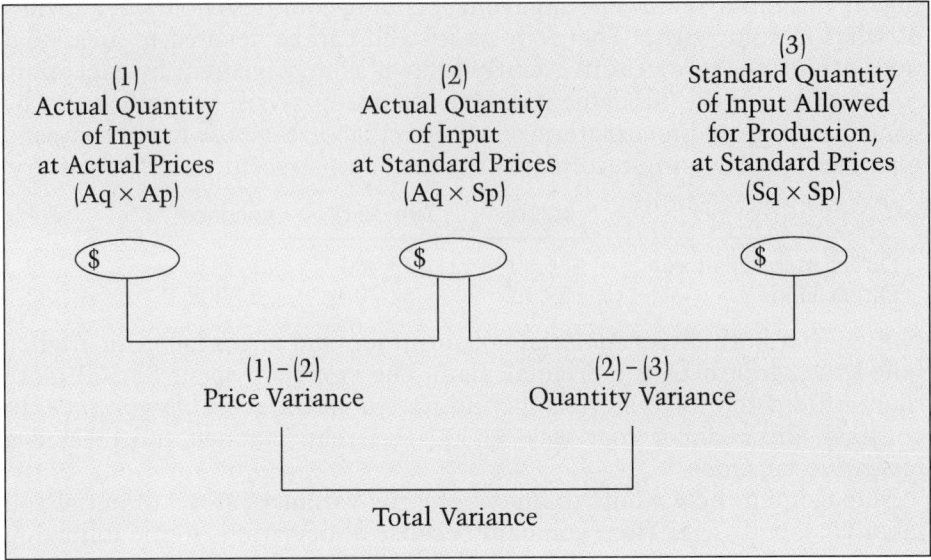

direct materials. Production totaled 4,000 completed units for the month just ended. If 11,800 pounds of materials were consumed, Aq would be 11,800 pounds and Sq would be 12,000 pounds (4,000 completed units × 3 pounds per unit).

The quantity variance is called the **materials quantity variance** when working with direct materials. For labor the name is changed to the **labor efficiency variance** to reflect the cause of the difference between actual and standard labor hours.

An Illustration of Direct Material Variances

To illustrate use of the preceding model, assume that Sanco, Inc., has developed a direct materials standard of 3 pounds per finished unit at $5.00 per pound. During a recent period the following activity took place:

■ Direct materials purchased and used in production: 6,000 pounds at $5.10 per pound
■ Production completed: 1,900 units

Exhibit 26-8 shows Sanco's price and quantity variances for direct materials, both of which are unfavorable. The unfavorable price variance arose because Sanco paid $0.10 in excess of the $5.00 standard price to acquire needed materials. The unfavorable quantity variance resulted from the company's usage of 300 pounds more than planned (6,000 versus 5,700) in manufacturing activities.

An Illustration of Direct Labor Variances

To explain the computation of direct labor variances, we will continue the previous example. Assume that Sanco has established the following labor standards for each unit of completed product:

■ Direct labor: 2 hours at $6.00 per hour

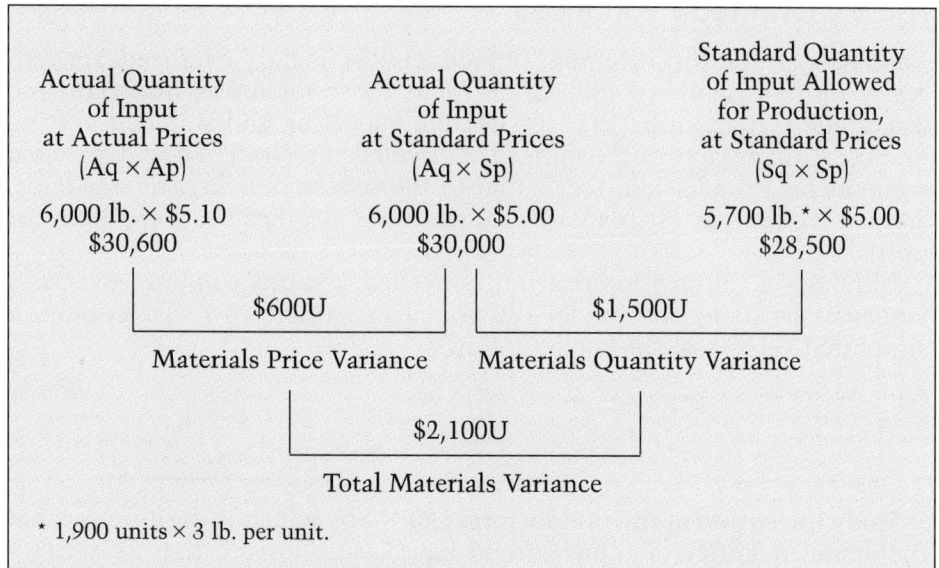

EXHIBIT 26-8
Sanco, Inc., Direct Materials Variances

In producing the 1,900 finished units, direct labor incurred totaled 4,100 hours at $5.80 per hour, or $23,780. The company's direct labor variances are shown in Exhibit 26-9.

As you can see, the labor variance computations are similar to those for materials. Rather than employ pounds and the material purchase price, labor calculations require the respective use of hours worked and the firm's wage rate. Sanco's labor rate variance was favorable because the actual rate paid ($5.80) was $0.20 less than standard. Labor efficiency was unfavorable, however, since actual hours worked exceeded the standard time allowed by 300 hours (4,100 − 3,800 = 300).

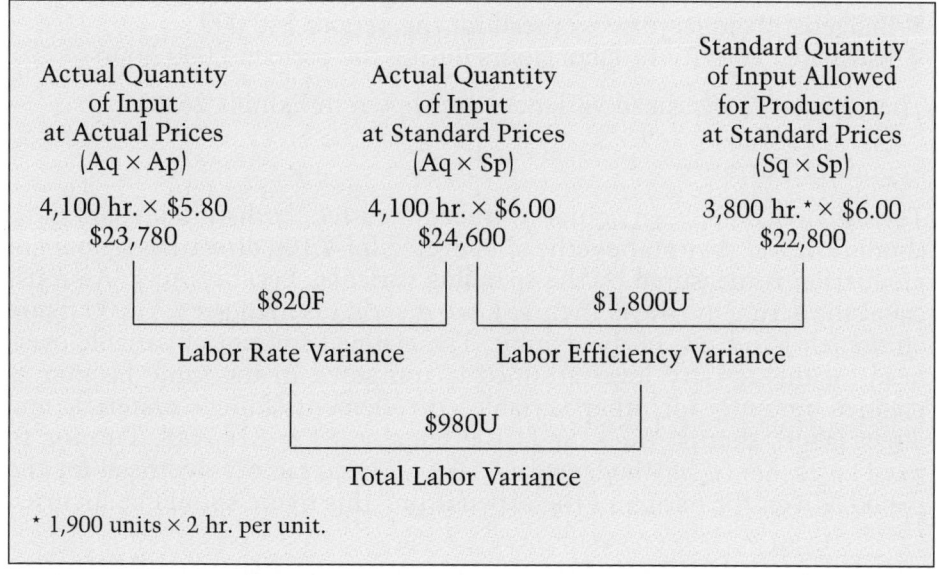

EXHIBIT 26-9
Sanco, Inc., Direct Labor Variances

Factory Overhead Variances

Variances for the third element of product cost, factory overhead, are generally more difficult to understand than those for direct materials and direct labor. Remember that for flexible budgeting and standard costing purposes, manufacturing overhead is divided into its fixed and variable components. In addition, recall that in the setting of overhead standards, an activity level is estimated to calculate the overhead rate per hour (or unit).

Although a minor modification is needed, we can compute overhead variances by using the model illustrated in Exhibit 26-7. To explain, a simplified version of the model follows.

$Aq \times Ap$ $\qquad\qquad\qquad$ $Aq \times Sp$ $\qquad\qquad\qquad$ $Sq \times Sp$

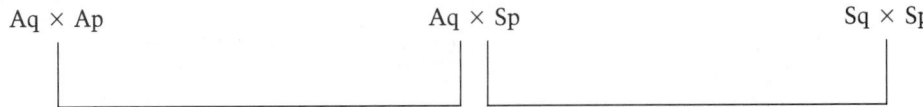

Study the nature of the middle term $(Aq \times Sp)$, which is the amount that the actual quantity of input should have cost. Observe that as activity increases or decreases, the $Aq \times Sp$ expression will fluctuate—a result that is easily seen by picturing the computations for direct materials and direct labor. As production increases, for example, the actual quantity of materials consumed and labor incurred will rise because of the variable nature of the cost functions. With *fixed costs*, however, it is an entirely different story. No matter what the actual level of activity, the same amount of cost should be incurred.[2] The $Aq \times Sp$ expression must therefore remain constant.

Given the foregoing, we can now proceed with the calculation of overhead variances for Sanco, Inc. Assume that Sanco applies overhead to products on the basis of direct labor hours. The following information is available:

- Actual factory overhead incurred (fixed plus variable): $73,000
- Standard variable overhead rate per direct labor hour: $7
- Standard fixed overhead rate per direct labor hour: $10
- Budgeted fixed factory overhead for the period: $40,000
- Estimated activity in labor hours during the period: 4,000 hours

The company's overhead variances are shown in Exhibit 26-10.

Spending Variance

The difference between actual overhead incurred (both variable and fixed combined) and the total overhead budgeted for 4,100 direct labor hours of production is measured by the **spending variance.** Because $Aq \times Ap$ must equal the actual overhead incurred, we merely inserted the $73,000 figure on the left-hand side of the exhibit. The planned amount of variable overhead for the activity level attained is computed in the same fashion as planned amounts for other variable cost elements (direct materials and direct labor), that is, $Aq \times Sp$ (4,100 hours $\times$ $7 = $28,700). Turning to fixed costs, Sanco has budgeted $40,000 of fixed factory overhead for the period. Given the nature of the expenditure, this figure should be incurred

---

[2] We are assuming that a firm is not moving from one activity range to another.

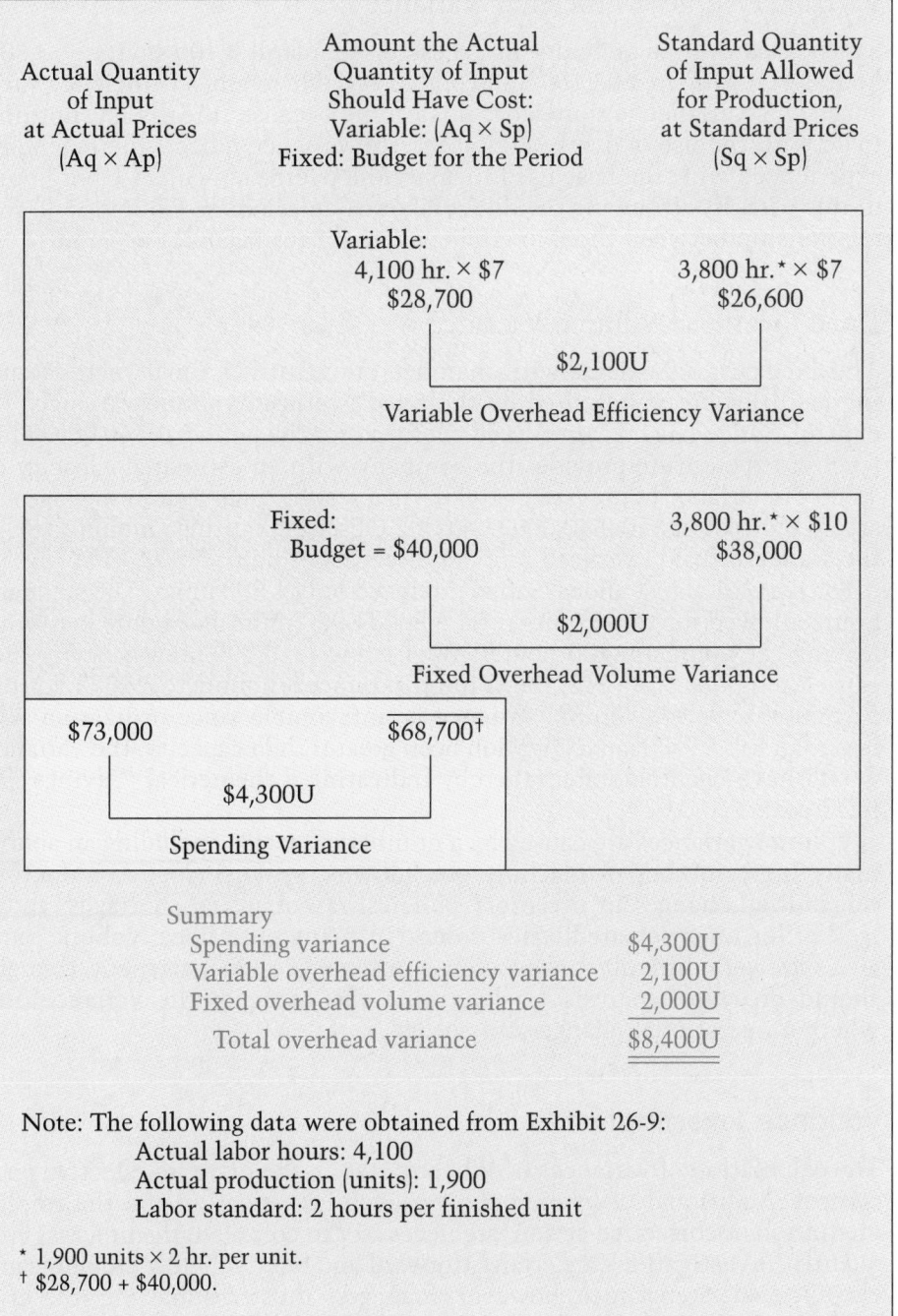

EXHIBIT 26-10
Sanco, Inc., Factory
Overhead Variances

Variable:
4,100 hr. × $7   3,800 hr.* × $7
$28,700 $26,600

$2,100U

Variable Overhead Efficiency Variance

Fixed:
Budget = $40,000   3,800 hr.* × $10
                     $38,000

$2,000U

Fixed Overhead Volume Variance

$73,000 $68,700†

$4,300U

Spending Variance

Summary
Spending variance $4,300U
Variable overhead efficiency variance   2,100U
Fixed overhead volume variance   2,000U

Total overhead variance $8,400U

Note: The following data were obtained from Exhibit 26-9:
        Actual labor hours: 4,100
        Actual production (units): 1,900
        Labor standard: 2 hours per finished unit

* 1,900 units × 2 hr. per unit.
† $28,700 + $40,000.

if direct labor input totals 4,100 hours, 4,200 hours, 4,000 hours, or for that matter, any level of activity within the relevant range.

Because the actual overhead exceeded budgeted amounts by $4,300 [$73,000 − ($28,700 + $40,000)], better control of overhead costs is needed. For effective control to occur, the variance must be further subdivided into its individual cost components (i.e., specific variable and fixed costs) and further related to the proper responsibility centers.

Variable Overhead Efficiency Variance

Sanco used 300 labor hours in excess of standard (4,100 hours − 3,800 hours), resulting in a $2,100 unfavorable **variable overhead efficiency variance.** This variance is somewhat misleading because it really has nothing to do with the use of overhead. Rather, the variance reflects inefficiencies experienced with the base used to apply the overhead—direct labor hours in this case. By reviewing the direct labor calculations in Exhibit 26-9, the relationship between the two efficiency variances becomes apparent.

Fixed Overhead Volume Variance

The fixed costs associated with an under- or overutilization of manufacturing facilities are represented by the **fixed overhead volume variance.** To explain, Sanco has budgeted fixed overhead for the period at $40,000. This level of expenditure provides the company with an estimated capacity of 4,000 direct labor hours (see p. 1088). As a result, each hour has an associated fixed cost of $10 ($40,000 ÷ 4,000). Observe that this amount is Sp— the standard fixed overhead rate per direct labor hour.

For the period just ended, Sanco produced only 1,900 units. The standard hours allowed for these units total 3,800 (1,900 units × 2 hours per unit), leaving the company 200 hours shy of using its 4,000-hour capacity. Because each hour costs $10, the volume variance amounts to $2,000. In this particular case the volume variance is unfavorable since utilization was less than capacity. Had utilization been greater than capacity, the variance would have been favorable, thereby indicating a theoretical "savings" in fixed costs.

Volume variances are caused by a number of factors, including an abnormally high number of machine breakdowns, strikes, sloppy production scheduling, changes in inventory policies, raw material shortages, and a lack of (or unanticipated) sales orders. In many situations, volume variances are very difficult to control or eliminate. Top management, though, should do some analysis to determine the cause of the variance and whether operational changes are needed.

Variance Investigation

OBJECTIVE
6
Describe the problems encountered in the variance investigation process.

The calculation of variances is only one step in the drive for effective cost control. Additional tasks, namely, variance investigation and the implementation of corrective action, are necessary to complete the process. Frequently, investigations are straightforward and relatively few problems are encountered. Sometimes, however, managers must assume the role of a detective to determine both the underlying cause and the correct party to hold accountable for a variance's creation.

In the simplest of cases, a variance arises because of problems directly identified with the production factor itself. For instance, a direct labor rate variance may be caused by a temporary change in the labor mix required for production. Because of illness or perhaps a rush order, workers who earn $7 per hour may be temporarily shifted to jobs that are normally performed by lower-paid employees. Turning to another example, a labor efficiency variance may arise from a lack of proper employee training or morale problems among the workers.

A variance investigation is often complicated by the strong interrelationships that exist among manufacturing activities. Difficulties with machine operation, for instance, can destroy labor efficiency and cause excessive use of raw materials. In a multidepartment setting, sloppy performance in a production department may lead to unfavorable efficiency and spending variances in subsequent assembly work. Furthermore, variance trade-offs may be a factor. A manager may purposely buy subpar materials and hope the accompanying favorable price variance will exceed the costs of any excess usage or additional labor time.

Our discussion thus far has taken the position that actual operations are to blame for the creation of variances. It is possible, of course, that the standard is the problem. Variance investigators should examine standards to determine whether the standards are set correctly and up-to-date. Standards should be reviewed periodically, usually once each year, and adjusted if necessary.

Tips & Techniques

Be aware that both unfavorable *and* favorable variances are candidates for investigation. Although a thorough examination of the latter may seem strange, such studies often prove beneficial. For instance, new production methods that have improved efficiency may be identified and implemented elsewhere in the plant. As another example, favorable spending variances may be investigated in an effort to avoid long-term problems. Such variances in advertising and maintenance could reveal a need to correct inadequate promotion and upkeep programs, respectively.

The Decision to Investigate

Realize that a variance is merely the mathematical difference between two numbers. Like ratios, which were discussed earlier in the text, these measures offer a hint that something is right or that something is wrong. Only in rare circumstances can they tell the complete story.

The decision to investigate normally depends on the size of the variance involved. Large variances are of obvious concern to management; small ones are not. Most firms establish a general guideline, such as, "Review all variances that differ from standard amounts by 10% or $1,000, whichever is lower."

Bear in mind that variance investigation costs money. The cost of determining the cause of a variance and taking the necessary corrective action may very well exceed the amount of the variance under study. Thus, variance review and correction should be based on the principle of cost-benefit analysis—making the evaluation and control of operations a profitable endeavor for the parties involved.

APPENDIX: JOURNAL ENTRIES FOR VARIANCES

OBJECTIVE
7

Integrate standard costs and variances into an accounting system.

Many companies have integrated standards and variances into their formal accounting systems to simplify bookkeeping. Firms can establish and carry a number of accounts at standard and need not keep track of daily fluctuations in input quantities and actual costs. The result is a reduction in record-keeping procedures.

To illustrate the journal entries used in a standard cost system, we will employ data from the Sanco, Inc., example that appears on pages 1086–1090.

Direct Materials

Sanco purchased and consumed 6,000 pounds of direct materials in current production activities. The entry to record the purchase follows.

Raw Materials	30,000	
Materials Price Variance	600	
Accounts Payable		30,600
To record purchase of direct materials		

The Accounts Payable account must be established at the actual amount owed to creditors, specifically, $30,600 (6,000 pounds × $5.10). The price variance is recognized at the time of acquisition to give management immediate feedback that a variance has occurred. Finally, the Raw Materials account is debited for $30,000: the actual quantity of materials purchased multiplied by the $5.00 standard price (6,000 pounds × $5.00 = $30,000).

Direct materials will eventually be taken out of the storeroom and used in manufacturing activities. Because the materials are carried in the accounts at the $5.00 standard price, the following entry is needed to record consumption of 6,000 pounds:

Work in Process	28,500	
Materials Quantity Variance	1,500	
Raw Materials		30,000
To record direct materials used		

The quantity variance is recorded at this time because the excess use of 300 pounds (6,000 − 5,700) is now known. The net result of these two entries is that Work in Process is debited for $28,500—the standard quantity of input times the standard price (5,700 pounds × $5.00 = $28,500).

Note that both the Raw Materials and Work in Process accounts are carried at the standard price and have debit balances. As a result, any amounts in excess of standard (i.e., unfavorable variances) are recorded as additional costs and debited to the proper variance accounts. In contrast, favorable variances are entered as credits.

Direct Labor

Consistent with the procedures just shown, Sanco would record direct labor incurrence in the following manner:

Work in Process	22,800	
Labor Efficiency Variance	1,800	
Labor Rate Variance		820
Wages Payable		23,780
To record direct labor for the period		

Once again, Work in Process is charged for the standard quantity of input multiplied by the standard price (3,800 hours × $6.00 = $22,800). In addition, Wages Payable is established at $23,780, which represents Aq × Ap (the wages actually owed to employees).

Factory Overhead

Actual factory overhead incurred is recorded as:

Factory Overhead	73,000	
Accounts Payable, Raw Materials, and so on		73,000
To record actual factory overhead charges		

Recall from Chapter 22 that because of difficulties in tracing overhead to finished products, each unit manufactured is charged with an estimated amount of overhead via an application rate. The application rate corresponds to the standard price (Sp), as described in the preceding pages. Sanco's variable and fixed overhead rates per direct labor hour amounted to $7 and $10, respectively. To achieve consistency with the accounting treatments for materials and labor, the Work in Process account is again charged with the amount obtained by multiplying the standard quantity of input by the standard price. From the variances computed in Exhibit 26-10, the journal entry to apply overhead to the 1,900 units produced is as follows:

Work in Process	64,600*	
Overhead Spending Variance	4,300	
Variable Overhead Efficiency Variance	2,100	
Fixed Overhead Volume Variance	2,000	
Factory Overhead		73,000
To apply overhead to production		

* Variable + fixed ($26,600 + $38,000 = $64,600).

Subsequent Entries

Upon conclusion of production, an entry is needed to transfer the cost of the completed units to the Finished Goods account. In addition, the variance accounts are either closed to Cost of Goods Sold or, if significant, allocated on a proportional basis among Work in Process, Finished Goods, and Cost of Goods Sold. The latter treatment restates these three accounts from standard cost to actual cost and prevents the generation of misleading financial statements.

When a company experiences significant variances, the cause of the variances should be determined prior to undertaking any allocation procedure. If large variances are caused by abnormal levels of inefficiency, spoilage, and similar factors, allocation to inventory accounts is inappropriate. Such a procedure would result in carrying waste and ineptness as assets on the balance sheet, a treatment that is incompatible with the principles of sound financial accounting. Charging the variances as a loss of the current period may be more appropriate.

END-OF-CHAPTER REVIEW

LEARNING OBJECTIVES: THE KEY POINTS

1 Explain the purpose and structure of a responsibility accounting system. Responsibility accounting involves the division of a company into various segments (e.g., divisions, territories, and so forth), with a manager appointed to oversee each segment's activities. The manager is held accountable for the unit's operating results and is evaluated accordingly.

The units in a responsibility accounting system may be organized as cost, profit, or investment centers. With a cost center, a manager is evaluated on the basis of costs incurred. Departmental heads strive to provide adequate service while keeping costs at a reasonably low level. In contrast, if the unit is organized as a profit center, the performance evaluation focuses on the level of profit generated. Finally, an investment center manager is concerned with the amount of income produced from a given level of asset investment, as measured by the segment's return on assets.

2 Construct and use a flexible budget. A flexible budget is a budget constructed for different levels of operation within the relevant range of activity. Costs are normally subdivided into variable and fixed categories, with amounts often integrated into performance reports once the actual level of activity is known. Flexible budgets are useful in performance evaluations because actual costs can be compared against budgeted amounts for the same volume level.

3 Explain what a standard cost is and how standards are developed. Standard costs are preset targets of performance—targets that are reachable under reasonably efficient operating conditions. These per-unit amounts are easily incorporated into budgets.

Standards are normally established by using a team approach. Engineering and production personnel, for example, are often consulted when determining the amount of direct material that is consumed in a product. Once the proper quantities are known, the standard cost is calculated by using information obtained from the purchasing department. In a similar manner, engineering and production staffs work jointly to compute the direct labor time needed to perform a particular task. The figures are then converted to dollars on the basis of wage rate data furnished by the personnel department.

4 Distinguish between ideal and attainable standards. An ideal standard is one that can be achieved in a perfect operating environment (i.e., maximum efficiency at minimum cost). By setting standards at such high levels, companies hope to improve output as employees increase their efforts to hit the target. Often, however, workers become frustrated in their attempts and morale may suffer. Most companies use attainable standards, or those achievable under efficient, not perfect, operating conditions. The standard is set high enough to motivate employees, but is not so unreasonably high as to cause frustration.

5 Calculate direct material, direct labor, and factory overhead variances. The variances for direct materials and direct labor are easily computed by use of the general model:

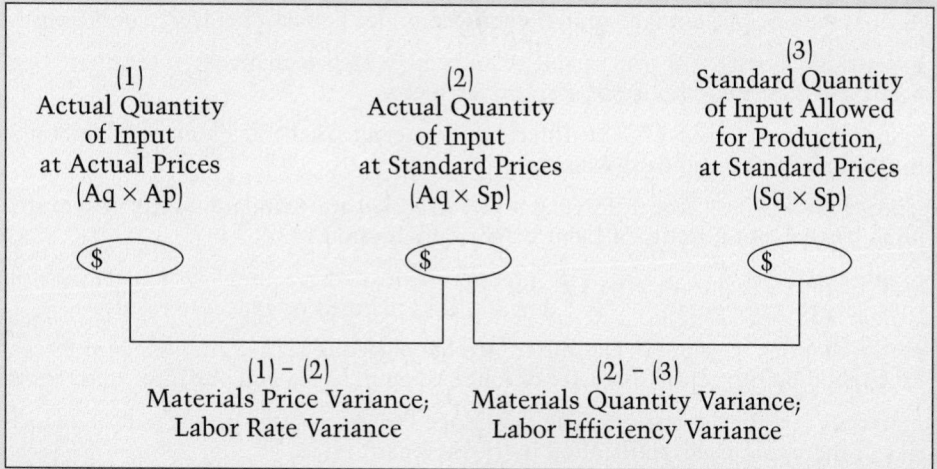

The calculations for factory overhead variances are slightly more complex and may be summarized as follows:

- *Spending variance*—The difference between the actual total overhead incurred (Aq × Ap) and the sum of the amounts budgeted for the actual hours worked (variable, Aq × Sp; fixed, budget for the period).
- *Variable overhead efficiency variance*—The difference between Aq × Sp and Sq × Sp for variable overhead.
- *Fixed overhead volume variance*—The difference between the fixed overhead budgeted for the period and the Sq × Sp computation.

6 Describe the problems encountered in the variance investigation process. A variance investigation involves a look at both actual *and* standard costs. Differences between these two amounts may arise from problems with the production factor itself (e.g., variable overhead) or interrelationships that exist among manufacturing activities. As an example of the latter, problems with labor efficiency may affect the amount of direct materials used during the period. Given that variance investigations are often time-consuming and costly, the decision to investigate is generally made on a cost-benefit basis.

7 (Appendix) Integrate standard costs and variances into an accounting system. Standard costs and variances are integrated into an accounting system by the use of journal entries. Variances are recorded in their own accounts (unfavorable variances by debits and favorable variances via credits). In addition, the entries are structured so that Work in Process, Finished Goods, and Cost of Goods Sold are normally carried at Sq × Sp amounts.

**KEY TERMS
AND CONCEPTS:
A QUICK OVERVIEW**

attainable standard   A standard that can be achieved by efficient, not perfect, operations; allows for normal scrap, waste, and spoilage.

cost center   A responsibility unit in which a manager is held accountable for cost incurrence.

fixed overhead volume variance   A variance that discloses the fixed costs associated with an under- or overutilization of manufacturing facilities.

flexible budget   A budget that covers a range of activity as opposed to a single level.

ideal standard   A standard that is achieved under perfect operating conditions.

investment center   A responsibility unit in which a manager is evaluated on profit and the effective use of asset investment.

labor efficiency variance   The difference between actual and standard labor hours, multiplied by the standard wage rate.

labor rate variance   The difference between actual and standard wage rates, multiplied by the actual hours of labor used in production.

management by exception   The practice of focusing a manager's attention on those aspects of operations that deviate from planned or expected results.

materials price variance   The difference between the actual and standard prices, multiplied by the actual quantity of materials purchased and put into production.

materials quantity variance   The difference between actual and standard quantities of materials used, multiplied by the standard price.

performance report   A report designed to provide the manager of a responsibility center with timely feedback of operating results.

profit center   A responsibility unit in which a manager is held accountable for profit.

responsibility accounting   A reporting system based on the organizational structure of a firm. Managers of each segment are held accountable for operating results and evaluated accordingly.

return on assets   A ratio that measures company profitability from a given level of asset investment. Also called return on investment (ROI).

spending variance   The difference between actual overhead incurred and the total amount of overhead budgeted for production.

standard   A norm used by businesses to measure what should occur under reasonably efficient operating conditions.

static budget   A budget developed for one level of activity.

variable overhead efficiency variance   A variance that reflects inefficiencies experienced with the base used to apply variable overhead cost to production.

CHAPTER QUIZ

The five questions that follow relate to several issues raised in the chapter. Test your knowledge of the issues by selecting the best answer. (The answers appear on p. 1114.)

1 Which of the following statements about responsibility accounting is false?
   a An investment center manager is usually evaluated on the basis of return on assets.
   b Managers should be held accountable for controllable costs.
   c Performance reports tend to be summarized at lower levels of an organization and more detailed at higher levels.
   d Normally, cost centers are not involved with revenue-generating activities.

2 Flexible budgets:
   a tend to result in improved performance reporting.
   b are the same as static budgets.
   c are constructed for one level of activity.
   d normally exclude fixed manufacturing costs.

3 Standard costs:
   a are inconsistent with budgets.
   b should be based on attainable levels of performance.
   c are normally calculated by the accountant without any other departmental input.
   d are calculated for direct materials and direct labor but not factory overhead.

4 Ace Corporation recently completed the manufacture of 4,000 computer tables. Each table's standard direct labor cost is $16 (2 hours at $8 per hour). If the actual payroll totaled $63,990 (8,100 hours at $7.90), the company's labor efficiency variance is:
   a $800F.   c $810F.
   b $800U.   d $810U.

5 The difference between the actual factory overhead incurred during the period and the overhead budgeted for the actual hours worked is known as the:
   a overhead spending variance.
   b variable overhead efficiency variance.
   c fixed overhead volume variance.
   d total overhead variance.

Mahoney, Inc., manufactures a single product and uses a standard costing system. A conversation with the firm's accountant revealed that each unit of finished product has the following material and labor standards:

SUMMARY PROBLEM

■ Direct materials: 4 units @ $2.50
■ Direct labor: 2 hours @ $6.50

Mahoney applies factory overhead on the basis of direct labor hours. Management estimates that budgeted production levels during the upcoming period will require a total of 50,000 direct labor hours. Variable and fixed overhead at this level of activity are estimated to be $150,000 and $275,000, respectively. Additional data follow.
1 Direct materials purchased and consumed during the period totaled 100,000 units at a cost of $2.65 per unit.
2 Direct labor incurred totaled 51,000 hours at a rate of $6.70 per hour.
3 Total overhead incurred amounted to $436,000.
4 Actual production totaled 26,000 units, all of which were completed.

Instructions

a Compute the company's variable and fixed overhead rates per direct labor hour.
b Compute the total standard cost of a finished unit.
c Determine Mahoney's direct materials variances.
d Determine Mahoney's direct labor variances.
e Determine Mahoney's factory overhead variances.

Solution

a Variable Overhead Rate $= \dfrac{\text{Estimated Variable Overhead}}{\text{Estimated Activity}}$

$= \dfrac{\$150,000}{50,000 \text{ direct labor hours}}$

$= \$3 \text{ per direct labor hour}$

$$\text{Fixed Overhead Rate} = \frac{\text{Estimated Fixed Overhead}}{\text{Estimated Activity}}$$

$$= \frac{\$275,000}{50,000 \text{ direct labor hours}}$$

$$= \$5.50 \text{ per direct labor hour}$$

b Direct materials: 4 units @ $2.50 $10.00
   Direct labor: 2 hours @ $6.50   13.00
   Variable overhead: 2 hours @ $3.00*   6.00
   Fixed overhead: 2 hours @ $5.50*   11.00
   Total standard cost per finished unit $40.00

   * From part (a).

c

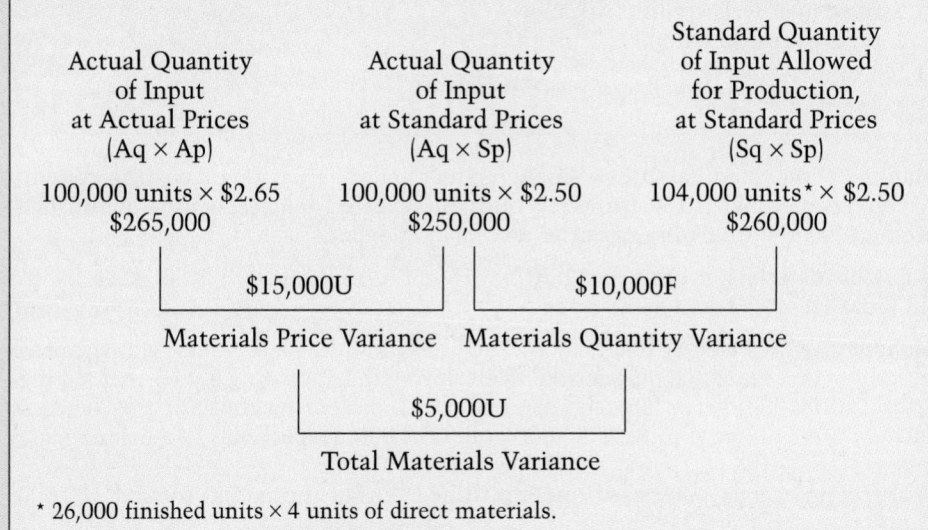

Actual Quantity of Input at Actual Prices (Aq × Ap)
100,000 units × $2.65
$265,000

Actual Quantity of Input at Standard Prices (Aq × Sp)
100,000 units × $2.50
$250,000

Standard Quantity of Input Allowed for Production, at Standard Prices (Sq × Sp)
104,000 units* × $2.50
$260,000

$15,000U
Materials Price Variance

$10,000F
Materials Quantity Variance

$5,000U
Total Materials Variance

* 26,000 finished units × 4 units of direct materials.

d

Actual Quantity of Input at Actual Prices (Aq × Ap)
51,000 hr. × $6.70
$341,700

Actual Quantity of Input at Standard Prices (Aq × Sp)
51,000 hr. × $6.50
$331,500

Standard Quantity of Input Allowed for Production, at Standard Prices (Sq × Sp)
52,000 hr.* × $6.50
$338,000

$10,200U
Labor Rate Variance

$6,500F
Labor Efficiency Variance

$3,700U
Total Labor Variance

* 26,000 finished units × 2 hr. per unit.

e

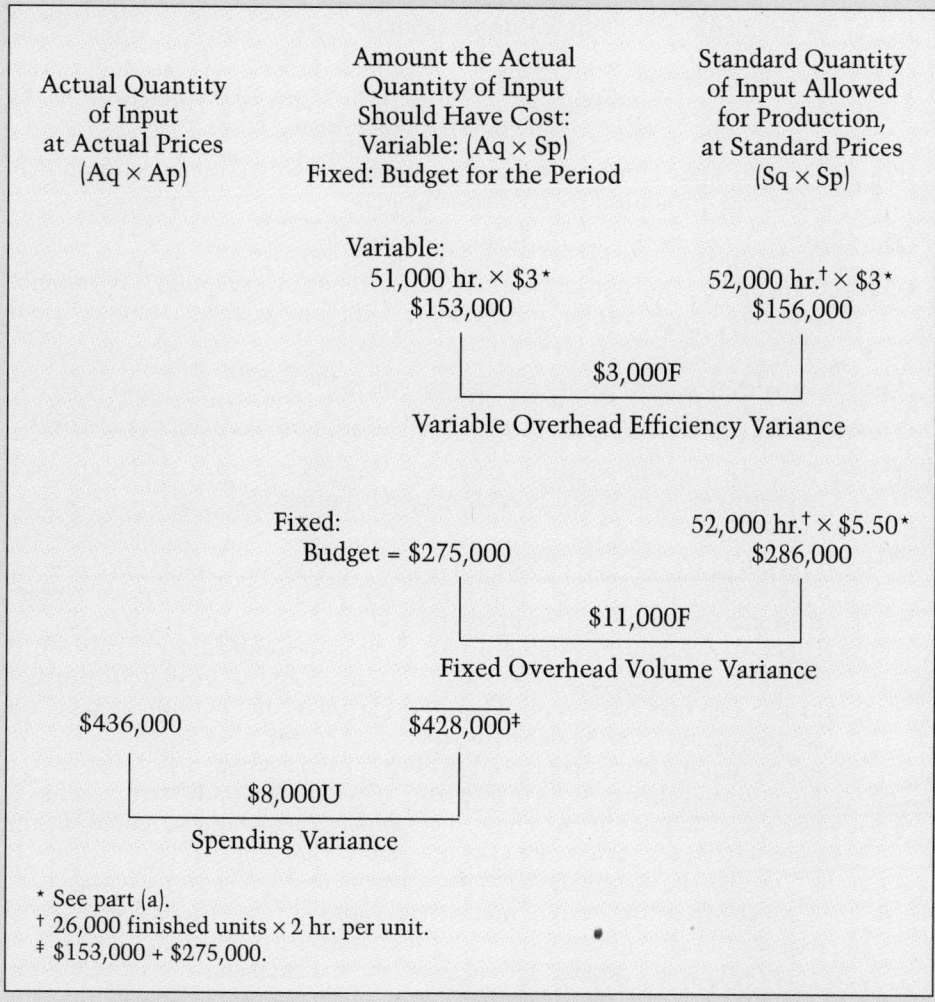

Actual Quantity of Input at Actual Prices (Aq × Ap)

Amount the Actual Quantity of Input Should Have Cost: Variable: (Aq × Sp) Fixed: Budget for the Period

Standard Quantity of Input Allowed for Production, at Standard Prices (Sq × Sp)

Variable:
51,000 hr. × $3*   52,000 hr.† × $3*
$153,000 $156,000

$3,000F

Variable Overhead Efficiency Variance

Fixed: 52,000 hr.† × $5.50*
Budget = $275,000 $286,000

$11,000F

Fixed Overhead Volume Variance

$436,000 $428,000‡

$8,000U

Spending Variance

* See part (a).
† 26,000 finished units × 2 hr. per unit.
‡ $153,000 + $275,000.

ASSIGNMENT MATERIAL

Q26-1 Briefly discuss the features associated with a responsibility accounting system.

Q26-2 Should a cost center manager strive for cost minimization? Why?

Q26-3 Differentiate between a profit center and an investment center.

Q26-4 Describe the flow of information in a typical responsibility reporting system.

Q26-5 Generally speaking, are performance reports more summarized at lower or higher levels of an organization?

Q26-6 Differentiate between a static budget and a flexible budget.

Q26-7 Explain the relationship, if any, between a standard cost and a flexible budget.

QUESTIONS

Q26-8 Identify the parties normally involved in establishing the following:
a Price standards for materials
b Efficiency standards for direct labor

Q26-9 An engineer once commented: "Standards must be based on a perfect operating environment, as anything less assumes inefficient working conditions." Evaluate the engineer's comment.

Q26-10 Why do some companies use ideal standards? What often occurs shortly after the introduction of ideal standards?

Q26-11 What is meant by an attainable standard?

Q26-12 Explain the concept known as "management by exception." Is variance analysis consistent or inconsistent with management by exception? Why?

Q26-13 Should managers investigate all variances? Why?

*__**Q26-14**__ Are favorable variances recorded in the accounts as debits or credits?

*__**Q26-15**__ List two possible methods of accounting for variances at the end of a reporting period. When is each method appropriate?

EXERCISES

E26-1 *Cost centers and profit centers* (L.O. 1)
Crest Manufacturing produces a single product at its Albany plant. Units are processed through departments A and B and then sent to finished goods. The firm has a maintenance department that performs repair jobs for the manufacturing departments.

The maintenance operation has always been evaluated as a cost center. Now with a change in management, a switch to a profit center setup is being considered. Prices charged for repair jobs would be based on the maintenance department's cost of operations.
a Discuss the difference between a cost center and a profit center.
b Mike Mizer, the head of maintenance, has always operated with a cost minimization philosophy. Will the change to a profit center likely alter the quality of service provided by the maintenance department? Explain your answer.
c What will be the reaction of the manufacturing departments to the change to a profit center? Consider the probable effect on the number of service requests when structuring your answer.

E26-2 *Flexible budgets and performance reports* (L.O. 2)
Ventura Headgear has experienced various labor problems in recent months, including two work stoppages during May. Management was therefore pleased to learn that May's production costs resulted in a $66,000 favorable variance, as follows:

	Budget	Actual	Variance
Direct materials used	$120,000	$ 99,000	$21,000F
Direct labor	180,000	148,000	32,000F
Variable factory overhead	90,000	72,000	18,000F
Fixed factory overhead	100,000	105,000	5,000U
Total production costs	$490,000	$424,000	$66,000F

---

* An asterisk preceding an item indicates that the material is covered in an appendix to this chapter.

The budget was based on an anticipated production level of 15,000 units, but only 11,000 units were manufactured.

a Prepare a performance report for Ventura by using the flexible budgeting approach.

b Compare the report prepared in part (a) with that originally given to management. Comment on (1) a major cause of the $66,000 favorable variance and (2) whether management should be pleased with May's performance.

E26-3 *Flexible budgets and performance reports* (L.O. 2)

Home Products, Inc., uses flexible budgeting for cost control and performance evaluations. A review of the company's master budget found that management expects to produce 8,000 units each month, resulting in annual expenditures for direct labor and supervisory salaries of $307,200 and $806,400, respectively. Supervisory salaries, a fixed cost, are spread evenly throughout the year. If October's production amounted to 7,800 units and a $2,900 unfavorable direct labor variance was reported, determine:

a The actual direct labor cost that appeared in the October performance report.

b The budgeted amount for supervisory salaries that appeared in the October performance report.

E26-4 *Variances for direct materials and direct labor* (L.O. 5)

Frank Wallace & Sons manufactures various products for industrial use. The following costs relate to the manufacture of the firm's leading product, a heavy-duty cleaner:

Direct materials
    Actual: 460,000 pounds purchased and consumed at a cost of $3.20 per pound
    Standard: 5 pounds per finished container at a cost of $3.25 per pound
Direct labor
    Actual: 17,800 hours at an average wage rate of $8.40 per hour
    Standard: 0.2 hours per finished container at an average wage rate of $8.50 per hour

Compute variances for direct materials and direct labor assuming that 90,000 finished containers were manufactured during the period.

E26-5 *Variances for direct materials and direct labor* (L.O. 5)

Banner Company manufactures flags of various countries. Each flag has a standard of eight square feet of fabric and three hours of direct labor time. Information about recent production activity follows.

Actual cost of fabric: $4.50 per square foot
Fabric consumed: 32,080 square feet
Standard price per square foot of fabric: $4.25
Standard direct labor rate: $10.00 per hour
Actual direct labor rate: $10.20 per hour
Actual labor hours worked: 11,940
Actual production completed: 4,000 flags

a Compute the materials price variance and the materials quantity variance.

b Compute the labor rate variance and the labor efficiency variance.

E26-6   *Variance analysis: Working backward* (L.O. 5)
Auto Lube performs oil changes and other minor maintenance services
(e.g., tire pressure checks, fluid checks, and so forth). The company advertises that all services are completed in 15 minutes. Eighty cars were
serviced on a recent Saturday, resulting in the following labor variances:
rate, $18U; efficiency, $64U. If the labor rate standard is $4 per hour,
determine the:
a Standard hours allowed for Saturday's work.
b Actual hours worked.
c Actual wage rate.

E26-7   *Computation and analysis of food variances* (L.O. 5, 6)
Executive Chefs provides food service to various airlines at New York's
LaGuardia Airport. The company uses a standard cost system and is very
concerned about cost control.
   During a recent two-day period, the firm prepared 1,600 seafood plat-
ters. Standards for the platter are 0.5 pounds of fresh fish at $4 per pound.
A performance report for this period follows and showed nothing un-
usual.

	Budget	Actual	Variance
Fresh fish	$3,200	$3,264	$64U

The company's purchasing director resigned shortly after the report was
distributed. A review of the accounting records showed that Executive
Chefs bought and consumed 1,020 pounds of seafood.
a Compute the company's price variance and quantity variance.
b Evaluate the company's activity over the two-day period. Include in
   your answer a possible reason behind the purchasing director's resignation.

E26-8   *Determining the effect on variances* (L.O. 5, 6)
Consider the following events that relate to Consolidated Industries:
a A machine malfunction caused higher-than-normal spoilage rates and
   required increased attention by the machine operator.
b The company had to absorb unexpected air freight charges on a rush
   order of direct materials.
c A slowdown occurred on the production line because of low morale
   among the workers.
d The local power company raised its rates by 5%.
e The firm hired 10 part-time workers to meet an increase in production
   levels. Consolidated had to pay premium wages because of a shortage
   of qualified help.

   Picture the nature of the materials variances (price and quantity) and
labor variances (rate and efficiency). Determine which variances, if any,
are affected by each event and whether the variance will be favorable or
unfavorable. *Note:* If a revision of standards is necessary, assume that no
revision occurs until the next accounting period.

E26-9   *Overview of standards and variances* (L.O. 3, 4, 5)
Evaluate the comments that follow as being True or False. If the comment is false, briefly explain why.
a The direct labor rate variance is computed as the difference between
   the actual and standard pay rates, multiplied by the actual hours
   worked.

b By hiring employees who possess below-average skill levels, a company is likely to generate favorable labor rate variances and unfavorable labor efficiency variances.
c In most cases, ideal standards are preferable to attainable standards.
d Standard costs are generally integrated into a company's budgets.
e An unfavorable volume variance indicates that fixed overhead incurred exceeded budgeted amounts.

E26-10 *Overhead variances* (L.O. 5)

Nova Manufacturing applies factory overhead to products on the basis of direct labor hours. At the beginning of the current year, the company's accountant made the following estimates for the forthcoming period:

- Estimated variable overhead: $500,000
- Estimated fixed overhead: $400,000
- Estimated direct labor hours: 40,000

It is now 12 months later. Actual total overhead incurred in the manufacture of 7,900 units amounted to $895,100. Actual labor hours totaled 39,800. Assuming a direct labor standard of five hours per finished unit, calculate the following:
a Variable overhead efficiency variance
b Fixed overhead volume variance
c Overhead spending variance

E26-11 *Overhead variances* (L.O. 5)

Chen Company employs a standard costing system. The standard cost sheet for one of its products follows.

Direct materials: 3 pounds @ $5.00	$ 15.00
Direct labor: 6 hours @ $6.50	39.00
Variable factory overhead: 6 hours @ $7.00	42.00
Fixed factory overhead: 6 hours @ $3.00	18.00
Total	$114.00

Total overhead incurred during June amounted to $445,000, of which $295,000 was variable. Budgeted fixed overhead of $1.8 million is spread evenly throughout the year. Finally, Chen's labor force worked a total of 40,000 hours during the month in producing 7,000 finished units.

Determine Chen's spending variance, variable overhead efficiency variance, and fixed overhead volume variance. Be sure to label the variances as favorable or unfavorable.

*E26-12 *Standard costs and journal entries* (L.O. 7)

Hutchins, Inc., has established the following standards for direct materials and direct labor for product no. 781:

Direct materials: 4 pounds @ $2.50 per pound	$10.00
Direct labor: 2 hours @ $8.00 per hour	16.00

The information below pertains to a recent month.
1 Purchases of direct materials amounted to 9,000 pounds at a total cost of $23,850.
2 Nine thousand pounds of direct materials were consumed in operations to manufacture 2,300 finished units.
3 Direct labor charges totaled 4,750 hours at $7.90 per hour.

a Compute the price and quantity variances for direct materials.

b Determine the rate and efficiency variances for direct labor.

c Prepare journal entries to record the transactions that relate to direct materials and direct labor.

PROBLEMS

Series A

P26-A1 Basic flexible budgeting (L.O. 2)

Centron, Inc., has the following budgeted production costs:

Direct materials	$0.40 per unit
Direct labor	1.80 per unit
Variable factory overhead	2.20 per unit
Fixed factory overhead	
Supervision	$24,000
Maintenance	18,000
Other	12,000

The company normally manufactures between 20,000 and 25,000 units each quarter. Should output exceed 25,000 units, maintenance and other fixed costs are expected to increase by $6,000 and $4,500, respectively.

During the recent quarter ended March 31, Centron produced 25,500 units and incurred the following costs:

Direct materials	$ 10,710
Direct labor	47,175
Variable factory overhead	51,940
Fixed factory overhead	
Supervision	24,500
Maintenance	23,700
Other	16,800
Total production costs	$174,825

Instructions

a Prepare a flexible budget for 20,000, 22,500, and 25,000 units of activity.

b Was Centron's experience in the quarter cited better or worse than anticipated? Prepare an appropriate performance report and explain your answer.

c Explain the benefit of using flexible budgets (as opposed to static budgets) in the measurement of performance.

P26-A2 Setting standards (L.O. 3, 4)

Starr Manufacturing Corporation is considering the implementation of a standard costing system. The information that follows pertains to one of the company's products, HD-24.

Direct materials used*		$1,020,000
Direct labor†		348,000
Other traceable variable costs		
Blending costs	$148,000	
Packaging materials	40,700	
Miscellaneous	74,000	262,700
Total variable costs		$1,630,700

* 240,000 gallons at $4.25 per gallon.
† 58,000 hours at $6.00 per hour.

These costs were incurred in the production of 185,000 gallons of HD-24, which were packaged four gallons to a case. Starr has been experiencing problems with the quality of materials used and plans to change suppliers in the forthcoming period. The price per gallon of direct materials is expected to rise to $4.40. The company anticipates that HD-24 output will total 80% of the direct materials used in production; the remainder is lost through evaporation.

Management estimates that abnormal production problems in the prior period led to the incurrence of an additional 2,500 labor hours. These problems have been corrected and are not expected to recur. Other variable costs are anticipated to remain stable, with the exception of packaging materials. Packaging cost is expected to increase by $0.04 per gallon.

Instructions

a By analyzing the data presented, compute an attainable standard variable cost for a case of HD-24.

b Compare and contrast ideal and attainable standards. What benefits normally result from the use of attainable standards?

c Discuss several problems that may be encountered in the standard-setting process by relying too heavily on past experience.

P26-A3 *Straightforward variance analysis* **(L.O. 5)**

AV Corporation manufactures a single product and uses a standard cost system. The following information was taken from the company's accounting records:

1-2-3

	Standard	Actual
Direct materials		
Cost per gallon	$6.50	$6.30
Gallons per finished unit	5	
Direct labor		
Cost per hour	$10.50	$10.70
Hours per finished unit	3.0	2.8
Factory overhead		
Total overhead incurred		$402,000
Variable overhead rate per hour	$3.00	
Fixed overhead rate per hour	$7.00	
Units produced		12,900

AV purchased and used 65,000 gallons of direct materials during the period. Budgeted fixed factory overhead was $280,000.

Instructions

a Compute the company's variances for direct materials.

b Compute the company's variances for direct labor.

c Compute the company's variances for factory overhead. AV applies factory overhead to products on the basis of direct labor hours.

P26-A4 *Variance analysis and interpretation* **(L.O. 1, 5, 6)**

Imtex Manufacturing uses a standard costing system. The variable cost standards for product no. 628 follow.

Direct materials: 3.2 pounds @ $5 $16.00
Direct labor: 8.5 hours @ $8   68.00
Variable overhead: 8.5 hours @ $3   25.50

The company has been experiencing rough times of late, with constant complaints from customers about poor product quality. In addition, the production supervisor is very unhappy with the performance reports that he receives to monitor factory operations. A typical report appears as shown.

IMTEX MANUFACTURING
Performance Report
For the Month Ended June 30, 19X3

	Actual	Standard	Variance
Direct costs*	$XX,XXX	$XX,XXX	$XX,XXX
Factory overhead	XX,XXX	XX,XXX	XX,XXX
Total	$XX,XXX	$XX,XXX	$XX,XXX

* Direct materials + direct labor.

In an effort to improve product quality, the supervisor has campaigned for a change to a better supplier and the hiring of more competent employees. He has recently been given permission to pursue both of these alternatives. Actual data follow.
1 Direct materials purchased and consumed amounted to 6,000 pounds at $5.80 per pound.
2 Direct labor incurred in the manufacture of 2,000 completed units totaled 15,400 hours at $10.50 per hour.
3 Variable overhead incurred totaled $47,200.

Instructions

a Suggest several ways that Imtex's performance report could be improved to provide better information for the supervisor.
b Prepare a complete variance analysis for direct materials, direct labor, and variable overhead. *Note:* Compute the overhead spending variance with regard to variable overhead only.
c Does the production supervisor's plan seem to be working? Discuss.

P26-A5 *Variance analysis: Working backward* (L.O. 5)

Marvel Company has a single manufacturing department that applies factory overhead on the basis of direct labor hours. Selected department information follows.

Cost of materials purchased and consumed	?
Materials standard per finished unit	3 pounds
Standard material cost per pound	$4
Materials price variance	$4,370U
Materials quantity variance	$8,600F
Actual labor hours worked	?
Labor standard per finished unit	5 hours
Standard labor rate per hour	$7

Labor rate variance	$22,800U
Labor efficiency variance	$14,000F
Total actual overhead incurred	?
Standard variable overhead rate	$2 per hour
Standard fixed overhead rate	$6 per hour
Budgeted fixed overhead	?
Variable overhead efficiency variance	?
Fixed overhead volume variance	$12,000U
Overhead spending variance	$4,800U
Number of units manufactured	8,000

Instructions

Determine each of the unknowns. *Hint:* It is helpful to solve separate models simultaneously for materials, labor, and overhead by filling in the given information.

*P26-A6 *Variance analysis and journal entries* (L.O. 7)

Southeast Manufacturing has integrated standard costs and variance reporting into its formal accounting system. The standard costs per finished unit follow.

Direct materials: 2 gallons @ $7.40	$14.80
Direct labor: 3 hours @ $10.00	30.00
Variable overhead*	6.00
Fixed overhead*	4.50
Total	$55.30

* Applied on the basis of direct labor hours.

Other data are:

- Purchases of direct materials: 20,000 gallons at $7.35 per gallon
- Direct labor incurred: 29,900 hours at a cost of $304,980
- Total overhead incurred amounted to $109,400; overhead variances were as follows:

Spending variance	$ 400F
Variable overhead efficiency variance	200F
Fixed overhead volume variance	5,000U

- Actual production amounted to 10,000 finished units, and direct materials consumption conformed to original predictions.

Instructions

a Determine Southeast's variances for direct materials.
b Determine Southeast's variances for direct labor.
c Prepare journal entries to record the following:
  (1) Direct materials purchases
  (2) Direct materials issued to production
  (3) Direct labor incurred
  (4) Factory overhead incurred
  (5) Factory overhead applied to production

Series B

P26-B1 *Basic flexible budgeting* (L.O. 2)

Paragon, Inc., normally manufactures between 36,000 and 42,000 units each month. A static budget based on 36,000 units and actual results for April follow.

	Budget	Actual
Direct materials	$172,800	$175,900
Direct labor	270,000	258,000
Variable factory overhead	115,200	109,000
Supervision	105,000	82,600
Insurance & taxes	60,000	61,500
Depreciation	84,000	88,000
	$807,000	$775,000

Conversations with Paragon's accountant revealed the following information:

1 April's production totaled 35,000 units.
2 Supervision, insurance and taxes, and depreciation are fixed costs.
3 Should production fall below 36,000 units, supervision costs are expected to be reduced by $20,000 because of temporary layoffs.

Instructions

a Prepare a flexible budget for 36,000, 39,000, and 42,000 units of activity.
b Prepare a performance report for April that can be used to judge Paragon's success or failure in meeting budgeted targets. Comment on your findings.
c Explain the flexibility that is associated with a flexible budget.

P26-B2 *Setting standards* (L.O. 3, 4)

Rencore, Inc., manufactures wooden bookends for office and home use. Wood is cut, shaped, and processed into the completed product. Just prior to completion and the attachment of felt pads that prevent scratches on furniture, the wood is inspected for defects. The following information is available:

■ Normally, 104 bookends must be processed for every 100 good units completed.

■ Each pair of bookends requires 2.5 board feet of lumber at $1.40 per board foot.

■ Each bookend has four felt pads on its base. Last year, when 15,000 pair were manufactured, pad cost amounted to $3,600. Rencore's management was just informed of a $0.01-per-pad price hike by the felt supplier.

■ All direct laborers are paid $12 per hour. Expected labor times for a pair of bookends are:

Cutting, shaping, and processing	15 minutes
Finishing (attaching felt pads, polishing)	1 minute

■ Actual packaging costs recently totaled $0.32 per pair, which was $0.02 higher than standard. Because of a change to a sturdier, more attractive box, the standard should be increased by 10%.

Instructions

a On the basis of the information presented, calculate an attainable standard cost for materials and labor for a pair of bookends.

b What parties would typically participate in the development of material and labor standards? What roles would these parties play?

c Assume that management is studying a decrease in labor time for the cutting, shaping, and processing operations to 14 minutes per pair even though the company's work force views 15 minutes as more realistic.

　(1) Would any benefits result from setting a tighter standard for Rencore's workers?

　(2) What problems might result from the change to a 14-minute standard?

P26-B3 *Straightforward variance analysis* (L.O. 5)

Arrow Enterprises uses a standard costing system. The standard cost sheet for product no. 549 follows.

Direct materials: 4 units @ $6.50	$ 26.00
Direct labor: 8 hours @ $8.50	68.00
Variable factory overhead: 8 hours @ $7.00	56.00
Fixed factory overhead: 8 hours @ $2.50	20.00
Total standard cost per unit	$170.00

The following information pertains to activity for December:

1 Direct materials acquired during the month amounted to 26,350 units at $6.40 per unit. All materials were consumed in operations.

2 Arrow incurred an average wage rate of $8.75 for 51,400 hours of activity.

3 Total overhead incurred amounted to $508,400. Budgeted fixed overhead totals $1.8 million and is spread evenly throughout the year.

4 Actual production amounted to 6,500 completed units.

Instructions

a Compute Arrow's direct material variances.

b Compute Arrow's direct labor variances.

c Compute Arrow's variances for factory overhead.

P26-B4 *Variance analysis and interpretation* (L.O. 1, 5, 6)

Cisco Industries uses a standard costing system to assist in the control of operations. The company's May performance report for variable manufacturing costs follows.

CISCO INDUSTRIES **Performance Report** **For the Month Ended May 31, 19X7**	
Direct materials variance, favorable	$ 300
Direct labor variance, favorable	600
Variable overhead variance, favorable	100
Total variances, favorable	$1,000

The president is extremely satisfied with the figures. He notes: "It looks like we've finally gotten operations under control. Apparently the change to a new supplier did the trick. In addition, I think the new supervisor is working out well. I've noticed a much happier and more efficient work force on my daily tours through the plant."

Assume that the following information has come to your attention.

1 Standard variable costs per unit of finished product:

Direct materials: 2.5 pounds @ $2.00	$ 5.00
Direct labor: 3.2 hours @ $7.00	22.40
Variable overhead: 3.2 hours @ $5.00	16.00
Total standard variable cost per unit	$43.40

2 Direct materials purchased and consumed amounted to 8,400 pounds at $1.75 per pound.
3 Direct labor incurred in the manufacture of 3,000 completed units totaled 11,100 hours at $6.00 per hour.
4 Variable factory overhead incurred amounted to $47,900.

Instructions

a Criticize the format and content of the performance report as currently constructed.
b Prepare a complete variance analysis for direct materials, direct labor, and variable overhead. *Note:* Compute the overhead spending variance with regard to variable overhead only.
c Explain the results of your findings to the president. Are things going as smoothly as the president believes? Discuss.

P26-B5 *Variance analysis: Working backward* (L.O. 5)

Hampton, Inc., has a single manufacturing department that applies factory overhead on the basis of direct labor hours. Selected departmental information follows.

Cost of materials purchased and consumed	$46,250
Materials standard per finished unit	4 pounds
Standard material cost per pound	?
Materials price variance	$5,550U
Materials quantity variance	$3,300F
Actual labor hours worked	6,000 hours
Labor standard per finished unit	1.5 hours
Standard labor rate per hour	$6
Labor rate variance	$4,500U
Labor efficiency variance	?
Total actual overhead incurred	$80,500
Standard variable overhead rate per hour	?
Standard fixed overhead rate	$8 per hour
Budgeted fixed overhead	$64,000
Variable overhead efficiency variance	$4,500F
Fixed overhead volume variance	?
Overhead spending variance	?
Number of units manufactured	5,000

Instructions

Determine each of the unknowns. *Hint:* It is helpful to solve separate models simultaneously for materials, labor, and overhead by filling in the given information.

*P26-B6 *Variance analysis and journal entries* (L.O. 7)

Evergreen Manufacturing has integrated standard costs and variance reporting into its formal accounting system. The standard costs per finished unit follow.

Direct materials: 2 pounds @ $3.25	$ 6.50
Direct labor: 0.75 hours @ $8.00	6.00
Variable overhead*	3.00
Fixed overhead*	5.25
Total	$20.75

* Applied on the basis of direct labor hours.

Other data are:

- Purchases of direct materials: 30,000 pounds at $3.35 per pound
- Direct labor incurred: 11,400 hours at a cost of $90,630
- Total overhead incurred amounted to $125,000; overhead variances were as follows:

Spending variance	$4,600F
Variable overhead efficiency variance	600U
Fixed overhead volume variance	5,250U

- Actual production amounted to 15,000 finished units, and direct materials consumption conformed to original predictions.

Instructions

a Determine Evergreen's variances for direct materials.
b Determine Evergreen's variances for direct labor.
c Prepare journal entries to record the following:
  (1) Direct materials purchases
  (2) Direct materials issued to production
  (3) Direct labor incurred
  (4) Factory overhead incurred
  (5) Factory overhead applied to production

BB26-1 *Responsibility accounting and variances* (L.O. 1, 3)

BEYOND THE BASICS

Burdick Manufacturing is a small producer of decorative accessories used in the home. Various materials are carefully shaped and formed by skilled craftsmen, with the final product being sold in fine furniture stores and specialty shops. The company uses responsibility accounting and has recently installed a new computerized standard cost system. The system has been tested thoroughly and is operating correctly.

Six weeks ago, the firm's sales manager accepted a large rush order for a nonstock item from a valued customer. The sales manager forwarded the order to Joe Perry, the production supervisor. Perry, in turn, filed the necessary paperwork with the purchasing department so that needed raw materials could be acquired. Unfortunately, a purchasing clerk temporarily lost the paperwork, and by the time it was located, it was too late to order from the normal supplier. A new supplier was found, who quoted a very attractive price. When the materials arrived, production personnel found them to be of poor quality.

Perry has recently returned from vacation, only to be confronted by Burdick's manufacturing vice-president about "inept performance in the period just ended." A heated discussion took place, with Perry being told to shape up or ship out.

Instructions

a Briefly explain the essence of a responsibility accounting system.
b What variances for materials and labor would *ordinarily* be controllable by and appear on a production supervisor's performance report?
c Briefly explain the probable reason behind the heated confrontation between Perry and the manufacturing vice-president. Does the manufacturing vice-president have a valid reason to be upset? Why?
d Given that the company has a responsibility accounting system, what could be done to correct the situation? Briefly discuss.

BB26-2 *Overview of chapter concepts: Multiple choice* (L.O. 1–6)
The following multiple-choice questions relate to various topics discussed in the chapter. Select the best answer.

1 Responsibility accounting:
   a focuses on the costs that a manager can control.
   b dictates that cost center managers minimize the amount of cost incurred.
   c requires a reporting system in which summarized information is used extensively by lower-level managers and detailed information is used by top executives.
   d prohibits the use of return on assets to evaluate investment centers.

Questions 2 and 3 are based on the following facts:
   Bryer Corporation developed a budget that included direct material costs of $200,000, direct labor of $50,000, variable factory overhead of $75,000, and fixed factory overhead of $107,000. Planned production was 50,000 units. Actual units manufactured totaled 60,000 and actual costs were: direct materials, $210,000; direct labor, $60,000; variable factory overhead, $100,000; and fixed factory overhead, $104,000.

2 If Bryer employed a static budget, the variance between total budgeted production costs and actual production costs would be:
   a $23,000 favorable.   c $42,000 favorable.
   b $23,000 unfavorable.   d $42,000 unfavorable.

3 If a performance report was prepared by using flexible budgeting concepts, the variance between total budgeted production costs and actual production costs would be:
   a $23,000 favorable.   c $42,000 favorable.
   b $23,000 unfavorable.   d $42,000 unfavorable.

4 Which of the following statements about standard costs is incorrect?
   a Standards are per-unit amounts, to be incorporated into a company's budget.
   b The development of standards is normally a team effort that involves the accountant, manufacturing personnel, engineers, and employees from the purchasing department.
   c Ideal standards usually result in a number of favorable variances.
   d Attainable standards are used to avoid behavioral problems on the part of employees.

5 Marion Manufacturing has set the standard rate per hour of direct labor at $6.00. During a recent period, the company's actual hourly labor rate was $5.75, standard hours worked totaled 10,000, and the labor effi-

ciency variance was $1,200U. The labor hours actually worked during the period were:

a 9,800.   c 10,200.

b 10,000.   d 10,209.

Questions 6 and 7 are based on the following facts:

Whitfield Company has developed standard overhead costs based on a capacity of 360,000 labor hours (or 90,000 completed units of production). The standard variable overhead rate is $3 per hour, and the standard fixed overhead rate is $5 per hour. During a recent period, only 80,000 finished units were produced. These units required 330,000 hours of labor time; actual total overhead was $2,756,000. Whitfield's budgeted fixed factory overhead was $1,800,000.

6 The company's overhead spending variance is:

a $34,000U.   c $76,000U.

b $34,000F.   d $76,000F.

7 Whitfield's fixed overhead volume variance is:

a $120,000U.   c $200,000U.

b $120,000F.   d $200,000F.

8 Variance investigation:

a requires a detailed look at all variances that arise.

b should focus only on unfavorable variances.

c is normally based on a cost-benefit analysis.

d is usually a fairly straightforward task.

CAI26-1 *The follow-up message* (L.O. 5, 6)

Communication Principle: Business relationships are carefully built and nurtured. Customers must be solicited and satisfied, and a quality network of suppliers must be established and monitored. Although considerable energy is typically expended in building such associations, continued *support* of the relationship is often neglected. This situation is mostly human nature—we grow content with the status quo or take a good thing for granted.

To help further these alliances, lines of communication should be opened and maintained in much the same way as a company does routine maintenance on equipment. The ongoing communications should have a theme. For example, when dealing with a supplier, an occasional note or phone call is in order and may take the following forms:

- Just wanted to thank you for a dependable delivery schedule.
- Checking in to make sure that our payments are in a form and timing that are convenient for you.
- We have been experiencing some difficulties with your sales representative and thought you might want some feedback.

In each case you are accomplishing multiple goals: strengthening the association; providing positive feedback; furnishing an early indication of a problem that might grow if unchecked; and so forth. In the long run, such communication paves the way for continued good relations and establishes a pool of goodwill that affected parties can draw upon if major difficulties arise.

■ ■ ■ ■ ■ ■ ■ ■

Consider the three scenarios that follow.

COMMUNICATION OF ACCOUNTING INFORMATION

- *Scenario A.* Adobe Company's material quantity variances reveal that excessive amounts of material are being used in production. The excess usage reflects a higher-than-normal defect rate associated with a part provided by Adobe's key supplier. The supplier should be notified and told that it is important for the situation to be corrected.
- *Scenario B.* The materials price variance of Heritage Corporation is favorable because of a supplier's special "customer appreciation" discount. The discount was totally unexpected.
- *Scenario C.* Fastrac Wholesale, a major supplier, has sent you a very nice personal gift. The gift must be returned because accepting it would violate your company's ethics policy.

Instructions

Draft an appropriate letter, note, or memo to the three suppliers. You may assume that prior dealings have put you on a "first-name" basis with a contact person in each of the firms.

Answers to Chapter Quiz

1 c

2 a

3 b

4 b [(Aq × Sp) − (Sq × Sp) = (8,100 hours × $8) − (8,000 hours × $8) = $800. The variance is unfavorable because actual hours exceeded standard hours.]

5 a

Decision Making and Contribution Reporting

LEARNING OBJECTIVES

After studying this chapter, you should be able to:

Demonstrate the effect of relevant costs and
sunk costs on decision making.

Evaluate different types of decision situations (e.g., make or buy).

Explain why the contribution margin must be analyzed
in terms of capacity constraints.

Distinguish between direct costs and indirect costs.

Prepare and use a contribution income statement.

Identify the features of direct (variable) costing and absorption
costing and prepare the related income statements.

Managers make a variety of decisions that are critical to the short- and long-term profitability and solvency of an enterprise. As evidence, examine the recent decisions of several well-known corporations that are shown in Exhibit 27-1. Future events will determine whether these actions were wise or whether alternatives would have been preferable.

Accountants play a significant role in decision making. Accounting information is continually generated to assist management in problem solving and in evaluating subsequent performance. Furthermore, in many firms the accountant actually assumes the role of a decision maker and selects from among alternative courses of action. The extent of this role is dependent on the overall philosophy of top management and the accountant's position in the organizational hierarchy.

This chapter is the first of a two-chapter sequence that explores the fundamentals of decision making. Although much of our presentation will focus on the decision process from a business viewpoint, many of the concepts illustrated are relevant to individuals as well. Students, employees, and family members are continually confronted with financial problems or issues that need attention. Knowing how to correctly evaluate alternatives can therefore be highly valuable in attempts made to improve one's financial position and well-being.

GENERAL APPROACH TO DECISION MAKING

OBJECTIVE
1

Demonstrate the effect of relevant costs and sunk costs on decision making.

EXHIBIT 27-1
Recent Business Decisions

Over time, management faces a number of different decisions. Certain decisions, such as the selection of a supplier for raw materials, are fairly routine; others occur with less regularity and are relatively complex (e.g., the addition or deletion of a product line). Some decisions affect only current operations, whereas others will have a significant impact for years to come. No matter what the decision, cost is bound to be a major factor. Stated simply, the costs related to one course of action must be compared against those of alternative strategies and policies.

Corporation	Decision
Blockbuster Entertainment	Acquired the largest home video retailer in the United Kingdom
Bristol-Myers Squibb	Entered into a research and development agreement with the National Cancer Institute
Colgate-Palmolive	Formed a joint venture to make and sell Colgate toothpaste in China
ITT Sheraton	Constructed new hotels in Africa and Southeast Asia
Mattel	Agreed to participate in attractions at three Disney theme parks and develop theme park toys
The Limited	Opened 434 new stores and hired 11,300 sales associates
Turner Broadcasting	Added more than 3,000 Hanna-Barbera cartoons to the company's programming base

Because of the variety inherent in the decision process, a general approach to decision making is extremely useful. The general approach first involves the identification of future costs, specifically, those associated with the decision at hand. To illustrate, assume that management is studying whether to replace an existing machine with a newer, more efficient model. Expected future costs must be evaluated, because these amounts will be the only ones incurred as a result of making the decision. Past historical costs may serve as a basis for predicting what the future costs will be, but *old costs are just memories and are not considered in the selection of alternatives.*

The next step in the general approach is to focus on **relevant costs,** or future costs that differ among alternative courses of action. In the replacement decision just cited, for example, any differences in maintenance costs between the old machine and the new machine are relevant and must be considered. Future costs that are identical for both pieces of equipment can be ignored, as such amounts have no impact on the ultimate selection.

Full Project or Incremental Approach?

Relevant costs can be studied by using either a full project or an incremental approach. As an example, assume that Merchants Company must make a delivery 150 miles from its warehouse (300 miles for a round trip). Two trucks are available: A and B. Truck A gets 10 miles per gallon and consumes one quart of oil every 100 miles. Truck B gets 7.5 miles per gallon and uses one quart of oil every 150 miles. Other data are as follows:

Gasoline	$1 per gallon
Oil	$2 per quart
Driver's wage	$6 per hour
Trip time	8 hours
Road tolls	$10

The costs of operating the two trucks are shown below.

	Truck A	Truck B	Difference
Gasoline*	$30	$ 40	$10
Oil†	6	4	(2)
Driver's wage (8 hours × $6)	48	48	—
Tolls	10	10	—
Total cost	$94	$102	$ 8

* Truck A: [(300 miles ÷ 10 miles per gallon) × $1] = $30.
  Truck B: [(300 miles ÷ 7.5 miles per gallon) × $1] = $40.

† Truck A: [(300 miles ÷ 100 miles per quart) × $2] = $6.
  Truck B: [(300 miles ÷ 150 miles per quart) × $2] = $4.

On the basis of the expected costs, the company should use truck A. Notice that the driver's wage and road tolls are the same for both vehicles, making these two items "nonfactors" in the selection process. Given this situation, the proper approach would have been to focus solely on the cost of gasoline and oil. These costs are relevant because they will be incurred in the future and will differ between the trucks.

If using the **full project approach,** management would compare $36 against $44 (gasoline + oil cost) to make the proper decision. Specifically, the total relevant costs associated with each alternative are evaluated. Conversely, with the **incremental approach,** only the net differences are considered. Management would therefore focus its attention on the $8 variation that appears in the right-hand column, which favors vehicle A.[1]

Although the incremental approach is often used in practice, it has two serious drawbacks. The method is cumbersome when more than two alternatives are being evaluated, and the act of netting often leads to mathematical errors. For these reasons we will stress the full project approach throughout the remainder of this chapter.

Decision Making: An Emphasis on the Future

Observe that the thrust of decision making is a focus on the future. Let us expand on this idea by concentrating on a problem faced by Malibu Construction, a builder of custom homes in southern California. Recently, the company agreed to build a spacious home for a valued customer. Work on the project began several months ago and is nearing completion. Most of the remaining work involves optional decorative accessories, landscaping, and the construction of a swimming pool and a tennis court. To date, Malibu has spent $650,000 on the project in the form of materials, labor, and overhead. Much to the dismay of management, the customer has just declared bankruptcy and must back out of the contract.

Malibu has conducted a thorough study of available alternatives and identified two courses of action:

1 Sell the unfinished residence as is for $610,000.

2 Make several design changes at a cost of $80,000 and complete the project. The company has found a buyer who is willing to pay $700,000 for the home if the changes are made.

A conventional "income statement" analysis reveals the undesirability of both alternatives. As the following figures show, losses will be incurred regardless of the selected option:

	Sell As Is		Redesign	
Revenue		$610,000		$700,000
Costs				
Existing	$650,000		$650,000	
Additional	—	650,000	80,000	730,000
Loss		$ (40,000)		$ (30,000)

Malibu's president, obviously displeased, was overheard saying: "We've already got $650,000 in this venture. Incurring a loss on top of all this would be foolish."

The Concept of Sunk Cost

A careful inspection of the preceding figures will reveal an inconsistency with the general approach to decision making that was illustrated earlier.

---

[1] Costs that differ among alternatives are sometimes called **differential costs.**

Notice that the existing cost of $650,000 is common to both alternatives and, therefore, should have no effect on the eventual selection.

This amount is considered a **sunk cost**—a past cost that has already been incurred. Regardless of whether Malibu sells the residence as is or pursues the redesign option, the existing costs are like "water under the bridge" and cannot be changed by management's actions. *Sunk costs are thus an irrelevant consideration in decision making.*

How, then, should the evaluation be made? A more appropriate analysis would be as follows:

	Sell As Is	Redesign
Revenue	$610,000	$700,000
Additional future costs	—	80,000
Net benefit from sale	$610,000	$620,000

With a focus on future revenues and costs that differ among the alternatives (i.e., those that are *relevant*), the analysis shows that Malibu should spend $80,000 for the redesign work and sell the estate for $700,000. In comparison with the "as is" sale, the company will be better off by $10,000 ($620,000 − $610,000).

Qualitative Factors

In addition to quantitative considerations, various qualitative factors must be addressed in the decision-making process. **Qualitative factors** are those whose evaluation in terms of dollars is impossible or, at best, difficult. As an example, the manager in the Merchants Company truck illustration may decide to send Truck B on the delivery because the vehicle is brand new and customer impressions are important. Or, in another situation, machine operators may rebel if they are not given a say in the proposed acquisition of new equipment. Such action would be detrimental to the firm and could lead to low morale and decreased productivity.

The preceding factors, although not quantifiable, can be important and should not be disregarded. Quite honestly, however, most business decisions are based primarily on dollars. Qualitative issues are perhaps most significant when the mathematical difference between alternatives is small and management needs a "tie breaker."

A Summary of the Decision-Making Approach

The general approach to decision making can be summarized as follows:

1 Identify each alternative and examine the future costs (and revenues).

2 Disregard items that are the same among the alternatives.

3 Identify and consider the qualitative factors.

4 Make a decision after studying both the quantitative analysis and the qualitative concerns.

These steps can be applied to many different decision-making areas. The next few sections of the chapter will explore several of these areas, including make or buy decisions, special order pricing, and the addition or deletion of products or departments.

ETHICS ISSUE

Your boss has promised a $20,000 bonus if you prepare a report showing that Division A is unprofitable and should be sold. To do so you would have to include several irrelevant costs that will probably go unnoticed. What would you do?

MAKE OR BUY DECISIONS

OBJECTIVE
2

Evaluate different types of decision situations (e.g., make or buy).

Manufacturing firms often purchase needed parts for their operations from outside suppliers. As an example, the roughly six million components of a Boeing 747-400 come from 1,500+ different companies. (About the only items Boeing itself makes are the wings.)[2] Even Burger King acquires its hamburger meat from outsiders. Interestingly, many of the firms that rely on external sources of supply have the technical abilities to produce the needed parts and materials themselves. Apparently, an analysis has deemed the purchase alternative preferable.

The choice to produce internally or to rely on external suppliers is commonly known as a *make or buy* decision. To illustrate the proper approach to follow in this decision situation, assume that Crane Company, a manufacturer of mopeds, is now producing all of its own motors. As shown in the following analysis, the motors cost $75 each, based on an output of 10,000 units per year.

	10,000 Motors	Per Motor
Direct materials	$180,000	$18
Direct labor	390,000	39
Variable factory overhead	100,000	10
Fixed factory overhead*	80,000	8
Total cost	$750,000	$75

* Allocated on the basis of capacity used.

Crane has solicited an offer from an external supplier to provide 10,000 motors at a set price of $72 each. To determine whether the motors should be manufactured internally or purchased externally, management must isolate the relevant costs. Future costs that differ between the make and buy alternatives must be studied. Sunk costs, in contrast, should be ignored.

In reviewing the previous information, we see that motor production was charged with $670,000 of variable costs, specifically, direct materials, direct labor, and variable factory overhead. Being variable, these costs will be eliminated if the motors are acquired from an outside supplier. The variable costs are thus relevant in an analysis of the make and buy alternatives. Turning to the fixed costs, Crane has allocated $80,000 of fixed factory overhead to motor production. In view of their fixed nature, these costs will be incurred even if the company decides in favor of an external purchase. As you already know, amounts that are the same among alternatives can be disregarded.

Avoidable Fixed Overhead

Frequently, when operations undergo a significant change, total fixed costs do not remain static. If manufacturing activities are discontinued, for example, it is conceivable that a production supervisor would be dismissed

---

[2] See "No More Weekend Stands," *Forbes*, September 17, 1990, pp. 191–92.

and some equipment leases terminated. Naturally, any future fixed costs that change should be included in the analysis.

In Crane's case, suppose that fixed factory overhead can be reduced by $20,000 if production is stopped. The following analysis indicates that management should reject the supplier's offer, because there is a $30,000 advantage in favor of manufacturing internally.

| | 10,000 Motors | |
	Make	Buy
Purchase		$720,000
Direct materials	$180,000	
Direct labor	390,000	
Variable factory overhead	100,000	
Avoidable fixed factory overhead	20,000	
Total cost	$690,000	$720,000
	$30,000 difference	

The preceding evaluation is straightforward with the possible exception of the avoidable fixed overhead. Realize that Crane will incur $80,000 of fixed overhead if the motors are produced internally and $60,000 of fixed overhead if they are acquired from suppliers. Thus, $20,000 of fixed costs must be associated with the manufacturing option.

Looking at the analysis from a slightly different perspective, we observe a $20,000 savings in fixed costs if the purchase alternative is selected. Therefore the net cost of dealing with an outside supplier is $700,000 ($720,000 − $20,000). Manufacturing costs would now consist solely of variable items and would total $670,000, which still maintains the $30,000 difference in favor of production ($700,000 − $670,000 = $30,000).

Qualitative Considerations

Given the quantitative outcome, we must also explore the qualitative factors that surround each alternative. In make or buy decisions, the decision to purchase externally means more dependence on suppliers and the attendant worry about product quality, strikes against suppliers, transportation strikes and hazards, personnel changes at suppliers' offices, and product discontinuance. To many companies, the quality concern alone would dictate rejection of the purchase alternative.

Opportunity Cost

In performing a complete analysis of make versus buy, management must also evaluate alternative uses of manufacturing facilities. If, for example, a decision is made to acquire goods externally, the purchaser's factory and equipment may remain idle. On the other hand, such decisions frequently release facilities for use in other production applications. In the Crane Company illustration, for instance, suppose the resources committed to motor production could be redirected toward making a new line of golf carts. Naturally, any income from the golf cart line would be lost if the firm continues its motor operation.

The cost of a forgone alternative is termed **opportunity cost.** If the golf carts promise to generate a *contribution margin* (i.e., sales minus variable costs) of $75,000, the make or buy decision will assume the following form:

	Make	Buy
Cost of buying		$720,000
Cost of making	$690,000	
Forgone contribution on golf carts	75,000	
Total cost	$765,000	$720,000

$45,000 difference

The analysis now shows that the company would benefit by $45,000 if it acquired the motors from the outside supplier. Explained differently, Crane is willing to pay an additional $30,000 per year to purchase the motors, in exchange for $75,000 of contribution margin provided by the golf carts.[3]

Tips & Techniques

Be aware that opportunity costs are not restricted to make or buy decisions. Such costs arise in many different settings (e.g., the evaluation of competing job offers) and must be considered if the proper alternative is to be selected. Despite their importance, opportunity costs are *not* entered in the accounting records nor do they appear on a company's financial statements. Financial accounting reports transactions and events that have occurred, not those that have been rejected.

SPECIAL ORDER PRICING

The pricing of special orders is another decision faced by many firms. Although businesses prefer to sell their products at the highest prices possible, economic conditions sometimes dictate otherwise. Various situations may arise where special orders are considered at prices that are less than optimum. In an effort to reach the proper decision, management must again focus on the differential (or incremental) costs and revenues involved.

As an example, assume that Smithfield Bicycle Company received an inquiry from a large national retailer to provide 20,000 R-18 racing bicycles at a price of $77 each. The bicycles will be marketed under the retailer's brand name. Although Smithfield has sufficient (idle) manufacturing capacity, management is reluctant to accept the order because the price is

---

[3] The same analysis in another format would show the net cost of buying to be $645,000 ($720,000 purchase cost − $75,000 contribution generated). The decision maker would then compare $645,000 against $690,000 and still note a $45,000 advantage in favor of the buy alternative.

well below the company's normal selling price of $119. The costs that follow pertain to the R-18 bicycle.

Materials	$ 42.80
Labor	24.50
Factory overhead*	24.70
Variable selling costs	10.00
Total	$102.00

* Eighty percent of the factory overhead represents fixed cost.

At first glance it appears that the retailer's offer should be rejected because it fails to cover the $102 total cost. However, further investigation reveals that variable selling costs will not be incurred on the order. Furthermore, in view of the fact that Smithfield currently has idle facilities, total fixed costs are not expected to change. Eighty percent of the factory overhead ($24.70 × 0.80 = $19.76) will therefore be present even if the offer is refused and can be disregarded. The following analysis shows that Smithfield would benefit by doing business with the retailer:

Special selling price		$77.00
Less variable costs		
Materials	$42.80	
Labor	24.50	
Variable factory overhead ($24.70 − $19.76)	4.94	72.24
Contribution margin per bicycle		$ 4.76

Recall from Chapter 24 that the contribution margin is the amount each unit generates toward covering fixed costs and producing net income. Given the preceding figures, acceptance of the special order will result in an overall profitability boost of $95,200 (20,000 bicycles × $4.76). Although each unit yields less than the normal R-18 sale, Smithfield has machines and other resources already in place that are not being used to the fullest extent possible. Thus, some extra business is really "icing on the cake."

Several qualitative issues must be addressed in this decision, including the following:

■ Will there be a decrease in sales of Smithfield's own brand of R-18 bicycle?
■ Are future orders from the retailer likely?
■ Will plant capacity devoted to the special order soon be needed for Smithfield's regular production activity?

Contribution Margin in Relation to Capacity

In addition to the special order situation, managers frequently study contribution margins when dealing with capacity constraints. Let us focus on a multiple-product company that is operating at capacity. The firm must evaluate which orders to accept and which to reject, and which products to

OBJECTIVE

3

Explain why the contribution margin must be analyzed in terms of capacity constraints.

EXECUTIVE BRIEFING
Orange Bowl Sponsorship: A Matter of Cost Versus Benefit

Carole Presley
Senior Vice-President
Federal Express Corporation

No matter what the form, companies make decisions by exploring the costs and benefits of decision alternatives. Consider, for instance, our firm's sponsorship of the Orange Bowl football game—a perfect example of reaping major benefit from the partnering of two highly compatible entities. The Orange Bowl has widespread appeal among the diverse groups in the FedEx customer base and reflects the high regard in which consumers generally hold the company.

Consequently, Federal Express realizes a far greater return than its investment in the big event. The return comes from the exposure it receives via commercials within the game and on-field graphics, as well as the incremental business the company gains by inviting key decision makers to attend a four-day seminar/sports entertainment gathering. While a little over $2 million per year is invested in sponsoring the event, the benefits in terms of exposure, incremental business, and stronger relationships can be measured by at least a tenfold annual return over the initial outlay.

promote and which to de-emphasize. The goal is to maximize contribution margin of the entire business, not just of one small facet. A common error in pursuing this goal is that given the resources available, items with the highest contribution margin per sales dollar are considered to be the most attractive.

To illustrate, assume that Beltline Manufacturing produces two models of computer furniture: Deluxe and Regular. The following information has been gathered:

	Deluxe	Regular
Selling price	$120	$80
Less variable cost	60	48
Contribution margin	$ 60	$32
Contribution margin ratio (contribution margin ÷ selling price)	50%	40%

It appears that the firm should concentrate its activity on the Deluxe model. Before we decide for certain, however, let us introduce some additional information. Suppose the furniture is extremely popular, with demand far exceeding the company's production capabilities. Further, it takes four hours to produce a Deluxe model and two hours to manufacture a Regular model. If only 30,000 labor hours are available during the period, Beltline would be better off to focus its efforts on the Regular model because of a higher payoff *per labor hour.*

	Deluxe	Regular
Contribution margin per labor hour		
Deluxe: $60 ÷ 4 hours	$15	
Regular: $32 ÷ 2 hours		$16
Available labor hours	30,000	30,000
Contribution margin per labor hour	× $15	× $16
Total contribution margin	$450,000	$480,000

The analysis shows that the Regular model provides the greatest total contribution given the firm's limited manufacturing resources. It should now be apparent that when a company is operating at capacity, management may be in error by emphasizing products or services that provide the greatest contribution per unit or per sales dollar. Stated simply, *contribution margin must be analyzed in terms of factors that limit its generation.*

Limiting factors assume many different forms, depending on the type of business. In heavily automated manufacturing companies, for example, the limiting factor is often the machine hours available for production. In entertainment situations it is the number of seats in a theater or an arena. Finally, in retail operations it is floor space.

ADDITION OR DELETION OF PRODUCTS OR DEPARTMENTS

Decisions to add or delete products, departments, and other major operating units (e.g., stores, plants, or divisions) are critical. Any errors that are made can normally be corrected only after suffering years of financial strife. In-depth analysis is therefore of utmost importance.

When a business unit is eliminated, the unit's sales are lost and there is a savings in variable costs. As a result, if a positive contribution margin is being generated and the unit is discontinued, overall profitability will suffer. One additional factor must be considered, however, and that is the behavior of fixed costs. As we noted earlier in the chapter, a significant change in operations will often influence the amount of fixed costs incurred by an enterprise. If a department or segment is eliminated, some fixed costs can normally be avoided. Those costs that can be avoided are really differential costs and, therefore, relevant to the decision.

To illustrate addition and deletion decisions, we will study the operations of Foodway, Inc., which owns a chain of supermarkets. Each Foodway store has four major departments: groceries, meat, produce, and hardware. Earnings data for store no. 175 during the past year are shown in Exhibit 27-2. On the basis of the reported $1.1 million loss, management believes that total profitability will increase if the hardware department is closed. A closer look at the figures and overall operation is needed, however, prior to any action being taken.

If customers remain loyal and sales in the other departments are not affected by the discontinuance of hardware, Foodway's profit will immediately decline by $1 million because of the loss in contribution margin. Notice, though, that the hardware department has four types of fixed costs: salaries, utilities, depreciation, and general and administrative. Specific information about these costs appears below the exhibit.

	Groceries	Meat	Produce	Hardware	Total
Sales	$42,000,000	$14,000,000	$7,000,000	$ 7,000,000	$70,000,000
Less variable costs	33,000,000	9,000,000	4,000,000	6,000,000	52,000,000
Contribution margin	$ 9,000,000	$ 5,000,000	$3,000,000	$ 1,000,000	$18,000,000
Less fixed costs					
Salaries	$ 2,000,000	$ 2,500,000	$1,900,000	$ 1,100,000	$ 7,500,000
Utilities	400,000	50,000	100,000	150,000	700,000
Depreciation	100,000	50,000	100,000	50,000	300,000
General & administrative	4,800,000	1,600,000	800,000	800,000	8,000,000
Total fixed costs	$ 7,300,000	$ 4,200,000	$2,900,000	$ 2,100,000	$16,500,000
Net income (loss)	$ 1,700,000	$ 800,000	$ 100,000	$(1,100,000)	$ 1,500,000

EXHIBIT 27-2
Foodway, Inc., Store no. 175:
Departmental Income
Statements

1 The salaries represent amounts paid to employees who work in the department. If hardware is dropped, employees who earn 40% of the salary amounts will be shifted to other areas. All other personnel in hardware will be discharged.

2 Utilities expense is allocated to each department on the basis of square feet. Total utilities cost is not expected to change significantly if the hardware operation is closed.

3 Depreciation relates to the building and also to the fixtures used in each department. If hardware is eliminated, the department's display racks and equipment will be utilized by other segments of the firm. Again, total cost is not expected to change.

4 General and administrative charges represent the costs of functions common to all departments, including purchasing, accounting, and personnel. These costs, allocated to each department on the basis of sales, will be reduced by $120,000 because of employee terminations.

In view of this information, the following analysis can be made:

Contribution margin lost if hardware is dropped		$1,000,000
Less avoidable costs		
Salaries ($1,100,000 × 0.60)	$660,000	
General & administrative	120,000	780,000
Decrease in total company income		$ 220,000

Although hardware's present bottom line indicates a loss of $1.1 million, it is still beneficial to retain the department, because the contribution produced is greater than the avoidable costs.

If desired, the same conclusion could have been reached by evaluating Foodway's earnings with and without the hardware department:

HIGHLIGHT

A College Student + Good Decisions = Million$

Shown his writeup in his 1983 high school yearbook, Michael Dell groans. He's hunched over a computer, his eyes hidden behind the glare of bottle-thick glasses. A nerd if ever there was one.

Nerd no longer, Dell at 26 wears contact lenses and fashionable suits. He and his wife, Susan, work out on mountain bikes and ski all the big resorts. Dell is also about $300 million richer than he was in 1983. Only in America. Only in computerland. Dell was one of the first to make inexpensive IBM clones. He pioneered the practice, now fairly widespread, of selling and servicing computers by telephone and through mail-order catalogs.

As a kid growing up on the west side of Houston, Michael wanted to "make more money than any other kid in school." Working after school selling subscriptions to the *Houston Post*, he found that recently married couples were the best prospects. He began collecting newlyweds' names from marriage licenses filed at the county courthouse, created a data base, and used personalized subscription solicitations. At 18, Dell was setting sales records and making $18,000 a year.

In the fall of 1983, Michael enrolled at the University of Texas. He regarded the campus more as a market than a source of learning. He bought an IBM PC and soon, between classes, was putting together kits to be used to upgrade IBM PCs and selling them to computer enthusiasts. Before his first semester was over, Michael was buying computer dealers' excess inventories of IBM PCs at cost and selling through the local newspaper and national computer magazines. With little or no overhead he could undercut retail stores. By the time his second semester rolled around, Dell was grossing big money— $30,000 in January, $80,000 by April. Dell was 19.

Then his parents paid him a surprise visit. He rushed to hide the computers stockpiled in his dorm room. Into his roommate's bathtub they went. Where are your schoolbooks, son, the parents wanted to know. He hadn't bothered to buy any. Dell and his parents came to an agreement: If Mi-

chael finished all his spring courses, he could run his business in the summer. If the business didn't fly, he'd have to return to school in the fall.

Dell started his new business as PC's Ltd., leasing 1,000 square feet of cheap office space and continuing to advertise. He was selling $180,000 worth of computers a month by September. Next came a small team of engineers to design his own IBM clone, a move to larger quarters, and the hiring of assembly workers. His telemarketers were soon offering machines for as little as $795, about 40% less than IBM charged. In fiscal 1986, his first year selling Dell-designed PCs by mail, revenues quintupled, to $34 million.

With cash in hand, Dell moved beyond mail order into selling machines to corporations. The corporate venture paid off, with nearly half of Dell's sales now generated by major corporate, government, and educational accounts. Skeptics said Europeans would never buy computers by mail. Again Dell proved the skeptics wrong. Recently, international sales were 34% of the firm's business. Dell has subsidiaries in 10 countries and recently began shipping from a new assembly plant in Ireland.

What now? Michael is pushing Dell Computer to add more value to the basic machines it sells. Salespeople, for example, now sell computer systems tailored to a customer's needs by adding software programs from Lotus, Microsoft, and other suppliers. "We want to be suppliers of entire systems," Dell says. At the same time he is moving to broaden his distribution by selling in stores. The goal is to sell in stores at prices not much higher than mail-order customers pay.

Can Dell Computer keep its position as a low-cost manufacturer and distributor in this more complex side of the business? That's the next big test Michael Dell faces. Regardless, he has already made quite a mark for himself in the history of the computer business. How? It's called one good decision, followed by another good decision, followed by yet one more.

Source: Adapted from "The Kid Who Turned Computers into Commodities," *Forbes 400*, October 21, 1991, pp. 318–19, 322. Excerpted by permission of *Forbes* magazine, © Forbes Inc., 1991.

	With Hardware	Without Hardware
Sales	$70,000,000	$63,000,000
Less variable costs	52,000,000	46,000,000
Contribution margin	$18,000,000	$17,000,000
Less fixed costs		
Salaries	$ 7,500,000	$ 6,840,000
Utilities*	700,000	700,000
Depreciation*	300,000	300,000
General & administrative	8,000,000	7,880,000
Total fixed costs	$16,500,000	$15,720,000
Net income (loss)	$ 1,500,000	$ 1,280,000

$220,000 difference

* These amounts are irrelevant to the decision and could have been omitted from the analysis.

Improvements in Performance Reporting

OBJECTIVE

4

Distinguish between direct costs and indirect costs.

The departmental income statements prepared for Foodway, Inc., are fairly traditional in scope and format. By a minor restructuring of the data, it is possible to improve the statements' usefulness in the evaluation of operations. Before we explain the underlying procedures, it is necessary to reintroduce (and slightly modify) a cost classification scheme that was discussed in Chapter 22.

Many costs within an organization are easily traced to and associated with a business segment, whereas other costs are not. Amounts that fall in the first category are called **direct costs;** those in the latter classification are **indirect costs.** A business segment normally refers to a responsibility center of the firm, such as a territory, division, department, and so on.

Because a segment can be defined in different ways, a given cost may be direct with respect to certain segments and indirect with respect to others. In the Foodway example, for instance, utilities expense was easily traced to store no. 175. However, it was an entirely different story when the store tried to associate the expense with smaller segments—in this case, departments. Tracing was much more difficult, leading management to adopt cost allocation procedures. Total utilities expense was related to the total square feet in the store, yielding a cost per square foot. Each department was then charged an appropriate amount, based on the area occupied.

Cost Allocations

Companies have adopted a variety of allocation procedures that range from the simple to the complex. The reason normally advanced for such procedures is that indirect costs are incurred to benefit multiple responsibility centers (e.g., departments). As such, each center should absorb its "fair share" of the expenditures.

Although this argument is sound, most accountants recognize that cost allocations have two serious deficiencies. First, as you saw earlier in the text with depreciation, the same cost can be allocated several different ways. At best, then, allocations are arbitrary. A given allocation method is generally viewed as adequate or inadequate by a responsibility center, depending on the amount charged. Large cost allocations are branded as unfair; small cost allocations, in contrast, receive few complaints. Turning to the second deficiency, the total cost to be allocated normally results from the decisions of other managers in the organizational hierarchy. Thus, to a large degree, the amount of cost charged to a center is beyond the center's control.

Contribution Income Statement

It appears that when costs are allocated to business segments, the final income figure does not present a clear measure of the segment's operating results. In recognition of this fact, accountants have developed the **contribution income statement.** This statement provides top management with an understanding of how individual centers affect total firm profitability and serves as a useful tool in performance evaluation and decision making. Consistent with responsibility accounting, the statement incorporates the following features:

OBJECTIVE

5

Prepare and use a contribution income statement.

1 The contribution margin is disclosed.

2 Fixed costs directly identifiable with a segment are divided into two classifications: controllable and uncontrollable.

3 Allocations of nontraceable costs are disregarded.[4]

To illustrate the contribution income statement, we will study EXOIL Corporation. EXOIL is divided into two divisions: Refining and Retailing. Retailing, in turn, has two major product lines: Parts and Fluids. Exhibit 27-3 contains the firm's contribution statements. The top half of the exhibit shows EXOIL's divisional operations; the bottom half displays Retailing's product lines.

The contribution statement begins with a display of a segment's contribution margin, that is, sales minus variable costs. Variable costs are considered to be controllable by (and traceable to) responsibility centers because the costs vary with center activity. The calculation of the contribution margin is helpful not only for performance evaluation but also for cost-volume-profit (CVP) analysis, such as determination of the break-even point.

Controllable Contribution Margin. Next, the **controllable contribution margin** is computed by subtracting fixed costs that are both controllable by the segment's management *and* directly traceable to the segment. Such costs are usually discretionary fixed costs (i.e., those that arise from management's decision-making process) and include certain supervisory salaries, local sales promotion costs, and outlays for research and development activities.

The controllable contribution margin is often considered the heart of the entire statement. This important measure represents the contribution to

---

[4] Although departmental contributions are disclosed, Exhibit 27-2 falls short of being a "true" contribution margin income statement. The upcoming discussion will clarify this point.

EXHIBIT 27-3
EXOIL Corporation
Contribution Income
Statements (in thousands)

	Total Company	Divisions	
		Refining	Retailing
Net sales	$3,000	$2,080	$920
Less variable costs			
Cost of goods sold	$2,000	$1,390	$610
Variable selling & administrative expense	240	85	155
Total variable costs	$2,240	$1,475	$765
Contribution margin	$ 760	$ 605	$155
Less controllable fixed costs	290	225	65
Controllable contribution margin	$ 470	$ 380	$ 90
Less uncontrollable fixed costs	210	168	42
Segment margin	$ 260	$ 212	$ 48
Less nontraceable costs	115		
Net income	$ 145		

	Retailing Division	Product Lines		Non-traceable Costs
		Parts	Fluids	
Net sales	$920	$645	$275	
Less variable costs				
Cost of goods sold	$610	$440	$170	
Variable selling & administrative expense	155	100	55	
Total variable costs	$765	$540	$225	
Contribution margin	$155	$105	$ 50	
Less controllable fixed costs	65	30	10	$ 25
Controllable contribution margin	$ 90	$ 75	$ 40	$(25)
Less uncontrollable fixed costs	42	13	7	22
Segment margin	$ 48	$ 62	$ 33	$(47)

profit that is under the direction of the responsibility center manager and is probably the best overall indicator of a manager's performance.

Segment Margin. The controllable contribution margin minus uncontrollable fixed costs yields the **segment margin.** The uncontrollable costs used in this calculation are incurred for the benefit of a specific responsibility center but are only minimally affected by the center's management. Typical examples of such costs include committed costs (such as property taxes and depreciation on factory buildings) and costs that result from decisions made at higher levels in the organization (e.g., the salary of the center's manager).

The segment margin shows the contribution of each responsibility center to company income after considering all traceable costs. Many accountants feel the segment margin is a good indicator of ongoing profitability because a center's entire fixed cost obligation is considered in the computation.

Controllable Margin Versus Segment Margin. Students often see little difference between the controllable contribution margin and the segment margin. Actually, these two performance measures serve distinctly different purposes. To explain, outstanding managers are frequently transferred to weak divisions to improve operations. Would you accept such an assignment if the company evaluated personnel and awarded bonuses on the basis of the "bottom line," namely, the segment margin? Probably not. No matter how hard you try, many uncontrollable factors would influence your performance appraisal. In addition, if the division was extremely weak, a heroic effort would be needed to show significant improvement in overall profitability. Thus, two performance measures are utilized. The controllable contribution margin is used for personnel decisions, such as raises and promotions. The segment margin, in contrast, is employed in exploring the long-run advisability of keeping a segment as an operating center of the business.

Nontraceable Costs. As we noted, the contribution approach disregards allocations of indirect costs. By studying the top half of Exhibit 27-3, you will notice that EXOIL incurred $115,000 of nontraceable costs. Also observe that not a single penny was charged against the segment margins of Refining and Retailing via allocations. These costs likely represent corporate administrative overhead incurred by the firm as a whole and not readily identifiable with either division.

In a similar manner, the bottom half of the exhibit reveals that Retailing's divisional manager had control over $65,000 of fixed costs. However, when the division was further segmented by product line, only $40,000 ($30,000 + $10,000) could be traced to Parts and Fluids. The remaining $25,000 was incurred jointly by the two product lines, making traceability difficult. As an example, the Retailing division may have employed an office manager who handled clerical work for both areas of activity. Once again, no attempt is made to charge indirect cost to segments; to do so would result in arbitrary, noncontrollable allocations.

By viewing Exhibit 27-3, you will notice that (1) cost of goods sold is included under the variable cost caption and (2) fixed costs are written off entirely in the current reporting period. This accounting treatment appears to contradict the material introduced in Chapters 21 and 22. Specifically, both variable *and* fixed overhead were included in the cost of a manufactured product and thus reflected in the cost-of-goods-sold calculation.

Over the years, two product costing methods have evolved: absorption costing and direct costing. The more traditional approach (and that illustrated in earlier chapters) is full or **absorption costing.** Under absorption costing, all manufacturing costs are considered product costs and included in the valuation of inventory.

DIRECT AND ABSORPTION COSTING

OBJECTIVE 6

Identify the features of direct (variable) costing and absorption costing and prepare the related income statements.

An alternate approach is the **direct costing** method. Direct costing is more accurately called **variable costing,** because only variable manufacturing costs (direct materials, direct labor, and variable factory overhead) are assigned to products. Fixed manufacturing costs are regarded as period costs and charged against revenues when incurred.

Fixed Manufacturing Overhead: The Key Difference

Observe that the treatment of fixed manufacturing overhead is the basic difference between direct and absorption costing. Companies that employ absorption costing place fixed overhead in inventory on the balance sheet. At the time of sale, product cost (including fixed overhead) is transferred from the balance sheet to the income statement via cost of goods sold. Firms that use direct costing, on the other hand, write off fixed manufacturing overhead immediately. This difference in timing is depicted in Exhibit 27-4.

A Basic Illustration

To illustrate the procedures that accompany these two methods, examine the following information (see p. 1133), which was obtained from the records of the Harris Corporation for the year ended December 31, 19X4.

EXHIBIT 27-4
Comparison of Absorption Costing and Direct Costing

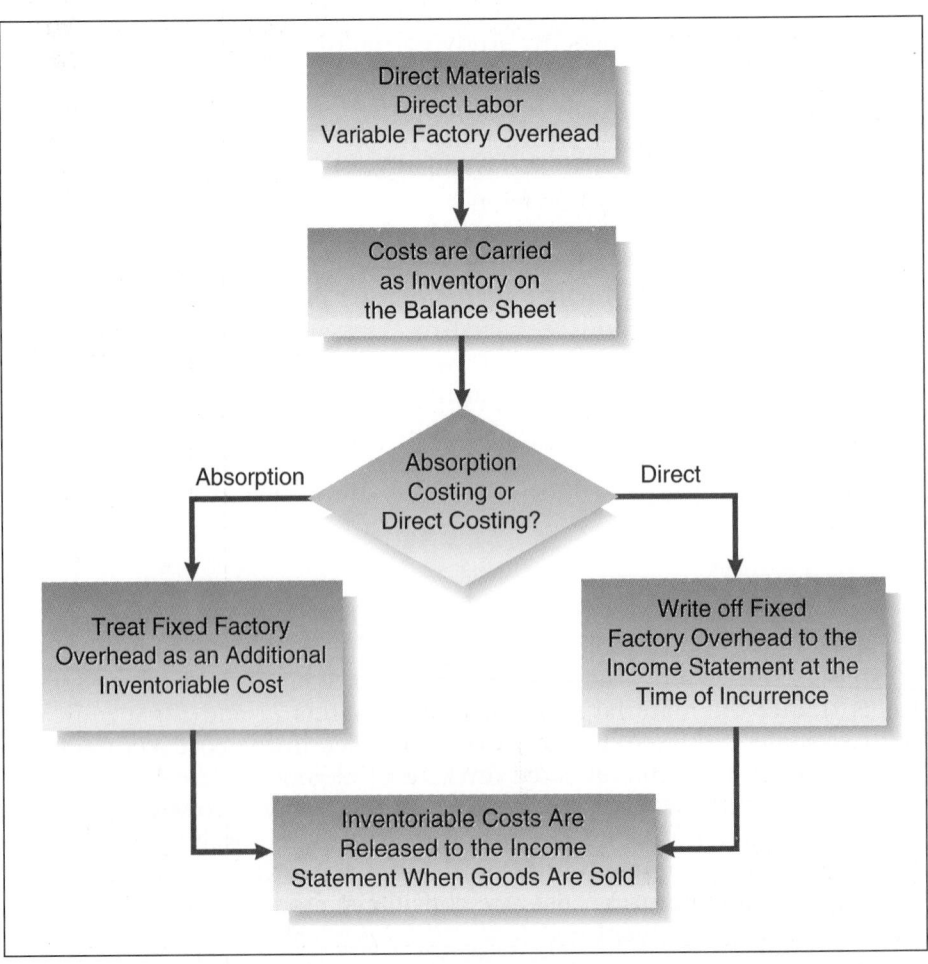

Sales: 9,500 units at $9
Selling and administrative costs: fixed, $5,000; variable, $2 per unit
Variable production costs per unit:

Direct materials	$1.00
Direct labor	1.50
Variable factory overhead	0.50
Total	$3.00

Fixed factory overhead: $10,000
Production: 10,000 units

Under absorption costing the unit product cost is $4.00:

Variable production costs	$3.00
Fixed factory overhead ($10,000 ÷ 10,000 units produced)	1.00
Total	$4.00

With direct costing the product cost per unit drops to $3.00, because only variable production costs are inventoried. Remember from previous chapters that selling and administrative costs are never attached to manufactured units. These amounts are treated as expenses of the period.

Given the preceding calculations, the company's income statements under both absorption costing and direct costing appear as shown in Exhibit 27-5. Two important observations should be made. First, notice the similarity between the direct costing income statement and the contribution approach shown earlier in the chapter. Direct costing produces a cost of goods sold that is comprised solely of variable costs, thereby giving management the ability to figure the contribution margin. In practice, the fixed costs that appear on the statement would be divided into two categories: those controllable by the segment manager and those that are uncontrollable.

Second, observe that a $500 difference arises between the two net income figures. Although both methods used the same data, keep the differing treatments of fixed manufacturing overhead in mind. Under direct costing, the entire pool of fixed production cost ($10,000) was deducted from current period revenues. With the absorption approach, however, $1 of fixed overhead ($10,000 ÷ 10,000 units manufactured) was attached to each unit produced. Because Harris completed 10,000 units but sold only 9,500, the fixed overhead charges were actually divided as follows:

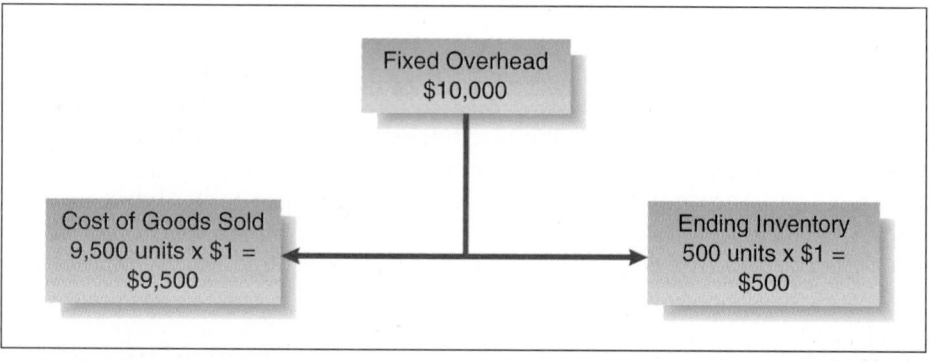

EXHIBIT 27-5
Absorption Costing and Direct
Costing Income Statements

HARRIS CORPORATION
Absorption Costing Income Statement
For the Year Ended December 31, 19X4

Sales (9,500 units × $9)		$85,500
Cost of goods sold (9,500 units × $4)		38,000
Gross profit		$47,500
Less selling & administrative costs		
Fixed	$ 5,000	
Variable (9,500 units × $2)	19,000	24,000
Net income		$23,500

HARRIS CORPORATION
Direct Costing Income Statement
For the Year Ended December 31, 19X4

Sales (9,500 units × $9)		$85,500
Less variable costs		
Cost of goods sold (9,500 units × $3)	$28,500	
Selling & administrative (9,500 units × $2)	19,000	47,500
Contribution margin		$38,000
Less fixed costs		
Manufacturing	$10,000	
Selling & administrative	5,000	15,000
Net income		$23,000

Cost of goods sold is written off in 19X4 and matched against sales. In contrast, the $500 of fixed overhead in ending inventory is carried as an asset on the balance sheet. The write-off of this latter amount is deferred until such time as the units are sold—probably 19X5. In sum, then, absorption costing would result in a higher income figure than direct costing because of the smaller charge against revenues ($9,500 versus $10,000). The opposite situation would occur in those periods where the number of units sold exceeds the number of units produced.

An Overview

Companies are free to use either of the preceding methods for internal reporting to management. Direct costing is generally preferred, however, because of its consistency with contribution reporting and the fact that the contribution margin is employed in performance evaluation and decision making—two internal management functions. Additionally, direct costing usually results in a "cleaner" measure of income than absorption costing, with the bottom line influenced by changes in sales and not by changes in inventory levels.

Despite these attributes, direct costing cannot be used for external financial reporting. The absorption method's approach of inventorying fixed manufacturing costs normally yields a better match on the income statement. At the time of sale, fixed costs are released to the income statement (via cost of goods sold) and matched against the sales revenues that have just been realized. In contrast, direct costing dictates that all fixed production costs be written off at the time of incurrence. This procedure thus ignores the fact that future revenues may result from the expenditure (and the units manufactured).

END-OF-CHAPTER REVIEW

1 **Demonstrate the effect of relevant costs and sunk costs on decision making.** Decision making is concerned with the future, as the past is history and cannot be changed. The focus is on relevant costs, or those future costs that differ among alternatives. Sunk costs, which are past costs that have already been incurred, are therefore ignored when reviewing possible options.

2 **Evaluate different types of decision situations (e.g., make or buy).** The evaluation of decisions such as make or buy and the acceptance of special orders requires an identification of relevant costs and qualitative factors. Such costs would normally include variable costs, opportunity costs, and any avoidable fixed costs. Both special orders and addition and deletion decisions focus on the contribution margin, or the amount that a unit contributes toward covering fixed costs and generating income. The unit in this case is an order or perhaps a department.

3 **Explain why the contribution margin must be analyzed in terms of capacity constraints.** When a business is constrained in terms of performing its activities, management should not focus on the contribution margin per unit of product. Rather, the emphasis should be on those products or activities that generate the highest contribution margin per constraining factor (labor hour, machine hour, square foot, and so forth). By following this strategy, a company will make the most profitable use of its available resources.

4 **Distinguish between direct costs and indirect costs.** The direct and indirect classification scheme deals with traceability. Direct costs are easily traced to a business segment, whereas indirect costs are not. A business segment may be defined in several different ways; for example, it may be a division, a department, or a product line. In an attempt to charge each segment with a fair share of the costs incurred, management often uses a chargeback procedure and allocates indirect costs to the units in question.

5 **Prepare and use a contribution income statement.** A contribution income statement discloses a segment's contribution toward the overall profit of the firm. All variable and direct fixed costs are charged to the segment where incurred, with the latter costs often categorized in terms of the degree of control exercised by the segment manager. Most important, the contribution statement contains no arbitrary allocations of indirect costs.

The statement reveals three performance measures: the contribution margin (sales minus variable costs), the controllable contribution margin, and the segment margin. The second measure, calculated by subtracting controllable fixed costs

**LEARNING OBJECTIVES:
THE KEY POINTS**

from the contribution margin, focuses on the margin controllable by a manager and is often used in personnel decisions (raises, bonuses, and so forth). The segment margin, a good indicator of long-run profitability, is the result of subtracting a segment's uncontrollable fixed costs from the controllable contribution margin.

6 Identify the features of direct (variable) costing and absorption costing and prepare the related income statements. These two methods of inventory costing differ in their treatment of fixed factory overhead. Under absorption costing, a specified amount of fixed overhead is attached to each unit produced. In contrast, with direct (i.e., variable) costing, fixed manufacturing charges are written off to the income statement when incurred. Direct costing is consistent with the contribution income statement and is therefore preferred for internal reporting. For external financial reporting, however, absorption costing must be used.

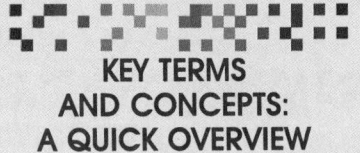

KEY TERMS
AND CONCEPTS:
A QUICK OVERVIEW

absorption costing A method under which all manufacturing costs are assigned to products; used for external financial reporting purposes.

contribution income statement An income statement that features disclosure of the contribution margin and fixed costs (both controllable and uncontrollable) directly identifiable with a segment.

controllable contribution margin A performance measure computed by subtracting controllable fixed costs from a segment's contribution margin.

differential cost A cost that differs among alternatives.

direct cost Any cost that is easily traced to and associated with a business segment.

direct costing A method that assigns only variable manufacturing costs (direct materials, direct labor, and variable manufacturing overhead) to products; more appropriately termed variable costing.

full project approach An evaluation of the total relevant costs associated with a decision alternative.

incremental approach An evaluation of the net difference in relevant costs associated with decision alternatives.

indirect cost A cost that is not easily traced to a business segment.

opportunity cost The cost of a forgone alternative.

qualitative factors Decision factors that cannot be evaluated in terms of dollars.

relevant cost A cost that must be considered in decision making because it differs among alternatives.

segment margin The controllable contribution margin minus uncontrollable fixed costs.

sunk cost A past cost that is irrelevant for decision making.

variable costing See "direct costing."

CHAPTER QUIZ

The five questions that follow relate to several issues raised in the chapter. Test your knowledge of the issues by selecting the best answer. (The answers appear on p. 1155.)

1 Which of the following statements is false?
   a Decision making focuses on future costs.
   b If a cost is identical for two alternatives under study, the cost can be ignored when making a decision.
   c Sunk costs are the key to decision making.
   d Fixed costs can be relevant when making a decision.

2 Martin Company has idle capacity and is studying whether to accept a special order for 1,000 units of its sole product. The product normally sells for $20 and has related variable and fixed manufacturing costs of $12 and $4, respectively. If the special order is accepted at a price of $15 per unit, Martin's overall profitability will:
   a decrease by $1,000.   c increase by $11,000.
   b increase by $3,000.   d increase by $15,000.

3 CEN Manufacturing has limited production time in its heavily automated factory. When determining which products to manufacture, management should study each product's:
   a contribution margin.   c total cost.
   b contribution margin ratio.   d contribution margin per machine hour.

4 Contribution income statements:
   a disclose a segment's controllable contribution margin and the segment margin.
   b contain allocations of nontraceable costs.
   c make no distinction between direct costs and indirect costs.
   d charge only controllable costs to the segment in question.

5 A company that uses absorption costing procedures:
   a is in violation of generally accepted accounting principles.
   b attaches fixed manufacturing overhead to each unit produced.
   c normally generates the same amount of net income as would be calculated by using direct costing.
   d attaches a selected amount of the firm's total fixed costs (including selling and administrative) to each unit manufactured.

Prestige of Ohio makes various parts for electric garage door openers. One of the subassemblies for the opener's gearbox has created a number of manufacturing problems, prompting management to obtain bids from an outside supplier. The following information is available:

SUMMARY PROBLEM

Variable manufacturing cost per gearbox	$ 14
Fixed manufacturing overhead	90,000

Units produced are expected to total 20,000. The subassembly can be purchased from Stevenson Electrical for $1.65 per unit. If Prestige decides in favor of Stevenson, variable costs of each gearbox will fall by 10% and fixed manufacturing overhead will decrease by $8,000.

Instructions

a Should Prestige make or buy the subassemblies? *Note:* There is one subassembly in each gearbox.
b Assume that the fixed manufacturing overhead of $90,000 can be subdivided as follows:

Costs traceable to the gearbox department and controllable by the department manager	$38,000

Costs traceable to the gearbox department and uncontrollable by
the department manager   29,000
Costs allocated to the gearbox department   23,000

Determine the amount of fixed manufacturing overhead:

(1) That would be included in the computation of the gearbox department's segment margin.

(2) That should be used to evaluate the gearbox manager in a promotion decision.

(3) That would appear on Prestige's contribution income statement.

c Disregard part (b) and assume that Prestige has decided to continue manufacture of the subassemblies. Further assume that in addition to the original data, the company has a $0.50-per-unit variable selling cost and fixed administrative costs that total $70,000. Calculate the inventoriable product cost for each gearbox under (1) direct costing and (2) absorption costing.

Solution

a Prestige's costs will decrease if the company discontinues production of the subassembly. This decrease therefore represents the cost of manufacturing.

Manufacture
    Variable: $14 × 0.10 × 20,000 units $28,000
    Fixed   8,000
        Total $36,000

Purchase
    20,000 units × $1.65 $33,000

Prestige will save $3,000 ($36,000 − $33,000) if it buys the subassemblies from Stevenson Electrical.

b (1) All traceable fixed costs would be included ($38,000 + $29,000 = $67,000).

  (2) Only controllable fixed costs would be included ($38,000).

  (3) The contribution income statement contains no cost allocations ($38,000 + $29,000 = $67,000).

c Selling and administrative costs are not inventoriable, as such amounts are written off as period expenses.

  (1) Direct: $14

  (2) Absorption: $14.00 + $4.50 ($90,000 ÷ 20,000 units) = $18.50

ASSIGNMENT MATERIAL

QUESTIONS

Q27-1   Discuss the general approach to decision making.

Q27-2   Are all future costs relevant for decision-making purposes? Explain.

Q27-3   An educator once commented, "Not all future costs are relevant to decisions, but costs are not relevant unless they occur in the future." Evaluate the educator's comment.

Q27-4   What is meant by the term "sunk cost"?

Q27-5   Should decisions be made "solely on the numbers"? Briefly discuss.

Q27-6 The Crandall Corporation has been offered $34 per unit for a one-time special order. Variable cost and fixed cost per unit amount to $27 and $10, respectively. If Crandall has available facilities, should the order be accepted? Why?

Q27-7 If a retailer has limited square footage in its store, what guideline should be used in deciding which new products to carry?

Q27-8 Differentiate between a direct cost and an indirect cost. As segments become smaller and smaller, what generally happens to cost traceability?

Q27-9 Should a departmental manager be held accountable for allocations of corporate overhead? Briefly discuss.

Q27-10 What features are associated with a contribution margin income statement?

Q27-11 Discuss the computations and meaning associated with the controllable contribution margin and the segment margin.

Q27-12 Differentiate between direct costing and absorption costing.

Q27-13 Creekside, Inc., began business on January 1 of the current year. The company produced 42,000 units but sold only 35,000 by December 31. Would direct costing net income be greater than absorption costing net income? Why?

Q27-14 Can direct costing be used for internal reporting? For external financial reporting?

EXERCISES

E27-1 *Relevant decision factors* (L.O. 1)
Consider the following:
a The cost of special electrical wiring, in an equipment acquisition decision.
b The sales revenues generated with an existing machine, which are not expected to change, in deciding whether to keep or replace the machine.
c Avoidable fixed manufacturing overhead, in a make or buy decision.
d The salary cost of a production supervisor who is already on the payroll, in a special order acceptance decision.
e The direct materials cost, in a make or buy decision.
f Product development costs incurred several months ago, in a product introduction decision.
g Alternative uses of your time, in a job acceptance decision.
h The cost of an old vehicle, in a keep-versus-disposal decision.
i Fixed corporate overhead, in the acceptance or rejection of a special order.

Evaluate each of the factors listed as being relevant or irrelevant to the decision situation noted. If the factor is irrelevant, briefly explain why.

E27-2 *Introductory decision making* (L.O. 1)
Metro Manufacturing recently produced 14,000 units at a cost of $18.40 per unit. The goods do not meet quality standards and can be sold as seconds to a discount chain for $14.75 each. Alternatively, Metro can reprocess the units at an additional cost of $5.60. The reprocessed units can then be sold for $21.00.
After evaluating the two alternatives, an assistant in the accounting

department concluded: "We'd be better off to keep the units. We'll incur a loss no matter which alternative is selected."

a Show the computations that formed the basis for the assistant's remarks.

b Is the assistant's conclusion correct? Why?

E27-3   *Make or buy* (L.O. 2)

1-2-3

The Ranco Corporation makes small plastic cases with built-in mirrors for sale to cosmetics manufacturers. The company's production costs for an annual volume of 300,000 cases (including mirrors) follow.

Direct materials	$ 45,000
Direct labor	18,000
Variable factory overhead	21,000
Fixed factory overhead	30,000
	$114,000

Because of various problems, Ranco desires to discontinue the mirror production and purchase the mirror from East Coast Glass for $0.11. If Ranco does business with East Coast Glass, material, labor, and variable overhead costs will decline by 40%, 30%, and 20%, respectively.

a Should Ranco make or buy the mirror? Why?

b Assume that if the mirror is purchased, the mirror's production space will be leased to a small manufacturer for $1,300 per month. Discuss the proper treatment of this revenue and its impact on Ranco's make or buy decision. *Note:* The amount of fixed overhead incurred will remain constant.

E27-4   *Special order* (L.O. 2)

Hudson River Enterprises manufactures and sells various types of athletic equipment. The company's most recent product-line income statement revealed the following selected information for the Ball Division:

Sales		$1,278,000
Cost of goods sold		
Variable	$432,000	
Fixed	282,000	714,000
Selling & administrative expenses		
Variable	$174,000	
Fixed	210,000	384,000

The figures relate to the production and sale of 60,000 soccer balls.

The National Soccer League (NSL) recently approached Hudson River about purchasing 4,800 balls through a special order. The balls would be of slightly higher quality than Hudson River is currently manufacturing, requiring an increase in direct material cost of $1.20 per ball. No variable selling and administrative costs will be incurred on this order, and fixed costs will continue at current levels. NSL is willing to buy the balls at $14.50 each.

a Will Hudson River's net income increase or decrease if the special order is accepted? By how much?

b Suppose you are given the additional information that the company's manufacturing capacity for soccer balls is 60,000 balls per year. If Hudson River's forecasts indicate a continuation of present sales trends, should the special order be accepted? Why?

E27-5 *Analysis of special order* (L.O. 2)

William Row builds custom homes that range in price from $125,000 to $300,000. The price of a home is determined by summing the estimated costs of materials, labor, and overhead, and then adding 15% for a profit margin. As an example, a home designed for Mr. and Mrs. David Presley was priced as follows:

Materials	$ 70,000
Labor	100,000
Overhead (20% of labor)	20,000
	$190,000
Profit—15%	28,500
Selling price	$218,500

Total overhead for the year has been estimated at $200,000, of which $120,000 is fixed and the remainder is variable in direct proportion to labor.

Business is currently very slow. The Presleys, feeling that the $218,500 price was too high, countered with an offer of $205,000.

a Determine the contribution margin on the home if Row accepted the Presleys' offer of $205,000.

b What is the minimum price that Row could have quoted without reducing or increasing his firm's net income?

E27-6 *Capacity constraint* (L.O. 3)

Moss Port Enterprises manufactures three products known as X, Y, and Z. Pertinent data about the products follow.

	X	Y	Z
Selling price	$50	$48	$80
Less variable costs			
Direct materials	$ 2	$24	$30
Direct labor	24	9	30
Variable factory overhead	8	3	10
Total	$34	$36	$70
Contribution margin	$16	$12	$10

Direct laborers are paid $6 per hour. The demand for these products is very strong; unfortunately, Moss Port has experienced a severe shortage of qualified workers. As a result, the company's labor force is working close to capacity, and only 2,000 hours of labor time are available in the upcoming accounting period.

a Determine the amount of labor time needed to manufacture a single unit of X, Y, and Z.

b Does Moss Port face any constraints that limit the amount of contribution margin it can generate? If so, what strategy should the company follow when deciding which product to manufacture.

c Determine which product should be selected for manufacture in the upcoming accounting period.

E27-7 *Dropping an unprofitable store* (L.O. 2)

Delmac, Inc., operates 35 pizza carry-outs in Ohio. The following information pertains to Akron's Bower Street carry-out for the year just ended:

Sales		$165,000
Cost of food & beverages		59,000
Gross profit		$106,000
Less operating expenses		
Equipment & building leases	$26,700	
Wages	73,400	
Utilities	4,800	
Pizza boxes, cups, supplies	6,800	
Share of allocated corporate overhead (e.g., executive salaries, etc.)	8,700	120,400
Net income (loss)		$ (14,400)

Management wants to close the Bower Street operation because of the loss. All equipment and building leases would be terminated. The manager (annual salary, $22,500) will be transferred to the nearby Fairlawn facility; other employees would be discharged.

Should the Bower Street carry-out be closed? Why?

E27-8 *Overview of decision making* (L.O. 1, 2)
Evaluate the comments that follow as being True or False. If the comment is false, briefly explain why.
a Decisions should be based solely on quantitative factors.
b Unavoidable fixed costs can be ignored in decision making.
c The cost of obsolete inventory can be disregarded when deciding whether to keep or dispose of the goods.
d If Dixon Company stops the production of a particular component, it can lease currently-used factory space to another firm. The lease revenue is properly viewed as an opportunity cost should Dixon continue its manufacturing activities.
e Special orders are frequently accepted even though an order's selling price may be less than the sum of direct material, direct labor, variable factory overhead, and fixed factory overhead charges.

E27-9 *Controllable costs* (L.O. 4, 5)
Consider the following costs of the Spirit Company:
a Allocated corporate overhead: $20,000.
b Local advertising expense: $6,600.
c Wages of part-time divisional workers: $3,200.
d Cost of goods sold (variable): $217,800.
e Salary of division manager: $23,600.
f Charges for divisional use of the corporate computer facility: $12,400.
g Sales commissions paid: $34,500.

Which of these costs would most likely be considered in the computation of the controllable contribution margin of a divisional manager? For those costs that are not considered, briefly explain why.

E27-10 *Contribution margin income statement* (L.O. 5)
The following information pertains to the Fairfax Division of Santa Monica Industries:

Net sales	$2,200,000
Controllable fixed costs traceable to the division	640,000
Allocated corporate overhead	150,000
Variable costs	
Cost of goods sold	510,000
Selling & administrative	440,000
Uncontrollable fixed costs traceable to the division	190,000

a Compute the Fairfax Division's:
  (1) Contribution margin.
  (2) Controllable contribution margin.
  (3) Segment margin.
b Which of the preceding measures (contribution margin, controllable contribution margin, or segment margin) should be used when making long-term decisions about divisional operations?
c Which of the preceding measures should be used in pay-raise decisions for divisional managers?

E27-11 *Direct and absorption inventory costing* (L.O. 6)

Milsap Industries began business on January 1 of the current year, manufacturing and selling a single product. Consider the data that follow.

1-2-3

	Units	Variable Cost Per Unit	Fixed Costs
Production volume	80,000		
Sales volume	72,000		
Direct materials		$1.30	
Direct labor		2.80	
Factory overhead		4.40	$540,000
Selling expenses		0.20	180,000

a Compute the cost of the company's ending inventory by using direct costing.
b Compute the cost of the company's ending inventory by using absorption costing.
c Suppose that Milsap's accountant had accidentally excluded straight-line depreciation on machinery from the data presented. Determine the effect of this error (overstate, understate, or no impact) on the company's:
  (1) Direct costing ending inventory.
  (2) Absorption costing ending inventory.

E27-12 *Direct and absorption income computations* (L.O. 6)

Crawford Company began operations on January 1 of the current year. The following information has been gathered from the accounting records:

Variable costs per unit
  Manufacturing: $12.50
  Selling & administrative: $1.10
Fixed costs
  Manufacturing: $120,000
  Selling & administrative: $60,000

Production and sales amounted to 80,000 units and 75,000 units, respectively. The selling price is $17.

a Compute net income for the year just ended by using the direct costing method.

b Compute net income for the year just ended by using the absorption costing method.

PROBLEMS

Series A

P27-A1 *Make or buy* (L.O. 2)

Anchor Manufacturing produces a full line of workshop tools. One of the company's products, a flat-head screwdriver, has a unit manufacturing cost of $6.85, computed as follows:

Direct materials	$2.40
Direct labor	0.90
Variable factory overhead	1.70
Fixed factory overhead	1.85 *
Total	$6.85

* Consists of factory supervision ($0.60), equipment depreciation ($0.20), and "other" fixed charges ($1.05).

All manufacturing fixed costs are computed by using a volume of 120,000 units per year.

Anchor's management has just been informed that a machine used in the production of screwdriver handles must soon be replaced—an expenditure that will increase annual straight-line depreciation by $50,400. To avoid the acquisition at this time, management has gathered the following information concerning an outside purchase of handles:

1 Injection Plastics will supply Anchor in lots of 30,000 units for $54,000. Anchor must pay freight, which should amount to $300 per shipment.

2 The current unit costs for direct materials, direct labor, and variable factory overhead will drop by 30%, 20%, and 20%, respectively.

3 Factory supervision and "other" fixed charges are not expected to change.

4 By dismantling handle production, Anchor will have added space and will be able to vacate rented storage facilities that cost $6,000 per year.

Instructions

a Should Anchor make or buy the plastic handles? On an annual basis, how much will the company save with the preferred alternative?

b The $6,000 rental charge could logically be called an opportunity cost. Explain the meaning of an opportunity cost and how the $6,000 charge qualifies.

c List several reservations that Anchor might have about dealing with an outside supplier such as Injection Plastics.

P27-A2 *Special order and pricing policy* (L.O. 2)

Hunter Corporation manufactures a variety of novelty items. Because of a weak economy, production and sales in the company's Leather Division are at an all-time low. The division's income statement revealed the following selected data:

Sales	$2,250,000
Fixed manufacturing & selling costs	420,000
Variable manufacturing & selling costs	70% of sales

Production and sales totaled 300,000 units.

An importer located in Sweden has approached Hunter about a special order arrangement. The importer would like to buy 25,000 leather key cases, the division's sole product, at $6.20 each. Although Hunter's normal 5% sales commission would not be paid on these units, several additional costs will be incurred:

1 Hunter must pay shipping charges and transfer taxes of $0.75 per case.
2 A special machine must be acquired to imprint the Swedish firm's logo. The machine will cost $6,000 and be of no use to Hunter once the order is completed. Materials, labor, and overhead costs will rise by $0.10 per case because of the related manufacturing operations.

Instructions

a Management says that the order should be rejected because "it is a loser, especially when the current fixed cost per unit is considered." Show computations that support management's claim.
b Should the order be accepted? Why?

P27-A3 *New product introduction* (L.O. 1, 2)

1-2-3

The FHR Corporation is engaged in the manufacture of communications equipment. During the past 18 months, two new products have been developed: a voice module and a decoder unit.

FHR recently conducted market surveys for the voice module and the decoder at a cost of $42,000 each. Although the surveys indicate that both products could be introduced at this time, the firm has encountered difficulty in obtaining the required electronic components. Thus, only one product will be manufactured. FHR's accounting department has gathered the information that follows.

	Voice Module	Decoder Unit
Development costs over the past 18 months	$115,000	$135,000
Production costs per unit		
Direct materials	$22.50	$27.80
Direct labor	$15.00	$20.00
Variable overhead	$18.00	$24.00
Sales commissions (expressed as a percentage of sales)	10%	5%
Selling price	$85	$95
Projected sales (units)	35,000	41,000
Projected advertising	$25,000	$30,000

Instructions

a List those costs that are irrelevant to the product introduction decision and explain why each is irrelevant.
b Compute the contribution margin per unit for each product.
c Which of the two products should be introduced at this time? Why?

P27-A4 *Dropping an unprofitable segment* (L.O. 2)

Bargain Mart operates a chain of discount stores in large metropolitan areas of the United States. An abbreviated income statement for store no. 2104 for the year just ended follows.

	Total	General Merchandise	Patio	Lunch Counter
Sales	$940,000	$500,000	$280,000	$160,000
Less variable expenses	598,000	310,000	168,000	120,000
Contribution margin	$342,000	$190,000	$112,000	$ 40,000
Less fixed expenses	256,000	130,000	77,000	49,000
Net income (loss)	$ 86,000	$ 60,000	$ 35,000	$ (9,000)

Because of poor performance, management wants to drop the lunch counter. If the lunch counter is closed, the vacated space will be divided between general merchandise and patio, with the following results:
1 General merchandise and patio sales are expected to increase by $35,000 and $12,000, respectively.
2 Fixed expenses include $31,000 of salaries earned by lunch counter employees. Employees who earn $19,000 would be transferred to other departments; remaining counter people will be terminated.
3 All other fixed costs incurred by the lunch counter will continue to be incurred.
4 The lunch counter's equipment will be removed and transferred to another store. Removal and transportation costs will amount to $2,700.

Instructions

a Should the lunch counter be dropped? Show computations to support your answer.
b Assume that Quality Caterers has approached Bargain Mart about running the lunch counter. Quality will pay Bargain Mart $1,400 per month and assume all costs of operation, with the exception of $12,200 of fixed costs. Should the lunch counter be retained in its present form or be turned over to Quality Caterers? Show computations to support your answer.

P27-A5 *Contribution income statement: Preparation and analysis* (L.O. 4, 5)
Marsha Warren, president of Warren Distributors, has just finished her review of the current year's operations. She noted, "We've been lucky. Given the state of the economy, I'm really pleased with these figures. A 3% return on sales will probably beat the competition."

Marsha's comments were based on the following income statement, which was prepared by a new employee. The employee summarized information that pertains to the company's three product lines: X, Y, and Z.

WARREN DISTRIBUTORS		
Income Statement		
For the Year Ended December 31, 19XX		
Net sales		$690,000
Less: Cost of goods sold	$444,000	
Sales commissions	63,300	
Local advertising	60,000	
Sales salaries	30,000	
Other	72,000	669,300
Net income		$ 20,700

Supplementary records revealed the following data:

1 Sales: X, 60,000 units at $5.00; Y, 70,000 units at $3.00; and Z, 40,000 units at $4.50.

2 Warren purchases units from various manufacturers. The prices paid per unit were as follows: X, $3.00; Y, $2.20; Z, $2.75.

3 Sales personnel of X and Z are paid on a commission basis. Commissions total 10% and 15% of each product's respective gross sales. Sales of Y are handled by one salesperson who receives a 3% commission plus a $30,000 salary. The salary is set by Y's management.

4 Local advertising is handled by product-line managers. Advertising costs for the product lines were: X, $25,000; Y, $20,000; Z, $15,000.

5 Other costs of $72,000 are subdivided as follows:
   Uncontrollable costs traceable to product lines: X, $20,000; Y, $16,000; and Z, $12,000.
   Administrative overhead not traceable to product lines: $24,000.

Instructions

a Give Warren more insight about operations by preparing a contribution income statement for the three product lines. Are things going as well as she believes or could operations be improved? Explain.

b If any of the product lines have a negative segment margin, present an analysis of the probable causes of poor performance.

P27-A6 *Direct and absorption costing* (L.O. 6)

The following information pertains to Turbo Enterprises for the year ended December 31, 19X8:

Variable cost per unit:	
Direct materials	$ 6
Direct labor	4
Factory overhead	9
Selling & administrative expense	3
Total	$22

Annual fixed costs:	
Factory overhead	$600,000
Selling & administrative expense	115,000
Total	$715,000

Other data (units):	
Sales	21,000
Production	25,000
Inventory, 12/31/X8	11,000

The unit selling price is $62. Assume that costs have been stable in recent years.

Instructions

a Compute the number of units in the beginning inventory on January 1, 19X8.

b Calculate the cost of the December 31 inventory assuming use of:
   (1) Direct costing.
   (2) Absorption costing.

c Prepare an income statement for the year ended December 31, 19X8, by using direct costing.

d Prepare an income statement for the year ended December 31, 19X8, by using absorption costing.

Series B

P27-B1 *Make or buy* (L.O. 2)

Micron, Inc., manufactures a full line of small home appliances. The manufactured cost of one of the company's products, a toaster oven, follows.

Direct materials	$ 5.60
Direct labor	9.00
Total factory overhead	13.50
Total	$28.10

Fixed overhead generally averages 70% of the total overhead charge.

Micron is currently producing all of the toaster oven's components. One of the components, part no. XY368, has created a number of manufacturing problems. The company is therefore considering an outside supplier. A supplier has agreed to provide XY368s in lots of 20,000 for $84,000. If Micron accepts the supplier's offer, it is estimated that the oven's direct labor and variable overhead cost will decline by 20%. In addition, direct material cost should fall by approximately 10%.

Instructions

a Should Micron make or buy the component? Show computations to support your answer. *Note:* Each oven uses one of the XY368 components.

b What is the maximum purchase price that Micron would be willing to pay an outside supplier for the 20,000 components?

c Assume that Micron can manufacture and sell 60,000 toaster ovens per year. To eliminate the production problems, top management has proposed transferring Phil Hartley from the company's microwave division to oversee manufacturing. Hartley is currently earning an annual salary of $43,000. In addition, new equipment would be leased at a cost of $3,100 per month. If both of these actions take place, should Micron make or buy the component? Show computations to support your answer.

d List several qualitative factors that Micron should consider in deciding whether to make or buy the component.

P27-B2 *Special order and pricing policy* (L.O. 2)

Regal Company makes several products that are used in the home. Revenues and costs of the Portable Vacuum System follow.

Sales		$290,000
Less:		
Direct materials used	$88,000	
Direct labor	80,000	
Total factory overhead	56,000	
Sales commissions, 10%	29,000	
Allocated administrative expense	15,500	268,500
Net income		$ 21,500

The figures shown are for the production and sale of 5,000 units. Factory overhead is applied on the basis of direct labor cost.

The Brower Corporation, which advertises heavily on television, has submitted an offer to purchase 2,200 vacuums at $51 each. Brower will market the product under its own brand name, and Regal's normal sales are not expected to suffer. Regal's president feels that the offer should be rejected because the price is below the current unit cost of $53.70 ($268,500 ÷ 5,000 units). An in-depth study revealed the following information:

1 Brower's units will require overtime at time and one-half the regular wage rate. *Note:* The overtime premium will be accounted for as direct labor.
2 Fixed factory overhead is applied by using a rate of 42% of direct labor cost.
3 No sales commissions will be paid on these units.
4 Administrative expenses are allocated to product lines on the basis of sales dollars. Because of the special order, an additional $6,000 will be charged to the vacuum line. Regal's total administrative costs will remain the same, however.

Instructions

Should Regal reject Brower's offer? Why?

P27-B3 *New product introduction* (L.O. 1, 2)

The Estrada Corporation is a small firm engaged in the manufacture of garden tools. During the past 12 months, two new products have been under development: a timer system for lawn watering and a lawn weeder. Research and development costs for the timer and the weeder have totaled $72,000 and $18,000, respectively.

Company policy is to introduce only one new product each year. Customer acceptability studies performed in the past few months indicate that both products would be successful. Estrada's accounting department has gathered the information that follows.

	Timer System	Lawn Weeder
Customer acceptability studies	$17,000	$24,000
Projected advertising	$30,000	$27,000
Projected sales (units)	10,000	18,000
Selling price	$48	$42
Sales commission (expressed as a percentage of sales)	5%	10%
Unit production costs		
Direct materials	$11.00	$12.00
Direct labor	$10.00	$10.50
Variable overhead	$15.50	$10.10

Instructions

a List those costs that are irrelevant to the product introduction decision and explain why each is irrelevant.
b Compute the contribution margin per unit for each product.
c Which of the two products should be introduced? Why?

P27-B4 *Dropping an unprofitable segment* (L.O. 2)

The Weekend Warrior sells running shoes, tennis shoes, and athletic apparel at a store on State Street. Product-line information for the year just ended follows.

	Sales	Variable Costs	Fixed Costs	Net
Running shoes	$120,000	$ 66,000	$28,000	$ 26,000
Tennis shoes	80,000	56,000	34,000	(10,000)
Athletic wear	250,000	150,000	64,000	36,000

Management is studying whether to drop tennis shoes because of the $10,000 loss. If the line is dropped, the following results are anticipated:

1 Fixed costs associated with tennis shoes will decrease by $7,000. All other fixed costs will continue to be incurred.

2 The space vacated by tennis shoes will be remodeled at a cost of $5,500. (This amount is considered immaterial and will be expensed when incurred.)

3 A vastly expanded line of running shoes will be offered for sale, especially lower-cost models. Sales of running shoes are expected to increase by $30,000, but the product line's contribution margin ratio (contribution margin ÷ sales) will fall by seven full percentage points.

4 Customers who shopped for tennis shoes often purchased athletic wear. Sales of athletic wear are anticipated to fall by 15%.

Instructions

a Determine if tennis shoes should be dropped.

b Suppose that management has decided to keep the tennis shoe line and run a promotional campaign. If the campaign will result in a fixed cost increase of $5,000, calculate:

(1) The additional contribution margin that must be generated to achieve a break-even operation with the tennis shoe line.

(2) The additional sales that must be generated to achieve a break-even operation with the tennis shoe line.

P27-B5 *Contribution income statement: Preparation and analysis* (L.O. 4, 5)

Harold Brandt, president of Brandt Distributing, has just finished a review of the current year's operations. He noted, "These figures look great. I was expecting overall performance to suffer, given the problems we've had with the Urbana Division. However, I believe we're now on sound footing and have few financial problems."

Harold's comments were based on the following income statement, which was prepared by a new employee. The employee summarized information that pertains to the firm's three divisions: Barrington, Springfield, and Urbana.

BRANDT DISTRIBUTING Income Statement For the Year Ended December 31, 19XX		
Net sales		$994,000
Less: Cost of goods sold	$632,000	
Sales commissions	49,700	
Salaries	130,000	
Advertising	80,000	
Other	75,000	966,700
Net income		$ 27,300

Supplementary records revealed the following information:
1 Sales: Barrington, 29,000 units at $10; Springfield, 34,000 units at $8; and Urbana, 48,000 units at $9.
2 Each division purchases units from various manufacturers. The prices paid per unit were as follows: Barrington, $6; Springfield, $5; Urbana, $6.
3 Each division pays a 5% commission to its sales force. In addition, the Urbana Division employs a sales manager who earns $30,000 per year. The sales manager's salary is set by Urbana's divisional manager. Other salaries for executives are established by Brandt and subdivided as follows:

Barrington	$ 25,000
Springfield	40,000
Urbana	35,000
Total	$100,000

4 Advertising is handled by divisional managers. The following costs were incurred: Barrington, $10,000; Springfield, $20,000; and Urbana, $50,000.
5 Other costs of $75,000 consisted of the following:
   Uncontrollable costs traceable to the divisions: Barrington, $8,000; Springfield, $6,000; and Urbana, $27,000.
   General corporate overhead: $34,000.

Instructions

a Give Brandt more insight about operations by preparing a contribution income statement for the three divisions. Are things going as well as he believes or could operations be improved? Explain.
b If any of the divisions have a negative segment margin, present an analysis of the probable causes of poor performance.

P27-B6 Direct and absorption costing (L.O. 6)
The information that follows pertains to Consumer Products for the year ended December 31, 19X6.

Inventory, 1/1/X6	24,000 units
Units manufactured	80,000
Units sold	82,000
Inventory, 12/31/X6	?　units

Manufacturing costs:	
Direct materials	$3 per unit
Direct labor	$5 per unit
Variable factory overhead	$9 per unit
Fixed factory overhead	$280,000

Selling & administrative expenses:	
Variable	$2 per unit
Fixed	$136,000

The unit selling price is $26. Assume that costs have been stable in recent years.

Instructions

a Compute the number of units in the ending inventory.
b Calculate the cost of a unit assuming use of:
  (1) Direct costing.
  (2) Absorption costing.
c Prepare an income statement for the year ended December 31, 19X6, by using direct costing.
d Prepare an income statement for the year ended December 31, 19X6, by using absorption costing.

BEYOND THE BASICS

BB27-1 *Analysis of costs; decision making** (L.O. 2)

Paradise, Inc., is a developer of hotels in Hawaii and other resort locations. The company is studying construction of a new facility on the island of El Reno, and two alternatives are under consideration:

- *Alternative A*—Build a "commercial class" hotel similar to Holiday Inn or Ramada, with an average room area of 550 square feet (including public spaces). There would be minimal meeting and banquet facilities.
- *Alternative B*—Build an "executive class" hotel similar to a Hyatt or a Hilton. The average room size would be 700 square feet; ample meeting and banquet facilities would be available for conventions, conferences, and so forth.

Paradise's accounting department has generated the following data:

Land cost: $25 per square foot of floor area
Construction cost: $80 per square foot
Real estate taxes, interest, and other overhead during construction: 30% of land and construction costs

Per-room outlays for furnishings and equipment, supplies, and opening advertising and marketing costs are estimated as follows:

	Commercial	Executive
Furnishings and equipment	$8,000	$12,500
Supplies	1,000	2,000
Advertising and marketing	2,000	4,000

The accounting department recommends adding 10% to the total of all preceding costs to allow for contingencies and estimation errors. Construction is expected to take two years.

Paradise sets a room rental rate equal to $1 per $1,000 of cost. Upon completion, the going rates for similar rooms are anticipated to be: commercial, $79 per day; executive, $135.

Instructions

a Compute the cost per room of building a commercial class hotel and an executive class hotel.
b Consider all information presented and determine the type of hotel that Paradise should construct. What factors should be evaluated in reaching the proper decision?

---

* This problem is adapted from "Room at the Top," *Forbes*, March 12, 1984, pp. 58, 59, 61.

BB27-2 *Overview of chapter concepts: Multiple choice* (L.O. 1, 2, 3, 5, 6)

The following multiple-choice questions relate to various topics discussed in the chapter. Select the best answer

1 Mercury, Inc., manufactures running shoes. A skilled worker is paid $25 per hour and can produce one pair of shoes every 30 minutes. In contrast, an apprentice who is paid $6.50 per hour can complete one pair every 120 minutes. A pair of shoes requires $20 of direct material. The skilled worker will waste an additional $1 of material for each pair produced; the apprentice will waste an additional $2. In a "full project approach" to evaluate the cost of a pair of shoes, the numbers that should be used for the worker and apprentice, respectively, would be:

a $12.50 versus $13.00.

b $13.50 versus $15.00.

c $33.50 versus $35.00.

d none of the above.

2 Parker manufactures 10,000 units per year of a part used in fuel systems. Production costs are: direct materials, $40,000; direct labor, $110,000; variable overhead, $90,000; and fixed overhead, $140,000. A-1 has offered to sell Parker the 10,000 units at $36 per unit. If Parker accepts the offer, facilities currently used in manufacturing could be leased to another company for $30,000 per year. Additionally, Parker will avoid $8 per unit of the fixed overhead. Should Parker accept A-1's offer?

a No, because it would be $10,000 cheaper to make the part.

b Yes, because it would be $20,000 cheaper to buy the part.

c Yes, because it would be $50,000 cheaper to buy the part.

d No, because it would be $30,000 cheaper to make the part.

3 Acme Company manufactures rugs. The forecasted income statement revealed anticipated sales of $8,400,000 (400,000 rugs at $21 each), gross profit of $2,000,000, and selling expenses of $600,000. Reflected in these amounts are $2,400,000 of fixed manufacturing overhead and $200,000 of fixed selling expenses.

A special order for 50,000 rugs at $12 each has been received. No additional fixed manufacturing costs will be incurred if the order is accepted, and no selling or administrative costs will result. If the order is accepted, overall profitability will:

a increase by $50,000.

b increase by $100,000.

c decrease by $200,000.

d change by an amount other than those listed.

4 Stillwater provided the following information about its three divisions:

	A	B	C
Sales	$1,000	$2,000	$2,500
Variable costs	500	1,700	2,700
Unavoidable fixed costs	200	200	100
Avoidable fixed costs	200	100	100

Can Stillwater improve overall profitability by closing any of the divisions?

a No, Stillwater can only hope to break even.

b Yes, by closing Division B.

c Yes, by closing Division C.

d Yes, by closing Divisions B and C.

5 In a decision that involves the use of scarce resources (say, machine hours), which of the following can safely be ignored?
  a The contribution margin per machine hour.
  b Opportunity costs.
  c Sunk costs.
  d Relevant costs.

6 When calculating the controllable contribution margin, fixed costs should be:
  a ignored.
  b subtracted from the contribution margin if such amounts are controllable by a segment's management.
  c subtracted from the contribution margin if such amounts are directly traceable to a segment.
  d subtracted from the contribution margin if such amounts are both controllable by a segment's management and directly traceable to the segment.

Questions 7 and 8 are based on the following facts:
  Cranston sells a product for $15 per unit. Variable manufacturing costs are $8 per unit, and variable selling and administrative costs are $3 per unit. Fixed manufacturing costs are $25,000 per year; fixed selling and administrative costs are $15,000. In the first year of operation, the company produced 12,500 units but sold only 10,000 units.

7 The ending inventory under absorption costing when compared to the ending inventory under direct costing is:
  a $5,000 smaller.   c the same.
  b $5,000 greater.   d $2,500 greater.

8 Under direct costing, the amount of fixed cost included in cost of goods sold for the first year of operation is:
  a $0.   c $25,000.
  b $20,000.   d $40,000.

COMMUNICATION OF ACCOUNTING INFORMATION

CAI27-1 *The flowchart as a communication tool* (L.O. 2)

Communication Principle: Businesses often use a variety of charts and graphs to convey information. A flowchart, for example, such as that shown in Exhibit 27-4, is frequently employed to simplify a sequential process. Various thoughts and/or processes are indicated by rectangular boxes, and decisions that must be made are depicted with diamonds. Finally, the arrows signify the sequence of events.

If you have ever studied computer programming or systems design, you probably know that flowcharts can display various degrees of sophistication. Some contain a vast assortment of symbols and connectors; others do not. The flowchart in Exhibit 27-4 is very basic in comparison with those encountered in practice. Nevertheless, it is still an effective tool—one that assists in the communication of a complex operation for better understanding of the task at hand.

■ ■ ■ ■ ■ ■ ■ ■

The management team at Gopher Company routinely rejects special orders. Carolyn Tsay, a staff accountant, is very concerned that profitable opportunities are being lost and has communicated this fact to her supervisor. The supervisor has arranged a special meeting with top management for Carolyn to explain her observations.

Instructions

Assume the role of Carolyn Tsay. In contemplation of the meeting, prepare a flowchart of the financial logic that should be used in evaluating whether a special order should be accepted or rejected. Given the nature of the situation (i.e., a presentation to top management), the flowchart's final draft should be polished and impressive.

Answers to Chapter Quiz

1 c

2 b [Each unit has a $3 contribution margin ($15 − $12); thus, 1,000 units × $3 = $3,000]

3 d

4 a

5 b

CHAPTER 28

Capital Budgeting

LEARNING OBJECTIVES

After studying this chapter, you should be able to:

Explain the nature of capital budgeting and identify the factors to consider in capital expenditure proposals.

Explain the concept of the time value of money.

Distinguish between compound interest and present value.

Use net present value, the internal rate of return, payback, and the accounting rate of return to evaluate long-term projects.

(Appendix) Demonstrate how income taxes complicate cash flow calculations.

Each year, American businesses spend vast sums of money on a variety of long-term investments. As evidence, consider the following excerpt from a recent annual report of General Electric:

> GE's total expenditures for new plant and equipment during [the year] were $2.3 billion, about the same level as previous years. . . . Total expenditures for the past five years were $10.9 billion, of which 30% was to increase capacity; 23% was to increase productivity; 14% was to replace and renew older equipment; 11% was to support new business start-ups; and 22% was for such other purposes as to improve research and development facilities and to provide for safety and environmental protection.

Most executives will agree that a company's long-term investments often spell the difference between financial prosperity or lengthy periods of unprofitable performance. Investments such as those cited by General Electric are costly and require the commitment of resources for many years. As a result, poor decisions are usually very difficult to reverse.

This chapter focuses on the evaluation of programs and projects that influence the financial performance of more than a single accounting period. Outlays for such undertakings are commonly called *capital expenditures*; the related planning and decision making is appropriately labeled **capital budgeting.**

CAPITAL BUDGETING DECISIONS

OBJECTIVE

Explain the nature of capital budgeting and identify the factors to consider in capital expenditure proposals.

Most firms face the same problem when evaluating long-term investments: too many investment opportunities and not enough money. Management must therefore exercise extreme care in the analysis of alternative courses of action. This analysis process gives rise to two basic types of capital budgeting decisions. The first type involves *project screening* to determine whether an investment proposal meets certain preset criteria. Examples of such criteria include a specified rate of return or perhaps the recovery of invested funds within a certain number of years. If the screening tests are met, the proposal is considered for acceptance; if not, rejection is in order.

The second type of decision concerns *ranking*. Given that a number of projects will probably be acceptable, ranking must occur because of the limited availability of investment dollars. A distinction is necessary to determine the most attractive project, the second most attractive project, and so forth. Our discussion will concentrate on screening decisions, with ranking decisions being left for advanced accounting and finance courses.

Decision Factors to Consider

Assume that you recently inherited $10,000 from a wealthy relative and are now exploring various investment possibilities. Three opportunities appear particularly attractive:

1 Purchase a six-month, $10,000 certificate of deposit that carries an interest rate of 8%.

2 Acquire $10,000 of stock in several so-called growth companies. The shares promise significant appreciation in market value but pay no dividends.

3 Purchase a $70,000 home by paying $9,000 down and securing a $61,000 mortgage loan. The loan will require payments over the next 30 years and carries a 10% interest rate.

Somehow you must decide which of the three investments to select. As a starting point, the following thoughts might be running through your mind:

- The first two investments require an immediate cash outlay of $10,000; the third requires only $9,000.
- The certificate of deposit yields a guaranteed interest rate of 8%.
- The stocks generate no dividends. However, the long-run income may be attractive if market prices increase substantially.
- The house requires monthly payments for mortgage principal and interest along with outlays for insurance, utilities, and property taxes. Furthermore, under the laws and regulations in effect at the time of this writing, interest and property taxes are deductible for federal income tax purposes. Homes have also appreciated in value over the years.

Although our list of decision factors is far from complete, these factors coincide with those studied by managers in the evaluation of capital expenditure proposals. Management is concerned with (1) the amount of an investment, (2) the periodic returns from an investment, and (3) the lowest rate of return acceptable to the company.

ETHICS ISSUE

X, Inc., requires that all capital projects in excess of $100,000 be approved by the board of directors. A remodeling project is estimated to cost roughly $120,000, subdivided as follows: building improvements, $80,000; new furniture, $25,000; and new computers, $15,000. To save time and avoid having to obtain board approval, you have been told to report the remodeling as three separate expenditures. How would you react?

Initial Investment

The amount of an investment is measured by the cash outlays necessary for acquisition. These outlays usually coincide with the purchase cost of the acquired assets (e.g., buildings, machinery, and so forth). Be aware, however, that in addition to this type of investment, some projects may require a further commitment of funds to simply get "up and running." Consider, for example, a company that desires to expand its market area and customer base. In most cases, this type of business decision is accompanied by a rise in the level of cash needed to support daily operations, along with buildups in accounts receivable and inventory levels. This situation requires an *investment in working capital* by the firm, with related dollar amounts treated as part of the project's initial cost.

Most companies are able to partially recover invested funds when a project's life is over. For instance, equipment and other assets may be sold in secondhand markets. In addition, the working capital investment just mentioned may be recovered by the sale of inventory, the collection of receivables, and the return of cash for use in other business activities. Amounts received from these events are properly treated as cash inflows in the year of occurrence.

Periodic Returns

Investments are made to increase an organization's profitability. Added profitability results from projects that (1) produce income by generating revenues in excess of expenses or (2) decrease costs. Income-producing investments include the addition of new product lines, an expansion of plant capacity, and the implementation of successful marketing programs. Cost reduction endeavors, on the other hand, often involve the installation of more efficient equipment and the acquisition of assets to perform services currently handled by outside entities. For example, a company could acquire its own truck to eliminate dependence on outside delivery firms.

For both income-producing and cost-saving projects, managers desire a return. That is, managers seek to recover their initial outlays *and* to provide the company with a reward for the risk associated with the investment. Returns can be measured in terms of accounting profits or net cash flows (cash inflows minus cash outflows). *For long-term decisions cash flow is preferred.* Bear in mind that accounting net income is accrual based and thereby focuses on when revenues are earned and expenses are incurred. The actual receipt and disbursement of cash are ignored.

As we explained in the Appendix to Chapter 17 and will explore later in this chapter, the timing of cash flows is extremely important. Stated simply, a dollar received today is worth more than a dollar to be received in the future. The dollar received today can be reinvested to earn additional returns for the enterprise. Naturally, additional returns are not possible with future dollars until such amounts are actually in hand. Given the time value of money and the fact that *cash* is invested and *cash* earns a return, cash flow is normally used for the evaluation of long-term investments.

The Cost of Capital

The analysis of investment opportunities requires the establishment of a cutoff rate for project acceptance or rejection. The cutoff rate (i.e., the minimum return acceptable to the firm) depends on the cost of obtaining investment funds. For example, if the cost of funds is 12%, a firm would ordinarily invest only in those projects that promise a return in excess of 12%.

As you are aware, funds for long-term investments are obtained from a variety of sources such as bonds, mortgages, stock issuances, and operations. The collective cost of these funds (which includes outlays for interest expense and dividends) is commonly referred to as the **cost of capital.**

Most managers will agree that proper determination of this measure is controversial and a topic related more to finance than to accounting. Thus, the underlying calculations are not considered here. Be aware, though, that the minimum desired return for investments is typically set several percentage points higher than the cost of capital. Such a procedure helps to offset any errors that may occur in the cost of capital's accompanying assumptions and estimates. The illustrations and problems that follow this discussion assume that the cost of capital has already been determined and is ready for use in the decision-making process.

Suppose that a manager has an option of receiving $1,000 today or $1,000 one year from now.[1] Virtually every executive would prefer the first alternative for two basic reasons. Receipt of the money today offers the advantage of reduced risk. The future, of course, is full of uncertainty. As time passes, more and more events can occur that jeopardize the inflow of future dollars. Because the $1,000 is in hand, the executive is exposed to less risk and becomes less concerned about changing conditions in the forthcoming months.

The first alternative is also preferred because of the **time value of money.** As explained earlier, a cash receipt today is worth more than an inflow that occurs in the future. Remember, money in hand can be reinvested to earn additional returns.

We caution that the preceding example is overly simplistic. When one compares equal sums of money (e.g., $1,000) at two different times, the preferred alternative is readily apparent. What happens, however, if we change the illustration? Assume that the second alternative now calls for an inflow of $1,050 or even $1,100 in one year. The decision becomes more difficult. Maybe the extra $50 or $100 is worth the wait; maybe not. An important consideration would surely be the investment opportunities available for the $1,000 just received.

Decisions such as those cited are facilitated if the time value of money is quantitatively incorporated into the evaluation process. This integration is accomplished by the use of present value, a derivation of compound interest.

Compound Interest

With **compound interest,** the interest is computed on principal plus previously accumulated interest. To illustrate, assume that you deposited $1,000 in a 6% savings account. If the interest is compounded annually, the deposit will grow to $1,191.02 by the end of three years, as the following figures show.

Year	Beginning Balance	+	Interest at 6%	=	Ending Balance
1	$1,000.00		$60.00		$1,060.00
2	1,060.00		63.60		1,123.60
3	1,123.60		67.42		1,191.02

Observe that the interest rate remains constant at 6%; however, the amount of interest earned each year has grown. This situation arises because the interest is based on principal and also on previously computed interest that is left on deposit.

Despite the apparent simplicity, the calculations become quite burdensome when many years are involved. Fortunately, a formula is available to determine the *future value* (i.e., ending value) of an investment at a given rate of interest (return). The formula is:

THE TIME VALUE OF MONEY

OBJECTIVE 2

Explain the concept of the time value of money.

OBJECTIVE 3

Distinguish between compound interest and present value.

---

[1] The presentation on the next few pages is an expansion of the Appendix to Chapter 17.

$$V = P(1 + r)^n$$

where

V = future value of the investment
P = present value of the investment
r = interest rate
n = number of periods

To calculate the value of the previous deposit at the end of, say, two years, the formula is used as follows:

$$
\begin{aligned}
V &= P(1 + r)^n \\
&= \$1,000(1 + 0.06)^2 \\
&= \$1,000(1.1236) \\
&= \$1,123.60
\end{aligned}
$$

Present Value

An investment can also be evaluated from a different perspective. Reconsider the preceding example and assume an opportunity is available that promises a $1,060 cash inflow at the end of one year. If you are willing to accept a 6% return on your money, how much would you spend today to receive this cash flow? The answer is $1,000. Why? If $1,000 is invested immediately at a 6% interest rate, the outlay will grow to the $1,060 that you can receive.

In essence we found this amount by working backward. Rather than take a present amount and extend it out to the future, as we would with compound interest, we took a future amount and brought it back to today. This latter process is often called **discounting.** The $1,000 is termed the **present value** of the investment, or the amount an investor is willing to pay to secure a specified cash flow ($1,060) on a future date (one year from now) at a given rate of return (6%). Compound interest and present value can be contrasted as shown in the accompanying graphic.

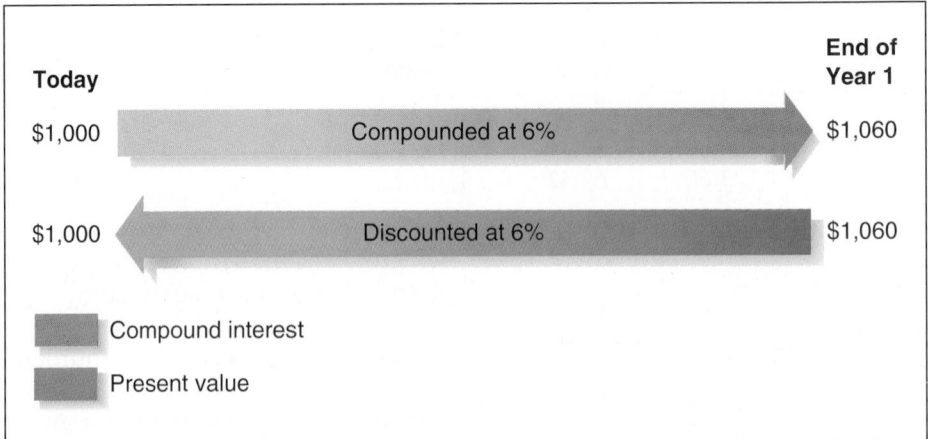

In view of this relationship, the present value of a future cash flow can be found by solving the compound interest formula for P. Since

$$V = P(1 + r)^n$$

then

$$P = \frac{V}{(1 + r)^n}$$

Using numbers from the preceding illustration, the $1,000 present value is determined as follows:

$$P = \frac{V}{(1 + r)^n}$$
$$= \frac{\$1,060}{(1.06)^1}$$
$$= \$1,000$$

Present Value Tables

Tables have been developed to assist in present value computations. Examine Table 1 in Appendix D at the end of the text. The table shows the present value factors of $1 at different rates of interest and for different time periods. Continuing our previous example, the factor for $1 to be received in one year given a 6% interest rate is 0.94340. Because we are trying to find the present value of $1,060, the calculation that follows is necessary.

Cash Flow		Present Value Factor		Present Value
$1,060	×	0.94340	=	$1,000

A quick review of the table reveals that as we go further into the future, the present value factors become smaller. Notice the impact of time on the receipt of $1,060.

If Received at the End of Year	The 6% Present Value Factor Would Be	Producing a Present Value of*
1	0.94340	$1,000
3	0.83962	890
5	0.74726	792
7	0.66506	705
9	0.59190	627

* $1,060 × present value factor.

These factors reflect the time value of money—the sooner cash inflows are received, the more valuable they are to the recipient. All other things being equal, companies are willing to pay greater sums of money for investments that promise quicker dollar returns.

Multiple Cash Flows and Annuities

Most long-term investments affect cash flows for more than a single year. To illustrate the necessary procedures, assume Target Industries acquired a machine that promised annual savings in cash operating costs of $2,000 over the next five years. Management requires a return on investment of 10%. For capital budgeting purposes, reductions in operating costs are viewed as cash inflows. Using the factors from Table 1, the present value of the machine's savings is $7,582:

Year	Cash Flow	× Present Value Factor	= Present Value
1	$2,000	0.90909	$1,818
2	2,000	0.82645	1,653
3	2,000	0.75132	1,503
4	2,000	0.68301	1,366
5	2,000	0.62092	1,242
Total present value			$7,582

These computations result in each of the individual cash flows being discounted back to the beginning of Year 1 (i.e., the "present"), as depicted in Exhibit 28-1.

A review of this process shows that in each year a present value factor is multiplied by the $2,000 cash flow. The calculations would have required less work had the savings been multiplied by the summation of the individual factors (0.90909 + 0.82645 + 0.75132 + 0.68301 + 0.62092 = 3.79079). As the following figures show, the same result is achieved:

$$\$2,000 \times 3.79079 = \$7,582$$

Our example has focused on an **annuity**—a series of equal cash flows over a number of years. To further simplify procedures in this type of situation, accountants often use an annuity table (see Table 2 in Appendix D). The factor in Table 2 for a $1 annuity over the next five years, discounted at 10%, is 3.79079. As before, the factor is multiplied by the cash flow to derive the appropriate present value.

An Added Complexity. Sometimes, annuity calculations are needed to discount cash flows that *begin* several years into the future. Suppose, for instance, that the machine in our illustration promises annual operating savings of $2,000 for the first two years and $1,000 for each of the next three years. Target now has two separate annuities, and the present value is found by using the procedures at the top of page 1165.

EXHIBIT 28-1
The Discounting of Multiple Cash Flows

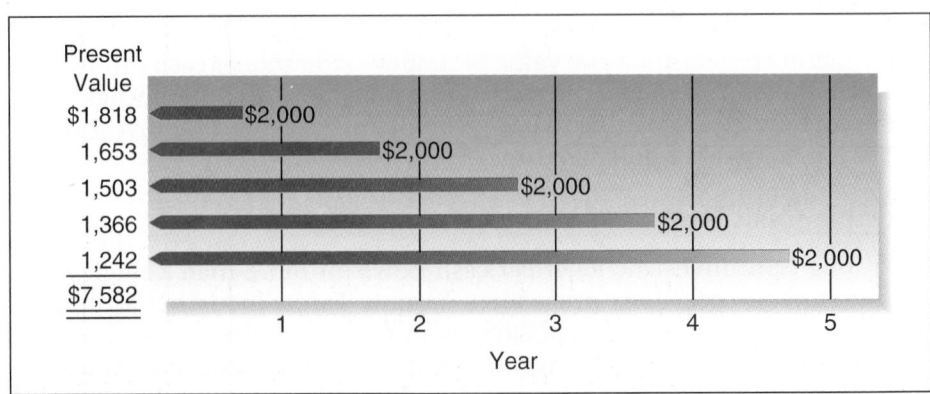

Years	Cash Flow	×	Present Value Factor	=	Present Value
1–2	$2,000		1.73554		$3,471
3–5	1,000		2.05525*		2,055
Total present value					$5,526

* 3.79079 − 1.73554.

Table 2 is once again the source of our data. The factor of 1.73554 is needed to discount the savings that occur during the first two years. The second factor, computed as the difference between 3.79079 (an annuity factor that covers Years 1–5) and 1.73554, permits Target to discount the cash flows for Years 3–5.

Tips & Techniques

The authors have found that many students disregard annuities in favor of a series of yearly multiplications with Table 1 factors. We feel this practice is unwise. Because an annuity factor is nothing more than the total of individual present value factors, problem solution time can be greatly reduced by mastering Table 2. Use the annuity factors whenever you are confronted with a series of equal cash inflows or outflows. The study time expended is more than offset by the benefits derived.

CAPITAL BUDGETING EVALUATION METHODS

Four methods of evaluating capital budgeting proposals are frequently encountered in practice:

1 Net present value

2 Internal rate of return

3 Payback

4 Accounting rate of return

Several recent surveys have shown that these evaluation tools are normally used in conjunction with one another. This situation occurs because each of the techniques listed has strengths and weaknesses and provides different information to management.

The majority of our discussion will center on the discounted cash flow methods of net present value and the internal rate of return. Both of these approaches have conceptual advantages over the others cited and have seen increased use in recent years.

Net Present Value

With the **net-present-value method**, the present value of an investment's cash inflows is netted against the present value of the cash outflows. The rate of return used for discounting corresponds to or is slightly in excess of the firm's cost of capital.

As an example of the necessary procedures, assume that Alpine Delivery

OBJECTIVE

4

Use net present value, the internal rate of return, payback, and the accounting rate of return to evaluate long-term projects.

is considering an expansion of service to the cities of High Point and Beeville. Two trucks must be acquired at a total cost of $95,000. The trucks have an eight-year life, will be depreciated by using the straight-line method, and are expected to generate annual net cash inflows of $18,000 from new business. Alpine requires a 10% minimum return on all investments.

Some managers may be tempted to evaluate the truck acquisition as follows:

Initial investment	$ (95,000)
Annual net cash inflows ($18,000 × 8 years)	144,000
Difference in favor of acquisition	$ 49,000

This analysis is incorrect for two reasons. First, the computations imply that all of the cash inflows are equivalent when, in fact, they are not. (As discussed in previous sections of the chapter, inflows that occur in earlier years can be reinvested for longer periods of time.) Second, we cannot compare an immediate cash outflow with cash inflows that are spread over the next eight years. Since the timing differs, the result is a comparison of dollars of unequal values—basically a study of apples and oranges.

The proper approach is to discount the cash flows at 10%. The correct computations follow.

	Cash Flow	×	Present Value Factor	=	Present Value
Initial investment	$(95,000)		1.00000		$(95,000)
Annual net cash inflows	18,000		5.33493		96,029
Net present value					$ 1,029

A factor of 1.0 is used for the initial investment because the outlay takes place immediately. The other factor (5.33493) is obtained from the annuity table (Table 2) at the intersection of the 8-period row and 10% column.

The net present value of $1,029 indicates the present value of the inflows exceeds the present value of the outflows. The trucks are therefore an attractive investment and should be acquired if funds are available. Projects that produce a positive net present value are acceptable; those with a negative net present value should be rejected. A positive net present value means the returns from an investment exceed a company's minimum desired rate of return (10% in Alpine's case).

Before leaving this example, it is important to note the impact of the discounting process on the decision. Actual cash inflows exceed actual cash outflows by $49,000; yet when discounting is introduced, the present value of the inflows and outflows differs by only $1,029. The time value of money has greatly diminished the attractiveness of the investment.

Omission of Depreciation Expense

Although the trucks have an eight-year life, management disregarded depreciation expense when making the acquisition decision. Depreciation is excluded from present value calculations because of the emphasis on cash flows and depreciation's noncash nature. The cost of the trucks took the form of a single, $95,000 cash outflow at the time of acquisition. An additional deduction for depreciation would therefore result in a double counting of the assets' cost.

Despite its noncash character, depreciation expense does affect the amount of income taxes paid to federal and state governments. Income taxes, which were ignored in the Alpine example, are discussed in the Appendix to this chapter.

An Expanded Example Using Net Present Value

The illustration that follows shows how a business can integrate present value into a keep-versus-replace decision. As you progress through the presentation, observe how the relevancy concept (as introduced in Chapter 27) continues to play an important role in the evaluation of alternatives.

Assume the Delicious Baking Company is studying the replacement of some equipment acquired four years ago at a cost of $55,000. The equipment is expected to provide six more years of service if $4,000 of major repairs are performed two years from now. Annual cash operating costs total $13,000 and are not expected to change in future periods. Delicious can sell the equipment now for $24,000; the estimated residual value in six years is $5,000.

Management can acquire new equipment that costs $62,000. The new equipment has a service life of six years, is expected to reduce cash operating costs by $6,000 annually, and has an estimated residual value of $18,000. Annual company sales will total $240,000 regardless of the decision.

If Delicious has a minimum desired rate of return of 14%, what should the firm do? To determine the proper course of action, we must first identify all relevant cash flows, namely, those that occur in the future and differ among the alternatives. Such an analysis reveals that we can disregard the $55,000 cost of the old equipment (it is sunk) and the future sales revenues of $1,440,000 ($240,000 × 6 years), which are common to both the keep and the replace options. Once the relevant cash flows are decided, the amounts are discounted by using the 14% present value factors that appear in Tables 1 and 2. The appropriate computations are shown in Exhibit 28-2.

The analysis reveals a negative net present value for both the keep and the replace alternatives. At first glance it appears that both options should be rejected, but such action is not possible. Given that one alternative must be selected in this type of situation, Delicious Baking should keep the present equipment. On a discounted cash flow basis, the company stands to benefit by $5,667 [$(51,353) versus $(57,020)].[2]

Internal Rate of Return

The net-present-value method is only one of several tools that a company can employ to evaluate capital budgeting proposals. Another tool that incorporates discounted cash flows is the **internal rate of return (IRR).** Some-

---

[2] The negative net present values arise because the company's sales revenues, a significant cash inflow, were omitted from the analysis.

	Year(s) of Occurrence	Cash Flow	× Present Value Factor =	Present Value
Keep the present equipment				
Cash operating costs	1–6	$(13,000)	3.88867	$(50,553)
Major repairs	2	(4,000)	0.76947	(3,078)
Disposal	6	5,000	0.45559	2,278
Net present value				$(51,353)
Replace the present equipment				
Initial investment	Immediate	$(62,000)	1.00000	$(62,000)
Sale of old equipment	Immediate	24,000	1.00000	24,000
Cash operating costs ($13,000 − $6,000)	1–6	(7,000)	3.88867	(27,221)
Disposal	6	18,000	0.45559	8,201
Net present value				$(57,020)
Net present value in favor of keeping the present equipment				$ 5,667

times called the time-adjusted rate of return, the IRR represents the actual yield on a project. It is computed by finding the discount rate that equates the present value of a project's cash inflows with the present value of the cash outflows. As a result of this calculation, the net present value is zero.

To illustrate the related procedures, let us assume that Kim Enterprises is confronted with an investment opportunity that costs $12,009 and promises net cash inflows of $5,000 for each of the next three years. The following computation, where F is defined as the discount factor that equates the present value of the inflows and outflows, is needed:

$$\$5,000 \times F = \$12,009$$

$$F = \frac{\$12,009}{\$5,000}$$

$$F = 2.4018$$

The return on Kim's investment can now be found by determining the rate represented by a factor of 2.4018. Because the investment involves a three-year annuity, we must examine Table 2, part of which is reproduced below.

Periods	8%	10%	12%	14%	16%
⋮	⋮	⋮	⋮	⋮	⋮
3	2.57710	2.48685	2.40183	2.32163	2.24589
⋮	⋮	⋮	⋮	⋮	⋮

Except for an extremely small rounding error, the 2.4018 discount factor coincides with a 12% interest rate. Thus, Kim's investment yields a 12%

rate of return. As noted earlier, this particular rate will produce a zero net present value:

Initial investment [$(12,009) × 1.00000]	$(12,009)
Annual net cash inflows discounted at 12% ($5,000 × 2.4018)	12,009
Net present value	$ —

Should the investment be pursued? Is a 12% return attractive to Kim? The answers to these questions depend on the company's cost of capital. If the internal rate of return is equal to or greater than the cost of capital, then the project should be considered for acceptance. If not, rejection is in order.

Two Complications

Two complications are normally encountered when figuring the internal rate of return. First, the factor that equates the present value of the inflows and outflows usually does not coincide with the factors that appear in the annuity table. Returning to the Kim example, suppose the investment called for an initial outlay of $11,775 rather than $12,009. The factor for the project would now be 2.355, calculated as follows:

$$\$5,000 \times F = \$11,775$$

$$F = \frac{\$11,775}{\$5,000}$$

$$F = 2.355$$

Scanning Table 2 for a three-period annuity, we find that the factor falls between a return of 12% and 14%. The actual return is found by using the mathematical process of *interpolation*, with the necessary procedures shown below.

	Present Value Factors	
12% return	2.40183	2.40183
Return on Kim's investment	2.35500	
14% return		2.32163
Difference	0.04683	0.08020

$$\text{Internal Rate of Return} = 12\% + \frac{0.04683}{0.08020}(2\%)^*$$

$$= 13.17\%$$

* 14% − 12%.

The second complication relates to uneven cash flows. The Kim illustration had an immediate single outflow followed by three inflows of $5,000 each. Picture the difficulties that would arise if there were additional flows of, say, an extra payment in the second year and the receipt of a residual value in the third year. Finding the one factor that equates the present value of all inflows and outflows would be burdensome, to say the least, and would require numerous rounds of trial and error. Fortunately, computer programs and hand-held calculators are available that perform the necessary computations. Most spreadsheets, for example, contain built-in functions that readily handle the discounting of both single-sum cash flows and annuities. The user can therefore concentrate on the analysis of results rather than the drudgery of procedure.

The Payback Method

Few accountants question the superiority of the discounted cash flow methods for investment analysis. Yet, as explained earlier in the chapter, methods other than net present value and the internal rate of return are in widespread use. Discounted cash flow began to gain popularity in the 1950s and is a relative newcomer on the project evaluation scene. For a number of reasons many managers still favor the older approaches, which ignore the time value of money. A brief overview of these approaches is therefore in order.

The **payback method** measures the amount of time it takes to recover a project's initial cash investment. To illustrate the necessary calculations, assume that Hill Corporation is examining the possibility of manufacturing a new product. Plant and equipment that cost $200,000 must be purchased and should result in net cash inflows of $60,000 for each of the next five years. When the cash flows are uniform, as they are in this example, the payback period is derived by use of the following formula:

$$\text{Payback Period} = \frac{\text{Initial Investment}}{\text{Annual Net Cash Inflow}}$$

$$= \frac{\$200,000}{\$60,000}$$

$$= 3.33 \text{ years}$$

Uneven Cash Flows

The formula just shown can only be used with uniform, or even, net cash inflows. In those situations where the annual inflows are unequal, the flows are summed until the amount of the original investment is reached. For example, assume the inflows associated with Hill's $200,000 investment are now as follows: Year 1, $70,000; Year 2, $70,000; Year 3, $80,000; Year 4, $50,000; and Year 5, $30,000. The required computations are:

Year	Annual Net Cash Inflow	Cumulative Net Cash Inflow
1	$70,000	$ 70,000
2	70,000	140,000
3	80,000	220,000
4	50,000	270,000
5	30,000	300,000

The computations reveal that $140,000 is recovered by the end of Year 2 and $220,000 by the conclusion of Year 3. Thus, the 200,000th dollar arrives sometime during Year 3 as a result of the $80,000 net cash inflow. The payback method assumes that cash flows are spread evenly through-out a period. Consequently, the additional $60,000 that must be recovered to reach the payback ($200,000 − $140,000) is assumed to be received three quarters of the way through the year ($60,000 ÷ $80,000). The payback, then, is 2.75 years.

Use of Payback: Pros and Cons

The payback method provides its users with a very simple tool for evaluation purposes. By comparing a project's payback period against a preestablished standard, a manager can easily determine project acceptability. This type of comparison is especially useful for companies that have limited cash balances and wish to recover their investment dollars rapidly. Short paybacks allow cash-starved businesses to undertake additional opportunities: the sooner cash is received, the sooner reinvestment can occur.

Unfortunately, the use of payback is not problem-free. In addition to ignoring the time value of money, the payback method exhibits a serious weakness by disregarding project profitability. As an example, assume that a company can invest in one of the following projects:

Project	Initial Investment	Annual Net Cash Inflow	Project Life
A	$100,000	$50,000	3 years
B	100,000	40,000	6 years

If the decision is based solely on payback, project A would be selected, because the initial investment is recovered more quickly.

$$\text{Project A Payback} = \frac{\$100,000}{\$50,000} = 2.0 \text{ years}$$

$$\text{Project B Payback} = \frac{\$100,000}{\$40,000} = 2.5 \text{ years}$$

Is this the correct choice, however? Most entities make investments to generate profit, not to see how fast funds can be returned.[3] Project B is really a better selection, because inflows *after* the payback period is reached will total $140,000 ($40,000 × 3.5 years) versus $50,000 ($50,000 × 1 year) for project A. Stated differently, the payback method considers net cash inflows up until the time the initial investment is recovered. Any receipts that occur after this point are disregarded in the computational process.

---

[3] As evidence, consider a recent competition won by Indianapolis for a new United Airlines maintenance facility. The city and the state of Indiana granted $294.6 million in incentives (such as tax breaks) to attract the center, which will create at least 6,300 jobs directly and another 11,000 jobs indirectly. State officials estimate a 16-year payback for Indiana's investment, while the city anticipates a 12- to 15-year recovery period. See "Ask and Your Company Shall Receive," *The Dallas Morning News*, February 4, 1992, pp. 1D, 6D.

HIGHLIGHT
Payback and a Midlife Crisis

Periodically, most everyone steps back and studies his or her career choice—especially when things are not going smoothly. Included in this group are lawyers who haven't made partner, teachers whose careers have peaked, and artists who grow tired of poverty. Many of these individuals think about dropping it all for a job switch, often by pursuing a graduate degree in business administration (more commonly known as an M.B.A.). Getting such a degree may well be a road to a new career. It might even be an intellectual challenge. But in financial terms, it may *not* be a good investment, especially for mid-career professionals.

The problem is the cost—and not just the cost of tuition. Getting an M.B.A. often means a career-switcher has to forgo two years of a substantial salary to study full-time, since part-time studies may be considered inadequate for students who need to be immersed in a new field. Analyzing the cost and return of investing in an M.B.A. degree, two tax planners with a large public accounting firm calculated how long it would take a career-switcher to pay for the degree with earnings from a new job. Their conclusion: Even with an above-average starting salary, the investment would be earned back only with superstar raises.

The conclusion is based on the following table, which shows the number of years required to recoup the two years of lost earnings and the cost of private-school education (the latter estimated at $28,000). The calculations assume that the career changers were 35 years old, had 10 years' work experience, and were earning $50,000 a year before the switch. Two further assumptions: their salaries would have increased 5% a year if they had stayed on the job, and the switchers could have earned 6%

a year on the forgone income. The table shows a range of starting salaries—and annual increases—after graduation.

Annual Salary Increases	Starting Salary		
	$40,000	$50,000	$60,000
5%	Never	Never	Never
10%	22 years	16 years	11 years
15%	17 years	11 years	9 years

As you can see, the fastest payback would be nine years—at a $60,000 starting salary and 15% annual raises. At a $40,000 starting salary and 10% annual raises, it would take 22 years to recoup the investment.

Not everyone would fare so badly, of course. Someone making a lower salary to begin with would lose less money by quitting work. And students at taxpayer-supported state schools would pay substantially less tuition than at a private school. Students who would have to leave home and live on campus, on the other hand, would face additional expenses that could run over $10,000 a year.

Some M.B.A. candidates are fortunate and can manage to keep income flowing while attending school full-time. Jeff Zahn, a 33-year-old New York musician, was earning between $45,000 and $50,000 annually as an electronic keyboard and cello player, but the unpredictability of the musician's life made him opt for business school. "A Broadway show can open and close in a night," he says. At the time this article was written, Zahn worked while studying full-time at New York University. During the day, he was a business student. At night, he played in the orchestra for the Broadway musical *Cats*.

Accounting Rate of Return

A fourth evaluation tool, the **accounting rate of return,** focuses on the average income generated by a project in relation to the initial investment outlay required for the project. Unlike the methods discussed earlier, *this capital budgeting technique emphasizes income and not cash flows.* A proper measure of profit, of course, includes a deduction for depreciation expense.

The accounting rate of return is computed by the following formula:

$$\text{Accounting Rate of Return} = \frac{\text{Average Annual Increase in Income}}{\text{Initial Investment}}$$

To illustrate the related calculations, assume that a company is considering the acquisition of some new machinery that costs $80,000. The machinery has a service life of 10 years, has no residual value, and will be depreciated by using the straight-line method. Average annual net cash inflows from operations are expected to increase by $28,000. The accounting rate of return is 25%, derived as follows:

$$\text{Accounting Rate of Return} = \frac{\$28,000 - \$8,000}{\$80,000} = 25\%$$

The numerator is computed by subtracting depreciation expense of $8,000 ($80,000 ÷ 10 years) from the operating cash flows.

Because the machinery will be depreciated, some companies feel the accounting rate of return is more appropriately based on an average investment figure rather than on the initial outlay. The average investment can be calculated by adding the beginning and ending investment and dividing by 2, specifically, ($80,000 + $0) ÷ 2, or $40,000.

Evaluation of the Accounting Rate of Return

The accounting rate of return remains popular primarily because of its consistency with the techniques employed to evaluate companywide and divisional performance. Further, most users agree that the accounting rate of return is a simple tool that is easy to understand. The calculated return on an investment is merely compared against a cutoff that has been established by management to judge project attractiveness.

Like payback, however, this method has several serious drawbacks. The time value of money is ignored as is the timing of an investment's earnings. Two projects, for example, may produce identical rates of return over a period of, say, three years. One of these projects may generate uniform earnings through the three-year period; the other may actually produce negative returns in the first two years and a substantial payoff in Year 3. These problems require that management closely study the data that underlie the calculation and not rely totally on the rate of return itself.

Businesses pay a substantial amount of their income to governmental authorities. In light of this fact, the revenues and expenses that accompany an investment must be examined to determine the effect on a company's taxes and related cash flows. In practice, the cash flows used with the

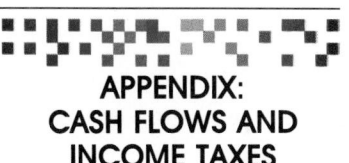

APPENDIX: CASH FLOWS AND INCOME TAXES

evaluation methods discussed earlier are normally calculated on an after-tax basis.

The Aftertax Concept

The aftertax concept is probably best explained by means of a simplified illustration. Assume that San Juan Enterprises, a service business, is studying the impact of adding a new administrative assistant to the payroll. Yearly salary and fringe benefit costs are expected to average $25,000; the company is subject to a 40% income tax rate. Management has prepared the following profitability analysis:

	Present Situation	Proposed Situation
Revenues	$200,000	$200,000
Operating expenses		
Existing	$130,000	$130,000
Administrative assistant	—	25,000
Total	$130,000	$155,000
Income before taxes	$ 70,000	$ 45,000
Income taxes at 40%	28,000	18,000
Net income	$ 42,000	$ 27,000

Observe the effect of the hiring decision on the company's income taxes. The increased salary and fringe benefit cost has reduced San Juan's taxes by $10,000 ($28,000 − $18,000). The true, *aftertax cost* of the administrative assistant, then, is $15,000 ($25,000 − $10,000).

In terms of cash flow, an analysis could have been made as follows:

Cash outflow for salaries and benefits	$(25,000)
Tax savings*	10,000
Net cash outflow	$(15,000)

* Recall that cost savings are treated as cash inflows.

The $15,000 net cash outflow would be employed in any type of capital budgeting analysis performed by the company (e.g., payback, net present value, and so forth).

Although our example has focused on an expense, the same concept could have been illustrated with an increase in revenue. Because revenues increase income (and related tax payments), we can say the following:

Cash inflow from added revenue	$ XX,XXX
Added taxes (a cash outflow)	(XX,XXX)
Net cash inflow	$ XX,XXX

The net cash flow computations just discussed can be simplified by use of the formula shown.

> (Cash Inflow or Outflow) × (1 − Tax Rate) = Net Cash Flow

In San Juan's case, for example, the $15,000 figure could have been derived as:

$$\$25,000 \times (1 - 0.40) = \$15,000$$

Depreciation: Why Special Treatment is Needed

On page 1166, we emphasized that depreciation is ignored in present value calculations because of its noncash nature. Bear in mind that depreciation (more specifically, a cost recovery write-off under the Modified Accelerated Cost Recovery System) is a deductible item when computing a company's tax obligation to the federal government. Such amounts, like the salary and fringe benefit costs shown earlier, therefore give rise to tax savings. However, special treatment is needed because depreciation itself is a noncash charge.

To illustrate this treatment, let us assume that San Juan's management is now considering an investment that will increase the firm's depreciation expense by $25,000. (This figure was purposely selected to coincide with the cost of the administrative assistant for ease in understanding.) Like the company's other expenditure, depreciation will produce a tax savings of $10,000. Unlike the earlier example, however, it would be improper to net the tax savings against the $25,000 figure—to do so would result in the offset of a cash flow against a noncash item. Hence, the only cash flow related to depreciation is the tax savings.

We can conclude that depreciation has given San Juan a *tax shield* of $10,000. That is, the deduction has shielded ("protected") the company's revenues from taxation and has lowered the firm's tax payments to the government. If desired, this concept could be expressed in a formula, as follows:

> Depreciation Deduction × Tax Rate = Cash Savings

$$\$25,000 \times 0.40 = \$10,000$$

END-OF-CHAPTER REVIEW

1 Explain the nature of capital budgeting and identify the factors to consider in capital expenditure proposals. Capital budgeting is concerned with the planning and decision making related to long-term investments. Examples of long-term investments include equipment acquisitions, building construction, and the addition of new product lines. Such projects are evaluated by comparing various project characteristics (e.g., the rate of return) against guidelines that have been estab-

LEARNING OBJECTIVES: THE KEY POINTS

lished by management. These evaluations are commonly known as screening decisions. Given that most companies have many acceptable projects but limited funds, management must determine the most attractive investment, the second most attractive investment, and so forth. This process is known as project ranking.

Three factors are normally considered when analyzing an investment. First, there is the amount of the initial investment, which may include an investment in working capital (e.g., buildups in cash, accounts receivable, and inventory). Second, the returns from the investment must be considered. Project returns are usually measured in terms of net cash flows, or cash inflows minus cash outflows. Finally, companies must consider the minimum rate of return acceptable on a project. This rate is typically set equal to or slightly in excess of the firm's cost of capital.

2 Explain the concept of the time value of money. The time value of money recognizes that a dollar received today is worth more to an investor than a dollar received in the future. Earlier inflows can be reinvested to generate additional returns. This concept is integrated in the evaluation of capital projects by the use of present value, as described by the next learning objective.

3 Distinguish between compound interest and present value. Compound interest and present value are two different tools that are used to evaluate an investment. Compound interest is employed to figure the amount to which a given sum will grow by the end of a designated time period. The underlying procedures involve the calculation of interest on the original amount invested as well as on previously computed interest that is left "on deposit."

Present value, on the other hand, discounts a future cash sum and figures its "current worth" to an investor. Stated differently, present value is the amount an investor is willing to pay today to receive specified future cash flows. The related computations recognize the time value of money by weighting the cash flows that occur in earlier years more heavily than those that occur in later years.

4 Use net present value, the internal rate of return, payback, and the accounting rate of return to evaluate long-term projects. As its name implies, the net-present-value method focuses on netting (i.e., offsetting) the present value of an investment's cash inflows against the present value of the cash outflows. If the result of this process is positive, the project should be considered for acceptance; if negative, rejection is in order. The internal rate of return is another present-value-based evaluation approach. This method finds the actual yield on an investment by equating the present value of an investment's cash inflows and cash outflows.

Unlike the first two approaches, payback and the accounting rate of return do not consider the time value of money. Payback shows how rapidly an initial investment is recovered. This method of project evaluation, although simple, ignores all cash flows that occur after the payback point has been reached. The accounting rate of return, also considered very easy to use, focuses on a project's return in relation to the amount invested or perhaps an average investment amount. The return in this case is measured in terms of income and not cash flow.

5 (Appendix) Demonstrate how income taxes complicate cash flow calculations. Capital budgeting models normally use aftertax amounts. Because many cash inflows and outflows (e.g., those from revenues and those for deductible expenses) affect a company's tax obligation, the tax implications for these items must be considered when analyzing a long-term investment. Deductible expenses result in a tax savings; conversely, revenues produce added tax for the firm. The tax effect is subtracted from the cash flow itself, with the net amount then used with the various capital budgeting evaluation tools. This netting procedure is not required for depreciation, which is a noncash expense.

accounting rate of return   A method of evaluating long-term projects that focuses on the average income generated in relation to the amount of the investment.

annuity   A series of equal cash flows over a number of years.

capital budgeting   Planning and decision making for long-term programs and projects.

compound interest   Interest that is calculated on both principal and previously accumulated interest.

cost of capital   The cost of investment funds.

discounting   The process of taking a future amount and bringing it back to its value today.

internal rate of return   A discounted cash flow method of evaluating long-term projects that derives the actual return on an investment.

net-present-value method   A method used to evaluate long-term investments in which the present value of an investment's cash inflows and outflows are netted against each other.

payback method   A method of analysis that measures the amount of time necessary to recover a project's initial cash investment.

present value   The amount an investor is willing to pay to secure a specified cash flow on a future date at a given rate of return.

time value of money   The concept that a dollar received today is worth more than a dollar received in the future.

The five questions that follow relate to several issues raised in the chapter. Test your knowledge of the issues by selecting the best answer. (The answers appear on p. 1191.)

1 Which of the following is rarely a consideration when analyzing a long-term project?
a The cost of the investment.
b The lowest rate of return acceptable to management.
c The company's current ratio.
d The investment's cash inflows and cash outflows.

2 The time value of money:
a is integrated in present value computations.
b weights cash flows that occur in five years more heavily than cash flows that occur in two years.
c is reflected by the accounting rate of return.
d should not be considered when analyzing an investment.

3 Hughes Corporation is considering a $200,000 machine that promises savings in cash operating costs of $40,000 over each of the next six years. The company requires a 10% return on its investments. Appropriate present value factors follow.

Present Value of $1	Present Value of a $1 Annuity
0.56447	4.35526

Ignoring income taxes, the machine's net present value is:
a $(5,790).
b $(25,790).
c $(177,421).
d some amount other than those listed above.

4 The internal rate of return:
a ignores the time value of money.
b is another name for the accounting rate of return.
c results in a net present value of zero.
d cannot be used when the payback period is less than three years.

5 The payback method:
a normally incorporates the use of discount factors.
b cannot be used with uneven cash flows.
c generally results in attractive projects from management's perspective, especially when the payback is "long" as opposed to "short."
d fails to consider all cash flows related to a project.

SUMMARY PROBLEM

The Ellison Corporation is studying the following investment opportunity:

Initial outlay required	$225,000
Net cash inflows, Years 1–5	75,000
Disposal value at the end of Year 5	5,000

Ellison desires a minimum return of 12% on all investments.

Instructions

a Compute the investment's payback period.
b Compute the net present value. Should the investment be considered for acceptance? Explain.
c Compute the internal rate of return. For simplicity, disregard the $5,000 disposal value.

Solution

a

Year	Annual Net Cash Inflow	Cumulative Net Cash Inflow
1	$75,000	$ 75,000
2	75,000	150,000
3	75,000	225,000
4	75,000	300,000
5	80,000	380,000

The payback period is three years.

b

	Cash Flow	×	Present Value Factor at 12%	=	Present Value
Initial investment	$(225,000)		1.00000		$(225,000)
Annual net cash inflows	75,000		3.60478		270,359
Disposal value	5,000		0.56743		2,837
Net present value					$ 48,196

The net present value is positive, which means the investment should be considered for acceptance.

c Let F = the discount factor that equates the present value of the investment's cash inflows and cash outflows

$$\$75,000 \times F = \$225,000$$
$$F = 3.0$$

Table 2 reveals that for a five-year annuity, a 3.0 factor lies between 18% and 20%. The internal rate of return is 19.86%, as shown by the following calculations:

	Present Value Factors	
18% return	3.12717	3.12717
Return on Ellison's investment	3.00000	
20% return		2.99061
Difference	0.12717	0.13656

$$\text{Internal Rate of Return} = 18\% + \frac{0.12717}{0.13656}(2\%)^{\star}$$
$$= 19.86\%$$

* 20% − 18%.

ASSIGNMENT MATERIAL

Q28-1 Why must businesses exercise extreme care in the selection of long-term investments?

Q28-2 Describe the screening and ranking processes related to capital budgeting.

Q28-3 What three factors should be considered in the evaluation of an investment opportunity?

Q28-4 What is meant by an investment in working capital? Are such investments ever recovered? Briefly explain.

Q28-5 In general, are net cash flows or accounting profits preferred in the evaluation of long-term investment proposals? Why?

Q28-6 What is the lowest rate of return acceptable to a company?

Q28-7 Explain what is meant by the time value of money.

Q28-8 Explain the relationship, if any, between compound interest and present value.

Q28-9 What is meant by the term "present value"?

Q28-10 What is an annuity?

Q28-11 Four methods are frequently used to evaluate capital budgeting proposals. Are these methods normally used by themselves or in conjunction with each other? Why?

Q28-12 Should depreciation be considered in a net-present-value computation if income taxes are ignored? Why?

Q28-13 When examining a project's cash inflows and outflows, what present value relationship holds true at the internal rate of return?

Q28-14 Aside from ignoring the time value of money, what is another inherent problem associated with the payback method?

Q28-15 Does the accounting rate of return focus on income or cash flows?

*Q28-16 Should cash flows used in a capital budgeting evaluation be expressed on a beforetax or an aftertax basis?

*Q28-17 Briefly discuss the concept of a depreciation tax shield.

EXERCISES

E28-1 *Basic present value calculations* (L.O. 3)
Calculate the present value of the following cash flows, rounding to the nearest dollar:
a A single cash inflow of $12,000 in five years, discounted at a 12% rate of return.
b An annual receipt of $16,000 over the next 12 years, discounted at a 14% rate of return.
c A single receipt of $15,000 at the end of Year 1 followed by a single receipt of $10,000 at the end of Year 3. The company has a 10% rate of return.
d An annual receipt of $8,000 for three years followed by a single receipt of $10,000 at the end of Year 4. The company has a 16% rate of return.

E28-2 *Present value analysis: Working backward* (L.O. 3)
The following information pertains to four independent investments:

	A	B	C	D
Present value	?	$19,646	$34,625	$50,852
Interest rate	10%	?	14%	12%
Investment period	4 years	5 years	?	10 years
Annual cash inflows	$8,000	$6,000	$7,000	?

Determine the unknown for each of the investments. (*Note:* Amounts have been rounded to the nearest dollar; please consider this procedure in your calculations. Do *not* interpolate.)

E28-3 *Straightforward net-present-value calculations* (L.O. 2, 4)
Contempo, Inc., is considering the acquisition of some new labor-saving equipment. Management estimates that the equipment will cost $42,000 and will produce the following savings in cash operating costs over the next five years: Year 1, $15,000; Year 2, $13,000; Year 3, $10,000; Year 4, $10,000; and Year 5, $6,000. The company uses the net-present-value method to analyze investments and desires a minimum rate of return of 12%.
a Compute the net present value of the proposed investment. Ignore income taxes and round to the nearest dollar.
b Considering the time value of money, should Contempo acquire the new equipment? Why?

---

* An asterisk preceding an item indicates that the material is covered in an appendix to this chapter.

E28-4 *Cash flow calculations and net present value* (L.O. 4)
On January 2, 19X1, Bruce Greene invested $10,000 in the stock market and purchased 500 shares of Heartland Development, Inc. Heartland paid cash dividends of $2.60 per share in 19X1 and 19X2; the dividend was raised to $3.10 per share in 19X3. On December 31, 19X3, Greene sold his holdings and generated proceeds of $13,000. Greene uses the net-present-value method and desires a 16% return on investments.

a Prepare a chronological list of the investment's cash flows. *Note:* Greene is entitled to the 19X3 dividend.

b Compute the investment's net present value, rounding calculations to the nearest dollar.

c Given the results of part (b), should Greene have acquired the Heartland stock? Briefly explain.

E28-5 *Straightforward net present value and internal rate of return* (L.O. 4)
The City of Bedford is studying a 600-acre site on Route 356 for a new landfill. The startup cost has been calculated as follows:

Purchase cost: $450 per acre
Site preparation: $175,000

The site can be used for 20 years before it reaches capacity. Bedford, which shares a facility in Bath Township with other municipalities, estimates that the new location will save $40,000 in annual operating costs.

a Should the landfill be acquired if Bedford desires an 8% return on its investment? Use the net-present-value method to determine your answer.

b Compute the internal rate of return on this project.

E28-6 *Payback and cash flow analysis* (L.O. 2, 4)
Elway and Associates uses the payback method to evaluate investment opportunities. Two investment proposals are under consideration, each requiring an initial outlay of $150,000. Cash flow information follows.

Investment A		Investment B	
Year	Net Cash Inflow	Year	Net Cash Inflow
1	$45,000	1–3	$35,000
2	60,000	4	40,000
3	35,000	5	10,000
4	10,000	6	40,000
5	15,000		
6	27,000		

a Compute the payback period of each investment.

b Solely on the basis of payback, which of the two investments is the more attractive? Why?

c From a total cash flow viewpoint, which of the two investments is really the more attractive? Disregard the time value of money.

d To provide the decision maker with additional information, what could Elway do to the cash inflows? Why would this process be helpful?

E28-7 *Payback and accounting rate of return* (L.O. 4)

Instant Change offers 10-minute oil changes from numerous facilities in Kansas and Nebraska. The company wants to expand into Illinois and has picked a site that is expected to have the following annual results:

Sales revenue		$310,000
Less operating expenses		
Oil & supplies	$105,000	
Wages	90,000	
Insurance	10,000	
Utilities	5,000	
Depreciation	25,000	235,000
Net income		$ 75,000

Land acquisition and building costs for the Illinois facility will require a $500,000 initial investment. Disregard income taxes.

a If management desires a payback of less than six years, should the Illinois facility be opened? Why?

b Compute the accounting rate of return on the initial investment.

c What do payback and the accounting rate of return have in common that the net-present-value method and the internal rate of return do not?

E28-8 *Comprehensive capital budgeting* (L.O. 4)

Usher Corporation is considering the purchase of a conveyor system that costs $92,133. The system has a 15-year life and will result in net cash inflows of $15,000 per year. Assume the use of straight-line depreciation, no residual value, and no income taxes, and round calculations to the nearest dollar.

a Determine the system's net present value if Usher has a 12% rate of return.

b Compute the system's internal rate of return.

c Determine the payback period.

d Determine the accounting rate of return on the company's initial investment.

E28-9 *Capital budgeting methods* (L.O. 4)

Consider the following capital budgeting evaluation tools:

1—Net present value
2—Internal rate of return
3—Payback method
4—Accounting rate of return

Match these tools with the comments that follow. In some cases more than one tool may apply.

_____a Focuses on income, not cash flows.

_____b Integrates the time value of money into the evaluation process.

_____c Equates the present value of a project's cash inflows and cash outflows.

_____d Stresses the recovery of the initial investment outlay.

_____e Discounts cash flows by employing factors that relate to a company's minimum acceptable return.

_____f A cash-flow-based approach that ignores selected cash flows on a project.

E28-10 *Overview of capital budgeting* (L.O. 1, 3, 4)

Evaluate the comments that follow as being True or False. If the comment is false, briefly explain why.

a Generally speaking, cash flows are preferred over accounting income when evaluating long-term investments.

b Present value is actually the "reverse" of compound interest.

c Annuity factors can be derived by summing the present value factors for individual, yearly cash flows.

d A project's internal rate of return will result in a zero net present value for the project.

e If income taxes are ignored, depreciation expense amounts should be used when figuring an investment's net present value.

*E28-11 *Aftertax cash flows and payback* (L.O. 4, 5)

Dayton Industries is considering the acquisition of a machine that costs $50,000. The machine is expected to provide annual beforetax savings in cash operating costs of $10,000 over its 10-year service life. Dayton uses straight-line depreciation on all assets and is subject to a 40% income tax rate.

a Determine the aftertax cash flows related to the machine. *Hint:* Be sure to include the tax savings from depreciation.

b Compute the machine's payback.

Series A

PROBLEMS

P28-A1 *Straightforward net-present-value and payback computations* (L.O. 4)

STL Entertainment is considering the acquisition of a sight-seeing boat for summer tours along the Mississippi River. The following information is available:

Cost of boat	$500,000
Service life	10 summer seasons
Disposal value at the end of 10 seasons	$100,000
Capacity per trip	300 passengers
Fixed operating costs per season (including straight-line depreciation)	$160,000
Variable operating costs per trip	$1,000
Ticket price	$5 per passenger

All operating costs, except depreciation, require cash outlays. On the basis of similar operations in other parts of the country, management anticipates that each trip will be sold out and that 120,000 passengers will be carried each season. Ignore income taxes.

Instructions

a Compute the payback period of the boat.

b By using the net-present-value method, determine whether STL Entertainment should acquire the boat. Assume a 14% desired return on all investments; round calculations to the nearest dollar.

P28-A2 *Make or buy; net present value; working capital investment* (L.O. 4)

Fairbanks, Inc., manufactures various components that are used in the production of motorcycle engines. The company is currently purchasing a particular valve assembly from Medford Machining for $14.80. Because of reliability problems with Medford and the fact that a price increase is imminent, Fairbanks is studying whether to produce the assembly itself. The following information is available:

a The company will need 7,500 valve assemblies annually over each of the next four years.

b Variable production costs are anticipated to be: direct materials, $1.10; direct labor, $1.50; and factory overhead, $0.60.

c A new supervisor would be hired to oversee production. Estimated annual wages will be $37,000, plus an additional 20% for fringe benefit costs.

d Specialized machinery that costs $140,000 would be acquired at the start of manufacturing. The machinery has a four-year life, a projected disposal value of $20,000, and will be depreciated by the straight-line method.

e Fairbanks must make an immediate $15,000 investment in working capital to acquire needed raw materials inventories. This investment will be recovered at the end of four years when production is anticipated to be discontinued. The machinery [see item (d)] will be sold at this time as well.

Management uses the net-present-value method to analyze investments, requiring a 14% rate of return. Ignore income taxes and round calculations to the nearest dollar.

Instructions

Determine whether Fairbanks should make or buy the valve assemblies.

P28-A3 *Basketball player decision* **(L.O. 4)**

The Phoenix Kings of the United Basketball League have a moody center by the name of Orlando Dawkins. Dawkins is under contract with the team and is scheduled to earn $650,000 in both 19X3 and 19X4. A $75,000 salary increase will take effect in 19X5.

Dawkins has not gotten along with several of his teammates and, as a result, management is exploring the possibility of a trade with the Philadelphia Rockets to acquire George Harper, a star player. The Kings would pay the Rockets $350,000 immediately for the trade to take place. Harper would be paid a $270,000 signing bonus at the beginning of 19X3 that management plans to expense over the next three years by using straight-line amortization. Harper's annual salary would be $950,000 from 19X3 through 19X5, highest on the team because of his ability to attract fans. The Kings expect that increased attendance will produce added annual net cash inflows of $525,000.

Phoenix officials feel that both players would play three more years for the Kings, at which time they would become free agents and move along to other clubs. The Kings would receive $380,000 compensation from the other club for Dawkins; for Harper the figure would increase to $500,000. Regardless of whether the trade takes place, the Kings are obligated to pay Dawkins $200,000 at the end of 19X4 under the terms of his original contract.

The Kings desire a rate of return of 14% and use the net-present-value method to analyze investments. Round all calculations to the nearest dollar and ignore income taxes.

Instructions

a Determine whether the Kings should keep Dawkins or trade for Harper. Assume the trade would occur on January 1, 19X3.

b Future cash flows are, in many cases, subject to change. List several events that could occur that might influence the cash flows in this situation.

P28-A4 *Accounting and internal rates of return* (L.O. 4)

Flowerville, Inc., is studying two investments in depreciable assets. Each asset requires an initial outlay of $60,000. The following schedules of cash flows are applicable:

	Investment A			Investment B	
Year	Cash Inflows	Cash Outflows	Year	Cash Inflows	Cash Outflows
1	$32,800	$11,800	1	$ —	$ —
2	35,000	14,000	2	—	—
3	38,700	17,700	3	—	—
4	40,000	19,000	4	186,800	102,800

The company will depreciate the assets by the straight-line method over a four-year life. Disregard residual values and income taxes.

Instructions

a Compute the accounting rate of return for each investment on the investment's initial acquisition cost. *Hint:* Be sure to calculate an average income figure for the numerator.
b Compute the internal rate of return for investment A.
c Assume that the internal rate of return on investment B is 8.8%. Compare the results obtained in parts (a) and (b). Comment on any differences that arose, and explain an underlying problem associated with the accounting rate of return.

P28-A5 *Payback analysis; accounting rate of return* (L.O. 4)

1-2-3

Scenic Ventures is studying the acquisition of a helicopter for tours of the Caribbean islands. The helicopter will cost $5 million, is expected to have a $1.4 million residual value, and will be depreciated over a 12-year service life by the straight-line method. The following annual cash operating costs are anticipated:

Fuel	$60,000
Wages	85,000
Maintenance	45,000
Insurance	58,000
Licenses	2,000

Tours will be provided on a year-round basis, with five trips being made each day. Operations will be shut down for selected holidays (Thanksgiving and Christmas), bad weather (six days), and major maintenance procedures (seven days). Scenic charges $75 per passenger, and the average tour is expected to have eight passengers.

Instructions

a Compute the annual net cash inflow from the new helicopter.
b If Scenic requires a payback of five years, should the helicopter be acquired?
c Calculate the helicopter's accounting rate of return.

*P28-A6 *Cash flow; taxes; net present value* (L.O. 4, 5)

Central Plains Freight Company is studying the possibility of adding a new truck to its fleet. The vehicle will cost $80,000 and is expected to generate annual sales revenues of $70,000. Central depreciates all vehicles by the straight-line method over a six-year service life. An $8,000 residual value is anticipated.

Management expects that the vehicle will be driven approximately 25,000 miles each year. Cash operating costs will average $0.22 per mile in Years 1–3 and then jump to $0.26 in Years 4–6. A driver will be paid a $35,000 annual salary.

Central Plains is subject to a 40% tax rate on all items of revenue and expense and requires a 16% return on all investments. The company employs the net-present-value method to evaluate long-term projects.

Instructions

a The following schedule has been designed to identify the net cash flows related to the truck. The first two items are done as examples.

Item	Amount	Tax Effect, If Any*	Aftertax Cash Flow
Truck cost	$(80,000)	None	$(80,000)
Revenues	70,000	$(28,000)	42,000

* Parentheses denote an increase in taxes.

Complete the schedule for the remaining items that result in an aftertax cash flow.

b Use the aftertax cash flow amounts in a net-present-value analysis and determine whether Central Plains should acquire the truck. Round all computations to the nearest dollar.

Series B

P28-B1 *Straightforward net-present-value and payback computations* (L.O. 4)

The Calgary Eskimos play in the Canadian Hockey League. Although the Eskimos will soon be moving to a modern arena, management is studying the possibility of expanding the team's present facility to accommodate increased crowds. A $2.4 million expansion is planned that has a $200,000 residual value and will be depreciated by the straight-line method over four seasons. Information about the expansion follows.

	Number of Seats	Occupancy Rate	Ticket Price
Class 1 seats	2,500	80%	$6
Class 2 seats	2,000	60	4

The team will play 50 home games each season. Total added operating costs per game (ushers, cleanup, and depreciation) are expected to average $11,800. All such costs, except depreciation, require cash outlays.

Instructions

a Compute the payback period of the expansion.
b By using the net-present-value method and a 16% desired rate of return, determine whether the expansion should be undertaken.
c In addition to the cash flows presented here, what other cash flows might change if the Eskimos add on to the arena?

P28-B2 *Make or buy; net present value; working capital investment* (L.O. 4)

1-2-3

Equity Products manufactures electronic components used in the appliance industry. The company currently purchases a particular part for $1.75. Because of problems with product quality and supplier reliability, Equity is studying whether to manufacture the part internally.

To begin production, new machinery must be acquired that costs $380,000. The machinery, which has a six-year life and an estimated residual value of $50,000, will be depreciated by the straight-line method. Art Sanchez, a current Equity employee, will oversee manufacturing activities and will be given a $7,000 raise because of increased responsibilities. Sanchez's original position will remain unfilled.

The company's cost accountants and engineers have estimated the unit variable production costs that follow.

Direct materials	$0.22
Direct labor	0.40
Variable factory overhead	0.32

Equity must make an immediate $30,000 working capital investment to build needed direct materials inventories. Annual production should total 120,000 units over each of the next six years. Manufacturing activities will then be discontinued and the materials inventories depleted (i.e., working capital recovered) because of a planned change in Equity's product line. The machinery will be sold because of its specialized nature.

Management uses the net-present-value method to analyze investment opportunities, requiring a 10% minimum rate of return. Ignore income taxes, and round calculations to the nearest dollar.

Instructions

Determine whether Equity should make or buy the part.

P28-B3 *Equipment replacement decision* (L.O. 2, 4)

Columbia Enterprises is studying the replacement of some equipment that originally cost $74,000. The equipment is expected to provide six more years of service if $8,700 of major repairs are performed in two years. Annual cash operating costs total $27,200. Columbia can sell the equipment now for $36,000; the estimated residual value in six years is $5,000.

New equipment is available that will reduce annual cash operating costs to $21,000. The equipment costs $103,000, has a service life of six years, and has an estimated residual value of $13,000. Company sales will total $430,000 per year with either the existing or the new equipment.

Columbia has a minimum desired return of 12% and depreciates all equipment by the straight-line method.

Instructions

a By using the net-present-value method, determine whether Columbia should keep its present equipment or acquire the new equipment. Round all calculations to the nearest dollar, and ignore income taxes.

b Columbia's management feels that the time value of money should be considered in all long-term decisions. Briefly discuss the rationale that underlies management's belief.

P28-B4 *Accounting and internal rates of return* (L.O. 4)

Triple-A Storage, Inc., is studying two investments in depreciable assets. Each asset requires an initial outlay of $180,000. The following schedules of cash flows are applicable:

	Investment No. 113			Investment No. 114	
Year	Cash Inflows	Cash Outflows	Year	Cash Inflows	Cash Outflows
1	$ —	$ —	1	$86,900	$35,600
2	—	—	2	94,300	43,000
3	—	—	3	98,000	46,700
4	—	—	4	90,000	38,700
5	501,900	245,400	5	80,000	28,700

The company will depreciate the assets by the straight-line method over a five-year life. Disregard residual values and income taxes.

Instructions

a Compute the accounting rate of return for each investment on the investment's initial acquisition cost. *Hint:* Be sure to calculate an average income figure for the numerator.

b Compute the internal rate of return for investment no. 114.

c Assume that the internal rate of return for investment no. 113 amounts to 7.4%. Explain why the internal rate of return differs between investments 113 and 114.

P28-B5 *Payback analysis; accounting rate of return* (L.O. 4)

1-2-3

Tasty Treats is studying the acquisition of a new vehicle to expand its fleet of ice-cream trucks for service in suburban neighborhoods. The truck, which has an eight-year service life and $2,000 residual value, is expected to cost $20,000. The company's owner anticipates that annual sales will increase by $25,000 if the truck is acquired. Annual operating costs will be: gasoline, $2,000; license, $100; maintenance and repair, $1,200; driver's salary, $6,800; and insurance, $900. The cost of ice cream generally averages 40% of sales. Ignore income taxes.

Instructions

a Compute the annual net cash inflow from operation of the additional truck.

b Determine the payback period.

c If Tasty Treats requires an accounting rate of return on initial investment of 12%, should the truck be acquired?

*P28-B6 *Cash flow; taxes; net present value* (L.O. 4, 5)

The Medstar Family Clinic currently has limited lab facilities for its patients. As a result, the practicing physicians have obtained a proposal from SurgiTech to supply new, state-of-the-art equipment. The equipment will cost $650,000 and will be depreciated by the straight-line method down to a $50,000 residual value. The following information is known:

Service life of equipment	8 years
Annual number of lab tests performed	
Years 1–2	2,900
Years 3–8	3,300
Average patient billing per test	$52
Annual wage of part-time lab assistant	$17,000
Maintenance cost at end of Year 5	$3,000

Medstar requires a 12% rate of return on all investments and will use the net-present-value method to analyze the SurgiTech proposal. The clinic is subject to a 30% income tax rate on all items of revenue and expense.

Instructions

a The following schedule has been designed to identify the net cash flows related to the equipment. The two items shown are done as examples.

Item	Amount	Tax Effect, If Any*	Aftertax Cash Flow
Equipment cost	$(650,000)	None	$(650,000)
Maintenance	(3,000)	$900	(2,100)

* Parentheses denote an increase in taxes.

Complete the schedule for the remaining items that result in an after-tax cash flow.

b Use the aftertax cash flow amounts in a net-present-value analysis and determine whether Medstar should acquire the equipment. Round all computations to the nearest dollar.

BB28-1 *Net present value; algebra; analysis* (L.O. 2, 4)

BEYOND THE BASICS

Ron Horstmann is considering various investment opportunities for his employer. One such opportunity involves obtaining a five-year franchise from CC Cookies to operate a store at Pepperwood Mall. CC Cookies requires a $40,000 immediate up-front payment. In addition, each store must be furnished with $200,000 of equipment that has a five-year life and a $20,000 disposal value. Additional information follows.

Anticipated annual sales	16,000 dozen
Annual franchise fee	5% of sales revenue
Variable cost per dozen	$2.25
Annual mall rent	
Years 1–2	$12,000
Years 3–5	13,500

CC Cookies will allow each franchise to set its own selling price on the basis of regional factors, local competition, and so forth. The price can range from $6.75 to $7.50 per dozen. In an effort to maximize sales, Horstmann's employer would charge $6.75.

Assume a 10% rate of return is required on all investments. Ignore income taxes.

Instructions

a Compute the net present value of the cookie franchise, rounding calculations to the nearest dollar. Should the store be opened? Why?

b At what selling price would the franchise produce a zero net present value? What has a strong possibility of changing if this selling price is charged?

c Would the net present value from part (a) increase or decrease if payment of the $40,000 franchise fee could be postponed until a later date? No calculations are necessary.

BB28-2 *Overview of chapter concepts: Multiple choice* (L.O. 1, 2, 3, 4)

The following multiple-choice questions relate to various topics discussed in the chapter. Select the best answer.

1 Assume that a company has a 12% cost of capital. Most managers:

  a would insist that long-term investments have a rate of return greater than 12%.

  b would expect the collective cost of funds to be less than 12%.

  c would have a cutoff rate for project acceptance of less than 12%.

  d would require an interest rate on borrowings of greater than 12%.

2 The present value of $100 to be received in one year, discounted at 10%, is:

  a more than $100.

  b less than $90.

  c equal to $90.

  d more than $90 but less than $100.

3 Consider the net-present-value method (NPV), the internal rate of return (IRR), the payback method (P), and the accounting rate of return (ARR). Which of the following choices is correct?

	Uses Discounted Cash Flows	Does Not Use Discounted Cash Flows
a	NPV, IRR, P	ARR
b	NPV, IRR	ARR, P
c	NPV, IRR, ARR	P
d	NPV	IRR, ARR, P

4 If a company uses the net-present-value method of capital budgeting, investments considered attractive would have:

  a a negative net present value.

  b a zero net present value.

  c a positive net present value.

  d total cash inflows greater than total cash outflows.

5 Genesis recently acquired an investment that will return the following cash inflows: Year 1, $10,000; Year 2, $11,000; Year 3, $12,000; and Year 4, $13,000. If the investment has a positive net present value of $2,500, computed by using a 10% rate of return, the original cost of the investment must have been:

  a $33,577.   c $38,577.

  b $36,077.   d $43,500.

6 If a $3,000 investment is scheduled to return $1,100 at the end of Year 1, $1,210 at the end of Year 2, and $1,331 at the end of Year 3, the investment's internal rate of return:

  a would be equal to 8%.

  b would be equal to 10%.

  c would be equal to 12%.

  d would be greater than 10% but less than 12%.

7 The payback period for a $1,000,000 investment that will return $150,000 annually:

  a is less than one year.

  b is 6 years, 8 months.

  c is 6 years, 9 months.

  d cannot be computed from the information presented.

8 The accounting rate of return:
  a is another name for the internal rate of return.
  b is one of several methods that rely on discounted cash flows to determine a project's attractiveness.
  c focuses on income (as opposed to cash flows) when evaluating a project.
  d is directly linked to an investment's payback period.

CAI28-1 *An overview of communication techniques* (L.O. 1)

Communication Principle: Effective communication is a key to business success. Memos, reports, charts, graphs, and oral presentations collectively convey information for a variety of purposes. Often, the ability to structure concise, understandable presentations has a significant impact on the situation at hand. Sloppy resumés, for example, are sure to eliminate a potential employee from consideration in a tight job market. A manager's report, to be reviewed by the board of directors, may be the major factor that underlies board acceptance or rejection of a given decision alternative.

In sum, the ability to communicate often makes the difference and should not be taken lightly. As you pursue a career in accounting, marketing, systems, or whatever your chosen profession may be, you no doubt will have many opportunities to experience the importance of effective delivery of information.

COMMUNICATION OF ACCOUNTING INFORMATION

■ ■ ■ ■ ■ ■ ■ ■ ■

In the next four weeks, Diane Horan must prepare a written and oral presentation for Fairfax Corporation's board of directors. The presentation focuses on the need for a new mainframe computer system, estimated to cost $2.7 million. Both the net-present-value and payback methods have found the computer to be an extremely attractive investment.

Because of other pressing obligations, Diane has enlisted the help of David Clark, a fellow employee. David is extremely bright and also very knowledgeable about the computer system. However, his communication skills are somewhat weak. Diane has therefore decided to prepare a list of "significant communication principles" for David's use.

Instructions

Assume the role of Diane Horan and prepare the list just mentioned. The principles should be taken from appropriate Communication of Accounting Information (CAI) problems in earlier chapters of this text.

Answers to Chapter Quiz

1 c

2 a

3 b $(200,000) × 1.00000 = $(200,000)
       40,000 × 4.35526 = 174,210
                     $ (25,790)

4 c

5 d

APPENDIX A

Special Journal Systems

As explained in Chapter 6, companies may choose from a variety of systems to process transactions and produce financial information. For those businesses that have rejected computerized systems in favor of manual accounting procedures, the use of special journals is a possible option. **Special journals** handle specialized (specific) types of high-frequency transactions. Careful study of Appendix A will show a distinct parallel between this form of transaction processing and the computerized modular systems that now abound in practice.

A review of many companies' business operations will often find that roughly 90% of the accompanying transactions fall into one of four categories. The special journal system is based on this finding, with the following four types of journals normally used to record business activity.

TYPES AND BENEFITS OF SPECIAL JOURNALS

Journal	Transactions Contained
Sales journal	Sales of merchandise on account
Purchases journal	Purchases of merchandise on account
Cash receipts journal	Receipts of cash
Cash payments journal	Payments of cash

Naturally, not all transactions and events will fit neatly into these classifications. Consider, for example, the need to record sales returns and allowances, purchases returns and allowances, adjusting entries, and closing entries. These and other similar items are therefore recorded in the general journal, which assumes a new role. Rather than being used to handle all business activity, the general journal is now employed *solely* for miscellaneous transactions and events (namely, those not accommodated in special journals).

Tips & Techniques

When first exposed to the operation of a special journal system, some students attempt to record a company's entire set of transactions in the general journal and also in the special journals just mentioned. This procedure is incorrect. A given transaction is entered in a special journal *or* the general journal, not both.

Companies that use special journals tend to receive two basic benefits. First, firms are able to spread their work load, since each journal can be maintained by a different employee. All credit sales can be accounted for by one person, all cash receipts by another, and so on. Second, special journals significantly reduce the amount of posting necessary to process transactions—an important consideration, especially in high-volume environments where this type of processing system is found.[1]

Sales Journal

The **sales journal** is employed to record sales of merchandise on account. We illustrate the journal's use by examining various transactions of Stereo Unlimited, a wholesale distributor of stereo equipment, records, tapes, and compact discs. The firm had the following credit sales during January:

Jan. 4 Sold $1,350 of stereo equipment on account (invoice no. 101) to House of Music.
    12 Opened an account for the Sound Center and sold $400 of records and tapes on account (invoice no. 102).
    18 Sold $150 of compact discs on account (invoice no. 103) to Treetops Lounge.
    25 Sold $1,200 of stereo equipment and $200 of records and tapes on account (invoice no. 104) to Walton's Music Store.

Stereo Unlimited's sales journal is shown in Exhibit A-1. The entries are taken from the data that appear on each sales invoice. Notice that only one line is necessary to record an individual transaction and the usual debit/credit format is absent. Furthermore, journal entry explanations are not used because all transactions are of the same type: a sale of merchandise on account.

To understand the journal's operation, let us keep our objectives in mind. The customer accounts in the subsidiary ledger must be updated to reflect the added amounts due the firm. Furthermore, the Accounts Receivable and Sales accounts must both be increased, the former to achieve the required control account/subsidiary ledger equality and the latter because the company has generated revenues from each of the four transac-

---

[1] If you have not already done so, please read the section in Chapter 6 entitled "Subsidiary Ledgers and Control Accounts" (pp. 228–229).

Sales Journal

				Page 1
Date	**Customer**	**Invoice No.**	**Post Ref**	**Amount**
19XX				
Jan. 4	House of Music	101	✓	1,350
12	Sound Center	102	✓	400
18	Treetops Lounge	103	✓	150
25	Walton's Music Store	104	✓	1,400
				3,300
				(110/410)

Total is posted monthly to general ledger accounts.

Individual amounts are posted daily to customer accounts in the subsidiary ledger.

General Ledger

Accounts Receivable   **Account No. 110**

Date	Ref	Debit	Credit	Balance
19XX				
Jan. 31	S1	3,300		3,300

Sales   **Account No. 410**

Date	Ref	Debit	Credit	Balance
19XX				
Jan. 31	S1		3,300	3,300

Accounts Receivable Subsidiary Ledger

House of Music

Date	Ref	Debit	Credit	Balance
19XX				
Jan. 4	S1	1,350		1,350

Sound Center

Date	Ref	Debit	Credit	Balance
19XX				
Jan. 12	S1	400		400

Treetops Lounge

Date	Ref	Debit	Credit	Balance
19XX				
Jan. 18	S1	150		150

Walton's Music Store

Date	Ref	Debit	Credit	Balance
19XX				
Jan. 25	S1	1,400		1,400

EXHIBIT A-1
Sales Journal and Related
Postings

tions. The preceding objectives are carried out through the posting process, which is illustrated in the exhibit.

Posting the Sales Journal

Exhibit A-1 reveals that individual sales are posted daily to the appropriate customer's account in the subsidiary ledger. Daily posting is necessary to keep up-to-date balances, which are helpful in both credit decisions and in responding to customer queries. To signify completion of this process and to provide an *audit trail* (i.e., a means to trace and access accounting information), one enters the notation S1 (sales journal, page 1) as a reference in the customer's account. Finally, a check mark is placed in the sales journal to indicate that the transaction was transferred to the subsidiary ledger.[2] These procedures are repeated until all transactions are posted.

Next, the control account is updated to maintain the necessary equality. Because the only type of transaction recorded in the sales journal is a sale of merchandise on account, the total of the amount column is posted periodically (e.g., monthly) as a debit to Accounts Receivable control and a credit to Sales. The notation S1 is then entered in these accounts in the general ledger. To finish the process, the numbers of the accounts to which the $3,300 was posted, 110 and 410, are written beneath the total.

A review of these procedures will find that the four transactions were transferred to the proper accounts by a total of six postings: Accounts Receivable control, Sales, and four subsidiary accounts. If Stereo Unlimited failed to employ a special journal system and instead used a general journal to record all of its transactions, the number of postings would increase considerably. Four separate journal entries would be constructed, each one containing a debit to Accounts Receivable control and a credit to Sales. Further, the individual transaction amounts would have to be charged to customer accounts in the subsidiary ledger, creating a total of 12 separate postings. As you can well imagine, the bookkeeping would become overwhelming as activity increases. Thankfully, the efficiency provided by a special journal accounting system is dramatic, thereby allowing manual data processing at a reasonable cost.

Journal Variations

The journals illustrated in this appendix are general models that can be altered to meet the needs of individual businesses. For example, if a company were charging its customers for sales taxes, an additional column could be added in the sales journal to record the taxes payable to the government. Or if management desired to report sales by product line, a minor design change would allow a firm to generate the necessary information. An expanded journal for Stereo Unlimited, for instance, might contain the following amount columns: Accounts Receivable debit, Stereo Equipment Sales credit, Record and Tape Sales credit, and Compact Disc Sales credit.

---

[2] Check marks are used because of the absence of account numbers in the subsidiary ledger. Companies that follow this practice arrange customer and creditor accounts alphabetically, thereby allowing for growth (or contraction) without having to modify numbering schemes.

A number of variations in journal design are possible. Generally speaking, separate amount columns are established when (1) more detailed accounting information is desired, as in the preceding case, or (2) transactions occur on a highly repetitive basis. These design "rules" will become more apparent in later sections of the appendix.

Purchases Journal

The procedures associated with the sales journal closely parallel those employed with the purchases journal. The **purchases journal** is used to record only one type of transaction: purchases of merchandise on account. Other types of acquisitions are recorded elsewhere. For example, a cash acquisition of merchandise would be entered in the cash payments journal, whereas a purchase of equipment on account would be placed in the general journal.

Every purchase of merchandise on account requires a debit to Purchases and a credit to Accounts Payable. In addition, because a business needs detailed information regarding the amounts owed to each supplier, a separate subsidiary ledger must be established. The sum of the individual creditor accounts in the subsidiary ledger must again equal the balance in the general ledger control account—Accounts Payable in this case.

Stereo Unlimited's purchases journal and related postings appear in Exhibit A-2. Individual amounts for purchases are credited daily to suppliers' accounts in the subsidiary ledger, because the balances owed have increased. Once again, completion of posting is denoted by placing a check mark in the journal. The journal's total is then posted at month-end as a debit to Purchases and a credit to Accounts Payable control. The P1 references in the ledger accounts indicate that the entries were transferred from page 1 of the purchases journal.

Overall, you should observe two important similarities in the operation of the sales and purchases journals, namely:

- Individual transaction amounts that affect subsidiary ledgers are posted daily to the appropriate subsidiary ledger accounts.
- Totals that affect control accounts are posted monthly to the general ledger.

Cash Receipts Journal

A company receives cash from many different sources, including cash sales, customer payments on account, the sale of old equipment, and bank loans. The possibilities are numerous. The **cash receipts journal** must therefore have multiple amount columns since all cash receipts are recorded here. Normally, separate columns are established for transactions that occur on a frequent basis.

Stereo Unlimited had the following cash receipts during January:

Jan. 2 Received $2,000 from Patricia Monroe, owner of Stereo Unlimited, as an investment in the business.
9 Sold $650 of stereo equipment and $150 of tapes for cash to Central Stereo.

Purchases Journal

		Invoice Information			Post Ref	Amount
Date	Supplier	Date	No.	Terms		
19XX						
Jan. 3	Able Electronics	Jan. 3	1721	—	✓	2,100
8	Columbia Records	7	1777	2/10, n/30	✓	750
16	Pioneer Associates	16	AF471	—	✓	420
26	Sony Corp.	26	9576	3/10, n/30	✓	2,060
						5,330
						(501/201)

Page 1

Total is posted monthly to general ledger accounts.

Individual amounts are posted daily to creditor accounts in the subsidiary ledger.

General Ledger

Accounts Payable — Account No. 201

Date	Ref	Debit	Credit	Balance
19XX				
Jan. 31	P1		5,330	5,330

Purchases — Account No. 501

Date	Ref	Debit	Credit	Balance
19XX				
Jan. 31	P1	5,330		5,330

Accounts Payable Subsidiary Ledger

Able Electronics

Date	Ref	Debit	Credit	Balance
19XX				
Jan. 3	P1		2,100	2,100

Columbia Records

Date	Ref	Debit	Credit	Balance
19XX				
Jan. 8	P1		750	750

Pioneer Associates

Date	Ref	Debit	Credit	Balance
19XX				
Jan. 16	P1		420	420

Sony Corp.

Date	Ref	Debit	Credit	Balance
19XX				
Jan. 26	P1		2,060	2,060

EXHIBIT A-2
Purchases Journal and
Related Postings

13 Received a check on account from the House of Music for the sale on January 4, minus the correct discount.

17 Received loan proceeds of $4,800 from California Trust Company to acquire several new display cases.

22 Sold $100 of records and $100 of compact discs to Burrows Music Company for cash.

28 Received a $280 check on account from the Sound Center in partial payment of the sale made on January 12.

Proper recording of these transactions is shown in Exhibit A-3. Assume that all credit sales were subject to terms of 2/10, n/30.

Operation of the Cash Receipts Journal

Transactions are entered in the cash receipts journal in accordance with accounting's normal debit/credit rules. To illustrate, examine the receipt on account from the Sound Center on January 28. An entry for $280 is placed in both the Cash debit column and the Accounts Receivable credit column. Sound Center appears in the Account space because the firm's subsidiary ledger account must be updated.

Transactions that do not arise often are recorded in the Sundry or miscellaneous column. On January 2, for example, Stereo Unlimited received $2,000 from Patricia Monroe as an investment in the business. The receipt requires a debit to Cash. Because owner investments are infrequent, the company has not established a separate capital column. Instead, $2,000 is placed in Sundry and Patricia Monroe, Capital, is entered in the Account space.

Note that the Account space is left blank for cash sales. Stereo Unlimited, like many other businesses, makes no attempt to gather the names of cash customers. An explanation of the transaction may be entered if desired (e.g., Daily Cash Sales).

Posting the Cash Receipts Journal

Individual amounts that appear in the Accounts Receivable and Sundry columns are posted throughout the month. Collections from credit customers are generally posted daily to the subsidiary ledger in an effort to maintain up-to-date account balances; entries in the Sundry column are transferred as they occur to minimize work during the hectic end of the period. As a result of this latter procedure, respective credits of $2,000 and $4,800 were posted to Patricia Monroe, Capital (account no. 301) and Loans Payable (account no. 210) in the general ledger. Entries in these accounts and others show a reference of CR1, indicating the amounts originated on page 1 of the cash receipts journal.

Upon conclusion of monthly activity, column totals are transferred to their respective ledger accounts. Before this process is performed, however, the equality of debits and credits must be evaluated. In the case of Stereo Unlimited, the required equality is maintained:

EXHIBIT A-3
Cash Receipts Journal and Related Postings

Cash Receipts Journal

Page 1

Date	Account	Post Ref	Cash Debit	Sales Discounts Debit	Accounts Receivable Credit	Sales Credit	Sundry Accounts Credit or (Debit)
19XX							
Jan. 2	Patricia Monroe, Capital	301	2,000				2,000
9	—		800			800	
13	House of Music	✓	1,323	27	1,350		
17	Loans Payable	210	4,800				4,800
22	—		200			200	
28	Sound Center	✓	280		280		
			9,403	27	1,630	1,000	6,800
			(101)	(413)	(110)	(410)	(X)

Totals, except Sundry, are posted monthly to general ledger accounts.

Individual amounts are posted daily to general ledger accounts.

Individual amounts are posted daily to customer accounts in the subsidiary ledger.

General Ledger

Cash   Account No. 101

Date	Ref	Debit	Credit	Balance
19XX				
Jan. 31	CR1	9,403		9,403

Accounts Receivable   Account No. 110

Date	Ref	Debit	Credit	Balance
19XX				
Jan. 31	S1	3,300		3,300
31	CR1		1,630	1,670

Loans Payable   Account No. 210

Date	Ref	Debit	Credit	Balance
19XX				
Jan. 17	CR1		4,800	4,800

Patricia Monroe, Capital   Account No. 301

Date	Ref	Debit	Credit	Balance
19XX				
Jan. 2	CR1		2,000	2,000

Sales   Account No. 410

Date	Ref	Debit	Credit	Balance
19XX				
Jan. 31	S1		3,300	3,300
31	CR1		1,000	4,300

Sales Discounts   Account No. 413

Date	Ref	Debit	Credit	Balance
19XX				
Jan. 31	CR1	27		27

Accounts Receivable Subsidiary Ledger

House of Music

Date	Ref	Debit	Credit	Balance
19XX				
Jan. 4	S1	1,350		1,350
13	CR1		1,350	—

Sound Center

Date	Ref	Debit	Credit	Balance
19XX				
Jan. 12	S1	400		400
28	CR1		280	120

Debits		Credits	
Cash	$9,403	Accounts receivable	$1,630
Sales discounts	27	Sales	1,000
	$9,430	Sundry accounts	6,800
			$9,430

All column totals are posted, with one exception: Sundry. As the X in Exhibit A-3 indicates, the total of the Sundry column is not posted, because its components ($2,000 and $4,800) have already been transferred to the proper accounts. The $6,800 total is generated only for use in determining whether total debits are equal to total credits.

Cash Payments Journal

The **cash payments journal** is used to record virtually all cash disbursements that are made by a business.[3] Because cash outlays are made for many different purposes, the journal utilized for their recording must be multicolumn in format. Separate columns are again established when the same type of transaction occurs frequently or when more detailed accounting information is desired.

Stereo Unlimited's cash disbursements during January were as follows:

Jan. 4 Paid January rent of $750 to Kraft Management by issuing check no. 101.

11 Issued check no. 102 for $100 to Central Stereo for the return of stereo equipment sold for cash on January 9.

14 Paid invoice no. 1777, dated January 7, of Columbia Records by issuing check no. 103. The invoice totaled $750 and was subject to terms of 2/10, n/30.

19 Paid $650 of sales commissions to John Harrison by issuing check no. 104.

27 Issued check no. 105 to Able Electronics for $2,100, in payment of the purchase made on January 3.

These transactions are recorded in the cash payments journal that appears in Exhibit A-4.

Observe that the journal possesses a Cash credit column since each payment reduces the company's cash balance. Furthermore, because the firm acquires its merchandise on credit, columns for Accounts Payable and Purchases Discounts are needed. Finally, a Sundry column is used to record disbursements that are made for other purposes. The journal has one additional feature: a check number column. All significant cash disbursements are made by check for reasons of safety and accountability. The check's number is entered in the journal to facilitate the audit trail (i.e., tracing) process.

---

[3] A minor exception occurs with small miscellaneous payments that are made from a petty cash system. The operation of a petty cash system is discussed in Chapter 7.

Cash Payments Journal

Page 1

Date	Check No.	Payee	Account	Post Ref	Cash Credit	Purchases Discounts Credit	Accounts Payable Debit	Sundry Accounts Debit or (Credit)
19XX								
Jan. 4	101	Kraft Management	Rent Expense	530	750			750)
11	102	Central Stereo	Sales Returns & Allowances	414	100			100)
14	103	Columbia Records		✓	735	15	750	
19	104	John Harrison	Sales Commissions	540	650			650)
27	105	Able Electronics		✓	2,100		2,100)	
					4,335	15	2,850	1,500
					(101)	(504)	(201)	(X)

Totals, except Sundry, are posted monthly to general ledger accounts.

Individual amounts are posted daily to general ledger accounts.

Individual amounts are posted daily to creditor accounts in the subsidiary ledger.

General Ledger

Cash — **Account No. 101**

Date	Ref	Debit	Credit	Balance
19XX				
Jan. 31	CR1	9,403		9,403
31	CP1		4,335	5,068

Accounts Payable — **Account No. 201**

Date	Ref	Debit	Credit	Balance
19XX				
Jan. 31	P1		5,330	5,330
31	CP1	2,850		2,480

Sales Returns & Allowances — **Account No. 414**

Date	Ref	Debit	Credit	Balance
19XX				
Jan. 11	CP1	100		100

Purchases Discounts — **Account No. 504**

Date	Ref	Debit	Credit	Balance
19XX				
Jan. 31	CP1		15	15

Rent Expense — **Account No. 530**

Date	Ref	Debit	Credit	Balance
19XX				
Jan. 4	CP1	750		750

Sales Commissions — **Account No. 540**

Date	Ref	Debit	Credit	Balance
19XX				
Jan. 19	CP1	650		650

Accounts Payable Subsidiary Ledger

Able Electronics

Date	Ref	Debit	Credit	Balance
19XX				
Jan. 3	P1		2,100	2,100
27	CP1	2,100		—

Columbia Records

Date	Ref	Debit	Credit	Balance
19XX				
Jan. 8	P1		750	750
14	CP1	750		—

Posting the Cash Payments Journal

Posting the cash payments journal is very similar to posting the cash receipts journal. Both journals are multicolumn in format, both have a Sundry column to record miscellaneous transactions, and both deal with a control account/subsidiary ledger arrangement. Throughout the month, individual amounts in the Sundry column are posted to the proper accounts in the general ledger (e.g., Rent Expense, Sales Returns & Allowances, and Sales Commissions). Similarly, entries in the Accounts Payable debit column are transferred daily to the Accounts Payable subsidiary ledger. At the end of the month, the columns are totaled, and the equality of debits and credits is checked. Then all column totals are posted to the general ledger, with the exception of Sundry. As before, individual elements of the Sundry column have already been transferred. The entries referenced by CP1 have come from the cash payments journal, page 1.

General Journal

Earlier in the appendix we noted that a business will have a number of transactions that cannot be accommodated in its special journals. Consider, for example, the journals that have been designed for Stereo Unlimited. Suppose that on January 19, the firm bought a piece of display equipment on account from Store Outfitters for $2,600. Because the purchases journal contains only purchases of merchandise, this acquisition must be recorded elsewhere, namely, in the general journal. The general journal is used to record transactions that cannot be placed in special journals (e.g., miscellaneous transactions, adjusting entries, and closing entries). The necessary entry follows.

General Journal

			Page 1	
19XX Jan. 19	Display Equipment Accounts Payable: Store Outfitters Purchased equipment on account	130 201/√	2,600	2,600

As the posting references indicate, the transaction was transferred to the Display Equipment account and the Accounts Payable control account in the general ledger. In addition, Store Outfitters was credited in the Accounts Payable subsidiary ledger. The effect of the latter two postings can be seen by viewing the accounts depicted on page A-12.

Several Final Comments

Once all postings are completed, a general ledger trial balance is constructed as the first step in summarizing the period's activity. The necessary procedures are identical to those discussed in Chapter 2 and are not

EXHIBIT A-5
Accounts Payable
Relationships for Stereo
Unlimited

Accounts Payable Subsidiary Ledger

Pioneer Associates

Date	Ref	Debit	Credit	Balance
19XX				
Jan. 16	P1		420	420

Sony Corp.

Date	Ref	Debit	Credit	Balance
19XX				
Jan. 26	P1		2,060	2,060

Store Outfitters

Date	Ref	Debit	Credit	Balance
19XX				
Jan. 19	J1		2,600	2,600

STEREO UNLIMITED
Schedule of Accounts Payable
January 31, 19XX

Pioneer Associates	$ 420
Sony Corp.	2,060
Store Outfitters	2,600
	$5,080

Control Account

Accounts Payable			Account No. 201	
Date	Ref	Debit	Credit	Balance
19XX				
Jan. 19	J1		2,600	2,600
31	P1		5,330	7,930
31	CP1	2,850		5,080

Note: The January 19th purchase is shown in the Accounts Payable control account here but not in those depicted in Exhibits A-2 and A-4. The reason is that the transaction had not yet been presented, making inclusion in the earlier exhibits inappropriate.

repeated here. In addition to preparing a trial balance, the subsidiary ledger/control account equality must be checked. The basic technique was introduced in Exhibit 6-1; it is shown for Stereo Unlimited's Accounts Payable account in Exhibit A-5.

To conclude, be aware that the transaction-recording and posting processes illustrated in the previous pages are performed by bookkeepers, not accountants. The accountant, however, is often requested to audit the output of information systems, review internal controls, and design new systems for clients. He or she must therefore possess a fundamental knowledge of how transactions are processed into the dollar amounts that appear on the financial statements.

END-OF-APPENDIX REVIEW

**KEY TERMS
AND CONCEPTS:
A QUICK OVERVIEW**

cash payments journal A special journal used to record virtually all cash disbursements made by a business.

cash receipts journal A special journal used to record all cash received by a business.

purchases journal   A special journal used to record purchases of merchandise on account.

sales journal   A special journal used to record sales of merchandise on account.

special journals   Journals that handle specialized (specific) types of transactions (cash receipts, sales, and so forth).

Your friend is a candidate for an office position at PC Stores. To qualify for the job, each candidate must successfully pass an examination that covers basic accounting and bookkeeping procedures. To prepare for the upcoming ordeal, all candidates were given a copy of last year's questions. Several of these questions follow.

SUMMARY PROBLEM

1 PC Stores uses a set of journals (sales, purchases, cash receipts, cash payments, and general) to record daily activity. In which journal would the following transactions and events be found?
   a Received $600 from the sale of old equipment used in the business.
   b Purchased a $75 calculator (to be used in the office) for cash.
   c Recorded the adjusting entry for supplies consumed during the month.
   d Recorded daily cash sales of $900.
   e Acquired $400 of merchandise on account from BMI, Inc.

2 PC Stores normally posts the total of its sales journal on a weekly basis. To what accounts should this total be posted?

3 Assume that a firm began operations on January 1 of the current year. Purchases of merchandise for the year just ended totaled $50,000, of which 30% were for cash. The company paid 80% of the amounts owed to suppliers.
   a Compute the balance in the Accounts Payable control account at the end of the period.
   b Compute the total of all account balances in the Accounts Payable subsidiary ledger at the end of the period.
   c Suppose that on December 29, the bookkeeper failed to record a $500 purchase of merchandise on account from Reliable Wholesale. Will the Accounts Payable control account still be in agreement with the subsidiary ledger? Briefly explain.

Instructions

In an effort to be well prepared for the examination, your friend has requested help in answering last year's questions. Draft a response to each of the questions listed.

Solution

1 a Cash receipts
   b Cash payments
   c General
   d Cash receipts
   e Purchases

2 The total should be posted as a debit to Accounts Receivable and a credit to Sales.

3 a

Beginning balance, Jan. 1	$ —
Add: Purchases on account ($50,000 × 0.70)	35,000
	$35,000
Deduct: Payments on account ($35,000 × 0.80)	28,000
Ending balance, Dec. 31	$ 7,000

b The account balances should total to $7,000.

c Yes. A failure to record the purchase means that the total posted to the Accounts Payable control account was understated by $500. Further, the bookkeeper failed to update Reliable Wholesale's account in the subsidiary ledger. Although both the control account and subsidiary ledger are understated, their balances will still be in agreement.

ASSIGNMENT MATERIAL

EXERCISES

EA-1 *Special journal selection and use*

Austin Office Supply employs the following journals:

Sales	Cash payments
Purchases	General
Cash receipts	

All journals are similar in format to those illustrated in this appendix. The following transactions and events occurred during February:

a Acquired merchandise on account from Texas Wholesalers.

b Sold merchandise to various customers for cash.

c Wrote check no. 118 in settlement of a past-due account payable.

d Acquired a new display counter on account for use in the store.

e Granted a cash refund to an irate customer for defective merchandise.

f Sold two new calculators on account to Tripro Auto Parts.

g Adjusted the Prepaid Advertising account to reflect February's advertising expense.

h Received $900 on account from Harris Enterprises, a customer.

i Returned merchandise acquired in error from Dean, Inc., Austin's chief supplier. Dean has agreed to reduce Austin's account.

Indicate the journal in which each of the preceding transactions and events would be recorded.

EA-2 *Operation of a special journal system*

Yum Yum Yogurt operates 10 frozen yogurt stores in Florida. The company uses special journals for sales, purchases, cash receipts, and cash payments, and a general journal. All are similar in format to those illustrated in this appendix. You have been requested to answer the following questions for an office clerk:

a In which journal would a store's daily cash sales be recorded?

b To which subsidiary ledger are the individual amounts in the purchases journal posted? How frequently should these amounts be posted?

c To which account is the total of the sales journal debited at the end of the month? To which account is the total credited?

d Where is the total of the Sundry column in the cash receipts journal posted at month-end?

e By month-end, which of the company's journals would probably contain the fewest transactions and events? Why?

EA-3 *Introduction to special journals*

Peartree Computing had the following credit sales during March 19X6:

Mar. 6   Sold $1,800 of computer equipment on account to Burger City.

     16   Sold $2,900 of computer equipment on account to Dave's Automotive.

     24   Sold $550 of computer equipment on account to Dallas Wallpaper.

The March 1 balance in Accounts Receivable was $300, which arose from a sale to Dave's Automotive on February 22. There were no receipts on account from customers during February or March.

a Record Peartree's March transactions in a journal similar to that shown in Exhibit A-1.

b Open T-accounts for Accounts Receivable (no. 110), Sales (no. 400), and the firm's customers. Post the sales journal and show how the accounts would appear as of March 31. Assume that credit sales transactions were posted from page 6 of the journal in February and page 7 in March.

c Prepare a schedule of accounts receivable as of March 31.

d What is the balance in the Accounts Receivable control account on March 31?

EA-4 *Understanding a purchases and cash payments journal*

On May 1 of the current year, the accounting records of Optical City revealed the following information:

Balance in Accounts Payable control account: $15,700

Balances in Accounts Payable subsidiary ledger: A-1 Labs, $3,700; NY Eye, $6,100; and Optica, $5,900

The following purchases and cash payments took place during the month:

Purchases on Account			Payments on Account		
Date	Supplier	Amount	Date	Supplier	Amount
May 7	NY Eye	$4,700	May 3	A-1 Labs	$ 3,700
15	Optica	3,500	9	Optica	5,782*
17	NY Eye	5,000	30	NY Eye	10,800
28	A-1 Labs	2,200			

* Payment of the company's May 1 balance minus a 2% discount.

a Determine the month-end total that would appear in Optical City's purchases journal. Where is this total posted?

b Determine the total of the Accounts Payable column in Optical City's cash payments journal. Is this total posted to the company's control account or the subsidiary ledger?

c Establish T-accounts for A-1 Labs, NY Eye, and Optica. Determine the amounts owed to each supplier at month-end.

d Compute the month-end balance in the Accounts Payable control account. Compare this balance with the total of the various supplier accounts from part (c) and comment on your findings.

EA-5 *Special journal/control account operation*

Summit Supply uses special journals similar to those illustrated in this appendix, along with a general journal to record miscellaneous transactions. On January 1 of the current year, the firm's Accounts Receivable and Accounts Payable control accounts revealed balances of $83,500 and $65,700, respectively.

The following information was obtained from a review of the journals on January 31:

Journal	Information
Sales	Total transactions, $24,300
Purchases	Total transactions, $19,900
Cash receipts	Collections from customers on account, $23,100
	Discounts taken by customers for prompt payment, $900
Cash payments	Payments to suppliers on account, $30,200
	Discounts taken on supplier invoices, $500
General	Purchases of machinery on account, $5,700
	Customer returns on account, $400

a Compute the balance in the Accounts Receivable control account on January 31 after all postings are made.
b Compute the balance in the Accounts Payable control account on January 31 after all postings are made. Assume that Summit uses the gross method of recording purchases.

PROBLEMS

PA-1 *Understanding a special journal system*

Reese Athletics Company furnishes athletic supplies and equipment to local retailers and schools. The firm maintains a sales journal, purchases journal, cash receipts journal, cash payments journal, and a general journal. Further, the bookkeeper has established subsidiary ledgers for both accounts receivable and accounts payable.

The following transactions occurred during a recent month:

1 Sold $2,600 of athletic supplies on account to Plano High School.
2 Processed a $5,000 cash withdrawal from the business for Vicki Reese, the owner.
3 Paid $6,800 on account to Wilson Sporting Goods, a supplier. The discount period had lapsed.
4 Acquired $9,800 of merchandise on account from NIKE, Inc.
5 Received $4,500 on account, net of the proper discount, from the Lakeside School District.
6 Paid $2,000 to acquire inventory at a competitor's going-out-of-business sale.
7 Acquired $2,900 of computing equipment on account from Dr. Computer for use in the business.
8 Returned $800 of defective merchandise acquired on account from Ball Four. Ball Four has agreed to reduce Reese's account.
9 Paid P&T Management $1,500 for the month's rent.
10 Made $3,700 of cash sales to various customers.

Instructions

Analyze the preceding transactions and determine:

A—The journal in which the transaction would be recorded.
B—Whether the transaction requires an immediate posting to a subsidiary ledger account.
C—Whether the transaction requires an immediate posting to a control account.
D—Whether the transaction requires an immediate posting to an account in the general ledger.

"Immediate" means that the posting occurs during the month as opposed to at month-end (e.g., as part of a total). Also, for items B, C, and D, if appropriate, indicate the name of the account. The first transaction is done as an example.

	(A) Journal	(B) Subsidiary Ledger Account	(C) Control Account	(D) General Ledger Account
1	Sales	Yes, Plano High	No	No
2				
etc.				

PA-2 *Detection of processing errors*

The Perez Company uses special journals to record sales, purchases, cash receipts, and cash payments. Perez also employs a general journal to record miscellaneous transactions and adjusting and closing entries. During March the following errors were made:

a A cash receipt on account from Joe Ellis was accidentally posted to Jay Elia's account in the Accounts Receivable subsidiary ledger.

b A clerk who also served as a part-time bookkeeper kept the cash received from a $100 cash sale and made no entry for the sale in the accounting records.

c The total of the purchases journal was accidentally underadded by $1,000.

d The $150 total of the Sales Discounts column in the cash receipts journal was posted to the Sales Discounts account as $1,500.

e A $600 sale on account to Jerry Avery was both entered in the sales journal and posted to Avery's account as $500.

f A cash receipt on account from Sue Cepeda was properly recorded in the cash receipts journal. The bookkeeper neglected to post the payment to Cepeda's account in the Accounts Receivable subsidiary ledger.

Instructions

State how each error is likely to be discovered. If discovery is unlikely, tell why.

PA-3 *Special journals, transaction processing, and schedules*

Casual Wear began business on July 1. Selected accounts (and account numbers) follow.

Cash	100	Sales returns	401
Accounts receivable	110	Purchases	510
Merchandise inventory	120	Purchases returns	511
Prepaid advertising	130	Purchases discounts	512
Office equipment	140	Rent expense	610
Accounts payable	200	Salaries expense	620
Loan payable	210	Utilities expense	630
Tina Sharp, capital	300	Interest expense	640
Sales	400		

The company uses special journals for sales, purchases, cash receipts, and cash payments, and a general journal to record miscellaneous transactions and events. The journals are similar in format to those illustrated in this appendix.

All merchandise is purchased on account, subject to terms of 2/10, n/30. Casual Wear uses a periodic inventory system. The transactions of July follow.

July 1 Secured $30,000 of financing from a $20,000 investment by the owner and a $10,000 bank loan.

1 Paid the first month's rent to Vantage Management; issued check no. 100 for $1,600.

2 Purchased $13,000 of merchandise on account from Jeans, Inc. (invoice no. 4421 dated July 2).

3 Purchased $3,000 of office equipment on account from Bronco Office Supply.

3 Paid $800 for five months of advertising in *Clothing Weekly*; issued check no. 101.

5 Sold $7,000 of goods on account to Denver Woman (invoice no. 2000).

7 Purchased $9,500 of merchandise on account from New York Fashions (invoice no. 2487 dated July 7).

10 Paid the balance owed to Jeans, Inc.; issued check no. 102.

11 Returned $900 of the merchandise purchased on July 7 from New York Fashions.

13 Sold $3,700 of goods on account to Nan's (invoice no. 2001).

14 Cash sales for the week ended July 14 amounted to $1,250.

15 Paid the amount owed to Bronco Office Supply; issued check no. 103.

16 Paid the proper amount owed to New York Fashions from the transactions of July 7 and July 11; issued check no. 104.

19 Purchased $6,600 of goods on account from Seaside Creations (invoice no. 1824 dated July 19).

21 Cash sales for the week ended July 21 amounted to $2,300.

24 Paid $520 to Colorado Light & Power for July utilities; issued check no. 105.

26 Sold $5,800 of goods on account to Wild One (invoice no. 2002).

27 Received the amount due from Denver Woman.

28 Cash sales for the week ended July 28 amounted to $1,300.

29 Accepted a $600 return of goods on account from Wild One. The goods were shipped in error on July 26.

29 Paid salaries of $3,300; issued check no. 106.

30 Obtained a $500 cash refund from Bronco Office Supply for the return of unneeded office equipment that was acquired on July 3.

31 Paid the first installment on the July 1 loan. Issued check no. 107 to Mountain Trust for $700, of which $150 is interest.

Instructions

a Record the transactions in the correct journals. Post the proper individual amounts and general journal entries daily; at the end of the month, post the appropriate totals.

b Prepare a trial balance of the general ledger accounts, a schedule of accounts receivable, and a schedule of accounts payable.

PA-4 *Special journals, transaction processing, and schedules*

Midtown Camera Distributors is a small proprietorship located in South Carolina. A recent review of the accounting records disclosed that Evertson Photo owes the firm $2,600 from a purchase of merchandise on November 28. Further, Midtown owes $3,700 to Tokyo Camera Works (a supplier) for a transaction on November 29. All credit sales and merchandise acquisitions are subject to terms of 2/10, n/30. The following transactions took place during December:

Dec. 2 Received a $5,000 cash investment from the owner, Diane Pettit.

3 Sold $500 of merchandise on account to Duke's Camera Shop (invoice no. 642).

5 Purchased $2,900 of merchandise on account from Polaroid Corporation (invoice no. 6847 dated December 5).

6 Paid the proper amount due Tokyo Camera Works for the purchase on November 29; issued check no. 4305.

7 Cash sales for the week amounted to $2,330.

9 Issued check no. 4306 for $520 to Smith and Son Printers for brochures to be used in January's advertising program.

12 Duke's Camera Shop paid the proper amount due in settlement of its account balance.

14 Cash sales for the week totaled $3,230.

14 Issued check no. 4307 to Polaroid Corporation in payment of the purchase on December 5.

15 Issued check no. 4308 to Susan Woodard in payment of her $1,800 salary.

17 Sold $2,200 of cameras and $650 of accessories on account to Dave's Studio (invoice no. 643).

19 Received $225 for consulting services rendered to a suburban newspaper's photography staff.

21 Cash sales for the week amounted to $1,120.

22 Sold a $580 camera on account to Hawthorne Photo Supply (invoice no. 644).

23 Purchased $1,950 of merchandise on account from Tokyo Camera Works (invoice no. 8041 dated December 23).

24 Hawthorne Photo Supply returned the camera purchased on December 22 and its account was adjusted.

24 Paid $85 for utilities to South Carolina Power and Light; issued check no. 4309.

26 Received a $50 check from Smith and Son Printers. An accompanying note stated that Midtown's bill for the printing job on December 9 had been computed incorrectly.

28 Sold a $620 camera on account to Hay Photography (invoice no. 645).

29 Cash sales for the week totaled $910.

30 Purchased a used delivery van from Savings National for $6,000; paid $2,000 down and secured a short-term loan for the remaining balance. Issued check no. 4310.

Midtown employs single-column sales and purchases journals and multi-column cash receipts and payments journals similar to those illustrated in this appendix. In addition, a general journal is used for miscellaneous transactions. The general ledger revealed the following balances on November 30 (account numbers appear in parentheses):

Cash (110)	$ 14,700	Sales discounts (420)	$ 2,200
Accounts receivable (120)	2,600	Sales returns (430)	3,700
Inventory (130)	56,700	Miscellaneous revenue	
Prepaid advertising (140)	1,600	(450)	—
Delivery van (150)	—	Purchases (510)	98,500
Accounts payable (210)	3,700	Purchases discounts (520)	1,600
Loan payable (220)	—	Wage expense (530)	24,400
Diane Pettit, capital (310)	85,300	Travel expense (540)	3,200
Diane Pettit, drawing		Rent expense (550)	11,500
(320)	15,000	Utilities expense (560)	3,100
Sales (410)	146,600		

Instructions

a Open Midtown's accounts in the general ledger and the Accounts Receivable and Accounts Payable subsidiary ledgers. *Note:* This step is not necessary if you are using the preprinted working papers that accompany the text.

b Record the December transactions in the correct journals. Post the proper individual amounts and general journal entries daily; at the end of the month, post the appropriate totals. All terms of sale are strictly followed.

c Prepare a trial balance of the general ledger accounts, a schedule of accounts receivable, and a schedule of accounts payable as of December 31.

APPENDIX B

An Introduction to Federal Income Taxes

The dates April 15 and May 5 have a unique meaning to many people in this country. April 15, of course, is the usual deadline for settling one's tax obligation with the U.S. government. May 5, on the other hand, represents a recent Tax Freedom Day—the day on which the average American will have earned enough money to pay his or her federal, state, and local tax bills for the year. The Tax Foundation, Inc., calculates Tax Freedom Day by assuming that every dollar the average worker earns starting on January 1 goes to the government.

Income taxes also have a "special meaning" to corporate management. Tax payments to various government authorities represent a significant cost of doing business and can severely limit an entity's plans for growth and expansion. In view of the magnitude of these assessments, companies (and individuals too) often devote considerable efforts to trying to reduce or postpone taxes. Tax planning and decision making are therefore of utmost importance.

This appendix presents an introduction to federal income taxes. Be aware while reading these pages that tax law is complex, full of exceptions, and often studied in advanced accounting courses. Our goal, thus, is to focus on the basic issues only.[1]

The first federal income tax was enacted to help finance the Civil War. Our present income tax, however, is derived from the Sixteenth Amendment to the Constitution, which was ratified in 1913. The amendment states:

FEDERAL INCOME TAX: BACKGROUND AND ADMINISTRATION

---

[1] Our discussion reflects the tax rules and rates that are in effect at the time of this writing.

> The Congress shall have power to lay and collect taxes on incomes, from whatever source derived, without apportionment among the several States, and without regard to any census or enumeration.

Over the years, Congress has passed various tax-related laws. Some of these laws have led to sweeping changes in our country's approach to the taxation of income. Not too long ago, for example, Congress enacted the Tax Reform Act of 1986—the culmination of efforts to provide "relief" for the taxpaying public. The Act called for substantial reductions in both individual and business income tax rates, while broadening the base on which taxes are computed. In addition, this legislation attempted to shift more of the tax burden from individuals to corporations.

Administration of the Tax Law

The tax laws passed by Congress are administered by the **Internal Revenue Service (IRS)**, an agency of the Treasury Department. Probably best known for the processing of tax returns, the IRS also interprets tax law, answers taxpayer questions, processes tax payments and refunds, and sometimes initiates legal action. Let us dwell on return processing for a moment, since this is the area of tax with which you may have had some interaction.

All returns filed with the IRS are checked for mathematical and mechanical accuracy. If a return is found to contain an error that overstates tax, any excess is either refunded or held as a credit against the next period's tax liability. When inaccuracies result in an underpayment of tax, a bill is sent to the erring taxpayer.

The IRS often goes one step further in the examination of returns by performing an audit. Returns are selected for audit on the basis of several factors, including errors contained within the return, requests for abnormally large refunds, disclosure of income and expenses in excess of certain specified limits, and simply on a random basis to encourage correct reporting by taxpayers. The number of returns selected for review varies and often depends on the availability of audit personnel. In a recent fiscal year, such examinations resulted in the assessment of $22.3 billion of additional taxes and penalties.[2]

CLASSES OF TAXPAYERS

According to tax law, there are four classes of taxpayers: individuals, corporations, estates, and trusts. Missing from this list are the proprietorship and partnership forms of business organization. These latter entity forms are not considered to be separate taxable units apart from their owners; thus, any income generated is taxed to the owner or partners whether or not such amounts have been withdrawn from the business. As we will show later in the discussion, the owner of a proprietorship reports business income from the enterprise on his or her individual tax return, together with salaries and income from other sources, and is taxed accordingly. Members of a partnership report their respective share of business income in a similar fashion.

---

[2] *Internal Revenue Service Annual Report: 1990* (Washington, D.C.: U.S. Government Printing Office, 1990), p. 7.

In contrast to the proprietorship and partnership, the corporation is a separate taxable entity and is required to pay taxes on its income. Additionally, individual stockholders must report any dividends received as part of their annual income. These procedures result in "double taxation" because income is taxed first to the corporation at the time of generation and later to stockholders when dividends are distributed. Taxation of corporations, as well as that for estates and trusts, is extremely specialized and will not be discussed in this appendix.

Taxpayer Accounting Methods: Cash Versus Accrual

Virtually all individual taxpayers and most small businesses use the **cash basis** of accounting when reporting to the IRS. Although not in accord with generally accepted accounting principles, the cash basis is often acceptable for figuring income subject to taxation. With the cash basis, revenues are recognized when cash is collected or *constructively received* (i.e., made available to the taxpayer). To explain constructive receipt, income is considered taxable when it is within the taxpayer's control. As a result, interest credited to a savings account on December 31, 19X1, is 19X1 income even if the amount is not entered in the savings passbook or withdrawn until 19X2.

Turning to expenses, the general rule under the cash basis is that expenses are recognized in the period of payment. There are exceptions, however. For example, disbursements for long-lived assets such as plant and equipment must be capitalized upon acquisition. Subsequently, if the assets are used for business purposes, a depreciation (i.e., cost recovery) deduction is allowed. Similarly, prepayments for business services (such as rent and insurance) are expensed not when paid but rather in the period(s) when benefits are received.

If they desire, taxpayers may elect to use the accrual basis of accounting. Under the **accrual basis,** revenues are recognized when earned, and expenses are entered in the records when incurred. Accrual accounting must be used by large corporations and businesses when inventories play a major role in operating activities.

Individual taxpayers generally voice a strong preference for cash-basis accounting because of the method's simplicity. In addition, cash-basis taxpayers are able to defer taxes into future accounting periods. A doctor, for instance, could delay billing patients seen in December until January and thereby transfer revenue into the next taxable year. Lower revenues give rise to lower taxes. Naturally, this action will catch up with the doctor in the next period; however, if the same practice is repeated, the postponement of taxes will continue. The end result is the generation of additional cash for investment purposes or to cover business expenses. Use of accrual accounting would prevent this postponement from occurring.

Forms and instructions for the computation and filing of income taxes are available from the IRS. Although the standard forms will not be illustrated here, the calculation of an individual's tax liability can be visualized in

TAX ACCOUNTING FOR INDIVIDUALS

terms of the general formula shown in Exhibit B-1. The manner in which the formula's components actually appear on a tax return varies somewhat from that shown in our illustration. Nevertheless, the formula is a useful tool for understanding the structure of our income tax system. Each of the components in the exhibit will now be explained.

Gross Income

A taxpayer can receive income from hundreds of different sources. In all likelihood even the most comprehensive listing of income sources would be incomplete. The Internal Revenue Code therefore presumes that all income is reportable and taxable *unless specifically excluded by law.* A taxpayer's **gross income,** then, is his or her total income less allowable exclusions. Typical items of gross income include, but are not limited to, compensation for services (e.g., wages, salaries, tips, and bonuses), interest, dividends, rents, alimony, pensions, most prizes and awards, income from a proprietorship or partnership, and gains from dealings in property and securities. Even proceeds from embezzlement, gambling winnings, and unemployment compensation are taxable!

Items excludable from gross income include certain life insurance proceeds, gifts and inheritances, certain scholarships, benefits from workers' compensation, and interest on state and local obligations such as municipal bonds. Thus, if a single taxpayer received a $24,000 salary, a $6,000 inheritance, $900 of dividends, and a $400 prize from a quiz show, gross income would be figured as follows:

	Income Received	Exclusions	Gross Income
Salary	$24,000	$ —	$24,000
Inheritance	6,000	6,000	—
Dividends	900	—	900
Prize	400	—	400
	$31,300	$6,000	$25,300

Deductions from Gross Income

As shown in Exhibit B-1, a taxpayer is entitled to several types of deductions. The first type, called **deductions from gross income,** are subtracted from gross income to yield **adjusted gross income.** These deductions often relate to an individual's trade or business and include certain expenses incurred in the generation of gross income. No matter where a deduction appears on a tax return, the rules for deductibility are the opposite of those for income. That is, nothing is deductible *unless specifically stated in the tax laws.*

Deductions from gross income include, but are not limited to, the following:

1 *Trade and business expenses*—Most ordinary and necessary expenses attributable to a taxpayer's trade or business are deductible. Such expenses include employee salaries, advertising, rent, utilities, and 80% of the amounts spent for business meals and entertainment. In the actual

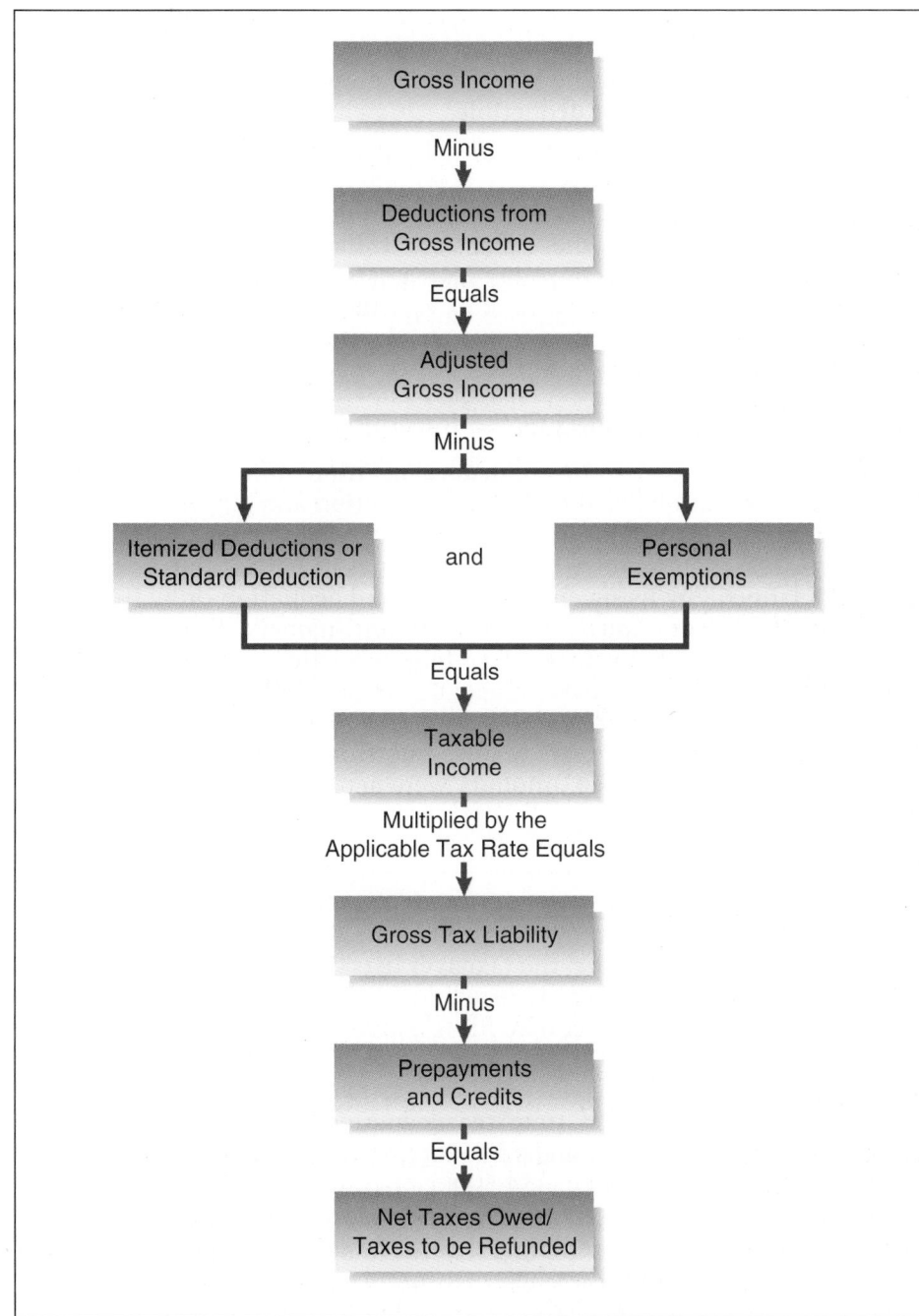

tax computation, business expenses are deducted from business revenues, and the net figure is reflected in the taxpayer's adjusted gross income.

2 *Losses on the sale or exchange of property and securities*—Subject to certain limits and conditions, losses incurred on the sale or exchange of selected assets are deductible from gross income if such assets were acquired and held for investment purposes. Examples of qualifying items include stocks, bonds, stamps, coins, and art. It is important to note that losses on the sale or exchange of *personal* property (e.g., a personal automobile or home) are not deductible.

3 *Contributions to retirement plans*—Taxpayers are eligible to establish their own retirement plans (such as an Individual Retirement Account, better known as an IRA). Subject to certain restrictions and limits, amounts contributed to these plans are deductible from gross income.

4 *Other deductions*—Other items that may be deducted from gross income include limited amounts of rental property expenses (e.g., repairs, interest, taxes, and depreciation) and certain alimony payments.

Deductions from Adjusted Gross Income

Exhibit B-1 reveals two groups of **deductions from adjusted gross income:** (1) itemized deductions or the standard deduction and (2) personal exemptions. Focusing on the first group, all taxpayers are given a tax break for selected expenses, most of which are personal in nature. These expenses may be "claimed" by using either the standard deduction or by itemizing.

The **standard deduction** is a preset amount, namely, $3,400 for single individuals and $5,700 for married couples who file a joint return.[3] These figures are raised if the taxpayers meet certain age and sight requirements. The benefit of using the standard deduction is that the deduction is automatic. Consequently, the taxpayer need not furnish proof that allowable expenses equal to the preset amounts were actually incurred.

Itemized Deductions

If taxpayers have allowable expenses that exceed the standard deduction, a lower taxable income is produced by using an alternate procedure known as **itemizing.** With itemizing, the taxpayer lists (i.e., deducts) *actual* allowable expenses that have been incurred during the year.

For example, if a married couple filing a joint return has allowable itemized deductions of $8,500, it would be advantageous to subtract this amount from adjusted gross income rather than use the $5,700 standard deduction. Alternatively, if itemized deductions total only $4,500, the couple should employ the standard deduction to reduce taxable income by an additional $1,200 ($5,700 − $4,500).

Unlike the standard deduction, itemizing is not automatic. Thus, the burden of proof shifts to the taxpayer to show that the expenses deducted were both incurred and allowable. Accurate record keeping along with retention of invoices, canceled checks, and other documentation is therefore necessary when using this method.

Deductions from adjusted gross income are permitted for the following:

1 *Medical and dental expenses*—Medical and dental expenses paid by the taxpayer are deductible to the extent such amounts exceed 7.5% of adjusted gross income. Deductible expenses include fees paid to hospi-

---

[3] A **joint return** reports the combined income and deductions of a husband and wife.

tals and doctors, outlays for medical appliances such as wheelchairs and glasses, the costs of any medical insurance premiums paid, and the costs of prescription drugs.

2 *Taxes*—Real-estate taxes, personal property taxes, and state and local income taxes are deductible. Nondeductible items include most federal taxes, taxes on gasoline and other motor fuels, state and local sales tax, and most licensing fees (such as driver's licenses).

3 *Interest*—Interest that results from a mortgage on a principal or second residence is typically deductible. In contrast, interest incurred on personal debt (e.g., car loans and credit card balances) cannot be deducted.

4 *Charitable contributions*—Subject to certain limits, contributions of money and property made to charitable, religious, educational, and other qualified organizations (usually nonprofit in nature) are deductible.

5 *Casualty losses*—A taxpayer can deduct the nonreimbursed portion of certain personal property losses that result from casualties such as fire and theft. A deduction is permitted to the extent that a given casualty loss exceeds $100 *and* the total of such net losses exceeds 10% of adjusted gross income. A taxpayer who has adjusted gross income of $25,000 and losses of $1,900 and $1,200 is therefore entitled to a $400 deduction: [($1,900 − $100 + $1,200 − $100) − 0.10($25,000)].

6 *Miscellaneous deductions and employee business expenses*—Itemized expenses related to investments and the production of income, such as those for safe deposit box rentals, certain legal and accounting fees, and investment counsel fees, are deductible. In addition, taxpayers can deduct some nonreimbursed costs that pertain to employment (e.g., uniform costs, union dues, dues to professional societies, subscriptions to professional journals, certain employment agency fees, job-related travel, 80% of entertainment costs, and moving expenses). With the exception of moving costs, the allowable deduction for the total of investment expenses, income-producing expenses, and employee expenses is limited to the portion that exceeds 2% of adjusted gross income.

Personal Exemptions

In addition to itemized deductions or the standard deduction, taxpayers are entitled to reduce adjusted gross income for **personal exemptions.** A $2,150 reduction is allowed for each exemption.[4] Tax laws permit one exemption for the taxpayer and additional exemptions for the taxpayer's spouse and each dependent claimed.

Generally stated, a **dependent** is a person who (1) has received over one-half of his or her support (food, clothing, lodging, and other similar expenses) from the taxpayer, (2) is closely related to the taxpayer or has lived in the taxpayer's home for the entire year, and (3) has less than $2,150 of gross income. This last test is waived for children of the taxpayer who are under nineteen years of age or full-time students.[5]

---

[4] The $2,150 amount is decreased on a graduated scale for certain "high-income" individuals and couples.

[5] Full-time students must be under age 24.

Taxable Income and the Gross Tax Liability

Adjusted gross income minus itemized deductions (or the standard deduction) and personal exemptions equals **taxable income.** Taxable income is used in conjunction with rate schedules similar to those shown in Exhibit B-2 to determine an individual's gross tax liability.[6]

A review of the exhibit reveals that single taxpayers attain higher tax rates faster (i.e., at a lower taxable income) than their married counterparts. For example, assuming $60,000 of taxable income, a single taxpayer would pay $14,476 to the federal government, whereas a married couple would pay $12,380. The computations follow.

Single taxpayer	
Tax on $49,300, per schedule	$11,159
Tax on $10,700 excess ($60,000 − $49,300) at 31%	3,317
Total tax	$14,476
Married couple	
Tax on $34,000, per schedule	$ 5,100
Tax on $26,000 excess ($60,000 − $34,000) at 28%	7,280
Total tax	$12,380

Prepayments and Tax Credits

Once the income tax is determined, two further items must be considered: tax prepayments and tax credits. Recall that our tax system operates on a pay-as-you-go basis, with income taxes being withheld from employees' wages throughout the period. These withholdings are made for two reasons. First, governmental expenditures occur during the year, so it is convenient to collect taxes on the same basis. Second, few taxpayers could (or would) pay their entire tax bill on a single date (usually April 15) because considerable savings would be necessary. Such withholdings are really tax prepayments and are therefore deducted from the gross tax liability when figuring the balance due the government.

EXHIBIT B-2
Tax Rate Schedules

SINGLE TAXPAYERS				MARRIED TAXPAYERS FILING A JOINT RETURN			
Taxable Income		Gross Tax Liability		Taxable Income		Gross Tax Liability	
From	To	Rounded Amount	Of Taxable Income in Excess of	From	To	Rounded Amount	Of Taxable Income in Excess of
$ 0	$20,350	$ 0 + 15%	$ 0	$ 0	$34,000	$ 0 + 15%	$ 0
20,350	49,300	3,053 + 28%	20,350	34,000	82,150	5,100 + 28%	34,000
49,300+		11,159 + 31%	49,300	82,150+		18,582 + 31%	82,150

---

[6] In certain instances, taxpayers use simplified tax tables to figure their tax obligation.

Taxpayers who anticipate owing large amounts of tax and who meet other requirements must pay estimated taxes in quarterly installments throughout the year. Estimated payments are also viewed as prepayments and are deducted from the taxpayer's gross liability.

In addition to withholdings and estimated payments, taxpayers are permitted certain **tax credits.** Such amounts are direct dollar-for-dollar reductions from a taxpayer's total tax bill. Credits currently exist, subject to specific limits and conditions, for low-income taxpayers, dependent child care expenses, and other selected items.

After withholdings, estimated payments, and tax credits are subtracted, the additional balance owed to the federal government or a taxpayer's expected refund becomes known. Sound money management dictates that requests for refunds be filed as soon as possible; taxes due should be paid as late as possible. By following these practices, the taxpayer has more funds available for longer periods of time.

Individual Tax Return Illustration

At this point it is helpful to review the preceding discussion in terms of a comprehensive illustration. Assume that George and Susan McGee and their three small children recently moved from another state for job-related reasons. Susan's father lives with the family and is totally dependent on the McGees for his support. George earned $64,000 working as an accountant. Susan operates a small gift shop that had sales of $57,000 and expenses (including cost of goods sold) of $39,500. The McGees earned $2,600 of interest on various savings accounts, $900 of dividends from a common stock investment, and $100 of interest on a municipal bond. During the year, they generated a $2,000 deductible loss on the sale of investment property. Itemized deductions included medical expenses of $4,000, mortgage interest of $10,000, $1,500 of state income taxes, non-reimbursed employee business expenses of $1,200, and moving costs of $2,400.

Total withholdings for federal income taxes amounted to $9,700. The McGees also paid estimated taxes of $2,800 and are entitled to a $75 tax credit for dependent child care expenses. On the basis of the preceding information and the filing of a joint return, the couple is due a tax refund of $1,259, as shown in Exhibit B-3.

A Further Probe of Tax Rates

The mechanics of using tax rates when determining an individual's tax obligation are fairly straightforward. A deeper understanding of rate structures and their impact is necessary, however, for achieving financial success. In discussing tax rates, we must distinguish between the average rate of tax and the marginal rate of tax. Assume, for a moment, that Linda Newton is a single taxpayer with taxable income of $49,300. Using the data that appear in Exhibit B-2, her tax obligation would amount to $11,159. Stated differently, the tax **averages** 22.6% of taxable income ($11,159 ÷ $49,300).

Suppose that Newton has been offered a new job with a $4,000 salary increase. Assuming her deductions remain fairly constant, the salary in-

EXHIBIT B-3
Individual Tax Return Filed Jointly by George and Susan McGee

Gross income			
George's salary		$64,000	
Gift shop sales	$57,000		
Less: Gift shop expenses	39,500	17,500	
Interest on savings		2,600	
Dividends		900	
Municipal bond interest (excluded)		—	
Total gross income			$85,000
Deductions from gross income			
Loss on investment property			2,000
Adjusted gross income			$83,000
Deductions from adjusted gross income			
Medical expenses	$ 4,000		
Less: 7.5% of adjusted gross income	6,225	$ —	
Mortgage interest		10,000	
State income taxes		1,500	
Employee business expenses	$ 1,200		
Less: 2% of adjusted gross income	1,660	—	
Moving expenses		2,400	
Total itemized deductions		$13,900	
Personal exemptions ($2,150 × 6)		12,900	26,800
Taxable income			$56,200
Tax computation based on rates in Exhibit B-2:			
Tax on $34,000, per schedule		$ 5,100	
Tax on $22,200 excess ($56,200 − $34,000) at 28%		6,216	
Gross tax liability			$11,316
Less: Child care tax credit		$ 75	
Taxes withheld		9,700	
Estimated payments		2,800	12,575
Taxes owed (refund)			$ (1,259)

crease would be taxed at the rate of 31% (from Exhibit B-2). Thirty-one percent is termed the **marginal rate of tax,** or the tax rate applied to each dollar of additional taxable income. From this simple example, you can see the importance of the marginal tax rate in planning and decision making. If the government has a 31% "bite," Newton would keep only 69¢ of each additional dollar earned. She could easily decide that the incremental take-home pay is simply too small, given the numerous problems associated with a change in employment. Should she be in a location where state and local income taxes have been enacted, these, too, must be considered, as such amounts further diminish the attractiveness of the increased salary.

The payment of income taxes often drains individuals (and businesses) of money needed for daily activities, growth, and perhaps even survival. As a result, taxpayers constantly strive to minimize their tax liability to the government by careful planning.

Tax liability may be reduced by following two courses of action: tax avoidance and tax evasion. **Tax avoidance** is achieved by the proper planning of financial events, affairs, and transactions within the legal confines of the tax statutes passed by Congress. In contrast, **tax evasion** represents a deliberate attempt to understate taxable income by the manipulation of income and expenses. For example, income may be intentionally understated, while fictitious deductions are claimed for expenses or exemptions. Tax evasion, of course, is illegal and accompanied by severe penalties.

Tax Avoidance: Areas to Consider

Taxpayers can reduce their liability to the government in many different ways. Small service businesses, for instance, that use the cash basis of accounting can delay the recording of revenue, thus reducing taxable income and postponing income taxes.

Taxes can be deferred into future periods by using accelerated cost recovery write-offs of long-term assets and, in periods of rising prices, the LIFO method of inventory costing. Under LIFO, the higher costs of recently acquired goods are matched against revenues, resulting in a lowering of taxable income. An additional method of avoidance is the acquisition of certain investments that generate tax-exempt income (such as state and local municipal bonds).

Suffice it to say that as long as there is an income tax, tax avoidance will be popular. Good business practice dictates that both individuals and companies conduct their activities mindful of tax implications. By so doing, significant strides will be made toward cash retention and economic prosperity.

END-OF-APPENDIX REVIEW

**KEY TERMS
AND CONCEPTS:
A QUICK OVERVIEW**

The accounting basis that recognizes revenues when earned and expenses when incurred.

Gross income of a taxpayer minus allowable deductions from gross income.

A taxpayer's gross tax liability divided by total taxable income.

The basis of accounting that focuses on the cash flows connected with revenues and expenses. Revenues are recognized when received, and expenses are recognized when paid. Used by most individual taxpayers.

Subtractions from adjusted gross income for certain personal expenses—specifically, itemized deductions (or the standard deduction) and personal exemptions.

deductions from gross income Subtractions from a taxpayer's income that typically relate to the generation of gross income.

dependent A person who (1) has received more than one-half of his or her support from the taxpayer, (2) is closely related to the taxpayer or has lived in the taxpayer's home for the entire year, and (3) has earned less than $2,150 of income (unless under 19 years of age or a full-time student).

gross income A taxpayer's total income minus allowable exclusions.

Internal Revenue Service (IRS) An agency of the U.S. Treasury Department that administers the tax laws passed by Congress and the rulings handed down by the courts.

itemizing A process performed by a taxpayer; involves listing the actual allowable personal expenses that have been incurred during the year.

joint return A filing status for tax purposes that combines the income and deductions of a husband and wife.

marginal rate of tax The tax rate applied to each additional dollar of taxable income.

personal exemption A $2,150 deduction from adjusted gross income that is allowed for the taxpayer, the spouse, and each dependent claimed.

standard deduction A preset amount that is used in place of a taxpayer's itemized deductions.

tax avoidance The planning of financial events, affairs, and transactions within the confines of tax laws to minimize the tax liability.

tax credit A direct dollar-for-dollar reduction from a taxpayer's total tax bill.

tax evasion The deliberate attempt to understate taxable income by the manipulation of revenues and expenses; an illegal activity.

taxable income Income reportable to the IRS; computed as adjusted gross income minus itemized deductions (or the standard deduction) and personal exemptions.

SUMMARY PROBLEM

Gayle Hopkins has just completed a review of the basic rules of federal income taxation for individuals. She is in the process of applying for a part-time position with H&R Sanderson, a local tax preparation service. Sanderson has asked Gayle to study data that pertain to Nancy and Fred Bishop and Stephanie and Harold Katz. The data follow.

Nancy and Fred Bishop	
Contribution to the United Way	$ 700
Interest on credit card balance	250
Repairs on rental property	1,900
Union dues	300
Federal income taxes owed	10,800

Stephanie and Harold Katz	
Gross income	$86,000
Deductions from gross income	5,000
Itemized deductions	15,000
Taxes withheld from salaries	9,700
Tax credits	500

Instructions

Assume the role of Gayle Hopkins and:

a Compute the Bishops' (1) deductions from gross income and (2) deductions from adjusted gross income. The couple will file a joint return and will itemize. Ignore any limitations on the amount of the deduction.

b Compute the amount of tax that the Katzes owe the federal government (or the refund due). The couple will file a joint return and claim four exemptions. Use the tax rates presented in Exhibit B-2.

Solution

a Deductions from gross income

Repairs on rental property	$1,900

Deductions from adjusted gross income

Contribution to the United Way	$ 700
Union dues	300
	$1,000

Note: Interest on credit cards and the couple's federal income taxes are not deductible.

b

Gross income		$86,000
Less: Deductions from gross income		5,000
Adjusted gross income		$81,000
Less: Itemized deductions	$15,000	
Personal exemptions ($2,150 × 4)	8,600	23,600
Taxable income		$57,400
Tax on $34,000, per schedule		$ 5,100
Tax on $23,400 excess ($57,400 − $34,000) at 28%		6,552
Gross tax liability		$11,652
Less: Taxes withheld from salaries	$ 9,700	
Tax credits	500	10,200
Taxes owed (refund)		$ 1,452

ASSIGNMENT MATERIAL

EXERCISES

EB-1 *Treatment of deductions and credits*
Classify items (a)–(h) as one of the following:

1— A deduction from gross income to arrive at adjusted gross income.
2— A deduction from adjusted gross income to arrive at taxable income.
3— A tax credit deductible from the gross tax liability.
4— A cost not deductible anywhere on the tax return.

Ignore possible limitations on the amount of the deduction or credit.

_____ a Amounts paid for dependent child care expenses.
_____ b Uninsured portion of fire loss on personal residence.
_____ c State income taxes.
_____ d Nonreimbursed moving expenses from New York City to Denver related to a change in employment.
_____ e Contribution to a retirement plan by a self-employed person.
_____ f Sales taxes paid on the purchase of a new fishing boat.
_____ g Subscription to a professional, work-related journal.
_____ h Dental expenses.

EB-2 *Itemized deductions versus standard deduction*
Dave and Susan Taylor, a married couple, file a joint return and have the following expenditures for the year just ended:

Hospital bills	$ 400
Medical insurance costs	750
Physician bills	150
Dentist bills	700
Prescription drugs	300
Cash donations to church	530
Real-estate taxes on personal residence	600
Miscellaneous employee expenses	250
Cost recovery (i.e., depreciation) on rental property	3,000
Mortgage interest on personal residence	1,100
Casualty loss on car accident (uninsured amount)	450

Assuming an adjusted gross income of $30,000, should the couple itemize their deductions? Show calculations to support your answer.

EB-3 *Calculation of key tax amounts*
Diane and Peter Martin have two small children. The following information was extracted from the couple's joint tax return:

Gross income	$50,000
Deductions from gross income	4,500
Itemized deductions	13,500
Taxes withheld from salaries	2,900
Estimated tax payments	500
Tax credits	600

Determine the following:
a Adjusted gross income.
b Taxable income.

c The couple's gross tax liability, using the rates presented in Exhibit B-2.

d The balance owed the federal government or the refund due. Indicate which and the amount.

EB-4 *Tax computation for individuals*

The following information was extracted from the accounting records of Susan and Tan Cheng:

Tan's salary	$91,000
Inheritance from deceased relative	5,000
Interest on savings account	1,100
Deductions from gross income	14,500
Itemized deductions	10,700
Income taxes withheld	12,400

The Chengs file a joint return and have three small children. Using the tax rates that appear in Exhibit B-2, compute the amount of tax the couple owes to the federal government (or the refund due).

EB-5 *Tax rate analysis*

Ted Baugh is married and the father of two small children. He and his wife have a total adjusted gross income of $97,000 and itemized expenses of $12,000.

a Ted files a joint return with his wife. Using the tax rate schedule that appears in Exhibit B-2, compute the couple's gross tax liability to the government.

b Compute the average tax rate.

c Compute the marginal tax rate.

d Assume that Ted is considering a new job that will pay an additional $1,000 per month. If itemized expenses remain fairly constant, how much additional cash will Ted have to meet living expenses during the upcoming year? Express your answer on an aftertax basis.

PROBLEMS

PB-1 *Tax computations for individuals*

Connie and Frank Jackson have three small children and file a joint tax return. Frank is employed as a manufacturer's representative and earns $70,000 per year. Connie is self-employed and conducts cooking classes in a rented facility across town. Revenues and expenses from her business, which is organized as a sole proprietorship, amounted to $29,900 and $26,100, respectively. (*Note:* No expenses were incurred for business meals or entertainment.) The couple earned $1,100 of interest and $700 of dividends from investments made throughout the year. The interest includes $100 from bonds issued by the state of Iowa. Additional information relating to the Jacksons follows.

Hospital and doctor bills	$ 2,600
Health insurance premiums	900
Prescription drugs	400
Interest on personal residence	6,100
Nonreimbursed moving expenses related to change in employment	2,200
Property taxes on personal residence	3,200
Contribution to Mid State University	500
Federal taxes withheld	10,300
Estimated tax payments during the year	1,900

Instructions

Compute the amount of tax the couple owes the federal government (or the refund due). Use the tax rate schedule that appears in Exhibit B-2.

PB-2 *Tax computations for individuals*

Leslie and Ronald Aikman are married and support four young children. The couple also provides all the support for Ron's father, who lives in a neighboring city. The following information has been extracted from the Aikmans' accounting records:

Ron's salary	$90,000
Rental income	7,200
Interest on savings accounts	2,400
Prize won at raffle	3,600
Dividends from stock investments	800
Expenses on rental property	5,000
Medical insurance premiums	1,800
Hospital costs	900
Prescription drugs	1,400
Property taxes on personal residence	1,900
State income taxes	400
Mortgage interest on personal residence	6,200
Charitable contributions	1,700
Food and clothing costs	9,700
Income tax withholdings	11,000
Estimated tax payments	2,000
Tax credits	400

The couple plans to file a joint tax return.

Instructions

Determine:

a Adjusted gross income. (*Hint:* The rental property transactions should be listed with other items of gross income.)

b Taxable income.

c The balance owed the federal government or the refund due. Indicate which and the amount; use the tax rate schedule that appears in Exhibit B-2.

APPENDIX C

Specimen Financial Statements

The next few pages contain recent financial statements of the Alberto Culver Company, a firm engaged in the manufacture and sale of consumer products. These statements are representative of those issued by other large corporations and reflect many of the topics discussed in this text.

Also included in these pages is a comprehensive set of statement notes. The notes expand upon the material presented in the statements and enlighten readers who desire further information about the firm's resources, obligations, transactions, and financial-reporting practices. In addition, on page C-9, you will find an audit report to Alberto Culver's stockholders from KPMG Peat Marwick, a large public accounting firm. The audit report indicates that the statements present fairly the company's financial position, cash flows, and results of operations.

Consolidated Statements of Earnings

Alberto-Culver Company and Subsidiaries

	Year ended September 30,		
	1991	1990	1989
Net sales	**$873,718,582**	795,824,968	717,438,433
Costs and expenses:			
Cost of products sold	**424,566,220**	383,410,005	344,539,260
Advertising, promotion, selling and administrative	**399,231,626**	353,737,155	320,587,961
Interest expense, net of interest income of $5,042,000 in 1991, $3,916,000 in 1990 and $2,895,000 in 1989	**1,779,656**	3,974,179	5,080,911
Total costs and expenses	**825,577,502**	741,121,339	670,208,132
Earnings before provision for income taxes and minority interest	**48,141,080**	54,703,629	47,230,301
Provision for income taxes (note 6)	**17,812,000**	19,694,000	17,792,000
Earnings before minority interest	**30,329,080**	35,009,629	29,438,301
Minority interest (notes 1 and 11)	**212,800**	—	—
Net earnings	**$ 30,116,280**	35,009,629	29,438,301
Net earnings per share	**$1.06**	1.30	1.12

See accompanying notes to consolidated financial statements.

Consolidated Statements of Retained Earnings

Alberto-Culver Company and Subsidiaries

	Year ended September 30,		
	1991	1990	1989
Retained earnings, beginning of year	**$167,731,681**	141,470,582	116,547,630
Net earnings	**30,116,280**	35,009,629	29,438,301
	197,847,961	176,480,211	145,985,931
Stock dividends (note 5)	**—**	(3,564,775)	—
Cash dividends (note 5)	**(6,092,578)**	(5,183,755)	(4,515,349)
Retained earnings, end of year	**$191,755,383**	167,731,681	141,470,582

See accompanying notes to consolidated financial statements.

Consolidated Balance Sheets

Alberto-Culver Company and Subsidiaries

	September 30,	
Assets	**1991**	1990
Current assets:		
Cash and cash equivalents	$ 80,103,407	79,582,846
Short-term investments	4,492,200	2,429,313
Receivables, less allowance for doubtful accounts		
(1991—$3,440,000; 1990—$2,996,000)	127,072,994	110,944,423
Inventories:		
Raw materials	29,212,029	23,194,353
Work-in-process	4,522,764	2,674,982
Finished goods	151,512,172	112,991,996
Total inventories	185,246,965	138,861,331
Prepaid expenses	7,025,850	4,588,524
Total current assets	403,941,416	336,406,437
Property, plant and equipment (note 7):		
Land	5,191,317	3,230,100
Buildings	61,994,267	43,610,734
Machinery and equipment	107,148,289	84,842,440
Total property, plant and equipment	174,333,873	131,683,274
Accumulated depreciation	59,423,578	49,911,018
Property, plant and equipment, net	114,910,295	81,772,256
Goodwill and trade names, net	45,214,566	15,465,337
Other assets	10,346,449	9,915,813
	$574,412,726	443,559,843

Liabilities and Stockholders' Equity

Current liabilities:		
Short-term borrowings	$ 4,939,052	4,449,473
Current maturities of long-term debt	10,763,683	634,633
Accounts payable	104,117,278	85,253,129
Accrued expenses (note 2)	57,814,661	42,093,491
Income taxes	14,038,310	11,360,154
Total current liabilities	191,672,984	143,790,880
Long-term debt (note 3)	97,819,452	60,728,041
Deferred income taxes	2,638,974	4,681,645
Other liabilities	10,747,321	3,491,628
Minority interest in consolidated subsidiary (notes 1 and 11)	22,102,800	—
Stockholders' equity (note 5):		
Common stock, par value $.22 per share:		
Class A authorized 25,000,000 shares;		
issued 13,261,624 shares	2,917,557	2,917,557
Class B authorized 25,000,000 shares;		
issued 20,945,424 shares	4,607,993	4,607,993
Additional paid-in capital	82,834,931	82,918,237
Retained earnings	191,755,383	167,731,681
Foreign currency translation (note 1)	(204,829)	344,111
	281,911,035	258,519,579
Less treasury stock, at cost (Class A common stock:		
1991—1,824,210 shares and 1990—1,558,139 shares; Class B common		
stock: 1991—4,143,482 shares and 1990—4,148,658 shares) (note 5)	32,479,840	27,651,930
Total stockholders' equity	249,431,195	230,867,649
	$574,412,726	443,559,843

See accompanying notes to consolidated financial statements, particularly note (11) pertaining to the acquisition of Cederroth International AB.

Consolidated Statements of Cash Flows

Alberto-Culver Company and Subsidiaries

	Year ended September 30,		
	1991	1990	1989
Cash Flows from Operating Activities:			
Net earnings	**$30,116,280**	35,009,629	29,438,301
Adjustments to reconcile net earnings to net cash provided by operating activities:			
Depreciation	**11,356,553**	10,125,430	7,704,200
Amortization of goodwill and other assets	**2,365,299**	2,376,403	2,471,854
Minority interest in net earnings	**212,800**	—	—
Receivables, net	**4,352,542**	(20,063,131)	(14,338,420)
Inventories	**(29,084,365)**	(12,175,582)	(7,560,343)
Prepaid expenses	**(1,122,674)**	(692,983)	982,621
Accounts payable and accrued expenses	**16,448,124**	10,250,255	9,224,740
Income taxes	**2,117,534**	7,220,204	(613,478)
Deferred income taxes	**(1,825,000)**	24,000	3,334,000
Other, net	**920,453**	692,734	123,205
Net cash provided by operating activities	**35,857,546**	32,766,959	30,766,680
Cash Flows from Investing Activities:			
Short-term investments	**(1,880,887)**	(2,314,122)	9,992,819
Capital expenditures	**(29,676,009)**	(14,397,876)	(17,761,522)
Other assets	**(2,077,385)**	2,215,000	(1,486,810)
Payments for purchased businesses, net of acquired company's cash	**(7,693,209)**	—	(15,715,953)
Proceeds from disposals of assets	**373,186**	452,247	345,993
Net cash used by investing activities	**(40,954,304)**	(14,044,751)	(24,625,473)
Cash Flows from Financing Activities:			
Short-term borrowings	**(2,611,174)**	579,471	(1,035,544)
Proceeds from long-term debt	**20,000,000**	375,000	20,855,150
Retirements of long-term debt	**(677,082)**	(11,802,293)	(8,352,488)
Net proceeds from issuance of common stock	**—**	34,045,046	—
Proceeds from exercise of stock options	**333,053**	3,305,595	499,698
Cash dividends paid	**(6,092,578)**	(5,183,755)	(4,515,349)
Stock purchased for treasury	**(5,097,674)**	(1,447,111)	—
Net cash provided by financing activities	**5,854,545**	19,871,953	7,451,467
Effect of foreign exchange rate changes on cash	**(237,226)**	724,128	76,404
Net increase in cash and cash equivalents	**520,561**	39,318,289	13,669,078
Cash and cash equivalents at beginning of year	**79,582,846**	40,264,557	26,595,479
Cash and cash equivalents at end of year	**$80,103,407**	79,582,846	40,264,557

See accompanying notes to consolidated financial statements.

Notes to Consolidated Financial Statements

(1) Summary of Significant Accounting Policies

PRINCIPLES OF CONSOLIDATION
The consolidated financial statements include accounts of the company and its subsidiaries, including Cederroth International AB (See "Minority Interest" below). All significant intercompany accounts and transactions have been eliminated.

CASH EQUIVALENTS
All highly liquid investments purchased with an original maturity of three months or less are considered to be cash equivalents. These investments are stated at cost which approximates market value.

SHORT-TERM INVESTMENTS
Short-term investments are stated at cost which is equal to market value at September 30, 1991 and 1990, respectively.

INVENTORIES
Inventories are stated at the lower of cost (first-in, first-out method) or market (net realizable value).

PROPERTY, PLANT AND EQUIPMENT
Property, plant and equipment are carried at cost. Depreciation is provided primarily on the straight-line method based on the estimated useful lives of assets. Expenditures for maintenance and repairs are expensed as incurred.

GOODWILL AND TRADE NAMES
The cost of goodwill and trade names is amortized over periods ranging from five to forty years.

MINORITY INTEREST
Minority interest represents the minority stockholders' proportionate share of the equity of Cederroth International AB. At September 30, 1991, the company owned 23.7 percent of Cederroth's capital stock, representing 74 percent voting control.

FOREIGN CURRENCY TRANSLATION
Foreign currency balance sheet accounts are generally translated at rates of exchange in effect at the balance sheet date. Results of operations are translated using the average exchange rates prevailing throughout the period.

Translation effects for operations in countries which do not have hyperinflationary economies are recorded as foreign currency translation in stockholders' equity. The following is an analysis of changes in the foreign currency translation account in 1991 and 1990:

	1991	1990
Balance, beginning of year	$ 344,111	(2,352,249)
Foreign currency translation gain (loss)	(548,940)	2,696,360
Balance, end of year	$(204,829)	344,111

Translation effects for operations in countries considered to be hyperinflationary and realized gains and losses from foreign currency transactions included in the consolidated statements of earnings resulted in losses of $335,000, $115,000 and $147,000 in 1991, 1990 and 1989, respectively.

INCOME TAXES
Provision is made for deferred income taxes resulting from timing differences in the recognition of revenue and expense for tax and financial statement purposes.

Statement of Financial Accounting Standards No. 96 ("FAS 96"), "Accounting for Income Taxes," requires a change from the deferred method of accounting for income taxes to the asset and liability method. FAS 96 must be adopted by the company no later than fiscal year 1994.

The company elected not to apply FAS 96 in fiscal year 1991 due to the uncertainty regarding proposed revisions to the statement. However, the company estimates the cumulative effect of adopting FAS 96 would not have had a material effect on the consolidated financial statements.

CALCULATION OF EARNINGS PER SHARE
Earnings per share are based on the following weighted average shares outstanding: 1991—28,303,000; 1990—26,831,000; 1989—26,175,000.

(2) Accrued Expenses

Accrued expenses consist of the following:

	1991	1990
Compensation and payroll taxes	$11,248,822	12,607,298
Promotional allowances	15,257,575	12,183,913
Other	31,308,264	17,302,280
	$57,814,661	42,093,491

(3) Long-Term Debt

Long-term debt, exclusive of current maturities, consists of the following:

	1991	1990
Term notes payable:		
7.875% due March, 1992	$ —	10,000,000
8.95% due February, 1993	10,000,000	10,000,000
9% due February, 1993	20,000,000	20,000,000
7.5% due September, 1994	20,000,000	—
9.73% due November, 1998	20,000,000	20,000,000
Foreign revolving credit agreements at 9.72%–10.53%	24,201,000	—
Other, principally foreign borrowings and capitalized leases at weighted average interest rates of 12.2% in 1991 and 9.2% in 1990.	3,618,452	728,041
	$97,819,452	60,728,041

Maturities of long-term debt are as follows:
1992—$10,764,000; 1993—$30,482,000; 1994—$20,759,000; 1995—$382,000; 1996—$146,000; 1997 and later—$46,050,000.

Notes Continued

(3) Long-Term Debt (continued)

The company has a revolving credit agreement for $100 million which can be increased to $300 million with the approval of the participating banks. Borrowings may be obtained at interest rates selected by the company using the bank base rate, rates determined through competitive bidding or at a certain percentage above the certificate of deposit rate or eurocurrency rate. The agreement expires in fiscal year 1992. There were no borrowings under the agreement at September 30, 1991.

Various borrowing arrangements impose restrictions on such items as total debt, working capital, dividend payments, treasury stock purchases and interest expense. At September 30, 1991, the company was in compliance with these arrangements and $55 million of consolidated retained earnings was not restricted as to the payment of dividends and purchases of treasury stock.

In addition to the revolving credit agreement, the company had unused lines of credit of approximately $125 million with various banks at September 30, 1991. The credit lines, which require no compensating balances, may be terminated at the option of the banks or the company.

(4) Stock Option Plans

The company has stock option plans which authorize the issuance of options to purchase a limited number of shares of the company's common stock at a price not less than the fair market value of the stock at the date of grant. Options under the plans expire five years from date of grant and are exercisable on a cumulative basis in four equal annual increments commencing one year after the date of grant.

Shares under option at September 30, 1991 are summarized below:

Year Granted	Shares Under Option	Per Share Option Price	Total Option Price
1987	55,500	$ 8.25-9.07	$ 474,375
1988	102,900	6.59-7.25	691,651
1989	198,250	13.25-14.57	2,679,812
1990	141,400	18.75-20.62	2,726,437
1991	68,600	19.88-21.86	1,403,165
	566,650		$7,975,440

Options for 44,177 shares were exercised in 1991 whereas options for 567,585 shares were exercised in the prior year. During 1991 and 1990, options for 13,050 and 65,000 shares, respectively, were terminated. Options for 103,150 shares were exercisable at September 30, 1991.

(5) Treasury Stock and Additional Paid-In Capital

Changes in treasury stock and additional paid-in capital during 1991, 1990 and 1989 were as follows (in thousands):

	Treasury Stock		Additional Paid-In Capital
	Shares	Amount	
Balance at September 30, 1988	6,311	$29,325	$46,231
Stock options exercised	(106)	(492)	8
Balance at September 30, 1989	6,205	28,833	46,239
Stock options exercised	(568)	(2,628)	677
Tax benefit on exercise of options	—	—	2,353
Stock purchased for treasury	70	1,447	—
Net proceeds from issuance of stock	—	—	33,649
Balance at September 30, 1990	5,707	27,652	82,918
Stock options exercised	(44)	(270)	63
Stock purchased for treasury	305	5,098	—
Other	—	—	(146)
Balance at September 30, 1991	5,968	$32,480	$82,835

The company has two classes of common stock, both of which are listed on the New York Stock Exchange. Except for voting, dividend and conversion rights, the Class A and Class B common stock are identical. Class A has one-tenth vote per share and Class B has one vote per share. No dividend may be paid on the Class B unless an equal or greater dividend is paid on the Class A, and dividends may be paid on the Class A in excess of dividends paid, or without paying dividends, on the Class B. All, and not less than all, of the Class A may at any time be converted into Class B on a share-for-share basis at the option of the company. The Class B is convertible into Class A on a share-for-share basis at the option of the holders.

Cash dividends for Class B common stock in 1991, 1990 and 1989 were $3,612,159 or $.215 per share, $3,262,522 or $.195 per share and $2,845,460 or $.1725 per share, respectively. Cash dividends for Class A common stock in 1991, 1990 and 1989 were $2,480,419 or $.215 per share, $1,921,233 or $.195 per share and $1,669,889 or $.1725 per share, respectively. Class A common stock dividends per share have been equal to those of Class B common stock since the Class A shares were issued in April, 1986.

The board of directors declared a two-for-one stock split in the form of a stock dividend on both Class A and Class B common stock effective February, 1990. An amount equal to the twenty-two cents per share par value of the additional shares was transferred from retained earnings to common stock. All common stock and per share figures included in this report, except the twenty-two cents per share par value, have been adjusted for the stock split.

In August, 1990, the Company sold 1.8 million shares of previously unissued Class A common stock. Net proceeds after related expenses were $34.0 million. An amount equal to the par value of the shares was credited to common stock with the remaining net proceeds being credited to additional paid-in capital.

Notes Continued

(6) Income Taxes

The provisions for income taxes consist of the following:

	1991	1990	1989
Currently payable:			
Federal	$14,226,000	12,341,000	9,121,000
Foreign	3,452,000	6,367,000	4,220,000
State	1,959,000	962,000	1,117,000
	19,637,000	19,670,000	14,458,000
Deferred:			
Federal	(3,478,000)	1,244,000	2,771,000
Foreign	1,653,000	(1,220,000)	563,000
	(1,825,000)	24,000	3,334,000
	$17,812,000	19,694,000	17,792,000

The deferred income tax provisions include the following components:

	1991	1990	1989
Accelerated tax depreciation	$ 1,658,000	1,588,000	2,696,000
Prepaid expenses	(1,011,000)	(763,000)	(114,000)
Inventory adjustments	(843,000)	(156,000)	255,000
Promotional accruals	(494,000)	(114,000)	135,000
Compensation accruals	(1,197,000)	—	—
Other	62,000	(531,000)	362,000
	$(1,825,000)	24,000	3,334,000

The difference between the effective income tax rate on earnings for financial statement purposes and the United States statutory federal income tax rate is summarized below:

	1991	1990	1989
Statutory tax rate	34.0%	34.0%	34.0%
Effect of foreign income tax rates	.5	.3	1.1
State income taxes, net of federal tax benefit	2.7	1.2	1.6
Other, net	(.2)	.5	1.0
Effective tax rate	37.0%	36.0%	37.7%

Domestic earnings before income taxes were $33.1 million, $42.5 million and $37.0 million in 1991, 1990 and 1989, respectively. Foreign operations had earnings before income taxes of $15.0 million, $12.2 million and $10.2 million in 1991, 1990, and 1989, respectively.

Undistributed earnings of the company's foreign operations amounting to $46.6 million are intended to remain permanently invested to finance future growth and expansion. Accordingly, no U.S. income taxes have been provided on those earnings at September 30, 1991. Should such earnings be distributed, the credit for foreign income taxes paid would substantially offset applicable U.S. income taxes.

(7) Lease Commitments

The major portion of the company's leases are for Sally Beauty Company stores. Other leases cover certain manufacturing and warehousing properties, office facilities, data processing equipment and automobiles. At September 30, 1991, future minimum payments under noncancellable leases are as follows:

	Operating Leases	Capital Leases
1992	$20,192,157	$724,328
1993	16,107,667	514,253
1994	13,334,861	397,222
1995	10,110,679	74,304
1996	6,486,424	56,572
1997 and later	15,276,123	65,389
Total minimum lease payments	$81,507,911	1,832,068
Less interest		400,140
Present value of net minimum lease payments		$1,431,928

Capital leases included in the consolidated balance sheets at September 30, 1991 and 1990 are summarized below:

	1991	1990
Machinery and equipment	$3,706,496	2,469,964
Accumulated depreciation and amortization	1,775,591	1,489,383
Obligations under capital leases:		
Current	566,683	456,141
Long-term	865,245	253,041

Certain leases require the company to pay real estate taxes, insurance, maintenance and special assessments.

Total rental expense for operating leases amounted to $31.2 million in 1991, $27.0 million in 1990 and $24.5 million in 1989.

Notes Continued

(8) Business Segments and Geographic Area Information

The principal business of Alberto-Culver Company and its subsidiaries is developing, manufacturing and marketing products designed for sale at retail and ultimately for personal use or use in the home (referred to as "mass marketed personal use products").

Another segment of the company's business is "institutional products" which includes hair care products sold through beauty and barber distributors to the professional trade, specialty foods sold to institutions and restaurants, and health and hygiene products intended for end-use by institutions and industries.

The "other products—Sally" business segment principally represents the operations of Sally Beauty Company which sells the company's and other manufacturers' professional beauty and barber products through Sally stores. This segment also includes contract packaging services performed for other companies.

Segment and geographic data for the years ended September 30, 1991, 1990 and 1989 are as follows:

Business Segments Information	1991	1990	1989
Net sales:			
Mass marketed personal use products	$387,297,031	378,552,032	354,028,171
Institutional products	99,258,293	98,979,192	86,346,901
Other products—Sally	395,898,751	325,836,276	284,103,009
Eliminations	(8,735,493)	(7,542,532)	(7,039,648)
	$873,718,582	795,824,968	717,438,433
Earnings before provision for income taxes:			
Mass marketed personal use products	$ 18,416,335	34,582,165	36,287,204
Institutional products	13,038,000	13,909,060	12,041,182
Other products—Sally	30,439,559	20,269,622	15,533,271
Operating profit	61,893,894	68,760,847	63,861,657
Unallocated expenses, net*	(11,973,158)	(10,083,039)	(11,550,445)
Interest expense, net of interest income	(1,779,656)	(3,974,179)	(5,080,911)
	$ 48,141,080	54,703,629	47,230,301
Identifiable assets:			
Mass marketed personal use products	$237,259,656	166,058,671	143,556,967
Institutional products	74,951,674	54,995,572	53,925,798
Other products—Sally	182,363,262	151,125,599	137,043,123
Corporate**	79,838,134	71,380,001	29,169,456
	$574,412,726	443,559,843	363,695,344
Depreciation and amortization expense:			
Mass marketed personal use products	$ 4,637,551	3,981,294	3,142,777
Institutional products	849,069	937,371	619,378
Other products—Sally	6,967,853	6,336,262	6,090,064
Corporate	1,267,379	1,246,906	323,835
	$ 13,721,852	12,501,833	10,176,054
Capital expenditures:			
Mass marketed personal use products	$ 19,250,116	7,095,526	7,185,165
Institutional products	2,916,417	1,705,966	1,400,679
Other products—Sally	8,052,497	5,597,429	7,055,523
Corporate	189,598	160,776	2,192,914
	$ 30,408,628	14,559,697	17,834,281

Geographic Area Information	1991	1990	1989
Net sales:			
United States	$661,126,235	610,645,823	552,202,008
Foreign	219,744,978	191,621,276	170,740,578
Eliminations	(7,152,631)	(6,442,131)	(5,504,153)
	$873,718,582	795,824,968	717,438,433
Operating profit:			
United States	$ 51,140,262	59,007,087	57,755,280
Foreign	10,753,632	9,753,760	6,106,377
	$ 61,893,894	68,760,847	63,861,657
Identifiable assets:			
United States	$294,471,285	268,723,966	239,021,689
Foreign	200,103,307	103,455,876	95,504,199
Corporate**	79,838,134	71,380,001	29,169,456
	$574,412,726	443,559,843	363,695,344

*The category "Unallocated expenses, net" principally consists of general corporate expenses and foreign exchange gains and losses.
**Corporate assets are primarily cash and cash equivalents, short-term investments and equipment.

Notes Continued

(9) Quarterly Financial Data

Unaudited quarterly statement of earnings information for the years ended September 30, 1991 and 1990 is summarized below (in thousands, except per share amounts):

1991	1st Quarter	2nd Quarter	3rd Quarter	4th Quarter
Net sales	$190,832	214,453	221,026	247,408
Cost of products sold	93,602	102,360	108,737	119,867
Net earnings	8,032	9,035	4,228	8,821
Earnings per share	.28	.32	.15	.31
1990				
Net sales	$176,330	194,726	201,732	223,037
Cost of products sold	87,338	93,616	97,342	105,114
Net earnings	6,574	7,457	9,624	11,355
Earnings per share	.25	.28	.36	.41

(10) Supplemental Cash Flow Information

	Year ended September 30,		
	1991	1990	1989
Cash paid for:			
Interest	$ 6,913,000	8,023,000	7,729,000
Income taxes	17,323,000	12,826,000	15,080,000
Capital lease obligations assumed	732,619	161,821	72,759
Liabilities assumed in conjunction with acquisitions:			
Fair value of assets acquired	$96,250,594	—	24,948,238
Cash paid	18,960,573	—	15,715,953
	$77,290,021	—	9,232,285

(11) Acquisition (Fiscal Year 1991)

In September 1991, the company purchased a 23.7% equity interest, representing 74.0% voting control, in Cederroth International AB, formerly Cederroth Nordic AB, for $17.4 million in cash. The acquisition was accounted for as a purchase. The excess of purchase price over historical cost, which is classified as goodwill at September 30, 1991, will be allocated to assets in fiscal year 1992.

The company's 74.0% controlling interest requires that Cederroth's operations since its acquisition be included in the consolidated financial statements. The 76.3% equity interest not acquired by the company is shown as "minority interest" in the 1991 consolidated statement of earnings and consolidated balance sheet. Had Cederroth been acquired at the beginning of fiscal year 1990, the pro-forma inclusion of its operating results would not have had a significant effect on reported consolidated net earnings for the years ended September 30, 1991 and 1990.

Significant accounts of Cederroth included in the company's consolidated balance sheet at September 30, 1991 were: cash and cash equivalents—$12 million; accounts receivable—$22 million; inventories—$17 million; property, plant and equipment—$15 million; goodwill and trade names—$20 million; accounts payable and accrued expenses—$20 million; long-term debt—$27 million; minority interest—$22 million.

(12) Acquisition (Fiscal Year 1989)

In October, 1988, the company purchased all of the assets of Save-Way Beauty Supply for cash and notes totaling approximately $23 million. The acquisition was accounted for as a purchase and accordingly, the results of operations of Save-Way have been included in the consolidated financial statements since its acquisition.

Auditors' Report

The Board of Directors and Stockholders
Alberto-Culver Company:

We have audited the accompanying consolidated balance sheets of Alberto-Culver Company and subsidiaries as of September 30, 1991 and 1990, and the related consolidated statements of earnings, retained earnings, and cash flows for each of the years in the three year period ended September 30, 1991. These consolidated financial statements are the responsibility of the company's management. Our responsibility is to express an opinion on these consolidated financial statements based on our audits.

We conducted our audits in accordance with generally accepted auditing standards. Those standards require that we plan and perform the audits to obtain reasonable assurance about whether the financial statements are free of material misstatement. An audit includes examining, on a test basis, evidence supporting the amounts and disclosures in the financial statements. An audit also includes assessing the accounting principles used and significant estimates made by management, as well as evaluating the overall financial statement presentation. We believe that our audits provide a reasonable basis for our opinion.

In our opinion, the consolidated financial statements referred to above present fairly, in all material respects, the financial position of Alberto-Culver Company and subsidiaries at September 30, 1991 and 1990, and the results of their operations and their cash flows for each of the years in the three year period ended September 30, 1991 in conformity with generally accepted accounting principles.

KPMG Peat Marwick

KPMG Peat Marwick

Chicago, Illinois
October 31, 1991

**Management's Discussion and Analysis of
Results of Operations and Financial Condition**

RESULTS OF OPERATIONS

Fiscal year 1991 marked the eighth consecutive year of record sales for Alberto-Culver Company. Net sales for the year ended September 30, 1991 were $873.7 million, an increase of 9.8% over prior year sales of $795.8 million. Net sales in 1989 were $717.4 million.

Net earnings were $30.1 million or $1.06 per share in 1991 compared to 1990 net earnings of $35.0 million or $1.30 per share. Net earnings in 1989 were $29.4 million or $1.12 per share. Comparing 1991 to 1990, the decline in current year earnings was primarily the result of lower sales of domestic hair care products and increased advertising and promotion spending for the "mass marketed personal use products" line of business. Earnings per share includes the effect of issuing 1.8 million shares of Class A common stock in the fourth quarter of fiscal year 1990. All earnings per share figures have been restated for the two-for-one stock split in February, 1990.

Sales of "mass marketed personal use products" were $387.3 million in 1991 versus $378.6 million in 1990. Product lines contributing to the current year's sales gain included Alberto VO5 Conditioning Hairdressing, TRESemmé retail hair care products and Papa Dash, a new lite salt blend introduced in fiscal year 1991. Sales of "mass marketed personal use products" increased 6.9% in 1990 compared to 1989.

"Institutional products" sales were $99.3 million in 1991 compared to $99.0 million in 1990 and $86.3 million in 1989. The higher sales in 1991 and 1990 were mainly due to Indola professional products.

Sales of the "Other Products—Sally" business segment increased to $395.9 million in 1991 compared to $325.8 million and $284.1 million in 1990 and 1989, respectively. The higher sales were due to the growth of Sally Beauty Company's operations. New store openings along with double digit sales gains for established stores accounted for Sally's impressive performance in 1991. The number of Sally stores increased 25.4% over the last two years to a total of 1,012 at the end of 1991 compared to 891 and 807 at the end of 1990 and 1989, respectively.

Cost of products sold as a percentage of sales was 48.6% in fiscal year 1991 compared to 48.2% in 1990 and 48.0% in 1989. The changes between years were primarily due to higher material costs, product mix and the growth of Sally Beauty Company, which has a relatively higher cost of products sold percentage.

Advertising, promotion, selling and administrative expenses increased 12.9% in 1991, 10.3% in 1990 and 15.9% in 1989. The higher costs were mainly attributable to increased investments in the advertising and promotion of "mass marketed personal use products" and higher administrative costs related to the growth of Sally Beauty Company. Advertising, promotion and market research expenditures were $146.1 million, $130.7 million and $120.5 million in 1991, 1990 and 1989, respectively.

Interest expense, net of interest income, was $1.8 million, $4.0 million and $5.1 million in 1991, 1990 and 1989, respectively. Interest expense was $6.8 million in 1991 versus $7.9 million in 1990 and $8.0 million in 1989. The reductions in interest expense between the periods were primarily due to fluctuations in the amount of debt obligations.

Interest income was $5.0 million, $3.9 million and $2.9 million in 1991, 1990 and 1989, respectively. The increases in interest income were principally due to higher levels of investments, partially offset by lower interest rates and the mix of taxable and tax-exempt securities.

The provision for income taxes as a percentage of earnings before income taxes was 37.0%, 36.0% and 37.7% in 1991, 1990 and 1989, respectively. Factors which influenced the effective tax rates for 1991, 1990, and 1989 are described in "note 6" to the consolidated financial statements.

The earnings of Cederroth International AB, which was acquired in September 1991, did not have a material effect on the company's 1991 consolidated statement of earnings. The acquisition of Cederroth is described in "note 11" to the consolidated financial statements.

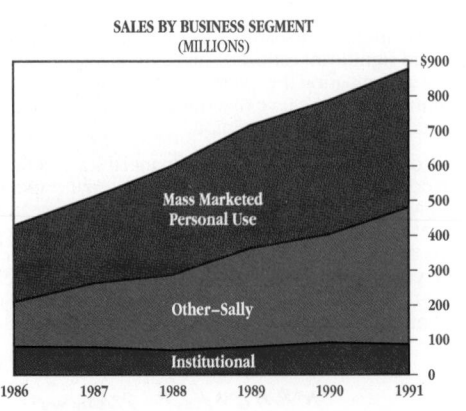

SALES BY BUSINESS SEGMENT
(MILLIONS)

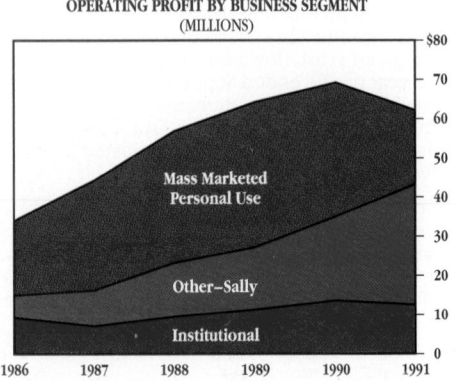

OPERATING PROFIT BY BUSINESS SEGMENT
(MILLIONS)

FINANCIAL CONDITION

The company's financial condition continued to strengthen from 1989 through 1991. The three year period was highlighted by significant sales growth from new products and established brands, business acquisitions and the expansion of Sally Beauty Company's operations.

The company's consolidated balance sheet at September 30, 1991 includes Cederroth International AB. Significant balance sheet accounts of Cederroth at that date were: cash and cash equivalents—$12 million; accounts receivable—$22 million; inventories—$17 million; property, plant and equipment—$15 million; goodwill and trade names—$20 million; accounts payable and accrued expenses—$20 million; long-term debt—$27 million and minority interest—$22 million. The acquisition of Cederroth is described in "note 11" to the consolidated financial statements.

Working capital at September 30, 1991 was $212.3 million, an increase of $19.7 million over September 30, 1990 working capital of $192.6 million. During the three year period ended September 30, 1991, working capital increased $117.5 million or 124%. Additionally, the company's current ratio improved to 2.11 to 1.00 at September 30, 1991 from 1.78 to 1.00 at the end of 1988.

The increase in working capital since 1988 was due to higher earnings, increased long-term borrowings, proceeds from the 1990 sale of 1.8 million shares of Class A common stock and the inclusion of working capital of acquired companies. Partially offsetting cash inflows were $61.8 million of capital expenditures, payments for acquired companies and $6.5 million for the purchase of common stock for the treasury. As to acquisitions, the Company paid $17.4 million to purchase a 23.7% equity interest, representing 74% voting control, in

Cederroth International AB in September 1991 and $23 million for the assets of Save Way Beauty Supply in October 1988. Capital expenditures include $14.0 million for a new manufacturing facility located in the United Kingdom completed in 1991.

Cash, cash equivalents and short-term investments grew to $84.6 million at September 30, 1991 from $36.7 million at September 30, 1988.

Accounts receivable and inventories less accounts payable were $208.2 million at September 30, 1991 compared to $108.2 million at September 30, 1988.

Short-term borrowings, including current maturities of long-term debt, increased $3.7 million since September 30, 1988 while long-term debt increased $53 million. At September 30, 1991, the company had available credit of $100 million under a revolving credit agreement and unused lines of credit with various banks of approximately $125 million.

Cash dividends per share increased 50.9% since 1988. Cash dividends paid on Class A and Class B common stock were 21.5 cents per share in 1991 compared to 19.5 cents in 1990 and 17.25 cents in 1989. During the three year period, dividends paid on both classes of common stock totaled $15.8 million.

INFLATION

The company was not significantly affected by inflation during the past three years. However, the cost of certain petro-chemical based materials did increase temporarily as a result of the 1990 conflict in the Middle East. Management continuously attempts to resist cost increases and counteract the effects of inflation through productivity improvements, cost reduction programs and price increases within the constraints of highly competitive markets.

ADVERTISING, PROMOTION & MARKET RESEARCH
(MILLIONS)

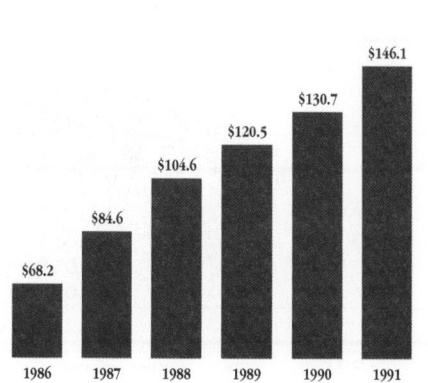

1986	1987	1988	1989	1990	1991
$68.2	$84.6	$104.6	$120.5	$130.7	$146.1

WORKING CAPITAL
(MILLIONS)

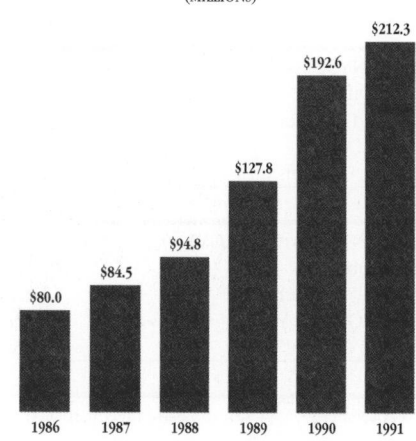

1986	1987	1988	1989	1990	1991
$80.0	$84.5	$94.8	$127.8	$192.6	$212.3

Selected Financial Data
Alberto-Culver Company and Subsidiaries

				Year ended September 30,	
	1991	1990	1989	1988	1987
Net sales	**$873,718,582**	795,824,968	717,438,433	604,708,002	514,491,442
Cost of products sold	**424,566,220**	383,410,005	344,539,260	284,842,795	246,834,940
Interest expense	**6,821,273**	7,890,653	7,975,819	5,926,771	4,509,732
Earnings before gain on sale of investment,* income taxes and minority interest	**48,141,080**	54,703,629	47,230,301	40,367,164	33,024,351
Provision for income taxes* and minority interest of $212,800 in 1991	**18,024,800**	19,694,000	17,792,000	15,745,000	14,861,000
Earnings before gain on sale of investment*	**30,116,280**	35,009,629	29,438,301	24,622,164	18,163,351
Earnings per share before gain on sale of investment*	**1.06**	1.30	1.12	.91	.64
Weighted average shares outstanding	**28,303,000**	26,831,000	26,175,000	26,999,000	28,404,000
Cash, cash equivalents and short-term investments	**$ 84,595,607**	82,012,159	40,379,748	36,703,489	41,177,543
Working capital	**212,268,432**	192,615,557	127,801,385	94,820,959	84,456,485
Current ratio	**2.11 to 1**	2.34 to 1	2.00 to 1	1.78 to 1	1.75 to 1
Property, plant and equipment, net	**114,910,295**	81,772,256	77,233,599	63,808,687	50,615,213
Total assets	**574,412,726**	443,559,843	363,695,344	305,923,607	275,996,071
Long-term debt	**97,819,452**	60,728,041	68,899,324	44,787,237	23,643,568
Stockholders' equity	**249,431,195**	230,867,649	160,088,384	134,690,160	132,937,440
Cash dividends per share**	**.215**	.195	.1725	.1425	.11625

Reference is made to notes (5) and (11) pertaining to changes in common stock and the acquisition of Cederroth International AB, respectively.

*In 1988, the sale of an investment resulted in a nonrecurring gain of $2,268,709 or $.08 per share after deducting income taxes of $1,408,000.

**Dividends per share on Class A common stock and Class B common stock have been equal since the Class A shares were issued in April, 1986.

Market Price of Common Stock and Cash Dividends Per Share
Alberto-Culver Company and Subsidiaries

The high and low sales prices of both classes of the company's common stock on the New York Stock Exchange and cash dividends per share in each quarter of fiscal year 1991 and 1990 are as follows:

	Market Price Range				Cash Dividends Per Share	
	1991		1990			
	High	**Low**	High	Low	**1991**	1990
Class A (NYSE symbol ACVA):						
First Quarter	**$23¹/₄**	**15⁷/₈**	20³/₄	16¹/₂	**$.050**	.045
Second Quarter	**24¹/₈**	**20¹/₄**	19³/₄	15³/₄	**.055**	.050
Third Quarter	**24⁷/₈**	**16³/₄**	20³/₈	16¹/₂	**.055**	.050
Fourth Quarter	**20**	**18**	22¹/₄	15¹/₈	**.055**	.050
					$.215	.195
Class B (NYSE symbol ACV):						
First Quarter	**$33¹/₄**	**20³/₈**	26³/₄	21³/₈	**$.050**	.045
Second Quarter	**34¹/₄**	**27³/₄**	25	20	**.055**	.050
Third Quarter	**31¹/₄**	**20¹/₄**	27¹/₄	20¹/₂	**.055**	.050
Fourth Quarter	**25¹/₄**	**21¹/₄**	27³/₄	19¹/₈	**.055**	.050
					$.215	.195

As of November 15, 1991, stockholders of record totaled 1,450 for Class A and 1,576 for Class B.

APPENDIX

D

Present Value Tables

TABLE 1
Present Value of $1

Periods	2%	4%	5%	6%	8%	9%	10%	12%	14%	16%	18%	20%
1	.98039	.96154	.95238	.94340	.92593	.91743	.90909	.89286	.87719	.86207	.84746	.83333
2	.96117	.92456	.90703	.89000	.85734	.84168	.82645	.79719	.76947	.74316	.71818	.69444
3	.94232	.88900	.86384	.83962	.79383	.77218	.75132	.71178	.67497	.64066	.60863	.57870
4	.92385	.85480	.82270	.79209	.73503	.70843	.68301	.63552	.59208	.55229	.51579	.48225
5	.90573	.82193	.78353	.74726	.68058	.64993	.62092	.56743	.51937	.47611	.43711	.40188
6	.88797	.79031	.74622	.70496	.63017	.59627	.56447	.50663	.45559	.41044	.37043	.33490
7	.87056	.75992	.71068	.66506	.58349	.54703	.51316	.45235	.39964	.35383	.31393	.27908
8	.85349	.73069	.67684	.62741	.54027	.50187	.46651	.40388	.35056	.30503	.26604	.23257
9	.83676	.70259	.64461	.59190	.50025	.46043	.42410	.36061	.30751	.26295	.22546	.19381
10	.82035	.67556	.61391	.55839	.46319	.42241	.38554	.32197	.26974	.22668	.19106	.16151
11	.80426	.64958	.58468	.52679	.42888	.38753	.35049	.28748	.23662	.19542	.16192	.13459
12	.78849	.62460	.55684	.49697	.39711	.35554	.31863	.25668	.20756	.16846	.13722	.11216
13	.77303	.60057	.53032	.46884	.36770	.32618	.28966	.22917	.18207	.14523	.11629	.09346
14	.75788	.57748	.50507	.44230	.34046	.29925	.26333	.20462	.15971	.12520	.09855	.07789
15	.74301	.55526	.48102	.41727	.31524	.27454	.23939	.18270	.14010	.10793	.08352	.06491
16	.72845	.53391	.45811	.39365	.29189	.25187	.21763	.16312	.12289	.09304	.07078	.05409
17	.71416	.51337	.43630	.37136	.27027	.23107	.19785	.14564	.10780	.08021	.05998	.04507
18	.70016	.49363	.41552	.35034	.25025	.21199	.17986	.13004	.09456	.06914	.05083	.03756
19	.68643	.47464	.39573	.33051	.23171	.19449	.16351	.11611	.08295	.05961	.04308	.03130
20	.67297	.45639	.37689	.31180	.21455	.17843	.14864	.10367	.07276	.05139	.03651	.02608
21	.65978	.43883	.35894	.29416	.19866	.16370	.13513	.09256	.06383	.04430	.03094	.02174
22	.64684	.42196	.34185	.27751	.18394	.15018	.12285	.08264	.05599	.03819	.02622	.01811
23	.63416	.40573	.32557	.26180	.17032	.13778	.11168	.07379	.04911	.03292	.02222	.01509
24	.62172	.39012	.31007	.24698	.15770	.12641	.10153	.06588	.04308	.02838	.01883	.01258
25	.60953	.37512	.29530	.23300	.14602	.11597	.09230	.05882	.03779	.02447	.01596	.01048

TABLE 2
Present Value of Ordinary Annuity of $1

Periods	2%	4%	5%	6%	8%	9%	10%	12%	14%	16%	18%	20%
1	.98039	.96154	.95238	.94340	.92593	.91743	.90909	.89286	.87719	.86207	.84746	.83333
2	1.94156	1.88609	1.85941	1.83339	1.78326	1.75911	1.73554	1.69005	1.64666	1.60523	1.56564	1.52778
3	2.88388	2.77509	2.72325	2.67301	2.57710	2.53130	2.48685	2.40183	2.32163	2.24589	2.17427	2.10648
4	3.80773	3.62990	3.54595	3.46511	3.31213	3.23972	3.16986	3.03735	2.91371	2.79818	2.69006	2.58873
5	4.71346	4.45182	4.32948	4.21236	3.99271	3.88965	3.79079	3.60478	3.43308	3.27429	3.12717	2.99061
6	5.60143	5.24214	5.07569	4.91732	4.62288	4.48592	4.35526	4.11141	3.88867	3.68474	3.49760	3.32551
7	6.47199	6.00205	5.78637	5.58238	5.20637	5.03295	4.86842	4.56376	4.28830	4.03857	3.81153	3.60459
8	7.32548	6.73274	6.46321	6.20979	5.74664	5.53482	5.33493	4.96764	4.63886	4.34359	4.07757	3.83716
9	8.16224	7.43533	7.10782	6.80169	6.24689	5.99525	5.75902	5.32825	4.94637	4.60654	4.30302	4.03097
10	8.98259	8.11090	7.72173	7.36009	6.71008	6.41766	6.14457	5.65022	5.21612	4.83323	4.49409	4.19247
11	9.78685	8.76048	8.30641	7.88687	7.13896	6.80519	6.49506	5.93770	5.45273	5.02864	4.65601	4.32706
12	10.57534	9.38507	8.86325	8.38384	7.53608	7.16073	6.81369	6.19437	5.66029	5.19711	4.79322	4.43922
13	11.34837	9.98565	9.39357	8.85268	7.90378	7.48690	7.10336	6.42355	5.84236	5.34233	4.90951	4.53268
14	12.01625	10.56312	9.89864	9.29498	8.24424	7.78615	7.36669	6.62817	6.00207	5.46753	5.00806	4.61057
15	12.84926	11.11839	10.37966	9.71225	8.55948	8.06069	7.60608	6.81086	6.14217	5.57546	5.09158	4.67547
16	13.57771	11.65230	10.83777	10.10590	8.85137	8.31256	7.82371	6.97399	6.26506	5.66850	5.16235	4.72956
17	14.29187	12.16567	11.27407	10.47726	9.12164	8.54363	8.02155	7.11963	6.37286	5.74870	5.22233	4.77463
18	14.99203	12.65930	11.68959	10.82760	9.37189	8.75563	8.20141	7.24967	6.46742	5.81785	5.27316	4.81219
19	15.67846	13.13394	12.08532	11.15812	9.60360	8.95012	8.36492	7.36578	6.55037	5.87746	5.31624	4.84350
20	16.35143	13.59033	12.46221	11.46992	9.81815	9.12855	8.51356	7.46944	6.62313	5.92884	5.35275	4.86958
21	17.01121	14.02916	12.82115	11.76408	10.01680	9.29224	8.64869	7.56200	6.68696	5.97314	5.38368	4.89132
22	17.65805	14.45112	13.16300	12.04158	10.20074	9.44243	8.77154	7.64465	6.74294	6.01133	5.40990	4.90943
23	18.29220	14.85684	13.48857	12.30338	10.37106	9.58021	8.88322	7.71843	6.79206	6.04425	5.43212	4.92453
24	18.91393	15.24696	13.79864	12.55036	10.52876	9.70661	8.98474	7.78432	6.83514	6.07263	5.45095	4.93710
25	19.52346	15.62208	14.09394	12.78336	10.67478	9.82258	9.07704	7.84314	6.87293	6.09709	5.46691	4.94759